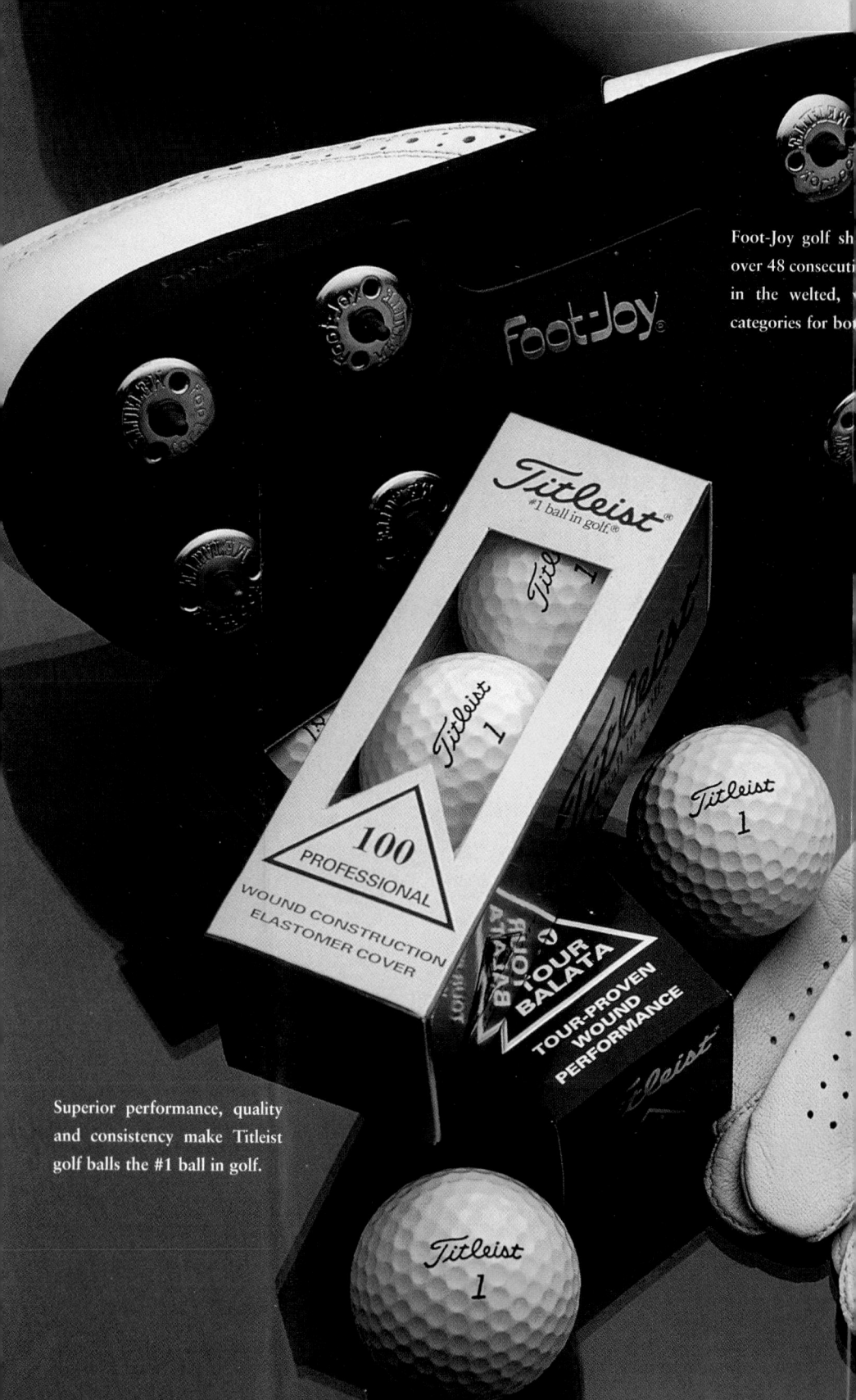

Foot-Joy golf sh
over 48 consecuti
in the welted,
categories for bo

Superior performance, quality
and consistency make Titleist
golf balls the #1 ball in golf.

A book filled with success stories should begin with two of golf's greatest.

shoe in golf for
m the #1 position
and lightweight
women.

90 HVC

TWO-PIECE DISTANCE
AND DURABILITY

Foot-Joy is the #1 glove in golf,
offering superior fit, feel and
grip within each glove category
in the market.

Titleist clubs and putters have
earned a reputation for superior
performance on tour and in the
golf shop.

The success stories of 1995 include many great individual performances from many different golfers around the world. Once again, one of the common threads among these players is the fact that more chose to play Titleist golf balls and wear Foot-Joy golf shoes while achieving their best than any other brand of balls or shoes.

The use and influence of Titleist and Foot-Joy products reaches the major professional tours like the U.S. PGA Tour, PGA European Tour, Japan PGA Tour, Australasian PGA Tour, South African PGA Tour, Asian Tour and Canadian Tour. It also extends to club professionals and top amateurs alike wherever golf is played.

Why do these knowledgeable golfers choose to trust their games to Titleist and Foot-Joy? It's because golfers worldwide have grown to understand the confidence that is gained through the superior quality and performance of our products.

That confidence is most apparent in Titleist's long-standing record of use on the U.S. PGA Tour. Since 1949, the Titleist golf ball has been the most played ball on the PGA Tour, year after year. It has also been the most played ball on the European PGA Tour for the last fifteen years. We're proud of the fact that golfers whose careers and livelihoods depend on the performance of the ball they use have selected Titleist. This confidence has helped make Titleist the most played ball in the world of golf.

A similar commitment to quality makes Foot-Joy the #1 Shoe in Golf. It continues as the shoe of choice by the majority of golfers on the major tours around the world.

On the U.S. PGA Tour, Foot-Joy shoes have been worn by more pros than any other brand, every year since 1945. The quality, design and craftsmanship that goes into a Foot-Joy shoe has continued to make it number one for all skill levels of players.

The Titleist and Foot-Joy brands have always stood for quality and performance. That's because the product has always been the most important part of each brand's history. And as the two brands move forward together, this mission remains our sole purpose. At Titleist and Foot-Joy Worldwide, this is more than a commitment, it's a tradition.

In this the 29th year of *The World of Professional Golf*, I felt it appropriate to make a particular dedication of this book to someone whose belief in this project over the years has been one of the main inspirations behind my efforts to bring to the sport of golf such a complete treatise. I would like, therefore, to dedicate this book to Johnny Carson without whose support and interest this publication would not have been possible.

Presents

Mark H. McCormack's The World of Professional Golf 1995

An IMG PUBLISHING Book

An IMG PUBLISHING Book

All rights reserved
First published 1995
© IMG Operations, Inc. 1995

Designed and produced by Davis Design
Appendixes prepared by Bronwyn Harris

ISBN 1-878843-12-5

Printed and bound in the United States of America.

Contents

1. The Sony Ranking

Seven victories in 1994 — for a total of 17 over three years — enabled Nick Price to reach No. 1 on the Sony Ranking. He achieved the top position, having risen from No. 24 in those three years, with his triumph in the PGA Championship, which came one month after he won the British Open title. He replaced Greg Norman, who had been No. 1 since February, when Norman ended Nick Faldo's record 81-week reign. Norman, who had three victories, ended the year ranked No. 2, and Faldo was No. 3 after winning two tournaments.

Bernhard Langer, who had two victories and has now won for 16 consecutive years, finished with the No. 4 ranking, ahead of Masters champion Jose Maria Olazabal at No. 5, who advanced from No. 15, and U.S. Open winner Ernie Els, who totalled five victories worldwide in climbing from No. 20 to No. 6.

These players were from six different countries — Price (Zimbabwe), Norman (Australia), Faldo (England), Langer (Germany), Olazabal (Spain) and Els (South Africa) — and none were from the United States. It was the first time since *The World of Professional Golf* began tracking world rankings in 1968 that no American was even among the top five players in the world. (See chart on page 10.)

There were just two Americans in the world's top 10 at the close of 1994, Fred Couples at No. 7 and Corey Pavin at No. 10. Others in the top 10 were No. 8 Colin Montgomerie of Scotland, the leading money winner in Europe, and No. 9 Masashi (Jumbo) Ozaki, who won seven tournaments in Japan. The depth of talent in American golf still was demonstrated over the next 20 places on the Sony Ranking, and players from the United States held 17 of the top 30 positions, 27 of the top 50 positions, and 52 of the top 100 positions.

The Sony Ranking was launched during the Masters week in 1986, and so it is now eight years since the Sony Corporation first announced this specially developed computerized method of evaluating the relative performances of the world's leading players. The Sony Ranking is sanctioned by the Championship Committee of the Royal and Ancient Golf Club of St. Andrews, and is endorsed by the major professional tours.

Some of the most respected people in golf worldwide bring their opinions to bear on the workings of the system. The Sony Ranking Advisory Committee meets at St. Andrews each October, and its recommendations are passed on to the R&A for approval. In addition to myself, the Sony Ranking Advisory Committee consists of:

Brenda Blumberg (advisor to South African PGA), Tim Finchem (U.S. PGA Tour), Peter Dobereiner (Association of Golf Writers), Taizo Kawata (Japan Golf Association), Kosaku Shimada (PGA of Japan), Colin Phillips (Australian Golf Union), Richard Rahusen (European Golf Association), Pat Rielly (PGA of America), Ken Schofield (PGA European Tour), Frank Tatum (past president, United States Golf Association), Colin Maclaine (past captain and chairman of the Championship Committee of the R&A), and Peter Townsend (PGA European Tour Policy Board).

All tournaments from the world's golf tours are taken into account and points are awarded according to the quality of the players participating in each event. The number of points distributed to each golfer is dependent upon his finishing position.

The four major championships (Masters Tournament, U.S. Open, British Open and PGA Championship) and the flagship events of the major tours (The Players Championship (U.S.), Volvo PGA Championship (Europe), Japan Open and Australian Open) are weighted separately to reflect the greater prestige of the events and strong fields participating.

The Sony Ranking is based on a three-year "rolling" average, weighted in favor of more recent results, and a divisor is used to take into account the number of tournaments played by each golfer. Points accumulated over the current 52-week period are multiplied by four, points earned over the previous 52-week period are multiplied by two, and points from the first 52-week period are simply added to the total.

Each player is then ranked according to his point average, which is determined by dividing his total number of points by the number of tournaments he has played over the three-year period. A player must, however, have a minimum divisor of at least 20 tournaments in each 52-week period, and a minimum divisor of at least 60 tournaments over the three-year period.

For example, if a golfer played in eight tournaments in the first 52-week period, played in 15 tournaments in the second 52-week period, and played in 32 tournaments in the most recent 52-week period, his divisor would be 72 (20 plus 20 plus 32). A golfer who played in 32 tournaments in each of the three 52-week periods would have a divisor of 96 (32 plus 32 plus 32).

Fifty points are awarded to the winner of a major championship, then 30 points for second place, 20 for third, 15 for fourth, 12 for fifth and down to at least one point for every player completing the final round. In The Players Championship, 40 points are awarded to the winner, then down to one point for 50th place.

In the Volvo PGA Championship, there is a minimum points level of 32 points for the winner, then down to one point for 41st place. The Australian Open and Japan Open are both assigned minimum points levels of 16 points for the winner, then down to one point for 21st place.

Minimum points levels for the winners of official tour events have been set at six points for events in Asia and South Africa, eight points in Japan, Australia and New Zealand, and 10 points in the United States and Europe. Points are reduced proportionately for events cut from 72 holes to 54 or 36 holes because of weather or other reasons.

Points to be awarded above the minimum levels for these events are determined by the strength of field. This is determined by the number and ranking of players in the tournaments who are among the top 100 golfers on the Sony Ranking. Each player ranked in the top 100 of the Sony Ranking is assigned "rating points" ranging from 50 points for the No. 1 player, then down to two points each for those ranked 81st to 100th.

The total of the rating points is then applied to the table on pages 8 and 9 to adjust the Sony Ranking points to reflect the quality of the field.

As a by-product, the Sony Ranking system is able to identify the strongest tournaments in the world. Many tournament organizers use the Sony Ranking to determine qualifiers or as a basis for issuing invitations. For example, the top 50 players on the Sony Ranking are exempt from having to qualify for the British Open. The PGA of America has also made effective use of the Sony Ranking in issuing invitations to the PGA Championship.

Once regarded as the least important of the four major events, the PGA Championship has in recent years drawn level with the other three. This has been the result of an upgrading of the venues and, in no small measure, to the use of the Sony Ranking in determining the participating fields. In 1994, the PGA Championship matched the British Opens of 1990 and 1993 for the highest ratings since the Sony Ranking was started. The top 10 finishers in the PGA Championship included seven from among the top 13 players on the Sony Ranking.

Following were the highest-rated tournaments in the world for 1994:

	Event	No. of Sony Ranked Players Participating					Sony Rating Points
		Top 5	Top 15	Top 30	Top 50	Top 100	
1	PGA Championship	5	15	30	47	75	754
2	British Open	4	13	27	45	74	696
3	U.S. Open	5	14	26	41	59	655
4	The Players Championship	4	13	26	36	65	627
5	Masters Tournament	4	13	25	37	61	622
6	The Nestle Invitational	3	10	19	26	54	496
7	NEC World Series of Golf	3	9	16	25	36	429
8	Johnnie Walker World Champ.	3	11	19	23	24	418
9	Doral-Ryder Open	4	7	15	18	41	392
9	Memorial Tournament	2	6	18	28	47	392
11	Buick Classic	2	7	18	25	41	385
12	Tour Championship	2	7	14	22	26	361
13	Sprint International	1	7	16	26	45	356
14	Honda Classic	3	7	12	17	35	343
15	Southwestern Bell Colonial	2	5	14	21	44	330
16	Johnnie Walker Asian Classic	4	6	9	15	27	329
17	GTE Byron Nelson Classic	2	5	13	19	35	324
18	Nedbank Million Dollar	3	9	12	12	12	306
19	Volvo PGA Championship	2	6	9	16	33	305
20	Trophee Lancome	3	6	9	17	35	300
21	Canon Greater Hartford Open	3	5	10	14	32	299
22	Volvo Masters	3	7	9	15	34	297
23	Dunhill British Masters	3	6	8	14	31	291
24	Buick Open	2	7	12	16	34	289
25	Nissan Los Angeles Open	1	5	12	19	39	282
26	Bell Canadian Open	2	4	12	17	36	281
27	Motorola Western Open	2	5	11	19	35	274
28	Murphy's Irish Open	2	5	7	13	26	271
29	MCI Heritage Classic	1	3	12	18	38	269
30	Mercedes German Masters	3	7	8	9	22	264

Age Groups of Top 100 Sony Ranked Players

Under 25	25-27	23-30	31-33	34-36	37-39	40-42	43-45	Over 45
					Price			
					Norman			
					Faldo			
					Langer			
					Ballesteros			
					Roberts			
				Couples	Cook			
		Olazabal		Pavin	Hoch			
		Love		Frost	Edwards			
		Maggert	Montgomerie	Woosnam	Stewart			
		Janzen	Singh	Lehman	Strange			
		Gilford	Faxon	Azinger	Simpson			
		Estes	Huston	Mize	Beck	Zoeller		
		Parnevik	Elkington	Nobilo	Rocca	McNulty		
		Jimenez	Fehr	Lane	Johnstone	Crenshaw		
	Els	Watts	Roe	Glasson	N. Ozaki	Torrance		
	Parry	Ogle	Gallagher	Calcavecchia	O'Meara	Nakajima		
	Haeggman	Daly	Forsbrand	Senior	Sluman	Haas		
	Johansson	Springer	Westner	Brand	Mackay	Romero	Kite	
	Clarke	Hamilton	Waldorf	Lowery	Allem	James	McCumber	M. Ozaki
	Baker	Henke	Magee	Forsman	Clements	Stadler	Watson	Irwin
Mickelson	Gamez	Andrade	Turner	Feherty	Ishii	Clark	Lietzke	Morgan
Allenby	Goosen	Rafferty	Triplett	Lyle	Bryant	Mason	Davis	Floyd

As the graph above illustrates, the wave of players who have dominated professional golf for the past decade appears to be cresting. At the peak are those in the 37-39 age group, including Price, Norman, Faldo, Langer and Seve Ballesteros, who have been No. 1 for 389 of the 455 weeks of the Sony Ranking's existence. Right behind them are the 34-36 age group, including Couples and Ian Woosnam, who were No. 1 for the other 66 weeks.

On the right side of the graph you see a dramatic dropoff as players enter their 40s, including Fuzzy Zoeller, Tom Kite and Ozaki. On the left side, there is evidence of the rise of players entering their late 20s and early 30s, including Els and Olazabal, two of the major championship winners of 1994, and other rising stars such as Montgomerie, Vijay Singh, Brad Faxon, Davis Love III, Jeff Maggert, Craig Parry, Phil Mickelson and Robert Allenby.

The top 200 players on the Sony Ranking as of December 31, 1994 are listed on pages 6 and 7, and in greater detail in the Appendixes. The opposite page makes note of the trends which occurred during the year.

As to be expected, the upward movements within the top 50 of the Sony Ranking were led by the major championship winners — Els, Olazabal and Price. On the downward list, three of the first four — Paul Azinger, Fred Couples and Steve Elkington — were out for varying times because of illness or injury.

Americans were most prominent in the movements into and out of the Sony Ranking's top 50, with Loren Roberts, Mark McCumber and Bob Estes gaining positions, and Payne Stewart, Rocco Mediate and Mark O'Meara dropping back.

Other major movements included Steve Lowery going from No. 246 to No. 69 on the Sony Ranking, and Brian Watts, with his five-victory year in Japan, advancing from No. 171 to No. 61. Three players went from the very bottom of the Sony Ranking (No. 949) into the top 200 — Carlos Franco (No. 128), Mike Heinen and Jonathon Lomas (tied for No. 150). On the downside, there were Steven Richardson (No. 60 to No. 120), Ian Baker-Finch (No. 66 to No. 170) and Lanny Wadkins (No. 73 to No. 179).

1994 Sony Ranking Review

Major Movements Within Top 50

Upward				Downward			
	Net Points	Position			Net Points	Position	
Name	Gained	1993	1994	Name	Lost	1993	1994
Ernie Els	832	20	6	Paul Azinger	572	6	21
Jose Maria Olazabal	504	15	5	Davis Love III	287	9	25
Nick Price	397	4	1	Fred Couples	270	5	7
Tom Lehman	340	48	17	Steve Elkington	249	19	43
Colin Montgomerie	313	14	8	Nick Faldo	230	1	3
Fuzzy Zoeller	297	46	12	Ian Woosnam	198	7	16
Seve Ballesteros	219	25	14	Lee Janzen	127	22	32
Masashi Ozaki	157	12	9	Bernhard Langer	125	4	4
Phil Mickelson	148	47	22	John Cook	111	18	24

Major Movements Into Top 50   Major Movements Out of Top 50

	Net Points	Position			Net Points	Position	
Name	Gained	1993	1994	Name	Lost	1993	1994
Loren Roberts	356	107	20	Payne Stewart	390	13	54
Mark McCumber	283	92	19	Rocco Mediate	241	41	102
Bob Estes	242	122	37	Mark O'Meara	235	28	83
Miguel Angel Jimenez	221	103	42	Ronan Rafferty	195	45	92
Scott Hoch	184	88	30	Chip Beck	183	23	62
Hale Irwin	182	89	29	Rodger Davis	179	40	81
Bill Glasson	175	109	36	Tony Johnstone	168	30	64
Robert Allenby	167	81	48	Peter Senior	167	27	53
Ben Crenshaw	94	64	34	Raymond Floyd	163	24	76
John Huston	93	68	40	Jim Gallagher, Jr.	158	34	65
Jesper Parnevik	90	72	39	Gordon Brand, Jr.	127	31	60
Rick Fehr	27	67	50	Costantino Rocca	119	33	63
Mark Calcavecchia	27	56	49	Mark James	109	35	55
Jay Haas	10	51	47	Scott Simpson	101	29	57
Tsuneyuki Nakajima	0	53	46	Craig Stadler	49	49	59

Other Major Movements

Upward				Downward			
	Net Points	Position			Net Points	Position	
Name	Gained	1993	1994	Name	Lost	1993	1994
Steve Lowery	248	246	69	Steven Richardson	265	60	120
Brian Watts	185	171	61	Ian Baker-Finch	246	66	170
Mike Springer	184	214	77	Lanny Wadkins	176	73	179
Lennie Clements	161	320	95	Fulton Allem	175	55	97
Carlos Franco	140	949	128	Dan Forsman	156	52	85
Andrew Coltart	138	801	143	Sandy Lyle	151	57	93
Mike Heinen	128	949	150	Nolan Henke	149	61	86
Jonathon Lomas	128	949	150	Paul Broadhurst	146	84	138
Hal Sutton	127	283	119	Chen Tze Chung	146	82	137
Eiji Mizoguchi	127	420	124	Joey Sindelar	131	79	127
Pierre Fulke	118	406	136	Peter Fowler	130	104	176
Kirk Triplett	117	207	99	Jamie Spence	125	98	174
Howard Clark	116	178	75	Billy Ray Brown	119	114	241
Brad Bryant	115	176	98	Jeff Sluman	115	71	90

The Sony Ranking

(As of December 31, 1994)

POS.	NAME, CIRCUIT	POINTS AVERAGE	POS.	NAME, CIRCUIT	POINTS AVERAGE
1	Nick Price, Afr 1	21.19	51	Mark Roe, Eur 12	4.68
2	Greg Norman, ANZ 1	20.57	52	Eduardo Romero, SAm 1	4.67
3	Nick Faldo, Eur 1	16.93	53	Peter Senior, ANZ 6	4.60
4	Bernhard Langer, Eur 2	15.32	54	Payne Stewart, USA 28	4.59
5	Jose Maria Olazabal, Eur 3	15.18	55	Mark James, Eur 13	4.54
6	Ernie Els, Afr 2	14.70	56	Joakim Haeggman, Eur 14	4.42
7	Fred Couples, USA 1	12.86	57	Scott Simpson, USA 29	4.41
8	Colin Montgomerie, Eur 4	12.19	58	Curtis Strange, USA 30	4.33
9	Masashi Ozaki, Jpn 1	11.39	59	Craig Stadler, USA 31	4.32
10	Corey Pavin, USA 2	10.87	60	Gordon Brand, Jr., Eur 15	4.30
11	David Frost, Afr 3	9.88	61	Brian Watts, USA 32	4.30
12	Fuzzy Zoeller, USA 3	9.73	62	Chip Beck, USA 33	4.18
13	Tom Kite, USA 4	9.03	63	Costantino Rocca, Eur 16	4.11
14	Seve Ballesteros, Eur 5	8.96	64	Tony Johnstone, Afr 5	4.09
15	Vijay Singh, Asa 1	8.49	65	Jim Gallagher, Jr., USA 34	4.07
16	Ian Woosnam, Eur 6	8.46	66	Gil Morgan, USA 35	4.01
17	Tom Lehman, USA 5	8.13	67	Brett Ogle, ANZ 7	3.93
18	Mark McNulty, Afr 4	8.01	68	Per-Ulrik Johansson, Eur 17	3.90
19	Mark McCumber, USA 6	7.68	69	Steve Lowery, USA 36	3.85
20	Loren Roberts, USA 7	7.46	70	Naomichi Ozaki, Jpn 3	3.83
21	Paul Azinger, USA 8	7.25	71	Anders Forsbrand, Eur 18	3.77
22	Phil Mickelson, USA 9	7.24	72	John Daly, USA 37	3.67
23	Tom Watson, USA 10	6.82	73	Wayne Westner, Afr 6	3.65
24	John Cook, USA 11	6.67	74	Darren Clarke, Eur 19	3.61
25	Davis Love III, USA 12	6.53	75	Howard Clark, Eur 20	3.49
26	Brad Faxon, USA 13	6.43	76	Raymond Floyd, USA 38	3.48
27	Jeff Maggert, USA 14	6.20	77	Mike Springer, USA 39	3.43
28	Larry Mize, USA 15	6.14	78	Duffy Waldorf, USA 40	3.37
29	Hale Irwin, USA 16	5.96	79	Andrew Magee, USA 41	3.30
30	Scott Hoch, USA 17	5.91	80	Todd Hamilton, USA 42	3.24
31	Frank Nobilo, ANZ 2	5.74	81	Rodger Davis, ANZ 8	3.24
32	Lee Janzen, USA 18	5.68	82	Peter Baker, Eur 21	3.22
33	David Gilford, Eur 7	5.59	83T	Mark O'Meara, USA 43	3.12
34	Ben Crenshaw, USA 19	5.58	83T	Carl Mason, Eur 22	3.12
35	Barry Lane, Eur 8	5.48	85	Dan Forsman, USA 44	3.11
36	Bill Glasson, USA 20	5.47	86	Nolan Henke, USA 45	3.11
37	Bob Estes, USA 21	5.36	87	Greg Turner, ANZ 9	3.08
38	Sam Torrance, Eur 9	5.23	88	Robert Gamez, USA 46	3.06
39	Jesper Parnevik, Eur 10	5.23	89	David Feherty, Eur 23	3.02
40	John Huston, USA 22	5.22	90	Jeff Sluman, USA 47	2.99
41	Bruce Lietzke, USA 23	5.22	91	Billy Andrade, USA 48	2.95
42	Miguel Angel Jimenez, Eur 11	5.20	92	Ronan Rafferty, Eur 24	2.92
43	Steve Elkington, ANZ 3	5.18	93	Sandy Lyle, Eur 25	2.91
44	Craig Parry, ANZ 4	5.14	94	Roger Mackay, ANZ 10	2.88
45	David Edwards, USA 24	5.07	95	Lennie Clements, USA 49	2.79
46	Tsuneyuki Nakajima, Jpn 2	5.00	96	David Ishii, USA 50	2.78
47	Jay Haas, USA 25	4.99	97	Fulton Allem, Afr 7	2.78
48	Robert Allenby, ANZ 5	4.94	98	Brad Bryant, USA 51	2.77
49	Mark Calcavecchia, USA 26	4.92	99	Kirk Triplett, USA 52	2.76
50	Rick Fehr, USA 27	4.82	100	Retief Goosen, Afr 8	2.73

POS.	NAME, CIRCUIT	POINTS AVERAGE	POS.	NAME, CIRCUIT	POINTS AVERAGE
101	Kenny Perry, USA 53	2.68	150T	Mike Heinen, USA 73	1.86
102	Rocco Mediate, USA 54	2.67	152	Sven Struver, Eur 38	1.85
103	Donnie Hammond, USA 55	2.63	153	Hajime Meshiai, Jpn 13	1.83
104	Tsukasa Watanabe, Jpn 4	2.62	154	Mike Harwood, ANZ 16	1.83
105	Jay Don Blake, USA 56	2.59	155	Jose Coceres, SAm 3	1.83
106	D.A. Weibring, USA 57	2.59	156	Gabriel Hjertstedt, Eur 39	1.82
107	Jose Rivero, Eur 26	2.59	157	Howard Twitty, USA 74	1.81
108	Peter Mitchell, Eur 27	2.58	158	Gary Hallberg, USA 75	1.79
109	Blaine McCallister, USA 58	2.56	159	Anthony Gilligan, ANZ 17	1.77
110	Fred Funk, USA 59	2.55	160	Mike Standly, USA 76	1.77
111	Yoshinori Mizumaki, Jpn 5	2.55	161	Paul McGinley, Eur 40	1.75
112	Michael Clayton, ANZ 11	2.53	162	Bob Lohr, USA 77	1.74
113	Mark Brooks, USA 60	2.53	163	Russell Claydon, Eur 41	1.71
114	Steve Pate, USA 61	2.52	164	Kiyoshi Murota, Jpn 14	1.71
115	Wayne Grady, ANZ 12	2.41	165	Stephen Ames, SAm 4	1.71
116	Masahiro Kuramoto, Jpn 6	2.39	166	Billy Mayfair, USA 78	1.69
117T	Keith Clearwater, USA 62	2.36	167	Dave Barr, Can 1	1.69
117T	Robert Karlsson, Eur 28	2.36	168	Paul Curry, Eur 42	1.68
119	Hal Sutton, USA 63	2.31	169	Des Smyth, Eur 43	1.68
120	Steven Richardson, Eur 29	2.30	170	Ian Baker-Finch, ANZ 18	1.68
121	Hsieh Chin Sheng, Asa 2	2.30	171	Tom Purtzer, USA 79	1.67
122	Frankie Minoza, Asa 3	2.27	172	Wayne Levi, USA 80	1.66
123	Peter Jacobsen, USA 64	2.26	173	Masayuki Kawamura, Jpn 15	1.66
124	Eiji Mizoguchi, Jpn 7	2.25	174	Jamie Spence, Eur 44	1.64
125	Patrick Burke, USA 65	2.24	175	Bruce Vaughan, USA 81	1.63
126	Glen Day, USA 66	2.21	176	Peter Fowler, ANZ 19	1.63
127	Joey Sindelar, USA 67	2.21	177	Hideki Kase, Jpn 16	1.63
128	Carlos Franco, SAm 2	2.19	178	Peter Hedblom, Eur 45	1.63
129	Greg Kraft, USA 68	2.18	179	Lanny Wadkins, USA 82	1.61
130	Russ Cochran, USA 69	2.18	180	Paul Moloney, ANZ 20	1.60
131	Jim McGovern, USA 70	2.16	181T	Eduardo Herrera, SAm 5	1.60
132	Terry Price, ANZ 13	2.09	181T	Johnny Miller, USA 83	1.60
133	Steve Stricker, USA 71	2.09	183	Mark Davis, Eur 46	1.60
134	Katsuyoshi Tomori, Jpn 8	2.09	184	Shigeki Maruyama, Jpn 17	1.59
135	Bradley Hughes, ANZ 14	2.08	185	Lucas Parsons, ANZ 21	1.58
136	Pierre Fulke, Eur 30	2.06	186	Miguel Angel Martin, Eur 47	1.57
137	Chen Tze Chung, Asa 4	2.02	187	Mats Lanner, Eur 48	1.57
138	Paul Broadhurst, Eur 31	1.99	188	John Bland, Afr 9	1.55
139	Katsunori Takahashi, Jpn 9	1.98	189	De Wet Basson, Afr 10	1.54
140	Jim Payne, Eur 32	1.98	190	Wayne Riley, ANZ 22	1.54
141	Hisayuki Sasaki, Jpn 10	1.95	191	Mike Hulbert, USA 84	1.54
142	Jean Van de Velde, Eur 33	1.95	192	Clark Dennis, USA 85	1.54
143	Andrew Coltart, Eur 34	1.95	193	Bob Gilder, USA 86	1.53
144	Phillip Price, Eur 35	1.93	194	Ken Green, USA 87	1.52
145T	Nobuo Serizawa, Jpn 11	1.92	195	Dudley Hart, USA 88	1.52
145T	Gene Sauers, USA 72	1.92	196	Teruo Sugihara, Jpn 18	1.52
147	Gary Orr, Eur 36	1.89	197T	Andrew Oldcorn, Eur 49	1.50
148	Peter O'Malley, ANZ 15	1.89	197T	Wayne Smith, ANZ 23	1.50
149	Isao Aoki, Jpn 12	1.87	199	Paul Eales, Eur 50	1.49
150T	Jonathon Lomas, Eur 37	1.86	200	Craig Warren, ANZ 24	1.48

Detailed Structure For Allocation of Sony Ranking Points

TOTAL RATING POINTS / Pos.	0	2	3	4	5 Asia & SAf Minimum	6-15	16-25 Austr/NZ & Japan Minimum	26-35	36-45 Eur & USA Minimum	46-55	56-65	66-75	76-85	86-95	96-105 Austr & Japan Opens Minimum	106-115	116-125	126-150	151-175	176-200	201-225	226-250	251-275	276-300	301-325	326-350	351-375	376-400	401-425	426-450	451-475 Europe PGA Champ. Minimum	476-500	501-525	526-575	576-625	626-675	676-725	726-775	776-825	Players Championship	MAJOR CHAMPIONSHIPS
1st	2	3	4	5	6	7	8	9	10	11	12	13	14	15	16	17	18	19	20	21	22	23	24	25	26	27	28	29	30	31	32	33	34	35	36	37	38	39	40	40	50
2nd	1	2	2	3	4	4	5	5	6	7	7	8	8	9	10	10	11	11	12	13	13	14	14	15	16	16	17	17	18	19	19	20	20	21	22	22	23	23	24	24	30
3rd	1	1	2	2	2	3	3	4	4	4	5	5	6	6	6	7	7	8	8	8	9	9	10	10	10	11	11	12	12	12	13	13	14	14	14	15	15	16	16	16	20
4th	1	1	1	2	2	2	2	3	3	3	4	4	4	5	5	5	5	6	6	6	7	7	7	8	8	8	8	9	9	9	10	10	10	11	11	11	11	12	12	12	15
5th		1	1	1	2	2	2	2	2	3	3	3	3	4	4	4	4	5	5	5	5	6	6	6	6	7	7	7	7	8	8	8	8	9	9	9	9	9	10	10	12
6th			1	1	1	2	2	2	2	2	2	3	3	3	3	3	4	4	4	4	4	5	5	5	5	5	6	6	6	6	6	7	7	7	7	7	8	8	8	8	10
7th				1	1	1	2	2	2	2	2	2	3	3	3	3	3	3	4	4	4	4	4	4	5	5	5	5	5	6	6	6	6	6	7	7	7	7	7	7	9
8th					1	1	1	2	2	2	2	2	2	2	3	3	3	3	3	3	4	4	4	4	4	4	4	5	5	5	5	5	6	6	6	6	6	6	6	6	8
9th					1	1	1	1	2	2	2	2	2	2	2	3	3	3	3	3	3	3	4	4	4	4	4	4	4	5	5	5	5	5	5	6	6	6	6	6	7
10th						1	1	1	1	2	2	2	2	2	2	2	2	3	3	3	3	3	3	3	4	4	4	4	4	4	4	4	5	5	5	5	5	5	5	5	7
11th							1	1	1	1	2	2	2	2	2	2	2	2	3	3	3	3	3	3	3	3	3	4	4	4	4	4	4	4	4	5	5	5	5	5	6
12th								1	1	1	1	2	2	2	2	2	2	2	2	2	3	3	3	3	3	3	3	3	3	4	4	4	4	4	4	4	4	5	5	5	6
13th									1	1	1	1	2	2	2	2	2	2	2	2	2	2	3	3	3	3	3	3	3	3	3	4	4	4	4	4	4	4	4	4	5
14th									1	1	1	1	1	2	2	2	2	2	2	2	2	2	2	3	3	3	3	3	3	3	3	3	3	3	4	4	4	4	4	4	5
15th										1	1	1	1	1	2	2	2	2	2	2	2	2	2	2	2	3	3	3	3	3	3	3	3	3	3	3	4	4	4	4	5
16th											1	1	1	1	1	1	2	2	2	2	2	2	2	2	2	2	2	3	3	3	3	3	3	3	3	3	3	3	4	4	4
17th												1	1	1	1	1	1	2	2	2	2	2	2	2	2	2	2	2	3	3	3	3	3	3	3	3	3	3	3	3	4
18th													1	1	1	1	1	1	2	2	2	2	2	2	2	2	2	2	2	2	3	3	3	3	3	3	3	3	3	3	4
19th													1	1	1	1	1	1	1	2	2	2	2	2	2	2	2	2	2	2	2	2	2	3	3	3	3	3	3	3	3	4

RATING POINTS

Current Rank of Players	Rating Points
1st	50
2nd	34
3rd	30
4th	27
5th	24
6th	21
7th	20
8th	19
9th	18
10th	17
11th	16
12th	15
13th	14
14th	13
15th	12
16th to 30th	11
31st to 34th	10
35th to 38th	9
39th to 43rd	8
44th to 50th	7
51st to 55th	6
56th to 60th	5
61st to 70th	4
71st to 80th	3
81st to 100th	2
Total Available	825

51st plus all making 36-hole cut in major championships

World Golf Rankings 1968-1994

Year	No. 1	No. 2	No. 3	No. 4	No. 5	No. 6	No. 7	No. 8	No. 9	No. 10
1968	Nicklaus	Palmer	Casper	Player	Charles	Boros	Coles	Thomson	Beard	Nagle
1969	Nicklaus	Player	Casper	Palmer	Charles	Beard	Archer	Trevino	Barber	Sikes
1970	Nicklaus	Player	Casper	Trevino	Charles	Devlin	Coles	Jacklin	Beard	Huggett
1971	Nicklaus	Trevino	Player	Palmer	Casper	Barber	Crampton	Charles	Devlin	Weiskopf
1972	Nicklaus	Player	Trevino	Crampton	Palmer	Jacklin	Weiskopf	Oosterhuis	Heard	Devlin
1973	Nicklaus	Weiskopf	Trevino	Player	Crampton	Miller	Oosterhuis	Wadkins	Heard	Brewer
1974	Nicklaus	Miller	Player	Weiskopf	Trevino	M. Ozaki	Crampton	Irwin	Green	Heard
1975	Nicklaus	Miller	Player	Irwin	Player	Green	Trevino	Casper	Crampton	Watson
1976	Nicklaus	Irwin	Miller	Player	Green	Watson	Weiskopf	Marsh	Crenshaw	Geiberger
1977	Nicklaus	Watson	Green	Irwin	Crenshaw	Marsh	Player	Weiskopf	Floyd	Ballesteros
1978	Watson	Nicklaus	Irwin	Green	Player	Crenshaw	Marsh	Ballesteros	Trevino	Aoki
1979	Watson	Nicklaus	Irwin	Trevino	Player	Aoki	Green	Crenshaw	Ballesteros	Wadkins
1980	Watson	Trevino	Aoki	Crenshaw	Nicklaus	Pate	Ballesteros	Bean	Irwin	Player
1981	Watson	Rogers	Aoki	Pate	Stadler	Ballesteros	Graham	Rogers	Floyd	Lietzke
1982	Watson	Floyd	Ballesteros	Kite	Kite	Pate	Nicklaus	Stadler	Aoki	Strange
1983	Ballesteros	Watson	Floyd	Norman	Langer	Nicklaus	Nakajima	Stadler	Aoki	Wadkins
1984	Ballesteros	Watson	Norman	Wadkins	Nakajima	Faldo	Nakajima	Strange	Kite	Peete
1985	Ballesteros	Langer	Norman	Watson	Bean	Wadkins	O'Meara	Strange	Pavin	Sutton
1986	Norman	Langer	Ballesteros	Nakajima	Strange	Tway	Sutton	Wadkins	Stewart	O'Meara
1987	Norman	Ballesteros	Langer	Lyle	Strange	Woosnam	Stewart	Frost	McNulty	Crenshaw
1988	Ballesteros	Norman	Lyle	Faldo	Stewart	Crenshaw	Woosnam	Calcavecchia	Azinger	Calcavecchia
1989	Norman	Faldo	Ballesteros	Strange	Stewart	Kite	Olazabal	Kite	Woosnam	Azinger
1990	Norman	Faldo	Olazabal	Woosnam	Norman	Azinger	Ballesteros	Stewart	McNulty	Calcavecchia
1991	Woosnam	Faldo	Olazabal	Ballesteros	Norman	Couples	Langer	Price	Azinger	Davis
1992	Faldo	Couples	Woosnam	Olazabal	Couples	Langer	Cook	Kite	Azinger	Love
1993	Faldo	Norman	Langer	Price	Olazabal	Azinger	Woosnam	Montgomerie	Love	Pavin
1994	Price	Norman	Faldo	Langer	Olazabal	Els	Couples	Montgomerie	M. Ozaki	Pavin

(*The World of Professional Golf* 1968-1985; Sony Ranking 1986-1994)

Sony Ranking of Leading Players 1986-1994

Player	1st Ranking	1986			1987			1988			1989			1990			1991			1992			1993			1994		
		April 27	August 31	December 31	April 26	August 30	December 31	May 1	August 28	December 31	April 30	August 27	December 31	April 29	August 26	December 31	April 28	August 25	December 31	April 27	August 30	December 31	April 25	August 29	December 31	May 1	August 28	December 31
Nick Price	52	41	40	54	57	46	47	50	33	41	27	43	38	45	47	38	43	41	24	20	10	8	5	4	4	3	1	1
Greg Norman	6	3	2	1	1	1	1	1	1	2	2	3	1	1	1	1	4	4	5	7	7	5	4	2	2	1	2	2
Nick Faldo	24	26	28	48	62	22	14	12	5	4	3	3	2	2	2	2	3	3	2	2	1	1	1	1	1	2	3	3
Bernhard Langer	1	2	3	2	3	3	3	4	9	15	18	20	16	14	17	14	9	8	7	6	4	6	2	3	3	4	4	4
Jose Maria Olazabal			166	43	46	38	49	49	36	20	8	9	7	9	3	3	2	2	3	6	3	4	7	8	15	7	6	5
Ernie Els																				95	80	40	53	27	20	14	7	6
Fred Couples	42	44	62	73	80	53	46	31	27	19	14	16	15	12	11	11	18	9	6	1	2	2	3	6	5	5	5	7
Colin Montgomerie													162	158	107	81	83	36	36	32	24	20	16	16	14	12	9	8
Masashi Ozaki	96	88	35	23	22	19	18	15	18	11	13	13	12	11	12	17	16	22	30	24	20	15	13	13	12	13	12	9
Corey Pavin	9	11	15	19	11	17	24	45	56	46	63	59	85	91	65	54	30	15	18	18	16	16	19	14	10	10	10	10
David Frost	39	45	37	39	31	21	22	11	12	8	16	14	13	13	18	24	33	52	82	101	92	26	20	15	11	9	8	11
Fuzzy Zoeller	20	16	19	20	26	45	39	56	63	39	44	46	49	55	52	64	42	33	34	42	82	90	80	40	46	18	17	12
Tom Kite	16	15	17	16	19	18	21	20	18	13	5	8	6	10	8	7	11	13	16	26	11	11	6	9	8	11	11	13
Seve Ballesteros	2	1	1	3	2	2	2	3	3	1	1	2	3	3	6	7	13	5	4	5	8	13	14	22	25	41	24	14
Vijay Singh											175	130	87	76	64	76	62	56	77	50	37	38	26	20	16	16	19	15
Ian Woosnam	32	30	32	30	21	16	6	5	7	7	12	6	9	6	4	4	1	1	1	4	5	3	8	7	7	8	13	16
Tom Lehman																				140	115	74	57	47	48	21	14	17
Mark McNulty	67	65	40	21	20	10	9	13	13	18	25	23	31	23	13	9	7	10	12	12	15	19	12	17	17	19	15	18
Mark McCumber	44	42	60	86	102	59	54	27	34	26	31	17	18	18	35	40	55	94	97	105	145	163	99	97	92	105	68	19
Loren Roberts											151	128	105	110	69	59	65	74	88	99	128	104	105	96	107	29	20	20

2. The Year In Retrospect

This was a time of change and challenge on the PGA Tour in the United States. In March, Deane Beman resigned as Commissioner. Twenty years earlier, as a struggling 36-year-old player, Beman had replaced Joseph C. Dey, Jr., as the head of what was then known as the Tournament Players Division of the PGA of America.

The American circuit in 1974 consisted of 43 primary and 14 "satellite" events with a total prize money of $8.3 million. In 1994, the three tours conducted by the restructured, independent PGA Tour — no longer a division of the PGA of America — were the regular PGA Tour, the Senior PGA Tour and the developmental Nike Tour, a total of 123 events and $103 million in prize money.

Tim Finchem was chosen in early May to replace Beman, effective at the end of the month. Finchem, age 47, joined the PGA Tour in 1988 as Vice President for Business Affairs and was promoted to Deputy Commissioner the next year. Those who knew Finchem, who had come from a political fund-raising and marketing background, had little doubt that he would receive excellent reviews, and would soon erase any notion that he was a clone of his predecessor, who never had much success in public relations. While trivial, note was made of Finchem taking a group of players to a Rolling Stones concert. Who could ever have imagined Beman doing that?

The continuing saga of John Daly presented an early test for Finchem, and in late November, came the headache of dealing with a proposed World Golf Tour, as well as an ongoing investigation by the Federal Trade Commission.

Daly began the year under suspension while undergoing alcoholic rehabilitation, and was widely praised for winning his first tournament while sober, the BellSouth Classic. Then Daly made some comments about drug abuse being a problem on the Tour to a tabloid writer before the British Open, which Daly could not verify to the Commissioner. (Perhaps Daly was trying to say he wasn't the only person out there with problems, but the response of the other players was such as that by Curtis Strange, who said, "He should crawl back under the rock he came from.")

Then, in a bizarre week at the NEC World Series of Golf, Daly persisted in hitting into the groups ahead of him until, in the final round, he encountered national club pro champion Jeff Roth and, after the round, Roth's parents as well. It was reported that there were exchanges of harsh words and curses, then the elder Roth wrestled Daly to the pavement outside the clubhouse. Daly said his back was injured, and withdrew from a tournament in Europe. Later, Daly and Finchem agreed that Daly would not play again in 1994.

For five years, the FTC Bureau of Competition has investigated the PGA Tour, considering in particular the Tour's rules regarding participation in conflicting events and releases for televised golf appearances. In August, the Bureau of Competition proposed that the Tour voluntarily eliminate these rules. The Tour refused, and said it planned to pursue the case through the FTC Commission, the courts and even Congress, if necessary, possibly to seek an antitrust exemption.

Then came the announcement of the World Golf Tour proposal, a 1995 series of eight (later six or four) tournaments, each with $3 million in prize money for 40 competitors, the top 30 players on the Sony Ranking and 10 invited players. These tournaments would conflict with existing events, with the players' agreements with the existing tours, and with the tours' agreements with sponsors and television networks.

Greg Norman was at the fore of this group, which included John and Scott, sons of John Montgomery, who has long been a tournament organizer, although the father said he had no role in this venture.

The idea of a world tour has been around at least since the time of Sam Snead and Fred Corcoran, including the primes of Arnold Palmer, Gary Player and Jack Nicklaus. Someone proposes it every 10 or 15 years, and it hasn't happened yet, although I believe it eventually will happen. As proposed, the World Golf Tour will not happen. The concept and execution was unprofessional and, certainly, the person leading the effort should not have been a player.

The organizers made a fundamental mistake. They expected the backing of the world's leading players. They failed to recognize the distinction between the words "support" and "commitment." Lots of people would "support" the idea of a world tour, but no sensible person would "commit" to such a tour if it would jeopardize the other tours or that person's corporate or individual interests. They had the "support" of Fox Television but that was not a "commitment" until all other elements — players, sponsors, venues, dates — were in place.

Despite a worldwide recession, golf has prospered over the past 15 years, and I'm a believer in that saying, "If it isn't broken, don't fix it." Golf works. We have the Royal and Ancient Golf Club and the United States Golf Association at the top, and beneath we have the various PGA organizations around the world. The merits of a world tour should have been discussed first with all of those groups. Instead, the folly of the World Golf Tour was quickly exposed.

While American professional golf awaited the arrival of Tiger Woods, which probably would not happen before 1998, the rest of the world continued to dominate the game. Never before in the history of the modern Grand Slam, starting in 1934 with the creation of the Masters Tournament, had golfers from the United States failed to win any of the four major championships. Spain's Jose Maria Olazabal, who would win four times, took the Masters. Ernie Els of South Africa won the U.S. Open, one of his five victories. Then Nick Price of Zimbabwe, who won seven tournaments for the year, claimed both the British Open and PGA Championship titles.

Those three golfers each earned over $2 million in prize money, as did three others, but none of them were Americans — Masashi (Jumbo) Ozaki of Japan, Greg Norman of Australia and Nick Faldo of England — and Els set a World Money List record with almost $2.9 million. According to the Sony Ranking, there were no Americans among the top six golfers in the world, and only two were in the top 10. The most prominent American golfer of 1994 was the 18-year-old Woods, who became the youngest-ever winner of the U.S. Amateur title before entering Stanford University in the autumn.

The leading American on the PGA Tour was 43-year-old Mark McCumber, who was third on the money list behind Price and Norman, and had three victories including the season-ending Tour Championship. Next on the money list were Tom Lehman and Loren Roberts, who both had passed their 35th birthdays before winning for the first time, and 43-year-old Fuzzy Zoeller, whose best for the year was six second-place finishes, including one in Japan.

It seemed that for every outstanding young American golfer, such as 24-year-old Phil Mickelson, the rest of the world was producing a couple more who were even better, such as 25-year-old Els and 28-year-old Olazabal.

In a *Sports Illustrated* article, Jaime Diaz wrote: "Something is seriously wrong with the top end of U.S. golf. For the last few years I've resisted committing to this position, reasoning that in golf the best view is the long one and that trends shouldn't be defined according to who won the last major. But now that is becoming irrefutable. Non-Americans have won eight of the last 10 major championships, 10 of the last 11 British Opens and six of the last seven Masters. It has been too long since the U.S. had a native star with any staying power."

Meanwhile, we heard once more the PGA Tour's party line that no one will ever dominate golf as some of the great players of the past, because going into the middle 1990s there were so many great players.

That analysis was nonsense.

First of all, the truly great players always rise to the top, outperform and beat down the competition. Furthermore, I think we can seriously question this abundance of great American players the PGA Tour likes to promote. It seems more likely that instead of producing an endless inventory of them, we've developed limitless numbers of very good to average golfers who hang on because of the prize money the PGA Tour has been able to provide.

A man can live quite comfortably by finishing in 20th place, whereas in earlier times he would have been looking for work. Consider this. Excluding limited-field events, in 1994 with a typical tournament with total prize money of $1.2 million, the average for 40 tournaments, a player who entered only 20 and placed 20th in each would have won approximately $320,000. He would have placed about 55th on the money list, and would have come back year after year.

Put the blame first on the American college golf programs for not producing stars. College golf is a team sport which encourages conservative play, and discourages individuals from playing to win. Then, the PGA Tour promotes sustained mediocrity with the all-exempt, top-125 money-winner system. It's a different story elsewhere in the world. Those golfers have become tougher by necessity, are more accustomed to varied conditions, have learned to win and are hungrier than most Americans to succeed.

These, then, were my top five golfers of the year:

NICK PRICE

Event	Position
Lexington PGA Championship	2
ICL International	1
Doral-Ryder Open	T-72

Event	Position
Honda Classic	1
The Nestle Invitational	T-2
The Players Championship	MC
Masters Tournament	T-35
Shell Houston Open	MC
BellSouth Classic	MC
GTE Byron Nelson Classic	T-20
Westinghouse-Family House Invitational	T-5
Southwestern Bell Colonial	1
U.S. Open Championship	MC
Canon Greater Hartford Open	T-33
Motorola Western Open	1
British Open Championship	1
Federal Express St. Jude Classic	4
PGA Championship	1
NEC World Series of Golf	T-10
Bell Canadian Open	1
Alfred Dunhill Cup	T-5
Texas Open	MC
Bridgestone Open	T-4
Tour Championship	T-20
PGA Grand Slam of Golf	2
Franklin Funds Shark Shootout	T-7
Nedbank Million Dollar Challenge	2
Johnnie Walker World Championship	T-12

Little did we know when Nick Price won the 1992 PGA Championship that it was the beginning of a phenomenal streak. Before winning the PGA Championship, Price, who had been a professional golfer since 1977, had won three times in the United States and 11 times worldwide, and had career earnings of $4,215,106. In the next 29 months, Price would play in 70 tournaments worldwide, record 17 victories and 45 top-10 finishes, and earn $6,579,182. He became No. 1 on the Sony Ranking.

"It's weird, a very strange turnaround. I went nearly eight years without winning," said Price, age 37, "and now I can't stop winning."

Price's seven victories this year — resulting in a World Money List total of $2,415,464, second only to Ernie Els — were major titles in the British Open and PGA Championship, the ICL International in South Africa, and PGA Tour triumphs in the Honda Classic, Southwestern Bell Colonial, Motorola Western Open and Bell Canadian Open. That was one more victory than his 1993 total, when he won four times in America and twice in South Africa, and three more than in 1992, when he followed the PGA Championship with two more U.S. wins and one in New Zealand.

At the start of 1994, Price said, "Last year just fueled my desire. It's a result of the 1980s when I was practicing hard and playing hard and just couldn't win. That hardened me. I don't want to back off now. I want very, very badly to win more majors. I've got to make up for lost time."

In the first round of the ICL International, Price shot a career-best, 11-under-par 61, but his year would be most noted for two spectacular putts, both on the 71st hole. He sank a 35-foot, double-breaking birdie putt to clinch the Honda Classic title and — the Shot of the Year — a 50-foot putt for eagle three to win the British Open. In the PGA Championship, Price shot 67-65-70-67–269, 11 under par, led every round and won by six strokes. He shot 64 in the final round to come from seven strokes behind in the Southwestern Bell Colonial, and had a one-stroke victory in the Bell Canadian Open, the result of a two-iron shot to two feet for an eagle on the 16th hole.

It was not Price's most consistent year. After winning in South Africa in January, Price suffered an inflamed left wrist which caused him to miss tournaments in Thailand and Australia after travelling there. He was near the bottom of the list, tied for 72nd place, in his first American start at the Doral-Ryder Open. After winning the Honda Classic and tieing for second in The Nestle Invitational, Price went into a five-event slump and missed the 36-hole cut three times. He would miss two more cuts, for a total of five, after missing a total of only two cuts in 1992 and 1993.

ERNIE ELS

Event	Position
Bell's Cup	T-2
Lexington PGA Championship	4
Dubai Desert Classic	1
Johnnie Walker Asian Classic	T-16
Mount Edgecombe Trophy	T-5
Microsoft Australian Masters	2
The Nestle Invitational	MC
The Players Championship	T-45
Freeport-McMoRan Classic	T-27
Masters Tournament	T-8
Benson & Hedges International Open	MC
Peugeot Open de Espana	T-6
Memorial Tournament	T-45
Volvo PGA Championship	2
Buick Classic	2
U.S. Open Championship	1
Murphy's Irish Open	T-8
Bell's Scottish Open	MC
British Open Championship	T-24
Heineken Dutch Open	T-7
PGA Championship	T-25
Sprint International	4
NEC World Series of Golf	T-26
European Open	T-14
Dunhill British Masters	T-5
Mercedes German Masters	T-2
Alfred Dunhill Cup	T-5
Toyota World Match Play Championship	1
Tour Championship	T-17
Gene Sarazen World Open	1

Event	Position
PGA Grand Slam of Golf	3
Dunlop Phoenix	T-16
Nashua Wild Coast Challenge	T-2
Nedbank Million Dollar Challenge	T-3
Johnnie Walker World Championship	1

In 1994, Ernie Els separated himself from other potential stars in his age group and rose to No. 6 on the Sony Ranking in only his third year in professional golf. Not 25 years old until October, Els not only won a major championship, the U.S. Open, but three other significant tournaments — Dubai Desert Classic, Toyota World Match Play Championship and Johnnie Walker World Championship — plus the unsanctioned Gene Sarazen World Open.

Els also had six second-place finishes in 35 starts worldwide — Bell's Cup, Microsoft Australian Masters, Volvo PGA Championship, Buick Classic, Mercedes German Masters and Nashua Wild Coast Challenge — and set a World Money List record with $2,862,854 — $37,163 more than Faldo won in 1993. "I have won a few bucks this year," he said, "but I don't think of it that way. I think of winning golf tournaments. It's great to win big money, but we play to win the tournaments, and that's the bottom line."

"I think I can reach a higher level," Els said at the year's end. "My driving, iron play, short game, everything can improve. I am a long way from being No. 1 in the world, and it is everyone's dream to be No. 1. Watching Nicky Price play this year, I think I am a long way behind him."

Els first gained serious notice in the early months of 1992, when he won four tournaments, including the notable trio of the South African Open, PGA and Masters events. He won twice more in South Africa later in the year, and significantly, tied for fifth place in the British Open. The next year, Els tied for sixth in the British Open and for seventh in the U.S. Open, and he tied for eighth in his first Masters in 1994. (By the end of 1994, Els had five top-10 finishes in nine major events as a professional. "It is always my goal to do well in the majors," he said. "That is where people really see how good you are.")

After his 1992 victories in South Africa, Els did not win again until late in November, 1993, but his triumphs came at a dazzling pace over the next 13 months. He started by winning the Dunlop Phoenix in Japan, with an impressive four-stroke victory over a strong international field. In January, he shot a course-record 61 in the first round and won by six strokes over another impressive field in Dubai. The U.S. Open title came after a playoff with Loren Roberts and Colin Montgomerie. Els beat Montgomerie again in the final of the Toyota World Match Play. He played his best golf of the year there in a second-round victory over Seve Ballesteros, having 10 birdies and two eagles over 35 holes to Ballesteros' 13 birdies. He won the Sarazen event by three strokes and walked away with the year-ending Johnnie Walker title by six.

JOSE MARIA OLAZABAL

Event	Position
Turespana Open de Tenerife	T-9
Turespana Masters Open de Andalucia	2
Turespana Open Mediterrania	1
The Players Championship	T-14
Freeport-McMoRan Classic	2
Masters Tournament	1
Tournoi Perrier de Paris	T-3
Benson & Hedges International Open	T-34
Peugeot Open de Espana	T-8
Tisettanta Italian Open	T-21
Volvo PGA Championship	1
Buick Classic	MC
U.S. Open Championship	MC
Peugeot Open de France	3
Murphy's Irish Open	T-4
British Open Championship	T-38
Heineken Dutch Open	T-26
PGA Championship	T-7
Sprint International	T-18
NEC World Series of Golf	1
European Open	T-2
Dunhill British Masters	T-16
Trophee Lancome	T-5
Mercedes German Masters	T-2
Toyota World Match Play Championship	3
Volvo Masters	T-8
PGA Grand Slam of Golf	4
Dunlop Phoenix	T-22
Casio World Open	T-3

As 1994 got underway, Jose Maria Olazabal was anxious for a victory. His best in 1993 had been two second-place finishes. He got the win in his third tournament in early March, the Turespana Open Mediterrania, which coincidentally was the last tournament he won in 1992. Olazabal had since fallen from No. 4 to No. 15 on the Sony Ranking. "I have started to see the light," said the 28-year-old Spaniard. "Now I can put the frustration and the bad memories behind me."

What a year it would become. He won the Masters among his four victories, placed fourth on the World Money List with $2,123,795, and finished at No. 5 on the Sony Ranking. He also won the Volvo PGA Championship in Europe, was fourth on that money list with £516,107, and added the NEC World Series of Golf title in the United States, where he was seventh with $969,900 in only eight events.

Olazabal also had four second-place finishes — including a playoff loss in the Mercedes German Masters — and 19 top-10 finishes in his 29 starts worldwide.

In the Masters, Olazabal became the sixth European winner in the past seven years and the ninth since 1980. He had great luck on the par-five 15th hole in the final round, when his five-iron approach shot hung on the bank in front of the green, rather than rolling back into the water, as gravity seemed to dictate it should. He scored an eagle which resulted in his two-stroke triumph. "When you see things like that happen," Olazabal said, "you think maybe it is your time to win."

There is an old saying that you have to lose the Masters before you can win, and if so, Olazabal was due. In 1991, he had taken a seven from just in front of the par-three sixth green, then bogeyed the final hole to lose to Ian Woosnam by one stroke.

COLIN MONTGOMERIE

Event	Position
Dubai Desert Classic	T-15
Johnnie Walker Asian Classic	T-6
Manila Southwoods Philippine Open	3
Kent Hong Kong Open	MC
The Nestle Invitational	MC
The Players Championship	T-9
Masters Tournament	MC
Air France Cannes Open	2
Benson & Hedges International Open	T-14
Peugeot Open de Espana	1
Volvo PGA Championship	T-37
Alfred Dunhill Open	T-3
Honda Open	T-20
U.S. Open Championship	T-2
Murphy's Irish Open	T-24
Bell's Scottish Open	4
British Open Championship	T-8
Heineken Dutch Open	T-4
Scandinavian Masters	T-12
PGA Championship	T-36
Murphy's English Open	1
Volvo German Open	1
Canon European Masters	MC
European Open	4
Dunhill British Masters	T-3
Trophee Lancome	4
Mercedes German Masters	MC
Alfred Dunhill Cup	T-5
Toyota World Match Play Championship	2
Volvo Masters	T-4
Alfred Dunhill Asian Masters	T-4
Nedbank Million Dollar Challenge	T-10
Johnnie Walker World Championship	T-10

Colin Montgomerie was close to having a year to match those of Ernie Els and Jose Maria Olazabal. The burly 31-year-old Scot ran head-on into Els on two of the most important occasions, the U.S. Open and Toyota World Match Play Championship, and was the runner-up both times. But Montgomerie won three PGA European Tour events and led the money list for the second consecutive year with £762,719.

He was eighth on the World Money List with $1,739,349, and improved from No. 14 to No. 8 on the Sony Ranking. He had 21 top-10 finishes in 33 tournaments.

The U.S. Open provided Montgomerie's greatest disappointment, for the second time in three years. In 1992, he placed third after the strong finishes of Tom Kite and Jeff Sluman. This year, he surged into the lead with his second-round 65, fell three strokes behind with 73 in the third round, then finished with 70 to tie Els and Loren Roberts at 279. He shot 78 in the playoff, while Els won in 20 holes after he and Roberts shot 74s. In the World Match Play, Montgomerie beat Yoshinori Mizumaki, Nick Faldo and Vijay Singh before losing 4 and 2 to Els.

Montgomerie's victories were in the Peugeot Open de Espana in May and the Murphy's English Open and Volvo German Open on successive weeks in August. He had excellent shots to the green on the 72nd hole to win the first two, a wedge to two feet in Spain and a four iron to eight for his first title on British soil. The next week, he held off Bernhard Langer, who was seeking his sixth German national championship.

GREG NORMAN

Event	Position
Mercedes Championship	10
Dubai Desert Classic	2
Johnnie Walker Asian Classic	1
Microsoft Australian Masters	T-18
Doral-Ryder Open	T-7
The Nestle Invitational	T-6
The Players Championship	1
Masters Tournament	T-18
MCI Heritage Classic	2
GTE Byron Nelson Classic	T-8
Memorial Tournament	2
Southwestern Bell Colonial	T-56
Buick Classic	T-16
U.S. Open Championship	T-6
Canon Greater Hartford Open	2
British Open Championship	T-11
PGA Championship	T-4
NEC World Series of Golf	T-8
Alfred Dunhill Cup	T-5
Las Vegas Invitational	T-49
Tour Championship	T-13
PGA Grand Slam of Golf	1
Franklin Funds Shark Shootout	T-7
Heineken Australian Open	T-4
Greg Norman's Holden Classic	T-2

The first three months held the promise that this might be one of Greg Norman's best years in professional golf, but it turned out to be just another very good one for the Great White Shark, although few golfers in the world were better.

Norman started the year impressively on the far-flung PGA European Tour, taking second place in the Dubai Desert Classic then winning the Johnnie Walker Asian Classic in Thailand, despite a lung infection which he developed on the trip that sapped his strength. After a 75-70 start in Thailand, Norman finished 64-68 to win by one stroke over a strong field. The victory ended Nick Faldo's 81-week hold on the Sony Ranking, as Norman returned to No. 1 in the world.

Returning to the PGA Tour in March, Norman blistered the Tournament Players Club at Sawgrass in 24 under par — which he called one of his "top three or four weeks of golf ever" — and won The Players Championship by four strokes. His opening-round 63 was a course record, as were his scores for 36 holes (130), 54 holes (197) and 72 holes (264).

His only other victory for the year was in the four-man PGA Grand Slam of Golf. He played well, but not well enough, in the major championships, having a tie for 18th place in the Masters, a tie for sixth in the U.S. Open, a tie for 11th in the British Open, and a tie for fourth in the PGA Championship. He finished the year No. 2 on the Sony Ranking and fifth on the World Money List with $2,117,307.

It's difficult to figure where to rate Jumbo Ozaki, who may well be the best currently active golfer who never won a major championship. The closest he has ever come was sixth place in the 1989 U.S. Open. This year in Japan was the 47-year-old Ozaki's best ever, with seven victories and earnings of over ¥200 million ($2,183,106 for third place on the World Money List). The calibre of opposition in Japan, however, was such that Ozaki was only 13th in Sony Ranking points earned for the year. Ozaki now has 69 career victories and over $10 million in earnings. But Ozaki has not fared very well outside Japan, and his best this year was a tie for 28th in the U.S. Open.

Three of the top six money winners in Japan this year were Brian Watts, David Ishii and Todd Hamilton, Americans who had not been successful on the U.S. PGA Tour, but who found riches there. Watts won five tournaments and $1,406,136. "The money is so much easier to make here, it's not even funny," said Watts, age 28, a former collegiate champion at Oklahoma State. "The quality of the field is so different. It's just not that deep."

Nick Faldo also was conspicuously absent from my list of the five best golfers of 1994. Starting the year No. 1 on the Sony Ranking, Faldo dropped behind Price and Norman on the final list. He won twice, the Alfred Dunhill Open in Europe and the Nedbank Million Dollar Challenge in South Africa. That $1 million first prize — plus $250,000 for a second-place tie in the Johnnie Walker World Championship — pushed his earnings for the year to $2,016,218, sixth on the World Money List. That might have been $62,100 more, but Faldo was disqualified in the final round of the Alfred Dunhill Asian Masters while holding a six-stroke lead, because he thought the tournament was being played under PGA European Tour rules.

The year for Faldo was much the same as 1993, a disappointment after his 1992 campaign with six victories including his fifth major title in the British Open. His coach, David Leadbetter, thinks Faldo's great 1992 record was a factor in his lack of success in 1993 and 1994. "He was hesitant to make changes, even when he got into some bad habits," Leadbetter said. "Now he is making changes again, and it's the best I have seen him swing in a couple of years. I think being passed by Price and Norman in the Sony Ranking will help Nick. All of a sudden, he isn't the one being shot at, he's the one doing the shooting. I firmly believe that Nick hasn't seen his best golf yet." At the year's end, Faldo was successfully experimenting with a cross-handed putting grip.

For 1995, Faldo said he would rejoin the U.S. PGA Tour — along with Els and Mark McNulty — and would play most of the required minimum of 15 events in the early part of the year. The PGA European Tour schedule before late May is not very appealing, and this will enable them to play against a higher level of competition, with better weather, course conditions and practice facilities. The U.S. PGA Tour considered reducing the minimum to 12 tournaments, but decided against it. This pleased the majority of American players, while not greatly reducing European participation. Olazabal, for example, declined but will still continue to play nine or 10 U.S. tournaments with invitations or exemptions.

Otherwise, the PGA European Tour for 1994 was most noted for a long list of two-event winners, including the resurgent Seve Ballesteros and Bernhard Langer, who extended his winning streak to 16 consecutive years, one year short of Ballesteros' Tour record. Other two-time winners were Els, Ian Woosnam, Vijay Singh, Eduardo Romero, David Gilford and Carl Mason. It was also a good year for the large Swedish contingent, with victories by Mats Lanner, Anders Forsbrand and Per-Ulrik Johansson, and a second-place finish in the British Open by Jesper Parnevik.

Langer was second to Montgomerie on the PGA European Tour money list with £635,483 ($1,333,036 for 15th place on the World Money List), and slipped only one notch on the Sony Ranking to No. 4. He won the Murphy's Irish Open and the season-ending Volvo Masters, where he shot 62, among 14 top-10 finishes in 27 tournaments.

Ballesteros won the Benson & Hedges International Open in May for his first victory since 1992, then had a great stretch in the autumn, including a victory in the Mercedes German Masters in a playoff against Els and Olazabal. Two weeks later, he was brilliant for two days of the Toyota World Match Play Championship, having 13 birdies in each match while beating David Frost and losing to Els. He was third in Europe with £590,101 ($1,212,862 for 16th place worldwide) and jumped from No. 25 to No. 14 on the Sony Ranking.

Less noticed, Frost also had a superb year, winning four times, the Canon Greater Hartford Open and the unsanctioned Westinghouse-Family House Invitational in the United States, Lexington PGA Championship in South Africa, and Kent Hong Kong Open. He had 13 top-10 finishes worldwide, maintained his No. 11 Sony Ranking and earned $1,371,889 for 12th place on the World Money List.

The play of Miguel Angel Jimenez was one of the year's biggest surprises in Europe. Jimenez, who went from No. 103 to No. 42 on the Sony Ranking, was fifth on the European money list with £437,403. He won the Heineken Dutch Open and was runner-up in two tournaments. Of no surprise was the European success of Australia's 23-year-old star Robert Allenby, who won the Honda Open and later took the Heineken Australian Open. His Aussie rival, 28-year-old Craig Parry, won the Microsoft Australian Masters. Parry maintained his No. 44 Sony Ranking, and Allenby improved from No. 81 to No. 48.

Any review of the 1994 U.S. PGA Tour should start with those who did not play, most notably Paul Azinger, winner of the 1993 PGA Championship and No. 6 (now No. 21) on the Sony Ranking. In December, 1993, Azinger was told he had lymphoma, a form of cancer, in his right shoulder. He required chemotherapy and radiation treatments, but made an inspirational return for five tournaments, starting with the Buick Open in August.

Not much was expected of Azinger on the golf course, and one of the lingering memories of the year must be his course-record 62 in the third round, and tie for fourth place, in the Johnnie Walker World Championship. "It means a lot to show everyone that I'm capable of doing what I could do in the past," he said. "Now my No. 1 goal for next year is to get on the Ryder Cup team."

Fred Couples began promisingly enough, with three second-places finishes in his first four tournaments. Then, in early March, Couples suffered back spasms while warming up in the Doral-Ryder Open, and did not play again until the Buick Classic in June. In the background was Couples' much-publicized divorce the previous autumn and his mother's death in April.

Couples took another month off after the Motorola Western Open in July, skipping the British Open, and when he came back he responded by shooting a final-round 67 to beat Corey Pavin in the Buick Open. His friend Davis Love III said, "I know he wasn't sitting at home, missing being out on the Tour. I think it was a sign he needed time off." Couples agreed, saying "I didn't miss golf at all."

Late in the year, Couples demonstrated why he was still the PGA Tour's best American player and No. 7 on the Sony Ranking. He won the Lincoln-Mercury Kapalua International, joined Love to become the first team to win the World Cup three years in a row, and claimed the Franklin Funds Shark Shootout with Brad Faxon. That thrust Couples into seventh place on the World Money List with $1,859,689.

Phil Mickelson won the season-opening Mercedes Championship but was injured in a skiing accident in early March — fracturing a femur and ankle — and did not play again until the Southwestern Bell Colonial in late May. His best after that were third place in the PGA Championship and a tie for third in the Las Vegas Invitational.

Mark Calcavecchia was also a skiing victim, injuring his knee in December and limping through two early tournaments before deciding to have arthroscopic surgery. One month later, Calcavecchia shot 65 in the final round and tied for ninth in the Buick Invitational of California, but for the year worldwide he was just as likely to miss the 36-hole cut (eight times) as he was to contend (second or third six times).

Others whose play was interrupted included Steve Elkington, who was out twice for hepatitis and nasal surgery but came back and won the Buick Southern Open. Rocco Mediate played just six tournaments, none after the

U.S. Open, because of herniated disks in his lower back, and Mark Wiebe was limited to nine starts after suffering a broken shoulder in yet another skiing accident.

Mark McCumber, who says he measures his success by victories, not by money, had plenty of both with the best year by an American in professional golf. He won three tournaments on the PGA Tour, including the Tour Championship, to finish third on the money list behind Price and Norman with $1,208,209. He added $250,000 with a tie for second place in the Johnnie Walker World Championship, and had a World Money List total of $1,463,376 for ninth place.

McCumber, who had not won for five years after a back injury, increased his career victory total to 10, and he advanced from No. 92 to No. 19 on the Sony Ranking. His first two victories were in the Anheuser-Busch Classic and Hardee's Classic, two tournaments with relatively weak fields. He beat America's best in the Tour's season-ending event, having a spectacular putt of "45 to 50 feet" to win a playoff against Fuzzy Zoeller, who placed fourth on the Tour's money list with $1,016,804 ($1,419,014 for 10th on the World Money List).

Two of the biggest stories of the year in America were Tom Lehman and Loren Roberts, ages 35 and 39, who had not won a tournament in a combined 31 years. Lehman almost won the Masters and won Jack Nicklaus' tournament, the Memorial. Roberts won Arnold Palmer's tournament, The Nestle Invitational, and went to a playoff in the U.S. Open.

They are friends, and Lehman was introduced to his future wife, Melissa, by Roberts' wife, Kim, at Pebble Beach in 1984. Lehman came to Roberts' press conference at Bay Hill and raised his arms in salute, and walked in the gallery during the U.S. Open playoff. "I wanted to be there for Loren, because he's been there for me so many times," Lehman said. After the Masters, Roberts had left him a note ("Don't get down ...") and left another before the last round at the Memorial ("This is your time ...").

Both earned over $1 million on the Tour, Lehman placing fourth with $1,031,144 and Roberts, sixth, with $1,015,671. And both had come a long, long way. Roberts went from No. 107 to No. 20 on the Sony Ranking, and Lehman, from No. 48 to No. 17. But in many ways, Lehman had come further. Roberts had maintained his Tour playing card since 1983 and had been a top-100 money winner for the previous six years. Lehman had been off the Tour since 1985, until returning and placing 24th and 33rd on the money list in the past two years.

Lehman told a great story to *Sports Illustrated* about his struggles in the intervening years as an international journeyman and mini-tour player, while failing six times in the Tour's qualifying tournament. He recalled an all-night trip home to California, where it started pouring rain, just short of the Arizona border. He saw a budget hotel and drove to the back of the parking lot. He stripped to his underwear, found a bar of soap in his baggage, climbed from his car into the rain, and showered then and there. "I just reeked, but I didn't want to stop and get a hotel room because I didn't want to spend $30 or $40 bucks," Lehman said. "... That pretty much sums it up, where I was just four years ago."

Other good news items of 1994 in America included unexpected victories by former stars Johnny Miller in the AT&T Pebble Beach National Pro-Am and by Hale Irwin in the MCI Heritage Classic, Andrew Magee's popular triumph at Tucson and, among the first-time winners, Mike Springer, who won twice. Corey Pavin backed up a victory in the Nissan Los Angeles Open with consecutive runner-up finishes in the Buick Open and PGA Championship, taking a top-10 place on the money list. Bruce Lietzke continued to roll on, winning the Las Vegas Invitational.

Jeff Maggert, while not winning, had 11 top-10 finishes and was ninth on the money list. Maggert also had a rare double eagle at the Masters. Robert Gamez did not win on the Tour, but was 44th on the money list and had an unofficial victory at Pebble Beach and another win in Japan, his first since the 1990 Nestle Invitational. Curtis Strange, who hasn't won in America since completing his back-to-back U.S. Opens in 1989, finished fourth in the Open, one stroke out of the playoff, and was 41st on the money list. "You accept the fact that you may not be the best in the world ever again," Strange said, "but I've also accepted that I can still contend and still win tournaments here and there."

On the downside, Jim Gallagher, Jr., went from fourth to 51st on the money list; Lee Janzen, from seventh to 35th, and Fulton Allem, from ninth to 109th. Of those from whom we might have expected more, Payne Stewart dropped from sixth to 123rd. Said Stewart, "If you're not thinking properly, you're just not going to beat the guys out here." Mark O'Meara fell from 43rd to 86th, but finished on a positive note, winning the Argentina Open. "This year has been a struggle," he said, "If you don't feel confident, you are going to struggle."

Among the many might-have-beens was the saga of Tom Watson, who finished one stroke behind Miller at Pebble Beach, and who had the lowest scoring average among the players who completed all four major championships. He was a particularly strong contender in the two Opens, tied for sixth in the U.S. Open and for 11th in the British Open.

Watson will always be judged by the standards he set from 1975 to 1984, when he won eight majors, was the leading money winner on the Tour five times and the Player of the Year six times. And he will always remember how abruptly the golden days ended. It was Sunday, July 22, 1984, along the wall behind the green on the Road Hole at St. Andrews, where he over-hit an approach shot and lost the British Open to Ballesteros.

Like Sam Snead, Watson's father's hero, his problem since has been putting. "I've talked about putting poorly too much publicly, and it's created its own momentum," he said. "I'm resigned that it can change. I can change."

Only one American, Calcavecchia, has won the British Open since Watson's heyday. The most notable failure among those whom Americans thought should have become major players has been Davis Love III. In 27 major championships as a professional, Love has yet to even place in the top 10. By comparison, one can't help but think of Ernie Els' record. Love did not win anywhere in 1994, other than the World Cup with Couples, and was 33rd on the money list. He missed the 36-hole cut in the Masters and PGA Championship, and finished 28th in the U.S. Open and 38th in the British Open.

Love admitted he was discouraged. "This year was the first time I was frustrated, knowing I wasn't playing anywhere near as well as I can," he said. At the British Open, Love attended Price's victory dinner, and had mixed emotions. "I was excited for Nick," he said. "On the other hand, I wanted to get as far away as I could. To see up close what it was like to win, being right there with Nick celebrating, made me want it more."

In senior golf, Lee Trevino matched Nick Price's total of seven victories, having six on the U.S. Senior PGA Tour and one in Japan, but had a neck ailment that required surgery in October. That enabled Dave Stockton, who had three victories and played in 32 official events to Trevino's 23, to repeat as the leading money winner with $1,402,519 ($1,446,864 for second place on the Senior World Money List). Trevino earned $1,202,369 for fourth place on the Tour and $1,318,501 for third place on the Senior World Money List.

With some of the older stars fading, and with Jack Nicklaus declining to play regularly, Trevino and Raymond Floyd were the only Senior PGA Tour leaders who were also major stars in their primes. Trevino's victories included the PGA Seniors Championship, when Floyd suffered the year's worst collapse, losing a four-stroke lead with 42 on the final nine holes.

At age 55, Trevino probably doesn't have many years left at the top. "Every year I keep saying that I'm going to cut back, I've got to stop, and it's enough for me," Trevino said. "But when it comes down to it, what else am I going to do? Claudia and I were talking at the breakfast table, and she said, 'You can't wait for '95 can you?' I looked at her and said, 'No.' So here I go again."

Floyd, who was 52 years old in September, won four times in 20 starts and was second to Stockton with $1,382,762, but led the Senior World Money List with $1,632,779, including a victory in the Diners Club Matches with Dave Eichelberger. He won a Senior PGA Tour major title at The Tradition, and won the Golf Magazine Senior Tour Championship on the fifth playoff hole, after shooting 66 to make up a six-stroke deficit to Jim Albus.

A 54-year-old former club pro, Albus played almost every week, a total of 34 tournaments, winning twice, placing second six times and earning $1,237,128 ($1,267,928 for fourth place worldwide). Before joining the Tour, Albus was pro at the exclusive Piping Rock Club in Westbury, New York, where he won two Metropolitan Opens and two Long Island Opens. "I've played more spectacular golf back in the Met Section, but I couldn't sustain it like I have here," Albus said, "and I'm not exactly sure why."

Jim Colbert and Tom Wargo, who won the Seniors British Open, were also over $1 million in official earnings, and other honors included Simon Hobday's victory in the U.S. Senior Open, for a South African double of the Open and Senior Open titles.

Nicklaus played in just six tournaments and won only the opening Mercedes Championship. Said Nicklaus of his game, "People have always said, 'Jack, I wish I could play like you.' Well, now they can." But Nicklaus and Arnold Palmer were teammates in the Diners Club Matches in December, and only two long putts by Dave Eichelberger, partner to Floyd, kept them from winning.

It was a year Nicklaus would like to forget for several reasons, especially because of the reaction to his quotes in a Canadian newspaper that "Blacks have different muscles that react in different ways." Later, in a prepared statement, Nicklaus said, "I have never knowingly or willingly made a statement that is racist."

Palmer would remember most his emotional farewell to the U.S. Open at Oakmont Country Club, near his home in western Pennsylvania, where he and Nicklaus staged a memorable duel in 1962. Palmer received a huge ovation down the 18th fairway, and then was so choked up that he could hardly speak at a press conference. "You never envision what a time like this might be like," he said later. "There's a lot of sports where I don't think you'll see what happened today. In most instances, in other sports, they would have booed me off. They gave me a standing ovation. I thought I could handle it better, but when I think about it, when I look back over the years, a lot of things have happened. And, a lot of thoughts and a lot of memories ... Whew!"

———————

Laura Davies had eight victories — the most by any golfer in the world — spread over five tours, and led the Women's World Money List with a record $1,006,143. The powerful English player won three times on the U.S. LPGA Tour (including a major title in the McDonald's LPGA Championship), twice in Europe, twice in Australasia and once in Japan. But Beth Daniel, with four victories, was the LPGA Rolex Player of the Year on a points system.

Davies also was a major contributor to the strengthening of the Women's Professional Golf European Tour. Last year, with many top players defecting to the LPGA, other players went to Davies with a plea for help. They asked Davies to support a plan to change executive directors, installing Terry Coates, a former marketing consultant with British Airways. In March, 1993, Coates took over and Davies became one of the WPGET's six player directors.

"Without her, we wouldn't have dragged the Tour out of the muck," said Coates, who credited Davies for the Tour's richer television contract and more sponsor support. "I think when she took on the responsibility of a leading player, she took on the mantle, too. I would like to think that made a contribution to the way she has played."

Other standouts included Donna Andrews, winner of the Nabisco Dinah Shore major title and two other tournaments. Patty Sheehan won the U.S. Women's Open, and Martha Nause got the other major victory in the du Maurier Ltd. Classic. Liselotte Neumann of Sweden won twice on the LPGA Tour and three times in Europe, where she led the money list with £102,750. The leader in Japan was Mayumi Hirase, who had ¥69,817,958 and four victories. Jae Sook Won won three times in Japan and once in Australasia, and Ikuyo Shiotani and Ayako Okamoto each won three times in Japan.

3. Masters Tournament

The Augusta National Golf Club course measures 6,925 yards, and whoever would win the Masters Tournament had better be able to handle every lovely, maddening pitch, roll and slope of it. But the 1994 Masters was decided, ultimately, over only 15 inches.

The first 12 inches were the distance between Jose Maria Olazabal's ball and the edge of the pond at the par-five 15th hole. No ball escaped the water from there, but this one did. It clung for dear life, and how it did is best left to magicians rather than students of gravity, staying obediently until Olazabal could make the dramatic eagle that carried him to the victory.

The other three inches were the cumulative distance by which Tom Lehman missed the critical putts that cost him this Masters. When all was said and done, that was pretty much it — the miracle that blessed Olazabal, and the fates that cursed Lehman.

There was Olazabal, himself an anguished Masters runner-up just three years earlier, and working his way out of a hole in this Masters. If the break he got at the 15th defied gravity — like Fred Couples' ball in the 1992 Masters, hanging on the bank at the 12th — well, that's golf, too.

"What can I say?" said Olazabal. "There are no words to express what I feel in a moment like this. I worked hard the last two years to get here. I cannot be a happier man."

Nor Lehman an unhappier one. If he had been able to beg, buy, borrow or steal a putt down the stretch, who knows? "I can accept not winning," Lehman said. "I feel I played well. I'm not ashamed I didn't win. If I can learn to putt a little better under pressure the final day, I'll do OK."

Olazabal, coming from behind, had rounds of 74, 67, 69 and 69 for a 279 total, nine under par in the four sunny, breezy spring days. Lehman, who led Olazabal by one stroke going into the final round, lost by two, totalling 281 on rounds of 70, 70, 69 and 72. Larry Mize, who scored one of the Masters' most dramatic victories with a long chip shot that beat Greg Norman in a playoff in 1987, led the first two rounds and finished third at 282. Tom Kite shot 283 and finished fourth, his 10th top-six finish in 18 Masters.

Olazabal made it the sixth Masters victory by a European in the last seven years. From the first Masters in 1934 through 1979, Gary Player was the only non-American golfer to win. But in the 15 years from 1980 on, this was the ninth Masters to fall into foreign hands. The last American to win was Couples in 1992, and before him, Mize, in 1987.

It was no surprise that on the eve of this Masters, the favorites were, by common consent, Norman, an Australian; Nick Faldo, an Englishman; Nick Price, a Zimbabwean, and Bernhard Langer, a German. No American was mentioned. "But it's pretty hard to say who's American and who isn't," said Norman, seeking his first green jacket. "A lot of us live in the U.S. now, and we're used to playing American courses."

Several of America's best golfers were ailing. Paul Azinger, the 1993 PGA champion, was being treated for lymphoma, a form of cancer, and Couples was out with a bad back. Said Raymond Floyd, "I think when the week is over, without Couples and Azinger, I'm looking for two spots in the top 10 that are going to be vacant. And very possibly the winning position."

Also absent was Phil Mickelson, the young left-hander who won the season-opening Mercedes Championship. He suffered a broken thigh and ankle in a skiing accident earlier in the year.

This Masters figured to have anything but an all-American finish. Norman had been impressive, winning the Johnnie Walker Asian Classic on the PGA European Tour two months ago, and only two weeks earlier running away with The Players Championship with a record 24-under-par score. Price was on a worldwide hot streak, and had just added the Honda Classic. Faldo, a two-time Masters winner, hadn't been on his game, but was due to break out.

Even two rookies were given a good chance — South Africa's Ernie Els and Fiji's Vijay Singh. "I'm in a daze," Els said, on his first visit to Augusta. "It's everything I thought, and better." Singh was trying the usual rookie's solution. "I'll try to treat this as just another golf tournament," Singh said. "We'll see if I can do that."

Olazabal was the leading money winner on the PGA European Tour, a month earlier winning the Turespana Open Mediterrania. He had had difficulty getting started in the Masters, however, and this one was no exception. He shot 74 and was six strokes off the lead. There were 24 players between him and Mize, the first-round leader.

Mize took a quick edge with a four-under-par 68 for a one-stroke lead over Kite and Fulton Allem of South Africa in a starting field of 85 (Doug Ford withdrew after nine holes). These were the only three rounds in the 60s on an Augusta National course that most said was playing the toughest they had ever seen it.

It seemed the Masters officials were trying to protect their course. Players were getting better and better, and so was their equipment. The wind was strong, the pin placements were wicked, the greens were fast. Scott Simpson (74) got a surprise introduction to the greens. His 25-foot putt for a birdie at No. 1 rolled across and off the green. His next shot was a 60-foot chip coming back.

Mize hit only 10 fairways, but logged six birdies, three in succession from No. 6 on putts of 10, five and 11 feet. He fell afoul of the 15th hole, a usually benign par five turned into a dragon with the green hard, the flag planted only 12 feet from the front edge, and the front slope cut short. "The way they've shaved it down there, it looks like a baby's rear-end," Norman cracked. His second shot had spun back into the water, but he escaped with a par.

Norman shot a wild 70 that consisted of six birdies, an eagle on a 12-foot putt at the 13th hole, six bogeys and just five pars. The six bogeys were five more than he made in the entire Players Championship. "Probably the worst I've played in my 14 Masters," he said, "and yet I walk off with 70."

The 15th was the pivotal hole. Nolan Henke made 10, and shot 77. Payne Stewart (78) and Costantino Rocca (79), the first Italian to play in the Masters, each made nine. The biggest victim of the day, though, was Tom Watson. He was four under par and leading the Masters when he came to the 15th. He laid up short of the pond, hit his third over the green, chipped back across and into the water, and finally two-putted for a triple-bogey eight and finished with 70. "It's a humbling game," Watson offered.

The talk of the day was about two-time winner Seve Ballesteros. He missed the greens on all the par-three holes, birdied all the par fives, had nine one-putts over the first 10 holes for one bogey, three birdies, six pars and one miracle — all for 70. The miracle came at the par-three No. 4, where he missed the green to the right, and floated a 25-yard shot over a bunker to a fast green sloping away from him. Floyd, his playing companion, said it would take an extraordinary shot just to stay on the green. Ballesteros put it about four feet from the hole, then made the putt. "That," Floyd said, "was the most fabulous par I've ever seen." Said Ballesteros, "That's the way it goes sometimes."

Some golfers would have welcomed a few pars, Jack Nicklaus among them. Nicklaus, the owner of a record six green jackets, hit only eight fairways and eight greens and shot 78. It was his worst start and his second-worst score in 36 Masters. "Disgusting," he said. His old friend and foe, four-time winner Arnold Palmer, also shot 78, and both were in danger of missing the 36-hole cut.

Kite teed off at 1:34 p.m. and knew it was a tougher Augusta National he would be facing. The early returns were already coming in. "They put some pin placements on us today that I haven't seen." said Kite, playing in his 18th Masters. "But the tougher the course, the better all the top players like it." Kite set the tone for his 69 with a bold par save, holing an 18-foot putt at No. 1 after driving into the deep fairway bunker. Allem, also with 69, made the turn at four under, then hit too much club at the 10th and 11th holes and bogeyed both. "I got greedy," he said. "They were unnecessary bogeys." But he made one of the great bogeys ever at the par-three 16th. He hit his tee shot so badly that it never even reached the pond in front of the green. He still had 101 yards of the 170 yards left, and he scraped out the bogey. "If you can't have fun at Augusta," Allem said, "you have to be dead from the shoulders up."

Olazabal had every right to feel haunted around the par-three No. 6, the hole that cost him the 1991 Masters. He missed the green to the right, hit two pitch shots that came rolling back to him, then popped the next across the green. He three-putted for a crippling seven. He finished second to Ian Woosnam, by one stroke. If the memory troubled him, it didn't show in the first round. He parred No. 6. But he bogeyed the first, 12th and 14th holes, then finished birdie, bogey, par and birdie for his 74. Lehman made the turn at two under par with birdies at Nos. 2 and 7, bogeyed No. 12, birdied the 15th and 16th, then bogeyed the 18th for his 70.

The first-round leaderboard was a cross-section of golf in the 1990s. It showed five Americans: Mize, Kite, Lehman, Floyd and Watson; plus a South African, Allem; a Spaniard, Ballesteros; a Fijian, Singh, and an Australian, Norman. To underline the value of experience, it also showed four former Masters champions — Mize, Floyd, Ballesteros and Watson.

Larry Mize	68	Seve Ballesteros	70
Fulton Allem	69	Vijay Singh	70
Tom Kite	69	Tom Watson	70
Tom Lehman	70	Greg Norman	70
Raymond Floyd	70		

The 36-hole cut was made at 149, five over par. Nicklaus shot 74 for a 152 total. This was only the third time he had missed the cut in his 36

Masters. "I've had a lot of good years here," Nicklaus said. "I can take a bad one." Palmer also missed, with 78–155. Since 1954, the Masters had either Palmer or Nicklaus or both for all four rounds. And now, for the first time since then — neither.

The Europeans also had a tough time of it. Missing the cut were Colin Montgomerie, Peter Baker, Anders Forsbrand and Barry Lane. Five of the past six Masters winners were Europeans and they just about put themselves out of contention. Woosnam shot 73–149, just making the cut. Sandy Lyle had a stroke to spare, with 73–148. Ballesteros, after that wild 70 on Friday, skied to a 76. Langer, the defending champion, who made only two birdies in the first 36 holes, shot 74–148, nine strokes off the lead. Faldo, a two-time champion, just made the cut with 73–149.

An American, Dan Forsman, shot 66, which would stand up as the low round of the tournament. This was a nice, ironic touch. In the final round of the 1993 Masters, Forsman closed to within one stroke of the lead, then took a devastating seven at the par-three 12th. He parred the 12th this time for the second consecutive day, and had six birdies and one bogey in his round. That put him at 140, tied for second place with Norman and Lehman.

Mize, the 36-hole leader at 139, was among those who bogeyed the 12th. He bunkered his seven-iron tee shot, hit out to 10 feet, and two-putted. "Man, what a hole," he said. "If 12 doesn't get your attention, you're not alive." He was leading by two strokes coming to the 18th, but he hit his drive into a bunker and bogeyed for his 71.

Norman missed the first and ninth greens and bogeyed both, but logged four birdies. He dared the nasty 11th and got away with it, firing his approach shot to about 18 inches. Then he lobbed a nine iron to a foot at the 17th, and shot 70–140. "Anybody within six or eight shots has got a chance," Norman said.

That included Lehman. He shot 70 for a share of second place at 140. Lehman was remembered, if at all, as one who took a run at the 1993 Masters title and tied for third place. "I'm not much of an attention-getter," he said, "but I do enjoy people respecting my game." Respect was coming to the likeable man who had known near-penniless struggles on mini-tours and overseas. Lehman, 35, played the PGA Tour from 1983 through 1985 but lost his playing card. He regained it with three victories on the developmental Hogan (now Nike) Tour in 1991, and had since won more than $1.2 million but no tournaments.

Lehman missed the greens at No. 5 and No. 10 and bogeyed both. His four birdies were classic Masters stuff. He birdied three of the par fives — two putts from long range at the second, eighth and 13th — and the 12th. "That's Russian Roulette at that hole," he said. "You just pick a club and swing." His choice was an eight iron, to 20 feet. Then he got a hint of what the fates had in store for him two days hence. At the 18th, his 15-foot birdie putt refused to drop. "Half the ball rolled over the hole," he said.

Kite was on one of his Masters forays — but only briefly. Kite took the lead with a birdie at No. 2, and birdied No. 7 to go to six under par. But he misclubbed himself at the 10th and left his approach 20 yards short. Then he needed two chip shots and double-bogeyed. It knocked him out of the lead. Ever get mad, like a 20-handicapper? someone asked. "Oh, I've never gotten mad in my life," Kite said. "Not calm, cool, collected Tom Kite." He also bogeyed the 18th, missing a four-foot par putt, and slipped two strokes off the lead with 72–141.

Watson joined the group at 141 with an interesting 71 that started with a wild tee shot at No. 1 that ended up far to the right, in the trees near the press building, and ended with a three-foot birdie putt at the 18th. It also included an amazing escape at the 15th. He had 162 yards to the green, and hit an eight iron. "I hit a good shot, and I was posing," he said, "and I heard the crowd going 'Oooooh,' and I thought, oh, no, not again." Yes, again. Only this time the ball spun back off the green and into the pond. He lobbed his next shot to 15 feet and holed the putt to save par.

Hale Irwin, bidding to become the oldest Masters winner at age 48, shot 68 but had the wildest round of the day — seven birdies and three bogeys, plus a routine save at the 17th and a brilliant one at the 18th, where he hit what he called a "pitch-and-run three iron, if that's possible." A wide tee shot left him under some trees, 201 yards from the hole. He smacked a low, hot three-iron shot that ended up on the bottom of the green, leaving him with a 40-foot putt that broke four feet. He holed it. "It wasn't an ordinary day," Irwin said.

Els, the big South African in his first Masters, noted that the par-five holes "are where you've got to do your scoring." Accordingly, he birdied all four in his 67–141.

If anything stamped Olazabal as the man to watch in this Masters, it was his second round — the only bogey-free round in the field that day. With the five-birdie 67, he leapfrogged 21 players into a tie for fifth place at 141, two strokes behind Mize. "The greens were firm, the wind was hard to judge and changed by the minute," Olazabal said. "But I was relaxed, and I really enjoyed the round. It was a nice present to myself." He made his first birdie at No. 6, with a six iron to six feet. He birdied No. 7 from 12 feet, saved par from seven feet at No. 10, then birdied the 11th from 18 feet. He two-putted the 15th from 25 feet (the second a six-footer), and holed a 12-footer at the 17th. "The main thing is to hit the ball like I did today," he said. "If I do that, I'll have a chance to win."

It was a day of extremes. Two South Africans suffered the worst collapses, eight strokes. Gary Player missed the cut, going from 71 to 79, and Allem, who tied for second in the first round, made it, despite shooting 77. Fred Funk and Rocca made it with the biggest comebacks, from 79 to 70. Davis Love III missed the cut, hurt by the double bogey at No. 7, where his ball hit the green and spun back down into the fairway. "I've never seen a tournament where luck plays such a huge part," he said. Mike Standly, in his first Masters, made the cut with 69 that included the first eagle at the 15th, while amateur Jeff Thomas' chance to eagle the 13th ended with a mistake. He forgot his putter back at the tee and had to use his two iron. On in two, he four-putted for a bogey.

As Irwin said, it wasn't an ordinary day.

The second-round leaderboard:

Larry Mize	71 - 139	Ernie Els	67 - 141
Dan Forsman	66 - 140	Hale Irwin	68 - 141
Greg Norman	70 - 140	Tom Watson	71 - 141
Tom Lehman	70 - 140	Tom Kite	72 - 141
Jose Maria Olazabal	67 - 141		

Lehman remained a name fairly well wrapped in obscurity. He had been in contention in the final round of the 1993 Masters, and he was on the leaderboard from the start of this year. Still, he was something of an unknown. Olazabal, with a little shrug, settled that matter with some fundamental logic. "I don't know much about him," Olazabal said. "But you don't have to know much about a guy who's shooting seven under par at this place, under these conditions."

All anyone needed to know about Lehman was that on a day that tested the sanity of all 51 players who made the cut, he hammered out a three-under-par 69 to take the lead at 209, seven under par. It was the highest total for the leader after three rounds since Ben Crenshaw's 213 in 1989. Olazabal matched Lehman's 69 and was one stroke behind. No one else broke 70, and only five others broke par, all with 71s — Kite, three behind at 212; Jim McGovern and Ian Baker-Finch, four behind; Floyd, six back, and Jeff Sluman, 11 behind. At the other extreme, the scores ranged crazily — Woosnam, the 1991 champion, 77; 1988 champion Lyle, 78, and Jeff Maggert, the day's worst, 82.

The conditions were maddening. The greens were hard and fast, and the warm Georgia winds, gusting to 20 miles an hour, may have refreshed the spectators, but they drove the golfers crazy. "The problem with the wind," said Brad Faxon, who shot 73 and was eight strokes off the lead at 217, "is that it blows hard when you're on top of the hills, but when you're in the valleys, it sometimes dies down and sometimes doesn't." So how does anyone read them? Faxon smiled patiently. "You have to guess," he said.

Then there were the pin placements. "They were the toughest pins ever," Faldo said. "They put it to the limit. You've got to hit it within two feet of the hole to have a chance. You've got to land it on the number." He didn't. He shot 73, his third consecutive round over par. Lanny Wadkins, making his 22nd Masters appearance, felt like a stranger. "They've got some pins I've never seen before," he said. He shot a 73 that left him 11 strokes off the pace. Big-hitting John Daly also struggled. He shot 77, and his 10-over-par 226 was the fourth-worst total.

The third round crimped some dreams, and ended others.

Mize, whose pursuit of a second Masters title looked promising as he led through the first two rounds, shot 72 and slipped two strokes behind Lehman's lead. Mize bogeyed No. 1 and was two over par through No. 5, but fought back to one under when he holed a 35-foot shot from the back bunker for a birdie at the par-three 12th. He was six under par for the tournament. He parred the next five holes, then two errors cost him a bogey at the 18th — a bunkered drive and a weak chip. "It's a fun week," Mize said, "but you sure use up all your patience."

Norman could say the same. He started the day one stroke behind Mize, bogeyed the sixth, seventh and ninth holes, then came up empty at the sure-birdie 13th. He reached the green in two, but three-putted for a par. He went through the entire round without a birdie, shot 75, and sat six behind Lehman at day's end. He had lost five strokes to the lead.

The third round wrote "The End" to two dreams. Irwin, a three-time U.S. Open champion, never got closer to the Masters title than a tie for fourth place twice in the 1970s. He soared from a second-round 68 to 79 in the third, and plunged from two strokes behind to 11 behind. Also dead were any hopes Dan Forsman had for making good on the promise of 1993. He shot 76.

Also out of the picture: Langer, 72–220; Ballesteros, 75–221, and Faldo, 73–222. Wadkins was also out of it with 73–220, but he left his mark. He went six-two-six from the 13th — bogey-eagle-bogey. (The eagle was a 156-yard seven iron into the cup at the 14th.) "Wild and wooly," Wadkins said. "Just like the rest of the day."

Elsewhere, it was a dogfight. By mid-afternoon, the leaderboard was in gridlock, with Lehman, Norman, Mize, Olazabal and Watson tied for the lead at five under.

Except for a few lapses, Lehman's 69 would have been two or more strokes better. There was the eight iron he hit over the green at the 12th. It cost him his first bogey of the day. He missed a three-foot birdie putt at the 17th, and then bunkered an easy seven-iron approach at the 18th and bogeyed. "I let up," he said. "You can't get ahead of yourself, and you can't get behind yourself. You have to stay in the now."

The "now" turned into a Lehman-Olazabal duel. Olazabal, playing ahead of Lehman, caught him with a brilliant eagle at the uphill No. 8. He fired a three iron 217 yards to the front of the green. The ball ended up six feet from the hole, and he dropped the putt. Then he took the lead with a birdie at the 10th, where he nearly holed his six-iron approach for another eagle. Then the downside. At the 13th, leading by two, he hit his five-iron approach into the water and took his first bogey in two days.

Behind him, Lehman erupted for three birdies in a four-hole stretch. He got the 13th after a cheeky blast out of the left bunker to 10 feet. He birdied the 500-yard 15th after a huge drive and a nine iron 160 yards to 15 feet. A nine iron, 160 yards? Lehman grinned. "It was downhill, downwind, down everything," he said. Then came his most dramatic birdie. He hit a nine iron at the par-three 16th, playing at 170 yards — "Downwind," he said — and faced a 50-foot putt with 20 feet of break. The ball rolled lazily, up over the rise, then down, and finally in. Lehman dropped his putter and raised his arms. He was eight under par and ahead by two strokes. "That was the greatest putt of my life," he said. Then his next putt had to be the worst. He had a three-foot putt for a birdie at the 17th. He missed it.

Olazabal was only one stroke off the lead, and he was feeling great. Even the devilish winds couldn't spoil his day. "We're used to it in Europe," he said. "It's not that bad to play in the wind."

And so as they came to the final round, Lehman was sitting prettier than he ever had in his career. Not only had he never won in the big leagues, this was the first time he had ever led going to the final round.

"There were times when I was walking up to the greens and people were standing and cheering, and I was getting a little water in the eyes," Lehman said. "Who would ever expect a kid from Minnesota to be leading the Masters?"

The third-round leaderboard:

Tom Lehman	69 - 209	Tom Watson	73 - 214
Jose Maria Olazabal	69 - 210	Raymond Floyd	71 - 215
Larry Mize	72 - 211	Loren Roberts	72 - 215
Tom Kite	71 - 212	Ernie Els	74 - 215
Jim McGovern	71 - 213	Greg Norman	74 - 215
Ian Baker-Finch	71 - 213		

The night before the final round of the Masters, Olazabal couldn't sleep and couldn't eat. "The food couldn't get down my throat," he said. The tension eased just a bit when he arrived at Augusta National. There was a note in his locker. "Be patient," it read. "You know exactly how to play this course. You are the greatest golfer in the world. Good luck." A tribute like that coming from none other than Ballesteros, a fellow Spaniard and himself the greatest not very long ago, was inspirational. Olazabal was a little calmer, a little more confident when he stepped out into the warm, sunny Georgia Sunday. He had his work cut out for him. Lehman wasn't the only problem in front of him. There was still the never-say-die Mize.

Kite, who has the best record of anyone who hasn't won the Masters, was turned away again. He started the final round three strokes off the lead. The rejection started at No. 1. He put his approach shot in close, but it spun back off the green. He played well, but couldn't catch up. He shot 71 for a 283 total, and was alone in fourth place. "A lot of could'ves, could'ves, could'ves," he said.

Others had their days, too, of various kinds. Maggert, leading off the final round, scored a double eagle at the par-five 13th, a 222-yard three iron that bounced twice and rolled in. "The people started jumping up and down and yelling so much," he said, "that I thought I was in the lead or something." He wasn't. He tied for last with U.S. Amateur champion John Harris, the only one of four amateurs to survive the cut. Maggert had the distinction of owning just the third double eagle in Masters history, after Gene Sarazen's immortal shot at No. 15 in 1935, and Bruce Devlin's at No. 8 in 1967.

Price hadn't been having a good Masters, and things only got worse. At the 12th, he put three balls into the water and made an eight (shooting 77–298). "Thank goodness there's another 24 weeks in the year," Price said. Mike Standly put two balls in the water, and also made eight. Langer, the 1993 champion, finished deep in the pack at 73–293.

The final round, then, settled into a three-man duel — Lehman, Olazabal and Mize, in that order on the leaderboard, one stroke apart. All three birdied the par-five No. 2, so Lehman was leading at eight under par, Olazabal was one stroke behind him, and Mize, two behind.

The first break in ranks came from Mize. His bogey at No. 5 dropped him three strokes off the lead. Then he charged into a share of the lead with a three-birdie burst — a 15-foot putt at No. 6, a three-footer at No. 7 and a chip-in from 40 feet at No. 8. That put him at eight under par and tied him for the lead with Lehman. Moments later, Olazabal also birdied No. 8, with two putts, and there was a three-way tie.

Mize stumbled at the 12th. His six-iron tee shot flew the green, leaving him a delicate downhill chip to the flag. "A bogey with that pin placement is real easy," he said. And he demonstrated. He flubbed the chip, knocking it only a few feet. He bounced back with a birdie at the 13th, two-putting from 20 feet to tie Olazabal at eight under par.

Then came the first real lurch. Lehman hit his tee shot over the green at No. 12 and took three to get down from the edge. The bogey knocked him out of the lead for good. Mize caught up with Olazabal with a two-putt birdie at the 13th to go to eight under. But Mize couldn't hold on, either. He bogeyed the 14th, three-putting, and Olazabal was alone in the lead, and for good. Mize's last try misfired. He bogeyed the 18th for 71 and took third place at six-under-par 282.

Ironically, Augusta's 15th, which baffled everyone early in the tournament, turned out to be the easiest hole both for the final round, a 4.549 average, and for the tournament, 4.775. It also turned out to be the decisive hole, where Olazabal, with a gift from gravity, made the eagle, and where fate denied Lehman.

At the 15th, Olazabal had 208 yards to the green. He hit a five iron. He watched the ball, his heart in his throat. "I thought it would clear the water," he said. "But when I saw it bounce, I thought, 'I hope it holds up.'" It did, but only because the fates had suspended the laws of gravity. The ball ended up on the bank in front of the green. It clung just about a foot above the water. "When you see things like that happen," Olazabal said, "you think maybe it is your time to win." Lehman couldn't believe it. "All it has to do is get on that grass," he said, "and it will go back in the water."

Lehman watched in disbelief when this one didn't, and then he turned to his own task. He hit a shot truer than Olazabal's. He fired a six iron 15 feet behind the flag. Olazabal, going first, faced a putt of 30 feet, slightly uphill, with a left-to-right break of about a foot. He cooly rolled it in.

Now Lehman had to match him to stay within one stroke. He tapped the ball, and it was tracking dead on for the hole — and then died, just short. Lehman, anguished, twisted and fell to his knees, then face down on the green, slapping the turf with both hands. "I put my whole heart and soul into it, and it just didn't go in," he said later. "It was like a stab in the heart."

Lehman tapped in for a birdie and trailed Olazabal by two strokes, but fate wasn't finished with him yet. At the 16th, where he had holed a huge 50-footer the day before, he had only four feet left for a birdie. He missed by a hair. At the 17th, Olazabal put his second shot over the green, then putted weakly up and over the mound, and then two-putted the last six feet. It was just his second bogey of the weekend. Lehman was on in two strokes, just 15 feet from the hole. A birdie would have tied him with Olazabal. He missed by a hair again. At least he was within one stroke with one hole left. It was his last chance. His strategy was sound, but his execution was flawed.

Lehman draws the ball, exactly the wrong shot for the 18th hole that requires, if anything, the left-to-right fade. The fairway bunkers, about 260 yards out, were well within reach of all of his woods. So for safety and accuracy, he decided to use his one iron, which he hits about 240 yards. His adrenaline was surging, and he didn't allow for the added force. He smacked the one-iron shot 265 yards into the lower bunker.

Second-guessers said he had become conservative. "I don't look at it as being conservative," he said. "The way the wind was blowing, I've got to hit an absolutely perfect drive to keep it in the fairway. I'm a right-to-left player. If I had to do it again, I'd hit the one iron. I'd just aim it further right." His lie in the bunker was not ideal, and his seven-iron shot was 30 yards short of the green. He bogeyed for a 72–281.

Olazabal had hooked his approach into the gallery above the hole, but his exquisite short game spared him the ignominy of winning the championship with a bogey. He chipped to within seven feet and salvaged the par for 69 and a two-stroke victory.

4. U.S. Open Championship

With a foreign golfer winning the Masters once again, speculation about whether or not an American could salvage his own national championship rose rather quickly as the United States Open Championship approached. It seemed probable one would, because through all the continued success of Europeans, Zimbabweans, South Africans and Australians in the other three major championships, when it came to the U.S. Open, American golfers had held firm. No foreign-born golfer had won the U.S. Open since Australia's David Graham in 1981, and only two others had won it since Ted Ray, an Englishman, in 1920. Gary Player of South Africa had broken the spell by winning the 1965 Open, and Tony Jacklin of England followed him, winning five years later.

There had been threats, certainly, but no victories.

Then along came Ernie Els, a tall and lanky, young South African. Just 24 years old and brimming with potential, Els became the seventh non-American-born U.S. Open champion since the end of the First World War. Four of those seven — Jim Barnes (1921), Cyril Walker (1924), Willie Macfarlane (1925) and Tommy Armour (1927) — had become citizens by the time they won the championship.

Els won in a playoff that included Colin Montgomerie of Scotland. Loren Roberts, a Californian, was the only American in the group. All three shot 279, five under par at the Oakmont Country Club on the outskirts of Pittsburgh. Els won with a par four on the second extra hole of the playoff after both he and Roberts had shot dismal scores of 74 over the scheduled 18 holes. Montgomerie had played so badly, he wasn't a factor after the first six holes and shot 78.

With four consecutive rounds of 70, Curtis Strange took third place, followed by John Cook, at 282. Tom Watson followed one stroke behind, at 283, along with Greg Norman and Clark Dennis, a 28-year-old Texan in his first year on the PGA Tour.

Lee Janzen, the 1993 Open champion, and Spain's Jose Maria Olazabal, who had won the Masters, missed the 36-hole cut, along with both Nick Faldo and, even more of a surprise, Nick Price, who played such wonderful golf through most of the year.

As the 1994 Open unfolded we were captivated by the probability we were watching the last gasp of the past and the awakening of the future, for while in the end the Open was won by Els, in the beginning it was monopolized by Watson, Jack Nicklaus and Hale Irwin, whose times had surely ended by then.

In their hearts the galleries must have known their old heroes wouldn't hold up through all four emotionally draining rounds, but simply to see their names atop the leaderboard delighted them and ignited the tantalizing prospect they might stay in the fight to the end. They couldn't of course; it was simply too much to ask. Nicklaus, who was 54 when the Open began, opened with 69 and 70, leaving him just three strokes off the lead at the halfway point; Watson opened with 68, which led, then slipped to 73 in the second, and Irwin, with two 69s, held second place, two strokes behind Montgomerie after 36 holes.

It was simply too much to ask for all three to continue playing at this level, and in the end they yielded to younger men. Nevertheless, they gave the galleries a thrill while they lasted. After his sensational opening, Nicklaus had no more to give, shot 77 and 76 in the last two rounds, and fell into a tie for 28th place. Irwin hung in the battle until the fourth round, when he shot 78 and dropped to a tie for 18th place.

Watson, who at the age of 44 was having a revival of spirit during 1994, hung in almost to the finish, but in the end he slipped to 74 in the closing round. Still, with 283, he tied for sixth place, just four strokes behind the leaders. A month later he was still playing at the top level and once again threatened to win the British Open.

There had been other championships where the past and the future have sharply defined themselves, and Els most certainly represented the future. He became the youngest Open champion since Jerry Pate won in 1976 when he was just 22, and he was just the eighth champion in his 20s since Nicklaus beat Arnold Palmer in 1962. It could hardly be called a trend, but Els was also the second consecutive Open champion in his 20s; Janzen won the 1993 Open at 28.

Like any champion, Els had standards most of us couldn't quite grasp. In the post-playoff interview with the press, he told of his introduction to the game by his father, a low-handicap amateur. Analyzing his own progress, he said, "I wasn't any good at all until I was 13 and won a pretty good junior tournament, and then came over here to San Diego and won the 13-14-year age group in the Junior World Championship." A year later, at 14, he lowered his handicap to scratch. By his reckoning, then, a golfer has accomplished nothing until he wins a championship.

That Els became only the seventh non-American-born player to have won the U.S. Open in 75 years seemed insignificant in the international flavor the game had taken on in the 1980s. Of the 18 major championships that had been played in the 1990s, Americans had won only seven, four of them U.S. Opens, two PGA Championships and one Masters. British golfers had won four, Australians three, and Zimbabwe, South Africa, Germany and Spain accounted for the other four.

Els, the latest of the international brigade to rise to the top of championship golf, first surfaced in 1992, winning six tournaments in South Africa. At the 1992 British Open, Els lit up the Muirfield scoreboard by opening with 66, and eventually placed fifth, seven strokes behind Faldo. While his opening score attracted interest, he held it with his length. He is very long, a quality that always draws a gallery. On some holes he drove farther than John Daly, who had amazed the world with his Brobdingnagian drives.

Ernie had earned his place in the Oakmont field by placing seventh at Baltusrol in 1993, seven strokes behind Janzen. He was especially impressive over the last two rounds, when he shot 68 and 67, very good scores under the circumstances, since this was, after all, his introduction to U.S. Open conditions.

In the autumn of 1993, Els won his first tournament outside South Africa with a four-stroke victory at the Dunlop Phoenix in Japan. The list of five runners-up was impressive: Jumbo Ozaki, Tommy Nakajima, Fred Couples,

Vijay Singh and Barry Lane. To start 1994, Els won for the first time on the PGA European Tour at the Dubai Desert Classic against a field that included all the European stars plus Norman and Price. He shot a course-record 61 in the first round, and led by five, six and eight strokes before winning by six over Norman with a 268 total, 20 under par.

Els had also placed eighth in the Masters earlier in 1994, another impressive performance under the pressures of a major championship. The Masters had been his fourth consecutive tournament in the United States, and his only first-class finish. He had missed the cut at The Nestle Invitational in Orlando, tied for 45th in The Players Championship, then improved to a tie for 27th in the Freeport-McMoRan Classic in New Orleans before coming to Augusta.

By the time of the Open, Els had hopscotched across the Atlantic five times. He began the year playing in Europe, flew to the United States for that string of four straight tournaments, skipped back to Europe for two more, flew back to Columbus for the Memorial, went back for the Volvo PGA Championship, then returned to the States for the Buick Open at Westchester, New York. He made those last three crossings within four weeks.

Rather than tiring him, this rather frenzied schedule seemed to inspire Els. After playing dull golf in the Memorial, he flew back to England, shot 272 at Wentworth and placed second to Olazabal in the Volvo PGA Championship, and after taking a week off shot 271 at Westchester and came in second to Janzen, who had temporarily revived after a disappointing first half of the year. Clearly Els was playing at the peak of his game and should have surprised no one by winning.

No one, though, had come into the Open with better credentials than Olazabal, who had played well throughout the year. He had won both the Masters and the Volvo PGA Championship, two of the biggest tournaments he plays, and in addition won the Turespana Open Mediterrania in his native Spain. He had also had two second-place finishes, first in the Turespana Masters Open de Andalucia and later in the Freeport-McMoRan Classic the week before the Masters. He returned home to Europe after Augusta, then came back in time for the Westchester.

Unlike Els, though, Olazabal had a disquieting time at Westchester. With rounds of 76 and 75, he missed the 36-hole cut and followed up with just as bleak an effort at Oakmont. With rounds of 76 and 74, he missed the cut.

Olazabal was not alone, though. Price, who at the time played the game better than anyone, failed abysmally, and so did Faldo. On the other hand, the championship saw the revival of both Seve Ballesteros and Watson, the first truly first-class effort by Strange in a good while, and the continued excellent golf of Norman.

All of this was played out over as testing a course as we have in the United States. Set in the rolling hills of western Pennsylvania, stretching 6,946 punishing yards, Oakmont might not be the best course we can offer in terms of strategic concepts and glorious surroundings, but it is certain that nowhere is there a more brutal test. Its greens are notoriously fast, usually the fastest the players ever see, and its rough has always grown thick and dense. Johnny Miller, who won the 1973 Open at Oakmont with his glorious final round of 63, calls it America's toughest course.

Adding to the normal difficulties, a heat wave had settled over the region the week of the Open. Temperatures lingered around 100 degrees, approaching records on some days, breaking them on others. The official temperature was listed at 97 on Thursday, the day of the first round, but it seemed hotter at Oakmont, and indeed became unbearable for 320-pound Chris Patton, the 1989 U.S. Amateur champion. After taking four putts on the seventh, Patton struggled through the eighth, then walked off the course, too exhausted to go further. Feeling sick and dizzy, Patton was taken to an emergency first aid station and given fluids.

With such high temperatures and correspondingly high humidity readings, we might have expected the older players to be affected most, especially with rounds taking more than five hours. Evidently the older men had lost little of their stamina, though. No one knew quite what to expect when Nicklaus started, particularly since he hadn't shot a round in par in a PGA Tour event all year and had missed the cut in all six he had entered. Asked about the condition of his game, Jack described it as "Absolute rubbish."

Others agreed. Irwin played a practice round with him on Wednesday and estimated he couldn't have broken 85 or 90. "He was just playing horribly," Irwin said. Something happens to Nicklaus, though, when he approaches one of the year's important events. "My game elevates," he explained, "especially my mental game."

Par is a good score on any Open course. Starting at 9:40 in the morning, paired with Miller and Larry Nelson, a grouping that sent the winners of the last three Oakmont Opens off together, Nicklaus reeled off five consecutive pars, giving hope to most of his fans, but then Jack had a glitch. He left his five-iron tee shot short of the sixth, a devilish par three of just under 200 yards, and bogeyed. Two holes later, though, on the eighth, a 245-yard par three that gave up only eight birdies all day, Jack rifled a glorious two iron within three feet of the hole and birdied. Back to even par.

He stood near the top of the leaderboard then, for others were starting off better, but while they faded, Nicklaus finished with a miracle birdie. A three wood from the tee and a five iron from the fairway left him perhaps 40 feet from the cup. He tried to do nothing more than roll his ball close, but it slipped into the proper groove and dived into the cup, giving him a score of 69, two under par.

As the putt fell, the gallery roared. Nicklaus dropped his putter, rolled his eyes, and looked heavenward, from whence the gift had come.

At about this time reporters scrambled to find if Nicklaus might have been the oldest man ever to lead the U.S. Open. He had turned 54 in January; could he be the oldest leader? Perhaps, but no one could be certain.

While his round filled his followers with hope, Nicklaus had reservations. He had been down this path before, opening the 1991 Masters with 68 before slipping into a tie for 35th place at the end, and shooting 69 in the first round a year later before falling to 42nd place. A realist, Nicklaus said, "It will surprise me if I can keep my game together for four days."

Despite the appalling pace of play, Nicklaus had almost finished when Watson teed off at one o'clock, grouped with Ian Woosnam and Larry Mize. Looking at the scoreboard, Watson saw Nicklaus' name up high and told himself, "No reason why Watson can't do it if Jack can do it."

At this stage of their lives, though, Watson had more in his favor than Nicklaus. For one thing, at 44 he was 10 years younger. For another, he had been playing quite well lately, placing second to Miller at Pebble Beach early in the season, following with a sixth-place finish in Los Angeles the following week, and taking eighth place in Orlando a month later. He had also tied for 14th place in The Players Championship and finished 13th at the Masters. Where Nicklaus hadn't ever threatened to break 70 all year, Watson had played 11 rounds in the 60s.

He had also played quite well in past events at Oakmont, placing second to Nelson in the 1983 Open and losing a playoff to John Mahaffey in the 1978 PGA Championship. Before turning professional, Watson had tied for fifth place in the 1969 U.S. Amateur at Oakmont, beaten by 10 strokes by Steve Melnyk.

Assessing the reason behind his improved play during 1994, Watson admitted, "Nothing is a substitute for having confidence in your swing. That is basically the reason why I am playing pretty well."

Never one of the great drivers, when he played at the top of his game during the middle 1970s to 1980s, Watson relied on his putting and on the little chips and pitches that can save a round. He played the first round like the old Watson and acknowledged that, "I turned 71 into 68 with some great saves. This is a very penal course. You have to make some good shots around the greens."

As he began, though, Watson looked a trifle shaky. He set himself up with birdie opportunities on both the first two holes, but he missed from 12 feet on the first and from four feet on the second. Then he overshot the third green, and suddenly everything changed. He chipped to two feet and saved par, then went for the green of the fourth hole with his second shot, found a bunker, but saved a birdie with an 80-foot bunker shot within three feet. Another good bunker shot saved a par three at the sixth, and after missing the seventh green he chipped in for another birdie.

Out in 34, he missed the 10th green but once again saved himself with a chip to 15 feet and a breaking putt that fell, and made his final save on the 12th, a long par five of 598 yards, the second longest hole on the Open rota (at 630 yards, Baltusrol's 17th is the longest). Short of the green with his third, Watson faced the same kind of shot he had played in the 1969 Amateur, a chip with about 30 feet of break. He played another delicate shot to six feet and once again holed the putt.

A final birdie at the 17th, an uphill par four of just 315 yards, and then a safe four at the last and Watson had his 68, three under par and just one stroke short of the best opening score ever in an Open at Oakmont.

A few minutes later Irwin played the last five holes in two under par and tied Nicklaus at 69, and at the end of the round they in turn were caught by Frank Nobilo, a New Zealander, and by Els, who had played the first 10 holes in two over par and the last eight in four under to salvage his 69.

Strange might have caught Watson except for some indecision on the final hole. Playing as well as he had in a long time, Strange had covered the first 17 holes in three under par, but he pushed his drive into the heavy rough on the 18th, then wavered between hitting a six iron or seven iron. As he said later, the club didn't matter. Long strands of grass whipped around the clubhead as he swung into the ball, the face closed, and the ball squirted left into a bunker. His third, played from sand, pulled up short, he chipped to about 15 feet, and took two putts. Instead of a par four and 68, he made six

and shot 70, one under par.
The first-round leaderboard:

Tom Watson	68	Jumbo Ozaki	70
Jack Nicklaus	69	Curtis Strange	70
Ernie Els	69	Scott Verplank	70
Frank Nobilo	69	Kirk Triplett	70
Hale Irwin	69		

The weather continued uncomfortably hot and humid for the second round, but the heat and the stifling humidity had no effect on scoring. Where only five men had broken 70 in the first round, 16 shot in the 60s in the second. At the end of the day, 14 players were under Oakmont's par of 142, and 22 men stood within six strokes of the lead.

Seldom had Oakmont been treated so harshly as it was this day. Montgomerie, Cook and David Edwards shot 65s, Steve Pate shot 66, five others shot 68 and seven more shot 69. An overnight storm had dumped half an inch of rain on Oakmont and softened the normally hard greens, which helped with the scoring, but when a morning fog caused a 10-minute delay at the start of the second round, it seemed certain that for the second consecutive day the entire field wouldn't finish. Six groups had failed to finish the first round, and six more were left on the course when the USGA stopped the second round a minute or two before eight o'clock Friday evening. They would have to finish at seven o'clock the following morning.

While the general level of scoring fell, not everyone bettered his performance from the first round. Watson, for example, played even better shots than he had on Thursday and yet got little from it. He missed only four fairways on driving holes, one fewer than he had in the first round, and he hit 15 greens, three more than in the first. Yet, where he had shot 68 on Thursday, he slipped to 73 on Friday and plunged to 11th place.

Following his opening 69 with another solid round of 70, Nicklaus clung to a share of fifth place, and Irwin, 49 years old then, continued to play as if he had shed 10 years. Out in 32, three under par, he looked as if he might take over the lead, but a double-bogey six on the 10th and a bogey six on the 12th nearly ruined his day. Recovering, he played the last six holes in one under par, climaxed by a birdie on the 18th, and earned another 69, giving him 138 for 36 holes.

With his blistering 65, Montgomerie took over first place at 136 and moved two strokes ahead of Irwin, Cook and Edwards. Others had joined the hunt by then. With 68, Jeff Maggert had tied Nicklaus at 139, and Nobilo, Pate, Strange and Els each had 140.

Montgomerie had been threatening to win major titles for some time. After a distinguished amateur career that saw him represent Britain in two Walker Cup matches and two World Amateur Team tournaments, he had turned to professional golf in 1987. Four years later he tied Ballesteros in the Volvo PGA Championship, but Ballesteros beat him on the second hole of the playoff with a marvelous 200-yard five iron within three feet of the second hole at Wentworth. To his credit, Montgomerie didn't wilt, even though he had missed the green. He nearly holed his chip that would have matched Seve's birdie.

The following year he shot 70 in the U.S. Open's windswept final round at Pebble Beach, the best score of the day, and finished third, two strokes behind Tom Kite and one behind Jeff Sluman.

He had been a model of consistency at Oakmont so far. In two rounds he had hit 18 fairways, not as many as Watson, who had hit 21, but both men had hit 27 greens. Montgomerie had reached 14 of his in the second round, but he had left himself so close he could putt on two of those he missed.

Out in 33 by holing birdie putts from 10 feet on the second and from five feet on the third, bogeying the eighth, then holing out from a bunker for an eagle three on the ninth, Montgomerie picked up another birdie on the 11th by holing from 20 feet, and still another on the long 12th, where a driver settled so deeply into the rough he had to chop his ball out with a five iron. A sand wedge pulled up 10 feet from the hole and the putt fell. Five under now, Montgomerie ran off five pars, then laid a seven iron 10 feet from the cup on the 18th and holed the putt. Thinking of his 65, Montgomerie said, "That's as good as I can do. That is about my limit — and a lot of people's limit."

By dropping the low score to 136, Montgomerie caused a few players to miss the cut. Janzen was among them. Practically shot out of the Open with his opening 77, Janzen snapped back with 71 in the second round, and with his 148 he thought he might finish within 10 strokes of the leader, which would keep him in the Open. Montgomerie's 65 ruined that hope, and Janzen was eliminated.

He wasn't alone. Price shot 148 as well, along with Faldo, who slipped to 75 in the second round; Nelson, the winner of the last previous Oakmont Open in 1983, and Mahaffey, who had won the 1978 PGA Championship there. Others who missed the cut included Payne Stewart, who had won the 1991 Open and placed second to Janzen in 1993; Olazabal; Corey Pavin, who had beaten Faldo in the final match of the Toyota World Match Play Championship the previous October; Miller, whose 63 in the final round of the 1973 Open remained an Oakmont landmark, and above all Palmer, who had decided this would be his last Open.

Everyone knew Arnold would not survive the cut, which fell at 147, five over par. He had opened with 77, and as it turned out would have needed 70 to survive. He lost any slim hope he had when he bogeyed both the third and fourth holes and went out in 37. Now he would need 33 to make it. No one truly believed he could do it, but no one was quite prepared for such a complete collapse of his game as they saw. It was a grim fadeout for one of the finest and most influential players the game has known. He parred only two holes on the second nine, bogeyed six and double-bogeyed the 17th. He had staggered home in 44 and shot 81. At 158, he missed the cut by 11 strokes.

None of this mattered. The closer he moved toward the final green, the bigger his gallery grew, applauding every move no matter how badly he played the shot. When he finally reached the 18th hole, the crowd stood five and six deep along the ropes, and as he walked that final long walk, they cheered and applauded every step.

His eyes glistening with tears, Palmer took off his straw hat and waved to the crowd as he walked, and as he stepped onto the front of the green, he bowed slightly.

After three-putting — his fourth three-putt green on the home nine — he waved once more to the gallery, then disappeared into the scorer's sanctum to check and sign his scorecard. A few minutes later, his voice wavering and cracking with the emotion of the moment, he could barely speak over national television.

He struggled to say, "It's been 40 years," but then his voice broke and he couldn't finish the sentence. Gathering himself once more but still choking over his words, he went on, "When you walk up the 18th and get an ovation like that ... I guess that says it all." Then he excused himself.

In the big press tent he faced the same crowd he had faced for more than 40 years, but now it was different. This would be his last press interview at a U.S. Open. He sat in front of the reporters, some of whom had seen him win many times, and tried to talk once more.

"I think you all know pretty much how I feel," he said. "It's been 40 years of work, fun and enjoyment."

Someone asked if he could name his greatest thrill. His eyes still glistening, Palmer said, "The whole experience." He paused to collect himself again, then again with a quaking voice muttered, "I haven't won all that much, I won a few tournaments, I won some majors. I suppose the most important thing is the game has been so good to me."

His emotions welling inside him, he lowered his head and covered his face with a towel, hoping to hide the tears. Then he said, "I think that's all I have to say."

He stood and walked toward an open seam in the tent, turned for a moment as the press corps stood and applauded, waved once more, then stepped out.

The second-round leaderboard:

Colin Montgomerie	65 - 136	Jack Nicklaus	70 - 139
Hale Irwin	69 - 138	Frank Nobilo	71 - 140
John Cook	65 - 138	Steve Pate	66 - 140
David Edwards	65 - 138	Curtis Strange	70 - 140
Jeff Maggert	68 - 139	Ernie Els	71 - 140

Although he had won it only once, Palmer had meant as much to the Open as any man who ever lived. Beyond that, even, he had meant more to golf than any player of his time. Now his Open career was over, and the game was left to younger men.

One of those was Els, 40 years younger than Palmer's 64 years. Playing clubs that no one would have believed possible when Palmer played in his first Open back in 1953, again at Oakmont, Els shot 66 in the third round and climbed from a tie for seventh place into a clear two-stroke lead on a day when Oakmont found itself under siege. Good as it was, Els' 66 wasn't the best score of the day. Roberts, a Californian just a week or so short of his 39th birthday, threatened the Open's scoring record by shooting 64 and jumping from 35th place into a tie for third. Watson regained his form of the opening round, added another 68, and matched Roberts, at 209, and Nobilo, who was playing in only his third tournament in the United States, shot 68 as well and took over second place alone, at 208.

Meanwhile, neither Montgomerie, Cook nor Edwards came anywhere near matching their 65s of the second round. Montgomerie fell back to 73 and dropped from first place into a tie for third, Cook shot 73 as well and fell back to a tie for ninth, and Edwards dropped even further after shooting 75. Pate, who had shot 66 on Friday, dropped back to 71, still a respectable score but hardly good enough to advance him. While Watson held his ground, though, Nicklaus began to slide. He shot 77, dropped 10 strokes behind Els, and was finished.

At the same time, Irwin continued to play first-class golf and might have shot a third consecutive 69 except for a misplayed drive on the 18th that led to a double-bogey six. He shot 71 instead and went into the last round tied with Watson, Roberts and Montgomerie, in third place.

Playing in temperatures that rose into the middle 90s once again, Roberts left the first tee a little after 11 o'clock, almost three hours ahead of Montgomerie and Irwin, the last off. Seemingly crippled by an opening round of 76, Roberts had fought back with 69 in the second round and, in the third round, reeling off seven birdies for his 64 without making a bogey.

It is safe to say he got everything possible out of his round. He drove the ball fairly well, hitting 11 of the 14 fairways on driving holes, which isn't bad, and at the same time missing five greens. Yet not one of those mistakes cost him a stroke. Except for the fourth, where he struggled after driving into shaggy rough, he played standard tee-to-green golf through the first nine, but he bunkered his approaches on both the 10th and 11th holes and still saved pars with nerveless putting. Bunkered twice more, on the 13th and 15th, he left himself with two more testing putts — a downhill three-footer on the 13th and another from 11 feet on the 15th and holed both.

Roberts had another tense moment on the 16th, the 228-yard par three, where he left his four wood 60 feet from the cup. This was three-putt distance, but with a stroke of luck he nursed it home for a birdie two. Six under par by then, and on his way to 65, Roberts hit a powerful drive on the 18th and followed with an exquisite six iron that dug into the green and pulled up 15 feet from the cup. Facing a slippery putt, he rolled it in.

Looking back on the round, Roberts claimed he had no expectations whatsoever of shooting such a low round, since he had been playing so poorly the last few weeks. "Today," he said, "I decided to go for broke."

Even though Roberts had shot the second lowest score ever in an Open, Els began as if he would beat it. With rough as formidable as Oakmont's the low scores normally are shot by those who hit fairways. Els missed five, but still he hit 16 greens, a high number under any circumstances. He played the first six holes with five threes, one of them on the fourth, a par five of 560 yards, and stood five under par after five holes. He reached the ninth, the other par five on the first nine, with an eight iron following a truly massive drive — the hole measured 474 yards uphill — and took two putts. He had played the first nine in 30 strokes, equaling the Open record.

He wasn't nearly so sharp coming home, and indeed looked as if he had thrown away all his good work on the first nine with some shoddy play on the second. He gave away two strokes with a double-bogey six on the 10th and lost another by three-putting the 16th from outside 50 feet, but he finished three, three by birdieing both the 17th and 18th from inside 10 feet. His 66 put some space between himself and Nobilo.

Like all good rounds, this could have been better. Along the way he had missed birdies from six feet, from eight feet, from 10 feet, from 12 feet and from 15 feet, all legitimate birdie opportunities for those who play at this level.

Not that he complained, but as the last round unfolded, it was clear he could have used them.

The third-round leaderboard:

Ernie Els	66 - 206	Steve Lowery	68 - 210
Frank Nobilo	68 - 208	Curtis Strange	70 - 210
Loren Roberts	64 - 209	Greg Norman	69 - 211
Tom Watson	68 - 209	Steve Pate	71 - 211
Hale Irwin	71 - 209	John Cook	73 - 211
Colin Montgomerie	73 - 209		

As it turned out, the fourth round was one of disappointment and frustration for everyone. After closing the third round with a double bogey, Irwin made another on the fifth the following day, shot 40 on the second nine and fell far behind. Watson had nothing left, either, shot 74, and dropped from the chase, and Nobilo, on his way to a 76, shot awful stuff. Strange had a chance after birdies on the third, fourth and fifth holes dropped him to six under par for the distance, and he was still in it after a birdie on the 14th, but then he stumbled, bogeying both the 15th and 16th and finishing with his fourth consecutive round of 70 and 280 for the 72 holes.

The Open, then, was left to Els, Roberts and Montgomerie. It was there to be taken, but no one could take command. They struggled throughout the day, each man leading at some stage, but always falling back.

Els, for example, stood seven under par after seven holes, but just as Roberts birdied the ninth, Els bogeyed the eighth. Now they were even with one another, six under par for 63 and 62 holes, but by then Montgomerie had rushed to the front with his own birdie at the ninth.

Montgomerie had been playing fine golf with three birdies through the first 10 holes, but then he bogeyed the 11th, 12th and 13th, picked up one more stroke coming home and finished with 70 for the day and a final score of 279, apparently out of reach of first place, leaving the final battle to Roberts and Els.

Roberts had dipped to seven under par with a marvelous four iron into the 13th that settled no more than five feet from the hole. He coaxed it home for the birdie two and now held a one-stroke lead over Els, who had followed his bogey at the eighth with a birdie at the 10th and another bogey at the 11th. Six under par again, Els birdied the 15th and bogeyed the 16th while Roberts bogeyed the 16th. They were even with one another again, with Roberts playing one hole ahead of Els.

The climax came on the last two holes. With Roberts playing the 18th, Els hooked his drive on the 17th behind a grandstand. He looked as if he were finished because his ball lay so deeply in a wooded tract he would have no shot even with line of sight relief from the grandstand. Or so it seemed. It didn't work out that way. Under a local rule in force, he was allowed to move his ball forward to a marked ball drop.

Although the procedure had been outlined early in the week, it caused some surprise and protest nonetheless. Bob Rosburg, a former PGA champion who was doing television commentary, could barely control himself.

His face flushed, he claimed Els had been allowed to move his ball 15 yards forward, violating one of the principal codes of the game that a player is never allowed to drop his ball closer to the hole when he takes relief. Others claimed the ball drop should have been used only for shots that actually went into the grandstand, not behind it.

That the procedure had been in place didn't matter. It seemed wrong that by taking a wild swing and trying to reach the green (the hole measured just 315 yards, and it could indeed be reached with a good shot) Els could escape punishment for missing. Nevertheless, he did, and he took advantage of the gift.

Now, with a clear run to the flagstick, he played a nice pitch-and-run that left him a putt of no more than five feet. If he holed it he would take the lead. He missed, and was still six under par and tied with Roberts.

Just then Roberts put too much into his approach shot to the 18th and knocked his ball over the back of the green, through the collar and into the deeper rough. He was clearly in trouble and might have given the Open away right there. Using a pitching wedge, he dug it out and left himself a reasonable putt for a par four, but he missed. Now he stood five under par for 72 holes, at 279, the same score as Montgomerie's. The Open belonged to Els if he could par the last hole.

Once again Els reached for his driver, and once again he hooked his shot deep into the trees. There would be no relief there, but as his caddie grew more and more nervous and pleaded with him to play safely back to the fairway, Ernie searched for an opening to the green. He could find nothing there, pitched out to the fairway and, after leaving his third 40 feet from the cup, holed from four or five feet to save a bogey. All three men tied at 279. There would be an 18-hole playoff the following day.

With all three obviously nervous and not playing their normal games, the playoff was not a pretty sight. Montgomerie, for example, parred the first hole then double-bogeyed the next two and went out in 42, six over par. After another double bogey at the 11th, he stood three under fives, the classic method of scoring used by 15-handicappers. He did collect himself and play the remaining holes in one under par, but he had fallen out of the chase long before then.

Els had an even rockier beginning. He pulled his opening drive into the rough behind a motorized crane holding a television camera and set off another rules controversy. The crane was a movable obstruction, but the referee — Trey Holland, the chairman of the USGA's Rules of Golf Committee — ruled by mistake that the crane was immovable and allowed Els line of sight relief and a free drop. Els bogeyed.

Holland, a urologist by profession, admitted his mistake later, but his candid admission hardly effected the amount of criticism heaped on him and the USGA. Some critics claimed that for an event as important as the U.S. Open the USGA should hire professional officials. Pure nonsense. How can a "professional official," whatever that might be, know the rules of golf better than the men who write and interpret them, which is what Holland and his colleagues do? But I digress.

After bogeying the first, Els made seven on the second, three over par on a hole of 342 yards. He overshot the green with his approach, hitting his ball into an unplayable lie in a bush, pitched back over and took three more strokes from there.

The hole seemed as if it would never end. Not only did Els make his seven, Montgomerie made six, and Roberts took a bogey five. Three men playing for one of the four most important titles in golf combined to play a little par four in six strokes over par. This playoff was indeed becoming anticlimactic. As they stood then, Els was four over par, Montgomerie was two over, and Roberts was one over, for he had bogeyed the second.

At about this time Els wanted to hide. He looked toward his caddie and said, "Why did I make that putt on the 18th and get into this thing?"

Within three holes, though, he and Roberts were tied, for Els had picked up one stroke with a birdie on the third and Roberts double-bogeyed the fifth. Quickly, though, Roberts moved ahead by birdieing the short sixth, but Els took back the stroke with a birdie of his own at the seventh. Both men bogeyed the eighth, birdied the ninth, and headed to the second nine still all square, each man two over par with 38s.

Roberts went ahead once more when Els bogeyed the long 12th, and in truth he had every chance to win. He had never been behind, and he still held a one-stroke lead as late as after the 15th hole. Then he made the big mistake where he couldn't afford one. Playing the 16th, Roberts had left his tee shot a good distance from the hole, but he lagged his putt nicely to about four or five feet. He had had approximately the same putt earlier in the week and he believed he knew how it would break. He played it poorly, though. The ball slipped past the hole, and now they were tied once more.

It stood even when both men birdied the 17th and made their pars on the 18th. Both Els and Roberts had shot 74 while Montgomerie had fallen to 78. Now Roberts and Els would go on to extra holes, beginning at the 10th rather than the first. Montgomerie, of course, would step aside.

Both men made standard pars on the 10th, but then Roberts' driver betrayed him. He hooked into rough so heavy that even though the hole measured just 378 yards he couldn't reach the green with his second shot. Els, meantime, played the hole perfectly, driving into the fairway and pitching on with his second.

Roberts hadn't given up, though. On with his third, he gave his putt a good run, and indeed hit the hole, but his ball spun out and he bogeyed. At the same time, Els had rolled his first putt three or four feet past and had no easy job left.

Still, he played the shot he had to play. He rolled it in and won with a par four. After the roughest sort of start — four over par after two holes, he had played the last 18 holes, including the two extra holes, in one under par.

By winning, Els had become the second South African to have won the U.S. Open. Whether he will turn out to be as durable as either Player, the 1965 U.S. Open champion, or Bobby Locke, another great South African golfer of an earlier time, could only be guessed at, but Roberts evidently had every confidence he could. "He has the whole game," he said. "He hits it long and he putts great. That usually works pretty well."

5. British Open Championship

The British Open Championship had been played at Turnberry three times through 1994, and each one of them had to stand among the more memorable in the long history of the event, the oldest tournament in golf. If Turnberry and its majestic hotel had been thought of only as an expensive resort in the past, it would be forever remembered as the site of the 1977 struggle between Tom Watson and Jack Nicklaus, principally for the last two rounds, when Watson shot 65-65 and Nicklaus 65-66 while the golf world held its breath.

In Turnberry's next British Open, nine years later in 1986, Greg Norman played stunning golf, shooting 63 in the second round, matching the lowest single round ever shot in one of the four major competitions, and beat Gordon J. Brand by five strokes.

In the latest visit to Turnberry, Nick Price, who had been having an erratic year, stormed home in birdie-eagle-par, shot 66 in the last round, and with a 268 total not only nipped Jesper Parnevik, the young Swede, by one stroke, he not only tied Watson's score from the 1977 British Open, he came within one stroke of tying the championship record of 267 that Norman had shot at Sandwich a year earlier.

Looking back on those three British Opens, a similar thread weaves among them. By winning, each of the three champions established himself firmly among the game's elite. While it is true that Watson had already won one British Open and a Masters Tournament before he arrived at Turnberry, his winning there was his second straight victory in a tight battle with Nicklaus (he had already outscored him in the Masters in April) and quite suddenly raised him to the same level as Jack.

Norman won the British Open after allowing the U.S. Open to slip away from him twice, first in 1984, when he lost a playoff to Fuzzy Zoeller, and again earlier in 1986, when he led after three rounds but closed with 75. Earlier that year he had led the Masters after three rounds and came to the 18th with a chance to tie Nicklaus, but he pushed his approach to the 18th into the crowd and bogeyed. He did not have a reputation as a strong finisher.

Price had a different kind of reputation. Through fierce determination and unrelenting drive he had developed into one of the five best players in the game by 1994, reliable in the ordinary PGA Tour events although not so reliable on the big occasions. When it mattered in the British Open, Price played the shots he had to play, and within one month, he would win not only at Turnberry but at Tulsa in the PGA Championship as well, leaving no doubt he had become the game's leading player.

The first of these was, of course, the British Open, a prize he had had within his reach twice in the past. Nick first surfaced as a player of international importance in 1982, when he stood on the 13th tee at Royal Troon leading Watson by two strokes. Then he bogeyed the 13th, double-bogeyed the 15th, and bogeyed the 17th. With 69 in sight, he shot 73 instead and finished one stroke behind Watson.

Price was 25 years old then. Six years later, a more mature golfer, he had gone into the last round at Royal Lytham and St. Annes leading Seve Ballesteros by two strokes; but in a struggle that had brought back memories of the battle between Watson and Nicklaus at Turnberry, Ballesteros closed with 65, Price shot 69, and Ballesteros won his third British Open. Price was thwarted again.

Nick finally broke through and won one of the four major competitions in 1992, when he took the PGA Championship, at Bellerive in St. Louis.

Winning the PGA seemed to give him a burst of confidence. Since then he had won eight tournaments in the United States, and that brought him into a direct conflict with Norman and Nick Faldo in the contest to determine the No. 1 player on the Sony Ranking. By winning at Turnberry and again at Southern Hills, he moved ahead of them.

It was not only his winning but his manner of winning which added a touch of romance, like something out of a Western movie, where the aging sheriff guns down the younger gunslinger bent on winning a reputation. Not that Price, at 37, could be called aging, but he did have Parnevik, the lanky Swede with the turned-up bill on his cap, by eight years. With the holes running out, Parnevik had the championship well in hand when Price decided he had better try to make something happen. He did. He birdied the 16th, eagled the 17th, and parred the 18th.

Parnevik helped by losing a stroke on the 18th through what must be called a poor decision. Refusing to look at the scoreboard, which would have shown him he needed nothing more than a par four, Parnevik decided he would need a birdie, played a risky shot designed to clear a bunker guarding the left front of the green, and underclubbed. Instead of the four, which, as it turned out, would have won him a place in the playoff, he made five.

Still, Price's eagle on the 17th, a par five of 498 yards, won the championship. On the green with his second shot, Price faced a putt of at least 50 feet from the left rear. After surveying the putt from every conceivable angle, he gave the ball a decisive rap. It ran toward the hole, took a slight break to the right, crept slowly toward the hole, and just as it seemed it would die, it tumbled into the cup. He had gauged the pace so truly, one was left with the impression that if the hole had been nothing but a circle drawn on the grass, his putt would have stopped inside it.

When the putt fell, Price leaped and raced around the green. The eagle had dropped him to 12 under par and moved him ahead of Parnevik, who had already blundered on the 18th. A final par four earned Price the championship.

That putt, so well struck and so perfectly played, will certainly take its place among great moments of the past. There have been other putts as telling as this, to be sure, but they have indeed been rare, so rare that only a few come easily to mind: Bobby Jones' from 40 feet on the final hole at Interlachen that settled the 1930 U.S. Open; Ben Hogan's from 30 feet on the 17th at Merion that assured he would win the playoff for the 1950 U.S. Open; Nicklaus' from 40 feet on the 16th at Augusta that won him the 1975 Masters; Watson's from about that same distance on Turnberry's 15th that tore the heart from Nicklaus in the last round of the 1977 British Open; Larry Nelson's from more than 60 feet on the 16th at Oakmont that beat Watson in the 1983 U.S. Open; and Hale Irwin's putt from 45 feet on the final green at Medinah that forced a playoff for the 1991 U.S. Open, which he won the following day.

Price's heroic moment lay ahead, of course, but as the starting date approached, no one could be sure of what to expect. A day or so before the opening round, Watson telephoned Nicklaus and told him he had "a couple of pigeons" lined up for a four-ball match in their final practice round.

"Who are they?" Nicklaus asked.

"Norman and Price," Watson answered, and they both laughed.

The following day, to their immense satisfaction, Watson and Nicklaus shot a better-ball score of 60 and wiped out Norman and Price.

While humbling the younger men had to be a pleasant experience for Watson and Nicklaus, at the same time it led to unreasonable expectations. Because the 1977 championship had been such a defining moment in the game's history, its memories command everyone's thoughts whenever the British Open returns to Turnberry, reminding us that on those four glorious days Watson and Nicklaus raised golf to levels we could have only dreamed of a few days earlier.

Seeing how those two old warriors handled the younger men, and remembering how well they had played during the early stages of the U.S. Open a month earlier, stirred some of the more devoted followers to dream that 1994 might turn out to be 1977 all over again. Of course it wasn't, nor could it hope to be. Nicklaus sensed the mood and, standing squarely on reality, cast it aside as only an illusion.

"A lot of people think you're going to be around forever," he said. "That can't happen. A lot of people out there today think this is 1977. It isn't."

Nicklaus turned out to be right about himself but only partly right about Watson. Playing late in the day under rainy conditions, Nicklaus fought his way around Turnberry in 72, two strokes over par. In the meantime, Watson shot 68, the same score he had opened with at Oakmont, but where he had led the U.S. Open, he found himself three strokes behind three unlikely players at Turnberry — Greg Turner, a 31-year-old New Zealander playing in only his third British Open; Jonathan Lomas, a young golfer from Shropshire, in England, just beginning a career on the PGA European Tour; and Andrew Magee, a veteran of the U.S. PGA Tour.

Magee had been in roughly this position before, but Turner and Lomas ranked as major surprises. In eight previous rounds in the British Open, Turner had shot only one round under 70. He had opened the 1993 championship by shooting 67 at Sandwich. At Turnberry he opened with 65. Lomas shot 66, and Magee 67. These were only the leaders. On a course unusually yielding, 30 men altogether shot scores under its par of 70. In addition to the three leaders, 11 men shot 68 and 16 more shot 69.

The low level of scoring shouldn't have come as much of a surprise since Turnberry was so ripe for ravaging. Weekend rains, which had dumped more than an inch of moisture on the ground, had softened the greens; the fairways had been widened somewhat from 1986, when the most generous measured little more than 22 yards, and the course overall, as everyone agreed, had never been better conditioned.

Those who feel more comfortable when the game's best players must struggle for their scores moaned that the championship needed a touch of weather. Weekend clouds had blown away, and Wednesday had been a warm and sunny day. The tenor had changed by Thursday morning, the day of the opening round. A brisk wind had risen as the first group teed off, and conditions worsened throughout the day, until those who went out after noon played through miserable conditions. Rain fell steadily, and the temperature plunged.

As a consequence, players found themselves using clubs they wouldn't ordinarily have played. Heading into a stiff wind on the third hole, a par four of 460 yards, both Payne Stewart and Bernhard Langer played their second shots with wooden clubs. Players of this caliber ordinarily reach the greens of 460-yard holes with clubs to spare. Even a 550-yard hole is reachable under calm conditions. Here, though, neither man hit the green.

Others ran into similar experiences on the 17th, which nearly everyone reached with irons in the later stages. Loren Roberts, Costantino Rocca and Lee James, the British Amateur champion, all fell short after playing wooden clubs. Watson had been playing his approach to the 16th with a nine iron in practice, and yet he needed a five iron in the first round.

At the same time the breeze shortened the downwind holes. Standing on the tee of the second, Turner pulled out his three wood and asked his caddie if he could reach a set of bunkers about 280 yards out. The caddie said, "No." Turner drove beyond them.

Without question those who played before the rain began falling in early afternoon had the advantage, and yet Turner had been among the late starters, beginning at 2:15 p.m., just behind Norman, Mark Calcavecchia, the 1989 British champion, and Ian Woosnam, and just as the rain began falling most heavily.

Not one of the consistent threats, Turner had joined the PGA European Tour in 1986, won the Scandinavian Enterprises Open later that year, and waited seven years to win his second, the 1993 Lancia Martini Italian Open. He had, however, shown signs of awakening in the weeks leading up to the British Open, shooting consecutive rounds of 73, 70, 69, 66 and tying for fourth place in the Murphy's Irish Open, then 65 and 67 in the qualifying rounds for the British Open.

His opening round at Turnberry qualified as bizarre. It was made up of two eagles, three birdies, two bogeys and 11 holes played in par. He began by running off five consecutive pars, then played the sixth, a downwind 222-yard par three, with a five iron. He laid it within 15 feet of the cup and holed the putt. Next, he reached the green of the seventh, which measured 528 downwind yards, with a three wood and a four iron that rolled within five feet of the cup. The putt dropped for an eagle three, and Turner had played two holes in three under par.

Out in 32, he faced the long battle home with so many holes playing dead into the wind and rain. He lost a stroke on the deceptive 12th, where he underclubbed. He won that stroke back with a birdie on the 14th, but bunkered his tee shot to the 15th and bogeyed again.

Just two under par then, Turner followed with the key hole of his round, the 16th, a par four of 410 yards that normally calls for nothing more than a drive and pitch. With the wind blowing directly at him, Greg fired a drive that left him 178 yards short of the flagstick. Feeling the strength of the wind, he knew he would need a substantial club to reach the green, perhaps even a two iron. Checking with his caddie, they both agreed this was indeed the club. The shot tore through the wind, hit short of the pin, ran directly at the hole, and dived in. Another eagle; now he stood four under par with two holes to play. More was coming.

Two woods left him short of the 17th green and a loose pitch shot ran 20 feet past the cup. Still, some scores are meant to be. He holed the putt and dipped to five under par. A drive and two iron to the 18th earned him a closing par and his 65.

Lomas, just 26 and playing in his first British Open, carries an unusual driver. Although he stands just 5-foot-9 inches, his driver measures 47 inches (the normal driver measures from 43½ to 44 inches). He said the bigger arc the long club creates had added perhaps 20 yards to his drives.

It was not his driving, though, but his work around the greens that led to his low score. Although he teed off at 9:15 a.m. under relatively mild conditions, Lomas still missed three of the first four greens and yet gave away nothing. He played delicate little chips on each of them and saved his pars. He made his first birdie on the seventh where a chip shot settled within a foot of the cup, then holed his only putt of any length on the ninth, where a 25-footer fell.

He had gone out in 33 with five one-putt greens, then one-putted three more coming home. He holed from 24 feet on the 10th — two from the same distance on consecutive holes — from six inches on the 14th for another birdie, then from 10 feet on the 16th to save a par four.

An engaging young man with sandy hair and a quick smile, Lomas floated off the final green on a cloud and said, "To do well in the Open was a dream."

Watson had the same dream, although he had set his goal at a higher level. He had already won five British Opens and had set his heart on winning a sixth, which would have matched Harry Vardon's record from early in the century. Off among the early starters, at 7:35 a.m., he had hardly slept through the night and had been up since five o'clock waiting to begin.

Tom began quietly enough with two routine pars, and almost pitched in for a birdie three after missing the third green. He had his first uncomfortable moment on the sixth, where he three-putted from 60 feet, but he won that stroke back on the seventh, where a big drive left him only a six iron to the green. Two putts and he had pulled back to even par.

He still stood even with par after the 12th, then picked up strokes by holing from 30 feet on the 13th and pitching to six feet on the 17th. These teasing, holeable putts have troubled Watson through his decline from the game's pinnacle. Where once they were hardly worth mentioning, they had bothered him for years. Here he rolled it in, but with a chance to add another birdie on the 18th, he missed from the same distance.

Still, Watson had at least left himself in good position for a serious run at the championship while other players of quality had not. Faldo, clearly not playing as well as he had a year earlier, had played an undistinguished Masters, placing 32nd, and had played so badly at the U.S. Open he had missed the 36-hole cut. Starting just before two o'clock grouped with Ernie Els, the U.S. Open champion, and Jim McGovern, a U.S. PGA Tour player, Faldo played the first 16 holes in two over par, then drove into the right rough on the 17th and made a huge mistake. He played McGovern's ball. Nick admitted later he hadn't checked but had assumed that since McGovern, who had hit into the rough as well, drives the ball longer than he and the ball he played had been the shortest drive, it must have been his.

With a two-stroke penalty, Faldo made an eight and shot 75, putting himself clearly at risk of missing the cut. He was not alone. Woosnam shot 79 and had no hope of playing through 72 holes, and Phil Mickelson, the young American who had shown much occasional promise, shot 78.

Jose Maria Olazabal, who had won the Masters in April, shot a dull 72, along with Colin Montgomerie, Langer and, of course, Nicklaus. Lee Janzen, the 1993 U.S. Open champion, and Stewart, who had won the U.S. Open in 1991 and placed second to Janzen in 1993, both shot 74s and were never heard from again.

The first-round leaderboard:

Greg Turner	65	John Daly	68
Jonathan Lomas	66	Jean Van de Velde	68
Andrew Magee	67	Peter Senior	68
Tom Watson	68	David Edwards	68
Loren Roberts	68	Wayne Grady	68
Jesper Parnevik	68	Brian Watts	68
David Feherty	68	Ross McFarlane	68

Friday, the day of the second round, was a day filled with contrasts. It was a day when Watson would arouse improbable dreams by roaring to the top of the standings with a glittering 65; when Price would shoot 66 and show he must still be reckoned with; when Parnevik would birdie three of the last four holes, shoot 66 as well, and make a move that would lead to a brush with glory; when Zoeller and Brad Faxon would begin their climbs, Faxon with a bogey-free 65 and Zoeller with 66 that sparkled with birdies on all four par-three holes, and a day when Faldo showed the value of pride.

Facing the inglorious prospect of being eliminated, Faldo rearranged his game and climbed back into the championship with a round of 66, another of his stunning bursts of scoring.

On the grim side, it was a day as well when John Daly ruined what had been a promising start with two badly played holes and never recovered, and when Magee went from the top of the leaderboard all the way out of the championship with a horrid 80.

It was a day as well when we would lose three of the greatest golfers who ever graced the championship. Lee Trevino missed the 36-hole cut by four strokes by shooting 147; Nicklaus missed by two, with 145, the same as Gary Player, who was playing his 40th consecutive British Open.

At the end of the day Watson led with 133, followed by Parnevik and Faxon, at 134, then Price, at 135, and Turner, Frank Nobilo, David Edwards and Lomas at 136.

Norman climbed within reach of the top with a blistering birdie-birdie finish that earned him a 67 and gave him 138, five strokes behind Watson. Norman, of course, is capable of shooting any score at all, so five strokes meant nothing with 36 holes still to play.

Even the weather had its contrast. Rain had given way to bright, clear skies, and the wind had veered to the northwest, creating different clubbing decisions. The holes that had played downwind on Thursday played into the breeze on Friday. The seventh, for example, had been easily reachable with medium irons during the opening round, but with the shift in the wind it called for much stronger clubbing in the second.

The shifting wind seemed to promote better scoring as well, for now the homeward holes played with the breeze rather than against it. Where 30 men had broken 70 in the first round, 47 shot in the 60s in the second. They were led by Mark Brooks, a Texan who shot 64 and climbed into a tie for 13th place where only a day earlier he had faced elimination following an opening round of 74. Three others shot 65, six more had 66, seven men shot 67, 10 others shot 68, and 20 shot 69. As a whole the field averaged 71.71 strokes, a little less than two over par.

As one of the early starters, off a few minutes before eight o'clock, Brooks birdied three of the first seven holes and went out in 32. Every hole had been an adventure. In addition to his birdies on the third, where he holed from 45 feet, the fifth and the seventh, Brooks had saved pars on the fourth, sixth and eighth with a combination of deft chipping and inspired putting. Over the six holes from the third through the eighth he had one-putted every green.

Starting back, Brooks holed from 18 feet on the 10th and from 15 feet on the 12th. Now he had one-putted eight of 10 greens. He would hole only one more, running in a 10-footer on the 16th for his final birdie of the day. Back in 32, he had his 64, the second lowest score ever shot in a British or U.S. Open.

While Brooks was driving scores to lower levels, Daly was moving in the opposite direction, turning a highly promising beginning into a disappointment. Playing only a hole behind Brooks, Daly had played some inspired golf on the outward nine. Three birdies had dropped him to five under par after 27 holes, but at the same time he had missed a number of opportunities that, had putts fallen from inside 15 feet, might have sent his scoring into the 20s. Then it all ended.

Out in 32, Daly stepped onto the 10th tee and played a dreadful hook down among the rocks and sand on the beach. Spectators, officials, players and caddies searched among the debris without finding the ball. Since it had clearly gone into the hazard, Daly dropped another ball, his second stroke, fell short with his third, pitched on with his fourth, and three-putted. He had made a seven and wiped out all the good work he had done on the first nine. More was coming.

A nice tee shot onto the 11th, a par three of 177 yards, settled just 20 feet from the hole, but Daly ran his first putt three feet past and lipped out his second. He still had two feet left, but a comfortable stance would have put his feet on Vijay Singh's line. Instead he took an awkward stance, balancing himself on the toe of his right foot, reached out with his putter, and missed again. On in one, down in four. A double-bogey five — five strokes thrown away on two holes.

Daly was done for. He played the next seven holes in one under par and shot 72 for the round. With 140, he qualified easily for the final two rounds, but he played no further part in the championship. Reaching the clubhouse, he climbed into his car and drove off saying, "I'm going home and pull the knife out of my heart."

Meantime, Turner birdied both the fourth and the sixth, and at that time stood seven under par, clearly in the lead. With another birdie within reach on the seventh, where a three-wood second shot reached the green, he three-putted, settling for a par five. That was the end of Turner. He lost three strokes over the next two holes, finished in 71, and fell steadily backward through the final 36 holes.

Lomas played a little better, shooting 70, but that wasn't good enough on a day like this, and, like Turner, he fell progressively behind.

This day belonged to Watson, who played as he had in his best years. The putts that hadn't fallen in the past fell. His irons were as crisp and decisive as he had ever played them, and his driving, although not always on line, sailed long and mostly true. While it wasn't a flawless round, Watson made no mistakes except to bogey the sixth and 13th holes.

He began by holing two sizable putts, one from 20 feet on the first and another from 50 feet on the third. One stroke slipped away when he missed the sixth green and bogeyed, but then he played five wonderful holes that combined impeccable ball-striking with the kind of nerveless putting he hadn't shown in years.

It began with the seventh, a hole where others had trouble reaching the green. After his drive drifted off the right of center, Watson played his metal driver once more and drilled a low-flying shot that knifed through the wind, hit short of the green, bounded up the hill, and pulled up perhaps 40 feet from the hole. Two putts and he had his birdie.

Playing into the wind once again on the eighth, Watson drove into the right rough, leaving him a difficult second shot. His ball sat above his feet in a classic hook lie, but Watson ripped into a three iron that settled on the green about eight feet to the right of the hole. It was a display of virtuoso shotmaking that inspired cheers from his growing gallery.

His gallery had grown with every hole, cheering every shot, good or not so good. It was easy to see he was pleased with his game. His face set in a tight grin, he looked at his fans occasionally, enough to let them know they and his awakening game had made him happy.

Now Watson stood three under par for the round and five under for 26 holes. A par four at the ninth and he was out in 32. On to the 10th. Another pushed drive left him a decent lie in the rough, and a nine iron aimed directly at the flagstick, set on the front left of the green, drifted slightly right in the crossing wind and came down within 15 feet of the cup. Another putt fell, and Watson had his fifth birdie in 10 holes.

Now for the 11th, where Daly had stumbled so badly. Watson's eight iron covered the flag all the way and braked within four feet. The putt dropped, and Watson went to six under par, but he could gain no more ground. A three-putt bogey cost him one stroke on the 13th, but he made it up with a two iron into the 17th and made his final birdie of the day.

In with 65, he faced the press a few minutes later and said, "Not bad for a 44-year-old has-been."

The second-round leaderboard:

Tom Watson	65 - 133	David Edwards	68 - 136
Jesper Parnevik	66 - 134	Jonathan Lomas	70 - 136
Brad Faxon	65 - 134	Fuzzy Zoeller	66 - 137
Nick Price	66 - 135	David Feherty	69 - 137
Greg Turner	71 - 136	Loren Roberts	69 - 137
Frank Nobilo	67 - 136	Ronan Rafferty	66 - 137

If Friday had been Watson's day, Saturday belonged to Zoeller, who stands among the more endearing golfers anyone has ever seen. In the heat of a tense battle, Zoeller acts like a man out walking his dog. He has an unhurried gait, although he plays his shots with a minimum of fuss, shares an occasional light comment with the gallery, and when he's not talking he's whistling, not always a recognizable tune.

Zoeller can lull you to sleep, but he woke everyone up with a third-round 64 that shot him into a tie for the lead, at 201, with Brad Faxon, who shot 67 to go with his 65 of the previous day.

Faxon's 132 for the second and third rounds was sensational scoring, but Zoeller had beaten him by two strokes. Combining his second round of 66 with his 64 in the third, he had played 36 holes in 130 strokes, which is about as well as anyone can play. The 201 total stood just two strokes over the record 199 that Nick Faldo had shot twice, first at St. Andrews in 1990, and two years later at Muirfield.

Once again we had a day of strikingly low scoring. Of the 81 players who had qualified for the last two rounds, 42 men, better than half the field, shot in the 60s. While Zoeller's 64 wasn't beaten that day, it was tied. Larry Mize, who had barely survived the cut after a 73-69 start, matched it. Meantime, Ronan Rafferty and Montgomerie shot 65s, nine others shot 66, eight more shot 67, seven shot 68, and 14 men shot 69.

Watson was among those at 69. By then he had shot three rounds in the 60s and suddenly found himself tied for third place at 202. Rafferty had caught him, and so had Price with his 67, and Parnevik with 68. David Feherty, the whimsical and impulsive Irishman, shot 66 and climbed into a threatening position at 203.

From the scores it is easy to see that Turnberry was at its least forbidding. The cold wind from the west had calmed to little more than a fresh breeze, the sun had burned away the overcast and sparkled on the Clyde estuary, and sailing craft rode the offshore wind. It was a day made for low scoring. Temperatures climbed once again, and the greens, still soft from the rains, remained inviting. Players could throw their shots directly at the flagsticks with little need to play the low running shots so common in the links golf.

The conditions were reflected by the results of the day's play as first one man and then another made his run at the leaders, placing Watson under siege from the start.

Starting off an hour and a half before Watson, Norman began with birdies on two of the first three holes, went out in 32, then tried to play a too-finely-gauged pitch to the 16th. Slightly underhit, his ball just missed carrying to the green, caught the top of a bank rising from a narrow brook, and tumbled down a steep grade into the water. He double-bogeyed, and his defense of the championship ended.

Meantime, others had taken up the challenge. Starting 40 minutes behind Watson and Parnevik, who were paired together at the end of the field, Zoeller moved off to a slow start, exchanging a birdie on the first with a bogey on the fifth. Faxon, though, just ahead of Watson and Parnevik, birdied the second and fell to seven under par; he had caught Watson.

Two holes later Watson surged ahead once more with a shot that brought back memories of the lobbed pitch he had holed on the 71st hole at Pebble Beach in the 1982 U.S. Open. His seven-iron approach rolled into the rough behind the third green, but Tom had never been uncomfortable with the little pitch shot. Taking his wedge, he dug the ball out of the grass and chopped it onto the green. Just as it had 12 years earlier, his ball ran to the hole and wedged itself between the pin and the lip edge of the cup.

Eight under par now, Watson had moved ahead once more. Sadly, though, for him and his fans, he would make no more headway. While he could hardly be said to struggle, he could make nothing happen on the greens, although he had a number of opportunities. He played the first nine in 34 in spite of a badly misplayed six iron on the fourth tee. He won it back with a birdie at the seventh, his third birdie there in three rounds, but then lost two more strokes through the 16th. Just six under par then, Watson birdied both the 17th and 18th and finished with 69.

It was turning into a wild and confusing day as first one, then another player made a move at the top. Feherty played the steadiest kind of golf, picking up birdies on the fifth, 10th, 15th and 17th as he came home in 32, shot 66, and dropped to seven under par. Price climbed from five under par when the round began to nine under after 17 holes, but he misplayed the 18th and missed a chance to tie Faxon and Zoeller. Rafferty had gone out in 32 with birdies on four of the first seven holes tempered by a bogey at the fifth, then came back in 34 with three more birdies and a bogey. And Faxon completed a run of 41 holes without a five on his scorecard. He had made his last five on the 12th hole of the first round, when he had shot 71.

The tensions of the day can only be imagined. At one stage a fluid situation became liquid, and no one could be sure of exactly what was going on. After dropping to six under par with a birdie on the 12th, Parnevik badly misjudged his approach to the 13th and bogeyed, and then Watson, who had holed a series of nerve-wracking putts, three-putted the 14th. With that mistake he dropped one stroke off the lead, behind Price and Faxon, who were playing just ahead of him, and Zoeller, two holes ahead.

Zoeller, who had shot 66 the previous day without once scoring a three — all twos, fours and fives — suddenly came to life after his bogey on the fifth and ran off six birdies over the next 13 holes. Still giving the appearance of a man in no hurry to go anywhere or do anything, Fuzzy played a series of undistinguished irons to 25 feet on the 12th and to 20 feet on the 13th, but a hot putter covers many sins. Both putts fell, and now he stood at seven under par, within one stroke of Watson and tied with both Price and Faxon.

The race remained tight the rest of the afternoon. Zoeller continued his relentless drive to a share of first place, Rafferty and Feherty picked up a further stroke each, Parnevik came back from some grim moments, and Watson signaled first that he would yield, and then bounced back once again to challenge.

Zoeller played both the 14th and 15th safely, then lofted a soft pitching wedge within 10 feet on the 16th and holed the putt. Eight under now, he had tied Watson and Faxon, and all three stood one stroke ahead of Price, Parnevik and Rafferty — six men within one stroke of one another.

At about the time Faxon and Price bunkered their approaches to the 14th but scraped out their pars, Zoeller two-putted the 17th from about 25 feet and birdied. Now Fuzzy stood alone at nine under par, one stroke ahead of the field.

After his unhurried stroll to the 18th tee, he played the hole as it was meant to be played. His drive ended in the absolute center of the fairway, and with the hole cut toward the right rear of the green, his pitch hit short of the pin, bounced once, dug in, and braked hole-high no more than 10 feet to the right of the cup.

Fuzzy was already six under par for the round; a birdie here would match the record. He took care lining up his putt and stroked it nicely, but he had misread his line. He had expected the ball to curl left toward the cup, but it rolled straight.

Nevertheless, he was in with 64 and had his 201 total.

This had been a wonderful pairing to watch, for Feherty had matched him almost stroke for stroke with his 66, and stood just two strokes back at 203.

Now everyone's thoughts turned to Watson, who was having a grim afternoon. The crowd was clearly pulling for him and he was playing his shots as well as he ever had, but somehow he couldn't score. After three-putting the 14th, he followed by three-putting the 16th as well, missing his second from four or five feet. Just as it had on the 14th, his ball had actually hit the inside of the hole then spun away and sat inches from the cup. With that bogey he went to six under par, three strokes off Zoeller's score, for Fuzzy had already played the 17th.

Watson, though, was a fighter; he wasn't through yet. After a three wood from the 17th tee, he played a marvelous two iron that carried to the top of the hill, ran onto the green, and rolled dead about 15 feet from the cup, within holing distance of an eagle three. Watson played a very fine putt that for one heart-stopping moment looked as if it might fall, but it missed. Still, Watson had his birdie, then played a one iron and a six iron to the 18th green about 10 feet from the cup and made another birdie. Once given up as finished, he had pulled himself back into the race, and with his two closing birdies not only revived memories of his past, but pulled himself within a stroke of the co-leaders as well.

The third-round leaderboard:

Fuzzy Zoeller	64 - 201	Jesper Parnevik	68 - 202
Brad Faxon	67 - 201	Ronan Rafferty	65 - 202
Tom Watson	69 - 202	David Feherty	66 - 203
Nick Price	67 - 202	Mark James	66 - 205

As the final round began, six men stood within one stroke of one another, with Feherty only one further stroke behind. It shaped up as a difficult day that would strain the nerves of even the strongest players. Looking over the standings as the third round finished, Price said, "There will be no sitting around waiting for par tomorrow because there is so much experience on the leaderboard. I hope my putter gets going because I think I'll need 65 to win." Nearly everyone agreed. Faxon predicted the winner would have to shoot three or four under par, "Particularly if it's a day like this."

Still dreaming of winning a sixth British Open, Watson said, "Nature has produced an easy course for us this year. It's going to take something in the middle 60s to win." Then, showing how he felt about the weather, he grinned and added, "I hope the wind blows 40 miles an hour."

His was a vain hope, because, if anything, the weather turned milder and even a touch warmer. The players put away their sweaters and windbreakers on this pleasant Scottish summer day and played in their shirtsleeves. The wind had shifted to the northeast, but it had negligible effect; this was another day made for low-scoring golf.

Perhaps it was the tension, but even though Turnberry had seldom seemed so vulnerable, the field scored nowhere nearly as well as it had the previous day. Where 42 men had broken 70 in the third round, only 29 men shot in the 60s in the last, raising the total to 148 for the championship, 32 more than the record that had been set only the previous year, at Royal St. George's.

Once again, some of those scores were indeed low. Both Faldo and the Swede Anders Forsbrand shot 64s early in the day, which moved them into the top 10 places; and Russell Claydon, a former Walker Cup player, shot 65.

When Faldo sped around the first nine in 32, everyone expected the year-old record of 267 might be broken. With 201, both Zoeller and Faxon would need 66 to match it, which wasn't out of the question, since each of them had already shot better scores than that; Price, Parnevik, Watson and Rafferty would need 65, and both Rafferty and Watson had done it while Price and Parnevik had missed by just one stroke.

Faldo came back in 32 as well for his 64. It is a measure of the man, though, that he wasn't satisfied. Hopelessly out of the running, he found a lofty goal to aim for. When he rifled a three iron about 20 feet from the cup on the 17th he said to himself, "If I hole this putt and then birdie the 18th I'll shoot 62. That's never been done before." That he didn't doesn't matter.

Two hours later Forsbrand came in with his own 64, confirming that it could indeed be done, but the lesson was evidently lost on everyone else. Throughout the first nine those close enough to make a run for the championship played a reserved sort of golf. The six men who began the day within a stroke of one another made more bogeys than birdies on the first nine, and the championship didn't come alive until they all turned for home.

Even so, there were a couple of interesting moments. Larry Mize holed his pitch to the first hole for an eagle two and followed up with a birdie on the third, which dropped him to seven under par, within two strokes of Zoeller and Faxon. After going out in 32, Mize lost his momentum, came back in 38, and at the end tied for 11th place. Then Watson gave everyone a thrill with a tentative move at the seventh, where he birdied for the fourth straight day. When his putt fell he held a share of first place for a brief moment. Then it ended quickly and sadly when his game collapsed utterly. Failing to hole the troublesome three- and four-footers that had bedeviled him so, Watson made sixes on both the eighth and ninth, a pair of par fours, and played no further part in the championship except to encourage Parnevik, his playing companion.

Nor could Zoeller or Faxon make something happen. After shooting a dull 70, Zoeller compared his round to sitting in a brown room watching the paint dry, and Faxon simply had no more to give. After a fine opening drive, he played a pitch that had nothing on it. His ball raced across the green into the rough beyond and he had his first bogey since the 13th hole of the first round. A few more followed; his finely tuned putting stroke could carry him no further. He shot 73 and fell to seventh place.

One of the wonders of this championship was that Zoeller hung on to claim third place, for the putts simply wouldn't fall for him. More than one singed the edge of the cup but slipped past, and yet he was never far from the lead. As late as the ninth hole when he missed a short putt for a par four, he shared first place with four others at eight under par — Zoeller, Price and Rafferty had played through the ninth, Parnevik through the 10th, and Feherty through the 11th.

At that stage no one could make up his mind who to follow because no one was playing first-class golf. How Price was managing to hang on defied logic because he was hitting the ball everywhere.

Now, with the others struggling to hold their ground, and indeed some dropping further behind, Parnevik made his move. He had made nothing but pars through the 10th hole, but then he played a solid six iron within six feet on the 11th and holed it for his first birdie of the day. Now he stood at nine under par and had moved ahead for the first time. Quickly, he laced a solid drive into the 12th fairway and followed with an eight iron that flew dead on line at the flagstick and pulled up just six feet short. One more putt fell; he stood at 10 under par then, ahead by two strokes.

Keeping up the pressure, he split the 13th fairway with another good drive and a nine iron to four feet. Again he holed and dipped 11 under par.

Parnevik was playing superb golf, but that last birdie had gained him no ground, for Price had birdied the 12th and Zoeller the 11th with a stunning five iron no more than a foot and a half from the cup. Both of them stood at nine under then, with Feherty at eight under.

After a regulation four at the 14th, Parnevik missed the 15th green and bogeyed, losing one stroke of his lead, and cutting it to a single stroke.

Price, meanwhile, had been living by the grace of the gods. He had gone out in even-par 35 with two birdies written off by a pair of bogeys. Starting back, he pulled his four-iron approach left of the 10th green, played an indifferent pitch to about 15 feet, then holed the putt for the par. After a routine par three on the 11th, an eight iron to 15 feet on the 12th set up his third birdie of the day. He would have to quicken his pace to shoot the 65 he said he needed.

Once again, though, he found trouble and looked as if he had ruined whatever hopes he might still hold. After missing the 13th green he played a nerveless pitch to four feet and saved one par, but then he played a pitiful five iron to the 14th that had nothing on it. Instead of biting and holding the green, the ball streaked across, through the gallery, and ran at least 25 feet beyond.

Then, with everything at stake, Price showed the fierce determination that had built up through years of experience. He played a wonderful running seven iron that bounced and rolled along the bare, uneven ground, hopped onto the green, and pulled up no more than four feet from the cup. He holed the putt and saved not only his round but the championship as well.

It was difficult at the time to estimate the importance of those two saves, but reflecting on them later Price claimed they were the keys to his winning. "The whole round was set up by 13 and 14," he said, and then admitted, "In previous years I might not have got them up and down. They were equally as important as my putts on 16 and 17."

Still, he lagged behind Parnevik, who was about to make his final run. Ten under par after the 15th, Jesper played a nice pitch into the 16th and holed from about 15 feet. Eleven under par then, he moved to the 17th, an almost certain birdie hole. It had already given up 38 birdies and seven eagles that day alone. Parnevik played a one iron off the tee and a four iron that turned slightly left and settled in the rough left and short of the green. Next he played a perfectly gauged little pitch-and-run about four feet from the hole and made the putt. When it fell, dropping him to 12 under par, just about everyone conceded he had won the championship.

Now, though, he made a mistake.

Although scoreboards were just about everywhere you looked, Parnevik didn't bother to check how he stood. He had heard constant bursts of cheering behind him and hadn't realized many of them were for hard-won pars. Now he assumed he needed a birdie on the final hole.

After a drive to the right edge of the fairway, he decided to go for the flagstick with a pitching wedge. He simply didn't have enough club. His ball dropped short and settled against a grassy bank in front of the green, his recovery fell short, and he bogeyed.

Against this backdrop, Price had holed from 14 feet on the 16th for a birdie, putting him at 10 under par, and then made his eagle three on the 17th, which dropped him to 12 under par and settled the championship. Clutching the gleaming silver claret jug, Price said, "In 1982 I had my left hand on this trophy. In 1988 I had my right hand on the trophy. Now I finally have it in both hands."

6. PGA Championship

Until Nick Price in 1994, no one had played the game on such a high level since Greg Norman in 1986, and no one since Tom Watson, in 1982, had won two of the game's major championships in succession. It is ironic, perhaps, that when Watson did win two in a row — the U.S. and British Opens — he beat Jack Nicklaus at Pebble Beach and who else but Price at Royal Troon. Watson will admit as well that the British Open was a gift, handed to him when Price butchered the final six holes while Tom sat in the Troon clubhouse assuming he had finished second. Watson won by one stroke.

Twelve years later, hardened by experience and driven to excel, Price won both the British Open and PGA Championship with forceful, attacking golf. He was the first since Walter Hagen in 1924 to win those two championships in the same year. While he barely squeaked by in the British Open, helped considerably by Jesper Parnevik's poor judgment on the last hole at Turnberry, he won the PGA Championship as few have ever won any of the major titles. He was overpowering. Playing at a level we hadn't seen since Norman shot 267 at Royal St. George's as he won the 1993 British Open, Price shot 67-65-70-67–269, 11 under par over the Southern Hills Country Club in Tulsa, Oklahoma, led every round, and beat Corey Pavin, the runner-up, by six strokes. Pavin shot only one round as high as 70. His 72-hole total of 275 would have won any of the previous four PGA Championships. In his best showing yet in a major tournament, Phil Mickelson placed third at 276, and Faldo, Norman and John Cook shared fourth place at 277, Faldo once again shifting into high gear at the end, as he had in the British Open, and closing with 66.

As a further indication of Price's consistency through the championship, on a very tough course that measured 6,834 yards with a strong par of 35-35–70, and had been the site of a number of important tournaments over the years — the U.S. Opens of 1958 and 1977 and the PGA Championships of 1970 and 1982 — he was never over par for nine holes, played the first nine in a collective four under par and the second nine in seven under. Anyone who followed him would have seen him birdie one of every four holes he played, on the average, and bogey one in every 10. He birdied 19 of the 72 holes and bogeyed seven, percentages of 26 percent for birdies and less than 10 percent for bogeys.

He also hit 51 of the 72 greens, which isn't all that impressive (Nicklaus hit 61 greens when he won the 1967 U.S. Open at Baltusrol), but at the same time he never needed as many as 30 putts in any of the four rounds. Only Pavin did better than that (he needed only 25 in two rounds and 27 in the other two), but he is generally accepted as a conjurer on the greens.

Even though Price opened the PGA Championship by bogeying the first hole, he became the sixth man since the championship converted from match play to stroke play in 1958 to have led after every round, and his total score of 269 beat the previous record of 271 by two strokes. The previous record had been set by Bobby Nichols at the Columbus (Ohio) Country Club in 1964, with perhaps the most bizarre golf within memory. Nichols hit the ball everywhere and still won. Once he hooked a drive that was clearly sailing into a major road but hit a tree instead, and while Ben Hogan watched with growing wonder, rebounded to the center of the fairway. Nichols' golf seemed so heaven-guided that Jay Hebert, himself a former PGA champion, was heard saying, "Sometimes somebody is *supposed* to win; the man upstairs says, 'There, that's the one; that man right there.'"

Price didn't play that kind of golf, but Norman remarked, "It seemed like every time somebody put some heat on him he just came back and birdied on top of us. Nobody was going to catch Nick."

Price's performance impressed even himself. Reflecting on his victory an hour after the finish he said, "I just have so much confidence in my ability, and it showed in the way I played today. My short game — my chipping and putting — won for me this week. Even though my long game was solid, my around-the-green play was flawless.

"I'm playing golf for the pure enjoyment of it now," he continued, "and there's nothing better, I can tell you that. I'm just a very content person right now, but I still have the desire to compete. I never want to lose that."

Someone asked him if he is now or expects to be the game's next dominant player, and he answered with candor, "I hope so. I really want to be. It's not a question of whether I want to be or not, it's just a question of whether I'll be able to do it."

That aside, it is true, though, that by winning in Tulsa he jumped to the top of the Sony Ranking.

It is fact that he had won two PGA Championships and a British Open over three years, which is better than anyone had done since Nicklaus won the 1978 British Open and then both the U.S. Open and PGA Championship in 1980. Before then Arnold Palmer had won five major tournaments in 1960 through 1962, and before then Hogan had won five from 1951 through 1953 — three of those in 1953 alone. (We should not overlook that Nicklaus won four within three years twice, three within two years twice, and three within three years another time.)

Price had won six events worldwide in 1994, and would win one more, short of the nine Norman won in 1986, but more impressive because of those two major titles. He had been playing like a dream over the previous month, winning the British Open with a score of 268, Motorola Western Open with 277 and PGA Championship with 269, and placing fourth in the Federal Express St. Jude Classic in Memphis, again shooting 268.

Meantime, the PGA Championship deserves worlds of credit for what it has done over the previous few years. It had been sort of a throw-in as one of the four principal competitions of the professionals' year, made part of the modern Grand Slam only because Bobby Jones had won four national championships in 1930, the year of his incomparable Grand Slam, when he won both the Open and Amateur championships of the United States and Britain. Had he not won four, would the modern slam be made up of the Masters, the two Opens, and the PGA? We can only wonder.

That it belonged with the other three could not be disputed after the three championships beginning with Price's victory at Bellerive. Then, in 1993, Norman, Nick Faldo, Paul Azinger and Vijay Singh together put on a stirring finish at the Inverness Club in Toledo, although both Singh and Faldo yielded in the end and left Azinger and Norman tied. Azinger won when Norman missed a makeable putt on the second playoff hole.

Finishes like those and Price's magnificent golf in the 1994 championship combined with the PGA's decisions to use the Sony Ranking to determine invitations, and to take its championship to courses more closely associated with the U.S. Open, have indeed raised the PGA to the levels it enjoyed for so many years as a match-play extravaganza, before is slunk into the doldrums through a series of lackluster venues and uninspiring winners.

In Azinger the PGA had an enormously popular champion, but not long after he won he found he had developed cancer in his right shoulder and had to drop out of golf for the better part of 1994. This was only his second appearance of the year. He had played in the Buick Open the week before, and although he had shot a respectable 70 in the second round he had missed the cut with 146.

In truth, he was never a factor in the PGA Championship. Beginning at 8:48 a.m. with Larry Nelson and Payne Stewart, two other former PGA champions, Azinger bogeyed five of the first nine holes and never recovered. He fought on, though, played the second nine in even-par 35 with two more bogeys offset by a pair of birdies and finished with 75 and very little hope of surviving the 36-hole cut.

The sky was clear and cloudless as play began at seven o'clock, and although the humidity remained fairly low, the temperature climbed throughout the day, reaching well into the 90s in mid-afternoon. It was indeed more comfortable at Southern Hills in August than it had been for the U.S. Open at Oakmont in June.

There was another difference between Oakmont and Southern Hills. Where Watson and Nicklaus had brought back memories of other days by moving to the top of the U.S. Open leaderboard, they were never really part of the PGA. Some omen of what lay ahead took place earlier in the week. In the last practice round before the British Open a month earlier, Watson and Nicklaus played a four-ball match against Norman and Price, shot a better-ball score of 60, and won a lot of money. They arranged a rematch before the PGA and lost it all back. Nicklaus opened the PGA with 79 and was doomed.

Watson, though, played almost as well as he had in both the U.S. Open and the British Open, shooting 69, just one stroke under par, and as the day ended, lurked only two strokes behind the leaders. Colin Montgomerie and Price shot 67s, followed by Ernie Els, the U.S. Open champion; Ian Woosnam, who had shown occasional returns of form during 1994, and Phil Mickelson and Fred Couples, who were considered the best hopes for an American victory. Of course, as someone pointed out, Mickelson was coming back from three months off the PGA Tour with a broken leg and Couples from a five-month absence because of a painful back condition, so their prospects weren't bright.

Southern Hills bared its teeth from the start. With 151 players taking their best shots at it under nearly perfect weather conditions, the course gave up only 14 rounds under its par of 70. Where it is only normal with players of this caliber to see one or two rounds at four or five under par at some point on the course, no one was ever lower than three under par at Southern Hills.

Continuing his pattern of excellent golf left over from the British Open, where he entered the final round at Turnberry in a tie for first place, Fuzzy

Zoeller was the first man in with a sub-par score. Off the first tee just a few minutes after eight o'clock paired with Faldo and Loren Roberts, Fuzzy went out in 36, dropping one stroke on the eighth, a par-three hole of 215 yards, then coming back in 33 with two birdies. Roberts, who had lost a playoff to Els for the U.S. Open, matched his 69, but Faldo continued to play indifferent golf and shot 73.

Half an hour later Mickelson came in with his 68, along with Watson and Ben Crenshaw, who had let a fine round slip away from him. Three under par after 11 holes, Ben stepped onto the tee of the 12th hole full of confidence. At 448 yards, the 12th is certainly the finest par-four hole Southern Hills can offer. Its fairway bends slightly left and its green sits behind a narrow brook that crosses the fairway just in front and then purls along the right side.

Crenshaw played a nice drive to the ideal spot on the fairway, then a soft pitch within five feet of the hole. For years one of the most reliable putters in the game, Crenshaw had every confidence he had holed it and moved to four under par. But the putt didn't fall, and everything went downhill from there. He pulled his drive on the 13th, a 537-yard par five, missed the green and bogeyed, then missed the 14th green and bogeyed there as well, then capped his entire frustrating day by three-putting the 18th. Stepping off the green he slammed his putter into his bag, something he rarely does. Instead of sharing the lead, he shot 70.

Mickelson, meanwhile, was playing very sound bogey-free golf. He missed only the 11th and 12th greens, and then by not very much, saved his pars on both, and birdied the 13th, where he played a nice pitch to 10 feet and holed the putt. He birdied again at the 16th, a long par four of 468 yards, where he holed from 40 feet. When he put up his 68, he held the first-round lead.

It didn't last long. About half an hour later Colin Montgomerie came in with his 67. He had started a little after nine o'clock grouped with Hale Irwin and Norman, whom everybody always expects to win these things. With 75, Irwin was never in it, and Norman shot a dull 71. Montgomerie, though, played wonderful golf, 18 holes over a trying course without bogeying a hole. He drove superbly, missing only the 16th fairway, where his ball drifted a foot into the light rough.

Montgomerie began quickly by rolling a 30-foot putt home on the first hole, then didn't make another until the 11th, a par three of 164 yards, where he almost made a hole-in-one. His tee shot, played with an eight iron, hit inside the cup on the fly but jumped out. Before he putted he had to ask the rules official at the scene to repair the edge of the cup, where his ball had hit (while players are allowed to fix their own pitch marks, they are not allowed to tamper with the hole itself).

He made his last birdie on the 13th, a par five, by reaching the back of the green with a powerful three wood and getting down in two from 30 feet. He had only one scare; his six-iron approach missed the 16th green and his chip left him five feet from the cup. He coaxed the putt home and played the remaining two holes without incident.

Price played later in the day, when the heat reached its worst, but it had no noticeable effect. Perhaps a touch unlucky at the start, Nick's drive picked up a daub of mud, and his six-iron approach turned a little left and hopped just off the green. He had to play his third shot with the mud still on the ball and ran it 15 feet past the hole. Two more putts and he had bogeyed. A birdie from 15 feet on the fifth brought him back to level par, and then he played the seventh, a 382-yard par four, with a two iron and a seven iron to 15 feet and holed the putt once more. One under par now.

He gave that stroke away by three-putting the ninth from 25 feet, but he played flawless golf from there in. He hit every green and missed only the 12th fairway, where he pounded his drive so hard it ran through the corner of the dogleg. Still, he played a downhill 180-yard six iron to 10 feet and holed the putt.

One under again, he picked up another birdie on the 13th. To demonstrate how far he was driving the ball, the 13th, one of only two par-five holes at Southern Hills, measures 537 yards. Price reached the back of the green with a two iron for his second shot, then two-putted from 45 feet or so. Two under.

He picked up his last birdie on the 17th, a nicely shaped par four of 352 yards, driving with his two iron once again and then playing a nice pitch to three or four feet with his nine iron.

The first-round leaderboard:

Nick Price	67	Loren Roberts	69
Colin Montgomerie	67	Sam Torrance	69
Phil Mickelson	68	Tom Watson	69
Ernie Els	68	D.A. Weibring	69
Fred Couples	68	David Gilford	69
Ian Woosnam	68	Lanny Wadkins	69
Fuzzy Zoeller	69	Raymond Floyd	69

It didn't take long to see that Southern Hills would be an easier course for the second round than it had for the first. Playing in the first group Friday morning, Ron Philo holed a 20-foot putt on the first hole. On Thursday it took seven groups and more than an hour for the first birdie to fall.

Further evidence: Where Price and Montgomerie had led the first round with 67, on Friday 67 was only the sixth best score of the day. Blaine McCallister shot 64, Price and Brian Henninger shot 65, Jose Maria Olazabal and Jay Haas shot 66s, and Crenshaw, Cook, Faldo, Corey Pavin, Frank Nobilo, Richard Zokol, Fulton Allem and Kenny Perry shot 67.

It was quite a day. With somewhat softer greens, Southern Hills gave up 34 rounds in the 60s against only 14 in the opening round, setting up remarkable shifts in the standings. McCallister bettered his score by 10 strokes, mated his 64 with an opening 74 and climbed into a tie for fifth place. Wayne Grady saved himself by shooting 68 to go with his opening 75 and moved into a tie for 38th; Zokol went from 77 to 67, Perry from 78 to 67, and Faldo from 73 to 66.

At the same time others were having dreadful problems. Montgomerie went from a share of the lead into a tie for 38th place by slipping to 76; Woosnam, only one stroke off the lead at the end of the first round, shot 72 and dropped into a tie for 14th place, and Singh, who had played so well at Inverness a year earlier, went from 70 right out of the tournament with 79.

After opening with 78, Seve Ballesteros began the second round as if he would never hit a fairway. He hit two trees on the first hole and another on the second, shot 76 and went home.

At the end of the day Price had the lead to himself, at 132, five comfortable strokes ahead of Pavin, Crenshaw and the surprising Haas, who hadn't often been this close to the lead in one of the important championships.

By then it looked as if Nick would run away with the championship. When he teed off, a little after nine o'clock, only Woosnam and Couples among the first-round leaders had begun, and neither man was having a good day. Couples bogeyed two of the first five holes on his way to 74 and a share of 28th place, and Woosnam had his share of problems after a highly promising start.

Very quickly he mounted a serious challenge to Price. Off about 15 minutes ahead of him, Woosie birdied the fourth hole and pulled into a tie with Nick, who was just beginning by then. Price struck back by rolling in a putt from 20 feet on the first hole and moving one stroke ahead, and then Woosnam birdied the fifth, catching Price once more. The second round was shaping up then as a tense and stirring battle.

Just then, though, Woosnam ran into trouble. Playing the seventh, which must be the easiest par-four hole on the course, Woosnam drove into the woods, nearly beheading a number of spectators, and into a spaghetti-like mess of television cables, dead behind a tree. From there he chipped out to open ground and followed with a miserable pitch that fell into a greenside bunker. Three more strokes and Woosnam had a double-bogey six. Then he compounded that horror by three-putting the eighth from 30 feet. He was finished, but he turned in 72 and fell into a tie for 14th place. He never figured again, though.

While Woosnam foundered, Price kept playing the steadiest kind of golf through the seventh. He ran into a little trouble when he missed the eighth green with his two-iron tee shot, but he chipped to six feet and holed the putt, then found a glob of mud on his ball once again when he drove into the rough on the ninth. His pitch ran off the back of the green, but he saved himself with a pretty chip within inches of the cup.

He had gone out in 34, but just ahead McCallister had played the first nine in 31, four under par. Well out of range of the leaders, McCallister had begun the day by holing an eight-foot putt on the first for a birdie, but then giving it back with a bogey on the second, where he bunkered his approach. He made no more mistakes after that as birdie followed birdie. A 10-footer fell at the third, and after a par four on the fourth, he ran off three consecutive birdies. He reached the green of the very long fifth, a par five of 614 yards, with a driver, three iron and wedge and holed from 12 feet; played a lovely seven iron inside a foot on the sixth, a 175-yard par three, and then holed from 20 feet or so on the seventh.

He stood at four under par then, and at that stage the fans didn't know who to follow — Price, who was actually leading the tournament, or McCallister, who might set a record.

McCallister was playing stunning irons. Two more quick birdies followed on the 10th and 11th, one from no more than two feet and the other from well inside 10 feet. He stood six under par then, and when he dropped a seven iron just outside 10 feet on the 15th and ran in the putt, he needed only three more pars to shoot 63 and match the lowest score ever shot in one of the four major championships.

He didn't make it, principally because of an inexcusably poor approach to the 17th and a worse third shot. After drilling a three wood into the ideal location in the fairway less than 100 yards from the green, he chunked a wedge into a bunker, played from there into another bunker, took two more to get down, and bogeyed. Par on the final hole gave him 64, still not a bad score but not what it might have been.

While McCallister was drawing raves, Price was playing almost as well. He had gone out in 34, then picked up his second birdie of the day at the 10th with a sand wedge to 15 feet. Two under for the day then, and five under for 28 holes. A sensational seven iron that pulled up within three feet of the cup on the 12th. When the putt fell, Price slipped to four under for the day and six under for the distance. He was pulling away, three strokes ahead of Montgomerie, who wouldn't begin for another hour, and Pavin, who had just birdied the 10th to go three under par for the day.

Another birdie putt fell for Price on the 13th, and still another on the 16th, the longest par four on the course, where he had driven so far he had only a sand wedge left. He pitched to 10 feet and holed the putt. Eight under par for 34 holes, he stood five strokes clear of Pavin, McCallister and Montgomerie, who would never be closer. Just before Price tapped in his second putt on the 18th, Montgomerie began his fall by bogeying the first.

Playing immediately behind Price, Pavin nearly holed his bunker shot on the 18th, but he made his par four, shot 67, and remained five strokes behind Price. McCallister had bogeyed the 17th by then and fallen a further stroke behind.

With Price playing such first-class golf, Olazabal's 66 drew less attention than it should have. He played a very steady round with all his five birdies crammed into the first 13 holes. He bogeyed the second, when he missed the green with an eight iron, but struck back by holing from 30 feet on the fourth and from five feet on the fifth, the long par five. Another putt fell from 15 feet on the ninth, another from 18 feet on the 11th, and he reached the 13th with a three-iron second shot and two-putted from 40 feet.

As with most rounds like this, it could have been lower. Olazabal had his 40-footer on the 13th dead on line but it pulled up short.

Still, Olazabal's 66 at least qualified him for the third and fourth rounds. He had missed the cut in both his previous two American tournaments. After winning the Masters, Olazabal missed the cut in both the U.S. Open and in the Buick Open the week before the PGA. Now, at 138 for 36 holes, he was solidly in contention.

The cut fell at 145 and caught a number of the game's foremost players, both past and current. Sadly, Azinger bowed out, along with Nicklaus, whose opening 79 had given him too much work to do; Ian Baker-Finch, who had been invisible since winning the 1991 British Open; Singh, who had been so impressive during 1993; Jesper Parnevik, who almost won the British Open a month earlier; Ballesteros, and Palmer, who had said this would probably be his last PGA. He went out in style, holing a 20-foot putt on the final hole. He shot 74, but again his opening 79 had left him much too far behind.

The second-round leaderboard:

Nick Price	65 - 132	Frank Nobilo	67 - 139
Corey Pavin	67 - 137	Ernie Els	71 - 139
Jay Haas	66 - 137	Glen Day	69 - 139
Ben Crenshaw	67 - 137	Gil Morgan	68 - 139
Blaine McCallister	64 - 138	Phil Mickelson	71 - 139
Jose Maria Olazabal	66 - 138	Craig Parry	69 - 139
John Cook	67 - 138		

With two rounds to go, it seemed obvious that only two developments could prevent Price from winning the PGA Championship. One, he would have to play a generally bad round and throw away his advantage, or, two, someone else would have to play two torrid rounds and catch him. While the 70 he shot in the third round couldn't be considered generally bad, it was, however, the worst he had played so far and indeed opened the way for others to catch him. Every time someone came close, though, he played a bad hole or two and fell back; and at the end of the day Price still held a three-stroke lead, not so comfortable as it had been, but good enough.

Haas, Pavin and Mickelson all had their opportunities, but they all fell short. Haas closed to within one stroke of Price at one stage, but he promptly triple-bogeyed the ninth hole and fell back. Pavin closed within two strokes and quickly dropped back as well, and Mickelson moved within two strokes of him as well, and just as quickly bollixed the 12th and couldn't advance further.

All of this played against a background of mounting heat and humidity under a blazing sun that sapped everyone's energy and sent hordes of people to first aid stations for relief. Volunteer doctors estimated more than 400 spectators been treated for heat-related problems during the first three rounds, and four or five were sent to hospitals for further treatment.

Scores, nevertheless, continued to run low. The 76 players who survived the 36-hole cut turned in 23 rounds in the 60s, but the lowest scores weren't as low as they had been in Friday's second round. Jeff Sluman, the 1988 PGA champion, and Steve Elkington each shot 66; Mickelson was among seven others who shot 67; Haas was among six at 68, and Pavin was among eight with 69.

Norman, one of the 67 shooters, climbed into a tie for fifth, along with Crenshaw, who shot 70, and Cook, with 69. Olazabal lost ground with his 70, falling from a tie for seventh into a tie for eighth. Watson continued his fine play of 1994 with 67 and climbed into a tie for eighth, along with Els, who shot 69, Loren Roberts, another of those with 67, Sluman and Olazabal.

At the same time, McCallister, who had blistered Southern Hills with his 64 on Friday, shot 75 on Saturday and dropped like a rock into a tie for 34th place with two others who had been much higher during the early rounds — Montgomerie, who shot 70, and Woosnam, with 73.

Both Elkington and Sluman played fairly early in the day, Elkington leaving the first tee at 10:18 a.m. and Sluman three groups later, at 10:54 a.m. Elkington played the steadier of the two, although both made more birdies on the second nine than the first. Elkington birdied both the fifth and seventh going out, dropped a stroke on the 10th, but then birdied both the 11th and 12th, not easy holes, and finished with another birdie on the 17th. He had gone out in 33 and back in 33 for his 66.

Sluman, though, appeared to be heading nowhere when he wiped out two hard-won birdies on the third and seventh with bogeys on the sixth and ninth. But he rallied on the second nine, picked up one birdie on the 13th, and after a nice par three on the 14th, ran off three more birdies on the 15th, 16th and 17th. Out in 35, he had stormed home in 31.

In the end Sluman's 66 had no effect. He shot 75 the next day and fell out of sight, but Elkington followed up with a closing 69 and finished with a respectable 278, good for a share of seventh place.

All of this was little more than entertainment for the fans who came early, since the main event didn't begin until after noon when first Mickelson and Gil Morgan teed off a little after 12.30 p.m., then Haas and Crenshaw at 1:09 p.m., followed by Pavin and Price, at 1:18 p.m.

The lesson taught by Elkington and Sluman that Southern Hills could be beaten wasn't lost on Mickelson. He began his round by birdieing three of the first four holes and five of the first eight. His first nine was marred only by a bogey five on the second, a particularly difficult driving hole where 14 balls had fallen into a lateral water hazard during the second round. With the hazard on the left, Mickelson pulled his drive into the right rough (he is left-handed, remember), and couldn't reach the green with his second shot. He missed his putt from eight feet after holing from six feet on the first for the birdie.

Two pitching wedges to 12 feet earned him birdies on both the third and fourth, and then a lovely eight-iron tee shot to six feet won him another at the sixth. He made his final birdie of the first nine with a terrific three iron to 15 feet on the eighth.

By then he stood four under par for the round and five under for the 44 holes. Price was well into his round by then and had already come under attack from Pavin, who holed a 35-foot putt on the second, cutting Price's lead over him from five strokes to four. At about that time, though, Mickelson had already birdied the sixth and moved ahead of Pavin into second place. Pavin's birdie tied him with Mickelson.

Then, when Mickelson birdied the eighth, he dropped to five under par; and with Price making nothing but pars through the opening holes, Phil had climbed within three strokes of him. This was one of those days when birdies were dropping so quickly it was hard to keep up with who stood where.

Except for Price. He simply could make nothing happen through the first nine holes, although he had some opportunities. After driving into the left rough, he had missed a birdie putt from 15 feet on the first hole, another from about the same distance on the sixth, and still another from little more than 10 feet on the ninth. He had missed two greens on the outward nine but had saved pars on both.

Pavin cut into Price's lead once more on the fifth, the par five. On the green with his third shot, Corey faced an unusual putt from 20 feet. When he stroked the ball, it broke from left-to-right toward the hole, but as it rolled along it looked as if he hadn't borrowed enough and that the ball would surely curl in front of the hole. Then, about six or eight feet from the hole, it straightened out and ran directly into the cup.

Now Pavin stood five under par, but two holes later he played a stunning seven iron inside two feet for his third birdie of the day. Six under par now, he had closed within two strokes of Price.

That, however, was as close as Pavin or Mickelson would come to catching Price. Pavin would pick up a couple of bogeys on the second nine, and a few minutes after Pavin holed his birdie on the seventh, Mickelson double-bogeyed the 12th. He pushed his drive into the left rough, overshot the green with a three-iron second shot that settled behind a grandstand, and after taking a free drop hit a poor pitch that didn't reach the green. A chip to 10 feet and two putts earned him a six and ended his threat.

Pavin then lost his momentum on the 12th and 14th holes. He missed the 12th green with a five-iron approach, costing him one stroke, then almost fell completely apart on the 13th, where he went for the green with a three-wood second and didn't make it. His ball splashed into a pond in front of the green.

Corey doesn't give up strokes easily, though. The ball lay fairly close to the bank, and after looking it over he realized he would have to stand in the water to play the shot. While the gallery cheered, he sat on his golf bag, took off his shoe and sock, then, in a shower of water, pitched his ball onto the green and saved his par.

He would have no such luck on the 14th, though. His tee shot nipped the overhanging branch of a tree on the right and dropped into the rough. When he walked up to his ball, Pavin found it close to a slight roll in the ground. Corey's pitch didn't make the green; instead it dropped into a bunker, and he played well to save a bogey.

Now Pavin stood at four under par, one stroke better than he had started but still four strokes behind Price, whose biggest worry then was Haas, who hadn't played this important a role in the PGA since the early 1980s when he came in fifth in 1982 and ninth in 1983. Forty years old, he had placed fifth in the Masters, but he had missed the cut in the U.S. Open and didn't play in the British Open. Now, though, he was threatening Price.

Beginning the round five strokes behind Price, tied with Pavin and Crenshaw, Haas dropped six strokes behind when he bogeyed the fourth hole. Right away he birdied the fifth with a fine sand wedge to eight feet, and closed within four strokes of Price with another birdie at the ninth, where he played a seven iron to 15 feet.

Playing torrid golf then, Haas birdied both the 10th and 11th, dropping to six under par and climbing within two strokes of Price. He wasn't through just yet. Both bogeyed the 12th, Haas with a six-iron approach that nipped a tree branch and fell short of the green, and Price with a mis-played drive that bounced into the right rough near the base of a tree and inside the fork of a broken twig lying on the ground. From this difficult lie he hit a wild shot that squirted across the fairway into the left rough and took three more strokes to hole out. Back to seven under par.

At the time Price was bogeying the 12th, Haas, playing one hole ahead of him, was birdieing the 13th with a nice pitch to five feet after laying up from about 230 yards. Now Haas stood at six under par once again, within one stroke of the lead. Then Haas committed a blunder that cost him dearly.

Playing the 15th hole, a par four with a fairway bunker sitting on the left about 250 yards out and a well-guarded green ringed by five bunkers, Haas pushed his drive slightly, possibly trying to avoid the bunker. His ball nicked a tree branch and dropped into the rough. Crenshaw had driven close by, and from the fairway cut a five iron around the tree and onto the green. Seeing how Crenshaw's five iron had behaved, Haas drew his seven iron, hoping to play the shot onto the green's lower level. It didn't work; the ball flew to the back of the green and hopped into one of the bunkers. Then Haas tried to play too cute a shot, hoping to pop the ball out and let it run downhill to the pin. He hit the shot too softly; the ball didn't even reach the green. He stubbed the chip, barely nudging the ball onto the green, took two putts, and made seven on a par-four hole, his second triple bogey of the tournament. Instead of putting pressure on Price, he had fallen four strokes behind, and Price was home free.

No other challenges materialized. Nick followed his bogey on the 12th with a birdie at the 13th, bogeyed the 15th, birdied the 17th and finished with 70.

Haas fought back with birdies on both the 16th and 17th, and Mickelson chipped in for a birdie at the 17th, but neither could catch up.

The third-round leaderboard:

Nick Price	70 - 202	John Cook	69 - 207
Jay Haas	68 - 205	Jose Maria Olazabal	70 - 208
Corey Pavin	69 - 206	Ernie Els	69 - 208
Phil Mickelson	67 - 206	Loren Roberts	67 - 208
Ben Crenshaw	70 - 207	Tom Watson	67 - 208
Greg Norman	67 - 207	Jeff Sluman	66 - 208

As he spoke with the press following the third round, Price said he felt that because Norman was capable of shooting any score at all, he was probably his most serious threat in the final round. Throughout the early holes, Price looked like a prophet.

The weather had changed overnight. The sun that had blazed down on Southern Hills through the first three rounds rode above a gray overcast, and the temperature fell from the mid to high 90s into the low 80s. It was much more comfortable than it had been, and it seemed at first to give Norman new life.

Greg did indeed look as if he might break into one of his wild rounds. He had improved his scoring by two strokes through each of the first three rounds, going from an opening 71 to 69 in the second round and then to 67 in the third. By then he stood five strokes behind Price, but then he opened the final round with two consecutive birdies, and before Price had quite finished the first hole, he found Norman breathing hard behind him, just three strokes back with 16 holes left to play.

Price, though, held his ground, birdied both the third and fourth, Norman cooled off, no one else made a serious run, and in the end Price won easily. Even though he won by so wide a margin, his round was worth watching, for he played wonderful golf. Instead of his tentative and occasional loose golf of the previous day, he played a forceful, attacking game, never allowing himself to be influenced by what the others ahead of him were doing and never letting his mind wander.

With supreme confidence in his swing, he seemed to hit every shot squarely on the face of the club, and on the occasional hole where his shot wandered from its target, he put the stroke behind him and got on with his mission.

He played an erratic last nine, with three bogeys, three birdies and three pars, but by then it hardly mattered, for he had many strokes in hand and had demoralized the competition.

Haas had begun the final round the closest to him, just three strokes back, but his threat had withered by the fourth hole, where he bogeyed for the second time. A double-bogey six at the sixth, and he was on his way to shooting 75 and falling well behind, at 280.

On a day when he needed birdies, Pavin could make nothing but pars; and even though Mickelson scored some birdies, he couldn't make enough of them, then ruined his chances of taking second place by double-bogeying the 16th.

Nevertheless, the day had its moments, the first of them when Norman ran off his opening birdies. He stood alone in second place then at five under par, but within minutes Mickelson holed from five feet on the third to catch Norman, then pulled ahead of him with another birdie on the fourth.

Mickelson stood six under par then, within two strokes of Price, but Price quickly played a stunning wedge into the third green that for a heart-stopping moment looked as if it might fall for an eagle two. Instead, it hopped about two feet from the pin for an easy birdie. Nine under par now and three strokes ahead. Another wedge to six feet on the fourth, another birdie, and now Price stood at 10 under par and four strokes ahead. No one would come closer through the day.

Still, there was hope, but not for Norman. He bogeyed the fifth and fell six strokes out of the lead. A bogey there was more troublesome that it might have been on another hole, for this was a par five, and players of Norman's quality should expect to birdie those holes. It seemed to take some of the fire out of him, for he could make nothing happen until the 13th hole, and by then it was far too late. A double-bogey six on the 17th and he finished with 70 instead of the 64 or 65 he could have used.

Price, meanwhile, plodded on, and within the next half hour he had it all won. Mickelson missed the seventh green and bogeyed, and then Price ripped a three iron into the eighth and holed from a little more than 20 feet. Now Price stood at 11 under par, Mickelson had gone to five under, and Pavin, still without a birdie, held steady at four under.

With a par four at the ninth, Price had played the first nine in 32, the kind of score he was concerned that Norman might shoot. He had played unbeatable golf, and had to do no more than hold steady through the home nine to claim the prize.

Now he played another glorious wedge within four feet on the 10th and of course birdied. Twelve under par, he opened his lead to seven strokes with eight holes to play. He gave that stroke away with his first really loose hole of the day, missing the 11th green with a six iron and then failing to make the putt from four feet after a very nice little chip. Back to 11 under par, but after once again playing a scary 12th hole by driving into the rough and holing from four feet after missing the green with an eight-iron approach, Price drove down the middle of the 13th fairway, laid up short of the water with a seven iron, then pitched to 12 feet. He holed it and went back to 12 under par.

Two holes later Pavin finally broke through by holing from 18 feet and birdieing the 15th just as Price bogeyed once again. Now Pavin stood at five under par, but it didn't matter. In truth nothing mattered now except for Price to stay on his feet. Pavin was closest to him, but six strokes behind, and Mickelson was next, fully seven strokes back after his six on the 16th.

Driving the ball enormous distances now, Price picked up his last birdie on the 16th, belting a driver out of sight and leaving himself nothing more than a solid six iron into the green of a hole that measures 468 yards. He hit the shot within eight feet of the hole and of course made the putt. Now he stood 12 under par, seven strokes ahead of Pavin and eight ahead of Mickelson.

After a standard par four on the 17th, Price stepped onto the 18th tee and played a two iron about as well as it could be played, far, far down the right side to the most treacherous spot in the drive zone, alongside a neck of a creek that knifes halfway across the fairway then burrows underground, and just short of two bunkers partway up the rise leading to the elevated green.

Price couldn't have walked ahead and dropped his ball in a better spot, nor could most of the field have hit the ball as far with their drivers. It was an enormous drive that left him only an eight iron into the green.

That he three-putted mattered not at all. As someone pointed out, he could have eight-putted and won. While it couldn't be considered one of the game's classic rounds, his 67, played under telling pressure, was at the least two strokes better than any of his closest challengers could put together.

This was an immensely satisfying victory for Price. As he said, "To lead every round of any major championship — or any tournament, for that matter — is very difficult, because you go to sleep thinking about all sorts of things. Had I not won there would have been a big question mark about my character. I would have been very depressed.

"But there is one thing I'm really happy about. I got my name on that trophy two out of three years, which is something very special."

7. The Players Championship

Throughout his career, Greg Norman has exhibited an Homeric, larger-than-life quality. His victories have been a touch more heroic, a little more awesome, slightly more overwhelming than anyone else's. The 1993 British Open Championship at Royal St. George's serves as an example. By the same token, his losses have been more epic, more cruel, more devastating. Even Homer, however, balked at having his heroes call their shots. That was left to Babe Ruth — and Greg Norman.

Norman added that Ruthian touch — he called his shot before the tournament started — in a record-breaking triumph in The Players Championship.

"I'm going to shoot 22 under on your golf course," Norman told Pete Dye, who designed and built the Tournament Players Club at Sawgrass as the home course for the PGA Tour. "You've got to come up with some harder courses, mate," Norman told the golf course architect whose layout once was cursed and vilified as being unplayably difficult.

(Dye blithely claimed to have forgotten Norman's prediction, however. Flying home after his run-away victory, Norman telephoned Dye to remind him, to tweak him just a bit. Dye was having none of it; said he put it out of his mind as the ravings of a lunatic. "Why should I pay attention to something crazy like that?" he asked.)

Norman did not, in fact, shoot 22 under par on Dye's course. He shot 24 under. He led all the way, set course scoring records in each round and threatened to play the entire tournament without a bogey. The attempt at a bogey-free performance fell short, however, on a poor swing with a five iron, a strong chip, a fluttering butterfly and a mis-read putt on the par-three 13th hole in the final round of the tournament billed as the annual championship of American golf's touring pros.

"I'm really disappointed I made a bogey," Norman said. "I've never gone 72 holes without one. That was my goal here. There are things you have an opportunity of doing maybe once or twice in a lifetime, and 72 holes without a bogey on a course like this would have been fabulous."

But that was about the only glitch, the only disappointment in a superlative effort that began with a course-record 63 and was followed by three consecutive 67s. He set course records for 36 holes (130) and 54 holes (197). He was 19 under par after three rounds, one more than the record 18-under total amassed by Nick Price for four rounds a year earlier. Norman's winning 264 total was 24 under par — six better than the old mark.

Quite simply, he was in a class by himself.

"I think this is in my top three or four weeks of golf ever," a deeply satisfied Norman said.

PGA Tour Commissioner Deane Beman was even more impressed. "I think this is one of those records that will never be beaten," Beman said. Fuzzy Zoeller, the happy-go-lucky 42-year-old who played the last two rounds with Norman and eventually finished second, tended to agree. "Greg did everything he needed to do to win," Zoeller said. "He played extremely well. In my 20 years out here, I haven't seen anyone play as well for 72 holes. I got beat by the best player in the world."

The Australian ace, then No. 1 on the Sony Ranking, was at the peak of his powers. He led by two strokes after the first round, by three after the second, by four after the third and won by four over Zoeller, the only man in the field able to keep him in sight. Zoeller had a closing 67 and a 268 total, better than the old scoring record and good enough to have won any of the 20 previous Players Championships. This time, however, it was second best, Zoeller's third runner-up finish in as many starts. "You know the old saying," he mused, "if you keep knocking on the door long enough, maybe it'll open. Maybe it won't. But I sure like the knocking."

Norman enjoyed it, too. Perhaps even more than Zoeller. After all, he had been knocking more frequently and with much greater success. In a 15-month period, going back to the start of the 1993 season, Norman had 26 top-10 finishes in 31 worldwide starts. Six of those were victories; 11 others were second, third or fourth. In that period, he won in the United States, Great Britain, Japan and Thailand and collected more than $3 million in worldwide earnings. And, with his first victory of the year, the Johnnie Walker Asian Classic in Thailand, Norman had regained the No. 1 spot on the Sony Ranking from Nick Faldo.

The Players Championship was Norman's 66th career victory around the world and his 12th official title on the American circuit. It was worth $450,000 from the total purse of $2.5 million. It increased his official season's earnings to $556,333 in the United States and put him on track for a bid at a third American money-winning title. He also slipped past Paul Azinger and into second place on the American career money-winning list at $7,173,986.

But his record-breaking accomplishments in this tournament came as no surprise to either Norman or the only man who has won more money on the American circuit, Tom Kite. Both predicted very low — possibly embarrassingly low — scores for an ambitious tournament that admittedly and unabashedly seeks a stature equal to that of the Masters, U.S. Open, British Open and PGA Championship.

Norman's prediction of a record score made to Dye and Kite's irate forecast of extremely low numbers were voiced after their first practice rounds on the course Tom Weiskopf once called "Donkey-Kong golf," a course so unplayably difficult that the embarrassed, anguished touring pros once forced Commissioner Beman to modify and ease the layout. Now, even before Norman's record assault began, some of the game's leading lights said it was too easy — certainly too easy for a tournament that, as Kite said, "wants to think of itself as a major."

The problem concerned the condition of the course. Player after player traipsed into the press interview area and called it "soft." The lush fairways kept tee shots from running into the rough. The yielding greens allowed players to attack the pins without fear. "Hopefully," Kite said, "the people in charge will try to do something about it." He admitted, however, there was little that could be done. "What they need right now is about a 60-mile-per-hour wind with zero humidity and dry this thing out."

But the wind did not blow, at least until the final round and relatively lightly then. Humidity remained high, and another saturating storm caused an overnight delay in the second round. And the course remained vulnerable. Nothing was changed. And, Beman said, nothing would be changed. The Commissioner took an unperturbed view of Norman's liberties with the course, rather than the more panic-stricken reaction of U.S. Open officials who hastily planted the "Hinkle tree" to block an opening to an adjacent fairway found by Lon Hinkle during the 1979 American national championship.

There were no plans, Beman said, to alter or toughen the TPC at Sawgrass. "This golf course was built for northeast Florida where, at this time of the year, the wind is going to blow," he said. "It's just that this year the wind blew only in the last round and not very much then. And the kind of golf we saw, you just don't see very often."

Zoeller was in complete agreement. "There's nothing wrong with the golf course. It was just the conditions and you can't do anything about that," he said. "They shouldn't make any changes. They should just pat us on the back, say 'Good playing,' and let us come back again next year."

On the closing holes, playing in the final twosome with Norman, Fuzzy followed his own advice: he patted his rival on the back, led the cheers for him in the march up the 18th fairway and acknowledged him as the premier player in the world.

But, true to his nature, the man who takes his nickname from his initials (Frank Urban Zoeller) had to clown around just a bit, too.

After Norman had missed a meaningless birdie putt on the final hole, Zoeller ambled up, towel in hand. "He was burning up the golf course," Fuzzy said later. "I just wanted to cool him off a little." Before Norman could tap in, Zoeller made a production of wiping the perspiration from Norman's face. Norman laughed, clapped his wide-brimmed hat on Fuzzy's head and tapped in the final putt. Zoeller threw an arm over Norman's shoulders as they walked away from one of the more significant triumphs of Norman's career.

"A very important win for me," he said. In addition to the more obvious values of the victory, the 39-year-old Australian also saw it as a confirmation of his change in approach to the game and an important alteration in his swing.

The flamboyant, go-for-broke Norman scored his first important triumph with a more compact, more conservative, more controlled swing. "I feel in total control," he said. And he's much more deliberate, taking more time over his shots, concentrating long and — he said — better. "I'm trying to see each shot twice now before I swing," he said. "It takes longer but that's my routine and I don't want to break it. I try to eliminate distractions and think positive thoughts."

While his pace may be slightly slower, Norman wasted no time in exerting his authority over a field that included Europe's Big Six of Faldo, Seve Ballesteros, Jose Maria Olazabal, Sandy Lyle, Ian Woosnam and Bernhard Langer, as well as defending titleholder Nick Price of Zimbabwe, the 1993 PGA Tour Player of the Year. The American contingent, however, was missing PGA titleholder Paul Azinger (receiving treatment for cancer), Fred Couples (back injury) and Phil Mickelson (broken leg).

Even if they had been healthy and on hand, however, it was not likely they could have matched strokes with Norman over the first round. With the fairways lush, the greens soft, the wind nothing more than a whisper of a breeze, and his game at a peak, Norman turned the once-feared TPC at Sawgrass into his personal plaything.

He missed only one green, didn't even come close to making a bogey and shot a nine-under-par 63 that tied the course record set by Fred Couples in 1992. This was one shot off Norman's career-best, a pair of 62s on the Blue Monster course at Doral. "I think I played better this round than those 62s," he said. "This was more under control. I've had 63s before, but sometimes you have to work hard for them. This was an under-control 63."

Norman, who started play from the 10th tee, made most of his move with a string of five consecutive birdies. After a birdie four on the 11th hole, he began the run with a 35-foot putt on the 13th. He hit a four iron to five feet on the 14th, birdied the 15th from 12 feet, reached the par-five 16th in two and two-putted and closed the string with a 15-foot birdie putt on the island green of the par-three 17th.

Going from the 18th green to the first tee "I just told myself to keep it going," Norman said. "On a long walk like that, it's easy to lose your momentum." But he didn't. He birdied the first and second, on putts of five and nine feet, and was eight under par for 11 holes. "I never really thought about shooting 59," he said in response to a question. "I wasn't thinking about a number. I was just trying to birdie them all." Of course he didn't. In fact, he only birdied one more, hitting a nine iron to five feet on the fifth. But that meant he had birdied half of them, nine of 18.

That effort, however, left him only two strokes in front of Kite, Colin Montgomerie, Lee Janzen and Jeff Maggert, all with 65s. Zoeller shot 66 in the exceptionally low overall scoring. In all, 38 of the 144-man field shot in the 60s, 93 were at par or better and the field average was under par, 71.4.

"You give us lush conditions," Norman said, "and see what we'll do." But he attempted to keep things in perspective. "I think we're taking this thing a little out of proportion," Norman said. "Nobody is really being controversial about the golf course. We're all being honest about it. The fact is it is a little softer than we like."

Kite, long a devotee of the tougher courses and more difficult conditions, was annoyed, however, and didn't appear to care who knew it. "I think most players would agree that if you have 63, you should be able to separate yourself from the field a little, more than one or two shots," he said. Montgomerie, on the other hand, was mystified. "In Europe, you shoot 65 and you're leading by three or four," he said, and shook his head. "Here, I'm two behind. I played the last four holes in par and felt like I dropped a shot or two. It's a different ball game."

The second round was a different kind of ball game, too. For one thing, it took two days to complete. For another, someone other than Greg Norman had an overnight lead. Not the lead at the end of a round, just the lead at the end of the day.

Play was held up for almost three hours by a thunderstorm that swept over the course promptly at nine a.m. Friday. The long delay eventually left half the field, 72 players, stranded on the course by darkness. Norman was among them. They marked their positions and came back at daylight Saturday to complete their second rounds.

Zoeller didn't have to get up early. He was in the half of the field that finished second-round play Friday. And Fuzzy had the overnight lead at 133,

11 under par, after an interrupted round of 67. It could have, probably should have, been better. But that three iron got him again.

Only a week earlier, at The Nestle Invitational, Zoeller missed a chance at victory when he sliced a three iron into the gallery on the 71st hole and watched the ball carom off a spectator's head into the water. This time, he had the 36-hole course and tournament record in sight before he hit that same three iron down a bank and into the water on the left of the 18th green. "I came over the top of it just a little bit. It was almost a good shot," Zoeller said. But it cost him a bogey. "Hey, I'm not a machine. I make mistakes," he said. Even with the mistake, he had an overnight lead of four over three-time U.S. Open winner Hale Irwin and Gary Hallberg, tied at 137. Irwin had 70, Hallberg 69.

Norman had played only 10 holes, and was two under par for the round, when darkness fell. And that presents one of the biggest challenges in golf, Norman said. "The hardest thing to do is to keep going when you have to stop in the middle of a round," he said.

He got away to the right start, however, and just kept rolling. "I started off making the right decision, going for No. 11 in two," he said. Norman got his second shot in a greenside bunker on that par-five hole then came out to tap-in distance for the birdie that put him back in front at 12 under par.

After missing a pair of birdie putts from about six feet on the 13th and 14th, he began to pull away with a six iron to four feet on the 15th and on the next hole, a par five, he again reached a greenside bunker in two and got it up and down for birdie. A save of par from a bunker on the 18th finished off the five-under-par effort and gave him a three-stroke advantage and a tournament record 130 at the tournament halfway point.

Zoeller held second while Davis Love III and Jeff Maggert, both of whom finished second-round play Saturday morning, shared third at 134. Maggert had a second-round 67, and Love shot 66.

A score of 144, par, was required to qualify for the final two rounds. Price, at 76–149, missed. Other prominent casualties were Ballesteros, Woosnam, Curtis Strange and John Daly.

After a brief lunch break, Norman found he was paired with Zoeller, his old friend and golfing foe and the man who beat him in an 18-hole playoff for the 1984 U.S. Open, for third-round play in the afternoon. And they quickly turned it into a two-man race. Maggert, Faldo and Love all got close at one time or another, but the real struggle remained concentrated in the final twosome.

Starting out with a three-stroke deficit, Zoeller made up one on the first nine then caught Norman with a nine iron to 18 inches on the 10th hole and an eight-foot birdie putt on the 11th. Norman, however, responded with birdies on the 12th, 13th and 16th, and Zoeller watched his eight-iron approach trickle over the retaining wall and into the water on the 17th. He managed to save bogey but lost still another shot to Norman, taking 68 against Norman's 67. Norman finished 54 holes, still without a bogey, in 197, 19 under par and another course record. Zoeller was at 201. The critical difference, Zoeller said, was Norman's "uncanny ability to scramble" after his few errant shots "and make something good happen out of a bad situation."

There were three examples in the third round. On the par-five second, he drove into the trees on the right, played out with a wedge, missed the green with a five iron, then chipped in for birdie.

He also missed the fifth with a five iron, the ball coming to rest on the downslope of a mound 20 yards right of the green. From an awkward stance, with the ball at chest height, he played a baseball swing up to 30 inches and made the par putt.

"My best shot of the day," he said, then reconsidered. "Well, there was 18," he said. There he drove into the gallery on the right and came up with another poor stance, again on a downhill lie, 173 yards from the pin. "I had to go over a dead stump, under a pine tree and slice it off the water. That was it. That's how the shot went," he said, and grinned: "and nothing but net." The remarkable par saved his four-shot lead and left Zoeller the only realistic challenger going into Sunday's final round. Maggert was third alone at 69–203. Faldo, with 68, and Love, with 70, were tied at 204 and were the only others within nine shots of the leader.

Zoeller went into the final round knowing he needed to play well, and Norman had to stumble. Zoeller accomplished the former, but Norman failed to provide the latter.

With four shots in hand, Norman needed only two holes to go seven in front and the tournament was, essentially, decided when the final round was only minutes old. Norman birdied the first two holes, each from about eight feet, while Zoeller missed the first green and made bogey.

At that point, only a few questions remained to be answered. One was whether Norman could get through the fourth round without a bogey. He answered that in the negative on the par-three 13th where he missed the green with "the only really bad swing I made all week," he said. He chipped to about eight feet and was standing over that putt when a butterfly fluttered across his line. He didn't flinch, didn't back away. But the putt missed on the left and he had his only bogey of the week.

He still led by five strokes with two holes to play, usually a margin that's safe enough. But with the island green of the 17th in front of him, and behind him a history of finding exotic methods of losing tournaments, Norman was taking nothing for granted. He was tight-lipped, unsmiling, intense, focused as he stood on the 17th tee, facing what he called "the toughest 141 yards under pressure in golf."

But when his nine-iron shot nestled in some two feet from the flag, a grinning Zoeller gave him a high-five. This game was over and Norman was a record-setting winner. He likened it to his brilliant British Open victory at Royal St. George's last year. "For the last two days I drew on Royal St. George's. At Royal St. George's I played with focus and dedication. That's the way I played today," he said.

Zoeller birdied three of the last four holes to match Norman's closing 67 and salvage second. Maggert once held that position but four-putted from long range for a bogey six on the 16th. He finished with 68 and a 271 total, the only other man within 12 shots of the winner.

8. Alfred Dunhill Cup

A little local knowledge can take you a long way. And perhaps at no other course in the world, fittingly since it was golf's very first layout, is that more true than at the Old Course in St. Andrews.

The first thing the Canadian team did when they arrived in this golfing Mecca in this eastern corner of Scotland was to go to the St. Andrews Caddie Master. Dave Barr's regular caddie is a Scot anyway, but Rick Stewart took on the help of his namesake Dod Stewart, and Rick Gibson hired the Caddie Master himself, Roy Mackenzie.

With this amount of local knowledge, the Canadians went a long way. All the way to the final of the Alfred Dunhill Cup — an event in which they had never got past the quarter-finals before — where they beat the United States, the defending champions.

They had arrived at St. Andrews unseeded and virtually unknown. Barr, 42, from Kelowna, British Columbia, is well enough known after 17 years on the U.S. PGA Tour where he has won twice. But his two companions were less easy to place.

Stewart, 40, spent six years on the U.S. Tour but now plays in Asia. He did not have a victory to his name. "I think I won a little pro am a couple years ago," he said. He hails from Matsqui, British Columbia, famed only as the home of the provincial penitentiary. His biggest check ever, he said, was £50,000, something he would double with his share of the £300,000 first prize.

Gibson, from Calgary and just coming up to his 33rd birthday, now lives in Manila, from where he led the Asian Tour money list in 1991 and now plays on the Japanese Tour. Like Stewart, he often played in the qualifying rounds, but never made the final team at St. Andrews.

Gibson may not have appreciated the invitation after shooting an 85 on the first, storm-hit day. "We nursed him along with a few glasses of wine that night," said captain Barr. "It shows great character to come back after an 85. But we played as a team and won as a team. The chemistry was good. When we saw that a guy was down, the others hung in there like dirty laundry. We didn't blow anyone out 3-0, but we got a lot of 2-1 wins.

"It's a fabulous feeling. We were by far the underdogs, but there was not an intimidation factor playing against the U.S., as some people might think. Everyone contributed. No one was the work horse."

Looking at the statistics, Barr was right. All three players won three of their individual matches and lost two. All three of Barr's victories were crucial wins and over classy opposition — Nick Price, ranked No. 1 in the world and captain of No. 2 seed Zimbabwe; Bernhard Langer of Germany, the world's No. 3-ranked golfer; and, in the final, Tom Kite, as gritty and hardened a competitor in head-to-head match-ups as you could find. The Americans were the titleholders, but only Fred Couples returned from the team that won in 1993. For Payne Stewart and John Daly, read Kite and Curtis Strange, both members of the 1987 winning U.S. team. Strange, like Couples of a year earlier, went through the week undefeated, but he was the only one of his countrymen to earn a win when it mattered most, in that final on Sunday afternoon.

Stewart knew the reason. "Dave was our work horse," he said. "He was the guy who took down the giants when we needed it. This is great for Canadian golf and shows all the small countries that they can go out and beat the big teams."

What helps to make the 500-year-ancient Old Course such a test, even for the modern-day professionals with their modern-day equipment and modern-day fitness programs, is the weather. The natural elements are even older than golf in St. Andrews and helped sculpt the very first golf course. Whether it be for a British Open Championship, played traditionally in July — as it will be at the Home of Golf for the 25th time in 1995 — or in October for the Alfred Dunhill Cup, the weather is an essential part of the day's talking points.

And it was a rare old day that greeted the competitors for the opening day of the 10th anniversary of the competition. It was a day that showed why the clubhouse of the Royal and Ancient Golf Club, perched intimidatingly behind the first tee, was built of the most solid-looking grey stone that the architects could find. Praise, too, should be given for the construction team who put up the row of tents, housing hospitality units, public catering and the press tent, along the right-hand side of the first fairway. With a gale measuring over 40 miles an hour and gusting to over 50 miles an hour, it was a miracle the whole lot did not end up in St. Andrews Bay just behind.

"You might as well throw away the yardage book on a day like this," said Price, who beat Langer 76-78 in the big showdown of the day. "We went through the motions of checking the yardages just so we didn't play any faster than normal. It was the hardest day to make a score I have ever played. I enjoy playing golf, but this is difficult to enjoy. You could make some big numbers out there."

Several players, including Price and Langer, faced the indignity of going to mark their ball, only to find it wander off with a will of its own. The tone of the Price-Langer match, and of the day, was set at the famous first hole, where the Swilcan Burn snakes dangerously in front of the green. Langer found the burn. "I hit a full eight iron and it didn't go 100 yards," he said. Price did not even reach the burn. The hole was halved in bogey fives. "I knew it was going to be difficult after that," Price said.

At the height of the gale, at lunch time, play was stopped for 15 minutes, but David Garland, the tournament director for the PGA European Tour, refused many players' requests for conditions to be called unplayable. Part of his reasoning lay in the format, head-to-head medal match play rather than a full stroke-play competition. He had one supporter in Greg Norman, who was loving every minute of it.

"I loved it, honestly," said Norman. "When it is head-to-head, the conditions are not such a big factor." While the field was a collective 276 over par, and the average score worked out to 77.5, Norman was one of only three men to match the par of 72. The others, Greg Turner and Darren Clarke in the New Zealand-Ireland match, played when the wind had eased a little at the end of the day. Norman played in the height of the storm. This was his first competitive outing in six weeks following a bout of intestinal problems that had seen him lose 13 pounds in five days and put him out of the

Presidents Cup. He had suggested that he might need to be given three shots on each nine due to his rustiness, which must have seemed a bit rich to his opponent Michel Besanceney of France, whose 76 would have won 16 of the other 23 matches.

"It becomes a bit of fun," Norman continued. "I was playing shots I remembered from when I grew up playing in Europe and which you don't get to play in the U.S. I don't think this was the worst conditions we have played in here, two years ago there was wind, rain, sleet and hail, and it was colder. But I think this is the toughest wind to play St. Andrews. It comes off the land and everything is a crosswind except for 18. You never get a wind like this for the Open, because then it comes off the sea."

The draw, always an eagerly anticipated event which takes place in the Old Course Hotel on Wednesday prior to play, seeded America, Zimbabwe, South Africa and Australia to win their groups and make the semi-finals. America and Zimbabwe were to meet in the final, although the draw did not rule out Australia and Zimbabwe meeting on Sunday afternoon, setting up a potential clash between the two best golfers in the world and firm friends who had just vacationed together in Belize, Price and Norman.

But the most interesting part of the draw was the pairing in group three, along with South Africa and the Republic of China, of Scotland and Paraguay. The two had met the year before, when Colin Montgomerie had declared "If we can't beat Paraguay, we deserve to go home." The unthinkable, as far as the home side was concerned, happened, Montgomerie losing the decisive match to Raul Fretes. In 1993, the Paraguay team of Fretes and the Franco brothers, Carlos and Angel, charted unknown depths of the Sony Ranking, but they also went home with a victory over Wales. All three returned in 1994, much improved, with Carlos Franco having led the Asian Tour money list and won a tournament on the Japan Tour.

Scotland again got off to a bad start. Gordon Brand, Jr., always trailed Angel Franco, whose 74 was one of the better scores of the day. Young Andrew Coltart was six ahead of Fretes after 10 holes before the Paraguayan launched a comeback. In the bottom match, Montgomerie birdied the first and was always just in front of Carlos Franco. He won 78-79. "Scoring didn't really matter as long as you were one ahead of your opponent," Monty said.

When Coltart bogeyed the 17th, to drop his sixth shot in seven holes, he wasn't even that. "When I was so far ahead, I was looking to put a point on the board, but in golf, especially in these conditions, it does not always follow," said the 23-year-old Scot. Both birdied the 18th and it was off to the 19th.

There, Fretes fell foul of the burn, his second shot landing on the green, but spinning back into the water. "I thought he hit a superb shot," said Coltart. "The wind just got it." The Scot was never going anywhere near the burn, and finished 60 feet past the flag. "Some people call it adrenaline, but it was fear." He still needed a good two-putt for the match. "I am proud of Andrew," said skipper Monty. "He put in a tremendous effort. It was a good win for us. Paraguay are a dangerous team."

In the other match in the group, South Africa crawled past the Republic of China 2-1. "I am embarrassed having won with an 81," said U.S. Open champion Ernie Els, who had two four-putts and three three-putts. Wayne

Westner lost to Chen Tze Chung after an 84 to an 83. "If I was playing cricket, it would have been a good score — I would nearly have made my first century. I three-putted the first five greens and had nine in all." In total, he had 44 putts.

In group one, America beat Japan 2-1, Strange shooting 78 but finding Tomohiro Maruyama the first of his victims. Couples found the perfect way of playing the first hole when he holed a seven iron from 130 yards for an eagle and a three-shot lead. Yoshinori Mizumaki did not have a chance to show a glimpse of his later form. Kite, however, went down to Nobuo Serizawa, 75-74. New Zealand's encounter with Ireland came down to the last match, where Philip Walton finished double bogey, bogey (driving out of bounds on the road on the right at the last) to lose by one shot to Grant Waite, 81-80.

Steve Elkington matched Norman's win in Australia's match with France, but they found themselves only second in group two after England white-washed Spain 3-0. Mark Roe was the most impressive, with 75 to Miguel Angel Jimenez's 80; and Barry Lane only escaped when Jose Rivero also drove out of bounds at the last, taking six to the Englishman's par four to lose by one.

Group four's top match between Zimbabwe and Germany hinged on the last encounter after Mark McNulty and Alexander Cejka coasted home in their matches. The key was Price's finish: four, four, four, three to Langer's six, four, five, three. "In these conditions, it would have been a good chance for us to cause an upset," Langer said. "It came down to putting. He holed a lot of 10-footers in the strong wind."

On the whole, it was not a good day for the eventual winners, losing 2-1 to Sweden. Gibson had the day's high round, 85, 13 over par, losing to Anders Forsbrand's 81. He bogeyed the entire back nine, something of an unfortunate record to hold. He had 46 putts, three-putting the last five. "I completely lost the feel for the speed of the greens," he admitted. "It came down to a total inexperience of playing in that kind of wind. I normally hit a low ball, but I had a tough day with every club in the bag."

Stewart shot 76 to beat the British Open runner-up, Jesper Parnevik. Quite an introduction to the Old Course. "Even in these conditions, she is a splendid little girl," he said. Gabriel Hjertstedt, enjoying a fine debut season on the PGA European Tour, however, took Barr to extra holes, at the second of which a Canadian bogey ended proceedings. "It was a good match," Barr said. "I would rather see rain than wind of this velocity. It was a day when you couldn't get too upset because everyone was facing the same conditions."

Friday dawned more quietly, there not quite being the howling wind of the day before. It was still difficult and while the upsets had not come the day before, now they did. First up was Ireland beating America 2-1 in group one. It was a dream win for the Irish, especially for captain Walton after his nightmare the day before. "I lay awake all night thinking about how I'd lost the match for us," he said. "I was so upset with myself. I just couldn't get back to sleep."

Strange, in the top match, continued on his winning way, with a 74-76 victory over McGinley. Next was Walton. Even with Kite with five to play, he finished two under to the American's two over. "It was nice to settle down and make a few bogeys and pars for a change, instead of the triple I started with yesterday," Walton said. "My whole attitude was better today. I was more aggressive."

That left Clarke, the 26-year-old prospective Ryder Cup player, to beat Couples. Clarke shot 71 to Freddie's 74. "I have played with Couples a couple of times, and outscored him on each occasion," said the confident young Irishman. Each of the Americans left for the practice range and some homework. With Japan beating New Zealand 2-1, each team in the group had one win and one loss.

Form was still obeyed in group two, however, where, in the best golf of the day, Australia slipped past Spain 2-1. Elkington and Rivero both won with 67s, while Jimenez, who had led at the turn, shot 72 in losing to Norman's 70. England again clocked up a 3-0 win, this time against France, thanks mainly to Howard Clark's overtime defeat of Besanceney at the 20th hole.

Scotland, which had never won the competition and, worse, lost to England in their two final appearances, continued on their way with a whitewash of the Republic of China. All three of the Scots shot two-under-par 70s. "I used to come here during the holidays when I was young," said Coltart, growing rapidly in confidence under the elevated pressure of playing for his country at home, "and that's the first time I have shot under par here."

And there was no surprise in South Africa beating Paraguay 2-1. It was no surprise, either, that it should be a tight squeeze. The surprise was that the lost point came from Els. Westner, improving 15 shots, and Frost had already secured the team victory, when Els was forced into extra holes by Angel Franco.

Els, a major champion but still just approaching his 25th birthday, comes from a country rich in golfing history, and enjoying prosperous times due to a more settled political situation. Franco, 36, has played on the Nike, Canadian and South American tours. In Paraguay there are 21 professionals at three clubs. The year before at St. Andrews he had beaten John Daly. He likes his opponents big. "I know Ernie is a great player, but on the course we are all equals. Nobody is less than any other," he said.

Mistakes at the 16th and 17th tied their match. They both birdied the first, then parred the second, third and fourth, then both birdied the par-five fifth. At the sixth, Els bunkered his tee shot and could only make a bogey, as is usually the case from Old Course bunkers. "Yes, I was determined not to lose," said Franco, who was playing only his second tournament after being out for six months with back trouble. "I am very happy to win and be the center of attention." Not so Els. "He was better than me on the day," said the South African, "I couldn't finish him off."

Price was having the same trouble with Barr. The whole shape of group four depended on the match. Germany had beaten Sweden thanks to Cejka, another promising young continental — born in then-Czechoslovakia, but as he put it "escaping" to Germany to pursue a golfing career — who beat Forsbrand at their second extra hole. Then the first two matches between Zimbabwe and Canada were split, particular honors going to Gibson, who shot 71 to beat Tony Johnstone by one. "It was nice to find the clubface again," said the Calgary man. "After yesterday's horror show anything would have felt good, but I was playing well, and the good thing was that I played well when I had to."

But Price just could not shake off Barr, who was about to make his 10th win (in 14 matches) in the competition a big one. Both went to the turn in 33, three birdies each, and then had bogeys at the short 11th. Barr edged in front with a birdie at the next. Price evened the match at the 14th. It was still level with the two to putt on the last green. Price went first, and couldn't believe it when his 16-footer stayed out. Then came Barr, from just two feet inside Price.

"I just saw my team sitting on the steps by the green and I thought: 'Let me just squeeze one in for my team,'" Barr said. It fell in. "It was a real nice feeling," Barr said. "I didn't want to go down that extra hole. It is a fantastic feeling to beat the No. 1 player in the world. Nick is a super guy and we are good friends. He is one of the genuine people in golf right now. We had a good time chatting together. But this win keeps our team alive. All three having won a match brings up our confidence. I'm glad for Rick Gibson after his 85 yesterday. I guess it puts everything into a real chaotic situation with everyone having won one match and lost one. It will be interesting to see what happens tomorrow."

The Saturday at the Alfred Dunhill Cup is an interesting day, especially since the change to the group format in 1992. Saturday is decision day. This time, two groups had straightforward head-to-head battles (two and three), in the other two anything could happen (one and four).

The Americans, in a "chaotic" group one, weren't leaving anything to chance, which necessitated a long breakfast meeting. "We had everything figured out, we talked about it, all the possibilities," Kite said. Added Strange: "The reason for us talking this morning was that we didn't want to be on the 16th tee figuring it out." What they realized was that they had to go out and beat New Zealand 3-0 and then sit back and hope.

Part one was accomplished, narrowly but successfully, against the largely off-form Kiwis. Kite beat Waite, 69-71; Strange beat Nobilo, 69-70; Couples beat Turner, 72-74. As Couples, still not happy with his putter said, "I was fortunate that Greg did not make any putts either."

Kite said, "It was a bit of a struggle this week. Teams you thought you could write off a few years ago, you can't write off any more. Competition is getting strong. We felt we should have beaten Ireland and here we were with our backs to the walls."

The significance of the Irish defeat was that if the Emerald Isle also won the match, against Japan, 3-0, then it would be Ireland into the semi-finals. McGinley, over Maruyama, and Clarke, remaining unbeaten with a win over Serizawa, completed two of the three legs. But it was obvious from early on that Ireland would not get three out of three. Not with Mizumaki in such scintillating form. Taking advantage of the now breathless and sunny conditions, the 36-year-old who has based himself on the U.S. PGA Tour shot 64 to win by six strokes over Walton. He came close to matching Strange's course-record 62 set in 1987.

His card was perfectly symmetrical, 32 out, 32 in. Birdies came at the second, third, fifth, seventh, 11th, 12th, 15th and 18th. "As I was playing, I wasn't thinking about who was going to qualify," he said. "I was so focused on my own game. From the 12th I started to think about the 62 and in the end I was disappointed for I had good chances at 14 and 16. But being the best score ever by a Japanese player on the Old Course is special to me. At the Open next year I am going to try to do a 63."

Walton's mood was rather different. "I am bitterly disappointed that we are not going through," said the Irish captain. "As a team we did well, and the U.S. are a bit lucky really. Once he parred 17 I knew I was gone. I needed him to stuff it up against the wall and take an eight, and then for me to birdie the last. It must have been in a dream that I saw that happening. I felt like kicking it up the last." As McGinley put it, philosophically: "Your man shooting 64 — what are the chances of that?"

Group four was also in a land of possibilities — and that man Barr was again at the center of a crucial match. To set the scene: Zimbabwe beat Sweden but could not manage the whitewash they needed due to Parnevik's 67-70 win over McNulty. Then in the Canada-Germany match, Stewart lost at the 19th to Sven Struver, while Gibson beat Cejka. This time Barr was up against Langer. And it was tight, again.

A birdie at the 13th put the Canadian level. At No. 16, he let his approach shot leak right and it ended in a devilish spot by the 17th tee board. "It was hard determining where the drop would be," Barr said, "so I played it from under the sign and chipped to two feet. A really great shot." Langer was in trouble at the 17th. Having pitched over the green, he tried to putt up the bank and ended up over the other side of the green. He chipped to 10 feet and holed the bogey putt. Barr had a first putt from 20 yards but got it safely down to two feet.

Langer then had a 15-foot birdie putt on the last green, but lipped out to lose by one. Had he holed it and then won in extra holes, it would have helped his side not at all, but it would have put Zimbabwe through. Instead, with the two sides level on matches won and games won, Canada's win the day before over Zimbabwe was the decider. "It was nerve-wracking at the last," said Barr. "I was ready to have a heart attack. It's the most nervous I have been. As an individual you can shrug off that sort of pressure, but not with two guys depending on you."

Matters were less confusing in the other sections. In group three, it was Scotland against South Africa. Coltart earned his third win 70-72 over Westner to complete a memorable week. But Els found his putting touch to defeat Brand, Jr., 68-70, and Montgomerie never recovered from four bogeys in a row from the fifth and lost to Frost. "It's a shame for Andrew," said Monty. "He played superbly all week and it's a pity for him. I should have been able to pull one through."

"I am thrilled to have beaten your favorite team," Frost told the Scottish press. "We knew we had a lot of work to do today. Our strategy worked. We considered all of us playing Montgomerie, but I didn't want to build up a U.S. Open rivalry between Ernie and Colin."

The last semi-final place came from the Australia-England encounter in group two. This is always serious business for the former Empire-builder and her former colony. This time it was England that wanted to win most, the team spirit working well between the former Ryder Cup veteran (Clark), the current Ryder Cup man (Lane) and the Ryder Cup wannabe (Roe). Though Clark shot 65 to beat Elkington, and Lane beat Allenby with 69 to 71, the best performance came from Roe, who defeated Norman 69-72. "It is great to beat one of your heroes," said the 31-year-old from Sheffield. "I went out there to shoot the best score I could. I knew on the first tee that if I shot par I would not win." Said Norman, "It was a flat day for me. Mark didn't make any mistakes. They beat us good. They deserve to be in the semis."

"It was quite surprising," admitted Clark. "I think we took them apart. We got so hyped up, and we let it come out on the golf course. That doesn't usually happen. We have got to try and relax this evening. We know we have a tough task tomorrow against the defending champions." For the first time, a team had gone through the group stages unbeaten, winning nine games out of nine. Explained Roe: "We were under orders from our wives — win 3-0 or don't come back to the room."

Clark's words were the ones to mark in Sunday morning's semi-final against the United States. England had no more to give. Having whitewashed everyone else, now it was their turn to suffer a 3-0 reverse. "It often happens that when you have such a good day, the next day is not so good," said Clark. "We got off to a bad start and it was tough to come back. They were very hot. We gave it our best shot and it was not good enough." Clark was three down after four holes and lost 68-74; Lane bogeyed the last to lose 71-70 to Strange, but the tie was already decided by then. The top match had been the most interesting. Kite rolled in a 15-footer on No. 16 to take a one-stroke lead.

What makes the medal-match play format so fascinating on this particular course is the 17th, the Road Hole, with its huge bunker guarding the front of the green, and a road, a wall and out of bounds behind. It measures 461 yards and is one of golf's most severe par fours. Roe came up short and could only chip and two-putt. Kite, however, hit a marvellous six iron to the heart of the green, two-putting from 10 feet. "As soon as I saw it in the air," Kite said of his second shot, "I said, 'How good is this!' How close it finished didn't really matter, it was the shot I needed to play at the time I needed it."

There was still No. 18 to go and Roe rammed in a birdie putt from 14 feet to put the pressure on Kite's par-saver. His long approach putt from the back of the green had come up five feet short. "Through the years, I have seen people leave that putt short," Kite said. "You know it is slower than it looks but you still can't hit it. But for the second putt I had a little look, and then stayed down and hit it in the heart of the hole.

"We were fortunate to get by England, because for the first three days they have played the best golf, and we didn't. We are looking forward to trying to defend the title. We didn't come over to go home early, and we didn't come over to finish second."

To achieve that they would have to beat Canada, whose lesser lights were the ones to see them by South Africa in the other semi-final. Stewart beat Frost by five, 70-75, and Gibson eased past Westner 70-74. The margins meant their matches were never in doubt, and left the bottom match, in which Els beat Barr 68-72, irrelevant.

"I am thrilled to death," said a delighted Stewart. "We have lots of work to do this afternoon, but this is thrilling — a career highlight. It is nice that Rick and I have come back to support Dave, for Dave is the guy who got us through to here."

In the absence of a World Series pitting the Maple Leaf against the Stars and Stripes, this would have to do. The draw came out so: Kite versus Barr, Strange versus Gibson, Couples versus Stewart.

Strange seemed to be playing better and better, and after 10 holes he was five under par and leading by five. One American point was assured. Eventually Strange won his fifth straight match 67-74. He said, "Winning all five is pleasing, but you hate to lose as a team, because you come as a team and leave as a team, that's what it's all about. When you are out there you can't be worrying about the other matches, just your own, but you're wondering all the same."

There was plenty for Strange to worry about. Barr was again battling magnificently. Two ahead after seven holes, three in front at the 10th, but there was a two-stroke swing at the next and Kite birdied No. 12 to go even. Barr was not done. He hit a six iron at the 15th which finished no more than two feet away. Then, there came the 17th.

Barr missed the green right, saw his chip flirt the dreaded bunker and then two-putted for a bogey. Kite, the memory of his morning approach shot still in his mind, now saw his four-iron shot pitch on the road and bounce way, way over the wall, out of bounds. To prove he had the right club, he hit another four iron on the green and two-putted for a six. "It's a great hole, isn't it?" he asked. "It's a great hole," he answered. "Sure does make you hit some shots." Kite birdied the last, but Barr had another famous win, and the match was even.

Eyes turned to the bottom match. The news registered with a smile only by Canadian hearts. Stewart was out in 34, birdied the 10th and was three ahead. He bogeyed the 14th, but got a helping hand from Couples, whose best play had arrived late in the morning, but had now escaped again in the afternoon, who two holes later missed a tiddler for par after his opponent had expertly gotten up and down from a bunker. "I was a little nervous of my position in the world at the time," Stewart said. "But I managed to knock in that 12-footer and that maybe stunned Freddie a bit." Stewart could afford to bogey the 17th and see Couples birdie the last, and still record the vital win 71-72.

"I'm stunned," Gibson said, still wearing the flat gray cap that had served him so well all week. "We didn't care about the ratings of this guy or that guy. We bucked the odds."

It was Kite who was buckled. "Yes, I thought we could win," he said. "I had some opportunities and it hurts because you have got a couple of teammates counting on you, and everyone who came over to support. It hurts a little bit."

But the Canadians were enjoying their moment in the spotlight, even though not a single Canadian journalist had made the trip over to see it happen. "We've had a couple of calls from home during the week," Barr said, "but I didn't expect to see anyone here."

"They'll be here next year," said Stewart.

9. Toyota World Match Play

It was not his winner's speech that Ernie Els was worried about. He gets enough practice at those. "My sister Carina is getting married on Saturday and I'm the best man," said the young South African. "I don't get to too many weddings. Actually, I missed my brother's. I'm looking forward to going home, but I've got to work on my speech."

The U.S. Open champion was speaking at the finale of the Toyota World Match Play Championship at the Wentworth Club, near London, having completed the formalities of the prize-giving and press conference after the 10th victory of his professional career, and his third of 1994. (He would make those totals 12 and five later in the year.)

The following day, Monday, October 17, would be his 25th birthday. Els likes to keep his feet on the ground, not easy for the stars of today. No one is remotely surprised that it has taken Els only 25 years to reach such stature.

Would he, Colin Montgomerie was asked after losing 4 and 2 in the final to Els, look back in years to come and think he was defeated that afternoon by one of the game's true greats? The answer was immediate and unhesitating. "Yes, I will," Montgomerie said. "Ernie has an old head on young shoulders. Everyone who has played him, and been beaten by him, will tell you that."

Montgomerie, on the verge of clinching his second successive PGA European Tour money title, had of course been beaten by Els in the playoff for the U.S. Open, in which the South African finally defeated Loren Roberts in sudden death. At Oakmont, Els had confirmed his major pedigree, winning in the manner of that legend of western Pennsylvania, Arnold Palmer. Els took out his driver and swung with might and courage, and showed equal valor on the greens.

Palmer, by coincidence, stands at the head of the roll of the World Match Play Championship as the first winner in 1964. Els was flattered by becoming the 31st winner. Palmer is one of four men to have won the title twice, Nick Faldo, Ian Woosnam and Hale Irwin being the other three. Greg Norman has three titles; Gary Player and Seve Ballesteros hold the record with five each. Jack Nicklaus, after five attempts, is one of now 10 players to have won once.

Els is hoping to move up the list. "There's a fellow countryman of mine," he said, "who has won this title five times. I've got some catching up to do."

Given the fact that the only younger player to win the title is Ballesteros (24 in 1981), Els has started the right way. His career has been a rapid succession. First, he dominated the South African amateur circuit, then his home professional tour; a fleeting passage through Europe — he won the Dubai Desert Classic at the start of 1994 by six shots over Norman — and then the world stage.

His short game, bunker play and chipping has passed postgraduate honors in an era when that part of golf is an exact science for the leading professionals, if still an incomprehensible one to the world's hackers. Yet if there is one thing that leaves his observers chattering in awe, it is the rhythm with which he harnesses the power of his long game; 300-plus-yard drives soaring into the sky with apparent ease.

It does not always click, of course. Two weeks before the World Match Play, Els had seemed to be coasting to a runaway victory in the Mercedes German Masters before first Jose Maria Olazabal and then Ballesteros hauled back the difference. Eventually, Ballesteros won a three-way playoff. Els would have revenge on both on his way to the final at Wentworth.

Before that could happen, it required the intervention of David Leadbetter. Leadbetter, the coach of two Nicks, Faldo and Price, has no such formal relationship with Els, but the young man has occasionally sought the Zimbabwean guru's advice and always has an ear for his comments. Wentworth is but a wedge shot from that other great Surrey course to the southwest of London, Sunningdale, where Els bases himself when in Europe.

After some inconsistent play at the Alfred Dunhill Cup the week before, Els headed over to Wentworth on Tuesday evening. He was hitting the ball anything but straight; one booming left, the next swinging right. A passing Leadbetter immediately spotted the error. "I was too far back on my heels," Els explained. "I'm trying to transfer my weight better. It's worked perfectly all week."

Els did not have to bring his newly spruced-up game to the course until Friday, as his U.S. Open win gave him a bye into the second round. Defending champion Corey Pavin, Masters champion Olazabal and Faldo also sat out the first day. Els would play the winner of the match which stole all the attention on Thursday: David Frost vs. Ballesteros.

The original lineup had not included the Spaniard, a fact that brought angry comments from the British newspapers and, not least, from Ballesteros himself. Shortly after the announcement, however, Seve telephoned the tournament director to say, should anyone drop out, he would still like to be considered for his 19th appearance and a chance to win a record sixth title. When John Daly withdrew following a skirmish at the NEC World Series, Ballesteros got his wish.

Ballesteros was in prime form. He had finished second at the Dunhill British Masters and third at the Trophee Lancome, before his victory in Berlin. A week at home in Spain saw him playing 18 holes early in the morning, then setting off for miles on his mountain bike. The only upset to his plans came when he took a spin, his laces caught in the spokes of a wheel, and he received a sore shoulder.

Wentworth's West Course was also in prime condition after late summer rain had given way to golden autumn sunshine. The splendor of the colors of the trees matched the quality of the greens. The scoring would be good, but no one expected it to be quite as good as it was. With an increased first-day gallery, most trying to fit around one match, the stage was well and truly set for a Ballesteros spectacular.

A 24-footer at the par-four third to go one up was just the start of a run of five consecutive birdies. Frost did well not to lose more than one more hole (the sixth) by the turn. To do so meant the South African holing a 15-footer at the seventh after Ballesteros had snuggled up his eight iron to a foot. The only dropped shot of the morning, by Frost at the short 10th, put Ballesteros three up, and when the South African failed to get the almost obligatory birdie at the 502-yard 18th, he found himself four down.

That after a round of five-under-par 67. No wonder Frost was dazzled. Ballesteros had shot nine-under-par 63, one stroke off Ronan Rafferty's record for the event.

Frost won the first hole in the afternoon, but bogeyed the third and again failed to match Ballesteros' birdie at the par-five fourth. There was the usual sorcery from the Spaniard, when he escaped from the trees at the seventh for a half, and then he finished the match off in a hurry with three birdies from the ninth. His 8-and-7 win more than made up for his 7-and-6 defeat by the same opponent a year before.

"It was my day," said Seve after totalling up his 13 birdies in 29 holes. "The 63 this morning was something special. That's the best I have played here. The reception of the people today was fantastic. I had great support all the way and I am very happy I played so well."

Ballesteros was as ecstatic as he had been despondent after his first-round humiliation the year before. He was sure of one thing that had made the difference in his game since then, indeed since the beginning of the year. "I am driving the ball very well," he said. "That's one thing that has not happened for a long time. Once you hit the fairway, the game becomes a lot easier. That has been the key point in the last month and a half. Last year I was hitting the ball on the shaft."

One other first-round match was a re-match from the year before. In 1993, Yoshinori Mizumaki took Montgomerie to the 37th hole. This time there was never more than a hole in it, the Scot lunching at one up after his 68 to Mizumaki's 70.

The Japanese player could never quite recapture the brilliance of his 64 at St. Andrews in the Alfred Dunhill Cup the week before, but he evened the match twice in the afternoon. The first time was thanks to an eagle at the fourth, but he immediately gave it back with a three-putt at the next. "I had my chances," Mizumaki said. "But my driving was particularly destructive. Usually it is very straight, but today it was left, right, left, right."

Montgomerie holed one of his few putts over 10 feet in the afternoon on the 13th, then took the match 2 and 1 at the 35th. "If I had lost today, I would only have had myself to blame," said the Scot. "I have never hit the ball better tee-to-green, but could not finish it off. It was depressing at times."

At lunch, Montgomerie had toyed with changing his putter, but it stayed in the bag by virtue of its handy record during the year, producing wins at the Spanish, English and German Opens. Still, he knew things would have to be better the following day. "No way I can go out and play Nick Faldo tomorrow putting the way I am."

Not that Montgomerie wasn't happy with the draw. "I think everybody is delighted not to be in the half of the draw with Seve," Monty said. "That was a tremendous performance. He's the best match player in the world, and to be beaten 8 and 7 says something for Seve."

Some of the best golf of the day, the Spaniard excepted, was played in the top match, an eclectic encounter between Fiji's Vijay Singh and Sweden's Jesper Parnevik. You had to get up early to catch all the fireworks in this one. Parnevik birdied the first two holes and was three up after seven and out in 31. Coming home, the roles were reversed, Singh holing from 45 feet to start a run of three closing birdies at the 16th. They were tied at lunch,

Singh shooting 66 and Parnevik 65. "I was a bit worried after Jesper's flying start," Singh admitted.

Parnevik, a par at the 18th away from tying Price for the British Open Championship, has had his share of monster putts holed against him. Singh, in prime form with two recent wins in Europe, sunk another 45-footer at the first hole after lunch. Singh never lost the lead again. Parnevik had to take a penalty drop from a ditch at the ninth, took a double-bogey six when his opponent was struggling to make par, and went three down. Singh was nine under par in winning 4 and 3 to the Swede's six under.

"There is not much I can say," Parnevik said of his World Match Play debut. "The double bogey really killed me when I had a chance to cut the gap. But the nine birdies he made in 14 holes really swung the game around."

"This is the first time I have reached the second round," Singh said, "so that in itself is a milestone. This morning I thought it was going to be one of those days. The long putt at 16 in the morning was the one that really gave me a boost."

In the final match, Brad Faxon had lost his only previous first-round match (to Norman in 1992), while Woosnam had never lost before the second round. Until now, much to the disappointment of the winner in 1987 and 1990. Woosnam's morning was soured by hooking two balls out of bounds from the middle of the 17th fairway.

He was two down at lunch, and fell further back at the first hole in the afternoon. He got back to one down when the American conceded the ninth, but Faxon was again three in front at the 11th and 13th.

But the West Course's long finish — the 380-yard 16th, the 571-yard 17th and the 502-yard 18th — offers both danger and the spectacular. Faxon missed the green at the 16th and failed to get up and down. Then, he drove out of bounds from the 17th tee, and then drove the bunker on the left at the last hole. On the green in three, however, Faxon holed from seven feet for a half and the match, by one hole.

The Welshman, who had flared just briefly in 1994 with two wins amid a number of average performances, was honest in his summing up. "I didn't deserve to win," he said. "I played shocking this afternoon, and not just with the putter. Every time I got one back, I gave it back at the next hole. I couldn't string the shots together, but that's how things are going — totally inconsistent."

"I enjoyed about 34 holes of that," said Faxon. "I missed a short one at 16 and then tried to give it away on 17. I choked like a dog." A look at the draw told him he would be facing Olazabal the following day. "It doesn't get any easier, does it?" Faxon said.

A spectacular first day promised an equally exciting second, and a record 16,120 crowd arrived early on Friday. They were not disappointed. Once the mist burnt off, the sunshine produced an idyllic scene. The fog still hung on the treetops when Els hit an eight iron from 145 yards at the third and saw the ball spin back into the cup. It was the first eagle two ever recorded in this competition at the hole.

"I knew I needed a great start," said Els. The previous evening he had sat in front of the television pondering the news of Ballesteros' 13 birdies against Frost. "I psyched myself up. Seve can do anything when he gets the magic going." The Spaniard was prepared, too. "Ernie is a great champion," Ballesteros said. "I have a lot of respect for someone who can win the U.S. Open. He is a great competitor."

Els was two up after only four holes when he added a birdie at the par five after his eagle. Ballesteros got one back at the 11th, but dropped his first shot of the tournament when he drove into the trees at No. 13. Similar waywardness at the last hole saw him chipping out left-handed — he has to do that somewhere along the line — and he was two down at lunch despite five birdies. "Another good match," he said.

Els went three up when Ballesteros misjudged his approach into the wrong tier at the seventh and three-putted. When the young South African bogeyed the 13th, and Ballesteros birdied the short 14th, it was back to one. Much to the frustration, but not surprise, of his followers, Seve now drove into the trees on the left of the 15th. His response was typical, birdieing the next hole.

But … there's always a but … the old generation of favorites has to give way to the new generation somewhere, and it happened on the 17th. Ballesteros, the master of the short game, left his pitch on the fringe, while Els chipped stone dead. "I had goose bumps at the end," Els said. "It was an unbelievable match. To beat a great man you have to play well, especially when he is on form. I just kept at it and did not give up. If he had got his nose in front it would have been very different."

Not the least significant feature of the match — in which Ballesteros again had 13 birdies to Els' 10 and two eagles — was the Spaniard's seven twos. Only the second hole in the morning escaped. Even more amazingly, four of them only earned a half. Said Seve, "I made seven twos, not bad. That's never happened to me before. It never happens to anyone. In the morning I played well, but in the afternoon I was really up and down. At 17 I did not produce the shot I needed."

Els said of the gallery, "Seve has won here five times and has been around a long time. I am a rookie. Obviously, he was the favorite. The crowd was for Seve, but I don't think it was against me. The match was played in a good spirit."

If the British crowd was won over by the South African, then Ballesteros knew the answer. "Ernie has everything," he explained. "He has all the shots in the bag. He is long, is a good iron player, has a good short game, is a good putter and has a good nerve. I don't think you could ask for anything else."

Faldo, the 1989 and 1992 winner, was about to have a similar experience with the next generation, although he could be forgiven for thinking his Ryder Cup partner would be more respectful. Not a bit. Montgomerie finished the morning round birdie, birdie, eagle to move from one up to three up. Faldo shot 68, and Monty 65.

Given Faldo's putting problems this year, it was a surprise that everything went well on the greens, but a swing malfunction let him down. Poor drives cost him the ninth hole (having got back to even), the 12th (to go three down again) and the last hole. His birdie, birdie finish was only good enough to get back one of the holes he needed, and despite a 66 to Monty's 70, the Scot halved the last hole to squeeze through by one. Monty said, "Coming home I was jaded and nervous but I just managed to hold on."

"I managed to get back into the game and then gave it away," said Faldo.

"I shot 10 under for 36 holes, which can't be bad, and lost, but that's match play. You would take that if it was the start of a 72-hole tournament." And, what of Montgomerie? "He is so confident in the way he is hitting the ball. He doesn't have a destructive shot. He is hitting fairways and putting well." So, the ideal Ryder Cup partner? "If he still wants me," Faldo said. "That's the ultimate compliment," was the Scotsman's reply.

Montgomerie has never hidden his admiration for Faldo. "I played Nick here in 1991 and took him to the 38th hole before losing. That was a good performance but I was not ready to win," Montgomerie said. "It was the same at the U.S. Open in 1992. If I had won, it might have hurt me in a negative way.

"I can now say to myself I can win, rather than saying to myself I can win, but not believing it. I have improved most years and today was an important win for me to show that I am still progressing."

Montgomerie added that he had learned a lot from playing with Faldo in the 1993 Ryder Cup. "It's not something you always get to see, but at the Ryder Cup there was the odd tip about putting and playing under pressure," he said. "It's all the little things that add up and probably helped me win today."

Once again, there was that feeling of the baton passing to the next wave of stars. It was enhanced by the day's other two winners. Olazabal was more troubled by the hip injury he had picked up in recent weeks, than with Faxon. Two up at lunch, with 67 to Faxon's 69 and with the aid of not one but two chip-ins, the Spaniard won three holes in a row from the 12th to complete a 6-and-4 win. "I putted fantastic this morning to keep in touch," admitted the American. "But this afternoon, when I missed a green I didn't make par, whereas when he missed a green he got up and down."

"I tried not to let my hip affect me, although it did hurt," Olazabal said. "I tried to swing the club as aggressively as usual. I am pleased to win. I did not play all that well, but it doesn't matter how you score or play if you win. The course is in good condition and the weather is fantastic: warm and not a breath of breeze."

The last man into the semi-finals, though in the first match out, was Singh, after beating Pavin at the 37th. That meant the American's campaign lasted 104 holes less than his victorious run the year before. Down early on, Singh shot a morning round of 66 to Pavin's 67 to be one up. The lead continued to oscillate after lunch, the Fijian squaring the match with a par at the 16th and again at the 18th, where Pavin failed to match his birdie.

Back at the first, Pavin was short of the green, Singh over the back. Pavin chipped 15 feet past; Singh got it to five feet and holed the putt. "He did what he needed to do and I didn't," Pavin said. "It irritates me that I had the game in my hands and let it go. I played well, but he hung on and took advantage of the mistakes I made."

Both players had played the previous week in Japan, where Pavin had experienced an earthquake which reminded him of growing up in Oxnard, California. The long-haul travelling, however, was catching up. "I was very surprised to get back to level at the 16th and also at the last," said Singh. "That was a good win, for it seems to have been a very long day."

Saturday, of necessity, was shorter after the usual morning fog obstinately refused to clear, causing a two-hour delay. But three-hour, 15-minute rounds, and a sandwich for lunch got the players through before dark. The semi-final lineup confirmed the changing of the guard: Olazabal, the Masters champion, against Els, the U.S. Open champion; Montgomerie, Europe's No. 1, against Singh, the world's No. 1 practicer.

By now, Olazabal was visibly limping. But with 69 to Els' 71, he was two up at the sandwich break. "Pathetic," was Els' halftime summing up. Olazabal contented himself by heading off to the physiotherapy van. It did the trick. Olazabal holed a 12-footer at the first, then glided his eight iron in to three feet at the short second. By now he was four up.

"He had me worried at four down with 16 to play," admitted Els. The South African's response was as rapid as it needed to be. He chipped in at the third — "Lucky No. 3 for me this week," he said — then got his birdie four at the next hole to cut the deficit to two. Olazabal would never win another hole. Two more Els birdies at the eighth and 11th squared the match.

Nothing was happening for Olazabal; worse, he bogeyed the 13th to go one down. The 17th, as for his countryman the day before, caused his downfall. Leaving his wedge approach on the fringe, he could not match Els' two-putt birdie. "I want to be able to say I lost to the champion on Monday," Olazabal told Els.

Olazabal had shot 65 to come from three behind to beat Els earlier in the year in the Volvo PGA Championship. Els was five under par for his 17 afternoon holes. "I have no excuses," said the Spaniard, referring to his hip. "After yesterday's match with Seve, it was difficult to pick up again trying to make so many birdies," said Els. "I felt a little down in the morning, but I played much better this afternoon. Tomorrow I'll have to be on my game from the off."

As Montgomerie said of the other semi-final, "While the scoring wasn't so good, with both of us making mistakes, it was a good match." The Scot won the 15th, 16th and 17th to go one up, but a two iron to four feet for a conceded eagle by Singh squared the match.

Montgomerie was up for most of the afternoon, until Singh produced another eagle at the 12th. "We got our act together coming in," said Singh. But he got on the wrong side of the 17th green, down the bank on the right, and could only make a par to Monty's birdie. While Singh did get up and down for birdie at the last hole, it was only good enough for a half. For the record, Singh lost the 18-hole playoff for third place to Olazabal, 2 and 1.

"I knew I needed to finish four, four not to let it go to the 37th," Montgomerie said. "I managed to play the last seven in three under par. It was getting cold and we were both tired, but concentration wasn't a problem. The prize is too great to lose your concentration."

So they went to a final which brought back memories of Oakmont. "Ernie, of course, beat me in the U.S. Open, but I am not concerned about that," said Montgomerie. Added Els, "I don't think we will be choking the way we choked at the U.S. Open."

One thing certainly wasn't reminiscent of Oakmont and that was the weather, now that the sunshine had deserted us and a more traditional autumnal dank had returned. It bothered Els not at all, as he went three up at the turn to Monty's two over. But Els drove into the trees at the 11th and could only move his recovery to the gorse. Monty rolled in a nice 16-footer at the 16th, and again birdied the 18th — its left-to-right curve perfectly suits his power fade — to even the match.

"I felt I was one up, not all-square," said Montgomerie. But Els came straight up and birdied the first hole in the afternoon and never lost the lead. Seven halves in par followed before, at the ninth, Els holed from outside Montgomerie to go two up. The Scot would later complain he never found the pace of the greens all day. He did get the next hole back, though, when Els missed the green, and with five holes to play there was still only one hole in it.

The end was quick. Els rolled in his birdie putt at the par-three 14th from 12 feet, then a par putt from over double that range at the next hole. Montgomerie had followed Els into the same bunker on the left off the tee, but couldn't get on the green in three. So far, he had played the last three holes in 13 under, but he would not get the chance to repeat his great finishes. Els hit hit eight-iron approach to the 16th to six feet; Monty missed the green and, when he failed to chip in, he conceded the match, 4 and 2.

"I got off to a great start in the afternoon and just needed to keep plugging away," Els said. "Colin is a great player and I did not want to give him too many chances." Both men are big and strong and well capable of coping with 36 holes a day, but the difference may have rested in the fact that the Scot was playing his 10th week in a row and his 15th in 16 weeks. "He was tired," said Els. "You could see it in his putting."

Montgomerie insisted, "I am not tired at all. I feel disappointed because I never gave myself a chance on the greens. He made the ball roll to the hole and I was not able to do that. That was the difference today. It has been positive for me to play well and battle on against four very good opponents. I am happy to have come out on top against three of them."

Montgomerie won £90,000, Els £160,000. "I guess you could say I have achieved all my dreams and more this year," Els said. "I wanted to be in contention in all the majors, to win on the European Tour and get my American Tour card."

Of course, there is now a lot for Els to live up to, not least the favorable comments from the likes of Nicklaus and Tom Watson. "It's nice to read what they say about you, but you don't want to start believing it," he said. "I still have a long way to go. But when I am hitting the ball well and my concentration is good, I feel I can win any tournament."

Starting in 1995, that is more likely to be on the U.S. PGA Tour, after his three-year sojourn in South Africa and Europe. "I have had a great time over here. The European Tour has been good to me. The public has been great, especially in Britain where they really know the game.

"When I came over here for the first time I was nowhere near the top 100 in the world. As I leave Europe, now I am in the top 10 and that speaks for itself. I think in America I can improve my game and become more consistent by playing on more consistent greens. I will always come back to Europe and play a couple of tournaments."

10. Johnnie Walker World Championship

Ernie Els stepped up on the interview platform, took his seat, and leaned forward, elbows on the table. It was the end of a hot day's work in the Johnnie Walker World Championship, just a week before Christmas. This was the same Ernie Els who had taken a similar seat after winning the U.S. Open at Oakmont back in June. Then, he had seemed a bit bewildered, possibly overwhelmed. Now, even though it was just the second round, he was more composed, perhaps more comfortable in the glare. Maybe just more accustomed to success, because goodness knows he had had plenty of it this year.

At all events, Els was going strong again. His face showed happiness, and maybe a trace of relief and even embarrassment. This was absurdly easy. Els was turning this gathering of the world's finest golfers into a rout. He had just shot another 64. Someone in the press asked, "Are you sure you're playing the same golf course as everyone else?" The big South African broke into a huge grin. "Every dog has his day," he said. But this dog — if one may borrow his own word — was having his year as well.

Two days later, after Els had wrapped up the six-stroke runaway victory, Nick Faldo would put everything in perspective with one simple, economic sentence. "When someone starts 64-64," Faldo said, with a shrug, "it's pretty hard to catch him." Faldo hadn't quite added to golf literature with that self-evident truism, but give him credit for summing up the 1994 Johnnie Walker World Championship.

Twenty-four of the finest assembled in Jamaica at Tryall Golf Club, an odd combination of topographies, with the first eight holes climbing through the lush, forested and flowery hills, the other 10 holes stretching across the flats along and near the sandy beach, and all of it hard by the blue and turquoise waters of Montego Bay and the Caribbean beyond. It was a lovely spot for Els' Christmas romp.

Even the weather smiled on Els. It didn't cause great problems or raise obstacles. The sun and heat lay heavy on Tryall for all four days, and although some troubling breezes rose now and then, there were none of the flag-bending winds like the ones Fred Couples battled when he won the inaugural in 1991. The greens stayed firm and dry, fast and hard to hold. The fairways were baked and bouncing. The rough was heavy in spots, and parched and scraggly in others. Hitting out of it wasn't the big problem, but guessing what the ball would do was. Imagine Mark McCumber's surprise at the 18th hole in the first round. He was just trying to advance his ball. His wedge shot flew 170 yards.

So here were Els' dog days on the Caribbean. He shot 64, 64, 71 and 69, for a 16-under-par 268 total. He led McCumber, Faldo and Colin Montgomerie by three strokes in the first round, then Faldo and Tom Lehman by six after two rounds, then Nick Price by seven after three rounds, and finally won by six over McCumber and Faldo.

The Johnnie Walker World Championship offered a $2.5 million purse with a $550,000 first prize, a $52,000 minimum and a small, elite field. There were 24 players, 14 who qualified by winning one or more of the designated events in the world, three from the Sony Ranking, six on invitations from the Championship's International Advisory Committee and defending champion Larry Mize. One of the IAC invitees was Paul Azinger, but his was as much a delayed appearance as a special invitation. Azinger was in the field for the 1993 Championship as the American PGA champion, but was forced to withdraw in November when he was diagnosed with lymphoma, a form of cancer. He returned to limited play in August.

All told, 19 of the 24 were from the Sony Ranking's top 30. Four other men who had qualified, all of them in the top 10, declined to play and were not replaced — Greg Norman, Corey Pavin, Jumbo Ozaki and Jose Maria Olazabal.

The Championship opened Thursday with two records — most players in the 60s for the first round, eight, and record low for the first round. That was Els with 64, breaking his own record of 66 in 1993. "Tryall is a resort course," Price would say, by way of explaining that it's not a hugely difficult course. Even so, under tournament conditions, Tryall is hardly a pushover. It had its generous moments, though.

McCumber greeted it with good humor. Humor and patience had been his strengths. McCumber, 43, hadn't won since he injured his back in 1989, but he came roaring back in 1994 with victories in the Anheuser-Busch Classic, Hardee's Classic and the Tour Championship. He had to soak his sore back in a hot bath for an hour before playing Tryall. Then he out-thought the course. "It favors a draw," McCumber said, and so on most driving holes, he used his three wood, since he could control it better for drawing the ball. The strategy helped him to a bogey-free 67 for the early lead. He missed a good chance at the par-five fourth, when he three-putted from 20 feet for a par, but he could hardly miss on the three birdies he did have: 30 inches, two feet and, at No. 7, a mere eight inches after he had been robbed of an eagle. His six-iron approach shot nicked the flagstick.

Then it was McCumber's turn to rob the course. At the par-five 17th, which would take a terrific beating all week, he tried to cut a soft five-iron shot into the green — "Should have been a six," he said — and ended up behind the green. He chipped 15 feet past the hole, but made the putt coming back. "A dramatic birdie which I shouldn't have made," he conceded. At the 18th, his three-wood tee shot got away from him, and the ball went sailing into high rough on the left. From there, he was trying to get downrange, and was startled to see his wedge shot fly 170 yards. "Must have been the Jamaican air," he said, "or the Red Stripe beer." He saved his par for the 67.

About a half-hour later, he was joined by the rejuvenated Faldo, who had had a very un-Faldo-like year, with only one victory, the Alfred Dunhill Open early in June. Otherwise, he wasn't much of a factor until he switched to cross-handed putting in September. Once he got comfortable with it, he was on his way back, as he showed early in December with a decisive victory in the Nedbank Million Dollar Challenge in South Africa. Not that the grip was infallible on Tryall's Bermuda greens. "Downgrain, they're quite quick, but upgrain, you've got to give it a whack," he said. "Apart from the four birdies, I had a couple of other chances." Five, at least. But he was superb on the four birdies. He holed 20-footers at the first and 16th holes, a 10-footer at No. 9, and chipped close at the par-five 14th.

Montgomerie was next in with 67, after rebounding from a double-bogey six at the dangerous 10th hole. The faintly dogleg-right par four, 392 yards, runs parallel to the sea, which is about only 100 yards away, to the left of play. Its principal charm is an elevated green sitting high behind a wide, deep drainage ditch. If it looks like a castle moat, the likeness isn't far off. The green is further defended by a naked little tree sitting high above the moat, about a third of the way in from the left of the green.

Montgomerie had just made a birdie at the ninth, holing from 20 feet, and was relieved to beat his nemesis, the front nine. "Last year, I had problems going out," he said, "so 33 this time was good. And I immediately relaxed." His approach at the 10th hit that little tree and dropped into the ditch. He scored a six. "A couple of years ago, I don't think I would have been able to recover from that, mentally," he said. He birdied the 12th from 20 feet, shook off a bogey at the par-three 13th, and birdied four of the last five holes, the last three in succession for his 67. "But if Ernie Els keeps doing what he's doing," Monty said, "we're all playing for second."

Els, in the pairing just behind Montgomerie and Price, had posted the 64 for a three-stroke lead. Els had nine birdies overall and a record-tying 31 on the second nine. He started with a birdie at the par-three No. 5 from eight feet, then devastated Tryall over the last 10 holes. He birdied the ninth and 10th holes, then took a double-bogey six at the 11th, where he put his approach shot over the back of the green, then putted down, 25 feet past the flag. "A little too hard," he explained.

"Normally, when I make double bogey, I get pretty hot under the collar," Els said. But, like Montgomerie, Els found inner reserve and proceeded to birdie six of the last seven holes. He got four in succession from No. 12, on putts of 12, one, 10 and six feet. He parred the 16th, then birdied the last two, the 17th on two putts from 35 feet and the 18th from 25 feet. "Probably my best run," Els said. "At least in the top two or three."

Life wasn't as simple for many others. Price, No. 1 on the Sony Ranking, was playing his first Johnnie Walker World Championship, having stayed home in Zimbabwe for the holidays in the first three. This time he brought a bad cold with him, and the best he could manage was 71. Tom Kite was two under par coming to the 18th, and double-bogeyed for his 71. Craig Parry was burned front and back, double-bogeying the first and 17th holes for 72. Seve Ballesteros had an indifferent 73, and things didn't improve for the struggling Vijay Singh. He made eight at the par-five 14th and shot the day's high of 75.

Faldo, by the way, revealed another secret, besides the cross-handed putting — builder's chalk. Heat and humidity ruin his touch, and so he dusts chalk on his hands the way a pool-shooter chalks the cue. "I've got chalk and cheese sandwiches in the bag," Faldo said. "I'm all right, as long as I don't eat the wrong one."

As the day drifted to a close, there was an odd sight on the practice green behind the little pro shop. There was Azinger, the man keeping a year-old date, who had shot a creditable 71, practicing his putting — cross-handed.

The long-awaited sea winds arrived for the second round about noon on Friday, though not with their usual muscle, but they were strong and capricious enough to cause problems. The place to watch from was the par-three 13th, a 191-yard hole with a nearly all-water carry across a placid backwater. The glassy surface was broken only by the leaves from bordering trees, floating like lily pads.

Friday was another hot day, and the breezes that helped relieve the heat also created problems for the golfers. One of the first victims was Brad Faxon, who opened with a bogey and a double bogey before he could get his game going. He had had five birdies since, including a 20-foot putt from off the green at the 12th. Now, on the 13th tee, the wind was behind him, quartering to the left, toward the sea. Just as Faxon swung, the wind gusted, and there went his ball, sailing well over the green and into the dense border of torch lily, a tall, sword-bladed plant with spikes of flame. That's out of bounds. He made six and shot 70.

Minutes later, along came Azinger, and the wind had come about and now was a slight headwind. His tee shot came down in the water. He salvaged a bogey with a 20-foot putt from above the hole and shot 74. Then Mize's hopes of repeating as champion ended when he suffered a seven and went on to shoot 78, the worst score of the week. And Montgomerie took a five that knocked him off the leaderboard and a 74 that put him out of the running.

Elsewhere, the double bogeys were flying. Among them: Fuzzy Zoeller (74) eagled No. 4, then had back-to-back sixes at Nos. 7 and 8; Kite (73) had sixes at the eighth and 10th; Carl Mason (74) at the ninth and 12th (on a stretch of six over par on four holes). The baffled Singh made five bogeys plus a double bogey at the 10th for 75, and Loren Roberts (71) made seven at the easy par-five 17th, which took another thrashing. It played more like a strong par-four hole, at an average of 4.33.

The second round could be described as a day of illusion. There was David Gilford with 64, and Couples and Lehman with 65s. But they couldn't pressure Els, who was moving out of reach, beyond pressure. He shot a second 64 and stretched his lead from three to six strokes. As Montgomerie observed after the first round, if Els kept it up, everyone was playing for second. Els was keeping it up.

Lehman, the big, friendly open-faced man from Minnesota, turned in a classic bogey-free 65 to join Faldo at 134, six strokes behind Els. He had three birdies on each nine, including a pair of 10-foot putts on the front, a deuce at the stubborn 13th and two putts from 45 feet at the 17th. He was travel-weary, having gone around the world in three weeks, playing in four events in Hawaii, Japan and South Africa. He confessed that he had lost his edge. But he seemed to have it this day. What brought it back? "Making some putts," he said. "That gets you going. For some reason, I'm seeing the line and reading the greens well the first two days."

Faldo had a day something like that, with his cross-handed putting style. "I tried it as much as 10, 12 years ago," he said. "This is the first time I've stuck with it." Once he became comfortable with it, the putts started dropping. He bogeyed twice this day, from the rough and from a bunker, but he made four birdies, one from six feet, two from 20 and one from 25. He made one other six-footer, but that was for an eagle at the 17th. "That made it a good score for the day," Faldo said. He was still six strokes behind Els. "He's played well all year, and he's not likely to do anything silly," Faldo said, "so you have to go out and do better."

Couples was a man bent on doing better than Els, and he almost did. The

65 was excellent, but nothing like what he had going. He was flirting with a course record until three crushing bogeys in four holes from the 10th stopped him. He tied his own record on the front nine with 30, getting three of his five birdies in succession from No. 7 on a two-foot putt, a 40-foot bunker shot and a 12-foot putt. Next the three bogeys, then four birdies over the last five holes, the last three in succession.

Azinger shot a pedestrian 74, but it was anything but pedestrian in action. He had become exasperated with his putting, and now he was trying the cross-handed style he had practiced the evening before. It was strange. "I don't know what I'm doing," he said. "But I'll figure something out."

Els, meanwhile, shot his second consecutive 64. As he had said, "Every dog has his day." Here was Els' day: A birdie from close range at No. 4 wiped out by a two-putt bogey at No. 5 after a poor bunker shot. A birdie from six feet at No. 7. And then Els continued to make Jamaican hay on Tryall's par-36 second nine. He had tied the record with 31 in the first round, and broke it with 30 in the second round, for a two-day aggregate of 11 under. He birdied the 11th and 12th from four and 12 feet, then birdied the last four holes, from eight feet at the 15th and 16th, two putts from 25 at the 17th and the 18th from 35. "The course is there to be taken," Els said. He would know.

Els had a large lead, but no one was conceding anything. "Tournaments are like marathons," Lehman said. "You keep on going, keep on going, and hope when you cross the finish line that you are ahead."

Els agreed. He remembered the Mercedes German Masters early in October. He led by four strokes with seven holes to play, and lost to Ballesteros in a playoff. No lead is safe, he noted. He remembered yet another, in his battle with Norman in the Dubai Desert Classic in January.

"I had an eight-shot lead," Els said.

"What happened?" came the question.

"I won by six," he said.

Two flashing stars just missed hitting head on. Els had those two blistering 64s, building up a hefty lead as though he had seen trouble coming. And there it came, in the third round. Azinger, with his new cross-handed putting grip, exploded back into the world of golf with a course-record, nine-under-par 62. "Was he cheating?" Faldo said in admiration. It was ironic. Azinger was supposed to be playing in the Johnnie Walker World Championship a year ago, but he had just undergone chemotherapy for the lymphoma diagnosed weeks earlier.

Azinger said he flirted briefly with the cross-handed grip at the PGA Tour qualifying tournament in 1982. Now it was working for others, he noted — Bernhard Langer, Couples, Kite, Faldo. What does it do for a golfer? For one thing, he said, moving the left hand below the right hand on the shaft lowers the left shoulder, and this improves control. The 62 rocketed him to a tie for third place after the third round. He needed just 25 putts, or 28 if you count using the putter from off the green, which the PGA Tour does not. He eagled the 17th from 30 feet, and made seven birdies from three, four, six, eight, 15, 18 and 20 feet.

Azinger and his putting were the talk of the day, especially since Els, paradoxically, lost ground and gained it at the same time. A hot sun and slightly brisker breezes baked the course further, and hardened it. After those two 64s, Els soared to a par 71, and had to birdie three of the last seven holes to do that. And then Els discovered that despite slipping, he was no longer leading by six strokes, but by seven. "Lucky for me nobody made a run," Els said. But he did feel a touch of hot breath, part of it wind, part of it Lehman, his playing companion.

Els was having his troubles. He bogeyed the par-three fifth hole, trying a soft five-iron shot instead of a hard six, and then bogeyed the eighth and 11th holes off poor sand shots. This from the man whose most grievous errors consisted of one double bogey in the first round and a single bogey in the second. Lehman, out with two birdies and two bogeys, birdied the dangerous 10th, and suddenly he was within three strokes. Els was down to 12 under par, and Lehman was at nine under. Then Lehman crashed. "I've had maybe one shot out-of-bounds all year," he said, "and now two OBs and one unplayable lie on the back nine." He bogeyed the 11th, double-bogeyed both the 12th and 17th, and shot his tournament-worst 75. He finished the day 10 strokes behind Els.

Price, still fighting a stuffed-head cold, birdied three holes in succession from the 15th for his 68 and felt a little empty. "I'm surprised everyone's going backward except Paul," he said. One other didn't go backward, but he started too far back to make a difference. It was Ballesteros, shooting a flawless, six-birdie 65, including a Ballesteros Special at No. 8. He hit his three-iron shot over the green, then holed a 20-yard pitching wedge coming back for the birdie. By coincidence, he played with his old and sometimes heated Ryder Cup foe, Azinger. "It was great to be with Paul, and walk the fairways with him and see him play so fantastic," Ballesteros said. "It's so good for the game."

The day ended on a question of conflicting ambitions. Azinger spoke of admiration for Els. "It might seem strange that a 34-year-old can learn from a 25-year-old, but I want to be more like Ernie," Azinger said. "Nothing rattles him." Els hadn't heard of this praise, and Azinger hadn't heard of Els' errors. "Somehow," said Els, confessing to being rattled by his three bogeys, "you've got to try to stay calm and play your own game."

Els went into the final round with that seven-stroke lead, and as Faldo had noted much earlier, he wasn't about to do anything silly. And he didn't. "I must say, the guys made it a little easier for me," Els said. It was just a matter of everybody playing out the string. For Faldo, it was a dress rehearsal for his coming assault on the U.S. PGA Tour. He shot 67 and tied for second place with McCumber, who also shot 67, but more to the point, he made five birdies over the last seven holes, and four of them in succession. It was just the sign he needed. "It was good to play under pressure," he said. "Now a rest and a start in Tucson in January," Faldo said.

They finished six strokes behind Els, who shot 69 for his 268 total, 16 under par, two strokes off Mize's tournament record in 1993. It was the end of a monumental year. This was his 1994: Five victories — the U.S. Open, Dubai Dessert Classic, Toyota World Match Play Championship, Gene Sarazen World Open and Johnnie Walker World Championship. He also had six second-place finishes, and won a total of $2,862,854. No one had ever won that much in a year before.

11. American Tours

Joyful beginnings and tearful endings, confrontation and controversy, injury and illness, positives and negatives all played roles on the 1994 U.S. PGA Tour.

The greater triumphs were scored by Paul Azinger, in his inspirational victory over cancer, and Nick Price in his continuing domination of the world game. A weeping Arnold Palmer said goodbye in his last U.S. Open appearance. Deane Beman stepped down after 20 years as Commissioner, while Jose Maria Olazabal and Ernie Els stepped up, each scoring his first major tournament victory.

A positive, new beginning occurred in the inaugural Presidents Cup matches in the suburbs of Washington, D.C., but a recurring negative attracted as much attention in the continuing, shabby saga of John Daly. After rolling around on the ground in a public scuffle with a 62-year-old tournament spectator in Akron, Ohio, the troubled young star — once again — spent the end of the season on the sidelines.

Beman was succeeded by Deputy Commissioner Tim Finchem. Beman's plans to join the Senior PGA Tour as a competitor were delayed by injuries that kept him out of action most of the year.

Azinger also missed most of the season while undergoing extensive, debilitating treatment for lymphoma — a form of cancer — in his right shoulder. The treatment was successful and the popular Azinger returned in defense of his title in the PGA Championship. That he missed the cut did nothing to detract from a comeback that made him a national symbol of hope against the disease.

He was one of three major figures who lost significant time to illness and injury, a factor that may have contributed to the first sweep of major titles by non-Americans. Phil Mickelson suffered a broken leg in a skiing accident and Fred Couples had a slow recovery from back spasms that forced him out of the Masters.

Still another medical problem was involved in the United States' major triumph of the season, a 20-12 victory over an International team in the Presidents Cup, a biennial competition patterned after the Ryder Cup competition. Greg Norman was afflicted with intestinal problems and was unable to compete with the team made up of players from countries not eligible for the Ryder Cup.

And, of course, there was the predictable trouble with the spring weather in North Texas. As usual, the GTE Byron Nelson Classic in Irving, Texas, and the Southwestern Bell Colonial, 30 miles away in Fort Worth, were hammered. The Nelson event was visited by a tornado, which reduced the tournament to 36 holes. Two weeks later, storms and flooding resulted in a rare Monday finish.

The amiable Price won that delayed tournament on the way to a dream season in which he collected two of the four major titles, went to No. 1 on the Sony Ranking, became the first since Tom Watson in 1980 to win five times on the PGA Tour, collected a second consecutive money title and wrapped up PGA Player of the Year honors as early as August. That came in his wire-to-wire, record-setting six-shot triumph with an 11-under-par 269 in the PGA Championship at Southern Hills, a performance that prompted Ben Crenshaw to enthuse, "He's a man in full flight. Striking the ball, I would say he's been as good as anyone since Ben Hogan and Byron Nelson. God, he's magnificent to watch."

And that was about all his would-be-competitors have been able to do — just watch — when Price was in the field. He also won the British Open (which combined with the U.S. Open victory by the South African Els and the Masters triumph of Spain's Olazabal for the first non-American sweep of the major titles). Price also won the Honda Classic, Motorola Western Open and Bell Canadian Open and finished the official season with a leading $1,499,927.

Other significant victories were scored by Norman, a record-breaking romp in The Players Championship, and Mark McCumber, who picked up his third title of the season in a playoff against Fuzzy Zoeller in the season-ending Tour Championship. That loss marked Zoeller's fifth runner-up finish in a winless season.

Mercedes Championship—$1,000,000
Winner: Phil Mickelson

Just when it looked like the seniors were going to embarrass the juniors, the most junior man in the field restored a sense of normalcy to the Mercedes Championship.

"I think the seniors are about where you would expect them to be. It's just that the guys on the regular tour maybe aren't playing quite as well as they usually do," Jack Nicklaus said, attempting to explain the unique situation that existed through the first three rounds of the two-tiered event formerly known as the Tournament of Champions.

For the first time in the decade since winners from the Senior PGA Tour joined champions from the regular tour — called "the juniors" by the over-50 set — in separate but simultaneous competition, both groups used the same tees at the La Costa Resort in Carlsbad, California. And, after 54 holes, golf's old folks were dead even with the kids. The lead in each section was 208, eight under par; Dave Stockton and Bob Murphy in the seniors, Fred Couples and Phil Mickelson in the juniors.

Nicklaus, as usual, was right in his appraisal. The seniors' leading score was about the same as the 10-year average for this tournament and the regular tour leaders were, unaccountably, four to five shots higher. Whatever the reason, the over-the-hill gang had a spring in the step and a twinkle in the eye — as well as a rooting section among the juniors — going into the final round. "I hope I win, and I hope the seniors beat me by five shots," Couples said. But flu caught up with Couples, and youth caught up with the seniors.

The lefty Mickelson needed only a par on the second extra hole to beat Couples in a playoff and, at 23 years, six months, become the youngest since Nicklaus to score four victories on the American tour. Mickelson and Couples each finished with 276 totals, 12 under par, slightly higher than the average winning score in this tournament but three shots better than the seniors' winning total.

United Airlines Hawaiian Open—$1,200,000
Winner: Brett Ogle

The strength of Brett Ogle's game cannot be doubted, not when it can rebound from the potential knockout punch of a 60, the third best score ever played on the U.S. PGA Tour. Ogle's rhymes, however, need a little work. "Clickity click, sixty-six," the chipper, gregarious Australian said, announcing his scores for each of the first two rounds of the United Airlines Hawaiian Open. "My game thrives on the par fives," Ogle said, explaining how he was able to stay in touch with the lead even when Davis Love III recorded a 12-under-par 60 — a score that has been bettered only twice and equalled eight times in PGA Tour history.

Love's second-round card:

Par	Out	544	344	345–36	In	434	544	435–36–72
Love	Out	344	344	243–31	In	323	444	423–29–60

For Love, the effort was both a blessing and a curse. It was, by two shots, the best of his career, was only one stroke off the Tour record, gave Love a four-shot advantage at the halfway point and included three eagles. Love could do no better than a pair of 71s over the last two days. The first involved an unhappy brush with a photographer and the second cost him the tournament. "First I got excited," Love said, reviewing his emotional roller-coaster. "Then I got angry. Then I got disappointed."

Ogle provided the disappointment when he engineered a two-stroke swing on the 71st hole — Ogle's 10-foot birdie putt with his 56-inch putter against Love's three-putt from the fringe — went two strokes up with one hole to play and beat Love by a single stroke with a closing 68 and a 269 total.

After 36 holes, Love was 16 under par at 128, but Ogle kept him in sight at 132. "I just tried to stay close and chip away," the Australian said. Much of that effort was accomplished on the par-five holes. Over the first two rounds, Ogle played them nine under par with an eagle and seven birdies. Even that paled in comparison with Love's second-round heroics. He played the long holes seven under par — in one day. Love missed a 15-foot eagle putt on the 508-yard 13th, and eagled the other three: a four iron to 18-foot putt on the 539-yard first, a seven iron to 15 feet on the 513-yard ninth, and a three wood to 10 feet on the 552-yard 18th.

Northern Telecom Open—$1,100,000
Winner: Andrew Magee

It was better than a good trade for Andrew Magee; more like two for one. He lost his standing as an answer to one of golf's most trivial of trivia questions but replaced it with (1) the fourth victory of his 10-season career, a front-running triumph in the Northern Telecom Open, and (2) a spot in the Masters.

The swap becomes even more attractive when it's considered that the distinction surrendered by Magee was hardly one of his most prized possessions. His name actually appeared in crossword puzzles as the correct response to: American pro golfer born in Paris. He is the son of an oil man who served a stint in France.

For the last couple of years, unfortunately, that was about the only distinction Magee could claim. Even that small claim to fame came to an end late in 1993 when native Parisian Thomas Levet made it through the U.S. PGA Tour's qualifying tournament. Magee was no more dismayed to see it end than he was to put behind him what he called "two weird years when I didn't have much direction."

Magee, who started his season in Tucson, found the path he wanted in the desert, opening with a round of 69 followed by three 67s, producing an 18-under-par 270 total and a two-stroke victory over Vijay Singh, Loren Roberts, Steve Stricker and Jay Don Blake. The most pressure, however, was applied by Olin Browne. Browne, three shots off the pace in the final round, made them up almost immediately, holing out a 217-yard, four-iron shot for a rare double eagle on the second hole before Magee got started. Browne, however, could not sustain the pace and dropped back to sixth alone with a closing 67 and 273 total. Magee took control of the lead with birdies on two of the first three holes and never looked back, playing the last 18 holes without a bogey.

Phoenix Open—$1,200,000
Winner: Bill Glasson

Bill Glasson used a two-day scoring burst to come from two shots back, climb over six players and collect a three-shot victory in the Phoenix Open. "Ten birdies in 15 holes; pretty cool," the laid-back, 33-year-old Glasson said after nailing down his sixth career triumph with a bogey-free, seven-under-par 64 over the final 18 holes at the TPC at Scottsdale. The decisive scoring explosion started in Saturday's third round: birdies on five of the last six holes, including the last four.

"I was anxious to play Sunday," Glasson said. "I wanted to keep the momentum going." The oft-injured man with the long blond hair did just that, reeling off three in a row at the start of the day's play for a string of seven consecutive birdies, just one short of the PGA Tour record. The birdie on No. 3 during the final round — a wedge shot to three feet — put him in the lead alone and he never looked back, playing the front in 30, then entering a comfort zone with birdies on the 15th and 16th. With a 268 total, 16 under par, Glasson collected $216,000, more than his yearlong earnings in six of his 10 previous seasons.

Glasson's last-round move to the top was aided by the varied misfortunes that beset the trio who shared the third-round lead. Rick Fehr, who said he "got distracted a couple of times on key shots by the TV cameras," could do no better than match par 71 over the last 18 holes. Dan Forsman and Andrew Magee, a winner in Tucson and shooting for an Arizona double, each crashed with 73. Bob Estes came on with a 10-footer on the last hole to claim second alone at 13 under par, one stroke in front of Jeff Maggert, Mike Springer and Blaine McCallister.

AT&T Pebble Beach National Pro-Am—$1,250,000
Winner: Johnny Miller

Johnny Miller searched for words to describe his turn-back-the-clock victory over Tom Watson in the AT&T Pebble Beach National Pro-Am. "A fluke," "a time warp," and "a touch of magic," were among his observations. But it was Watson, whose collapse over the last three holes paved the way for Miller's triumph, who best summed up the drama that developed on the cliffs and crags overlooking the Pacific. "In my early career, I lived by the putter," Watson said. "Today, I died by the putter."

Watson missed putts of four, three and six feet on the last three holes. Any one of them would have forced a playoff between the two middle-aged masters, each of whom was attempting to end a non-winning string that stretched back to 1987. Miller, 46, was the more unlikely candidate. After scoring his last previous victory in this event seven years earlier, Miller had retreated to the television commentators booth. "Winning that one gave me the chance to say goodbye," he said. Miller played in only five official events in the 90s. And he came to his favorite playground "to have some fun. I didn't come here to win," he said. He did both, acquiring his third Pebble Beach title with a 281 total, seven under par.

Miller and Watson, 44, took charge over the last 18 holes, played in miserable weather — wind, cold and occasional rain — at Pebble Beach. Watson, a Hall of Famer and the last American Ryder Cup captain, took command on the back nine and held a one-stroke lead with three holes to go over the links that provided him with the 1982 U.S. Open title.

On the 16th, he hit his approach to 15 feet and, attempting to go two up with two to play, hammered his first putt four feet long. And he missed the come-backer for a bogey that dropped him back into a tie. At the 17th, he hit a four iron to the middle of the green and grazed the cup with his birdie attempt from 35 feet. But the man who made so many clutch putts in his glory years pulled his three-foot second putt just a bit and the ball spun out. It was a second consecutive three-putt bogey and now he trailed by one.

Two three woods put him in the front bunker on the par-five 18th. Needing a birdie four to tie and force a playoff, Watson's sand shot was about six feet long. He left the putt one-half inch short, dead in the heart of the cup. Needing a par five to win, Miller played it conservatively, four wood, five-iron lay up, wedge to 20 feet and two putts, completing a round of 74 for the 24th — and most surprising — victory of his career.

Watson was waiting to shake his hand when Miller came off the 18th green. "I told him to get his rear end back in the television booth," said Watson, who also shot 74 and dropped back into a tie for second at 282 with Jeff Maggert, Corey Pavin and Kirk Triplett.

Nissan Los Angeles Open—$1,000,000
Winner: Corey Pavin

Put him in match play and gritty, fiercely competitive little Corey Pavin is among the world's best. He proved it with critical contributions to the last two American Ryder Cup victories — contested under a match play format. He proved it again in 1993, beating Nick Price, Nick Faldo and others on his way to a victory in the prestigious Toyota World Match Play Championship in England. And he proved it still again in the Nissan Los Angeles Open, vaulting over Fred Couples in a head-to-head last-round confrontation and going on to a two-shot triumph.

No one else was closer than five strokes over the final 18 holes at the Riviera Country Club and both principals agreed it was, indeed, match play. And, although he was 60 yards and more ahead of his opponent off the tee, the powerful Couples was — at least this time — overmatched by the wiry, wily little Pavin who found himself in his element. "I love match play," Pavin said. "It is the essence of golf. It is what golf was meant to be. It is golf in its purest form."

Their confrontation was along classic lines: the power-hitter vs. the finesse player. It was set up by Couples pounding out scores of 67, 67, 68 and a one-shot lead over the first three days and Pavin staying close on the strength of a brilliant no-bogey, seven-under-par 64 in the second round. The effort was even more remarkable in that it came over highly suspect, spiky, bumpy young greens. Riviera's putting surfaces, laid down in 1926, in recent years had encountered drainage and growing problems. The club hired Ben Crenshaw as a consultant to oversee a rebuilding project. The greens were dug up and — aided by computer readings — rebuilt and restored to their original configurations and contours.

The match turned on putting. Couples, who used 33 putts on the last round, missed two par-savers from less than 30 inches. Pavin, who had only 25 putts in his final 68, made two from about 25 feet. One of Couples' short misses came on the 14th in a three-putt bogey. It went against Pavin's 12-foot birdie putt on the same hole for a two-stroke swing that pulled them even. One of Pavin's long ones came on the 16th, giving him a two-stroke lead with two holes to play.

He went on to acquire his 11th victory in as many years on the PGA Tour with a 271 total, 13 under par. For Couples, it was his third runner-up finish in four worldwide starts for the season. He lost to Greg Norman by one shot the week before in Thailand and was second in the season-opening Mercedes Championship.

Bob Hope Chrysler Classic—$1,100,000
Winner: Scott Hoch

Scott Hoch had a problem. He was alone on the road and facing a long evening. After five years without an American victory, he suddenly found himself with a four-shot lead going into the last 18 holes of the Bob Hope Chrysler Classic.

"When you haven't won in so long," Hoch said, "you really don't know how to go about it." So, in order to take his mind off golf, Hoch went to the movies. Plural. He saw three of them the night before the final round. One was *On Deadly Ground*, starring action hero Steven Seagal. "That got me in the mood to kick some butt, 'cause that's what he does," Hoch said after converting his big lead and a hard-won, scrambling round of 70 into the fifth victory of his 15-year PGA Tour career. The three-shot triumph snapped a non-winning string that stretched back to the 1989 Las Vegas Invitational, like this one a multiple-course, five-day, 90-hole tournament played under a pro-am format.

Hoch led by two strokes or more throughout the chilly final round at Indian Wells and won with a 334 total, 26 under par. His task was eased when no one within striking range of the lead was able to apply any appreciable pressure. Lennie Clements, Jim Gallagher and Billy Glasson had a combined total of two birdies on the back nine of the easiest of the four desert resort courses used in this event. That enabled Hoch to survive his own mistakes. He saved par from behind a palm tree on the 12th. He missed the green on the 13th and 15th, but saved par on both.

Even the shot that sealed the victory came from trouble. On the par-five 14th, he drove behind the gallery in the left rough, found an opening through the trees and got his second into a bunker short of the green. In a difficult position, with one foot on the lip of the bunker, Hoch played a 60-foot sand shot to within inches of the flag and turned potential trouble into a birdie. It gave him a five-shot lead with four to go and, despite a three-putt bogey on the 17th, he brought it home with relative ease.

A couple of veterans, Fuzzy Zoeller and Payne Stewart, made the best runs at Hoch, but each was too far back to have any realistic hopes of overtaking the man who lost a playoff for the 1989 Masters. Zoeller, who started the last round seven shots back, shot 66 for 337 and tied for second with Gallagher and Clements, each of whom had a closing 68. Stewart was 11 back, too much to overcome even with a nine-under-par 63 that left him alone at 338.

Buick Invitational of California—$1,100,000
Winner: Craig Stadler

Even though the Great White Shark was swimming in foreign waters, and the Golden Bear hasn't prowled this area in many years, a homegrown Walrus and a critical eagle combined to impart a certain zoological aspect to the Buick Invitational of California. With Greg Norman and Jack Nicklaus among the many missing — nine of the top 10 money winners from 1993 and 22 of the top 30 bypassed the last stop on the Western swing — the tournament again turned to local products for credibility. With the aid of a go-ahead eagle, Craig Stadler, "The Walrus," a native and resident of San Diego, obliged.

"This is very special," Stadler said after rounds of 67, 67, 68, 66 produced a one-stroke victory at 268, 20 under par. It was the 11th triumph of a 19-season career for the 40-year-old Stadler, and his first in two years. "I've played here so long (he estimated between 300 and 400 career rounds at the Torrey Pines Golf Club) and had so many chances. I'm very happy. I think it's well-earned," he said.

Perhaps his best previous chance in his hometown tournament produced the most heartbreaking moment of his career, a day-late disqualification. In the third round of the 1987 tournament, Stadler had to go to his knees to play his second shot from beneath the limbs of a tree on the 14th hole. He put a towel on the ground to keep his trousers from getting wet. A day later Stadler was on the course competing in fourth-round play when national television aired videotape of the towel/tree third-round shot. A viewer called. After Stadler completed fourth-round play, one shot out of the lead, he was informed he had been disqualified for building a stance.

"I've learned to hate that hole over the years," Stadler said. His lack of affection was reinforced this time by 14th-hole bogeys in both the third and fourth rounds. In this case, however, it really didn't matter. He came back to birdie the 15th each day, dropping a curling, 20-foot putt in the final round that put him back in front alone. He had taken the lead initially with a 20-foot eagle putt after hitting a driver from the fairway on the par-five ninth. Stadler also birdied the 17th, hitting a wedge to four feet. That one gave him a two-shot lead and the margin he needed when Steve Lowery birdied the final hole to close within one at 68–269. Phil Mickelson, the young lefty who was the defending titleholder, closed with a 64 and was third alone at 270.

Doral-Ryder Open—$1,400,000
Winner: John Huston

John Huston — call him Lonesome John — walked down the fairways in something approaching solitude. For 11 holes of the final round in the Doral-Ryder Open, he was accompanied only by his caddie, a walking scorer and, outside the ropes, some slightly confused spectators. Their confusion escalated late in the day when Huston was joined by good friend Brian Claar. "It was a weird feeling," Claar said. "People were looking at me like, 'Hey, that's not Fred Couples.' They thought I was just some guy who jumped out of the crowd."

Couples, scheduled in the same twosome with Huston, was not to be found on Doral's Blue Monster course. Warming up on the range, "I hit one ball and it felt like my back exploded," Couples said. He was forced to withdraw, his future in doubt, and left Huston playing as a onesome. And it was Huston, not Claar, who jumped out of the crowd, the group of five players four shots back of third-round leader Billy Andrade. Playing alone and trampling on the heels of the group ahead of him, Huston birdied three holes in a row and reached the lead just before Claar finished competition, turned around and joined him as a marker on the 12th tee.

It was something of a relief for Huston, who played about a half hour in front of the other contenders. "I'd never played by myself before — not ever," he said. "When Brian came out, it kind of helped me pace myself coming home." Now in a more familiar role with a playing partner on hand, Huston, 32, found a comfortable rhythm, birdied the 15th from 25 feet and gave himself some breathing room with an eight iron to six feet on the 17th. He preserved the margin with par from a bunker on the 18th, completing a final-round 66 and a 274 total, 14 under par.

That score became a three-shot victory — the third of his career, all of which have come in Florida — when Andrade was unable to answer Huston's stretch run. Andrade, a non-winner since scoring consecutive victories in 1991, saw his last chance disappear on the 17th hole. He hit a seven iron to three feet and needed that birdie putt to close to within one with one hole to go. But he missed it to the right.

Honda Classic—$1,100,000
Winner: Nick Price

Both Nick Price and John Daly were trying to make up for lost time in the Honda Classic. Both succeeded. Making his first start after coming off a four-month suspension imposed by PGA Tour Commissioner Deane Beman, Daly celebrated his return to competition with a solid fourth-place finish that could have been even better. The longest hitter in captivity, Daly, as usual, drew the lion's share of the huge gallery and rewarded them with a last-round challenge for the title. "When I got to four under (par) and looked at the leaderboard and saw Nick was six under, I thought I had a chance to win the tournament," Daly said. But he was unable to get his irons close enough to have legitimate birdie chances and finished with a string of 10 consecutive pars.

Pars were of little value in an attempt to overtake Price, who confirmed a return to his 1993 Player of the Year form with a closing 66 in blustery winds and a one-shot triumph in only his second American start of the season. This one, secured on a 276 total, eight under par at Weston Hills, marked his 12th international triumph in 18 months, going back to his 1992 PGA Championship. But it was a little different from the others. "Usually, I've had a little cushion going into the last round," noted Price, who was four strokes back going into the last 18. "I did all the right things. Today I went out there and won the tournament. I played well for three days and kept making mistakes. Today, all I tried to do was not make mistakes."

He succeeded, hitting all 18 greens. The only glitch came on a three-putt bogey on the back nine. But he more than made up for that with an 18-foot birdie putt that curled in on the 13th and the clinching, 35-foot, double-breaking putt that found the cup on the 17th and sent Price leaping into the air in glee. "I've never been so excited in my life," he said.

The 17th hole putt gave him the margin he needed. Craig Parry, playing behind Price, followed with a 40-foot chip-in birdie on the same hole, but was unable to birdie the par-five finishing hole and came up one stroke short at 67–277. Brandel Chamblee, the journeyman who led or shared the lead through the first three rounds, was third alone — his career-high finish — at 278 after a closing 71. Daly, who shot 68 over the last round, tied for fourth with Bernhard Langer, Davis Love III and Curtis Strange.

The Nestle Invitational—$1,200,000
Winner: Loren Roberts

At age 38, Loren Roberts became a first-time winner as the beneficiary of
(1) a bad bounce off a spectator's head, (2) a drive that dribbled into the
rough, and (3) a missed putt. All three, as well as his own bogey-free finishing round of 67, were necessary for Roberts to rid himself of a title he
termed "of dubious distinction" with a victory in The Nestle Invitational.
With the triumph, he happily surrendered designation as the player with the
most U.S. career money-winnings who had not won a tournament. "It was
beginning to bother me," said the veteran of 13 years on the pro tour.
   But he had to have some help. And he got it from Fuzzy Zoeller, Vijay
Singh and Nick Price over the last few holes at Arnold Palmer's Bay Hill
Club. Roberts finished play about a half-hour ahead of the other contenders.
His day's work done and a 13-under-par total of 275 on the board, he was
standing by the 18th green and, he said, thinking "I had no chance because
I hadn't birdied" the vulnerable par-five 16th.
   Zoeller birdied it. So did Singh. Each went 14 under par, one ahead of
Roberts. But Zoeller sliced his three-iron shot on the par-three 17th and
watched the ball bounce hit off a spectator's head. The man wasn't seriously
injured. But when the ball caromed 10 yards into the water, Zoeller was on
his way to a double bogey that killed his chances. "A bad shot at the wrong
time. It had ugly written all over it," Zoeller said. Next up was Price, at 12
under par, who faced an 18-foot putt to force a playoff. He missed it. And
then there was Singh, the native of Fiji who opened his American career
with a runner-up finish in this tournament a year earlier. From the lead, he
three-putted for bogey on the 17th, dropping back into a tie. His tee shot on
the 18th ran into the rough. He was unable to reach the green and also
bogeyed, handing the title to Roberts, who said "If you're dreaming, you
win by four or five. But I'll take it any way I can get it."
   Zoeller, with 69, Price 70 and Singh 71 all tied for second at 277.

The Players Championship—$2,500,000
Winner: Greg Norman

See Chapter 7.

Freeport-McMoRan Classic—$1,200,000
Winner: Ben Crenshaw

Sitting in an interview area after his three-stroke victory, Ben Crenshaw had
a slightly embarrassed smile on his face. From time to time, he would duck
his head a little, as if chagrined. "I made a lot of putts," Crenshaw said, then
realized what a massive understatement he had just uttered. He corrected
himself. "I made the ones I should have," he said, paused, offered that
sheepish grin again and continued, "and then I made some others. And that
made the difference."
   It also made for a last-round 68, one of the great putting exhibitions of

the season and the 18th victory of Crenshaw's 22-year career. This one came on a 273 total, 15 under par at English Turn and extended a peculiar, inexplicable streak for the 42-year-old Crenshaw. Going back to 1992, his last three top-10 finishes all have been victories: the Western Open in 1992, the Nestle in 1993 and now the Freeport-McMoRan Classic. "I don't understand it," he said of the all-or-nothing streak. "I can't explain it." It could be that "Li'l Ben," his putter, has more than a little to do with it. When the putter gets hot, he wins. When it doesn't, he isn't in contention.

He entered the final round in a tie for the lead with Sam Torrance of Scotland. Crenshaw pulled two strokes ahead over the front nine, then blew the lead with a double bogey on the 10th. "Terrible," he said. "It was terribly unsettling at that point." But he came back quickly with birdies on the 11th and 13th, then applied the clincher on the 14th, a 30-footer from the back fringe, wide-breaking, up and over a crest. Torrance, using an elongated putter that he anchors under his chin, missed a six-foot par-saving putt, and Crenshaw had a three-shot lead.

Torrance got one back with a two-putt birdie four on the 15th. For a moment, on the 16th, it appeared as if Torrance would pull even. From the rough, Crenshaw hit the front bunker. Torrance had a 12-footer for birdie. Crenshaw came out to eight feet and made the par putt. Torrance missed his birdie and remained two behind with two holes to play. He missed the green and bogeyed the 17th, then blew second place when he hit into the water on the 18th.

Jose Maria Olazabal, who had a first-round 63, holed a bunker shot on the 18th for a birdie-birdie finish and was runner-up at 69–276. "I kind of got a shock from him," Torrance said after slipping to third at 73–278. "I thought second place was secure. He deserved it. He made a tough shot on 18 for birdie."

Masters Tournament—$1,700,000
Winner: Jose Maria Olazabal

See Chapter 3.

MCI Heritage Classic—$1,250,000
Winner: Hale Irwin

By his own estimate, Hale Irwin climbed out of a self-dug grave to score his third victory in the Heritage Classic. "The first six holes I buried myself," Irwin said. "I had not one foot, but both feet in the grave. Then, somehow, the burial vault opened." It opened on the strength of his rallying, last-round 68 and sent the sprightly, 48-year-old veteran on a third triumphant march toward the lighthouse beyond the 18th green at the Harbour Town Golf Links. It was a march he first made 23 years earlier when he turned back Arnold Palmer and Jack Nicklaus and scored his first career victory. This one was a little more comfortable, but, at the same time, slightly disturbing.

His scrambling start along with Greg Norman's early move over the opening holes of the final round produced more than a little doubt that he would win this one. But Irwin's rally made up a three-shot deficit and sent him to the final hole with a two-shot advantage. The man who has made a career out of consistency, preserved it with a solid, safe, two-putt par on the last hole, completing a course-record 18-under-par 266 total. His 20th career victory and first since 1990 was worth $225,000 and made him the oldest winner since Raymond Floyd won the 1992 Doral-Ryder Open at age 49.

Irwin owned a two-shot lead starting the final round but lost two shots to par over the first six holes, including a poor sand wedge and a three-putt bogey six on the fifth and, in his words "a stinking drive off the toe," setting up a sixth-hole bogey. At the same time, Norman birdied three of the first five holes and suddenly held a three-stroke lead. He was to par in from that point, however, and Irwin started back. A four iron to 12 feet on the eighth, a seven iron to 15 feet on the 12th and seven iron to three feet on the 13th brought him even. He hit wedges to tap-in distance on the 15th and 16th and brought it home. "I got the bit in my teeth and felt like I could run forever," he said.

But he recognized he had help. "I was fortunate Greg leveled out," Irwin said. Norman, who matched Irwin's closing 68, was second alone at 268. Loren Roberts' last-round 62 lifted him into third place at 69. David Frost, whose second-round 61 broke the course record, was one of three tied for fourth at 270.

Kmart Greater Greensboro Open—$1,500,000
Winner: Mike Springer

When your golf ball hits a tree, it's hardly ever considered a good thing. When your golf ball hits the pin, it's almost always very, very good. But neither was necessarily so in the protest-marred final round of the Kmart Greater Greensboro Open. Mike Springer hit a tree. In this case it was a good break, an answer to a prayer. Hale Irwin hit a pin. While it wasn't necessarily a bad break, it did constitute half of a two-shot swing in Springer's favor, a critical portion of a three-stroke, wire-to-wire run for the first victory of his four-season career. He won with a closing round of par 72 and a 275 total, 13 under par.

The triumph was worth $270,000, more than he had won in any of his three previous full seasons. And it was the first step toward his annual target: "Win three tournaments, play solid, be a top-30 money winner," he said. He's done it only once, in the inaugural Ben Hogan Tour season. Springer won three on the 1990 Ben Hogan Tour, finished fourth on the money list and gained a spot on the regular tour. Until Greensboro, however, his record among the big boys was littered with near-misses, no victories. He tied for third place after leading with seven holes to play in Atlanta in 1991. In 1992, he led with two holes to go in San Diego and tied for sixth. In 1993, there were four top-10 finishes.

This time, however, he seized the tournament lead and never let go. He took the first-round lead with 64 at Forest Oaks, increased it to four shots with a second-round 69 and maintained the margin with a third-round 70. "I feel like I am in control," he said, going into the final round. "They have to come out and take it from me. This is my tournament to lose and I have been looking forward to that (position) for a long, long time." And he had to wait just a little longer. Just before his tee time, people protesting against the sponsors ran onto the 10th fairway and sat down. About 60 were arrested and led away in handcuffs.

Springer kept his lead in the three- to four-stroke range until late in the day. After missing a six-foot birdie putt on the 15th, Irwin, 48, seeking a second consecutive victory, hit the flagstick with his seven-iron approach on the 16th. The ball disappeared into the cup, then spun out. It was a tap-in birdie but "a two would have been nice," Irwin said. Springer, playing behind Irwin, hooked his tee shot off the 16th tee and saw the ball heading out of bounds. "Hit a tree," he begged. The ball obliged. It hit a tree and dropped straight down, some six feet from the white out-of-bounds stakes. He made a welcome bogey and saw his margin cut to two strokes. When Irwin missed the 18th green and bogeyed, however, Springer was able to cruise in as a winner. Irwin, with a closing 69, tied for second with Brad Bryant and Ed Humenik.

Shell Houston Open—$1,300,000
Winner: Mike Heinen

On the practice green before the final round of the Shell Houston Open, rookie Mike Heinen walked up to the man with whom he was paired in the final twosome. He introduced himself. He had never before met Tom Kite. A few hours later, however, Kite, Hal Sutton, Jeff Maggert and a national television audience were very much aware of the identity of the young man from the Cajun country of southern Louisiana. His father, Bill Heinen, summed it up. "That boy done surprised me," he said. "I never dreamed this. I knew he had talent, but I figured the first time he went up against the big boys, they'd knock him on his butt. But he done knocked them on their butts."

The 27-year-old rookie, a product of Southwestern Louisiana, the Nike Tour and the Canadian Tour, used a bogey-free, four-under-par 68 in the last round to break out of a tie with Maggert and Kite, turned back an eight-birdie challenge by Sutton and become the fifth player in as many years to score his first PGA Tour triumph in this tournament. His three-stroke victory with a 16-under-par 272 total followed first-time triumphs in Houston by Jim McGovern (1993), Fred Funk (1992), Fulton Allem (1991) and Tony Sills (1990). None were more obscure than Heinen.

Heinen showed no trace of nerves in a steady run over the last 18 holes. He dropped a 20-footer on the fourth hole, had a clutch par-saving putt on the eighth, then made 15-footers on the ninth and 11th and seemed blissfully unaware of Sutton's charge. He pulled to within one stroke of the lead on the 16th with a 25-foot birdie, but missed the green and bogeyed the 17th, enabling Heinen to complete the upset with a solid, two-putt par on the last hole. Maggert and Kite, each with a closing 71, tied for second with Sutton.

BellSouth Classic—$1,200,000
Winner: John Daly

John Daly's roller-coaster career reached its greatest peak since his 1991 PGA triumph with the last-hole birdie that brought golf's longest hitter a one-shot victory in the BellSouth Classic at the Atlanta Country Club. Daly was fighting back tears after dropping the five-foot putt that capped a comeback from personal adversity.

"This is the first tournament I've won on the PGA Tour in a sober manner," he said. "I'm still shaking. Thank God it's over. Nothing could mean more than winning sober. To win again is a great feeling. But the best feeling is that I know I can win a golf tournament sober. You always wonder. You always think, 'Hey, can I do that?'"

The questions arose during his suspensions from Tour activity, first during an alcohol rehabilitation program, then a four-month sit-down for improper conduct. Daly, a non-winner since 1992 but one of the Tour's most popular players and greatest gate attractions, answered with a closing round of par 72 and a 14-under-par 274 total. Needing a birdie on the 499-yard, par-five finishing hole to win, Daly pounded his drive more than 300 yards down the fairway. His approach caught bunker on the left, but he got it up and down for the victory and an answer to the questions.

The third victory of his career served as a personal landmark for the troubled Daly, but it did not come easily. Daly led through the second and third rounds, but a string of three consecutive bogeys opened the door in the fourth. There were challengers aplenty. David Peoples led until a bogey-bogey finish. Blaine McCallister was in the hunt until scoring his second double bogey of the round. And Daly used his favorite weapon, the driver, to win it. He challenged the water on the left with the massive tee shot that set up an eight-iron second shot to the par-five 18th hole, then got it up and down from the sand for the needed birdie. Defending champion Nolan Henke and Brian Henninger, who made an eight-foot eagle putt on the final hole, tied for second at 275.

GTE Byron Nelson Classic—$1,200,000
Winner: Neal Lancaster

Problems. The GTE Byron Nelson Classic caused problems for players, for spectators, for PGA Tour officials, for tournament sponsors. Even for local television stations. They had to decide whether their coverage should go in the sports section of their telecast, or the weather. Or even straight news. After all, when thousands of spectators are evacuated before a tornado skips from one golf course to another, it's news. When the weather-plagued tournament — weather has caused disruptions in 20 of the last 28 years — finally sloshed and slogged to a close, Neal Lancaster was the winner of the largest playoff (six men) in one of the shortest (36 holes) tournaments in PGA Tour history.

The first two days of scheduled play were nearly identical. Heavy overnight rains flooded the TPC at Las Colinas. Starting times were delayed, and delayed again and, in early afternoon, play was abandoned. By Friday night, not a shot had been played by the 156-man field. On Saturday morning, officials hastily brought into play the adjacent Cottonwood Valley course and scheduled a double round of 36 holes. The first 18 went off as scheduled, but another storm hit in late afternoon. This one included a tornado that skipped from one course to another, touching down briefly on each shortly after players and spectators were ordered to evacuate. No injuries were reported, but the tournament schedule was disrupted again. Only a handful of players completed second-round play, half the field had not even teed off and officials reluctantly revised the format to 36 holes.

Lancaster, a 33-year-old journeyman who had not finished higher than fifth in a five-season career, returned Sunday morning to birdie his two remaining second-round holes, completing a 65 and a 132 total. He then waited around a few hours before David Ogrin, David Edwards, Mark Carnevale, Tom Byrum and Japan's Yoshi Mizumaki matched that total after one round on each course and set up the six-man playoff.

On the 37th hole of the tournament, Lancaster hit his approach to five feet, with Carnevale just outside of that. None of the other four could do better than par. Carnevale missed his birdie try and Lancaster literally shook his in. "I was so nervous my hands were shaking on the putter," he said of the stroke that ended one of the more bizarre events of the year.

Memorial Tournament—$1,500,000
Winner: Tom Lehman

Jack Nicklaus had to search back through history for the words to describe the brilliance of Tom Lehman's overwhelming, run-away victory in the Memorial Tournament Nicklaus created and now hosts. "Bob Jones said years ago at Augusta that I played a game with which he was not familiar," Nicklaus recalled. "Times have changed. Tom Lehman definitely played a game this week with which I am not familiar. This is a golf course we thought would be a pretty challenging test. It was for everyone but Mr. Tom Lehman."

In the most outstanding performance of the American season to this point, Lehman shot four consecutive 67s for a 20-under-par total — by three strokes a record on the Muirfield Village Golf Club course built by Nicklaus and generally considered one of the best in the country — won by the largest margin of the year, five shots, over the then No. 1 player in the world, Greg Norman.

The first PGA Tour victory of a career than included six unsuccessful attempts at the qualifying tournament, tours in Asia, South Africa and on the Ben Hogan circuit, also helped ease the pain of Lehman's loss in the Masters only six weeks earlier. Just as he did then, Lehman took a lead into the final round. Instead of letting it get away as he did in the Masters, the husky, 35-year-old Lehman simply built on it this time, steadily pulling away from the field.

"My whole game plan was to torch the front nine," Lehman said. And he did, playing it in 32. From a four-shot advantage starting the round, he went to seven ahead at the turn and, essentially, this game was over even though Norman was playing his best and throwing a last-round 64 at Lehman. All it did was get him second place at 273. John Cook, at 276, and Donnie

Hammond, also at 276, were the only others within 10 shots of the leader.

Southwestern Bell Colonial—$1,400,000
Winner: Nick Price

After a one-week visit to the midwest, the PGA Tour returned to Texas and the Southwestern Bell Colonial, some 30 miles west of Las Colinas, where violent weather cut the GTE Byron Nelson Classic to a 36-hole event. The weather did not improve appreciably in the Tour's absence, this time extending the tournament to a rare Monday finish, the first in three years. The storms and the day-late finish did little to detract from Nick Price's brilliant last-round comeback from a seven-shot deficit and his eventual playoff decision over Scott Simpson.

A nine-foot birdie putt on the first extra hole provided the popular man from Zimbabwe with his second victory of the season and brought an end to a peculiar record. Price became the first double winner of the year in the United States, in the 21st tournament of the season. Never before had the Tour gone so deep in the schedule without a two-time winner.

He won with a six-under-par 64 in the final round that included five consecutive birdies. Both the round and the birdie string were interrupted by a thunderstorm late Sunday afternoon and caused the overnight delay. Simpson, who appeared to have the title in his pocket with a course record, 15-under-par 195 and a four-stroke lead after 54 holes, Price and 16 others were stranded on the course.

When they returned Monday morning, Price ran in a 20-foot putt on the 14th hole — his fourth consecutive birdie — to pull to within one stroke. He made up that one on the next hole, scoring from 17 feet, then parred in. Simpson, who did not have a birdie in the final round, did the same and the playoff was on. Simpson put his approach on the 18th, the first extra hole, about 20 feet from the flag and Price got his to about nine feet. Simpson's birdie try was a foot short. Price ran his into the heart of the cup and was back in the spotlight again.

Kemper Open—$1,300,000
Winner: Mark Brooks

Given the gift of a snowman in May, Mark Brooks cruised to a three-shot victory in the Kemper Open. Brooks, 33, acquired his fourth title in an 11-season PGA Tour career, and his first in three years, after distraught Bobby Wadkins blew a last-round lead with a triple-bogey eight — in golfers' parlance, a "snowman." It was a gift, pure and simple. And Brooks knew it. "Maybe somewhere in college" someone may have given him one like that, Brooks said, "but never out here."

Brooks took the gift and ran with it, playing a surprisingly — for him — solid and conservative two-under-par 69 over the last round for a 271 total. It all turned on the eight at the 529-yard sixth. Wadkins, 42, the younger brother of Lanny Wadkins, was nursing the remains of a two-stroke third-round lead when he went to the tee. A drive down the right side left him with 193 yards to the pin, but 100-foot-tall oak trees hung over the right side. A high fade, the shot he had played there in earlier rounds, was needed. But Wadkins, seeking the first victory in more than 20 seasons on the PGA Tour, hit it into the trees. After a frantic, 50-person, five-minute search, the ball was ruled lost. He hit the next into a bunker behind the green, failed to reach the green, chipped to eight feet and missed it. Any realistic chance of a recovery disappeared on bogeys at the eighth and 12th holes.

Wadkins' triple bogey sent Brooks from one stroke behind to two in front and he made certain no one else got any closer. Frequently an erratic player whose birdies and bogeys often outnumber his pars, Brooks made 16 pars for the day, including 13 over one stretch and 11 in a row after Wadkins' eight. The streak ended with a last-hole birdie that really wasn't necessary but served as a punctuation mark to Brooks' rebuttal to a media question following the first round, in which Brooks played with the two top gate attractions in the tournament, Phil Mickelson and John Daly.

After shooting a pace-setting 65 in the company of those stars, Brooks was asked if he "felt like chopped liver" out there. He delivered an icy glare to the questioner and his voice rose as he said, "I'm leading this golf tournament," he said. "They were lucky to be paired with me." And he confirmed the observation with his winning performance three days later.

Buick Classic—$1,200,000
Winner: Lee Janzen

Going into the Buick Classic, Lee Janzen was wondering if he had struck a bargain he had forgotten, a bargain that would make the 1993 U.S. Open title the last he would ever win. Eleven months and three weeks after that victory, Janzen went to the Westchester Country Club in the northern suburbs of New York City in a full-fledged slump, without a top-10 finish since his triumph at Baltusrol. "During the (U.S.) Open, I must've told God that if He would help me make this putt I would never ask for another, because I haven't made one since," Janzen joked.

It really wasn't a joking matter, however. Questions began to arise as to whether he had reached a career peak in the U.S. Open. Those questions were answered in a head-to-head last-round shootout with Ernie Els of South Africa. In a tie for the lead, Janzen dropped a curling, 35-foot birdie putt on the par-three 16th while Els made bogey from a bunker, a two-shot swing that propelled Janzen to a three-stroke triumph. He ended the long drought with a five-under-par 66 over the last 18 holes on the hilly course and a 16-under-par 268 total.

Els, a runner-up to Masters champion Jose Maria Olazabal of Spain two weeks earlier in the Volvo PGA Championship in England, was the only man within reach after a closing 68 and a 271 total. "At Wentworth, Jose was holing everything," Els said. "And today I got Lee on one of his best days." The $129,600 second-place check insured Els of a place in the top 125 money winners and an exemption on the American tour next year. Brad Faxon tied for third after a birdie, birdie, birdie, eagle, birdie string beginning on the sixth hole of the final round.

In addition to answering any questions about his slump, Janzen also avenged a 1993 defeat that had troubled him for a year. Janzen held a three-shot lead going into the last round of this tournament a year ago. He blew it, finishing third. "Sometimes you dwell on those instead of thinking about your good rounds or your wins," Janzen said. "Even after winning the U.S. Open the week after, I still felt I had let this one get away. But now I've taken care of that."

Fred Couples tied for 29th at 282 in his return to competition after a three-month absence with a back injury.

U.S. Open Championship—$1,700,000
Winner: Ernie Els

See Chapter 4.

Canon Greater Hartford Open—$1,200,000
Winner: David Frost

David Frost found himself in the extremely rare and highly unenviable position of winning a PGA Tour event and playing in the shadow of a man who tied for third. Perhaps not since 1945 — when Byron Nelson's 11-tournament winning string ended with his placing behind Fred Haas and George Low — has a third-place finisher commanded as much attention as did Dave Stockton, Jr., in the Canon Greater Hartford Open.

Stockton, a rookie and son of the two-time former PGA champion, was attempting to join his father as the only father-son combination to win the same tournament. The elder Stockton won this event in 1974. The run at his first title took on even greater significance for young Dave in the final round after his father scored a run-away triumph in the Ford Senior Players Championship, and Dave Jr. was left with the chance to join his father in a never-accomplished double: father and son with victories on the same day.

It was not to be, however. Young Stockton led at the tournament halfway point, but the veteran Frost tied him at 11-under-par 199 through 54 holes, moving up with a third-round 66. Over the last 18, Stockton was unable to keep up the pace and the race quickly developed into a struggle between the South African Frost and golf's then No. 1 player, Australian Greg Norman.

Stockton, whose quest for a couple of doubles kept him in the spotlight for three rounds, could do no better than 72 over the final round and surrendered center stage to the two stars. Their duel was resolved on the 12th hole of the Tournament Players Club at River Highlands, where Norman went from bunker to bunker and made double bogey. The steady Frost shot 69 over the last round and scored the ninth victory of his 10-year American career with a 268 total, 12 under par. Norman finished one shot back at 69–269.

Motorola Western Open—$1,200,000
Winner: Nick Price

It wasn't pretty. In fact, it was downright ugly. But it counted. And, while Nick Price's victory in the Motorola Western Open may have been something less than artistic, it served as confirmation that the affable man from Zimbabwe has reached a level attained by only a handful of golf's greatest players: he can win even when he is not at his best.

"I just gutted it out," Price said after his successful title defense. Significantly, he won this time with a 277 total, 11 under par on the Dubsdread course at Cog Hill in the suburbs of Chicago. Under almost identical conditions, he was eight shots better in his 1993 victory. "I didn't play as well, but I was able to draw on my experiences of the last four years, maybe my whole career. Winning even though I wasn't at the top of my game has to give me a lot of confidence," he said. It also gave him his third victory of the season on the American tour — at this stage no one else had won more than once — and his 14th around the world going back to his 1992 PGA Championship.

Greg Kraft, 169th on the money list and seeking his first official victory, carried a one-shot lead into the final round. A 10-foot birdie putt on the 11th and a 30-foot sand shot for birdie on the 12th put him three in front. Then it all went wrong. He bogeyed the next from a bunker and three-putted the 14th. He managed a birdie four on the 15th, but the door had been opened. Price caught him with birdies on the 15th and 16th but had trouble putting him away. In the end, Price won it with a par-bogey finish and a 71 against Kraft's bogey-bogey completion of a 73. Price, playing in front of Kraft, missed a five-foot par putt on the final hole and Kraft needed a par to tie. But he went from bunker to bunker for the bogey that made Price the winner.

Anheuser-Busch Classic—$1,100,000
Winner: Mark McCumber

In the parlance of golf's touring pros, the Anheuser-Busch Classic is known as the ABC, a tournament in which rookies learn their lessons. Almost all the leading lights usually skip the tournament on the banks of the James River in Williamsburg, Virginia — as well as the sweltering heat (the temperature-humidity index hit 118 one day during this tournament) — to prepare for the British Open. In their absence the younger players and also-rans frequently are in their element. This time, however, it was a 42-year-old veteran and winner of eight Tour titles who learned a lesson.

Mark McCumber picked up his ball from the fourth green at Kingsmill in the third round and forgot to mark it. "I can't believe I forgot to mark it," McCumber said. "I've never done that before and, believe me, I'll never do it again." The incident, which incurred a one-stroke penalty, proved to be more embarrassing than significant. Scores of 65 and 66 over the last two rounds more than compensated for the lapse as McCumber broke a five-year non-winning string with a three-shot victory on a 17-under-par 267 total. "This is the longest I've gone without a win," McCumber said. "It almost makes you think, 'Am I going to win again?'"

In answering his own question, he got some help and helped himself. Bob Lohr hit into the water and made double bogey on the 54th hole, passing the third-round lead to McCumber. Then McCumber took things into his own hands in the final round, crushing the hopes of any would-be challengers with consecutive chip-in birdies on the 15th and 16th holes.

Rookie Glen Day shot 66 over the last 18 holes and was second alone at 270. He won $118,800, assuring him of an exemption for next year. "This takes a load off my back," he said. "Now I can say, 'I can do this.'"

Deposit Guaranty Classic—$700,000
Winner: Brian Henninger

For its first 26 years, the Deposit Guaranty Classic (formerly the Magnolia Classic) was played in Hattiesburg, as a satellite to the Masters. This year it moved north to larger Jackson, Mississippi's capital. The purse was more than doubled. For the first time, it had full, official status on the PGA Tour. New dates put it opposite the British Open, and a larger, stronger field responded. Then the rains came.

A series of storms dumped more than 12 inches of rain on the Annandale course Monday through Saturday. The second round was completed Saturday just before a dangerous storm flooded the saturated course with five inches of rain; strong winds blew down trees, tents and skyboxes. Officials had no choice but to cancel the last two scheduled rounds.

Sunday afternoon officials found one hole, the par-five 18th, dry enough to stage a playoff between Brian Henninger and Mike Sullivan, who shared the 36-hole lead at 135. Henninger twice dropped out of casual water in the fairway, made birdie and scored his first victory. "I don't know how to describe it," Henninger said. "I'm proud to be the champion, but I won't feel like a true champion on the PGA Tour until I win a 72-hole event."

New England Classic—$1,000,000
Winner: Kenny Perry

Thunderstorms stopped play in both the second and third rounds of the New England Classic. But the rain and wind and lightning at Pleasant Valley was mild compared to the storm of controversy that blew up over the withdrawal of John Daly, the tournament's top drawing card, after the first round.

Only a week after his comments on drug use on the PGA Tour drew a visit from PGA Commissioner Tim Finchem at the British Open, Daly shot a 75 — including a four-putt double bogey on the 17th and a careless, fast-played bogey on the last — and told tournament chairman Ted Mingolla he was withdrawing. "He said he is mentally and physically completely drained, totally exhausted," Mingolla said. "He said, 'When I get like this I cannot play the game of golf.'" About an hour later, Finchem, also on the scene, said "John has had some problems along the way. He continues to have to deal with those problems."

When Daly, who had played in six consecutive tournaments, gave way to fatigue, a man playing in his 11th event in 12 weeks stepped forward. Kenny

Perry admitted he was pushing himself with his schedule, but insisted there was a reason for it: seven finishes in the top 30 in his last nine starts. "In the past, when I've played well, I've taken some time off, then it's taken me a couple of months to get back to playing well again. This time I wanted to keep playing," he said.

He had more than his share of playing on Sunday, six holes of the rain-delayed third round, then 18 of the last. He played the first six one under and trailed David Feherty of Northern Ireland and Ed Fiori by one through 54 holes. After a two-hour break, Perry came back to play the front nine in 31, taking a three-shot lead over Feherty. The fast-talking Irishman cut the margin to one with birdies on the 16th and 17th, but was unable to birdie the par-five finishing hole. Perry scored the second victory of his eight-season career with a closing 65 and a 268 total.

Federal Express St. Jude Classic—$1,250,000
Winner: Dicky Pride

Nearing the two-thirds mark of the season, Dicky Pride's rookie year on the PGA Tour had been something less than a smashing success. He had made only five cuts in 18 starts. His confidence was such that he was convinced he would have to return to the late-season qualifying tournament and talked his fiancee, Kim Shearer, into changing their scheduled wedding date from December 10 to December 17 to make way for the qualifying.

His playing plans — but not the wedding arrangements — underwent a quick revision in Memphis, when the 25-year-old longshot from Tuscaloosa, Alabama, dropped two critical putts on the 18th hole at the Tournament Players Club at Southwind, scored the first victory of his young career in a three-man playoff, collected $225,000 and suddenly found himself in possession of a two-year exemption.

After opening rounds of 66, 67 and 67, Pride went into the final round in a three-way tie for the lead. His first hole of the day may have been as critical as his last two. "I was very, very nervous and I didn't feel too good on the range," Pride said. "Then at the first tee, I hit the worst drive of the week. Then I hit the worst recovery shot of the week. Then I hit the greatest chip I've probably ever hit in my life. I had to carry it about 30 feet over the bunker and then run it about 40, 50 feet." It went in the hole and Pride was off and running. But he had to roll in a 20-foot, 72nd-hole birdie putt to complete another 67 and tie Hal Sutton and Gene Sauers at 267. Sutton got into the playoff with a last-round 64 and Sauers with a 66. British Open champion Nick Price missed the playoff by a single shot after a closing 64.

The playoff lasted only one hole. Sauers was away, about 30 feet, on the 18th green and left his birdie try just short. Then it was the rookie Pride. "I was below the hole about 25 feet, dead uphill to the right lip the whole way. It broke right in the middle of the cup" for a birdie, he said. Sutton, who hasn't won since 1986, had a 15-footer to prolong the playoff. When it slid by on the left Pride became a winner.

Buick Open—$1,100,000
Winner: Fred Couples

America's two leading golfers, Paul Azinger and Fred Couples, each accomplished a comeback in the Buick Open. The pre-tournament activities and the first two rounds of the event in Grand Blanc, Michigan, centered around Azinger and his return to competition after successfully battling the cancer that was diagnosed shortly after he won the 1993 PGA Championship. After countless press conferences and interviews, Azinger received a five-minute ovation when he went to the first tee. That he eventually missed the cut after rounds of 76, 70, mattered not at all. "Teeing off was the big victory for me," said the man whose comeback from the disease captured the admiration of millions of fans around the world.

After Azinger departed, the tournament belonged to Couples, the casual, easy-going guy who missed three months of the season following a serious back injury in March. He went into the double-round wind-up — necessitated by a rain-out on Thursday — with large question marks about how his back would stand up to a 36-hole finale. He came out of it with an 11-under-par 133 for the two rounds, a two-stroke triumph and a return to the winners circle that even he didn't expect.

"I wasn't blowing the year off," said Couples, who returned to competition a month earlier, "but I had the feeling, 'Go out and play. Don't hurt yourself. Don't think of the tournament.' It's hard for me to believe I won," he said following his first victory in 17 months. "It's a weird game. Am I surprised that I won? You bet."

Couples was six back going into Sunday's play, but 65 in the morning round brought him to within one of front-runner Corey Pavin, who played the first two rounds in 131. Couples' chip-in birdie on the first hole of the afternoon brought him even, however, and Pavin dropped back with bogeys on the second and third. The gritty Pavin stayed within striking range, however, even though Couples eagled the par-five 13th for the third time in four rounds, but could not answer Fred's decisive seven-iron pitch to tap-in distance for birdie on the final hole. Pavin's closing 71 left him two shots off the winning pace at 272.

PGA Championship—$1,700,000
Winner: Nick Price

See Chapter 6.

Sprint International—$1,410,000
Winner: Steve Lowery

After nine years of adjusting and tinkering with an unusual format, the modified Stableford scoring system used for the Sprint International finally produced precisely what tournament founder Jack Vickers envisioned and desired: a down-to-the-wire shootout of the first magnitude. And there was no mistake about it over the last 18 holes at Castle Pines, it was the format and scoring system that set up the drama in the foothills of the Rockies south of Denver.

Under this system, medal scores do not count; only points. Players are awarded (or penalized) for their performance on each hole: five for eagle, two for birdie, zero for par, minus one for bogey, minus three for double bogey or higher. So the 10 points gained by Steve Lowery for a pair of last-round eagles, on the 14th and 17th, proved to be critical as Lowery came from nowhere to tie Rick Fehr after 72 holes. Lowery, 33, then collected his career-first PGA Tour title in a playoff when Fehr hit his drive into the water on the first extra hole.

Points accumulated over all four rounds with cuts to 72 players after 36 holes and to 24 players after the third round. Lowery led after two rounds, but Keith Clearwater held the advantage after 54 holes. He faded quickly in the final round, however, and U.S. Open champion Ernie Els moved in front. Lowery wasn't even close. After three consecutive bogeys, the last on the 13th, he was 10 points back.

Lowery hit a three-iron second shot 240 yards in the 7,000-foot altitude, curling it around pine trees to the green, some 25 feet from the cup on the par-five 14th. The putt dropped for eagle and he was back in the race. By the time he reached the 17th, another par five, Els had drifted back into the pack. This time Lowery had a 211-yard, uphill five iron for his second, and stuck it in less than two feet from the flag. That gave him 35 points for the tournament, a total that was matched by Fehr with a late push that produced birdies on the 13th, 14th, 15th and 17th holes. Tom Kite, Duffy Waldorf and Dave Stockton, Jr. also made back-nine runs that fell short.

NEC World Series of Golf—$2,000,000
Winner: Jose Maria Olazabal

While Jose Maria Olazabal of Spain was enhancing his career with a victory in the NEC World Series of Golf on the north side of Werner Road in Akron, Ohio, John Daly was — once again — placing his in jeopardy, rolling around on the ground in a public scuffle with a spectator just south of the street that separates the two courses at the Firestone Country Club.

Olazabal's one-stroke victory over Scott Hoch enabled the Masters champion to join Nick Price of Zimbabwe as the only multiple winners on the PGA Tour this year. The Spanish star came from three shots off the pace in the last round, shooting a three-under-par 67 — by two strokes the best of the day — in difficult, windy, occasionally showery conditions. He took the lead with a two-shot swing on the ninth hole — his seven iron to three feet for a birdie against Hoch's bogey — and wasn't headed again, winning with a 269 total, 11 under par on the North course. Hoch, who missed a birdie putt of less than two feet on the 17th hole, birdied the last hole from about six feet to match par 70 and take second place alone at 270. Third-round leader Steve Lowery slipped to 72 over the last 18 and tied for third at 271 with Brad Faxon.

The victory was worth $360,000 and boosted Olazabal's American earnings for the year to $969,900 in only eight starts. Olazabal also won this title in 1990, then at the South course, the long-time venue for this exclusive event. The North was hastily pressed into service when, a month before the tournament dates, the South lost its greens to a mysterious blight.

The clubhouse is on the South course and it was there — while Olazabal and Hoch and others were trying to win the tournament a few hundred yards away — that Daly was involved in the altercation with Bob Roth, 62. Roth's son, national club pro champion Jeff Roth of Flint, Michigan, played in front of Daly in the final round and, after Daly completed his 83, accused the former PGA champion of hitting into his group. Andrew Magee and Greg Norman's caddie made similar, separate accusations earlier in the week.

After an exchange of words with Jeff Roth, Daly was leaving the clubhouse when he was confronted by the elder Roth. More words were exchanged. The elder Roth grabbed Daly and the two men fell to the ground. They were separated by caddies and spectators. Daly, who was suspended two times by former Commissioner Deane Beman, left the scene without comment. Commissioner Tim Finchem said he would review staff reports and talk with the principals before making any public statements. Later, Finchem announced that he and Daly had agreed that Daly would play no more tournaments in 1994.

Greater Milwaukee Open—$1,000,000
Winner: Mike Springer

The need for a knack and a postponed vacation turned into a surprise Greater-Greater double for Mike Springer. Reaping the benefit of a last-hole bogey six by Mark Calcavecchia, Springer hung on for a one-shot victory in the Greater Milwaukee Open. That combined with his triumph in the Kmart Greater Greensboro Open earlier in the year to make Springer the first American to win two tournaments this season.

He took this one, being played for the first time at the municipal Brown Deer Golf Club, with a 16-under-par 268 total and a closing 67 in cool, windy weather. But the seeds of the victory were sown a week earlier when the weary Springer made a last-minute decision to enter the tournament, delaying a family vacation by a week. He holed three 30-footers in his opening round at the NEC World Series of Golf, just beat the Friday deadline for entering Milwaukee and told his wife by telephone, "I'm just putting too good to take the week off."

It did not come easily, however. Springer came from two shots back to establish a one-stroke lead going to the 72nd hole, a reachable par-five hole. After a good drive, he had the opportunity to go for the green and all but wrap it up. But he pushed his three wood far to the right, pitched on and two-putted for par.

That opened the door for Calcavecchia, playing in the group behind Springer. Calcavecchia, apparently on the brink of breaking a two-and-a-half-year non-winning string, vaulted into contention with a 40-foot eagle putt on the 18th hole in Saturday's third round. He went to the 18th on Sunday, needing a birdie to tie, but drove into deep rough on the left, slashed out, pitched short into a bunker, blasted out and two-putted for bogey. "It's kind of weird about winning tournaments," Calcavecchia said. "You need a knack. I had that knack in the '80s. Now, maybe I'm trying too hard."

His last-hole lapse enabled Loren Roberts to claim second at 68–269. Calcavecchia tied for third at 270 with Bob Estes, Tom Purtzer and Joey Sindelar.

Bell Canadian Open—$1,300,000
Winner: Nick Price

Mark Calcavecchia gave voice to a sentiment that was becoming prevalent among his fellow touring pros. "I'm going to sneak a look at his schedule, and when this guy is playing, I'm taking a week off," Calcavecchia said after his last hole eagle had been nullified by Nick Price's career-best two-iron shot, the critical blow in the Zimbabwean's fifth PGA Tour victory of the year, a one-stroke triumph in the Bell Canadian Open.

"For so long, it was so hard for me to win, and suddenly — I wouldn't say it's easy to win — but I'm winning," Price said. "It's weird, a very strange turn-around. I went nearly eight years without winning and now I can't stop winning."

Price had to work hard for this one, however. Weary from a frantic schedule that went back to his British Open victory two months earlier, he was urged by his wife to skip this event. After declining her advice, he found his swing was slightly out of sync. "My hips are too fast and I'm leaving everything out to the right," he said.

But two good breaks, both on the 11th hole, some clutch putting and the decisive two-iron shot pulled him through. "My putter saved me," Price said of the mallet called "the Fat Lady Swings," that required only 118 strokes — many of them par-saving six-footers — for the week on Glen Abbey's greens. He also got lucky, bouncing an approach off a rock in Sixteen Mile Creek and onto the green on one occasion, and on another scoring a birdie on the same hole after his drive caromed off a tree to within 50 yards of the green.

In the final round, Calcavecchia — playing well in front of Price — grabbed a share of the lead with a 40-foot eagle putt on the 18th hole. Only moments later, however, Price lashed a two iron 217 yards to the par-five 16th and watched the ball run to within two feet of the flag for an easy eagle, the decisive stroke in his closing 68 and 13-under-par 275 total.

B.C. Open—$900,000
Winner: Mike Sullivan

After scoring only his third victory in a 17-season career in the B.C. Open, Mike Sullivan said he considered — briefly — picking the ball out of the cup on the final hole at the En-Joie Golf Club and throwing the ball into the gallery at Endicott, New York. But the 39-year-old veteran restrained himself. "As old and decrepit as I'm getting, I thought I might hurt myself," he said.

Sullivan, whose career has been marked by a variety of injuries and ailments, was hampered last year by two herniated discs, finished 167th on the money list and was playing this season on a medical exemption. But he had collected checks in only eight of 21 previous starts and, with the season winding down, was looking at the probable need to return to the Tour's qualifying tournament if he was to be able to play next year. On top of that, he came into this tournament with a stiff neck, spent the first three days of the week in the traveling fitness trailer and was unable to get in a practice round.

"There's a lot of truth in the fact that a guy who is hurt or sick doesn't have a lot of expectations," he said. But he birdied the first three holes of the tournament, shot 65 and, with scores of 67 and 68 in the next two rounds, stayed within two shots of leader Jeff Sluman going into the last 18 holes. Sluman, sniffling and sneezing from a heavy summer cold, surrendered the lead to Sullivan's one-under-par 35 on the front and Mike never looked back. He didn't look at a scoreboard either, and was unaware of how he stood until he drove into the rough on the 18th and asked his caddie for the pin position.

"He said I didn't have to worry about shooting for the pin, that I had a four-stroke lead. Then it was just a matter of fighting back the tears," Sullivan said after his closing 66 and 266 total produced a four-stroke victory. It also produced a $162,000 check — more than he had made in all but one of his 16 previous full seasons — and provided him entry to the 1995 World Series of Golf, the Masters and the Mercedes Championship.

The Presidents Cup
Winner: United States

The targets and expectations for the hastily arranged Presidents Cup, as voiced by PGA Tour Commissioner Tim Finchem at the opening ceremonies, were lofty in the extreme. Speaking to the teams, diplomats and dignitaries — including honorary tournament chairman President Gerald Ford — Finchem called for "the best inaugural of a significant competition in the history of golf."

"I think we achieved that," the Commissioner said after an apparent American run-away became a nail-biter of classic proportions in Lake Manassas, Virginia.

American team captain Hale Irwin said, "I've never felt intimidated in my life, but some shots I saw here this week intimidated me. It was a fantastic display of golf." International team captain David Graham concurred. "Unbelievable," he said. "That was some of the most awesome golf I've had the pleasure of watching." And he called the shot that finally secured the cup for the United States, Fred Couples' nine iron from a fairway bunker, "one of the top three golf shots I've ever seen in my life."

The Americans won 20-12, but the score hardly indicates the level of competition. Late Sunday afternoon, with eight of the 12 final singles matches still out, the outcome was in doubt. The U.S. needed only one more point, but four matches were in playoffs, two others were tied and the International team — made up of players from countries not eligible for Ryder Cup play — was leading in the other two. Couples clinched it with his 147-yard shot from a fairway bunker that caught the slope of a ridge on the 18th green at the Robert Trent Jones Golf Club and curled back to within a foot of the cup.

Nick Price, the weary Zimbabwean who held the world's No. 1 ranking but was the only one of the 24 players who did not score a victory, conceded the putt and the Americans had an unbeatable 17-9 lead. It also made moot the four playoffs in progress and the matches were declared halved, immediately boosting the score to 19-11.

The singles playoffs, as well as the possibility of a two-man playoff for the team title in the event the matches ended in a 16-16 tie, were two of the changes introduced to make this new event at least slightly different from the Ryder Cup, the enormously popular biennial competition that prompted the formation of this new event and served as the model for its format.

Much remained the same, 12-man teams and, most importantly, the match-play format that produces the greatest drama in golf. Ten of the 12 Americans came off a money list, with Irwin making two additional picks. Ten of the International team came from the Sony Ranking, with Graham making two picks.

One change produced an unexpected problem. Five fourball and five foursome matches were scheduled both Friday and Saturday, as opposed to four of each in the Ryder Cup. The additional match left the captains with little flexibility in resting players and resulted in both squads nearing exhaustion when the matches were over. Price, who had an extremely heavy schedule since his British Open victory two months earlier, reached his physical and mental limit and asked to be sat down in alternate-shot play Saturday afternoon.

Another problem was anticipated. "We were so late in pulling the trigger (making a firm decision to go ahead with the new event), we were aware that some players may have made commitments they could not break," Finchem said.

U.S. Open champion Ernie Els of South Africa and Japanese stars Jumbo Ozaki and Tommy Nakajima used that excuse in passing up the event. The International team received another pre-tournament jolt when Greg Norman developed intestinal problems, was ordered by his physician to cease all activity for three weeks and was forced to withdraw.

The United States jumped off to a 5-0 sweep of the opening fourball matches, with only one match reaching the 18th, then split the afternoon matches, retaining a five-point lead. The International team rallied to take three and a half of a possible five points Saturday morning, pulling to within three at 9-6 going into the afternoon alternate shot matches.

The pairings of David Frost and Peter Senior, and Vijay Singh and Steve Elkington quickly won their matches, the Internationals trailed at 10-8 and, with American duos of Corey Pavin and Loren Roberts, and Phil Mickelson and Tom Lehman in deep trouble, a 10-10 tie going into Sunday's singles seemed possible, even probable.

That's when the gritty little Pavin took over. He and Roberts were two-down playing the 15th when Pavin holed a bunker shot for birdie to go one-down. On the 17th, he holed a four-foot birdie putt to pull even, then won the match with a pitch to four feet on the final hole. Lehman and Mickelson also pulled out their match, and the Americans went into Sunday's play with a 12-8 margin.

Irwin, Jim Gallagher and Jay Haas quickly won their singles matches and Senior got a point for the Internationals, setting the score at 15-9. Jeff Maggert beat Australian Bradley Hughes 2 and 1, and the U.S. was within a point of clinching. But the next four matches went into playoffs before Couples' last-hole heroics settled things.

Davis Love III, with a 4-0-1 won-lost-tied record, was the Americans' leading point-scorer. Couples was 3-0-0. Gallagher and Pavin, who seems to thrive on match play, were 3-1-1 and 2-2-1, respectively. Singh led the International team at 3-1-1.

Hardee's Classic—$1,000,000
Winner: Mark McCumber

After David Frost's last-gasp try for a triple fell short, Mark McCumber was more than happy to complete a double, claiming the Hardee's Classic for his second title of the year. "It's a unique year. I don't base my years on money; that's a poor criteria. But winning twice in a year is an accomplishment," McCumber, 43, said after a closing string of seven consecutive pars produced a three-under-par 67, a 265 total and a one-stroke victory over Kenny Perry.

While it may not be a personal measuring stick, the $180,000 first prize also clinched a seasonal goal for McCumber, a spot in the 30-man field for the Tour Championship.

McCumber, who broke a five-year non-winning string in the Anheuser-Busch Classic earlier in the season, led or shared the lead all the way over the last 18 holes at Oakwood in Coal Valley, Illinois. His bogey-free final round was necessary to withstand a variety of challenges, principally from Perry, Frost and Mike Bradley, who got in position with a third-round 62, then tied McCumber for the lead 12 holes into the final round. A double bogey on the 13th and a triple bogey on the last sent him back into the pack.

Like Bradley, Frost and Perry also self-destructed. Frost, who won this tournament the last two years and was attempting to become only the 10th man in PGA Tour history to score three consecutive victories in the same tournament, moved to within one of the lead with an eagle-birdie burst beginning on the 10th, but bogeyed the 12th and finished in a tie for third. Perry had a share of the lead going to the final hole, then blew it with a pull-hook two-iron tee shot into the trees. He had to play out, pitched on and one-putted for the bogey that dropped him back to second at 266.

Buick Southern Open—$700,000
Winner: Steve Elkington

Everyone knew the bad weather was coming. And there wasn't a thing they could do about it. But it really didn't matter. The chances of anyone overtaking Steve Elkington in the Buick Southern Open were not much better than the odds on stopping the heavy rain that washed out the fourth round and cut the tournament to 54 holes.

"The chances of catching a player five shots ahead and playing some of the best golf in the world are pretty slim, rain, hail or shine," Steve Rintoul said after the last-round cancelation left him a distant second to fellow

Australian Elkington. "He had 32 putts on Saturday and still shot 68. It would have been almost impossible to catch him," Rintoul said.

And that was just what Elkington was trying to do, establish the largest possible lead before the well-advertised rains arrived on Sunday. "I tried to play the (third) round like it was the last round because I knew the rain was coming," Elkington said. "I knew everyone wanted to catch me and I put more distance between me and the field. I don't know what it was, but I just played flawless golf for 54 holes." It included a pair of 66s in the opening rounds, a 68 despite six missed putts of 10 feet or less over his last nine holes and a 200 total, 16 under par on the Callaway Gardens, Georgia, Mountain View course.

"It doesn't surprise me to play good golf, but I didn't expect to come out and play perfect golf like I did this week. If I play like I am now, I'm going to feel like I can win every week, and I haven't felt like that for a while," Elkington said after his first victory in two years. He was sidelined much of the season, first with hepatitis, then in a recovery period following extensive nasal surgery. "A lot of guys are just trying to finish out their years," he said. "I'm trying to get mine cranked up."

Walt Disney World/Oldsmobile Classic—$1,100,000
Winner: Rick Fehr

A wait of eight years, one month and two days between victories is tough enough for anyone, anytime. But for Rick Fehr, the last 30 minutes of his long dry spell were, by far, the most anxious, the most difficult, the most nerve-wracking. "I'm making phone calls and thinking, 'Well, there goes another chance to win down the drain,'" Fehr said after his two-stroke decision in the Walt Disney World/Oldsmobile Classic in Lake Buena Vista, Florida.

Since his only previous victory in the B.C. Open in his rookie year of 1986, Fehr had compiled an impressive list of near-misses, an 0-4 playoff record and eight runner-up finishes. He had a share of the third-round lead in this one — and very nearly missed his last-round starting time. A courtesy car driver failed to arrive at a pre-arranged time at Fehr's hotel on the huge Magic Kingdom resort. He was told a taxi could not be arranged in time. Panic was setting in when a car and driver appeared. Just in time.

After that, the tournament was relatively easy. "Walking down the first fairway with my caddie, we said, 'Boy, this is going to be a good story,'" Fehr said. "Maybe it helped. I didn't have time to think about the final round. Actually, I felt relaxed. I felt like the biggest challenge of the day was already behind me."

Still remaining, however, were challenges from Fuzzy Zoeller, Craig Stadler, Robert Gamez and Steve Stricker. The last of those disappeared when Stadler three-putted the 15th and Fehr hit a six-iron second shot to two feet for birdie on the 17th. A par on the 18th finished off a round of 68 on the Magnolia course, and his 269 total put him two ahead of Stadler and Zoeller. The victory not only broke Fehr's long non-winning string, the $198,000 winner's check also boosted him to 25th on the money list and virtually assured him of a place in the season-ending Tour Championship.

Texas Open—$1,000,000
Winner: Bob Estes

Shortly after scoring the first victory of a seven-season career in a wire-to-wire triumph in the Texas Open, poker-faced young Bob Estes decided apologies were in order. "I want to apologize to my family, friends, the marshals, the gallery and camera crews," Estes said, expressionless as ever. Then he explained. "When I stop to smile and talk to people, I don't concentrate as well as I should. I was taking care of business," he said, then let a little smile flit around the corners of his mouth. "I'll work on my image a little later."

While he led all the way, opening with a nine-under-par 62 on the tight, tree-lined Oak Hills Country Club course in San Antonio, then set seasonal marks with a 127 for two rounds and 195 for three, Estes' career-first victory required all his concentration, all the mental toughness he could muster. "It's tough, sleeping on the lead every night, especially when you haven't won before," he said. "But now that it's over, I couldn't pick a better way to win my first tournament than leading every round."

Estes had a four-stroke lead going into the final round, but first Don Pooley and then Gil Morgan closed to within one. Estes was equal to each challenge. He responded to Pooley's move with consecutive birdies of his own, and answered Morgan with a 257-yard three-wood shot on the 15th that set up a two-putt birdie and gave him a two-stroke lead and virtually clinched it. He went on to a closing 70 and a 19-under-par 265. Morgan finished one back after a final-round 67, and Pooley, on a comeback from career-threatening back surgery, was third at 68–267.

Las Vegas Invitational—$1,400,000
Winner: Bruce Lietzke

Bruce Lietzke marches to the beat of a different drummer. And the rhythm he pursues is a mystery to most of his contemporaries on the PGA Tour. The veteran has little or no interest in golf's major championships and occasionally — as he did this year — skips them all. He plays 16 or 17 tournaments a year and never, ever practices. But he has won more than $5 million in a 20-year, part-time career and notched his 13th victory in the five-day, three-course, 90-hole Las Vegas Invitational.

"Actually, I have mixed emotions," Lietzke said after his decisive two-iron shot set up the go-ahead eagle on the 16th hole at the TPC at Summerlin, a shot that vaulted the 43-year-old Lietzke over Robert Gamez, age 26, and dashed the hopes of 24-year-old Phil Mickelson and rookies Paul Stankowski and Jim Furyk. "I'd planned on this being my last day of golf for the year," Lietzke said. "You don't know how much I was looking forward to putting the clubs away for an extended period."

The victory, however, was worth $270,000 and boosted Lietzke into the top 30 money winners for the year, thus providing him with a place in the season-ending, $3 million Tour Championship and necessitating a change in his vacation plans. "Two weeks ago, that was the furthest thing from my mind," said Lietzke, who won $318,000 of his season's $486,431 in his last two starts.

Lietzke won this one with a closing, seven-under-par 65, built around a 232-yard two-iron shot on the 560-yard, par-five 16th. The ball nestled in about four feet from the cup and, using his elongated putter, Lietzke rapped it home to wrest the lead away from Gamez, who birdied the last five holes for 64 and a 333 total. "You can't really complain when you play solid and get beat. That's what Bruce did. He beat me. He beat everybody," Gamez said. Mickelson, who scored 10 birdies in a round of 63, tied for third at 335 with Billy Andrade, who shot 67. Stankowski and Furyk were tied at 336 with Bill Glasson.

Tour Championship—$3,000,000
Winner: Mark McCumber

Easy-going Fuzzy Zoeller has a habit of scattering one-line quips around the courses of the PGA Tour. But the one line he provided Mark McCumber proved to be decisive in the final official event of the American season, the Tour Championship. "It helped enormously," McCumber said after Fuzzy gave him the line and the speed of a monster putt on the first hole of their playoff. "Not only did he give me the line, he got it so close I knew he was in for four and that made me go for it," McCumber said after dropping the winning birdie putt that he estimated at "45 to 50 feet." That one plunged into the heart of the hole just seconds after Zoeller — on the same line — had run up an even longer putt to tap-in distance.

McCumber, 43, and Zoeller, 42, each played the final round at San Francisco's Olympic Club in 68 and finished regulation play at 274, 10 under par. McCumber led by two strokes with two holes to go, but Zoeller birdied the 17th and McCumber three-putted from the back fringe on the 18th. A few minutes later he won on the same hole, the first of the playoff, when both he and Zoeller kept their approaches far below the pin on the sharply sloping green.

McCumber's victory, his third of the season and 10th of his career, was worth $540,000 from the total purse of $3 million and made him one of six men to go past $1 million in official season earnings. He finished at $1,208,209. Zoeller collected $324,000 but took little consolation in also going over $1 million for the first time. "Hey, I'm trying to get my name on trophies," said Zoeller, who had five runner-up finishes in a winless season. "By the time I'm dead, all the money will be gone, but the trophies will still be there."

Brad Bryant, with a closing 68, missed the playoff by a single stroke at 275. David Frost and Bill Glasson, who led or shared the lead through the first three rounds, were next at 276.

Special Events

Westinghouse-Family House Invitational—$700,000
Winner: David Frost

David Frost held off fast-closing Scott Hoch and Joey Sindelar for a two-stroke victory in the Westinghouse-Family House Invitational. Frost was seven under par with rounds of 69 and 68 at The Club at Nevillewood in Carnegie, Pennsylvania, and collected $140,000. Hoch and Sindelar each mounted a second-round charge with 67s and tied for second at 139 with Curtis Strange.

Jerry Ford Invitational—$94,500
Winner: Jay Don Blake

Jay Don Blake compiled a pair of five-under-par 67s at the Country Club of the Rockies in Vail, Colorado, and scored a two-shot victory in the Jerry Ford Invitational, preceding the Sprint International. Kirk Triplett had a second-round 65 that put him in a tie for second at 136 with Ed Fiori, Bob Lohr, Lon Hinkle and Jerry Pate.

Ernst Championship—$680,000
Winner: Billy Andrade

Billy Andrade birdied the second extra hole to beat host Fred Couples in the Ernst Championship at the Overlake Golf and Country Club at Medina, Washington. Andrade came from three strokes back with a four-under-par 66 to tie Couples at 134, then collected $150,000 with his playoff victory. Couples, who gathered 25 other touring pros to the Seattle area for the benefit affair, set the first-round pace with 65.

Fred Meyer Challenge—$700,000
Winners: John Cook and Mark O'Meara

Mark O'Meara came into the Fred Meyer Challenge on a downer. He was involved in probably the worst slump of his career. "Golf is a game with up and down cycles. I'm in one of those down cycles," he said before the start of the two-day event at the Oregon Golf Club. But he proved his own point, leaving West Linn, Oregon, on a high after teaming with John Cook in a two-hole playoff victory worth $50,000 to each winner.

Cook and O'Meara combined for scores of 63, 62 and were tied at 17-under-par 125 with master putters Ben Crenshaw and Phil Mickelson. O'Meara provided the winner on the second playoff hole, the 499-yard, par-four 18th, getting up and down from in front of the green with a six-foot par putt after Crenshaw had missed from about the same distance. Host Peter Jacobsen and Arnold Palmer were third at 64-62–126.

Guadalajara Invitational—$175,000
Winner: Loren Roberts

Loren Roberts closed with three consecutive birdies to win the Guadalajara Invitational by two strokes over Hale Irwin. Roberts shot a seven-under-par 65 for a 266 total, and Irwin had 67 after entering the final round tied for the lead. Irwin missed a six-foot birdie putt, and a chance to tie Roberts, on the 15th hole. He then had a birdie-bogey-eagle finish.

Gene Sarazen World Open—$1,900,000
Winner: Ernie Els

From five strokes behind midway through the final round, Ernie Els rode what he called "the best shot I've ever hit in my life," to a three-stroke victory in the Gene Sarazen World Open at Chateau Elan in Braselton, Georgia. Els hooked a 230-yard three-iron shot about 15 yards around trees to within seven feet of the flag on the par-five 14th hole and made the putt for an eagle that gave him the lead for the first time.

He went on to 30 on the back nine, a seven-under-par 65 over the final 18 holes and a 273 winning total. Fred Funk, a five-stroke leader after eight holes in the final round, could do no better than match par 72 and was second at 276. In addition to the winners of the major championships, national open champions for the last three years from 55 countries around the world were invited to this new tournament. There were 74 acceptances, but of the Grand Slam winners from the last two years, only Els and Lee Janzen competed.

Lincoln-Mercury Kapalua International—$1,000,000
Winner: Fred Couples

Just as George Foreman did a few hours earlier, Fred Couples delivered a knockout punch in the final round of the Lincoln-Mercury Kapalua International. Couples' blow came in the form of his first competitive hole-in-one, a 168-yard eight-iron shot on the 11th hole at the Plantation course at the Kapalua Resort in Maui, Hawaii. It was the centerpiece of Couples' three-under-par 70 that produced a 279 total and a successful defense of the title he won a year earlier.

"That shot was almost as shocking as watching Foreman win last night," Couples said, referring to the knockout by the 45-year-old Foreman of Michael Moorer for one version of the world heavyweight boxing championship. It was almost as decisive. Second-round leader Tom Lehman was tied with Couples after nine holes of the final round. But, playing ahead of Fred, he made double bogey on the 11th. Couples' ace made it a four-shot swing on the hole. It also gave Couples a three-shot lead over Bob Gilder, and the defending champion led the rest of the way. Gilder was second at 73–281.

PGA Grand Slam of Golf—$1,000,000
Winner: Greg Norman

Greg Norman's last-hole eagle sealed a three-stroke victory over Nick Price in the PGA Grand Slam of Golf at the Poipu Bay Resort course on the Hawaiian island of Kauai. Norman and Price were tied after 32 holes of the two-round event that brings together the winners of the Masters, U.S. and British Opens and the PGA Championship. Norman, the defending champion, got in the field only because Price won two of the four qualifying events.

Norman went ahead with a 375-yard drive and a wedge that set up a birdie on the 15th. Knowing he needed an eagle on the 18th, Price overswung and mis-hit his drive. That mistake became meaningless after Norman hit a five-iron second shot to three feet and made the eagle putt, finishing off rounds of 70 and 68 worth $400,000. Price, at 139, won $250,000. Ernie Els, the U.S. Open champion from South Africa, followed at 143 ($200,000) and Masters titleholder Jose Maria Olazabal of Spain trailed at 144 ($150,000).

World Cup of Golf—$1,200,000
Winners: United States/Fred Couples

Fred Couples and Davis Love III teamed for an unprecedented third consecutive victory in the World Cup of Golf by Heineken at Dorado Beach in Puerto Rico. With Couples doing most of the damage, they romped to a 16-stroke margin on a 40-under-par total of 536 — both records for the international event which began 39 years earlier as the Canada Cup. Mark McNulty and Tony Johnstone of Zimbabwe were distant seconds at 550.

Couples and Love began building their huge lead with opening scores of 65 and 67, respectively, in the first round that was delayed overnight by a tropical rainstorm. After a brief break and a change of clothes, they came back in the afternoon to take the tournament out of reach, Couples scoring an eagle and seven birdies in a round of 63. He went on to take individual honors at 265, five strokes ahead of Costantino Rocca of Italy.

Mexican Open—$600,000
Winner: Chris Perry

Chris Perry birdied the first three holes of the final round and went on to a six-under-par 66 and a one-stroke victory over Bob Tway in the Mexican Open at Mexico City. Perry finished with a 274 total and collected $100,000, the largest check of his 11-season career as a touring pro. Tway, the third-round leader, had a closing 69 and 275 total.

Pebble Beach Invitational—$175,000
Winner: Robert Gamez

Robert Gamez, who had never before played the Pebble Beach Golf Links in competition, shot an opening 65 and went on to a front-running victory in the Pebble Beach Invitational over a field that included seniors, sons and some LPGA players. Gamez's lead went as high as 11 strokes in the last round before he finished with a six-shot margin at 10-under-par 206. It was his first victory since his rookie season of 1990.

Franklin Funds Shark Shootout—$1,100,000
Winners: Fred Couples and Brad Faxon

Fred Couples, this time combining with Brad Faxon in the Franklin Funds Shark Shootout, continued his blitz of the PGA Tour's "second season." Their two-shot victory over Curtis Strange and Mark O'Meara provided Couples with his third triumph in as many weeks in the late-season events. In the two previous weeks Couples had successfully defended his title in the Lincoln-Mercury Kapalua International and (with Davis Love III) the World Cup. With $150,000 as his share of the winning prize in this one, Couples pushed his three-week earnings to $580,000.

The 10 two-man teams in the Shark Shootout played one round each of alternate shot, better-ball and scramble at Sherwood Country Club in Thousand Oaks, California. Couples and Faxon played the first two rounds in 68 and 64, then came from behind with eight consecutive birdies leading off the final round. Faxon's four-iron second shot and Couples' eight-foot putt on the 16th provided the clinching eagle in a closing round of 14-under-par 58. They finished at 190, 26 under par.

Diners Club Matches—$1,850,000
Winners: Jim McGovern and Jeff Maggert
Raymond Floyd and Dave Eichelberger
Kelly Robbins and Tammie Green

The tongue very definitely was in the cheek when Dave Eichelberger gave voice to a world-class understatement. "I think," Eichelberger said, "that's the first time I've ever beaten Nicklaus and Palmer." The journeyman Eichelberger, a rookie on the Senior PGA Tour, made the observation after his two critical birdie putts provided him and partner Raymond Floyd with a 19-hole upset victory over Jack Nicklaus and Arnold Palmer in the senior final in the inaugural Diners Club Matches.

After trailing most of the day, Nicklaus and Palmer won four of five holes beginning on the 12th and were one-up going to the 18th. Eichelberger, however, rolled in an 18-foot birdie putt on the 18th to draw even, then won it with a 15-footer on the first extra hole, stealing the match from Palmer and Nicklaus and center stage from the teams of Jim McGovern and Jeff Maggert, and Kelly Robbins and Tammie Green.

McGovern and Maggert came back from four down with five holes to play to beat Rocco Mediate and Lee Janzen one-up on the 19th hole on Maggert's eight-foot birdie putt for the regular tour title, while Robbins and Green won the LPGA portion of the better-ball match play event 2 and 1 over Juli Inkster and Dottie Mochrie. Each member of the three winning teams received $125,000.

Nike Tour

A great thing about the Nike Tour is that one victory does not mean very much, unlike the PGA Tour, where too many players consider themselves successful even when they have won nothing. Twelve players won tournaments on the 1994 Nike Tour but were not among the 10 leading money winners who received players cards for next year's PGA Tour. Nine players, who won a total of 15 tournaments, received their cards, as did one player who did not have a victory on the American developmental circuit that runs from February through October.

The average earnings of the leading 10 players was in the $130,000 range, led by Chris Perry, an eight-year veteran of the PGA Tour, with $167,148. He had one victory, a Tour-best 10 top-10 finishes, and made the 36-hole cut in 24 consecutive tournaments. Perry, age 32, said he had "sought help from a lot of people and become too mechanical. Now I'm focused on returning to the Tour. I have returned to my old ways, and it may not be pretty, but I feel I'm ready for 1995."

Jerry Haas, whose brother Jay is on the PGA Tour, had three victories, including two in a row. Scott Gump, Skip Kendall, Bruce Vaughan and Tommy Armour III won twice each, while David Duval, Pat Bates and Jim Carter won once each. Emlyn Aubrey, who had won the 1994 Indian Open on the Asian Tour, took the final qualifying position for the 1995 PGA Tour despite not having a victory. Former Tour player Keith Fergus won two tournaments, yet did not qualify.

Although the Nike Tour did not get into full swing until April, there was one tournament in February and two in March. Kendall, who narrowly lost his player's card after the 1993 PGA Tour, was on track for the first event, taking a six-stroke victory in Moreno Valley, California. Aubrey was runner-up, as he would be two more times. Gump used a final-hole birdie to also start his season well by winning the second event in Monterrey, Mexico.

Two champions from the African Tours were among the winners in April. Vaughan, who earlier in the year won the Mount Edgecombe Trophy, won in Pensacola, Florida, and Omar Uresti, winner of the Hollard Insurance Royal Swazi Sun Classic, took the title in Shreveport, Louisiana, in a playoff with Bates. Vaughan won a second Nike title, his third overall, in August in Odessa, Texas.

Fergus, who resigned as golf coach at the University of Houston to join the Nike Tour, was another early winner in Panama City, Florida, and won again in September in Boise, Idaho. But Fergus placed 13th on the qualifying list, less than $7,000 behind Aubrey. For Fergus, in the final tournament of the year, three strokes made the difference.

Gump won his second title in late May in Greenville, South Carolina, then Armour took charge for two weeks, winning both in Ohio, in Springboro and Concord. Kendall followed two weeks later with his second triumph of the year in Cary, North Carolina.

The Nike Tour progressed through the summer into Missouri, Kansas, South Dakota, Texas and New Mexico with no repeat winners, the most notable triumph probably being that by Carter who, having finished second three times, finally won with a last-round 66 in Albuquerque, by one stroke over Aubrey. The next week in Provo, Utah, Perry moved to the top of the money list after winning by one stroke over Duval.

Haas won back-to-back in Richland, Washington, and Windsor, California, leading into the Nike Tour Championship in Cornelius, Oregon. Mike Schuchart, who did not qualify for the 1995 PGA Tour, won the closing tournament, while Aubrey, Sonny Skinner and Lee Rinker battled for the final qualifying position. Skinner had reason to be the most disappointed, as he shot closing rounds of 75 and 78 to miss qualifying by only $1,741.

Canadian Tour

The Canadian Tour, which produced the Alfred Dunhill Cup champions, was less hospitable than St. Andrews' Old Course for the Canadian-born players on the 1994 circuit. Golfers from the United States and South Africa dominated, winning seven times over the 10 tournaments held from June through August. Americans won four events; South Africans, three; Canadians, two; and Australians, one. There were no multiple individual winners, and less than C$4,000 separated the top four finishers on the money list, which was led by Eric Woods, from Corona Del Mar, California, with C$44,083.

The first three tournaments were in British Columbia, and Americans won the first two, Matt Jackson in the Payless Open in Parksville and Robert Meyer in the Morningstar Classic in Victoria, where Woods double-bogeyed the last hole to let Meyer into a playoff. Next, Australian Craig Jones, who won the AMP New Zealand Open earlier in the year, won the B.C. Tel Pacific Open in Vernon.

When the Tour moved to Ponoka for the Alberta Open, Canadian Jim Rutledge won for the first time in five years, shooting 68 in the last round for a 271 total and a come-from-behind victory by one stroke over Roger Wessels of South Africa. Both Wessels and American Scott Dunlap had 62s, eight under par, in an earlier round, but shot 72 and 73, respectively, on the last day.

In the Klondike Open in Edmonton, Ian Hutchings of South Africa sank a 10-foot birdie putt on the fourth extra hole to defeat Arden Knoll of Canada after both finished with 68s and 275 totals.

Dunlap's turn to win came at the Xerox Manitoba Open in Winnipeg, where the young man from Sarasota, Florida, battled strong winds and came from seven strokes behind in the final round to win by two strokes with 70, one under par, and a 276 total. Runner-up Mike Weir of Canada, who had a closing-round 78, led the field by four strokes when the day began and was still four ahead of Dunlap with six holes to play.

The Canadian Tour continued with two Ontario tournaments. At the Infiniti Tournament Players Championship in King City, Derek James of South Africa shot a final-round 65, including 30 on the first nine, for a 271 total to win by two strokes over Ray Stewart, one of Canada's Alfred Dunhill Cup players.

Stewart was runner-up again the next week in the inaugural Canadian Masters in Ancaster. South Africa's Wessels, who placed second in the Alberta Open, won by one stroke with a closing 70 and 272 total. Stewart, who finished with 69, bogeyed three par-three holes on the last nine. Wessels holed a 132-yard shot for eagle at No. 7 and birdied No. 17 to secure the victory.

Woods became the first Canadian Tour player in six years to successfully defend a title when he won the Export "A" Inc. Ontario Open in London, winning by four strokes with a final 71 and 278 total after a spirited head-to-head battle with Wessels.

Stuart Hendley gave Canada a second victory in the season's final event, the Trafalgar CPGA Championship in Bromont, Quebec, despite a shaky last round. Hendley started the last day with a four-stroke lead, shot 73 for a 275 total and won by one stroke.

South American Tour

Professional golf in South America — a nine-event South American Tour and three independent tournaments in Argentina — was dominated by the Argentinians and a group of Americans without U.S. PGA Tour players' cards. There were two exceptions. Raul Fretes of Paraguay won two tournaments and led the South American Tour money list with $57,770. Mark O'Meara made a one-event stop at the Argentina Open and won by six strokes.

With that victory, O'Meara joined a short list of players — along with Gary Player, Hale Irwin, David Graham and Bernhard Langer — who had won in the United States, Europe, Japan, Australia and South America in their careers.

The South American Tour began in late September, when Miguel Guzman of Argentina won the Bogota Open. American Ron Wuensche then won the Los Andes Open in Colombia and, after an off week, Mauricio Molina of Argentina won the T.C. Ecuador Open. It was on to the Los Inkas-Peru Open, where another American, David Ogrin, was the champion.

After another off week, the Tour moved into November with the Litoral Open in Argentina, won by an Argentinian, Cesar Monasterio. Fretes won his first at the Uruguay Open, and American Mike Cunning won the Paraguay Open. The final two events were held in December in Chile, with Jose Maria Cantero of Argentina winning the Prince of Wales Open, and Fretes winning the Los Leones-Chile Open.

The independent events in Argentina were the Argentina Open, with a $200,000 purse, the largest on the continent, the Argentina Tournament of Champions, won by Jose Coceres, and Argentina PGA, won by Armando Saavedra, both of Argentina.

12. European Tour

The statisticians were kept busy on the PGA European Tour in 1994. There were, for example, 24 holes-in-one, four playoffs, eight first-time winners, eight multiple winners, and 12 course records. The record-shooters were led by that dynamic youngster, South Africa's Ernie Els, age 24, who joined the first-time winners in the Dubai Desert Classic. Els led off the tournament with an 11-under-par 61 and won by six strokes over Greg Norman. That was the start of a year that would include the U.S. Open Championship for Els.

Professional golf went behind the old Iron Curtain for the first time, with the Mercedes German Masters being moved to Motzen, in the former East Germany, and a new tournament, the Chemapol Trophy Czech Open, being played in the Czech Republic.

Nick Faldo had been atop the Sony Ranking for a record 81 consecutive weeks, and then was dragged down by a misfiring game. Faldo won once in Europe, in the Alfred Dunhill Open in June. But as he turned 37, the season went by without a major scalp to call his own, without another European victory, without much of a stir. Not that he wasn't trying. He had practiced barefooted in the Johnnie Walker World Championship in December, 1993, and he adopted the cross-handed putting style in September. Something paid off. He won the Nedbank Million Dollar Challenge in December. It may not have been an official victory, but it sure made him feel better. "Yes," he said, "a million times better." There was a bonus: The way he was playing, the 1995 season looked brighter.

For a while, 1994 looked like the Year of the Swede on the PGA European Tour. Mats Lanner, who had gone dormant for so long, took the season-opening Madeira Island Open, and Anders Forsbrand followed him with the Moroccan Open the following week. These were the first back-to-back victories ever by Swedes.

It was also the Year of the Spaniard, or at least the return of the same. Seve Ballesteros, who hadn't won since 1992, beat Faldo by three strokes in the Benson & Hedges International Open in May. He capped his year by winning the Mercedes German Masters and by almost winning the season finale, the Volvo Masters. He finished second to Bernhard Langer, who was scoring his second win of the year, after the Murphy's Irish Open. It marked the 16th consecutive year in which Langer had won on the PGA European Tour.

The "other" Spaniard, Jose Maria Olazabal, also hadn't won since 1992. He resurfaced in the Turespana Open Mediterrania, then added the Volvo PGA Championship. Oh, yes — he went to Augusta and won the Masters, too, launching the first year in which the four major championships would go without an American winner.

Nick Price saw to that, thanks to Jesper Parnevik, the young Swede who preferred to look the other way. Parnevik was on the verge of winning the British Open Championship at Turnberry when he dared not glance at the leaderboard coming down the stretch. He didn't know he was winning, and he gambled at the 18th and lost. Price did his part, with a sensational 50-

foot eagle putt at the 17th. The crown that had eluded him in 1982 and 1988 was his. That wasn't all that was his. He also won the American PGA Championship for a double-major year, along with five other events.

Colin Montgomerie, a two-time winner in 1993, added to his record in 1994 with three victories. He took the Peugeot Open de Espana in May, and then after a U.S. Open he would rather forget, he won the Murphy's English Open and Volvo German Open back-to-back in August. That put him atop the money list for the second consecutive year.

Montgomerie showed a sense of drama in the Peugeot Open de Espana. He was so vexed by his putting that he took five putters with him. The putt he really needed, though, was one that broke four hearts — a mere two-footer at the final hole. Then at the Murphy's English Open, it was another final-hole heartbreaker, this time an eight-footer for his first win on British soil.

"I'm playing well enough to win any tournament I enter," Monty said. That ought to set off a nervous alarm for 1995.

Madeira Island Open—£250,000
Winner: Mats Lanner

The 1994 PGA European Tour season opened in fits and starts in mid-January, with the Madeira Island Open shortened to three rounds and fragmented across four days by stubborn fog, but in the end an old name returned to the top. It was Mats Lanner, one of the early Swedish threats, scoring his first victory in seven years with a 206 total, 10 under par at Campo de Golfe. He won by two strokes over countrymen, Mathias Gronberg and Peter Hedblom, and Howard Clark. It was Lanner's second career victory. His first was the 1987 Epson Grand Prix, a match-play event.

"Obviously, sometimes you have doubts," Lanner said, "but deep down inside I always thought that someday I'm going to crack it and win a stroke-play event." This one was almost match play, the way he and Clark duelled down the stretch.

The leaders began the third round on Saturday, but fog and rain stopped play at 3:15 p.m., leaving them to finish the round — and the tournament — on Sunday. Clark, looking for his first victory since 1988, began the round with a two-stroke lead over Lanner, Paul Broadhurst and Jeremy Robinson. Lanner, who resumed play on Sunday at No. 10, was tied for the lead at nine under par with Clark and Hedblom. He then logged three birdies in six holes — the 10th from 30 feet, the 13th from 12 and the 15th from from eight.

With the others suffering a series of errors, Lanner led by three with three holes to play and seemed to have things locked up. But he didn't. He three-putted the 16th for one bogey, missed the green at the 17th for another, but he pulled himself together for a birdie at the 18th, with a driver, eight iron and two putts. He had a final-round 69, following his 70 and 67.

Moroccan Open—£350,000
Winner: Anders Forsbrand

Anders Forsbrand made it two in succession for the Swedes — the first Swedish back-to-back victories ever on the PGA European Tour — with a late spurt that carried him to a four-stroke victory in the Moroccan Open. He played Golf Royal de Agadir in 276, 12 under par, making Howard Clark a runner-up again. It was Forsbrand's first win since his three-victory year in 1992.

It was a Swedish festival. Robert Karlsson and Peter Hedblom joined a five-way tie for the first-round lead at 68. Clark shot 67 in the second round for a three-stroke lead over Forsbrand and Gordon Brand, Jr. But Clark started to slip, and a third-round 72 left him tied with Forsbrand (69) at 207, three strokes clear of the field going into the final round. Then it turned into match play.

Forsbrand bogeyed No. 3, but bounced back with birdies at the next two holes, from 25 and 20 feet, respectively. Clark kept pace with a 20-footer and a five-footer, and led by one after nine holes. Then trouble set in. Forsbrand tied when Clark bogeyed the 13th, then took a one-stroke lead at the 15th with a birdie from 15 feet to Clark's bogey.

At the par-five 17th, Forsbrand two-putted from 60 feet after a long, straight drive, while Clark bunkered his drive, and another birdie-bogey swing put Forsbrand out of reach. Forsbrand finished with 69. He then pointed to the growing Swedish strength, noting three others in the top 10, and offered rhetorically, "If we can win two out of two, why not three out of three?" Said the groggy Clark, headed for the AT&T Pro-Am at Pebble Beach, "I suppose I'll run into another Swede out there, too."

Dubai Desert Classic—£450,000
Winner: Ernie Els

Big, blond Ernie Els, 24, had won almost at will on his native South African Tour, and if anyone wondered whether he had the stuff to win on the PGA European Tour as well, he dispelled all doubts with a whistles-bells-and-fireworks victory in the Dubai Desert Classic. Starting with a course-record 61 in the first round, Els lit up the late January sky with a 268 total, 20 under par. More to the point, Els led successively by five, six and eight strokes before winning by six over Greg Norman.

"That's the best golf I've ever played," said Els, whose other scores were 69, 67 and 71. "It's taken me 18 months to win in Europe, and now I hope I can win a couple more." Who could doubt that he will?

He survived his tense moments — if they could remotely be described as tense. In the third round, he hooked his tee shot at No. 1 almost out of bounds, then hooked again at No. 2 into a bunker. But he salvaged par both times. Before anyone could get any false hopes, he birdied No. 3 on two putts, then No. 5, firing a five iron to five feet, and then No. 6, where he put a four iron to six feet. In all, he had five birdies in his 67. Norman recognized Els' growing strengths. "If he was going to get scared, it was going to be today," Norman said.

Els' 61, 11 under par, broke Eamonn Darcy's record by three strokes. Els also tied Fred Couples' PGA European Tour record of 12 birdies in 18 holes. He was devastating with the putter. He needed only 21 putts in the round, and he played the back nine in 29. The most telling compliment came from Norman. Els has often been compared to him, both being tall, blond and strong. But they are very different in one respect. "Ernie has a lot calmer temperament than I had 14 years ago," Norman said. "It's taken me 14 years to get where he is now."

Johnnie Walker Asian Classic—£600,000
Winner: Greg Norman

"I guess the saying, 'Beware the sick golfer,' is sometimes true," Greg Norman noted. Fred Couples couldn't agree more. Norman, fighting off a strength-sapping lung infection, and deep in the pack after the second round, came charging through with two dazzling closing rounds to win the Johnnie Walker Asian Classic, shooting 277, 11 under par at Blue Canyon Country Club in Phuket, Thailand.

Norman, who became ill after the Dubai Desert Classic the previous week, needed sleep and antibiotics. Too weak to practice, he surveyed the course from a golf cart on Wednesday. His 75 was nine behind Couples' lead in the first round. With a second-round 70, he was seven behind Couples and Bernhard Langer after 36 holes. Then he crashed through in the third with a course-record 64 that left him just one stroke off the lead, behind Couples and Ian Woosnam. The battle was on in the final round.

Norman, who made six bogeys in his first 27 holes and only one in the last 45, caught Couples at 10 under par with a birdie from 12 feet at No. 16. The end was in sight, but not yet within reach. "I knew if I could birdie 18, then 11 would be the magic number," Norman said. Then playing to his own script at the 18th, he flipped a pitching wedge to 10 feet and dropped the putt to finish at 11 under with a closing 68. Now Couples, who had last birdied at No. 6, needed a birdie at the 18th to tie. But he couldn't get it.

"I had the wedge in my hand six times on the back nine, but didn't make a birdie," Couples lamented. Langer bogeyed the 17th and finished third, two behind. The long-slumping Woosnam made six at the 18th and finished fourth, four strokes back. Nick Faldo missed the 36-hole cut, and it cost him the top spot in the world. Norman went to No. 1 on the Sony Ranking with the victory.

Turespana Open de Tenerife—£250,000
Winner: David Gilford

The Turespana Open de Tenerife was the Nostalgia Open for a while — at least until a frazzled putter overtook Brian Barnes, age 49. Barnes, who hadn't won on the PGA European Tour in 13 years, thrilled his fans with a record-tying 64 in the third round, and took a one-stroke lead into the fourth round. That's where the dream ended. He three-putted seven times and closed with 77. Up stepped David Gilford, for a two-stroke victory at

10-under-par 278 on the Golf del Sur course. Gilford shot 72, 70, 66 and 70 to win by two strokes over Wayne Riley, Andrew Murray and Juan Quiros. Barnes sank to a tie for fifth place at 281.

Barnes said it wasn't his nerves that did him in. "I got to the stage where I was uncomfortable on the greens, and it was bloody annoying," he said. "Basically, I didn't stand up to the challenge."

But Gilford did, in a manner of speaking. He started the day four strokes behind Barnes, and he was still one stroke behind with six holes to play. It was at the par-five 14th that he turned the tournament around. He fired a seven-iron approach to eight feet and holed the putt for an eagle three and the lead. He wobbled coming in, taking bogeys at the 16th and 17th holes, but it didn't cost him any ground. Barnes three-putted four of the last five holes, and finished with two double bogeys.

Extremadura Open—£250,000
Winner: Paul Eales

Paul Eales may never have seen anything like it in his career, and he certainly never did anything like it — an explosion of five under par over four holes. He himself was the author, and that bit of pyrotechnics hurled him into the Extremadura Open championship, his first victory in six years on the PGA European Tour. Eales, 30, trailed successively by five strokes, then five, then one, before going headlong into the winner's circle at Golf del Guadiana at Badajoz, Spain. He played the par-72 course in 281, seven under par. He won by one stroke over Peter Hedblom and by two over Andrew Coltart and Jose Maria Canizares. His scores were 72, 69, 69 and 71.

Eales didn't seem destined for any great reward here when he opened the final round with a three-putt six. That kept him one stroke behind the third-round leaders, Nic Henning and Miguel Angel Jimenez. He started his breathtaking stretch at No. 5, holing a 30-footer for a two. He got another two at No. 6, only this was an eagle, on a five-iron shot from 157 yards. He followed that with birdies at the seventh and eighth, from three and 12 feet. Eales was leading by four coming to No. 9, and he needed the cushion. He three-putted Nos. 9 and 11 for bogeys, and he still led by two when he reached the par-five 18th. Good thing. He bogeyed it, too.

Turespana Masters Open de Andalucia—£300,000
Winner: Carl Mason

When Carl Mason's dream finally came true, he was speechless. "For 21 years I have dreamed of this moment," Mason told the gallery, after winning the Turespana Masters Open de Andalucia, "and now that it's arrived, I can't think of anything to say."

Maybe words wouldn't fit the occasion. Mason was 40, he had joined the PGA European Tour in 1974, and maybe he had reached the point where it seemed victory wasn't in the cards for him. He had been runner-up six times. When victory did finally come, it came with a flourish at the par-72 Montecastillo

Golf Club at Jerez de la Frontera in Spain. On rounds of 67, 70, 71 and 70, he shared the first-round lead in a five-way tie, fell two behind in the second round, and then was tied with Jose Maria Olazabal going into the final round. A performance chart would tell you which was more likely to lose, and the chart would have been wrong. Mason, with a 10-under-par 278 total, beat Olazabal by two.

It was hardly automatic. Mason three-putted for a bogey at No. 3, and Gordon Brand, Jr., moved into the lead with birdies at the fourth and fifth. But he fell back with bogeys at the next two holes, both after bunker trouble. Meanwhile, Mason broke out in a rash of great putting, holing 30-footers for birdies at Nos. 4, 6 and 7. He also holed a six-footer for a birdie at the par-five 16th, where Brand's chances died with a bogey. Olazabal, after a great scrambling par at the 17th, trailed by one stroke coming to No. 18. But he bogeyed, and Mason negotiated two bunkers to make his par and take his long-awaited victory.

Turespana Open Mediterrania—£300,000
Winner: Jose Maria Olazabal

One minute, Paul McGinley had his first victory firmly in hand. The next, it was gone, in a puff of anticipation. While he was starting to enjoy the victory, Jose Maria Olazabal, a man in a slump, snatched the Turespana Open Mediterrania away. The memory will be one of McGinley's bitterest. He was leading by three strokes with two holes to play, and ended up losing in a playoff. "I had it on a plate today, and didn't win it," McGinley said. "After 16 holes, I thought to myself, 'I'm three ahead and I've done all the hard work.' My concentration dropped."

The wind had come up, making club selection even more critical at the 235-yard, par-three 17th. It was ordinarily a two-iron shot for McGinley, but with the wind in his face, he needed a one iron, which he didn't have. So he opted for his five wood. It was too much club. He went long and to the left, down the bank. "I never thought I could win until then," Olazabal said. "I knew it was the wrong club. He knew I could not make a birdie and he should have gone for a four. It was nerves. With more experience, it may not have happened."

McGinley, thwarted by a stone behind his ball, could chip only about five yards, and then he hit his next shot over the green. He chipped back and made the putt for a double-bogey five, losing two strokes of his lead to Olazabal's par. He lost the rest of it at the 18th, making bogey after hooking his tee shot. Olazabal parred, and they were tied at 12-under-par 276. McGinley played the par-72 Villa Martin course in rounds of 70, 68, 68 and 70, and Olazabal in 70, 65, 71 and 70. They halved the first playoff hole, the 17th, and at the 18th, McGinley drove into the rough and parred, and Olazabal birdied from 25 feet for the victory, his first since this event in 1992.

"I have started to see the light," Olazabal said. "Now I can put the frustration and the bad memories behind me."

Turespana Open de Baleares—£250,000
Winner: Barry Lane

Barry Lane spent a restless night before the final round of the Turespana Open de Baleares, not because his lead was so small, but because it was so big — five strokes. "It was a nightmare, defending a big lead," he said. "It is the hardest way to win. I had to block out everything and just play the course. But if I could shoot 69, I knew someone would need 63."

Lane did shoot 69, but nobody could manage the 63, and so he had the fifth victory of his career. It was a sterling performance for other reasons as well. He had to take painkillers for an injury, his children were home with the chicken pox, and defending champion Jim Payne was on his heels all the way. Even so, Lane led wire-to-wire with a 269 total, 19 under par on the Son Vida course on Majorca.

Lane rocketed through the field. In the first round, he birdied seven of the last 11 holes for a course-record 64 and a three-stroke lead. In the third round, he birdied six of the last 11 holes in a 66 that kept Payne at bay. But Payne wouldn't stay put. In the final round, he birdied three in succession from No. 2 and charged through the middle of the last nine — a birdie at the 12th from 20 feet, long putts for an eagle three at the 13th and a birdie three at the 15th against Lane's bogey. "But when I overshot the 17th green, I knew it was all over," Payne said, after the bogey.

Portuguese Open—£300,000
Winner: Phillip Price

By Phillip Price's accounting, that bottle of champagne was already one year too old. He had bought it a year earlier, in anticipation of scoring his first PGA European Tour victory. "I was beginning to wonder if I would ever open it," Price said, after the Portuguese Open. "But now I can." A tie for second in the 1993 GA European Open was the best previous finish by the 27-year-old Welshman since he joined the Tour in 1989. Price could pop that cork at last, after holding off a host of challengers, including defending champion David Gilford, for a wire-to-wire victory.

Price burst into a one-stroke lead with a course-record 64 in the first round, then had 71, 71 and 72 for a six-under-par 278 total at the Penha Longa Golf Club near Lisbon. He enjoyed a luxurious four-stroke victory over Gilford, Retief Goosen and Paul Eales. Price had eight birdies in his first-round 64, needing only 26 putts. In the second, Goosen, with 66, tied him at 135. But Price wouldn't crack, as evidenced by his 25 consecutive pars from the second round to the third.

He was a little shaky early in the final round. A pair of bogeys on the front nine cut his lead over Gilford to one stroke. Gilford tied him with a birdie at the par-five 12th, but not for long. Price regained the lead there minutes later with a birdie of his own, from 15 feet. Gilford's bid ended with a seven at the par-four 14th, where he bunkered his drive, barely got out, and topped a three wood. He closed with 73. Goosen couldn't coax a putt down and shot 74. Eales got within a stroke with birdies at the 11th and 12th, then slipped back with bogeys at the 17th and 18th for 73.

Open V33 du Grand Lyon—£225,000
Winner: Stephen Ames

The PGA European Tour got its first champion from Trinidad and Tobago when Stephen Ames came from behind in the stinging rain and near-gale winds of the final day to win the Open V33 at Les Sangliers Golf Club in Lyon, France. Ames shot a closing two-over-par 74. That's not an impressive figure until one discovers that Gordon Manson's 71 was the only sub-par round in the unrelenting wind and rain, and that there were only 12 other scores under 74. For all of that, however, Ames came from two strokes behind Wayne Riley going into the final round, and outran him to the finish.

Ames, never closer than two to the lead after the first three rounds, shot 282, six under par. Spain's Pedro Linhart closed with 72 and Sweden's Gabriel Hjerstedt 77 to tie for second place, two strokes behind. Riley crashed to a disastrous 79 and ended up fourth at 285. Ames, in his third year on the PGA European Tour, took five cracks at the European qualifying tournament before finally making it in 1992. His perseverance paid off handsomely in the brutal weather of the tournament's final day.

Tournoi Perrier de Paris—£350,000
Winners: Peter Baker and David J. Russell

Conventional wisdom is that any time the firm of Ballesteros and Olazabal Ltd. enters a team event, everyone else can start playing for second place. But that wasn't the case for the Spanish Ryder Cup players in the inaugural Tournoi Perrier de Paris, in a wintry mid-April week at the Saint-Cloud Golf Club in Saint-Cloud, France. The British partnership of Peter Baker and David J. Russell squandered a big lead but escaped with a one-stroke victory over Mark Mouland and Jamie Spence. Seve Ballesteros and Jose Maria Olazabal, the newly crowned Masters champion, tied for third place.

It was a scorekeeper's nightmare: Baker and Russell opened with a dazzling 58 in fourballs, then shot 68 in foursomes, 65 in greensomes, and then 69 in fourballs for a 20-under-par total of 260. Their closing 69 was the highest score among the contenders, but was enough to beat Mouland and Spence by one stroke.

Baker and Russell started the final round with a six-stroke lead, and headed straight for trouble. They made the turn in one-over-par 36, bogeyed the 10th hole, and got caught when Mouland and Spence birdied the 10th and 12th. Russell responded with birdies at the 13th, from seven feet, and the 14th, from 18 feet. But the hounds would not be put off. Spence dropped a four-footer for birdie at the 16th to cut the deficit to one, and Mouland holed from five feet at the par-five 17th. But Russell matched him — with some outside help. His tee shot was headed for the trees, but hit a limb and came down. He reached the green from there and two-putted for a birdie, and then Baker locked up the victory with an up-and-down par at the 18th.

Heineken Open Catalonia—£300,000
Winner: Jose Coceres

Jean Louis Guepy, something of a prodigy in golf, did everything at the Heineken Open Catalonia but win it. Guepy made 21 birdies and two eagles, usually enough to win most tournaments, but his reward was second place. This race went to the steadier, Argentina's Jose Coceres, on rounds of 70, 69, 67 and 69 for a 275 total, 13 under par at Pals Golf Club. Coceres broke free on the second nine in the final day for a three-stroke victory.

"I could see victory clearly after the 14th," said Coceres, 30, six-year veteran of the PGA European Tour. That's where he eagled to all but wrap it up. Before that, it had been a struggle all the way. Guepy shot and shared the first-round lead with Gavin Levenson and Thomas Levet. He shot 68 and led Wayne Riley and Rolf Muntz by two strokes after the second round. Coceres surfaced in the third round and led Guepy, who had 72, by one stroke going into the final round.

Guepy regained the lead at the ninth hole with a birdie from 18 feet, then slipped back with a bogey at the 10th. Coceres jumped at the opportunity. He birdied the par-three 11th to pull one stroke ahead, then sprinted with the eagle at the 14th from 12 feet. Guepy had to settle for second, finishing with 71, gilding his reputation as possibly the most unlikely character on the Tour. A native of New Hebrides, a French island between Tahiti and Australia, Guepy was a crack junior tennis player. He didn't take up golf until he was 20, and six short years later, he's a contender.

Air France Cannes Open—£300,000
Winner: Ian Woosnam

Ian Woosnam, the king of Riviera golf — three Monte Carlo Opens, one Mediterranean — added to his total there with the Air France Cannes Open, but this was a flight he almost missed. Woosie came to Cannes-Mougins Golf Club still struggling with his game. After 26 holes, he was 14 strokes off the lead and on his way to missing the 36-hole cut (which would come at even-par 144). Then he took off like a rocket. Beginning at No. 9 in the second round, the 27th hole, he raced over the final 46 holes in 20 under par with 19 birdies and an eagle, including a six-birdie stretch in the fourth round, to win by five strokes over a marveling Colin Montgomerie.

"When Ian starts playing like that, you just have to play for second place," Monty said. As for a relieved Woosie, he looked at his 72-70 start, then the 63-66 finish, for a 17-under-par 271 total, and noted, "It's been a long time since I've played so well. When I get fed up, I seem to play better." In the second round, after bogeying three of the first seven holes, he came to No. 9 in a slow burn, hooked his drive around the rocky dogleg-left, pitched to 25 feet, and holed the putt. He also birdied the 10th from six feet, the 13th from 10, and eagled the 14th after a 225-yard two iron to eight feet, and shot 70.

Woosie shot 63 in the third round for a one-stroke lead over Monty and Pierre Fulke going into the final round. They tied him briefly when he bogeyed the fourth, then he zoomed away with the six consecutive birdies.

He two-putted Nos. 7 and 8, both par fives, got the next four on putts of 18, four, 18 and 12 feet, and then tacked on another at the par-five 14th from 15 feet. Montgomerie took second with two long birdie putts, a 20-footer at the 12th and a 30-footer at the 18th for 276, five behind Woosie.

Benson & Hedges International Open—£650,000
Winner: Seve Ballesteros

Seve Ballesteros lit up golf, lit up the smile in his own eyes, and put the doomsayers to rest with a going-away victory in the Benson & Hedges International Open. "It is nice to win again," he said. "I am now more consistent and more confident." It was his first victory since 1992, and he shared the credit with Mac O'Grady, the former American golfer. "He has changed a couple things, which means my shots stay in play more," said Ballesteros, who had rounds of 69, 70, 72 and 70 for a 281 total, seven under par at St. Mellion Golf and Country Club in Plymouth, England.

Ballesteros led through the first two rounds, trailed by one stroke in the third, then closed with a bogey-free 70, moving past Gary Orr to a three-stroke win over Nick Faldo. "Under Mac, Seve seems to have found something," said Faldo, who got within one stroke in the final round with birdies at Nos. 3 and 5, then gave them back with bogeys at the eighth and 10th. He battled down the stretch, making birdies at the 15th and 16th to get to four under par. His birdie putts at the 14th and 17th lipped out, and a 10-footer at the 18th narrowly missed. "I was trying to shoot 65," Faldo said.

Wayne Westner also got to four under, but he bogeyed the 17th after an errant drive, then committed one of golf's greatest sins. Trying to tap in a ball hanging on the lip at the 18th, he missed completely. He double-bogeyed.

Ballesteros was playing for more than the victory. The U.S. Open was about a month away and he wasn't qualified. He would need a special exemption. Some thought winning here would earn it for him. "It is up to them now," he said.

Peugeot Open de Espana—£500,000
Winner: Colin Montgomerie

Colin Montgomerie had taken five putters with him to the Peugeot Open de Espana, for the obvious and painful reason. But when he faced the most important putt of the tournament, he could have used a gravy ladle. A five-man chase the final day came down to Montgomerie's wedge shot to two feet at the final hole. His putting had been spooking him, but not this time.

So Montgomerie, a two-time winner a year earlier, scored his first victory of 1994 in mid-May and returned to the top of the money list, where he had finished in 1993. He posted a 277 total, 11 under par, beating Richard Boxall, Mark Roe and Mark McNulty by one, and Bernhard Langer by two. Monty, who shot rounds of 70, 71, 66 and 70 at Club de Campo at Madrid, broke from the pack with his third-round 66 to tie for the lead with McNulty and Roe. He noted with some wry self-criticism, "I just had to hole a putt over four feet, and I did that on the first green — after leaving my birdie putt eight feet short." Then he birdied four holes in succession from No. 6.

It wasn't business as usual for Montgomerie's winning birdie at the 18th. He was about to hit his tee shot when his caddie, Alastair McLean, yelled "Stop!" A squirrel had come out on the tee, sending snickers through the gallery. He stopped, regrouped, then drove perfectly to set up the birdie. McNulty sliced into the trees at the 10th and had to chip out sideways, then "over-corrected" and missed the green at the par-three 11th and bogeyed again. "One bad shot cost me the tournament," McNulty said. Roe bogeyed the 13th and 15th, and bounced back for birdies at the last two holes from eight and four feet. Boxall birdied three of the last seven, but three-putted the 16th.

Tisettanta Italian Open—£450,000
Winner: Eduardo Romero

The man they call El Gato — "The Cat" — at home in Argentina, went for the jugular in the Tisettanta Italian Open. Eduardo Romero came into the final round one stroke off the lead, and after parring the first hole, he launched a birdie-eagle-birdie strike that catapulted him to a one-stroke victory over New Zealand's Greg Turner. It was Romero's first European victory in three years and his fifth overall. And it didn't come easily.

"I was nervous all day, but I played well," Romero said, as he showed with the clutch par at the final hole for the victory. Turner set the pace with a final-round 65, seven under par at the new Marco Simone club in Rome, for a 273 total. Romero came through like a champion. At the final hole, he pulled his drive into the left rough, hit a seven iron to the front of the green, 45 feet from the flag, and rammed his first putt seven feet past the hole. That seven-footer was what he needed for the winning par, and that's what he got, wrapping up 67 and 272 total, 16 under par.

Alexander Cejka of Germany, bolted into the first-round lead with 64. He shot 74 in the second round and was replaced by Sweden's Fredrik Lindgren, who made his bid with 64 and 69 in the middle rounds. It was looking promising for him until Romero, who had earlier scores of 69, 67 and 69, exploded over the final round. After the opening par, he birdied No. 2 from 10 feet, eagled No. 3 on a six iron to seven feet, and birdied No. 4 from 10 feet. Turner applied the heat with a birdie at the par-five 16th, and birdied the short 17th from 40 feet for his eighth birdie of the day. Then he saved par at the 18th, forcing Romero to do the same behind him.

Volvo PGA Championship—£800,000
Winner: Jose Maria Olazabal

The Volvo PGA Championship went to Jose Maria Olazabal on a brilliant last-round 65 that edged the nearly wire-to-wire leader Ernie Els. Seve Ballesteros, who had to finish first or second to maintain his No. 2 position on the PGA European Tour money list to gain an automatic berth in the U.S. Open, finished sixth. His only chance now was a special exemption from the

U.S. Golf Association — which he received.

"I did it more with the heart and the stomach than anything else," Olazabal said. "The way I was striking the ball earlier in the week, I would never have thought I could do it." Olazabal shot 67, 68, 71 and 65 for a 271 total, 17 under par, but the tournament was in doubt until the end. "I knew I could win at the 18th, but not before," Olazabal said. He started the final round tied for second place, three strokes behind Els. He was out in 33 with an eagle from 18 feet at No. 4, gaining a stroke on Els, and the duel was on.

Olazabal chipped in from 45 feet at the 11th and birdied the 12th on two putts to tie Els. Els surged ahead by two strokes with birdies at the 12th and 13th, then bogeyed the 14th on three putts. Olazabal jumped at the opportunity, dropping a 21-foot putt for another birdie at the 15th. They were tied coming to No. 17. Olazabal birdied the tough par five with an approach to two feet while Els saved par after hooking his drive into the trees. Els then birdied the par-five 18th, but so did Olazabal.

Alfred Dunhill Open—£600,000
Winner: Nick Faldo

"You need luck and the run of the greens to win tournaments," Nick Faldo said, and he got plenty of both to ring up his first victory in 11 months in the Alfred Dunhill Open. Speaking of luck: "It was surprising that Monty and Bernhard, two great wind players, should blow out the same day," he said. "But that's golf."

Colin Montgomerie opened the final round at Royal Zoute Golf Club in Knokke, Belgium, leading Bernhard Langer by two strokes and Faldo by five. Then Montgomerie plunged into a nightmarish stretch, losing four strokes in three holes from the 14th, including a double bogey at the par-three 16th. He shot 77 and tied for third. Langer four-putted for a triple-bogey seven at No. 1, en route to 75 and a share of third.

With them out of the way, Faldo needed one final bit of luck. Joakim Haeggman obliged. He bogeyed the 18th, needing three to get down from the back of the green, for a one-over-par 72. That lowered him into a tie with Faldo at five-under-par total. Faldo, who never led until that final putt fell, trailed by as much as six. After rounds of 67, 74 and 67, he battled the pounding winds to a standoff for a rocky par 71. He took the playoff with a par five.

His final round was a masterpiece of survival. He three-putted the first for a bogey, birdied the second from 12 feet, and bogeyed the par-three No. 8. He also bogeyed No. 10, then eagled the par-five 12th after a two iron to 35 feet. He bogeyed the 16th out of a bunker, then birdied the par-five 17th from 10 feet. He had done his best. He needed some luck, and that's when Haeggman bogeyed the 18th.

Honda Open—£500,000
Winner: Robert Allenby

"I've won three times in Australia, but this is different," said Robert Allenby, a slender 22-year-old. "I've been dreaming about this for a long time." This dream came true the hard way.

Allenby, latest in the line of young Australian stars, staked his breakthrough victory in the Honda Open at Gut Kaden, near Hamburg, Germany. Allenby trailed all the way until he tied Miguel Angel Jimenez in the final round and then beat him on the third playoff hole. It was his first victory in three years on the PGA European Tour.

Allenby trailed by six strokes in the first round, five in the second, and then — after leader Rodger Davis suffered a 76 — was one behind Jimenez and Russell Claydon to start the fourth round. Jimenez moved ahead with two birdies going out, and escaped with a chip-in par at the 13th. Allenby closed in on the second nine. He birdied No. 11 from 25 feet, and got another birdie at the par-five 15th, but bogeyed the par-three 16th after scuffing a chip shot just six inches. He bounced right back, pitching to one foot for a birdie at the par-five 17th. Jimenez's last chance to win outright died when his 18-foot birdie putt at the 18th tailed off.

In the playoff, Allenby stayed alive at the first extra hole by saving par, missed the victory when he three-putted the second, then won at the third hole, the 18th again, with a par after Jimenez hit twice into bunkers. They had tied at 12-under-par 276 in regulation, Allenby shooting rounds of 72, 67, 68 and 69 to Jimenez's 70, 71, 65 and 70.

Jersey European Airways Open—£350,000
Winner: Paul Curry

While Ernie Els was winning his first major championship, the U.S. Open, Paul Curry was winning a major of his own at La Moye, Jersey. Curry, age 33 and 15 years on the PGA European Tour, finally broke through in the Jersey European Airways Open, becoming the eighth first-time winner of the season. And he did it in style, with two stunning rounds — 62 in the second round, 63 in the fourth — for a 266 total, and a tournament-record 22 under par. Curry trailed all the way, but with a sensational 12-hole charge, came from three strokes behind in the final round to sweep past 54-hole leader Mark James by three.

"When I holed out for an albatross two at the 16th in the third round, I felt it could be my week," Curry said. It was a three iron from 203 yards. He birdied the 18th as well for a solid 68.

Curry, trailing by three strokes, started the final round with a bogey at the par-three first hole. He bounced back with a birdie at No. 2, and then raced 12 holes in nine under par. He birdied No. 5, eagled No. 6 on a four wood to 15 feet, then made five consecutive birdies from No. 9, including a 20-footer at the 10th and a 30-footer at the 12th.

Peugeot Open de France—£550,000
Winner: Mark Roe

The home stretch of the National Golf Club at Versailles, so often the grave-yard of the hopeful, claimed another victim in the Peugeot Open de France. Just as the young Swede, Gabriel Hjerstedt, was about to notch his first victory, Mark Roe put on a strong drive and won on the final hole.

"It's not fun to watch someone bogey the last for you to win," said Roe, who won with a 274 total, 14 under par. "But Gaby had not won before, and it's very rare the first time you are really in contention."

Five players tied for the first-round lead with 66s, but Hjerstedt was one stroke behind, Roe four. Malcolm Mackenzie took the second-round lead with 66–136. Hjerstedt was at 137, Roe 141. Then Hjerstedt led by one stroke in the third round with 68–206, and Roe was three behind.

Roe, playing two groups ahead of Hjerstedt, birdied twice on the first nine, then birdied the 10th, 13th and the par-five 14th, even after bunkering his second shot. Hjertstedt, after four birdies in a row from No. 10, hit the same bunker at the 14th and bogeyed. The two-stroke swing cut his lead to one. Roe birdied the fateful 16th from eight feet, parred the 17th, then at the 18th, after reaching from rough, he two-putted from 90 feet for his par and closing 66. Hjerstedt was scrambling his way home. At No. 16, his tee shot was over the green, but he saved par. At the 17th, he was bunkered but got out and saved par. And at the 18th, he duck-hooked his drive into the lake and bogeyed, and the title belonged to Roe.

Murphy's Irish Open—£592,593
Winner: Bernhard Langer

Bernhard Langer withstood a furious charge by John Daly to win the Murphy's Irish Open, making it 16 consecutive years that Langer had won on the PGA European Tour. They both brushed past third-round leader Robert Allenby in their dash to the finish. Langer started four strokes off Allenby's lead, Daly seven. Daly put the pressure on immediately. He began the final round with six successive threes, three for birdies, one for an eagle, on his way to tying the course record with seven-under-par 65.

"I was aware of what John was doing," Langer said, "but I came out of the blocks pretty fast myself."

Langer made five birdies to the turn, including a 40-footer at No. 4, and matched Daly with 31 on the first nine. He went on to a one-stroke victory with 67 and 275, 13 under par at Mount Juliet. "Dropping only one shot in the last 36 holes was very pleasing," Langer said, "although I shouldn't have even dropped one." That was in the final round, at the 15th, where he bunkered an eight-iron shot. Then he birdied No. 16 from 30 feet.

Allenby, who scored his breakthrough victory in the Honda Open a month earlier, started the final round leading Jose Maria Olazabal and Nick Faldo by three strokes. Olazabal closed with 71 and tied for fourth place, and Faldo shot 73 and tied for eighth. Allenby lost the lead at No. 8, tied with a birdie at No. 10, then bogeyed the 11th en route to 72 to tie for second with Daly.

Bell's Scottish Open—£600,000
Winner: Carl Mason

Winning came as such a shock the first time, Carl Mason didn't know how to act. He did the second time, though. The instant the Bell's Scottish Open was safely in his bag, he hurled his cap to the ground and punched the air. "I'm gobsmacked — I didn't think the second one would come so soon," said Mason, practically dumbstruck when he won the Turespana Masters Open de Andalucia in February. After 21 years of frustration, he had won twice in one season.

Mason, who trailed from the start, set up this win with a blistering nine-under-par 61 in the third round, a run of eight birdies and an eagle at the Gleneagles King's Course. It was the jewel in a 15-under-par 265 total that beat Peter Mitchell by one stroke. Mason's closing-round 68 was another jewel, coming in a furious wind and rain storm.

"In those conditions, you know it's going to be a battle," Mason said. He started the final round one stroke behind Mitchell and two ahead of Jesper Parnevik and Howard Twitty. Mason birdied the third and fourth holes, bogeyed No. 5 and birdied No. 6. Parnevik's bid ran out of gas after birdies at the 13th and 14th. He finished in third place. Twitty, the first-round leader with 64, double-bogeyed the par-three 16th, shot 74, and dropped to 16th.

Mason picked up speed at the turn, chipping in at the 10th and 11th holes, and told himself, "This must be your day." He was leading by four strokes until Mitchell drove the 310-yard 14th, to within five feet, and made the eagle two. Both bogeyed the short 16th, and Mason also bogeyed the 17th, missing his par from four feet. Then a six iron to six feet set up a birdie at the 18th. He had his second victory. "It wasn't any easier," he said.

British Open Championship—£1,100,000
Winner: Nick Price

See Chapter 5.

Heineken Dutch Open—£650,000
Winner: Miguel Angel Jimenez

In a tournament in which par was utterly destroyed, and in a field that contained such notables as Colin Montgomerie, Ian Woosnam and Jose Maria Olazabal, it was a lesser-known Spaniard, Miguel Angel Jimenez, who solved the Hilversum course in Utrecht, The Netherlands, for a two-stroke victory in the Heineken Dutch Open. Jimenez, 30, a former caddie in his seventh season on the PGA European Tour, made a splash himself when he turned back Nick Faldo to win the 1992 Piaget Open. This time his toughest opponent was himself.

Jimenez led the first round, trailed by one stroke in the second, and regained the lead and entered the final round with a two-stroke lead on Peter Mitchell, and was out in a solid two-under-par 34. Then the tournament almost got away from him. He stumbled to three consecutive bogeys from the 11th, and Howard Clark slipped through the opening and took the lead. "I was worried after the 13th," Jimenez said, "but then my putt at the 15th gave me a lot of confidence and I felt then I could win." Jimenez birdied three of the last four holes, first holing a 20-foot putt for a two at the 15th, then getting the 16th and 18th, both par fives, wrapping up a tournament card of 65-68-67-70–270, 18 under par. It was a strong win against a strong field. Clark closed with a 67 and finished second by two strokes. Montgomerie finished fourth, Ernie Els seventh, Woosnam 23rd and Olazabal 26th.

Scandinavian Masters—£650,000
Winner: Vijay Singh

It was billed as the Scandinavian Masters, but for a while it looked like a preview of the future of European golf. Bernhard Langer nearly missed the 36-hole cut when he bogeyed four of his last 12 holes, but there was Sven Struver, the "other German" despite his Nordic name, sharing the second-round lead with Pierre Fulke, 23, a Swede despite his French-German-sounding name. And Per Haugsrud, one of the rarest of tournament golfers — a Norwegian — was crowding the lead in the third round.

But after the spectators got a glimpse of the future, the present took over, and the irony was almost too ironic. The old adage, "Beware the sick golfer," was practically created for oft-injured Mark McNulty, but he was the victim this time. Vijay Singh, whose back ached so badly he contemplated withdrawing, charged to a final-round 64 for a three-stroke victory over McNulty, whose own charge was too little and came too late.

"This is one of the best victories I've ever had," said Singh, who trailed by three strokes entering the final round. He crushed the Drottningholm course near Stockholm with a 20-under-par total of 268. McNulty, who started four strokes back, surged with three successive birdies from the 15th hole.

Singh was on pace for a course record when he birdied four of the first five holes and eagled the par-five seventh with a 20-foot chip. He birdied the 10th and 11th, both from 12 feet. But big drives at those holes triggered a painful twitch in his back. "Fortunately, the next few holes I could take irons," he said. "I wasn't worried about records. I just wanted to win."

BMW International Open—£525,000
Winner: Mark McNulty

There's nothing like Germany and a chart full of medical woes to bring out the best in oft-afflicted Mark McNulty. This time McNulty, four-time German Open champion, playing with a delicate neck (a cricket injury) and painful and swollen mosquito bites, outran the field and rejuvenated strongman Seve Ballesteros to take the BMW International Open at St. Eurach in Munich. It was his 13th European victory. "I'm old as the wind, but the wind is still blowing," said McNulty, 40.

McNulty and Ballesteros trailed all the way and opened the final round five strokes off Darren Clarke's lead. Ballesteros threw down the gauntlet with birdies on the first three holes. McNulty responded with a chip-in eagle at No. 1 and then three birdies en route to a seven-under-par 65 that edged Ballesteros by a stroke. McNulty posted rounds of 70, 71, 68 and 65 for a 274 total, 14 under par, to Ballesteros' 69-68-72-66–275. Ballesteros, warned against slow play in the first and fourth rounds, carded seven birdies and one bogey in his closing 66.

The tournament was decided down the final stretch. McNulty had birdied No. 8 from 20 feet to make the turn in 31, matching Ballesteros. McNulty locked up the victory at the 219-yard 17th, where he dropped a 20-foot birdie putt for his third two. Ballesteros, meanwhile, had to save par from seven feet at the 17th, and caught the rough with his tee shot at the 18th.

It helped everyone that Clarke refused to rein in his aggressive game in the final round. He made five more birdies, for a total of 28 in the tournament, but he also suffered four bogeys and a double bogey for a 73 and fourth place. Mark Roe birdied four of the first six holes and finished with a 69 for third place alone.

Hohe Brucke Austrian Open—£250,000
Winner: Mark Davis

It's in the books as a two-stroke victory, but Mark Davis' win over Philip Walton in the Hohe Brucke Austrian Open actually was much tighter. In fact, it was decided by Walton's error on the final tee. Davis, trailing by two strokes, exploded into the lead with a run of two birdies and an eagle. Then Walton, who led through the second and third rounds, misclubbed at the 18th, drove out of bounds, and Davis had the second victory of his eight-year career, both in this event.

"I have no idea why I play so well in Austria," said Davis, who had scores of 68, 69, 69 and 64 for a 270 total, 18 under par. Davis trailed England's Phil Golding by two strokes in the first round, then trailed Walton by four in the next two rounds. He started fast in the fourth round. He birdied the first and fifth holes, and gained more ground at No. 9, dropping a 12-footer for a birdie. Walton, playing behind him, suffered a three-putt bogey there. Then Davis birdied the 14th off a wedge to eight feet; birdied the 15th, from 20 feet, and eagled the par-five 16th, a three-wood second to three feet, for a two-stroke lead. Just as crucial, it turned out, was his par-saving 15-footer at the 17th. Walton had come to life and caught him with birdies at the 16th and 17th.

Now the fatal 18th. Most golfers were hitting a two iron off the tee, but Walton pulled his three wood to the surprise of many. He sliced the tee shot out of bounds and took a double-bogey six. "I had played so well all week, and I fancied the three wood," he said, puzzled. "It's a great pity to lose like that."

Murphy's English Open—£600,000
Winner: Colin Montgomerie

Colin Montgomerie has this dramatic way of ringing down the curtain. In the Peugeot Open de Espana in May, it was a wedge to two feet at the final hole. Now, at Murphy's English Open in mid-August, it was a four iron to eight feet — once again at the final hole. Two great shots, two victories. But this one, his fifth career victory, was different. "It's very special to win for the first time on British soil," he said.

Montgomerie, trailing all the way, entered the final round two strokes behind Des Smyth, who promptly opened the door by refusing to tone down his game after taking the lead with a third-round 66. "I'll play aggressively tomorrow, and to hell with the consequences," Smyth said. He was steady until the back nine. There, he bogeyed the 13th and 14th holes, played the Forest of Arden course in Warwickshire in two-over-par 74, and tied for fourth place.

The battle was between Montgomerie and Barry Lane. Lane, with four birdies going out, made the turn in three-under 33. Monty, with birdies at three of the first six holes, was out in 35. They were tied at 12 under, one stroke behind Smyth. Lane moved in front with two clutch birdies, from 20 feet at the 13th and 15 feet at the 15th. Monty and Smyth both bogeyed the 13th and 14th. Monty got one stroke back with a birdie at the 15th, where he fired a seven iron to 20 feet. He then birdied the par-five 17th on two putts, and Lane bogeyed the hole. They were tied at 13 under par.

Then came Montgomerie's curtain-dropper, the 210-yard, par-three 18th. Monty launched a four iron to eight feet, dropped the putt, and picked up his second title of the year on a card of 70-67-68-69–274, 14 under par. Said an exuberant Monty, "I'm playing well enough to win any tournament I enter."

Volvo German Open—£650,000
Winner: Colin Montgomerie

Colin Montgomerie didn't wait until the 18th hole this time, but he was just as dramatic, chalking up his second consecutive victory and his third of the season, a one-stroke win over hard-closing Bernhard Langer in the Volvo German Open in Dusseldorf. Earlier, Montgomerie was calling his work "stupid, crazy and totally unacceptable." That was after a double-bogey six at No. 9, his final hole in the second round. Two rounds later, he was talking about the 1995 Ryder Cup. "I want to win one of the 10 automatic spots," he said. "I can't rely on getting picked."

Montgomerie had rounds of 65, 68, 66 and 70 for a 19-under-par 269 total that held off Langer, who was seeking his sixth German Open. Langer's closing 68 fell one stroke short. Monty's earlier battle was with Welshman Phillip Price, the second-round leader, whom he caught in the third round with an eagle-birdie-birdie burst starting at the 12th hole, against a birdie-bogey-bogey stretch.

Price took a three-putt bogey at No. 1 in the fourth round, and Montgomerie widened the gap with a birdie at No. 3 from 10 feet, and sent a wedge to one foot at No. 8 for another birdie. Meanwhile, Langer, who had started three strokes behind, was making his move with three birdies in five holes from No. 2. He also birdied the 12th to go to 18 under par, but Monty birdied the 12th and the 13th — the latter with another wedge to one foot — and got to 21 under. Montgomerie then faltered, with two bogeys over the last five holes, including the 18th, but Langer couldn't capitalize on his lapse.

Canon European Masters—£668,000
Winner: Eduardo Romero

The calendar said September, 1994, but the golfers said it was Ryder Cup, 1995. The Canon European Masters at Crans-sur-Sierre in the Swiss Alps was the first PGA European Tour event counting for 1995 Ryder Cup points. But the European chase failed. Argentinian Eduardo Romero, the Tisettanta Italian Open winner in May, beat Sweden's Pierre Fulke, 23, by one stroke. It was Fulke's best finish ever.

"I put pressure on Eduardo at the start and I felt I could still beat him when I birdied at 12 and he bogeyed," Fulke said. But he missed a birdie at the 17th in a hot finish and had to settle for a Ryder Cup windfall, with such players as Sam Torrance, Nick Faldo, Bernhard Langer and Seve Ballesteros chasing him.

"This is one of the best wins of my career, because of the strength of the field," Romero said, after his rounds of 64, 68, 66 and 68 for a 266 total, 22 under par. Fulke, two strokes behind going into the final round, passed Romero with three birdies in the first four holes, two of them from 15 feet. Romero answered with three in succession from No. 5, all from inside five feet, and led by three strokes. Fulke wedged to two feet and birdied the long eighth, but Romero's lead was back to three when he birdied the 10th from four feet to Fulke's bogey out of a bunker.

At the 12th, Fulke made a tap-in birdie and Romero missed the green and bogeyed. Then Romero birdied the par-five 14th, hitting a three wood 265 yards out of the rough to 15 feet and two-putting. He also birdied the 15th to go to 23 under par. Fulke pressed on. He birdied the 16th from eight feet and the 18th from 10, but just missed from six feet at the 17th. So Romero's closing bogey merely cut his margin to one.

European Open—£600,000
Winner: David Gilford

David Gilford, lover of Hereford cattle and the solitude of the country, is anything but retiring with his golf clubs. In February, he won the Turespana Open de Tenerife with a late move, and he made the point again, with a runaway victory in the European Open in mid-September. He showed his heels most of the way, trailing Colin Montgomerie by four strokes in the first round, and Jose Maria Olazabal briefly in the fourth round. "I thought I would need a good score, and to do a 67 from the front is the perfect way to win," Gilford said. His scores were 70, 68, 70 and 67 for a 13-under-par total of 275 at the East Sussex National course in England. Costantino Rocca (70) and Jose Maria Olazabal (69) tied for second place, a distant five strokes back.

"The way David scored this week is unbelievable," said Olazabal, who knew first-hand. He exploded into the fourth round, scoring birdies at the first and second holes from five and 12 feet, and at the fifth and sixth from 12 and five feet. That put him nine under par and one stroke ahead of Gilford. Not for long. Gilford, playing behind him, popped a sand wedge to 18 inches at No. 6 for the birdie that tied Olazabal, then regained the lead with one from 12 feet at No. 8. Olazabal helped by three-putting the ninth for a bogey. Coming home, Gilford locked it up with birdies at the 12th from 10 feet, the 15th from eight and the 16th from 10.

It was the sixth win in Gilford's nine seasons, and the most satisfying. "This is one of the best events on Tour, probably only behind the PGA and Volvo Masters," Gilford said.

Dunhill British Masters—£650,000
Winner: Ian Woosnam

As Ian Woosnam was saying back in May, on winning the Air France Cannes Open. "When I get fed up, I seem to play better." He must have been fed up again here in mid-September, judging from the way he took the Dunhill British Masters title after trailing Seve Ballesteros by seven strokes after the second round and by one after the third. He won by four on a 17-under-par total of 271, touring the famed par-72 Woburn course in rounds of 71, 70, 63 and 67, leaving Ballesteros, Colin Montgomerie, Bernhard Langer and Ernie Els behind.

"I think this will prove a point — don't ever write me off," Woosnam said, explaining it was a bad back, not disinterest, that caused his recent slump. He visited a physiotherapist two weeks before the Dunhill British Masters and came back a new man, as his card suggested — 14 under par for the last 36 holes. Woosie got within one stroke of the lead with a course record-tying 63 in the third round Sunday morning, and the door opened the rest of the way when Ballesteros' putter cooled off. He had nine one-putt greens in his second-round 65, but made only two birdies in his closing 72.

Woosnam started the final round with four successive birdies, and got another on a 12-foot putt at No. 7, and faced just one more threat. Miguel Angel Martin got to 17 under par and made a dazzling save after a drive next to a tree at the 13th. But he didn't survive a visit to the gorse at the 14th. He double-bogeyed. And after Woosie birdied the 16th from 15 feet for a two-stroke lead, Martin went from bad to awful. He bogeyed the 16th from the trees, and drove out of bounds and made eight at the par-five 18th for a 73 and a tie for seventh place.

Trophee Lancome—£600,000
Winner: Vijay Singh

"It was probably the best round I have ever played," Vijay Singh was saying, after a wild finish to a three-man duel gave him the victory by one stroke over Miguel Angel Jimenez and by two over Seve Ballesteros in the Trophee Lancome near Paris. It was his second victory of the season and the sixth in seven years on the PGA European Tour, and few came harder. Singh led or shared the lead in all four rounds at St. Nom la Breteche, but in the superheated fourth round, the lead changed hands at 12 of the 18 holes. Singh settled matters with a birdie at the 17th and a beautifully saved par at the 18th, wrapping up a tournament record 263 total, 17 under par, on scores of 65, 63, 69 and 66. Jimenez shot 67–264, and Ballesteros 65–265. Colin Montgomerie was next in the 66-man field, five strokes behind Ballesteros.

Ballesteros, co-leader in the first round, held the lead after eight holes of the final round, thanks to a three-birdie spurt. And then in the leapfrogging stretch: Singh tied for first place with a chip-in birdie at the 14th. Jimenez went ahead with a 30-foot birdie putt at the 15th. Ballesteros and Singh tied him with birdies at the par-five 16th, where Jimenez stayed with them, saving par with a chip over a sign and a 15-foot putt coming back.

The crack came at the 17th. Ballesteros pulled his drive and bogeyed. Jimenez parred the last two holes, and Singh then won with a birdie at the 17th, on a 15-foot putt, and a tap-in save after a lipped-out bunker escape at the par-three 18th.

Mercedes German Masters—£625,000
Winner: Seve Ballesteros

If Seve Ballesteros' Benson & Hedges victory in May didn't say it convincingly enough, then his whirlwind triumph in the Mercedes German Masters in October did. Ballesteros, at age 37, is not washed up. He conquered this one, coming from six strokes behind in the final round to tie for the lead, then beat two of the game's brightest, Ernie Els and Jose Maria Olazabal, in a playoff.

A bit of history was made in the process. The former Stuttgart-based tournament became the first PGA European Tour event played behind what used to be the Iron Curtain, at the Motzener See Club in the former East Germany. Els led by seven strokes at the halfway mark off a hot 63-64 start, but he cooled to a 70-73 finish. Olazabal (67-67-66-70) and Ballesteros (68-70-65-67) tied him at 270, 18 under par.

Els led by four strokes with seven holes left, but squandered two of them when he double-bogeyed the par-three 12th. Olazabal had a ragged front nine, with two birdies, an eagle, a bogey and a double bogey, for a net gain of one stroke. Then he moved to within one stroke of Els with a birdie at the 13th. Ballesteros, gaining steam with three birdies on the first nine, then birdied the 10th, 13th and 16th and was waiting at 18 under par while the other two missed the victory by missing the 18th green. Olazabal got a chip-and-putt par, and Els a chip-and-two-putt bogey. In the playoff at the 18th, Els and Olazabal parred, but Ballesteros fired a six iron to about 30 inches.

"I didn't think there was much chance for me," said Ballesteros, who was 13 under par for the last 37 holes. "I needed to test myself."

Alfred Dunhill Cup—£1,000,000
Winner: Canada

See Chapter 8.

Toyota World Match Play Championship—£600,000
Winner: Ernie Els

See Chapter 9.

Chemapol Trophy Czech Open—£500,000
Winner: Per-Ulrik Johansson

For those who like their golf history scrambled, the Chemapol Trophy Czech Open was the place to be. This was the easy part: It was the first new tournament held behind the old Iron Curtain, but the second event ever (the Mercedes German Masters was moved earlier this year). It was held at Marianske Lazne Golf Club in the Czech Republic. And then the scores told another story. Per-Ulrik Johansson, the 1991 PGA European Tour Rookie of the Year, took his second career victory, with scores of 61, 56, 54 and 66 for a 237 total, 11 under par, and won by three strokes over fellow Swede Klas Eriksson in a week filled with sub-60 scoring.

This was a 63-hole tournament. The course, usually 6,753 yards and a par of 71, was played at 15 holes (par 59) for the first three rounds because the 11th, 13th and 14th greens were frozen.

Still, everyone played the same course, and it was a long climb for Johansson. He trailed Gordon Brand, Jr., Sam Torrance and Frank Nobilo (54s) by seven strokes in the first round; trailed Robert Allenby (112) by five in the second, and Nobilo and Sven Struver (178) by one in the third. The final round was played at 18 holes, but with a shotgun start to beat the weather. Johansson's putter was hot. He birdied from 60 feet at No. 2 and 40 feet at No. 8. He drove the green at the 299-yard 10th and two-putted. He holed from 10 feet at the 14th and from 12 feet at the 15th, and he two-putted the par-five 17th after reaching the green in two with a three wood.

Volvo Masters—£750,000
Winner: Bernhard Langer

This was the Volvo Masters, final event of the 1994 PGA European Tour, at Valderrama, Spain, with an elite field of 54 players. The moment screamed for a great finish, and that's what it got, a shootout to the end. Bernhard Langer — who shot nine-under-par 62 in the second round and who had come from behind in the fourth round — wasn't going to win this title without one last fight. Seve Ballesteros needed a par at the 18th hole to tie him, and Colin Montgomerie needed a birdie. But both bogeyed, and Langer had his first Volvo Masters, his second victory of the year.

"Anyone who can shoot 62 round this course," said Montgomerie, "deserves to win any tournament." That was the tribute to Langer for the jewel in his card of 71-62-73-70–276, eight under par. Langer needed only 23 putts after an alignment tip from Anders Forsbrand. Langer chipped in at No. 1, birdied Nos. 5 and 9 from seven and four feet, and roared home with birdies at the 10th, 11th, 13th, 16th, 17th and 18th from five, 12, 35, 12, 12 and 25 feet. "I didn't think it was possible to score a 62 at Valderrama," Langer said.

The final round was a mad dash. Ballesteros led Montgomerie and Langer by two strokes, and Miguel Angel Jimenez by three. Jimenez tied for the lead briefly, then faded with 71 made up of two eagles, two birdies, four bogeys and a double bogey. Vijay Singh charged with five birdies for a front-nine 32. Langer birdied the par-five 17th from eight feet to tie Ballesteros, then saved par from a bunker at the 18th. A cranky driver stopped Ballesteros. A stray shot cost him a birdie chance at the 17th. Another at the 18th forced him to chip sideways, then he bunkered his approach, blasted to three feet, and bogeyed for 73 and a tie for second place with Singh, one shot behind. Jimenez and Montgomerie tied for fourth place.

Johnnie Walker World Championship—$2,500,000
Winner: Ernie Els

See Chapter 10.

13. Asia/Japan Tours

An apt description of the 1994 season in Japan borrows from the Bible. David and Goliath. In this scenario, though, Goliath wins ... and wins big. David, in this modern switch on the fabled battle, is Brian Watts, a 28-year-old American from Oklahoma whose once-promising career had been going nowhere until his lack of success elsewhere led him to Asia in early 1993. Goliath is 47-year-old Masashi (Jumbo) Ozaki, almost without argument now considered Japan's greatest player ever.

That Watts was even in a position to threaten Ozaki's preeminent position in Japanese golf was hairbreadth. He was invited to play on the Japan PGA Tour only because he led the 1993 Asian Tour money list, and he finished first by an eyelash. Watts made the most of the opportunity, particularly in his second season in Japan in 1994. Winning more often than any American since David Ishii, Watts moved into the month of October seemingly on the verge of seizing the Japan PGA Tour's No. 1 position and depriving Ozaki, just as Hajime Meshiai had done the year before.

When Watts scored back-to-back victories in the Bridgestone Open and rich Philip Morris Championship for his fourth and fifth wins of the season, he was right on the heels of Ozaki on the money list. The stone had been hurled from the sling. But, Jumbo ducked, and reacted. In three consecutive weeks, in the heart of the toughest, most lucrative part of the season in Japan, Ozaki won the Daiwa International by 15 strokes, Visa Taiheiyo Masters by five, and Dunlop Phoenix, against a truly powerful international field, by one over Tom Watson.

With that seventh victory of the season and 69th of his career in late November, Ozaki adjourned for the year, his record earnings at ¥215,468,000 — $2,183,106 on the World Money List — and his No. 9 position on the Sony Ranking. Journalists in Japan credit Jumbo with an eight-victory season "in the mid-1970s," presumably in one of his first two of six No. 1 seasons, but no edition of *The World of Professional Golf* for that decade lists him with more than five victories in any one season.

Regardless, 1994 was clearly Ozaki's best year ever. Despite his marvelous record, though, we may never know just how good he is. On the few occasions that he has ventured overseas some years, he has never made much of an impression. Ozaki indicated he intended to work hard and take a serious run at the world's four major championships in 1995. Time will tell.

Watts pretty much forfeited his chances of overhauling Ozaki in the late season when he returned to America for two weeks after his fifth win, but he told *Sports Illustrated's* Tom Verducci that his success in Japan would not prompt him to again try the U.S PGA Tour, for which he qualified only once in five tries and lost his card after a single season. Instead, he planned to play at least one more season in Japan.

Tsuneyuki (Tommy) Nakajima, regaining much of his old form over the past two seasons, was the only other player with more than two wins in Japan in 1994. He picked up three victories in the first two months of the season, then was nothing more than a frequent contender the rest of the year.

Americans Ishii, the Hawaiian who was the No. 1 money winner in Japan in 1987, and Todd Hamilton, the Asian Tour leader in 1992, each won twice, along with Japan's Yoshinori Mizumaki, the only other multiple winner.

Because of Ozaki's exploits in the late season, foreign visitors did not fare as well as usual. Other than the non-Japanese regulars on the circuit, the only foreigners who won titles were Corey Pavin in the Tokai Classic and Robert Gamez in the Casio World Open.

One other overseas player won in Japan. Carlos Franco of Paraguay, who followed directly in the footsteps of Hamilton and Watts onto the Japan Tour via the invitation he earned as the 1994 Asian Tour champion, won the Gene Sarazen Jun Classic in September. Back in February, he set up his finest season with victory in the opener of the Asian Tour season — the Manila Southwoods Philippine Open.

That started a string of seven victories by players from all parts of the world ... except Asia. In order, David Frost of South Africa at Hong Kong, Emlyn Aubrey and Brandt Jobe of the United States in India and Thailand, Joakim Haeggman of Sweden in Malaysia, Frank Nobilo of New Zealand in Indonesia and Craig McClellan of the United States in the Sabah Masters. Hong Chia Yuh broke the spell for Asia when he scored a rare victory by an amateur in his homeland in the Republic of China Open. A native son — Jong Duck Kim — won again in the Korea Open; and Ozaki made the Dunlop Open, the season-ending event on the Asia circuit as well as an early stop on the Japan PGA Tour, the first of his 1994 victories

Manila Southwoods Philippine Open—US$250,000

Winner: Carlos Franco

Carlos Franco got off to a fast start on his big season on the Newsweek Asian Tour with a playoff victory in the Southwoods Philippine Open at Manila. Franco, who helped put theretofore-obscure Paraguay on the world golfing map in 1993 when his team shocked Scotland in the opening round of the Alfred Dunhill Cup at St. Andrews, came from three strokes off the pace with 71 in the final round at Southwoods Country Club to force the playoff. He caught South Korea's Sang Ho Choi, winner of the 1991 Korean Open on the Asian Tour and 37 other events in his native country, at 280 and won the first title ever on the circuit by a Paraguayan.

Both players lingered close to the pace throughout as American Mike Cunning, Michael Blewett and Chul Sang Cho led the first day with 67s. Choi shot 68 Friday and joined Cunning at the top at 138. Franco, one of five golf pro brothers from Asuncion, shot 69 for 141 and remained three shots behind Choi when both posted 68s Saturday. The two men handed the lead back and forth all day Sunday, finally ending in the tie when Franco three-putted the 17th and Choi birdied the 18th. However, the Korean was in two bunkers on the playoff hole and Franco won easily with a par. Scotland's Colin Montgomerie, with a 70-70 finish, placed third.

Kent Hong Kong Open—US$250,000
Winner: David Frost

Nothing obscure about the second winner on the 1994 Asian Tour. Unlike Carlos Franco, South Africa's David Frost ranks among the leading players in the world and he joined a distinguished roster of past champions when he won the Kent Hong Kong Open at Fanling's Royal Hong Kong Golf Club in late February. Frost, whose excellent credentials include eight victories on the U.S. PGA Tour and two in Africa's Million Dollar Challenge, had to go the same route as Franco, landing the title when he defeated Craig McClellan on the first hole of a playoff. Both men closed with 67s for 274 totals. McClellan got his when he holed a seven-iron approach for an eagle at the 18th hole.

Frost and McClellan, 38, winless in his 10 years on the Asian Tour, trailed Barry Lane, the British Ryder Cupper, by two strokes entering the final round with four lesser lights in between. Lane had taken the lead at 205 with 67 Saturday, supplanting Taiwan's Chen Tze Chung, who took 75 after a 66-68–134 start. Chen, in turn, had replaced Canadian Philip Jonas, whose opening 65 was the best among a horde of low scores. Corey Pavin looked like the winner most of the round Sunday, but a bogey at the last hole dropped him to nine under par, where he finished with Lane, one shot behind Frost and McClellan. McClellan hit his approach shot into a bunker in the playoff and lost to Frost's solid par.

Classic Indian Open—US$200,000
Winner: Emlyn Aubrey

Emlyn Aubrey, unsuccessful in his brief stint on the U.S. PGA Tour, returned to the arena of earlier triumph and picked up his second career victory on the Asian Tour in early March. The 30-year-old Aubrey, who lost his playing privileges in America after the 1992 season, staged a strong finish at Royal Calcutta Golf Club to win the Classic Indian Open by one stroke over fellow American Brandt Jobe.

Aubrey, who won the Philippine Open in 1989, started strongly at hot, steamy Royal Calcutta, taking sole possession of first place Friday after rounds of 69-70 for 139, three ahead of South Korean Young Il Kim. He let the field back into the game Saturday, though retaining a one-shot lead, when he plummeted to 76. He was at 215, just one stroke ahead of Jobe and Paraguay's Pedro Martinez and only two in front of seven others. At one time or another in the early going Sunday, Jobe and Martinez led or were part of a six-way tie for first place. Then, Aubrey took charge. He birdied the 11th and 12th holes to move two strokes ahead, and subsequent birdies at the 15th and 17th protected the final margin when he bogeyed the 18th for 70 and a 285 total, three under par.

Thai International Thailand Open—US$300,000
Winner: Brandt Jobe

Although this time Brandt Jobe made off with the title, the competition for victory in the Thai International Thailand Open seemed like a continuation of the previous week's Classic Indian Open. Jobe, the runner-up at Royal Calcutta, opened in front with 65 at Bangkok's Tanah City Country Club and went on to a 12-under-par 276 total and a four-shot victory over Lee Porter. Emlyn Aubrey, the winner in India, tied for third with Carlos Franco, who had tied for third with Porter the previous Sunday.

The only interloper was Englishman John Gould, a golf academy operator in France who played on the PGA European Tour 10 years ago. Gould, who started at Tanah City with a pair of 68s and led Jobe by one shot at that point, tied for third with Aubrey and Franco. Jobe, an All-American at UCLA in the late 1980s, regained the lead from Gould and raced five strokes in front of Franco and Australian Chris Gray with 69 Saturday and finished up with 70 Sunday to become the sixth American winner of the Thailand Open. His U.S. predecessors include U.S. PGA Tour regulars Howard Twitty (1975) and Tom Sieckmann (1981).

Benson & Hedges Malaysian Open—US$250,000
Winner: Joakim Haeggman

In the first four weeks of the Asian Tour, the continents of North America, South America and Africa were represented in the winners' circle. It was Europe's turn when the circuit reached Kuala Lumpur for the Benson & Hedges Malaysian Open — in the person of Joakim Haeggman, Sweden's first-ever Ryder Cup player, making his first visit to Asia. Haeggman had a lot of work to do to acquire that title. He went eight extra holes before winning the season's third playoff, in which he faced New Zealand's Frank Nobilo, a fast-rising international standout, and Malaysia's own Periasamy Gunasagaran at Royal Selangor Golf Club. The three had tied at nine-under-par 279.

The first three rounds created a major logjam for the Sunday finale. Craig McClellan opened with 66. Then Carlos Franco, the money list leader and Philippine Open winner, shot 65 Friday, taking a two-stroke lead over McClellan (71) and Gunasagaran (68-69). When the shooting ended Saturday, Franco and Nico Van Rensburg of South Africa were ahead at 208, but 18 others were within three strokes. Haeggman shot 69, Nobilo 68 and Gunasagaran 70 to force overtime play. Nobilo missed a couple of chances before a bogey took him out at the sixth extra hole and Haeggman got the victory when Gunasagaran missed a three-foot par putt.

Sampoerna Indonesian Open—US$250,000
Winner: Frank Nobilo

Disappointed but not discouraged by a playoff loss the previous Sunday in Malaysia, Frank Nobilo made his brief visit pay off with his first victory on the Asian Tour and ninth of his career. Moving in front Friday in the middle of three wet and windy rounds, Nobilo, who was to make an excellent showing in the U.S. Open two months later, followed with solid rounds of 68 and 69 for a 15-under-par 273 total in the Sampoerna Indonesian Open at Kapuk Indah Golf Club in Jakarta and an easy three-stroke triumph.

The New Zealand pro's 69, the first of four rounds in the 60s, put him two strokes off the lead, which he took over Friday with a 67–136, two better than the 69-69–138 of American Gary Webb and three in front of Philip Jonas, Scott Frisch and Scotland Ryder Cupper Sam Torrance, one of the first-round leaders. Although his leading margin slipped to one when he shot 68 Saturday, Nobilo's opposition thinned. Webb shot 67 for 205 and Robert Meyer, another American, 66 for 207, but no one else was within five strokes. Nobilo put the other two contenders away on the back nine, opening a good lead on the first two holes, later adding three consecutive birdies. It was plenty of cushion for two bogeys on the last three holes to fend off runner-up Jerry Smith who closed with 66–276.

Sabah Masters—US$260,000
Winner: Craig McClellan

It was a long time in coming for Craig McClellan. The 38-year-old Michigan native had been playing the Asian Tour for a decade with some success but without a victory before capturing the Sabah Masters, the new addition to the circuit in 1994. The eventual win involved a playoff, as McClellan came from five strokes off the pace at Sabah Golf and Country Club in Kota Kinabalu, Malaysia, to forge a tie and defeat Burma's Kyi Hla Han on the second extra hole.

Things were not promising for McClellan after the first round. He had shot 75 and faced the prospect of missing the 36-hole cut. Canadian Rick Todd had the first-round lead with 68, the only round under 70 the first day. Rob Moss and Pedro Martinez led the second day with 141 as McClellan recovered with 71. Another 71 Saturday left him five shots behind Asia Tour leader Carlos Franco; Jerry Smith, the previous week's runner-up, and Kyi Hla Han. McClellan's final-round 67 put him in the clubhouse with a four-under-par 284 total and the lead, which held up until the Burma pro made par 72 for the tie. McClellan won the playoff at the par-five 18th, the second playoff hole, when he reached the back of the green in two and two-putted for the winning birdie.

Chin Fong Republic of China Open—US$300,000
Winner: Hong Chia Yuh

Who would have thought it would be an unheralded, 20-year-old amateur who would score the first victory of the 1994 Asian Tour season by an Asian golfer? That's what happened in the Chin Fong Republic of China Open when, after the circuit's first seven tournaments went to pros from the United States, Sweden, South Africa, New Zealand and Paraguay, Hong Chia Yuh, a university student from Taipei, survived a late bid by Thailand's Boonchu Ruengkit and registered a one-stroke victory at Taiwan Golf and Country Club. He finished with 68 for a 276 total, 12 under par. It was the first win in 12 years on the Asian Tour by an amateur.

Hong Chia Yuh entered the picture with a seven-under-par 65 in the second round after trailing first-round leader Taichi Teshima of Japan — 66 — by four. Hong's 135 gave him a two-stroke lead over Hsieh Chin Sheng and three over Teshima. The young amateur slipped to 73 Sunday, yielding a one-stroke lead to Hsieh. Ruengkit was one behind him at 209. Hong started with a birdie Sunday and built a four-stroke lead. Back came Ruengkit with four birdies in a row, starting at the 13th, to take the lead. Hong countered marvelously with birdies at the last two holes to secure the victory. The lucrative consolation for the Thai runner-up was the US$50,000 first prize.

Maekyung Korean Open—US$350,000
Winner: Jong Duck Kim

Jong Duck Kim carried on his homeland's tradition with his hard-won victory in the Maekyung Korean Open, next-to-last leg of the Asian Tour. Pitted against strong players from all parts of the world, Korean pros have experienced impressive success in their country's national championship. Since the Korean Open became a stop on the circuit in 1970, South Korean pros have taken the title 11 times. Kim's 1994 victory was the fourth in five years for the home pros. It came the hard way — in a three-man playoff, the fifth in nine weeks on the Asian Tour.

Kim, Canadian Jim Rutledge and American Mike Tschetter finished their 72 holes at Nam Seoul Country Club deadlocked at four-under-par 284 totals after a rather remarkable final round, in which Taiwan's Hsieh Yu Shu let a five-stroke lead (70-66) after 36 holes and a three-stroke lead (70-66-74) after 54 holes escape. Kim and Tschetter, brother of LPGA Tour player Kris, went into the final round trailing by six strokes and Rutledge was eight back at 218. Hsieh fell to 75 Sunday and finished one shot behind Kim, Tschetter (68s) and Rutledge (66). In the playoff, Rutledge went out with a par to birdies by the other two at the par-five 16th and Kim won with a par at the par-three 17th.

Token Corporation Cup—¥75,000,000
Winner: Craig Warren

The 1994 Japan PGA Tour got off to a watery start, which may have worked to the benefit of the winner, Craig Warren of Australia, and to the detriment of the runner-up, Masashi (Jumbo) Ozaki. Heavy rains washed out the third round of the Token Corporation Cup at Kedoin Country Club at Kagoshima. Warren, 30, won for the first time in his three years on the circuit, nipping the fast-closing Ozaki by one stroke with his eight-under-par 208 total. Who knows what might have happened if Ozaki had had that lost round to work with against Warren and the lead.

Yoshitaka Yamamoto and Daisuke Serizawa shared the first-round lead with 69s, one shot ahead of Warren and four others. The Aussie came back with 68 Friday, moving a stroke in front of countryman Brian Jones and Hisayuki Sasaki with his 138. Ozaki, who had started with 74, shot 69 Friday, but still trailed by five when the weather wiped out Saturday play. Ozaki exploded with 66 Sunday for 209 but fell one stroke short.

Daido Drinco Shizuoka Open—¥100,000,000
Winner: Tsuneyuki Nakajima

David Ishii made a spirited defense of his Daido Drinco Shizuoka Open title, but in the end he and the others succumbed to another former winner — Tsuneyuki (Tommy) Nakajima — who won the long-standing tournament in 1983. Nakajima's second Shizuoka victory came on the first hole of a play-off after he and Toru Nakamura, another Japan PGA Tour veteran, tied with eight-under-par 280 totals at Shizuoka Country Club at Hamaoka.

The tournament had a different leader each day — Takaaki Fukuzawa Thursday with 69, Yoshinori Mizumaki Friday with 72-68—140 and Hideki Kase (70-74-66) with Ishii (71-70-69) Saturday at 210. Nakajima trailed by one with his 71-71-69, and Nakamura was three off the pace with his 73-73-67. Nakamura repeated the 67 and Nakajima fashioned 69 to forge the deadlock as Kase shot 72 and Ishii 73 to fall back. Nakajima won with a three-foot par putt in the overtime after Nakamura missed his from six feet. The win was Nakajima's 42nd on the circuit.

United Airlines KSB Sentonaikai Open—¥70,000,000
Winner: Kazuhiro Takami

Kazuhiro Takami put himself in such a strong position after the first three rounds of the United Airlines KSB Sentonaikai Open that he had the luxury of shooting a one-over-par 73 in the final round and not even feeling threatened. In fact, Takami finished the last day just as he had started it — six strokes ahead of everyone else at Kinojyo Golf Club at Sojya. He was seven under par at 281, and runner-up Yoshinori Kaneko, at 287, was the only other par-breaker.

Kaneko led for the first two days with rounds of 66 and 74, Takami sitting just a stroke back after 36 holes. Then, Takami blistered Kinojyo with 67 to establish the six-stroke lead he carried to victory Sunday. Tsuneyuki Nakajima, the previous week's winner at Shizuoka, finished in a four-way tie for third at par 288.

Descente Classic Munsingwear Cup—¥80,000,000
Winner: Brian Watts

Nobody expected it then, but Brian Watts signalled what was in store for him and the Japan PGA Tour when he won the Descente Classic Munsingwear Cup in early April. American Watts didn't exactly come out of the blue, having led the 1993 money list on the Asian Tour and played well enough in Japan to retain his privileges for 1994. He opted to play in Japan rather than defend his Asian Tour title in early 1994, but didn't make much of a splash until the Japan circuit reached Miki and the Century Miki Golf Club.

There, Watts jockeyed with the lead for three rounds, then, just as happened with Kazuhiro Takami in winning the KSB Sentonaikai the previous Sunday, Watts got home with the victory easily Sunday with a one-over-par 73. His 280 total gave him a three-stroke triumph, his first in Japan, over Hideki Kase, Frankie Minoza, Hisao Inoue and Tsukasa Watanabe. Watts led the first day with 67, slipped one behind Tsuyoshi Yoneyama Friday and regained the lead with 69–207, two strokes in front of Australian Roger Mackay, a seven-time winner in Japan over the years. Mackay shot 76 Sunday.

Pocari Sweat Open—¥60,000,000
Winner: Yoshinori Mizumaki

Yoshinori Mizumaki's triumph in the Pocari Sweat Open bordered on the remarkable. After heavy rains had washed out the scheduled first round at Hiroshima Hakuryuko Country Club and shortened the tournament to 54 holes, Mizumaki began play with a par 72 Friday. Normally, 72 is not a bad score, but in this case it left him in a tie for 52nd place.

That's a lot of players to pass in two rounds, but pass them he did. On Saturday, he blazed a 65 and soared into a three-way tie for fourth with Shigeki Maruyama and Seiki Okuda, three behind leader Tsukasa Watanabe, who also shot 65 that day for 134. Mizumaki followed with 66 Sunday, enough to ease him one stroke in front of Watanabe, who shot 70 for 204. Final-round 67s put Richard Backwell and Masayuki Kawamura into a third-place tie at 206.

Tsuruya Open—¥100,000,000
Winner: Tsuneyuki Nakajima

Tsuneyuki (Tommy) Nakajima became the first multiple winner on the 1994 Japan PGA Tour when he captured the Tsuruya Open, a new event replacing the long-standing Bridgestone Aso Open in that spot on the schedule. The talented Nakajima, winning for the 43rd time in his long career, landed his second 1994 title the same way as he did the first — in a playoff.

After starting the week at Sports Shinko Country Club at Yamanohara, site of the 1993 Japan PGA Championship, with 68, two behind co-leaders Hsieh Min Nan, the aging veteran, and Yeh Chang Ting, both from Taiwan, Nakajima moved into a four-way tie for first place with Yeh, Richard Backwell and Kiyoshi Murota at 138. A second 70 Saturday enabled Nakajima to inch into the lead by a stroke over Murota, Chen Tze Chung and Shigeki Maruyama. His closing 71 Sunday was not enough to settle things right away. Tsutomu Higa climbed into a deadlock at 279 with his 67, but lost on the second hole of the subsequent playoff. The two parred the first extra hole, then the 39-year-old Nakajima took the title with a birdie on the next hole.

Dunlop Open—¥100,000,000
Winner: Masashi (Jumbo) Ozaki

Masashi (Jumbo) Ozaki translated international disappointment into domestic tranquility as he launched what was to be his greatest season ever. Enduring an early exit from the famed Masters in America in early April when he missed the 36-hole cut by one stroke, Ozaki made his first 1994 start on familiar ground and won the Dunlop Open for the fourth time in his overwhelming career, edging Taiwan's Hsieh Chin Sheng by one stroke with his 67-68-70-69—274 total, 14 under par on Ibaragi Country Club's East Course, on which he scored all four Dunlop victories.

Besides being an important early stop on the Japan PGA Tour, the Dunlop was also the final destination of the Asian Tour and it settled the Asian Order of Merit in quiet fashion. Although finishing 40th at Ibaragi, Paraguay's Carlos Franco wrapped up the 1994 title and reaped its benefits — playing privileges on the Japan Tour and an invitation to the British Open.

Ozaki started effectively on the long East Course with the 67-68 rounds, building a three-stroke lead over Frankie Minoza and Peter Senior of Australia. Minoza, the top player from the Philippines who won the Dunlop title in 1990, fired 66 Saturday and slipped into a one-shot lead over Ozaki, who shot 70 for 205. Minoza built his lead to three strokes on the first five holes Sunday before Ozaki came alive. Ozaki followed a Minoza bogey at No. 8 with an eagle at No. 9, took the lead with a birdie at the 10th and rode it to victory. Minoza fell four shots away after a double bogey at the 15th and Hsieh got within one stroke with a birdie at the last hole.

Chunichi Crowns—¥120,000,000
Winner: Roger Mackay

His ambition whetted by a near-miss a month earlier, Roger Mackay chose the Chunichi Crowns, one of the early-season's richest events, to play his best golf of the year and roll to his eighth victory on the Japan PGA Tour. The Australian, a regular in Japan for years, opened with a six-under-par 64 at Nagoya Golf Club's Wago course. That gave him a one-stroke lead over Naomichi (Joe) Ozaki and Peter Senior, and he never looked back the rest of the way, posting an 11-under-par 269 total and a two-stroke win over Ozaki.

Mackay widened his leading margin to four over Tsukasa Watanabe and Masanobu Kimura with 67–131 Friday. Ozaki shot 66 Saturday to take over second place, three behind Mackay and his second 67 for 198. Mackay started the day with a bogey and took four against three birdies for 71 Sunday, enough for the two-shot victory. Of note, 57-year-old Teruo Sugihara shot 65 Sunday and finished third at 272.

Fuji Sankei Classic—¥120,000,000
Winner: Kiyoshi Murota

Kiyoshi Murota, who has been around the Japan PGA Tour for many years, chose a lucrative time to seize just the third victory of his career. The 38-year-old Murota, holding his own on a blustery Sunday, came from two strokes off the pace in the Fuji Sankei Classic and, with a one-over-par 72, breezed to a four-stroke win at the Kawana Hotel Golf Club at Ito. His 284 total brought him a ¥21.6 million check.

Defeat was a bitter pill for Toshiaki Odate, who led after the second (71-66–137) and third (73–210) rounds. He was in the thick of the battle Sunday as late as the 16th hole, where he birdied the par five to overtake Murota, who bogeyed there. Abruptly, Toshiaki collapsed, taking a seven on the par-three 17th and a double-bogey six at the last hole for 79. Murota bogeyed the 17th and parred the 18th for the winning 72. Nobuo Serizawa took second place, even though shooting a two-over 73 for 289. Even with 79, Odate salvaged a share of third place with Shigeki Maruyama, who had 69, the day's best round, and Frankie Minoza of the Philippines.

Japan PGA Championship—¥100,000,000
Winner: Hiroshi Goda

A non-exempt, winless pro, Hiroshi Goda had to play his way into the Japan PGA Championship at Lake Green Golf Club in Gifu. His victory prospects seemed nil, since no player who had emerged from a qualifier had ever won the important championship. So, this was the first time as Goda survived the final-round charge of five-time champion Masashi (Jumbo) Ozaki and won by one stroke with his five-under-par 279 total.

Goda, 29, in his 10th season on the Japan PGA Tour, began his victory quest at Lake Green with a five-under-par 66, leading Seiji Ebihara and Yutaka Hagawa by one stroke, and Ozaki by three. A 73 slowed down Goda Friday, Masanobu Kimura slipping into first place a stroke ahead of Goda, Ebihara and Kouki Idoki with a pair of 69s. Back came Goda Saturday with a sparkling 67 that shot him five strokes in front of Ebihara, the runner-up, who put up 72 for a 211 total as Kimura faded with 75. Goda's advantage was peeling away Sunday as Ozaki closed the gap with birdies at the 11th and 12th, but he missed a four-footer for bogey at the 14th. His eventual 68 gave him 280, one shot shy of Goda but five ahead of third-place finishers Ebihara and Noboru Sugai.

Pepsi Ube-Kosan Tournament—¥80,000,000
Winner: Tsuneyuki Nakajima

The 44th victory of Tsuneyuki Nakajima's career had to have been one of the easiest. Nakajima, the leader on the Japan PGA Tour's money list, scored his third 1994 triumph from the front, never behind as he fired four rounds in the 60s and won the Pepsi Ube-Kosan Tournament by three with his 16-under-par 268. It was his second win in three years at Ube Country Club at Ajisucho.

Successive rounds of 65-67-67 can do a lot of damage to the opposition. That's what Nakajima put on the board as he went from a first-place tie with Minoru Hatsumi Thursday to a four-stroke lead over Nobuo Serizawa Friday to an eight-shot lead over five players — Hideto Shigenobu, Kiyoshi Murota, Takaaki Fukuzawa, Tsukasa Watanabe and Brent Franklin — at the end of play Saturday. Nakajima played a steady, sedate round Sunday — two birdies, 16 pars, for 69 and the 268 total. He won by three over Watanabe, five over Samson Gimson, both of whom moved up with 64s.

Mitsubishi Galant Tournament—¥75,000,000
Winner: Katsuyoshi Tomori

Katsuyoshi Tomori obviously wasn't fazed by what he saw over his shoulder as he advanced toward victory in the Mitsubishi Galant Tournament at Hokkaido Hayakita Country Club. Even though he had not won on the Japan PGA Tour in four years, the 39-year-old Tomori had no problem with the pressure of Jumbo Ozaki, Tommy Nakajima and Chen Tze Ming in hot pursuit in the final round and rolled to a six-stroke victory in the season's third rain-abbreviated tournament. It was the fifth victory for Tomori in his long career.

Chen and Eduardo Herrera led the first day with 68s before the weather claimed the Friday round. When play resumed Saturday, Katsuyoshi fired 66 for 135 and took a three-stroke lead over Chen, Nakajima and Norikazu Kawakami. A chip-in birdie at the par-three second hole gave Tomori an early boost Sunday. He followed with three more birdies, took two bogeys and shot 70, widening his margin to a final six strokes over Nakajima, who posted 72 for 211. Chen finished at 212, and Ozaki at 213.

JCB Sendai Classic—¥100,000,000
Winner: Masahiro Kuramoto

It had been a long dry spell for Masahiro Kuramoto. Never before in his 12-year career on the Japan PGA Tour had Kuramoto, with 26 titles on his fine record, gone without a victory for so long. The 26th win had come in the season-ending Daikyo Open in December of 1992. After the unsuccessful 1993 season, which he split between Japan and the U.S. PGA Tour, and the first three months of action on the 1994 Japan PGA Tour, Kuramoto broke through with his 27th win, a two-stroke triumph over Roger Mackay and Toshiaki Sudo in the JCB Sendai Classic at Omote Zoe Golf Club at Shibata.

Little was proved the first day as five players shared the first-round lead with 67s, only one of whom, Frankie Minoza, would remain a contender through the weekend. Kuramoto, who had opened with 71, jumped into third place with a six-under-par 65 Friday, then tied with Minoza and Sudo, one shot behind leaders Craig Warren, the Australian who won the Token Corporation Cup that began the season in March, and Ken Kusumoto. Kuramoto seized the lead Saturday with 67–203, one ahead of Sudo, who shot 68. Mackay took a run Sunday with a front-nine 32, but Kuramoto produced a 31 coming in for 68 and the two-shot win with his 13-under-par 271 total. Nakajima, continuing his fine form, tied for fourth at 275 with Minoza, Warren and Shigenori Mori.

Sapporo Tokyu Open—¥100,000,000
Winner: Yoshinori Mizumaki

Yoshinori Mizumaki became just the year's second multiple winner when he grabbed the Sapporo Tokyu Open in Hokkaido in mid-June. Only Tsuneyuki (Tommy) Nakajima, with three victories, had won more than once when Mizumaki added the Sapporo Tokyu title to his Pocari Sweat victory in early April.

In and out of the lead during the first three rounds, Mizumaki survived a final-round 74 to edge Colombia's Eduardo Herrera by one stroke with his 11-under-par 277 total at Sapporo International Country Club. Yoshinori's seesaw travels to the title began with 65 as he shared the first-round lead with Seiji Ebihara. When he shot 70 Friday, Mizumaki slipped a stroke behind Yoshimi Niizeki, but promptly regained first place with 68 Saturday that projected him three strokes in front of Chen Tze Ming, five ahead of Niizeki and Craig Warren. He needed the padding Sunday when Herrera surged into contention and shot 69, falling the one stroke short. Chen shot 73, but took third place at 279.

Yomiuri Open—¥100,000,000
Winner: Tsukasa Watanabe

The perennial bridesmaid shed that negative distinction in the Yomiuri Open at Osaka's Yomiuri Country Club. Tsukasa Watanabe, who has had more chances to win tournaments than he cares to remember, scored the second victory of his extensive career with the unintentional assistance of runner-up Anthony Gilligan. Watanabe posted a 14-under-par 270 total and won by two over Gilligan.

Watanabe and Gilligan went to the front Friday after Eduardo Herrera, coming off a second-place finish the week before, opened with 64. Gilligan added 64 to his first-round 65 for a 129 total and a three-stroke lead over Watanabe at the end of Friday's play. The two traded places Saturday as Watanabe, who had started with rounds of 68 and 64, fashioned a 67 for 199 to lead Gilligan by one stroke going into the final round. Gilligan's birdie at the 10th and Watanabe's bogey at the 13th put the Aussie in front by a shot, but Watanabe birdied the 15th and Gilligan bogeyed the last two holes to set the final outcome.

Mizuno Open—¥100,000,000
Winner: Brian Watts

His second 1994 victory in Japan came the hard way for Brian Watts, the former NCAA champion out of Oklahoma State. Watts, who had scored a three-shot victory in the early season in the Descente Classic Munsingwear Cup, got win No. 2 in a four-man playoff in the Mizuno Open at Tokinodai Country Club, becoming just the third multiple winner of the season at that point in late June.

The deadlock occurred when Yoshinori Kaneko and Koichi Suzuki overtook Watts and Colombia's Eduardo Herrera, who had carried the lead into the final round with scores of 209 and shot 71s Sunday. Kaneko recorded 68 and Suzuki 71 Sunday. The other three had chances for birdies on the first extra hole — the 433-yard 18th — but only Watts converted ... from 33 feet out of a bunker. Richard Backwell led the first day with 65, then Anthony Gilligan, the previous week's runner-up, took over with 69-66–135 Friday. He floundered to 76 Saturday. Watts, who had trailed Gilligan by one stroke, shot 73 after a pair of 68s to tie for the lead with Herrera.

PGA Philanthropy Cup—¥100,000,000
Winner: Todd Hamilton

How little things changed from one week to the next at the end of June on the Japan PGA Tour. One Sunday after Brian Watts, 28, American, Oklahoma State All-American, Asian Tour season champion won a playoff in the Mizuno Open, Todd Hamilton, 29, American, Oklahoma State All-American, Asian Tour season champion won a playoff in the PGA Philanthropy Cup tournament. Hamilton, who scored two victories in Japan after winning the 1992 Asian Tour money title, picked up No. 3 when he birdied the first extra hole at Golden Valley Golf Club to defeat Eiji Mizoguchi.

Both staged final-round rallies to create the deadlock and force the playoff. Nobuo Serizawa, 34, a 10-time career winner, was in first place after the middle rounds. He shot 66–135 and shared the lead with Tetsu Nishikawa and Yoshimi Niizeki Friday, then took sole possession of first place with 70–205 Saturday, two shots in front of the remarkable, 57-year-old Teruo Sugihara. Hamilton soared on the front nine Sunday with five birdies and an eagle for 29, but shot 38 coming in for 67–278, matching Mizoguchi's 67. He dropped a 12-footer for the winning birdie. Serizawa shot 76 Sunday, but Sugihara missed the playoff by just a single stroke with his 72, tying Chen Tze Chung, Yoshinori Kaneko and Shigeki Maruyama.

Yonex Open Hiroshima—¥80,000,000
Winner: Masashi Ozaki

Masashi (Jumbo) Ozaki launched the major segment of what was to be his greatest of many outstanding seasons with a decisive, come-from-behind victory in the Yonex Open Hiroshima in early July. Ozaki, who had played in only five Japan PGA Tour tournaments in the early season and won the

Dunlop Open, picked on another event in which he had an outstanding track record when he scored his three-stroke victory with his 14-under-par 274 on the Happonmitsu course of Hiroshima Country Club. The win, his career 64th, was his sixth at Hiroshima.

Ozaki quickly erased the four-stroke deficit he faced when he teed off Sunday. Trailing little-known Toyotake Nakao, the leader at 205, and three others, Jumbo birdied the first five holes and went on to a 65 and the three-shot win. Nobuo Serizawa, who had faltered in the final round of the PGA Philanthropy the week before, also made a strong final-round move with 66 and grabbed second place. A second-round 74 had delayed Ozaki's run, as Shinsaku Maeda led the first day and four players — Tsutomu Higa, Yoshitaka Yamamoto, Kouki Idoki and Nakao — held the top spot with 137s after 36 holes. Despite 67 Saturday, Ozaki still trailed by four entering the final round.

Nikkei Cup Torakichi Nakamura Memorial—¥80,000,000
Winner: Toru Suzuki

Toru Suzuki made a long-distance move up the standings over the four rounds of the Nikkei Cup Torakichi Nakamura Memorial tournament, reaching the top and victory the final day with his 20-under-par 268 total, matching the then low 72-hole score of the Japan PGA Tour season shot by Tommy Nakajima in the Pepsi Ube-Kosan in May. It was Suzuki's first Japan PGA Tour victory, as was the Nikkei Cup win in 1993 at Tomakomai Golf Club for Samson Gimson of Singapore.

With an opening 72, Suzuki was tied for 74th place as little-known Zaw Moe of Burma shot a course-record 63 and took a two-stroke lead over Harumitsu Hamano. Suzuki made up a lot of ground Friday with 67, jumping to 24th place as Ikuo Shirahama and Stewart Ginn, the Australian veteran, overtook Moe at 135. Saturday belonged to Yoshinori Kaneko, a strong contender in recent events. Kaneko broke Moe's two-day-old record with a 10-under-par 62 and soared into a one-stroke lead at 201. Suzuki, with 65, was then three back at 204. He capped his surge with 64 Sunday, coasting to a five-stroke final margin over Katsunari Takahashi as Kaneko faded to 73–274, tied for third with Yoshitaka Yamamoto and Satoshi Higashi.

NST Niigata Open—¥60,000,000
Winner: Pete Izumikawa

Pete Izumikawa's career on the Japan PGA Tour seemed to have peaked in 1984 when he won the ANA Sapporo Open and two unofficial 36-hole events. He enjoyed only moderate success over the next 10 years until re-emerging with his fourth title in the NST Niigata Open at Nakajo Golf Club in Niigata the first week of August when the regular Japan PGA Tour schedule resumed after an off-week for sectional action. Izumikawa held off a late threat from Kiyoshi Maita and won by two with his final-round 69 and 12-under-par total.

After trailing leader Hiroshi Ueda by one stroke after the first round with his 67, Izumikawa followed with 70 and moved a stroke in front of Hisashi Nakase and Hiroya Kamide with his 137. Mitsutaka Kusakabe joined Izumikawa and Kamide in first place at 207 Saturday, then Izumikawa moved to the victory Sunday. Maita provided the only serious challenge. He birdied three holes in a row, starting at the 13th, to catch Izumikawa, but he bogeyed the 17th and the winner's last of six birdies wrapped up the title.

Acom International—¥100,000,000
Winner: Naomichi Ozaki

Maybe a change of pace was what Naomichi (Joe) Ozaki needed. Certainly one of Japan's leading players, Ozaki had gone through the first five months of the Japan PGA Tour season without making even a strong run, let alone registering a victory. Up on the schedule came the Acom International, the Stableford-style points tournament at the Seve Ballesteros Golf Club, and Ozaki broke through with that initial 1994 win, the 25th of his career.

Ozaki never led until the final day, but was always within range. Satoshi Higashi compiled 22 points to lead after the first round, then Yasunobu Kuramoto took command for two days. With 16 and 11 points in the first two rounds, he was five ahead of Hirofumi Miyase. He jumped his total to 33 Saturday, leading Miyase and Ozaki (14-2-12) by five. The wheels came off for Kuramoto Sunday. He lost five points and Ozaki charged to a six-point victory with 13 Sunday for a 41 total. Masayuki Kawamura, with the best final round gathering 17 points, was the runner-up.

Maruman Open—¥120,000,000
Winner: David Ishii

David Ishii, the Japanese-American from Hawaii who was the first U.S. citizen to make serious inroads into the spoils of the Japan PGA Tour, added another victory to his record when he prevailed in a playoff for the Maruman Open title. The 39-year-old Ishii, the leading money winner in Japan in 1987 when he scored six of his 13 wins, had not acquired a title since early in the 1993 season before he tied Hirofumi Miyase and Nobuo Serizawa at nine-under-par 279 at Narita Springs Country Club near Tokyo and brought about Maruman's third playoff in the last four years.

The lead changed hands each day at Narita Springs with none of the eventual playoff participants involved. The first day, Anthony Gilligan, Kazunari Matsunaga and Takanori Hano posted 66s. On Friday, Matsunaga was one of five men on top with 137s, among them Carlos Franco, the Asian Tour champion, and Zaw Moe of Burma. Veteran Saburo Fujiki took over Saturday with 206. Ishii was one of three players within a stroke, while Serizawa was at 209 and Miyase at 210. Fujiki plummeted to 78 Sunday, as Ishii shot par, Serizawa 70 and Miyase 69 to forge the deadlock, the latter two both missing fairly short birdie putts at the last hole. Ishii grabbed the title when he dropped a four-foot birdie putt on the first extra hole.

Hisamitsu KBC Augusta Tournament—¥100,000,000
Winner: Brian Watts

Now he was getting worldwide attention. When Brian Watts grabbed his third title of the season on the Japan PGA Tour in the Hisamitsu KBC Augusta Tournament at Shimacho and stood off the late challenge of Masashi (Jumbo) Ozaki in the process, golf followers back home in the United States and elsewhere began to take notice of the hitherto name-in-a-crowd. The 28-year-old Watts led from the second round to the finish at Keya Golf Club and registered a 17-under-par 271 total. Ozaki shot 66 the last day, but fell two strokes short of the winner.

Watts began the tournament with 66, trailing leaders Masayuki Kawamura and Jin Han Lim by a shot. His second-round 67 moved him into the lead by one stroke over Kawamura, then he slipped into a three-way tie at the top with Hsieh Chin Sheng and Tadashi Ezure all at 204 after his 71 Saturday. Hsieh shot 63, the week's best round. Watts was nearly flawless Sunday, clicking off five birdies and taking no bogeys in his closing 67 to keep Ozaki at bay. Hsieh and Ezure had 72s to tie Kawamura at 276, one stroke behind third-place finisher Hiroshi Ueda.

Japan Match Play Championship—¥80,000,000
Winner: Todd Hamilton

Todd Hamilton joined David Ishii as the only overseas players ever to capture the Japan Match Play Championship in the 20th renewal of the event in early September at the Hokkaido Nidom Classic course at Tomakomai. Hamilton smashed Ikuo Shirahama in the 36-hole championship match, 8 and 7, to score his second victory of the year and fourth of his career on the Japan PGA Tour.

Several of Japan's top stars, including former winners Jumbo Ozaki and Tommy Nakajima, did not play in the limited-field event which features the previous year's top 32 money winners, so the top first-round casualties were Naomichi Ozaki and Masahiro Kuramoto. Hamilton defeated Tsuyoshi Yoneyama, 2 up, and Shirahama advanced with a 3-and-1 win over Tsukasa Watanabe. In the second round, Hamilton tripped Katsuyoshi Tomori, 2 and 1, and Shirahama took out Nobuo Serizawa, 4 and 3. The two finalists reached that plateau with 36-hole victories over two Nihon University graduates, Hamilton defeating Shigeki Maruyama, 3 and 2, and Shirahama dropping Ryoken Kawagishi, 4 and 3.

Suntory Open—¥100,000,000
Winner: David Ishii

The American monopoly on Japan PGA Tour victories continued at the Suntory Open. David Ishii made it four in a row for American players as he won his second title in four weeks and the 14th of his career in Japan. It took him an extra hole to do it, though. He tied for first with Hisayuki Sasaki at 11-under-par 277, then deprived Sasaki of his first-ever victory when he dropped a seven-foot birdie putt on the playoff, par-five 18th hole at Narashino Country Club in Inzai.

The lead changed hands every day. Australians Brent Franklin and Bradley Hughes led the first day with 67s, then yielded to Seiki Okuda and Masayuki Kawamura and their 136s. Jumbo Ozaki made his considerable presence felt Saturday, shooting 66 to join Hughes and Kawamura at the top with 206s. Ishii was three strokes back and Sasaki four back at that point. Ishii shot 68 and Sasaki 67 in the final round as Ozaki and Kawamura fell back with 73s and Hughes took a 75. Five players, including Andrew Magee, visiting from the U.S. PGA Tour, missed the playoff by one stroke with 278s.

ANA Open—¥100,000,000
Winner: Masashi Ozaki

Masashi (Jumbo) Ozaki was not about to let another one get away. The Japanese star, who had led and lost the previous week, made a shambles of the opposition in the rain-impaired ANA Open. No surprise there. Ozaki had won the tournament twice in the previous four years and three times in a row in the early 1970s, but never as decisively as he did this mid-September at Sapporo Golf Club. He won by nine strokes, the year's biggest margin to that date, and did so despite double bogeys at the last two holes.

Eiichi Itai had a momentary moment of glory when he shot 65 the first day. Then, it was all Ozaki after rain washed out the Friday round and ordained a 36-hole finish Sunday. Jumbo fired his second 68 Saturday for 136 and a two-stroke lead over Masahiro Kuramoto, three over Itai and Tsuneyuki Nakajima. Basically, it was all over after the morning 18 holes Sunday. Ozaki walloped Sapporo with a nine-under-par 63 for a 199 total and raced to an eight-stroke lead over Kiyoshi Murota, the eventual runner-up. Coasting and perhaps, at age 47, tiring a bit, Ozaki finished with 69–268 and the nine-stroke win his third of the season and 65th career victory in Japan. Murota shot 70 for 277, edging Yoshitaka Yamamoto by one stroke.

Gene Sarazen Jun Classic—¥110,000,000
Winner: Carlos Franco

Once again, an Asian Tour champion proved himself worthy of the one-year exemption it brings on the Japan PGA Tour. Following in the recent footsteps of Brian Watts and Todd Hamilton, Carlos Franco, the 1994 Asian Tour leader, triumphed on the richer, tougher circuit in Japan. With three of Japan's best players and Hamilton in pursuit, the Paraguayan Franco scored a two-stroke victory in the Gene Sarazen Jun Classic at the Rope Club in Shioya.

Franco, the first player from Paraguay to win on any of the six major world tours when he triumphed in the Manila Southwoods Philippine Open in February, led all the way in the Jun Classic. He began with 65 in the rain-interrupted first round and held a one-stroke lead over Lin Chie Hsiang with his 132 total midway through the tournament. His 68 Saturday stretched his lead to five strokes over Hamilton, who came up with 65–205. Even though he wavered with a par 72 Sunday, Franco had enough cushion to withstand, by two strokes, the closing 65 of Tsuneyuki (Tommy) Nakajima, who finished second. Joe Ozaki shot 67 and Jumbo Ozaki 68, tying for third with Hamilton, who had 71.

Japan Open Championship—¥100,000,000
Winner: Masashi Ozaki

If Carlos Franco had any illusions about two wins in a row in Japan, Masashi (Jumbo) Ozaki made short work of those ideas. As one might expect from this great player who numbered four earlier victories in the championship, Ozaki broke from a first-place tie with Jun Classic winner Franco and rumbled to a monstrous, 13-stroke victory in the Japan Open at Yokkaichi Country Club. He broke, by four strokes, the championship's 72-hole record with his 18-under-par 270 total. The margin was believed to be the biggest in the 59-event history of Japan's national championship.

Ozaki and Franco shot 68s in a windy first round before Jumbo took total command. He shot 66 for 134 Friday, taking his first bogey of the tournament on the 36th hole. The winds from the fringes of a typhoon continued to blow Saturday, but didn't faze Ozaki, whose 69–203 elevated him six strokes in front of runner-up Hideki Kase. Todd Hamilton shot 66 and was the only other player with a remote chance. Jumbo ran off five birdies, took no bogeys, shot 67 and chalked up the 13-stroke victory over Kase, who fell to 74, and David Ishii, who shot 70. Franco, who floundered in the middle rounds, closed with a 67 to tie for fifth place at 285.

Tokai Classic—¥110,000,000
Winner: Corey Pavin

Corey Pavin, a major money winner again on the 1994 U.S. PGA Tour but with just one victory to show for it, went title-hunting in Japan in October and came back with the Tokai Classic, a tournament won by Larry Nelson and Mark O'Meara in years gone by. It was not easy pickings. Pavin clung to an overnight lead and beat Taiwan's Hsieh Chin Sheng by one stroke on Miyoshi Country Club's West Course.

Pavin opened the Tokai Classic with 68, one stroke ahead of Hisayuki Sasaki, who lost the Suntory Open to David Ishii in a playoff. The two traded places Friday as Corey shot 69 for 137 and Hisayuki added 67 to his first-round 69 in a wild round that included an eagle and a double bogey. Pavin went ahead to stay Saturday, making four birdies in the middle of the round to shape his 68–205 and a two-stroke lead over Hiroshi Ueda. Hsieh was third at 210 and advanced Sunday with 68–278. Pavin had three birdies and three bogeys for a par 72 and his winning 277. Ueda (73) finished third at 280 with Akiyoshi Omachi and Vijay Singh.

Asahi Beer Golf Digest Tournament—¥150,000,000
Winner: Eiji Mizoguchi

There was no denying Eiji Mizoguchi at the Asahi Beer Golf Digest Tournament. After six seasons of futility on the Japan PGA Tour, Mizoguchi got himself on a roll at Tomei Country Club and staged the lowest-scoring finish of the season to capture his first title by a runaway five strokes. His 19-under-par 265 total was the lowest 72-hole score of the season.

Neither Mizoguchi or Hiroshi Ueda were in sight during the first two rounds. Five players — Masayuki Kawamura, Hisayuki Sasaki, Stewart Ginn, Eiichi Itai and Ken Kusumoto — shot 66s Thursday, then Pete Izumikawa and Hiroya Kamide moved in front Friday with 133s. At that point, Mizoguchi was at 70-68–138 and Ueda at 69-68–137. Ueda then produced a sizzling 63 and Mizoguchi fell in two behind with Ginn. Mizoguchi never slowed down, firing an eight-birdie 63 Sunday to put the long-sought victory on ice. Ginn, with 68, and Ueda, with 70, tied for second at 270.

Bridgestone Open—¥120,000,000
Winner: Brian Watts

One of the most remarkable stretches in the history of the Japan PGA Tour began with the Bridgestone Open and the fourth 1994 victory of previously unheralded American Brian Watts. Skeptics had been expecting the bubble to burst, but the only bubbles that were bursting in Watts' face were from the champagne of victory. The Bridgestone triumph was Watts' most impressive because the field that week was enhanced by the presence of a group of U.S. PGA Tour stars, led by Nick Price.

After sitting two strokes off the lead Thursday behind Kiyoshi Maita's 66, Watts moved three strokes into the lead Friday with 67 for 135. Seven regulars were at 138, with the likes of Price and Jumbo Ozaki lurking at 139. Those two played together, packed the gallery and remained in contention. But the day belonged to Watts, who shot 67 and widened his margin to five strokes with his 202 total. Ozaki, with 68, was next at 207, and Price was among three players at 209. Watts responded to the final-round pressure and a double bogey at the 11th hole that cut seriously into his lead with two birdies on the last four holes to get back to par for the round and a 274 total, 14 under par, for the week. Mark Calcavecchia charged Sunday with 66 to pick off second place with 277, one shot ahead of Roger Mackay.

Philip Morris Championship—¥200,000,000
Winner: Brian Watts

Now, Brian Watts constituted a genuine threat to Jumbo Ozaki's supremacy on the 1994 Japan PGA Tour. By winning the Philip Morris Championship, the richest tournament of the season, Watts moved a victory ahead of Ozaki and within close striking range of Jumbo on the money list. The Philip Morris event, successor to the ABC Lark Cup at the ABC Golf Club in Tojo, put up ¥200 million, by far the biggest purse of the year, and the streaking

American picked up the ¥36 million first-place check with his 12-under-par 276 total and one-stroke victory over Jumbo Ozaki, brother Joe and Duffy Waldorf, the U.S. PGA Tour regular.

Hot rounds put the lead in different hands each of the first three days. Kiyoshi Murota was in front Thursday after 66, then Joe Ozaki took over Friday with 68-66–134. Waldorf took a share of the lead when he shot 68 Saturday, joining Tsuyoshi Yoneyama (65) and Masahiro Kuramoto (70) at 206. The Ozakis were at 207 and Watts, after rounds of 71-66-71 was at 208. Brian was steady for victory Sunday with his four-birdie 68. The Ozakis both shot 70s to tie Waldorf and his 71 for 277.

Daiwa International—¥170,000,000
Winner: Masashi Ozaki

Perhaps all Jumbo Ozaki needed was a serious challenge. Whether or not the run that Brian Watts had taken the previous two weeks had any effect on Ozaki's approach to the remaining sequence of rich events on the Japan PGA Tour, he went after them with a vengeance, starting with the Daiwa International at Hatoyama Country Club in Saitama. When he was finished with that opposition, which included a small contingent of overseas players, Ozaki had destroyed them with a 15-stroke victory.

Jumbo was in charge from start to finish. He first put 65 on the board to lead by three over brother Joe and Todd Hamilton, then widened the gap to four over Joe on Friday, shooting just a par round in strong winds that day. The margin went to seven Saturday with his 70–207. Mike Reid of the United States and Peter McWhinney of Australia were at 214. Jumbo saved the best for last, shooting 63 that tied the Hatoyama course record Sunday. The lead soared to a final 15 over Fuzzy Zoeller, whose 68 jumped him into his sixth second-place finish of the season. It was win No. 67 for Ozaki, his fifth of 1994, and the ¥30.6 million prize gave him a good cushion over Watts, who had returned to the United States for a two-week break.

Sumitomo Visa Taiheiyo Masters—¥150,000,000
Winner: Masashi Ozaki

By the end of the week of the Sumitomo Visa Taiheiyo Masters, Jumbo Ozaki had taken on the resemblance of a steamroller or, as he later put it, of George Foreman, the American boxer of the same age, who had just won the heavyweight championship of America. For the second week in a row, Ozaki never gave the opposition a chance, again leading from wire to wire. At the Taiheiyo Club's picturesque Gotemba course near Mount Fuji, he settled for a five-stroke margin, although shooting a duplicate 18-under-par 270 total. He again left an American, this time Bob Estes, well behind in second place after Estes had shared first place with him midway through the tournament.

Ozaki birdied five of his last eight holes Thursday for 66 to take a one-stroke lead over five other players, including Tommy Nakajima, Roger Mackay, Toru Nakamura, Satoshi Higashi and American Larry Mize. Estes caught

Jumbo at 135 the second day with a 67, Ozaki retaining the share of the lead with an eagle at the par-five 18th. Another strong finish the next day — birdies on the last four holes — gave Ozaki a three-shot lead over Yoshinori Mizumaki and Eiichi Itai. Estes moved within two shots after 12 holes Sunday, but Jumbo pulled away after Bob bogeyed the 14th, finished with 67 for the 270 and the five-shot win. With the ¥27 million prize, he broke the Japan PGA Tour money record, his own, with earnings of ¥188,468,000.

Dunlop Phoenix—¥150,000,000
Winner: Masashi Ozaki

Typically, the Dunlop Phoenix had the strongest foreign contingent of the Japan PGA Tour season, but that didn't matter to Jumbo Ozaki, who completed his splendid three-in-a-row victory run with a one-stroke victory in the rain-shortened, 54-hole tournament at Phoenix Country Club in Miyazaki. The seventh 1994 victory, which carried his earnings over the ¥200 million mark, also completed his season, his No. 1 position assured for the fourth time in the last six years and sixth time in his long career.

Ozaki needed all of his skills in the Dunlop Phoenix, and a final-round 65 to take a one-stroke victory over Tom Watson, who led the two rounds that surrounded the Friday washout. Actually, Watson shared first place Thursday with Barry Lane, Ernie Els and Todd Hamilton. Then, after the rain Friday, Watson came back with 68 Saturday and took a one-stroke lead over Lane and Nobuo Serizawa. Ozaki sat two shots off the lead at 136 with brother Joe and David Ishii. On Sunday, he fired the lowest fourth-round score by a winner in Dunlop Phoenix history — 65 — for a 201 total, 15 under par, yet he just defeated Watson by one stroke. Watson had reasonable birdie chances at three of the last four holes and left an eagle putt short for the tie at the last hole. Lane double-bogeyed the 17th and finished in a tie for third place at 204 with Serizawa and Scott Hoch of the United States, who shot a final-round 64. Brian Watts, who returned from America and posted a 209 total, tied for 16th place.

Casio World Open—¥150,000,000
Winner: Robert Gamez

The Casio World Open has been dominated over its 14-year history by American and European winners. Add Robert Gamez, the 26-year-old Las Vegas resident who caught fire at the end of the 1994 season with victories in an unofficial event at Pebble Beach and the Casio World Open, which he won by four strokes at Ibusuki Golf Club at Kaimoncho. His 17-under-par 271 total established that margin over Scott Hoch, who finished third the previous Sunday at Phoenix and won the Casio World in 1982 and 1986. Until those victories, Gamez had come up an also-ran since his rookie year of 1990, when he won at Tucson and in The Nestle Invitational, where he holed a seven-iron shot for an eagle two on the last hole.

Graham Marsh, a familiar foreign face in Japan, with 25 wins, who is now playing on the Senior PGA Tour in the United States, returned to Japan at year's end and led the first day with 66. When he fell back with 73 Friday, Gamez charged into first place with his 68-66–134 total, one stroke ahead of Hisayuki Sasaki and Shinji Ikeuchi. Gamez built his lead to two over Wayne Smith of Australia with 68–202 Saturday as Hoch and Eiji Mizoguchi moved into third place with 67s for 206. Hoch caught Gamez with three birdies on the first seven holes, but Gamez birdied four holes after that to match Hoch with 69s. Jose Maria Olazabal tied Mizuguchi for third at 277.

Japan Series Hitachi Cup—¥100,000,000
Winner: Hisayuki Sasaki

Half of the 24 players in the Japan Series Hitachi Cup qualified as 1994 winners on the Japan PGA Tour. The rest were among the top 20 money winners of the season and among the latter was Hisayuki Sasaki, who had never won at all. Not until that week at the Yomiuri Member Golf Club at Nishinomiya, when he came from behind in the final round with a sparkling 66 and picked off a one-stroke victory with his 14-under-par 270 total. That finish edged two favorites — Naomichi (Joe) Ozaki at 271 and Tsuneyuki (Tommy) Nakajima, a three-time 1994 winner.

Ozaki, a two-time Series winner whose only 1994 victory was in the Acom International, had things well in hand for three days. He opened blazing with a course-record 62 — nine birdies on the par-71 course — and took a two-stroke lead on Eiji Mizoguchi. On Friday, Ozaki again shot the day's best round — 66 — and stretched his margin to five strokes with his 128 total. He still seemed solid with a one-bogey 69 Saturday, although his lead dropped to three strokes over Yoshinori Kaneko. Sasaki was seven back at 204 with Mizoguchi after rounds of 68, 66 and 70. Ozaki, in trouble and losing ground Sunday, was unable to counter Sasaki's 65, the product primarily of four birdies on the last five holes. Ozaki fell to 74 for his 271 and the runner-up slot.

Daikyo Open—¥120,000,000
Winner: Hideki Kase

Hideki Kase almost ran out of real estate in his successful bid to salvage his 1994 season with a victory. He got it in the year's last event — the Daikyo Open on Okinawa — slipping past Seiji Ebihara in the final round with 67 for a 268 total, 16 under par. It had been more than four years since Kase had his big, and only other, victory in the 1990 Japan PGA Championship.

Ken Kusumoto was the hot player in the first round, shooting 63 for a two-stroke lead over Hisayuki Sasaki, fresh from his Japan Series victory. Hirofumi Miyase took over first place Friday with his pair of 66s to lead Kusumoto and Yoshitaka Yamamoto by one stroke. Ebihara shot 64 Saturday to establish his one-stroke lead over Kase, who had followed an opening 69 with two 66s. Ebihara had a 69 Sunday for 269. Masahiro Kuramoto, with 65, and Kusumoto, with 68, tied Ebihara for second place.

14. Australasian Tour

The highlight of the 1994 Australasian Tour was almost the lowlight, when Robert Allenby, this region's brightest young star, won the Heineken Australian Open after narrowly avoiding a disastrous finish. Allenby dropped five shots over the last four holes at Royal Sydney Golf Club, but salvaged the victory when Brett Ogle missed a 12-foot putt to tie him. Thus, Allenby won the national championship that eluded him three years earlier as an amateur, when he was second to Wayne Riley by one stroke.

That same year, 1991, Allenby won the Victorian Open as an amateur and has now won five more titles as a professional. He won three times on the Australasian Tour in 1992 and 1993, and took his first victory this year on the PGA European Tour in the Honda Open in Germany, winning a three-hole playoff against Miguel Angel Jimenez. Three weeks later, Allenby led the Murphy's Irish Open by three strokes entering the final round, only to tie for second place when Bernhard Langer shot a closing 67.

For the year, Allenby, now age 23, had 10 finishes in the top-10 in 32 worldwide starts, and advanced from No. 81 to No. 48 on the Sony Ranking. On the PGA European Tour, where Allenby played 22 events, he won £240,174 for 17th place on the money list. There were only four native Australasian players ahead of him on the Sony Ranking: No. 2 Greg Norman, No. 31 Frank Nobilo, No. 43 Steve Elkington and No. 44 Craig Parry.

Allenby led the 1994 Australasian money list with A$199,644, followed by Parry with A$185,919 and American Patrick Burke with A$182,570. Rounding out the top five were two more Australians, Michael Clayton with A$177,662 and Anthony Gilligan with A$136,327.

Parry was the only one of the four listed higher than Allenby on the Sony Ranking to win in 1994 on the Australasian Tour. It was an important victory indeed, the Microsoft Australian Masters, which was a qualifying event for the Johnnie Walker World Championship, along with the Heineken Australian Open. Parry shot a final-round 68 and won by three strokes over Ernie Els, after Els held a two-stroke lead through 54 holes. Parry went on to play most of the year in the United States, where he was second in his first start and placed 46th on the money list with US$354,602.

Two golfers won twice each in 1994 on the Australasian Tour, Clayton and Burke. When Clayton won the Heineken Classic in Perth early in the year, he was using a long-shafted putter, but had switched back to an old Ping model for his second win in the season-ending Schweppes Coolum Classic. Consistency, if not spectacular performances, was the most significant feature of Clayton's year, as he made the 36-hole cut in 32 of 35 tournaments.

Burke, who came to this circuit after losing his player's card in the United States, started well, with a victory in the second event, the Optus Players Championship. For much of the year, however, Burke fought a virus and he had to borrow US$10,000 to return for the later tournaments. He was able to repay the loan and show a profit by winning the Victorian Open and placing second in the Alfred Dunhill Asian Masters.

The Alfred Dunhill tournament, played in Bali, featured perhaps the most bizarre result of the year anywhere, when Nick Faldo was disqualified while holding a six-stroke lead in the final round, which enabled Canada's Jack Kay to take first place. The disqualification was for signing an incorrect scorecard in the third round. Faldo mistakenly removed a loose impediment, a piece of coral, in a bunker. The error was not discovered until the next day.

In other Australasian tournaments, Craig Jones started the year with his first professional victory in the AMP New Zealand Open, Peter Senior won the Canon Challenge, Lucas Parsons won the Foodlink Queensland Open, Andrew Coltart won the Reebok Australian PGA Championship, Gilligan won Greg Norman's Holden Classic, Shane Robinson won the Air New Zealand-Shell Open, and Darren Chivas won the unsanctioned New South Wales Open.

AMP New Zealand Open—A$243,000
Winner: Craig Jones

Nine consecutive pars were all Craig Jones of Australia needed to win his first professional tournament in the AMP New Zealand Open, but Frank Nobilo was left to wonder what it would take to win his national title. Runner-up for the third time, Nobilo had an eagle putt from 25 feet slide past the hole at the 18th, and Nobilo finished one stroke behind Jones. The champion had a 277 total, seven under par at Remuera Golf Club in Auckland, including 72 in the final round. Nobilo finished with 70 for his 278 total.

"I don't know what I have to do to win this Open," said Nobilo, who had his back treated by a chiropractor before the final round and started with two bogeys. "I like silver medals, but to hell with coming second. I want to win."

Jones, a 24-year-old from Queensland, played solidly for all four rounds, with earlier scores of 69, 71 and 65. He was four strokes behind David Iwasaki-Smith in the first round and seven off the pace of Zoran Zorkic after 36 holes. Jones took the lead with his third-round 65 on a hot and steamy day when Zorkic shot 73 after a 67-66 start. Zorkic closed with 74 and tied for third place at 280 with Steve Conran and Tony Maloney.

Optus Players Championship—A$300,000
Winner: Patrick Burke

A three-stroke lead on the final hole was barely enough for Patrick Burke to secure his first professional victory in the Optus Players Championship at Kingston Health Golf Club in Melbourne. He finished with a double bogey after pushing his drive into bushes on the right of the fairway and taking a penalty for an unplayable lie. He two-putted for an even-par 72 and 280 total, eight under par, to win by one stroke over Bradley Hughes.

A 31-year-old Californian, Burke had placed 144th on the 1993 U.S. PGA Tour money list, 19 positions too high to retain his player's card. The victory provided Burke with a five-year exemption on the Australasian Tour, and Burke delighted the gallery by saying he would live in Queensland in order to play both this and the American circuits.

Burke entered the final round with a two-stroke lead after shooting 69, 67 and 72. Hughes had rounds of 78, 73, 70 and 70 for his 281 total, while

Ossie Moore took third place at 282, one stroke ahead of a group of six golfers including Peter Senior, leader of the 1993 Australasian Order of Merit.

Heineken Classic—A$350,000
Winner: Michael Clayton

Michael Clayton had mixed feelings about whether the long-shafted putter should be legal, but he put that club to good use and won the Heineken Classic at The Vines Resort in Perth. "My own view is that it's cheating to use it," Clayton said, "but so long as the authorities say it is completely legal, it will remain in my bag."

Clayton was a three-stroke winner over Wayne Smith, with Patrick Burke and Robert Allenby one stroke further behind. The champion had a 279 total, nine under par, on rounds of 67, 71, 71 and 70. He and Smith were tied after 54 holes, then Smith finished with 73. Allenby also finished with 73, and Burke recovered from his third-round 78 to shoot 69.

Through nine holes of the final round, Allenby was tied for the lead with Smith, one stroke ahead of Clayton. Allenby's approach shot to No. 10 was right of the green, sitting up perfectly in what seemed a natural hollow but in fact was a dried-out lateral water hazard. Allenby moved some twigs, and the resulting penalty and double bogey left Clayton and Smith to fight out the remaining holes.

Clayton secured the victory on the 17th and 18th holes. He was unable to see the 17th green on his approach shot because of a group of trees, but managed to hit the ball within three feet of the hole. Smith had an errant drive and bogeyed the 18th, and Clayton birdied the hole with a four iron to 10 feet.

New South Wales Open—A$50,000
Winner: Darren Chivas

Darren Chivas slipped through to win the unofficial New South Wales Open at Manley Golf Club in Sydney by one stroke after the 54-hole leaders, Michael Campbell and Grant Kenny, faded in the final round. Chivas shot two-under-par 70 for a 283 total, five under par, and won by one stroke over David Ecob, who also finished with 70.

Kenny led the first two rounds and was tied at 212 with Campbell after the third round. Campbell shot 74 and tied for third place at 286, and Kenny shot 77 and fell to a sixth-place tie at 289.

Microsoft Australian Masters—A$750,000
Winner: Craig Parry

It was for good reason if Craig Parry had a sense of victory before the Microsoft Australian Masters. When Parry won this tournament in 1992, his wife, Jenny, was pregnant; his brother, Glenn, caddied for him; and he won the pro-am event. All of that was true this year. Parry came from behind then, and he did so again, winning by three strokes over Ernie Els after trailing Els by two entering the final round.

The difference in the two victories was Greg Norman. In 1992, Parry came from five strokes behind Norman to win by three. This time, Norman, who had just won the Johnnie Walker Asian Classic in Thailand, knocked himself from contention with 77 and tied for 18th place at 292 after starting the last round three strokes behind Els and one behind Parry.

Els, a late replacement for the injured Nick Price, impressed the gallery at Huntingdale Golf Club in Melbourne on his first visit to Australia. The young South African shot rounds of 70, 70 and 72 to enter the final day two strokes clear of Parry, with Norman, Wayne Grady and rookie Grant Kenny three strokes behind. Kenny started with 65 but was over par in two of the next three rounds, and his final 79 left him 12 strokes back at 294. Grady shot 73 in the last round for his 288 total.

Parry had rounds of 74, 70, 70 and a closing 68 for his 282 total, 10 under par, while Els finished with 73 and a 285 total. Peter Senior, with a final-round 68, and Peter Teravainen tied for third place at 286, then came Wayne Smith in fifth place at 287.

On the opening hole of the final round, Parry birdied and Els bogeyed, and they were tied. Els recovered the lead and faltered again. Parry then made an eagle three on the 10th hole, holing a 30-foot putt after a drive and five iron to the green. "I knew I just didn't have to make any silly errors after that," Parry said. He did have a bogey at the 17th hole, however.

Parry viewed his victory as a reward for a swing change under the direction of noted teacher David Leadbetter. Parry shortened his backswing to eliminate the occasional snap hook that crept into his game, which Parry felt would enable him "to get to the next level."

Canon Challenge—A$300,000
Winner: Peter Senior

The reputations of the world's best golfers are based upon their play in the major championships, but those playing outside the U.S. PGA Tour have great difficulty obtaining invitations to the three events in America. That means for many their only chance of the year is the British Open Championship.

Peter Senior is one of those. He was not invited to the Masters Tournament despite having led the 1993 Australasian money list. Senior's position in the top 50 of the Sony Ranking assured him of playing in the British Open, and Senior acknowledged that he was eyeing that title, after winning the Canon Challenge for his first victory of the year. "I think I'm a very good player," he said, "and hopefully, in the next couple of years, I can climb those extra rungs."

The triumph at Castle Hill Country Club in Sydney advanced Senior to No. 28 on the Sony Ranking. He was the third-ranked Australian player, behind only Greg Norman and Steve Elkington.

Senior won the Canon Challenge in a playoff over Chris Gray, a former Australian Amateur champion. He entered the final round one stroke ahead of Gray and shot 69 to Gray's 68, both finishing with 276 totals, 12 under par. Gray holed a nine-iron shot for an eagle two on the seventh hole for a two-stroke lead, but Senior won with his play on the 18th. He made a 14-foot putt for a birdie to force the playoff, then sank another 14-footer to win.

Foodlink Queensland Open—A$200,000
Winner: Lucas Parsons

"This one's for you, Dad," Lucas Parsons said after he had won the Foodlink Queensland Open. Parsons' father died a month earlier after a long illness.

Parsons won by two strokes over his good friend Michael Campbell after Campbell entered the last round with a two-stroke lead. Parsons started with a six-under-par 66, then was overtaken by Campbell in the windy conditions of the second and third rounds. Parsons shot 72 and 75, while Campbell posted 68, 77 and then matched Parsons' opening 66.

In the fourth round, Parsons shot 69 for a 282 total at Windaroo, and Campbell finished with 73–284, taking second place by three strokes over Michael Clayton and Glenn Joyner. Parsons drew even with birdies on the first two holes, then there was a three-stroke swing on the 13th and 14th holes, with Parsons making two birdies and Campbell, a bogey after hitting a drive into a hazard.

Not only the victory, but also the party was at Campbell's expense, since he and Parsons have a wager of two bottles of vintage champagne at each tournament they play.

Epson Singapore Open—A$546,040
Winner: Kyi Hla Han

After a decade on the Australasian Tour, Kyi Hla Han scored his first victory there, winning the Epson Singapore Open in a final-round battle with two Australians, former U.S. PGA champion Wayne Grady and Chris Gray. Han, a 33-year-old Burmese, entered the last day with a three-stroke lead and withstood a tense struggle that ended when Gray double-bogeyed the final hole to fall from a tie for first place.

Han came into Singapore on a hot streak, having won two minor events, the Hong Kong PGA and Johor Masters. He shot rounds of 67, 69, 68 and 71 for a 275 total, 13 under par at Tanah Merah Country Club, where the very hot and humid days were occasionally interrupted by thunderstorms, which provided soft, receptive greens for the golfers. Grady placed second at 276 and Gray was third at 277. Grady started with 68 and Gray, 69, then they posted identical scores of 70, 69 and 69.

A highlight of the tournament was the hole-in-one by a local golfer, Mardan Mamat. Although Mamat missed the 36-hole cut, he was rewarded for his ace with a Jaguar convertible valued at A$350,000.

Alfred Dunhill Asian Masters—$466,216
Winner: Jack Kay

A certain victory became a sudden disqualification for Nick Faldo, when the English star was removed during the final round of the Alfred Dunhill Asian Masters because of a rules infraction which occurred in the third round but went undetected for a day. Thus, Canadian Jack Kay, who was six strokes behind before Faldo was eliminated, acquired a bizarre victory in exotic Bali.

In the third round, while playing in the company of Craig Parry, Faldo removed a piece of coral from behind his golf ball in a bunker on the second hole. The next day, Parry found a piece of coral behind his ball in a bunker on the seventh hole. Parry was about to pick up the coral when he was told by his marker, Michael Campbell, that removing loose impediments in bunkers was not allowed under Australasian Tour rules.

That, of course, is also among the Rules of Golf, but a rule on the PGA European Tour allows players to remove loose impediments from bunkers, and Faldo and Parry had incorrectly assumed the same exception also applied on the Australasian Tour. Once Parry was corrected, he was bound to report Faldo's error. "I felt lousy reporting Nick and I was just a basket case after that," Parry said. "The real problem is that rules vary all over the world."

Chief referee Trevor Herden had the thankless task of going to the 12th tee to advise Faldo that he had been disqualified — technically, for reporting a score lower than his actual score on that second hole, since a penalty stroke should have been added at the time of the infraction. "I was on automatic, thinking it was European rules," Faldo said. "Obviously, I broke the rules, but it is the first time I have done so and been called for it the following day." Two years ago, Faldo was disqualified after a round at Sun City for a similar infraction.

The disqualification nullified Faldo's brilliant play at the par-71 Bali Golf and Country Club, where he posted rounds of 67, 63 and 69 for a 199 total after 54 holes. Kay won by one stroke over Patrick Burke with a 277 total on scores of 73, 66, 66 and 72. "We all know who really won the tournament," Kay said. "As far as I'm concerned I finished second and received first-place money (A$83,918). I have never played in Europe, though, and so I would never dream of touching anything in a bunker."

Victorian Open—A$200,000
Winner: Patrick Burke

American journeyman Patrick Burke, playing on US$10,000 in borrowed money, hit the jackpot on consecutive weeks. First, Burke benefited from Nick Faldo's disqualification in Bali to win A$47,554 for second place, then he earned A$36,000 with a victory in the Victorian Open.

The winner of the Optus Players Championship early in the year, Burke had been battling a strength-sapping virus for much of 1994, and said he had run out of money before obtaining a loan for this trip. Burke birdied the last three holes at the Victoria Golf Club for a final-round 67 and 278 total to win by two strokes over Australians Rob Willis, who had led for two days, and Tim Elliott.

Willis finished with 72 after earlier rounds of 69, 69 and 70, while Elliott had a closing 69. Willis said he lost his momentum with a bogey on the 12th hole after an unlucky bounce into the rough. "Burke then made three birdies and that killed me," Willis said. Taking fourth place at 281, including a final-round 67, was Stuart Appleby, the 24-year-old former Australian Amateur champion who had won four times earlier this year on the Australasian developmental circuit.

Reebok PGA Championship—A$200,000
Winner: Andrew Coltart

When Andrew Coltart made a double bogey on the first hole of the final round, hitting a wedge shot across the first green and into an unplayable lie, the 24-year-old Scotsman undoubtedly thought this would not be his day. "That's it," Coltart said. "Nice professional shot." He took six, and said then he was "lucky to get it." But less than four hours later, Coltart won the Reebok PGA Championship at New South Wales Club in Sydney.

From five strokes behind the leaders, Coltart began his comeback with an eagle three on the fifth hole, and surged through the last nine holes in 33 for his 70 and seven-under-par 281 total, completing a two-stroke victory over Terry Price. There were strong winds over the last two rounds, and Coltart shot 77 in the third round after starting with two 67s.

Through 54 holes, Paul Devenport led at 208, two strokes in front of Mike Harwood and three ahead of Coltart. Devenport finished with 78 for a share of sixth place, and Harwood shot 74 to place third, three strokes behind Coltart. A birdie at the 12th hole tied Coltart with Price, and they shared the lead until Price bogeyed the par-three 17th. Both missed the green there, but Coltart recovered to six feet and sank the putt. Price made bogey again at the 18th.

Elliott Boult had 64 in the first round, the best score of the tournament, but followed with rounds of 71, 78 and 73 and tied for sixth place.

Heineken Australian Open—A$850,000
Winner: Robert Allenby

Regarded for several years as Australia's brightest young star, Robert Allenby came home from a successful European campaign to win the great prize that eluded him three years ago, the Heineken Australian Open. Despite a faltering finish, Allenby completed his fourth successive 70 for a 280 total, eight under par at Royal Sydney Golf Club, and won by one stroke over Brett Ogle, who rimmed out a potential par putt to tie on the final hole from 12 feet.

In 1991, as an amateur, Allenby nearly won his national championship, but Wayne Riley took it with a long putt across the 18th green at Royal Melbourne. Now age 23, Allenby secured his sixth professional victory and his second of the year, to go with his win in the Honda Open in Europe.

In a duel of thin men, Allenby held a three-stroke lead over Ogle with four holes to play, then Allenby finished bogey, double bogey, bogey, bogey. Fortunately for Allenby, Ogle didn't play much better than that, having bogey, par, bogey, bogey, and then threw down his hat on the 18th green in frustration. Ogle finished with 74 and a 281 total, after having started the fourth round with a two-stroke lead over Peter Baker and Paul Devenport, and a three-stroke margin over Allenby.

Allenby burst out with 31 for the first nine holes on the last day, then made two more birdies before disaster struck. "I can't explain it," Allenby told the press. "Just don't say I choked." Regardless, Allenby managed to win the prize and the honor of having his name on the Stonehaven Cup, along with such others as Arnold Palmer, Jack Nicklaus, Peter Thomson and Greg Norman. "Great names," he said, "and now I'm part of them. It is a dream I had as a young amateur come true."

Baker shot a final-round 73 and was third at 282, then came a tie for fourth with Norman, defending champion Brad Faxon and Gary Orr, all three of whom had poor starts. Norman had 74 and Orr, 76, in the first round and Faxon, 76, in the second round. Devenport finished with 75 and tied for seventh place at 284.

Greg Norman's Holden Classic—A$700,000
Winner: Anthony Gilligan

Anthony Gilligan, a 32-year-old Queenslander, had won in Japan and Canada, but never in his native Australia, until he shot a five-under-par 67 in the final round for a 274 total to win Greg Norman's Holden Classic by two strokes at Royal Melbourne Golf Club's Composite Course. Gilligan, however, spoke with the determination of an experienced winner when he told his caddie with two holes to play, "Let's finish birdie, birdie and we'll bury them."

It was a brave statement, since Gilligan was referring to the host, Norman, Mark Calcavecchia, both major championship winners, and Paul Moloney, who tied for second place at 276 after Gilligan came through with those two birdies. He had a pitch-and-run shot and a one-putt birdie on the par-five 17th hole, then a 25-foot birdie putt on the 18th, after a two-iron shot to the green. "Nothing could match the thrill of winning in Australia," Gilligan said afterwards.

Norman and Calcavecchia were in the final group, behind Gilligan and Glenn Joyner, with Calcavecchia having gone to the final round with a one-stroke advantage over the other three. Calcavecchia finished with 70, Norman shot 69, and Moloney moved up with 67 to tie them for second place. Moloney had five birdies, no bogeys, and thrilled the crowd at the 18th green with a 50-foot birdie when it appeared he had a real chance of winning. Joyner shot 75 and tied for 11th place.

Gilligan, who had earlier rounds of 71, 66 and 70, was not without problems on the last day. He bogeyed the 10th and 12th holes, and Norman took the lead alone after 10 holes before bogeying the 11th and 12th. Gilligan then seized his chance, first birdieing the 13th, then hitting his second shot to the middle of the green on the par-five 14th for another birdie.

Among the other notable performances were those of Lucas Parsons, who was under par each day while tieing for fifth place at 278, and of Gary Simpson, recently voted *Australian Golf Digest*'s Amateur of the Year, who tied Brett Ogle and Wayne Grady for seventh place at 280.

Air New Zealand-Shell Open—A$244,050
Winner: Shane Robinson

A professional golfer for five years, Shane Robinson had only one top-10 finish to his credit, but the 30-year-old Australian pulled a big surprise in winning the Air New Zealand-Shell Open when Lucas Parsons encountered trouble in the final round. Parsons, holding a one-stroke lead over Robinson and Andre Stolz, shot 74 while Robinson finished with 71 and a 274 total, six under par at the Grange Golf Club in Auckland.

Robinson was boosted by his 64 in the second round, which enabled him to share the lead at 134 with Parsons, who had 64 on the opening day. Parsons then shot 68 to Robinson's 69 to carry the lead into the final 18 holes. There was a tense battle on the last day, and three contenders shot 66s, including David McKenzie, who placed second at 275. There were six players tied for third at 276 — Parsons, Terry Price, Don Fardon, Peter Fowler, David Small and Anthony Christie.

Battling his nerves over the closing stretch, Robinson made pars on the last five holes to secure the victory. He hit his drive under a tree at the 17th hole and needed a six-foot putt to save par, then safely two-putted the 18th to win.

Schweppes Coolum Classic—A$200,000
Winner: Michael Clayton

Michael Clayton closed out a two-victory year by winning the Schweppes Coolum Classic on the weekend before Christmas in Queensland. He was not well-placed after starting with 69 and 73, but his six-under-par 66 in the third round provided a two-stroke lead over Andre Stolz and Andrew Bonhomme. Clayton expanded that to a four-stroke victory over Stolz with 69 in the last round for a 277 total, 11 under par.

Clayton, who missed the 36-hole cut in only three of 35 tournaments worldwide in 1994, used his putter to great advantage after switching from a long-shafted model to a favorite old Ping putter. In the final round, he sank a 40-foot putt on the 14th hole and another putt almost as long at the 16th hole to set up the victory, after Stolz had tied him through 11 holes. Stolz finished with 71 and a 281 total for second place, and American Jack O'Keefe, from Little Rock, Arkansas, had 67, the best score of the last day, to take third place at 285.

15. African Tours

Nick Faldo was reported missing from the PGA European Tour, but not to worry — Faldo turned up alive and more than well in South Africa, at the Nedbank Million Dollar Challenge at Sun City early in December, to be precise. Maybe Faldo couldn't forget the poor (for him) year he had just had in Europe, but he could cushion the blow with his performance at Sun City, with the one million U.S. dollars he won and the promise it held for the future.

Faldo, 37 now, had been fussing with his game all year. At the Johnnie Walker World Championship at Jamaica a year earlier, in December, 1993, he took to practicing barefooted, for better feel or balance. And then at Sun City, in December, 1994, he was putting cross-handed, which he had adopted in September. The results added up fast: 66 and a two-stroke lead in the first round, and 64 and a whopping seven-stroke lead in the second round. True, he tailed off and got caught, but he had enough steam to win by three strokes. Did this make him feel better? "Yes, a million times better," Faldo cracked. "It's pretty tough to say I've had a rough year after that."

Elsewhere in Africa, the 1994 season played to the extremes, a mixture of the old and new.

From the old came Tony Johnstone, kicking off the 1994 segment of the First National Bank Tour with a victory in the Bell's Cup in January. "I don't want this to end," Johnstone said, and he wasn't referring to the head-to-head battle he had with Ernie Els. The Bell's Cup was merely Johnstone's fourth victory in four FNB starts, dating to late 1993.

Also from the old came something of an Alphonse-and-Gaston act by David Frost and Nick Price.

Frost went first in the Lexington PGA Championship. For all of his successes, he had never been able to nail down the PGA title. He got this one with a 50-foot birdie putt on the final hole for 63. Not that birdies are ever wasted, but all this one did was boost his margin to seven strokes. Second place went to his old foe, Price, who started the final round two strokes behind and ended up seven behind. "I'm not complaining," Price said. "I'm very happy with the way I played."

But of course. Price was merely the hottest golfer in the world. Then it was his turn in the ICL International. A seven-stroke victim one week, a nine-stroke winner the next. And who was second to him by that awesome margin? Frost, of course, co-runner-up with American Bruce Vaughan. Price wasn't all that happy about how he played this time. "All that good golf, and I come out and play badly in the final round," Price said. In this case, that meant 72 in the fourth round, which was bound to look bad after his 61 in the first round. Even his nine-stroke victory looked common. After all, when he started the final round, he was 13 strokes ahead of Frost.

The new arrived first in the person of Omar Uresti, an American Nike Tour hopeful, who won his spurs in the Hollard Insurance Royal Swazi Sun Classic. He had to finish the first round under automobile headlights, and the final round in the rain, for his win as a professional. Vaughan scored his first FNB victory in the Autopage Mount Edgecombe Trophy, at the expense of Johnstone.

The streaking Johnstone was about to chalk up another victory when Vaughan tore through the final nine with six birdies, tied him with 63, and beat him in a playoff. Said Vaughan: "I'm almost speechless."

Add England's Martin Gates to the first-timers, and add Ernie Els to golf's weird victims. The Hassan II Trophy is not an official sanctioned event, but don't try to explain the difference to Gates. It felt the same to him when he won the classy invitational in Morocco. And as for Els, the rocketing young talent — he came to the Nashua Wild Coast Challenge in November with the U.S. Open crowning his big year. When he got rolling, few could stand up to him, and he was rolling down the final stretch of the Wild Coast when a strange thing happened at the 16th. He nearly stepped on a deadly night adder that had picked that moment to slither across his path. Els bogeyed the hole, and double-bogeyed the next.

Someone — or some thing — had finally found a way to stop Els.

Bell's Cup—R525,000
Winner: Tony Johnstone

"I just don't want this to end," Tony Johnstone was saying, and small wonder. Playing a breathtaking iron game, Johnstone, the 37-year-old Zimbabwean who plies South Africa before heading for the PGA European Tour, made the Bell's Cup his fourth victory in four starts on the First National Bank Tour. From about 100 to 200 yards out, he put 10 shots to within three feet of the pin, and played the Fancourt course in rounds of 65, 68, 68 and 70 for a 271 total, 17 under par. That put him an incredible 66 under par for the four victories.

But this one, leading off the FNB Tour for 1994, the first week of January, didn't come easy. It was three strokes on paper, but on the course Johnstone had to hold off Ernie Els in a stretch drive. Johnstone didn't have a real grip on the victory until the 15th hole, after some scary moments. Els tied for second place at 274 with David Frost, who closed with 67.

"I must admit it was nerve-wracking out there, with just a one-shot difference between Els and myself until the 15th," Johnstone said. Johnstone's two-stroke lead going into the final round evaporated immediately when Els started birdie-birdie and took a one-stroke lead against Johnstone's par-bogey. It was the hound-and-the-hare the rest of the way, until the 15th where Johnstone leaped into a commanding three-stroke lead. He fired one of those marvelous approaches, an eight iron stiff to the pin, and tapped in for the birdie three while Els drove badly, then three-putted for a bogey.

Lexington PGA Championship—R575,000
Winner: David Frost

David Frost marched up onto the 72nd and final green and rolled home a 50-foot putt for a birdie that did little more than stamp an exclamation point on the Lexington PGA Championship. It was unnecessary because he had come to that final hole at the Wanderers already ahead by a luxurious six strokes. And so after leading wire-to-wire, he stepped off with his first Lexington

PGA title with a whopping seven-stroke victory. That final birdie gave him a closing seven-under-par 63 to add to a start of 64, 67 and 65, completing a 21-under-par total of 259. That broke the previous record by six strokes. Nobody even came close. "Frosty just played great," said Nick Price, runner-up at 14-under-par 266, who last played a month earlier when he won the Million Dollar Challenge. He entered the final round two strokes behind Frost. "I knew it was going to be a tall order to beat him," Price said. "But I'm not complaining. I'm very happy with the way I played." Price knew that helpless feeling in the final round. Frost began opening the gap in a hurry with a birdie at No. 2, then got another from about 25 feet at No. 4. All told, he made eight birdies against only one bogey in that final round.

Wayne Westner matched Frost's closing 63 to take third place at 267, edging Ernie Els (67) by one stroke.

ICL International—R500,000
Winner: Nick Price

It's almost as if they were playing my turn/your turn. Nick Price, distant runner-up to David Frost in the Lexington PGA the week before, took his turn this time, running away with the ICL International by a record nine strokes. In second place was Frost, co-runner-up with American Bruce Vaughan. Price had a royal time of it in winning his second consecutive ICL title. After a career-low, 11-under-par 61 in the first round, only a par 72 in the fourth round kept him from matching or breaking the tournament record 266 at Zwartkop, set in 1988 when the course wasn't as severe.

"All that good golf and then I come out and play badly in the final round," said Price, Player of the Year on the American PGA Tour in 1993. "I guess that's the great challenge of this game. You never get it completely licked." Price came pretty close, though, shooting a 21-under-par total of 267 on rounds of 61, 69, 65 and 72. The final round was played under gray skies, with a bit of rain and a switch in the wind that caused Price some problems in club selection. He made four bogeys, after he had earlier gone 47 holes without one. "I was a little disappointed with the way I played the final day," Price said. "I just was really happy I birdied the final hole. I didn't want to shoot over par."

Telkom South African Masters—R575,000
Winner: Chris Davison

As Chris Davison walked up the final fairway, there was only one thing left to do, and he did it. He let the tears come. The English-born Davison, 32, who had had his troubles since being named FNB Tour Rookie of the Year for the 1989-90 season, fulfilled that early promise by winning the Telkom South African Masters.

"It's something I've worked hard for — it's just unbelievable," said Davison after coming from behind to post his first victory, a two-stroke triumph at the tough new Lost City course. Davison played the par-72 course in rounds of 69, 74, 68 and 70, a seven-under-par 281 total to overrun American Bruce

Vaughan (69-70-71-73–283), who led by one going into the final round. Davison, trailing Vaughan by one stroke, started the fourth round without fanfare, parring the first three holes. Then he exploded, getting birdies at the fourth, fifth, seventh and ninth. That had him out in 32 and nine under par for the tournament. Vaughan, meanwhile, went in the other direction, slipping from six under par to four under at the turn. "I tried not to look at the score," Davison said, "and instead play the course like in match play." He stuck to his guns and fought off the stubborn bad memories — like the six or seven times he threatened, only to wobble down the final stretch. "I can breath again," Davison said. "You get so many doubts in your mind when you're in winning situations and fail to pull it off. You think to yourself — will it ever happen? Today, it did. I'm a happy man."

Hollard Insurance Royal Swazi Sun Classic—R400,000
Winner: Omar Uresti

Omar Uresti, 25-year-old visitor from the American Nike Tour, started in the dark and finished in the rain to score his first victory as a professional in the Hollard Insurance Royal Swazi Sun Classic. His trials merely underlined a trying week for the entire field at the par-72 Royal Swazi Country Club. Of the 71 finishers, only four had three rounds in the 60s, and Uresti, a former University of Texas player, was one of them. He shot 65, 73, 68 and 68 for a 274 total, 14 under par, for a two-stroke victory over fellow American Andrew Pitts.

Play was so slow in the first round, approaching six hours, that Uresti had to wrap up his leading 65 in the glow of auto headlights at the 18th green. "I wanted to finish," he said. "Everything was going so well, and I didn't want to lose my rhythm." Then in the fourth round, he had to fight off a downpour and challenges from fellow Pitts and big-hitting South African Wayne Westner.

The final round began as an all-American shootout, with Uresti tied at 206 for the lead with James Becker and Scott Dunlap, along with Westner. Becker and Dunlap faded, and then came the rain. "I saw the scoreboard at the 14th tee, and I knew I needed to make some birdies," Uresti said. Which he promptly did — at the 14th, 15th and 16th holes. Westner's chances died with a bogey at the par-five 17th.

Standard Chartered Kenya Open—£70,000
Winner: Paul Carman

It was an all-England finale in the Standard Chartered Kenya Open at Nairobi in February, but it took a long and stubborn battle to get it settled. Paul Carman shot rounds of 67, 70, 68 and 71 for 276 total, and Glenn Ralph tied him with scores of 69, 67, 69 and 71. They struggled through a playoff that ended at the fourth extra hole when Carman dropped a two-foot putt for his par, while Ralph hit into a bunker and suffered a bogey. Carman could have won in regulation play, but three-putted the 16th hole.

The field was spread out behind them. Tied for third, three strokes off the lead at 279 were Philip Harrison of England and Mark Litton of Wales. Peter Njiru was a stroke further back in fifth place. Scotland's Craig Maltman was sixth at 281, and England's Chris Platts closed with a two-under-par 67 for seventh place at 282. Kenyan amateur Joseph Okello turned in a tournament-best 66 in the third round and tied for 10th at 287.

Autopage Mount Edgecombe Trophy—R500,000
Winner: Bruce Vaughan

Bruce Vaughan, runner-up in the ICL International and the Telkom South African Masters back-to-back, was so accustomed to second place that he was willing to settle for it in the Autopage Mount Edgecombe Trophy at Mount Edgecombe Country Club. That's how well Tony Johnstone was playing. Then, not to stretch an old saying too far, a funny thing happened to this bridesmaid on the way to the altar. Vaughan, 37-year-old American trying to make it on the Nike Tour, caught fire down the stretch, tied Johnstone, and beat him in a playoff for his first FNB Tour victory.

Johnstone, looking for his fourth win in five starts, had reached the final turn in 32, with two birdies and an eagle. He looked like a shoo-in. "I didn't think I had a chance," Vaughan said. "I was quite content to play for second place." Vaughan, out in 32 with two birdies, an eagle and a bogey, was about to settle for second place when the magic hit. He struck for six birdies on the second nine — four in succession, from Nos. 10 through 13, on a 12-foot putt, a 60-footer and a pair of 12-footers. Then he birdied the 17th and 18th for a nine-under-par 63 (including a two and 10 threes) to tie Johnstone at 13-under-par 275. Vaughan won with a par four on the second extra hole.

Hassan II Trophy—$402,000
Winner: Martin Gates

Martin Gates, a 30-year-old Englishman, got a taunting glimpse from atop the leaderboard in the first round of the Dunhill British Masters in mid-September. He wasn't able to stay up there, but he liked what he saw, and a little while later, in early November, his persistence paid off in the Hassan II Trophy in Morocco, for the first victory of his career. The tournament played at Royal Golf Dar es Salam at Rabat, Morocco, the first week of November, isn't part of any tour, but with a strong invitational field, it was a testing event.

Gates led or shared the lead all the way on a par-73, 7,300-yard course that played even longer after heavy rains. Gates got a battle from Sweden's Robert Karlsson in the final round. They started out tied at nine under par and pulled away from the pack. They traded birdies around the turn, and Gates steamed home with four birdies over the last six holes. The crucial moment came at the par-four 16th, where Karlsson drove into the trees and Gates dropped an 18-foot putt for a birdie and a two-stroke swing. Gates then finished in style, with a birdie at the par-five 18th, for a three-stroke win on a card of 68-67-75-69—279, 13 under par. Gates' timing couldn't have been better. The win served as a wedding gift for his bride two weeks later.

Zimbabwe Open—R350,000
Winner: Chris Williams

The Zimbabwe Open at Royal Harare was decided by two short putts — one that was made, one that wasn't. American Andrew Pitts had the first crack, a three-footer at the final hole. He missed. Then Chris Williams, an Englishman living in South Africa, faced a four-footer on the first playoff hole. Williams didn't miss, and he had his first victory in five years and the third of his career.

"I thought I'd lost the tournament at the last," said Williams. "I really did expect Andrew to hole his putt for the title." Williams had rounds of 65, 68, 70 and 69, and Pitts shot 67, 67, 68 and 70. They tied at 272, 16 under par. Pre-tournament favorite Mark McNulty, who missed two late birdie chances, closed with 66, and fell one stroke short of them. Tony Johnstone, another former champion, led in the second round, faltered in the third, and got back within range before bogeying the 14th and 15th to finish tied for fifth.

Williams, trailing going into the final round, either led or shared the lead from the fifth to the 17th holes. There, he three-putted, missing his second from less than two feet, and fell one stroke behind. At the par-four 18th, Williams hit the green in two, about 25 feet from the flag. Pitts was just short with his second shot and chipped to about three feet. Williams missed his long birdie try, and now Pitts could win with a par, but he missed. At the first playoff hole, the par-five 16th, both missed the green. Pitts chipped to eight feet, and Williams chipped well inside him, to about four feet. This time, Pitts missed with his first putt, and Williams sank his for the win.

Nashua Wild Coast Challenge—R500,000
Winner: Hendrik Buhrmann

Ernie Els, newly 25 and just setting out on what promises to be an outstanding career, will discover many more ways that golf tournaments can be lost. But this one will do for now.

Els was battling Hendrik Buhrmann down the final stretch of the Nashua Wild Coast Challenge at Port Edward, and had just slugged a 300-yard drive on the par-five 16th hole. As he was leaving the tee, he noticed something moving in the grass, slithering toward him. It turned out to be a poisonous three-foot night adder. Els abruptly changed course. He proceeded to hit a wedge shot into a greenside pond and bogeyed, then hooked his tee shot at the par-three 17th and double-bogeyed. He shot 70 for a three-under-par 277 total and lost by five strokes to Buhrmann. But he refused to use the snake as an alibi.

"The snake shook me up, but it's no excuse," Els said. "This is Africa, and I've seen enough before. I just played a bad approach shot." Buhrmann led wire-to-wire on rounds of 64, 67, 72 and 69 for a 272 total, eight under par. He led Phil Simmons by two strokes in the first round, Els and Trevor Dodds by four in the second round, and shared the third-round lead with Dodds, by two strokes over Els. Dodds and Els finished tied for second place, five ahead of Ian Palmer and Warren Schutte.

Nedbank Million Dollar Challenge—$2,510,000
Winner: Nick Faldo

By any other standards, it was a splendid year — one victory, an eighth-place finish at the British Open, and enough other high finishes to lock up eighth place on the PGA European Tour's money list. But Nick Faldo's standards are not the same as others, and so he was delighted with a year-end victory in the 12-man Nedbank Million Dollar Challenge at Sun City. The victory, which looked like a cakewalk for a while, paid him U.S. $1 million.

"It's pretty tough to say I've had a rough year after that," said Faldo, a three-time runner-up at Sun City. He telegraphed this victory at the Gary Player Country Club with an eight-under-par 64 in the second round. He made eight birdies for the second consecutive day, and he burned the back nine with seven birdies — five in succession — for 29. "That was the best nine holes I have ever played," he said. The 64 gave him a seven-stroke lead over Nick Price and Bernhard Langer after 36 holes.

"Faldo is going to have to make some mistakes before anyone can catch him," Price said. It almost happened. Whatever the cause, defensive play or stale putting, Faldo shot 73 in the third round, allowing Price and Ernie Els to close in. Els caught Faldo in the third and fourth rounds but never took the lead. Faldo said his gamble at the 14th hole in the final round won the tournament for him. He hit his second shot through a bush to save his par.

Faldo then turned in a card of 66-64-73-69–272, 16 under par, beat Price by three strokes, and finally got something off his chest. Said Faldo, "I've always wanted to say this — Sun City, Thanks a million."

16. Senior Tours

This was the year that was for Dave Stockton, the year that might have been for Lee Trevino, and the year that almost was for Raymond Floyd on the Senior PGA Tour. Stockton, again accelerating his game as the months rolled by, repeated as the season's leading money winner and Player of the Year.

Rarely out of contention all season, Stockton won the Ford Senior Players and Nationwide Championships in June and the Burnet Classic in August amid a stretch of 17 tournaments from mid-June to mid-October in which he was seventh or better in all except four of them and never worse than 19th. Little wonder that he accumulated $1,402,519 in official prize money, a record, and was voted the year's top senior by the Golf Writers Association of America. Stockton then had $3,247,885 in Senior Tour earnings in just over three years.

Yet, for all of Stockton's heroics, it could be argued that he won those year-end honors by the default of Trevino. For the second year in a row, Trevino's season was cut short by an injury. In 1994, a neck ailment allowed him to play only three times after August and required surgery in late October. He had already won nearly $1.2 million, six Senior PGA Tour tournaments and the American Express Grand Slam in Japan when he first experienced the disc problem in late August.

The U.S. victories included Trevino's second PGA Seniors Championship and the sixth one tied him with Miller Barber at 24 atop the total wins list on the Tour. He finished fourth on the 1994 money list with $1,202,369, one of six players who exceeded the million-dollar mark. His fellow pros voted him their Player of the Year honor.

Floyd fell only $200,000 short of Stockton on the money list when he won the season-ending Golf Magazine Senior Tour Championship in November, and played 12 fewer events than Stockton in winning $1,382,762. Think what he might have had if he had played a few more events. His worst finish was a tie for 18th in Los Angeles and he was out of the top 10 only one other time all year. Or if he hadn't blown the PGA Seniors on the heels of his win in the Tradition, his first of four 1994 victories.

Jim Colbert spurted in mid-summer with two wins and two seconds in four weeks on his way to a $1,012,115 season, but the man who gave the others fits most of the season was Jim Albus, the 54-year-old former club pro, who first attracted Senior PGA Tour headlines when he won the 1991 Senior Players Championship. Playing almost every week — 34 events in all — Albus won twice (Vantage at the Dominion and Bank of Boston) and was second six other times, including two playoff losses, in compiling $1,237,128.

It was by far the best season ever among players with little or no experience on the PGA Tour in their younger days, although it should be noted that Tom Wargo, a man of similar background who won the 1993 PGA Seniors, was the other millionaire with $1,005,344. Wargo won the Doug Sanders Celebrity Classic and the Seniors British Open, the latter adding some £40,000 to his bankroll.

South Africa's Simon Hobday, who won the Senior Players title in 1993, captured the U.S. Senior Open Championship at Pinehurst, one of his two

1994 victories. He, Albus and Colbert were among six double winners. The others: Bob Murphy, 1993's top newcomer who won twice in three weeks at the end of the season; Larry Gilbert, another ex-club pro who was one of seven first-time winners, and Japan's Isao Aoki, the only back-to-back victor.

The varied list of first-time winners besides Gilbert included Tom Weiskopf, who played a limited schedule his first two seasons; Jack Kiefer, also a former club pro; Dave Eichelberger, who came on strong late in the season; Kermit Zarley, after nearly four years of trying; Tony Jacklin, the British star of the 1960s and 1970s playing his first partial season in America as a senior, and Jay Sigel. Sigel, the former outstanding amateur who won from 10 strokes back in the GTE West, was quite consistent with 14 top-10 finishes and more than $600,000 in earnings and clearly was the top rookie of the year.

Jack Nicklaus won the season-opening Mercedes Championship but nothing else. Mike Hill, who had won 15 times the previous four seasons, had just one title in 1994. Bob Charles and George Archer, who placed second and third on the 1993 money list and had never had winless seasons before on the Senior PGA Tour, were shut out in 1994. Tom Shaw, also otherwise winless in 1994, took the Senior Grand Slam title in February, and Floyd and Eichelberger defeated Nicklaus and Arnold Palmer in an exciting finale in the inaugural Diners Club Matches in December.

In a rather surprising development, John Morgan, a journeyman in his younger days in European golf, dominated the European Seniors Tour. Morgan, who had turned 50 in late 1993, won three of the circuit's 13 events, including the Forte PGA Seniors at Sunningdale, and was the leading money winner with £57,209. Tommy Horton, the 1993 European Seniors champion, and Ireland's Liam Higgins each won twice in 1994, finishing third and sixth on the money list.

Seiichi Kanai continued his domination of the Japan Senior Tour in 1994. He was the only multiple winner, capturing the TPC Starts, Nagoya TV and Ho-Oh Cup. Aoki returned to his native land after campaigning successfully in America with two victories and took the Japan Senior Open Championship in late November.

Mercedes Championship—$500,000
Winner: Jack Nicklaus

Who would have thought, even with the limited schedule he plays on the Senior PGA Tour, that Jack Nicklaus' victory in the season-opening Mercedes Championship in early January would be his only win of the season? Particularly since the triumph in what had always been known as the Tournament of Champions at the La Costa Resort in Southern California was typical Nicklaus.

Nicklaus lurked just off the pace for three rounds, then hammered home the victory, his seventh as a senior, with a closing, four-under-par 68 for a 279 total, edging Bob Murphy by one stroke. Dave Stockton, attempting to pick up where he left off as the No. 1 man on the 1993 Senior PGA Tour, was headed in that direction for three rounds. He led for two days with his

67-72 start before Murphy caught him at 208 after the third round. Nicklaus had overcome a 73 start with a pair of 69s and began Sunday three strokes behind Stockton and Murphy.

Surprisingly, Stockton fell out of contention early on his way to 75 and third place. Murphy gave Nicklaus an opening when he double-bogeyed the seventh hole. Jack finally drew even with a birdie at the 16th, matched birdies with Murphy at No. 17 and put a solid par on the board at the 18th. Murphy mis-clubbed, flew the green and had virtually no chance to salvage par out of the heavy rough. He didn't, leaving the tough chip short of the green and taking a bogey for 72 and 280.

Royal Caribbean Classic—$800,000
Winner: Lee Trevino

Lee Trevino made the first move toward the big year he had in mind for 1994 when he captured the Royal Caribbean Classic, the first full-field event of the Senior PGA Tour season, landing his 19th title and depriving Kermit Zarley of his first in a four-hole playoff at The Links of Key Biscayne near Miami, Florida. Trevino birdied the 54th hole with a tap-in for 66 and a 205 total, going to the playoff with Zarley, one of four second-round co-leaders, who made a good par from sand at the 18th for 68 and his matching total.

Trevino, vowing to improve on his fourth-place finish on the 1993 money list, trailed Zarley, J.C. Snead, Bob Charles and George Archer by two strokes at 139 after two rounds on the remodeled Key Biscayne course. He had led by one after an opening 66, but shot 73 Saturday, blaming it on inconsistent putting. Snead and Charles remained in contention Sunday until each bogeyed a hole in the stretch and took 70s for 207. Archer shot 71 for 208.

Trevino and Zarley, winless in his three seasons on the Senior PGA Tour, both parred the first extra hole and birdied the second. Zarley left short a birdie putt for the win at the 17th, then in their third visit of the day to the 18th, hooked his tee shot into a lake to hand the victory to Trevino. It was a bit of history revisited for Trevino, who won his first Senior PGA Tour title in the 1990 Royal Caribbean Classic when Jim Dent drove into the water at the 18th and took a fatal double bogey.

Senior Grand Slam of Golf—$500,000
Winner: Tom Shaw

Tom Shaw's strong finish provided the most exciting touch to a somewhat lackluster Senior Grand Slam of Golf that figured to be better, considering it brought together the winners of 1993's four most prestigious Senior PGA Tour events in a 36-hole shootout in Queretaro, Mexico. Shaw, the Tradition champion, bounced back from near disaster with birdies on two of the last four holes for 69, a 139 total and a two-stroke victory at Club de Campestre Queretaro. It was the highlight of an otherwise unproductive season.

Surprisingly, Jack Nicklaus had a terrible start, never got going and finished last just a month after winning the Mercedes Championship. With 75, the reigning U.S. Senior Open champion trailed Shaw, Jim Colbert (Senior

Players) and Tom Wargo (PGA Seniors) by five strokes after the first round. Shaw built a three-stroke lead over the first 13 holes only to lose it all when Wargo eagled the par-five 14th and Shaw, dumping a pitch shot in a bunker, bogeyed. Shaw recovered with birdies at the 15th and 17th and beat Colbert (70-71) by two strokes. Wargo shot 70-72–142 and Nicklaus wound up with 75-70–145. Shaw collected $250,000 for the victory.

GTE Suncoast Classic—$700,000
Winner: Rocky Thompson

Rocky Thompson figured it out that Saturday night in his hotel room. "I thought 61 would do it ... five under on the front and five under on the back. I can't say I expected it but I was damn well trying," Thompson recalled after he did just that in the final round and scored an astonishing victory in the GTE Suncoast Classic, his first in three years and third of his 30-year pro career. Thompson, the mayor of the Texas town of Toco, came virtually from nowhere to do something only one other man — Johnny Miller at Tucson in 1975 — ever did on either PGA Tour, shoot a final-round 61 for a victory. The 61 tied the Senior PGA Tour's 18-hole record.

No one was paying any attention Sunday morning to Thompson. He was seven strokes off the pace and no one in senior history had won from that far back. Besides, Mike Hill, one of the Tour's stalwarts, had taken the second-round lead with 64 for a 133 total. Orville Moody was at 135 and George Archer, who had shared the first-round lead at 66 with Moody, was at 136 with Raymond Floyd.

Thompson, who had started 73-67–140, began his Sunday charge with consecutive birdies at the third, fourth and fifth holes. He started another birdie run at the eighth, turned in 30 and added two more at the 10th and 11th. Hill was not doing much and, when he double-bogeyed the 10th, dropped into a first-place tie with Thompson. Hill continued to fade from there and Floyd became the Thompson pursuer as the birdie at the 11th put Rocky in front to stay. He made a good par putt at No. 12, birdied No. 14 from 22 feet and the last two holes from eight feet for 30-31–61–201. Floyd birdied only No. 15 in the stretch and his fine 66 still left him one stroke short.

IntelliNet Challenge—$500,000
Winner: Mike Hill

Mike Hill wasn't going to let another one get away, injured back or not. Hill, who had blown a two-stroke lead the previous Sunday in Tampa, shook off an early-morning back spasm with a big assist from tour-traveling Centinela fitness trailer personnel and rolled to a three-stroke victory in the IntelliNet Challenge at The Vineyards course in Naples, Florida. In the process, he broke the Vineyards record with his closing 63, which gave him a 15-under-par 201 total. It was Hill's 16th victory in five years on the Senior PGA Tour and 19th of his career.

The victory was a reversal of the Tampa loss. After his wife and son helped him to the course and a Centinela therapist popped a rib into place,

Hill teed off four strokes off the pace of George Archer (67-67) and two behind Tom Wargo, Dick Goetz and former amateur great Jay Sigel, who had begun his third pro tournament with 65 and the lead. With Archer floundering toward an outgoing 38, the contenders bunched up. Wargo went one shot in front of Hill, Goetz, Sigel and Archer when he birdied the fifth hole, then moved to 13 under par with birdies at the seventh and 10th.

Meanwhile, Hill, who birdied six times in the nine-hole stretch through the 13th after not being sure he could get off the therapist's table, was thinking about "shooting in the 50s." He made that a possibility when he birdied the 13th, 15th and 16th, but ended that chance when he bogeyed the par-three 17th. His 10-foot birdie at the 18th ensured the win. Wargo had lost his last chance with a bogey at the 16th, finishing second at 204, one stroke ahead of Archer, Goetz and Dave Stockton.

Chrysler Cup—$600,000
Winners: International Team/George Archer

In what was to prove to be the dominant pattern on the world golf scene in 1994, the International team was victorious in the Chrysler Cup. The triumph, amid controversy surrounding the event's frequently changing format, was the first in seven years for the Internationals and just the second in its nine-year history. For the second year, the Chrysler Cup was contested in a variation of stroke play, with the best five of each team's eight scores counting each day. All scores counted in the concurrent individual competition, which George Archer won with his 68-63-72–203 total and a birdie three on the first hole of a playoff against South African Simon Hobday, who had 67-67-69–203.

The Internationals' victory — 58 under par to 56 under — was checkered by the absence of Lee Trevino, who declared it was because of the change from match play, which sponsors defended as being beneficial for spectators and television and, without saying so, the talent-thin International team. Jack Nicklaus and Raymond Floyd also declined to play, reasons unannounced.

The U.S. team fell 12 strokes behind the first day — 25 under to 13 under — and spent the weekend in a vain effort to catch up. Surprising Bruce Devlin paced the fast start of the Internationals with 65 as his team had five of the day's seven best scores. Even though Archer fired his record-tying 63, the Americans only made up two strokes Saturday and trailed by 10. At one point late Sunday, the U.S. team had drawn within one shot of the leaders. However, 67 by Gary Player and 69s by Bob Charles and Hobday gave their team a 13-under day and the 58-under final total.

GTE West Classic—$550,000
Winner: Jay Sigel

Few, if any, observers doubted that Jay Sigel would be a successful player on the Senior PGA Tour when he abandoned his amateur status and joined the circuit in 1994. It's doubtful, though, that anybody expected that success to come so quickly and with such an impact as it did in the GTE West

Classic at Ojai Valley Inn in Southern California.

Sigel won in just his fourth start on the Senior PGA Tour and came from 10 strokes off the pace with an eight-under-par 62 in the final round to overtake Jim Colbert, then beat him on the fourth hole of a playoff. No winner on either PGA Tour ever made as big a final-18 comeback. Rocky Thompson had just set the Senior PGA Tour mark three weeks earlier when he made up seven strokes with 61 in the GTE Suncoast Classic.

Sigel, who was the first-round leader and finished sixth two weeks earlier in Naples, was thinking 65 and another top-10 finish when he teed off Sunday at Ojai. Colbert, seemingly in the driver's seat after his Tour-record 62-64–126 start gave him a four-shot lead over Tom Wargo, ran out of birdies Sunday. "It's hard to play the game when you can't putt," said Colbert, noting that he made just one birdie in his 72, and missed from three feet for the win at the 18th. Sigel, on the other hand, had eight birdies, including a tap-in for the 62. Both birdied the 18th to start the playoff, then Sigel wrapped up the victory with a three-footer after Colbert missed from seven feet when they played the 18th again after matching pars at the 16th and 17th.

Vantage at the Dominion—$650,000
Winner: Jim Albus

Jim Albus went wire to wire and won the Vantage at the Dominion tournament, but it wasn't as easy as it might sound. Albus, who is proving to be the best of the Senior PGA Tour players from the club pro ranks, had to grind out pars on the last seven holes on a damp Sunday to salvage a 73–208 total and a one-stroke victory over Lee Trevino, George Archer and Graham Marsh. It was his third win on the circuit and first in little more than a year.

Despite poor putting, Albus seized a one-stroke lead in the opening round at Dominion Country Club in San Antonio, shooting 68 with an eagle, five birdies and three bogeys. Archer and Dave Stockton had 69s. Albus widened his lead to three Saturday with 67 for 135, as his putting turned around. He had five birdies, including a 40-foot putt at the par-three fifth. At that point, his closest competitors were Archer and Gibby Gilbert at 138. Marsh was at 139 and Trevino at 140.

Albus thought he would suffer the fate of recent final-round front-runners on the Senior PGA Tour when he had four bogeys and a birdie on the first eight holes and yielded the lead to Archer. However, he birdied the par-five ninth and 11th holes to regain first place by one stroke over five players and clung to the lead with the seven closing pars. Gilbert and Rocky Thompson fell back with bogeys, while the other three, to the winner's astonishment, could score nothing better than pars on the way in.

Doug Sanders Celebrity Classic—$500,000
Winner: Tom Wargo

Tom Wargo got an unexpected assist from the rulebook on the way to his second victory on the Senior PGA Tour. Wargo, the 1993 PGA Seniors champion, had barely started the final round of the Doug Sanders Celebrity Classic, playing with Isao Aoki and Chi Chi Rodriguez in the final group. Suddenly, Aoki, who led Wargo by one shot, Rodriguez by two at the time, was gone, the victim of an inadvertent rules violation the previous day.

That turned the lead over to Wargo, who nursed it to the win. He shot an even-par 72 for a 209 total to edge Bob Murphy, who charged home with a 66 for 210. Rodriguez stayed in contention until he double-bogeyed the par-five 16th hole. He wound up with 73 and placed third with 211.

Wargo started the tournament with 71, three behind leaders Aoki and Larry Gilbert, then moved within a shot of the long-time Japanese star Saturday with a 66 that included a hole-in-one. It was during that round that Aoki erred, allowing his caddie to rake a fairway bunker after a search for his plugged ball, which he found, declared unplayable and was about to drop. No one at the time realized it was a rules violation and two-stroke penalty. He signed his scorecard for 68 (should have been 70) and the lead. Tour officials learned of the infraction the next day and advised a stunned Aoki as he played the second hole.

The Tradition at Desert Mountain—$850,000
Winner: Raymond Floyd

One mark of a truly outstanding golfer is the ability to make the most out of bad shots and win when his game has deserted him. Raymond Floyd is a truly outstanding golfer and he demonstrated that scrambling ability to an impressive degree in early April when he captured the Tradition title in the Arizona desert highlands outside Phoenix. It was his sixth victory in just 24 starts since joining the Senior PGA Tour in September, 1992, and came on the first hole of a playoff against Dale Douglass.

Floyd played solidly until the very end of his third round at Desert Mountain. He opened with 65, leading Gibby Gilbert by one stroke, four others by two. When Raymond followed with 70, Gilbert and Charles Coody caught up, Gilbert with 69, Coody with 67. Floyd pulled away again Saturday, but two wild tee shots at the par-five 18th cost him a bogey and all but a stroke of his lead.

The poor drives signalled more trouble Sunday. He needed eight birdies to blunt the effect of four bogeys and get into the playoff. Still, Floyd turned with a two-stroke lead over Jim Colbert and three over Douglass. Five holes later, after back-to-back bogeys at the 13th and 14th, he trailed them by a stroke. He and Douglass birdied the 15th, then Raymond holed a 32-foot birdie chip at the 16th to catch up. Both birdied the 18th, Douglass missing the win when his eagle chip nudged the flagstick and stayed out. In the playoff, Floyd reached the green in two and his two-putt birdie ended it as Douglass bogeyed.

PGA Seniors Championship—$850,000
Winner: Lee Trevino

Never did the term "watery grave" apply more aptly than it did to Raymond Floyd in the PGA Seniors Championship. Just when it appeared that Floyd was about to win senior golf's oldest national title, he buried that prospect in two ponds at PGA National Golf Club's Champion course and gave the championship to playing companion Lee Trevino. The shocked Trevino accepted, edging Jim Colbert by one stroke to win his second PGA Seniors in three years and his second Senior PGA Tour title of 1994.

Floyd, the co-leader with Larry Mowry at 138 after the second round, had entered the windy final day with a two-shot lead over Trevino (70-69-70) after his third straight 69 for a 207 total. Out in 33 Sunday, Floyd had four strokes in hand over Trevino. Five holes later, his lead was down to one, a combination of his bogey and two birdies by Trevino. Disaster struck at the par-three 15th. His five-iron tee shot went right, as had been happening to him all day, and the ball plunked in the water. From the drop zone, he pumped another into the water behind the green and finished with a seven to Trevino's par. Then, after coming back with a 40-foot birdie putt at the 16th, Raymond sank when he put his seven-iron tee shot at the 17th in the water again.

Trevino parred Nos. 16 and 17 and three-putted the 18th from 50 feet for a 70–279 total and the one-stroke victory over Colbert, who closed with 67. Floyd wound up with 75 and tied for third place with Dave Stockton at 282.

Dallas Reunion Pro-Am—$500,000
Winner: Larry Gilbert

First, it was Jay Sigel, a long-time amateur, picking up his first win on the Senior PGA Tour at Naples. Next, it was Larry Gilbert, a long-time club pro, landing his first title on the circuit in the Dallas Reunion Pro-Am in late April. Neither man was a regular who grew up on the PGA Tour. In Gilbert's case, he might have, but for an ailing young son many years ago who could not get proper care on the road. Gilbert opted for club pro work, exhibiting his talent over the years with 13 state titles in Kentucky and three national PGA Club Pro Championships, the last one in 1991.

He won more than $500,000 in his initial season in 1993, finishing second in the year-ending Senior Tour Championship before winning in Dallas. He came from three shots off the pace at Oak Cliff Country Club to edge Rocky Thompson and George Archer by one stroke with his eight-under-par 202 total.

Jerry McGee, a second-year senior whose last wins came in a pair on the 1979 PGA Tour, fired 66 twice to establish a two-stroke lead going into the final round. However, he faltered in the middle of the round and fell from contention. The battle came down to Gilbert, Archer and Thompson in the stretch. Archer finished first, leaving a 25-foot birdie putt inches short at the final hole, posting 68 for his 203. Thompson led Archer and Gilbert by one at that point, but drove into trees at the 16th and took a bogey while Gilbert was lofting an eight-iron approach a foot from the hole to birdie the 17th. The title was his when Thompson lipped out a tying putt on the final green.

Las Vegas Senior Classic—$900,000
Winner: Raymond Floyd

Raymond Floyd was glad that he changed his mind. He had not planned to play in the two events following the PGA Seniors Championship and he still skipped Dallas, but when Floyd had one of the most mortifying collapses in his career at Palm Beach Gardens, "I didn't feel very good about it and that's the reason why I elected to play" in the Las Vegas Senior Classic. Raymond was as solid in Las Vegas as he was tentative in the final stages of the PGA Seniors and rolled to a three-stroke victory, tying the tournament record with his 13-under-par 203 total at the TPC at Summerlin.

Floyd missed only five greens over the 54 holes and his only bogeys were two three-putts. "That's as good as I've played a tournament tee to green in a number of years," he reflected afterward. Still, it took him two rounds to get into high gear. His opening 68 left him two behind Kermit Zarley and Larry Gilbert. He shot 70–138 and still trailed by two, then behind Jim Dent (70-66), going into the final round.

Though a seven-time winner on the Senior PGA Tour, Dent had never won when he led on Sunday morning ... and it happened again. Floyd launched a string of five birdies at the 12th hole, passed Dent with the second one at the 13th and was home free with 65. Tom Wargo, who also started the day at 138, grabbed second place with 68–206 and Dent shot 71–207.

Liberty Mutual Legends of Golf—$1,100,000
Winners: Dale Douglass and Charles Coody

None were happier than Dale Douglass and Charles Coody when creator Fred Raphael called off the trial run of individual play after one year and restored the team format of the Liberty Mutual Legends of Golf in 1994. Good friends through most of their careers on the PGA Tour, Coody and Douglass, unspectacular individually, had proved a formidable team in earlier years in the Legends and in 1990 had run off to a seven-stroke victory with a tournament-record of 39 under par in the then 72-hole event. Douglass and Coody picked up their second Legends title at Barton Creek in Austin, Texas, this time by a hard-earned single shot. Their winning total of 28-under-par 188 was one better than the postings of Chi Chi Rodriguez and Jim Dent, and Bob Murphy and Jim Colbert.

The winners rode in front the first two days, sharing the Friday lead with Rodriguez and Dent at nine-under-par 63, then moving two strokes ahead Saturday with 61–124. Murphy and Colbert, and Dent and Rodriguez were at 126. Their outgoing 33 Saturday dropped them out of the lead for the first time, one behind Murphy and Colbert, and Rodriguez and Dent. Then Coody drove the 270-yard 12th and two-putted from 25 feet, launching a string of five birdies that restored a one-stroke advantage that he and Douglass nursed to victory with Coody's par from the rough at the last hole. Dent's eagle at the 18th had come too late, and Colbert and Murphy tied him and Rodriguez at 189 with Murphy's birdie at the 18th.

PaineWebber Invitational—$750,000
Winner: Lee Trevino

They can't say Lee Trevino didn't warn them. Trevino got the week of the PaineWebber Invitational in Charlotte, North Carolina, off to a roaring start with a course-record 63 in the Pro-Am at the TPC at Piper Glen and finished it with the tournament title in hand. The finish wasn't as easy as the prelude, though. Trevino needed a birdie at the last hole to pick off a one-shot victory, his third of the Senior PGA Tour season and 21st in his four-plus years on the circuit.

Trevino emerged from a bunched-up pack of contenders Sunday, as Piper Glen, in superb condition, yielded a multitude of low rounds all week. He was tied with Jimmy Powell, DeWitt Weaver and Jerry McGee at 135 after two rounds, having fired an outgoing 29 Saturday en route to 65, and 18 others were within four shots of the top. Four of them were tied at the turn Sunday. McGee, who had won the last Kemper Open in Charlotte in 1979, led briefly early in the final round and was still close until he bogeyed the par-three 17th.

That little hole — 142 yards below a hillside tee — did even more damage to Powell, a strong contender at Piper Glen for the second year in a row. Powell had just taken the lead back from Trevino with a birdie at the par-five 16th, only to watch as his comfortable nine-iron shot jumped over the green into the lake behind. Now, he and Trevino were tied at 12 under par with Jim Colbert, already finished after shooting 66. Lee nearly reached the green on the water-lined, par-five 18th, almost holed his chip, and won when Powell missed his 10-foot birdie putt.

Cadillac NFL Classic—$900,000
Winner: Raymond Floyd

Raymond Floyd regained the upper hand in his running duel with Lee Trevino for supremacy of the Senior PGA Tour in the Cadillac NFL Classic at New Jersey's venerable Upper Montclair Country Club. Floyd matched Trevino's three 1994 victories and inched ahead of him on the money list, but, as happened with the first win in the Tradition and with his shocking loss in the PGA Seniors a month earlier, Raymond had trouble with his game at the end. At soggy Upper Montclair, Floyd sailed into the final round with a five-stroke lead, yet had to make a par from the trees on the final hole to squeeze out a one-shot victory.

The golf pros shared the stage with many of the top NFL stars through Friday, when Floyd launched his title bid with an eight-under-par 64. He led George Archer by three, Larry Gilbert by five. Floyd followed with 68–132 and widened the gap to five over Archer, who shot 70–137. However, it was Gary Player from 138 and Bob Murphy from 139 who most nearly took advantage of Floyd's faltering finish Sunday.

In the end, it all rode on the 18th hole, a 590-yard par five. Murphy, playing just ahead of Floyd and Player and trailing by one, missed a five-foot birdie putt and posted 69–207. Player did birdie the hole, but he had been two back. Floyd went from right rough to left rough behind a tree, hit a 200-yard two iron through the green, but laid his 25-foot downhill chip a foot from the hole to save the par, shoot 74 and win with 206, his eighth triumph in 28 Senior PGA Tour starts.

Bell Atlantic Classic—$700,000
Winner: Lee Trevino

Back came Lee Trevino, who, with one exception, had been trading victories and the No. 1 money list spot on the Senior PGA Tour with Raymond Floyd for the last two months. In that period, each won three times, but Trevino's victory in the Bell Atlantic Classic at Philadelphia was his fourth on the circuit and fifth overall for 1994. When he finished up at Chester Valley, a difficult, rolling, par-70 course, with a four-under-par 206 and a two-stroke victory over Mike Hill, a relaxed Trevino effused, "I don't have to prove anything else. If I don't win another tournament, I've had a heck of a year. I'm playing with the other guys' money."

Trevino, who had won the Bell Atlantic title in 1992, had two of his four bogeys on the windy first day, when he shot 71 and trailed Tom Wargo, Jim Dent and Larry Ziegler by three. After running off eight pars on the front nine Saturday, Lee put together a 67 with four birdies and a bogey the rest of the way, taking a one-stroke lead over Dent and Tommy Aaron.

Trevino started strongly Sunday, opening a three-stroke lead with birdies on the second and third holes. The potential runaway stalled, though, and Dent caught him with a birdie at the seventh hole. Aaron was just two back. Lee remained steady the rest of the way and Dent fell back with a double bogey at the 13th and a bogey at the 15th. Trevino was home free then with a four-stroke lead. Hill, seemingly out of the picture after an early double bogey, birdied the last two holes for 68–208, the only other sub-par 54-hole score. Aaron, with 71, finished at 210.

Bruno's Memorial Classic—$1,000,000
Winner: Jim Dent

A two-year dry spell, replete with wasted chances that he had consigned to "past history," ended for Jim Dent with a finish in the Bruno's Memorial Classic that was a turnaround from the performances that had frustrated his title efforts during the winless period. Last-round woes, most often associated with poor putting, had cost him several victories in 1993 and early 1994. At Birmingham, Alabama's Greystone Golf Club, he emerged from a pack of final-round contenders with a blazing finish to capture his eighth Senior PGA Tour title, and a hot putter was the instigator.

Dent, 55, had started the Bruno's Memorial 66-68 and trailed Bob Charles by two strokes entering the Sunday round. Larry Gilbert was in between and three others — Jay Sigel, Kermit Zarley and George Archer — joined them in a free-for-all on the front nine. Then, Dent found putter magic to go with his booming tee shots. Aiming for a back-nine 30, he began with a 20-footer for birdie at No. 10, added another birdie at No. 11 and caught the leader, Charles, with a 10-foot birdie at No. 13. Then, he put the field away with birdies at Nos. 15 and 16 from 20 and 11 feet, respectively.

He came up one short of his desired 30, but the 31 for 67 handled the case nicely. With his 15-under-par 201 total, he won by two over Charles, who had an unusually unproductive time with his putter and shot 71–203. Gilbert holed a 125-yard eight-iron shot for eagle and Zarley closed with 68 to share second place with Charles, as Dent picked up his first victory since the 1992 Newport Cup.

Nationwide Championship—$1,150,000
Winner: Dave Stockton

Where have you gone, Dave Stockton? Those who so wondered about the absence of Stockton, 1993's leading money winner and Player of the Year on the Senior PGA Tour, from the 1994 winners' circle forgot to check the calendar. The 52-year-old Californian never has enjoyed much early-season success. In 1993, he didn't win his first of five tournaments until the end of April. It was time when the Tour reached Atlanta for the rich Nationwide Championship, and Stockton, in one way, did it with a vengeance. He shot 63 in the second round at the Country Club of the South to take the lead and went on to a final 198 total, the season's lowest.

Yet, he won by just one stroke over Bob Murphy, his only close pursuer, and preserved that slim margin with a remarkable par after he topped his tee shot on the final hole. Murphy mustered a 64 Saturday to stay within one stroke of Stockton, who posted 130. No one else was close nor entered the picture Sunday — Jim Albus and Jim Dent finished third at 203, Albus with his second 64 in two weeks.

Murphy stayed right on Stockton's heels and was ready to pounce from one back when Dave struck "the worst 18th hole tee shot ever hit." Envisioning a playoff, Murphy played a cautious shot to the green. Stockton had hit a 226-yard four wood far short of the green, then hit his wedge third shot three feet from the hole. The par won when Murphy failed to drop his 35-foot birdie putt.

BellSouth Senior Classic at Opryland—$1,050,000
Winner: Lee Trevino

Dave Stockton came close to making the BellSouth Senior Classic at Opryland an instant replay of his victory the previous Sunday in Atlanta, but a slight deviation in the action opened the way for Lee Trevino's fifth Senior PGA Tour victory of the 1994 season, a one-stroke decision over Stockton and Jim Albus.

Fresh from his Atlanta triumph, Stockton began the circuit's newest tournament with a 10-under-par 62 in the humid 90-degree weather of Nashville, Tennessee, yet only led Jim Dent by one stroke. He shot a third straight 31 on Saturday on the front nine of Springhouse Golf Club in the shadows of Opryland, then unintentionally slowed down the rest of the weekend. He came in with 38 for 69–141 and still had a one-stroke lead, but then over Tour leader Trevino, who had shot 67-65. Trevino inched ahead on the front nine Sunday as Dave shot 36.

Trevino seemed destined to win after he made a weird par at the 11th hole, where he drove poorly, skipped his "missed" second shot off a lake, hit a bad third shot 45 feet short of the cup, and watched a fast-moving putt hit the center of the hole, jump into the air and drop in. "Then I thought it was mine," Lee said later. He made a hard par off a poor tee shot at the par-three 17th to hold a tie with Stockton, then won at the 18th when Dave, for the second week in a row, hit a bad drive at the 72nd hole. This one went into the water and he bogeyed. Trevino made a two-putt par for 67–199 and had the victory when Albus missed a five-foot birdie putt.

Ford Senior Players Championship—$1,400,000
Winner: Dave Stockton

"This may be a fun summer." This very logical comment came from Dave Stockton after he had run away from the field and won the Senior Players Championship for the second time in three years, this time with Ford rather than Mazda as the sponsor. Not only had Stockton blitzed the opposition with a six-stroke victory and a course-record, 17-under-par 271 total, but he maintained a torrid, three-week pace in which he won twice and finished second by one shot, 51 under par all told. The only damper that day came when son Dave, Jr., didn't win at the PGA Tour stop in Hartford and achieve a first in pro golf — concurrent father and son victories.

Stockton made 24 birdies and was the only player with four sub-par rounds on the TPC of Michigan course in Dearborn, where he won his first tournament as a senior in 1992. He opened with a pair of 66s. The first one put him one shot behind leader Tom Weiskopf and the second gave him a three-stroke lead over Lee Trevino after rain delayed the start of play until nearly noon. Stockton shot 71 on a drizzly Saturday, cranking up his lead to five over Jim Albus (67-69-72), the former club pro who launched his fine career on the Senior PGA Tour by winning the Players title in 1991.

Albus picked up two strokes on Stockton with birdies at the first two holes Sunday, then lightning forced a 90-minute delay. Stockton promptly returned the favor with two birdies when play resumed and was never challenged after that. He shot 68 for the 271 and Albus 69 for 277, second by one shot over Trevino, Raymond Floyd and Isao Aoki.

U.S. Senior Open—$800,000
Winner: Simon Hobday

The 1994 U.S. Open went to South Africa in the hands of rising star Ernie Els. Three weeks later, the 1994 U.S. Senior Open also went to South Africa, this time in the hands of Simon Hobday, a 54-year-old journeyman of considerable talent but not one who ever populated the upper echelons of the game. A two-time winner on the Senior PGA Tour since arriving in America in 1991, Hobday captured the final major event of the year with a finish at famed Pinehurst, North Carolina's No. 2 Course that did not reflect the near-record score of 274 that he posted. Admitting afterward that he was choking,

Hobday struggled to 75 Sunday and held off Graham Marsh and Jim Albus by one stroke.

Until Sunday, though, Hobday outclassed all of the Senior PGA Tour's biggest names. He opened with 66 and shared the first-round lead with Albus, who had been on a tear with two seconds, a third and a fifth in his last four starts. Hobday, who had done little since early in the season, jumped two shots in front of Albus with 67 Friday, when a long rain delay stranded 33 players at day's end.

It happened again Saturday, this time catching the 18 contenders at the end of the field. At that point, Hobday had five holes left in his third round and led Albus by two strokes. He still had that margin after finishing up that round early Sunday. He began the final round with three bogeys on a day when he hit only seven fairways and six greens in regulation. Albus didn't do any better, and Marsh took little advantage until finally catching Hobday at the 71st hole. But Marsh overshot the 18th green and Hobday's two-putt par brought him the prized title.

Kroger Classic—$850,000
Winner: Jim Colbert

Jim Colbert and Raymond Floyd were the pick of the somewhat-feeble Kroger Classic field that was depleted by its scheduled position following three million-dollar tournaments and the Senior Players and U.S. Senior Open championships. Fittingly, those two provided the closing drama in Cincinnati, Ohio, as Floyd, seeking his fourth title of the season, made a vain effort to overtake Colbert, who carried a six-stroke lead into the final round. Colbert won by two strokes, shooting 69 for a 199 total, but it wasn't as tight as it sounds because he bogeyed and Floyd birdied the last hole for 65–201. The next four finishers were at 205.

Colbert, who had not won in more than a year, built a six-stroke lead over the first two rounds, starting two behind Kermit Zarley's 64 and adding a 64 of his own Saturday for 130. Floyd, Zarley, Bob Murphy, DeWitt Weaver and Rocky Thompson were next at 136. Mindful of his painful loss early in the season when Jay Sigel beat him from 10 shots back, Colbert fashioned a strong final round against a charging Floyd.

Colbert birdied five of the first seven holes with a bogey thrown in and had stretched his lead to 10 when he holed a 60-foot eagle putt at the ninth to turn in 30, 18 under par. Floyd came alive there with a matching eagle and four successive birdies. Colbert three-putted the 11th. Floyd drove into the water and bogeyed the next hole, so that, even when Colbert three-putted the 15th and 16th, he still had a four-stroke cushion.

Ameritech Open—$650,000
Winner: John Paul Cain

In 1989, John Paul Cain made a little history when he became the first career-amateur-turned-pro to win a tournament on the Senior PGA Tour. No one else had done that since then until Jay Sigel landed the GTE West title in early 1994 in his first season as a pro. Nor had Cain himself fared very well since that victory at Grand Rapids in 1989. In fact, the Houston stockbroker had lost his exempt status and was added to the Ameritech Open field in late July as a last-minute sponsor invitee. He made the most of it, prevailing in a tight finish to edge Simon Hobday and Jim Colbert, the two most recent winners on the circuit, by one stroke. He had a 14-under-par 202 total at Chicago's Stonebridge Country Club.

Cain's game, aided by a practice-round tip from Hobday, was solid all week. He missed only one fairway and three greens over the 54 holes and took just three bogeys. He began with 66, trailing J.C. Snead and Marion Heck by a stroke, then took the lead Saturday with 67–133. Colbert, shooting for his second win in a row, forged ahead late in the round, but Cain kept his chances alive when he topped a Colbert birdie at the 16th hole with a 15-footer of his own. He caught up with a good par to Colbert's bogey at the 17th and snagged the title with another par at the par-five 18th when Colbert went for the green despite a weak drive and put the ball in the water in front. Hobday missed a birdie putt there, and settled for second place with Colbert.

Southwestern Bell Classic—$700,000
Winner: Jim Colbert

Jim Colbert clearly was the Senior PGA Tour's hottest player in July after sandwiching victories in the Kroger and Southwestern Bell Classics around a second-place finish (by one) in the Ameritech Open. Colbert, a local favorite who was an athletic star in nearby Kansas City, won the Southwestern Bell by two strokes with a 196 total, the low 54-hole score to that point of the season, but he had his hands full Sunday as each of his playing companions — Isao Aoki and Larry Gilbert — matched his 65.

Gilbert and Aoki tied for second at 198. Graham Marsh, who finished fourth at 200, jumped off in the lead Friday with a four-under-par 66. Colbert shot 68, then singed the Loch Lloyd course with a 63 Saturday amid holes-in-one by Tommy Aaron and Dick Hendrickson. Aoki shot 64 and Gilbert 66 that day to share second place with Marsh (67), two behind Colbert.

Gilbert challenged early and Aoki late in the final round, but couldn't catch the hometowner, who had made the Southwestern Bell his first senior victory in 1991. He pulled away from Gilbert when he birdied the last three holes on the front nine. Aoki birdied the 11th and just missed an eagle at the 13th, but Colbert matched the birdie at 13 and opened his final margin with another at 15. Aoki had birdie chances on each of the last three holes, but missed them all.

Northville Long Island Classic—$650,000
Winner: Lee Trevino

To the competitive delight of none of the other players on the Senior PGA Tour, Lee Trevino returned to action after a three-week absence. In the lead from start to finish in the Northville Long Island Classic, Trevino registered his sixth win of the Senior PGA Tour season (seventh overall). The seven-stroke victory at Meadow Brook Country Club lifted Trevino into a tie with Miller Barber for the most career wins on the circuit, 24.

Playing with a driver he put together in his home workshop in Florida during his time away from the Tour, Trevino launched the tournament with a six-under-par 66 and shared the lead with Jimmy Powell. Although erratic early, he settled down and posted 69. That left him tied for the lead, this time with Jay Sigel ... until the next morning. Sigel had posted 68-67–135 after his Saturday round, but Tournament Director Brian Henning decided over-night that a penalty stroke had to be added to his score because of an incorrect ruling by a Tour rules official on a putting situation involving a moving ball.

This seemed to unnerve Sigel badly during the round Sunday. He three-putted four times while shooting 72. Jerry McGee, just two back after 36 holes, shot 73. That made things easy for Trevino, who blazed to a 65. That tied the tournament record and his 200 total set a new Northville mark by two strokes. Jim Colbert also shot 65 Sunday to jump into second place at 207, giving him two wins and two seconds in four weeks.

Bank of Boston Classic—$750,000
Winner: Jim Albus

Jim Albus had a streak in June and early July in which he did everything except win a second 1994 tournament. A month later, he launched another run, but this time he started it was a victory in the Bank of Boston Classic at Concord, Massachusetts. He did it under the most difficult of circum-stances, playing head-to-head with Raymond Floyd and Lee Trevino in Sunday's final grouping. Albus, now the most successful of the ex-club pros on the Senior PGA Tour, mustered a final-round 70 and his 13-under-par 203 total gave him a two-stroke victory over Floyd and a fast-closing Bob Brue.

As he did when he won the Vantage at the Dominion tournament in San Antonio, Albus led at Nashawtuc Country Club from the drenched first round to the title. In the first round that was completed in a heavy rain after eight o'clock, Albus opened with a solid 67, sharing the lead with Brue, who has never won in his many years on both PGA Tours. Albus followed with 66 Saturday for 133, making his first bogey of the tournament. Floyd and Trevino both shot 67s, Floyd then second at 136 and Trevino with Butch Baird at 137.

Albus maintained his two-stroke lead against the thrusts of those two, Brue and Mike Hill, running off a birdie and 12 pars before encountering his first trouble. He drove through the dogleg into trees on the short, par-four 14th, had to chip out and bogeyed, tightening things up. Then, he missed a three-foot birdie putt at the 15th. But, he birdied the next two holes and was home free. Floyd's putter remained cold, Brue's 65 was too little too late, and Trevino bogeyed the last two holes to tie for fourth with Hill and Dick Lotz.

First of America Classic—$650,000
Winner: Tony Jacklin

Out of competitive golf for years but prominent as captain of the European Ryder Cup team for eight years, Tony Jacklin decided to return to America once more, this time to play on the Senior PGA Tour. He went to Florida eight months before his 50th birthday (July 7th) and honed his game in mini-tour competition.

Though a former winner of both the U.S. and British Opens (1969), Jacklin was not eligible for an automatic spot on the Senior PGA Tour. He needed sponsors' invitations, which he received easily. The fourth one came from the First of America Classic and he turned it into a victory, his first since 1982 in Europe. He put in just 36 holes in winning the title at Egypt Valley Country Club at Grand Rapids, Michigan, as rain washed out the Saturday round. It was the first weather-shortened event of the season.

Jacklin had finished no better than 34th in his first three starts in America and had an embarrassing 81 and disqualification in the Seniors British Open two weeks earlier. His swing rhythm returned at Egypt Valley and he started with 68, his first sub-70 score as a senior. That left him two behind Isao Aoki, Jimmy Powell, Graham Marsh and Jim Albus, the previous week's winner. The key to the winning 68 he shot on a rainy Sunday was an eagle-birdie spurt at the 13th and 14th holes that gave him the room he needed to edge Dave Stockton. Albus and Lee Trevino (66) were at 138.

Burnet Classic—$1,050,000
Winner: Dave Stockton

Consistently high finishes and victories in three of the richest events on the Senior PGA Tour boosted Dave Stockton over the million-dollar mark in official earnings for the second year in a row, the first time this has been accomplished on the circuit. The win that put 1993's Player of the Year over the top came in the second Burnet Classic at Bunker Hills Country Club outside of Minneapolis.

The $1,059,045 moved Stockton into second place on the Tour's money list and within range of leader Lee Trevino, who had his worst finish of the season — 32nd — and gave the first real hint of the neck trouble that would later take him out of action and into surgery. Trevino, by the way, has earned over a million dollars three times but never consecutively.

Stockton's competition at the Burnet Classic Sunday came solely from Jim Albus, continuing his outstanding season and moving within million-dollar range himself. They had positioned themselves one-two Saturday after Dick Rhyan, the first-round leader at 66, skied to 77. Stockton was at 68-66–134 and Albus at 69-66–135. Albus took the lead momentarily with birdies on three of the first five holes. But Stockton moved back in front to stay with birdies at the sixth and eighth holes as Albus was three-putting twice. Stockton widened the gap to three, then three-putted the 17th to leave the door slightly ajar. Albus reached the green on the par-five 18th in two, Stockton in three. Stockton two-putted for par and had the title and $157,500 in prize money when Albus missed his 15-foot eagle putt for the tie. Stockton posted

69 for 203, 13 under par, and Albus 69 for 204.

Franklin Quest Championship—$500,000
Winner: Tom Weiskopf

Under other circumstances, Tom Weiskopf would have been a delighted man when he won the Franklin Quest Championship, particularly since it was his first official victory in the year and a half that he had played on the Senior PGA Tour. Instead, his pleasure was tempered by the pall cast over the tournament by the death of his good friend, Bert Yancey, who succumbed to a cardiac arrest attack within minutes of his tee time for the first round of the tournament.

Emotionally spent after winning the tournament in overtime against Dave Stockton, Weiskopf attributed his victory to divine guidance from his old friend and asked that Yancey's name accompany his on the championship trophy. "I didn't win this tournament," Weiskopf said. "Bert Yancey made me win it. He was with me every step of the way."

Weiskopf, who had played a limited schedule on the Senior PGA Tour since turning 50 in November of 1992, staged a tremendous finish to capture the victory at Park Meadows Golf Club outside Salt Lake City in late August. Although he was in contention from the start, Weiskopf had to birdie the last three holes to overtake Stockton and force a playoff. He shared the first-round lead with Stockton and Jack Kiefer at 68, then trailed Stockton and his 10-under-par 134 by one stroke after a 67, tied at that point with Bob Murphy.

Weiskopf fell back early in the final round as Stockton, Kiefer and Murphy jockeyed with the lead, then came alive when he holed an 80-footer at the 16th, two-putted the par-five 17th and sank an 18-footer at the 18th for 69 that tied Stockton, who posted 70 for his 204. Weiskopf made the deciding birdie when the two played No. 18 again, holing an 18-footer. Stockton then missed from six feet.

GTE Northwest Classic—$550,000
Winner: Simon Hobday

Overtime became necessary for the second week in a row when a rain-plagued GTE Northwest Classic wound up in a tie between Senior Open champion Simon Hobday and hot-handed Jim Albus. Hobday prevailed on the third hole of the year's fourth playoff, landing his second 1994 title and fourth in his four years on the Senior PGA Tour.

Albus, the ex-club pro, continuing to play as if he had been on the Tour throughout his career, began the tournament in front with 66, one stroke in front of Tony Jacklin, the First of America winner. Then, history repeated itself. Hobday and Albus were among 15 players called in off the Inglewood Country Club course when darkness set in Saturday after a three-hour rain delay.

As was the case in the Senior Open in which Hobday and Albus finished one-two, they had to wrap up that round Sunday before the start of the final round. Hobday posted 69–139 to take the lead and Albus finished with 75 for 141. Albus finished first in the regular round with a two-putt birdie at the par-five 18th for 68–209 and Hobday matched that 18th hole birdie moments later when he got down in two from a greenside bunker for 70 and his 209.

In the playoff, they both birdied the 18th again and parred the 15th — Albus lipped out an eight-footer for a win — before the South African ended it by holing a 20-footer at the par-three 16th after Albus, who overclubbed, missed from 40 feet.

Quicksilver Classic—$1,050,000
Winner: Dave Eichelberger

Dave Eichelberger blind-sided the field at the Quicksilver Classic, the rich, second-year event at the club of the same name outside Pittsburgh. Eichelberger had come to the Senior PGA Tour toward the end of 1993. He hadn't won since 1981 and didn't make a cut in his last three years. The ineptitude continued on the over-50 circuit. He didn't make a decent showing until July, and made his first big check when he tied for third in the Burnet Classic in late August.

Eichelberger was not given a serious chance of winning at the testing Quicksilver course, even though he carried a one-stroke lead into the final round. Neither was Ben Smith, a non-winner, who opened with 68 and led Raymond Floyd, Bob Dickson and Jim Colbert by a shot. He was gone after an 81 Saturday as Eichelberger moved in front by a stroke, thanks to a fortunate bounce and birdie at the 18th hole. He shot 67 for 138, one ahead of Graham Marsh, two in front of Miller Barber. Those two fell back Sunday, but Eichelberger was still in front coming down the stretch. He three-putted the 14th, then birdied the 15th; bogeyed the 16th, then birdied the 17th. "I wasn't comfortable until I chipped that one to six inches at 18." It gave him 71–209 and a two-shot win over Floyd and Homero Blancas.

Bank One Classic—$550,000
Winner: Isao Aoki

Back in America for his final stay of the Senior PGA Tour season, Isao Aoki found the key to his two-year victory drought on the circuit. "I was pressing too hard," he explained, noting this had been especially true at the Bank One Classic at Lexington, Kentucky, where he had his own nationalistic rooting section from the major Toyota operations nearby. A more relaxed Aoki scored a 14-under-par 202 total at the Kearney Hills Links for a three-stroke victory, his first on the Senior PGA Tour since his 36-hole win in the 1992 Nationwide Championship in Atlanta.

The ever-present Jim Albus and Jimmy Powell showed the way in the first round with 66s, a stroke ahead of Dale Douglass and DeWitt Weaver. Aoki, who had opened with 69, came back Saturday with 64 — the product of a chip-in eagle and eight birdies — and took the lead at 133 by one over Albus and Powell, who both shot 68s.

Aoki maintained the upper hand all day Sunday, getting into the comfort zone when he eagled the par-five third hole and Albus took an eight with two balls in the water. He secured the victory with a tough, downhill 20-foot birdie at the 15th and finished with 69 for the 202. Chi Chi Rodriguez, also experiencing a long spell without victory, eagled the last hole for 66 and finished second at 205. Albus, who steadied after the early triple bogey, tied for sixth and the $18,700 check carried his official earnings over the $1 million mark.

Brickyard Crossing Championship—$700,000
Winner: Isao Aoki

"Winning the first one was hard, but winning the second was even harder," said Isao Aoki, evaluating his victories two years apart on the Senior PGA Tour after recording the latter in the Bank One Classic. "Maybe the third will be easier." It was — and came much sooner than expected. Aoki followed the Kentucky victory with another in the Brickyard Crossing Championship, successor to the GTE North event in Indianapolis, the next week in a 36-hole event at the remodeled course at the famous Indianapolis Speedway. He was the first back-to-back winner of the season.

Heavy rains washed out Friday's scheduled first round at Brickyard Crossing. Larry Gilbert and Jim Dent, two 1994 winners, came to the fore Saturday with 65s, leading five other players, including Aoki, by one shot. Dent had a bogey-free, seven-birdie round, while Gilbert had a run of six birdies amid his two-bogey round.

Aoki had two early birdies, but figured the turning point in the round was his 15-foot par putt at the 13th that preserved his bogey-free tournament. He won it at the par-three 17th, where he put his four-iron tee shot three feet from the cup. That birdie tied him at 11 under par with Tom Wargo, playing behind him, and he had his victory margin moments later when Wargo three-putted the 17th. Jimmy Powell, in ahead of both men with a back-nine 30 for 66–134, tied for second with Wargo (66-68) as Aoki posted 67 for the winning 133 total.

Vantage Championship—$1,500,000
Winner: Larry Gilbert

With his competitive second-place finish in the 1993 Senior Tour Championship and his first senior victory in April in the Dallas Reunion Pro-Am, Larry Gilbert had proved to himself that he could play on even terms with "those guys." But, he still had something to do. "You have to win the second one to prove it's no fluke," Gilbert insisted.

Prove it he did in a down-to-the-wire battle with one of golf's premier players, Raymond Floyd, in the Vantage Championship at Winston-Salem, North Carolina's Tanglewood Park course. Gilbert's third straight 66 was just enough to nip Floyd by one stroke and collect the $225,000 first prize in the Senior PGA Tour's richest event. He was 18 under par with a 198 total and made 19 birdies.

Dave Stockton, who was to take over the money-list lead off his tie-for-third, $99,000 finish, looked like the winner when he smashed the course record Friday with a nine-under-par 63, though he led Bob Murphy by just one stroke. Stockton ruined his title chances Saturday with 74 as Gilbert and Jim Dent, who also had a pair of 66s, took over first place at 132. Floyd was two back with four others.

Gilbert faced heavy pressure from Floyd on the back nine Sunday. He bounced back from his only bogey of the day at No. 10 with birdies on the next two holes. Floyd caught him with birdies of his own at the 14th and 15th, only to doom his bid at the par-three 16th, where he pulled his tee shot into the bleachers and eventually muffed a three-footer for double bogey. Gilbert made it a three-stroke swing when he holed his 22-footer from the fringe for his last birdie. Floyd fought back with birdies at the last two holes, forcing Gilbert to two-putt the 18th green for the win.

The Transamerica—$600,000
Winner: Kermit Zarley

Kermit Zarley, a two-time winner during his career on the PGA Tour, had been flirting with victory during his first three years on the Senior PGA Tour and had come away unrewarded. The victory finally came in early October in The Transamerica at Silverado Country Club in the Napa Valley of Northern California where he had captured his first pro title 26 years earlier, though on Silverado's other course. It didn't come easily. Zarley beat Isao Aoki on the first playoff hole and became the year's sixth first-time winner.

Neither player figured strongly among the contenders through the first two rounds. Butch Baird and Bob E. Smith shot first-round 65s to lead Jay Sigel by two strokes. Baird and Sigel shared first place with Gary Player and Tommy Aycock at 136. Zarley was at 138, Aoki at 141 at that point. Player and Jim Dent dominated the early going Sunday. Dent, who started at 140, surged into a three-shot lead before taking a triple bogey at the par-five 13th. Player got close with five birdies in the middle of the round, but closed with five pars.

Meanwhile, Aoki, who had won two in a row in mid-September, was blazing. He eagled the ninth hole and followed with eight birdies and a par at the 12th hole for 63–204. More than an hour later, Zarley forged the tie with a two-putt birdie for 66 at the par-five 18th. Nearly two hours after he finished the regular round, Aoki drove into the trees on the 18th, the first playoff hole. Zarley again hit the green in two and his two-putt birdie was the winner as Aoki had to settle for par.

Raley's Gold Rush—$650,000
Winner: Bob Murphy

Thirteen years earlier, Dave Eichelberger had won his last title on the PGA Tour in a playoff in the Tallahassee Open. One of his two victims that day was Bob Murphy. Murphy enacted a bit of revenge on Eichelberger when the two wound up in another playoff in the Raley's Gold Rush on the Senior

PGA Tour late in the 1994 season. The two had tied at 208 at the end of 54 holes at Rancho Murieta, outside Sacramento. So, they played the 18th hole again ... and again ...and again ...and again ... and one final time, once too many for Eichelberger, who drove that fifth extra tee shot out of bounds, making it easy for Murphy, the 1993 Rookie of the Year on the senior circuit, to finally win his first 1994 title after five runner-up finishes.

Eichelberger, continuing his strong late-season play that included victory in the Quicksilver Classic, carried a three-stroke lead into the final round. He opened with 68, tied with Simon Hobday and trailing Gibby Gilbert by a shot. Always noted as a fine bad-weather player, Eichelberger shot 69 amid winds gusting to 35 m.p.h. Saturday to establish the three-shot margin over Chi Chi Rodriguez and Murphy.

On Sunday, Eichelberger shot 39 on the front nine. That opened the door not only to Murphy, who was out in 34, but also to J.C. Snead, winless in 1994 despite several strong bids. Snead, who had begun the day 10 strokes off the pace, shot 63 and had the lead momentarily, but eventually finished two back with Jim Albus. Murphy holed a 20-foot birdie putt at No. 18, then Eichelberger made a four-footer for the tie.

Ralph's Classic—$750,000
Winner: Jack Kiefer

Yet another club pro hit it big on the Senior PGA Tour when Jack Kiefer climaxed a steadily improving record in his four years on the circuit by winning the Ralph's Classic at Rancho Park in Los Angeles. The 54-year-old Kiefer came from three strokes off the pace in the final round with an eight-under-par 63 and 197 total to snatch a one-shot victory over Dale Douglass, who tied the Senior PGA Tour record with 61 in the final round.

Low scores were commonplace all week. Bobby Nichols shot 64 Friday and led by one shot over Tony Jacklin. Jim Dent, for whom 6,340-yard Rancho Park was a drive-and-wedge course, fired 63 Saturday, yet barely managed a one-stroke lead at 11-under-par 131 over Dave Eichelberger, who shot 62. Kiefer, who honed his game in sectional play in New Jersey and eastern Pennsylvania before trying the Senior PGA Tour, posted 69-65 the first two days.

When Dent got stuck on pars Sunday, the focus swung to Kiefer and Douglass. When Douglass birdied the 17th, he tied Kiefer for the lead. He also birdied the 18th, but Kiefer had birdies at the 14th and 15th to regain a one-shot margin and he carried that to the finish with three pars. He had been watching the scoreboard as he neared the finish. "I'm glad Dale ran out of holes," he remarked.

Hyatt Regency Maui Kaanapali Classic—$550,000
Winner: Bob Murphy

The Senior PGA Tour season was ending too soon for Bob Murphy. Only the Golf Magazine Senior Tour Championship remained on the schedule after Murphy annexed his second victory in three weeks in the Hyatt Regency Maui Kaanapali Classic. With a fourth-place finish at Los Angeles sandwiched in between, he was the hottest player on the circuit going to Myrtle Beach for the season-ending championship.

Murphy, who had exchanged the microphone for his golf clubs to join the Senior PGA Tour in 1993, fired an opening-round, nine-under-par 62, never trailed and won by two strokes with his 18-under-par 195 total, a tournament record and the lowest 54-hole score of the season. He had never won in Hawaii, coming closest 22 years earlier with a playoff loss in the Hawaiian Open.

It wasn't exactly a breeze. Murphy led by four strokes after the 62. Jerry McGee and Jack Kiefer, the winner at Los Angeles, followed at 66. McGee shot 64 Saturday and pulled within one stroke of Murphy and his 67–129 total. The issue remained in doubt after the front nine Sunday with Kiefer, Dale Douglass and defending champion George Archer still within striking distance. Archer went out in 29 and Kiefer in 30. Both Archer and Douglass shot 65s for 199 and 200 respectively. Murphy put away Kiefer at the start of the back nine when he birdied the 11th after Jack bogeyed the 10th. Kiefer never got closer than two, shooting 65 for 197.

Golf Magazine Senior Tour Championship—$1,350,000
Winner: Raymond Floyd

The Golf Magazine Senior Tour Championship ended appropriately with a duel between two of the year's most successful players — Raymond Floyd and the surprising Jim Albus. When the shooting ended, five holes into overtime, Floyd had the title and just missed snatching the No. 1 spot on the Senior PGA Tour money list from Dave Stockton, whose sixth-place finish earned him enough to stay ahead of Floyd, despite his $240,000 first-place winnings at the Dunes Golf and Beach Club in Myrtle Beach, South Carolina.

Albus, the ex-club pro who won twice in 1994 and second or third in nine other events, had the upper hand over the first three rounds at the testing oceanside Robert Trent Jones course that launched the golfing boom on the famed Carolina Grand Strand in the 1950s. The native New Yorker staked himself to a two-stroke lead the first day with 64, then slipped into a tie for first place Friday as he shot 71 and Rocky Thompson put 70 with his opening 65. Albus then went 15 under par and six strokes ahead Saturday with 66–201, Floyd advancing to second place with 67-73-67–207.

Anything but confident, Albus was "not sure what I'll do tomorrow." What he did was lose all of the lead by the 10th hole, where he took his third bogey and Floyd made his fifth birdie. Both played in strongly and tied at 273 when Albus birdied from 15 feet for 72 and Floyd from eight feet for 66. Then came a near repeat of the playoff four weeks earlier — five excursions over the Dunes' 18th hole. Both survived some challenges the first four times they played it before Floyd dunked a 15-footer for the winning birdie, winning the sixth of his 16 career playoffs.

European Seniors Tour

St. Pierre Classic—£50,000
Winner: Tommy Horton

Tommy Horton, the leading player on the 1993 PGA European Seniors Tour, picked up where he left off with a three-stroke victory in the St. Pierre Classic, the opening event of the 1994 season. The 52-year-old Englishman won the last two events of the 1993 campaign among his three titles that season. The St. Pierre victory, his fifth as a senior, was particularly sweet for Horton, who blew a two-stroke lead after 50 holes in the predecessor Gary Player Classic in 1993 and finished third to Neil Coles.

Three steady rounds brought Horton his second victory at St. Pierre in Chepstow, Wales — his first 16 years earlier in the Dunlop Masters among his 17 wins on the regular circuit. He opened with par 71, and was tied for the lead with defender Coles, David Snell and Peter Green, and was still deadlocked for first place after another 71 Saturday. Coles also had a par round, and David Butler joined them with the week's best round, 67, for his 142 total.

Horton, who tuned up for the European season by playing four weeks on the U.S. Senior PGA Tour, trailed briefly Sunday with an early three-putt, but established a two-shot lead over Coles when he birdied the eighth hole. Butler faded quickly with a double bogey-bogey start. Horton clearly took the driver's seat when he holed a bunker shot for two at the par-three 13th after Coles had made six at the 12th. Avoiding the watery pitfalls that ruined him in 1993 at the 15th and 17th holes, Horton posted 70 for a 212 total and his three-stroke victory margin over Brian Huggett, the 1992 winner at Chepstow. Coles had 74 and was third at 216.

La Manga Club Spanish Open—£100,000
Winner: Brian Huggett

Brian Huggett moved up a notch when the PGA European Seniors Tour moved to Spain for the La Manga Club Spanish Open, one of the richest events of the season. Runner-up to Tommy Horton in the opener in Britain, the 57-year-old Huggett captured the La Manga title at Cartegena with a sensational eagle on the first hole of a playoff, the fifth senior victory for the Welshman, who also was second to Horton on the 1993 money list.

David Snell, an early contender the week before, started his move toward the playoff with the best opening round, 69. The 60-year-old tumbled to 78 Saturday, falling three shots behind leaders Brian Waites (72-72) and American Chick Evans (71-73). Huggett was at 146 after rounds of 72 and 74.

Huggett, Snell and the other playoff participant, Malcolm Gregson, had brilliant stretches Sunday in forging the tie at one-under-par 215. Huggett, the frequent Ryder Cupper, birdied the last three holes for 69. Snell finished

3-3-3-3-4 — four birdies — for 68. Gregson, 50, six shots back entering the last round, had six birdies and an eagle for 65. Gregson, a reformed gadabout from his younger days, one-putted nine times, from 20 feet at the first hole and 65 feet at the seventh.

The playoff ended quickly when Huggett put a five-wood second shot on the par-five 18th three feet from the cup and dropped the winning putt. Evans and Waites missed the playoff by one stroke with 72s, with Antonio Garrido and Horton another shot back at 217.

D-Day Open—£50,000
Winner: Brian Waites

It had been a tough fight for Brian Waites to regain his health and his golf game after a severe car accident in 1991, so perhaps it was appropriate that he would win his first tournament on the PGA European Seniors Tour in the D-Day Open at historic Omaha Beach, scene of one of the bloodiest battles of the Allied invasion in World War II.

Actually, the 54-year-old Waites won with relative ease, a far cry from the struggles endured by the servicemen who fought and died on the sands and bluffs of Normandy in northern France. He opened with 69 and never trailed, eventually winning by six strokes with his 10-under-par 202 total. He put it away Saturday with a brilliant 66, when he carded seven birdies en route to a five-stroke lead over Tony Grubb.

Unshaken by a poor tee shot and an early bogey Sunday, Waites matched birdies and bogeys for a par 36 on the outgoing nine. He dropped a seven-foot birdie putt at the par-five 11th and parred in for 71 and the 206 total. Antonio Garrido, the only man in the field who had previously played the Omaha Beach Golf Club course at Port en Bessin, used his course knowledge to grab second place by one stroke from Grubb and Tommy Horton. He shot 71 for 212. Horton holed a 155-yard eight-iron shot at the 17th hole for an eagle two as he posted 68, the best round Sunday.

Northern Electric Seniors—£50,000
Winner: John Morgan

It required a record six extra holes against one of Britain's finest players of the 1960s era for John Morgan to join the ranks of tournament winners on the PGA European Seniors Tour. Morgan, a seniors rookie whose last victory had come in the 1986 Jersey Open, landed the Northern Electric title in that overtime battle against 64-year-old Bernard Hunt, the veteran Ryder Cupper, at Slaley Hall Golf and Country Club in Northumberland.

Hunt, whose starting 70 was never bettered in the tournament, led the first day, one stroke in front of Phil Ferranti and two ahead of John Fourie. Irishman Liam Higgins took charge Saturday, shooting 71 for a 144 total and a one-stroke lead over Morgan (74-71) and two ahead of Hunt (70-76), Fourie (72-74) and Ferranti (71-75). Gale-force winds struck Sunday, and Hunt's 73 for 219 stood up as the lead until Morgan bogeyed the last hole for 74 to tie the three-over-par total and Higgins drove wildly to take six and finish one shot shy with 76, in at 220 with Tommy Horton.

Hunt had the upper hand on his 50-year-old opponent through most of the playoff, lipping out with three birdie putts and a chip on the first four holes. But the determined Morgan, who had arrived early and "wheeled" the course to confirm yardages, made a 20-footer at the sixth extra hole for the winning birdie, succeeding Brian Huggett as the Northern Electric champion. Huggett won the first two stagings of the event.

Tandem Open—£52,000
Winner: Malcolm Gregson

Youth was served again on the PGA European Seniors Tour in the Tandem Open when 50-year-old Malcolm Gregson followed 50-year-old John Morgan into the winners' circle. Gregson, who joined the circuit at just about the same time as Morgan late in the 1993 season, hung on to score a one-stroke victory with his 11-under-par 205 total at Stockley Park, outside of London.

Much more benign weather greeted the seniors after the heavy stuff at Northumberland and the scores reflected it. American David Jimenez shot 67 in Friday's opening round to lead Jimmy Kinsella and Phil Ferranti by one shot and seven others, including Gregson, by two. Gregson came back with 67 Saturday and took first place, one shot ahead of Liam Higgins (70-67). Jimenez had 72 for 139, good for third place.

Gregson, who was one of the playoff losers to Brian Huggett in the La Manga Club Spanish Seniors Open in May, started fast Sunday. He sank short birdie putts at the third and fourth holes and had a four-shot lead when Higgins hit a six iron out of bounds at the fifth. Morgan, starting the round five back and bogeying the first hole, surged into contention with an outgoing 33. Despite another shot out of bounds at the 10th, Higgins hung tough, drove the 306-yard 14th with a three iron and made an eagle two. Morgan, with four back-nine birdies, finished up a 65, not quite enough as Gregson parred the last hole for 69 for the one-shot victory. Higgins birdied the 18th to tie Morgan for second.

Seniors British Open—£220,000
Winner: Tom Wargo

Tom Wargo did what none of the more prominent career tournament pros from America had accomplished in eight years. The long-time club pro, who has been a popular success on the Senior PGA Tour in the United States, became the first American victor in the Seniors British Open, the cornerstone event of the PGA European Seniors Tour, with his two-stroke triumph at famed Royal Lytham and St. Annes in late July. His eight-under-par 280 total provided that margin over Bob Charles, the defender and two-time winner.

Six years earlier, when the British Open was last played at Royal Lytham, unknown Wargo tried and failed to qualify, but stayed and watched as Seve Ballesteros won his third title. This time, he came as a two-time winner on the U.S. senior circuit and the 1993 PGA Seniors champion, riding a hot streak in America. He opened with 73, four shots off the pace of Liam Higgins, Alberto Croce and Arnold Palmer. Charles took the second-round lead with 70 and 69 for a 139 total, two in front of Doug Dalziel (75-66) and Wargo (73-68). Wargo moved ahead midway through the third round and was never behind after that. He shot another 68 for a 209 total, seven under par.

Two ahead of Charles and three in front of Dalziel, an American transplant from Scotland, the 51-year-old Wargo fought them on even terms on the closing Saturday. When the three reached the par-four 17th, Wargo had a one-stroke margin over the other two, thanks primarily to an eagle at the 11th. All three missed the green, but Wargo made par from the sand with a 20-foot putt while Charles and Dalziel bogeyed. Wargo preserved that two-stroke margin with a par at the 18th for 71.

Dalziel had 70, Charles 71 for their 282s and two-time winner Gary Player and Brian Huggett were next, five shots further back at 287. Palmer, making his best showing of the season, was at 288 with John Morgan. Tony Jacklin's senior debut in his native England came to an early conclusion. He posted an erroneous 80 at the end of a disastrous first round, had actually shot 81 and was disqualified.

Lawrence Batley Seniors—£65,000
Winner: John Morgan

Little had been seen of Peter Butler during the early stages of the 1994 PGA European Seniors Tour, but he turned his game up several notches when it came time to defend his Lawrence Batley Seniors title at Woodsome Hall in Huddersfield. Unfortunately for Butler, his improvement ran afoul of the season's hottest player, John Morgan, who parried Butler's middle-round 64 with a 65 of his own and went on to a four-stroke triumph with his eight-under-par 202 total. He became the first multiple winner of 1994, the title coupled with the Northern Electric crown.

Scoring was low on the well-groomed acres of Woodsome Hall through the weekend. Alberto Croce of Italy opened with 66 over the par-70 layout, but led by only one over Morgan and David Butler, by two over the reliable Neil Coles and David Talbot. Enter Peter Butler, who had been "practicing and practicing ... I knew my luck would change eventually." He broke the course record Saturday with 64 for a 135 total, carding five birdie threes, but that only moved him up to second place as Morgan added 65 to his opening 67 for 132 and a three-stroke lead. Morgan twice pitched and chipped to tap-in range and sank a 20-footer for one of his other birdies.

Morgan was never in trouble Sunday. Brian Huggett shot 66, but had begun the day 10 shots back. Nobody else could mount a challenge to Morgan's solid 70. Butler slipped to 72 and finished in a tie for third with Tommy Horton at 207, a stroke behind Spain's Jose Maria Roca, whose 68 was the day's second-best round.

Forte PGA Seniors Championship—£75,000
Winner: John Morgan

Though professing to be in awe of the Ryder Cup icons against whom he was competing on the PGA European Seniors Tour, John Morgan continued to leave them in his wake when the circuit arrived at Sunningdale Golf Club. The first-season oldster made it two in a row with his one-stroke victory in the Forte PGA Seniors Championship, the oldest event in European senior golf, dating back to 1957 and carrying the Forte banner since 1981. The victory, on the heels of his win in the Lawrence Batley the previous Sunday along with his earlier Northern Electric title, strengthened Morgan's hold on first place on the money list.

Rather than the likes of Neil Coles, Bernard Hunt and Christy O'Connor whom he respects so much, Morgan drew his stiffest opposition at Sunningdale from an unlikely group of challengers, led by David Creamer, a former table tennis champion no less. Alberto Croce, the Italian World Cupper, opened with the lead for the second successive week, shooting 67, one stroke ahead of Morgan and Tommy Horton. Creamer, a recent winner of the German Seniors who still had to qualify to make the Forte PGA field, fired a four-under-par 66 Saturday, tying for the lead with Morgan, who repeated his opening 68. A shot back were American stranger Terry Fine, fresh from a spell on the Japanese Senior Tour, and Croce.

Sunday's hot round, 65, came from Italy's Renato Campagnoli, but the spurt to 206 merely earned him third-place money as Morgan fashioned his third straight sub-par round. Morgan's decisive play came when he chipped in for an eagle at the 14th hole. He followed a succeeding bogey with three pars for 67 and his seven-under-par 203. Creamer shot 69 for 205, Fine 70 for 207.

Belfast Telegraph Irish Senior Masters—£60,000
Winner: Tommy Horton

Look out for Tommy Horton when he gets to a course where he was a winner in his regular tour days. First, he wins the St. Pierre Seniors Classic in May, 16 years after he took the Dunlop Masters there. Then, he picks up his second 1994 victory in the Belfast Telegraph Irish Senior Masters at Malone Golf Club in Belfast, where he won the Gallaher Ulster Open in 1971. Both victories came hard — by one stroke over Neil Coles 23 years ago, and in a playoff in the PGA European Seniors Tour triumph, his sixth on the over-50 circuit.

Renato Campagnoli, who had closed with 65 the previous Sunday in the Forte PGA, carried his momentum to Belfast. The former Italian World Cupper led the Irish Senior Masters Friday and Saturday at Malone. He started with 67, one shot ahead of Horton and two in front of Brian Waites and David Snell; then followed with 70 for a 137 total, five under par, and a two-stroke lead over Horton (68-71) and Malcolm Gregson, the Tandem winner (70-69). Campagnoli remained in the driver's seat Sunday, leading by five strokes after 12 holes, prompting Horton to feel "victory was out of my reach." Then, the Italian missed a three-foot birdie putt at No. 13 and double-bogeyed the next two water holes. He came back with two birdies, but had to sink a 12-foot par putt after nearly putting his approach out of bounds at the 18th. The 71 forced the playoff with Horton, who had three birdies and a bogey in the 69 for his 208 total.

The two played the 18th two more times after that. They matched pars the first time, then Renato three-putted from 30 feet on the next visit and lost the tournament to Horton's par.

Joe Powell Memorial Classic—£52,000
Winner: Liam Higgins

Liam Higgins, the PGA European Seniors Tour's longest hitter who came up just a bit short a couple of times in the middle of the 1994 season, broke through with his first victory in late August. The powerful Irishman mastered some nasty weather at Collingtree Park in the Joe Powell Memorial Classic and rolled to a four-stroke victory in the three-year-old event.

The 51-year-old Higgins pieced together three 70s for his six-under-par 210 total, but the second 70 was more important than it would seem. Four strokes behind Peter Butler, whose opening 66 at the Northampton course was the day's best and his second course record of the season, Higgins seized the lead with the Saturday 70, the low round on a windy, wet afternoon on a course dotted with water hazards. A three-putt bogey was his only miscue of the day as he moved one stroke ahead of Neil Coles and two in front of Malcolm Gregson. Butler, who had a run of five straight birdies in his 66 Friday, skied to 80 and out of contention Saturday.

Higgins started fast Sunday and virtually sewed up the victory with a magnificent eagle at the 533-yard fourth hole, where he reached the green with a one iron and three iron — "two of the greatest shots I ever hit" — and sank a 30-foot putt. That put him five strokes in front. By the time he reached the 15th hole, he was nine under par and leading by eight. From there in, he gave back three shots to card the third 70 and the four-stroke victory over Gregson, to whom he had lost by a shot in the Tandem Open. Coles, playing with Higgins, faded to 75 and third place at 216.

Shell Scottish Seniors Open—£100,000
Winner: Antonio Garrido

Another strong 1994 contender became a winner when Antonio Garrido, the experienced Spaniard, scored a decisive victory in the Shell Scottish Seniors Open at Royal Aberdeen. Like other first-time 1994 winners John Morgan, Malcolm Gregson and Liam Higgins new to the senior ranks, Garrido outplayed the best of the older stars of the PGA European Seniors Tour and registered an easy, five-stroke victory with his nine-under-par 201 total.

Garrido, whose impressive record in his 33 seasons includes five victories on the regular European circuit, a Ryder Cup appearance in 1979 and a World Cup victory for Spain as partner to Seve Ballesteros, drew his strongest challenge the first two days from Doug Dalziel, the America-based Scot who has played extensively on the U.S. Senior PGA Tour. Dalziel blazed to

64 on Friday and 70 on Saturday while Garrido was shooting 66 and 68, so they entered the final round in a first-place tie.

The experience of the 50-year-old Spaniard played a major role, as he rolled to 67 that included three-putt bogeys on the 16th and 18th holes. Dalziel dropped into a tie for seventh place with 75, allowing five others to pass him in the standings. Neil Coles and Renato Campagnoli bounced back from weak opening rounds to tie for second place at 206. Coles added 65 and 68 to his opening 73, and Campagnoli 68 and 66 to his starting 72. Brian Huggett, Tommy Horton and Malcolm Gregson deadlocked for fourth at 208. Dalziel shared seventh with Brian Waites.

Zurich Senior Pro-Am: Lexus Trophy—£47,000
Winner: Liam Higgins

Liam Higgins became the third multiple winner on the 1994 PGA European Seniors Tour, but it took the best final score of the circuit's three-year history to do it in the season finale in the Swiss Alps. Higgins needed every stroke of his 16-under-par 200 total in the Zurich Senior Pro-Am: Lexus Trophy at Breitenloo Golf Club to post his second senior win.

The big reason was that Antonio Garrido, who had won the previous event in Scotland, was shooting a record score himself. Higgins and Neil Coles had matched the Breitenloo course record with opening 67s, then Garrido shattered the mark in the second round with 64. Garrido, who had begun with 68, took the lead, but only by one shot, as Higgins shot 66. Coles stayed close with 68 for 135.

Misfortune plagued Garrido Sunday. He had lost a night's sleep with a severe toothache and played the final round under sedation. It showed, although he shot 71. However, this was no match for the game of Higgins, who shot 67 for the 200 total and awed the gallery and his fellow pros when he hit the 517-yard 12th with two one-iron shots. Coles also had physical problems Sunday, injuring a thumb at the ninth hole. He, too, shot 71 for 206, finishing third, one stroke in front of Brian Huggett, who had an eagle two in his 70 that secured his second-place finish on the money list. John Morgan tied for sixth at 212, clinching the money title for 1994.

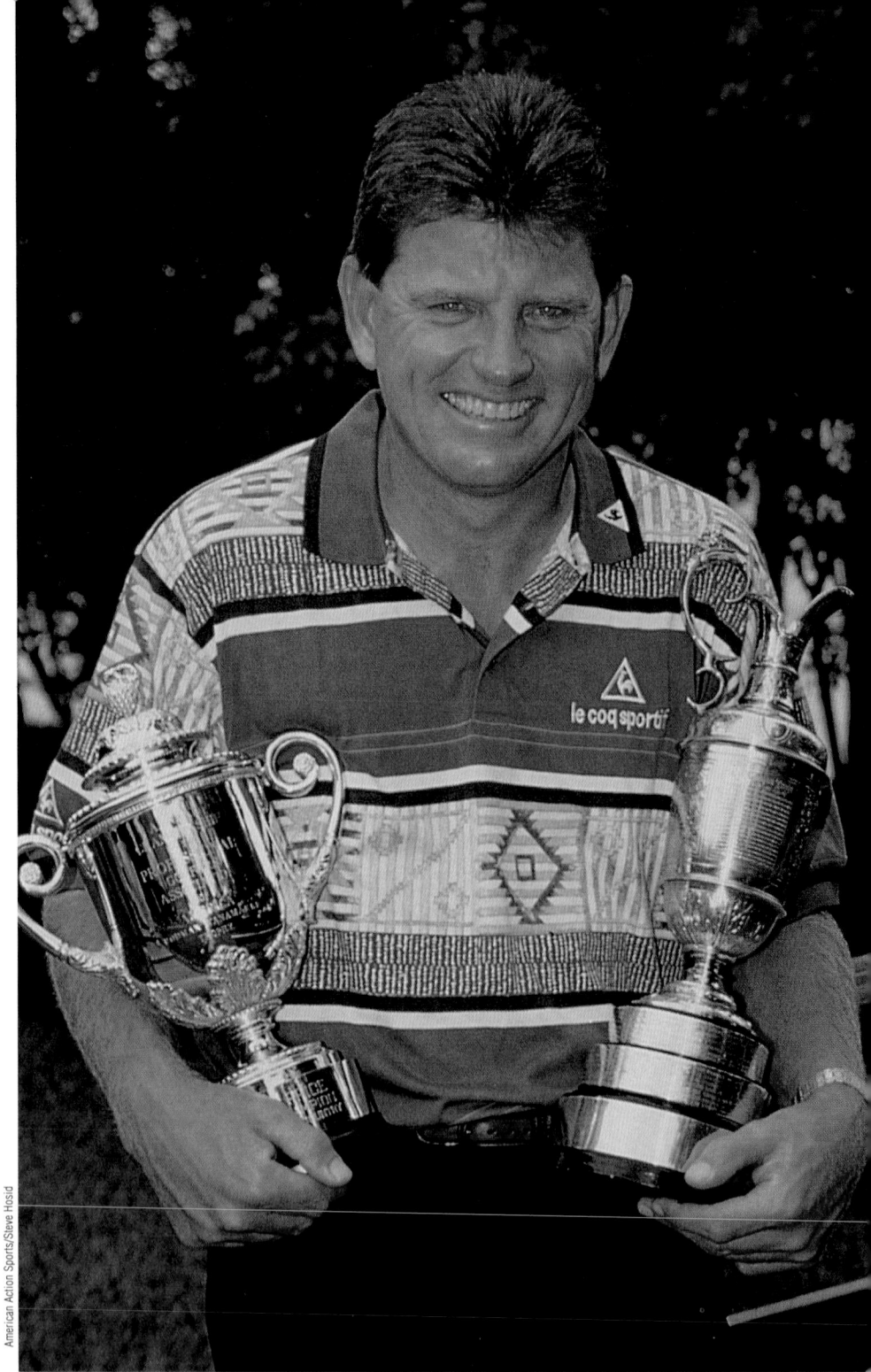

Seven victories, including two major titles, enabled Nick Price to become No. 1 in the world on the Sony Ranking.

Masters Tournament

Spain's Jose Maria Olazabal scored the sixth Masters victory by a PGA
European Tour player in the last seven years.

Larry Mize was two strokes shy of a second Masters title.

Tom Lehman couldn't believe his fate at No. 15.

Loren Roberts tied for fifth after his opening 75.

Tom Kite was again denied a Masters victory.

U.S. Open

It took 92 holes before South Africa's Ernie Els could hoist the U.S. Open trophy.

Loren Roberts barely missed a 35-foot putt in the playoff.

Colin Montgomerie was eliminated with 78 in the playoff.

With four 70s, Curtis Strange was runner-up by one stroke.

A second-round 65 helped John Cook place fourth.

British Open

Jesper Parnevik's approach shot was short on the 18th, relegating the Swede to second place by one stroke in the British Open.

Tom Watson led after 36 holes.

Fuzzy Zoeller (left) and Brad Faxon were tied after three rounds. Zoeller placed third and Faxon, seventh.

Michael C. Cohen

Nick Price celebrates the Shot of the Year, his 50-foot eagle putt at No. 17 to win the British Open.

PGA Championship

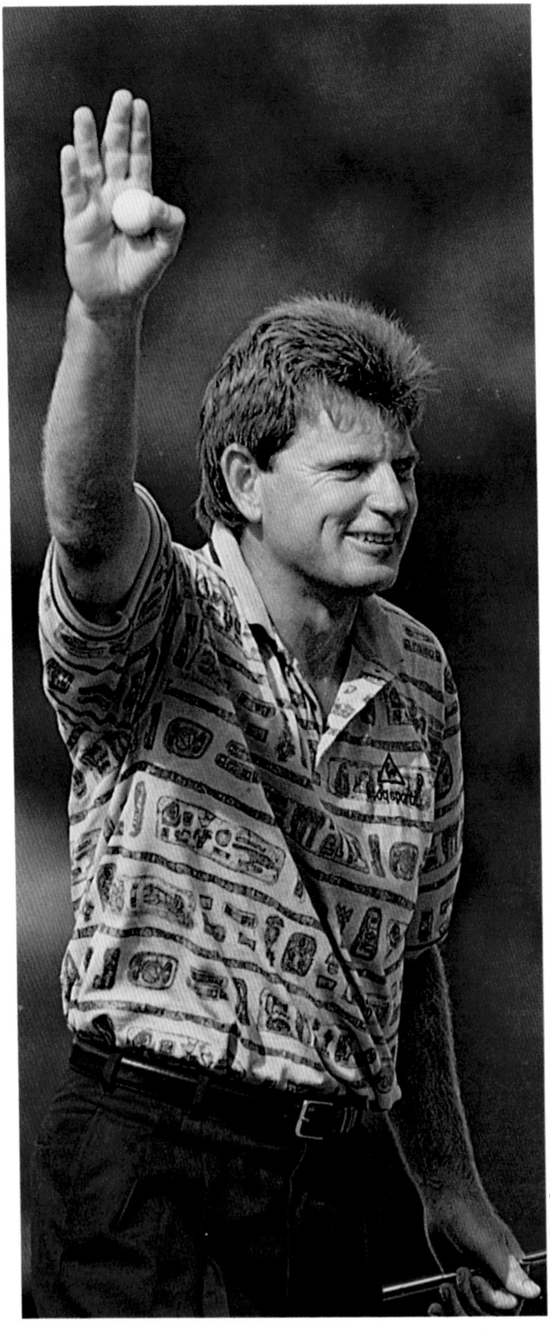

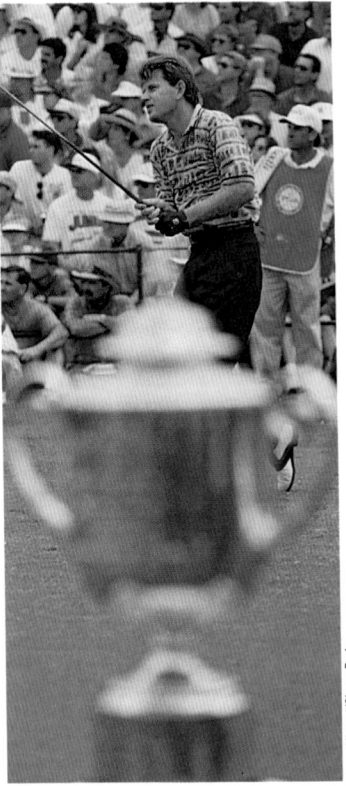

Allsport/Simon Bruty

Allsport/Simon Bruty

Nick Price led or shared the lead all the way in winning the PGA Championship for the second time by six strokes.

Corey Pavin was the distant runner-up.

Young Phil Mickelson placed third.

Nick Faldo's 66 shared fourth place.

Paul Azinger got a hero's welcome.

Alfred Dunhill Cup

The Alfred Dunhill Cup went to Canada's team of Ray Stewart, Rick Gibson and Dave Barr over the United States in the championship match.

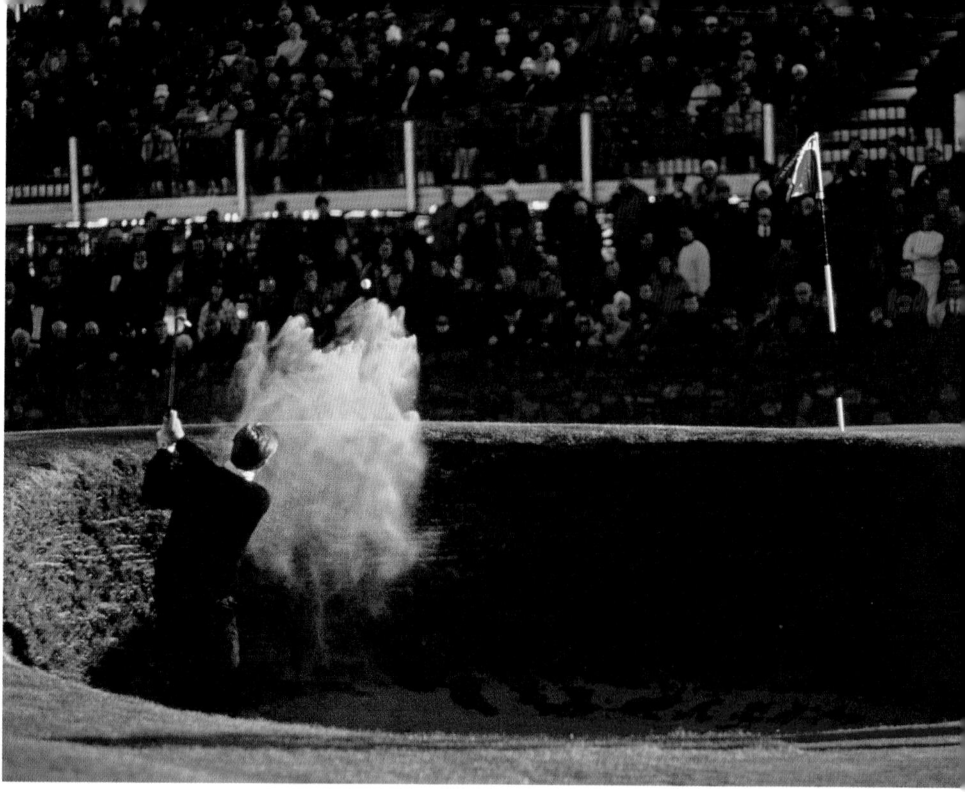

Allsport/Stephen Munday

Germany's Sven Struver blasts from the Road Bunker on St. Andrews' 17th hole.

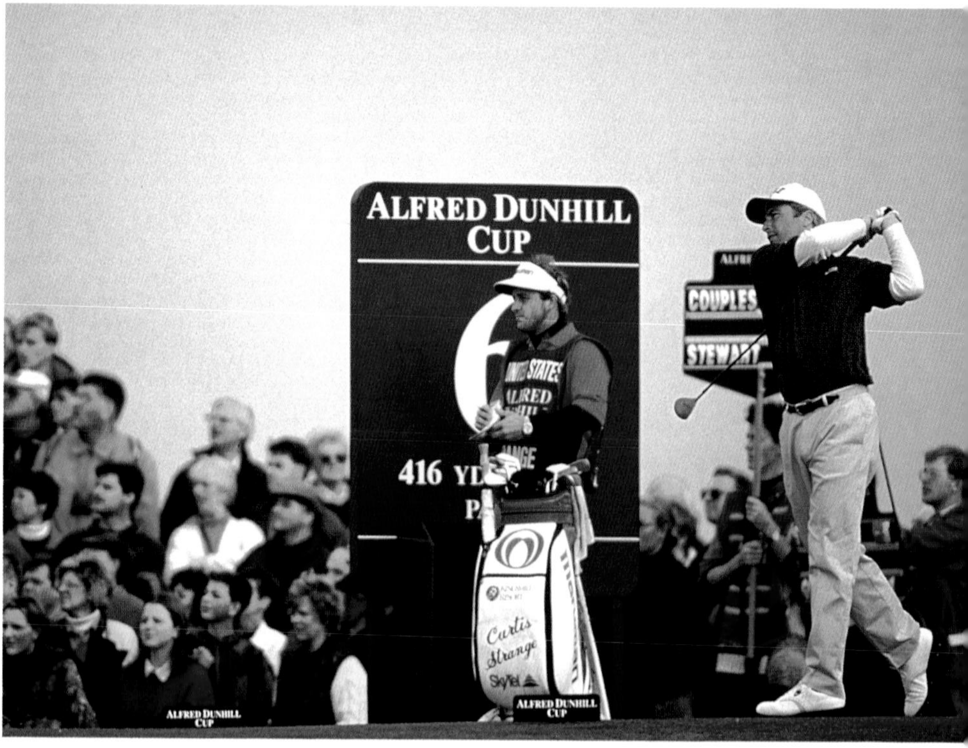

Allsport/Stephen Munday

Curtis Strange was unbeaten, but needed more help from his American teammates.

Toyota World Match Play

Allsport/David Cannon

Ernie Els tees off with the distinctive Wentworth clubhouse in the background.

Allsport/Stephen Munday

Allsport/Stephen Munday

The Toyota World Match Play was the third of Els' five 1994 victories.

As at the U.S. Open, Colin Montgomerie was second to Els in the World Match Play.

Vijay Singh lost to Montgomerie, 1 up in the semi-finals.

Jose Maria Olazabal won the third-place match.

Johnnie Walker World Championship

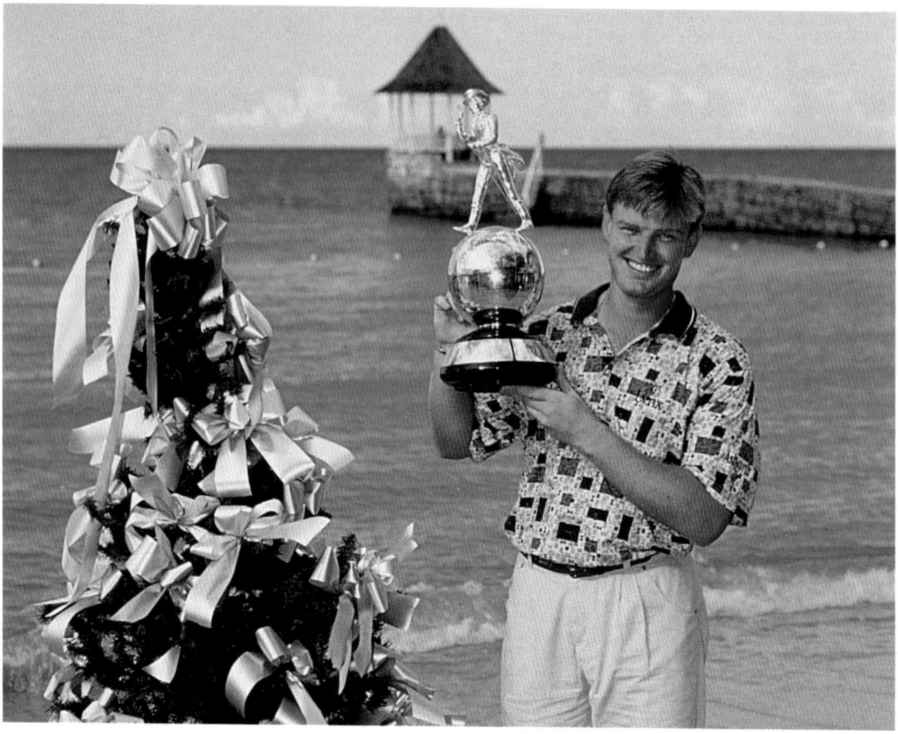

Allsport/Gary Newkirk

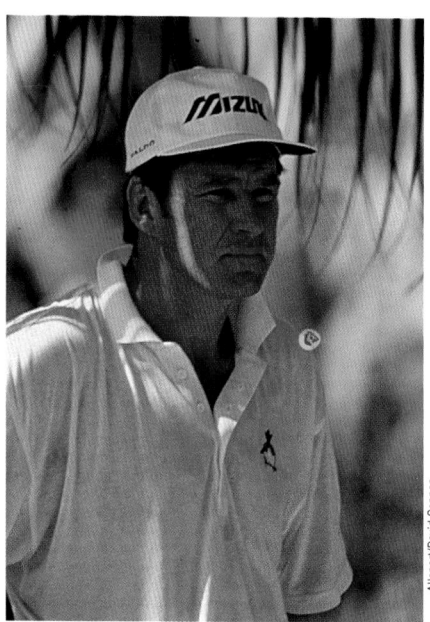

For Ernie Els, it was a six-stroke Christmas romp in Jamaica.

Allsport/David Cannon

Allsport/David Cannon

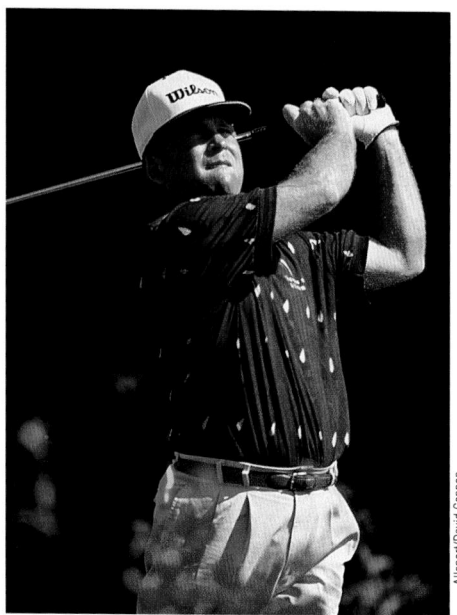

Nick Faldo (left) and Mark McCumber shared second place at 274.

Allsport/David Rogers

Allsport/David Rogers

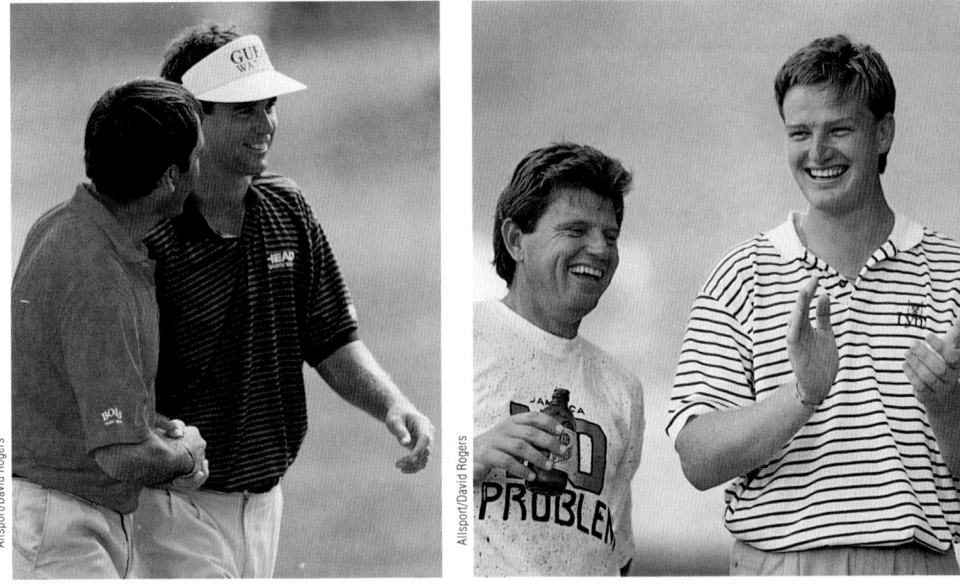

Seve Ballesteros (left) welcomed back Paul Azinger after his 64. Nick Price (right) and Els enjoyed the year's finale.

Allsport/David Cannon

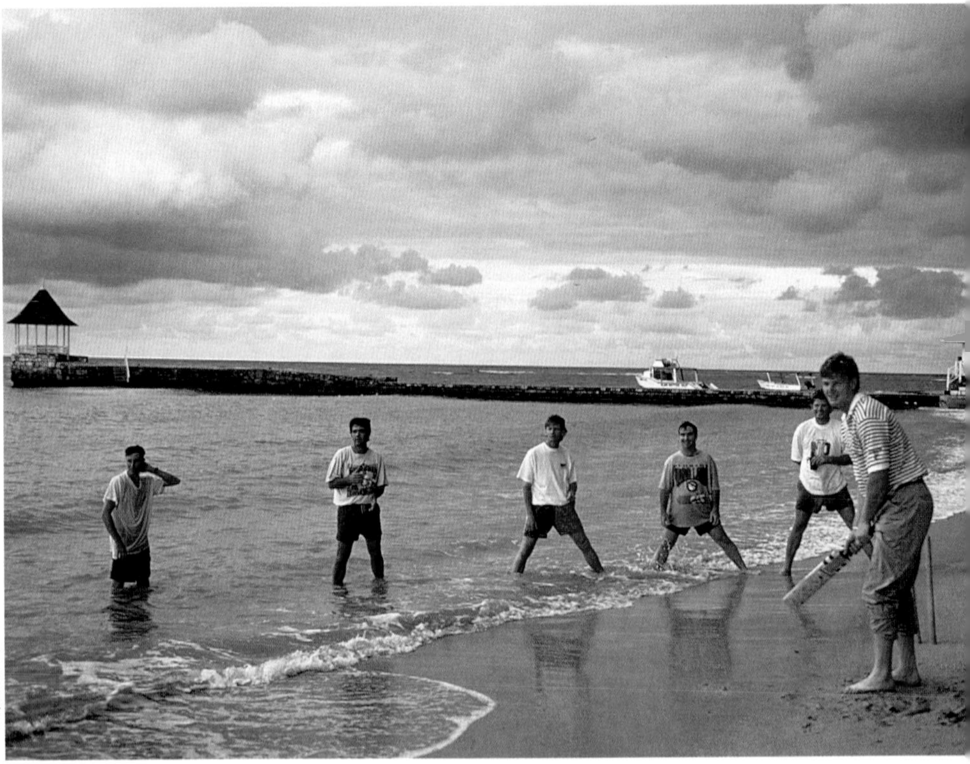

An all-around sportsman, Els also excelled in cricket on the beach with the other golfers.

A Last Hurrah at U.S. Open

Golf Magazine/Fred Vuich

Arnold Palmer acknowledges a tremendous ovation in his final U.S. Open appearance at Oakmont Country Club in his native western Pennsylvania.

Japan Senior Tour

American Express Grand Slam—¥60,000,000
Winner: Lee Trevino

Another corporation wrote it, but the name on the winner's check at the annual Grand Slam tournament, the international highlight of the seniors season in Japan, was the same — Lee Trevino. The American star accepted ¥9 million in prize money from the tournament's new sponsor, American Express, with his repeat victory at Japan's Oak Hills Country Club near Tokyo, continuing a multiple-winner pattern in the 12-year-old event. Bob Charles won three years in a row; Gene Littler, Miller Barber, Lee Elder and now Trevino twice each. Raymond Floyd (1992) is the only one-timer.

Trevino also repeated his winning score in the 1994 opener of the Japan Senior Tour, but this time his nine-under-par 207 total routed the opposition, Gary Player finishing seven strokes back at 214. Trevino won by two in 1993. The 1994 win was the second of the year for Trevino.

The leaderboard was crowded at the top Friday. Taiwan's Chen Chien Chung's 69 put him a stroke ahead of Trevino and four others — fellow Americans Jay Sigel and Bill Hall and Japan's Masaru Amano and Kesahiko Uchida — with seven more at 71. Trevino took charge Saturday with 68, moving two strokes in front of Haruo Yasuda and three ahead of Player. Both shot 69s. Hall and Tom Weiskopf stayed close at 142. Trevino was never threatened Sunday. His 69 blew up the big final gap as Yasuda fell to 76 and Player mustered just 73, enough to hold onto second place. Amano was at 215, and Weiskopf tied Hisashi Suzumura (69) for fourth at 216.

TPC Starts Senior—¥50,000,000
Winner: Seiichi Kanai

Seiichi Kanai picked up where he left off in 1993, in the driver's seat on the Japan Senior Tour after the international players departed the scene and the domestic circuit got underway. Kanai, the 1993 money list leader with ¥39,813,750, duplicated one of his four 1993 victories when he captured the TPC Starts Senior, defeating Hsieh Min Nan and Hiroshi Ishii in a playoff after they finished in a three-way tie with six-under-par 282s at Garden Golf Club. Kanai birdied the first extra hole to secure the victory.

Kanai, winner of 16 titles in earlier days on the regular circuit, was five strokes back after an opening-round 72 as Kikuo Arai led with 67. Hsieh was at 68 with Shoji Kikuchi and Ishii at 69 with Ryosuke Ota. Kanai narrowed the gap Friday with 69 for 141, two behind Hsieh (71) and Ota (70), the new leaders at 139. Ishii shot 71 for 140. Hsieh, the long-time Taiwanese star who won three times on the Japan circuit in 1993, took a two-stroke lead Saturday with 69 for 208. Ota fell back with 75, leaving Kanai (69) and Ishii (70) the closest pursuers at 210. The tie was forged Sunday when Hsieh took a 74 and Kanai and Ishii had 72s.

Daiichi Seimei Cup —¥50,000,000
Winner: Hiroshi Ishii

Hiroshi Ishii rebounded from a playoff loss in his last previous start on the Japan Senior Tour six weeks earlier to win the Daiichi Seimei Cup at Tomisato Golf Club in Chiba Prefecture. He produced a dazzling, eight-under-par 64 and claimed a four-stroke victory with his 203 total.

Ishii moved up each day after his first-round 71 left him in 17th place, five behind leader Billy Dunk, the Australian who won twice on the Japan Tour in 1993. Ishii's second-round 68 jumped him into a third-place tie with the fabled Chen Ching Po at 139 as Haruo Yasuda, the Grand Slam contender, went ahead with 66 for 136. Eleuterio Nival of the Philippines settled in the runner-up slot with 68–138. That's where Nival finished Sunday, four shots behind winner Ishii with 69 and 207, as Yasuda faded to 73 and tied Hsieh Min Nan for third at 209.

Mizuno Senior Classic—¥30,000,000
Winner: Tetsuhiro Ueda

Tetsuhiro Ueda joined the winners' ranks on the Japan Senior Tour in late May, scoring a come-from-behind victory in the Mizuno Senior Classic at Daiei Country Club in Chiba Prefecture. Ueda, who never won on Japan's regular circuit, picked off the Mizuno Senior title with his closing 66 for a 204 total, 12 under par, and a two-stroke margin over Hiroshi Ishii, the previous week's winner, and Ichiro Teramoto.

Although close for two days, Ueda never led until he went in front the last day. Teramoto, Takeo Abe and Mitsuhiro Kitsuta shared the first-round lead with 68s as six players, including Ueda, had 69s. Teramoto duplicated his opening round Saturday and his 136 gave him a one-shot lead over Teruo Suzumura and Ryosuke Ota. Ueda had another 69 and was two back with Ishii and Kitsuta entering the final round. Ishii shot 68 and Teramoto 70 Sunday.

Japan PGA Senior Championship—¥50,000,000
Winner: Shigeru Uchida

Shigeru Uchida got his hands on the PGA Senior Championship in 1993 and liked the idea. He did it again when the championship was staged at Shimoakima Country Club in Gunma Prefecture the first week of June. In command for all except one round, Uchida closed with a steady 70 for a seven-under-par 281 and a two-shot victory over Fujio Kobayashi.

Uchida probably won the tournament the first day when he grabbed the lead with a strong 66. Seiji Ogawa, who eventually tied for third, three strokes back at 284, was the only other player to break 70 the first day with 68. A 71 Friday widened Uchida's margin to three over Ogawa (68-72), but he slipped a stroke off the pace Saturday when he shot 74 for 211. Masaru Amano moved a stroke in front with 69–210 and Ichiro Teramoto, the Mizuno co-runner-up, joined Uchida at 211 with his 68. Both had 74s Sunday.

Komatsu Open—¥30,000,000
Winner: Ryosuke Ota

Ryosuke Ota fulfilled earlier threats in the Komatsu Open. Ota, the winner of the 1993 Ho-Oh Cup, got what he deserved in the final round at Sahara Springs Country Club in Chiba Prefecture. He shot the day's second-best round — 68 — and it gave him a one-stroke victory at eight-under-par 208. He edged Billy Dunk, Seiji Ogawa and Masaru Amano, three others who had been in contention in earlier events, by one stroke.

Ogawa, a third-place finisher the previous week, led the first day at Sahara Springs with 66, two strokes ahead of Ota and five others, and retained first place Saturday with 70–136. Norihiko Matsumoto was at 138, Dunk at 139 and Ota and three others at 140. Ogawa was the big loser Sunday with 73 for his 209 total. Amano shot 69 and Dunk 70. Haruo Yasuda, far back after two rounds, shot 65 Sunday.

HTB Senior Classic—¥30,000,000
Winner: Masaru Amano

Another frequent contender in the early season, Masaru Amano, put a win on his record as the Japan Senior Tour concluded the first half of its season and headed for a three-month hiatus. Amano captured the HTB Senior Classic title at Chitose Kuko Country Club in Hokkaido, but barely survived a final-round 74. His eight-under-par 208 total edged Kikuo Arai and Seiji Ogawa by one stroke.

Amano set up the victory with back-to-back 67s. The first gave him a one-stroke lead over Shigeru Uchida and Namio Takasu, and the second one elevated him four strokes ahead of Uchida, the two-time Japan Senior PGA champion, and five strokes in front of five others, including Ogawa, who had led for two rounds the week before in the Komatsu Open. Once again, Ogawa came up one short as he shot 70 to the winner's 74. Arai came from far back with 67 to share the runner-up slot with Ogawa.

Tokyu Senior Cup—¥30,000,000
Winner: Norihiko Matsumoto

A new winner surfaced when the players on the Japan Senior Tour reassembled to continue their season in late September. Norihiko Matsumoto, who had made a minimal impact on the circuit up to that point, was impressive in his victory in the Tokyu Senior Cup at Grand Oak Golf Club in Hyogo Prefecture. Matsumoto shot 65 to take the lead the first day and was never seriously threatened the rest of the way. He finished with a 14-under-par 202 total and a five-stroke margin.

The first-round 65 put Matsumoto three strokes ahead of Hsiung Kuo Chie, Seiichi Kanai, Kiyokuni Kimoto and Seiji Ogawa, a second-place finisher in his last two starts. When he followed with 67 Saturday, Matsumoto widened his advantage to four strokes over Teruo Suzumura, who shot 65 for 136. Eight players were at 138 and one of them, Yoshihiro Takada, eventually occupied the runner-up slot at 207 as Matsumoto closed with 70. Ageless Teruo Sugihara tied for third at 208 with Hsiung and Haruo Yasuda.

Nagoya TV Cup—¥40,000,000
Winner: Seiichi Kanai

The parade of different winners every tournament came to an end when the Japan Senior Tour reached Hananoki Golf Club at Mizunami in Gifu Prefecture for the Nagoya TV Cup in late October. Not surprisingly, Seiichi Kanai was the string breaker. Kanai, who had won the TPC Starts tournament in early April, had the best of a barrage of low scores Sunday at Hananoki and emerged with a nine-under-par 207 total and a one-stroke victory over Hsiung Kuo Chie.

Mitsutaka Kono was the first-round leader with 68 as Kanai settled for a par round. Hsiung, the defending champion, strengthened his bid for a repeat with a second-round 69 that gave him 139 and a one-stroke lead over Mitsuhiro Kitsuta and two over the omnipresent Seiji Ogawa. Kanai was then three strokes back after 70 for a 142 total. A 65 and three 66s went up on the scoreboard Sunday, and Kanai had the lowest number, scoring his sixth victory in two years on the senior circuit. Hsiung fell a stroke short with his 69, Haruo Yasuda had one of the 66s and finished third at 210.

Ho-Oh Cup—¥35,000,000
Winner: Seiichi Kanai

Riding a hot hand, Seiichi Kanai made it two in a row on the Japan Senior Tour, capturing the Ho-Oh Cup on the golf course of the same name the Sunday after he landed the Nagoya TV Cup title. It was another tight squeeze for the circuit's most successful player, winning a head-to-head battle by one shot over Ichiro Teramoto, who had a couple of near-misses in the early season.

Par took a beating at Ho-Oh Friday as Billy Dunk of Australia fired an eight-under-par 64 and Hiroshi Ishii, the Daiichi Seimei winner, and Hsieh Yung Yo, the great Taiwanese player, opened with 65s. Kanai and Hsieh Min Nan shot 66s and eight others broke 70. Kanai went ahead by one stroke Saturday with 67–133, in front of Teramoto, who matched Dunk's 64, and Ishii. Both Kanai and Teramoto shot 69s Sunday. Masaru Amano, with three 68s, placed third. Ishii had 71 Sunday and tied for fourth with Ryosuke Ota.

Asahi Kokusai Vintage Classic—¥30,000,000
Winner: Haruo Yasuda

Haruo Yasuda, who made several unsuccessful runs on the Japan Senior Tour earlier in the season, prevailed in a four-man scramble for the title in the Asahi Kokusai Vintage Classic in early November. Yasuda carried a one-stroke lead into the final round at the Hamamura Onsen Golf Club and won by that margin with his nine-under-par 207 total.

Taiwan's Hsu Chie San opened the tournament with 65 and a three-stroke lead over Fujio Kobayashi, but slipped slowly down the ladder after that. Yasuda, who started with 71, fired 66 Saturday to take his one-stroke lead over Kobayashi (68-70), Hsieh Min Nan (71-67) and Hsu (65-73). Kikuo Arai was at 72-67–139 and gave Yasuda his stiffest test Sunday, shooting 69 while taking 35 putts. Yasuda had better putting luck, shooting 70 with 31 putts for the one-stroke triumph. Kobayashi and Hsieh, with 71, tied for third at 209.

Japan Senior Open—¥50,000,000
Winner: Isao Aoki

The players on the Senior Japan PGA Tour could look at it two ways. With Isao Aoki playing full-time on the Senior PGA Tour in America, they all had better chances of winning. However, they also recognized how much his presence would have added to the prestige and financial well-being of the circuit. Aoki proved the first point when he made his initial appearance on the Senior Japan Tour in the Senior Open championship in late November and made it the 64th victory of his marvelous career.

Aoki, who won twice earlier in the year in America, came from five strokes off the pace at Nara Kokusai Golf Club to score a one-stroke victory over third-round leader Mitsuhiro Kitta. He shot a final-round 67 for a 279 total, nine under par. Aoki caught Kitta at the turn Sunday, shooting 34 while Kitta was absorbing two double bogeys en route to a 39. Kitta recovered and played the back nine in 34, but fell one stroke shy as Aoki came home with 33 for the winning 67. Gary Player competed in the Japan Senior Open and placed third at 284.

Ryokuei Group Cup—¥40,000,000
Winner: Hsieh Min Nan

Hsieh Min Nan went from contender to champion at the end of the Japan Senior Tour season. After third- and fifth-place finishes the two previous weeks, the talented Taiwanese veteran captured the Ryokuei Group Cup, the final event of the year, with his seven-under-par 209 total. His only serious challenger in the final round was Seiichi Kanai, the season's top performer who was gunning for his fourth 1994 title. Kanai finished two behind Hsieh at 211, four shots ahead of Sadao Ogawa in third place.

Masaru Amano launched an erratic weekend at the Onahama Springs Hotel and Golf Club with 67 to lead Ogawa by one, Kikuo Arai and American Art Proctor by two. Hsieh then raced to a three-stroke lead with a 67 Saturday for 137. Kanai, with 72-68, was next at 140 and gave Hsieh his only competition Sunday. He shot 72, but picked up just the single stroke as Hsieh clinched victory with 71.

17. Women's Tours

The Player of the Year on the LPGA Tour in the United States was Beth Daniel. Liselotte Neumann led the Women's Professional Golf European Tour, and Mayumi Hirase was No. 1 on the Japan LPGA circuit. On a worldwide basis, however, none could touch England's Laura Davies, who had eight victories spread over five Tours, including a major title in the McDonald's LPGA Championship. She also would have won the Nabisco Dinah Shore, but for a two-stroke swing on the final hole.

Davies' other victories were the Standard Register Ping and Sara Lee Classic in America, Irish Holidays Open and Skoda Scottish Open in Europe, Thailand Open, Itoen Ladies in Japan, and Alpine Australian Ladies Masters.

In the Australian victory, which was the final tournament, only a week before Christmas, Davies equalled an all-time scoring record with a 20-under-par performance at the par-73 Royal Pines Resort in Queensland. It had been done previously by Daniel and Nancy Lopez in the United States and by Dale Reid in Europe.

Davies' victories on five Tours in one year matched the 1974 accomplishment of Gary Player, who won nine times including the Masters and British Open. That was also the year he shot 59 in the Brazil Open. He won three tournaments in South Africa, two in America, two in Europe, and one each in Australia and Brazil.

Davies' earnings on the U.S. LPGA Tour were $687,201, which were $27,775 more than Daniel earned with four victories. But Daniel won the Rolex Player of the Year award, based on a points system, 48 points to 47. The contest literally came down to the last putt, with Davies leaving short an eight-foot putt in the Toray Japan Queens Cup that would have given her fourth place in the tournament, worth two points.

Age 31, Davies now has 31 victories worldwide, including the 1987 U.S. Women's Open. "This is the best season I've ever had," she said. "Maybe when the merry-go-round starts again in January, I will win the Player of the Year title. The money title was the one I wanted this year."

Standing 5-10 and weighing 180 pounds, she is one of the strongest players ever in women's golf. Until this year, however, her power hadn't translated into dominance. "Now she's taken the game by the scruff of the neck," said Terry Coates, executive director of the WPG European Tour. Her problem was not physical, but temperamental. "Because I hit it such a long way," Davies said, "everyone assumed the game was easy for me."

Daniel began the year with 27 career victories, but none since 1991. She earned her third Player of the Year title with victories in the Corning Classic, Oldsmobile Classic, JAL Big Apple Classic and World Championship of Women's Golf. Other LPGA headliners included major championship winners Donna Andrews in the Nabisco Dinah Shore, Patty Sheehan in the U.S. Women's Open, and Martha Nause in the du Maurier Ltd. Classic. Andrews had a total of three victories.

Betsy King and Amy Alcott both went without a victory, each needing just one more to have 30 career triumphs and qualify for the LPGA Hall of Fame. Alcott had not won since 1991, and King continued to come agonizingly close to her milestone victory. In the final tournament of the year, the Toray Japan Queens Cup, which King won in 1993, she lost a playoff to Woo Soon Ko of Korea.

It must also be noted among the year's highlights that the Americans won back the Solheim Cup, which they lost to the Europeans two years earlier.

The Swedes again had several outstanding performers, led by Liselotte Neumann, who won twice on the U.S. LPGA Tour and three times on the WPG European Tour, where she led the money list with £102,750. She was third in the U.S. with $505,701. Helen Alfredsson let the U.S. Women's Open slip from her grasp for the second consecutive year after holding a commanding lead, but she won the next week and also had a victory in Europe. Annika Sorenstam was the Rookie of the Year in America and later took her first professional victory in the Holden Australian Open.

Hirase led the Japan LPGA Tour with ¥69,817,958 and four victories, earning ¥4,006,342 more than Ikuyo Shiotani, who won three times. Jae Sook Won had three victories in Japan and one in Australasia, and Ayako Okamoto won three events in Japan.

Women's golf lost one of its greatest supporters in 1994, when Dinah Shore died at age 76. She was elected as the first honorary member of the LPGA Hall of Fame. She had been associated with the LPGA since 1971. She had no interest in golf until David Foster, then chairman of Colgate Palmolive, ask her to lend her name to a tournament. She later became a keen golfer.

HealthSouth Palm Beach Classic—$400,000
Winner: Dawn Coe-Jones

After winning only once in 10 seasons, Dawn Coe-Jones decided it was time to do something about it. She won the first event of the year on the LPGA Tour, the HealthSouth Palm Beach Classic.

Coe-Jones had consistent rounds of 67, 69 and 65 for a 209 total and a one-stroke victory over Lauri Merten and two strokes better than Laura Davies. "In the last three years, I've been playing more in the off-season, since I moved to Tampa," Coe-Jones said. "When I lived in Houston, I didn't play that much. I think in playing more since I moved to Florida, I come out to the first tournament ready to go."

Lisa Walters took the first-round lead with 66 and shared first place with Davies after 36 holes. For a while on Sunday, it appeared Merten, the U.S. Women's Open champion, would spoil Coe-Jones' effort. Coe-Jones would have none of it, however. After making the turn in 31 to lead by one stroke, she birdied Nos. 11 and 12. Then, after a bogey at No. 16 dropped her into a tie with Merten, Coe-Jones ran in an 18-foot birdie at No. 17 for the victory.

Hawaiian Open—$500,000
Winner: Marta Figueras-Dotti

After 10 years of congratulating other players on their victories, Marta Figueras-Dotti finally received her champagne shower by winning the Hawaiian Open.

A final-round 71 and 209 total, seven under par, gave Figueras-Dotti a one-stroke victory over Jane Geddes.

Figueras-Dotti had to work hard for it. A two-stroke swing at the par-three 16th ultimately decided the outcome. Geddes, playing in the next-to-last group, hit into a bunker and made bogey. Figueras-Dotti took advantage, making birdie from eight feet, to lead by two strokes and had the luxury of bogeying the last hole. "After all I've been through, both mental and physical, this is wonderful," Figueras-Dotti said. "In the past, there was always something happening to me. The last four years have been horrendous."

Val Skinner led the first round with 67, then shared the lead with Figueras-Dotti after 36 holes, with Betsy King just one stroke back in search of victory No. 30 and entry into the LPGA Hall of Fame. King faded with a closing 76, and Skinner couldn't get any putts to fall, shooting 74.

Chrysler-Plymouth Tournament of Champions—$700,000
Winner: Dottie Mochrie

When the final round of the Chrysler-Plymouth Tournament of Champions began, Nancy Lopez was the sentimental favorite and Betsy King the lady-in-waiting to enter the LPGA Hall of Fame. But it was Dottie Mochrie who beat one of the best LPGA fields ever assembled to win this inaugural event for tournament winners of the past two years. Mochrie started the last round trailing Lopez by two strokes, finished with a three-under-par 69 and a 287 total, and beat Lopez and Lauri Merten by two. King was no factor this week at the Grand Cypress Resort in Orlando, Florida. After holding a four-shot lead through 36 holes, she followed with 74 and 76 to tie for seventh place.

"Oh, what a feeling. This is the best field you can put together," said Mochrie, the only player to finish under par. "I feel fortunate to have been here." Mochrie came out of the gate at a gallop in the last round. She holed out at No. 1 for eagle to catch Lopez, then birdied the second, eighth, 11th and 12th holes to take a three-shot lead over Merten. Even with bogeys at Nos. 17 and 18, Mochrie was unchallenged because Lopez did the same.

The wind eliminated all but the hardy the first two days when the average scores were 75 and 78. There were more sub-par rounds (12) in the final round than in the first three (nine). "I've always been intense," Mochrie said. "I enjoy my job, but it is a job. It's like (husband) Doug said when someone in the gallery told me to smile. 'This is not the Ice Capades. You don't fall on a double axel and get up and smile, and everything's okay, you know.'"

Ping/Welch's Championship—$425,000
Winner: Donna Andrews

To understand how Donna Andrews won the Ping/Welch's Championship in Tucson, you have to go back to 1990 and the Women's Kemper Open in Hawaii, where she opened with a pair of 70s, then shot 81. How could that happen? Trade winds. They came up in the third round and blew Andrews, who had never played in such breezes, off the leaderboard.

"I had never played in those conditions and when I got back from that experience I told my instructor, Jack Lumpkin, to teach me how to hit the knock-down shot," Andrews said. Lumpkin must have done a good job, because Andrews made the Ping/Welch's Championship her second LPGA victory. She shot 73 for a 12-under-par 276 total in 40 mile-an-hour winds on Sunday and won by three strokes over Brandie Burton and Judy Dickinson.

"It was anywhere from a three- to five-club wind," Andrews said. "It's a good thing I started out with 66, because my score went up every day." Only 10 of the 71 players who made the cut broke par the last day and eight soared into the 80s.

Andrews' opening 66 was only good for second place behind Michelle Estill, but a second-round 68 put her up by two strokes and she moved three up on a third-round 69.

Standard Register Ping—$700,000
Winner: Laura Davies

When Laura Davies is on her game, other members of the LPGA Tour roll their eyes toward the heavens and wonder aloud, "Now, why can't I do that?" The Standard Register Ping tournament in Phoenix was one of those occasions, especially the final two rounds, when Davies shot 66 and 70 to blitz the field on the way to a four-shot victory over Beth Daniel and Elaine Crosby.

Leaving her driver in the bag in the last round, Davies went to her two iron, and hit every fairway while completing a 15-under-par 277 total. "I was swinging out of my shoes (with my driver) and barely keeping up with her two iron," said Kelly Robbins, the 36-hole leader. "When she keeps it in play, nobody's going to catch her."

Davies had a simple explanation for down-shifting. "There was no reason to hit the driver. The fairways were running well and I used the irons to protect my lead," she said. That lead was established early in the final round. Back-to-back birdies at the third and fourth holes, along with third-round leader Crosby's bogey at No. 4, gave Davies a four-stroke advantage. Crosby got back within two strokes with a birdie at No. 16, but bogeyed the 17th hole.

Nabisco Dinah Shore—$700,000
Winner: Donna Andrews

This was the first Nabisco Dinah Shore after the death of its namesake, and in the grand tradition of show business, the show went on. What a show it was, with the LPGA Tour's two most recent winners, Donna Andrews and Laura Davies, bringing the house down on the final two holes.

Tied with Davies at 12 under par, Andrews hit a five iron into the front bunker of the 175-yard, par-three 17th hole, then blasted out and missed a 20-footer for par. Davies made par and appeared to have a grip on the victory, with a one-shot lead and a par-five hole left to play.

Davies took a conservative approach, choosing to hit a four iron off the tee. She blocked the shot, had to lay up in the left rough, then didn't get her approach to the crest of the green and saw the shot trickle back, 60 feet from the flagstick. Andrews hit a couple of three-wood shots, then a six iron that stopped six feet behind the hole. Davies left her first putt eight feet short. Andrews made her birdie, then Davies missed the par putt.

After the awards presentation, Andrews jumped into the lake, continuing a tradition begun by Amy Alcott some years before. Dinah Shore always went in with the winner. "I wish Dinah could have been here, but I'm sure she's looking down and laughing and saying, 'Well done,'" Andrews said. "I didn't think I had it in me coming down the stretch. This is just wonderful."

Andrews had rounds of 70, 69, 67 and 70 for a 276 total, 12 under par in winning her first major title. For Davies, it was bitter disappointment. "On a scale of 1 to 10, this is a 10," Davies said in measuring her disappointment. "You just have to say, 'Well done, Donna.' Seems like I always three-putt that (18th) hole. But it never mattered that much until today."

Atlanta Championship—$650,000
Winner: Val Skinner

When Val Skinner started the final round of the Atlanta Championship two strokes behind Liselotte Neumann, her plan was to be patient and not do anything that would take her out of contention.

Little did she know that Neumann would make the fatal mistake. She made a triple-bogey seven on the first hole. Skinner made par and protected the lead on the way to her first victory since the 1993 Lady Keystone Open.

Skinner won with a closing round of 68, and a 10-under-par 206 total. "I wasn't prepared for what happened so early in the round," Skinner said. "I felt bad for Liselotte. You don't want to see any player do that."

What Neumann did was miss the first green from the middle of the fairway, hit her third shot into a bunker, blast out to 15 feet and three-putt. "Everything happened so quickly out there," Neumann said. "All of a sudden, I'm standing there with a seven on my scorecard. It wasn't devastating. There were 17 holes left, but Val didn't open any doors for me."

Judy Dickinson, the other member of the final group, started one stroke behind Neumann, but faded with 39 over the first nine holes. Beth Daniel moved into a tie for the lead early in the final round, but she bogeyed the ninth hole, then ran off seven straight pars and never threatened the leaders in finishing three strokes behind Skinner.

Sprint Championship—$1,200,000
Winner: Sherri Steinhauer

Sherri Steinhauer arrived for the LPGA Tour's richest event, the Sprint Championship in Daytona Beach, Florida, with one victory in eight years. This time, she had a psychological edge, an audio tape supplied by Bob Rotella, and it proved to be what Steinhauer needed for a one-stroke victory over Kelly Robbins.

"I was sweating it out after taking a three-shot lead into Sunday," Steinhauer said. "My mind was wandering with all sorts of dumb thoughts. But this time I played through them, started thinking about birdies. It was a big relief to win again."

When the tournament reached the last round, only Steinhauer and Robbins were left in contention. Trish Johnson led after 36 holes, but shot 75 on Saturday. Michelle McGann, only one stroke behind heading into the weekend, faded with 73. By the 14th hole of the last round, Robbins had moved to within one stroke of Steinhauer. That's when Steinhauer's tape recorded message dominated her thoughts. "My thought was birdies," she said.

Steinhauer made a 30-foot birdie at No. 15 to increase her lead to two strokes, held that margin with another birdie at No. 16, and took a one-shot lead to the 18th hole after making bogey at No. 17. "When I made the 30-footer at 15, it gave me a big lift," Steinhauer said. "Kelly was only one back. After I made the putt at 16, there were no dumb thoughts coming in."

She birdied the 18th from 20 feet. "Making that putt, after the three-putt at the 17th, was really big for me," said Steinhauer, who had rounds of 68, 68, 67 and 70 for a 273 total, 15 under par.

Sara Lee Classic—$525,000
Winner: Laura Davies

When Laura Davies is on her game, there's not much her LPGA Tour foes can do but admire it. Such was the case at the rain-plagued Sara Lee Classic, where Davies posted rounds of 70 and 68 on Sunday for a one-stroke victory over defending champion Meg Mallon.

Half the field was forced into a 36-hole finale after Saturday's second round was twice delayed. "All I want to do now is go to bed," said Davies, who added the Sara Lee crown to her Standard Register Ping title seven weeks before. "I didn't think I would get so tired. I've played 36 holes many times. But I'm 30 now, maybe getting too old for 36 holes a day."

Mallon almost turned the day into a longer one. She barely missed a six-foot putt for birdie at No. 18 that would have sent the tournament into a playoff.

The final round began with Davies and Mallon only one shot ahead of Jane Crafter, who led the first round with 64. Davies and Mallon quickly pulled away. Things turned Davies' way on the 11th hole, a 480-yard par five, where she made an improbable birdie. She drove into a bunker, hit a two iron 200 yards over water onto the fringe of the green, then made a six-foot putt for birdie. She increased her lead to two strokes with another birdie at No. 16.

Davies may have won at No. 17, where she chipped in for par and Mallon made a birdie to cut her lead to a single shot. "I've seen Laura do some amazing things, so I wasn't surprised at anything she did today," Mallon said. "If you get caught up in that, you'll lose your concentration."

McDonald's LPGA Championship—$1,100,000
Winner: Laura Davies

The word "dominating" came to mind at Du Pont Country Club in Wilmington, Delaware, after Laura Davies shot 137 over the last two rounds to win the McDonald's LPGA Championship for her second consecutive victory, third of the LPGA season and fourth of the year worldwide. "I'll ride it as long as I can," Davies said, after her three-stroke victory over Alice Ritzman on rounds of 70, 72, 69 and 68 for a 279 total, nine under par. "I'll just keep playing and enjoying it."

Davies trailed Ritzman and Dottie Mochrie by two strokes after the first round and was two behind Patty Sheehan and Robin Walton going to the weekend. A 69 on Saturday gave Davies a share of the lead with Meg Mallon, one stroke ahead of Sheehan and Ritzman.

Mallon battled a balky putter all week and it caught up with her on Sunday. She limped home with 75. Sheehan took up the charge and led by one stroke after nine holes, but her lead was short-lived. Bogeys at Nos. 12 and 13, and a double bogey at No. 14 sent her reeling. Ritzman tied Davies with birdies at Nos. 10 and 12, but Davies made a birdie at No. 12 to regain the lead, then added two more birdies at Nos. 14 and 15.

"I hit some bad shots, but got away with them," Davies said. "There were a lot of players who had a chance to win today, but those two birdies in the middle of the back nine were what did it for me."

Lady Keystone Open—$400,000
Winner: Elaine Crosby

It was the last round of a tournament, Betsy King was holding a one-stroke lead and had the LPGA Hall of Fame in her sights. But she missed again. This time Elaine Crosby shot a final-round 70 to King's 73 and spoiled King's party at Hershey Country Club in Pennsylvania, less than an hour from where King grew up.

Crosby emerged from a tightly bunched pack with back-to-back birdies at Nos. 16 and 17 to win for the second time in her career with a 54-total of 211. That was one stroke less than Laura Davies, and King tied for third place with Val Skinner. "I always thought I had the ability to do it," Crosby said.

"Last year, I didn't have the confidence needed to win. I worried about my swing on every hole. But last night I told myself to go out there and shoot the lowest number you can. Not paying attention to what others are doing is success in itself."

King had only herself to blame. She hit only six fairways in the last round and gave herself precious few birdie opportunities on the firm, fast greens. It was the ninth time in 18 months that she entered the last round either leading or tied and didn't win. She was neither depressed nor disgusted. "I feel fine. I didn't drive the ball well enough to win, but this is the best tournament I've had all year, so I'm not disappointed," King said. "I look at it as a positive."

Corning Classic—$500,000
Winner: Beth Daniel

When the final putt dropped on Sunday in the Corning Classic, Beth Daniel owned a one-stroke victory over Nancy Ramsbottom for her first title since 1991.

This was Ramsbottom's tournament to lose, and she did. She was ahead by three strokes with six holes to play. Then she made a double bogey at No. 13, a bogey at No. 14 and a three-putt bogey at No. 17 after regaining a share of the lead with a 22-foot birdie at No. 15. "I was having a hard time breathing," Ramsbottom said. "It's not easy, when you've never won, to have a lead like that. It's like you're not in control."

Still, it took a great shot from Daniel to deny Ramsbottom her first victory. Under and between trees from 97 yards out, Daniel hit a punch shot to 18 feet and made the birdie putt. "If you believe in fate, that was it," Daniel said. "There's a fine line between winning and losing, and a lot of people might say I shouldn't have won, but I did."

Oldsmobile Classic—$600,000
Winner: Beth Daniel

When Beth Daniel made a five-foot putt on the 18th hole to seal a four-stroke Oldsmobile Classic victory, it served as an exclamation point to the theory that she was entering another of her streaks. Daniel's final-round 68 gave her a record-equalling, 20-under-par 268 total, a second consecutive victory and the 29th of her 16-year LPGA career.

Daniel was tied with Ellie Gibson after the first round, led Meg Mallon by four strokes at the halfway point and led by four over Lisa Kiggens, who would finish second, going into the last round. Her scores were 67, 63, 70 and 68.

The only disappointment for Daniel was a closing bogey Friday that denied her a personal-best 62. "I'm a real goal-setter, and to have an opportunity for a personal best slip away gets to me," she said.

Daniel was threatened only once. Meg Mallon caught her after seven holes in the third round. Daniel shot five-under-par 31 on the second nine, and the rest of the field faded. By the time she walked off the 18th green, her lead was back up to four strokes, where it remained for most of the last round.

Minnesota LPGA Classic—$500,000
Winner: Liselotte Neumann

At the Minnesota LPGA Classic, Liselotte Neumann made the most of her opportunities and Amy Alcott did not. Neumann closed out her third LPGA Tour victory, and first since 1991, with a solid 66.

There was more at stake for Alcott, who has been stalking her 30th victory and Hall of Fame status to cap her exceptional career.

The turning point was the 12th hole, a 467-yard par five, where the two players came tied for the lead. Alcott's second shot landed short of the green and looked as if it would finish close to the hole. But the ball caught a ridge and rolled right, ending up in the far corner of the green. Neumann's shot caught the same ridge, but it rolled left and settled 10 feet from the hole. Alcott three-putted for par; Neumann made her putt for eagle. The two-shot swing was more than Alcott could overcome, and she faded away to fourth place.

"If golf was would-haves, could-haves and should-haves, I would have everything by now," said Alcott. "But my golf shot goes one way, somebody else's goes another. At least I gave myself a chance."

"After the eagle, there were a lot of holes left and Hiromi (Kobayashi) was coming up," Neumann said. "But I felt my game was really good." She finished out the 66 for a 205 total, nine under par, and won by four strokes.

Rochester International—$500,000
Winner: Lisa Kiggens

On a day when Betsy King's friends had 30 roses boxed and ready for an 18th hole presentation, 21-year-old Lisa Kiggens won her first LPGA tournament. Kiggens, who was five years old when King joined the LPGA, made a birdie on the final hole for a flawless 66 and won by one stroke over Dawn Coe-Jones and by two over King.

Kiggens, second youngest player on the Tour, had rounds of 67, 69, 71 and 66 for a 273 total, 15 under par. It was the third lowest total in tournament history.

King has been so close to her 30th victory so many times, this one left her unfazed. "When you have a chance to win, it comes to your mind," King said. "But I'm just trying to win, whether it's 30th, 45th or whatever. I don't plan on winning just one more. This is the best I've played in a final round when I had a chance to win. So, I'm gaining on it."

Kiggens played one year at UCLA then turned pro at age 19. She lost her players' card the first year, but made $64,851 a year ago and brought new confidence into 1994. She began the final round two strokes behind four players and with one thought in mind, to do the best she could. She also decided to avoid peeking at the leaderboards. "With so many players so close, it made no sense," Kiggens said. "I never looked all day."

Kiggens made her move with birdies on all three par-three holes on the first nine and took the lead, then birdied Nos. 11 and 13. Coe-Jones came on in a flurry with birdies at No. 11, 12, 16 and 17 to tie her, but all she could manage was a par at No. 18, where Kiggens won it.

ShopRite Classic—$500,000
Winner: Donna Andrews

For someone who had just won her third tournament of the year and fourth in nine months, Donna Andrews wore a haggard look as she walked off the 18th green with a two-stroke victory over Michelle Estill in the ShopRite Classic in Somers Point, New Jersey. She wasn't looking to jump into a lake, as she did at the Nabisco Dinah Shore. Rather a hole. "Jumping in the lake is my nature," Andrews said. "But mentally, I'm exhausted."

Andrews was breezing along, leading by five strokes with four holes to go, when suddenly nothing went right. She bogeyed the 15th hole, double-bogeyed the 16th and bogeyed the 17th before wrapping up the victory with a two-putt par at the 18th. "I really had to work hard coming down the stretch," said Andrews, who finished with 74 and a six-under-par 207 total. "I felt comfortable," she said. "If you have five shots over four holes, you darn well better win."

Andrews had the look of a winner all week. She opened with 67 to trail Missie McGeorge by one stroke. She added 66 on Saturday and led Barb Bunkowsky by three. Andrews' lead looked so solid that Estill, who shot a final-round 65, had packed up and headed for Norfolk, Virginia, for a Monday pro-am. Estill avoided an embarrassing situation when Andrews righted her game.

"That would have been something, huh?" Andrews said. "I don't know who would have been more embarrassed if I had lost that five-shot lead, me or Michelle. A two-way tie settled by default."

Youngstown-Warren Classic—$550,000
Winner: Tammie Green

Tammie Green was beginning to feel like she was stuck in the mud when the LPGA Tour headed to Youngstown, Ohio, for the Youngstown-Warren Classic. In 11 starts, she had made money in all, but won none.

Youngstown is home for Green, meaning her mother's cooking and her three horses, on which to ride her cares away. It must have worked. Green shot 67, 69 and 70 for a 206 total, leading wire-to-wire at Avalon Lakes, and winning by two strokes over Colleen Walker. "This year was beginning to grind on me. I wasn't having much fun," Green said. "But this week was just what the doctor ordered."

Green's victory was overshadowed by the news that fellow pro Kim Williams had been shot the night before while walking in the parking lot of a nearby drugstore. She was struck in the neck by a bullet, which lodged in her shoulder just below her collarbone. Williams wasn't seriously injured, however, which lifted the pall that settled on the tournament.

Green had to win this one the hard way. After opening with 67, she had to play 32 holes Sunday because rain had interrupted Saturday's play. She finished the second round with 69 to lead Walker by one stroke. Walker knew it wasn't going to be her day when she made a hole-in-one on the sixth hole and gained only one shot after Green sank a 15-foot putt for birdie. Green then birdied the ninth and 13th holes.

Jamie Farr Toledo Classic—$500,000
Winner: Kelly Robbins

Kelly Robbins had been on the LPGA Tour only three years, but after winning the Jamie Farr Toledo (Ohio) Classic, she felt like a seasoned veteran. The victory was her second, both in playoffs. The first time, in the 1993 Corning

Classic, the victim was Alison Nicholas. This time it was good friend Tammie Green, who was working on back-to-back victories in her home state.

Robbins prevailed by hitting a pitching wedge to within five feet and making the putt on the first extra hole after the two players had finished with nine-under-par 204 totals at Highland Meadows Golf Club.

Robbins won the hard way, recovering from two potentially disastrous mistakes in the final round. At the ninth hole, she made a bogey due to a lack of patience. A bug buzzed around her head as she prepared to hit her second shot. Rather than backing away, she played on, and missed the green. Birdies on three of the next four holes enabled Robbins to take a two-shot lead. At the 16th, her second shot nestled against the fringe. She tried to choke down on a five wood and putt the ball. It scooted 15 feet past the pin, but she saved par.

As it turned out, that putt made the difference, as Green birdied three of the last four holes for 67 to force the playoff. "I was preparing for a playoff the last few holes because I figured Tammie would birdie one of the last two," Robbins said.

JAL Big Apple Classic—$650,000
Winner: Beth Daniel

Beth Daniel knew how Betsy King and Amy Alcott felt after Daniel won the JAL Big Apple Classic in New Rochelle, New York, with a birdie on the first playoff hole to beat Laura Davies. It was Daniel's 30th career victory, leaving her one major championship shy of qualifying for the Hall of Fame. King and Alcott each need one victory of any kind to qualify.

"There's going to be a lot of pressure on me at the Open because I need another major to get in the Hall," Daniel said. "I know, like Betsy and Amy, that's the question I'm going to hear until I get it. Somehow, I have to forget all that and try to go out and have some fun."

The JAL Big Apple Classic was Daniel's third victory of the year after going winless for the previous two years. This one was hardly routine. Daniel shot a bogey-free 66 in the third round to take a three-stroke lead, then blew that advantage in the final round with 71. She holed a seven-footer for birdie on the final hole to force the playoff, then made a six-footer to win.

JoAnne Carner opened with rounds of 68 and 67 to lead by two strokes and awaken hopes that, at age 55, she might break Sam Snead's record as the oldest winner on the non-senior tours. On the weekend rounds, she shot 76 and 77.

U.S. Women's Open—$850,000
Winner: Patty Sheehan

It is said you have to be able to handle the agony of falling short in a U.S. Women's Open before you can enjoy a victory. Patty Sheehan understands. She experienced defeat in Atlanta in 1990, having an 11-shot lead early in the final round and losing by one stroke to Betsy King.

Her victory came in 1992, when she birdied the last two holes to catch

Juli Inkster, then won in a playoff. She won again this year, holding off
Tammie Green at Indianwood Golf Club in Lake Orion, Michigan. Sheehan
had rounds of 66, 71, 69 and 71 for a 277 total, which tied the 72-hole
scoring record.

This year's hard-luck loser was Helen Alfredsson, for a second time. A
year ago Alfredsson lost after holding a two-stroke lead with three holes to
play. This time the loss was more devastating. She led by eight strokes after
43 holes, only to finish tied for ninth place, eight shots behind.

Alfredsson's opening-round 63 broke by two strokes the record for the
Women's Open, and tied the men's mark held by Jack Nicklaus, Tom Weiskopf
and Johnny Miller. Her 36-hole total of 132 broke the previous marks for
men and women. But the Open is about staying power. Sheehan had it.
Alfredsson did not. "I've been there. I know how she feels," Sheehan said
later. "But she's going to win her Open. She has too much talent not to."

For the first 43 holes, Alfredsson was 13 under par. For the last 29 holes,
she was 14 over par. "This is a game you never try to understand," Alfredsson
said. "I don't know what happened. It kept getting worse and worse and
there was nothing I could do about it." Maybe Alfredsson's problem was
Sheehan. She wouldn't go away, saying after the second round, "Unless
Helen goes crazy, this tournament is not over." Sheehan was steady. She
played the first two rounds five under par, and took the lead by one stroke
over Green with a third-round 69.

In the final round, Donna Andrews got within three strokes with a couple
of early birdies, but bogeyed three of the next six holes and wasn't heard
from again.

When Sheehan birdied the third hole to take a three-stroke lead, the championship appeared to be hers to lose. She nearly did, with a shaky stretch
late on the back nine. Green pulled to within one stroke after nine holes, tied
for the lead with a birdie at No. 12 and could have moved in front at No.
15, but her birdie putt stopped inches short. Sheehan birdied No. 16 to
regain the lead, and when Green missed a 12-footer to tie at No. 18, it was
over. "It was a great fight, it just didn't end up the way I would like," Green
said. "I had my chances, but Patty is as tough as they come in these things."

Sheehan couldn't argue with that. "I've had so many near-misses and so
many disappointments in the Open that stick out in my mind," she said. "To
come back from all that is gratifying."

Ping/Welch's Championship—$450,000
Winner: Helen Alfredsson

It is said that when you fall off a horse the best thing is to climb back onto
the beast. So it was for Helen Alfredsson. After taking the big tumble in last
week's U.S. Women's Open, the mercurial Swede climbed back onto the
LPGA saddle in Canton, Massachusetts, exorcised the demons and won the
Ping/Welch's Championship. Alfredsson went around the Blue Hill Country
Club course for a 274 total and won by four strokes over Pat Bradley and
Juli Inkster. In winning for the second time in her three-year career, Alfredsson
earned $67,500 and the admiration of those who figured it would take weeks
for her to pick up the pieces from her Open crash.

"My favorite football team, the 49ers, had a coach (Bill Walsh) who said if you give up you never had a chance," Alfredsson said at the awards ceremony. "If I had come here feeling sorry for myself, I would have had no chance. Winning here means I don't have to answer any more questions about the Open."

Alfredsson answered all the questions in the final round, when Bradley and Inkster stayed with her until the last nine, even overcoming a one-stroke deficit to Inkster. She answered the challenge with birdies at Nos. 10, 12, 14, 15 and 18, finishing with 66.

Bradley and Inkster were early pacesetters. Bradley led the first round with 67, then Inkster added 69 to her opening 67 to move ahead at the halfway point. But they couldn't shake Alfredsson. "To her credit, Helen didn't crash," Bradley said. "You have to tip your hat to her. She went through a lot of adversity and stood up to it."

McCall's Classic at Stratton Mountain—$500,000
Winner: Carolyn Hill

Fourteen years ago, Carolyn Hill came to the LPGA Tour as a can't-miss prospect. She did not win until 1994, when she blitzed the McCall's Classic field with a 275 total, 13 under par over the Stratton Mountain Country Club course in Vermont for a three-stroke victory over Nancy Ramsbottom.

Her share of the purse ($75,000) was more than she had won in all but one of her 14 years. "I can't explain why it took me so long," said Hill, who had come close once before, finishing second to Nancy Lopez in the 1981 Nabisco Dinah Shore. "For a long time, I think I forgot why I was out here or even played the game."

Tied with Ramsbottom after six holes in the final round, Hill took command with birdies on four of the next seven holes and finished with 69, her third sub-70 score of the week.

Betsy King opened with 64, but succumbed again to the pressure of the elusive 30th victory to enter the LPGA Hall of Fame. King then shot 73, 72 and 76 and tied for eighth place. "It seems the harder I try, the worse I get," King said. "I don't know how a person can shoot 64 one day and not make anything the next three."

Children's Medical Center Classic—$350,000
Winner: Maggie Will

When Maggie Will decided in the winter of 1993 to overhaul her swing, she didn't know where it would take her. To a victory? That's where Will finished after she made a 15-foot putt for birdie on the second playoff hole against Jill Briles-Hinton and Alicia Dibos in the Children's Medical Center Classic in Beavercreek, Ohio.

The 29-year-old Will was an unlikely winner in a strong field that included Beth Daniel, Tammie Green, Kelly Robbins, Meg Mallon and Nancy Lopez on the same week when the Weetabix Women's British Open was being held. "The last two or three months I was getting frustrated," Will said. "Any time you make a change, it takes a long time to get comfortable with it."

Will's victory, the third of her career, was courtesy of Briles-Hinton, who carried a two-stroke lead to the final hole. She bogeyed from a greenside bunker while Will and Dibos made birdies. They tied at six-under-par 210, and Daniel almost made it a playoff foursome, but her 16-footer for birdie came up short.

The three bogeyed the first playoff hole and Will ended it quickly on the second hole with a wedge shot to 15 feet while the other two missed the green.

Chicago Challenge—$500,000
Winner: Jane Geddes

When Jane Geddes came to the Chicago Challenge in Naperville, Illinois, she was 30th on the money list and had only two top-10 finishes. She was looking for more than money and found it, a three-stroke victory over Dale Eggeling and Robin Walton. It was her first win since 1991. "I had such a fast start after I won the Open and seven tournaments in 12 months," she said. "I got on a fast track, then lost track. I really never worked hard at it."

She finished at 16-under-par 272 on rounds of 68, 69, 68 and 67. It was the first time she had four rounds under par in two years. Her only tense moment came when she bogeyed the 16th hole and led Walton by one stroke, then she birdied the 17th and 18th. "With the big lead she had, someone would have to shoot lights out to catch her, low to mid 60s," said Walton, who shot 65 and found it wasn't enough. "If she played too conservatively, I thought I could catch her, but she obviously didn't."

When Geddes shot 68 to take the third-round lead, it put her in position to do something for the first time — to win after leading through 54 holes. "I wanted to see if my swing would work under pressure," Geddes said. "I wanted to make birdies. I wanted to do all the things I did when I was playing well. I feel like I stepped up to that level again."

du Maurier Ltd. Classic—$800,000
Winner: Martha Nause

As defining moments go, few could match Martha Nause's one-stroke victory in the du Maurier Ltd. Classic in Ottawa, Canada, the last of the LPGA's major championships.

Nause's 17-year career to this point had been drab, with just two victories. Two years ago, she came down with an inner ear viral infection that so damaged her balance that she couldn't walk or drive a car. Everything came together for Nause at the du Maurier. She followed an opening-round 65 with solid scores of 71, 72 and 71 for a 279 total, and edged Michelle McGann by one stroke. "I don't think I believed in myself until now," said the 39-year-old Nause. "I always knew I had the physical skills, but I suffered from low self-esteem. Now I know I can win. There's no reason to think less of myself."

At the halfway point, Nause was tied for first place with Betsy King and

Kelly Robbins, who consistently out-drove her by 30 yards. Neither King nor Robbins were heard from again, but Nause hung tough. She was tied with Liselotte Neumann, Leigh Ann Mills and McGann after three rounds.

Nause started poorly in the final round, bogeying two of the first four holes to slip two strokes behind. She pulled even again after nine holes, and was undaunted the remainder of the day. Wind gusts of up to 40 miles an hour sent Mills soaring to 80 and Robbins to 75, and Neumann didn't make a birdie until No. 18. Nause birdied No. 13 to pull even with McGann, then holed a 15-footer for birdie at No. 14 and a 20-footer at No. 15 to pull away by two strokes. She bogeyed the 17th, but McGann failed to birdie the par-five 18th, hitting her second shot into a bunker 20 yards short of the green.

State Farm Rail Classic—$525,000
Winner: Barb Mucha

It is said that there's no such thing as a sure thing. Laura Davies started the final round of the State Farm Rail Classic in Springfield, Illinois, with a four-stroke lead — and lost. The victory went to Barb Mucha, who was five strokes behind before shooting 67. Davies shot 77 and finished tied for 14th place.

"Everyone was saying, 'What do you think it's going to take to catch Laura?'" Mucha said. "As it turned out, she wasn't the one to beat. The course was the one to beat. Golf is like that."

Mucha, whose best finish in 1994 had been a tie for 12th place, took the lead after a birdie at No. 8. Davies, playing one group ahead, went five over par on the fifth through eighth holes. She didn't get her first birdie until No. 10, and by then she trailed Mucha by three strokes. The fight for first place was instead between Mucha and Kim Shipman, who had a chance to force a playoff at No. 18, but her 30-foot birdie try ran past the cup.

"That's the way it goes," Davies said. "I've done well this year. This is just one that got away. It matters, obviously, but it's not that big a deal."

Ping-Cellular One Championship—$500,000
Winner: Missie McGeorge

While destiny again denied two stars the one victory they needed for Hall-of-Fame status, it shined on someone who had waited 11 years for her first victory. Betsy King and Amy Alcott, the Hall's ladies-in-waiting, were on the brink of their 30th victories in the Ping-Cellular One Championship in Portland, Oregon, but Missie McGeorge broke their hearts this time.

McGeorge shot a final-round 66 for a three-stroke victory, exorcising a demon of sorts. Just a year ago, McGeorge bogeyed the final hole in this event, handing the title to Donna Andrews. As for King and Alcott, King started playing well too late and finished second, while Alcott led after two rounds but wilted on the final afternoon with 76 and drifted well back into the pack.

"I learned a lot from last year's final nine," McGeorge said. "I went out there today and said, 'What the heck. Let's have fun and enjoy it.'" McGeorge zipped to the front with birdies on Nos. 7, 9, 10 and 11. With that, she broke away from King, who, like McGeorge, started the round trailing Alcott by three strokes. McGeorge finished with a nine-under-par 207 total, tying the tournament record set by Ayako Okamoto in 1986.

Safeco Classic—$500,000
Winner: Deb Richard

Few would have blamed Deb Richard if she had packed away her clubs after failing to make the United States team for the Solheim Cup. Her play in the last three weeks — a tie for 47th place and two missed cuts — had cost her a place on the team. "It was easy, really," said Richard, after posting rounds of 71, 68, 70 and 67 for a 276 total to win the Safeco Classic in Kent, Washington. "At first I worked myself into a real funk, then I decided it's over, it's done, it's time to move on. And I played so calm this week."

Richard made a birdie on the last hole to finish one stroke ahead of Tammie Green, Chris Johnson, Michelle Estill and Rosie Jones. It was the fourth straight year that Jones had finished second here, but the saddest players had to be Johnson and Swede Annika Sorenstam. Johnson missed an 18-inch putt at No. 17, and Sorenstam took a one-stroke lead into the last round, then blew to 74 and tied for sixth place.

Richard started the final round six strokes behind Sorenstam and five behind Johnson, but she birdied five of the first nine holes and trailed Johnson by two strokes after 15 holes. Johnson then bogeyed the 16th and 17th holes, while Richard birdied the 16th and 18th to win. "I just got careless and rushed it," Johnson said of the missed putt at No. 17. "Who knows where my mind was."

It was Richard's fourth career victory, and her first since 1991, when she won twice and finished fifth on the money list. "I think I took my 1991 success for granted," Richard said. "It won't happen again. I really relish being on the Tour."

Heartland Classic—$500,000
Winner: Liselotte Neumann

Laura Davies may be the most imposing of all the European women who play the LPGA Tour, but in the past four months Liselotte Neumann had given her a run for the money. In June, the 28-year-old Swede won the Minnesota Classic; in August, she captured the Weetabix Women's British Open and, in early October, she took another title in the Heartland Classic in St. Louis, Missouri.

Neumann exploded past 36-hole leader Pearl Sinn in the third round, stretched her lead to as many as five strokes midway through the final round, and held on for a three-stroke victory over Sinn and Elaine Crosby. Her 10-under-par 278 total came on rounds of 70, 71, 67 and 70 over the Forest Hills Country Club course. "Winning three times in Europe and twice in the U.S. helps tremendously leading into the World Championship and Solheim Cup," said Neumann, who came onto the American scene as a rookie to win the U.S.

Women's Open six years ago.

Neumann got hot early on the second nine Saturday, moving past Sinn with three consecutive birdies beginning at the 12th hole. The last round was almost a replay, as Neumann birdied the ninth, 10th and 12th holes, pushing her lead to five strokes. Crosby had a chance to win when she birdied the 16th hole, and Neumann bogeyed Nos. 16 and 17, but there would be no more Neumann mistakes or Crosby birdies. "You have to be impressed," Crosby said. "I think she's one of the best players in the world. In my book, she's probably No. 1 or No. 2 in the world."

World Championship of Women's Golf—$425,000
Winner: Beth Daniel

Golf is not always about winning money, but when the World Championship of Women's Golf reached the final round, the LPGA's money-winning title was on the minds of Beth Daniel and Laura Davies.

As Davies lined up a 15-foot birdie putt on the final hole, it wasn't to win the tournament. It was to retain her hold on first place on the 1994 money list. Davies made the putt, then jokingly implored Beth Daniel, who won the tournament, not to take her sparkling game to the next week's season-ending Toray Japan Queens Cup. "Let me have it," Davies said. "Because I want it."

No way was Daniel going to oblige Davies. Not the way she was playing. She shot a flawless final round of 65 for a 14-under-par 274 total and a three-stroke victory over Elaine Crosby, worth $105,000 that moved her to within $10,965 of Davies. The victory was the 31st of Daniel's career, her fourth of the year, and it moved her into the lead for Player of the Year honors, one point ahead of Davies.

Daniel started the final round four strokes out of the lead held by Crosby, but she birdied the first hole and the seventh, then made four birdies in a row starting at No. 10 to blow everyone away. "That wasn't good golf, it was great golf," Davies said. "Only one person could hurt me in this tournament for the money title, and Beth went out and did it."

"I've had a great year," Daniel said. "I have won four times and come back from a very bad year. I've won enough regular tournaments now to be eligible for the Hall of Fame, but I've got to work a little harder in the majors. I still need a couple of those."

In addition to being in the hunt for the money title with one event left, Daniel's play solidified her position atop the Vare Trophy race, which goes to the player with the lowest scoring average. "I'm still thinking about the money title, Player of the Year and the Vare," Daniel said. "Winning the triple crown would be something. Yes, I'm definitely going to Japan."

Solheim Cup
Winner: United States

There was no swagger in the Americans' steps, as there had been two years ago, when the United States LPGA Tour team met the WPG European Tour team in the Solheim Cup at The Greenbrier in White Sulphur Springs, West Virginia. After being humbled in Scotland, the Americans simply wanted to reclaim the crystal trophy. That, they did, although it was no runaway, as the score of 13 points to seven might indicate.

The score was tied at five points each after two days of fourball and foursomes matches, then the Americans won eight of the 10 singles matches on the final afternoon. All but two of the 10 matches went at least 17 holes. "I really believe both teams played extremely well," said JoAnne Carner, the American captain. "It was touch-and-go there. Some of the matches could have gone either way. I'm proud of both teams."

Dottie Mochrie and Brandie Burton were the American stars, together producing six points. They defeated two of the Europeans' best pairings, Liselotte Neumann and Helen Alfredsson, and Laura Davies and Alison Nichols. Meg Mallon and Beth Daniel redeemed themselves, each winning two of three matches. Mallon, who surrendered the Cup-winning point in 1992, had the point this time to clinch the victory.

Alfredsson led off the singles for the Europeans, defeating Betsy King, then the Americans won the next four matches, with Mochrie romping past Catrin Nilsmark with seven birdies in 10 holes. Mallon won a tense match against Pam Wright for the deciding point. "Pam is tough," Mallon said. "After she won the 15th to be one down, my only thought was to stay aggressive, to put the pressure on her." Mallon made par putts from six and 12 feet on the next two holes, and two-putted for par at the 18th.

JC Penney Classic—$1,200,000
Winners: Marta Figueras-Dotti and Brad Bryant

After 17 years of struggle, Brad Bryant finally rid himself of the non-winner tag, but his four-hole playoff victory with Marta Figueras-Dotti of Spain in the JC Penney Classic did nothing to change Bryant's perspective. "Winning doesn't mean that much to me," said Bryant, who has more than $2 million in career earnings. "The important things to me are my wife and kids. I can win 42 golf tournaments next year and if that's all I do, I'm a pretty terrible person."

Bryant and Figueras-Dotti, who had won only once in an 11-year career, tied Helen Alfredsson of Sweden and Robert Gamez at the end of the regulation 72 holes at 262, 22 under par, then won with a par on the fourth extra hole when Alfredsson missed a three-foot second putt. Each of the winners received $150,000.

Women's European Tour

Ford Classic—£100,000
Winner: Catrin Nilsmark

In front of a large crowd at Woburn's Duchess Course, Sweden's Catrin Nilsmark clinched her first Women's Professional Golf European Tour victory in the season-opening Ford Classic. Leading by three strokes going to the final round, Nilsmark withstood challenges from Trish Johnson, Mardi Lunn, Annika Sorenstam and rookie Joanne Morley, not to mention No. 1-ranked Laura Davies, who started her round with an eagle three.

Nilsmark secured the victory with birdies on four of the last six holes for a four-under-par 70 and 284 total. Johnson and Morley shared second place at 288 and Davies was fourth at 289. Nilsmark, who sank the putt to win the Solheim Cup for the Europeans at Dalmahoy in 1992, was previously acknowledged as one of the best players on the Tour not to have won, although she had three runner-up finishes since starting in 1989.

Ladies Open Costa Azul—£50,000
Winner: Sandrine Mendiburu

A late flurry of birdies enabled Sandrine Mendiburu to sweep past Britain's Lora Fairclough for her first victory in the weather-hit Ladies Open Costa Azul at Aroeira in Lisbon, Portugal. Rain washed out two of the four rounds and delayed the final round by an hour. Mendiburu, the 1992 Rookie of the Year, scored three birdies starting from the 15th hole. After hitting a five iron short of the 18th green, she struck a wedge from 60 yards to four feet for her second 70 to finish at four-under-par 140, one stroke ahead of Fairclough.

"I would like to play like this for the rest of the season," said Mendiburu, who twice had to settle for second place. Fairclough, a winner in Sweden last year, conceded, "You can't take it away from Sandrine. That was a fantastic finish and she deserved to win."

Evian Masters—£232,500
Winner: Helen Alfredsson

Helen Alfredsson ended a 15-month winless streak with an impressive sixth European title when she won the inaugural Evian Masters at the Royal Golf Club on the shores of Lake Geneva in France. Alfredsson thrilled a large crowd with a closing-round 70 for a one-under-par 287 total to finish three strokes ahead of Lora Fairclough and Australia's Sarah Gautrey. It was Alfredsson's first victory since the 1993 Nabisco Dinah Shore.

The Swede staged a spectacular late rally to collect £34,875 in the richest tournament on the WPG European Tour. Alfredsson was two strokes behind

Fairclough when they reached the final turn. "I dropped shots at the first two holes, which was not a happy start," Alfredsson said. "I told myself to be patient and not try to force the birdies because I knew that everyone would be having a hard time." Her first two birdies came with putts of 35 and 45 feet at the 11th and 13th, and she made another two birdies at the final two holes, from 15 and four feet.

Trish Johnson and Sally Prosser had shared the third-round lead with Alfredsson and Fairclough, but both stumbled in the last round. Johnson shot 77 and Prosser, 79.

OVB Damen Open—£100,000
Winner: Florence Descampe

Florence Descampe gave herself and Solheim Cup captain Mickey Walker a timely boost when she ended a two years' lean spell with a victory in the inaugural OVB Damen Open at Zell am See, near Salzburg, Austria. Descampe made up four strokes on American Tracy Hanson with a final-round 68 which left them tied at 15-under-par 277, two strokes ahead of Australian Loraine Lambert.

Descampe won on the second hole of the playoff, when she struck a two-iron shot to 25 feet for a birdie four. "I am so happy. It feels great, fantastic, and I know that this will get me going again," said Descampe. It was the Belgian's sixth WPG European Tour victory and her first win since the McCall's Classic in America two years ago.

BMW European Masters—£160,000
Winner: Helen Wadsworth

The leader for the last three rounds, Helen Wadsworth shook off early nerves with a late burst of birdies to complete an impressive first victory in the BMW European Masters at Bercuit near Brussels, Belgium. Wadsworth had a closing-round 73 for a 14-under-par 278 total to finish three strokes ahead of Tracy Hanson, who also finished with 73. Laura Davies and Sweden's Annika Sorenstam shared third place at 283.

Wadsworth said, "I was so nervous last night that I hardly slept and I didn't have a great start today, but making three birdies in a row got me going." She started with a bogey, par and double bogey and two of her three-stroke lead had disappeared. But at the ninth Wadsworth gathered the first of five birdies over her last 10 holes. The last of those birdies at the 16th left Hanson in the runner-up spot for the second week running.

Hennessy Cup—£220,000
Winner: Liselotte Neumann

With a course-record 65 in the final round, Liselotte Neumann defended her title and gave Sweden a fourth consecutive victory in the Hennessy Cup at the Golf und Landclub Koln in Cologne, Germany.

It was the eighth WPG European Tour win for Neumann, who just three weeks earlier won the Minnesota LPGA Classic. Her 11-under-par 277 total left her one stroke ahead of Britain's Alison Nicholas, the 54-hole leader, who finished with 71. Kristal Parker of the United States was two strokes behind. "This golf course does something to me," Neumann said. "It is great to defend a title with the extra pressure involved and good to finish with a great round."

Irish Holidays Open—£70,000
Winner: Laura Davies

Laura Davies lived up to her ranking as the world's No. 1 woman golfer when she swept to an impressive victory in the Irish Holidays Open at St. Margaret's Golf & Country Club near Dublin. In a testing wind, Davies produced a closing-round 71 for a six-under-par 282 total to win by eight strokes over Helen Wadsworth of Wales and Carin Hjalmarsson of Sweden.

Davies led by three strokes entering the final round, and over the closing holes she sprinted to the victory. She holed a chip from 40 feet for a birdie at the 13th then, after another birdie at the 16th, holed from 20 feet for an eagle three at the 17th hole. "This is an important victory for me. It means that I have won at least one European Tour event in each of the last 10 years," said Davies, who leads the WPG European Tour career money list.

Skoda Scottish Open—£75,000
Winner: Laura Davies

Another chapter to Laura Davies' staggering season was written when she completed a sixth victory of the year by winning the Skoda Scottish Open with a closing-round 72 at Dalmahoy. Davies held off a challenge from Karina Orum, and her 10-under-par 278 total left her one stroke ahead of the Dane, who finished with 70. Spain's Laura Navarro and American Jane Geddes shared third place at 280.

After starting the final round with a three-stroke lead, Davies bogeyed three of the first six holes, and Orum made two birdies, taking a two-shot advantage. Davies squandered a birdie chance at the 10th hole, but holed a 25-footer for a birdie at the 12th. At the 14th, Orum bogeyed and Davies birdied again to regain the lead.

"I thought this one had slipped away after the 10th hole, but all year I have drilled myself to accept disappointments and keep plugging away. I was so impressed by the way Karina played and I am sure her turn will come," said Davies after the 31st triumph of her career.

Weetabix Women's British Open—£335,000
Winner: Liselotte Neumann

When Sweden's Liselotte Neumann soared to a five-stroke lead in the Weetabix Women's British Open, there was little doubt she would not duplicate the actions of her countryman Jesper Parnevik. Unlike Parnevik, who may have lost the British Open because he didn't look at leaderboards on the last day, Neumann anxiously checked every one in sight as she marched to victory.

Neumann started the final round three strokes ahead of the field at Woburn Golf and Country Club. When she bogeyed both the 15th and 16th holes after moving in front by five strokes with four holes to play, she was ever attentive to her standing. "I don't think I've ever had a round not looking at the board," Neumann said. "I always think it's important to know what's going on. Today, being a couple of shots ahead, I wanted to know if anyone was catching up."

No one was. Neumann's closing 72, her fourth round under par on the Duke's Course, was enough to maintain her overnight lead over Cindy Figg-Currier. Neumann had earlier rounds of 71, 67 and 70, and finished with a 280 total, 12 under par. Sharing second place were Dottie Mochrie and Sweden's Annika Sorenstam, who had final-round 70s for their 283 totals.

Trygg-Hansa Open—£100,000
Winner: Liselotte Neumann

There was no stopping Liselotte Neumann, who led every round and stormed to a four-stroke victory in the Trygg-Hansa Open at Haninge Golf Club in Stockholm. A week after taking the Weetabix Women's British Open crown, Neumann posted an 18-under-par 274 total to win over Australia's Corinne Dibnah.

"It is so exciting to win here in Sweden again," said Neumann, who won over the same course in 1991. Her final-round 67 was her 10th consecutive round below par. A winner's check for £15,000 helped Neumann set a WPG European Tour record by becoming the first player to break the six-figure barrier.

Waterford Dairies English Open—£60,000
Winner: Patricia Meunier

Patricia Meunier of France surged to an impressive first victory when she won the Waterford Dairies English Open at The Tytherington Club in Cheshire, England, home of the WPG European Tour. Meunier battled through heavy rain for a final-round 71 which left her with an even-par 288 total to finish two strokes ahead of Marie Laure de Lorenzi, another French golfer, who also shot 71 and shared second place with Australia's Corinne Dibnah.

Dibnah and Lora Fairclough shared the third-round lead, one stroke ahead of Sofia Gronberg Whitmore of Sweden and two ahead of Meunier, but only Meunier was close to par on the last day. Dibnah shot 75, Fairclough had 76 and Gronberg Whitmore, 79.

"If someone had told me this morning that I would win, I would never have believed them. When I saw the leaderboard at the 14th hole I was so nervous and excited," Meunier said. From Dijon, Meunier, age 21, joined Sandrine Mendiburu, Catrin Nilsmark and Helen Wadsworth to become the fourth first-time WPG European Tour winner of the year.

Sens Dutch Open—£55,000
Winner: Liz Weima

Women's golf in Holland received a timely boost when Liz Weima became the fifth first-time winner of the season with a stunning victory in the Sens Dutch Open at Rijk van Nijmegen. It was the first Dutch success on the WPG European Tour, and Weima more than doubled her 1994 winnings when she collected a check for £8,250 after her two-under-par 214 performance left her two strokes ahead of Sweden's Sofia Gronberg Whitmore. Weima took a three-stroke lead at 142 with 68 in the second round, and finished with even-par 72.

Weima, age 25, only took up the game seven years ago. "I took up a two-year course to become a teaching professional and made such good progress that I decided to become a playing professional, but it has all been faster than I imaged," she said. Only one week earlier, Weima had the best finish of her two-year career when she shared 12th place in the Waterford Dairies English Open.

BMW Italian Open—£70,000
Winner: Corinne Dibnah

Australia's Corinne Dibnah recaptured the title she last held in 1991 and her 13th WPG European Tour victory, when she beat Scotland's Dale Reid at the second extra hole to win the BMW Italian Open at Lignano. Dibnah and Reid had stormed home with final-round 66s to finish tied at 11-under-par 277, one stroke ahead of American Susan Moon, with third-round leader Lora Fairclough one stroke further behind, after her closing 70.

The Queenslander birdied three of her last four holes to draw even with the Scot and clinched the victory with a par four at the 18th, the second playoff hole. Both Dibnah and Reid drove into a fairway bunker. From 120 yards, Dibnah played a recovery to 20 feet to settle the issue. "I don't feel elated beating my best friend," Dibnah said. "Dale needed it more than I did, but she is coming into form at the right time before the Solheim Cup match."

La Manga Club Spanish Open—£60,000
Winner: Marie Laure de Lorenzi

French golfer Marie Laure de Lorenzi had no regrets about turning down captain Mickey Walker's invitation to be the reserve for the European Solheim Cup team after her victory in the La Manga Club Spanish Open. De Lorenzi gained her 15th WPG European Tour victory success when she beat Sweden's

Sofia Gronberg Whitmore at the second playoff hole after they had finished in a tie at six-under-par 282, two strokes ahead of Karina Orum of Denmark. "The Solheim Cup for me is over. I didn't play well enough this year, but I will be trying to make it in a couple of years' time," she said.

Gronberg Whitmore led through the first three rounds. She started with 68 and 69 and was five strokes clear of Trish Johnson and six ahead of de Lorenzi. Gronberg Whitmore shot 73 in the third round, including a two-stroke penalty for grounding her club in a hazard at the 18th hole, and de Lorenzi climbed within one stroke with her 68.

In the final round, de Lorenzi shot 71 to force the playoff and won with a bogey six when Gronberg Whitmore double-bogeyed the 18th again.

Var Open de France Feminin—£55,000
Winner: Julie Forbes

The final event of the 1994 WPG European Tour produced the year's sixth first-time winner, as Scotland's Julie Forbes made her breakthrough in a three-way playoff to win the Var Open de France Feminin at St. Endreol. Forbes, who turned professional in 1990, had come from behind with a closing-round 70 to finish in a deadlock with Dale Reid and Suzanne Strudwick at three-under-par 213, two strokes ahead of defending champion Marie Laure de Lorenzi.

Forbes settled the issue when she rolled home an 18-foot birdie putt at the second playoff hole. "I putted well all week and holed single putts at three of the last four holes to get into the playoff," Forbes said. "I knew I had a chance because I had the same putt on the last green earlier in the week. This time it went in, and I can't believe that I won." Forbes had a final-round 70 while Strudwick, the 36-hole leader, shot 74 and Reid shot 72.

Princess Lalla Meriem Cup—FF250,000
Winner: Gillian Stewart

Scotland's Gillian Stewart, who had not won in seven years, had a seven-stroke victory in the unofficial Princess Lalla Meriem Cup in Rabat, Morocco. Stewart shot a six-under-par 67 in the final round for a 210 total to overtake Denmark's Karina Orum, who finished with 75.

Women's Australasian Tours

Thailand Open—US$90,000
Winner: Laura Davies

Laura Davies defended her title in the Thailand Open to launch the Women's Asian Tour in January, just a month after she had concluded the 1993 circuit by winning in Australia. Davies had a 206 total, 10 under par, for a seven-stroke victory over Mardi Lunn. In 1993, Davies won the Thailand Open in a playoff over Lunn's sister, Karen. She was tied for the lead after an opening-round 70 at Thana City Golf and Country Club near Bangkok, then pulled away with another 70 and her closing 66.

Malaysian JAL Open—US$85,000
Winner: Jae Sook Won

Korea's Jae Sook Won held off Tracy Hanson of the United States and won the Malaysian JAL Open by two strokes at Bukit Jambul Country Club in Penang. Won shot 75-75-70 for her 220 total, four over par. Hanson led by two strokes with her 75-73 start, then Won posted the only sub-par round of the tournament. The turning points were the 13th and 14th holes. Hanson double-bogeyed the par-three 13th, while Won parred, then Won chipped in for an eagle on the par-four 14th.

Indonesian Open—US$80,000
Winner: Tracy Hanson

Tracy Hanson avenged her loss to Jae Sook Won in Malaysia by winning a playoff for the Indonesian Open over Won and England's Sally Prosser the following week at Handara Kosaido Country Club in Bali. Hanson birdied the first extra hole after they had tied at 212, four under par. Prosser led Hanson by two strokes and Won by five entering the last round. Won finished with 68, then waited as Hanson completed her 71 and Prosser shot 73, with bogeys on two of the last three holes.

Republic of China-Taiwan Open—US$110,000
Winner: Karen Weiss

American Karen Weiss birdied the first three holes of the final round and continued to a one-stroke victory over hard-charging Carin Hjalmarsson of Sweden in the Republic of China-Taiwan Open with a three-under-par 213 total at Chang Gung Golf Club in Taipei, Taiwan. Weiss and Li Wen Lin were tied at 145 after 36 holes, with Hjalmarsson five strokes behind. Li shot 74 in the last round, while Weiss had 68 and Hjalmarsson was close behind with 64.

Holden Australian Open—A$200,000
Winner: Annika Sorenstam

Annika Sorenstam, coming off a Rookie-of-the-Year season in the United States, scored her first professional victory with ease in the Holden Australian Open in December. The biggest problem for the 24-year-old Swede was the sunburn on her feet during a heat wave in Adelaide, where she went for a walk on the beach before the tournament.

Sorenstam started with 68 and was tied for the lead with amateur Kate Macintosh, then pulled away in the following rounds, shooting 72, 72 and 74 for a 286 total, 10 under par at Royal Adelaide Golf Club, for a five-stroke triumph over Rachel Hetherington. Jane Crafter and Kris Tschetter tied for third place at 292. No one got closer than four strokes to Sorenstam's lead on the last day, and birdies on the 15th and 16th holes clinched the title.

Alpine Australian Ladies Masters—A$250,000
Winner: Laura Davies

In the final women's tournament of 1994, Laura Davies capped her superb year with her eighth victory, spanning five Tours, and did so with a 20-under-par score, equalling the lowest on record in women's golf. In doing so, Davies defended her title in the Alpine Australian Ladies Masters, winning by four strokes over 19-year-old Karrie Webb, who was playing in only her second professional tournament.

Davies led from start to finish at the Royal Pines Resort in Queensland, shooting a course-record, nine-under-par 64 in the first round, and continuing with scores of 68, 73 and 67 for her 272 total on the par-73 layout. Yet Webb surged to a one-stroke lead over Davies with eight holes to play, having shot 32 for the first nine. There was a two-stroke swing at the par-three 14th, where Davies birdied and Webb bogeyed. Webb finished with 69, after earlier rounds of 67, 70 and 70.

Davies missed a 15-foot birdie putt on the final hole that would have put her at 21 under par, one stroke better than the best ever recorded on the U.S. LPGA Tour by Nancy Lopez and Beth Daniel and in Europe by Dale Reid.

Japan LPGA Tour

Daikin Orchid—¥60,000,000
Winner: Akiko Fukushima

Youth was served early on the 1994 Japan LPGA Tour when 20-year-old Akiko Fukushima won the Daikin Orchid tournament, the opening event of the season at Ryukyu Golf Club in southern Japan in early March. Fukushima, a long-hitting golfer whose father was a pro baseball player, eased to her first career title with a four-stroke victory even with a final-round par 72 that included an out-of-bounds tee shot.

An opening 71 left Fukushima four shots off the pace of Yuri Kawanami after 18 holes, but her following 70 pushed her into a one-stroke lead over Kawanami and Kayoko Ikoma. Fukushima, who was averaging 270 yards with her drives, had three birdies, a bogey and a double bogey, the latter when she knocked her tee shot out of bounds at the par-five 11th hole. The par 72 set her final score at three-under-par 213. Ayako Okamoto and Hiromi Takamura tied for second at 217.

Chiyoda Ladies—¥50,000,000
Winner: Wu Ming Yueh

Wu Ming Yueh led from start to finish in the Chiyoda Ladies tournament at Koyu-gun, but it was a shorter-than-normal trip. Saturday's second round was rained out, so Wu's combination of an opening-round 68 and final-round 71 produced her two-stroke win over Mayumi Murai. The 44-year-old pro from Taiwan led by one over Jeong Soo Kim and Murai by three after the first 18 holes before locking up the seventh victory of her nine-year pro career with four birdies and three bogeys in the final round.

Saishunkan Ladies—¥60,000,000
Winner: Ikuyo Shiotani

Ikuyo Shiotani, who went winless in 1993 after leading the Japan LPGA Tour's money list the previous season, insured that it wouldn't continue through another campaign. Shiotani came from six strokes off the pace in the final round to score a one-stroke victory with her two-under-par 214 total at Takayubaru Country Club at Mashiki. It was her seventh career triumph.

Young Akiko Fukushima positioned herself for a second victory of the new season with a 68-69 start, establishing a two-shot lead over Kaori Harada (68-71) as Shiotani opened with 71-72. Scores soared Sunday and Ikuyo won the title with a one-under-par 71 and 214 total. Harada shot 76, but finished second, one stroke ahead of Fukushima, who fell apart and shot 79 on the tough Takayubaru greens.

Kibun Classic—¥50,000,000
Winner: Woo Soon Ko

Ikuyo Shiotani made a strong run at her second consecutive victory on the Japan LPGA Tour but yielded to Korea's Woo Soon Ko in the final round of the Kibun Classic. Ko came from two strokes behind with a 74 on a day of extremely high scoring, eking out a one-shot victory over Norimi Terazawa with her 221 total. The winner had earlier rounds of 73 and 74. Shiotani endured a horrendous 84 after a 71-74 start that had given her a one-stroke lead over Chieko Nishida and two over a half dozen others, including Ko.

Mitsukoshi Cup—¥60,000,000
Winner: Yuko Moriguchi

The season's first playoff decided the winner of the Mitsukoshi Cup at Segovia Golf Club in Chiyoda. Yuko Moriguchi, winner of the Stanley tournament in 1993, emerged victorious after four extra holes against Akiko Fukushima, who was trying to become the season's first double winner. The two players finished regulation with one-under-par 287 totals. Ikuyo Shiotani, who had bounced back from her staggering finish the week before, was tied with Fukushima after 54 holes at 218, one stroke behind leader Moriguchi. However, Shiotani again finished weakly with 73 as Fukushima shot 69 and Moriguchi 70 to forge the tie and force the playoff.

Kenshoen Ladies—¥50,000,000
Winner: Ikuyo Shiotani

It could very easily have been four in a row for Ikuyo Shiotani. On consecutive Sundays after winning the Saishunkan tournament, the experienced Shiotani frittered away victory chances with faltering finishes. Then, in the Kenshoen Ladies event at Dogo Golf Club at Matsuyama the following week, she notched her second 1994 title and eighth of her career, coming from a stroke off the pace of Norimi Terazawa to win by two strokes with her seven-under-par 209 total.

Ikuyo trailed Terazawa, Kikuko Shibata and Kim Man Soo by two strokes after opening with 71. A 69 Saturday moved her within one shot of Terazawa, who had 70 for her 139 total, and another 69 Sunday wrapped up the triumph. Aki Nakano climbed into second place with 71-70-70–211.

Nasu Ogawa—¥50,000,000
Winner: Marnie McGuire

New Zealand's Marnie McGuire cracked the Oriental monopoly on the 1994 Japan LPGA Tour, squeezing out a one-stroke victory in the Nasu Ogawa tournament at Ogawamachi in Tochigi Prefecture in late April. Her victim was the red hot Ikuyo Shiotani, winner of two and strong contender in the other two of the previous four events.

They both shot one-under-par 71s after entering Sunday's final round separated by a single stroke. McGuire's 71 gave her a 210 total. The first-round co-leaders with 69s — Hiromi Takamura, Toshimi Kimura and Mayumi Hirase — all finished well off the pace.

Satake Japan Classic—¥50,000,000
Winner: Chieko Nishida

A winner in Australia, Thailand and the United States during the previous five months, Laura Davies, the brilliant English pro, came within one stroke of adding a Japanese title to her collection.

Carrying a two-stroke lead into the final round of the Satake Japan Classic at Hiroshima Country Club, Davies slipped to 76, opening the door for Chieko Nishida, the 1993 Chukyo Bridgestone champion. Nishida faltered, too, with four back-nine bogeys, but her par 72 and 218 total enabled her to pick off first place from Davies, Akiko Fukushima and Miyuki Shimabukuro, who had trailed Davies by two after 36 holes. Disaster struck Hisako Higuchi, who opened in front with 68 and followed with 83, eventually finishing 17th.

Gunze World Cup—¥60,000,000
Winner: Jae Sook Won

Jae Sook Won joined the ranks of South Korean winners on the Japan LPGA Tour, stepping into the breach when countrywoman Shin Sora collapsed in the final round of the Gunze World Cup tournament at Tokyo's renowned Yomiuri Country Club. The 24-year-old Won, landing the first title of her three-year career in Japan to go with her January victory in the Malasian Open, shot a final-round 71 for a 287 total, one under par, and won by three over Yuko Moriguchi and Kumiko Hiyoshi.

Fukumi Tani led the first day with 70, in front by two strokes over five others, including Vicki Goetze, one of four Americans in the field. The Koreans dominated from there in. Jae Sook Won overtook Tani at 143 the second day with a 68–143, then slipped a shot behind Shin Sora Saturday, 215-216. Sora stumbled to 81 Sunday, leaving the door open for Won.

Yakult Ladies—¥60,000,000
Winner: Kaori Higo

It was not a classic par round, but Kaori Higo's 72 on the final day of the Yakult Ladies tournament at Fukuoka Kokusai Country Club did the job. It gave the 25-year-old a 211 score and a one-stroke victory, her first of the season. Nayoko Yoshikawa, the first-round leader with Huang Bie Shyun (68s), Suzuko Maeda and Hisako Takeda tied for second place at 212. In a three-way deadlock with Yoshikawa and Hiromi Takamura at 139, one behind Takeda, Higo put together a wild final round with five bogeys, three on the last four holes, three birdies and an eagle to gain the narrow victory.

Chukyo TV Bridgestone—¥50,000,000
Winner: Akemi Yamaoka

The wait finally ended for Akemi Yamaoka. The 43-year-old pro, in her 11th season on the Japan LPGA Tour, came from four strokes off the lead in the final round with a five-under-par 67 to snatch the victory, the first of her career, from South Korea's Ok Hee Ku. One of the most prominent of the Korean golfers, Ku had taken the lead after 36 holes at 71-72–143, one stroke in front of Hiromi Takamura. Yamaoka was at 147. She came out firing Sunday with birdies on the first two holes, later adding three others in her solid finishing round at Kasugai Country Club in Aichi Prefecture. Ku, shooting for her first victory since the late-season Itsuki tournament in 1993, had a birdie and a bogey in the 72 that dropped her into second place at the finish.

Toto Motors—¥50,000,000
Winner: Jae Sook Won

Won went to two in the Toto Motors tournament at Toto Hanno Country Club in Saitama. That is, Jae Sook Won scored her second victory of the 1994 campaign on the Japan LPGA Tour, rallying from a four-stroke deficit with a final-round 68 to score a one-stroke victory. Winner of the Gunze World Cup three weeks earlier, Won was little noticed as she shot 73 and 70 the first two days.

Shin Sora, another strong Korean pro, led the first day with 69, then Michiko Hattori, the American-trained, three-time winner on the 1993 circuit, took over at 70-69–139 and led three others by two strokes. The South Korean victor took command Sunday with three birdies on the front nine en route to her winning 68–211 as Hattori slumped to 75. Kumiko Hiyoshi shot 70 for 212, and Akemi Yamaoka, the previous week's winner in the Chukyo TV Bridgestone, tied for third at 213 with Aiko Hashimoto.

Mitsubishi Electric Ladies—¥50,000,000
Winner: Suzuko Maeda

Suzuko Maeda got better every day and that produced her first victory in almost a year on the Japan LPGA Tour. Maeda, who won the Suntory the previous June, started with 74, five strokes behind the 20-year-old leader, Akiko Fukushima, one of the season's leading players who won the opening Daikin Orchid tournament. While Fukushima headed downhill, Maeda moved up to a fourth-place tie Saturday with 69. She tied with Jae Sook Won and Fukushima, two shots off the lead shared by Toshimi Kimura and Aiko Hashimoto, the 1986 Japan Amateur champion who has not won in her six years on the circuit. Not this time, either. Maeda fashioned Sunday's best round, 68, and won the tournament by three strokes with her five-under-par 211 total. Hashimoto shot 73 and finished second.

Suntory Ladies Open—¥50,000,000
Winner: Akemi Yamaoka

Riding the best streak of her long career, Akemi Yamaoka scored her second victory in four weeks on the Japan LPGA Tour in the Suntory Ladies Open, this time being the first player of the season to lead from start to finish in a 72-hole event. Yamaoka won by six strokes with her 13-under-par 275 total. It was a far cry from the Chukyo TV Bridgestone, in which she captured her first victory in 11 years on the circuit. In scoring that victory in May, the 43-year-old Yamaoka came from four strokes behind in the final round.

Yamaoka's dominating performance in the Suntory went this way: She shot 67 and led by one stroke the first day, added 66 to open a four-stroke lead the second day, widened the gap to seven Saturday with 70 for a 203 total and coasted home with 72 for the 275 total Sunday. Ikuyo Shiotani, one of two others who had won twice in 1994, finished second, six strokes back at 281. Five others finished a distant third at 285.

Dunlop Twin Lakes Ladies—¥50,000,000
Winner: Toshimi Kimura

Decisive victory followed decisive victory on the Japan LPGA Tour when Toshimi Kimura, a three-time winner in 1993, picked up her first title of 1994 in the Dunlop Twin Lakes Ladies Open at Twin Lakes Country Club in Fujioka. As was the case with Akemi Yamaoka the previous week, Kimura never trailed at Twin Lakes and eventually posted a six-stroke victory with her four-under-par 284 total, even though taking 77 in a final round in which only one player in the field broke par. Michiko Hattori shot 71 Sunday and tied Akiko Fukushima (78) for second at 290.

Kimura opened with 68, sharing first place with Keiko Suzuki and Nobuko Kizawa; followed with 72 and retained the top position, tied with Ayako Okamoto at 140. She broke ahead Saturday with 67, forging a four-stroke lead over Yumiko Akagi. In horrid conditions Sunday, Toshimi's 77 actually widened the gap by two, as Hattori made a huge move with her 71.

Japan Women's Open Championship—¥60,000,000
Winner: Michiko Hattori

Michiko Hattori telegraphed the victory the Sunday before she won the Japan Women's Open Championship. The 1985 U.S. Women's Amateur champion leaped to second place in the preceding Twin Lakes tournament with the best final-round score and carried that momentum onto the Japan Women's Open at Musashi Country Club at Saitama. The three-time 1993 winner shook off one weak round, 76 the second day, and rolled to a three-stroke victory with her one-under-par 287 total.

The lead changed hands three times through the third round. Yuka Irie opened on top with 67, then Ikuyo Shiotani, the season's most consistent player, jumped in front with 69–140. Hattori shot 71 Saturday to share first place with Toshimi Kimura with 216s. Michiko shot a one-under-par 71 Sunday for the winning 287 total. Kimura faded and Hiromi Kobayashi, a regular in 1994 on the U.S. LPGA Tour, posted 72 and claimed second place with her 290.

Tohato Ladies—¥50,000,000
Winner: Ayako Okamoto

It was only a matter of time before Ayako Okamoto tacked a 1994 title to her wonderful record. One would not expect the winner of 56 tournaments to go too long in the season before landing another victory. Okamoto nailed No. 57 in the Tohato Ladies, defeating Hiromi Takamura in a playoff after the two tied at 214 in regulation. This was no particular surprise, since Okamoto had won the Tohato event at Oak Village Golf Club outside of Tokyo two times previously.

Three players — Satake Classic winner Chieko Nishida, Korean Ok Hee Ku and Takamura — shared the second-round lead at 142, supplanting first-round leader Chikako Matsuzawa (69). Okamoto, two off the pace with 73 and 71, overtook Takamura with 70 to her 72 Sunday, forcing overtime. Ayako won with a two-putt par on the first extra hole as Hiromi sacrificed a stroke after a wild drive.

Toyo Suisan Ladies—¥50,000,000
Winner: Hiromi Takamura

Hiromi Takamura showed great heart when she rebounded from the playoff defeat in the Tohato Classic one Sunday to score a two-stroke victory the next Sunday in the Toyo Suisan Ladies at Kosaido Sapporo Country Club in Hokkaido. The triumph was the seventh of Takamura's career and the first in two years for the 1990 champion of the Japan LPGA Tour.

Kumiko Hiyoshi, a two-time winner in 1993 and twice a runner-up earlier in the 1994 season, showed the way at Sapporo the first two days. She opened with 67, added 68 for a 135 total and led by two strokes over Takamura, and by six or more over everyone else. But Hiyoshi couldn't hold the pace Sunday, shooting 76, and Takamura jumped in with 72–209 for the victory. Mayumi Murai and Jae Sook Won tied for third at 215.

Resort Trust Cleanup Ladies—¥50,000,000
Winner: Feng Tseng Hsiu

Feng Tseng Hsiu didn't take long. Two weeks after she arrived from Taiwan to play on the Japan LPGA Tour, Feng had a victory, her first in the country. The third-year pro, the second Taiwanese winner of 1994 on the circuit, came from two shots off the pace in the final round and registered a three-stroke win with her three-under-par 213 total.

The Taiwan contingent made a particularly strong showing in the Resort Trust Cleanup Ladies at Maple Point Golf Club at Kitatsuru. Huang Yueh

Chin shot 67 for the first-round lead. Wu Ming Yueh and Japan's Aki Takamura shared the lead the second day at 141 with three other Taiwanese pros, including Feng, just two off the pace. Feng started with a bogey Sunday, but shot 70, one of the day's best scores, to post her three-stroke win over Reiko Kashiwado, Natsuko Noro and Kaori Harada.

Katokichi Queens Cup—¥50,000,000
Winner: Ikuyo Shiotani

Ikuyo Shiotani's outstanding season continued in the Katokichi Queens Cup. Shiotani surged to her third victory of the season and it carried her to the top of the money list. She posted a six-under-par 213 total and won by three over Kazumi Takada. It was the ninth win of her 11-year career.

Shiotani led the first day by two strokes with 68, then slipped one stroke behind Taiwan's Huang Hui Fan (73-68–141) Saturday before bouncing back with 71 Sunday. Takada also closed with 71 for her 216 total, and took second place. Miyuki Shimabukuro was third at 217.

SC Ladies—¥50,000,000
Winner: Yuko Moriguchi

Yuko Moriguchi kept adding to her record the hard way in 1994. Moriguchi went the playoff route successfully for the second time in the season, capturing the SC Ladies at Kosaido Saitama Golf Club with a par on the second extra hole. It took her four overtime holes to win her 40th career title in the Mitsukoshi Cup in April.

The loser at Saitama was Aiko Hashimoto, who had carried a one-stroke lead into the final round with 67 and 70 for a 137 total. Toshimi Kimura and Akemi Yamaoka were at 138, and Moriguchi was at 139. Yamaoka, a two-time 1994 winner, had opened on top with 66. Moriguchi shot a one-under-par 71, Hashimoto 73 to forge the final tie at 210.

Asahi Kokusai Ladies—¥50,000,000
Winner: Young Mi Lee

The ladies from South Korea chalked up their third 1994 title when Young Mi Lee held off Ikuyo Shiotani's bid for a fourth victory and won the Asahi Kokusai Ladies tournament at the Asahi Kokusai Hamamura Onsen Golf Club. Lee, 31, who had won twice before on the Japan LPGA Tour but not for two years, posted an eight-under-par 208 total.

Lee and Shiotani, the money list leader, entered the final round tied at 137 after identical starts of 68 and 69. The Korean bogeyed the first hole Sunday but steadied, picked up two subsequent birdies for 71 and a one-stroke victory over Shiotani, who shot 72, and Hiromi Hirakata, who closed with the day's best score, 69.

NEC Karuizawa 72—¥60,000,000
Winner: Mayumi Hirase

Mayumi Hirase, a double winner on the 1993 Japan LPGA Tour, scored her first 1994 victory in the NEC Karuizawa 72, knocking off one of the circuit's titans, Ayako Okamoto, on the first hole of a playoff at Karuizawa 72 Golf Club at Nagano.

Hirase led from the start until Okamoto overhauled her at the wire Sunday. With her 68-69–137 start for 36 holes, Hirase seized a five-stroke lead on the strong field and was six ahead of Okamoto going into the final round. However, she slipped to 74 and the veteran international star caught her at 211 with her 68. Five players, including Ikuyo Shiotani and three other 1994 winners, tied for third at 215.

Itoki Classic—¥50,000,000
Winner: Ayako Okamoto

Ayako Okamoto turned the tables on Mayumi Hirase the week after losing a playoff to her at Nagano. Okamoto dominated the Itoki Classic from start to its abbreviated finish and recorded a three-stroke victory. Thunderstorms forced the shortening of the final round to nine holes, so Okamoto's winning total was an unusual 172.

Hirase, who began the tournament with 75 and trailed the eventual winner by nine after 18 holes, shot 67 the second day and added a 33 Sunday to vault into second place at 175. Okamoto's first-round 66 staked her to a three-stroke lead and she went four ahead of Aki Nakano Saturday with 68–134. They played the back nine of Glen Oaks Country Club at Kurimoto Sunday. Okamoto gave away three strokes with bogeys before a final-hole birdie for 38 and the 172 total.

Goyo Kensetsu Cup—¥60,000,000
Winner: Chikako Matsuzawa

Chikako Matsuzawa broke the stranglehold of the leading lights who had been monopolizing the titles on the Japan LPGA Tour at the Goyo Kensetsu Cup. Matsuzawa, who had one moment of glory two months earlier when she led the Tohato Ladies after the first round, became a rare first-time winner on the circuit with a bit of a hair-breadth, one-stroke victory at seven-under-par 209.

She started with 70, two behind leader Kumiko Hiyoshi, then moved into second place with 66–136, one shot behind Suzuko Maeda, the Mitsubishi Electric winner in June. Chikako had a rather shaky 73 Sunday, but grabbed the title when Maeda struggled to 75 and fast-closing Akemi Yamaoka and Kaori Higa fell a shot short with 68s.

Fuji Sankei Classic—¥45,000,000
Winner: Huang Yueh Chin

Wet weather curtailed action for the second time in three weeks on the Japan LPGA Tour and Huang Yueh Chin was the apparent beneficiary in the Fuji Sankei Classic. When play resumed Saturday after an afternoon thunderstorm wiped out the first round, Huang launched her move to a third 1994 victory for Taiwanese players. She and three others — Nayoko Yoshikawa, Junko Yasui and amateur Chika Aritoh — scored 69s and shared the lead. Of that group, only Huang broke par Sunday and her 71 for 140 gave her a one-stroke victory over Yoshikawa, Fuki Kido and Young Mi Lee, the Asahi Kokusai winner.

A few players had finished Friday before the storm hit, but the purse was reduced by one quarter when the round was cancelled.

Japan LPGA Championship—¥65,000,000
Winner: Kumiko Hiyoshi

Kumiko Hiyoshi, who had been beating around the victory bush quite often since scoring two early-season victories in 1993, won a major title in September in the Japan LPGA Championship at Hodaka Country Club in Nagano. The 30-year-old pro rallied from a two-stroke deficit and won by that same margin with her 285 total, picking up the fourth title of her career.

Hiyoshi put herself in a hole Friday when she skied to 77 after sharing the first-round lead at 69 with Fuki Kido and Aiko Hashimoto, two players who had been on the verge of winning several times earlier in the season. Kaori Higo, the Yakult winner, was the midway leader with 142. Kumiko bounced back Saturday with 68 to move within two strokes of co-leaders Mayumi Hirase (70-76-66) and Jae Sook Won (74-69-69). Hirase, the NEC Karuizawa 72 winner and 1993's leading money winner with three victories, still had the lead Sunday until Hiyoshi birdied the 14th hole and hung on for 71. Her 285 beat Hirase by two strokes and Aiko Hashimoto by three.

Kosaido Asahi Cup—¥60,000,000
Winner: Ayako Okamoto

Ayako Okamoto joined Ikuyo Shiotani, the money list leader, as a three-time winner on the 1994 Japan LPGA Tour when she came from three strokes off the pace to capture the Kosaido Asahi Cup at Chiba Kosaido Country Club. The victory boosted her career total to 41 wins, including 17 on the U.S. LPGA Tour.

Woo Soon Ko, the Kibun Classic winner in April, was headed for a second victory for two days. She began the tournament with 68 and added 70 for a 138 total and a three-stroke lead over Okamoto. The Korean fell behind early on Sunday when she bogeyed four of the first five holes and never fully recovered. Okamoto was just good enough with her two-birdie, one-bogey 71 for a 212 total, four under par, to edge Ko, who wound up with 75 for 213. Tracy Hanson, the former U.S. Curtis Cup player who won the

Indonesian Open in January, shot a final-round 69 for 214 to finish third.

Miyagi TV Cup—¥37,500,000
Winner: Jae Sook Won

Bad weather dealt the Japan LPGA Tour its most severe blow when the circuit when to Ohira for the Miyagi TV Cup. For the second time, rain washed out an opening round. Then, more rain forced a nine-hole finish on Sunday. Jae Sook Won scored a 27-hole victory, her third on the 1994 circuit and fourth of the year.

The South Korean shared the first-round lead with Ikuyo Shiotani and Wu Ming Yueh at 69, then nipped Shiotani in the abbreviated Sunday round with 34 to Shiotani's 35. The odd winning total was 103.

Yukijirushi Tokai Classic—¥60,000,000
Winner: Michiko Hattori

Michiko Hattori, who hit the high spot of her young professional career when she won the Japan Women's Open in June, put the fifth victory of her three-year pro career onto her record when she won the Yukijirushi Tokai Classic title. It was a one-stroke victory at Ryosen Golf Club as two of the early leaders self-destructed in their victory bids.

Hisako Higuchi, the first-round leader, disappeared after starting with a dazzling 65. Then, in the second round, Kaori Higo took a two-stroke lead over Higuchi and Mitsuko Hamada with 140, only to fumble to 79 Sunday. Meanwhile, Hattori was sitting close to the pace with 143 and followed with 69 Sunday for 212 that brought a one-stroke victory over Fuki Kido, who closed with 68 for 213 and tied for second with Hamada.

Takara World Invitational—¥65,000,000
Winner: Mayumi Hirase

Mayumi Hirase upheld the prestige of Japan's women pros when she over-whelmed an international field in the rich Takara World Invitational at Caledonian Golf Club and scored a two-stroke victory. Hirase, one of Japan's leading players who had traded victories with the No. 1 talent Ayako Okamoto two months earlier, held off the challenge of Sweden's Liselotte Neumann and several other stars of the U.S. women's circuit, finishing with 278, 10 under par, to post her second 1994 victory.

Neumann, who won the 1988 U.S. Women's Open, established a five-stroke lead after 36 holes when she fired 65 for a 134 total. Hirase, with 68 and 71, was the only player within eight strokes. Then, an eight-stroke swing followed on Saturday as Neumann shattered to 75 while Hirase was shooting 67 and taking a three-shot lead into the final round. Hirase's closing 72 gave her a two-stroke victory over Neumann. Brandie Burton, one of the Ameri-cans in the invitational field, finished a distant third at 286.

Fujitsu Ladies—¥60,000,000
Winner: Kikuko Shibata

Kikuko Shibata snuck up on the field and surprised all with a one-stroke victory in the Fujitsu Ladies tournament at Hamono Golf Course at Ichihara, Chiba Prefecture. Never in the contending picture during the first two rounds, Shibata shot a modest, two-under-par 70 Sunday to finish one shot ahead of Aki Nakano, Chikayo Yamazaki, Shin Sora of South Korea and Akane Ohshiro.

Wu Ming Yueh was the first-round leader with 67. Shibata was then five strokes behind. Mayumi Murai and Ohshiro took over first place Saturday with 139s. Shibata was at 143. Her closing 70 for a 213 total was all she needed Sunday.

Nichirei International—$618,750
Winner: United States

As an alternate on the U.S. Solheim Cup team, Michelle McGann walked the course with captain JoAnne Carner and cheered her LPGA teammates to a resounding victory against the Europeans. McGann got her chance to make a difference in the Nichirei International, making the transition from sideline to spotlight in leading the Americans to a convincing 22½ to 13½ triumph over the Japanese LPGA team.

McGann teamed with Donna Andrews for two victories in the better-ball matches and thrashed 1985 U.S. Women's Amateur champion Michiko Hattori by 10 strokes (66 to 76) in the singles. The performance earned McGann Most Valuable Player honors and a bracelet worth $15,000 to go with the $22,000 she earned as a member of the winning team.

In addition to the two victories with McGann, Andrews shot 66 in the singles to easily defeat Young Mi Lee of South Korea by seven shots. Tammie Green and Sherri Steinhauer were undefeated in the three-day competition. Elaine Crosby, another Solheim cheerleader, teamed with Dawn Coe-Jones for two victories and each won her singles match.

After the first day, the U.S. led 7½ to 1½, which was no surprise considering the lopsided history of these matches, which the U.S. leads 13-2. But on the second day, Japan closed to within three points, winning six of the better-ball matches. When Woo Soon Ko opened Sunday's singles with a victory over Martha Nause, it served as a wake-up call for the Americans. When McGann finished off Hattori, the U.S. had won 12 of the 18 matches.

Toray Japan Queens Cup—$700,000
Winner: Woo Soon Ko

Poor Betsy King. Needing to make an eight-foot putt on the final hole of regulation to win the Toray Japan Queens Cup and step into the LPGA's Hall of Fame, King missed. To make matters worse, she then three-putted the first playoff hole and lost to Woo Soon Ko of Korea.

Joining King on the woe-is-me list was Laura Davies, who missed an eight-footer at No. 18 for 73 that cost her Player of the Year honors and the

Vare Trophy for lowest scoring average, both to Beth Daniel, who opened the door for Davies with rounds of 72, 71 and 76. Davies, however, did hold onto her money lead by tying for seventh place and earning $19,549.

King garnered the most sympathy. She started the final round two strokes ahead on rounds of 67 and 67, but finished with 72. "I had a good feeling all week," King said. "I was confident because I always play well here." King ran afoul of Murphy's Law that says anything that can go wrong will go wrong. First, she mis-read the eight-footer to win, right, then she three-putted from 50 feet on the playoff hole, leaving her first putt eight feet short, and badly missing it.

"This is the closest I've come to winning my 30th," King said. "But I guess I'm gaining on it. I've never been in a playoff before. I wish I could have done it, gotten it out of the way and been able to have a nice off-season. Now it'll make for a long winter."

Ko, the first-round leader and the winner of 16 events in Korea, finished with a solid 70 but inwardly conceded the victory to King. When King missed the putt to win, Ko breathed easier. She hit her approach shot on the playoff hole to 20 feet and calmly two-putted for par.

Itoen Ladies—¥60,000,000
Winner: Laura Davies

Laura Davies continued a remarkable international season with a one-stroke victory in the Itoen Ladies tournament at the Great Island Club at Chonanmachi. Clearly the world's No. 1 woman golfer of the year with previous 1994 victories on the U.S. (three), European (two) and Asia (one) circuits, the long-hitting Englishwoman led the Itoen all the way and it became close only at the end.

Davies opened with 64 and added 66 for a 130 total, establishing a five-stroke lead over Nayoko Yoshikawa and Kaori Higo. With four birdies on the front nine Sunday, it looked like a runaway for Davies. Enter Mayumi Murai, winless in 1994 after three victories the year before. Murai was closing the gap on her way to a career-best 66 and Davies contributed with four bogeys on the next seven holes. But Davies holed a short birdie putt at the 17th to shoot 71 and edge Murai by one shot with her 15-under-par total. It was the 31st victory of Davies' outstanding career.

Daio Seishi Elleair Open—¥60,000,000
Winner: Mayumi Hirase

Mayumi Hirase matched her 1993 victory total on the Japan LPGA Tour when she won the Daio Seishi Elleair Open. Hirase, the 1993 money list leader who didn't win her first 1994 title until mid-August, picked up her third at Matsuyama in mid-November, coming from a stroke off the pace with a final-round 70 for a 211 total and a two-stroke victory over Michiko Hattori, a two-time winner earlier in the season, and Nayoko Yoshikawa, twice a 1994 runner-up. Hirase, a second-place finisher twice in the weeks shortly after the Karuizawa 72 win in August, scored her 12th career victory with a seven-birdie, five-bogey final round for the two-under-par 70 after a 71-70 start had left her a stroke behind Norimi Terazawa (72-68).

Meiji Nyugyo Cup—¥50,000,000
Winner: Mayumi Hirase

On a roll, Mayumi Hirase followed up her Elleair victory with an impressive, wire-to-wire triumph in the Meiji Nyugyo Cup, notching her fourth title of 1994, the 13th of her career, and taking over the No. 1 position on the Japan LPGA Tour. The ¥9 million prize jumped her season earnings to ¥69,300,000, inching her ahead of Ikuyo Shiotani, the 1992 leading money winner and leader in the 1994 standings since mid-season. Hirase opened with 68, tied for the lead with Ayako Okamoto and Nayoko Yoshikawa, then moved two shots ahead of Marnie McGuire with a 70–138 Saturday. Her final-round 70 and eight-under-par 208 total stretched her winning margin to four over Aiko Hashimoto, runner-up for a third time in 1994.

Mizuno Ladies Open—¥60,000,000
Winner: Mitsuyo Hirata

Mitsuyo Hirata, who had enjoyed much success on the Japan LPGA Tour through the season, ended it on a high note when she captured the Mizuno Ladies Open at Kumamoto Chuo Country Club at Kyokushimura. Hirata, who posted rounds of 69-67 the first two days and took a one-stroke lead over Nayoko Yoshikawa in the final round, survived a double bogey Sunday, shot 71 for a nine-under-par 207 total and a three-stroke victory over Yoshikawa and Aiko Hashimoto, both second-place finishers in the preceding two weeks who went winless for the year. Mayumi Murai, a three-time winner in 1993 and the first-day leader with 68, wound up in fourth place with her 212. Though far off the pace at 29th place, Mayumi Hirase clinched the money list title for the second year in a row.

APPENDIXES

The Sony Ranking
(As of December 31, 1994)

Pos.		Player	Circuit	Points Average	Total Points	No. of Events	91/93 Total	91/93 Minus	1994 Plus
1	(4)	Nick Price	Afr 1	21.19	1716	81	1319	-707	1104
2	(2)	Greg Norman	ANZ 1	20.57	1399	68	1334	-711	776
3	(1)	Nick Faldo	Eur 1	16.93	1236	73	1466	-794	564
4	(3)	Bernhard Langer	Eur 2	15.32	1164	76	1289	-729	604
5	(15)	Jose Maria Olazabal	Eur 3	15.18	1199	79	695	-424	928
6	(20)	Ernie Els	Afr 2	14.70	1382	94	550	-276	1108
7	(5)	Fred Couples	USA 1	12.86	939	73	1209	-694	424
8	(14)	Colin Montgomerie	Eur 4	12.19	1182	97	869	-483	796
9	(12)	Masashi Ozaki	Jpn 1	11.39	797	70	640	-343	500
10	(10)	Corey Pavin	USA 2	10.87	891	82	834	-479	536
11	(11)	David Frost	Afr 3	9.88	968	98	917	-469	520
12	(46)	Fuzzy Zoeller	USA 3	9.73	603	62	306	-183	480
13	(8)	Tom Kite	USA 4	9.03	677	75	765	-412	324
14	(25)	Seve Ballesteros	Eur 5	8.96	681	76	462	-329	548
15	(16)	Vijay Singh	Asa 1	8.49	925	109	908	-487	504
16	(7)	Ian Woosnam	Eur 6	8.46	660	78	856	-516	320
17	(48)	Tom Lehman	USA 5	8.13	756	93	416	-208	548
18	(17)	Mark McNulty	Afr 4	8.01	561	70	550	-309	320
19	(92)	Mark McCumber	USA 6	7.68	507	66	224	-121	404
20	(107)	Loren Roberts	USA 7	7.46	597	80	241	-136	492
21	(6)	Paul Azinger	USA 8	7.25	522	72	1094	-600	28
22	(47)	Phil Mickelson	USA 9	7.24	492	68	344	-184	332
23	(26)	Tom Watson	USA 10	6.82	409	60	367	-210	252
24	(18)	John Cook	USA 11	6.67	500	75	611	-339	228
25	(9)	Davis Love III	USA 12	6.53	568	87	855	-479	192
26	(36)	Brad Faxon	USA 13	6.43	585	91	500	-275	360
27	(50)	Jeff Maggert	USA 14	6.20	552	89	463	-243	332
28	(21)	Larry Mize	USA 15	6.14	491	80	554	-295	232
29	(89)	Hale Irwin	USA 16	5.96	399	67	217	-142	324
30	(88)	Scott Hoch	USA 17	5.91	455	77	271	-168	352
31	(32)	Frank Nobilo	ANZ 2	5.74	471	82	476	-277	272
32	(22)	Lee Janzen	USA 18	5.68	545	96	672	-347	220
33	(43)	David Gilford	Eur 7	5.59	464	83	424	-240	280
34	(64)	Ben Crenshaw	USA 19	5.58	430	77	336	-186	280
35	(38)	Barry Lane	Eur 8	5.48	553	101	564	-299	288
36	(109)	Bill Glasson	USA 20	5.47	350	64	175	-89	264
37	(122)	Bob Estes	USA 21	5.36	466	87	224	-118	360
38	(37)	Sam Torrance	Eur 9	5.23	455	87	467	-260	248
39	(72)	Jesper Parnevik	Eur 10	5.23	387	74	297	-158	248
40	(68)	John Huston	USA 22	5.22	475	91	382	-215	308
41	(42)	Bruce Lietzke	USA 23	5.22	313	60	318	-197	192
42	(103)	Miguel Angel Jimenez	Eur 11	5.20	478	92	257	-139	360
43	(19)	Steve Elkington	ANZ 3	5.18	399	77	648	-361	112
44	(44)	Craig Parry	ANZ 4	5.14	473	92	495	-310	288
45	(39)	David Edwards	USA 24	5.07	380	75	431	-239	188
46	(53)	Tsuneyuki Nakajima	Jpn 2	5.00	430	86	430	-244	244
47	(51)	Jay Haas	USA 25	4.99	434	87	424	-222	232
48	(81)	Robert Allenby	ANZ 5	4.94	459	93	292	-153	320

( ) : Figures in brackets indicate 1991/93 positions.

Pos.		Player	Circuit	Points Average	Total Points	No. of Events	91/93 Total	91/93 Minus	1994 Plus
49	(56)	Mark Calcavecchia	USA 26	4.92	487	99	460	-261	288
50	(67)	Rick Fehr	USA 27	4.82	366	76	339	-185	212
51	(85)	Mark Roe	Eur 12	4.68	393	84	295	-158	256
52	(65)	Eduardo Romero	SAm 1	4.67	350	75	349	-211	212
53	(27)	Peter Senior	ANZ 6	4.60	437	95	604	-331	164
54	(13)	Payne Stewart	USA 28	4.59	376	82	766	-442	52
55	(35)	Mark James	Eur 13	4.54	313	69	422	-237	128
56	(63)	Joakim Haeggman	Eur 14	4.42	349	79	333	-172	188
57	(29)	Scott Simpson	USA 29	4.41	335	76	436	-245	144
58	(74)	Curtis Strange	USA 30	4.33	316	73	283	-163	196
59	(49)	Craig Stadler	USA 31	4.32	350	81	399	-245	196
60	(31)	Gordon Brand, Jr.	Eur 15	4.30	370	86	497	-267	140
61	(171T)	Brian Watts	USA 32	4.30	318	74	133	-67	252
62	(23)	Chip Beck	USA 33	4.18	364	87	547	-311	128
63	(33)	Costantino Rocca	Eur 16	4.11	370	90	489	-263	144
64	(30)	Tony Johnstone	Afr 5	4.09	372	91	540	-300	132
65	(34)	Jim Gallagher, Jr.	USA 34	4.07	346	85	504	-286	128
66	(62)	Gil Morgan	USA 35	4.01	277	69	344	-187	120
67	(76)	Brett Ogle	ANZ 7	3.93	299	76	290	-163	172
68	(97)	Per-Ulrik Johansson	Eur 17	3.90	308	79	233	-137	212
69	(246)	Steve Lowery	USA 36	3.85	323	84	75	-40	288
70	(75)	Naomichi Ozaki	Jpn 3	3.83	375	98	361	-206	220
71	(59)	Anders Forsbrand	Eur 18	3.77	347	92	445	-242	144
72	(96)	John Daly	USA 37	3.67	286	78	294	-188	180
73	(54)	Wayne Westner	Afr 6	3.65	307	84	362	-187	132
74	(58)	Darren Clarke	Eur 19	3.61	303	84	371	-188	120
75	(178)	Howard Clark	Eur 20	3.49	227	65	111	-60	176
76	(24)	Raymond Floyd	USA 38	3.48	209	60	372	-211	48
77	(214)	Mike Springer	USA 39	3.43	302	88	118	-68	252
78	(83)	Duffy Waldorf	USA 40	3.37	293	87	309	-164	148
79	(90)	Andrew Magee	USA 41	3.30	297	90	314	-201	184
80	(91)	Todd Hamilton	USA 42	3.24	308	95	274	-138	172
81	(40)	Rodger Davis	ANZ 8	3.24	272	84	451	-287	108
82	(70)	Peter Baker	Eur 21	3.22	290	90	367	-189	112
83T	(28)	Mark O'Meara	USA 43	3.12	268	86	503	-299	64
83T	(127)	Carl Mason	Eur 22	3.12	268	86	204	-112	176
85	(52)	Dan Forsman	USA 44	3.11	252	81	408	-216	60
86	(61)	Nolan Henke	USA 45	3.11	264	85	413	-245	96
87	(106)	Greg Turner	ANZ 9	3.08	240	78	233	-133	140
88	(162)	Robert Gamez	USA 46	3.06	245	80	158	-97	184
89	(69)	David Feherty	Eur 23	3.02	263	87	366	-215	112
90	(71)	Jeff Sluman	USA 47	2.99	293	98	408	-239	124
91	(80)	Billy Andrade	USA 48	2.95	274	93	348	-218	144
92	(45)	Ronan Rafferty	Eur 24	2.92	277	95	472	-251	56
93	(57)	Sandy Lyle	Eur 25	2.91	239	82	390	-231	80
94	(110)	Roger Mackay	ANZ 10	2.88	190	66	206	-132	116
95	(320T)	Lennie Clements	USA 49	2.79	204	73	43	-23	184
96	(154)	David Ishii	USA 50	2.78	253	91	172	-91	172
97	(55)	Fulton Allem	Afr 7	2.78	250	90	425	-231	56
98	(176)	Brad Bryant	USA 51	2.77	271	98	156	-89	204
99	(207T)	Kirk Triplett	USA 52	2.76	232	84	115	-63	180
100	(86)	Retief Goosen	Afr 8	2.73	235	86	249	-126	112
101	(143)	Kenny Perry	USA 53	2.68	225	84	170	-109	164
102	(41)	Rocco Mediate	USA 54	2.67	192	72	433	-253	12
103	(115)	Donnie Hammond	USA 55	2.63	197	75	198	-105	104
104	(118)	Tsukasa Watanabe	Jpn 4	2.62	283	108	282	-151	152

( ) : Figures in brackets indicate 1991/93 positions.

Pos.		Player	Circuit	Points Average	Total Points	No. of Events	91/93 Total	91/93 Minus	1994 Plus
105	(101)	Jay Don Blake	USA 56	2.59	205	79	243	-158	120
106	(87)	D.A. Weibring	USA 57	2.59	176	68	240	-148	84
107	(78)	Jose Rivero	Eur 26	2.59	194	75	284	-162	72
108	(145)	Peter Mitchell	Eur 27	2.58	258	100	202	-116	172
109	(105)	Blaine McCallister	USA 58	2.56	220	86	245	-153	128
110	(123)	Fred Funk	USA 59	2.55	250	98	246	-136	140
111	(142)	Yoshinori Mizumaki	Jpn 5	2.55	260	102	212	-116	164
112	(204)	Michael Clayton	ANZ 11	2.53	256	101	139	-75	192
113	(95)	Mark Brooks	USA 60	2.53	273	108	334	-205	144
114	(77)	Steve Pate	USA 61	2.52	237	94	349	-228	116
115	(112)	Wayne Grady	ANZ 12	2.41	222	92	252	-146	116
116	(111)	Masahiro Kuramoto	Jpn 6	2.39	208	87	258	-142	92
117T	(93)	Keith Clearwater	USA 62	2.36	236	100	320	-172	88
117T	(99)	Robert Karlsson	Eur 28	2.36	177	75	209	-112	80
119	(283)	Hal Sutton	USA 63	2.31	199	86	72	-57	184
120	(60)	Steven Richardson	Eur 29	2.30	246	107	511	-309	44
121	(229)	Hsieh Chin Sheng	Asa 2	2.30	147	64	72	-37	112
122	(139)	Frankie Minoza	Asa 3	2.27	168	74	167	-87	88
123	(136)	Peter Jacobsen	USA 64	2.26	167	74	169	-102	100
124	(420)	Eiji Mizoguchi	Jpn 7	2.25	153	68	26	-13	140
125	(392)	Patrick Burke	USA 65	2.24	152	68	32	-16	136
126	(151)	Glen Day	USA 66	2.21	177	80	146	-81	112
127	(79)	Joey Sindelar	USA 67	2.21	168	76	299	-159	28
128	(949T)	Carlos Franco	SAm 2	2.19	140	64	0	0	140
129	(152T)	Greg Kraft	USA 68	2.18	190	87	148	-74	116
130	(94)	Russ Cochran	USA 69	2.18	192	88	296	-184	80
131	(150)	Jim McGovern	USA 70	2.16	222	103	210	-108	120
132	(155)	Terry Price	ANZ 13	2.09	155	74	118	-63	100
133	(338T)	Steve Stricker	USA 71	2.09	138	66	36	-18	120
134	(209)	Katsuyoshi Tomori	Jpn 8	2.09	167	80	87	-44	124
135	(100)	Bradley Hughes	ANZ 14	2.08	152	73	200	-104	56
136	(406T)	Pierre Fulke	Eur 30	2.06	146	71	28	-14	132
137	(82)	Chen Tze Chung	Asa 4	2.02	182	90	328	-178	32
138	(84)	Paul Broadhurst	Eur 31	1.99	159	80	305	-174	28
139	(135)	Katsunori Takahashi	Jpn 9	1.98	186	94	222	-116	80
140	(128)	Jim Payne	Eur 32	1.98	174	88	206	-104	72
141	(284)	Hisayuki Sasaki	Jpn 10	1.95	129	66	50	-25	104
142	(144)	Jean Van de Velde	Eur 33	1.95	183	94	198	-111	96
143	(801T)	Andrew Coltart	Eur 34	1.95	142	73	4	-2	140
144	(247)	Phillip Price	Eur 35	1.93	158	82	83	-45	120
145T	(197)	Nobuo Serizawa	Jpn 11	1.92	175	91	133	-74	116
145T	(117)	Gene Sauers	USA 72	1.92	150	78	203	-121	68
147	(163)	Gary Orr	Eur 36	1.89	157	83	130	-65	92
148	(124)	Peter O'Malley	ANZ 15	1.89	170	90	227	-129	72
149	(138)	Isao Aoki	Jpn 12	1.87	114	61	150	-92	56
150T	(949T)	Jonathon Lomas	Eur 37	1.86	128	69	0	0	128
150T	(949T)	Mike Heinen	USA 73	1.86	128	69	0	0	128
152	(250)	Sven Struver	Eur 38	1.85	137	74	67	-34	104
153	(102)	Hajime Meshiai	Jpn 13	1.83	165	90	283	-146	28
154	(147)	Mike Harwood	ANZ 16	1.83	174	95	183	-133	124
155	(130)	Jose Coceres	SAm 3	1.83	130	71	156	-78	52
156	(286)	Gabriel Hjertstedt	Eur 39	1.82	120	66	49	-25	96
157	(108)	Howard Twitty	USA 74	1.81	163	90	255	-140	48
158	(149)	Gary Hallberg	USA 75	1.79	154	86	174	-104	84
159	(282)	Anthony Gilligan	ANZ 17	1.77	126	71	62	-32	96
160	(132)	Mike Standly	USA 76	1.77	163	92	209	-106	60

( ) : Figures in brackets indicate 1991/93 positions.

Pos.		Player	Circuit	Points Average	Total Points	No. of Events	91/93 Total	91/93 Minus	1994 Plus
161	(170)	Paul McGinley	Eur 40	1.75	147	84	135	-68	80
162	(129)	Bob Lohr	USA 77	1.74	150	86	193	-119	76
163	(266)	Russell Claydon	Eur 41	1.71	156	91	82	-50	124
164	(171T)	Kiyoshi Murota	Jpn 14	1.71	185	108	189	-100	96
165	(180)	Stephen Ames	SAm 4	1.71	116	68	104	-52	64
166	(121)	Billy Mayfair	USA 78	1.69	166	98	255	-137	48
167	(237)	Dave Barr	Can 1	1.69	137	81	87	-50	100
168	(263T)	Paul Curry	Eur 42	1.68	128	76	73	-41	96
169	(157)	Des Smyth	Eur 43	1.68	143	85	168	-89	64
170	(66)	Ian Baker-Finch	ANZ 18	1.68	153	91	399	-274	28
171	(120)	Tom Purtzer	USA 79	1.67	127	76	205	-150	72
172	(140)	Wayne Levi	USA 80	1.66	128	77	166	-98	60
173	(307T)	Masayuki Kawamura	Jpn 15	1.66	126	76	48	-26	104
174	(98)	Jamie Spence	Eur 44	1.64	143	87	268	-153	28
175	(328T)	Bruce Vaughan	USA 81	1.63	98	60	38	-20	80
176	(104)	Peter Fowler	ANZ 19	1.63	158	97	288	-162	32
177	(325T)	Hideki Kase	Jpn 16	1.63	127	78	56	-37	108
178	(898T)	Peter Hedblom	Eur 45	1.63	104	64	1	-1	104
179	(73)	Lanny Wadkins	USA 82	1.61	119	74	295	-192	16
180	(252T)	Paul Moloney	ANZ 20	1.60	109	68	60	-31	80
181T	(338T)	Eduardo Herrera	SAm 5	1.60	96	60	42	-22	76
181T	(949T)	Johnny Miller	USA 83	1.60	96	60	0	0	96
183	(296)	Mark Davis	Eur 46	1.60	139	87	66	-43	116
184	(200T)	Shigeki Maruyama	Jpn 17	1.59	110	69	84	-42	68
185	(270)	Lucas Parsons	ANZ 21	1.58	95	60	54	-27	68
186	(186)	Miguel Angel Martin	Eur 47	1.57	132	84	124	-80	88
187	(152T)	Mats Lanner	Eur 48	1.57	127	81	176	-105	56
188	(175)	John Bland	Afr 9	1.55	110	71	127	-85	68
189	(116)	De Wet Basson	Afr 10	1.54	117	76	182	-93	28
190	(195)	Wayne Riley	ANZ 22	1.54	143	93	142	-87	88
191	(119)	Mike Hulbert	USA 84	1.54	149	97	250	-165	64
192	(679)	Clark Dennis	USA 85	1.54	109	71	8	-7	108
193	(182)	Bob Gilder	USA 86	1.53	139	91	137	-86	88
194	(126)	Ken Green	USA 87	1.52	117	77	197	-116	36
195	(134)	Dudley Hart	USA 88	1.52	135	89	199	-104	40
196	(281)	Teruo Sugihara	Jpn 18	1.52	97	64	64	-39	72
197T	(164)	Andrew Oldcorn	Eur 49	1.50	90	60	109	-55	36
197T	(221T)	Wayne Smith	ANZ 23	1.50	105	70	78	-41	68
199	(425T)	Paul Eales	Eur 50	1.49	118	79	28	-14	104
200	(241T)	Craig Warren	ANZ 24	1.48	98	66	64	-34	68

( ) : Figures in brackets indicate 1991/93 positions.

World's Winners of 1994

U.S. PGA TOUR

Mercedes Championship	Phil Mickelson
United Airlines Hawaiian Open	Brett Ogle
Northern Telecom Open	Andrew Magee
Phoenix Open	Bill Glasson
AT&T Pebble Beach National Pro-Am	Johnny Miller
Nissan Los Angeles Open	Corey Pavin
Bob Hope Chrysler Classic	Scott Hoch
Buick Invitational of California	Craig Stadler
Doral-Ryder Open	John Huston
Honda Classic	Nick Price (2)
The Nestle Invitational	Loren Roberts
The Players Championship	Greg Norman (2)
Freeport-McMoRan Classic	Ben Crenshaw
Masters Tournament	Jose Maria Olazabal (2)
MCI Heritage Classic	Hale Irwin
Kmart Greater Greensboro Open	Mike Springer
Shell Houston Open	Mike Heinen
BellSouth Classic	John Daly
GTE Byron Nelson Classic	Neal Lancaster
Memorial Tournament	Tom Lehman
Southwestern Bell Colonial	Nick Price (3)
Kemper Open	Mark Brooks
Buick Classic	Lee Janzen
U.S. Open Championship	Ernie Els (2)
Canon Greater Hartford Open	David Frost (4)
Motorola Western Open	Nick Price (4)
Anheuser-Busch Classic	Mark McCumber
Deposit Guaranty Classic	Brian Henninger
New England Classic	Kenny Perry
Federal Express St. Jude Classic	Dicky Pride
Buick Open	Fred Couples
PGA Championship	Nick Price (6)
Sprint International	Steve Lowery
NEC World Series of Golf	Jose Maria Olazabal (4)
Greater Milwaukee Open	Mike Springer (2)
Bell Canadian Open	Nick Price (7)
B.C. Open	Mike Sullivan
The Presidents Cup	United States
Hardee's Classic	Mark McCumber (2)
Buick Southern Open	Steve Elkington
Walt Disney World/Oldsmobile Classic	Rick Fehr
Texas Open	Bob Estes
Las Vegas Invitational	Bruce Lietzke
Tour Championship	Mark McCumber (3)

SPECIAL EVENTS

Westinghouse-Family House Invitational	David Frost (3)
Jerry Ford Invitational	Jay Don Blake
Ernst Championship	Billy Andrade
Fred Meyer Challenge	Mark O'Meara/John Cook
Guadalajara Invitational	Loren Roberts (2)
Gene Sarazen World Open	Ernie Els (4)
Lincoln-Mercury Kapalua International	Fred Couples (2)

PGA Grand Slam of Golf	Greg Norman (3)
World Cup of Golf	United States/Fred Couples (3)
Mexican Open	Chris Perry (2)
Pebble Beach Invitational	Robert Gamez
Franklin Funds Shark Shootout	Fred Couples (4)/Brad Faxon
Diners Club Matches	Jeff Maggert/Jim McGovern

NIKE TOUR

Inland Empire Open	Skip Kendall
Monterrey Open	Scott Gump
Louisiana Open	Bill Porter
Pensacola Open	Bruce Vaughan (2)
Mississippi Gulf Coast Classic	John Elliott
Panama City Beach Classic	Keith Fergus
Shreveport Open	Omar Uresti (2)
Alabama Classic	Tommy Tolles
South Carolina Classic	Charlie Rymer
Central Georgia Open	Rick Pearson
Knoxville Open	Vic Wilk
Greater Greenville Classic	Scott Gump (2)
Miami Valley Open	Tommy Armour
Cleveland Open	Tommy Armour (2)
Dominion Open	Sonny Skinner
Carolina Classic	Skip Kendall (2)
Gateway Classic	Brad Fabel
Wichita Charity Classic	Dennis Postlewait
Dakota Dunes Open	Pat Bates
Ozarks Open	Jerry Haas
Texarkana Open	Mike Brisky
Permian Basin Open	Bruce Vaughan (3)
New Mexico Charity Classic	Jim Carter
Utah Classic	Chris Perry
Boise Open	Keith Fergus (2)
Tri-Cities Classic	Jerry Haas (2)
Sonoma County Open	Jerry Haas (3)
Nike Tour Championship	Mike Schuchart

CANADIAN TOUR

Payless Open	Matt Jackson
Morningstar Classic	Robert Meyer
B.C. Tel Pacific Open	Craig Jones (2)
Alberta Open	Jim Rutledge
Klondike Klassic	Ian Hutchings
Xerox Manitoba Open	Scott Dunlap
Infiniti Tournament Players Championship	Derek James
Canadian Masters	Roger Wessels
Export "A" Inc. Ontario Open	Eric Woods
Trafalgar CPGA Championship	Stuart Hendley
International Team Matches	International Team

SOUTH AMERICAN TOUR

Bogota Open	Miguel Guzman
Los Andes Open	Ron Wuensche
T.C. Ecuador Open	Mauricio Molina
Los Inkas-Peru Open	David Ogrin
Litoral Open	Cesar Monasterio
Uruguay Open	Raul Fretes
Argentina Tournament of Champions	Jose Coceres (2)
Paraguay Open	Mike Cunning
Argentina PGA	Armando Saavedra

286 / WORLD'S WINNERS OF 1994

Prince of Wales Open	Jose Maria Cantero
Argentina Open	Mark O'Meara (2)
Los Leones-Chile Open	Raul Fretes (2)

PGA EUROPEAN TOUR

Madeira Island Open	Mats Lanner
Moroccan Open	Anders Forsbrand
Dubai Desert Classic	Ernie Els
Johnnie Walker Asian Classic	Greg Norman
Turespana Open de Tenerife	David Gilford
Extremadura Open	Paul Eales
Turespana Masters Open de Andalucia	Carl Mason
Turespana Open Mediterrania	Jose Maria Olazabal
Turespana Open de Baleares	Barry Lane
Portuguese Open	Phillip Price
Open V33 du Grand Lyon	Stephen Ames
Tournoi Perrier de Paris	Peter Baker/David J. Russell
Heineken Open Catalonia	Jose Coceres
Air France Cannes Open	Ian Woosnam
Benson & Hedges International Open	Seve Ballesteros
Peugeot Open de Espana	Colin Montgomerie
Tisettanta Italian Open	Eduardo Romero
Volvo PGA Championship	Jose Maria Olazabal (3)
Alfred Dunhill Open	Nick Faldo
Honda Open	Robert Allenby
Jersey European Airways Open	Paul Curry
Peugeot Open de France	Mark Roe
Murphy's Irish Open	Bernhard Langer
Bell's Scottish Open	Carl Mason (2)
British Open Championship	Nick Price (5)
Heineken Dutch Open	Miguel Angel Jimenez
Scandinavian Masters	Vijay Singh
BMW International Open	Mark McNulty
Hohe Brucke Austrian Open	Mark Davis
Murphy's English Open	Colin Montgomerie (2)
Volvo German Open	Colin Montgomerie (3)
Canon European Masters	Eduardo Romero (2)
European Open	David Gilford (2)
Dunhill British Masters	Ian Woosnam (2)
Trophee Lancome	Vijay Singh (2)
Mercedes German Masters	Seve Ballesteros (2)
Alfred Dunhill Cup	Canada
Toyota World Match Play Championship	Ernie Els (3)
Chemapol Trophy Czech Open	Per-Ulrik Johansson
Volvo Masters	Bernhard Langer (2)
Johnnie Walker World Championship	Ernie Els (5)

ASIA TOUR

Manila Southwoods Philippine Open	Carlos Franco
Kent Hong Kong Open	David Frost (2)
Classic Indian Open	Emlyn Aubrey
Thai International Thailand Open	Brandt Jobe
Benson & Hedges Malaysian Open	Joakim Haeggman
Sampoerna Indonesian Open	Frank Nobilo
Sabah Masters	Craig McClellan
Chin Fong Republic of China Open	Hong Chia Yuh
Maekyung Korean Open	Jong Duck Kim

JAPAN TOUR

Token Corporation Cup	Craig Warren
Daido Drinco Shizuoka Open	Tsuneyuki Nakajima

United Airlines KSB Sentonaikai Open	Kazuhiro Takami
Descente Classic Munsingwear Cup	Brian Watts
Pocari Sweat Open	Yoshinori Mizumaki
Tsuruya Open	Tsuneyuki Nakajima (2)
Dunlop Open	Masashi Ozaki
Chunichi Crowns	Roger Mackay
Fuji Sankei Classic	Kiyoshi Murota
Japan PGA Championship	Hiroshi Goda
Pepsi Ube-Kosan Tournament	Tsuneyuki Nakajima (3)
Mitsubishi Galant Tournament	Katsuyoshi Tomori
JCB Sendai Classic	Masahiro Kuramoto
Sapporo Tokyu Open	Yoshinori Mizumaki (2)
Yomiuri Open	Tsukasa Watanabe
Mizuno Open	Brian Watts (2)
PGA Philanthropy Cup	Todd Hamilton
Yonex Open Hiroshima	Masashi Ozaki (2)
Nikkei Cup Torakichi Nakamura Memorial	Toru Suzuki
NST Niigata Open	Pete Izumikawa
Acom International	Naomichi Ozaki
Maruman Open	David Ishii
Hisamitsu KBC Augusta Tournament	Brian Watts (3)
Japan Match Play Championship	Todd Hamilton (2)
Suntory Open	David Ishii (2)
ANA Open	Masashi Ozaki (3)
Gene Sarazan Jun Classic	Carlos Franco (2)
Japan Open Championship	Masashi Ozaki (4)
Tokai Classic	Corey Pavin (2)
Asahi Beer Golf Digest Tournament	Eiji Mizoguchi
Bridgestone Open	Brian Watts (4)
Philip Morris Championship	Brian Watts (5)
Daiwa International	Masashi Ozaki (5)
Sumitomo Visa Taiheiyo Masters	Masashi Ozaki (6)
Dunlop Phoenix	Masashi Ozaki (7)
Casio World Open	Robert Gamez (2)
Japan Series Hitachi Cup	Hisayuki Sasaki
Daikyo Open	Hideki Kase

AUSTRALASIAN TOUR

AMP New Zealand Open	Craig Jones
Optus Players Championship	Patrick Burke
Heineken Classic	Michael Clayton
New South Wales Open	Darren Chivas
Microsoft Australian Masters	Craig Parry
Canon Challenge	Peter Senior
Foodlink Queensland Open	Lucas Parsons
Epson Singapore Open	Kyi Hla Han
Alfred Dunhill Asian Masters	Jack Kay
Victorian Open	Patrick Burke (2)
Reebok PGA Championship	Andrew Coltart
Heineken Australian Open	Robert Allenby (2)
Greg Norman's Holden Classic	Anthony Gilligan
Air New Zealand-Shell Open	Shane Robinson
Schweppes Coolum Classic	Michael Clayton (2)

AFRICAN TOURS

Bell's Cup	Tony Johnstone
Lexington PGA Championship	David Frost
ICL International	Nick Price
Telkom South African Masters	Chris Davison
Hollard Insurance Royal Swazi Sun Classic	Omar Uresti
Standard Chartered Kenya Open	Paul Carman

Autopage Mount Edgecombe Trophy   Bruce Vaughan
Hassan II Trophy   Martin Gates
Zimbabwe Open   Chris Williams
Nashua Wild Coast Challenge   Hendrik Buhrmann
Nedbank Million Dollar Challenge   Nick Faldo (2)

U.S. SENIOR PGA TOUR

Mercedes Championship	Jack Nicklaus
Royal Caribbean Classic	Lee Trevino
Senior Grand Slam of Golf	Tom Shaw
GTE Suncoast Classic	Rocky Thompson
IntelliNet Challenge	Mike Hill
Chrysler Cup	International Team/George Archer
GTE West Classic	Jay Sigel
Vantage at the Dominion	Jim Albus
Doug Sanders Celebrity Classic	Tom Wargo
The Tradition at Desert Mountain	Raymond Floyd
PGA Seniors Championship	Lee Trevino (3)
Dallas Reunion Pro-Am	Larry Gilbert
Las Vegas Senior Classic	Raymond Floyd (2)
Liberty Mutual Legends of Golf	Dale Douglass/Charles Coody
PaineWebber Invitational	Lee Trevino (4)
Cadillac NFL Classic	Raymond Floyd (3)
Bell Atlantic Classic	Lee Trevino (5)
Bruno's Memorial Classic	Jim Dent
Nationwide Championship	Dave Stockton
BellSouth Senior Classic at Opryland	Lee Trevino (6)
Ford Senior Players Championship	Dave Stockton (2)
U.S. Senior Open	Simon Hobday
Kroger Classic	Jim Colbert
Ameritech Open	John Paul Cain
Southwestern Bell Classic	Jim Colbert (2)
Northville Long Island Classic	Lee Trevino (7)
Bank of Boston Classic	Jim Albus (2)
First of America Classic	Tony Jacklin
Burnet Classic	Dave Stockton (3)
Franklin Quest Championship	Tom Weiskopf
GTE Northwest Classic	Simon Hobday (2)
Quicksilver Classic	Dave Eichelberger
Bank One Classic	Isao Aoki
Brickyard Crossing Championship	Isao Aoki (2)
Vantage Championship	Larry Gilbert (2)
The Transamerica	Kermit Zarley
Raley's Gold Rush	Bob Murphy
Ralph's Classic	Jack Kiefer
Hyatt Regency Maui Kaanapali Classic	Bob Murphy (2)
Golf Magazine Senior Tour Championship	Raymond Floyd (4)
Diners Club Matches	Raymond Floyd (5)/
	Dave Eichelberger (2)

EUROPEAN SENIORS TOUR

St. Pierre Classic	Tommy Horton
La Manga Club Spanish Open	Brian Huggett
D-Day Open	Brian Waites
Northern Electric Seniors	John Morgan
Tandem Open	Malcolm Gregson
Seniors British Open	Tom Wargo (2)
Lawrence Batley Seniors	John Morgan (2)
Forte PGA Seniors Championship	John Morgan (3)
Belfast Telegraph Irish Senior Masters	Tommy Horton (2)
Joe Powell Memorial Classic	Liam Higgins

Shell Scottish Seniors Open   Antonio Garrido
Zurich Senior Pro-Am: Lexus Trophy   Liam Higgins (2)

JAPAN SENIOR TOUR

American Express Grand Slam	Lee Trevino (2)
TPC Starts Senior	Seiichi Kanai
Daiichi Seimei Cup	Hiroshi Ishii
Mizuno Senior Classic	Tetsuhiro Ueda
Japan PGA Senior Championship	Shigeru Uchida
Komatsu Open	Ryosuke Ota
HTB Senior Classic	Masaru Amano
Tokyu Senior Cup	Norihiko Matsumoto
Nagoya TV Cup	Seiichi Kanai (2)
Ho-Oh Cup	Seiichi Kanai (3)
Asahi Kokusai Vintage Classic	Haruo Yasuda
Japan Senior Open	Isao Aoki (3)
Ryokuei Group Cup	Hsieh Min Nan

U.S. LPGA TOUR

HealthSouth Palm Beach Classic	Dawn Coe-Jones
Hawaiian Open	Marta Figueras-Dotti
Chrysler-Plymouth Tournament of Champions	Dottie Mochrie
Ping/Welch's Championship	Donna Andrews
Standard Register Ping	Laura Davies (2)
Nabisco Dinah Shore	Donna Andrews (2)
Atlanta Championship	Val Skinner
Sprint Championship	Sherri Steinhauer
Sara Lee Classic	Laura Davies (3)
McDonald's LPGA Championship	Laura Davies (4)
Lady Keystone Open	Elaine Crosby
Corning Classic	Beth Daniel
Oldsmobile Classic	Beth Daniel (2)
Minnesota LPGA Classic	Liselotte Neumann
Rochester International	Lisa Kiggens
ShopRite Classic	Donna Andrews (3)
Youngstown-Warren Classic	Tammie Green
Jamie Farr Toledo Classic	Kelly Robbins
JAL Big Apple Classic	Beth Daniel (3)
U.S. Women's Open	Patty Sheehan
Ping/Welch's Championship	Helen Alfredsson (2)
McCall's Classic at Stratton Mountain	Carolyn Hill
Children's Medical Center Classic	Maggie Will
Chicago Challenge	Jane Geddes
du Maurier Ltd. Classic	Martha Nause
State Farm Rail Classic	Barb Mucha
Ping-Cellular One Championship	Missie McGeorge
Safeco Classic	Deb Richard
Heartland Classic	Liselotte Neumann (5)
World Championship of Women's Golf	Beth Daniel (4)
Solheim Cup	United States
JC Penney Classic	Marta Figueras-Dotti (2)/ Brad Bryant
Diners Club Matches	Kelly Robbins (2)/ Tammie Green (2)

WOMEN'S EUROPEAN TOUR

Ford Classic	Catrin Nilsmark
Ladies Open Costa Azul	Sandrine Mendiburu
Evian Masters	Helen Alfredsson
OVB Damen Open	Florence Descampe
BMW European Masters	Helen Wadsworth

Hennessy Cup	Liselotte Neumann (2)
Irish Holidays Open	Laura Davies (5)
Skoda Scottish Open	Laura Davies (6)
Weetabix Women's British Open	Liselotte Neumann (3)
Trygg-Hansa Open	Liselotte Neumann (4)
Waterford Dairies English Open	Patricia Meunier
Sens Dutch Open	Liz Weima
BMW Italian Open	Corinne Dibnah
La Manga Club Spanish Open	Marie Laure de Lorenzi
Var Open de France Feminin	Julie Forbes
Princess Lalla Meriem Cup	Gillian Stewart

WOMEN'S AUSTRALASIAN TOURS

Thailand Open	Laura Davies
Malaysian JAL Open	Jae Sook Won
Indonesian Open	Tracy Hanson
Republic of China-Taiwan Open	Karen Weiss
Holden Australian Open	Annika Sorenstam
Alpine Australian Ladies Masters	Laura Davies (8)

JAPAN LPGA TOUR

Daikin Orchid	Akiko Fukushima
Chiyoda Ladies	Wu Ming Yueh
Saishunkan Ladies	Ikuyo Shiotani
Kibun Classic	Woo Soon Ko
Mitsukoshi Cup	Yuko Moriguchi
Kenshoen Ladies	Ikuyo Shiotani (2)
Nasu Ogawa	Marnie McGuire
Satake Japan Classic	Chieko Nishida
Gunze World Cup	Jae Sook Won (2)
Yakult Ladies	Kaori Higo
Chukyo TV Bridgestone	Akemi Yamaoka
Toto Motors	Jae Sook Won (3)
Mitsubishi Electric Ladies	Suzuko Maeda
Suntory Ladies Open	Akemi Yamaoka (2)
Dunlop Twin Lakes Ladies	Toshimi Kimura
Japan Women's Open Championship	Michiko Hattori
Tohato Ladies	Ayako Okamoto
Toyo Suisan Ladies	Hiromi Takamura
Resort Trust Cleanup Ladies	Feng Tseng Hsiu
Katokichi Queens Cup	Ikuyo Shiotani (3)
SC Ladies	Yuko Moriguchi (2)
Asahi Kokusai Ladies	Young Mi Lee
NEC Karuizawa 72	Mayumi Hirase
Itoki Classic	Ayako Okamoto (2)
Goyo Kensetsu Cup	Chikako Matsuzawa
Fuji Sankei Classic	Huang Yueh Chin
Japan LPGA Championship	Kumiko Hiyoshi
Kosaido Asahi Cup	Ayako Okamoto (3)
Miyagi TV Cup	Jae Sook Won (4)
Yukijirushi Tokai Classic	Michiko Hattori (2)
Takara World Invitational	Mayumi Hirase (2)
Fujitsu Ladies	Kikuko Shibata
Nichirei International	United States
Toray Japan Queens Cup	Woo Soon Ko (2)
Itoen Ladies	Laura Davies (7)
Daio Seishi Elleair Open	Mayumi Hirase (3)
Meiji Nyugyo Cup	Mayumi Hirase (4)
Mizuno Ladies Open	Mitsuyo Hirata

Multiple Winners of 1994

PLAYER	WINS	PLAYER	WINS
Laura Davies	8	Nick Faldo	2
Masashi Ozaki	7	Keith Fergus	2
Nick Price	7	Marta Figueras-Dotti	2
Lee Trevino	7	Carlos Franco	2
Ernie Els	5	Raul Fretes	2
Raymond Floyd	5	Robert Gamez	2
Liselotte Neumann	5	Larry Gilbert	2
Brian Watts	5	David Gilford	2
Fred Couples	4	Tammie Green	2
Beth Daniel	4	Scott Gump	2
David Frost	4	Todd Hamilton	2
Mayumi Hirase	4	Michiko Hattori	2
Jose Maria Olazabal	4	Liam Higgins	2
Jae Sook Won	4	Simon Hobday	2
Donna Andrews	3	Tommy Horton	2
Isao Aoki	3	David Ishii	2
Jerry Haas	3	Craig Jones	2
Seiichi Kanai	3	Skip Kendall	2
Mark McCumber	3	Woo Soon Ko	2
Colin Montgomerie	3	Bernhard Langer	2
John Morgan	3	Carl Mason	2
Tsuneyuki Nakajima	3	Yoshinori Mizumaki	2
Greg Norman	3	Yuko Moriguchi	2
Ayako Okamoto	3	Bob Murphy	2
Ikuyo Shiotani	3	Mark O'Meara	2
Dave Stockton	3	Corey Pavin	2
Bruce Vaughan	3	Chris Perry	2
Jim Albus	2	Kelly Robbins	2
Helen Alfredsson	2	Loren Roberts	2
Robert Allenby	2	Eduardo Romero	2
Tommy Armour	2	Vijay Singh	2
Seve Ballesteros	2	Mike Springer	2
Patrick Burke	2	Omar Uresti	2
Michael Clayton	2	Tom Wargo	2
Jose Coceres	2	Ian Woosnam	2
Jim Colbert	2	Akemi Yamaoka	2
Dave Eichelberger	2		

World Money List

This list of the 300 leading money winners in the world of professional golf in 1994 was compiled from the results of all men's (excluding seniors) tournaments carried in the Appendixes of this edition.

In the 29 years during which World Money Lists have been compiled, the earnings of the player in the 200th position have risen from a total of $3,326 in 1966 to $226,995 in 1994. The top-200 players in 1966 earned a total of $4,680,287. In 1994, the comparable total was $113,088,699.

Because of fluctuating values of money throughout the world, it was necessary to determine an average value of non-American currency to U.S. money to prepare this listing. The conversion rates used for 1994 were: British pound = US$1.53; Japanese yen = US$0.00997; South African rand = US$0.29; Australian dollar = US$0.74; Canadian dollar = US$0.72.

POS.	PLAYER, COUNTRY	TOTAL MONEY
1	Ernie Els, South Africa	$2,862,854
2	Nick Price, Zimbabwe	2,415,464
3	Masashi Ozaki, Japan	2,183,106
4	Jose Maria Olazabal, Spain	2,123,795
5	Greg Norman, Australia	2,117,307
6	Nick Faldo, England	2,016,218
7	Fred Couples, U.S.	1,859,689
8	Colin Montgomerie, Scotland	1,739,349
9	Mark McCumber, U.S.	1,463,376
10	Fuzzy Zoeller, U.S.	1,419,014
11	Brian Watts, U.S.	1,406,136
12	David Frost, South Africa	1,371,889
13	Tom Lehman, U.S.	1,367,308
14	Corey Pavin, U.S.	1,354,819
15	Bernhard Langer, Germany	1,333,036
16	Seve Ballesteros, Spain	1,212,862
17	Tsuneyuki Nakajima, Japan	1,182,784
18	Vijay Singh, Fiji	1,159,646
19	Loren Roberts, U.S.	1,150,369
20	Scott Hoch, U.S.	1,121,042
21	Jeff Maggert, U.S.	1,112,713
22	Brad Faxon, U.S.	1,070,018
23	Naomichi Ozaki, Japan	1,061,408
24	Hale Irwin, U.S.	1,027,836
25	Davis Love III, U.S.	969,943
26	Bob Estes, U.S.	951,515
27	Tom Kite, U.S.	917,806
28	Mark Calcavecchia, U.S.	903,273
29	David Ishii, U.S.	901,296
30	Todd Hamilton, U.S.	885,003
31	John Huston, U.S.	864,985
32	Brad Bryant, U.S.	860,953
33	Mark McNulty, Zimbabwe	848,517

POS.	PLAYER, COUNTRY	TOTAL MONEY
34	Phil Mickelson, U.S.	831,734
35	Steve Lowery, U.S.	818,440
36	Mike Springer, U.S.	817,354
37	Ben Crenshaw, U.S.	801,262
38	Eiji Mizoguchi, Japan	795,318
39	Yoshinori Mizumaki, Japan	778,788
40	Bill Glasson, U.S.	771,535
41	Miguel Angel Jimenez, Spain	770,774
42	Hisayuki Sasaki, Japan	768,460
43	Robert Gamez, U.S.	762,543
44	Nobuo Serizawa, Japan	707,108
45	Tsukasa Watanabe, Japan	689,510
46	Jay Haas, U.S.	667,586
47	Ian Woosnam, Wales	654,682
48	Kiyoshi Murota, Japan	648,567
49	Curtis Strange, U.S.	645,048
50	Bruce Lietzke, U.S.	643,176
52	Dave Barr, Canada	639,823
52	Robert Allenby, Australia	625,840
53	Masahiro Kuramoto, Japan	624,674
54	Lee Janzen, U.S.	615,759
55	Rick Fehr, U.S.	614,130
56	Barry Lane, England	612,442
57	Rick Gibson, Canada	608,079
58	Kenny Perry, U.S.	600,941
59	John Cook, U.S.	597,749
60	Hideki Kase, Japan	596,017
61	Craig Parry, Australia	595,662
62	Mark Roe, England	590,340
63	David Gilford, England	584,943
64	Mark Brooks, U.S.	573,972
65	Craig Stadler, U.S.	572,876
66	Katsuyoshi Tomori, Japan	568,373
67	Larry Mize, U.S.	564,825
68	Tom Watson, U.S.	559,508
69	Jesper Parnevik, Sweden	555,468
70	Masayuki Kawamura, Japan	549,919
71	Hsieh Chin Sheng, Taiwan	546,345
72	Hal Sutton, U.S.	540,162
73	Fred Funk, U.S.	536,155
74	Yoshinori Kaneko, Japan	535,346
75	Billy Andrade, U.S.	522,223
76	Eduardo Romero, Argentina	515,266
77	David Edwards, U.S.	514,184
78	Andrew Magee, U.S.	508,459
79	Carlos Franco, Paraguay	507,191
80	Frank Nobilo, New Zealand	504,620
81	Roger Mackay, Australia	497,472
82	Peter Senior, Australia	479,732
83	Kirk Triplett, U.S.	471,507
84	Lennie Clements, U.S.	456,756
85	Sam Torrance, Scotland	454,692
86	Steve Elkington, Australia	454,649
87	Howard Clark, England	454,449

POS.	PLAYER, COUNTRY	TOTAL MONEY
88	Brett Ogle, Australia	453,481
89	John Daly, U.S.	450,836
90	Hiroshi Ueda, Japan	443,912
91	Duffy Waldorf, U.S.	437,039
92	Katsunari Takahashi, Japan	436,273
93	Jim McGovern, U.S.	434,983
94	Anthony Gilligan, Australia	428,156
95	Joakim Haeggman, Sweden	420,398
96	Mike Heinen, U.S.	420,005
97	Eduardo Herrera, Colombia	418,260
98	Craig Warren, Australia	413,330
99	Costantino Rocca, Italy	411,590
100	Carl Mason, England	406,272
101	Frankie Minoza, Philippines	403,680
102	Per-Ulrik Johansson, Sweden	397,728
103	Shigenori Maruyama, Japan	394,118
104	Satoshi Higashi, Japan	393,779
105	Mark O'Meara, U.S.	389,070
106	Jim Gallagher, Jr., U.S.	386,315
107	Kazuhiro Takami, Japan	380,602
108	Peter Mitchell, England	374,692
109	Glen Day, U.S.	372,223
110	Chen Tze Ming, Taiwan	371,560
111	Blaine McCallister, U.S.	367,925
112	Masanobu Kimura, Japan	364,205
113	Chip Beck, U.S.	359,549
114	Toru Suzuki, Japan	357,166
115	Greg Turner, New Zealand	356,508
116	Scott Simpson, U.S.	355,658
117	Hirofumi Miyase, Japan	348,937
118	Brian Henninger, U.S.	346,580
119	Jay Don Blake, U.S.	344,171
120	Steve Stricker, U.S.	343,576
121	Peter Jacobsen, U.S.	341,114
122	Seiji Ebihara, Japan	339,513
123	David Feherty, Northern Ireland	338,975
124	Steve Pate, U.S.	335,808
125	Neal Lancaster, U.S.	332,488
126	Jeff Sluman, U.S.	329,907
127	Dicky Pride, U.S.	326,707
128	Yoshitaka Yamamoto, Japan	326,208
129	Donnie Hammond, U.S.	323,486
130	Anders Forsbrand, Sweden	323,479
131	Gordon Brand, Jr., Scotland	323,409
132	Ray Stewart, Canada	320,096
133	Bob Gilder, U.S.	316,471
134	Hiroshi Goda, Japan	313,917
135	Michael Clayton, Australia	312,883
136	Pierre Fulke, Sweden	312,095
137	Gil Morgan, U.S.	310,608
138	Kiyoshi Maita, Japan	309,917
139	Ikuo Shirahama, Japan	305,983
140	Mike Sullivan, U.S.	303,586
141	Tony Johnstone, Zimbabwe	299,396

POS.	PLAYER, COUNTRY	TOTAL MONEY
142	Clark Dennis, U.S.	298,885
143	Stewart Ginn, Australia	297,712
144	Chen Tze Chung, Taiwan	289,879
145	Richard Backwell, Australia	289,115
146	Greg Kraft, U.S.	288,240
147	Chris Perry, U.S.	286,988
148	Nolan Henke, U.S.	286,444
149	Andrew Coltart, Scotland	285,956
150	Jim Furyk, U.S.	284,514
151	Wayne Westner, South Africa	283,892
152	Saburo Fujiki, Japan	281,679
153	Tomohiro Maruyama, Japan	280,428
154	Tsuyoshi Yoneyama, Japan	279,842
155	Russell Claydon, England	278,963
156	Peter Baker, England	270,400
157	Paul Eales, England	270,076
158	Darren Clarke, Northern Ireland	268,849
159	Bob Lohr, U.S.	268,705
160	D.A. Weibring, U.S.	268,675
161	Mike Hulbert, U.S.	268,174
162	Ryoken Kawagishi, Japan	267,633
163	Mark Davis, England	266,937
164	Daisuke Serizawa, Japan	262,123
165	Phillip Price, Wales	262,057
166	Keith Clearwater, U.S.	260,882
167	Nobumitsu Yuhara, Japan	258,225
168	Wayne Smith, Australia	257,150
169	Ted Tryba, U.S.	256,301
170	Mark James, England	255,950
171	Paul Curry, England	255,842
172	Seiki Okuda, Japan	255,814
173	Akiyoshi Omachi, Japan	254,965
174	Tommy Armour III, U.S.	253,498
175	Jonathan Lomas, England	253,489
176	Samson Gimson, Singapore	252,865
177	Paul Goydos, U.S.	250,927
178	Gene Sauers, U.S.	250,654
179	Pete Izumikawa, Japan	247,799
180	Toshiaki Odate, Japan	246,395
181	Guy Boros, U.S.	245,942
182	Ken Kusumoto, Japan	245,381
183	Wayne Grady, Australia	245,228
184	Shigenori Mori, Japan	243,483
185	Hideto Shigenobu, Japan	240,566
186	Kouki Idoki, Japan	240,381
187	Gary Hallberg, U.S.	240,139
188	Russ Cochran, U.S.	239,827
189	Lin Chie Hsiang, Taiwan	236,223
190	Sven Struver, Germany	235,660
191	Retief Goosen, South Africa	233,989
192	Peter Hedblom, Sweden	231,706
193	Johnny Miller, U.S.	230,330
194	Dave Stockton, Jr., U.S.	229,474
195	Jose Rivero, Spain	229,421

POS.	PLAYER, COUNTRY	TOTAL MONEY
196	Tom Purtzer, U.S.	228,964
197	Gabriel Hjertstedt, Sweden	228,437
198	Paul McGinley, Ireland	227,809
199	David Ogrin, U.S.	227,249
200	Fulton Allem, South Africa	226,995
201	Peter McWhinney, Australia	225,323
202	Chris DiMarco, U.S.	225,174
203	Robin Freeman, U.S.	220,896
204	Hiroya Kamide, Japan	218,538
205	Hiroshi Makino, Japan	217,612
206	Wayne Levi, U.S.	217,425
207	Yoshimi Niizeki, Japan	214,619
208	Emlyn Aubrey, U.S.	214,189
209	Miguel Angel Martin, Spain	212,442
210	Gary Orr, Scotland	212,020
211	Bobby Wadkins, U.S.	210,311
212	Doug Tewell, U.S.	208,658
213	Mark Carnevale, U.S.	206,093
214	Mike Harwood, Australia	204,932
215	Sandy Lyle, Scotland	204,108
216	Jean Van de Velde, France	204,091
217	Lee Westwood, England	201,513
218	Rodger Davis, Australia	201,407
219	Philip Walton, Ireland	200,664
220	Robert Karlsson, Sweden	200,179
221	Jim Thorpe, U.S.	198,664
222	Eiichi Itai, Japan	195,225
223	Scott Gump, U.S.	194,716
224	Toshiaki Sudo, Japan	192,411
225	Kohichi Suzuki, Japan	192,192
226	Mike Standly, U.S.	192,050
227	Howard Twitty, U.S.	191,140
228	Brian Claar, U.S.	189,670
229	Martin Gates, England	188,954
230	Scott Verplank, U.S.	188,335
231	Bruce Vaughan, U.S.	187,484
232	Ed Humenik, U.S.	186,832
233	Klas Eriksson, Sweden	185,800
234	Mike Reid, U.S.	183,959
235	Bob Burns, U.S.	182,139
236	Brian Kamm, U.S.	181,884
237	Bob Tway, U.S.	181,176
238	Michael Bradley, U.S.	178,737
239	Wayne Riley, Australia	177,509
240	Billy Mayfair, U.S.	177,459
241	Steve Rintoul, Australia	176,789
242	Yutaka Hagawa, Japan	174,175
243	Joey Sindelar, U.S.	172,230
244	Dillard Pruitt, U.S.	171,866
245	Shinji Ikeuchi, Japan	170,724
246	Takaaki Fukuzawa, Japan	170,640
247	David Duval, U.S.	170,436
248	Paul Stankowski, U.S.	170,393
249	Pat Bates, U.S.	169,662

POS.	PLAYER, COUNTRY	TOTAL MONEY
250	Tsutomu Higa, Japan	168,744
251	Shoichi Kuwabara, Japan	168,243
252	John Wilson, U.S.	168,225
253	Kinpachi Yoshimura, Japan	167,352
254	Mitsutaka Kusakabe, Japan	166,611
255	Harumitsu Hamano, Japan	165,984
256	Tom Byrum, U.S.	163,379
257	Des Smyth, Ireland	161,196
258	Brandel Chamblee, U.S.	161,018
259	Dan Forsman, U.S.	160,805
260	Jay Delsing, U.S.	156,895
261	Stephen Ames, Trinidad & Tobago	156,368
262	Jose Coceres, Argentina	156,204
263	Patrick Burke, U.S.	155,811
264	Ken Green, U.S.	155,156
265	Richard Boxall, England	154,966
266	Hideyuki Sato, Japan	154,223
267	Teruo Nakamura, Japan	152,595
268	Ignacio Garrido, Spain	151,241
269	Jeff Woodland, Australia	151,206
270	David Peoples, U.S.	150,418
271	John Bland, South Africa	149,689
272	Peter Teravainen, U.S.	149,095
273	Toru Nakamura, Japan	149,039
274	Justin Leonard, U.S.	148,780
275	Payne Stewart, U.S.	146,758
276	Tetsu Nishikawa, Japan	146,260
277	John Morse, U.S.	146,137
278	Jim Payne, England	144,956
279	Ross McFarlane, Scotland	144,248
280	Hajime Meshiai, Japan	143,418
281	Terry Price, Australia	143,217
282	Curt Byrum, U.S.	142,754
283	Jim Carter, U.S.	142,750
284	Dennis Paulson, U.S.	142,515
285	Paul Moloney, Australia	141,635
286	Ronan Rafferty, Northern Ireland	141,374
287	Andrew Sherborne, England	140,274
288	Ronnie Black, U.S.	139,822
289	Skip Kendall, U.S.	139,459
290	Joel Edwards, U.S.	139,141
291	Jamie Spence, England	138,906
292	Michel Besanceney, France	138,207
293	Noboru Sugai, Japan	137,926
294	Brandt Jobe, U.S.	135,192
295	Paul Azinger, U.S.	135,089
296	Kelly Gibson, U.S.	134,841
297	Keith Fergus, U.S.	133,852
298	Shoichi Yamamoto, Japan	132,411
299	Mike Donald, U.S.	132,035
300	Peter Jordan, U.S.	130,363

Career World Money List

The following is a listing of the 50 leading money winners for their careers through the 1994 season. It includes active and inactive players. The World Money List from this and the 28 previous editions of this annual and a table prepared for a companion book, *The Wonderful World of Professional Golf* (Atheneum, 1973), form the basis for this compilation. Additional figures were taken from official records of major golf associations, although the shortcomings in records-keeping in professional golf outside the United States in the 1950s and 1960s and exclusions from U.S. records in a few cases during those years prevent these figures from being completely accurate. Conversions of foreign currency figures to U.S. dollars are based on average values during the particular years involved.

POS.	PLAYER, COUNTRY	TOTAL MONEY
1	Greg Norman, Australia	$14,411,816
2	Bernhard Langer, Germany	12,544,089
3	Fred Couples, U.S.	12,467,216
4	Nick Faldo, England	12,390,787
5	Tom Kite, U.S.	11,618,408
6	Masashi Ozaki, Japan	11,530,850
7	Lee Trevino, U.S.	10,816,204
8	Nick Price, Zimbabwe	10,794,288
9	Seve Ballesteros, Spain	10,738,159
10	David Frost, South Africa	10,485,760
11	Raymond Floyd, U.S.	10,060,154
12	Ian Woosnam, Wales	9,964,170
13	Payne Stewart, U.S.	9,070,431
14	Curtis Strange, U.S.	8,965,801
15	Tsuneyuki Nakajima, Japan	8,841,776
16	Isao Aoki, Japan	8,801,355
17	Paul Azinger, U.S.	8,319,808
18	Jose Maria Olazabal, Spain	8,307,317
19	Tom Watson, U.S.	8,153,308
20	Jack Nicklaus, U.S.	8,003,864
21	Bob Charles, New Zealand	7,819,973
22	Ben Crenshaw, U.S.	7,771,290
23	Lanny Wadkins, U.S.	7,691,670
24	Corey Pavin, U.S.	7,591,468
25	Gary Player, South Africa	7,503,191
26	Craig Stadler, U.S.	7,258,948
27	Naomichi Ozaki, Japan	7,257,342
28	Chi Chi Rodriguez, U.S.	7,190,247
29	George Archer, U.S.	7,131,237
30	Mark Calcavecchia, U.S.	7,103,965
31	Hale Irwin, U.S.	7,074,968
32	Mark O'Meara, U.S.	6,790,209
33	Chip Beck, U.S.	6,720,168
34	Davis Love III, U.S.	6,693,556
35	Miller Barber, U.S.	6,643,073

POS.	PLAYER, COUNTRY	TOTAL MONEY
36	Sandy Lyle, Scotland	6,402,898
37	Larry Mize, U.S.	6,211,690
38	Scott Hoch, U.S.	6,171,051
39	Bruce Lietzke, U.S.	6,003,431
40	Mike Hill, U.S.	5,890,394
41	Mark McNulty, Zimbabwe	5,888,642
42	Jim Colbert, U.S.	5,726,595
43	Bruce Crampton, Australia	5,721,022
44	Fuzzy Zoeller, U.S.	5,717,522
45	Graham Marsh, Australia	5,587,193
46	Colin Montgomerie, Scotland	5,530,485
47	Masahiro Kuramoto, Japan	5,505,155
48	Dale Douglass, U.S.	5,458,985
49	John Cook, U.S.	5,384,323
50	Mark McCumber, U.S.	5,322,115

These 50 players have won $401,048,367 in their lifetimes playing professional tournament golf.

Senior World Money List

This list includes official earnings on the U.S. PGA Tour, U.S. Senior PGA Tour, European Seniors Tour and Japan Senior Tour, along with other winnings in established unofficial events when reliable figures could be obtained.

POS.	PLAYER, COUNTRY	TOTAL MONEY
1	Raymond Floyd, U.S.	$1,632,779
2	Dave Stockton, U.S.	1,446,864
3	Lee Trevino, U.S.	1,318,501
4	Jim Albus, U.S.	1,267,928
5	Jim Colbert, U.S.	1,218,865
6	Tom Wargo, U.S.	1,171,419
7	Jim Dent, U.S.	1,027,141
8	Bob Murphy, U.S.	897,112
9	Larry Gilbert, U.S.	883,544
10	Isao Aoki, Japan	867,098
11	George Archer, U.S.	807,408
12	Simon Hobday, South Africa	718,221
13	Chi Chi Rodriguez, U.S.	671,348
14	Dave Eichelberger, U.S.	670,417
15	Dale Douglass, U.S.	648,886
16	Jay Sigel, U.S.	647,402

POS.	PLAYER, COUNTRY	TOTAL MONEY
17	Mike Hill, U.S.	625,621
18	J.C. Snead, U.S.	608,364
19	Graham Marsh, Australia	597,745
20	Bob Charles, New Zealand	595,487
21	Jimmy Powell, U.S.	589,638
22	Kermit Zarley, U.S.	538,274
23	Jack Kiefer, U.S.	532,467
24	Rocky Thompson, U.S.	529,073
25	Tom Shaw, U.S.	498,124
26	Gary Player, South Africa	444,991
27	Tom Weiskopf, U.S.	420,561
28	Gibby Gilbert, U.S.	405,842
29	Jerry McGee, U.S.	398,219
30	Tommy Aaron U.S.	397,515
31	Jack Nicklaus, U.S.	395,426
32	Teruo Sugihara, Japan	373,915
33	Charles Coody, U.S.	329,295
34	DeWitt Weaver, U.S.	318,387
35	John Paul Cain, U.S.	291,868
36	Seiichi Kanai, Japan	268,121
37	Bob Dickson, U.S.	264,701
38	Walter Zembriski, U.S.	246,412
39	Terry Dill, U.S.	232,306
40	Larry Laoretti, U.S.	232,001
41	Tony Jacklin, England	226,551
42	Orville Moody, U.S.	217,490
43	Tommy Aycock, U.S.	212,660
44	Richard Rhyan, U.S.	210,183
45	Homero Blancas, U.S.	209,550
46	Harry Toscano, U.S.	207,508
47	Dick Goetz, U.S.	202,657
48	Arnold Palmer, U.S.	196,977
49	Hsieh Min Nan, Taiwan	195,068
50	Bob Smith, U.S.	186,502
51	Calvin Peete, U.S.	186,432
52	Larry Ziegler, U.S.	185,644
53	Harold Henning, South Africa	185,394
54	Bob Brue, U.S.	184,693
55	Masaru Amano, Japan	183,786
56	Hiroshi Ishii, Japan	183,468
57	Ben Smith, U.S.	180,943
58	Butch Baird, U.S.	178,831
59	Haruo Yasuda, Japan	172,546
60	Dick Lotz, U.S.	167,152
61	Brian Waites, England	166,684
62	Rives McBee, U.S.	166,177
63	Don January, U.S.	161,976
64	Shigeru Uchida, Japan	160,382
65	Gay Brewer, U.S.	156,064
66	Miller Barber, U.S.	154,327
67	Dick Hendrickson, U.S.	153,155
68	Larry Mowry, U.S.	149,923
69	Don Bies, U.S.	147,185
70	Tommy Horton, England	147,134

POS.	PLAYER, COUNTRY	TOTAL MONEY
71	Bobby Nichols, U.S.	140,695
72	Bill Hall, U.S.	138,712
73	Kikuo Arai, Japan	136,079
74	Ichiro Teramoto, Japan	129,204
75	Bruce Crampton, Australia	128,860
76	Jim Ferree, U.S.	127,463
77	Al Geiberger, U.S.	119,902
78	Ryosuke Ota, Japan	117,718
79	Norihiko Matsumoto, Japan	116,759
80	Fujio Kobayashi, Japan	114,909
81	Seiji Ogawa, Japan	113,294
82	Joe Jimenez, U.S.	112,106
83	Marion Heck, U.S.	110,097
84	Billy Dunk, Australia	100,237
85	Mitsuhiro Kitsuta, Japan	99,455
86	Hsiung Kuo Chie, Taiwan	97,016
87	Tetsuhiro Ueda, Japan	96,441
88	Bruce Devlin, Australia	93,557
89	John Morgan, England	87,530
90	Eleuterio Nival, Philippines	87,140
91	Robert Zimmerman, U.S.	82,882
92	Teruo Suzuki, Japan	82,100
93	Gene Littler, U.S.	80,592
94	Robert Gaona, U.S.	74,873
95	Brian Huggett, Wales	74,477
96	Yoshihiro Takada, Japan	72,724
97	Randy Petri, U.S.	70,669
98	Hisashi Suzumura, Japan	69,639
99	Art Proctor, U.S.	69,150
100	Babe Hiskey, U.S.	68,720

Women's World Money List

This list includes official earnings on the U.S. LPGA Tour, Women's European Tour, Women's Australasian Tour and Japan LPGA Tour, along with other winnings in established unofficial events when reliable figures could be obtained.

POS.	PLAYER, COUNTRY	TOTAL MONEY
1	Laura Davies, England	$1,006,143
2	Beth Daniel, U.S.	764,246
3	Mayumi Hirase, Japan	696,085
4	Liselotte Neumann, Sweden	683,076

POS.	PLAYER, COUNTRY	TOTAL MONEY
5	Ikuyo Shiotani, Japan	656,142
6	Jae Sook Won, Korea	609,184
7	Dottie Mochrie, U.S.	607,921
8	Tammie Green, U.S.	565,969
9	Michiko Hattori, Japan	550,191
10	Akiko Fukushima, Japan	547,748
11	Kelly Robbins, Japan	543,278
12	Ayako Okamoto, Japan	536,328
13	Akemi Yamaoka, Japan	495,581
14	Helen Alfredsson, Sweden	486,293
15	Kumiko Hiyoshi, Japan	477,357
16	Aiko Hashimoto, Japan	473,596
17	Donna Andrews, U.S.	471,182
18	Yuko Moriguchi, Japan	462,420
19	Sherri Steinhauer, U.S.	443,401
20	Meg Mallon, U.S.	410,385
21	Betsy King, U.S.	400,646
22	Hiromi Takamura, Japan	388,222
23	Kaori Higo, Japan	384,498
24	Toshimi Kimura, Japan	377,564
25	Elaine Crosby, U.S.	375,199
26	Val Skinner, U.S.	363,184
27	Suzuko Maeda, Japan	361,626
28	Young Mi Lee, Korea	350,781
29	Fuki Kido, Japan	350,558
30	Mayumi Murai, Japan	342,140
31	Patty Sheehan, U.S.	338,562
32	Jane Geddes, U.S.	333,701
33	Mitsuyo Hirata, Japan	309,004
34	Woo Soon Ko, Korea	307,207
35	Michelle McGann, U.S.	306,936
36	Miyuki Shimabukuro, Japan	300,990
37	Chieko Nishida, Japan	288,586
38	Junko Yasui, Japan	281,427
39	Marta Figueras-Dotti, Spain	273,513
40	Judy Dickinson, U.S.	272,879
41	Hiromi Kobayashi, Japan	272,126
42	Marnie McGuire, New Zealand	267,573
43	Deb Richard, U.S.	266,127
44	Pat Bradley, U.S.	258,774
45	Martha Nause, U.S.	258,297
46	Aki Nakano, Japan	249,592
47	Annika Sorenstam, Sweden	249,422
48	Wu Ming Yueh, Taiwan	237,280
49	Dawn Coe-Jones, U.S.	233,988
50	Chikako Matsuzawa, Japan	231,923
51	Kikuko Shibata, Japan	222,525
52	Brandie Burton, U.S.	222,485
53	Alicia Dibos, Peru	222,244
54	Huang Bie Shyun, Taiwan	221,088
55	Kaori Harada, Japan	214,824
56	Alice Ritzman, U.S.	213,955
57	Nancy Lopez, U.S.	212,952
58	Chris Johnson, U.S.	212,528

POS.	PLAYER, COUNTRY	TOTAL MONEY
59	Aki Takamura, Japan	211,755
60	Nancy Ramsbottom, U.S.	209,842
61	Huang Yueh Chin, Taiwan	209,006
62	Ok Hee Ku, Korea	206,421
63	Lauri Merten, U.S.	203,212
64	Amy Alcott, U.S.	202,923
65	Lisa Kiggens, U.S.	200,609
66	Akane Ohshiro, Japan	192,112
67	Ae Sook Kim, Korea	190,921
68	Missie McGeorge, U.S.	181,281
69	Barb Bunkowsky, U.S.	172,421
70	Juli Inkster, U.S.	166,229
71	Dale Eggeling, U.S.	166,001
72	Michelle Estill, U.S.	162,986
73	Colleen Walker, U.S.	162,700
74	Shin Sora, Korea	161,158
75	Barb Mucha, U.S.	157,852
76	Aiko Takasu, Japan	152,950
77	Ray Bell, Australia	152,499
78	Rosie Jones, U.S.	150,850
79	Feng Tseng Hsiu, Taiwan	148,689
80	Norimi Terazawa, Japan	145,916
81	Kristi Albers, U.S.	140,628
82	Tracy Hanson, U.S.	140,306
83	Chikayo Yamazaki, Japan	138,188
84	Miki Oda, Japan	135,297
85	Fukumi Tani, Japan	134,551
86	Kris Tschetter, U.S.	132,859
87	Nayoko Yoshikawa, Japan	130,989
88	Natsuko Noro, Japan	127,575
89	Hisako Higuchi, Japan	125,858
90	Gail Graham, Canada	124,551
91	Cheng Mei Chi, Taiwan	124,500
92	Amy Benz, U.S.	124,189
93	Mariko Ohtani, Japan	123,913
94	Carolyn Hill, U.S.	123,660
95	Florence Descampe, Belgium	123,298
96	Dana Dormann, U.S.	123,215
97	Yuka Irie, Japan	123,196
98	Missie Berteotti, U.S.	123,161
99	Julie Larsen, U.S.	121,402
100	Yuko Saitoh, Japan	121,345

American Tours

Mercedes Championship

La Costa Country Club, Carlsbad, California
Par 36-36—72; 7,022 yards

January 6-9
purse, $1,000,000

	SCORES				TOTAL	MONEY
Phil Mickelson	70	68	70	68	276	$180,000
Fred Couples	69	70	69	68	276	120,000
(Mickelson defeated Couples on second playoff hole.)						
Tom Kite	73	68	69	68	278	80,000
Jay Haas	71	71	69	69	280	46,625
Davis Love III	71	69	72	68	280	46,625
Jeff Maggert	72	74	65	69	280	46,625
Scott Simpson	70	72	70	68	280	46,625
David Edwards	75	68	66	72	281	34,000
Howard Twitty	72	73	67	69	281	34,000
Greg Norman	70	73	69	70	282	31,000
Ben Crenshaw	71	70	69	73	283	28,250
Brett Ogle	69	72	71	71	283	28,250
Jim Gallagher, Jr.	73	69	73	70	285	25,000
Billy Mayfair	72	68	72	73	285	25,000
Mike Standly	75	72	67	71	285	25,000
Fulton Allem	71	76	72	67	286	23,000
Nolan Henke	69	74	71	73	287	21,500
Blaine McCallister	74	74	68	71	287	21,500
Vijay Singh	69	70	76	72	287	21,500
Lee Janzen	71	74	74	70	289	20,250
Grant Waite	70	69	77	73	289	20,250
Jim McGovern	73	71	73	73	290	19,500
John Inman	71	70	76	74	291	19,000
Rocco Mediate	72	71	77	72	292	18,500

United Airlines Hawaiian Open

Waialae Country Club, Honolulu, Hawaii
Par 36-36—72; 6,975 yards

January 13-16
purse, $1,200,000

	SCORES				TOTAL	MONEY
Brett Ogle	66	66	69	68	269	$216,000
Davis Love III	68	60	71	71	270	129,600
John Huston	70	68	67	67	272	81,600
Corey Pavin	68	70	70	65	273	57,600
Jesper Parnevik	71	66	74	63	274	48,000
Craig Parry	66	70	72	67	275	41,700
Ted Tryba	69	71	68	67	275	41,700
Lennie Clements	69	66	70	71	276	31,200
Paul Goydos	67	73	69	67	276	31,200
David Ishii	70	67	69	70	276	31,200
Jeff Maggert	69	67	68	72	276	31,200
David Ogrin	72	69	68	67	276	31,200
Seiki Okuda	71	69	72	64	276	31,200
Jay Don Blake	70	65	71	71	277	19,800

	SCORES				TOTAL	MONEY
Tom Lehman	68	67	68	74	277	19,800
John Morse	69	69	69	70	277	19,800
Dave Rummells	69	69	72	67	277	19,800
Steve Stricker	68	69	69	71	277	19,800
Bob Tway	70	71	69	67	277	19,800
Clark Dennis	70	69	71	68	278	14,480
Naomichi Ozaki	71	68	72	67	278	14,480
Scott Simpson	69	69	71	69	278	14,480
Robin Freeman	63	69	75	72	279	11,040
John Inman	69	68	70	72	279	11,040
Billy Mayfair	73	68	69	69	279	11,040
Hal Sutton	70	69	67	73	279	11,040
Fred Funk	68	73	68	71	280	8,520
Larry Silveira	70	70	72	68	280	8,520
Mike Smith	73	66	74	67	280	8,520
Jim Thorpe	70	69	69	72	280	8,520
Richard Zokol	72	67	72	69	280	8,520
Steve Brodie	71	67	75	68	281	5,840
Mark Brooks	68	72	73	68	281	5,840
Olin Browne	71	69	70	71	281	5,840
David Edwards	70	69	69	73	281	5,840
Wayne Grady	69	70	74	68	281	5,840
Morris Hatalsky	67	66	75	73	281	5,840
Nolan Henke	69	71	72	69	281	5,840
Hale Irwin	67	72	72	70	281	5,840
Skip Kendall	73	66	68	74	281	5,840
Mike Reid	68	67	75	71	281	5,840
Vijay Singh	74	67	72	68	281	5,840
Mike Sullivan	68	69	75	69	281	5,840
Dave Barr	67	70	70	75	282	3,628
Bill Britton	68	73	71	70	282	3,628
Brad Lardon	69	69	75	69	282	3,628
Wayne Levi	69	70	69	74	282	3,628
Craig Stadler	69	68	76	69	282	3,628
Esteban Toledo	69	72	73	68	282	3,628
Dudley Hart	71	69	73	70	283	2,818.67
Yoshinori Mizumaki	70	71	73	69	283	2,818.67
Jack Renner	73	68	73	69	283	2,818.67
Jeff Sluman	70	71	72	70	283	2,818.67
Lanny Wadkins	71	69	73	70	283	2,818.67
John Wilson	68	69	75	71	283	2,818.67
Russ Cochran	70	70	71	72	283	2,818.66
Steve Lamontagne	70	69	73	71	283	2,818.66
Dave Stockton, Jr.	72	68	72	71	283	2,818.66
Brad Bryant	70	71	75	68	284	2,628
Tom Garner	67	71	73	73	284	2,628
Sean Murphy	67	69	74	74	284	2,628
Mike Standly	68	70	74	72	284	2,628
Ed Dougherty	73	68	73	71	285	2,544
Steve Jurgensen	67	74	71	73	285	2,544
Gene Sauers	70	70	73	72	285	2,544
Chris DiMarco	70	70	69	77	286	2,448
Kelly Gibson	68	70	75	73	286	2,448
Brian Henninger	72	66	74	74	286	2,448
Pete Jordan	71	70	75	70	286	2,448
David Peoples	68	70	75	73	286	2,448
John Flannery	71	67	74	75	287	2,376
Bill Kratzert	72	68	75	73	288	2,328
Dillard Pruitt	71	70	77	70	288	2,328
David Toms	71	70	76	71	288	2,328

	SCORES				TOTAL	MONEY
John Mahaffey	71	70	77	73	291	2,280
Ty Armstrong	73	67	81	72	293	2,244
Rocky Walcher	68	73	76	76	293	2,244

Northern Telecom Open

Tucson National Golf Course, Tucson, Arizona
Par 36-36—72; 7,148 yards

January 20-23
purse, $1,100,000

Starr Pass Golf Course, Tucson, Arizona
Par 36-36—72; 7,010 yards

	SCORES				TOTAL	MONEY
Andrew Magee	69	67	67	67	270	$198,000
Jay Don Blake	68	69	67	68	272	72,600
Loren Roberts	68	68	72	64	272	72,600
Vijay Singh	67	68	72	65	272	72,600
Steve Stricker	68	69	68	67	272	72,600
Olin Browne	70	70	66	67	273	39,600
Jim Furyk	68	68	67	71	274	35,475
Robert Gamez	66	71	71	66	274	35,475
Bob Burns	70	72	69	65	276	22,400
David Feherty	70	69	67	70	276	22,400
Rick Fehr	73	68	69	66	276	22,400
John Huston	68	71	70	67	276	22,400
Billy Mayfair	69	71	68	68	276	22,400
Rocco Mediate	70	70	71	65	276	22,400
Phil Mickelson	69	70	70	67	276	22,400
Dillard Pruitt	64	71	68	73	276	22,400
Mike Springer	70	65	73	68	276	22,400
Jim Thorpe	69	70	70	67	276	22,400
Kirk Triplett	69	69	70	68	276	22,400
Ted Schulz	71	71	68	67	277	13,750
Ted Tryba	71	67	71	68	277	13,750
Mark Brooks	72	68	71	67	278	9,915.72
Russ Cochran	71	70	69	68	278	9,915.72
Wayne Grady	72	66	73	67	278	9,915.72
Morris Hatalsky	69	73	66	70	278	9,915.71
Mike Heinen	69	70	68	71	278	9,915.71
Gil Morgan	70	69	73	66	278	9,915.71
David Toms	70	68	70	70	278	9,915.71
Keith Clearwater	71	66	71	71	279	6,413
Jay Delsing	68	68	70	73	279	6,413
Fred Funk	67	71	68	73	279	6,413
Larry Nelson	65	72	71	71	279	6,413
Christian Pena	68	73	70	68	279	6,413
Gene Sauers	70	70	68	71	279	6,413
Tom Sieckmann	73	69	71	66	279	6,413
Mike Standly	71	69	69	70	279	6,413
Stan Utley	71	69	70	69	279	6,413
Willie Wood	70	71	71	67	279	6,413
Curt Byrum	71	71	70	68	280	4,730
John Morse	70	70	73	67	280	4,730
Dave Rummells	70	72	69	69	280	4,730
Lennie Clements	70	72	72	67	281	3,960
Robin Freeman	70	71	70	70	281	3,960
Payne Stewart	71	67	71	72	281	3,960

	SCORES				TOTAL	MONEY
Fuzzy Zoeller	69	71	74	67	281	3,960
Ronnie Black	71	69	71	71	282	2,992
Guy Boros	69	73	71	69	282	2,992
Glen Day	69	70	70	73	282	2,992
Ken Green	69	73	71	69	282	2,992
Yoshinori Mizumaki	71	70	70	71	282	2,992
Naomichi Ozaki	66	69	73	74	282	2,992
Brandel Chamblee	70	68	72	73	283	2,539.43
Brian Claar	71	71	71	70	283	2,539.43
John Flannery	68	72	73	70	283	2,539.43
Bruce Fleisher	69	70	69	75	283	2,539.43
John Inman	71	69	70	73	283	2,539.43
Curtis Strange	71	66	71	75	283	2,539.43
Brad Bryant	76	65	75	67	283	2,539.42
Billy Andrade	71	71	74	68	284	2,409
Bill Britton	71	71	74	68	284	2,409
Chris DiMarco	68	74	70	72	284	2,409
Lee Janzen	71	69	73	71	284	2,409
Peter Jordan	70	72	71	72	285	2,310
Bill Kratzert	72	70	72	71	285	2,310
Bob May	69	71	71	74	285	2,310
Doug Tewell	70	71	70	74	285	2,310
Jim Woodward	73	68	75	69	285	2,310
Gary McCord	65	74	76	71	286	2,244
Neal Lancaster	69	72	71	75	287	2,222
Jim McGovern	72	70	75	73	290	2,200
Grant Waite	70	71	83	68	292	2,178
Brett Ogle	67	72	74	WD		

Phoenix Open

TPC of Scottsdale, Scottsdale, Arizona
Par 35-36—71; 6,992 yards

January 27-30
purse, $1,200,000

	SCORES				TOTAL	MONEY
Bill Glasson	68	68	68	64	268	$216,000
Bob Estes	66	68	69	68	271	129,600
Jeff Maggert	70	68	69	65	272	62,400
Blaine McCallister	67	69	69	67	272	62,400
Mike Springer	68	68	71	65	272	62,400
Rick Fehr	66	67	69	71	273	41,700
Tom Lehman	67	68	73	65	273	41,700
Fred Funk	69	69	70	66	274	32,400
Scott Hoch	72	66	67	69	274	32,400
Phil Mickelson	67	70	71	66	274	32,400
Steve Pate	68	69	69	68	274	32,400
Curtis Strange	71	70	69	64	274	32,400
Dave Barr	72	65	69	69	275	21,840
Bob Burns	67	69	67	72	275	21,840
Dan Forsman	65	70	67	73	275	21,840
Bruce Lietzke	69	68	68	70	275	21,840
Andrew Magee	68	65	69	73	275	21,840
Billy Andrade	69	65	69	73	276	14,100
Mark Calcavecchia	71	69	69	67	276	14,100
Gary McCord	65	70	70	71	276	14,100
Larry Rinker	69	65	72	70	276	14,100
Tim Simpson	68	67	70	71	276	14,100

	SCORES			TOTAL	MONEY
Vijay Singh	68	69	72	67	276	14,100
Ted Tryba	72	66	68	70	276	14,100
Grant Waite	70	70	67	69	276	14,100
Gil Morgan	68	69	70	70	277	9,420
Steve Stricker	70	70	71	66	277	9,420
Ed Fiori	69	72	67	70	278	8,700
Neal Lancaster	71	70	67	70	278	8,700
Brian Claar	72	69	70	68	279	7,620
Mike Hulbert	66	69	74	70	279	7,620
Lee Janzen	68	69	68	74	279	7,620
Dillard Pruitt	69	71	70	69	279	7,620
Clark Dennis	70	70	69	71	280	6,192
Trevor Dodds	70	70	68	72	280	6,192
Robert Gamez	75	66	70	69	280	6,192
Tom Sieckmann	69	71	69	71	280	6,192
Willie Wood	70	68	72	70	280	6,192
Chip Beck	69	70	73	69	281	4,324.80
Jay Don Blake	70	70	71	70	281	4,324.80
Brandel Chamblee	66	74	72	69	281	4,324.80
Brad Faxon	74	67	69	71	281	4,324.80
Jim Furyk	68	71	70	72	281	4,324.80
Jim Gallagher, Jr.	69	72	71	69	281	4,324.80
Kelly Gibson	70	70	73	68	281	4,324.80
David Ogrin	68	72	69	72	281	4,324.80
Tom Purtzer	68	73	70	70	281	4,324.80
Tom Watson	71	69	72	69	281	4,324.80
David Feherty	70	70	72	70	282	2,961.60
Hale Irwin	69	70	75	68	282	2,961.60
Peter Jacobsen	71	68	72	71	282	2,961.60
Greg Kraft	67	73	71	71	282	2,961.60
Mark Lye	65	73	73	71	282	2,961.60
Michael Bradley	73	68	70	72	283	2,724
Jay Delsing	71	70	71	71	283	2,724
Bruce Fleisher	70	71	72	70	283	2,724
Larry Mize	71	70	70	72	283	2,724
Kenny Perry	69	70	72	72	283	2,724
Mike Standly	71	69	73	70	283	2,724
Marco Dawson	69	69	70	76	284	2,604
Ken Green	73	63	75	73	284	2,604
Naomichi Ozaki	70	69	72	73	284	2,604
Mark Wiebe	70	71	70	73	284	2,604
*Todd Demsey	75	66	73	70	284	
Mark Carnevale	70	71	77	67	285	2,508
Russ Cochran	71	70	71	73	285	2,508
Dan Pohl	70	70	71	74	285	2,508
Scott Watkins	69	72	69	75	285	2,508
Brad Bryant	68	71	72	75	286	2,436
Billy Mayfair	71	70	72	73	286	2,436
Brian Kamm	72	68	75	73	288	2,388
Scott Simpson	69	70	73	76	288	2,388
R.W. Eaks	70	70	73	76	289	2,352

AT&T Pebble Beach National Pro-Am

Pebble Beach Golf Links, Pebble Beach, California
Par 36-36—72; 6,799 yards

February 3-6
purse, $1,250,000

Spyglass Hill Golf Links, Pebble Beach, California
Par 36-36—72; 6,810 yards

Poppy Hills Golf Club, Pebble Beach, California
Par 36-36—72; 6,865 yards

	SCORES				TOTAL	MONEY
Johnny Miller	68	72	67	74	281	$225,000
Jeff Maggert	68	72	72	70	282	82,500
Corey Pavin	69	71	71	71	282	82,500
Kirk Triplett	69	74	67	72	282	82,500
Tom Watson	69	67	72	74	282	82,500
Tom Lehman	69	68	73	73	283	45,000
Keith Clearwater	70	70	71	73	284	36,375
Jay Delsing	66	75	70	73	284	36,375
Dudley Hart	65	71	70	78	284	36,375
Blaine McCallister	68	71	72	73	284	36,375
Ted Tryba	70	70	70	74	284	36,375
Dan Forsman	77	68	70	70	285	23,035.72
Dennis Paulson	72	67	75	71	285	23,035.72
Mike Standly	70	74	71	70	285	23,035.72
Chip Beck	74	68	70	73	285	23,035.71
Clark Dennis	70	70	73	72	285	23,035.71
Paul Goydos	71	70	70	74	285	23,035.71
Larry Silveira	73	69	69	74	285	23,035.71
David Edwards	69	70	73	74	286	15,150
Raymond Floyd	70	71	70	75	286	15,150
Bob Lohr	73	71	67	75	286	15,150
Jesper Parnevik	71	69	73	73	286	15,150
Esteban Toledo	70	74	69	73	286	15,150
Bob Gilder	67	71	72	77	287	10,375
Gary Hallberg	70	72	71	74	287	10,375
Davis Love III	69	66	78	74	287	10,375
Andrew Magee	70	69	72	76	287	10,375
Vijay Singh	70	70	72	75	287	10,375
Bill Britton	70	69	73	76	288	7,609.38
Jim Furyk	67	70	77	74	288	7,609.38
Jim Gallagher, Jr.	70	70	73	75	288	7,609.38
Charles Raulerson	72	68	73	75	288	7,609.38
Jay Haas	69	73	75	71	288	7,609.37
Hale Irwin	76	72	69	71	288	7,609.37
Mike Reid	68	73	71	76	288	7,609.37
Dennis Trixler	71	70	70	77	288	7,609.37
Guy Boros	68	71	76	74	289	4,435
Brad Bryant	74	71	69	75	289	4,435
Mark Cato	71	71	72	75	289	4,435
David Duval	69	72	75	73	289	4,435
David Frost	70	73	73	73	289	4,435
Morris Hatalsky	70	72	74	73	289	4,435
Brian Henninger	72	70	75	72	289	4,435
Peter Jacobsen	68	77	71	73	289	4,435
Brian Kamm	69	70	77	73	289	4,435
Tom Kite	68	70	72	79	289	4,435
Jim Nelford	70	73	71	75	289	4,435
Mark O'Meara	72	71	71	75	289	4,435

	SCORES				TOTAL	MONEY
Kenny Perry	73	72	72	72	289	4,435
Craig Stadler	72	69	72	76	289	4,435
Phil Tataurangi	67	73	75	74	289	4,435
Brian Claar	69	75	73	73	290	2,915
Brad Faxon	73	69	75	73	290	2,915
Bill Glasson	74	69	73	74	290	2,915
Larry Rinker	74	70	71	75	290	2,915
Willie Wood	75	70	69	76	290	2,915
Lennie Clements	74	72	70	75	291	2,800
Larry Mize	69	73	73	76	291	2,800
Payne Stewart	68	73	73	77	291	2,800
Ed Dougherty	68	77	72	75	292	2,712.50
Roger Maltbie	69	71	77	75	292	2,712.50
D.A. Weibring	73	73	71	75	292	2,712.50
Mark Wurtz	73	71	73	75	292	2,712.50
Steve Lamontagne	72	75	69	77	293	2,637.50
Jeff Woodland	73	71	71	78	293	2,637.50
Robin Freeman	69	74	74	77	294	2,575
Ted Goin	76	71	70	77	294	2,575
Lon Hinkle	68	73	72	81	294	2,575
Glen Day	73	69	75	79	296	2,512.50
Tom Garner	71	72	74	79	296	2,512.50

Nissan Los Angeles Open

Riviera Country Club, Pacific Palisades, California
Par 35-36—71; 6,946 yards

February 10-13
purse, $1,000,000

	SCORES				TOTAL	MONEY
Corey Pavin	67	64	72	68	271	$180,000
Fred Couples	67	67	68	71	273	108,000
Chip Beck	66	71	72	68	277	68,000
Brad Faxon	70	71	68	69	278	48,000
David Frost	67	74	71	67	279	40,000
Peter Jacobsen	69	71	68	72	280	34,750
Tom Watson	69	71	71	69	280	34,750
Lennie Clements	68	74	68	71	281	28,000
Jay Delsing	67	72	69	73	281	28,000
Craig Stadler	68	69	71	73	281	28,000
Kirk Triplett	68	76	69	68	281	28,000
Mike Hulbert	70	71	70	71	282	21,000
Tom Purtzer	64	74	74	70	282	21,000
Fuzzy Zoeller	67	73	72	70	282	21,000
Donnie Hammond	69	74	72	68	283	16,000
Tom Lehman	69	73	73	68	283	16,000
Mark O'Meara	69	73	70	71	283	16,000
Jeff Sluman	72	70	71	70	283	16,000
Mike Springer	69	70	74	70	283	16,000
Scott Hoch	69	73	72	70	284	10,428.58
Robin Freeman	71	68	71	74	284	10,428.57
Paul Goydos	69	73	69	73	284	10,428.57
Blaine McCallister	70	76	70	68	284	10,428.57
Kiyoshi Murota	69	67	73	75	284	10,428.57
Jesper Parnevik	66	73	72	73	284	10,428.57
Mike Reid	71	73	68	72	284	10,428.57
Michael Allen	68	76	71	70	285	6,245.46
Brian Claar	72	72	71	70	285	6,245.46

	SCORES				TOTAL	MONEY
Phil Mickelson	70	73	73	69	285	6,245.46
Scott Verplank	71	74	70	70	285	6,245.46
Duffy Waldorf	70	71	74	70	285	6,245.46
Tom Kite	72	72	71	70	285	6,245.45
Naomichi Ozaki	72	71	68	74	285	6,245.45
Dan Pohl	73	72	71	69	285	6,245.45
Larry Rinker	70	71	73	71	285	6,245.45
Hal Sutton	71	68	70	76	285	6,245.45
Jim Woodward	71	75	71	68	285	6,245.45
Steve Lowery	73	72	69	72	286	4,600
Vijay Singh	72	71	73	70	286	4,600
Bob Estes	72	72	72	71	287	3,800
Bruce Lietzke	71	75	69	72	287	3,800
Dick Mast	71	73	70	73	287	3,800
Larry Mize	70	74	72	71	287	3,800
Yoshinori Mizumaki	72	72	77	66	287	3,800
Richard Zokol	69	75	71	72	287	3,800
Ronnie Black	70	74	72	72	288	3,000
Nolan Henke	67	73	74	74	288	3,000
Jim Furyk	70	76	75	68	289	2,620
Greg Kraft	71	72	75	71	289	2,620
David Peoples	70	76	72	71	289	2,620
Ben Crenshaw	71	73	72	74	290	2,353.34
Brian Kamm	74	68	75	73	290	2,353.34
Phil Blackmar	69	73	78	70	290	2,353.33
Gene Sauers	71	73	74	72	290	2,353.33
Ted Schulz	70	74	74	72	290	2,353.33
Jeff Woodland	68	76	75	71	290	2,353.33
Billy Andrade	71	72	73	75	291	2,230
Bob Burns	73	73	71	74	291	2,230
Gary Hallberg	71	74	72	74	291	2,230
Jim McGovern	69	76	75	71	291	2,230
Neal Lancaster	68	75	74	75	292	2,140
Steve Pate	71	73	75	73	292	2,140
Mike Standly	70	74	78	70	292	2,140
Dave Stockton, Jr.	70	75	73	74	292	2,140
Willie Wood	70	74	75	73	292	2,140
Jeff Maggert	72	74	72	75	293	2,070
Payne Stewart	70	74	74	75	293	2,070
Mark Carnevale	74	72	76	72	294	2,010
David Edwards	70	71	73	80	294	2,010
Bruce Fleisher	73	71	76	74	294	2,010
Joey Rassett	69	75	74	76	294	2,010
Brandel Chamblee	70	76	75	74	295	1,960
Robert Gamez	70	72	75	81	298	1,930
Tim Simpson	73	73	76	76	298	1,930
Ty Armstrong	72	73	76	81	302	1,900

Bob Hope Chrysler Classic

Indian Wells Country Club, Indian Wells, California
Par 36-36—72; 6,478 yards

February 16-20
purse, $1,100,000

PGA West, Palmer Course, La Quinta, California
Par 36-36—72; 6,931 yards

Bermuda Dunes Country Club, Indian Wells, California
Par 36-36—72; 6,927 yards

La Quinta Country Club, La Quinta, California
Par 36-36—72; 6,911 yards

			SCORES			TOTAL	MONEY
Scott Hoch	66	62	70	66	70	334	$198,000
Fuzzy Zoeller	70	67	66	68	66	337	82,133.34
Lennie Clements	67	69	61	72	68	337	82,133.33
Jim Gallagher, Jr.	66	67	74	62	68	337	82,133.33
Payne Stewart	67	69	71	68	63	338	44,000
Guy Boros	66	67	68	69	69	339	36,850
Keith Clearwater	67	64	70	68	70	339	36,850
Paul Stankowski	67	66	69	68	69	339	36,850
Bob Estes	66	69	70	67	68	340	30,800
John Huston	66	68	66	68	72	340	30,800
Glen Day	67	67	68	69	70	341	25,300
Bruce Lietzke	68	69	65	67	72	341	25,300
Andrew Magee	67	67	71	70	66	341	25,300
Michael Allen	66	68	70	67	71	342	19,250
Bruce Fleisher	68	70	66	70	68	342	19,250
Fred Funk	66	70	68	69	69	342	19,250
Bill Glasson	70	66	66	66	74	342	19,250
Jay Delsing	65	69	66	73	71	344	15,400
Robert Gamez	72	67	68	65	72	344	15,400
Bob Gilder	69	69	66	69	71	344	15,400
Rick Fehr	73	68	69	68	67	345	10,638.58
Dave Barr	69	65	70	72	69	345	10,638.57
John Cook	68	72	68	67	70	345	10,638.57
Robin Freeman	69	73	68	69	66	345	10,638.57
David Peoples	68	68	71	71	67	345	10,638.57
Hal Sutton	63	70	72	69	71	345	10,638.57
Jeff Woodland	68	67	71	71	68	345	10,638.57
Donnie Hammond	65	69	70	72	70	346	7,810
Kiyoshi Murota	69	71	71	67	68	346	7,810
Craig Stadler	75	66	71	66	68	346	7,810
Michael Bradley	72	71	65	68	71	347	6,380
Bob Burns	67	66	72	73	69	347	6,380
Paul Goydos	69	69	71	70	68	347	6,380
Peter Jordan	67	67	74	68	71	347	6,380
Costantino Rocca	69	71	67	69	71	347	6,380
Jeff Sluman	72	70	64	69	72	347	6,380
Russ Cochran	72	69	69	68	70	348	4,730
Marco Dawson	70	67	72	71	68	348	4,730
Trevor Dodds	67	70	70	69	72	348	4,730
Gary McCord	72	74	67	65	70	348	4,730
Gene Sauers	68	71	68	74	67	348	4,730
Tim Simpson	68	69	76	69	66	348	4,730
Curtis Strange	70	70	73	67	68	348	4,730
Andy Bean	69	70	71	70	69	349	3,179
Mark Brooks	72	68	68	72	69	349	3,179

	SCORES					TOTAL	MONEY
Clark Dennis	65	72	69	72	71	349	3,179
Brad Fabel	67	68	75	70	69	349	3,179
Peter Jacobsen	69	68	71	68	73	349	3,179
Doug Martin	67	66	76	71	69	349	3,179
David Ogrin	68	69	69	74	69	349	3,179
Scott Simpson	68	69	69	73	70	349	3,179
Jay Don Blake	73	70	71	64	72	350	2,579.50
Davis Love III	68	70	72	71	69	350	2,579.50
Loren Roberts	69	68	74	72	67	350	2,579.50
Steve Stricker	67	70	72	72	69	350	2,579.50
Steve Lowery	73	70	69	71	68	351	2,497
Dick Mast	67	72	70	72	70	351	2,497
Jay Haas	69	68	67	77	71	352	2,409
Tommy Moore	67	68	74	72	71	352	2,409
Jodie Mudd	66	66	71	76	73	352	2,409
Mac O'Grady	71	72	69	69	71	352	2,409
Joey Rassett	69	72	72	70	69	352	2,409
John Wilson	67	72	73	69	71	352	2,409
Brad Bryant	71	72	71	69	70	353	2,299
Ed Dougherty	69	67	73	71	73	353	2,299
Greg Kraft	71	66	71	73	72	353	2,299
Mark O'Meara	69	68	70	76	70	353	2,299
Curt Byrum	70	72	69	70	73	354	2,189
Mark Carnevale	70	69	72	69	74	354	2,189
Mike Heinen	71	69	75	68	71	354	2,189
Steve Pate	70	71	71	71	71	354	2,189
Steve Rintoul	71	71	70	70	72	354	2,189
Dave Rummells	69	70	72	70	73	354	2,189
Dennis Paulson	71	73	68	68	75	355	2,101
Bobby Wadkins	67	72	68	75	73	355	2,101
Todd Barranger	74	69	73	66	75	357	2,057
Dan Pohl	73	68	72	70	74	357	2,057
Blaine McCallister	73	69	68	73	75	358	2,024

Buick Invitational of California

Torrey Pines Golf Course, La Jolla, California
South Course: Par 36-36—72; 7,000 yards
North Course: Par 36-36—72; 6,592 yards

February 24-27
purse, $1,100,000

	SCORES				TOTAL	MONEY
Craig Stadler	67	67	68	66	268	$198,000
Steve Lowery	67	68	66	68	269	118,800
Phil Mickelson	68	69	69	64	270	74,800
Hal Sutton	68	68	67	69	272	52,800
Mark Carnevale	67	69	70	67	273	44,000
Bob Estes	70	67	67	70	274	36,850
Robin Freeman	68	67	71	68	274	36,850
Kirk Triplett	71	63	68	72	274	36,850
Mark Calcavecchia	69	72	69	65	275	28,600
Lennie Clements	66	69	68	72	275	28,600
Paul Goydos	68	70	70	67	275	28,600
Doug Martin	65	73	68	69	275	28,600
Ronnie Black	65	68	69	74	276	22,000
Tom Lehman	68	70	67	71	276	22,000
Tom Byrum	70	64	71	72	277	18,150
Bob Lohr	69	67	71	70	277	18,150

	SCORES				TOTAL	MONEY
Scott Simpson	70	70	70	67	277	18,150
David Toms	65	65	72	75	277	18,150
Russ Cochran	67	72	68	71	278	13,332
Glen Day	68	67	72	71	278	13,332
Ed Dougherty	66	70	73	69	278	13,332
Payne Stewart	70	66	68	74	278	13,332
Jim Thorpe	72	69	69	68	278	13,332
Brandel Chamblee	67	73	71	68	279	8,705.72
Donnie Hammond	72	66	71	70	279	8,705.72
Monte Montgomery	70	71	68	70	279	8,705.72
Jay Don Blake	69	66	76	68	279	8,705.71
Gary Hallberg	67	70	70	72	279	8,705.71
Wayne Levi	69	71	68	71	279	8,705.71
Jeff Woodland	71	69	68	71	279	8,705.71
Dave Barr	69	67	75	69	280	6,105
Bob Boldt	69	69	72	70	280	6,105
Guy Boros	72	66	71	71	280	6,105
John Cook	71	69	71	69	280	6,105
Steve Pate	71	70	70	69	280	6,105
Dennis Paulson	68	73	68	71	280	6,105
Paul Stankowski	67	68	75	70	280	6,105
John Wilson	71	69	70	70	280	6,105
*Todd Demsey	67	74	67	72	280	
Bobby Clampett	73	68	70	70	281	4,510
Brad Fabel	69	71	71	70	281	4,510
Brad Faxon	68	66	76	71	281	4,510
D.A. Russell	69	70	71	71	281	4,510
Mark Wurtz	69	64	71	77	281	4,510
John Adams	72	69	70	71	282	3,325.67
Mark Brooks	74	67	70	71	282	3,325.67
Steve Lamontagne	68	70	72	72	282	3,325.67
Scott Verplank	66	71	72	73	282	3,325.67
Todd Barranger	67	71	70	74	282	3,325.66
Steve Brodie	68	69	69	76	282	3,325.66
Ed Fiori	69	70	71	73	283	2,569.60
Fred Funk	67	73	70	73	283	2,569.60
Jay Haas	71	68	74	70	283	2,569.60
Morris Hatalsky	71	68	72	72	283	2,569.60
Gary McCord	70	69	70	74	283	2,569.60
Naomichi Ozaki	69	68	76	70	283	2,569.60
David Peoples	68	73	71	71	283	2,569.60
Charles Raulerson	70	70	66	77	283	2,569.60
Costantino Rocca	69	69	74	71	283	2,569.60
Tim Simpson	72	68	71	72	283	2,569.60
Brad Bryant	70	70	71	73	284	2,343
Scott Gump	69	70	73	72	284	2,343
Mark Lye	69	71	71	73	284	2,343
Billy Mayfair	71	69	69	75	284	2,343
Dave Rummells	69	72	71	72	284	2,343
Larry Silveira	68	72	74	70	284	2,343
Vijay Singh	67	73	72	72	284	2,343
Phil Tataurangi	68	68	73	75	284	2,343
Bruce Fleisher	70	71	72	72	285	2,200
Thomas Levet	73	66	73	73	285	2,200
Brad Sherfy	74	67	74	70	285	2,200
Dave Stockton, Jr.	70	71	72	72	285	2,200
Ted Tryba	67	74	71	73	285	2,200
J.C. Anderson	71	70	70	75	286	2,112
Roger Gunn	66	70	77	73	286	2,112
Mike Smith	67	74	74	71	286	2,112

	SCORES				TOTAL	MONEY
Esteban Toledo	73	68	75	71	287	2,068
Keith Clearwater	68	73	75	74	290	2,046
Robert Wrenn	69	72	77	75	293	2,024
Shaun Micheel	70	70	77	79	296	2,002

Doral-Ryder Open

Doral Resort & Country Club, Blue Course, Miami, Florida   March 3-6
Par 36-36—72; 6,939 yards   purse, $1,400,000

	SCORES				TOTAL	MONEY
John Huston	70	68	70	66	274	$252,000
Billy Andrade	70	68	66	73	277	123,200
Brad Bryant	70	69	69	69	277	123,200
Jim Thorpe	68	72	68	71	279	57,866.67
D.A. Weibring	74	69	65	71	279	57,866.67
Lennie Clements	72	70	66	71	279	57,866.66
Bruce Lietzke	74	69	71	67	281	43,633.34
Greg Norman	71	74	69	67	281	43,633.33
Loren Roberts	73	70	69	69	281	43,633.33
Mike Hulbert	72	74	70	66	282	35,000
Mark McCumber	76	69	68	69	282	35,000
Larry Nelson	73	64	69	76	282	35,000
Curtis Strange	73	72	70	68	283	27,066.67
Mike Sullivan	71	75	71	66	283	27,066.67
Raymond Floyd	68	76	69	70	283	27,066.66
Bob Burns	70	73	69	72	284	19,640
Mark Calcavecchia	74	72	68	70	284	19,640
Tom Kite	72	73	69	70	284	19,640
Andrew Magee	75	73	69	67	284	19,640
Dick Mast	69	69	74	72	284	19,640
Naomichi Ozaki	75	69	71	69	284	19,640
Jeff Sluman	74	71	70	69	284	19,640
Chip Beck	74	71	68	72	285	12,880
Jay Don Blake	74	71	69	71	285	12,880
David Frost	74	70	69	72	285	12,880
Craig Stadler	71	73	69	72	285	12,880
Michael Bradley	75	68	74	69	286	9,520
Scott Hoch	72	73	67	74	286	9,520
Bob Lohr	72	72	73	69	286	9,520
Jim McGovern	75	70	68	73	286	9,520
Jesper Parnevik	73	72	71	70	286	9,520
Gene Sauers	72	74	69	71	286	9,520
Hal Sutton	76	71	67	72	286	9,520
Ben Crenshaw	73	70	73	71	287	7,224
David Edwards	70	76	71	70	287	7,224
Jim Furyk	72	73	70	72	287	7,224
Gary Hallberg	71	73	72	71	287	7,224
Lee Janzen	74	74	68	71	287	7,224
Dave Barr	78	70	70	70	288	5,600
Mark Carnevale	72	72	72	72	288	5,600
Brian Claar	75	69	71	73	288	5,600
Keith Clearwater	75	73	72	68	288	5,600
Tom Purtzer	72	72	70	74	288	5,600
Bob Tway	71	73	71	73	288	5,600
Bruce Fleisher	77	71	68	73	289	4,214
Ken Green	72	73	73	71	289	4,214

	SCORES				TOTAL	MONEY
Kenny Perry	73	73	71	72	289	4,214
Tom Watson	73	74	71	71	289	4,214
Mark Brooks	73	74	72	71	290	3,344.45
Ed Dougherty	76	71	73	70	290	3,344.45
Rick Fehr	77	71	72	70	290	3,344.45
Mike Reid	73	75	75	67	290	3,344.45
Bob Gilder	74	73	70	73	290	3,344.44
Paul Goydos	72	74	71	73	290	3,344.44
Mark O'Meara	77	71	68	74	290	3,344.44
Larry Rinker	73	73	72	72	290	3,344.44
Ted Tryba	75	73	69	73	290	3,344.44
Fred Funk	73	71	72	75	291	3,108
Neal Lancaster	71	71	77	72	291	3,108
John Morse	74	73	74	70	291	3,108
Tom Cleaver	75	71	73	73	292	2,954
Steve Elkington	76	70	74	72	292	2,954
Ed Fiori	75	71	73	73	292	2,954
Steve Lowery	74	72	72	74	292	2,954
David Peoples	72	76	73	71	292	2,954
Steve Stricker	73	69	78	72	292	2,954
Lanny Wadkins	79	67	71	75	292	2,954
Jim Woodward	74	73	72	73	292	2,954
Davis Love III	75	68	73	77	293	2,800
David Toms	72	75	75	71	293	2,800
Richard Zokol	76	71	74	72	293	2,800
Nick Price	75	73	73	73	294	2,716
Dillard Pruitt	73	73	76	72	294	2,716
Paul Trittler	77	71	72	74	294	2,716
Brandel Chamblee	72	75	75	73	295	2,646
Vijay Singh	72	74	71	78	295	2,646
Fred Couples	74	70	67	WD		

Honda Classic

Weston Hills Golf & Country Club, Ft. Lauderdale, Florida
Par 36-36—72; 7,069 yards

March 10-13
purse, $1,100,000

	SCORES				TOTAL	MONEY
Nick Price	70	67	73	66	276	$198,000
Craig Parry	68	73	69	67	277	118,800
Brandel Chamblee	67	68	72	71	278	74,800
John Daly	69	70	73	68	280	43,312.50
Bernhard Langer	67	72	73	68	280	43,312.50
Davis Love III	68	71	70	71	280	43,312.50
Curtis Strange	71	67	72	70	280	43,312.50
David Edwards	70	72	69	71	282	34,100
Bruce Fleisher	68	73	70	72	283	27,500
Jim Gallagher, Jr.	68	71	74	70	283	27,500
Tom Kite	71	72	71	69	283	27,500
Sandy Lyle	71	74	72	66	283	27,500
Hal Sutton	71	72	70	70	283	27,500
Gary Hallberg	74	70	71	69	284	19,250
Steve Lamontagne	72	75	68	69	284	19,250
Andrew Magee	68	75	73	68	284	19,250
Mark McCumber	68	72	75	69	284	19,250
Fred Funk	70	68	78	69	285	12,466.67
Ed Humenik	70	71	77	67	285	12,466.67

	SCORES	TOTAL	MONEY
Hale Irwin	72 69 75 69	285	12,466.67
Tom Purtzer	68 74 73 70	285	12,466.67
Tim Simpson	74 67 75 69	285	12,466.67
Jeff Woodland	68 75 72 70	285	12,466.67
Ed Dougherty	70 65 77 73	285	12,466.66
Paul Goydos	73 71 71 70	285	12,466.66
Bruce Lietzke	68 68 74 75	285	12,466.66
Billy Andrade	73 73 71 69	286	8,140
Jim McGovern	70 71 74 71	286	8,140
Vijay Singh	77 67 72 70	286	8,140
Mark Carnevale	75 71 71 70	287	6,831
Brad Fabel	70 73 75 69	287	6,831
Scott Hoch	68 71 75 73	287	6,831
Naomichi Ozaki	68 76 72 71	287	6,831
Joey Rassett	72 74 71 70	287	6,831
Glen Day	72 72 72 72	288	5,541.25
John Huston	70 71 79 68	288	5,541.25
Peter Jordan	70 75 75 68	288	5,541.25
Scott Verplank	73 74 71 70	288	5,541.25
Bill Britton	75 72 71 71	289	3,864
Mark Brooks	74 73 71 71	289	3,864
Russ Cochran	70 74 75 70	289	3,864
John Cook	72 72 71 74	289	3,864
Nick Faldo	70 70 73 76	289	3,864
Yoshinori Mizumaki	74 72 70 73	289	3,864
Kenny Perry	72 68 75 74	289	3,864
Esteban Toledo	69 74 73 73	289	3,864
Paul Trittler	76 71 73 69	289	3,864
Bob Tway	71 73 76 69	289	3,864
Richard Zokol	72 74 73 70	289	3,864
Jay Delsing	69 76 72 73	290	2,583.78
Clark Dennis	75 70 70 75	290	2,583.78
Mike Hulbert	74 72 72 72	290	2,583.78
Brian Kamm	71 76 70 73	290	2,583.78
Neal Lancaster	71 72 77 70	290	2,583.78
Dave Stockton, Jr.	74 72 71 73	290	2,583.78
David Toms	70 74 75 71	290	2,583.78
Blaine McCallister	73 72 70 75	290	2,583.77
John Morse	73 74 68 75	290	2,583.77
Chris DiMarco	71 73 75 72	291	2,387
Mike Donald	71 71 78 71	291	2,387
Wayne Grady	71 75 72 73	291	2,387
Charles Raulerson	72 75 71 73	291	2,387
Paul Stankowski	73 73 73 72	291	2,387
Ian Woosnam	72 71 72 76	291	2,387
Howard Twitty	72 75 73 72	292	2,310
Brian Claar	68 77 76 72	293	2,277
Keith Clearwater	72 73 74 74	293	2,277
Joel Edwards	72 75 76 71	294	2,233
Steve Pate	71 74 76 73	294	2,233
Jesper Parnevik	71 75 74 75	295	2,178
Jeff Roth	74 73 72 76	295	2,178
Tom Sieckmann	71 71 79 74	295	2,178
Guy Boros	74 73 76 73	296	2,123
Dan Oschmann	73 72 75 76	296	2,123
Dave Bishop	74 72 78 73	297	2,057
Mike Heinen	75 70 79 73	297	2,057
John Mahaffey	69 74 76 78	297	2,057
David Ogrin	70 77 76 74	297	2,057
Kelly Gibson	70 77 78 73	298	2,002

	SCORES				TOTAL	MONEY
Mark O'Meara	72	69	76	82	299	1,980
Gary McCord	73	73	84	72	302	1,958

The Nestle Invitational

Bay Hill Club & Lodge, Orlando, Florida
Par 36-36—72; 7,114 yards

March 17-20
purse, $1,200,000

	SCORES				TOTAL	MONEY
Loren Roberts	70	70	68	67	275	$216,000
Nick Price	66	72	68	70	276	89,600
Vijay Singh	68	69	68	71	276	89,600
Fuzzy Zoeller	72	68	67	69	276	89,600
Larry Mize	68	69	71	69	277	48,000
Tom Lehman	72	67	68	71	278	41,700
Greg Norman	68	72	71	67	278	41,700
Tom Watson	69	70	67	73	279	37,200
Andrew Magee	70	67	69	74	280	34,800
Glen Day	70	68	72	71	281	30,000
Bill Glasson	70	72	71	68	281	30,000
D.A. Weibring	71	73	70	67	281	30,000
Bob Estes	72	73	70	67	282	19,950
Paul Goydos	70	69	70	73	282	19,950
Wayne Grady	71	70	71	70	282	19,950
Jay Haas	70	74	72	66	282	19,950
Donnie Hammond	72	72	68	70	282	19,950
Bob Lohr	70	70	72	70	282	19,950
Blaine McCallister	74	73	69	66	282	19,950
Mark McCumber	71	74	67	70	282	19,950
Jay Don Blake	74	69	70	70	283	11,265
Mark Brooks	72	70	69	72	283	11,265
Ben Crenshaw	70	69	73	71	283	11,265
John Daly	73	72	72	66	283	11,265
Dan Forsman	75	69	68	71	283	11,265
Bernhard Langer	75	69	65	74	283	11,265
Scott Simpson	68	75	69	71	283	11,265
Kirk Triplett	69	76	67	71	283	11,265
Mark Carnevale	70	75	67	72	284	7,980
John Huston	73	68	68	75	284	7,980
Curtis Strange	71	72	70	71	284	7,980
Grant Waite	69	72	72	71	284	7,980
David Frost	73	71	70	71	285	6,780
Jim Gallagher, Jr.	69	74	73	69	285	6,780
Jesper Parnevik	73	74	66	72	285	6,780
Keith Clearwater	77	70	70	69	286	5,530
Bruce Fleisher	72	72	73	69	286	5,530
Ed Humenik	78	69	71	68	286	5,530
Davis Love III	70	73	70	73	286	5,530
Masashi Ozaki	74	72	71	69	286	5,530
Dan Pohl	70	69	74	73	286	5,530
Billy Andrade	71	72	71	73	287	4,200
Brad Bryant	72	72	72	71	287	4,200
Mark Calcavecchia	70	74	70	73	287	4,200
John Cook	72	74	74	67	287	4,200
Brad Faxon	74	70	72	71	287	4,200
Peter Jacobsen	72	73	71	72	288	3,172.80
Jeff Maggert	76	71	69	72	288	3,172.80

	SCORES				TOTAL	MONEY
Mark O'Meara	73	72	70	73	288	3,172.80
Craig Parry	73	72	70	73	288	3,172.80
Dicky Pride	72	73	69	74	288	3,172.80
Michael Allen	69	70	73	77	289	2,798.40
Steve Lowery	69	76	72	72	289	2,798.40
Billy Mayfair	75	70	67	77	289	2,798.40
Ted Schulz	71	68	77	73	289	2,798.40
Joey Sindelar	74	73	68	74	289	2,798.40
Chris DiMarco	73	73	73	71	290	2,676
Scott Hoch	72	72	73	73	290	2,676
Mike Springer	69	74	73	74	290	2,676
Leonard Thompson	73	70	76	71	290	2,676
*John Harris	77	67	76	70	290	
Peter Baker	74	72	74	71	291	2,592
Payne Stewart	73	71	73	74	291	2,592
Jim Thorpe	75	72	74	70	291	2,592
Clark Dennis	75	69	78	70	292	2,508
Jodie Mudd	71	73	73	75	292	2,508
Steve Stricker	72	73	73	74	292	2,508
Ian Woosnam	71	72	74	75	292	2,508
Patrick Burke	68	74	75	76	293	2,436
Jay Delsing	70	75	73	75	293	2,436
Robin Freeman	72	73	75	74	294	2,376
Jerry Pate	73	71	77	73	294	2,376
Mike Sullivan	69	75	77	73	294	2,376
Larry Nelson	72	73	75	75	295	2,316
Robert Wrenn	74	71	70	80	295	2,316
John Inman	72	75	72	78	297	2,280
David Duval	71	74	76	78	299	2,256

The Players Championship

TPC at Sawgrass, Ponte Vedra, Florida
Par 36-36—72; 6,896 yards

March 24-27
purse, $2,500,000

	SCORES				TOTAL	MONEY
Greg Norman	63	67	67	67	264	$450,000
Fuzzy Zoeller	66	67	68	67	268	270,000
Jeff Maggert	65	69	69	68	271	170,000
Hale Irwin	67	70	70	69	276	120,000
Nick Faldo	67	69	68	73	277	100,000
Brad Faxon	68	68	70	72	278	83,750
Davis Love III	68	66	70	74	278	83,750
Steve Lowery	68	74	69	67	278	83,750
Gary Hallberg	68	69	69	73	279	65,000
Nolan Henke	73	69	69	68	279	65,000
Tom Kite	65	71	70	73	279	65,000
Colin Montgomerie	65	73	71	70	279	65,000
Mike Springer	68	68	72	72	280	52,500
Dave Barr	68	69	72	72	281	42,500
Jose Maria Olazabal	69	69	73	70	281	42,500
Craig Parry	69	66	73	73	281	42,500
Loren Roberts	68	71	71	71	281	42,500
Tom Watson	71	72	71	67	281	42,500
Ben Crenshaw	72	72	68	70	282	31,375
Dillard Pruitt	70	71	68	73	282	31,375
Mike Standly	72	71	68	71	282	31,375

		SCORES			TOTAL	MONEY
Hal Sutton	67	68	74	73	282	31,375
Mark Calcavecchia	70	72	69	72	283	23,000
John Cook	70	71	72	70	283	23,000
Tim Simpson	69	71	70	73	283	23,000
Steve Stricker	72	70	70	71	283	23,000
Lennie Clements	68	71	74	71	284	16,640.63
Ed Fiori	70	68	74	72	284	16,640.63
Jim Gallagher, Jr.	76	68	70	70	284	16,640.63
Wayne Levi	72	68	72	72	284	16,640.63
Chip Beck	73	71	67	73	284	16,640.62
Jay Delsing	67	73	71	73	284	16,640.62
Bernhard Langer	74	68	70	72	284	16,640.62
John Mahaffey	71	73	65	75	284	16,640.62
Jay Don Blake	70	73	69	73	285	11,037.50
Bob Estes	70	71	70	74	285	11,037.50
Bob Gilder	71	71	70	73	285	11,037.50
Mike Hulbert	71	71	70	73	285	11,037.50
John Huston	68	73	72	72	285	11,037.50
Lee Janzen	65	75	70	75	285	11,037.50
Neal Lancaster	71	68	72	74	285	11,037.50
Roger Maltbie	71	69	73	72	285	11,037.50
Joey Sindelar	70	74	70	71	285	11,037.50
Ted Tryba	68	73	69	75	285	11,037.50
Ernie Els	69	73	72	72	286	7,150
Rick Fehr	70	73	68	75	286	7,150
Wayne Grady	67	73	71	75	286	7,150
Andrew Magee	72	71	70	73	286	7,150
Naomichi Ozaki	71	72	70	73	286	7,150
Kirk Triplett	71	72	70	73	286	7,150
David Edwards	69	70	72	76	287	5,962.50
Steve Elkington	71	72	75	69	287	5,962.50
Gene Sauers	73	69	75	70	287	5,962.50
Grant Waite	74	68	71	74	287	5,962.50
Fulton Allem	70	71	72	75	288	5,600
Brian Claar	68	76	72	72	288	5,600
Keith Clearwater	70	72	70	76	288	5,600
Jay Haas	75	69	71	73	288	5,600
Jim McGovern	72	72	71	73	288	5,600
Larry Nelson	70	67	76	75	288	5,600
Vijay Singh	71	69	69	79	288	5,600
Michael Allen	74	69	73	73	289	5,250
Joel Edwards	68	75	73	73	289	5,250
Paul Goydos	72	72	71	74	289	5,250
Mark McCumber	73	71	75	70	289	5,250
Kenny Perry	69	75	73	72	289	5,250
Jim Thorpe	73	69	73	74	289	5,250
Howard Twitty	69	75	72	73	289	5,250
Ian Baker-Finch	73	69	74	74	290	4,950
Brandel Chamblee	70	72	72	76	290	4,950
Russ Cochran	70	73	78	69	290	4,950
Donnie Hammond	68	73	75	74	290	4,950
D.A. Weibring	75	69	70	76	290	4,950
Brad Bryant	75	69	75	72	291	4,725
Sandy Lyle	71	72	71	77	291	4,725
Dick Mast	73	70	74	74	291	4,725
Tom Sieckmann	73	68	69	81	291	4,725
John Adams	72	70	76	74	292	4,525
Fred Funk	73	71	73	75	292	4,525
Greg Kraft	72	71	72	77	292	4,525
Corey Pavin	69	73	73	77	292	4,525

	SCORES				TOTAL	MONEY
Masashi Ozaki	68	76	75	74	293	4,400
Dan Forsman	67	77	73	77	294	4,350
Robert Gamez	70	72	81	72	295	4,300
Denis Watson	74	69	80	74	297	4,250

Freeport-McMoRan Classic

English Turn Golf & Country Club, New Orleans, Louisiana   March 31-April 3
Par 36-36—72; 7,116 yards   purse, $1,200,000

	SCORES				TOTAL	MONEY
Ben Crenshaw	69	68	68	68	273	$216,000
Jose Maria Olazabal	63	74	70	69	276	129,600
Sam Torrance	67	71	67	73	278	81,600
Dennis Paulson	74	62	75	68	279	49,600
Kenny Perry	69	72	68	70	279	49,600
Mike Springer	73	69	69	68	279	49,600
Steve Brodie	71	67	72	71	281	36,150
Bobby Clampett	70	68	72	71	281	36,150
Chris DiMarco	76	70	66	69	281	36,150
Dick Mast	71	69	74	67	281	36,150
Jim Furyk	70	72	66	74	282	30,000
Glen Day	72	68	72	71	283	25,200
John Flannery	73	72	69	69	283	25,200
John Morse	72	71	67	73	283	25,200
Michael Bradley	72	74	69	69	284	18,000
Bob Burns	71	72	69	72	284	18,000
Lennie Clements	73	67	73	71	284	18,000
Ed Dougherty	74	70	66	74	284	18,000
Mike Standly	68	71	77	68	284	18,000
Ted Tryba	72	70	67	75	284	18,000
Duffy Waldorf	71	72	68	73	284	18,000
Donnie Hammond	73	70	68	74	285	11,520
Peter Jordan	72	71	67	75	285	11,520
Doug Martin	75	70	71	69	285	11,520
Hal Sutton	72	68	73	72	285	11,520
Mark Wurtz	73	71	71	70	285	11,520
Ian Baker-Finch	71	70	72	73	286	7,987.50
Trevor Dodds	75	68	69	74	286	7,987.50
Joel Edwards	70	75	68	73	286	7,987.50
Ernie Els	69	76	69	72	286	7,987.50
Kelly Gibson	72	69	69	76	286	7,987.50
Ted Schulz	72	67	73	74	286	7,987.50
Joey Sindelar	72	69	69	76	286	7,987.50
Greg Twiggs	76	66	68	76	286	7,987.50
Russ Cochran	70	71	73	73	287	5,665.72
Larry Rinker	70	72	72	73	287	5,665.72
Nick Faldo	72	71	70	74	287	5,665.71
Chris Kite	71	70	72	74	287	5,665.71
Bob Lohr	70	72	71	74	287	5,665.71
Naomichi Ozaki	71	68	74	74	287	5,665.71
Gene Sauers	71	75	70	71	287	5,665.72
Gary Hallberg	71	69	76	72	288	4,560
Steve Lamontagne	69	74	70	75	288	4,560
Joey Rassett	68	76	73	72	289	3,541.72
Dave Rummells	74	69	75	71	289	3,541.72
Scott Verplank	76	68	77	68	289	3,541.72

	SCORES				TOTAL	MONEY
Mark Brooks	72	67	75	75	289	3,541.71
Mike Hulbert	74	71	70	74	289	3,541.71
Sean Murphy	72	73	71	73	289	3,541.71
John Wilson	71	70	73	75	289	3,541.71
Jesper Parnevik	73	69	73	75	290	2,862
Tim Simpson	69	70	73	78	290	2,862
Kirk Triplett	73	72	72	73	290	2,862
Richard Zokol	76	70	74	70	290	2,862
Marco Dawson	72	74	70	75	291	2,736
Eddie Kirby	71	74	73	73	291	2,736
Lanny Wadkins	71	70	70	80	291	2,736
Clark Dennis	73	70	75	74	292	2,652
David Frost	74	72	71	75	292	2,652
Tommy Moore	72	73	75	72	292	2,652
Stan Utley	72	72	74	74	292	2,652
Guy Boros	77	69	73	74	293	2,568
Steve Gotsche	74	72	71	76	293	2,568
Dillard Pruitt	73	72	70	78	293	2,568
Todd Barranger	76	70	70	78	294	2,496
Buddy Gardner	73	73	74	74	294	2,496
Brad Lardon	72	71	74	77	294	2,496
Russell Beiersdorf	72	74	73	76	295	2,448
Brad King	74	72	77	74	297	2,424
Lance Ten Broeck	72	74	75	77	298	2,400
Rocky Walcher	76	68	78	77	299	2,376
Payne Stewart	72	70	77	81	300	2,352

Masters Tournament

Augusta National Golf Club, Augusta, Georgia
Par 36-36—72; 6,905 yards

April 7-10
purse, $1,700,000

	SCORES				TOTAL	MONEY
Jose Maria Olazabal	74	67	69	69	279	$360,000
Tom Lehman	70	70	69	72	281	216,000
Larry Mize	68	71	72	71	282	136,000
Tom Kite	69	72	71	71	283	96,000
Jay Haas	72	72	72	69	285	73,000
Jim McGovern	72	70	71	72	285	73,000
Loren Roberts	75	68	72	70	285	73,000
Ernie Els	74	67	74	71	286	60,000
Corey Pavin	71	72	73	70	286	60,000
Ian Baker-Finch	71	71	71	74	287	50,000
Raymond Floyd	70	74	71	72	287	50,000
John Huston	72	72	74	69	287	50,000
Tom Watson	70	71	73	74	288	42,000
Dan Forsman	74	66	76	73	289	38,000
Chip Beck	71	71	75	74	291	34,000
Brad Faxon	71	73	73	74	291	34,000
Mark O'Meara	75	70	76	70	291	34,000
Seve Ballesteros	70	76	75	71	292	24,343
Ben Crenshaw	74	73	73	72	292	24,343
David Edwards	73	72	73	74	292	24,343
Bill Glasson	72	73	75	72	292	24,343
Hale Irwin	73	68	79	72	292	24,343
Greg Norman	70	70	75	77	292	24,343
Lanny Wadkins	73	74	73	72	292	24,343

	SCORES				TOTAL	MONEY
Bernhard Langer	74	74	72	73	293	16,800
Jeff Sluman	74	75	71	73	293	16,800
Scott Simpson	74	74	73	73	294	14,800
Vijay Singh	70	75	74	75	294	14,800
Curtis Strange	74	70	75	75	294	14,800
Lee Janzen	75	71	76	73	295	13,300
Craig Parry	75	74	73	73	295	13,300
Nick Faldo	76	73	73	74	296	12,400
Russ Cochran	71	74	74	78	297	11,550
Sam Torrance	76	73	74	74	297	11,550
David Frost	74	71	75	78	298	10,300
Nick Price	74	73	74	77	298	10,300
Fuzzy Zoeller	74	72	74	78	298	10,300
Fulton Allem	69	77	76	77	299	9,000
Fred Funk	79	70	75	75	299	9,000
Sandy Lyle	75	73	78	73	299	9,000
Wayne Grady	74	73	73	80	300	7,400
Andrew Magee	74	74	76	76	300	7,400
Hajime Meshiai	71	71	80	78	300	7,400
Costantino Rocca	79	70	78	73	300	7,400
Mike Standly	77	69	79	75	300	7,400
John Cook	77	72	77	75	301	6,000
Ian Woosnam	76	73	77	75	301	6,000
John Daly	76	73	77	78	304	5,250
Howard Twitty	73	76	74	81	304	5,250
Jeff Maggert	75	73	82	75	305	5,000
*John Harris	72	76	80	77	305	

Out Of Final 36 Holes

Mark Calcavecchia	75	75	150
Rick Fehr	77	73	150
Nolan Henke	77	73	150
Johnny Miller	77	73	150
Colin Montgomerie	77	73	150
Gil Morgan	74	76	150
Masashi Ozaki	76	74	150
Gary Player	71	79	150
Craig Stadler	76	74	150
Jim Gallagher, Jr.	74	77	151
Dudley Hart	76	75	151
Billy Mayfair	74	77	151
Brett Ogle	74	77	151
Danny Ellis	78	74	152
John Inman	76	76	152
Jack Nicklaus	78	74	152
Grant Waite	74	78	152
Peter Baker	78	75	153
Bob Estes	77	76	153
John Adams	76	78	154
Billy Casper	77	77	154
Charles Coody	80	74	154
Anders Forsbrand	80	74	154
Scott Hoch	75	79	154
Davis Love III	76	78	154
Steve Elkington	81	74	155
Arnold Palmer	78	77	155
Tommy Aaron	76	80	156
Payne Stewart	78	78	156
Jeffrey Thomas	78	78	156

	SCORES		TOTAL
Blaine McCallister	79	78	157
Barry Lane	76	82	158
Iain Pyman	82	79	161
Gary Brewer	84	79	163
Doug Ford	85	WD	

(Professionals who did not complete 72 holes received $1,500.)

MCI Heritage Classic

Harbour Town Golf Links, Hilton Head Island, South Carolina   April 14-17
Par 36-35—71; 6,916 yards   purse, $1,250,000

	SCORES				TOTAL	MONEY
Hale Irwin	68	65	65	68	266	$225,000
Greg Norman	67	66	67	68	268	135,000
Loren Roberts	69	70	68	62	269	85,000
David Edwards	70	71	65	64	270	51,666.67
David Frost	70	61	72	67	270	51,666.67
Nolan Henke	69	69	66	66	270	51,666.66
Russ Cochran	67	67	66	71	271	40,312.50
Bob Estes	65	70	68	68	271	40,312.50
Larry Mize	67	65	75	65	272	35,000
Jesper Parnevik	68	68	69	67	272	35,000
Jim McGovern	67	65	73	70	275	31,250
Fred Funk	65	70	71	70	276	27,500
Peter Jacobsen	68	68	71	69	276	27,500
Dan Forsman	72	66	75	64	277	23,750
Marco Dawson	70	70	66	72	278	21,250
Jeff Maggert	67	72	67	72	278	21,250
Vijay Singh	68	75	68	67	278	21,250
Dave Barr	72	65	71	71	279	15,750
John Cook	72	70	69	68	279	15,750
Barry Jaeckel	66	73	69	71	279	15,750
Tom Lehman	66	69	73	71	279	15,750
Tim Simpson	68	72	72	67	279	15,750
Robert Wrenn	71	69	71	68	279	15,750
Rick Fehr	69	72	69	70	280	11,000
John Inman	77	64	73	66	280	11,000
Wayne Levi	67	70	69	74	280	11,000
Chip Beck	73	69	70	69	281	9,250
Mark McCumber	70	70	74	67	281	9,250
Willie Wood	70	68	70	73	281	9,250
Jay Haas	71	69	73	69	282	7,265.63
Mark Lye	71	69	74	68	282	7,265.63
Don Pooley	70	67	74	71	282	7,265.63
Jim Thorpe	71	68	74	69	282	7,265.63
Jay Don Blake	73	67	69	73	282	7,265.62
Brad Faxon	69	69	73	71	282	7,265.62
Steve Pate	69	70	72	71	282	7,265.62
Mike Standly	71	69	66	76	282	7,265.62
Dick Mast	72	68	70	73	283	5,500
Tom Purtzer	71	69	73	70	283	5,500
Mike Reid	70	71	70	72	283	5,500
Bobby Wadkins	71	72	68	72	283	5,500
Brian Claar	69	71	73	71	284	4,021.88
Keith Clearwater	70	73	70	71	284	4,021.88

	SCORES				TOTAL	MONEY
Ken Green	70	70	75	69	284	4,021.88
Howard Twitty	68	72	72	72	284	4,021.88
Ronnie Black	71	71	68	74	284	4,021.87
Michael Bradley	68	72	71	73	284	4,021.87
Ed Humenik	69	72	71	72	284	4,021.87
Blaine McCallister	70	71	70	73	284	4,021.87
Fulton Allem	75	68	71	71	285	3,015
Bob Gilder	69	73	68	75	285	3,015
Mike Springer	72	69	75	69	285	3,015
Steve Stricker	72	70	72	71	285	3,015
Joey Sindelar	72	67	73	73	285	3,015
Jay Delsing	74	67	74	71	286	2,825
John Flannery	72	69	75	70	286	2,825
Andrew Magee	70	73	67	76	286	2,825
Gil Morgan	70	70	71	75	286	2,825
Jerry Pate	74	68	70	74	286	2,825
Joel Edwards	70	72	73	72	287	2,712.50
Scott Hoch	70	73	73	71	287	2,712.50
Steve Lowery	69	67	74	77	287	2,712.50
Kenny Perry	67	72	73	75	287	2,712.50
Ian Baker-Finch	70	72	72	74	288	2,612.50
Bob Lohr	68	74	77	69	288	2,612.50
Charles Raulerson	74	69	75	70	288	2,612.50
Tom Watson	72	70	72	74	288	2,612.50
Hubert Green	68	72	73	76	289	2,550
Dudley Hart	71	67	76	76	290	2,512.50
Dave Rummells	70	72	74	74	290	2,512.50
Neal Lancaster	70	72	73	76	291	2,462.50
Larry Nelson	75	66	74	76	291	2,462.50
Grant Waite	71	72	76	73	292	2,425
Brett Ogle	72	71	72	78	293	2,400
Doug Tewell	72	70	75	81	298	2,375

Kmart Greater Greensboro Open

Forest Oaks Country Club, Greensboro, North Carolina April 21-24
Par 36-36—72; 6,958 yards purse, $1,500,000

	SCORES				TOTAL	MONEY
Mike Springer	64	69	70	72	275	$270,000
Brad Bryant	68	71	68	71	278	112,000
Ed Humenik	72	65	73	68	278	112,000
Hale Irwin	65	73	71	69	278	112,000
Bob Lohr	69	71	69	70	279	60,000
Donnie Hammond	70	71	69	70	280	52,125
John Morse	72	68	67	73	280	52,125
David Edwards	71	74	68	68	281	42,000
Joel Edwards	69	69	73	70	281	42,000
Dudley Hart	75	69	67	70	281	42,000
Mike Smith	69	73	69	70	281	42,000
Gil Morgan	68	71	69	74	282	34,500
Jay Haas	69	73	71	70	283	30,000
Howard Twitty	72	69	71	71	283	30,000
Guy Boros	71	73	69	71	284	22,500
Lennie Clements	71	69	72	72	284	22,500
Marco Dawson	70	74	72	68	284	22,500
Brad Faxon	68	73	73	70	284	22,500

		SCORES			TOTAL	MONEY
Bill Kratzert	69	72	72	71	284	22,500
Steve Lowery	71	72	71	70	284	22,500
Roger Maltbie	69	75	70	70	284	22,500
John Cook	72	72	71	70	285	13,521.43
Bill Glasson	68	73	72	72	285	13,521.43
John Huston	73	65	75	72	285	13,521.43
Lee Janzen	68	72	73	72	285	13,521.43
Brett Ogle	72	70	71	72	285	13,521.43
Mike Reid	70	73	72	70	285	13,521.43
Dave Barr	72	71	68	74	285	13,521.42
Mark Brooks	68	74	69	75	286	9,975
Jay Delsing	69	75	69	73	286	9,975
Mike Hulbert	71	72	68	75	286	9,975
Blaine McCallister	70	70	74	72	286	9,975
Mark Calcavecchia	71	70	71	75	287	8,287.50
Peter Jacobsen	72	73	72	70	287	8,287.50
Craig Parry	69	71	75	72	287	8,287.50
Gene Sauers	71	71	74	71	287	8,287.50
Chip Beck	71	73	71	73	288	6,450
Steve Brodie	72	73	74	69	288	6,450
Robert Gamez	70	74	71	73	288	6,450
Kelly Gibson	70	73	73	72	288	6,450
Ken Green	71	73	70	74	288	6,450
Steve Stricker	72	73	71	72	288	6,450
Willie Wood	73	72	74	69	288	6,450
Billy Andrade	71	73	72	73	289	4,062.50
Brandel Chamblee	71	73	74	71	289	4,062.50
Bobby Clampett	74	71	70	74	289	4,062.50
Glen Day	69	73	73	74	289	4,062.50
Brad Fabel	72	71	75	71	289	4,062.50
Jim Furyk	70	73	73	73	289	4,062.50
Mark O'Meara	72	73	74	70	289	4,062.50
David Peoples	67	75	74	73	289	4,062.50
Joey Sindelar	70	75	73	71	289	4,062.50
Ted Tryba	70	73	73	73	289	4,062.50
Duffy Waldorf	69	74	73	73	289	4,062.50
Fuzzy Zoeller	74	68	74	73	289	4,062.50
John Adams	69	72	76	73	290	3,330
Chris DiMarco	69	73	78	70	290	3,330
Steve Elkington	76	69	71	74	290	3,330
David Feherty	70	74	71	75	290	3,330
Steve Pate	73	72	76	69	290	3,330
Jeff Sluman	73	72	73	72	290	3,330
Jeff Woodland	73	69	76	72	290	3,330
Brian Claar	70	71	75	75	291	3,210
Bob Gilder	73	72	76	71	292	3,165
Vijay Singh	71	73	76	72	292	3,165
Larry Nelson	71	72	76	74	293	3,120
Chris Smith	71	74	78	71	294	3,075
Kirk Triplett	74	70	76	74	294	3,075
Phil Tataurangi	71	74	73	77	295	3,015
Bobby Wadkins	75	69	75	76	295	3,015
Trevor Dodds	69	76	77	74	296	2,940
Peter Jordan	66	77	75	78	296	2,940
Grant Waite	74	71	77	74	296	2,940
Russ Cochran	73	72	79	74	298	2,880
Bob Burns	70	74	81	75	300	2,850
Charles Raulerson	74	68	81	78	301	2,820

Shell Houston Open

TPC at the Woodlands, The Woodlands, Texas
Par 36-36—72; 7,042 yards

April 28-May 1
purse, $1,300,000

	SCORES				TOTAL	MONEY
Mike Heinen	67	68	69	68	272	$234,000
Jeff Maggert	70	66	68	71	275	97,066.67
Hal Sutton	68	70	68	69	275	97,066.67
Tom Kite	68	65	71	71	275	97,066.66
Bob Gilder	66	76	69	67	278	49,400
Vijay Singh	72	67	69	70	278	49,400
John Daly	68	74	70	67	279	40,516.67
Gil Morgan	70	71	72	66	279	40,516.67
Peter Jacobsen	68	73	69	69	279	40,516.66
Dave Barr	66	72	71	71	280	32,500
Fred Funk	71	67	71	71	280	32,500
Curtis Strange	71	72	66	71	280	32,500
Clark Dennis	65	71	72	69	281	25,133.34
Fulton Allem	72	70	69	70	281	25,133.33
Jeff Woodland	69	72	66	74	281	25,133.33
Jay Haas	72	67	73	70	282	18,237.15
Bob Lohr	70	66	74	72	282	18,237.15
Rick Fehr	71	68	68	75	282	18,237.14
Robert Gamez	69	68	71	74	282	18,237.14
Wayne Levi	72	67	69	74	282	18,237.14
Doug Martin	71	66	70	75	282	18,237.14
John Morse	71	70	69	72	282	18,237.14
Keith Clearwater	72	67	75	69	283	12,480
Donnie Hammond	70	69	71	73	283	12,480
Mark McCumber	70	69	70	74	283	12,480
Peter Jordan	68	71	71	74	284	9,425
Brian Kamm	70	69	73	72	284	9,425
Loren Roberts	70	72	69	73	284	9,425
Mike Sullivan	70	71	70	73	284	9,425
Doug Tewell	71	68	71	74	284	9,425
Stan Utley	71	69	73	71	284	9,425
Marco Dawson	70	72	74	69	285	7,193.34
Dicky Pride	74	69	73	69	285	7,193.34
Lennie Clements	68	71	72	74	285	7,193.33
P.H. Horgan III	71	70	74	70	285	7,193.33
David Toms	71	68	73	73	285	7,193.33
Tray Tyner	68	71	72	74	285	7,193.33
Curt Byrum	71	72	70	73	286	5,070
Brad Fabel	71	71	71	73	286	5,070
Mark Lye	69	74	70	73	286	5,070
Andrew Magee	65	78	71	72	286	5,070
Dick Mast	67	76	69	74	286	5,070
Jim McGovern	71	72	71	72	286	5,070
Yoshinori Mizumaki	68	72	73	73	286	5,070
Steve Rintoul	73	70	70	73	286	5,070
Robert Wrenn	70	66	74	76	286	5,070
Kelly Gibson	68	74	74	71	287	3,298.75
Mike Hulbert	75	68	72	72	287	3,298.75
J.L. Lewis	69	71	76	71	287	3,298.75
Steve Pate	70	69	73	75	287	3,298.75
Joey Rassett	68	71	74	74	287	3,298.75
Dave Rummells	69	72	72	74	287	3,298.75
D.A. Weibring	71	71	71	74	287	3,298.75
John Wilson	69	73	71	74	287	3,298.75

	SCORES				TOTAL	MONEY
Steve Elkington	67	74	72	75	288	2,925
Steve Lamontagne	74	68	72	74	288	2,925
Neal Lancaster	73	68	74	73	288	2,925
Shaun Micheel	72	68	74	74	288	2,925
Larry Rinker	70	72	75	71	288	2,925
Phil Tataurangi	69	73	73	73	288	2,925
Ronnie Black	71	72	77	69	289	2,769
Steve Brodie	70	70	70	79	289	2,769
Ben Crenshaw	72	70	75	72	289	2,769
Keith Fergus	70	72	74	73	289	2,769
Paul Goydos	68	72	75	74	289	2,769
Dan Pohl	70	72	74	73	289	2,769
John Adams	71	71	72	76	290	2,639
Michael Allen	69	74	73	74	290	2,639
Bill Britton	70	70	76	74	290	2,639
Brad Lardon	72	71	76	71	290	2,639
Russell Beiersdorf	71	70	79	71	291	2,535
Steve Gotsche	71	71	75	74	291	2,535
Tim Simpson	73	69	72	77	291	2,535
Ted Tryba	71	72	71	77	291	2,535
Mark Brooks	72	69	75	76	292	2,470
Mike Brisky	68	75	75	75	293	2,418
Ed Humenik	69	71	71	82	293	2,418
Duffy Waldorf	68	69	79	77	293	2,418
Tom Sieckmann	72	70	78	75	295	2,366
Ed Dougherty	71	70	82	74	297	2,340

BellSouth Classic

Atlanta Country Club, Marietta, Georgia
Par 36-36—72; 7,018 yards

May 5-8
purse, $1,200,000

	SCORES				TOTAL	MONEY
John Daly	69	64	69	72	274	$216,000
Nolan Henke	70	67	69	69	275	105,600
Brian Henninger	68	67	69	71	275	105,600
Bob Estes	71	69	68	68	276	52,800
David Peoples	73	65	68	70	276	52,800
Lennie Clements	68	69	72	68	277	38,850
Russ Cochran	69	69	69	70	277	38,850
Tom Kite	66	72	68	71	277	38,850
Blaine McCallister	69	68	69	71	277	38,850
Clark Dennis	71	66	72	69	278	32,400
Paul Goydos	68	72	70	69	279	28,800
Davis Love III	70	70	70	69	279	28,800
Olin Browne	73	71	65	71	280	21,840
Dave Rummells	69	67	71	73	280	21,840
Paul Stankowski	69	69	70	72	280	21,840
Hal Sutton	66	71	71	72	280	21,840
Mark Wurtz	68	68	72	72	280	21,840
Brian Kamm	70	69	74	68	281	16,800
Larry Mize	71	71	70	69	281	16,800
Corey Pavin	68	71	70	72	281	16,800
Jay Don Blake	72	71	68	71	282	12,480
Bill Britton	71	70	71	70	282	12,480
Fred Funk	72	69	73	68	282	12,480
Mark McCumber	72	69	68	73	282	12,480

	SCORES				TOTAL	MONEY
Scott Verplank	69	72	68	73	282	12,480
John Adams	72	69	70	72	283	9,060
Michael Bradley	69	75	71	68	283	9,060
Yoshinori Mizumaki	72	72	70	69	283	9,060
Bobby Wadkins	71	69	70	73	283	9,060
Billy Andrade	70	73	70	71	284	7,452
Hale Irwin	71	72	69	72	284	7,452
Wayne Levi	68	68	71	77	284	7,452
Joey Sindelar	73	69	71	71	284	7,452
Rocky Walcher	69	70	71	74	284	7,452
Dave Barr	74	70	70	71	285	5,665.72
Mike Hulbert	73	71	70	71	285	5,665.72
Peter Persons	71	70	72	72	285	5,665.72
Mark Brooks	70	69	75	71	285	5,665.71
Craig Parry	67	74	73	71	285	5,665.71
Steve Stricker	73	70	67	75	285	5,665.71
Esteban Toledo	68	72	71	74	285	5,665.71
Steve Rintoul	74	65	73	74	286	4,560
Jeff Woodland	70	69	72	75	286	4,560
Russell Beiersdorf	70	73	70	74	287	3,541.72
Ed Humenik	71	73	70	73	287	3,541.72
Doug Tewell	71	71	71	74	287	3,541.72
Joel Edwards	74	69	71	73	287	3,541.71
Greg Kraft	73	71	73	70	287	3,541.71
Neal Lancaster	73	70	71	73	287	3,541.71
David Toms	73	69	74	71	287	3,541.71
Ed Dougherty	76	68	68	76	288	2,888
Steve Lowery	74	67	73	74	288	2,888
Mark Lye	70	69	72	77	288	2,888
John Morse	71	72	71	75	289	2,736
Kenny Perry	71	70	74	74	289	2,736
Larry Silveira	70	74	73	72	289	2,736
Mike Springer	76	68	73	72	289	2,736
Duffy Waldorf	73	70	73	73	289	2,736
Michael Allen	69	73	71	77	290	2,604
Tripp Isenhour	72	71	73	74	290	2,604
Billy Mayfair	74	69	76	71	290	2,604
Larry Nelson	75	69	69	77	290	2,604
Tom Sieckmann	71	71	76	72	290	2,604
Jeff Sluman	72	71	72	75	290	2,604
Ty Armstrong	73	70	73	75	291	2,496
Brad Bryant	75	69	74	73	291	2,496
Jim McGovern	72	71	76	72	291	2,496
David Ogrin	72	72	73	75	292	2,436
Willie Wood	71	73	76	72	292	2,436
Brandel Chamblee	71	69	78	76	294	2,388
David Feherty	70	74	73	77	294	2,388
Morris Hatalsky	76	68	72	79	295	2,352
Tommy Brannen	75	67	78	76	296	2,316
Eddie Kirby	73	69	76	78	296	2,316
Marco Dawson	72	72	76	77	297	2,280
Brad King	71	72	79	77	299	2,256

GTE Byron Nelson Classic

TPC at Los Colinas, Irving, Texas
Par 35-35—70; 6,742 yards
(Third and fourth rounds cancelled — rain.)

May 12-15
purse, $1,200,000

	SCORES		TOTAL	MONEY
Neal Lancaster	67	65	132	$216,000
Tom Byrum	68	64	132	72,000
Mark Carnevale	65	67	132	72,000
David Edwards	67	65	132	72,000
Yoshinori Mizumaki	66	66	132	72,000
David Ogrin	64	68	132	72,000
(Lancaster defeated five others on first extra hole.)				
Brad Bryant	66	67	133	40,200
Ronnie Black	70	64	134	31,200
Mark Brooks	67	67	134	31,200
Ben Crenshaw	66	68	134	31,200
Bob Gilder	67	67	134	31,200
Greg Norman	66	68	134	31,200
Jeff Woodland	69	65	134	31,200
Tommy Armour	65	70	135	19,800
Chip Beck	72	63	135	19,800
Billy Mayfair	68	67	135	19,800
Naomichi Ozaki	69	66	135	19,800
Kenny Perry	67	68	135	19,800
Loren Roberts	71	64	135	19,800
Guy Boros	66	70	136	12,105
Mark Calcavecchia	70	66	136	12,105
Mark O'Meara	69	67	136	12,105
Nick Price	65	71	136	12,105
Dicky Pride	70	66	136	12,105
Craig Stadler	69	67	136	12,105
Doug Tewell	69	67	136	12,105
Jim Thorpe	68	68	136	12,105
Jesper Parnevik	65	72	137	6,737.15
Tim Simpson	67	70	137	6,737.15
Ted Tryba	71	66	137	6,737.15
Willie Wood	70	67	137	6,737.15
Perry Arthur	69	68	137	6,737.14
Jay Don Blake	68	69	137	6,737.14
Michael Bradley	67	70	137	6,737.14
Bob Eastwood	71	66	137	6,737.14
Tom Garner	67	70	137	6,737.14
Morris Hatalsky	73	64	137	6,737.14
Tom Kite	68	69	137	6,737.14
Corey Pavin	69	68	137	6,737.14
Larry Silveira	68	69	137	6,737.14
D.A. Weibring	68	69	137	6,737.14
Brandel Chamblee	68	70	138	3,861
Chris DiMarco	67	71	138	3,861
Dan Forsman	72	66	138	3,861
Ken Green	69	69	138	3,861
Donnie Hammond	68	70	138	3,861
Larry Mize	67	71	138	3,861
Steve Rintoul	67	71	138	3,861
Bob Tway	70	68	138	3,861
Todd Barranger	72	67	139	2,732.80
Trevor Dodds	70	69	139	2,732.80
Bob Estes	73	66	139	2,732.80

	SCORES				TOTAL	MONEY
Rick Fehr	70	69			139	2,732.80
Robin Freeman	70	69			139	2,732.80
Robert Gamez	69	70			139	2,732.80
Paul Goydos	73	66			139	2,732.80
Jay Haas	71	68			139	2,732.80
Jeff Maggert	68	71			139	2,732.80
Sean Murphy	71	68			139	2,732.80
Dennis Paulson	73	66			139	2,732.80
Dave Rummells	72	67			139	2,732.80
D.A. Russell	70	69			139	2,732.80
Mike Sullivan	71	68			139	2,732.80
Billy Tuten	70	69			139	2,732.80
Ty Armstrong	68	72			140	2,304
Billy Ray Brown	70	70			140	2,304
Russ Cochran	70	70			140	2,304
Ed Dougherty	70	70			140	2,304
David Frost	72	68			140	2,304
Hubert Green	71	69			140	2,304
Gary Hallberg	69	71			140	2,304
Brad King	69	71			140	2,304
Brad Lardon	72	68			140	2,304
Steve Lowery	69	71			140	2,304
Doug Martin	70	70			140	2,304
Dillard Pruitt	68	72			140	2,304
Joey Rassett	73	67			140	2,304
Mike Standly	69	71			140	2,304
Hal Sutton	73	67			140	2,304
Grant Waite	70	70			140	2,304
Mark Wurtz	68	72			140	2,304
Richard Zokol	72	68			140	2,304
Bobby Wadkins	72	75			147	2,304

Memorial Tournament

Muirfield Village Golf Club, Dublin, Ohio
Par 36-36—72; 7,104 yards

May 19-22
purse, $1,500,000

	SCORES				TOTAL	MONEY
Tom Lehman	67	67	67	67	268	$270,000
Greg Norman	70	69	70	64	273	162,000
John Cook	67	69	69	71	276	102,000
Donnie Hammond	69	69	70	69	277	72,000
David Edwards	69	67	72	70	278	60,000
Robert Gamez	77	69	66	67	279	54,000
Mark Brooks	64	75	70	71	280	48,375
Ben Crenshaw	72	66	74	68	280	48,375
Brad Faxon	72	68	72	69	281	42,000
Jeff Maggert	71	74	66	70	281	42,000
David Frost	69	71	71	71	282	34,500
Gary Hallberg	77	66	68	71	282	34,500
Steve Lowery	71	70	69	72	282	34,500
Chip Beck	72	70	70	71	283	25,500
Scott Hoch	71	73	71	68	283	25,500
Hale Irwin	73	70	70	70	283	25,500
Scott Simpson	68	72	72	71	283	25,500
Curtis Strange	74	69	73	67	283	25,500
Bob Estes	71	68	70	75	284	18,180

	SCORES				TOTAL	MONEY
Jay Haas	72	70	74	68	284	18,180
Bruce Lietzke	72	71	73	68	284	18,180
Larry Mize	74	67	71	72	284	18,180
Yoshinori Mizumaki	72	73	69	70	284	18,180
Kenny Perry	71	73	71	70	285	13,800
Kirk Triplett	72	71	69	73	285	13,800
Billy Andrade	74	71	73	68	286	11,325
Mike Heinen	71	73	76	66	286	11,325
John Huston	73	74	68	71	286	11,325
Loren Roberts	71	74	70	71	286	11,325
Lennie Clements	71	71	72	73	287	9,315
David Duval	73	73	72	69	287	9,315
Hajime Meshiai	73	74	71	69	287	9,315
Larry Nelson	72	74	69	72	287	9,315
Corey Pavin	76	69	70	72	287	9,315
Clark Dennis	72	74	73	69	288	7,725
Jim Thorpe	70	75	72	71	288	7,725
Tom Watson	77	69	70	72	288	7,725
Fulton Allem	74	70	72	73	289	6,150
Peter Jacobsen	72	75	70	72	289	6,150
Bob Lohr	74	74	68	73	289	6,150
Jim McGovern	72	69	74	74	289	6,150
Jesper Parnevik	70	75	72	72	289	6,150
Steve Stricker	72	75	69	73	289	6,150
Bob Tway	71	77	69	72	289	6,150
Steve Elkington	69	72	72	77	290	4,392
Ernie Els	72	74	68	76	290	4,392
Davis Love III	71	70	73	76	290	4,392
Mike Springer	72	71	78	69	290	4,392
Ted Tryba	70	76	76	68	290	4,392
Fred Funk	73	72	74	72	291	3,652.50
Brian Henninger	74	69	72	76	291	3,652.50
Ed Humenik	74	74	74	69	291	3,652.50
Billy Mayfair	69	71	72	79	291	3,652.50
Mark Calcavecchia	74	74	68	76	292	3,435
Rick Fehr	75	72	71	74	292	3,435
Nolan Henke	72	71	73	76	292	3,435
Mark O'Meara	75	69	74	74	292	3,435
Bradley Hughes	74	73	74	72	293	3,345
Wayne Levi	72	76	68	77	293	3,345
Wayne Grady	73	70	70	81	294	3,255
Lee Janzen	72	75	75	72	294	3,255
John Mahaffey	73	75	72	74	294	3,255
Craig Stadler	71	73	73	77	294	3,255
Paul Goydos	74	72	71	78	295	3,165
Andy North	76	71	72	76	295	3,165
*Allen Doyle	75	72	75	73	295	
Keith Clearwater	73	73	72	78	296	3,105
Doug Martin	72	75	75	74	296	3,105
Mike Standly	76	72	74	75	297	3,060
Naomichi Ozaki	72	76	75	75	298	3,030
John Daly	74	74	73	78	299	3,000
Andy Bean	76	71	70	83	300	2,955
Bill Kratzert	73	74	78	75	300	2,955
Dave Rummells	74	71	77	80	302	2,910

Southwestern Bell Colonial

Colonial Country Club, Forth Worth, Texas
Par 35-35—70; 7,010 yards

May 26-29
purse, $1,400,000

	SCORES				TOTAL	MONEY
Nick Price	65	70	67	64	266	$252,000
Scott Simpson	66	65	64	71	266	151,200
(Price defeated Simpson on first extra hole.)						
Hale Irwin	64	70	68	65	267	95,200
Peter Jordan	68	70	66	66	270	67,200
Brad Faxon	70	66	67	68	271	51,100
Gary Hallberg	67	67	65	72	271	51,100
Tom Lehman	66	66	69	70	271	51,100
Phil Mickelson	68	68	71	65	272	43,400
John Cook	66	71	67	70	274	37,800
Mark McCumber	68	69	67	70	274	37,800
Corey Pavin	68	67	69	70	274	37,800
Mark Calcavecchia	68	69	71	67	275	29,400
Ben Crenshaw	69	69	69	68	275	29,400
Fuzzy Zoeller	68	70	68	69	275	29,400
Clark Dennis	69	69	67	71	276	23,800
David Edwards	72	67	68	69	276	23,800
David Frost	65	68	75	68	276	23,800
Ken Green	67	66	69	75	277	18,900
Naomichi Ozaki	70	69	71	67	277	18,900
Kenny Perry	73	67	69	68	277	18,900
Kirk Triplett	71	68	69	69	277	18,900
Guy Boros	70	63	71	74	278	14,560
Bob Estes	67	71	71	69	278	14,560
John Huston	70	68	65	75	278	14,560
Lennie Clements	70	68	67	74	279	10,920
Wayne Grady	71	65	68	75	279	10,920
David Ogrin	70	68	68	73	279	10,920
Steve Pate	69	64	74	72	279	10,920
Tom Purtzer	71	69	70	69	279	10,920
Lee Janzen	70	70	71	69	280	7,478.34
Andrew Magee	67	73	71	69	280	7,478.34
Roger Maltbie	69	67	72	72	280	7,478.34
Mike Springer	67	71	73	69	280	7,478.34
Glen Day	69	68	71	72	280	7,478.33
Mike Heinen	70	70	68	72	280	7,478.33
Scott Hoch	68	70	69	73	280	7,478.33
Bruce Lietzke	67	72	69	72	280	7,478.33
Mike Reid	67	66	71	76	280	7,478.33
Loren Roberts	70	65	71	74	280	7,478.33
Dave Stockton, Jr.	69	68	68	75	280	7,478.33
D.A. Weibring	69	70	68	73	280	7,478.33
Mark Brooks	68	67	72	74	281	4,900
Davis Love III	72	69	71	69	281	4,900
Brett Ogle	72	70	67	72	281	4,900
Joey Sindelar	71	70	72	68	281	4,900
Steve Stricker	71	67	67	76	281	4,900
Steve Lowery	71	71	71	69	282	3,845.34
Mike Hulbert	70	67	71	74	282	3,845.33
Dave Stockton	70	68	71	73	282	3,845.33
Tom Byrum	72	69	72	70	283	3,409
Keith Clearwater	70	68	67	78	283	3,409
Donnie Hammond	68	70	69	76	283	3,409
Jodie Mudd	70	71	72	70	283	3,409

	SCORES				TOTAL	MONEY
*John Harris	69	72	71	71	283	
Brian Henninger	69	71	70	74	284	3,248
Dave Barr	71	71	69	74	285	3,136
Jay Don Blake	69	65	74	77	285	3,136
David Feherty	67	72	68	78	285	3,136
Bruce Fleisher	71	70	71	73	285	3,136
Jeff Maggert	71	66	75	73	285	3,136
Greg Norman	70	69	71	75	285	3,136
Howard Twitty	70	68	73	74	285	3,136
Mark Carnevale	69	73	67	77	286	2,996
Hajime Meshiai	66	74	72	74	286	2,996
Jeff Sluman	73	68	74	71	286	2,996
Fred Funk	68	71	70	78	287	2,912
John Inman	68	72	74	73	287	2,912
Hal Sutton	72	70	70	75	287	2,912
Billy Mayfair	71	71	72	74	288	2,856
Michael Allen	69	73	72	76	290	2,828
Paul Goydos	70	72	75	74	291	2,786
Doug Tewell	68	70	75	78	291	2,786
Rick Fehr	71	70	77	75	293	2,744

Kemper Open

TPC at Avenel, Potomac, Maryland
Par 36-35—71; 7,005 yards

June 2-5
purse, $1,300,000

	SCORES				TOTAL	MONEY
Mark Brooks	65	68	69	69	271	$234,000
Bobby Wadkins	68	67	65	74	274	114,400
D.A. Weibring	70	68	68	68	274	114,400
Lee Janzen	70	71	68	66	275	57,200
Phil Mickelson	70	69	67	69	275	57,200
Joel Edwards	71	70	68	69	278	46,800
Craig Parry	69	71	69	70	279	40,516.67
Kenny Perry	72	72	68	67	279	40,516.67
Mark Lye	70	70	69	70	279	40,516.66
Michael Bradley	70	71	67	73	281	26,975
Robert Gamez	72	66	69	74	281	26,975
Kelly Gibson	75	64	71	71	281	26,975
Scott Hoch	69	72	67	73	281	26,975
Brian Kamm	69	71	68	73	281	26,975
Wayne Levi	68	70	72	71	281	26,975
Tim Simpson	71	72	70	68	281	26,975
Kirk Triplett	72	73	67	69	281	26,975
Rob Boldt	70	68	73	71	282	16,380
Mark Carnevale	71	69	68	74	282	16,380
Mike Donald	71	70	72	69	282	16,380
Greg Kraft	74	70	70	68	282	16,380
Bob May	71	71	66	74	282	16,380
Bobby Clampett	73	71	65	73	282	16,380
Scott Verplank	72	72	69	70	283	10,288.58
Morris Hatalsky	74	69	67	73	283	10,288.57
Andrew Magee	69	72	72	70	283	10,288.57
Mark O'Meara	69	68	69	77	283	10,288.57
Dennis Paulson	72	70	70	71	283	10,288.57
Steve Rintoul	70	73	70	70	283	10,288.57
Leonard Thompson	71	70	71	71	283	10,288.57

	SCORES				TOTAL	MONEY
Jay Don Blake	71	68	70	75	284	7,540
Brian Claar	75	70	69	70	284	7,540
John Daly	73	71	69	71	284	7,540
Robin Freeman	73	70	69	72	284	7,540
Mike Hulbert	71	70	71	72	284	7,540
Dave Rummells	71	70	67	76	284	7,540
Bill Britton	73	71	71	70	285	5,590
Keith Clearwater	73	68	71	73	285	5,590
Ed Dougherty	68	74	70	73	285	5,590
Brad Fabel	74	69	74	68	285	5,590
Tommy Moore	71	69	72	73	285	5,590
Joey Rassett	72	68	72	73	285	5,590
Jeff Sluman	70	73	70	72	285	5,590
Clark Dennis	71	71	69	75	286	4,040.40
Brad Faxon	70	69	73	74	286	4,040.40
Steve Lamontagne	77	68	70	71	286	4,040.40
Dick Mast	75	69	70	72	286	4,040.40
Dillard Pruitt	71	73	67	75	286	4,040.40
Russell Beiersdorf	71	68	74	74	287	3,126.50
Marco Dawson	76	67	74	70	287	3,126.50
Gary Hallberg	74	69	68	76	287	3,126.50
Ed Humenik	73	72	75	67	287	3,126.50
Dicky Pride	72	69	71	75	287	3,126.50
Paul Stankowski	70	72	70	75	287	3,126.50
Doug Tewell	74	71	70	72	287	3,126.50
Esteban Toledo	71	70	73	73	287	3,126.50
John Flannery	72	73	71	72	288	2,860
Bradley Hughes	71	73	68	76	288	2,860
John Inman	75	70	70	73	288	2,860
Roger Maltbie	74	70	74	70	288	2,860
David Peoples	72	71	70	75	288	2,860
Payne Stewart	73	68	72	75	288	2,860
Mark Wurtz	74	70	70	74	288	2,860
Shaun Micheel	72	70	75	72	289	2,756
Fred Funk	74	71	73	72	290	2,691
Neal Lancaster	74	68	74	74	290	2,691
Howard Twitty	71	71	74	74	290	2,691
Lanny Wadkins	71	74	68	77	290	2,691
Gene Sauers	74	71	71	75	291	2,626
Willie Wood	74	69	73	76	292	2,600
Billy Mayfair	71	72	74	76	293	2,574
Tom Garner	74	70	70	80	294	2,548
Olin Browne	73	70	71	81	295	2,509
Ted Schulz	74	71	76	74	295	2,509
Chris DiMarco	70	72	76	78	296	2,470
Lance Ten Broeck	75	70	81	75	301	2,444

Buick Classic

Westchester Country Club, Harrison, New York
Par 36-35—71; 6,779 yards

June 9-12
purse, $1,200,000

	SCORES				TOTAL	MONEY
Lee Janzen	69	69	64	66	268	$216,000
Ernie Els	68	66	69	68	271	129,600
Brad Faxon	70	68	70	66	274	69,600
Jay Haas	68	70	69	67	274	69,600

	SCORES				TOTAL	MONEY
Billy Andrade	70	71	66	69	276	43,800
Bob Burns	71	67	70	68	276	43,800
Steve Pate	66	72	69	69	276	43,800
Mark Brooks	71	70	66	70	277	32,400
Robin Freeman	69	69	69	70	277	32,400
Hale Irwin	70	72	65	70	277	32,400
Jeff Maggert	72	72	64	69	277	32,400
Naomichi Ozaki	69	67	69	72	277	32,400
Dillard Pruitt	66	71	68	73	278	24,000
John Wilson	68	68	69	73	278	24,000
Tom Kite	68	74	64	73	279	21,600
Brad Bryant	70	67	73	70	280	17,400
Bob Estes	66	71	70	73	280	17,400
Greg Norman	73	67	69	71	280	17,400
Hal Sutton	71	71	66	72	280	17,400
Phil Tataurangi	71	71	67	71	280	17,400
Ted Tryba	71	71	66	72	280	17,400
Gary Hallberg	71	67	72	71	281	11,520
Jim Thorpe	71	71	67	72	281	11,520
Esteban Toledo	71	73	67	70	281	11,520
Tom Watson	71	71	70	69	281	11,520
Jim McGovern	73	71	70	67	281	11,520
Ronnie Black	70	71	65	76	282	7,494.55
Brian Claar	71	73	68	70	282	7,494.55
David Frost	67	77	71	67	282	7,494.55
John Huston	70	72	75	65	282	7,494.55
John Mahaffey	71	73	68	70	282	7,494.55
Mark McCumber	69	72	70	71	282	7,494.55
Lennie Clements	73	68	72	69	282	7,494.54
Fred Couples	70	69	70	73	282	7,494.54
John Flannery	72	68	70	72	282	7,494.54
Fred Funk	69	70	69	74	282	7,494.54
Brett Ogle	69	70	75	68	282	7,494.54
Fulton Allem	72	69	68	74	283	5,040
Dave Barr	71	73	69	70	283	5,040
Mark Carnevale	72	69	72	70	283	5,040
Davis Love III	71	71	69	72	283	5,040
Rocco Mediate	74	67	71	71	283	5,040
Mike Reid	65	70	73	75	283	5,040
Rob Boldt	73	71	72	68	284	3,628
Ben Crenshaw	73	70	68	73	284	3,628
Jay Delsing	74	68	70	72	284	3,628
Blaine McCallister	72	67	73	72	284	3,628
Corey Pavin	72	69	68	75	284	3,628
Scott Verplank	71	70	69	74	284	3,628
Phil Blackmar	68	72	68	77	285	2,922
Russ Cochran	69	74	69	73	285	2,922
Wayne Levi	66	74	74	71	285	2,922
Doug Tewell	68	72	73	72	285	2,922
David Ogrin	73	69	71	73	286	2,760
Steve Rintoul	72	71	75	68	286	2,760
Bob Tway	71	70	75	70	286	2,760
Howard Twitty	71	73	72	71	287	2,712
Steve Brodie	66	76	72	74	288	2,652
Dudley Hart	77	67	70	74	288	2,652
Mike Hulbert	73	68	73	74	288	2,652
Joey Rassett	75	69	71	73	288	2,652
Nolan Henke	70	73	73	73	289	2,568
Dave Stockton, Jr.	72	70	71	76	289	2,568
Jeff Woodland	72	71	71	75	289	2,568

	SCORES				TOTAL	MONEY
Bob May	72	70	77	71	290	2,508
Payne Stewart	72	72	72	74	290	2,508
Todd Barranger	71	73	68	79	291	2,460
Bill Britton	71	73	76	71	291	2,460
Seve Ballesteros	71	73	75	73	292	2,424
David Feherty	74	70	75	76	295	2,400

U.S. Open Championship

Oakmont Country Club, Oakmont, Pennsylvania
Par 36-35—71; 6,946 yards

June 16-19
purse, $1,700,000

	SCORES				TOTAL	MONEY
Ernie Els	69	71	66	73	279	$320,000
Loren Roberts	76	69	64	70	279	141,827.50
Colin Montgomerie	71	65	73	70	279	141,827.50
(Els (74) defeated Roberts (74) on 20th hole. Montgomerie (78) eliminated after 18 holes.)						
Curtis Strange	70	70	70	70	280	75,728
John Cook	73	65	73	71	282	61,318
Clark Dennis	71	71	70	71	283	49,485.34
Greg Norman	71	71	69	72	283	49,485.33
Tom Watson	68	73	68	74	283	49,485.33
Jeff Maggert	71	68	75	70	284	37,179.75
Frank Nobilo	69	71	68	76	284	37,179.75
Jeff Sluman	72	69	72	71	284	37,179.75
Duffy Waldorf	74	68	73	69	284	37,179.75
Scott Hoch	72	72	70	71	285	29,767.34
David Edwards	73	65	75	72	285	29,767.33
Jim McGovern	73	69	74	69	285	29,767.33
Fred Couples	72	71	69	74	286	25,899.50
Steve Lowery	71	71	68	76	286	25,899.50
Seve Ballesteros	72	72	70	73	287	22,477.67
Scott Verplank	70	72	75	70	287	22,477.67
Hale Irwin	69	69	71	78	287	22,477.66
Steve Pate	74	66	71	77	288	19,464
Sam Torrance	72	71	76	69	288	19,464
Bernhard Langer	72	72	73	72	289	17,223
Kirk Triplett	70	71	71	77	289	17,223
Chip Beck	73	73	70	74	290	14,705.67
Mike Springer	74	72	73	71	290	14,705.67
Craig Parry	78	68	71	73	290	14,705.66
Lennie Clements	73	71	73	75	292	11,514.20
Jim Furyk	74	69	74	75	292	11,514.20
Davis Love III	74	72	74	72	292	11,514.20
Jack Nicklaus	69	70	77	76	292	11,514.20
Masashi Ozaki	70	73	69	80	292	11,514.20
Mark Carnevale	75	72	76	70	293	9,578.34
Ben Crenshaw	71	74	70	78	293	9,578.34
Fulton Allem	73	70	74	76	293	9,578.33
Brad Faxon	73	69	71	80	293	9,578.33
Tom Kite	73	71	72	77	293	9,578.33
Tom Lehman	77	68	73	75	293	9,578.33
Peter Baker	73	73	73	75	294	8,005.75
Gordon Brand, Jr.	73	71	73	77	294	8,005.75
Bradley Hughes	71	72	77	74	294	8,005.75
Brandt Jobe	72	74	68	80	294	8,005.75
Francis Quinn	75	72	73	75	295	7,222
Don Walsworth	71	75	73	77	296	6,595.34

	SCORES				TOTAL	MONEY
Fred Funk	74	71	74	77	296	6,595.33
Paul Goydos	74	72	79	71	296	6,595.33
Olin Browne	74	73	77	73	297	5,105.38
Tim Dunlavey	76	70	78	73	297	5,105.38
Michael Emery	74	73	75	75	297	5,105.38
Barry Lane	77	70	76	74	297	5,105.38
David Berganio	73	72	76	76	297	5,105.37
Jim Gallagher, Jr.	74	68	77	78	297	5,105.37
Wayne Levi	76	70	73	78	297	5,105.37
Phil Mickelson	75	70	73	79	297	5,105.37
Tommy Armour	73	73	79	73	298	4,324.67
Scott Simpson	74	73	73	78	298	4,324.67
Hugh Royer III	72	71	77	78	298	4,324.66
Steven Richardson	74	73	76	76	299	4,105
Fuzzy Zoeller	76	70	76	77	299	4,105
Doug Martin	76	70	74	81	301	3,967
Dave Rummells	71	74	82	74	301	3,967
Michael Smith	74	73	78	77	302	3,800.34
Emlyn Aubrey	72	69	81	80	302	3,800.33
Ed Humenik	74	72	81	75	302	3,800.33

Out of Final 36 Holes

Bill Britton	76	72	148
Mark Brooks	75	73	148
Brad Bryant	76	72	148
Mark Calcavecchia	71	77	148
Nick Faldo	73	75	148
Stephen Flesch	74	74	148
Ken Green	76	72	148
Jay Haas	75	73	148
Lee Janzen	77	71	148
John Mahaffey	78	70	148
Hajime Meshiai	71	77	148
Larry Nelson	75	73	148
Mark O'Meara	72	76	148
Chris Perry	78	70	148
Nick Price	76	72	148
Mark Wurtz	71	77	148
*Buddy Alexander	75	74	149
Jay Don Blake	79	70	149
Michael Bradley	74	75	149
David Frost	72	77	149
Wayne Grady	75	74	149
Jimmy Green	74	75	149
Mike Hulbert	74	75	149
Eric Johnson	77	72	149
Mark Lye	73	76	149
Baker Maddera	75	74	149
Billy Mayfair	76	73	149
Larry Mize	77	72	149
Payne Stewart	74	75	149
Mike Sullivan	75	74	149
Harry Taylor	76	73	149
Bob Tway	78	71	149
John Adams	75	75	150
Joakim Haeggman	77	73	150
Jose Maria Olazabal	76	74	150
Paul Stankowski	75	75	150
Brent Studer	76	74	150

	SCORES		TOTAL
Glen Day	75	76	151
Rick Fehr	78	73	151
Jacob Ferenz	75	76	151
Robert Friend	78	73	151
Robert Gamez	76	75	151
Masahiro Kuramoto	79	72	151
Andy North	78	73	151
David Ogrin	74	77	151
Corey Pavin	78	73	151
Sam Randolph	74	77	151
Costantino Rocca	77	74	151
John Stacey	78	73	151
Jim Thorpe	71	80	151
Trevor Dodds	77	75	152
John Huston	76	76	152
Gil Morgan	79	73	152
John Morse	77	75	152
Tim Simpson	79	73	152
Craig Stadler	78	74	152
Ian Woosnam	77	75	152
Todd Barranger	76	77	153
Willy Burnitz	79	74	153
Darren Clarke	78	75	153
Nolan Henke	75	78	153
Arden Knoll	77	76	153
Marty Schiene	74	79	153
Mike Small	77	76	153
Howard Twitty	78	75	153
Brian Craig	73	81	154
John Daly	81	73	154
Mark Mielke	80	74	154
Mick Soli	78	76	154
P.H. Horgan III	79	76	155
Brian Kamm	79	76	155
Frank Lickliter, Jr.	79	76	155
*Duke Delcher	78	78	156
Mike Grant	80	76	156
Chris Haarlow	82	74	156
Gary Hallberg	78	78	156
*John Harris	79	77	156
Ian Baker-Finch	83	74	157
Johnny Miller	81	76	157
*Randy Sonnier	82	75	157
Bart Bryant	76	82	158
Packard Dewitt	80	78	158
Douglas DuChateau	79	79	158
Arnold Palmer	77	81	158
Javier Sanchez	79	80	159
*Craig Barlow	80	80	160
Thomas Garner	79	81	160
Mark Mason	83	77	160
Scott Medlin	79	82	161
*Joey Ferrari	82	79	161
Michael Weeks	83	83	166
Rocco Mediate	76	70	WD
Michael Allen	77		DQ
David Lundstrom	80		WD
Chris Patton			WD

(Professionals who did not complete 72 holes received $1,000.)

Canon Greater Hartford Open

TPC at River Highlands, Cromwell, Connecticut
Par 35-35—70; 6,820 yards

June 23-26
purse, $1,200,000

	SCORES				TOTAL	MONEY
David Frost	65	68	66	69	268	$216,000
Greg Norman	69	65	66	69	269	129,600
Corey Pavin	65	73	66	67	271	57,600
Dave Stockton, Jr.	66	66	67	72	271	57,600
Steve Stricker	70	67	67	67	271	57,600
Dave Barr	68	70	68	65	271	57,600
Kirk Triplett	71	66	69	67	273	38,700
Wayne Levi	68	66	71	68	273	38,700
Mike Reid	66	68	69	72	275	28,800
John Cook	71	67	64	73	275	28,800
Glen Day	72	65	70	68	275	28,800
Clark Dennis	65	72	66	72	275	28,800
Ken Green	69	70	68	68	275	28,800
Peter Jacobsen	68	68	70	69	275	28,800
Kenny Perry	67	68	69	72	276	19,200
Mike Standly	70	71	64	71	276	19,200
Doug Tewell	67	68	70	71	276	19,200
Fred Couples	71	68	71	66	276	19,200
Brad Faxon	71	69	64	72	276	19,200
Larry Silveira	67	73	71	66	277	15,000
Steve Lowery	71	66	70	70	277	15,000
Ted Tryba	68	66	69	75	278	12,000
Rocky Walcher	69	69	72	68	278	12,000
Tom Byrum	69	68	69	72	278	12,000
Scott Hoch	69	67	68	74	278	12,000
Fuzzy Zoeller	72	64	73	70	279	8,520
Brandel Chamblee	71	68	66	74	279	8,520
Jay Delsing	74	67	69	69	279	8,520
David Feherty	73	68	69	69	279	8,520
Ed Humenik	69	70	69	71	279	8,520
Brian Kamm	75	66	69	69	279	8,520
Phil Mickelson	65	72	70	72	279	8,520
Trevor Dodds	71	69	70	70	280	6,205.72
Andrew Magee	69	71	69	71	280	6,205.72
Gil Morgan	68	73	68	71	280	6,205.72
Nick Price	70	70	67	73	280	6,205.71
Mike Springer	73	67	67	73	280	6,205.71
Peter Jordan	66	71	68	75	280	6,205.71
Mark O'Meara	67	72	69	72	280	6,205.71
Dillard Pruitt	70	71	64	76	281	4,440
Gene Sauers	73	68	66	74	281	4,440
Scott Simpson	70	68	69	74	281	4,440
Jeff Sluman	70	71	71	69	281	4,440
Roger Maltbie	68	70	67	76	281	4,440
Yoshinori Mizumaki	70	70	69	72	281	4,440
John Morse	69	69	71	72	281	4,440
Mike Sullivan	69	68	74	71	282	3,228
Ed Dougherty	71	70	72	69	282	3,228
Dudley Hart	69	69	72	72	282	3,228
Brian Henninger	69	71	72	70	282	3,228
Ty Armstrong	71	70	68	74	283	2,862
John Elliott	72	69	71	71	283	2,862
Dan Forsman	70	70	71	72	283	2,862
Morris Hatalsky	69	72	68	74	283	2,862

	SCORES			TOTAL	MONEY
David Toms	66	68	74	76	284	2,700
Michael Allen	72	69	72	71	284	2,700
Billy Andrade	71	69	69	75	284	2,700
Guy Boros	69	71	72	72	284	2,700
Steve Brodie	73	68	72	71	284	2,700
Paul Goydos	71	70	67	76	284	2,700
Bill Britton	72	65	70	78	285	2,604
Olin Browne	74	67	72	72	285	2,604
Greg Kraft	66	71	73	76	286	2,568
Mark Wurtz	69	69	72	77	287	2,532
Steve Elkington	66	73	75	73	287	2,532
Esteban Toledo	69	70	76	73	288	2,484
Chip Beck	70	70	69	79	288	2,484
Naomichi Ozaki	69	70	71	79	289	2,448
Brad Lardon	72	69	71	78	290	2,424
Chris Kite	68	71	74	79	292	2,400

Motorola Western Open

Cog Hill Golf & Country Club, Lemont, Illinois
Par 36-36—72; 7,073 yards

June 30-July 3
purse, $1,200,000

	SCORES			TOTAL	MONEY
Nick Price	67	67	72	71	277	$216,000
Greg Kraft	67	70	68	73	278	129,600
Mark Calcavecchia	67	70	72	70	279	62,400
Bill Glasson	66	70	72	71	279	62,400
Scott Hoch	67	69	73	70	279	62,400
Kelly Gibson	69	72	72	67	280	41,700
Jeff Sluman	68	69	69	74	280	41,700
David Duval	73	70	70	68	281	28,000
David Frost	71	68	74	68	281	28,000
Jim Gallagher, Jr.	72	68	68	73	281	28,000
Andrew Magee	71	70	69	71	281	28,000
Tom Purtzer	68	72	73	68	281	28,000
Larry Silveira	73	71	68	69	281	28,000
Doug Tewell	69	72	71	69	281	28,000
Jim Thorpe	71	72	71	67	281	28,000
Mark Wurtz	70	70	70	71	281	28,000
Rob Boldt	69	71	72	70	282	14,667.67
Brad Bryant	70	72	70	70	282	14,667.67
Bob Estes	68	73	70	71	282	14,667.67
John Mahaffey	71	72	72	67	282	14,667.67
Mike Standly	70	72	73	67	282	14,667.67
Scott Verplank	71	72	72	67	282	14,667.67
Peter Jacobsen	71	69	71	71	282	14,667.66
Jeff Maggert	70	70	71	71	282	14,667.66
Tom Watson	69	68	73	72	282	14,667.66
Fred Couples	68	71	69	75	283	8,800
Morris Hatalsky	72	71	72	68	283	8,800
Justin Leonard	70	69	74	70	283	8,800
Sean Murphy	66	72	74	71	283	8,800
Craig Stadler	71	73	68	71	283	8,800
John Flannery	70	73	71	70	284	7,116
Tom Kite	69	70	72	73	284	7,116
Bob Lohr	69	73	71	71	284	7,116
Mark McCumber	69	71	74	70	284	7,116

		SCORES			TOTAL	MONEY
Yoshinori Mizumaki	73	69	70	72	284	7,116
Michael Allen	69	73	72	71	285	5,166.67
Dave Barr	69	74	70	72	285	5,166.67
Ben Crenshaw	68	73	72	72	285	5,166.67
Clark Dennis	70	71	72	72	285	5,166.67
Mark O'Meara	68	74	71	72	285	5,166.67
Joey Rassett	72	72	68	73	285	5,166.67
Bob Gilder	66	71	72	76	285	5,166.66
Steve Lamontagne	67	73	71	74	285	5,166.66
Ted Tryba	70	70	72	73	285	5,166.66
Olin Browne	70	70	74	72	286	3,363.43
Curt Byrum	70	70	71	75	286	3,363.43
Bill Kratzert	69	70	71	76	286	3,363.43
Jodie Mudd	71	73	71	71	286	3,363.43
David Ogrin	70	72	70	74	286	3,363.43
Scott Simpson	72	70	74	70	286	3,363.43
Glen Day	70	67	75	74	286	3,363.42
Ed Fiori	71	72	73	71	287	2,856
Tom Lehman	71	73	71	72	287	2,856
Andy Bean	67	71	80	70	288	2,676
Steve Elkington	69	74	73	72	288	2,676
Brian Henninger	74	70	68	76	288	2,676
Hale Irwin	72	70	73	73	288	2,676
Larry Mize	69	67	76	76	288	2,676
Steve Pate	73	71	72	72	288	2,676
Steve Rintoul	73	70	77	68	288	2,676
Joey Sindelar	72	72	73	71	288	2,676
Curtis Strange	70	74	74	70	288	2,676
Dave Rummells	67	71	74	76	288	2,676
Brian Claar	71	73	74	71	289	2,520
Phil Mickelson	66	69	77	77	289	2,520
Steve Stricker	69	75	73	72	289	2,520
Russ Cochran	71	73	71	75	290	2,400
Ed Dougherty	72	72	76	70	290	2,400
Joel Edwards	71	72	76	71	290	2,400
Robin Freeman	73	71	73	73	290	2,400
Tim Simpson	72	71	79	68	290	2,400
Phil Tataurangi	70	74	73	73	290	2,400
Steve Brodie	71	72	77	70	290	2,400
Robert Gamez	72	68	75	76	291	2,268
Tom Garner	74	70	76	71	291	2,268
John Huston	66	75	74	76	291	2,268
Dennis Paulson	71	72	73	75	291	2,268
Dan Forsman	70	69	72	81	292	2,196
D.A. Weibring	69	75	74	74	292	2,196
Peter Jordan	74	69	72	78	293	2,136
Brian Kamm	72	71	78	72	293	2,136
Hal Sutton	71	69	80	73	293	2,136
Ken Green	70	74	71	80	295	2,088
Jim McGovern	73	71	79	73	296	2,064
Paul Goydos	70	74	76	77	297	2,040

Anheuser-Busch Classic

Kingsmill Golf Club, Riverside Course, Williamsburg, Virginia   July 7-10
Par 36-35—71; 6,797 yards   purse, $1,100,000

	SCORES				TOTAL	MONEY
Mark McCumber	67	69	65	66	267	$198,000
Glen Day	64	68	72	66	270	118,800
Justin Leonard	67	69	67	69	272	74,800
Michael Bradley	68	69	69	67	273	45,466.67
John Wilson	64	70	72	67	273	45,466.67
Scott Verplank	71	69	66	67	273	45,466.66
Jay Haas	69	73	65	67	274	34,283.34
Tommy Armour III	69	71	67	67	274	34,283.33
Bob Lohr	61	68	73	72	274	34,283.33
Jim Furyk	70	70	66	69	275	28,600
Yoshinori Mizumaki	68	70	70	67	275	28,600
Ken Green	67	69	71	69	276	24,200
Mike Hulbert	68	70	67	71	276	24,200
Bobby Clampett	70	70	70	67	277	18,700
Ben Crenshaw	71	67	70	69	277	18,700
Scott Hoch	65	72	70	70	277	18,700
Kenny Perry	70	69	68	70	277	18,700
Tom Purtzer	66	69	70	72	277	18,700
Ty Armstrong	68	70	69	71	278	14,300
Stan Utley	67	71	71	69	278	14,300
Richard Zokol	69	69	69	71	278	14,300
Keith Fergus	69	71	74	65	279	9,411.12
Ronnie Black	67	69	74	69	279	9,411.11
Steve Lamontagne	68	69	69	73	279	9,411.11
John Mahaffey	69	71	70	69	279	9,411.11
Joey Sindelar	71	70	68	70	279	9,411.11
Hal Sutton	68	72	70	69	279	9,411.11
Ted Tryba	74	68	69	68	279	9,411.11
Robert Wrenn	69	69	71	70	279	9,411.11
Mark Wurtz	69	73	64	73	279	9,411.11
Gene Sauers	68	72	71	69	280	6,238.58
Joe Dailey	69	70	69	72	280	6,238.57
Ed Dougherty	66	75	70	69	280	6,238.57
Kelly Gibson	74	67	68	71	280	6,238.57
P.H. Horgan III	71	69	69	71	280	6,238.57
Charles Raulerson	70	72	69	69	280	6,238.57
Steve Stricker	68	68	72	72	280	6,238.57
J.C. Anderson	69	70	69	73	281	4,400
Russell Beiersdorf	69	68	72	72	281	4,400
Jay Don Blake	70	72	70	69	281	4,400
Bill Britton	69	73	70	69	281	4,400
Jim Gallagher, Jr.	69	71	72	69	281	4,400
Brian Henninger	73	69	68	71	281	4,400
Davis Love III	68	69	74	70	281	4,400
Doug Tewell	71	68	72	70	281	4,400
Todd Barranger	72	67	75	68	282	2,992
Brian Claar	72	70	70	70	282	2,992
Robin Freeman	71	71	69	71	282	2,992
Brad Lardon	72	66	74	70	282	2,992
Dennis Paulson	67	73	72	70	282	2,992
Clarence Rose	67	71	72	72	282	2,992
Rob Boldt	68	72	71	72	283	2,552
Skip Kendall	71	69	74	69	283	2,552
Naomichi Ozaki	66	71	75	71	283	2,552

		SCORES			TOTAL	MONEY
Dillard Pruitt	72	67	74	70	283	2,552
Dave Stockton, Jr.	72	69	68	74	283	2,552
Curtis Strange	70	69	76	68	283	2,552
Michael Allen	72	69	71	72	284	2,431
Brandel Chamblee	71	70	73	70	284	2,431
John Flannery	72	70	67	75	284	2,431
Bill Kratzert	72	70	73	69	284	2,431
Steve Gotsche	71	70	74	70	285	2,376
Chris Kite	72	70	69	75	286	2,321
Larry Rinker	71	68	79	68	286	2,321
Steve Rintoul	70	72	71	73	286	2,321
Lance Ten Broeck	68	73	71	74	286	2,321
Brad Bryant	73	69	73	72	287	2,255
Don Reese	74	68	73	72	287	2,255
Vance Heafner	73	67	73	75	288	2,189
John Inman	71	70	75	72	288	2,189
Ron Streck	70	72	73	73	288	2,189
Jim Thorpe	69	73	73	73	288	2,189

Deposit Guaranty Classic

Annadale Golf Club, Madison, Mississippi
Par 36-36—72; 7,157 yards
(Third and fourth rounds cancelled — rain.)

July 14-17
purse, $700,000

	SCORES		TOTAL	MONEY
Brian Henninger	67	68	135	$126,000
Mike Sullivan	66	69	135	75,600
(Henninger defeated Sullivan on first extra hole.)				
Tommy Armour III	71	65	136	31,570
Guy Boros	69	67	136	31,570
Chris DiMarco	70	66	136	31,570
Scott Hoch	69	67	136	31,570
Dave Stockton, Jr.	69	67	136	31,570
Bobby Clampett	68	69	137	20,300
Dicky Pride	73	64	137	20,300
Stan Utley	67	70	137	20,300
Mike Brisky	66	72	138	14,840
Curt Byrum	66	72	138	14,840
Brandel Chamblee	66	72	138	14,840
Ernie Gonzalez	68	70	138	14,840
Chris Perry	68	70	138	14,840
John Flannery	68	71	139	10,850
Hal Sutton	70	69	139	10,850
Leonard Thompson	71	68	139	10,850
Esteban Toledo	71	68	139	10,850
Bobby Wadkins	71	69	140	7,583.34
Jeff Woodland	68	72	140	7,583.34
Russell Beiersdorf	70	70	140	7,583.33
Steve Lamontagne	71	69	140	7,583.33
Ed Sneed	73	67	140	7,583.33
Scott Verplank	69	71	140	7,583.33
David Ogrin	69	72	141	4,569.10
Phil Blackmar	71	70	141	4,569.09
Marco Dawson	71	70	141	4,569.09
Brad Fabel	69	72	141	4,569.09
Keith Fergus	69	72	141	4,569.09

	SCORES				TOTAL	MONEY
Bruce Fleisher	69	72			141	4,569.09
Robin Freeman	72	69			141	4,569.09
Shaun Micheel	72	69			141	4,569.09
David Peoples	72	69			141	4,569.09
Kenny Perry	72	69			141	4,569.09
Don Reese	70	71			141	4,569.09
Todd Barranger	72	70			142	2,597.54
Patrick Burke	71	71			142	2,597.54
Tom Byrum	71	71			142	2,597.54
Clark Dennis	70	72			142	2,597.54
Bob Gilder	70	72			142	2,597.54
Donnie Hammond	70	72			142	2,597.54
Steve Lowery	70	72			142	2,597.54
Dillard Pruitt	74	68			142	2,597.54
Tony Sills	71	71			142	2,597.54
David Toms	74	68			142	2,597.54
John Wilson	71	71			142	2,597.54
Brad Lardon	70	72			142	2,597.53
Harry Taylor	72	70			142	2,597.53
Ty Armstrong	69	74			143	1,618.17
Rob Boldt	72	71			143	1,618.17
Olin Browne	69	74			143	1,618.17
John Elliott	66	77			143	1,618.17
Joe Inman	72	71			143	1,618.17
Steve Rintoul	74	69			143	1,618.17
Gene Sauers	72	71			143	1,618.17
Lance Ten Broeck	73	70			143	1,618.17
Chad Ginn	72	71			143	1,618.16
P.H. Horgan III	73	70			143	1,618.16
Kenny Knox	73	70			143	1,618.16
Rocky Walcher	72	71			143	1,618.16
John Adams	73	71			144	1,435
Steve Brodie	72	72			144	1,435
Brian Claar	72	72			144	1,435
Russ Cochran	72	72			144	1,435
Frank Conner	72	72			144	1,435
Jon Diggetts	73	71			144	1,435
Steve Gotsche	73	71			144	1,435
Mark Pfeil	70	74			144	1,435
Dave Rummells	73	71			144	1,435
Grant Waite	75	69			144	1,435
Jim Woodward	71	73			144	1,435
Richard Zokol	73	71			144	1,435

New England Classic

Pleasant Valley Country Club, Sutton, Massachusetts
Par 36-35—71; 7,110 yards

July 21-24
purse, $1,000,000

	SCORES				TOTAL	MONEY
Kenny Perry	67	66	70	65	268	$180,000
David Feherty	65	69	68	67	269	108,000
Ed Fiori	66	66	70	70	272	68,000
Chris DiMarco	67	68	70	68	273	48,000
Steve Gotsche	68	70	69	67	274	40,000
Billy Downes	71	68	69	67	275	33,500
Fred Funk	68	66	75	66	275	33,500

		SCORES			TOTAL	MONEY
Justin Leonard	69	68	70	68	275	33,500
Bill Glasson	68	68	71	69	276	23,142.86
Ken Green	68	72	68	68	276	23,142.86
Jeff Maggert	68	69	71	68	276	23,142.86
Blaine McCallister	68	73	69	66	276	23,142.86
Francis Quinn	67	72	66	71	276	23,142.86
Guy Boros	65	69	70	72	276	23,142.85
Wayne Levi	66	71	68	71	276	23,142.85
John Adams	71	68	72	66	277	14,500
Mark Calcavecchia	68	71	69	69	277	14,500
Lennie Clements	70	69	71	67	277	14,500
Brad Faxon	70	70	71	66	277	14,500
Donnie Hammond	70	69	71	67	277	14,500
Dick Mast	66	69	70	72	277	14,500
Tommy Armour III	66	69	72	71	278	9,600
Jim Furyk	71	69	71	67	278	9,600
Paul Goydos	72	67	70	69	278	9,600
Dave Rummells	71	70	68	69	278	9,600
Gene Sauers	70	69	72	67	278	9,600
Bob Lohr	68	72	68	71	279	7,400
Tony Sills	67	72	72	68	279	7,400
Jeff Sluman	70	71	71	67	279	7,400
Trevor Dodds	71	69	70	70	280	5,688.89
Jay Haas	73	68	70	69	280	5,688.89
Morris Hatalsky	66	72	73	69	280	5,688.89
P.H. Horgan III	68	69	71	72	280	5,688.89
John Morse	70	70	69	71	280	5,688.89
Dennis Paulson	66	73	71	70	280	5,688.89
Greg Twiggs	70	71	67	72	280	5,688.89
Robert Wrenn	71	70	69	70	280	5,688.89
Michael Bradley	71	65	73	71	280	5,688.88
Brad Bryant	70	71	70	70	281	3,512.73
Bobby Clampett	71	70	71	69	281	3,512.73
Steve Elkington	72	69	73	67	281	3,512.73
Bob Gilder	73	68	74	66	281	3,512.73
Eddie Kirby	70	71	70	70	281	3,512.73
Kenny Knox	70	71	68	72	281	3,512.73
Sean Murphy	71	70	70	70	281	3,512.73
Sam Randolph	69	72	69	71	281	3,512.73
Ronnie Black	65	70	72	74	281	3,512.72
Leonard Thompson	67	72	74	68	281	3,512.72
Mark Wurtz	64	73	73	71	281	3,512.72
Olin Browne	70	71	72	69	282	2,348.89
Curt Byrum	66	73	73	70	282	2,348.89
Jay Delsing	70	69	73	70	282	2,348.89
Joel Edwards	69	72	71	70	282	2,348.89
Robin Freeman	69	72	72	69	282	2,348.89
Brad Lardon	68	73	67	74	282	2,348.89
Mark Lye	69	72	69	72	282	2,348.89
David Toms	72	68	71	71	282	2,348.89
Jim Thorpe	67	72	75	68	282	2,348.88
Billy Andrade	69	70	71	73	283	2,200
Larry Rinker	68	71	72	72	283	2,200
Stan Utley	71	68	71	73	283	2,200
Mike Donald	70	70	73	71	284	2,150
Bob Estes	66	75	70	73	284	2,150
Brian Henninger	64	74	72	75	285	2,060
Mike Hulbert	71	70	71	73	285	2,060
Steve Lamontagne	69	70	73	73	285	2,060
Billy Mayfair	72	69	72	72	285	2,060

	SCORES				TOTAL	MONEY
Steve Pate	71	69	74	71	285	2,060
Payne Stewart	70	70	75	70	285	2,060
Lance Ten Broeck	70	68	75	72	285	2,060
Mike Brisky	71	70	73	72	286	1,980
Billy Ray Brown	69	69	77	72	287	1,950
Tommy Moore	70	71	70	76	287	1,950
Dana Quigley	70	71	72	76	289	1,920

Federal Express St. Jude Classic

TPC at Southwind, Memphis, Tennessee   July 28-31
Par 36-35—71; 7,006 yards   purse, $1,100,000

	SCORES				TOTAL	MONEY
Dicky Pride	66	67	67	67	267	$225,000
Gene Sauers	67	66	68	66	267	110,000
Hal Sutton	67	68	68	64	267	110,000
(Pride defeated Sauers and Sutton on first extra hole.)						
Nick Price	72	66	66	64	268	60,000
Dave Barr	66	69	67	67	269	45,625
Russ Cochran	67	68	65	69	269	45,625
Wayne Grady	70	66	67	66	269	45,625
Paul Stankowski	68	67	69	66	270	37,500
Fuzzy Zoeller	66	65	70	69	270	37,500
Brian Claar	69	67	68	67	271	28,750
John Cook	67	70	65	69	271	28,750
Jim Gallagher, Jr.	71	68	65	67	271	28,750
Gil Morgan	70	67	63	71	271	28,750
Duffy Waldorf	67	70	67	67	271	28,750
Chris DiMarco	67	73	65	67	272	20,625
Jay Haas	67	66	68	71	272	20,625
Craig Parry	73	65	66	68	272	20,625
Payne Stewart	66	68	69	69	272	20,625
John Adams	71	67	65	70	273	15,150
Peter Jacobsen	68	70	67	68	273	15,150
David Ogrin	70	70	66	67	273	15,150
Mike Reid	72	67	67	67	273	15,150
Doug Tewell	69	66	68	70	273	15,150
Robin Freeman	71	68	69	66	274	9,671.88
Jim Furyk	68	69	70	67	274	9,671.88
Bob Gilder	69	71	66	68	274	9,671.88
Ken Green	67	67	75	65	274	9,671.88
Lennie Clements	73	66	65	70	274	9,671.87
Bob Estes	72	67	63	72	274	9,671.87
Mike Hulbert	70	65	70	69	274	9,671.87
Mark McCumber	70	66	68	70	274	9,671.87
John Huston	67	71	72	65	275	7,396.67
Jodie Mudd	70	68	71	66	275	7,396.67
Bob Lohr	70	68	70	67	275	7,396.66
Billy Andrade	71	69	69	67	276	5,901.43
Donnie Hammond	69	67	72	68	276	5,901.43
Morris Hatalsky	68	68	73	67	276	5,901.43
Loren Roberts	68	71	72	65	276	5,901.43
Tony Sills	70	64	72	70	276	5,901.43
Jim Woodward	67	70	71	68	276	5,901.43
Steve Pate	70	68	67	71	276	5,901.42
Joel Edwards	69	69	67	72	277	4,625

	SCORES				TOTAL	MONEY
Scott Hoch	71	67	70	69	277	4,625
Kirk Triplett	70	69	69	69	277	4,625
Tom Purtzer	69	68	73	68	278	3,503.58
Steve Brodie	71	68	66	73	278	3,503.57
Jay Delsing	68	67	71	72	278	3,503.57
Neal Lancaster	71	65	73	69	278	3,503.57
Yoshinori Mizumaki	71	69	70	68	278	3,503.57
Steve Rintoul	69	70	68	71	278	3,503.57
Grant Waite	75	65	69	69	278	3,503.57
Michael Allen	71	69	67	72	279	2,915
Phil Blackmar	69	71	70	69	279	2,915
David Feherty	70	68	74	67	279	2,915
Bill Glasson	70	70	68	71	279	2,915
David Peoples	71	68	68	72	279	2,915
Peter Jordan	67	72	71	70	280	2,825
Guy Boros	70	70	71	70	281	2,775
Michael Bradley	67	70	74	70	281	2,775
Bob Tway	71	68	71	71	281	2,775
Tom Sieckmann	72	67	73	70	282	2,712.50
Howard Twitty	69	71	74	68	282	2,712.50
John Inman	71	69	73	71	284	2,625
Dan Pohl	68	69	75	72	284	2,625
Ted Schulz	66	69	73	76	284	2,625
Larry Silveira	70	69	73	72	284	2,625
Stan Utley	72	67	75	70	284	2,625
Trevor Dodds	67	73	73	73	286	2,537.50
John Mahaffey	73	67	73	73	286	2,537.50
Robert Gamez	67	73	72	77	289	2,500

Buick Open

Warwick Hills Golf & Country Club, Grand Blanc, Michigan
Par 36-36—72; 7,105 yards

August 4-7
purse, $1,100,000

	SCORES				TOTAL	MONEY
Fred Couples	72	65	65	68	270	$198,000
Corey Pavin	66	65	70	71	272	118,800
Greg Kraft	71	72	67	66	276	57,200
Steve Pate	71	67	69	69	276	57,200
Curtis Strange	71	70	67	68	276	57,200
Keith Clearwater	71	67	69	70	277	38,225
Ben Crenshaw	72	68	69	68	277	38,225
Fred Funk	65	70	71	72	278	31,900
Tom Lehman	71	67	70	70	278	31,900
Duffy Waldorf	69	67	74	68	278	31,900
Steve Elkington	71	68	69	71	279	22,550
Nick Faldo	70	67	73	69	279	22,550
Tom Kite	69	68	72	70	279	22,550
Davis Love III	69	67	72	71	279	22,550
Dennis Paulson	70	71	67	71	279	22,550
Tom Purtzer	69	71	65	74	279	22,550
Chip Beck	70	71	70	69	280	16,500
Peter Jacobsen	69	71	71	69	280	16,500
Hal Sutton	70	71	69	70	280	16,500
David Feherty	71	71	70	69	281	11,916.67
Kenny Knox	71	72	69	69	281	11,916.67
David Ogrin	71	71	71	68	281	11,916.67

	SCORES				TOTAL	MONEY
Ted Tryba	71	70	70	70	281	11,916.67
Gil Morgan	73	68	70	70	281	11,916.66
Howard Twitty	69	70	68	74	281	11,916.66
Joel Edwards	70	73	71	68	282	8,635
Fuzzy Zoeller	70	71	71	70	282	8,635
Guy Boros	72	68	73	70	283	7,005.63
Yoshinori Mizumaki	69	69	73	72	283	7,005.63
Mike Reid	71	69	73	70	283	7,005.63
John Wilson	70	68	73	72	283	7,005.63
Brad Faxon	72	71	72	68	283	7,005.62
David Frost	70	71	68	74	283	7,005.62
Paul Goydos	71	72	71	69	283	7,005.62
Kenny Perry	72	69	69	73	283	7,005.62
Jay Don Blake	69	70	73	72	284	4,957.86
Jim Furyk	71	69	72	72	284	4,957.86
Craig Parry	69	69	74	72	284	4,957.86
David Toms	72	71	70	71	284	4,957.86
Bobby Wadkins	73	69	70	72	284	4,957.86
Curt Byrum	73	70	74	67	284	4,957.85
Ken Green	72	70	75	67	284	4,957.85
Robin Freeman	70	70	76	69	285	3,850
Sandy Lyle	70	73	71	71	285	3,850
D.A. Weibring	70	72	71	72	285	3,850
Dave Barr	69	74	70	73	286	3,118.50
Ed Fiori	71	71	75	69	286	3,118.50
Eddie Kirby	72	68	76	70	286	3,118.50
Larry Mize	76	66	70	74	286	3,118.50
Billy Mayfair	72	71	76	68	287	2,772
Chris DiMarco	75	66	73	74	288	2,604.80
Dan Forsman	75	66	76	71	288	2,604.80
Wayne Levi	72	70	75	71	288	2,604.80
Larry Silveira	72	70	74	72	288	2,604.80
Esteban Toledo	69	70	73	76	288	2,604.80
Olin Browne	71	69	74	75	289	2,486
Sean Murphy	70	73	76	70	289	2,486
Richard Zokol	72	70	76	71	289	2,486
Mike Heinen	71	70	70	79	290	2,420
Sam Torrance	75	68	74	73	290	2,420
Rocky Walcher	73	70	73	74	290	2,420
Jay Delsing	72	71	74	75	292	2,365
Brian Kamm	70	72	72	78	292	2,365
Grant Waite	72	71	76	74	293	2,332
John Traub	72	71	77	78	298	2,310

PGA Championship

Southern Hills Country Club, Tulsa, Oklahoma
Par 35-35—70; 6,834 yards

August 11-14
purse, $1,700,000

	SCORES				TOTAL	MONEY
Nick Price	67	65	70	67	269	$310,000
Corey Pavin	70	67	69	69	275	160,000
Phil Mickelson	68	71	67	70	276	110,000
Nick Faldo	73	67	71	66	277	76,666.67
Greg Norman	71	69	67	70	277	76,666.67
John Cook	71	67	69	70	277	76,666.66
Steve Elkington	73	70	66	69	278	57,500

	SCORES				TOTAL	MONEY
Jose Maria Olazabal	72	66	70	70	278	57,500
Ben Crenshaw	70	67	70	72	279	41,000
Tom Kite	72	68	69	70	279	41,000
Loren Roberts	69	72	67	71	279	41,000
Tom Watson	69	72	67	71	279	41,000
Ian Woosnam	68	72	73	66	279	41,000
Jay Haas	71	66	68	75	280	32,000
Glen Day	70	69	70	72	281	27,000
Mark McNulty	72	68	70	71	281	27,000
Larry Mize	72	72	67	70	281	27,000
Kirk Triplett	71	69	71	70	281	27,000
Bill Glasson	71	73	68	70	282	18,666.67
Mark McCumber	73	70	71	68	282	18,666.67
Craig Stadler	70	70	74	68	282	18,666.67
Curtis Strange	73	71	68	70	282	18,666.67
Craig Parry	70	69	70	73	282	18,666.66
Fuzzy Zoeller	69	71	72	70	282	18,666.66
Ernie Els	68	71	69	75	283	13,000
David Frost	70	71	69	73	283	13,000
Barry Lane	70	73	68	72	283	13,000
Bernhard Langer	73	71	67	72	283	13,000
Jeff Sluman	70	72	66	75	283	13,000
Brad Faxon	72	73	73	66	284	8,458.34
Richard Zokol	77	67	67	73	284	8,458.34
Bob Boyd	72	71	70	71	284	8,458.33
Lennie Clements	74	70	69	71	284	8,458.33
Wayne Grady	75	68	71	70	284	8,458.33
Sam Torrance	69	75	69	71	284	8,458.33
Chip Beck	72	70	72	71	285	7,000
Blaine McCallister	74	64	75	72	285	7,000
Colin Montgomerie	67	76	70	72	285	7,000
Fred Couples	68	74	75	69	286	6,030
Hale Irwin	75	69	68	74	286	6,030
Tom Lehman	73	71	68	74	286	6,030
Billy Mayfair	73	72	71	70	286	6,030
Gil Morgan	71	68	73	74	286	6,030
David Edwards	72	70	74	71	287	5,200
David Gilford	69	73	73	72	287	5,200
Neal Lancaster	73	72	72	70	287	5,200
Fulton Allem	74	67	74	73	288	4,112.50
Billy Andrade	71	71	78	68	288	4,112.50
Bob Estes	72	71	72	73	288	4,112.50
Greg Kraft	74	69	70	75	288	4,112.50
Andrew Magee	70	74	71	73	288	4,112.50
Frank Nobilo	72	67	74	75	288	4,112.50
Masashi Ozaki	71	69	72	76	288	4,112.50
D.A. Weibring	69	73	70	76	288	4,112.50
Kenny Perry	78	67	70	74	289	3,158.34
Mike Springer	77	66	69	77	289	3,158.34
Tom Dolby	73	68	75	73	289	3,158.33
Fred Funk	76	69	72	72	289	3,158.33
Dudley Hart	72	71	75	71	289	3,158.33
Hal Sutton	76	69	72	72	289	3,158.33
Bruce Fleisher	75	68	72	75	290	2,800
Raymond Floyd	69	76	73	72	290	2,800
Ron McDougal	76	69	72	73	290	2,800
Tsuneyuki Nakajima	73	71	74	72	290	2,800
Lanny Wadkins	69	73	73	75	290	2,800
Jay Don Blake	72	71	74	74	291	2,600
John Inman	70	72	73	76	291	2,600

	SCORES				TOTAL	MONEY
Lee Janzen	73	71	73	74	291	2,600
Todd Smith	74	69	71	77	291	2,600
Payne Stewart	72	73	72	74	291	2,600
Donnie Hammond	74	69	76	73	292	2,512.50
Peter Senior	74	71	70	77	292	2,512.50
Sandy Lyle	75	70	76	76	297	2,462.50
Dicky Pride	75	69	73	80	297	2,462.50
Brian Henninger	77	65	78	78	298	2,412.50
Hajime Meshiai	74	71	74	79	298	2,412.50

Out of Final 36 Holes

Bob Ackerman	72	74	146
Brad Bryant	76	70	146
Mark Calcavecchia	74	72	146
John Daly	73	73	146
Jim Gallagher, Jr.	77	69	146
Tony Johnstone	75	71	146
Davis Love III	73	73	146
John Mahaffey	72	74	146
Larry Nelson	75	71	146
Jeff Roth	73	73	146
Peter Baker	76	71	147
Dave Barr	71	76	147
Anders Forsbrand	73	74	147
Mike Gove	72	75	147
Joakim Haeggman	72	75	147
Nolan Henke	72	75	147
Scott Hoch	74	73	147
Mark James	71	76	147
Darrell Kestner	73	74	147
Jim McGovern	73	74	147
Ted Tryba	74	73	147
Ian Baker-Finch	74	74	148
Mark Brooks	78	70	148
Gary Hallberg	70	78	148
Mike Heinen	75	73	148
Scott Simpson	75	73	148
Paul Azinger	75	74	149
John Deforest	74	75	149
David Graham	75	74	149
Hubert Green	74	75	149
Steve Lowery	72	77	149
Ron Philo	76	73	149
Vijay Singh	70	79	149
Bob Tway	77	72	149
Jim White	81	68	149
John Bermel	72	78	150
Walt Chapman	75	75	150
Russ Cochran	72	78	150
Rick Fehr	71	79	150
Robert Hoyt	76	74	150
Gregg Jones	71	79	150
Bob Lohr	77	73	150
Jack Nicklaus	79	71	150
Lonnie Nielsen	73	77	150
Costantino Rocca	73	77	150
Wes Smith	72	78	150
Mel Baum	77	74	151
Denny Hepler	77	74	151

	SCORES		TOTAL
John Huston	78	73	151
John Lee	77	74	151
Rod Nuckolls	74	77	151
Brett Ogle	75	76	151
Jerry Wisz	74	77	151
Rick Acton	76	76	152
Jesper Parnevik	79	73	152
Barry Redmond	77	75	152
Bruce Zabriski	78	74	152
Thomas Gray	75	78	153
Jeff Maggert	78	75	153
Pat O'Brien	76	77	153
Pete Oakley	77	76	153
Arnold Palmer	79	74	153
Brad Sherfy	79	74	153
Seve Ballesteros	78	76	154
Kevin Cashman	75	79	154
Will Frantz	78	76	154
J.L. Lewis	77	77	154
Scott Steger	81	74	155
Tom Cleaver	77	80	157
Steve Smitha	83	74	157
Ed Terasa	78	79	157
Miguel Biamon	82	76	158
Scott Mahlberg	79	79	158
Scott Williams	77	81	158
George Bowman	87	88	175

(Professionals who did not complete 72 holes received $1,500.)

The Sprint International

Castle Pines Golf Club, Castle Rock, Colorado
Par 36-36—72; 7,559 yards

August 18-21
purse, $1,400,000

FINAL ROUND

	POINTS				TOTAL	MONEY
Steve Lowery	7	14	5	9	35	$252,000
Rick Fehr	10	5	9	11	35	151,200
(Lowery defeated Fehr on first extra hole.)						
Duffy Waldorf	7	6	8	13	34	95,200
Ernie Els	5	7	17	4	33	67,200
Tom Kite	4	12	10	6	32	56,000
John Adams	6	6	9	10	31	48,650
Chris DiMarco	4	2	14	11	31	48,650
Mark Calcavecchia	0	8	11	11	30	42,000
Dave Stockton, Jr.	6	14	5	5	30	42,000
Phil Mickelson	0	11	9	9	29	36,400
Mike Reid	14	6	5	4	29	36,400
Jay Haas	10	4	8	6	28	32,200
Tom Lehman	6	9	4	7	26	28,000
Gene Sauers	4	13	5	4	26	28,000
Lee Janzen	11	4	4	6	25	23,800
Hal Sutton	10	5	5	5	25	23,800
Ted Tryba	5	8	9	3	25	23,800
Keith Clearwater	4	9	6	5	24	20,300

	POINTS				TOTAL	MONEY
Jose Maria Olazabal	7	12	11	-6	24	20,300
Mark McNulty	8	6	5	4	23	18,200
Bruce Lietzke	16	-2	9	-1	22	16,800
Bradley Hughes	8	4	9	0	21	15,680
Steve Pate	2	6	12	-1	19	14,560
Mark Carnevale	8	0	12	-6	14	13,440

IN THE MONEY

	POINTS			TOTAL	MONEY
Richard Zokol	9	5	5	19	12,320
Brad Bryant	2	9	7	18	10,570
Dudley Hart	5	3	10	18	10,570
Roger Maltbie	-3	12	9	18	10,570
Steve Elkington	6	6	6	18	10,570
Dicky Pride	3	4	10	17	9,310
Morris Hatalsky	7	4	6	17	9,310
Fred Funk	5	4	7	16	7,580
Chip Beck	7	1	8	16	7,580
Mark Wurtz	9	2	5	16	7,580
Fulton Allem	10	-3	9	16	7,580
Ronnie Black	7	1	8	16	7,580
D.A. Weibring	-3	9	10	16	7,580
David Edwards	3	8	5	16	7,580
Bob Tway	7	4	4	15	5,880
Guy Boros	9	2	4	15	5,880
Hale Irwin	5	10	0	15	5,880
Tom Watson	-3	12	6	15	5,880
Brad Faxon	2	10	2	14	4,900
Joey Sindelar	-2	10	6	14	4,900
Lennie Clements	-1	11	4	14	4,900
Ken Green	12	1	0	13	3,808
Brett Ogle	7	3	3	13	3,808
Clark Dennis	3	7	3	13	3,808
Scott Simpson	1	5	7	13	3,808
David Peoples	2	3	8	13	3,808
Paul Stankowski	2	5	6	13	3,808
Sean Murphy	3	2	6	11	3,304
Grant Waite	6	0	5	11	3,304
Craig Parry	5	8	-2	11	3,304
David Toms	0	5	5	10	3,150
Fred Couples	11	-3	2	10	3,150
Jeff Maggert	1	8	1	10	3,150
Robin Freeman	8	2	0	10	3,150
Davis Love III	3	4	3	10	3,150
Steve Stricker	0	5	5	10	3,150
Bob Burns	3	3	3	9	3,052
Bob Estes	7	0	1	8	2,996
Willie Wood	6	1	1	8	2,996
Craig Stadler	3	4	1	8	2,996
Larry Silveira	2	7	-2	7	2,926
Ian Baker-Finch	7	-2	2	7	2,926
Brian Henninger	4	1	1	6	2,884
Tom Purtzer	-3	9	-2	4	2,842
Jay Don Blake	-2	10	-4	4	2,842
Mark Wiebe	5	1	-3	3	2,800
Dan Forsman	1	5	-5	1	2,758
Brandel Chamblee	8	1	-8	1	2,758

NEC World Series of Golf

Firestone Country Club, North Course, Akron, Ohio
Par 35-35—70; 6,918 yards

August 25-28
purse, $2,000,000

	SCORES				TOTAL	MONEY
Jose Maria Olazabal	66	67	69	67	269	$360,000
Scott Hoch	71	64	65	70	270	216,000
Brad Faxon	69	68	65	69	271	116,000
Steve Lowery	67	66	66	72	271	116,000
John Huston	73	64	64	71	272	76,000
Mark McNulty	69	68	65	70	272	76,000
Mike Heinen	71	67	65	70	273	67,000
Fred Couples	69	70	65	70	274	60,000
Greg Norman	67	67	68	72	274	60,000
Hale Irwin	70	65	71	70	276	52,000
Nick Price	68	66	69	73	276	52,000
Tom Lehman	72	69	64	72	277	40,500
Davis Love III	68	72	67	70	277	40,500
Larry Mize	69	68	68	72	277	40,500
Loren Roberts	65	70	68	74	277	40,500
Jim Gallagher, Jr.	70	68	70	70	278	30,000
Bill Glasson	71	73	64	70	278	30,000
Jeff Maggert	66	74	65	73	278	30,000
Corey Pavin	70	70	69	69	278	30,000
Craig Stadler	65	78	64	71	278	30,000
Jay Haas	75	64	70	70	279	22,400
Billy Mayfair	67	72	69	71	279	22,400
Kenny Perry	69	72	70	68	279	22,400
Tsuneyuki Nakajima	69	71	66	74	280	18,400
Craig Parry	69	69	71	71	280	18,400
Mark Brooks	71	65	69	76	281	15,110
Ernie Els	68	66	71	76	281	15,110
John Inman	70	67	69	75	281	15,110
Phil Mickelson	75	70	68	68	281	15,110
Curtis Strange	69	71	68	73	281	15,110
Neal Lancaster	70	73	69	70	282	14,400
Mark McCumber	66	67	72	77	282	14,400
Blaine McCallister	69	74	67	73	283	14,250
Andrew Magee	71	72	70	71	284	14,150
Ben Crenshaw	70	73	70	72	285	14,000
Lee Janzen	70	71	69	75	285	14,000
Fulton Allem	68	77	68	74	287	13,800
Jeff Roth	74	68	70	75	287	13,800
David Frost	67	71	75	76	289	13,650
Ikuo Shirahama	73	70	77	70	290	13,550
Mike Springer	75	68	69	80	292	13,450
Carl Mason	72	74	71	76	293	13,350
Brian Henninger	71	73	70	80	294	13,250
John Daly	69	73	70	83	295	13,150
Seiki Okuda	70	72	74	80	296	13,050
Dicky Pride	78	73	70	77	298	12,950
Ian Baker-Finch	67	82	77	76	302	12,850
Hiroshi Goda	75	78	73	80	306	12,750

Greater Milwaukee Open

Brown Deer Golf Course, Milwaukee, Wisconsin
Par 35-36—71; 6,716 yards

September 1-4
purse, $1,000,000

	SCORES				TOTAL	MONEY
Mike Springer	69	67	65	67	268	$180,000
Loren Roberts	70	63	68	68	269	108,000
Mark Calcavecchia	67	68	64	71	270	48,000
Bob Estes	67	66	65	72	270	48,000
Tom Purtzer	70	69	67	64	270	48,000
Joey Sindelar	67	68	66	69	270	48,000
Dave Barr	69	64	70	68	271	32,250
Marco Dawson	68	66	69	68	271	32,250
Mark O'Meara	68	69	67	68	272	28,000
Steve Pate	68	70	65	69	272	28,000
Jay Don Blake	68	68	66	71	273	24,000
Jay Haas	67	66	69	71	273	24,000
Michael Allen	66	72	69	67	274	18,200
Bill Britton	71	64	65	74	274	18,200
Kelly Gibson	68	68	71	67	274	18,200
John Inman	68	67	66	73	274	18,200
Tom Sieckmann	67	72	64	71	274	18,200
Mark Brooks	69	69	69	68	275	12,171.43
Mike Donald	72	68	65	70	275	12,171.43
Bruce Lietzke	71	68	66	70	275	12,171.43
Gil Morgan	71	67	68	69	275	12,171.43
Dennis Paulson	68	67	69	71	275	12,171.43
Joey Rassett	69	68	69	69	275	12,171.43
David Toms	66	69	67	73	275	12,171.42
John Flannery	69	66	73	68	276	7,975
Scott Hoch	69	70	70	67	276	7,975
Doug Tewell	70	70	65	71	276	7,975
D.A. Weibring	65	66	71	74	276	7,975
Brandel Chamblee	68	70	69	70	277	6,087.50
David Feherty	69	67	70	71	277	6,087.50
Bruce Fleisher	69	70	73	65	277	6,087.50
Roger Maltbie	69	68	70	70	277	6,087.50
David Peoples	68	69	67	73	277	6,087.50
Charles Raulerson	73	67	65	72	277	6,087.50
Howard Twitty	69	70	71	67	277	6,087.50
Duffy Waldorf	67	68	71	71	277	6,087.50
Curtis Strange	68	71	67	72	278	4,600
Steve Stricker	71	68	67	72	278	4,600
Jim Thorpe	68	69	69	72	278	4,600
David Ogrin	69	69	68	72	278	4,600
Glen Day	68	72	65	74	279	3,315.56
Dave Stockton, Jr.	71	69	70	69	279	3,315.56
Harry Taylor	72	68	70	69	279	3,315.56
Bobby Wadkins	68	71	66	74	279	3,315.56
Willie Wood	68	70	70	71	279	3,315.56
Jim Furyk	68	68	69	74	279	3,315.55
Eddie Kirby	71	69	69	70	279	3,315.55
Wayne Levi	69	71	65	74	279	3,315.55
Robert Wrenn	72	68	68	71	279	3,315.55
John Adams	71	66	68	75	280	2,362.50
Ronnie Black	70	70	71	69	280	2,362.50
Lennie Clements	71	67	68	74	280	2,362.50
Clark Dennis	70	70	68	72	280	2,362.50
Bob Gilder	69	71	67	73	280	2,362.50

	SCORES				TOTAL	MONEY
Ken Green	69	71	68	72	280	2,362.50
Tim Simpson	69	71	69	71	280	2,362.50
John Wilson	68	71	71	70	280	2,362.50
Tom Garner	71	69	67	74	281	2,210
P.H. Horgan III	68	71	70	72	281	2,210
Bill Kratzert	67	73	71	70	281	2,210
Leonard Thompson	72	68	70	71	281	2,210
Steve Brodie	70	68	67	77	282	2,120
Olin Browne	66	73	74	69	282	2,120
Tony Sills	69	71	70	72	282	2,120
Mike Standly	70	69	70	73	282	2,120
Ben Walter	71	69	71	71	282	2,120
Sean Murphy	71	69	69	74	283	2,050
Dillard Pruitt	72	68	71	72	283	2,050
Richard Zokol	69	71	70	74	284	2,020
Morris Hatalsky	70	70	70	75	285	1,980
Blaine McCallister	67	71	74	73	285	1,980
Dave Rummells	70	69	72	74	285	1,980
Brook Schmitt	72	68	77	81	298	1,940

Bell Canadian Open

Glen Abbey Golf Club, Oakville, Ontario
Par 35-37—72; 7,112 yards

September 8-11
purse, $1,300,000

	SCORES				TOTAL	MONEY
Nick Price	67	72	68	68	275	$234,000
Mark Calcavecchia	67	71	71	67	276	140,400
Tom Lehman	69	69	70	69	277	88,400
Jay Don Blake	74	63	73	68	278	57,200
Mark McCumber	74	65	67	72	278	57,200
Fulton Allem	69	69	71	70	279	43,550
Brian Kamm	71	71	69	68	279	43,550
Steve Stricker	69	70	69	71	279	43,550
Mark O'Meara	66	72	72	70	280	37,700
Bob Estes	72	73	68	68	281	32,500
Greg Kraft	72	70	70	69	281	32,500
Payne Stewart	68	72	72	69	281	32,500
Bob Tway	69	73	71	69	282	26,000
Scott Verplank	75	67	71	69	282	26,000
Rick Fehr	72	70	67	74	283	21,450
Dick Mast	66	76	74	67	283	21,450
Curtis Strange	74	68	68	73	283	21,450
Roger Wessels	68	72	72	71	283	21,450
Billy Andrade	71	69	71	73	284	15,756
Guy Boros	69	73	73	69	284	15,756
Glen Day	69	71	69	75	284	15,756
David Edwards	73	69	70	72	284	15,756
Bill Glasson	71	72	73	68	284	15,756
Phil Tataurangi	71	73	73	68	285	10,288.58
Brad Bryant	69	72	75	69	285	10,288.57
Steve Elkington	69	76	70	70	285	10,288.57
Doug Martin	70	74	69	72	285	10,288.57
Gil Morgan	69	72	69	75	285	10,288.57
Rocky Walcher	74	70	70	71	285	10,288.57
Duffy Waldorf	68	72	72	73	285	10,288.57
Keith Clearwater	69	73	72	72	286	7,215

	SCORES				TOTAL	MONEY
Clark Dennis	71	66	74	75	286	7,215
David Frost	73	69	71	73	286	7,215
Ken Green	74	70	72	70	286	7,215
Dan Halldorson	71	70	69	76	286	7,215
Mike Hulbert	73	69	71	73	286	7,215
Davis Love III	71	73	74	68	286	7,215
Phil Mickelson	69	71	71	75	286	7,215
Dave Barr	68	77	70	72	287	5,200
Fred Couples	70	70	77	70	287	5,200
Jim Furyk	69	73	72	73	287	5,200
Steve Lamontagne	70	75	71	71	287	5,200
John Morse	74	68	74	71	287	5,200
Mike Sullivan	73	72	69	73	287	5,200
Bill Kratzert	75	70	73	70	288	4,030
Jesper Parnevik	71	69	75	73	288	4,030
Howard Twitty	70	72	73	73	288	4,030
Chip Beck	72	69	73	75	289	3,307.20
Steve Lowery	71	71	72	75	289	3,307.20
Dillard Pruitt	74	71	71	73	289	3,307.20
Larry Silveira	73	70	72	74	289	3,307.20
Doug Tewell	73	72	70	74	289	3,307.20
Ted Schulz	74	71	73	72	290	2,981.34
Grant Waite	69	76	73	72	290	2,981.34
Robin Freeman	68	68	75	79	290	2,981.33
P.H. Horgan III	71	74	72	73	290	2,981.33
Larry Mize	72	71	70	77	290	2,981.33
Dennis Paulson	73	72	72	73	290	2,981.33
Brandel Chamblee	68	69	78	76	291	2,782
Bob Gilder	73	72	76	70	291	2,782
Gary Hallberg	67	76	71	77	291	2,782
Ed Humenik	72	69	76	74	291	2,782
Jeff Maggert	70	70	72	79	291	2,782
John Mahaffey	71	74	68	78	291	2,782
Bob May	69	76	75	71	291	2,782
Jodie Mudd	70	75	70	76	291	2,782
Sean Murphy	71	72	76	72	291	2,782
Olin Browne	70	75	74	74	293	2,639
Curt Byrum	71	72	74	76	293	2,639
Ronnie Black	71	74	73	77	295	2,561
Kelly Gibson	73	71	73	78	295	2,561
Lee Janzen	67	76	76	76	295	2,561
Bob Lohr	71	73	75	76	295	2,561
David Feherty	70	74	76	76	296	2,496
Ty Armstrong	71	72	76	78	297	2,457
Brad Faxon	70	75	80	72	297	2,457
Paul Stankowski	74	71	77	78	300	2,418
Mike Standly	70	72	84	80	306	2,392

B.C. Open

En-Joie Golf Club, Endicott, New York
Par 37-34—71; 6,966 yards

September 15-18
purse, $900,000

	SCORES				TOTAL	MONEY
Mike Sullivan	65	67	68	66	266	$162,000
Jeff Sluman	63	68	67	72	270	97,200
Brian Claar	68	68	65	71	272	52,200

	SCORES				TOTAL	MONEY
Mike Hulbert	67	67	68	70	272	52,200
Russell Beiersdorf	69	66	68	70	273	34,200
Curt Byrum	67	69	66	71	273	34,200
Bill Glasson	70	65	68	71	274	28,050
Paul Goydos	68	68	67	71	274	28,050
Blaine McCallister	67	70	65	72	274	28,050
Robin Freeman	68	65	69	73	275	22,500
Mike Heinen	65	70	68	72	275	22,500
P.H. Horgan III	68	67	69	71	275	22,500
Todd Barranger	65	71	69	71	276	16,875
David Edwards	66	70	71	69	276	16,875
Lee Janzen	67	67	72	70	276	16,875
Mark O'Meara	65	73	67	71	276	16,875
Brad Bryant	71	65	72	69	277	12,600
Sean Murphy	67	68	72	70	277	12,600
Steve Pate	70	68	70	69	277	12,600
Joey Rassett	71	68	67	71	277	12,600
John Wilson	71	68	69	69	277	12,600
Steve Brodie	67	71	72	68	278	8,112.86
Joel Edwards	64	72	70	72	278	8,112.86
Kelly Gibson	71	66	69	72	278	8,112.86
Eddie Kirby	71	68	69	70	278	8,112.86
Kirk Triplett	70	68	67	73	278	8,112.86
Glen Day	64	69	73	72	278	8,112.85
David Peoples	70	65	71	72	278	8,112.85
Marco Dawson	65	70	69	75	279	6,120
Bruce Fleisher	67	70	68	74	279	6,120
Greg Kraft	70	67	69	73	279	6,120
Ronnie Black	66	73	69	72	280	4,770
Keith Clearwater	69	68	72	71	280	4,770
Chris DiMarco	67	72	67	74	280	4,770
Mike Donald	70	69	70	71	280	4,770
Tom Kite	68	71	68	73	280	4,770
Steve Lamontagne	70	69	65	76	280	4,770
Neal Lancaster	69	67	72	72	280	4,770
Scott Verplank	67	69	68	76	280	4,770
Rob Boldt	70	68	68	75	281	3,420
Ed Fiori	69	68	73	71	281	3,420
Steve Jones	67	70	70	74	281	3,420
Dick Mast	68	70	73	70	281	3,420
David Ogrin	70	68	72	71	281	3,420
Howard Twitty	70	66	71	74	281	3,420
Chip Beck	67	71	71	73	282	2,494.80
Tom Byrum	65	72	71	74	282	2,494.80
Dillard Pruitt	66	73	74	69	282	2,494.80
Tony Sills	67	72	74	69	282	2,494.80
Dave Stockton, Jr.	68	69	73	72	282	2,494.80
Michael Allen	67	72	73	71	283	2,094.75
Bobby Clampett	66	72	71	74	283	2,094.75
Steve Lowery	69	69	74	71	283	2,094.75
Don Reese	71	67	73	72	283	2,094.75
Doug Tewell	71	69	71	72	283	2,094.75
Leonard Thompson	66	73	70	74	283	2,094.75
Ted Tryba	68	71	75	69	283	2,094.75
Bobby Wadkins	71	65	77	70	283	2,094.75
Jesper Parnevik	69	71	70	74	284	1,980
Esteban Toledo	69	71	72	72	284	1,980
Olin Browne	72	68	71	73	284	1,980
Guy Boros	66	74	74	71	285	1,908
Peter Jordan	67	70	69	79	285	1,908

	SCORES				TOTAL	MONEY
Tony Saraceno	69	70	76	70	285	1,908
Steve Stricker	69	71	70	75	285	1,908
Willie Wood	70	70	71	74	285	1,908
Lon Hinkle	68	72	72	74	286	1,836
Larry Silveira	69	71	71	75	286	1,836
Harry Taylor	71	68	75	72	286	1,836
Billy Andrade	70	68	70	79	287	1,782
Mike Brisky	69	70	69	79	287	1,782
John Flannery	64	72	74	77	287	1,782
Morris Hatalsky	72	67	72	78	289	1,737
Bob May	70	69	71	79	289	1,737
Tom Hearn	71	68	70	82	291	1,710

The Presidents Cup

Robert Trent Jones Golf Club, Lake Manassas, Virginia   September 16-18
Par 36-36—72; 7,238 yards

FIRST DAY
Morning Fourballs

Corey Pavin and Jeff Maggert (USA) defeated Steve Elkington and Vijay Singh
(International), 2 and 1
Jay Haas and Scott Hoch (USA) defeated Fulton Allem and David Frost (International), 6 and 5
Fred Couples and Davis Love III (USA) defeated Nick Price and Bradley Hughes
(International), 1 up
John Huston and Jim Gallagher, Jr. (USA) defeated Craig Parry and Robert Allenby
(International), 4 and 2
Tom Lehman and Phil Mickelson (USA) defeated Frank Nobilo and Peter Senior
(International), 3 and 2

Afternoon Foursomes

Hale Irwin and Loren Roberts (USA) defeated Frost and Allem (Int.), 3 and 1
Haas and Hoch (USA) defeated Parry and Tsukasa Watanabe (Int.), 4 and 3
Nobilo and Allenby (Int.) defeated Pavin and Maggert (USA), 2 and 1
Elkington and Singh (Int.) defeated Mickelson and Lehman (USA), 2 and 1
Love and Gallagher (USA) halved with Price and Mark McNulty (Int.)

SECOND DAY
Morning Fourballs

Allem and McNulty (Int.) defeated Gallagher and Huston (USA), 4 and 3
Watanabe and Singh (Int.) defeated Haas and Hoch (USA), 3 and 1
Parry and Hughes (Int.) defeated Roberts and Lehman (USA), 4 and 3
Love and Couples (USA) defeated Nobilo and Allenby (Int.), 2 up
Price and Elkington (Int.) halved with Mickelson and Pavin (USA)

Afternoon Foursomes

Frost and Senior (Int.) defeated Irwin and Haas (USA), 6 and 5
Roberts and Pavin (USA) defeated Parry and Allem (Int.), 1 up
Singh and Elkington (Int.) defeated Maggert and Huston (USA), 3 and 2
Love and Gallagher (USA) defeated Nobilo and Allenby (Int.), 7 and 5
Mickelson and Lehman (USA) defeated Hughes and McNulty (Int.), 3 and 2

THIRD DAY
Singles

Irwin (USA) defeated Allenby (Int.), 1 up
Haas (USA) defeated McNulty (Int.), 4 and 3
Gallagher (USA) defeated Watanabe (Int.), 4 and 3
Allem (Int.) halved with Mickelson (USA), 21 holes
Singh (Int.) halved with Lehman (USA), 20 holes
Senior (Int.) defeated Huston (USA), 3 and 2
Frost (Int.) halved with Hoch (USA)
Maggert (USA) defeated Hughes (Int.), 2 and 1
Nobilo (Int.) halved with Roberts (USA)
Couples (USA) defeated Price (Int.), 1 up
Love (USA) defeated Elkington (Int.), 1 up
Parry (Int.) defeated Pavin (USA), 1 up

FINAL RESULTS: United States 20, International 12

Hardee's Classic

Oakwood Country Club, Coal Valley, Illinois
Par 35-35—70; 6,755 yards

September 22-25
purse, $1,000,000

	SCORES				TOTAL	MONEY
Mark McCumber	66	67	65	67	265	$180,000
Kenny Perry	67	66	65	68	266	108,000
Mike Donald	70	66	64	67	267	58,000
David Frost	68	67	67	65	267	58,000
Russ Cochran	67	66	70	65	268	40,000
Curt Byrum	69	65	65	70	269	32,375
John Huston	71	66	67	65	269	32,375
Tom Lehman	71	67	65	66	269	32,375
Robert Wrenn	63	70	67	69	269	32,375
Michael Bradley	72	67	62	69	270	23,000
Mark Calcavecchia	66	69	69	66	270	23,000
Wayne Levi	67	70	65	68	270	23,000
Doug Tewell	65	69	69	67	270	23,000
Kirk Triplett	67	65	70	68	270	23,000
Steve Brodie	68	69	71	63	271	17,000
Billy Mayfair	73	66	65	67	271	17,000
Scott Verplank	69	71	66	65	271	17,000
Tim Conley	68	67	68	69	272	13,040
Bob Estes	66	65	72	69	272	13,040
Blaine McCallister	69	67	67	69	272	13,040
David Peoples	69	68	67	68	272	13,040
Willie Wood	68	68	66	70	272	13,040
Neal Lancaster	65	65	71	72	273	9,600
Steve Rintoul	71	66	65	71	273	9,600
Lanny Wadkins	69	68	70	66	273	9,600
Michael Allen	68	67	70	69	274	7,400
Brian Henninger	71	67	67	69	274	7,400
John Inman	72	68	65	69	274	7,400
Gil Morgan	66	72	67	69	274	7,400
Steve Stricker	67	68	73	66	274	7,400
Brad Bryant	72	65	68	70	275	5,320
Brandel Chamblee	68	66	70	71	275	5,320
Trevor Dodds	68	69	68	70	275	5,320
Nolan Henke	69	68	71	67	275	5,320
Steve Jones	69	70	67	69	275	5,320

	SCORES				TOTAL	MONEY
Brad King	68	70	66	71	275	5,320
Kenny Knox	69	68	72	66	275	5,320
Peter Persons	70	68	66	71	275	5,320
Dave Rummells	69	70	67	69	275	5,320
Bobby Wadkins	67	70	69	69	275	5,320
Ed Dougherty	67	69	69	71	276	3,900
Tom Purtzer	70	65	68	73	276	3,900
Gene Sauers	71	68	68	69	276	3,900
Todd Barranger	71	69	70	67	277	3,108
Chip Beck	71	69	70	67	277	3,108
Vance Heafner	67	68	72	70	277	3,108
Don Reese	68	69	70	70	277	3,108
Esteban Toledo	70	69	66	72	277	3,108
Fulton Allem	69	68	68	73	278	2,495
Brian Claar	69	67	75	67	278	2,495
Joel Edwards	67	71	71	69	278	2,495
Steve Lamontagne	72	66	72	68	278	2,495
Mike Brisky	71	67	70	71	279	2,293.34
Tony Sills	69	68	72	70	279	2,293.34
John Flannery	69	71	68	71	279	2,293.33
Robert Gamez	70	69	71	69	279	2,293.33
D.A. Russell	71	67	67	74	279	2,293.33
Dave Stockton, Jr.	70	65	73	71	279	2,293.33
Mark Brooks	66	70	75	69	280	2,180
Chris Kite	69	68	73	70	280	2,180
Tom Sieckmann	70	67	71	72	280	2,180
Phil Tataurangi	74	66	72	68	280	2,180
David Toms	71	68	72	69	280	2,180
Rob Boldt	70	68	72	71	281	2,090
Brian Kamm	68	71	71	71	281	2,090
Charles Raulerson	68	68	71	74	281	2,090
Jeff Woodland	68	70	70	73	281	2,090
Robin Freeman	72	64	74	72	282	2,040
Ernie Gonzalez	69	71	71	72	283	2,020
Warren Schutte	69	70	76	69	284	1,990
Jerry Smith	72	68	72	72	284	1,990

Buick Southern Open

Callaway Gardens Resort, Pine Mountain, Georgia
Par 36-36—72; 7,057 yards
(Fourth round cancelled — rain, high winds.)

September 29-October 2
purse, $800,000

	SCORES			TOTAL	MONEY
Steve Elkington	66	66	68	200	$144,000
Steve Rintoul	70	65	70	205	86,400
Brad Bryant	70	68	69	207	54,400
Buddy Gardner	71	69	68	208	33,066.67
Steve Pate	69	71	68	208	33,066.67
Gene Sauers	72	67	69	208	33,066.66
Blaine McCallister	69	71	69	209	24,100
Larry Mize	69	73	67	209	24,100
Jeff Sluman	69	70	70	209	24,100
Bobby Wadkins	69	72	68	209	24,100
Phil Blackmar	71	73	66	210	15,400
Mike Brisky	67	71	72	210	15,400
Curt Byrum	71	65	74	210	15,400

	SCORES			TOTAL	MONEY
Brian Claar	70	66	74	210	15,400
Bob Estes	70	70	70	210	15,400
Bill Glasson	68	73	69	210	15,400
Donnie Hammond	71	72	67	210	15,400
Steve Lamontagne	66	69	75	210	15,400
Mike Donald	67	74	70	211	7,733.34
Justin Leonard	69	74	68	211	7,733.34
Harry Taylor	74	70	67	211	7,733.34
David Toms	70	72	69	211	7,733.34
Paul Azinger	71	70	70	211	7,733.33
David Ogrin	69	72	70	211	7,733.33
Don Reese	68	69	74	211	7,733.33
Dave Rummells	70	68	73	211	7,733.33
Tom Sieckmann	72	66	73	211	7,733.33
Kirk Triplett	68	70	73	211	7,733.33
Willie Wood	70	69	72	211	7,733.33
Richard Zokol	67	70	74	211	7,733.33
Ronnie Black	68	73	71	212	4,256
Rick Fehr	69	73	70	212	4,256
Mike Hulbert	71	73	68	212	4,256
Bruce Lietzke	71	73	68	212	4,256
John Mahaffey	74	69	69	212	4,256
Jim McGovern	66	73	73	212	4,256
Kenny Perry	67	72	73	212	4,256
Lee Porter	70	73	69	212	4,256
Dicky Pride	70	67	75	212	4,256
Hal Sutton	70	73	69	212	4,256
Mark Brooks	71	73	69	213	2,532.37
Glen Day	70	74	69	213	2,532.37
Dan Forsman	73	70	70	213	2,532.37
Ted Schulz	71	73	69	213	2,532.37
Rob Boldt	72	70	71	213	2,532.36
Brandel Chamblee	71	72	70	213	2,532.36
Marco Dawson	72	70	71	213	2,532.36
Jim Gallagher, Jr.	72	69	72	213	2,532.36
Bob Lohr	72	71	70	213	2,532.36
Doug Tewell	69	72	72	213	2,532.36
Bob Tway	70	69	74	213	2,532.36
Billy Andrade	73	71	70	214	1,838
Olin Browne	69	71	74	214	1,838
Bob Gilder	69	73	72	214	1,838
Scott Gump	70	72	72	214	1,838
Neal Lancaster	72	72	70	214	1,838
Sean Murphy	76	66	72	214	1,838
Mike Standly	72	71	71	214	1,838
John Wilson	73	69	72	214	1,838
John Adams	71	69	75	215	1,712
Michael Allen	70	72	73	215	1,712
Todd Barranger	65	77	73	215	1,712
Steve Gotsche	69	73	73	215	1,712
Eddie Kirby	69	70	76	215	1,712
Davis Love III	72	66	77	215	1,712
Don Pooley	72	72	71	215	1,712
Russell Beiersdorf	72	72	72	216	1,608
Tom Byrum	69	74	73	216	1,608
Paul Goydos	71	69	76	216	1,608
Ed Humenik	70	73	73	216	1,608
Paul Stankowski	73	70	73	216	1,608
Mike Sullivan	69	73	74	216	1,608
Russ Cochran	70	73	74	217	1,504

	SCORES			TOTAL	MONEY
Ed Dougherty	71	72	74	217	1,504
P.H. Horgan III	71	70	76	217	1,504
Brian Kamm	71	72	74	217	1,504
Kenny Knox	69	73	75	217	1,504
Charles Raulerson	70	73	74	217	1,504
Mark Wurtz	72	72	73	217	1,504
Chris Kite	74	70	74	218	1,416
Dick Mast	68	76	74	218	1,416
Mike Smith	73	71	74	218	1,416
Ted Tryba	72	72	74	218	1,416
Leonard Thompson	73	71	75	219	1,360
Stan Utley	67	73	79	219	1,360
Rocky Walcher	71	72	76	219	1,360
Robert Wrenn	71	73	77	221	1,328
Jerry Pate	73	71	79	223	1,312

Walt Disney World/Oldsmobile Classic

Magnolia Course
Par 36-36—72; 7,190 yards

Palm Course
Par 36-36—72; 6,976 yards

Eagle Pines
Par 36-36—72; 6,772 yards
Orlando, Florida

October 6-9
purse, $1,100,000

	SCORES				TOTAL	MONEY
Rick Fehr	63	70	68	68	269	$198,000
Craig Stadler	68	66	67	70	271	96,800
Fuzzy Zoeller	66	70	69	66	271	96,800
Trevor Dodds	68	66	70	68	272	48,400
Steve Stricker	72	67	66	67	272	48,400
Robert Gamez	68	69	68	68	273	39,600
Glen Day	65	68	72	69	274	33,137.50
Donnie Hammond	68	72	67	67	274	33,137.50
Brian Kamm	69	69	68	68	274	33,137.50
Doug Tewell	69	66	71	68	274	33,137.50
Clark Dennis	67	67	72	70	276	24,200
Jim Gallagher, Jr.	65	68	74	69	276	24,200
John Huston	68	72	70	66	276	24,200
Mark McCumber	69	70	71	66	276	24,200
Steve Brodie	72	67	66	72	277	15,473.34
Mike Donald	70	70	72	65	277	15,473.34
Davis Love III	69	69	71	68	277	15,473.34
Ronnie Black	68	72	69	68	277	15,473.33
Curt Byrum	67	69	72	69	277	15,473.33
Greg Kraft	70	68	68	71	277	15,473.33
Larry Mize	69	70	69	69	277	15,473.33
Dave Stockton, Jr.	68	64	72	73	277	15,473.33
Bobby Wadkins	70	71	68	68	277	15,473.33
Dudley Hart	67	71	71	69	278	8,323.34
Lee Janzen	72	65	67	74	278	8,323.34
Duffy Waldorf	68	71	71	68	278	8,323.34
Bob Lohr	63	71	74	70	278	8,323.33
Billy Mayfair	68	75	67	68	278	8,323.33

	SCORES				TOTAL	MONEY
Dillard Pruitt	70	72	70	66	278	8,323.33
Mike Reid	69	71	71	67	278	8,323.33
Joey Sindelar	69	69	70	70	278	8,323.33
Payne Stewart	69	70	69	70	278	8,323.33
Gene Sauers	73	69	67	70	279	5,688.58
Paul Azinger	72	68	68	71	279	5,688.57
Olin Browne	72	69	71	67	279	5,688.57
Brad Bryant	64	72	70	73	279	5,688.57
Fred Funk	70	70	70	69	279	5,688.57
Larry Rinker	66	69	72	72	279	5,688.57
Hal Sutton	71	71	68	69	279	5,688.57
Chip Beck	66	76	69	69	280	4,070
Sean Murphy	74	68	69	69	280	4,070
David Ogrin	71	69	71	69	280	4,070
Bob Tway	69	72	69	70	280	4,070
Howard Twitty	68	72	69	71	280	4,070
Stan Utley	68	71	70	71	280	4,070
Lanny Wadkins	72	69	68	71	280	4,070
Ed Dougherty	66	74	71	70	281	2,762.23
Wayne Levi	71	70	69	71	281	2,762.23
Fulton Allem	73	67	70	71	281	2,762.22
Mark Calcavecchia	71	71	67	72	281	2,762.22
John Flannery	70	70	62	79	281	2,762.22
Ed Humenik	71	71	69	70	281	2,762.22
Bob May	71	72	68	70	281	2,762.22
Jim McGovern	71	72	68	70	281	2,762.22
Steve Rintoul	72	71	68	70	281	2,762.22
Michael Allen	65	75	69	73	282	2,442
Brad Faxon	69	70	72	71	282	2,442
Kelly Gibson	70	72	67	73	282	2,442
Dick Mast	67	72	70	73	282	2,442
Steve Pate	71	71	68	72	282	2,442
Ted Tryba	71	69	71	71	282	2,442
Mark Wiebe	71	73	67	71	282	2,442
Michael Bradley	70	75	66	72	283	2,288
Chris DiMarco	70	73	69	71	283	2,288
Gary Hallberg	70	73	68	72	283	2,288
Mike Hulbert	70	68	69	76	283	2,288
Peter Jacobsen	68	74	70	71	283	2,288
John Morse	67	71	74	71	283	2,288
Mike Standly	70	71	69	73	283	2,288
John Cook	68	73	71	72	284	2,178
Jim Furyk	71	70	69	74	284	2,178
Mike Heinen	73	75	64	72	284	2,178
Jay Haas	70	72	70	75	287	2,134
Loren Roberts	74	68	69	77	288	2,101
Scott Simpson	68	72	69	79	288	2,101
David Peoples	75	69	68	77	289	2,068
Buddy Gardner	64	72	75	79	290	2,046

Texas Open

Oak Hills Country Club, San Antonio, Texas
Par 35-36—71; 6,650 yards

October 13-16
purse, $1,000,000

	SCORES				TOTAL	MONEY
Bob Estes	62	65	68	70	265	$180,000
Gil Morgan	66	68	65	67	266	108,000
Don Pooley	69	65	65	68	267	68,000
Bruce Lietzke	68	69	64	69	270	48,000
Mark McNulty	70	65	67	69	271	36,500
Craig Stadler	68	66	69	68	271	36,500
John Wilson	66	68	67	70	271	36,500
J.C. Anderson	67	64	70	71	272	25,000
Brad Bryant	66	67	70	69	272	25,000
Bob Burns	65	69	68	70	272	25,000
Ben Crenshaw	70	69	68	65	272	25,000
Blaine McCallister	70	65	72	65	272	25,000
Mark O'Meara	70	69	67	66	272	25,000
Dillard Pruitt	70	68	67	67	272	25,000
Fred Couples	67	69	68	69	273	15,500
Jim Furyk	70	67	67	69	273	15,500
John Inman	66	69	68	70	273	15,500
Brian Kamm	65	67	68	73	273	15,500
Justin Leonard	67	69	68	69	273	15,500
David Ogrin	70	69	65	69	273	15,500
Ed Dougherty	67	70	67	70	274	9,133.34
Nolan Henke	71	67	66	70	274	9,133.34
Jim McGovern	68	69	67	70	274	9,133.34
John Cook	69	69	67	69	274	9,133.33
Marco Dawson	68	68	68	70	274	9,133.33
Lee Janzen	69	69	72	64	274	9,133.33
Steve Rintoul	65	68	69	72	274	9,133.33
Bob Tway	63	67	72	72	274	9,133.33
Bobby Wadkins	69	66	69	70	274	9,133.33
Michael Bradley	66	69	72	68	275	6,500
Steve Gotsche	69	68	70	68	275	6,500
Dave Rummells	67	67	69	72	275	6,500
Mark Calcavecchia	70	69	70	67	276	5,171.43
Jay Haas	70	69	70	67	276	5,171.43
Donnie Hammond	67	68	70	71	276	5,171.43
Dick Mast	69	69	69	69	276	5,171.43
Mark Wiebe	68	68	70	70	276	5,171.43
Richard Zokol	70	67	70	69	276	5,171.43
Sean Murphy	68	65	70	73	276	5,171.42
Guy Boros	71	67	67	72	277	3,800
Dudley Hart	68	69	70	70	277	3,800
P.H. Horgan III	68	70	69	70	277	3,800
Neal Lancaster	67	69	69	72	277	3,800
Andrew Magee	66	70	69	72	277	3,800
Howard Twitty	70	65	72	70	277	3,800
Brandel Chamblee	69	68	74	67	278	2,600
Chris DiMarco	70	67	68	73	278	2,600
David Edwards	71	66	72	69	278	2,600
Paul Goydos	69	69	70	70	278	2,600
Bob May	69	66	72	71	278	2,600
Tim Simpson	67	70	71	70	278	2,600
Phil Tataurangi	70	69	67	72	278	2,600
Ted Tryba	70	69	68	71	278	2,600
D.A. Weibring	70	67	72	69	278	2,600

	SCORES				TOTAL	MONEY
Russ Cochran	67	69	71	72	279	2,260
Brian Henninger	68	70	71	70	279	2,260
David Peoples	72	65	70	72	279	2,260
Scott Simpson	70	68	73	68	279	2,260
Jeff Woodland	70	68	70	71	279	2,260
Bill Britton	70	68	68	74	280	2,150
Steve Brodie	69	70	71	70	280	2,150
Mike Heinen	69	68	71	72	280	2,150
Dicky Pride	70	69	69	72	280	2,150
Joey Rassett	69	67	72	72	280	2,150
Jim Woodward	69	70	70	71	280	2,150
Billy Mayfair	70	69	72	70	281	2,070
Curtis Strange	69	69	74	69	281	2,070
Larry Rinker	70	68	70	74	282	2,030
Duffy Waldorf	70	69	70	73	282	2,030
Rocky Walcher	67	71	71	74	283	2,000
Mark Brooks	67	70	74	73	284	1,980
David Feherty	68	71	74	74	287	1,950
Brad King	68	71	70	78	287	1,950
Eddie Kirby	68	69	77	76	290	1,920

Las Vegas Invitational

Las Vegas Country Club
Par 36-36—72; 7,164 yards

October 19-23
purse, $1,500,000

TPC at Summerlin
Par 36-36—72; 7,243 yards

Las Vegas Hilton Country Club
Par 36-35—71; 7,111 yards
Las Vegas, Nevada

	SCORES					TOTAL	MONEY
Bruce Lietzke	66	67	68	66	65	332	$270,000
Robert Gamez	66	70	64	69	64	333	162,000
Billy Andrade	66	68	67	67	67	335	87,000
Phil Mickelson	70	66	66	70	63	335	87,000
Jim Furyk	67	64	69	66	70	336	54,750
Bill Glasson	67	68	70	65	66	336	54,750
Paul Stankowski	70	66	66	69	65	336	54,750
Guy Boros	70	63	67	68	69	337	42,000
Scott Hoch	66	63	70	70	68	337	42,000
Sean Murphy	64	69	67	69	68	337	42,000
Kirk Triplett	69	65	65	68	70	337	42,000
Jay Don Blake	66	69	66	69	68	338	33,000
Jim Gallagher, Jr.	69	70	67	64	68	338	33,000
Mike Heinen	66	66	68	71	68	339	27,750
Mark Brooks	68	69	67	70	65	339	27,750
Steve Elkington	70	67	66	66	71	340	21,750
Dan Forsman	67	64	68	70	71	340	21,750
Gil Morgan	72	67	65	69	67	340	21,750
Dillard Pruitt	70	66	67	68	69	340	21,750
Bob Tway	69	70	67	67	67	340	21,750
Duffy Waldorf	68	69	72	64	67	340	21,750
Brad Bryant	71	67	67	68	68	341	15,600
Clark Dennis	68	67	67	73	66	341	15,600

	SCORES					TOTAL	MONEY
John Flannery	68	70	66	69	68	341	15,600
Tommy Armour III	71	67	65	69	70	342	13,200
Bob Burns	72	67	65	68	71	343	10,875
Dudley Hart	65	66	75	70	67	343	10,875
Steve Rintoul	71	69	68	67	68	343	10,875
Craig Stadler	71	70	67	68	67	343	10,875
Willie Wood	70	67	68	68	70	343	10,875
Rick Fehr	68	69	67	69	70	343	10,875
Brian Henninger	67	70	68	70	69	344	8,121.43
Peter Jordan	71	68	68	68	69	344	8,121.43
Brian Kamm	64	70	66	72	72	344	8,121.43
Brett Ogle	68	69	68	68	71	344	8,121.43
Dave Stockton, Jr.	70	66	72	66	70	344	8,121.43
Fuzzy Zoeller	71	68	68	68	69	344	8,121.43
Dave Rummells	67	68	69	68	72	344	8,121.42
Michael Bradley	67	68	69	69	72	345	6,000
Fred Funk	68	69	67	71	70	345	6,000
Lee Janzen	70	65	72	69	69	345	6,000
Jodie Mudd	67	69	70	68	71	345	6,000
Mike Standly	66	68	67	72	72	345	6,000
Howard Twitty	66	67	73	68	71	345	6,000
Michael Allen	69	70	67	66	74	346	4,515
Brian Claar	66	69	70	69	72	346	4,515
Neal Lancaster	66	69	67	69	75	346	4,515
John Wilson	67	72	70	70	67	346	4,515
Greg Norman	67	69	71	71	69	347	3,742.50
Dicky Pride	73	67	68	70	69	347	3,742.50
Tim Simpson	67	69	68	71	72	347	3,742.50
Keith Clearwater	66	70	69	73	69	347	3,742.50
J.C. Anderson	71	70	66	71	70	348	3,510
Mike Sullivan	68	68	70	69	73	348	3,510
Ken Green	70	68	64	72	75	349	3,405
Donnie Hammond	68	70	71	68	72	349	3,405
Morris Hatalsky	68	69	72	72	68	349	3,405
Peter Jacobsen	70	71	66	74	68	349	3,405
Nolan Henke	65	73	66	71	75	350	3,255
Mike Hulbert	71	67	69	68	75	350	3,255
Tom Lehman	69	71	69	72	69	350	3,255
Andrew Magee	68	72	68	71	71	350	3,255
Blaine McCallister	72	68	69	70	71	350	3,255
David Toms	74	66	69	72	69	350	3,255
Jay Haas	70	66	70	71	75	352	3,105
Jim McGovern	69	72	68	73	70	352	3,105
David Peoples	68	70	68	71	75	352	3,105
Payne Stewart	70	69	69	71	73	352	3,105
Larry Mize	69	67	71	76	73	356	3,015
Mark Wiebe	71	67	71	72	75	356	3,015
David Edwards	72	67	70	72	77	358	2,970
Wayne Levi	67	71	71	72	80	361	2,940
Brandel Chamblee	70	69	70	74	79	362	2,910
Fulton Allem	75	65	69	74	81	364	2,865
Mark Wurtz	68	73	67	72	84	364	2,865
Curt Byrum	68	67	69	69	DQ		

Tour Championship

The Olympic Club, Lake Course, San Francisco, California
Par 35-36—71; 6,812 yards

October 27-30
purse, $3,000,000

		SCORES			TOTAL	MONEY
Mark McCumber	66	71	69	68	274	$540,000
Fuzzy Zoeller	71	69	66	68	274	324,000
(McCumber defeated Zoeller on first extra hole.)						
Brad Bryant	72	68	67	68	275	207,000
David Frost	66	69	75	66	276	132,000
Bill Glasson	66	68	71	71	276	132,000
Jay Haas	69	71	71	66	277	108,000
Jeff Maggert	72	66	70	70	278	102,000
Steve Lowery	66	69	72	72	279	93,000
Loren Roberts	71	70	68	70	279	93,000
John Huston	74	68	66	72	280	81,000
Bruce Lietzke	69	71	71	69	280	81,000
Corey Pavin	69	69	70	72	280	81,000
Ben Crenshaw	72	70	69	70	281	71,400
Greg Norman	69	75	66	71	281	71,400
Bob Estes	71	70	73	68	282	64,800
Rick Fehr	67	69	77	69	282	64,800
Ernie Els	68	67	72	76	283	60,000
Phil Mickelson	68	71	70	74	283	60,000
Mike Springer	72	67	73	71	283	60,000
Scott Hoch	74	74	68	68	284	57,000
Nick Price	71	74	67	72	284	57,000
Hale Irwin	70	74	67	74	285	54,600
Tom Kite	69	72	72	72	285	54,600
Mark Calcavecchia	73	68	74	71	286	52,200
Hal Sutton	73	70	74	69	286	52,200
Brad Faxon	71	71	73	73	288	50,100
Kenny Perry	75	69	72	72	288	50,100
Tom Lehman	73	70	72	74	289	49,200
Mark Brooks	69	72	72	77	290	48,300
Fred Couples	70	72	74	74	290	48,300

Special Events

Westinghouse-Family House Invitational

The Club at Nevillewood, Carnegie, Pennsylvania
Par 36-36—72; 7,210 yards

May 23-24
purse, $700,000

	SCORES		TOTAL	MONEY
David Frost	69	68	137	$140,000
Curtis Strange	69	70	139	57,666.67
Scott Hoch	72	67	139	57,666.67
Joey Sindelar	72	67	139	57,666.67
Nick Price	70	70	140	34,000
Brett Ogle	68	72	140	34,000
Grant Waite	68	73	141	23,000
Craig Parry	74	67	141	23,000
Bruce Lietzke	70	72	142	18,000
Jeff Maggert	72	71	143	15,000
Keith Clearwater	69	76	145	12,000
D.A. Weibring	71	74	145	12,000
Mike Heinen	71	74	145	12,000
Rocco Mediate	73	72	145	12,000
Jim Gallagher, Jr.	73	72	145	12,000
Billy Andrade	73	72	145	12,000
Andrew Magee	73	73	146	12,000
Mike Hulbert	72	74	146	12,000
Steve Pate	73	74	147	12,000
Craig Stadler	77	70	147	12,000
Mark Calcavecchia	79	69	148	12,000
David Edwards	72	76	148	12,000
Bob Tway	72	77	149	12,000
Ian Baker-Finch	77	73	150	12,000
Fulton Allem	76	75	151	12,000
Billy Ray Brown	76	82	158	12,000
Les Botkins	80	80	160	12,000

Jerry Ford Invitational

Country Club of the Rockies
Par 36-36—72; 7,354 yards

August 15-16
purse, $350,000

Vail Golf Club
Par 35-36—71; 7,064 yards
Vail, Colorado

	SCORES		TOTAL	MONEY
Jay Don Blake	67	67	134	$25,000
Bob Lohr	69	67	136	6,500
Jerry Pate	65	71	136	6,500
Lon Hinkle	67	69	136	6,500
Kirk Triplett	71	65	136	6,500
Ed Fiori	70	66	136	6,500
Lennie Clements	69	68	137	5,000

	SCORES		TOTAL	MONEY
Craig Stadler	70	67	137	5,000
David Peoples	68	70	138	5,000
Jim Thorpe	70	69	139	5,000
Charles Coody	68	71	139	5,000
Dave Eichelberger	70	69	139	5,000
Tom Purtzer	71	69	140	5,000
Keith Clearwater	69	71	140	5,000
Chris Perry	70	70	140	5,000
Dave Stockton, Jr.	71	69	140	5,000
Mark Calcavecchia	74	67	141	5,000
Andy Bean	68	73	141	5,000
John Schroeder	66	75	141	5,000
Howard Twitty	73	68	141	5,000
Dow Finsterwald	72	70	142	5,000
Donnie Hammond	71	71	142	5,000
Robert Wrenn	71	71	142	5,000
Barry Jaeckel	73	69	142	5,000
Andrew Magee	70	72	142	5,000
John Huston	70	72	142	5,000
Leonard Thompson	76	68	144	5,000
Gary McCord	70	74	144	5,000
Clarence Rose	70	74	144	5,000
Dan Pohl	72	72	144	5,000
Morris Hatalsky	71	73	144	5,000
Bill Kratzert	73	72	145	5,000
J.C. Snead	74	71	145	5,000
Richard Zokol	74	71	145	5,000
Deane Beman	74	72	146	5,000
Andy North	76	70	146	5,000
Gary Hallberg	72	74	146	5,000
Tom Clary	77	70	147	5,000
George Burns	75	72	147	5,000
Mark Lye	73	74	147	5,000
Greg Twiggs	72	75	147	5,000
Jim Nelford	69	79	148	5,000
Buddy Gardner	74	74	148	5,000
Ted Schulz	74	75	149	5,000
Mike Sullivan	74	75	149	5,000
Steve Satterstrom	77	79	149	5,000
Dale Douglass	78	72	150	5,000
Lee Elder	72	78	150	5,000
Denis Watson	73	80	153	5,000
Tom Apple	78	78	156	5,000

Ernst Championship

Overlake Golf & Country Club, Medina, Washington
Par 35-35—70; 6,616 yards

August 15-16
purse, $680,000

	SCORES		TOTAL	MONEY
Billy Andrade	68	66	134	$150,000
Fred Couples	65	69	134	75,000
(Andrade defeated Couples on second extra hole.)				
Davis Love III	67	69	136	50,000
John Cook	67	71	138	27,500
Phil Mickelson	67	71	138	27,500
Jay Haas	68	71	139	19,000

	SCORES		TOTAL	MONEY
Mike Hulbert	71	68	139	19,000
Steve Pate	69	70	139	19,000
Keith Clearwater	73	67	140	15,000
Dave Feherty	71	69	140	15,000
Corey Pavin	69	71	140	15,000
Ian Baker-Finch	76	65	141	15,000
Tom Lehman	68	74	142	15,000
Fulton Allem	68	74	142	15,000
Hale Irwin	71	72	143	15,000
Blaine McCallister	72	71	143	15,000
Jeff Sluman	70	73	143	15,000
Rick Fehr	75	69	144	15,000
Wayne Grady	75	70	145	15,000

Fred Meyer Challenge

Oregon Golf Club, West Linn, Oregon
Par 35-36—71; 6,889 yards

August 22-23
purse, $700,000

	SCORES		TOTAL	MONEY
				(Team)
Mark O'Meara/John Cook	63	62	125	$100,000
Ben Crenshaw/Phil Mickelson	62	63	125	80,000
(O'Meara/Cook defeated Crenshaw/Mickelson on second extra hole.)				
Arnold Palmer/Peter Jacobsen	64	62	126	70,000
Bob Gilder/Fulton Allem	64	64	128	57,500
Davis Love III/Fred Couples	65	63	128	57,500
Jay Haas/Craig Stadler	66	63	129	50,000
Bruce Lietzke/Jim Gallagher, Jr.	63	66	129	50,000
Brian Henninger/Lee Janzen	62	67	129	50,000
Jack Nicklaus/Gary Nicklaus	65	65	130	47,000
Steve Elkington/Tom Purtzer	64	66	130	47,000
John Daly/Jim McGovern	65	66	131	46,000
Tom Weiskopf/Vijay Singh	68	68	136	45,000

Guadalajara Invitational

Guadalajara Country Club, Guadalajara, Mexico
Par 36-36—72; 6,897 yards

October 13-16
purse, $175,000

	SCORES				TOTAL	MONEY
Loren Roberts	69	68	64	65	266	$45,000
Hale Irwin	64	67	70	67	268	35,000
Jay Don Blake	74	64	66	65	269	17,000
Fred Funk	68	69	67	65	269	17,000
Rafael Alarcon	73	68	68	67	276	10,333
Patrick Burke	70	70	68	68	276	10,333
Ed Fiori	71	69	67	69	276	10,333
Greg Turner	66	71	69	72	278	7,000
Brett Ogle	71	68	66	74	279	6,000
Gary Orr	73	70	71	67	281	5,000
Peter Persons	72	68	71	71	282	4,000
Jeff Hart	71	71	69	72	283	2,750
Sixto Torres, Jr.	68	70	71	74	283	2,750
Ernesto Perez	72	74	72	73	291	1,500
Victor Regalado	84	80	73	80	317	1,000

Gene Sarazen World Open

The Legends at Chateau Elan, Braselton, Georgia
Par 36-36—72; 6,900 yards

November 3-6
purse, $1,900,000

	SCORES				TOTAL	MONEY
Ernie Els	67	73	68	65	273	$350,000
Fred Funk	69	69	66	62	276	200,000
Tom Sieckmann	67	69	71	73	280	106,400
Mark Calcavecchia	69	73	68	70	280	106,400
Eduardo Romero	69	73	71	68	281	72,200
Mark McNulty	71	67	73	71	282	56,525
Joakim Haeggman	72	70	69	71	282	56,525
Mark Roe	69	72	71	70	282	56,525
Costantino Rocca	73	72	67	70	282	56,525
Miguel Angel Jimenez	72	71	68	72	283	45,600
Jesper Parnevik	65	76	71	72	284	36,575
Steve Elkington	74	67	73	70	284	36,575
Greg Turner	74	72	71	67	284	36,575
Ian Woosnam	72	71	72	69	284	36,575
Tony Johnstone	71	72	70	73	286	26,600
Brandt Jobe	71	72	74	69	286	26,600
Emlyn Aubrey	74	69	73	70	286	26,600
Carl Mason	72	70	68	76	286	26,600
Frank Nobilo	74	70	71	71	286	26,600
Lee Janzen	70	75	71	72	288	19,760
Armando Saavedra	71	74	73	70	288	19,760
Clinton Whitelaw	69	76	72	71	288	19,760
Phillip Price	74	71	72	72	289	15,960
Craig Stadler	71	78	69	71	289	15,960
Darren Clarke	69	73	69	79	290	14,060
Peter Mitchell	70	73	75	72	290	14,060
Rick Parker	72	77	73	68	290	14,060
Bill Israelson	72	75	70	74	291	12,065
Anders Forsbrand	74	71	74	72	291	12,065
Raul Fretes	74	72	76	69	291	12,065
Mikael Piltz	68	76	77	70	291	12,065
Gene Fieger	73	72	75	72	292	10,450
Brian Watts	71	69	76	76	292	10,450
Gerry Norquist	73	68	73	79	293	9,500
Peter Fowler	72	74	71	76	293	9,500
Tom Gillis	76	70	74	74	294	8,740
Pedro Martinez	74	74	71	75	294	8,740
Jamie Spence	76	74	72	73	295	8,170
Jeff Wagner	75	76	74	71	296	7,477
Gary Webb	71	74	75	76	296	7,477
Eduardo Caballero	77	79	73	68	297	7,068
Gordon Brand, Jr.	70	75	75	77	297	7,068
Craig Jones	77	72	74	74	297	7,068
Per Nyman	71	74	74	78	297	7,068
Jeff Lewis	79	69	75	75	298	6,783
Paul Carman	75	76	72	76	299	6,546
Frank Edmonds	75	75	74	75	299	6,546
Christian Post	74	73	77	75	299	6,546
Gordon Manson	73	74	76	76	299	6,546
Darren Barnes	72	78	75	76	301	6,308
Craig Maltman	73	75	75	79	302	6,166
John Wade	75	75	80	72	302	6,166
Vicente Fernandez	74	74	82	73	303	5,985
Jesus Amaya	78	72	77	76	303	5,985

Lincoln-Mercury Kapalua International

Kapalua Resort, Maui, Hawaii
Par 36-37—73; 7,263 yards

November 3-6
purse, $1,200,000

	SCORES				TOTAL	MONEY
Fred Couples	66	71	72	70	279	$180,000
Bob Gilder	70	67	71	73	281	104,000
Tom Lehman	66	69	76	72	283	65,000
Ben Crenshaw	71	73	70	71	285	39,925
Bill Glasson	74	67	73	71	285	39,925
Peter Jacobsen	71	72	72	71	286	32,000
John Cook	71	69	74	73	287	25,333.34
Keith Clearwater	72	67	72	76	287	25,333.33
Barry Lane	72	67	71	77	287	25,333.33
Davis Love III	72	69	73	75	289	18,500
Jim McGovern	66	73	72	78	289	18,500
David Peoples	76	67	75	71	289	18,500
Sam Torrance	68	74	74	73	289	18,500
Kirk Triplett	68	72	76	73	289	18,500
Duffy Waldorf	69	72	75	73	289	18,500
Steve Pate	72	68	78	72	290	13,157.15
Scott Simpson	70	71	77	72	290	13,157.15
Jay Delsing	72	67	74	77	290	13,157.14
Robert Gamez	70	78	73	69	290	13,157.14
Bob Lohr	72	70	74	74	290	13,157.14
Gary McCord	66	79	70	75	290	13,157.14
Tom Purtzer	72	73	73	72	290	13,157.14
Mike Hulbert	71	74	74	72	291	11,000
Ed Humenik	68	74	75	74	291	11,000
Billy Andrade	73	75	72	72	292	9,820
Glen Day	72	71	73	76	292	9,820
Clark Dennis	68	75	74	75	292	9,820
Paul Goydos	70	73	78	71	292	9,820
Ted Tryba	71	73	74	74	292	9,820
Jay Don Blake	73	76	77	67	293	9,820
Andy Bean	72	72	77	73	294	8,850
Donnie Hammond	72	72	75	75	294	8,850
Jack Nicklaus	69	71	76	78	294	8,850
Lennie Clements	73	72	76	75	296	8,600
Mike Standly	69	72	81	74	296	8,600
Mark Brooks	75	72	77	73	297	8,366.67
David Feherty	74	71	74	78	297	8,366.67
Justin Leonard	71	76	77	73	297	8,366.67
David Ogrin	75	67	80	77	299	8,250
Brad Bryant	72	76	75	77	300	8,150
Hale Irwin	73	73	79	75	300	8,150
Neal Lancaster	77	75	71	77	300	8,150
Dave Barr	72	75	75	79	301	8,025
Nolan Henke	76	73	78	74	301	8,025
Jim Thorpe	70	71	83	78	302	7,950
Chris DiMarco	78	76	77	72	303	7,875
Mike Heinen	72	70	85	76	303	7,875
Dicky Pride	72	76	86	77	311	7,800
Deane Beman	77	74	82	80	313	7,750
Mark Rolfing	82	84	86	86	338	7,700

PGA Grand Slam of Golf

Poipu Bay Resort, Kauai, Hawaii
Par 36-36—72; 6,957 yards

November 8-9
purse, $1,000,000

	SCORES		TOTAL	MONEY
Greg Norman	70	66	136	$400,000
Nick Price	70	69	139	250,000
Ernie Els	72	71	143	200,000
Jose Marie Olazabal	74	70	144	150,000

World Cup of Golf

Dorado Beach Golf Club, Dorado, Puerto Rico
Par 36-36—72; 7,005 yards

November 10-13
purse, $1,200,000

	INDIVIDUAL SCORES				TOTAL
UNITED STATES (536)—$300,000					
Fred Couples	65	63	68	69	265
Davis Love III	67	66	69	69	271
ZIMBABWE (550)—$150,000					
Mark McNulty	68	67	67	70	272
Tony Johnstone	67	72	66	73	278
SWEDEN (551)—$100,000					
Jesper Parnevik	69	69	70	67	275
Joakim Haeggman	71	65	70	70	276
NEW ZEALAND (553)—$75,000					
Frank Nobilo	70	66	67	69	272
Greg Turner	72	70	68	71	281
SCOTLAND (557)—$45,666					
Gordon Brand, Jr.	73	69	72	65	279
Andrew Coltart	71	68	69	70	278
PARAGUAY (557)—$45,666					
Pedro Martinez	71	69	69	69	278
Angel Franco	69	68	72	70	279
JAPAN (557)—$45,666					
Masayuki Kawamura	71	67	65	73	276
Toru Suzuki	75	68	66	72	281
GERMANY (558)—$24,000					
Bernhard Langer	71	71	65	69	276
Sven Struver	71	69	73	69	282
AUSTRALIA (559)—$18,000					
Steve Elkington	69	68	71	66	274
Michael Clayton	75	65	75	70	285
ITALY (559)—$18,000					
Costantino Rocca	68	66	68	68	270
Silvio Grappasonni	69	71	75	74	289

	INDIVIDUAL SCORES				TOTAL

MALAYSIA (559)—$18,000

Periasamy Gunasegaran	73	69	71	73	286
Marimuthu Ramayah	66	64	69	74	273

ARGENTINA (560)—$14,000

Eduardo Romero	72	66	66	70	274
Miguel Guzman	72	70	73	71	286

MEXICO (563)—$12,000

Esteban Toledo	69	72	69	68	278
Rafael Alarcon	73	73	70	69	285

CANADA (565)—$11,000

Dave Barr	72	68	71	72	283
Rick Gibson	71	66	71	74	282

FRANCE (568)—$8,700

Michel Besanceney	74	71	75	69	289
Jean Van de Velde	73	67	68	71	279

SOUTH AFRICA (568)—$8,700

Roger Wessels	70	68	74	70	282
Wayne Westner	70	72	73	71	286

IRELAND (568)—$8,700

Darren Clarke	69	70	76	71	286
Paul McGinley	69	70	72	71	282

ENGLAND (568)—$8,700

Mark Roe	69	71	72	72	284
Barry Lane	72	70	68	74	284

REPUBLIC OF KOREA (570)—$7,400

Young Kun Han	75	72	68	72	287
Sang Ho Choi	74	66	72	71	283

HOLLAND (570)—$7,400

Chris Van Der Velde	71	71	70	71	283
Joost Steenkammer	73	67	74	73	287

THAILAND (570)—$7,400

Prayad Marksaeng	69	71	67	75	282
Boonchu Ruengkit	70	71	75	72	288

BRAZIL (577)—$7,000

Acacio Pedro	77	70	73	75	295
Antonio Barcellos	69	68	70	75	282

FINLAND (578)—$6,700

Mikael Piltz	72	74	67	71	284
Anssi Kankkonen	72	75	73	74	294

DENMARK (578)—$6,700

Jacob Rasmussen	78	70	69	75	292
Steen Tinning	71	73	70	72	286

WALES (579)—$6,400

Phillip Price	77	72	72	81	302
Ian Woosnam	73	69	66	69	277

		INDIVIDUAL SCORES			TOTAL
CHINESE TEAM TAIPEI (581)—$6,200					
Yu Chin Han	75	66	73	74	288
Lu Chien Soon	72	73	73	75	293
SPAIN (583)—$6,000					
Jose Rivero	73	71	74	78	296
Miguel Angel Jimenez	73	70	74	70	287
SWITZERLAND (592)—$5,800					
Andre Bossert	71	71	70	73	285
Marco Scopetta	72	81	72	82	307
PUERTO RICO (595)—$5,600					
*Wilfredo Morales	71	74	72	74	291
Manuel B. Camacho	75	73	78	78	304
HONG KONG (598)—$5,400					
Richard Kan	79	74	77	74	304
Dominuque Boulet	78	76	67	73	294
NORWAY (624)—$5,200					
Hans Strom-Olsen	84	84	76	80	324
Thomas Nielsen	76	71	79	74	300
JAMAICA (DQ)—$5,000					
Ralph Mairs	77	77	77	79	310
Seymour Rose	DQ				

INTERNATIONAL TROPHY

WINNER: Couples - 265 - $100,000. RUNNER-UP: Rocca - 270 - $50,000. ORDER OF FINISH: Love - 271 - $25,000; Nobilo, McNulty - 272 - $7,500 each.

Mexican Open

Club de Golf Mexico, Mexico City, Mexico
Par 36-36—72; 7,145 yards

November 17-20
purse, $600,000

	SCORES				TOTAL	MONEY
Chris Perry	69	69	70	66	274	$100,000
Bob Tway	69	67	70	69	275	55,000
John Cook	71	68	69	68	276	38,000
Howard Twitty	64	68	75	70	277	34,000
Tom Byrum	72	67	72	67	278	30,000
Bob Lohr	70	73	69	67	279	24,000
Doug Tewell	73	65	68	73	279	24,000
Jose Rivero	70	70	71	69	280	18,000
Fred Funk	69	71	72	70	282	15,750
David Feherty	69	73	69	71	282	15,750
Tommy Armour III	71	68	74	70	283	14,100
John Mahaffey	74	71	70	68	283	14,100
Dave Stockton, Jr.	70	72	68	74	284	12,900
Miguel Guzman	73	67	71	73	284	12,900
Jay Don Blake	74	73	66	72	285	12,000
Jay Haas	72	75	69	70	286	10,200
Jerry Haas	71	72	67	76	286	10,200
Donnie Hammond	72	72	71	71	286	10,200

	SCORES				TOTAL	MONEY
Lennie Clements	71	73	72	70	286	10,200
Miguel Angel Martin	70	70	70	76	286	10,200
Tom Weiskopf	75	70	72	70	287	8,600
Willie Wood	71	72	74	71	288	7,400
Frank Conner	71	71	74	72	288	7,400
Jaime Gomez	72	72	73	71	288	7,400
Mike Mitchell	73	69	70	76	288	7,400
Juan Brito	71	74	73	70	288	7,400
Don Reese	73	74	71	71	289	6,000
Jorge Perez	70	71	73	75	289	6,000
Scott Verplank	71	71	72	76	290	5,100
Pat Sharpe	74	71	73	72	290	5,100
Rafael Alarcon	75	71	71	74	291	4,300
Alberto Kaneda	76	65	71	79	291	4,300
Rodolfo Cazaubon	74	76	70	71	291	4,300
Ricardo Samar	73	73	69	76	291	4,300
Sandy Lyle	72	74	74	72	292	3,700
Carlos Espinosa	72	74	71	75	292	3,700
Carlos Larrain	73	72	75	73	293	3,400
Andy Bean	72	73	73	76	294	2,900
Andy North	74	74	73	73	294	2,900
Tom Sieckmann	78	73	70	73	294	2,900
Cesar Perez	69	76	74	75	294	2,900
Billy Ray Brown	71	71	77	76	295	2,200
Angel Cabrera	72	75	74	74	295	2,200
Pablo Del Olmo	73	72	73	77	295	2,200
Ed Fiori	72	74	72	78	296	1,400
Tim Hobby	69	79	76	73	297	1,400
Sixto Torres, Fr.	74	71	74	78	297	1,400
Antonio Pilar	72	74	77	74	297	1,000
Carlos Perez	76	73	72	78	299	1,000

Pebble Beach Invitational

Pebble Beach Golf Links, Pebble Beach, California
Par 36-36—72; 6,799 yards

November 17-20
purse, $200,000

	SCORES				TOTAL	MONEY
Robert Gamez	65	71	70	71	277	$40,000
Kirk Triplett	73	71	68	71	283	22,500
Bob Gilder	73	74	70	68	285	10,050
Keith Fergus	70	70	72	73	285	10,050
Lisa Kiggens	72	74	70	72	288	5,330
Steve Jones	74	74	68	72	288	5,330
Dave Eichelberger	75	71	71	71	288	5,330
George Archer	69	73	71	75	288	5,330
James Furyk	72	72	70	74	288	5,330
Johnny Miller	71	67	72	79	289	5,330
Rob Boldt	77	71	68	73	289	3,125
Brian Mogg	73	76	68	72	289	3,125
Gary Hallberg	72	66	76	75	289	3,125
Bob May	69	75	76	70	290	2,400
Bob Ford	69	73	76	72	290	2,400
Juli Inkster	73	71	71	75	290	2,400
Shawn Kelly	76	70	74	71	291	2,150
Tommy Masters	73	70	70	78	291	2,150
Jeff McMillian	72	74	76	70	292	1,883

	SCORES				TOTAL	MONEY
Shawn McEntee	74	74	73	71	292	1,883
Danny Edwards	71	72	72	77	292	1,883
Butch Baird	72	73	73	75	293	1,800
Brett Upper	74	72	77	71	294	1,700
Mark Wiebe	75	77	68	74	294	1,700
Don Pooley	76	71	70	77	294	1,700
Jeff Wilson	74	75	74	72	295	1,575
Val Skinner	74	69	74	78	295	1,575
Todd Fischer	74	78	72	72	296	1,418
Ronnie Black	75	73	74	74	296	1,418
Laird Small	69	78	75	74	296	1,418
Terry Foreman	71	76	73	76	296	1,418
Charles Gibson	74	74	71	77	296	1,418
Lonnie Neilsen	70	73	75	78	296	1,418
Al Geiberger	76	73	74	74	297	1,340
Brent Geiberger	69	80	75	75	299	1,310
Roger Maltbie	74	76	71	78	299	1,310
Kris Tschetter	77	76	75	72	300	1,260
Jimmy Powell	78	75	72	75	300	1,260
Terry Dill	78	71	73	78	300	1,260
Laurie Merten	75	75	78	73	301	1,210
Marion Dantzler	75	76	71	79	301	1,210
Barry Jaeckel	77	74	75	76	302	1,160
Cindy Rarick	74	78	74	76	302	1,160
Johnny Miller, Jr.	74	78	74	77	303	1,110
Rick Rhoads	75	78	75	75	303	1,110
Mike Jick	74	77	76	77	304	1,080
Scott Hoyt	74	78	73	80	305	1,050
Chuck Milne	78	74	75	78	305	1,050
Bruce Soulsby	77	82	68	79	306	1,020
Dudley Hart	72	83	73	WD		

Franklin Funds Shark Shootout

Sherwood Country Club, Thousand Oaks, California
Par 36-36—72; 7,025 yards

November 18-20
purse, $1,100,000

	SCORES			TOTAL	MONEY (Each)
Fred Couples/Brad Faxon	68	64	58	190	$150,000
Curtis Strange/Mark O'Meara	70	64	58	192	85,000
Chip Beck/Jeff Maggert	68	65	60	193	57,500
Lanny Wadkins/Andrew Magee	66	66	62	194	44,500
Ben Crenshaw/Mark Calcavecchia	69	62	64	195	41,500
Arnold Palmer/Peter Jacobsen	73	64	59	196	39,000
Greg Norman/Nick Price	72	63	62	197	35,250
Hale Irwin/Bruce Lietzke	70	67	60	197	35,250
David Frost/Fuzzy Zoeller	71	67	66	204	32,000
Raymond Floyd/Steve Elkington	73	69	63	205	30,000

Diners Club Matches

PGA West, Jack Nicklaus Course, La Quinta, California
Par 36-36—72; 6,546 yards

December 8-11
purse, $2,100,000

FIRST ROUND

John Huston and Brian Claar defeated Ben Crenshaw and Phil Mickelson, 19 holes.
Lee Janzen and Rocco Mediate defeated Lanny Wadkins and Paul Azinger, 4 and 2.
Scott Hoch and Chip Beck defeated Mike Springer and Neal Lancaster, 1 up.
Fuzzy Zoeller and Curtis Strange defeated Ronnie Black and Brad Bryant, 3 and 2.
Rick Fehr and Loren Roberts defeated Kenny Perry and Leonard Thompson, 2 and 1.
Hale Irwin and Jay Haas defeated Mark Calcavecchia and Billy Mayfair, 3 and 2.
Bill Glasson and David Edwards defeated Mark Brooks and Andrew Magee, 1 up.
Jeff Maggert and Jim McGovern defeated Jim Gallagher, Jr. and Steve Lowery, 1 up.

(Losers in first round received $15,000 each.)

SECOND ROUND

Janzen and Mediate defeated Hoch and Beck, 1 up.
Zoeller and Strange defeated Huston and Claar, 20 holes.
Maggert and McGovern defeated Fehr and Roberts, 3 and 1.
Glasson and Edwards defeated Irwin and Haas, 4 and 2.

(Losers in second round received $20,000 each.)

THIRD ROUND

Janzen and Mediate defeated Zoeller and Strange, 1 up.
Maggert and McGovern defeated Glasson and Edwards, 19 holes.

(Losers in third round received $35,000 each.)

FOURTH ROUND

Maggert and McGovern defeated Janzen and Mediate, 19 holes.

(Winners in fourth round received $125,000 each; losers received $50,000 each.)

Nike Tour

Inland Empire Open

Moreno Valley Ranch Golf Club, Moreno Valley, California
Par 36-36—72; 6,880 yards
(Second round cancelled — rain.)

February 3-6
purse, $200,000

	SCORES			TOTAL	MONEY
Skip Kendall	65	67	65	197	$36,000
Emlyn Aubrey	67	67	69	203	22,700
Bill Murchison	66	68	71	205	16,500
Jeff Barlow	69	68	69	206	10,000
Jack Ferenz	67	69	70	206	10,000
Bryan Gorman	68	67	71	206	10,000
David Jackson	70	71	65	206	10,000
R.W. Eaks	69	67	71	207	5,100
John Elliott	69	65	73	207	5,100
Jeff Hart	67	70	70	207	5,100
Chris Peddicord	66	71	70	207	5,100
Mike Smith	73	67	67	207	5,100
Robert Meyer	68	70	70	208	3,300
David Kirkpatrick	70	71	68	209	2,713.34
Mike Schuchart	70	71	68	209	2,713.34
Jon Fiedler	67	66	76	209	2,713.33
Matt Peterson	68	71	70	209	2,713.33
Thomas Scherrer	68	69	72	209	2,713.33
Sonny Skinner	69	70	70	209	2,713.33
George Bowman	71	72	67	210	2,100
Chris Hunsucker	74	67	69	210	2,100
John Ross	69	67	74	210	2,100
Monte Scheinblum	68	72	70	210	2,100
Lance Ten Broeck	71	69	70	210	2,100
Mark Mielke	71	72	68	211	1,508.58
Jerry Foltz	69	72	70	211	1,508.57
Tim Loustalot	70	70	71	211	1,508.57
Chris Perry	71	68	72	211	1,508.57
Kevin Sutherland	69	72	70	211	1,508.57
Mike Tschetter	73	69	69	211	1,508.57
Bob Wolcot	68	70	73	211	1,508.57

Monterrey Open

Club Campestre, Monterrey, Mexico
Par 36-36—72; 6,869 yards

March 3-6
purse, $200,000

	SCORES				TOTAL	MONEY
Scott Gump	67	67	68	67	269	$36,000
Brian Henninger	67	70	66	67	270	22,700
Robert Friend	68	65	68	70	271	16,500
Clark Burroughs	69	68	70	65	272	12,500
Tim Loustalot	69	67	74	64	274	7,583.34
Chris Perry	67	70	68	69	274	7,583.34

	SCORES				TOTAL	MONEY
J.P. Hayes	68	68	68	70	274	7,583.33
Bill Porter	66	68	69	71	274	7,583.33
Larry Rentz	70	64	69	71	274	7,583.33
Monte Scheinblum	69	68	66	71	274	7,583.33
P.H. Horgan III	70	69	67	69	275	3,475
David Jackson	68	71	65	71	275	3,475
Charles Rymer	72	65	69	69	275	3,475
Jade Work	70	66	66	73	275	3,475
Tom Byrum	68	68	69	71	276	2,695
John Kennaday	65	75	67	69	276	2,695
Gary Rusnak	71	66	69	70	276	2,695
Mike Sposa	70	70	67	69	276	2,695
Jeff Brehaut	69	66	74	68	277	2,100
Steve Haskins	70	71	68	68	277	2,100
Dean Hiers	68	68	72	69	277	2,100
Jim Kane	69	68	71	69	277	2,100
Lee Rinker	72	68	68	69	277	2,100
Lance Ten Broeck	69	67	71	70	277	2,100
Tommy Tolles	68	70	69	70	277	2,100
Rob Boldt	73	66	68	71	278	1,550
Danny Briggs	71	68	70	69	278	1,550
John Elliott	71	70	67	70	278	1,550
Skip Kendall	72	67	71	68	278	1,550
Jeffrey Peck	69	72	74	64	279	1,253.34
Woody Austin	70	68	71	70	279	1,253.33
Jeff Wilson	69	70	72	68	279	1,253.33

Louisiana Open

Le Triomphe Country Club, Broussard, Louisiana
Par 36-36—72; 6,798 yards

March 24-27
purse, $175,000

	SCORES				TOTAL	MONEY
Bill Porter	68	67	71	70	276	$31,500
Brad Fabel	71	67	70	70	278	19,862.50
Thomas Scherrer	71	66	68	74	279	14,437.50
Sonny Skinner	74	69	70	68	281	10,937.50
Jeff Woodland	73	68	71	70	282	8,020.84
Jeff Cook	69	69	71	73	282	8,020.83
Buddy Gardner	73	67	71	71	282	8,020.83
J.C. Anderson	67	72	74	70	283	4,812.50
Tom Byrum	72	65	74	72	283	4,812.50
Mike Donald	70	70	71	72	283	4,812.50
Mike Smith	70	66	72	75	283	4,812.50
Skip Kendall	68	73	70	73	284	2,975
Omar Uresti	72	71	68	73	284	2,975
J.P. Hayes	72	70	68	75	285	2,374.17
Matt Peterson	69	74	69	73	285	2,374.17
Joey Rassett	69	70	72	74	285	2,374.17
Phil Tataurangi	72	71	74	68	285	2,374.17
Scott Gump	67	71	77	70	285	2,374.16
Chris Perry	68	69	74	74	285	2,374.16
Rex Caldwell	65	72	80	69	286	1,881.25
Steve Haskins	66	76	75	69	286	1,881.25
Jim Lemon	69	72	73	72	286	1,881.25
Esteban Toledo	69	68	75	74	286	1,881.25
Jeff Coston	66	71	75	75	287	1,402.50

	SCORES				TOTAL	MONEY
David Duval	66	71	75	75	287	1,402.50
Dean Hiers	69	73	76	69	287	1,402.50
Peter Jordan	67	72	75	73	287	1,402.50
Franklin Langham	70	70	74	73	287	1,402.50
Harry Rudolph	71	71	69	76	287	1,402.50
Roger Salazar	71	69	77	70	287	1,402.50

Pensacola Open

The Moors Golf Club, Milton, Florida
Par 35-36—71; 6,912 yards

March 31-April 3
purse, $200,000

	SCORES				TOTAL	MONEY
Bruce Vaughan	68	66	66	71	271	$36,000
Ron Philo	62	70	69	71	272	22,700
Pat Bates	69	67	66	71	273	14,500
Skip Kendall	71	69	63	70	273	14,500
Webb Heintzelman	70	72	65	67	274	7,583.34
Harry Rudolph	72	70	67	65	274	7,583.34
David Duval	72	69	65	68	274	7,583.33
Robert Friend	71	67	68	68	274	7,583.33
Scott Gump	70	66	70	68	274	7,583.33
Franklin Langham	68	65	69	72	274	7,583.33
Keith Fergus	70	68	67	70	275	3,600
Ralph Howe III	71	67	69	68	275	3,600
Steve Isley	69	67	69	70	275	3,600
Mitch Adcock	72	69	66	69	276	3,000
Sam Randolph	72	69	69	66	276	3,000
Clark Burroughs	70	68	69	70	277	2,690
Peter Persons	69	68	70	70	277	2,690
Jeff Klein	68	69	72	69	278	2,500
Joe Durant	68	73	66	72	279	1,950
Jim Estes	72	70	68	69	279	1,950
Steve Ford	70	69	69	71	279	1,950
Jimmy Green	71	68	70	70	279	1,950
J.P. Hayes	71	69	69	70	279	1,950
Craig Kanada	72	69	71	67	279	1,950
David Kirkpatrick	71	67	71	70	279	1,950
Lee Rinker	68	68	75	68	279	1,950
Harry Taylor	73	68	67	71	279	1,950
Jade Work	69	71	67	72	279	1,950
Mike Schuchart	68	72	71	69	280	1,217.15
Sonny Skinner	73	68	71	68	280	1,217.15
Tommy Armour	72	68	65	75	280	1,217.14
Tom Byrum	70	71	65	74	280	1,217.14
Greg Cesario	69	71	69	71	280	1,217.14
Matt Mitchell	74	68	66	72	280	1,217.14
Chris Perry	72	67	70	71	280	1,217.14

Mississippi Gulf Coast Classic

Windance Golf & Country Club, Gulfport, Mississippi
Par 35-37—72; 6,735 yards

April 7-10
purse, $175,000

		SCORES			TOTAL	MONEY
John Elliott	68	71	68	69	276	$31,500
Chris Perry	67	69	71	69	276	19,862.50
(Elliott defeated Perry on second extra hole.)						
Skip Kendall	70	67	67	73	277	12,687.50
Rick Pearson	74	68	68	67	277	12,687.50
Craig Kanada	72	68	72	67	279	7,546.88
Tim Loustalot	69	74	69	67	279	7,546.88
Buddy Gardner	67	71	72	69	279	7,546.87
Bob Wolcot	66	68	75	70	279	7,546.87
Jeff Coston	70	69	72	69	280	3,815
David Duval	72	67	72	69	280	3,815
Jim Furyk	70	70	69	71	280	3,815
Hugh Royer III	73	70	69	68	280	3,815
Dave Stockton, Jr.	71	67	71	71	280	3,815
J.C. Anderson	68	72	69	72	281	2,177
Ben Bates	70	69	71	71	281	2,177
David Berganio, Jr.	67	72	71	71	281	2,177
Robert Friend	71	68	69	73	281	2,177
Jimmy Green	71	69	72	69	281	2,177
Ralph Howe III	70	73	69	69	281	2,177
Rich Parker	71	70	69	71	281	2,177
Dicky Pride	70	71	70	70	281	2,177
Jeff Wilson	71	70	69	71	281	2,177
Mark Wurtz	72	70	71	68	281	2,177
Woody Austin	72	71	71	68	282	1,443.75
Clark Burroughs	72	71	68	71	282	1,443.75
Jim Kane	71	71	69	71	282	1,443.75
Brad Lardon	68	72	75	67	282	1,443.75
Peter Persons	70	73	70	69	282	1,443.75
Sam Randolph	72	70	72	68	282	1,443.75
Scott Gump	73	68	72	70	283	1,038.34
Roger Salazar	74	69	71	69	283	1,038.34
Tommy Armour	70	70	68	75	283	1,038.33
Pat Bates	69	72	71	71	283	1,038.33
Steve Gotsche	71	71	70	71	283	1,038.33
Omar Uresti	69	69	70	75	283	1,038.33

Panama City Beach Classic

The Hombre Golf Club, Panama City, Florida
Par 36-36—72; 6,885 yards

April 15-17
purse, $175,000

		SCORES		TOTAL	MONEY
Keith Fergus	66	64	72	202	$31,500
Tommy Armour	67	68	69	204	19,862.50
Robert Friend	68	66	72	206	14,437.50
Mike Brisky	71	67	69	207	9,333.34
Tom Byrum	73	65	69	207	9,333.33
Scott Gump	69	67	71	207	9,333.33
Woody Austin	72	67	69	208	7,000
Patrick Burke	72	67	70	209	3,987.50
Jeff Gallagher	74	68	67	209	3,987.50

	SCORES			TOTAL	MONEY
John Maginnes	70	69	70	209	3,987.50
Lee Rinker	72	66	71	209	3,987.50
Steve Rintoul	71	69	69	209	3,987.50
Chris Rule	69	68	72	209	3,987.50
Sonny Skinner	69	69	71	209	3,987.50
Greg Cesario	72	67	71	210	2,306.50
Frank Conner	71	70	69	210	2,306.50
Steve Haskins	72	67	71	210	2,306.50
Skip Kendall	73	68	69	210	2,306.50
Rick Pearson	72	68	70	210	2,306.50
Mike Donald	70	71	70	211	1,793.75
Tom Garner	71	69	71	211	1,793.75
Bill Murchison	71	68	72	211	1,793.75
Dicky Pride	73	69	69	211	1,793.75
Lance Ten Broeck	70	70	71	211	1,793.75
Jeff Woodland	71	68	72	211	1,793.75
Jorge Berendt	72	70	70	212	1,316
Tom Carr	71	68	73	212	1,316
David Kirkpatrick	70	69	73	212	1,316
Roger Rowland	74	67	71	212	1,316
Gary Rusnak	71	70	71	212	1,316

Shreveport Open

Southern Trace Country Club, Shreveport, Louisiana
Par 36-36—72; 6,916 yards

April 21-24
purse, $175,000

	SCORES				TOTAL	MONEY
Omar Uresti	65	71	63	71	270	$31,500
Pat Bates	67	67	69	67	270	19,862.50
(Uresti defeated Bates on sixth extra hole.)						
Tommy Armour	71	68	67	66	272	14,437.50
Mike Schuchart	70	66	70	67	273	10,937.50
Chris Perry	69	68	68	69	274	8,531.25
Lance Ten Broeck	69	66	71	68	274	8,531.25
Jay Cooper	72	68	70	66	276	5,687.50
Steve Ford	66	71	69	70	276	5,687.50
Steve Rintoul	68	71	67	70	276	5,687.50
Bruce Vaughan	68	70	73	65	276	5,687.50
Tim Herron	69	68	72	68	277	2,699.38
Gary Rusnak	72	66	69	70	277	2,699.38
Sonny Skinner	69	70	69	69	277	2,699.38
Mike Sposa	70	69	69	69	277	2,699.38
Chad Ginn	66	70	70	71	277	2,699.37
Perry Moss	70	66	70	71	277	2,699.37
Sam Randolph	70	69	67	71	277	2,699.37
Tommy Tolles	71	65	68	73	277	2,699.37
Frank Conner	66	67	79	66	278	1,968.75
Mike Donald	64	69	74	71	278	1,968.75
David Duval	69	67	67	75	278	1,968.75
Jerry Kelly	69	68	71	70	278	1,968.75
Danny Briggs	68	73	68	70	279	1,618.75
Steve Haskins	70	69	73	67	279	1,618.75
Barry Jaeckel	65	73	70	71	279	1,618.75
Peter Persons	70	70	67	72	279	1,618.75
Greg Bruckner	69	72	70	69	280	1,204.59
Mike Small	72	69	69	70	280	1,204.59

	SCORES				TOTAL	MONEY
Brian Henninger	67	70	73	70	280	1,204.58
Skip Kendall	66	73	69	72	280	1,204.58
Clarence Rose	71	69	69	71	280	1,204.58
Jim Schuman	68	72	67	73	280	1,204.58

Alabama Classic

Cherokee Ridge Country Club, Union Grove, Alabama
Par 36-36—72; 6,867 yards

April 28-May 1
purse, $200,000

	SCORES				TOTAL	MONEY
Tommy Tolles	66	69	70	69	274	$36,000
Clark Burroughs	69	71	66	69	275	22,700
Jeff Brehaut	67	70	72	67	276	14,500
David Duval	73	66	65	72	276	14,500
Jerry Kelly	69	67	71	70	277	10,500
David Kirkpatrick	69	69	69	72	279	9,000
Greg Bruckner	70	68	70	72	280	7,000
Robert Friend	72	67	73	68	280	7,000
Tim Loustalot	72	70	68	70	280	7,000
Barry Fabyan	71	69	69	72	281	3,950
Jeff Gallagher	70	68	69	74	281	3,950
Peter Persons	67	68	72	74	281	3,950
Lee Rinker	72	65	72	72	281	3,950
Jim Carter	71	71	69	71	282	2,713.34
Ron Philo	73	70	71	68	282	2,713.34
Danny Briggs	73	68	68	73	282	2,713.33
John Kennaday	69	70	70	73	282	2,713.33
Bill Murchison	68	73	70	71	282	2,713.33
Mike Schuchart	69	71	68	74	282	2,713.33
Frank Conner	70	68	70	75	283	2,000
Steve Haskins	70	69	70	74	283	2,000
Chris Perry	69	71	70	73	283	2,000
Roger Salazar	67	72	70	74	283	2,000
Sonny Skinner	71	70	71	71	283	2,000
Ron Streck	68	73	69	73	283	2,000
Bruce Vaughan	70	73	68	72	283	2,000
Joe Durant	71	70	70	73	284	1,345.72
Rich Parker	73	70	68	73	284	1,345.72
Matt Peterson	69	72	68	75	284	1,345.72
Ralph Howe III	71	69	70	74	284	1,345.71
Rick Smallridge	69	71	69	75	284	1,345.71
Brian Smith	71	68	74	71	284	1,345.71
Bob Wolcott	71	66	68	79	284	1,345.71

South Carolina Classic

Country Club of South Carolina, Florence, South Carolina
Par 36-36—72; 7,150 yards

May 5-8
purse, $175,000

	SCORES				TOTAL	MONEY
Charles Rymer	67	67	72	68	274	$31,500
Pat Bates	69	67	72	67	275	19,862.50
Craig Kanada	67	71	69	69	276	12,687.50
Bruce Vaughan	65	71	73	67	276	12,687.50

		SCORES			TOTAL	MONEY
Mike Schuchart	72	68	69	68	277	9,187.50
Woody Austin	70	72	70	66	278	6,125
Tom Carr	68	71	75	64	278	6,125
Rich Parker	68	69	70	71	278	6,125
Mike Sposa	68	71	70	69	278	6,125
Tommy Tolles	66	71	73	68	278	6,125
Mark Allen	70	69	69	71	279	2,772.50
Tom Byrum	70	68	69	72	279	2,772.50
Ricky Gonzalez	69	68	71	71	279	2,772.50
Chris Hunsucker	71	71	67	70	279	2,772.50
Jerry Kelly	71	65	76	67	279	2,772.50
Chris Perry	68	71	71	69	279	2,772.50
Thomas Scherrer	68	72	71	68	279	2,772.50
Mike Donald	71	69	69	71	280	2,012.50
Joe Durant	69	67	73	71	280	2,012.50
Mike Emery, Jr.	70	70	71	69	280	2,012.50
Joey Gullion	67	71	72	70	280	2,012.50
Christian Pena	68	66	74	72	280	2,012.50
Tommy Armour	69	67	74	71	281	1,750
Greg Bruckner	70	68	72	72	282	1,402.50
Steve Cartano	67	72	73	70	282	1,402.50
Jim Carter	68	70	74	70	282	1,402.50
Frank Conner	71	71	72	68	282	1,402.50
Tad Holloway	71	69	73	69	282	1,402.50
Karl Kimball	70	69	72	71	282	1,402.50
Dicky Thompson	71	68	70	73	282	1,402.50

Central Georgia Open

River North Country Club, Macon, Georgia
Par 36-36—72; 6,714 yards

May 12-15
purse, $175,000

		SCORES			TOTAL	MONEY
Rick Pearson	71	68	65	69	273	$31,500
Bill Murchison	65	72	67	69	273	15,079.17
Charles Rymer	73	66	65	69	273	15,079.17
Danny Briggs	69	67	66	71	273	15,079.16
(Pearson defeated Murchison, Rymer and Briggs on second extra hole.)						
Emlyn Aubrey	67	72	70	65	274	8,020.84
Jim Schuman	70	67	70	67	274	8,020.83
Tommy Tolles	69	71	66	68	274	8,020.83
Barry Fabyan	69	68	70	68	275	5,687.50
Tim Loustalot	66	69	73	67	275	5,687.50
Jerry Kelly	71	67	71	67	276	3,937.50
Hugh Royer III	68	69	68	71	276	3,937.50
Jose Cantero	71	68	67	71	277	2,585
Jim Carter	67	68	72	70	277	2,585
Joe Durant	71	72	65	69	277	2,585
Chris Hunsucker	71	73	64	69	277	2,585
Skip Kendall	71	69	65	72	277	2,585
Francis Quinn	72	66	71	68	277	2,585
Mike Smith	69	71	70	67	277	2,585
Jorge Berendt	72	70	72	64	278	2,056.25
Perry Moss	69	71	69	69	278	2,056.25
Greg Bruckner	71	67	71	70	279	1,750
Brad Fabel	71	68	72	68	279	1,750
Joe Inman	72	68	70	69	279	1,750

	SCORES	TOTAL	MONEY
Steve Isley	73 71 68 67	279	1,750
Jade Work	68 73 72 66	279	1,750
David Duval	74 70 66 70	280	1,316
Buddy Gardner	74 69 70 67	280	1,316
Clarence Rose	72 65 70 73	280	1,316
Gary Rusnak	70 70 71 69	280	1,316
Tom Shaw	73 71 70 66	280	1,316

Knoxville Open

Willow Creek Golf Club, Knoxville, Tennessee
Par 35-36—71; 6,869 yards

May 19-22
purse, $200,000

	SCORES	TOTAL	MONEY
Vic Wilk	70 71 68 66	275	$36,000
Bill Murchison	72 66 70 68	276	22,700
Rick Pearson	71 70 66 70	277	16,500
Tom Garner	73 65 70 70	278	10,666.67
Gary Rusnak	69 69 70 70	278	10,666.67
Frank Conner	73 70 65 70	278	10,666.66
Emlyn Aubrey	72 69 67 71	279	4,987.50
Clark Burroughs	70 73 70 66	279	4,987.50
Joe Durant	74 70 67 68	279	4,987.50
Barry Fabyan	73 69 67 70	279	4,987.50
Scott Gump	69 70 69 71	279	4,987.50
Jerry Kelly	69 69 70 71	279	4,987.50
Jeff Klein	70 72 69 68	279	4,987.50
Thomas Scherrer	73 71 65 70	279	4,987.50
Steve Haskins	68 71 68 73	280	2,636
Brad King	67 73 70 70	280	2,636
Chris Perry	72 67 71 70	280	2,636
Lee Rinker	71 71 68 70	280	2,636
Mike Sposa	72 69 69 70	280	2,636
Robert Friend	70 73 69 69	281	2,000
Craig Kanada	71 69 72 69	281	2,000
Chris Peddicord	70 71 70 70	281	2,000
Sonny Skinner	73 71 67 70	281	2,000
Mike Smith	74 70 70 67	281	2,000
Lance Ten Broeck	71 68 74 68	281	2,000
Tray Tyner	69 71 72 69	281	2,000
Franklin Langham	76 68 68 70	282	1,500
Francis Quinn	74 70 68 70	282	1,500
Hugh Royer III	74 70 70 68	282	1,500
David Kirkpatrick	74 70 68 71	283	1,280
Gerry Norquist	69 71 72 71	283	1,280

Greater Greenville Classic

Verdae Greens Golf Club, Greenville, South Carolina
Par 36-36—72; 6,798 yards

May 25-28
purse, $175,000

	SCORES	TOTAL	MONEY
Scott Gump	71 67 66 68	272	$31,500
Tim Conley	65 72 67 69	273	19,862.50
Rafael Alarcon	70 68 67 69	274	14,437.50

	SCORES				TOTAL	MONEY
Chris Tucker	69	71	70	67	277	9,333.34
Tommy Armour	68	70	68	71	277	9,333.33
Thomas Scherrer	69	68	71	69	277	9,333.33
Rob Boldt	71	67	70	70	278	6,562.50
Craig Kanada	69	69	72	68	278	6,562.50
Joe Hamorski	70	67	72	70	279	4,375
Skip Kendall	71	65	72	71	279	4,375
Karl Zoller	67	69	73	70	279	4,375
Brad Fabel	71	69	73	67	280	2,975
Mark Lye	70	71	69	70	280	2,975
Mark Allen	70	70	70	71	281	2,555
Sam Randolph	70	72	70	69	281	2,555
Lee Rinker	70	71	70	70	281	2,555
David Kirkpatrick	75	68	70	69	282	2,193.34
Keith Fergus	68	72	73	69	282	2,193.33
Chris Perry	72	71	68	71	282	2,193.33
Steve Haskins	74	70	70	69	283	1,925
Dennis Postlewait	75	69	71	68	283	1,925
Tommy Tolles	70	69	72	72	283	1,925
Emlyn Aubrey	65	73	71	75	284	1,370.25
Pat Bates	72	72	71	69	284	1,370.25
Michael Christie	74	66	72	72	284	1,370.25
Bobby Doolittle	71	69	75	69	284	1,370.25
Joe Durant	72	71	73	68	284	1,370.25
Buddy Gardner	73	70	72	69	284	1,370.25
Matt Peterson	68	67	77	72	284	1,370.25
Bill Porter	72	70	74	68	284	1,370.25
Mike Sposa	75	69	71	69	284	1,370.25
Vic Wilk	74	70	72	68	284	1,370.25

Miami Valley Open

Heatherwoode Golf Club, Springboro, Ohio
Par 36-35—71; 6,730 yards

June 2-5
purse, $200,000

	SCORES				TOTAL	MONEY
Tommy Armour	68	67	66	65	266	$36,000
Jim Carter	69	69	66	65	269	22,700
Clark Burroughs	69	68	63	70	270	14,500
Chris Perry	69	69	64	68	270	14,500
Craig Kanada	70	61	72	68	271	9,750
Lee Rinker	68	68	67	68	271	9,750
Glen Hnatiuk	70	70	63	69	272	7,500
Jim Kane	69	69	65	69	272	7,500
Mark Allen	72	68	66	67	273	5,000
Woody Austin	71	67	68	67	273	5,000
Tim Loustalot	69	68	70	66	273	5,000
Emlyn Aubrey	70	68	68	68	274	3,030
Tom Carr	68	65	70	71	274	3,030
Scott Gump	70	69	66	69	274	3,030
Skip Kendall	70	68	66	70	274	3,030
Bill Murchison	72	67	65	70	274	3,030
Don Walsworth	68	72	64	70	274	3,030
David Berganio, Jr.	73	69	69	64	275	2,450
Greg Cesario	69	72	65	69	275	2,450
David Duval	67	67	76	66	276	2,100
Tom Gillis	67	70	67	72	276	2,100

	SCORES				TOTAL	MONEY
Steve Isley	73	68	64	71	276	2,100
Chris Peddicord	72	70	65	69	276	2,100
Bill Porter	69	70	68	69	276	2,100
Frank Conner	72	69	69	67	277	1,470
John Dal Corobbo	69	73	67	68	277	1,470
Joe Durant	69	68	70	70	277	1,470
Jeff Klein	69	70	66	72	277	1,470
Hicks Malonson	71	70	69	67	277	1,470
Francis Quinn	67	73	66	71	277	1,470
Jim Schuman	68	72	66	71	277	1,470
Sonny Skinner	68	70	66	73	277	1,470

Cleveland Open

Quail Hollow Resort, Concord, Ohio
Par 36-36—72; 6,712 yards

June 9-12
purse, $200,000

	SCORES				TOTAL	MONEY
Tommy Armour	68	68	70	69	275	$36,000
Scott Gump	72	70	64	69	275	19,600
Thomas Scherrer	70	69	69	67	275	19,600
(Armour defeated Gump and Scherrer on first extra hole.)						
Russell Beiersdorf	69	72	67	69	277	11,500
Buddy Gardner	67	71	66	73	277	11,500
Danny Briggs	70	65	76	67	278	9,000
Webb Heintzelman	71	70	70	68	279	5,583.34
Chris Perry	73	68	72	66	279	5,583.34
Sam Randolph	71	70	69	69	279	5,583.33
Lee Rinker	71	70	67	71	279	5,583.33
Hugh Royer III	68	74	66	71	279	5,583.33
Mike Smith	73	68	68	70	279	5,583.33
J.P. Hayes	71	73	68	69	281	3,100
Rick Pearson	70	71	71	69	281	3,100
Jim Schuman	70	72	69	70	281	3,100
Emlyn Aubrey	74	67	70	71	282	2,570
Jeff Barlow	74	67	70	71	282	2,570
Jeff Gallagher	69	74	69	70	282	2,570
Don Reese	70	70	69	73	282	2,570
Robert Friend	69	71	69	74	283	2,200
Tim Straub	71	69	70	73	283	2,200
Bob Wolcott	74	68	71	70	283	2,200
Tom Carr	70	71	71	72	284	1,850
Mike Emery, Jr.	73	70	73	68	284	1,850
Chris Hunsucker	72	69	70	73	284	1,850
David Jackson	71	71	69	73	284	1,850
Craig Kanada	71	73	72	69	285	1,345.72
Clarence Rose	74	68	73	70	285	1,345.72
Mike Schuchart	69	73	74	69	285	1,345.72
David Berganio, Jr.	69	72	73	71	285	1,345.71
Joe Hamorski	70	73	69	73	285	1,345.71
Steve Haskins	72	72	69	72	285	1,345.71
Sonny Skinner	69	73	73	70	285	1,345.71

Dominion Open

The Dominion Club, Glen Allen, Virginia
Par 36-36—72; 7,040 yards

June 16-19
purse, $175,000

		SCORES			TOTAL	MONEY
Sonny Skinner	70	65	67	69	271	$36,000
Jim Carter	65	68	68	70	271	22,700
(Skinner defeated Carter on second extra hole.)						
Barry Fabyan	72	68	69	63	272	13,166.67
John Wilson	67	69	69	67	272	13,166.67
John Riegger	70	69	65	68	272	13,166.66
Peter Persons	67	69	67	70	273	8,500
Jeff Wilson	69	72	66	66	273	8,500
Pat Bates	68	70	66	70	274	7,000
Rob Boldt	69	70	68	68	275	3,971.43
Greg Cesario	65	70	70	70	275	3,971.43
Jerry Kelly	72	67	66	70	275	3,971.43
Franklin Langham	70	67	73	65	275	3,971.43
Bill Porter	68	71	72	64	275	3,971.43
Don Reese	68	71	68	68	275	3,971.43
Bob Burns	67	69	68	71	275	3,971.42
Clarence Rose	65	71	68	72	276	2,690
Mike Schuchart	68	68	70	70	276	2,690
J.C. Anderson	69	69	65	74	277	2,000
Wayne Defrancesco	68	70	70	69	277	2,000
Brad Fabel	72	69	67	69	277	2,000
Chad Ginn	69	69	70	69	277	2,000
John Kennaday	68	70	66	73	277	2,000
Tim Loustalot	70	68	69	70	277	2,000
Perry Moss	68	68	69	72	277	2,000
Rich Parker	69	66	72	70	277	2,000
Matt Peterson	69	69	67	72	277	2,000
Bruce Vaughan	71	69	68	69	277	2,000
Bob Wolcott	70	71	69	67	277	2,000
Greg Bruckner	71	70	64	73	278	1,195
Tom Carr	70	69	70	69	278	1,195
Jeff Cook	69	69	68	72	278	1,195
Scott Gump	70	70	66	72	278	1,195
John Maginnes	71	69	71	67	278	1,195
Jim Schuman	68	72	70	68	278	1,195
Lance Ten Broeck	70	69	69	70	278	1,195
Robert Wrenn	70	71	67	70	278	1,195

Carolina Classic

Prestonwood Country Club, Cary, North Carolina
Par 36-36—72; 6,879 yards

June 23-26
purse, $200,000

		SCORES			TOTAL	MONEY
Skip Kendall	65	72	70	69	276	$36,000
Pat Bates	66	68	70	74	278	22,700
Emlyn Aubrey	67	73	69	70	279	14,500
Chris Perry	70	70	70	69	279	14,500
Jeff Barlow	68	72	67	73	280	9,750
David Duval	70	69	69	72	280	9,750
Tripp Isenhour	72	70	68	71	281	7,000
Thomas Scherrer	67	72	69	73	281	7,000

	SCORES				TOTAL	MONEY
Bruce Vaughan	71	71	71	68	281	7,000
Steve Jones	68	71	71	72	282	3,950
Bill Murchison	69	71	70	72	282	3,950
Sonny Skinner	69	69	71	73	282	3,950
Tommy Tolles	72	69	71	70	282	3,950
Tim Conley	68	74	71	70	283	2,845
Barry Fabyan	69	73	70	71	283	2,845
Vance Heafner	68	74	70	71	283	2,845
Bill Porter	69	74	70	70	283	2,845
Jim Carter	68	74	75	67	284	2,500
John Kennaday	71	69	71	74	285	2,300
Rich Parker	69	74	72	70	285	2,300
Sam Randolph	65	75	76	69	285	2,300
Bob Boyd	69	70	69	78	286	1,950
Scott Gump	68	72	74	72	286	1,950
Hicks Malonson	72	71	73	70	286	1,950
Gary Rusnak	72	71	73	70	286	1,950
Tom Carr	71	73	74	69	287	1,390
Jeff Cook	66	75	70	76	287	1,390
John Dal Corobbo	73	72	71	71	287	1,390
Oswald Drawdy	68	72	73	74	287	1,390
Jeff Gallagher	72	71	72	72	287	1,390
Kelly Mitchum	73	66	73	75	287	1,390
Jim Schuman	72	70	76	69	287	1,390
Omar Uresti	67	73	74	73	287	1,390

Gateway Classic

Lake Forest Country Club, Lake St. Louis, Missouri
Par 36-36—72; 7,141 yards

July 21-24
purse, $200,000

	SCORES				TOTAL	MONEY
Brad Fabel	70	68	71	70	279	$36,000
Jim Carter	71	69	71	69	280	19,600
Chris Perry	69	72	69	70	280	19,600
Jeff Cook	71	70	72	68	281	9,400
Scott Gump	67	75	70	69	281	9,400
Chris Patton	71	69	72	69	281	9,400
Lee Rinker	71	71	70	69	281	9,400
Tommy Tolles	70	68	73	70	281	9,400
Keith Fergus	72	68	70	72	282	5,500
Jerry Kelly	71	69	69	73	282	5,500
Emlyn Aubrey	68	77	68	70	283	3,600
Woody Austin	70	71	69	73	283	3,600
Chris Hunsucker	74	68	68	73	283	3,600
David Duval	73	68	71	72	284	2,920
Jim Schuman	73	70	68	73	284	2,920
Mike Sposa	70	73	73	68	284	2,920
Rafael Alarcon	73	72	72	68	285	2,152
Kyle Coody	74	71	70	70	285	2,152
Joe Durant	71	71	74	69	285	2,152
Craig Kanada	73	70	71	71	285	2,152
David Kirkpatrick	73	70	71	71	285	2,152
Bill Porter	71	67	74	73	285	2,152
John Ross	68	69	75	73	285	2,152
Gary Rusnak	72	70	75	68	285	2,152
Charles Rymer	69	69	75	72	285	2,152

	SCORES				TOTAL	MONEY
Tray Tyner	70	74	68	73	285	2,152
Jeff Gallagher	74	70	70	72	286	1,455
Rick Pearson	70	70	73	73	286	1,455
Mike Schuchart	73	71	73	69	286	1,455
Don Walsworth	69	72	73	72	286	1,455

Wichita Charity Classic

Reflection Ridge Country Club, Wichita, Kansas
Par 36-36—72; 6,730 yards

July 28-31
purse, $175,000

	SCORES				TOTAL	MONEY
Dennis Postlewait	66	66	69	70	271	$31,500
Clark Burroughs	67	68	71	66	272	19,862.50
Tom Carr	65	70	69	69	273	12,687.50
Tommy Tolles	68	65	69	71	273	12,687.50
Greg Bruckner	68	72	70	64	274	8,020.84
Hugh Royer III	68	71	67	68	274	8,020.83
Bruce Vaughan	63	71	71	69	274	8,020.83
Pat Bates	68	70	68	69	275	5,250
Jeff Freeman	64	70	70	71	275	5,250
Mike Sposa	67	68	72	68	275	5,250
Chad Ginn	70	69	68	69	276	2,772.50
Scott Gump	67	70	68	71	276	2,772.50
Skip Kendall	70	68	73	65	276	2,772.50
Jeff Klein	69	69	68	70	276	2,772.50
Matt Peterson	72	63	71	70	276	2,772.50
Lee Rinker	69	68	71	68	276	2,772.50
Gary Webb	68	70	69	69	276	2,772.50
Jeff Barlow	66	72	70	69	277	2,100
Steve Isley	70	69	70	68	277	2,100
Thomas Scherrer	66	72	68	71	277	2,100
Tom Garner	67	72	71	68	278	1,750
Joey Gullion	71	67	68	72	278	1,750
J.P. Hayes	68	67	71	72	278	1,750
Bob Heintz	68	70	68	72	278	1,750
Greg Whisman	70	68	69	71	278	1,750
Jeff Brehaut	69	68	70	72	279	1,245
John Elliott	66	72	69	72	279	1,245
Robert Friend	73	65	69	72	279	1,245
Steve Jones	72	68	67	72	279	1,245
Craig Kanada	70	68	71	70	279	1,245
Jerry Kelly	65	71	68	75	279	1,245
Chris Perry	69	70	71	69	279	1,245

Dakota Dunes Open

Dakota Dunes Country Club, Dakota Dunes, South Dakota
Par 36-36—72; 7,165 yards

August 4-7
purse, $200,000

	SCORES				TOTAL	MONEY
Pat Bates	74	68	69	65	276	$36,000
Rex Caldwell	71	70	69	68	278	19,600
Gary Webb	73	69	72	64	278	19,600
Jeff Brehaut	71	70	69	69	279	11,500

	SCORES				TOTAL	MONEY
Vic Wilk	70	70	72	67	279	11,500
Tim Loustalot	69	67	71	73	280	9,000
Scott Gump	70	70	70	71	281	8,000
Greg Bruckner	66	72	74	70	282	6,500
Sonny Skinner	71	70	70	71	282	6,500
Jeff Barlow	69	70	75	69	283	4,166.67
Thomas Scherrer	73	66	75	69	283	4,166.67
Don Reese	67	72	72	72	283	4,166.66
Frank Lickliter	72	72	72	68	284	3,200
Bruce Vaughan	69	75	70	70	284	3,200
Tom Carr	70	70	75	70	285	2,636
Keith Fergus	70	70	71	74	285	2,636
Jerry Kelly	71	71	72	71	285	2,636
Lee Rinker	71	67	76	71	285	2,636
Omar Uresti	69	70	74	72	285	2,636
Jeff Freeman	72	71	71	72	286	2,150
Bill Murchison	72	68	76	70	286	2,150
Rich Parker	70	72	74	70	286	2,150
Matt Peterson	72	69	73	72	286	2,150
Steve Isley	73	69	70	75	287	1,750
Peter Persons	69	70	77	71	287	1,750
Dennis Postlewait	71	70	74	72	287	1,750
Charles Rymer	70	73	75	69	287	1,750
Woody Austin	76	68	73	71	288	1,332
Skip Kendall	72	72	73	71	288	1,332
Chris Perry	68	77	74	69	288	1,332
Hugh Royer III	70	72	78	68	288	1,332
Tommy Tolles	72	68	73	75	288	1,332

Ozarks Open

Highland Springs Country Club, Springfield, Missouri
Par 36-36—72; 7,038 yards

August 11-14
purse, $200,000

	SCORES				TOTAL	MONEY
Jerry Haas	69	65	69	69	272	$36,000
Frank Conner	68	71	70	64	273	22,700
Pat Bates	66	70	70	68	274	14,500
David Duval	69	66	67	72	274	14,500
Charles Rymer	71	70	69	65	275	7,583.34
Sonny Skinner	71	69	69	66	275	7,583.34
Clark Burroughs	68	67	67	73	275	7,583.33
Buddy Gardner	71	69	66	69	275	7,583.33
David Jackson	67	71	67	70	275	7,583.33
Vic Wilk	66	66	72	71	275	7,583.33
Bill Murchison	69	71	69	67	276	3,600
Chris Perry	70	68	71	67	276	3,600
Matt Peterson	66	70	73	67	276	3,600
Peter Persons	68	71	73	65	277	3,000
Thomas Scherrer	68	71	72	66	277	3,000
Emlyn Aubrey	69	68	72	69	278	2,570
Rex Caldwell	69	71	71	67	278	2,570
Mike Schuchart	69	69	72	68	278	2,570
Tray Tyner	68	71	72	67	278	2,570
Scott Gump	73	68	68	70	279	2,150
Skip Kendall	69	71	70	69	279	2,150
Don Reese	73	67	70	69	279	2,150

		SCORES			TOTAL	MONEY
Tommy Tolles	66	68	70	75	279	2,150
Woody Austin	70	72	63	75	280	1,800
Steve Jurgensen	67	67	78	68	280	1,800
Tony Sills	68	70	70	72	280	1,800
Mike Emery, Jr.	68	70	71	72	281	1,376.67
Jack Ferenz	69	71	69	72	281	1,376.67
Todd Parks	70	70	72	69	281	1,376.67
Stan Utley	68	72	72	69	281	1,376.67
John Elliott	69	71	73	68	281	1,376.66
Omar Uresti	68	72	68	73	281	1,376.66

Texarkana Open

Texarkana Country Club, Texarkana, Texas
Par 36-36—72; 6,588 yards

August 18-21
purse, $200,000

		SCORES			TOTAL	MONEY
Mike Brisky	66	65	68	67	266	$36,000
Sonny Skinner	67	66	68	72	273	22,700
David Duval	69	69	69	67	274	14,500
David Kirkpatrick	68	65	72	69	274	14,500
Ralph Howe III	68	67	70	70	275	8,625
Franklin Langham	70	69	72	64	275	8,625
John Maginnes	71	66	72	66	275	8,625
Tray Tyner	69	67	66	73	275	8,625
Jim Carter	71	66	67	72	276	4,625
Robert Friend	70	67	68	71	276	4,625
Thomas Scherrer	70	70	66	70	276	4,625
Tommy Tolles	67	68	68	73	276	4,625
Bill Porter	67	72	68	70	277	3,200
Ron Whittaker	68	69	67	73	277	3,200
Frank Conner	67	72	72	67	278	2,695
Tony Sills	71	70	69	68	278	2,695
Bruce Vaughan	68	70	71	69	278	2,695
Zoran Zorkic	69	70	69	70	278	2,695
J.C. Anderson	72	71	71	65	279	2,050
Ben Bates	69	70	67	73	279	2,050
Pat Bates	67	70	73	69	279	2,050
Chad Ginn	70	67	72	70	279	2,050
Dennis Postlewait	70	69	72	68	279	2,050
Cade Stone	73	69	67	70	279	2,050
Omar Uresti	71	65	68	75	279	2,050
Kim Young	68	68	71	72	279	2,050
Steve Ford	70	69	70	71	280	1,455
Jerry Haas	72	68	71	69	280	1,455
Tom Loustalot	73	63	73	71	280	1,455
Bill Murchison	69	72	71	68	280	1,455

Permian Basin Open

The Club at Mission Dorado, Odessa, Texas
Par 36-36—72; 7,135 yards

August 25-28
purse, $175,000

	SCORES				TOTAL	MONEY
Bruce Vaughan	68	67	67	67	269	$31,500
Gary Rusnak	67	68	70	68	273	17,150
Bob Wolcott	71	64	70	68	273	17,150
Chris Perry	70	72	67	65	274	9,333.34
Jeff Barlow	68	66	69	71	274	9,333.33
T. Gene Jones	70	67	69	68	274	9,333.33
Bill Porter	67	67	72	69	275	6,562.50
Zoran Zorkic	69	68	68	70	275	6,562.50
Greg Cesario	69	68	68	71	276	3,815
Rick Dalpos	73	67	66	70	276	3,815
R.W. Eaks	70	70	69	67	276	3,815
Ricky Gonzalez	70	70	68	68	276	3,815
Jerry Haas	70	68	70	68	276	3,815
Rafael Alarcon	73	69	67	68	277	2,322.50
Shane Bertsch	71	71	68	67	277	2,322.50
Clark Burroughs	70	68	71	68	277	2,322.50
Buddy Gardner	70	69	68	70	277	2,322.50
Alan Pate	70	68	68	71	277	2,322.50
Mike Smith	69	70	69	69	277	2,322.50
Rick Todd	67	72	69	69	277	2,322.50
Tommy Armour III	70	69	69	70	278	1,750
Kawika Cotner	71	71	67	69	278	1,750
Glen Hnatiuk	70	70	67	71	278	1,750
Chris Hunsucker	70	67	72	69	278	1,750
Mike Sposa	70	71	68	69	278	1,750
J.C. Anderson	70	66	70	73	279	1,190
John Elliott	69	67	70	73	279	1,190
Keith Fergus	71	69	71	68	279	1,190
Steve Isley	66	73	72	68	279	1,190
Franklin Langham	68	74	68	69	279	1,190
Todd Parks	72	69	72	66	279	1,190
Christian Pena	69	68	71	71	279	1,190
Hugh Royer III	67	73	68	71	279	1,190
Tony Sills	65	68	73	73	279	1,190

New Mexico Charity Classic

University of New Mexico Championship Golf Course,
Albuquerque, New Mexico
Par 36-36—72; 7,248 yards

September 1-4
purse, $175,000

	SCORES				TOTAL	MONEY
Jim Carter	69	68	71	66	272	$31,500
Emlyn Aubrey	65	71	71	66	273	17,150
Chad Ginn	67	71	71	64	273	17,150
David Duval	65	74	69	66	274	10,937.50
Bruce Vaughan	69	71	71	64	275	8,020.84
R.W. Eaks	70	70	66	69	275	8,020.83
Chris Perry	67	68	71	69	275	8,020.83
Woody Austin	69	72	68	67	276	4,200
Keith Fergus	69	71	68	68	276	4,200
John Maginnes	71	71	68	66	276	4,200

	SCORES				TOTAL	MONEY
Matt Peterson	71	71	66	68	276	4,200
Bill Porter	67	73	68	68	276	4,200
Gary Rusnak	68	73	70	65	276	4,200
Scott Gump	72	65	73	67	277	2,555
Lee Rinker	65	72	73	67	277	2,555
Mike Schuchart	70	69	70	68	277	2,555
Harry Rudolph	70	69	71	68	278	2,292.50
Greg Cesario	70	72	71	66	279	2,056.25
David Jackson	70	67	69	73	279	2,056.25
Thomas Scherrer	73	67	66	73	279	2,056.25
Greg Whisman	69	71	68	71	279	2,056.25
Pat Bates	70	72	71	67	280	1,575
Danny Briggs	69	72	71	68	280	1,575
Jack Ferenz	72	70	66	72	280	1,575
Ricky Gonzalez	70	72	69	69	280	1,575
Tim Herron	69	72	69	70	280	1,575
Chris Peddicord	73	69	69	69	280	1,575
Eric Rustand	71	70	69	70	280	1,575
Greg Bruckner	71	71	70	69	281	1,128.75
John Elliott	66	71	71	73	281	1,128.75
Tom Shaw	68	72	71	70	281	1,128.75
Bob Wolcott	66	74	72	69	281	1,128.75

Utah Classic

Riverside Country Club, Provo, Utah
Par 36-36—72; 7,001 yards

September 9-11
purse, $175,000

	SCORES			TOTAL	MONEY
Chris Perry	69	68	68	205	$31,500
David Duval	70	65	71	206	19,862.50
Tom Garner	68	71	69	208	14,437.50
Jim Carter	72	68	69	209	10,937.50
Jeff Barlow	71	71	68	210	8,020.84
Buddy Gardner	70	69	71	210	8,020.83
Jerry Kelly	68	71	71	210	8,020.83
Craig Kanada	74	71	66	211	6,125
Clark Burroughs	72	71	69	212	4,046.88
Gary Rusnak	69	74	69	212	4,046.88
Don Reese	68	68	76	212	4,046.87
Thomas Scherrer	65	72	75	212	4,046.87
T. Gene Jones	66	73	74	213	2,712.50
Tommy Tolles	69	71	73	213	2,712.50
Bob Wolcott	69	72	72	213	2,712.50
Danny Briggs	72	72	70	214	2,110
Rick Dalpos	70	70	74	214	2,110
Tim Herron	73	71	70	214	2,110
Ryan Rhees	74	69	71	214	2,110
Lee Rinker	66	73	75	214	2,110
Mike Schuchart	69	71	74	214	2,110
Jade Work	70	74	70	214	2,110
Rex Caldwell	69	70	76	215	1,618.75
Glen Hnatiuk	73	71	71	215	1,618.75
Sonny Skinner	71	74	70	215	1,618.75
Tray Tyner	68	74	73	215	1,618.75
Jerry Haas	73	69	74	216	1,177.50
Tad Holloway	69	70	77	216	1,177.50

	SCORES			TOTAL	MONEY
Franklin Langham	70	70	76	216	1,177.50
Tim Loustalot	72	73	71	216	1,177.50
Clarence Rose	69	74	73	216	1,177.50
Mike Sposa	70	72	74	216	1,177.50
Jeff Thomsen	73	71	72	216	1,177.50

Boise Open

Hillcrest Country Club, Boise, Idaho
Par 36-35—71; 6,773 yards

September 16-18
purse, $200,000

	SCORES			TOTAL	MONEY
Keith Fergus	65	69	64	198	$36,000
Bill Murchison	66	64	68	198	22,700
(Fergus defeated Murchison on second extra hole.)					
Woody Austin	68	71	61	200	13,166.67
Scott Gump	67	68	65	200	13,166.67
J.P. Hayes	69	61	70	200	13,166.66
Lee Rinker	66	71	64	201	9,000
John Maginnes	68	68	66	202	8,000
Emlyn Aubrey	68	67	68	203	5,500
Jerry Haas	67	67	69	203	5,500
Jerry Kelly	69	70	74	203	5,500
Bruce Vaughan	68	65	70	203	5,500
David Duval	68	68	68	204	3,300
Chris Perry	65	72	67	204	3,300
Bill Porter	67	67	70	204	3,300
Jaime Gomez	69	67	69	205	2,830
David Jackson	64	68	73	205	2,830
Glen Hnatiuk	69	72	65	206	2,353.34
Rick Pearson	74	67	65	206	2,353.34
Chris Patton	69	69	68	206	2,353.33
Dennis Postlewait	69	68	69	206	2,353.33
Mike Schuchart	69	67	70	206	2,353.33
Omar Uresti	69	65	72	206	2,353.33
Pat Bates	72	65	70	207	1,750
Rick Dalpos	72	66	69	207	1,750
Robert Friend	69	71	67	207	1,750
Rich Parker	68	67	72	207	1,750
Monte Scheinblum	68	68	71	207	1,750
Tray Tyner	70	68	69	207	1,750
Tommy Armour III	67	68	73	208	1,110
Danny Briggs	64	73	71	208	1,110
Greg Bruckner	71	70	67	208	1,110
Clark Burroughs	70	69	69	208	1,110
Croy Cochran	66	74	68	208	1,110
Mike Emery, Jr.	70	68	70	208	1,110
Ralph Howe III	74	66	68	208	1,110
Jim Kane	74	66	68	208	1,110
Skip Kendall	69	69	70	208	1,110
John Kennaday	74	67	67	208	1,110
Franklin Langham	71	68	69	208	1,110
Vic Wilk	70	71	67	208	1,110

Tri-Cities Classic

Meadow Springs Country Club, Richland, Washington
Par 36-36—72; 6,926 yards

September 23-25
purse, $175,000

	SCORES			TOTAL	MONEY
Jerry Haas	69	67	67	203	$31,500
Brad Fabel	70	66	68	204	19,862.50
Lee Rinker	67	68	70	205	14,437.50
Jim Carter	69	67	71	207	7,729.17
Jeff Cook	70	70	67	207	7,729.17
Charles Rymer	69	66	72	207	7,729.17
Kevin Sutherland	70	70	67	207	7,729.17
David Duval	68	66	73	207	7,729.16
Harry Rudolph	67	67	73	207	7,729.16
Steve Haskins	74	65	69	208	4,375
Greg Bruckner	74	67	68	209	2,699.38
Clark Burroughs	71	71	67	209	2,699.38
John Dowdall	68	73	68	209	2,699.38
J.P. Hayes	67	73	69	209	2,699.38
Pat Bates	72	68	69	209	2,699.37
Danny Briggs	71	67	71	209	2,699.37
Webb Heintzelman	70	70	69	209	2,699.37
Bill Porter	68	71	70	209	2,699.37
Bill Murchison	69	72	69	210	1,925
Chris Peddicord	70	71	69	210	1,925
Matt Peterson	70	70	70	210	1,925
Gary Rusnak	72	71	67	210	1,925
Omar Uresti	67	73	70	210	1,925
R.W. Eaks	69	68	74	211	1,487.50
Skip Kendall	71	70	70	211	1,487.50
John Maginnes	68	69	74	211	1,487.50
Chris Perry	70	69	72	211	1,487.50
Sam Randolph	67	71	73	211	1,487.50
Tommy Armour III	68	72	72	212	1,106
Rick Dalpos	76	67	69	212	1,106
Ralph Howe III	72	71	69	212	1,106
Jerry Kelly	72	68	72	212	1,106
Bob Wolcott	73	67	72	212	1,106

Sonoma County Open

Windsor Golf Club, Windsor, California
Par 36-36—72; 6,650 yards

September 29-October 2
purse, $175,000

	SCORES				TOTAL	MONEY
Jerry Haas	67	68	71	71	277	$31,500
Woody Austin	68	68	69	74	279	19,862.50
Keith Fergus	70	76	69	65	280	11,520.84
Lee Rinker	70	67	71	72	280	11,520.83
Mike Schuchart	74	68	69	69	280	11,520.83
John Dowdall	70	76	66	69	281	7,000
David Jackson	67	71	71	72	281	7,000
Christian Pena	70	72	66	73	281	7,000
Emlyn Aubrey	70	74	70	69	283	4,046.88
Bob Wolcott	73	70	71	69	283	4,046.88
Jerry Kelly	66	73	72	72	283	4,046.87
Dave Sutherland	77	65	69	72	283	4,046.87
Danny Briggs	73	71	70	70	284	2,800

	SCORES				TOTAL	MONEY
Bill Porter	71	68	71	74	284	2,800
Webb Heintzelman	71	72	72	70	285	2,476.25
John Maginnes	70	71	72	72	285	2,476.25
Chris Patton	70	72	72	72	286	2,292.50
Jeff Barlow	72	73	71	71	287	1,925
Ben Bates	70	75	75	67	287	1,925
Jeff Gallagher	72	71	74	70	287	1,925
Jim Lemon	74	70	70	73	287	1,925
Matt Peterson	73	73	70	71	287	1,925
John Ross	71	74	71	71	287	1,925
Hugh Royer III	72	74	70	71	287	1,925
Rick Dalpos	73	72	73	70	288	1,359.17
Joe Durant	72	75	73	68	288	1,359.17
Sam Randolph	74	72	71	71	288	1,359.17
Vic Wilk	69	75	74	70	288	1,359.17
Tom Carr	68	72	73	75	288	1,359.16
Gerry Norquist	69	73	72	74	288	1,359.16

Nike Tour Championship

Pumpkin Ridge Golf Club, Cornelius, Oregon
Par 35-36—72; 6,839 yards

October 13-16
purse, $225,000

	SCORES				TOTAL	MONEY
Mike Schuchart	69	67	68	73	277	$40,500
Emlyn Aubrey	72	69	67	70	278	19,762.50
Jeff Cook	73	70	67	68	278	19,762.50
Lee Rinker	69	70	69	70	278	19,762.50
John Maginnes	68	69	68	74	279	12,375
Jim Carter	69	68	71	72	280	9,562.50
David Duval	67	73	69	71	280	9,562.50
Brad Fabel	68	74	69	70	281	7,875
Keith Fergus	69	73	72	68	282	5,625
J.P. Hayes	70	72	69	71	282	5,625
Tim Loustalot	71	72	74	65	282	5,625
Pat Bates	73	72	72	66	283	3,993.75
Vic Wilk	73	73	68	69	283	3,993.75
Jeff Brehaut	68	73	76	68	285	3,375
Jerry Haas	74	71	67	73	285	3,375
Scott Gump	70	72	76	68	286	2,955
Bill Porter	72	76	67	71	286	2,955
Thomas Scherrer	76	70	75	65	286	2,955
Woody Austin	73	71	70	73	287	2,700
Omar Uresti	75	74	72	67	288	2,587.50
Robert Friend	73	71	70	75	289	2,418.75
Craig Kanada	76	71	67	75	289	2,418.75
David Jackson	74	75	72	69	290	2,081.25
Skip Kendall	68	72	76	74	290	2,081.25
Mike Sposa	76	76	71	67	290	2,081.25
Tommy Tolles	75	73	70	72	290	2,081.25
Tommy Armour III	70	73	74	74	291	1,665
Tom Carr	72	72	72	75	291	1,665
Frank Conner	72	69	75	75	291	1,665
Bob Wolcott	78	72	72	69	291	1,665

Canadian Tour

Payless Open

Cordova Bay Golf Course, Parksville, British Columbia
Par 36-36—72; 6,628 yards

June 2-5
purse, C$100,000

	SCORES				TOTAL	MONEY
Matt Jackson	71	67	69	69	276	C$18,000
David DeLong	72	69	69	68	278	8,000
Jim Rutledge	69	69	72	68	278	8,000
Marty Roberts	70	74	68	67	279	3,975
Ian Leggatt	72	71	70	66	279	3,975
Eric Woods	67	73	70	69	279	3,975
Scott Geroux	70	69	72	68	279	3,975
Rick Todd	73	70	68	69	280	2,450
Frank Edmonds	75	67	67	71	280	2,450
Craig Marseilles	70	68	73	69	280	2,450
Don Fardon	72	69	71	69	281	1,800
David Bolton	69	71	72	69	281	1,800
Michael Tschetter	69	71	71	70	281	1,800
Dean Wilson	67	71	72	71	281	1,800
Matthew Lane	68	69	75	69	281	1,800
Blair Piercy	73	72	66	71	282	1,500
John Randle, Jr.	79	67	67	70	283	1,425
Arden Knoll	70	74	69	70	283	1,425
Dan Halldorson	74	71	69	70	284	1,250
Guy Hill	72	72	73	67	284	1,250
Scott Dunlap	74	70	70	70	284	1,250
Stuart Hendley	74	67	70	73	284	1,250
Jerry Springer	73	68	72	71	284	1,250
Nick Goetze	75	69	70	71	285	1,043.75
Danny Ellis	72	66	74	73	285	1,043.75
Robert Meyer	73	66	75	71	285	1,043.75
Craig Howard	68	67	73	77	285	1,043.75
Jeff Bloom	76	70	71	69	286	887.50
Carlos Espinosa	71	75	72	68	286	887.50
Cam Emerson	72	73	70	71	286	887.50
Ian Hutchings	75	70	68	73	286	887.50
Stephen Leaney	77	67	71	71	286	887.50
Kent Jones	71	72	71	72	286	887.50
Todd Doohan	74	68	73	71	286	887.50
Ray Stewart	72	68	72	74	286	887.50

Morningstar Classic

Morningstar International Golf Course, Victoria, British Columbia
Par 36-36—72; 7,018 yards

June 9-12
purse, C$100,000

	SCORES				TOTAL	MONEY
Robert Meyer	67	70	66	73	276	C$18,000
Eric Woods	70	67	68	71	276	10,000

(Meyer defeated Woods on first extra hole.)

	SCORES				TOTAL	MONEY
Duane Bock	69	73	68	67	277	6,000
Rick Todd	73	69	67	69	278	4,800
Paul Devenport	68	71	68	72	279	3,450
Scott Geroux	69	69	69	72	279	3,450
Michael Tschetter	68	70	70	71	279	3,450
Craig Marseilles	71	66	69	73	279	3,450
Dean Wilson	74	68	62	76	280	2,216.67
Daniel Pelczarski	70	70	71	69	280	2,216.67
Carlos Espinosa	71	66	71	72	280	2,216.67
Ray Stewart	72	72	65	72	281	1,800
Jeff Bloom	73	70	70	68	281	1,800
Ray Freeman	69	71	72	69	281	1,800
Derek Fung	71	71	68	72	282	1,460
Ian Leggatt	70	72	72	68	282	1,460
Brian Slevin	72	69	69	72	282	1,460
Derek James	69	72	72	69	282	1,460
Perry Parker	70	68	75	69	282	1,460
Stuart Hendley	69	72	68	74	283	1,275
Don Fardon	72	68	67	76	283	1,275
Tim Herron	70	74	68	72	284	1,041.67
Steve Schneiter	74	70	68	72	284	1,041.67
Todd Fanning	71	72	69	72	284	1,041.67
Remi Bouchard	72	70	71	71	284	1,041.67
Norm Jarvis	73	69	73	69	284	1,041.67
Bruce Heuchan	73	68	76	67	284	1,041.67
Mike Weir	70	71	72	71	284	1,041.67
Arden Knoll	72	69	73	70	284	1,041.67
Jean-Louis Lamarre	69	68	70	77	284	1,041.67

B.C. Tel Pacific Open

Predator Ridge Golf Resort, Vernon, British Columbia
Par 36-35—71; 6,641 yards

June 16-19
purse, C$100,000

	SCORES				TOTAL	MONEY
Craig Jones	67	66	67	68	268	C$18,000
Guy Hill	73	66	65	68	272	8,000
Brent Franklin	70	68	67	67	272	8,000
Ray Stewart	69	67	69	68	273	4,233.33
Jim Rutledge	67	69	67	70	273	4,233.33
Eric Woods	69	65	69	70	273	4,233.33
Derek James	69	69	67	69	274	2,783.33
Stuart Hendley	71	67	67	69	274	2,783.33
Ian Leggatt	65	72	68	69	274	2,783.33
Tim Herron	70	68	68	69	275	2,033.33
Scott Dunlap	70	68	66	71	275	2,033.33
Ian Hutchings	67	68	66	74	275	2,033.33
Kent Jones	67	70	70	69	276	1,800
Richard Zokol	68	70	65	74	277	1,600
Daniel Pelczarski	67	70	71	69	277	1,600
Kip Byrne	72	65	66	74	277	1,600
Dean Wilson	69	69	68	72	278	1,375
Duane Bock	71	66	69	72	278	1,375
Dave Miley	67	68	68	75	278	1,375
Scott Ford	68	67	69	74	278	1,375
Paul Devenport	70	72	67	70	279	1,093.75
John Restino	71	70	69	69	279	1,093.75

	SCORES				TOTAL	MONEY
Perry Parker	72	67	68	72	279	1,093.75
Frank Edmonds	70	68	67	74	279	1,093.75
Dave Barr	71	67	68	73	279	1,093.75
Jean-Louis Lamarre	72	66	71	70	279	1,093.75
David DeLong	69	68	67	75	279	1,093.75
Robert Meyer	72	65	71	71	279	1,093.75
Ray Freeman	72	70	72	66	280	925
Marty Roberts	69	71	68	72	280	925
Dave Pashko	72	67	68	73	280	925

Alberta Open

Wolf Creek Golf Resort, Ponoka, Alberta
Par 35-35—70; 6,516 yards

June 23-26
purse, C$100,000

	SCORES				TOTAL	MONEY
Jim Rutledge	68	66	69	68	271	C$18,000
Roger Wessels	71	67	62	72	272	10,000
Scott Dunlap	68	62	70	73	273	6,000
Mike Weir	69	69	69	67	274	4,800
David DeLong	71	68	66	70	275	3,700
Eric Woods	66	71	68	70	275	3,700
Ian Hutchings	71	67	68	69	275	3,700
Carlos Espinosa	71	70	67	68	276	2,575
Craig Jones	71	67	70	68	276	2,575
Remi Bouchard	69	71	67	71	278	2,033.33
Nick Goetze	71	66	72	69	278	2,033.33
Stephen Leaney	66	69	72	71	278	2,033.33
Brian Wright	68	72	69	70	279	1,650
Matt Jackson	69	70	72	68	279	1,650
Hank Baran	68	69	73	69	279	1,650
Kent Jones	65	69	72	73	279	1,650
Derek James	75	70	67	68	280	1,275
Guy Hill	70	73	67	70	280	1,275
Joe Cioe	69	74	68	69	280	1,275
Bob Rannow	67	75	68	70	280	1,275
Dan Dupuis	71	70	68	71	280	1,275
Daniel Pelczarski	66	74	70	70	280	1,275
Matthew Lane	71	68	73	68	280	1,275
Ray Freeman	65	70	73	72	280	1,275
Mark Telerico	71	72	68	70	281	1,037.50
Arden Knoll	72	66	71	72	281	1,037.50
Kevin Baker	70	74	73	65	282	975
Bruce Bulina	75	69	70	68	282	975
Stuart Hendley	70	70	69	73	282	975
George Andrews	76	69	66	72	283	862.50
John Randle	75	70	68	70	283	862.50
Mike Pero	73	70	67	73	283	862.50
Don Graham	72	71	73	67	283	862.50
Tom Jackson	72	68	69	74	283	862.50
Jeff Bloom	66	70	72	75	283	862.50

Klondike Klassic

The Ranch Golf and Country Club, Edmonton, Alberta
Par 35-35—70; 6,664 yards

June 31-July 3
purse, C$100,000

		SCORES			TOTAL	MONEY
Ian Hutchings	70	71	66	68	275	C$18,000
Arden Knoll	65	68	74	68	275	10,000
(Hutchings defeated Knoll on fourth extra hole.)						
Duane Bock	70	70	66	70	276	6,000
Jeff Bloom	68	72	69	68	277	4,500
Rick Todd	69	70	70	68	277	4,500
Michael Tschetter	71	71	68	68	278	3,200
Scott Ford	68	72	65	73	278	3,200
Matthew Lane	69	67	72	70	278	3,200
Brett Liddle	67	73	70	69	279	2,325
Eric Woods	67	70	70	72	279	2,325
Rob Willis	68	72	71	69	280	1,800
John McMullen	66	72	67	75	280	1,800
Scott Dunlap	68	70	73	69	280	1,800
Jim Rutledge	67	70	73	70	280	1,800
Derek James	67	66	73	74	280	1,800
Todd Fanning	68	75	68	70	281	1,400
Craig Jones	71	72	68	70	281	1,400
Ian Leggatt	68	75	67	71	281	1,400
Frank Edmonds	69	73	69	70	281	1,400
Tim Herron	71	71	73	66	281	1,400
Ben Weir	67	74	69	72	282	1,129.17
Ben Fouchee	67	72	73	70	282	1,129.17
Cam Emerson	65	73	72	72	282	1,129.17
Kent Jones	68	70	74	70	282	1,129.17
Marty Roberts	71	66	69	76	282	1,129.17
David DeLong	67	69	71	75	282	1,129.17
Oswald Drawdy	67	76	72	68	283	950
Drew Hartt	71	72	68	72	283	950
Mike Weir	69	73	71	70	283	950
Daniel Pelczarski	68	71	72	72	283	950
Perry Parker	67	72	72	72	283	950

Xerox Manitoba Open

Pine Ridge Golf Course, Winnipeg, Manitoba
Par 35-36—71; 6,618 yards

July 7-10
purse, C$100,000

		SCORES			TOTAL	MONEY
Scott Dunlap	68	70	68	70	276	C$18,000
Mike Weir	66	70	64	78	278	10,000
Matthew Lane	68	69	67	75	279	6,000
Ben Weir	73	71	65	74	283	3,720
Oswald Drawdy	72	70	66	75	283	3,720
David Robinson	73	68	68	74	283	3,720
Frank Edmonds	66	72	70	75	283	3,720
Todd Doohan	69	67	73	74	283	3,720
Kevin Baker	72	70	67	75	284	2,325
Ray Freeman	69	70	68	77	284	2,325
Derek James	70	74	66	75	285	1,900
Robert Meyer	67	76	67	75	285	1,900
Daniel Pelczarski	69	70	70	76	285	1,900

	SCORES				TOTAL	MONEY
Mike Pero	71	70	73	72	286	1,562.50
Jim Rutledge	72	69	71	74	286	1,562.50
Bruce Bulina	70	70	70	76	286	1,562.50
Todd Fanning	69	69	75	73	286	1,562.50
Roger Wessels	72	73	71	71	287	1,300
Tom Harding	73	70	70	74	287	1,300
Adam Kase	67	75	69	76	287	1,300
Danny Ellis	70	72	72	73	287	1,300
Brett Liddle	70	69	73	76	287	1,300
Jerry Anderson	71	74	69	74	288	1,021.88
Dave Miley	71	74	69	74	288	1,021.88
Trey Maples	70	74	70	74	288	1,021.88
Tom Inskeep	69	75	70	74	288	1,021.88
Ian Hutchings	71	73	72	72	288	1,021.88
Michael Tschetter	70	73	69	76	288	1,021.88
Joe Cioe	71	72	69	76	288	1,021.88
Tim Herron	67	75	71	75	288	1,021.88

Infiniti Tournament Players Championship

King Valley Golf Course, King City, Ontario
Par 35-36—71; 6,446 yards

July 21-24
purse, C$100,000

	SCORES				TOTAL	MONEY
Derek James	69	70	67	65	271	C$18,000
Ray Stewart	69	63	72	69	273	10,000
Ray Freeman	69	73	67	68	277	6,000
Roger Wessels	70	71	66	71	278	4,500
Adam Kase	66	71	73	68	278	4,500
Craig Howard	72	72	67	68	279	2,850
Cam Emerson	76	64	66	73	279	2,850
Bruce Bulina	71	69	70	69	279	2,850
Duane Bock	64	74	71	70	279	2,850
Dan Dupuis	64	73	71	71	279	2,850
Stephen Leaney	70	73	73	64	280	1,950
Stuart Hendley	68	69	74	69	280	1,950
Todd Fanning	65	73	71	72	281	1,800
Blair Piercy	77	65	70	70	282	1,562.50
Joe Cioe	72	69	73	68	282	1,562.50
Eric Woods	72	69	71	70	282	1,562.50
Ian Leggatt	67	70	76	69	282	1,562.50
John Restino	70	74	66	73	283	1,325
Rick Todd	73	71	70	69	283	1,325
Phillip Hatchett	71	70	71	71	283	1,325
Daniel Pelczarski	71	68	73	71	283	1,325
Lee Chill	67	74	70	73	284	1,200
Ben Weir	70	74	67	74	285	1,050
Guy Hill	75	68	70	72	285	1,050
Darryl James	69	73	72	71	285	1,050
Mike Lee	71	71	70	73	285	1,050
Jean-Louis Lamarre	74	67	73	71	285	1,050
Andy Beal	67	72	72	74	285	1,050
Mark Telerico	68	76	77	65	286	862.50
Dave Pashko	76	67	72	71	286	862.50
Tim Balmer	70	72	76	68	286	862.50
Ian Doig	71	70	74	71	286	862.50
Jerry Anderson	72	69	74	71	286	862.50

	SCORES				TOTAL	MONEY
Trey Maples	72	69	73	72	286	862.50
Greg Petersen	64	76	78	68	286	862.50
Craig Marseilles	70	69	77	70	286	862.50

Canadian Masters

Heron Point Golf Links, Ancaster, Ontario
Par 36-35—71; 6,841 yards

July 28-31
purse, C$100,000

	SCORES				TOTAL	MONEY
Roger Wessels	63	70	69	70	272	C$18,000
Ray Stewart	67	67	70	69	273	10,000
Ian Hutchings	69	69	70	67	275	5,400
Tim Straub	65	71	67	72	275	5,400
Duane Bock	68	67	71	70	276	4,200
Scott Dunlap	73	69	69	66	277	3,450
Jim Rutledge	71	68	70	68	277	3,450
Dan Dupuis	75	66	70	67	278	2,700
Ray Freeman	70	70	68	72	280	2,450
Dean Wilson	68	71	73	69	281	2,100
Matthew Lane	67	67	73	74	281	2,100
Kent Jones	75	68	69	70	282	1,750
Rob Sullivan	72	70	67	73	282	1,750
Jerry Anderson	70	70	71	71	282	1,750
Danny Ellis	69	70	73	70	282	1,750
David Wettlaufer	72	72	71	68	283	1,300
Derek James	69	73	70	71	283	1,300
Paul Devenport	69	73	71	70	283	1,300
David DeLong	72	70	70	71	283	1,300
Daniel Pelczarski	67	75	70	71	283	1,300
Perry Parker	70	71	72	70	283	1,300
Ian Leggatt	70	70	67	76	283	1,300
Frank Edmonds	71	69	73	70	283	1,300
Ben Weir	71	68	74	70	283	1,300
Dan Halldorson	70	72	76	66	284	987.50
John Restino	71	71	73	69	284	987.50
Phillip Hatchett	70	72	72	70	284	987.50
Trey Maples	73	68	71	72	284	987.50
Tim Balmer	67	72	69	76	284	987.50
Arden Knoll	68	69	77	70	284	987.50

Export "A" Inc. Ontario Open

Forest City National, London, Ontario
Par 36-36—72; 6,820 yards

August 11-14
purse, C$100,000

	SCORES				TOTAL	MONEY
Eric Woods	69	69	69	71	278	C$18,000
Ian Hutchings	71	69	72	70	282	8,000
Matthew Lane	67	68	78	69	282	8,000
Greg Petersen	74	72	65	72	283	4,500
David Morland	69	68	77	69	283	4,500
Stuart Hendley	72	72	73	69	286	3,012.50
Duane Bock	72	73	72	69	286	3,012.50
Roger Wessels	73	67	69	77	286	3,012.50

	SCORES				TOTAL	MONEY
Ray Stewart	70	68	75	73	286	3,012.50
Cam Emerson	72	71	71	73	287	2,100
Bruce Bulina	73	68	72	74	287	2,100
Ian Leggatt	73	71	70	74	288	1,750
Jim Rutledge	70	72	73	73	288	1,750
Tom Inskeep	72	74	70	72	288	1,750
Rick Todd	70	67	78	73	288	1,750
Blair Piercy	70	73	73	73	289	1,475
Tony Mollica	72	68	73	76	289	1,475
John Restino	70	75	70	75	290	1,275
Jean-Louis Lamarre	73	71	72	74	290	1,275
Ray Freeman	72	72	75	71	290	1,275
Todd Fanning	71	72	71	76	290	1,275
Robert Meyer	68	74	71	77	290	1,275
Arden Knoll	68	71	75	76	290	1,275
Mike Grob	74	71	75	71	291	1,058.33
Tim Straub	77	68	74	72	291	1,058.33
Philip Jonas	74	69	72	76	291	1,058.33
Dave Hamilton	74	70	73	75	292	912.50
John McMullen	72	73	77	70	292	912.50
Phillip Hatchett	72	71	71	78	292	912.50
Kent Jones	75	70	72	75	292	912.50
Angel Franco	75	70	74	73	292	912.50
Dan Dupuis	71	72	71	78	292	912.50
Frank Edmonds	76	69	71	76	292	912.50
Pat Sharpe	73	73	75	71	292	912.50

Trafalgar CPGA Championship

Le Royal Bromont Golf Club, Bromont, Quebec   August 18-21
Par 36-36—72; 6,681 yards   purse, C$100,000

	SCORES				TOTAL	MONEY
Stuart Hendley	67	68	67	73	275	C$18,000
Scott Ford	73	66	70	67	276	10,000
Matthew Lane	70	67	69	71	277	5,400
Scott Dunlap	70	67	71	69	277	5,400
Mark Telerico	69	73	70	66	278	3,950
Roger Wessels	70	72	68	68	278	3,950
Perry Parker	69	74	67	69	279	2,950
Danny Ellis	72	67	70	70	279	2,950
Dave Pashko	71	71	71	67	280	2,216.67
Ray Stewart	67	71	71	71	280	2,216.67
Arden Knoll	70	67	73	70	280	2,216.67
Mike Small	70	70	67	74	281	1,900
John Restino	70	72	71	69	282	1,610
Ben Weir	73	69	68	72	282	1,610
Pete McCutcheon	69	72	69	72	282	1,610
Remi Bouchard	73	68	69	72	282	1,610
Blair Piercy	67	69	71	75	282	1,610
Joe Cioe	70	73	69	71	283	1,325
Dan Dupuis	68	74	74	67	283	1,325
Ray Freeman	70	70	71	72	283	1,325
Jim Rutledge	67	71	72	73	283	1,325
Ian Hutchings	75	69	68	72	284	1,087.50
Rick Todd	74	68	71	71	284	1,087.50
Duane Bock	71	71	71	71	284	1,087.50

	SCORES			TOTAL	MONEY
Derek James	70	71	71	72	284	1,087.50
Brian Wright	68	72	71	73	284	1,087.50
Norm Jarvis	69	72	71	72	284	1,087.50
Frank Edmonds	73	71	70	71	285	912.50
Kevin Baker	72	71	73	69	285	912.50
Davidson Matyczuk	74	69	68	74	285	912.50
Ben Fouchee	73	69	71	72	285	912.50
David DeLong	72	70	69	74	285	912.50
Matt Jackson	71	68	73	73	285	912.50

International Team Matches

National Pines Golf and Country Club, Barrie, Ontario
Par 36-36—72; 7,040 yards

August 23-25
purse, C$18,000

FIRST DAY
Singles

Arden Knoll (Canada) defeated Derek James (International), 3 and 2
Darryl James (Canada) defeated Ray Freeman (International), 3 and 1
Jim Rutledge (Canada) halved with Eric Woods (International)
Mike Weir (Canada) halved with Scott Dunlap (International)
Matthew Lane (International) defeated Dan Dupuis (Canada), 4 and 2
Robert Meyer (International) defeated Blair Piercy (Canada), 1 up
Scott Ford (International) defeated Frank Edmonds (Canada), 1 up
Ian Hutchings (International) defeated Cam Emerson (Canada), 4 and 2
Perry Parker (International) defeated Ian Leggatt (Canada), 4 and 2
Duane Bock (International) defeated Bruce Bulina (Canada), 3 and 2

SECOND DAY
Alternate Shot (Foursomes)

Rutledge and Piercy (Canada) halved with Bock and Lane (International)
Knoll and Edmonds (Canada) halved with Dunlap and Freeman (International)
Meyer and Ford (International) defeated Emerson and James (Canada), 1 up
Hutchings and James (International) defeated Bulina and Leggatt (Canada), 4 and 2
Woods and Parker (International) defeated Weir and Dupuis (Canada), 3 and 1

THIRD DAY
Better Ball (Fourballs)

Rutledge and Bulina (Canada) defeated Lane and Bock (International), 5 and 3
Weir and Dupuis (Canada) defeated James and Hutchings (International), 1 up
Knoll and James (Canada) halved with Meyer and Woods (International)
Dunlap and Freeman (International) defeated Leggatt and Piercy (Canada), 1 up
Parker and Ford (International) defeated Emerson and Edmonds (Canada), 5 and 3

FINAL RESULTS: International Team 13½, Canada 6½

(Each member of the International Team received C$1,200; each member of the
Canadian Team received C$600.)

South American Tour

Bogota Open

Bogota Country Club, Bogota, Colombia
Par 36-36—72; 7,161 yards

September 29-October 2
purse, $80,000

		SCORES			TOTAL	MONEY
Miguel Guzman	66	69	71	70	276	$14,400
Pedro Martinez	71	72	74	65	282	7,760
Jose Maria Cantero	75	66	68	73	282	7,760
Gustavo Mendoza	70	69	74	70	283	5,120
Jorge Benedetti	69	71	73	71	284	3,760
Angel Franco	74	71	67	72	284	3,760
Raul Fretes	73	72	70	72	287	2,480
Diego Serna	74	70	70	73	287	2,480
Eduardo Martinez	70	75	74	69	288	1,920
Armando Redondo	72	71	74	71	288	1,920
Clay Devers	71	68	75	74	288	1,920
Luis Felipe Graf	73	73	71	72	289	1,485
Anai Fuentes	66	76	73	74	289	1,485
Eleuterio Solls	68	71	75	75	289	1,485
Rigoberto Velasquez	71	67	76	75	289	1,485
Jesus Amaya	73	71	75	71	290	1,280
Scott Taylor	72	73	71	75	291	1,120
Ramon Franco	70	73	71	77	291	1,120
Jeff Schmid	72	70	68	81	291	1,120
Antonio Barcellos	73	75	73	72	293	920
Angel Cabrera	72	77	72	72	293	920
Miguel Fernandez	72	75	78	69	294	756
Colin Woods	72	78	72	72	294	756
Joey Rassett	71	75	73	75	294	756
Thomas Cleaver	76	72	70	76	294	756
Erik Andersson	75	72	78	70	295	608
Mauricio Molina	75	74	74	72	295	608
Angel Romero	74	74	75	72	295	608
Armando Saavedra	72	78	73	72	295	608
Juan Pablo Velasco	74	74	73	74	295	608
Cesar Serna	74	72	73	76	295	608

Los Andes Open

Los Andes Golf Club, Cali, Colombia
Par 36-36—72; 7,060 yards

October 6-9
purse, $80,000

		SCORES			TOTAL	MONEY
Ron Wuensche	74	70	67	67	278	$14,400
Gustavo Rojas	67	73	68	71	279	7,760
Antonio Barcellos	70	66	72	71	279	7,760
Joao Corteiz	70	71	71	68	280	4,213.33
Mike Cunning	71	72	69	68	280	4,213.33
Rafael Alarcon	71	69	70	70	280	4,213.33
Pedro Martinez	70	72	71	68	281	2,346.67
Ramon Franco	70	74	68	69	281	2,346.67
Mark Strickland	71	70	69	71	281	2,346.67

	SCORES				TOTAL	MONEY
Pablo Benzadon	71	70	70	71	282	1,760
Luis Felipe Graf	69	69	71	73	282	1,760
Angel Cabrera	69	71	69	74	282	1,760
Mauricio Molina	72	71	72	68	283	1,480
Roberto Coceres	71	71	70	71	283	1,480
Guillermo Encina	71	72	73	68	284	1,280
Jorge Benedetti	73	70	72	69	284	1,280
Bill Faeth	71	70	70	73	284	1,280
Erik Andersson	70	74	70	71	285	1,120
Acacio Pedro	71	70	76	69	286	1,000
Juan Antonio Massal	74	73	68	71	286	1,000
Miguel Fernandez	70	70	71	76	287	880
Jeff Schmid	74	71	72	71	288	722.67
Rafael Barcellos	69	71	77	71	288	722.67
Clay Devers	69	76	71	72	288	722.67
Rafael Gomez	72	72	71	73	288	722.67
Scott Taylor	74	66	74	74	288	722.67
Eduardo Martinez	70	75	69	74	288	722.67
Gustavo Acosta	72	72	74	71	289	608
Jay Hunter	72	75	72	71	290	560
Cesar Serna	71	72	74	73	290	560
Pedro Gomez	71	72	74	73	290	560
Roberto Herrera	73	71	72	74	290	560
Sebastian Fernandez	74	69	72	75	290	560

T.C. Ecuador Open

Guayaquil Country Club, Guayaquil, Ecuador
Par 36-36—72; 6,760 yards

October 20-23
purse, $100,000

	SCORES				TOTAL	MONEY
Mauricio Molina	68	72	69	71	280	$18,000
Clay Devers	71	74	68	69	282	11,400
Antonio Barcellos	68	76	69	70	283	8,000
Guillermo Encina	70	72	73	70	285	6,400
Pedro Martinez	74	70	71	71	286	4,700
Jeff Schmid	70	73	69	74	286	4,700
Jean-Louis Lamarre	76	74	69	68	287	3,100
Angel Franco	73	74	70	70	287	3,100
Frank Edmonds	71	74	70	73	288	2,600
Ramon Franco	72	68	76	73	289	2,300
Rodolfo Rodriquez	74	70	71	74	289	2,300
Scott Taylor	71	75	74	70	290	1,850
Angel Romero	75	74	69	72	290	1,850
Marco Ruiz	71	73	73	73	290	1,850
Ruben Alvarez	70	71	71	78	290	1,850
*E. Penaredonda	69	75	74	72	290	
Jesus Amaya	74	77	70	70	291	1,350
Rigoberto Velasquez	75	73	72	71	291	1,350
Rafael Barcellos	76	72	72	71	291	1,350
Ron Wuensche	70	76	71	74	291	1,350
Gustavo Rojas	72	71	74	74	291	1,350
Luis Felipe Graf	74	69	73	75	291	1,350
Juan Pablo Velasco	75	74	71	72	292	966.67
Miguel Fernandez	72	74	73	73	292	966.67
Brad Klapprott	70	75	73	74	292	966.67
Carlos Dluhosh	76	74	72	72	294	860
Gustavo Mendoza	71	76	74	73	294	860

	SCORES				TOTAL	MONEY
Jay Hunter	74	75	76	70	295	744
Gaston Reartes	73	71	78	73	295	744
Jerry Smith	68	73	81	73	295	744
Joao Corteiz	75	71	76	73	295	744
Miguel Guzman	74	70	76	75	295	744

Los Inkas-Peru Open

Los Inkas Country Club, Lima, Peru   October 27-30
Par 36-36—72; 7,013 yards   purse, $110,000

	SCORES				TOTAL	MONEY
David Ogrin	66	73	65	68	272	$19,800
Raul Fretes	68	70	69	70	277	10,670
Gustavo Rojas	72	67	67	71	277	10,670
Brad Klapprott	68	71	68	71	278	7,040
Ron Wuensche	68	69	73	69	279	5,720
Luis Felipe Graf	72	70	70	68	280	4,620
Roy Mackenzie	68	71	72	70	281	3,740
Jeff Bloom	73	69	71	69	282	2,640
Ramon Franco	73	69	69	71	282	2,640
Pedro Martinez	68	75	68	71	282	2,640
Jerry Smith	74	67	66	75	282	2,640
Scott Taylor	66	70	71	75	282	2,640
Angel Franco	69	72	73	69	283	1,925
Angel Romero	72	70	71	70	283	1,925
Jorge Benedetti	74	70	69	70	283	1,925
Diego Ventureira	71	68	72	72	283	1,925
Howie Johnson	69	72	77	66	284	1,485
Rafael Barcellos	74	68	73	69	284	1,485
Roberto Coceres	72	71	70	71	284	1,485
Guillermo Encina	69	71	73	71	284	1,485
Erik Andersson	71	71	72	71	285	1,129.33
Rigoberto Velasquez	74	68	67	76	285	1,129.33
Mauricio Molina	71	66	72	76	285	1,129.33
Antonio Barcellos	73	73	71	69	286	946
Miguel Fernandez	71	71	73	71	286	946
Omar Peralta	71	70	73	72	286	946
Carlos Dluhosh	71	68	72	75	286	946
Raul Albarasin	72	71	73	71	287	781
Acacio Pedro	73	71	70	73	287	781
Doug Johnson	69	72	73	73	287	781
Jeff Schmid	71	71	72	73	287	781
Jean-Louis Lamarre	70	74	69	74	287	781
Jose Cardenas	71	70	72	74	287	781

Litoral Open

Rosario Golf Club, Rosario, Argentina   November 10-13
Par 35-36—71; 6,388 yards   purse, $80,000

	SCORES				TOTAL	MONEY
Cesar Monasterio	66	69	69	67	271	$14,400
Brad Klapprott	69	67	70	68	274	7,760
Gustavo Rojas	73	62	70	69	274	7,760
Raul Fretes	63	71	70	66	276	4,640
Ruben Alvarez	70	69	70	67	276	4,640

	SCORES	TOTAL	MONEY
Jose Maria Cantero	68 72 66 71	277	3,360
Angel Cabrera	69 73 71 66	279	2,480
Scott Taylor	70 66 71 72	279	2,480
Luis Carbonetti	73 67 69 71	280	2,000
Jorge Soto	66 67 70 77	280	2,000
Roberto Coceres	70 71 71 69	281	1,680
Carlos Almaraz	71 69 69 72	281	1,680
Armando Saavedra	72 70 74 66	282	1,400
Clay Devers	73 71 70 68	282	1,400
Kevin Wentworth	73 68 71 70	282	1,400
Adan Sowa	70 67 70 75	282	1,400
Horacio Carbonetti	75 67 71 70	283	1,160
Miguel Fernandez	73 70 68 72	283	1,160
Jerry Smith	72 74 69 69	284	924
Mauricio Molina	71 73 71 69	284	924
Ricardo Coceres	74 72 69 69	284	924
Ruben Saya	75 67 72 70	284	924
Daniel Lobos	74 72 71 68	285	736
Jay Hunter	74 73 70 68	285	736
Gaston Reartes	69 66 78 72	285	736
Eduardo Argiro	71 76 70 69	286	656
Jeff Schmid	72 68 70 76	286	656
Raul Albarasin	67 73 79 68	287	576
Omar Solis	73 72 70 72	287	576
Fabian Montovia	74 70 71 72	287	576
Marcelo Isla	76 69 70 72	287	576
Jeff Bloom	75 72 68 72	287	576

Uruguay Open

Golf Club of Uruguay, Montevideo, Uruguay
Par 37-36—73; 6,458 yards

November 17-20
purse, $70,000

	SCORES	TOTAL	MONEY
Raul Fretes	71 67 69 68	275	$12,600
Ron Wuensche	77 72 63 65	277	7,980
Fabian Montovia	71 68 71 68	278	5,600
Mark Strickland	72 69 70 69	280	4,480
Pedro Martinez	68 69 77 67	281	3,290
Brad Klapprott	70 73 71 67	281	3,290
Angel Franco	70 73 69 70	282	2,053.33
Scott Taylor	69 70 73 70	282	2,053.33
Patrick Horgan	68 70 69 75	282	2,053.33
Clay Devers	74 72 67 70	283	1,680
Kevin Wentworth	78 69 68 69	284	1,470
Frank Edmonds	68 72 69 75	284	1,470
Miguel Fernandez	76 72 69 69	285	1,330
Luis Felipe Graf	72 70 73 71	286	1,225
Jorge Benedetti	71 69 70 76	286	1,225
Gustavo Rojas	76 74 69 68	287	980
Rafael Barcellos	72 73 72 70	287	980
Doug Johnson	71 75 69 72	287	980
Antonio Barcellos	76 68 71 72	287	980
Antonio Nascimento	71 72 70 74	287	980
Acacio Pedro	74 72 70 72	288	742
Eduardo Caballero	71 73 70 74	288	742
Jeff Schmid	72 74 70 73	289	672
Erik Andersson	75 73 71 71	290	616
Jerry Smith	73 72 72 73	290	616

	SCORES				TOTAL	MONEY
Joao Corteiz	69	76	70	75	290	616
Emmanuel Dussart	70	77	72	72	291	546
Mauricio Molina	69	74	69	79	291	546
Jay Hunter	73	74	73	72	292	511
Ramon Franco	75	72	70	75	292	511

Argentina Tournament of Champions

Olivos Golf Club, Buenos Aires, Argentina
Par 36-35—71; 6,692 yards

November 17-20
purse, $157,500

	SCORES				TOTAL	MONEY
Jose Coceres	69	67	65	71	272	$25,600
Sam Torrance	72	66	69	69	276	13,850
Eduardo Romero	74	70	67	65	276	13,850
Paul Eales	73	70	70	65	278	9,100
Ignacio Garrido	74	70	67	68	279	7,400
Stephen Ames	68	75	66	71	280	6,000
Santiago Luna	72	67	66	76	281	4,183
Fulton Allem	74	69	70	68	281	4,183
Cesar Monasterio	72	72	70	67	281	4,183
Domingo Hospital	74	70	66	72	282	3,400
Ruben Alvarez	71	69	71	72	283	3,000
Vicente Fernandez	68	73	72	70	283	3,000
Wayne Westner	69	72	70	73	284	2,700
Ricardo Coceres	71	73	71	71	286	2,495
Jose Maria Cantero	72	72	72	70	286	2,495
Omar Peralta	71	71	71	74	287	2,210
Roberto Coceres	77	66	75	69	287	2,210
Jorge Berendt	79	69	70	70	288	1,608
Daniel Lobos	73	70	74	71	288	1,608
Rick Hartmann	70	74	70	74	288	1,608
Luis Carbonetti	73	74	68	73	288	1,608
Chris Moody	73	71	71	73	288	1,608
Jorge Soto	75	72	71	70	288	1,608
Adan Sowa	73	73	73	69	288	1,608
Antoine LeBouc	71	72	74	72	289	1,225
Philip Walton	75	72	73	69	289	1,225
Carlos Perez	73	73	73	71	290	1,075
Johan Rystrom	72	69	71	78	290	1,075
Diego Ventureira	79	70	72	69	290	1,075
Moreno Marcos	76	73	72	69	290	1,075

Paraguay Open

Yacht and Golf Club, Asuncion, Paraguay
Par 36-35—71; 6,537 yards

November 24-27
purse, $70,000

	SCORES				TOTAL	MONEY
Mike Cunning	72	67	68	69	276	$12,600
Carlos Franco	75	70	70	64	279	6,020
Angel Franco	71	70	69	69	279	6,020
Eduardo Caballero	70	68	72	69	279	6,020
Gustavo Rojas	72	74	69	67	282	3,640
Antonio Barcellos	69	69	72	73	283	2,940
Scott Taylor	73	72	70	69	284	2,170

	SCORES				TOTAL	MONEY
Michael Krantz	71	72	72	69	284	2,170
Raul Fretes	77	68	68	72	285	1,820
Colin Woods	73	74	69	70	286	1,680
Ron Wuensche	67	77	75	68	287	1,382.50
Jeff Schmid	78	73	66	70	287	1,382.50
Ramon Franco	73	70	73	71	287	1,382.50
Joao Corteiz	75	70	69	73	287	1,382.50
Rigoberto Velasquez	74	75	70	69	288	1,155
Jeff Bloom	70	76	72	70	288	1,155
Frank Edmonds	73	73	71	72	289	980
Jerry Smith	73	74	69	73	289	980
Pedro Martinez	73	73	68	75	289	980
Rafael Barcellos	75	76	71	68	290	749
Kevin Wentworth	74	75	72	69	290	749
Mauricio Molina	77	70	70	73	290	749
Alvaro Ortiz	69	77	68	76	290	749
Clay Devers	71	70	74	76	291	644
Luis Felipe Graf	78	70	75	69	292	588
Mark Strickland	74	74	72	72	292	588
Eladio Franco	73	70	72	77	292	588
Jay Hunter	73	73	76	71	293	525
Aaron Meeks	71	74	75	73	293	525
Erik Andersson	71	70	78	75	294	504

Argentina PGA

Los Lagartos Golf Club, Buenos Aires, Argentina
Par 36-36—72; 6,806 yards

November 24-27
purse, $165,000

	SCORES				TOTAL	MONEY
Armando Saavedra	69	65	69	70	273	$25,000
Cesar Monasterio	65	66	72	71	274	14,000
Eduardo Romero	67	72	72	67	278	10,000
Craig Stadler	70	66	71	72	279	8,500
Jorge Berendt	70	69	69	71	279	8,500
Vicente Fernandez	68	77	67	69	281	6,000
Paul Eales	71	71	70	70	282	5,500
Domingo Hospital	72	74	67	71	284	4,500
Steven Bottomley	73	71	66	74	284	4,500
Roberto Coceres	68	74	70	73	285	3,633
Daniel Lobos	71	73	70	71	285	3,633
Stephen Ames	70	71	72	72	285	3,633
Jose Coceres	67	73	70	76	286	3,050
Rick Hartmann	74	71	69	72	286	3,050
Antoine LeBouc	70	71	74	71	286	3,050
Angel Cabrera	74	70	72	70	286	3,050
Ricardo Gonzalez	73	70	77	67	287	2,650
Antonio Garrido	72	69	73	73	287	2,650
Ignacio Garrido	76	71	70	71	288	2,333
Sam Torrance	71	73	73	71	288	2,333
Ricardo Coceres	73	74	71	70	288	2,333
Michel Besanceney	74	71	71	73	289	2,050
Omar Solis	72	72	75	70	289	2,050
Omar Peralta	74	67	72	77	290	1,375
Gustavo Acosta	72	73	73	72	290	1,375
Ricardo Montenegro	71	70	78	71	290	1,375
Carlos Perez	75	72	73	70	290	1,375
Adan Sowa	74	70	75	72	291	1,000

	SCORES				TOTAL	MONEY
Miguel Romero	76	70	70	76	292	1,000
Miguel Guzman	70	75	75	72	292	1,000

Prince of Wales Open

Prince of Wales Country Club, Santiago, Chile   December 1-4
Par 36-36—72; 6,708 yards   purse, $120,000

	SCORES				TOTAL	MONEY
Jose Maria Cantero	66	65	70	74	275	$21,600
Raul Fretes	68	68	71	70	277	11,160
Aaron Meeks	73	68	66	70	277	11,160
Eduardo Caballero	69	66	72	71	278	6,720
Guillermo Encina	70	70	67	71	278	6,720
Rigoberto Velasquez	73	70	69	67	279	3,920
Antonio Barcellos	72	72	66	69	279	3,920
Kevin Wentworth	66	68	71	74	279	3,920
Luis Berrios	72	70	68	70	280	2,652
Gustavo Rojas	65	66	74	75	280	2,652
Gavin Levenson	70	70	73	68	281	2,220
Pedro Martinez	69	70	73	69	281	2,220
Roy Mackenzie	71	72	69	69	281	2,220
Erik Andersson	70	66	72	73	281	2,220
Brian Mogg	71	74	70	67	282	1,824
Ramon Franco	71	69	70	72	282	1,824
Luis Felipe Graf	71	71	68	72	282	1,824
Angel Franco	69	73	73	68	283	1,560
Harry Rudolph	76	68	69	70	283	1,560
Juan Pablo Velasco	70	73	68	72	283	1,560
Emmanuel Dussart	72	72	66	74	284	1,416
Joao Corteiz	71	74	71	69	285	1,236
Jeff Schmid	74	69	72	70	285	1,236
Mike Cunning	73	69	72	71	285	1,236
Howie Johnson	71	70	67	77	286	1,236
Angel Romero	73	72	70	71	286	940.80
Acacio Pedro	73	70	72	71	286	940.80
Fabian Montovia	69	70	75	72	286	940.80
Scott Taylor	70	67	75	74	286	940.80
Alvaro Ortiz	70	70	71	75	286	940.80

Argentina Open

Buenos Aires Golf Club, Buenos Aires, Argentina   December 1-4
Par 36-36-72   purse, $200,000

	SCORES				TOTAL	MONEY
Mark O'Meara	71	67	69	71	278	$40,000
Cesar Monasterio	70	71	70	73	284	20,000
John Cook	71	70	73	70	284	20,000
Roberto Coceres	69	71	76	71	287	12,000
Craig Stadler	72	70	76	70	288	10,000
Jorge Berendt	72	74	72	71	289	8,000
Frank Nobilo	74	71	75	71	291	6,000
Sebastian Fernandez	73	71	75	74	293	5,025
Jeff Maggert	73	69	75	76	293	5,025
Rick Hartmann	76	69	77	71	293	5,025
Jesper Parnevik	76	68	77	72	293	5,025

	SCORES				TOTAL	MONEY
Vicente Fernandez	77	70	76	72	295	4,200
Angel Cabrera	77	70	76	72	295	4,200
Ronnie Damm	73	71	72	80	296	3,900
Steve Bottomley	72	70	75	80	297	3,700
Jose Coceres	82	69	76	71	298	3,400
Stephen Hamill	76	70	79	73	298	3,400
Rafael Gomez	79	73	77	72	301	2,900
Ricardo Mareorati	77	70	78	76	301	2,900
Pedro R. Lopez	76	72	79	74	301	2,900
Miguel Guzman	76	75	75	76	302	2,400
Michel Besanceney	78	72	76	76	302	2,400
Chris Moody	72	75	83	74	304	1,900
Ricardo Coceres	78	70	78	78	304	1,900
Antonio Ortiz	80	72	76	76	304	1,900
Armando Saavedra	81	71	78	75	305	1,337.50
Dionicio Rios	74	71	84	76	305	1,337.50
Daniel Lobos	72	81	74	78	305	1,337.50
Andres Coceres	73	73	81	78	305	1,337.50
Antoine LeBouc	82	73	75	76	306	1,203.33
Gustavo Acosta	72	70	84	80	306	1,203.33
Carlos Perez	74	72	80	80	306	1,203.34

Los Leones-Chile Open

Golf Club of Los Leones, Santiago, Chile
Par 36-36—72; 6,676 yards

December 8-11
purse, $80,000

	SCORES				TOTAL	MONEY
Raul Fretes	66	69	71	68	274	$14,400
Fabian Montovia	68	68	73	66	275	7,760
Gustavo Rojas	65	68	73	69	275	7,760
Jean-Louis Lamarre	65	72	69	71	277	5,120
Chris Davison	70	66	73	69	278	3,760
Roberto Coceres	66	72	67	73	278	3,760
Carlos Franco	73	66	74	66	279	2,480
Angel Franco	70	71	67	71	279	2,480
Eric Shaffer	67	71	71	71	280	1,840
Roy Mackenzie	68	69	72	71	280	1,840
Rafael Ponce	67	69	71	73	280	1,840
Marco Ruiz	68	75	64	73	280	1,840
Doug Johnson	65	68	72	76	281	1,520
Stephen Novarro	66	78	69	69	282	1,280
Jeff Schmid	69	73	69	71	282	1,280
Rigoberto Velasquez	71	71	69	71	282	1,280
Luis Carbonetti	69	72	69	72	282	1,280
Eduardo Caballero	65	69	73	75	282	1,280
Juan Pablo Velasco	72	72	69	70	283	960
Ron Wuensche	71	70	70	72	283	960
Gavin Levenson	70	70	70	73	283	960
Antonio Barcellos	72	70	70	72	284	739.20
Guillermo Encina	68	72	71	73	284	739.20
Luis Felipe Graf	70	68	72	74	284	739.20
Armando Saavedra	69	70	71	74	284	739.20
Clay Devers	68	69	73	74	284	739.20
Dusti Watson	67	71	72	75	285	640
Mark Strickland	74	69	75	68	286	584
Angel Romero	73	70	71	72	286	584
Angel Fernandez	67	73	72	74	286	584
Jose Maria Cantero	69	73	68	76	286	584

European Tour

Madeira Island Open

Madeira Golf Club, Madeira, Spain
Par 36-36—72; 6,606 yards
(Sunday was an extra day to finish Round 3.)

January 13-16
purse, £250,000

	SCORES			TOTAL	MONEY
Mats Lanner	70	67	69	206	£41,660
Mathias Gronberg	69	70	69	208	18,640
Peter Hedblom	69	69	70	208	18,640
Howard Clark	68	67	73	208	18,640
Miguel Angel Martin	71	69	71	211	8,950
Gabriel Hjertstedt	71	67	73	211	8,950
Jeremy Robinson	71	66	74	211	8,950
Paul Eales	69	73	70	212	5,616.67
Diego Borrego	69	70	73	212	5,616.67
Paul Broadhurst	70	67	75	212	5,616.67
Jay Townsend	67	74	72	213	4,600
Alexander Cejka	72	71	71	214	3,864
David Curry	71	71	72	214	3,864
Carl Mason	71	70	73	214	3,864
Terry Price	70	70	74	214	3,864
Keith Waters	71	68	75	214	3,864
Nick Godin	69	76	70	215	3,300
Pedro Linhart	74	68	73	215	3,300
Jean Louis Guepy	74	70	72	215	2,815.63
Paul Curry	74	72	70	216	2,815.63
Lee Westwood	72	69	75	216	2,815.63
David Williams	73	68	75	216	2,815.63
Danny Mijovic	68	73	75	216	2,815.63
Paul Mayo	70	70	76	216	2,815.63
Sven Struver	70	70	76	216	2,815.63
Scott Watson	72	67	77	216	2,815.63
Paul Moloney	75	69	73	217	2,253.57
Russell Claydon	70	74	73	217	2,253.57
Paul McGinley	74	71	72	217	2,253.57
Gordon J. Brand	71	75	71	217	2,253.57
Roger Chapman	68	74	75	217	2,253.57
Steven Richardson	71	71	75	217	2,253.57
Anders Sorensen	72	69	76	217	2,253.57
Phillip Price	72	73	73	218	1,950
Des Smyth	76	69	73	218	1,950
Colin Brooks	72	74	72	218	1,950
Andrew Coltart	74	70	75	219	1,550
Ian Garbutt	73	71	75	219	1,550
Steven Bottomley	71	73	75	219	1,550
Anders Forsbrand	72	72	75	219	1,550
Brian Marchbank	74	71	74	219	1,550
Craig Cassells	74	71	74	219	1,550
Fredrik Larsson	72	73	74	219	1,550
Heinz P. Thul	72	74	73	219	1,550
Ricky Willison	75	71	73	219	1,550
Michel Besanceney	75	68	76	219	1,550
Stephen McAllister	72	70	77	219	1,550

	SCORES			TOTAL	MONEY
Martin Gates	74	68	77	219	1,550
Steve Van Vuuren	70	71	78	219	1,550
Carl Magnus Stromberg	71	73	76	220	1,075
Paul Affleck	73	71	76	220	1,075
Thomas Gogele	75	70	75	220	1,075
Andrew Murray	76	69	75	220	1,075
Ralf Berhorst	71	72	77	220	1,075
Andrew Sherborne	72	69	79	220	1,075
Robert Lee	70	75	76	221	785.71
Paul Lawrie	74	71	76	221	785.71
Giuseppe Cali	73	72	76	221	785.71
Patrick Bates	74	72	75	221	785.71
Ross McFarlane	77	69	75	221	785.71
Olle Nordberg	71	75	75	221	785.71
Jeff Hall	70	72	79	221	785.71
Derrick Cooper	74	72	76	222	650
Mikael Piltz	70	73	79	222	650
Paul Way	70	72	80	222	650
Mark Mouland	71	75	77	223	400
David Gilford	71	75	78	224	396
Jose Manuel Carriles	71	75	78	224	396
Mark Nichols	73	73	78	224	396
Mikael Krantz	74	70	81	225	391
Massimo Scarpa	74	72	79	225	391
Antoine LeBouc	72	71	83	226	388

Moroccan Open

Golf Royal de Agadir, Morocco
Par 36-36—72; 6,657 yards

January 20-23
purse, £350,000

	SCORES				TOTAL	MONEY
Anders Forsbrand	70	68	69	69	276	£58,330
Howard Clark	68	67	72	73	280	38,880
Robert Karlsson	68	72	70	71	281	21,910
Peter Hedblom	68	72	73	69	282	16,165
Frank Nobilo	72	72	68	70	282	16,165
Jonathan Sewell	68	72	74	69	283	10,500
Scott Watson	73	72	68	70	283	10,500
Jean Van de Velde	72	68	71	72	283	10,500
Andrew Coltart	74	69	75	66	284	7,820
Pierre Fulke	75	68	73	69	285	6,720
Gordon Brand, Jr.	70	68	75	72	285	6,720
Alexander Cejka	71	75	71	69	286	5,666.67
Philip Walton	69	71	75	71	286	5,666.67
Jeremy Robinson	71	70	73	72	286	5,666.67
Ruben Alvarez	76	68	74	69	287	5,035
David Williams	74	67	69	77	287	5,035
Wayne Westner	72	75	72	69	288	4,310.83
Wayne Riley	73	72	74	69	288	4,310.83
Jonathan Lomas	72	75	70	71	288	4,310.83
Gabriel Hjertstedt	69	72	75	72	288	4,310.83
Mark Roe	71	68	76	73	288	4,310.83
Silvio Grappasonni	70	73	68	77	288	4,310.83
Steven Richardson	74	68	74	73	289	3,832.50
Jon Robson	71	69	73	76	289	3,832.50
Juan Quiros	75	69	74	72	290	3,213

	SCORES				TOTAL	MONEY
Ian Garbutt	72	72	76	70	290	3,213
Paul Affleck	78	68	75	69	290	3,213
Ricky Willison	70	76	72	72	290	3,213
Paul Moloney	74	71	72	73	290	3,213
Andre Bossert	75	72	70	73	290	3,213
Jeff Hall	71	70	75	74	290	3,213
Patrick Bates	71	74	71	74	290	3,213
Paul Mayo	70	73	72	75	290	3,213
Pedro Linhart	73	68	73	76	290	3,213
Michel Besanceney	73	71	75	72	291	2,625
Joakim Haeggman	72	72	76	71	291	2,625
Nic Henning	71	70	76	74	291	2,625
Jay Townsend	75	72	70	74	291	2,625
Klas Eriksson	77	69	73	73	292	2,275
Ralf Berhorst	76	69	76	71	292	2,275
Massimo Scarpa	73	72	73	74	292	2,275
Steve Bowman	75	72	71	74	292	2,275
Martin Gates	72	74	71	75	292	2,275
Gary Orr	72	72	72	76	292	2,275
Manuel Pinero	74	70	74	75	293	1,960
Sven Struver	74	73	74	72	293	1,960
Torsten Giedeon	75	69	74	75	293	1,960
Des Smyth	75	71	73	75	294	1,610
Paul Broadhurst	73	74	73	74	294	1,610
Gordon J. Brand	72	75	75	72	294	1,610
Mike McLean	73	73	76	72	294	1,610
Marcus Wills	77	70	77	70	294	1,610
Russell Claydon	73	70	81	70	294	1,610
Phillip Price	74	69	72	79	294	1,610
Manny Zerman	70	76	73	76	295	1,197
Marc Farry	73	73	73	76	295	1,197
Stephen Hamill	73	70	77	75	295	1,197
Mathias Gronberg	73	72	76	74	295	1,197
Miguel Angel Martin	71	75	77	72	295	1,197
Gordon Manson	73	72	74	77	296	1,032.50
Paul Eales	68	75	80	73	296	1,032.50
Heinz P. Thul	73	74	75	75	297	945
Antoine LeBouc	73	73	76	75	297	945
Fredrik Larsson	73	72	78	74	297	945
Glenn Ralph	75	72	78	76	301	875
Carl Magnus Stromberg	75	72	79	78	304	524
Keith Waters	74	72	83	75	304	524

Dubai Desert Classic

Emirates Golf Club, Dubai, United Arab Emirates
Par 35-37—72; 7,100 yards

January 27-30
purse, £450,000

	SCORES				TOTAL	MONEY
Ernie Els	61	69	67	71	268	£75,000
Greg Norman	68	69	68	69	274	50,000
Wayne Westner	70	68	69	68	275	28,170
Jonathan Lomas	66	73	70	67	276	19,103.33
Isao Aoki	67	72	70	67	276	19,103.33
Tsukasa Watanabe	70	70	67	69	276	19,103.33
Per-Ulrik Johansson	70	71	69	67	277	12,375
Gary Evans	67	69	71	70	277	12,375
Craig Cassells	68	69	69	72	278	9,525

	SCORES				TOTAL	MONEY
Klas Eriksson	69	69	70	70	278	9,525
Mark Roe	66	71	74	68	279	7,753.33
Sam Torrance	69	67	75	68	279	7,753.33
Jim Payne	68	73	71	67	279	7,753.33
Anders Forsbrand	69	72	74	65	280	6,800
Jeremy Robinson	71	70	71	69	281	6,338.33
Gary Orr	68	69	74	70	281	6,338.33
Colin Montgomerie	71	67	74	69	281	6,338.33
Magnus Sunesson	69	71	69	73	282	5,595
Richard Boxall	69	70	71	72	282	5,595
Barry Lane	69	70	75	68	282	5,595
Retief Goosen	72	71	73	67	283	4,995
Russell Claydon	69	71	71	72	283	4,995
Stephen Ames	69	69	74	71	283	4,995
Mark Davis	75	66	72	70	283	4,995
Miguel Angel Martin	72	72	67	72	283	4,995
Darren Clarke	69	71	70	74	284	4,252.50
Bernhard Langer	71	73	69	71	284	4,252.50
Ricky Willison	69	70	74	71	284	4,252.50
David Gilford	70	74	71	69	284	4,252.50
Paul Broadhurst	69	67	77	71	284	4,252.50
Sandy Lyle	72	70	71	71	284	4,252.50
Paul Curry	70	69	73	73	285	3,735
Jeff Hawkes	70	73	70	72	285	3,735
Mark Mouland	71	72	70	73	286	3,150
Jay Townsend	73	72	73	68	286	3,150
David Ray	71	73	72	70	286	3,150
Pierre Fulke	74	69	71	72	286	3,150
David Curry	70	70	75	71	286	3,150
Andrew Murray	70	75	70	71	286	3,150
Ruben Alvarez	72	70	72	72	286	3,150
Peter Baker	72	72	73	69	286	3,150
Tony Johnstone	73	72	72	69	286	3,150
Carl Mason	71	71	72	72	286	3,150
Silvio Grappasonni	71	73	72	70	286	3,150
Olle Nordberg	71	74	72	70	287	2,385
De Wet Basson	74	66	73	74	287	2,385
Roger Chapman	71	70	70	76	287	2,385
Peter Fowler	72	70	71	74	287	2,385
Joakim Haeggman	71	72	71	73	287	2,385
Philip Walton	76	69	71	71	287	2,385
Paul McGinley	75	70	71	72	288	1,980
Steen Tinning	70	74	68	76	288	1,980
Sven Struver	74	69	75	70	288	1,980
Peter Teravainen	72	73	70	74	289	1,710
Andrew Sherborne	71	74	70	74	289	1,710
Martin Gates	72	73	72	72	289	1,710
Olle Karlsson	69	72	72	77	290	1,455
Andrew Oldcorn	74	71	72	73	290	1,455
Lee Westwood	74	71	72	73	290	1,455
Jamie Spence	74	71	72	74	291	1,305
Nicklas Fasth	70	73	75	73	291	1,305
Gavin Levenson	70	75	73	73	291	1,305
Fredrik Lindgren	70	72	74	76	292	1,192.50
Mike Miller	73	72	76	71	292	1,192.50
Miguel Angel Jimenez	72	71	75	75	293	900
Malcolm Mackenzie	72	73	76	72	293	900
Paul Way	69	75	73	77	294	672
Adam Hunter	72	72	74	76	294	672
Johan Rystrom	72	72	75	77	296	668

	SCORES				TOTAL	MONEY
Derrick Cooper	75	70	76	75	296	668
Paul Mayo	70	73	79	75	297	665
Frederic Regard	70	72	77	80	299	663

Johnnie Walker Asian Classic

Blue Canyon Country Club, Phuket, Thailand
Par 36-36—72; 7,049 yards

February 3-6
purse, £600,000

	SCORES				TOTAL	MONEY
Greg Norman	75	70	64	68	277	£100,000
Fred Couples	66	72	70	70	278	66,660
Bernhard Langer	68	70	71	70	279	37,560
Ian Woosnam	68	72	68	73	281	30,000
Mike Harwood	71	72	69	70	282	25,400
Colin Montgomerie	70	72	71	70	283	19,500
Hsieh Chin Sheng	70	69	70	74	283	19,500
Frankie Minoza	72	74	67	71	284	14,220
David Feherty	69	71	73	71	284	14,220
Pierre Fulke	74	70	72	69	285	11,106.67
Isao Aoki	70	71	71	73	285	11,106.67
Sven Struver	77	70	69	69	285	11,106.67
Frank Nobilo	77	69	70	70	286	9,213.33
Ray Stewart	75	72	68	71	286	9,213.33
De Wet Basson	72	73	71	70	286	9,213.33
Ernie Els	71	73	74	69	287	8,100
Peter Senior	71	73	70	73	287	8,100
Jean Van de Velde	72	72	72	71	287	8,100
Miguel Angel Martin	74	73	69	72	288	7,220
Peter Baker	69	72	72	75	288	7,220
Fredrik Larsson	71	74	72	71	288	7,220
Scott Watson	76	70	72	71	289	6,570
Miguel Angel Jimenez	71	70	77	71	289	6,570
Robert Karlsson	74	73	69	73	289	6,570
Paul McGinley	71	75	74	69	289	6,570
Barry Lane	75	69	71	75	290	6,030
Peter O'Malley	76	72	70	72	290	6,030
Andre Bossert	72	76	71	72	291	5,320
Choi Sang Ho	73	71	76	71	291	5,320
Mats Lanner	70	74	70	77	291	5,320
Mike Clayton	77	69	75	70	291	5,320
Darren Clarke	73	71	73	74	291	5,320
Tony Johnstone	70	71	71	79	291	5,320
Maian Nasim	70	75	73	74	292	4,440
Ian Palmer	72	73	74	73	292	4,440
Steve Bowman	75	69	76	72	292	4,440
Jim Payne	71	73	75	73	292	4,440
Ronan Rafferty	71	69	71	81	292	4,440
Steven Bottomley	70	76	72	74	292	4,440
Des Smyth	72	74	74	72	292	4,440
*Tiger Woods	74	71	74	73	292	
Robert Allenby	76	72	68	77	293	3,480
Kevin Wentworth	75	73	69	76	293	3,480
Klas Eriksson	71	75	75	72	293	3,480
Carlos Espinosa	71	75	75	72	293	3,480
Gary Orr	73	75	74	71	293	3,480
Gavin Levenson	74	71	76	72	293	3,480

	SCORES				TOTAL	MONEY
Peter Teravainen	74	74	75	70	293	3,480
David Ray	74	72	75	72	293	3,480
Sandy Lyle	73	72	70	78	293	3,480
Manny Zerman	76	70	73	75	294	2,760
Lee Westwood	69	77	77	71	294	2,760
Jonathan Lomas	75	72	74	73	294	2,760
Magnus Sunesson	76	72	73	74	295	2,400
Anthony Gilligan	76	71	74	74	295	2,400
Carl Mason	75	72	74	74	295	2,400
Gordon J. Brand	71	76	74	75	296	2,100
Todd Hamilton	73	70	73	80	296	2,100
Adam Hunter	73	74	74	76	297	1,860
Ruben Alvarez	72	76	70	79	297	1,860
Gary Evans	75	73	77	72	297	1,860
John McHenry	73	72	78	75	298	1,710
Paul Way	74	74	77	73	298	1,710
Eoghan O'Connell	75	72	75	77	299	1,590
Craig Cassells	73	75	77	74	299	1,590
Andrew Coltart	74	73	78	76	301	1,200
David R. Jones	72	74	75	80	301	1,200
Philip Walton	72	75	79	78	304	898
Ali Sher	75	73	79	DQ		

Turespana Open de Tenerife

Golf del Sur, Tenerife, Canary Islands
Par 36-36—72; 6,384 yards

February 10-13
purse, £250,000

	SCORES				TOTAL	MONEY
David Gilford	72	70	66	70	278	£41,660
Wayne Riley	68	71	70	71	280	18,640
Andrew Murray	73	67	68	72	280	18,640
Juan Quiros	70	68	67	75	280	18,640
Bill Malley	69	76	69	67	281	8,275
Jose Maria Canizares	67	70	73	71	281	8,275
David Ray	70	70	69	72	281	8,275
Brian Barnes	73	67	64	77	281	8,275
Jonathan Sewell	74	67	73	69	283	4,555
Paul Curry	69	71	72	71	283	4,555
Jose Davila	74	68	70	71	283	4,555
Des Smyth	70	71	70	72	283	4,555
Jose Maria Olazabal	73	69	69	72	283	4,555
Ruben Alvarez	72	65	73	73	283	4,555
John Metcalfe	71	68	76	69	284	3,521.67
Jose Rivero	73	68	73	70	284	3,521.67
Diego Borrego	68	70	72	74	284	3,521.67
Jon Robson	71	72	72	70	285	2,861.11
Haydn Selby-Green	72	73	69	71	285	2,861.11
Greg Turner	73	70	71	71	285	2,861.11
Santiago Luna	74	69	70	72	285	2,861.11
Ralf Berhorst	72	71	70	72	285	2,861.11
Russell Claydon	71	71	70	73	285	2,861.11
Jose Manuel Carriles	71	71	69	74	285	2,861.11
Miguel Angel Jimenez	74	70	67	74	285	2,861.11
Ignacio Garrido	75	67	66	77	285	2,861.11
Paul Affleck	72	71	71	72	286	2,475
Christian Cevaer	70	74	72	71	287	2,127.78

	SCORES				TOTAL	MONEY
Antoine LeBouc	72	72	72	71	287	2,127.78
Steven Bottomley	73	71	72	71	287	2,127.78
Colin Brooks	70	75	72	70	287	2,127.78
David Curry	72	68	74	73	287	2,127.78
Mikael Krantz	72	72	70	73	287	2,127.78
Heinz P. Thul	70	70	73	74	287	2,127.78
Manuel Pinero	71	69	73	74	287	2,127.78
Paul Lawrie	72	72	69	74	287	2,127.78
Thomas Gogele	71	69	76	72	288	1,800
David Williams	72	73	72	71	288	1,800
Chris Williams	71	74	69	74	288	1,800
Philip Talbot	72	71	72	74	289	1,650
Glenn Ralph	72	73	72	72	289	1,650
Keith Waters	73	71	69	76	289	1,650
Pedro Linhart	76	64	75	75	290	1,475
Mark Roe	71	72	74	73	290	1,475
Ian Spencer	73	72	75	70	290	1,475
Michel Besanceney	70	71	73	76	290	1,475
Mathias Gronberg	71	72	72	76	291	1,275
Andrew Sandywell	72	71	72	76	291	1,275
Christy O'Connor, Jr.	72	72	73	74	291	1,275
David J. Russell	72	70	75	74	291	1,275
Philip Walton	76	70	70	76	292	1,050
Craig Cassells	73	71	73	75	292	1,050
Stuart Cage	70	73	75	74	292	1,050
Lee Westwood	72	74	73	73	292	1,050
Martin Gates	77	69	75	71	292	1,050
Fernando Roca	74	70	73	76	293	850
Andrew Collison	71	74	73	75	293	850
Peter Hedblom	71	72	76	74	293	850
Mikael Piltz	72	73	73	76	294	750
Gordon J. Brand	71	74	77	72	294	750
Miles Tunnicliff	75	69	71	79	244	750
Carl Magnus Stromberg	72	72	74	77	295	675
Tomas Jesus Munoz	74	72	73	76	295	675
Manuel Moreno	76	69	78	72	295	675
Carlos Larrain	73	73	74	76	296	512.50
Gordon Manson	73	71	71	81	296	512.50
Eoghan O'Connell	72	74	75	79	300	397
Jeff Hall	73	72	81	74	300	397
Robin Mann	67	75	80	79	301	393
Mark James	71	73	80	77	301	393

Extremadura Open

Golf del Guadiana, Badajoz, Spain
Par 36-36—72; 6,980 yards

February 17-20
purse, £250,000

	SCORES				TOTAL	MONEY
Paul Eales	72	69	69	71	281	£41,600
Peter Hedblom	72	69	71	70	282	27,770
Andrew Coltart	68	74	71	70	283	14,075
Jose Maria Canizares	70	73	68	72	283	14,075
Ian Spencer	74	71	68	71	284	7,283.33
Lee Westwood	68	72	72	72	284	7,283.33
Peter Mitchell	69	69	74	72	284	7,283.33
Jim Payne	72	70	70	72	284	7,283.33

	SCORES				TOTAL	MONEY
Miguel Angel Jimenez	67	73	69	75	284	7,283.33
Nic Henning	72	71	66	75	284	7,283.33
Per-Ulrik Johansson	73	70	71	71	285	4,080
Klas Eriksson	72	72	70	71	285	4,080
David Williams	71	74	69	71	285	4,080
Ignacio Gervas	73	68	72	72	285	4,080
Mathias Gronberg	73	67	72	73	285	4,080
Stephen McAllister	71	73	73	69	286	3,305
Robin Mann	70	76	68	72	286	3,305
Paul Mayo	70	71	71	74	286	3,305
Jose Rivero	71	70	70	75	286	3,305
Miguel Angel Martin	74	72	73	68	287	2,887.50
Andrew Sherborne	72	74	69	72	287	2,887.50
Terry Price	69	71	74	73	287	2,887.50
Alexander Cejka	76	68	70	73	287	2,887.50
Jesus Maria Arruti	72	73	71	72	288	2,587.50
Michel Besanceney	76	70	70	72	288	2,587.50
Adam Hunter	73	70	72	73	288	2,587.50
Keith Waters	71	72	72	73	289	2,287.50
Heinz P. Thul	71	76	71	71	289	2,287.50
Ricky Willison	77	69	73	70	289	2,287.50
Ian Garbutt	69	76	75	69	289	2,287.50
Steven Bottomley	71	72	71	75	289	2,287.50
Massimo Scarpa	73	74	71	72	290	1,900
Paul Richard Simpson	76	72	71	71	290	1,900
Philip Talbot	69	76	74	71	290	1,900
Mikael Piltz	76	72	72	70	290	1,900
David Curry	70	73	72	75	290	1,900
Paul Moloney	72	73	70	75	290	1,900
Ruben Alvarez	73	75	67	75	290	1,900
Ignacio Garrido	71	74	69	76	290	1,900
Giuseppe Cali	71	68	72	79	290	1,900
Ian Palmer	73	73	74	71	291	1,500
Jeremy Robinson	74	72	74	71	291	1,500
Steve Van Vuuren	73	73	74	71	291	1,500
Haydn Selby-Green	74	74	72	71	291	1,500
Frank Nobilo	74	74	72	71	291	1,500
Gabriel Hjertstedt	72	74	75	70	291	1,500
Stephen Hamill	77	70	71	73	291	1,500
Juan Pinero	73	74	71	74	292	1,175
Bill Malley	74	71	73	74	292	1,175
Mikael Krantz	73	72	73	74	292	1,175
David R. Jones	73	71	76	72	292	1,175
Ross Drummond	72	76	67	77	292	1,175
Christian Cevaer	70	77	67	78	292	1,175
Antoine LeBouc	74	73	72	74	293	860.71
Steen Tinning	74	73	72	74	293	860.71
Jose Manuel Carriles	74	71	74	74	293	860.71
Jon Robson	70	73	76	74	293	860.71
Juan Quiros	76	72	74	71	293	860.71
Carlos Larrain	73	73	72	75	293	860.71
Marcus Wills	71	73	73	76	293	860.71
Nicolas Joakimides	72	71	75	76	294	687.50
Andrew Collison	75	72	72	75	294	687.50
Pedro Linhart	74	72	74	74	294	687.50
Antonio Garrido	75	73	73	73	294	687.50
Jose Rozadilla	76	71	71	77	295	625
Thomas Gogele	75	73	74	74	296	400
Brian Barnes	75	70	75	77	297	396
Daniel Lozano	74	73	74	76	297	396

	SCORES				TOTAL	MONEY
Eric Giraud	78	68	77	74	297	396
Yago Beamonte	75	71	74	78	298	390
Diego Borrego	72	76	75	75	298	390
Manuel Moreno	74	73	77	74	298	390
Nick Godin	70	78	75	76	299	386
Eduardo Romero	71	77	77	77	302	384

Turespana Masters Open de Andalucia

Montecastillo Golf Resort, Jerez, Spain
Par 36-36—72; 7,024 yards

February 24-27
purse, £300,000

	SCORES				TOTAL	MONEY
Carl Mason	67	70	71	70	278	£50,535.89
Jose Maria Olazabal	69	68	71	72	280	33,670.37
Gordon Brand, Jr.	71	69	69	72	281	18,988.88
Per-Ulrik Johansson	69	72	71	70	282	15,166.84
Miguel Angel Jimenez	70	73	72	68	283	12,861.48
Ian Palmer	69	71	72	72	284	8,523.76
Jay Townsend	67	74	71	72	284	8,523.76
Peter Teravainen	70	73	68	73	284	8,523.76
Ross Drummond	69	69	73	73	284	8,523.76
Patrick Bates	71	68	77	69	285	5,278.06
Jose Coceres	70	72	69	74	285	5,278.06
Peter Fowler	67	68	75	75	285	5,278.06
Jim Payne	67	69	75	74	285	5,278.06
Ross McFarlane	68	70	73	74	285	5,278.06
Roger Chapman	68	74	72	72	286	4,277.05
Mark Roe	72	70	70	74	286	4,277.05
David R. Jones	75	66	71	74	286	4,277.05
David Williams	71	72	70	74	287	3,566.37
Seve Ballesteros	70	71	72	74	287	3,566.37
Sandy Lyle	74	70	72	71	287	3,566.37
Eduardo Romero	68	75	70	74	287	3,566.37
Paul Eales	72	68	75	72	287	3,566.37
Ricky Willison	72	72	71	72	287	3,566.37
Silvio Grappasonni	73	69	74	71	287	3,566.37
Antoine LeBouc	74	68	71	75	288	3,003.03
Miguel Angel Martin	71	73	72	72	288	3,003.03
Frank Nobilo	68	73	74	73	288	3,003.03
Ignacio Garrido	73	67	71	77	288	3,003.03
Paul Curry	69	71	72	76	288	3,003.03
Nic Henning	72	71	72	74	289	2,405.46
Glenn Ralph	70	73	73	73	289	2,405.46
Greg Turner	68	73	74	74	289	2,405.46
Richard Boxall	74	69	68	78	289	2,405.46
Russell Claydon	71	71	71	76	289	2,405.46
Pierre Fulke	70	73	72	74	289	2,405.46
Klas Eriksson	69	70	76	74	289	2,405.46
David Ray	68	73	75	73	289	2,405.46
Mathias Gronberg	72	70	73	74	289	2,405.46
Manny Zerman	71	71	76	71	289	2,405.46
Paul McGinley	71	72	74	73	290	1,971.69
Jose Maria Canizares	69	69	78	74	290	1,971.69
Andre Bossert	71	73	75	71	290	1,971.69
Gordon Manson	71	70	72	77	290	1,971.69
Paul Mayo	70	73	69	79	291	1,729.02

	SCORES				TOTAL	MONEY
Nick Godin	70	73	73	75	291	1,729.02
Scott Watson	72	69	76	74	291	1,729.02
Alberto Binaghi	68	75	72	76	291	1,729.02
Brian Nelson	74	70	74	74	292	1,456.02
Mark Mouland	70	73	72	77	292	1,456.02
Phillip Price	70	70	75	77	292	1,456.02
Magnus Sunesson	70	68	77	77	292	1,456.02
David Curry	74	70	72	76	292	1,456.02
Ian Spencer	69	73	71	80	293	1,213.35
Juan Quiros	67	70	77	79	293	1,213.35
Tomas Jesus Munoz	69	73	75	76	293	1,213.35
Paul Lawrie	71	70	76	77	294	1,061.68
Jonathan Lomas	69	73	78	74	294	1,061.68
Gary Nicklaus	72	72	74	77	295	940.34
Mike McLean	74	67	79	75	295	940.34
Terry Price	71	73	79	72	295	940.34
Andrew Sherborne	69	75	76	76	296	864.51
Retief Goosen	70	74	78	74	296	864.51
Martin Gates	70	71	82	75	298	803.85
Adam Hunter	69	71	85	73	298	803.85
Alexander Cejka	73	70	80	77	300	758.34

Turespana Open Mediterrania

Villa Martin, Torrevieja, Spain
Par 36-36—72; 6,696 yards

March 3-6
purse, £300,000

	SCORES				TOTAL	MONEY
Jose Maria Olazabal	70	65	71	70	276	£50,000
Paul McGinley	70	68	68	70	276	33,330
(Olazabal defeated McGinley on second extra hole.)						
Peter Baker	73	71	65	69	278	16,890
Gordon J. Brand	68	66	70	74	278	16,890
Klas Eriksson	67	72	70	70	279	10,733.33
Robert Allenby	70	68	71	70	279	10,733.33
Tony Johnstone	68	68	68	75	279	10,733.33
Phil Golding	68	73	70	69	280	7,095
Juan Quiros	67	67	71	75	280	7,095
Robert Karlsson	72	68	71	70	281	5,560
De Wet Basson	71	69	68	73	281	5,560
Miguel Angel Jimenez	70	69	70	72	281	5,560
Frederic Regard	72	71	69	70	282	4,610
Mike Clayton	72	70	65	75	282	4,610
Ignacio Garrido	72	69	71	70	282	4,610
Ross McFarlane	74	69	71	69	283	3,771.43
Terry Price	75	69	71	68	283	3,771.43
Brian Nelson	68	74	75	66	283	3,771.43
Andrew Coltart	71	71	69	72	283	3,771.43
Howard Clark	72	68	71	72	283	3,771.43
Peter Mitchell	72	67	72	72	283	3,771.43
Lee Westwood	68	69	71	75	283	3,771.43
Pierre Fulke	73	70	70	71	284	3,105
David R. Jones	76	66	67	75	284	3,105
Antonio Garrido	66	75	68	75	284	3,105
Domingo Hospital	72	68	71	73	284	3,105
Roger Chapman	74	66	74	70	284	3,105
Frank Nobilo	68	70	70	76	284	3,105

		SCORES			TOTAL	MONEY
Philip Walton	72	70	74	69	285	2,512.50
John McHenry	72	71	69	73	285	2,512.50
Mats Lanner	73	70	70	72	285	2,512.50
Andre Bossert	70	70	72	73	285	2,512.50
Jose Rivero	69	71	70	75	285	2,512.50
Steven Bottomley	72	68	69	76	285	2,512.50
Manny Zerman	70	70	73	72	285	2,512.50
David A. Russell	69	69	70	77	285	2,512.50
Richard Boxall	74	70	71	71	286	2,070
Peter Fowler	69	72	72	73	286	2,070
Silvio Grappasonni	71	70	74	71	286	2,070
Mathias Gronberg	69	72	72	73	286	2,070
Mark Nichols	70	70	72	74	286	2,070
Russell Claydon	72	65	72	77	286	2,070
Martin Gates	70	72	75	70	287	1,650
Ian Palmer	71	71	74	71	287	1,650
Jean Van de Velde	72	71	71	73	287	1,650
Thomas Levet	73	70	70	74	287	1,650
Jamie Spence	72	71	74	70	287	1,650
Gavin Levenson	73	71	69	74	287	1,650
Robert Lee	70	72	70	75	287	1,650
Scott Watson	69	72	69	77	287	1,650
Santiago Luna	72	71	67	78	288	1,230
Jose Coceres	75	68	70	75	288	1,230
Gabriel Hjertstedt	69	74	73	72	288	1,230
Anders Gillner	73	71	72	72	288	1,230
Yago Beamonte	69	75	72	72	288	1,230
Eduardo Romero	67	72	71	78	288	1,230
Wayne Riley	71	71	72	75	289	936
Magnus Sunesson	74	69	72	74	289	936
Anders Sorensen	72	72	72	73	289	936
Olle Nordberg	74	70	76	69	289	936
Mike Harwood	68	71	75	75	289	936
Darren Clarke	71	72	77	70	290	679.67
Peter Teravainen	73	70	72	75	290	679.67
Stephen McAllister	74	69	71	76	290	679.67
Alberto Binaghi	72	72	73	73	290	679.67
Johan Rystrom	72	72	72	74	290	679.67
David J. Russell	74	70	68	78	291	679.67
Paul Lawrie	71	71	70	79	291	442
Michel Besanceney	68	75	73	75	291	442
Ignacio Gervas	73	71	75	72	291	442
Manuel Pinero	73	71	71	76	291	442
David Ray	69	68	74	80	291	442
Malcolm Mackenzie	74	70	71	79	294	436
Mark Roe	72	72	74	87	305	434
Ruben Alvarez	73	71	77	DQ		431
Steen Tinning	72	72	77	DQ		431

Turespana Open de Baleares

Son Vida Golf Club, Palma de Mallorca, Spain
Par 35-37—72; 6,500 yards

March 10-13
purse, £250,000

		SCORES			TOTAL	MONEY
Barry Lane	64	70	66	69	269	£41,616.31
Jim Payne	67	68	70	66	271	27,727.55

Fuzzy Zoeller (left) and Greg Norman amuse the gallery after Norman's four-stroke romp in The Players Championship.

Johnny Miller had a win for the ages.   Mark McCumber scored three victories.

Loren Roberts' big year began at Bay Hill with   Andrew Magee had a trophy to
host Arnold Palmer.   wear at Tucson.

Tom Lehman celebrates his
Memorial victory.

Phil Mickelson won the first event, the
Mercedes Championship.

Fuzzy Zoeller was second five
times — and once in Japan.

Fred Couples was the American hero of the
Presidents Cup.

Steve Lowery got his first win.

Hale Irwin won the Heritage again.

Mike Springer had two victories.

Corey Pavin was the L.A. champion.

New Orleans winner Ben Crenshaw.

Jeff Maggert was top-10 on the money list.

Popular John Daly began and ended
1994 off the PGA Tour.

David Frost had four worldwide victories.

European Tour

Allsport/Stephen Munday

Colin Montgomerie won three events in Spain, Germany and England, and led the European money list for the second year in a row.

Allsport/Anton Want

Nick Faldo's only European win was the Alfred Dunhill Open.

Allsport/Stephen Munday

Jose Maria Olazabal's four worldwide victories included the Volvo PGA.

Honda Open winner Robert Allenby.

Moroccan Open winner Anders Forsbrand.

European Masters winner Eduardo Romero.

British Masters winner Ian Woosnam.

Allsport/Stephen Munday

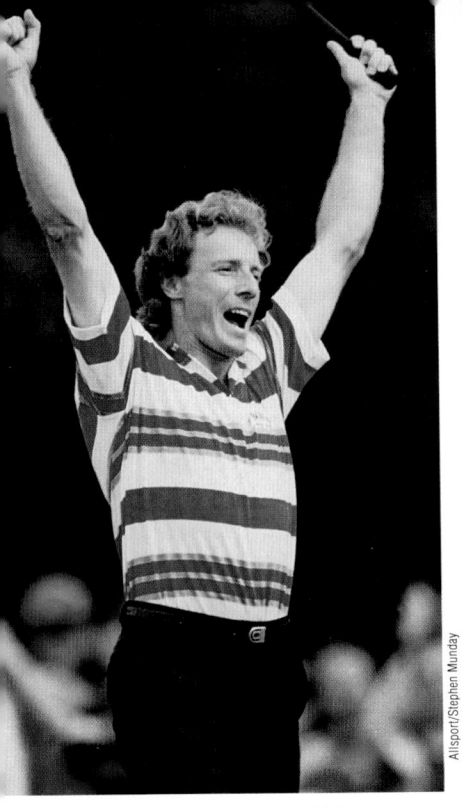

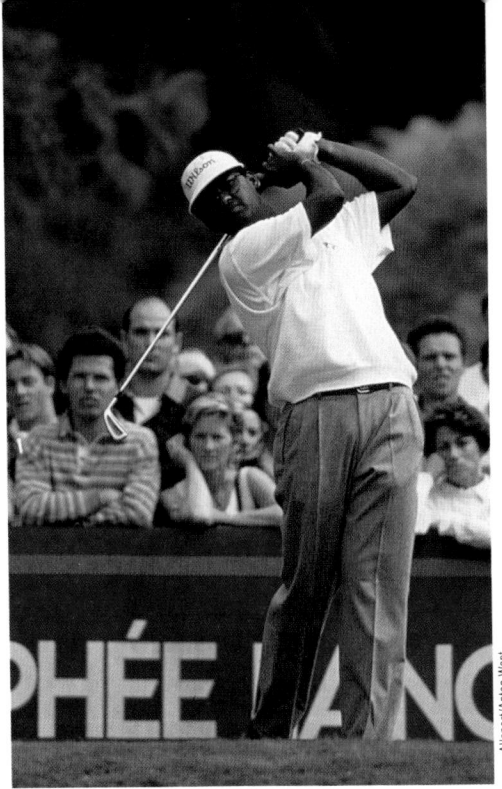

Bernhard Langer had 62 in winning the Volvo Masters.

Allsport/Anton Want

The Trophee Lancome was one of Vijay Singh's two European victories.

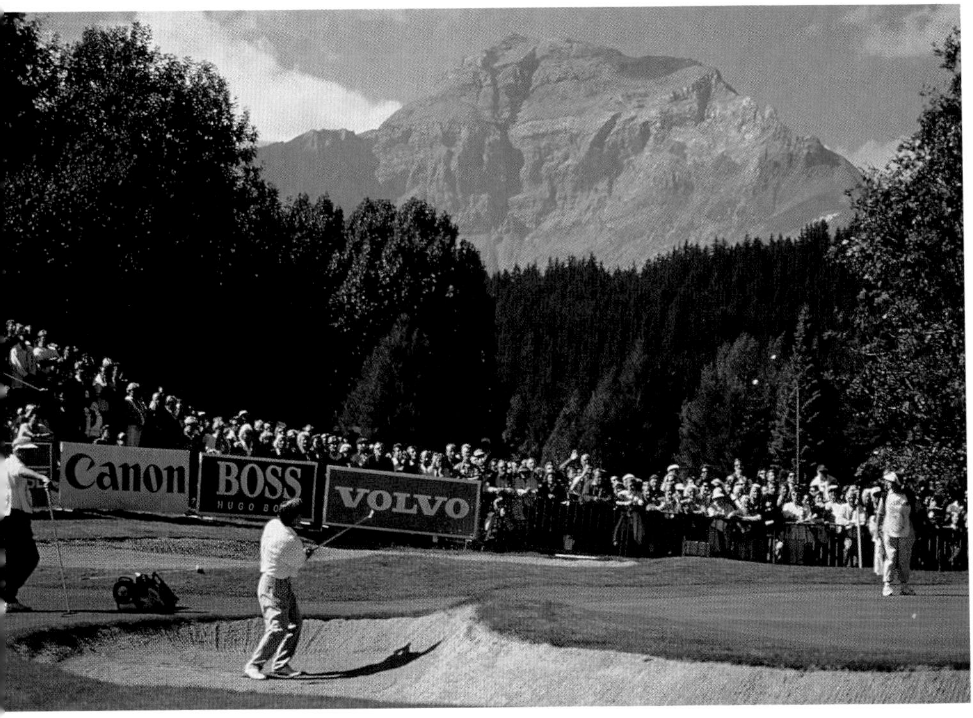

Allsport/David Cannon

Barry Lane plays against a majestic backdrop in the Canon European Masters.

David Gilford won in Spain and Britain.

Seve Ballesteros had two European triumphs in England and Germany.

Mark McNulty won the BMW title.

Miguel Angel Jimenez holes the winning Heineken Dutch Open putt.

Mark Roe celebrates his victory in the Peugeot Open de France.

Australasian/Japan Tours

Craig Parry won the Microsoft
Australian Masters.

With seven victories, Masashi (Jumbo)
Ozaki became the first to win over
¥200 million in Japan.

Heineken Australian Open champion
Robert Allenby.

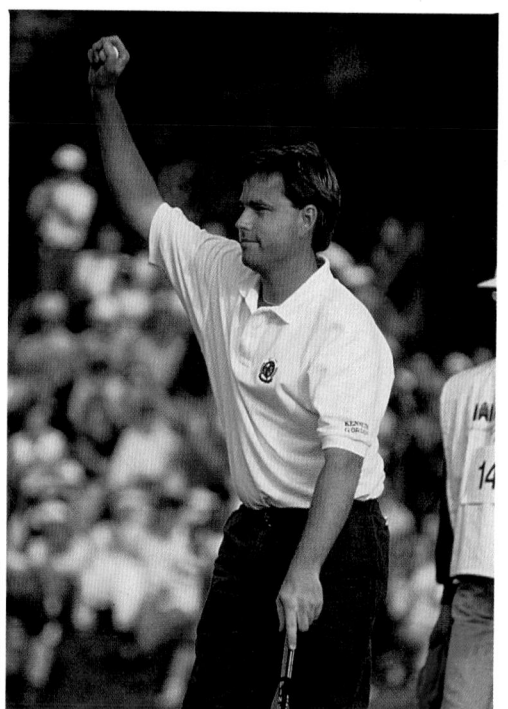

American Brian Watts won five events.

Tommy Nakajima had three wins.

Yoshinori Mizumaki won twice.

Joe Ozaki won the Acom International.

Senior Tours

Tom Wargo won the Seniors British Open Championship.

Lee Trevino's seven wins included the PGA Seniors title.

South Africa's Simon Hobday was the U.S. Senior Open champion.

Dave Stockton led the U.S. money list.

Jim Albus had two victories.

Raymond Floyd won four titles.

July was Jim Colbert's month.

Women's Tours

Laura Davies had eight worldwide victories and led the LPGA money list.

Beth Daniel won the World Championship of Women's Golf.

Patty Sheehan was the U.S. Women's Open champion.

Liselotte Neumann's five wins included the Weetabix British title.

Michael C. Cohen

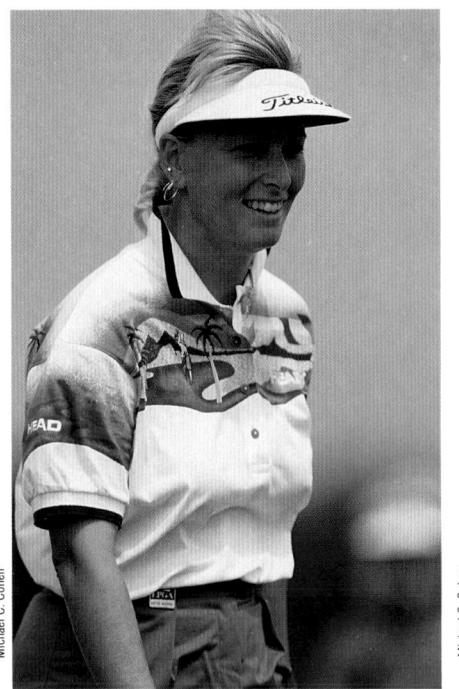

Dottie Mochrie was fourth on the LPGA money list.

Michael C. Cohen

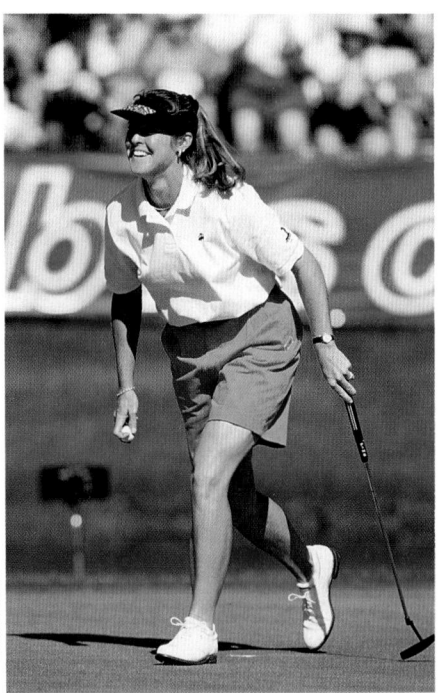

Donna Andrews won the Nabisco Dinah Shore Championship.

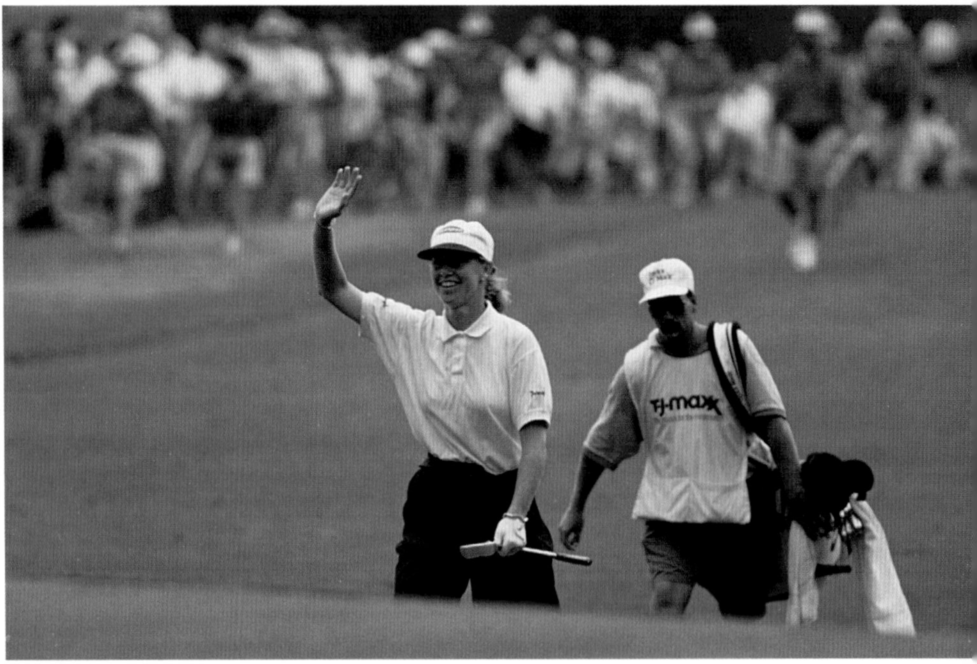

Michael C. Cohen

Helen Alfredsson won in the United States and Europe.

Allsport/Stephen Dunn

Allsport/Stephen Dunn

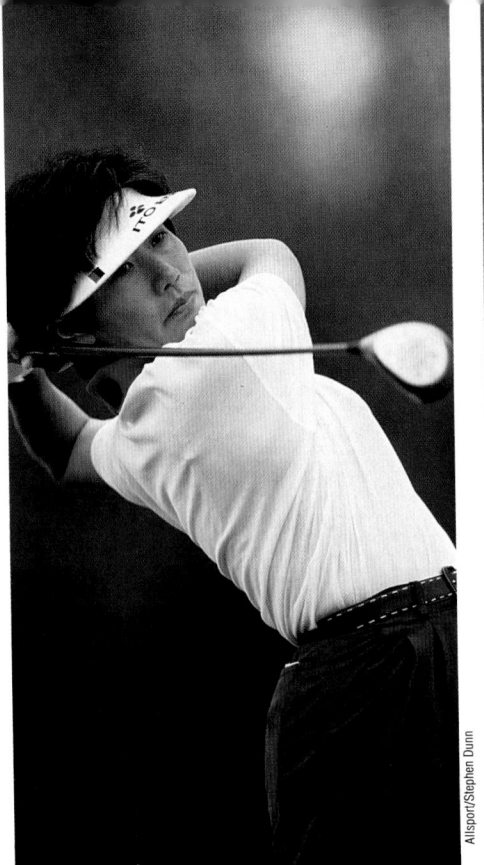

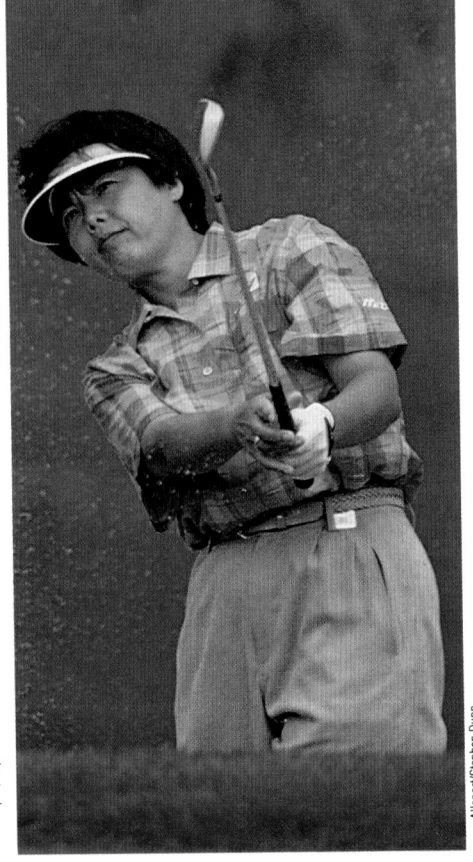

Ikuyo Shiotani (left) and Ayako Okamoto each won three events in Japan.

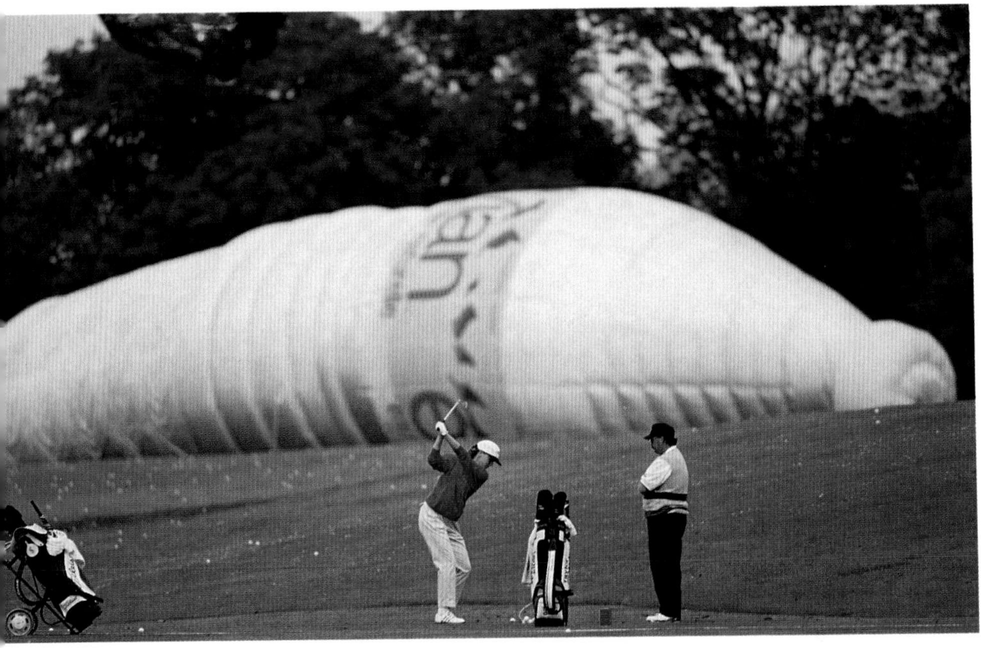

Chicot Agency

The Evian Masters offered an unusual target on the practice range.

	SCORES				TOTAL	MONEY
Wayne Westner	68	70	67	68	273	15,637.34
Paul Lawrie	74	65	69	67	275	11,540.66
Lee Westwood	69	67	71	68	275	11,540.66
Sven Struver	71	67	72	67	277	7,493.93
Andrew Coltart	73	69	67	68	277	7,493.93
Jose Rivero	72	67	66	72	277	7,493.93
Peter Hedblom	72	71	68	67	278	5,062.57
Terry Price	71	71	68	68	278	5,062.57
Pedro Linhart	71	71	64	72	278	5,062.57
Alexander Cejka	74	70	70	65	279	4,159.13
Robert Karlsson	68	71	71	69	279	4,159.13
Miguel Angel Jimenez	75	69	69	67	280	3,746.97
Ross McFarlane	73	70	69	68	280	3,746.97
Adam Hunter	73	71	69	68	281	3,522.15
Jeff Hawkes	69	74	73	66	282	2,910.14
Fredrik Lindgren	72	69	76	65	282	2,910.14
Jean Van de Velde	70	72	71	69	282	2,910.14
Andrew Collison	69	71	72	70	282	2,910.14
Jeremy Robinson	73	68	71	70	282	2,910.14
Ian Spencer	74	68	70	70	282	2,910.14
Santiago Luna	68	72	71	71	282	2,910.14
Jose Rozadilla	71	71	69	71	282	2,910.14
Mike Clayton	67	73	70	72	282	2,910.14
Gabriel Hjertstedt	70	69	70	73	282	2,910.14
Glenn Ralph	73	69	74	67	283	2,398.06
Retief Goosen	69	73	74	67	283	2,398.06
Mark Davis	73	67	77	66	283	2,398.06
De Wet Basson	71	74	74	65	284	2,173.24
Jonathan Lomas	71	73	69	71	284	2,173.24
Eric Giraud	69	71	71	73	284	2,173.24
Derrick Cooper	73	72	70	70	285	1,848.50
Gordon J. Brand	70	74	70	71	285	1,848.50
Keith Waters	69	74	71	71	285	1,848.50
Mark Roe	74	69	71	71	285	1,848.50
Anders Sorensen	72	68	73	72	285	1,848.50
Peter Teravainen	71	69	72	73	285	1,848.50
Ignacio Garrido	74	71	67	73	285	1,848.50
Adam Mednick	70	71	70	74	285	1,848.50
Michel Besanceney	68	74	67	76	285	1,848.50
Paul Eales	76	69	70	71	286	1,423.85
Antoine LeBouc	72	69	74	71	286	1,423.85
Ian Garbutt	69	72	75	70	286	1,423.85
Martin Poxon	71	72	74	69	286	1,423.85
Mike Miller	70	75	74	67	286	1,423.85
Carl Magnus Stromberg	70	71	72	73	286	1,423.85
Paul McGinley	75	70	68	73	286	1,423.85
Robert Allenby	70	74	69	73	286	1,423.85
Richard Boxall	68	76	71	72	287	1,174.05
Jose Manuel Carriles	71	70	75	71	287	1,174.05
Roger Chapman	74	68	74	72	288	999.19
Phillip Price	70	71	76	71	288	999.19
Juan Quiros	71	71	76	70	288	999.19
Gary Orr	72	70	77	69	288	999.19
Jon Robson	70	71	72	75	288	999.19
Stephen Hamill	71	72	73	73	289	766.04
Mats Lanner	72	73	71	73	289	766.04
Brian Nelson	73	69	74	73	289	766.04
David Ray	69	73	74	73	289	766.04
David R. Jones	72	71	77	69	289	766.04
Domingo Hospital	70	73	71	75	289	766.04

	SCORES				TOTAL	MONEY
David Williams	73	70	74	73	290	661.96
Ignacio Gervas	70	75	75	70	290	661.96
Des Smyth	73	71	73	74	291	474.16
Ulrich Eckhardt	73	69	76	73	291	474.16
Manuel Pinero	71	72	77	71	291	474.16
Eduardo Romero	75	69	71	77	292	394
Phil Golding	71	70	74	77	292	394
Marcus Wills	71	68	81	72	292	394
Steven Bottomley	75	70	76	72	293	390
Paul Curry	75	68	73	78	294	388
Jose Coceres	71	72	72	81	296	385
Heinz P. Thul	73	72	73	78	296	385
Justin Hobday	69	76	75	78	298	382

Portuguese Open

Penha Longa Golf Club, Linho, Sintra, Lisbon, Portugal
Par 35-36—71; 6,865 yards

March 17-20
purse, £300,000

	SCORES				TOTAL	MONEY
Phillip Price	64	71	71	72	278	£50,000
David Gilford	71	69	69	73	282	22,370
Retief Goosen	69	66	73	74	282	22,370
Paul Eales	66	71	72	73	282	22,370
Costantino Rocca	65	73	74	71	283	11,600
Ignacio Garrido	69	69	73	72	283	11,600
Miguel Angel Jimenez	70	68	74	72	284	8,250
Glenn Ralph	71	69	71	73	284	8,250
Ronan Rafferty	69	68	73	75	285	5,842.50
Michel Besanceney	69	71	72	73	285	5,842.50
Mike Clayton	66	74	73	72	285	5,842.50
Howard Clark	67	73	74	71	285	5,842.50
David J. Russell	69	69	77	71	286	4,515
Carl Mason	67	69	79	71	286	4,515
Domingo Hospital	70	71	73	72	286	4,515
Brian Barnes	69	67	73	77	286	4,515
Gary Evans	69	73	75	70	287	3,642.86
Jean Van de Velde	68	68	76	75	287	3,642.86
Stephen Ames	74	69	74	70	287	3,642.86
Gary Orr	68	70	75	74	287	3,642.86
Mike Miller	71	68	74	74	287	3,642.86
Sam Torrance	70	73	70	74	287	3,642.86
Robert Karlsson	70	70	72	75	287	3,642.86
Gavin Levenson	71	73	71	73	288	3,015
Gordon J. Brand	69	71	79	69	288	3,015
Sven Struver	68	71	74	75	288	3,015
Russell Claydon	74	66	77	71	288	3,015
Gordon Brand, Jr.	67	73	74	74	288	3,015
Ross McFarlane	75	69	70	74	288	3,015
Lee Westwood	69	70	73	77	289	2,505
Steven Richardson	71	72	73	73	289	2,505
De Wet Basson	72	71	75	71	289	2,505
Andre Bossert	71	69	74	75	289	2,505
Richard Boxall	73	71	75	70	289	2,505
Alberto Binaghi	73	69	74	73	289	2,505
Nick Godin	71	73	71	75	290	2,040
Jose Manuel Carriles	69	73	78	70	290	2,040

	SCORES				TOTAL	MONEY
Paul Lawrie	69	74	71	76	290	2,040
Greg Turner	69	73	73	75	290	2,040
Peter Fowler	72	68	75	75	290	2,040
Anders Forsbrand	71	69	74	76	290	2,040
Steven Bottomley	67	72	79	72	290	2,040
Mark Mouland	74	70	74	72	290	2,040
Andrew Coltart	73	68	73	76	290	2,040
Philip Walton	70	70	74	77	291	1,620
Terry Price	72	68	75	76	291	1,620
Thomas Levet	70	70	75	76	291	1,620
Adam Hunter	71	73	76	71	291	1,620
Peter Teravainen	69	75	75	72	291	1,620
Tony Johnstone	70	73	75	74	292	1,320
Robert Allenby	71	70	75	76	292	1,320
Steve Bowman	68	74	78	72	292	1,320
Gordon Manson	68	73	75	76	292	1,320
Gabriel Hjertstedt	71	70	74	77	292	1,320
Olle Nordberg	71	72	75	75	293	1,080
Brian Marchbank	69	72	73	79	293	1,080
Phil Golding	71	72	76	74	293	1,080
Peter Mitchell	72	71	74	77	294	945
Jose Maria Canizares	70	71	82	71	294	945
Mark Davis	75	69	75	76	295	885
Fredrik Larsson	72	70	79	74	295	885
Chris Moody	71	70	82	74	297	840
David A. Russell	72	72	77	77	298	795
Carl Suneson	72	72	77	77	298	795
Massimo Scarpa	71	70	78	84	303	750
*Almerindo Sequeira	74	69	80	86	309	
Eduardo Romero	69	71	78	WD		

Open V33 du Grand Lyon

Golf Course de Lyon, Villette d'Anthon, Lyon, France
Par 36-36—72; 7,289 yards

April 1-4
purse, £225,000

	SCORES				TOTAL	MONEY
Stephen Ames	70	67	71	74	282	£37,500
Pedro Linhart	72	68	72	72	284	19,535
Gabriel Hjertstedt	68	68	71	77	284	19,535
Wayne Riley	69	68	69	79	285	11,250
Gary Orr	69	66	76	75	286	9,500
Michel Besanceney	69	75	68	75	287	7,275
David Gilford	70	73	71	73	287	7,275
Philip Walton	72	71	72	73	288	5,030
Gordon J. Brand	70	69	73	76	288	5,030
Miles Tunnicliff	72	68	75	73	288	5,030
Santiago Luna	72	71	73	73	289	3,903.33
Lee Westwood	73	71	72	73	289	3,903.33
Torsten Giedeon	71	72	70	76	289	3,903.33
Jim Payne	71	69	74	76	290	3,266
Heinz P. Thul	72	72	69	77	290	3,266
Ronan Rafferty	73	70	71	76	290	3,266
Keith Waters	71	72	75	72	290	3,266
Alexander Cejka	70	77	71	72	290	3,266
Russell Claydon	74	67	76	74	291	2,810
Peter Mitchell	73	69	73	76	291	2,810

	SCORES				TOTAL	MONEY
Carl Mason	75	70	70	77	292	2,481.67
Mark Mouland	71	73	74	74	292	2,481.67
Andrew Sherborne	69	72	77	74	292	2,481.67
Gordon Manson	73	71	77	71	292	2,481.67
Adam Hunter	70	75	75	72	292	2,481.67
Jeremy Robinson	72	69	74	77	292	2,481.67
Miguel Angel Martin	77	68	73	75	293	2,010
John McHenry	73	71	71	78	293	2,010
Marc Farry	69	73	73	78	293	2,010
Brian Marchbank	70	70	79	74	293	2,010
Paul Eales	75	72	70	76	293	2,010
Ross McFarlane	75	71	74	73	293	2,010
Robin Mann	73	70	74	76	293	2,010
Paul Affleck	71	75	74	74	294	1,642
Michael Campbell	73	73	76	72	294	1,642
Magnus Sunesson	74	73	73	74	294	1,642
Phillip Price	67	76	79	72	294	1,642
Anders Gillner	72	73	74	75	294	1,642
Malcolm Mackenzie	73	72	69	81	295	1,520
Eric Giraud	70	74	70	82	296	1,320
Gordon Brand, Jr.	73	69	73	81	296	1,320
Paul Lawrie	73	71	75	77	296	1,320
Thomas Gogele	76	70	72	78	296	1,320
Fabrice Honnorat de Mal	73	70	75	78	296	1,320
Jacob Rasmussen	69	76	72	79	296	1,320
Silvio Grappasonni	74	71	77	74	296	1,320
Emmanuel Dussart	75	70	75	76	296	1,320
Jeff Remesy	71	71	76	78	296	1,320
Mike Miller	73	71	75	78	297	1,080
David Williams	71	73	75	78	297	1,080
Phil Golding	71	75	71	80	297	1,080
Liam White	72	72	72	82	298	940
Mark Davis	76	87	74	81	298	940
Jean Louis Guepy	74	70	75	79	298	940
Ricky Willison	71	72	76	79	298	940
Steen Tinning	73	73	72	81	299	780
Laurent Lassalle	74	71	80	74	299	780
Andrew Hare	76	69	77	77	299	780
Domingo Hospital	75	72	71	81	299	780
Steven Bottomley	74	72	75	79	300	660
Paul Mayo	73	73	76	78	300	660
Eoghan O'Connell	76	70	75	79	300	660
David Curry	74	73	75	79	301	527.50
Brian Barnes	76	71	77	77	301	527.50
Raymond Russell	71	71	76	83	301	527.50
Tim Planchin	74	72	78	77	301	527.50
Gavin Levenson	73	73	78	78	302	397
Colin Brooks	71	76	78	77	302	397
Andre Bossert	74	70	77	83	304	394
Andrew Collison	75	70	74	87	306	391
Peter Fowler	74	73	83	76	306	391
Martin Poxon	74	73	75	WD		
Ignacio Garrido	72	75	DQ			

Tournoi Perrier de Paris

Golf de Saint-Cloud, Paris, France
Par 35-36—71; 6,540 yards

April 14-17
purse, £350,000

	SCORES				TOTAL	MONEY
						(Each)
Peter Baker/David J. Russell	58	68	65	69	260	£35,000
Mark Mouland/Jamie Spence	62	69	66	64	261	25,000
Russell Claydon/Paul Eales	60	66	71	66	263	15,000
Seve Ballesteros/Jose Maria Olazabal	63	67	67	66	263	15,000
Miguel Angel Jimenez/Jose Rivero	66	70	64	64	264	9,000
Mark Davis/David R. Jones	66	68	67	64	265	5,583.34
Andrew Sherborne/Paul Curry	65	68	67	65	265	5,583.34
Thomas Levet/Marc Pendaries	62	71	66	66	265	5,583.34
Steven Richardson/Peter Mitchell	65	69	65	67	266	4,375
Manuel Pinero/Jose Maria Canizares	63	68	67	68	266	4,375
Gordon J. Brand/Glenn Ralph	65	69	68	65	267	4,000
Des Smyth/Paul McGinley	68	68	64	68	268	3,750
Paul Lawrie/Stephen McAllister	66	68	70	65	269	2,964.29
Jesus Maria Arruti/Tomas Jesus Munoz	65	69	70	65	269	2,964.29
Gary Evans/Retief Goosen	66	69	68	66	269	2,964.29
Frederic Regard/Jeff Remesy	65	67	70	67	269	2,964.29
Ignacio Gervas/Domingo Hospital	66	69	67	67	269	2,964.29
Jonathan Lomas/Miles Tunnicliff	65	71	66	67	269	2,964.29
Robin Mann/Keith Waters	65	69	67	68	269	2,964.29
Antonio Garrido/Ignacio Garrido	65	70	69	66	270	2,400
Haydn Selby-Green/Jon Robson	66	70	68	66	270	2,400
Ralf Berhorst/Alexander Cejka	65	69	68	68	270	2,400
Jean Van de Velde/Christian Cevaer	66	67	68	70	271	2,200
Juan Quiros/Diego Borrego	63	73	69	68	273	2,100
Michel Besanceney/Jean Louis Guepy	67	69	73	66	275	1,850
Mark Roe/Robert Lee	64	69	75	67	275	1,850
Olivier Edmond/Frederic Cupillard	65	66	75	69	275	1,850
Anders Forsbrand/Vilhelm Forsbrand	66	69	71	69	275	1,850
Marcus Wills/Raymond Burns	66	70	71	71	278	1,550
Ove Sellberg/Nicklas Fasth	64	71	72	71	278	1,550

Heineken Open Catalonia

Pals Golf Club, Costa Brava, Spain
Par 36-36—72; 6,713 yards

April 21-24
purse, £300,000

	SCORES				TOTAL	MONEY
Jose Coceres	70	69	67	69	275	£50,000
Jean Louis Guepy	67	68	72	71	278	33,330
Russell Claydon	72	73	69	65	279	18,780
Sam Torrance	70	73	70	67	280	15,000
Wayne Riley	68	69	74	70	281	9,925
Adam Hunter	70	72	69	70	281	9,925
Pierre Fulke	71	71	69	70	281	9,925
Gordon Brand, Jr.	70	72	69	70	281	9,925
Mark Mouland	70	72	71	69	282	6,690
Ignacio Garrido	74	73	70	66	283	5,560
Frank Nobilo	71	68	71	73	283	5,560
Retief Goosen	74	65	69	75	283	5,560
Paul Affleck	72	70	71	71	284	4,610
Steven Bottomley	71	75	67	71	284	4,610

		SCORES			TOTAL	MONEY
Miguel Angel Jimenez	70	70	72	72	284	4,610
Lee Westwood	72	75	70	68	285	4,050
Howard Clark	69	72	74	70	285	4,050
Gordon J. Brand	69	72	70	74	285	4,050
Roger Chapman	70	77	69	70	286	3,470
Jim Payne	69	73	69	75	286	3,470
Fredrik Lindgren	71	72	71	72	286	3,470
Jay Townsend	73	67	77	69	286	3,470
Christy O'Connor, Jr.	70	70	73	73	286	3,470
Anders Gillner	73	71	72	70	286	3,470
Andrew Collison	72	69	74	72	287	2,925
Gabriel Hjertstedt	71	75	73	68	287	2,925
Juan Quiros	72	68	73	74	287	2,925
Klas Eriksson	73	71	72	71	287	2,925
Jose Maria Canizares	71	76	68	72	287	2,925
Jose Manuel Carriles	74	68	72	73	287	2,925
Miguel Angel Martin	72	75	68	73	288	2,466
Juan Anglada	72	74	73	69	288	2,466
Gavin Levenson	67	78	72	71	288	2,466
Jean Van de Velde	73	72	73	70	288	2,466
Ignacio Feliu	72	75	68	73	288	2,466
Peter O'Malley	72	75	72	70	289	2,070
Greg Turner	75	72	74	68	289	2,070
Andrew Coltart	73	73	72	71	289	2,070
Pedro Linhart	72	73	73	71	289	2,070
Jose Rozadilla	73	67	74	75	289	2,070
Ross Drummond	75	71	73	70	289	2,070
Michel Besanceney	73	72	73	71	289	2,070
Gary Orr	73	72	71	73	289	2,070
Peter Fowler	70	75	69	76	290	1,770
Alberto Binaghi	74	72	72	72	290	1,770
Brian Barnes	73	71	73	74	291	1,590
Adam Mednick	74	70	75	72	291	1,590
Colin Brooks	74	67	78	72	291	1,590
Des Smyth	71	73	74	73	291	1,590
Ruben Álvarez	73	74	71	74	292	1,230
Sven Struver	72	74	76	70	292	1,230
Stephen Ames	71	76	74	71	292	1,230
Jose Rivero	73	72	76	71	292	1,230
Phillip Price	76	69	74	73	292	1,230
Brian Marchbank	73	71	77	71	292	1,230
Rolf Muntz	72	65	77	78	292	1,230
Phil Golding	74	72	74	72	292	1,230
Derrick Cooper	71	73	75	74	293	885
Patrick Burke	72	75	76	70	293	885
Terry Price	74	73	73	73	293	885
Thomas Levet	67	80	73	73	293	885
Craig Cassells	70	73	78	72	293	885
Mike McLean	74	71	75	73	293	885
Per-Ulrik Johansson	71	74	80	69	294	607
Andrew Sherborne	73	71	79	71	294	607
Frederic Regard	72	74	78	70	294	607
Gordon Manson	73	70	76	75	294	607
Peter Mitchell	71	74	75	75	295	443
De Wet Basson	71	75	73	76	295	443
Fredrik Larsson	72	75	75	73	295	443
Olle Nordberg	69	76	78	72	295	443
Brian Nelson	75	72	75	74	296	437
Robert Lee	74	71	75	76	296	437
Steve Bowman	71	74	74	78	297	433

	SCORES				TOTAL	MONEY
Ignacio Gervas	73	73	77	74	297	433
Mark Davis	71	76	77	74	298	428
Anders Sorensen	70	75	77	76	298	428
Eduardo Romero	72	73	79	74	298	428
Justin Hobday	73	73	76	77	299	424
Ralf Berhorst	71	71	83	75	300	422
Thomas Gogele	75	72	83	75	305	420
David Gilford	75	72	DQ			

Air France Cannes Open

Cannes Mougins Golf Club, Cannes, France
Par 36-36—72; 6,263 yards

April 28-May 1
purse, £300,000

	SCORES				TOTAL	MONEY
Ian Woosnam	72	70	63	66	271	£50,000
Colin Montgomerie	70	69	67	70	276	33,330
Jean Van de Velde	73	71	68	65	277	16,890
Wayne Riley	69	69	73	66	277	16,890
Pierre Fulke	68	69	69	72	278	12,700
Terry Price	69	71	70	71	281	7,195.71
Santiago Luna	69	69	76	67	281	7,195.71
Tony Johnstone	69	69	74	69	281	7,195.71
Russell Claydon	72	67	73	69	281	7,195.71
Darren Clarke	69	69	72	71	281	7,195.71
Sam Torrance	65	68	76	72	281	7,195.71
Per-Ulrik Johansson	73	70	69	69	281	7,195.71
Ross Drummond	69	70	72	71	281	4,515
Robert Karlsson	67	71	70	74	282	4,515
Jim Payne	72	68	69	73	282	4,515
Greg Turner	72	68	72	70	282	4,515
Peter Baker	72	71	70	70	283	4,050
Barry Lane	68	71	75	70	284	3,624
Fredrik Lindgren	70	74	70	70	284	3,624
Silvio Grappasonni	68	72	73	71	284	3,624
Gary Evans	69	70	70	75	284	3,624
Gordon Brand, Jr.	70	68	70	76	284	3,624
Ignacio Garrido	75	68	73	69	285	3,195
De Wet Basson	74	69	74	68	285	3,195
Peter O'Malley	72	69	72	72	285	3,195
Klas Eriksson	70	74	70	71	285	3,195
Anders Gillner	70	74	73	69	286	2,704.29
Peter Hedblom	72	71	72	71	286	2,704.29
Gary Orr	69	71	75	71	286	2,704.29
Rodger Davis	71	69	74	72	286	2,704.29
Jonathan Lomas	75	69	75	67	286	2,704.29
Howard Clark	70	69	76	71	286	2,704.29
David Gilford	71	71	72	72	286	2,704.29
Jay Townsend	68	69	71	79	287	2,220
Jeremy Robinson	66	74	72	75	287	2,220
Michael Campbell	74	69	69	75	287	2,220
Andrew Coltart	68	71	76	72	287	2,220
Brian Marchbank	70	71	72	74	287	2,220
Costantino Rocca	70	71	76	70	287	2,220
Des Smyth	73	68	70	76	287	2,220
Brian Nelson	71	69	77	71	288	1,830
Lee Westwood	73	69	74	72	288	1,830

	SCORES				TOTAL	MONEY
Miguel Angel Martin	68	73	73	74	288	1,830
Mike Clayton	72	71	74	71	288	1,830
Robert Allenby	73	70	71	74	288	1,830
Quentin Dabson	72	71	69	76	288	1,830
Ian Spencer	70	72	72	75	289	1,440
Carl Magnus Stromberg	70	74	73	72	289	1,440
Manny Zerman	67	77	69	76	289	1,440
Mark McNulty	72	69	74	74	289	1,440
Peter Teravainen	72	71	71	75	289	1,440
Mike McLean	72	71	71	75	289	1,440
Peter Mitchell	68	75	74	72	289	1,440
Anders Forsbrand	74	68	76	72	290	1,140
Malcolm Mackenzie	71	70	75	74	290	1,140
Richard Boxall	71	72	71	76	290	1,140
Steen Tinning	71	71	77	72	291	952.50
Paul Way	71	72	74	74	291	952.50
Derrick Cooper	73	71	75	72	291	952.50
Ian Palmer	72	72	69	78	291	952.50
Mark Mouland	70	71	74	77	292	825
David J. Russell	69	70	78	75	292	825
Peter Fowler	74	68	77	73	292	825
Ralf Berhorst	70	73	75	74	292	825
Jamie Spence	71	72	77	73	293	600
Stephen Ames	72	66	78	77	293	600
Keith Waters	70	74	74	77	295	448
Jeff Remesy	71	72	77	76	296	446
Steve Bowman	73	70	77	77	297	444
Nic Henning	72	72	77	77	298	441
Phil Golding	75	69	77	77	298	441

Benson & Hedges International Open

St. Mellion Golf & Country Club, Plymouth, England
Par 36-36—72; 7,054 yards

May 5-8
purse, £650,000

	SCORES				TOTAL	MONEY
Seve Ballesteros	69	70	72	70	281	£108,330
Nick Faldo	75	69	70	70	284	72,210
Jonathan Lomas	74	70	69	72	285	36,595
Gary Orr	70	70	70	75	285	36,595
Wayne Westner	70	74	69	74	287	20,108
Phillip Price	69	73	71	74	287	20,108
Robert Karlsson	73	72	70	72	287	20,108
Sam Torrance	75	68	69	75	287	20,108
Paul Curry	76	69	70	72	287	20,108
Alexander Cejka	76	72	67	73	288	11,650
Mark Roe	73	72	71	72	288	11,650
Howard Clark	70	72	75	71	288	11,650
Jose Rivero	70	73	75	70	288	11,650
Malcolm Mackenzie	73	72	73	71	289	9,356.25
Gordon Brand, Jr.	76	71	72	70	289	9,356.25
Colin Montgomerie	73	70	77	69	289	9,356.25
Bernhard Langer	70	77	70	72	289	9,356.25
Barry Lane	77	72	68	73	290	7,540
Darren Clarke	73	73	67	77	290	7,540
Steen Tinning	75	74	70	71	290	7,540
Sven Struver	72	73	72	73	290	7,540

	SCORES				TOTAL	MONEY
Eduardo Romero	75	73	70	72	290	7,540
Paul McGinley	72	69	75	74	290	7,540
Rodger Davis	78	71	67	74	290	7,540
Andrew Sherborne	74	70	72	74	290	7,540
Retief Goosen	71	76	73	71	291	5,955.63
Per-Ulrik Johansson	75	70	71	75	291	5,955.63
Mark James	72	73	75	71	291	5,955.63
Stephen Ames	70	72	79	70	291	5,955.63
Peter Fowler	71	74	70	76	291	5,955.63
Jean Van de Velde	71	74	75	71	291	5,955.63
Fredrik Lindgren	73	74	70	74	291	5,955.63
Mike Clayton	74	72	70	75	291	5,955.63
Jose Maria Olazabal	76	72	71	73	292	4,940
Frank Nobilo	75	71	73	73	292	4,940
Andrew Murray	74	69	75	74	292	4,940
Mark Davis	72	75	76	69	292	4,940
Paul Mayo	72	74	75	71	292	4,940
Terry Price	76	73	70	74	293	4,225
David Ray	73	74	72	74	293	4,225
Paul Affleck	74	75	73	71	293	4,225
Sandy Lyle	75	72	74	72	293	4,225
Lee Westwood	72	72	74	75	293	4,225
Domingo Hospital	77	70	71	75	293	4,225
Andrew Oldcorn	76	73	72	73	294	3,445
Paul Eales	73	72	78	71	294	3,445
Manuel Pinero	75	72	72	75	294	3,445
Gavin Levenson	74	74	75	71	294	3,445
Jim Payne	74	74	72	74	294	3,445
Ian Spencer	75	72	71	76	294	3,445
Philip Walton	72	75	71	77	295	2,600
Gary Evans	77	72	71	75	295	2,600
David Curry	73	75	71	76	295	2,600
Bernhard Gallacher	72	74	76	73	295	2,600
John Bland	72	75	74	74	295	2,600
Jamie Spence	75	69	77	74	295	2,600
Mike McLean	72	74	71	78	295	2,600
Gordon J. Brand	73	75	78	70	296	1,917.50
Richard Boxall	75	72	76	73	296	1,917.50
Miguel Angel Jimenez	77	71	76	72	296	1,917.50
Mathias Gronberg	77	70	74	75	296	1,917.50
Andre Bossert	74	74	74	74	296	1,917.50
Gabriel Hjertstedt	76	70	75	75	296	1,917.50
*David Howell	75	72	73	76	296	
Pierre Fulke	74	71	77	75	297	1,430
Robert Allenby	74	72	73	78	297	1,430
Peter Teravainen	79	70	74	74	297	1,430
Roger Chapman	71	74	75	78	298	972
Carl Mason	75	74	77	72	298	972
De Wet Basson	73	75	72	79	299	968
John McHenry	74	75	75	75	299	968
Peter Hedblom	73	74	74	79	300	965
Jeff Hawkes	76	73	80	73	302	960
Justin Hobday	73	72	82	75	302	960
Michel Besanceney	78	69	80	75	302	960
Des Smyth	72	76	83	71	302	960

Peugeot Open de Espana

Club De Campo, Madrid, Spain
Par 36-36—72; 6,928 yards

May 12-15
purse, £500,000

	SCORES				TOTAL	MONEY
Colin Montgomerie	70	71	66	70	277	£83,330
Mark Roe	70	68	69	71	278	37,283.33
Richard Boxall	69	69	70	70	278	37,283.33
Mark McNulty	68	69	70	71	278	37,283.33
Bernhard Langer	70	69	69	71	279	21,200
Jonathan Lomas	74	73	67	67	281	16,250
Ernie Els	67	74	73	67	281	16,250
Phillip Price	72	72	67	71	282	9,911.67
Steen Tinning	74	69	71	68	282	9,911.67
Seve Ballesteros	72	71	73	66	282	9,911.67
Jose Maria Olazabal	71	70	69	72	282	9,911.67
Gordon Brand, Jr.	69	72	71	70	282	9,911.67
Frederic Regard	69	71	71	71	282	9,911.67
Manny Zerman	70	73	70	70	283	7,500
Peter Mitchell	68	74	69	72	283	7,500
Santiago Luna	73	73	71	67	284	6,383.33
Ross McFarlane	71	74	72	67	284	6,383.33
Stuart Little	71	74	71	68	284	6,383.33
Jesus Maria Arruti	69	74	73	68	284	6,383.33
Peter Teravainen	73	69	71	71	284	6,383.33
David Curry	71	69	72	72	284	6,383.33
Domingo Hospital	72	73	70	70	285	5,550
Silvio Grappasonni	75	72	71	67	285	5,550
Ricky Willison	71	71	72	71	285	5,550
De Wet Basson	73	72	71	70	286	5,025
Jose Coceres	69	74	69	74	286	5,025
Costantino Rocca	73	69	74	70	286	5,025
Stephen Field	70	70	69	77	286	5,025
Andrew Sherborne	69	75	73	70	287	4,650
Andrew Collison	76	69	73	70	288	4,350
Steven Bottomley	71	75	71	71	288	4,350
Stephen Ames	72	75	72	69	288	4,350
Alfonso Pinero	73	72	71	73	289	3,700
Paul McGinley	74	73	72	70	289	3,700
Phil Golding	73	71	71	74	289	3,700
Mike Harwood	75	69	73	72	289	3,700
Mariano Aparicio	72	72	75	70	289	3,700
Ignacio Garrido	71	72	71	75	289	3,700
John Bland	70	73	75	71	289	3,700
Jose Rivero	73	70	74	72	289	3,700
David Ray	74	69	73	73	289	3,700
Paul Mayo	78	68	72	72	290	3,100
Paul Way	73	74	69	74	290	3,100
Jay Townsend	70	74	73	73	290	3,100
Mikael Krantz	71	75	72	73	291	2,800
Peter Baker	74	74	74	70	291	2,800
Antoine LeBouc	73	74	73	71	291	2,800
Steven Richardson	68	77	74	73	292	2,350
Michel Besanceney	75	70	73	74	292	2,350
David J. Russell	72	74	76	70	292	2,350
Tom Pernice	75	71	74	72	292	2,350
Eric Giraud	71	76	76	69	292	2,350
Yago Beamonte	71	74	75	72	292	2,350
Ian Garbutt	70	75	73	75	293	1,900

	SCORES				TOTAL	MONEY
Manuel Pinero	74	71	74	74	293	1,900
Alberto Binaghi	71	73	75	74	293	1,900
Peter Fowler	71	74	75	74	294	1,587.50
Robert Lee	74	72	79	69	294	1,587.50
Miguel Angel Jimenez	73	74	74	73	294	1,587.50
Nick Godin	72	70	76	76	294	1,587.50
Nic Henning	72	74	79	70	295	1,400
Andre Bossert	73	74	75	73	295	1,400
Carl Magnus Stromberg	75	72	72	76	295	1,400
Chris Williams	76	70	74	77	297	1,300
Paul Moloney	78	68	74	78	298	916
Andrew Hare	73	74	77	74	298	916
Ralf Berhorst	73	72	77	76	298	916
Jeff Hawkes	69	77	74	79	299	746
Brian Barnes	72	74	78	76	300	744
Robert Karlsson	76	71	79	76	302	742
Magnus Sunesson	72	75	77	79	303	740
Jose Rozadilla	74	73	79	DQ		

Tisettanta Italian Open

Marco Simone Golf Club, Rome, Italy
Par 36-36—72; 6,937 yards

May 19-22
purse, £450,000

	SCORES				TOTAL	MONEY
Eduardo Romero	69	67	69	67	272	£75,000
Greg Turner	69	69	70	65	273	50,000
Fredrik Lindgren	71	64	69	71	275	28,170
Anders Forsbrand	73	69	66	68	276	16,412
Peter Teravainen	71	73	65	67	276	16,412
Robert Allenby	70	71	69	66	276	16,412
Paul Eales	65	70	70	71	276	16,412
John Bland	70	67	69	70	276	16,412
Robert Lee	71	68	69	69	277	10,050
Mike Harwood	71	72	69	66	278	8,340
Frank Nobilo	70	66	72	70	278	8,340
Terry Price	73	67	68	70	278	8,340
Paul Affleck	71	70	69	69	279	7,240
Jamie Spence	70	72	71	67	280	6,740
Ronan Rafferty	67	71	73	69	280	6,740
Richard Boxall	68	71	69	73	281	5,950
Malcolm Mackenzie	72	67	73	69	281	5,950
Howard Clark	70	69	73	69	281	5,950
Brian Nelson	69	70	72	70	281	5,950
Stephen Bennett	70	69	72	71	282	5,400
Olle Karlsson	72	73	69	69	283	4,995
Jose Maria Olazabal	70	71	74	68	283	4,995
De Wet Basson	71	70	70	72	283	4,995
Wayne Riley	68	70	73	72	283	4,995
Ruben Alvarez	73	72	70	68	283	4,995
Peter O'Malley	67	71	71	75	284	4,455
Carl Magnus Stromberg	72	72	71	69	284	4,455
Silvio Grappasonni	70	72	72	70	284	4,455
Jose Coceres	75	69	70	71	285	4,117.50
Steve Bowman	69	76	72	68	285	4,117.50
Manny Zerman	74	71	72	69	286	3,699
Colin Brooks	72	72	73	69	286	3,699

	SCORES				TOTAL	MONEY
Gary Orr	68	75	72	71	286	3,699
Peter Mitchell	72	72	72	70	286	3,699
Ian Spencer	72	71	72	71	286	3,699
Scott Watson	70	74	71	72	287	3,195
Antoine LeBouc	71	74	72	70	287	3,195
Alexander Cejka	64	74	75	74	287	3,195
Rodger Davis	71	69	77	70	287	3,195
Torsten Giedeon	72	73	75	67	287	3,195
Jim Payne	70	73	75	69	287	3,195
Barry Lane	74	71	73	70	288	2,655
Alberto Binaghi	73	71	73	71	288	2,655
Peter Hedblom	72	70	73	73	288	2,655
Miles Tunnicliff	75	70	71	72	288	2,655
David Curry	75	70	71	72	288	2,655
Glenn Ralph	71	72	72	73	288	2,655
Thomas Gogele	73	71	75	70	289	2,295
Mark Nichols	74	71	76	68	289	2,295
Mathias Gronberg	73	72	79	66	290	1,935
Jean Louis Guepy	70	73	70	77	290	1,935
Costantino Rocca	72	73	74	71	290	1,935
Liam White	69	72	72	77	290	1,935
Lee Westwood	71	74	73	72	290	1,935
Andrea Canessa	74	69	76	71	290	1,935
Ian Garbutt	73	71	70	77	291	1,467
Sven Struver	72	71	76	72	291	1,467
Chris Moody	68	75	74	74	291	1,467
Andrew Hare	68	75	72	76	291	1,467
Massimo Florioli	72	71	77	71	291	1,467
Paolo Quirici	70	75	74	73	292	1,237.50
Chris Williams	76	68	74	74	292	1,237.50
Ignacio Gervas	69	72	79	72	292	1,237.50
Baldovino Dassu	72	73	75	72	292	1,237.50
Diego Borrego	72	73	75	75	295	900
Michel Besanceney	72	70	79	74	295	900
*Matteo Zaretti	71	73	78	73	295	
Heinz P. Thul	70	75	80	73	298	672
Anders Gillner	74	70	80	74	298	672

Volvo PGA Championship

Wentworth Club, Surrey, England
Par 35-37—72; 6,957 yards

May 27-30
purse, £800,000

	SCORES				TOTAL	MONEY
Jose Maria Olazabal	67	68	71	65	271	£133,330
Ernie Els	66	66	71	69	272	88,880
Bernhard Langer	69	70	67	68	274	50,070
Joakim Haeggman	69	69	70	68	276	36,940
Miguel Angel Jimenez	68	66	72	70	276	36,940
Seve Ballesteros	73	66	70	68	277	28,000
Mark James	68	72	71	67	278	24,000
Adam Hunter	71	65	72	71	279	20,000
Sandy Lyle	68	71	70	71	280	17,840
Malcolm Mackenzie	73	70	69	69	281	14,340
Frank Nobilo	73	66	69	73	281	14,340
Peter Hedblom	69	69	71	72	281	14,340
Kevin Stables	71	71	71	68	281	14,340

	SCORES				TOTAL	MONEY
Jonathan Lomas	74	68	69	71	282	11,280
Costantino Rocca	67	70	72	73	282	11,280
Eduardo Romero	69	72	68	73	282	11,280
Howard Clark	73	69	70	70	282	11,280
Paul Lawrie	69	70	71	72	282	11,280
Vijay Singh	72	69	70	72	283	9,760
Peter Baker	73	67	73	70	283	9,760
Lee Westwood	75	70	67	72	284	8,520
Mark Roe	71	70	68	75	284	8,520
Paul Way	72	72	71	69	284	8,520
Barry Lane	70	70	73	71	284	8,520
Miguel Angel Martin	71	74	71	68	284	8,520
Mike Clayton	70	73	72	69	284	8,520
Mats Lanner	70	70	69	75	284	8,520
Nick Faldo	72	70	70	72	284	8,520
Des Smyth	74	71	70	70	285	6,880
Anders Forsbrand	69	70	75	71	285	6,880
Rodger Davis	70	73	74	68	285	6,880
Jose Coceres	71	72	72	70	285	6,880
Mike McLean	75	70	70	70	285	6,880
Wayne Riley	68	76	69	72	285	6,880
Gordon Brand, Jr.	69	74	73	70	286	6,160
Silvio Grappasonni	72	71	69	74	286	6,160
David Gilford	71	74	71	71	287	5,200
Colin Montgomerie	74	69	75	69	287	5,200
Philip Walton	76	68	71	72	287	5,200
Richard Boxall	70	74	74	69	287	5,200
Jose Rivero	72	72	69	74	287	5,200
Vicente Fernandez	73	71	71	72	287	5,200
Retief Goosen	72	73	70	72	287	5,200
Gordon J. Brand	70	69	70	78	287	5,200
David R. Jones	69	71	74	73	287	5,200
Alberto Binaghi	72	71	71	73	287	5,200
Ronan Rafferty	68	73	70	77	288	4,320
Robert Allenby	71	71	75	72	289	3,760
Peter Teravainen	70	69	78	72	289	3,760
John Bland	72	73	72	72	289	3,760
Jim Payne	71	74	70	74	289	3,760
Paul Curry	70	74	73	72	289	3,760
Peter Mitchell	72	72	70	75	289	3,760
David A. Russell	72	71	73	74	290	3,120
Thomas Levet	71	73	73	73	290	3,120
Pierre Fulke	72	67	74	78	291	2,880
Andrew Oldcorn	75	67	75	75	292	2,540
Stephen Ames	73	69	72	78	292	2,540
Christy O'Connor, Jr.	71	72	73	76	292	2,540
Martin Gates	73	71	76	72	292	2,540
Gary Evans	74	69	74	76	293	2,240
David Curry	72	73	73	75	293	2,240
Ross Drummond	73	72	73	75	293	2,240
Steve Bowman	72	71	76	78	297	1,760
Johan Rystrom	76	69	72	80	297	1,760
John McHenry	71	73	76	77	297	1,760
David Jones	70	74	72	82	298	1,198

Alfred Dunhill Open

Royal Zoute Golf Club, Knokke, Belgium
Par 34-37—71; 6,964 yards

June 2-5
purse, £600,000

	SCORES				TOTAL	MONEY
Nick Faldo	67	74	67	71	279	£100,000
Joakim Haeggman	73	68	66	72	279	66,660
(Faldo defeated Haeggman on first extra hole.)						
Peter Hedblom	69	73	65	73	280	30,986.67
Bernhard Langer	69	68	68	75	280	30,986.67
Colin Montgomerie	67	70	66	77	280	30,986.67
Ignacio Garrido	67	70	71	73	281	19,500
Philip Walton	73	67	69	72	281	19,500
Mike Clayton	68	70	73	71	282	14,220
Andrew Murray	69	71	69	73	282	14,220
Barry Lane	65	70	76	72	283	11,106.67
Des Smyth	72	75	68	68	283	11,106.67
Rodger Davis	73	71	68	71	283	11,106.67
Olle Karlsson	69	74	70	71	284	9,640
Retief Goosen	73	73	71	68	285	8,820
Gordon Brand, Jr.	69	74	70	72	285	8,820
Stephen McAllister	72	70	70	73	285	8,820
Mark Roe	69	69	74	74	286	7,760
Greg Turner	71	74	70	71	286	7,760
Jeff Hawkes	72	71	73	70	286	7,760
Gary Orr	71	73	72	71	287	6,840
David Gilford	74	70	72	71	287	6,840
Vijay Singh	69	70	75	73	287	6,840
David Williams	68	75	73	71	287	6,840
Mike McLean	70	71	75	71	287	6,840
Mike Harwood	73	70	73	72	288	5,940
Per-Ulrik Johansson	74	69	72	73	288	5,940
Peter Mitchell	72	73	73	70	288	5,940
Frank Nobilo	73	72	70	73	288	5,940
Chris Davison	70	74	73	71	288	5,940
Domingo Hospital	67	76	70	76	289	4,882.50
Lee Westwood	73	74	71	71	289	4,882.50
Gordon Manson	73	73	74	69	289	4,882.50
Jose Rivero	70	75	68	76	289	4,882.50
Ronan Rafferty	74	72	71	72	289	4,882.50
Roger Wessels	69	72	74	74	289	4,882.50
Klas Eriksson	70	76	71	72	289	4,882.50
Anders Forsbrand	73	70	69	77	289	4,882.50
Andrew Sherborne	69	72	74	75	290	4,260
Sandy Lyle	72	74	71	73	290	4,260
Sven Struver	76	71	71	73	291	3,840
Paul McGinley	72	71	71	77	291	3,840
David R. Jones	72	73	73	73	291	3,840
Tony Johnstone	73	70	73	75	291	3,840
Paul Curry	69	71	78	73	291	3,840
Wayne Riley	71	75	73	73	292	3,300
Michel Besanceney	71	76	69	76	292	3,300
Ian Woosnam	70	75	74	73	292	3,300
Gordon J. Brand	73	71	74	74	292	3,300
Steven Richardson	71	75	73	74	293	3,000
Fredrik Lindgren	74	71	71	78	294	2,640
Ben Fouchee	72	71	77	74	294	2,640
Anders Gillner	71	73	74	76	294	2,640
Ian Palmer	74	70	78	72	294	2,640

	SCORES				TOTAL	MONEY
Costantino Rocca	74	70	72	78	294	2,640
Jim Payne	73	71	77	74	295	1,971.43
Peter Fowler	73	74	74	74	295	1,971.43
Mathias Gronberg	72	71	76	76	295	1,971.43
Robert Lee	73	72	73	77	295	1,971.43
Derrick Cooper	71	74	74	76	295	1,971.43
Robert Karlsson	71	73	76	75	295	1,971.43
Manuel Pinero	70	75	75	75	295	1,971.43
Pierre Fulke	69	75	79	73	296	1,452
Sam Torrance	74	70	75	77	296	1,452
Alexander Cejka	70	74	76	76	296	1,452
Phillip Price	75	72	73	76	296	1,452
Brian Marchbank	72	74	74	76	296	1,452
Craig Cassells	74	73	75	75	297	897
Paul Mayo	74	73	74	76	297	897
Peter Teravainen	70	77	76	75	298	892
Wayne Westner	69	78	80	71	298	892
Magnus Sunesson	72	74	74	78	298	892
Carl Mason	72	74	72	81	299	888
Jose Manuel Carriles	65	81	79	77	302	885
David Ray	74	72	77	79	302	885

Honda Open

Gut Kaden, Alveslohe, Hamburg, Germany
Par 36-36—72; 7,073 yards

June 9-12
purse, £500,000

	SCORES				TOTAL	MONEY
Robert Allenby	72	67	68	69	276	£83,330
Miguel Angel Jimenez	70	71	65	70	276	55,550
(Allenby defeated Jimenez on third extra hole.)						
Rodger Davis	66	68	76	68	278	31,300
David Gilford	70	70	68	71	279	25,000
Bernhard Langer	70	72	72	66	280	16,550
Gabriel Hjertstedt	69	71	73	67	280	16,550
Andrew Coltart	69	69	69	73	280	16,550
Paul Lawrie	68	71	72	69	280	16,550
Barry Lane	73	72	70	66	281	8,852.86
Russell Claydon	73	70	63	75	281	8,852.86
Andrew Hare	73	70	68	70	281	8,852.86
Stephen Field	71	69	68	73	281	8,852.86
Silvio Grappasonni	68	74	70	69	281	8,852.86
Steen Tinning	75	67	68	71	281	8,852.86
Domingo Hospital	69	72	73	67	281	8,852.86
Carl Mason	71	69	72	70	282	6,612.50
Anders Gillner	74	69	74	65	282	6,612.50
Mike Harwood	73	71	69	69	282	6,612.50
Ian Palmer	71	71	70	70	282	6,612.50
Pierre Fulke	70	71	71	71	283	5,700
Colin Montgomerie	69	69	74	71	283	5,700
Miles Tunnicliff	74	69	71	69	283	5,700
Mathias Gronberg	73	70	69	71	283	5,700
Robert Lee	72	71	71	69	283	5,700
Paul Broadhurst	69	69	72	74	284	5,100
Paul Moloney	71	72	71	70	284	5,100
Juan Quiros	72	72	71	69	284	5,100
Jonathan Lomas	73	66	73	73	285	4,575

	SCORES				TOTAL	MONEY
Jeremy Robinson	73	71	71	70	285	4,575
Alberto Binaghi	74	70	70	71	285	4,575
Mark Mouland	73	71	72	69	285	4,575
Mark Davis	71	71	70	74	286	3,950
Tony Johnstone	70	73	73	70	286	3,950
Marc Farry	72	69	74	71	286	3,950
Jon Robson	69	74	71	72	286	3,950
Ian Woosnam	73	71	69	73	286	3,950
Glenn Ralph	70	71	75	70	286	3,950
Eoghan O'Connell	71	71	71	74	287	3,250
Craig Cassells	74	71	75	67	287	3,250
Ralf Berhorst	70	72	72	73	287	3,250
Stuart Little	72	73	70	72	287	3,250
Jose Rivero	73	71	71	72	287	3,250
Ruben Alvarez	73	70	70	74	287	3,250
Ignacio Garrido	75	70	71	71	287	3,250
Santiago Luna	71	72	71	73	287	3,250
Alexander Cejka	72	71	73	72	288	2,400
Andrew Sherborne	76	68	73	71	288	2,400
Iain Pyman	76	69	71	72	288	2,400
Gordon Manson	72	70	75	71	288	2,400
Jonathan Sewell	69	76	73	70	288	2,400
David J. Russell	74	68	76	70	288	2,400
Mats Lanner	72	68	72	76	288	2,400
Steve Van Vuuren	72	71	74	71	288	2,400
Bill Malley	75	69	68	76	288	2,400
Chris Moody	73	71	72	73	289	1,527.27
Mike Miller	75	67	73	74	289	1,527.27
Fredrik Lindgren	73	72	72	72	289	1,527.27
Michel Besanceney	71	73	70	75	289	1,527.27
David A. Russell	72	69	74	74	289	1,527.27
Gordon J. Brand	75	69	73	72	289	1,527.27
David R. Jones	74	70	71	74	289	1,527.27
Ross Drummond	71	74	71	73	289	1,527.27
Ulrich Zilg	68	74	72	75	289	1,527.27
Frederic Regard	72	72	74	71	289	1,527.27
Mike McLean	71	74	71	73	289	1,527.27
Oliver Eckstein	72	73	69	76	290	748
Roger Chapman	72	73	73	72	290	748
Brian Marchbank	70	72	71	77	290	748
Thomas Gogele	73	71	74	73	291	743
Mark McNulty	69	75	75	72	291	743
Andre Bossert	72	73	73	74	292	739
Gavin Levenson	71	74	73	74	292	739
Ove Sellberg	71	72	77	75	295	736
Antoine LeBouc	71	74	76	76	297	733
Ignacio Gervas	73	71	75	78	297	733

Jersey European Airways Open

La Moye Golf Club, St. Brelade, Jersey
Par 36-36—72; 6,813 yards

June 16-19
purse, £350,000

	SCORES				TOTAL	MONEY
Paul Curry	73	62	68	63	266	£58,330
Mark James	69	63	68	69	269	38,880
Iain Pyman	66	67	68	70	271	21,910

	SCORES				TOTAL	MONEY
Rodger Davis	69	66	66	72	273	13,770
Jim Payne	70	69	67	67	273	13,770
Peter Mitchell	70	68	66	69	273	13,770
Tommy Horton	71	65	70	67	273	13,770
Des Smyth	68	69	65	72	274	8,750
Andrew Oldcorn	66	66	70	73	275	7,820
Gabriel Hjertstedt	67	68	68	73	276	6,486.67
Andrew Murray	70	69	68	69	276	6,486.67
Mark Davis	68	67	71	70	276	6,486.67
Ronan Rafferty	67	69	68	73	277	5,490
Ross Drummond	70	70	68	69	277	5,490
Stephen Field	68	68	70	72	278	5,140
Mark Roe	69	69	72	69	279	4,467.50
Andrew Coltart	69	68	69	73	279	4,467.50
Steven Bottomley	74	68	70	67	279	4,467.50
David Gilford	69	72	69	69	279	4,467.50
Magnus Sunesson	71	66	72	70	279	4,467.50
Manny Zerman	70	68	70	71	279	4,467.50
David J. Russell	71	71	69	69	280	3,990
Gavin Levenson	66	69	75	71	281	3,727.50
Mike Clayton	69	69	76	67	281	3,727.50
Michel Besanceney	73	67	71	70	281	3,727.50
Bernard Gallacher	74	65	74	68	281	3,727.50
David R. Jones	71	71	68	72	282	3,155
Brian Marchbank	71	71	69	71	282	3,155
Keith Waters	69	72	75	66	282	3,155
David Williams	72	66	74	70	282	3,155
Howard Clark	68	67	69	78	282	3,155
Phillip Price	69	71	71	71	282	3,155
Stephen Bennett	69	72	70	71	282	3,155
Gordon J. Brand	67	73	68	75	283	2,555
Ian Spencer	70	73	69	71	283	2,555
Paul McGinley	72	70	69	72	283	2,555
Anders Forsbrand	72	75	69	70	283	2,555
Robert Karlsson	67	75	71	70	283	2,555
Jorge Berendt	73	69	68	73	283	2,555
Gordon Manson	67	71	74	71	283	2,555
Malcolm Mackenzie	71	69	73	70	283	2,555
Pedro Linhart	72	70	70	72	284	2,135
Mike Miller	71	72	74	67	284	2,135
Chris Moody	68	73	73	70	284	2,135
Frederic Regard	71	69	72	72	284	2,135
Paul Lawrie	68	68	71	78	285	1,820
Jamie Spence	69	73	75	68	285	1,820
Wayne Riley	72	70	68	75	285	1,820
Philip Walton	70	71	71	73	285	1,820
De Wet Basson	71	73	70	71	285	1,820
Christy O'Connor, Jr.	72	71	71	72	286	1,435
Eoghan O'Connell	72	71	75	68	286	1,435
Paul Eales	70	70	72	74	286	1,435
Andrew Hare	68	70	77	71	286	1,435
Scott Watson	72	69	72	73	286	1,435
Paul Way	74	70	67	75	286	1,435
Andre Bossert	73	71	69	74	287	1,055
Jose Manuel Carriles	72	72	74	69	287	1,055
David A. Russell	72	70	73	72	287	1,055
Carl Suneson	72	70	72	73	287	1,055
Roger Chapman	69	74	70	74	287	1,055
Paul Mayo	70	73	73	71	287	1,055
David Ray	69	75	70	73	287	1,055

	SCORES				TOTAL	MONEY
Paul Moloney	73	71	70	74	288	892.50
Gary Evans	70	70	73	75	288	892.50
Ruben Alvarez	74	70	71	74	289	525
Miguel Angel Martin	71	70	72	77	290	522
Ross McFarlane	75	67	78	70	290	522
Eamonn Darcy	71	70	76	74	291	519
Jeremy Robinson	75	69	74	74	292	517
John Morgan	73	69	77	76	295	515

Peugeot Open de France

National Golf Club, Paris, France
Par 36-36—72; 7,122 yards

June 23-26
purse, £550,000

	SCORES				TOTAL	MONEY
Mark Roe	70	71	67	66	274	£91,660
Gabriel Hjertstedt	67	70	68	70	275	61,100
Jose Maria Olazabal	68	72	69	69	278	34,430
Lee Westwood	66	74	68	71	279	27,500
Andrew Coltart	68	70	71	71	280	19,683.33
Robert Allenby	71	71	71	67	280	19,683.33
Paul McGinley	70	72	67	71	280	19,683.33
John Bland	66	71	74	70	281	12,343.33
Ignacio Garrido	67	70	70	74	281	12,343.33
Per-Ulrik Johansson	72	73	66	70	281	12,343.33
Paul Eales	66	74	70	72	282	8,223.33
Malcolm Mackenzie	70	66	70	76	282	8,223.33
Mike Miller	66	73	73	70	282	8,223.33
Jay Townsend	72	67	70	73	282	8,223.33
Stephen Ames	73	71	71	67	282	8,223.33
Steven Richardson	70	72	69	71	282	8,223.33
Miguel Angel Martin	69	73	70	70	282	8,223.33
Glenn Ralph	73	70	69	70	282	8,223.33
David Gilford	67	70	70	75	282	8,223.33
Paul Moloney	75	68	69	71	283	5,940
Marc Farry	70	70	70	73	283	5,940
Mark James	73	69	71	70	283	5,940
Jose Rivero	69	70	73	71	283	5,940
Mike Clayton	69	74	70	70	283	5,940
Domingo Hospital	73	70	68	72	283	5,940
Mark McNulty	70	67	70	76	283	5,940
Sven Struver	69	70	73	71	283	5,940
Nicklas Fasth	68	74	71	70	283	5,940
David Williams	69	71	70	74	284	4,867.50
Barry Lane	71	73	69	71	284	4,867.50
Olle Nordberg	67	77	70	70	284	4,867.50
Jim Payne	70	74	71	69	284	4,867.50
Alberto Binaghi	72	73	72	68	285	4,235
Peter Mitchell	66	74	72	73	285	4,235
Eoghan O'Connell	70	71	70	74	285	4,235
Frank Nobilo	70	71	74	70	285	4,235
Gordon Brand, Jr.	70	70	73	72	285	4,235
Wayne Westner	70	72	69	74	285	4,235
Diego Borrego	71	71	69	75	286	3,685
Chris Davison	68	74	72	72	286	3,685
Martin Gates	70	68	71	77	286	3,685
Olivier Edmond	70	73	69	74	286	3,685

	SCORES			TOTAL	MONEY
Alexander Cejka	71	73	71	72	287	3,135
Ronan Rafferty	69	72	72	74	287	3,135
Paul Affleck	70	73	72	72	287	3,135
Carl Suneson	70	74	70	73	287	3,135
David Curry	72	71	71	73	287	3,135
Silvio Grappasonni	70	72	74	71	287	3,135
Howard Clark	71	74	71	72	288	2,530
Robert Karlsson	70	72	70	76	288	2,530
Torsten Giedeon	70	71	68	79	288	2,530
Mark Mouland	72	70	72	74	288	2,530
Eric Giraud	68	75	67	78	288	2,530
Phil Golding	71	73	73	72	289	2,035
Ian Spencer	68	72	75	74	289	2,035
Greg Turner	69	74	71	75	289	2,035
Juan Quiros	73	72	73	71	289	2,035
Andre Bossert	70	74	72	74	290	1,622.50
Jonathan Lomas	67	74	77	72	290	1,622.50
Mikael Krantz	74	71	70	75	290	1,622.50
Thomas Levet	68	77	72	73	290	1,622.50
Manny Zerman	68	76	73	73	290	1,622.50
Paul Curry	71	74	73	72	290	1,622.50
Vicente Fernandez	71	70	73	77	291	1,210
Sandy Lyle	75	70	70	76	291	1,210
Steve Van Vuuren	75	68	71	77	291	1,210
Ross Drummond	69	76	73	74	292	822
David R. Jones	72	70	73	77	292	822
Michel Besanceney	70	74	72	77	293	818
Philip Walton	72	72	75	74	293	818
Mark Nichols	73	71	72	79	295	814
Iain Pyman	72	70	76	77	295	814
Colin Brooks	71	74	77	75	297	811
Jeremy Robinson	72	73	68	86	299	809
Jean Charles Cambon	74	71	78	79	302	807

Murphy's Irish Open

Mount Juliet Country Club, Kilkenny, Ireland
Par 36-36—72; 7,143 yards

June 30-July 3
purse, £592,593

	SCORES			TOTAL	MONEY
Bernhard Langer	70	68	70	67	275	£98,765.43
Robert Allenby	68	68	68	72	276	51,466.67
John Daly	70	68	73	65	276	51,466.67
Greg Turner	73	70	69	66	278	27,358.03
Jose Maria Olazabal	68	68	71	71	278	27,358.03
Peter Baker	70	68	71	70	279	19,259.26
Steven Richardson	71	70	69	69	279	19,259.26
Alberto Binaghi	69	70	70	71	280	11,369.31
Mike Harwood	69	69	70	72	280	11,369.31
Paul Moloney	71	70	67	72	280	11,369.31
Ernie Els	71	73	67	69	280	11,369.31
Sam Torrance	65	73	73	69	280	11,369.31
Craig Parry	70	69	70	71	280	11,369.31
Nick Faldo	69	71	67	73	280	11,369.31
John McHenry	73	71	66	71	281	8,011.85
Mike Clayton	68	71	72	70	281	8,011.85
Mike McLean	70	70	73	68	281	8,011.85

	SCORES				TOTAL	MONEY
Per-Ulrik Johansson	72	69	67	73	281	8,011.85
Rodger Davis	74	69	68	70	281	8,011.85
Diego Borrego	68	74	72	68	282	6,844.45
Tony Johnstone	68	69	76	69	282	6,844.45
Frank Nobilo	73	72	67	70	282	6,844.45
Ruben Alvarez	71	71	71	69	282	6,844.45
Sandy Lyle	71	71	71	70	283	6,133.33
Domingo Hospital	69	71	71	72	283	6,133.33
Colin Montgomerie	70	70	72	71	283	6,133.33
Mathias Gronberg	68	72	75	68	283	6,133.33
Martin Gates	70	74	66	74	284	5,511.11
Sven Struver	69	74	71	70	284	5,511.11
Paul Lawrie	68	73	69	74	284	5,511.11
Russell Claydon	73	69	74	69	285	5,066.67
Eduardo Romero	69	71	72	73	285	5,066.67
Wayne Riley	72	72	69	73	286	4,740.74
Gary Evans	70	68	73	75	286	4,740.74
Seve Ballesteros	67	76	71	72	286	4,740.74
Ian Palmer	69	72	71	75	287	4,148.15
Retief Goosen	74	70	73	70	287	4,148.15
Peter Hedblom	71	71	74	71	287	4,148.15
Thomas Levet	71	69	71	76	287	4,148.15
Stephen Hamill	72	72	74	69	287	4,148.15
Craig Cassells	67	75	72	73	287	4,148.15
Brian Nelson	69	71	74	73	287	4,148.15
Olle Nordberg	71	72	74	71	288	3,555.56
Lee Westwood	68	71	75	74	288	3,555.56
Jose Maria Canizares	75	68	70	75	288	3,555.56
Nic Henning	73	68	72	76	289	3,259.26
Ignacio Garrido	69	74	73	73	289	3,259.26
Jay Townsend	71	71	75	73	290	2,903.70
Ronan Rafferty	72	71	73	74	290	2,903.70
Manuel Pinero	72	71	73	74	290	2,903.70
Santiago Luna	71	71	75	73	290	2,903.70
Mike Miller	70	71	77	73	291	2,311.11
Stephen Ames	72	73	74	72	291	2,311.11
Anders Gillner	70	72	71	78	291	2,311.11
Andre Bossert	71	71	74	75	291	2,311.11
Peter O'Malley	70	68	80	73	291	2,311.11
Mark Mouland	71	74	76	70	291	2,311.11
Andrew Sherborne	73	72	76	71	292	1,896.30
*Keith Nolan	71	73	73	75	292	
Robert Karlsson	69	73	77	74	293	1,718.52
David Feherty	76	68	76	73	293	1,718.52
Gary Orr	70	74	74	75	293	1,718.52
Jimmy Heggarty	71	69	77	76	293	1,718.52
Brian Marchbank	69	75	72	77	293	1,718.52
Robert Lee	72	73	74	75	294	1,511.11
Steve Bowman	70	74	74	76	294	1,511.11
Darren Clarke	72	73	76	74	295	888.89
David Errity	72	73	77	75	297	885.93
Pedro Linhart	71	74	77	75	297	885.93
Jeremy Robinson	71	74	73	80	298	882.96
John Bland	74	71	80	74	299	880.99
Haydn Selby-Green	73	72	76	79	300	879.01
Phil Golding	74	71	77	81	303	877.04

Bell's Scottish Open

Gleneagles Hotel, King's Course, Perthshire, Scotland
Par 35-35—70; 6,739 yards

July 6-9
purse, £600,000

	SCORES				TOTAL	MONEY
Carl Mason	67	69	61	68	265	£100,000
Peter Mitchell	67	64	65	70	266	66,660
Jesper Parnevik	70	65	64	68	267	37,560
Colin Montgomerie	67	66	69	66	268	30,000
Darren Clarke	67	67	67	69	270	23,200
Jonathan Lomas	66	66	68	70	270	23,200
Andrew Oldcorn	70	63	67	71	271	13,892
Paul Curry	72	64	67	68	271	13,892
Jim McGovern	71	65	68	67	271	13,892
Miguel Angel Martin	70	65	65	71	271	13,892
Brett Ogle	72	66	66	67	271	13,892
Brian Marchbank	68	68	69	67	272	9,485
Peter Senior	69	69	64	70	272	9,485
Mark Roe	72	67	69	64	272	9,485
David A. Russell	68	65	67	72	272	9,485
Howard Twitty	64	70	65	74	273	8,100
Miguel Angel Jimenez	68	68	65	72	273	8,100
Paul Moloney	69	68	70	66	273	8,100
Howard Clark	69	69	65	71	274	6,940
Peter Baker	69	69	71	68	274	6,940
Paul Broadhurst	67	69	65	73	274	6,940
Nicklas Fasth	70	66	70	68	274	6,940
Per-Ulrik Johansson	66	66	69	73	274	6,940
Peter Jacobsen	71	67	65	71	274	6,940
Santiago Luna	67	67	70	71	275	5,850
Wayne Westner	68	66	70	71	275	5,850
Ian Woosnam	66	71	70	68	275	5,850
Paul Eales	71	68	68	68	275	5,850
Mike Springer	70	67	66	72	275	5,850
Terry Price	72	67	65	71	275	5,850
David Feherty	67	69	68	72	276	4,870
Eduardo Romero	69	64	68	75	276	4,870
Ruben Alvarez	69	64	69	74	276	4,870
Andrew Sherborne	73	66	66	71	276	4,870
Peter Hedblom	72	67	67	70	276	4,870
Alberto Binaghi	72	67	68	69	276	4,870
Jay Townsend	69	68	69	71	277	4,080
Andrew Murray	70	68	67	72	277	4,080
Mark Mouland	72	66	67	72	277	4,080
Gary Orr	70	69	69	69	277	4,080
Anders Gillner	70	67	70	70	277	4,080
Stephen Ames	69	69	69	70	277	4,080
Sam Torrance	73	66	68	70	277	4,080
Jamie Spence	70	68	68	72	278	3,420
Gary Nicklaus	69	69	66	74	278	3,420
David J. Russell	70	63	71	74	278	3,420
Magnus Sunesson	70	69	66	73	278	3,420
Vijay Singh	68	70	64	77	279	3,000
Adam Hunter	69	70	65	75	279	3,000
Mark McNulty	67	69	69	74	279	3,000
Pierre Fulke	70	68	64	78	280	2,520
Gary Evans	71	67	68	74	280	2,520
Mark James	73	65	63	79	280	2,520
Barry Lane	67	71	68	74	280	2,520

	SCORES				TOTAL	MONEY
Gordon J. Brand	73	63	71	73	280	2,520
Tom Lehman	68	69	71	73	281	1,995
Lennie Clements	66	68	68	79	281	1,995
John Bland	70	69	69	73	281	1,995
Steve Bowman	71	68	67	75	281	1,995
Vicente Fernandez	67	71	68	76	282	1,710
Mike Miller	68	71	71	72	282	1,710
Derrick Cooper	74	65	71	72	282	1,710
Jose Manuel Carriles	70	69	74	69	282	1,710
Ignacio Garrido	68	68	71	76	283	1,320
Domingo Hospital	70	68	72	73	283	1,320
John Daly	68	71	69	75	283	1,320
Malcolm Mackenzie	73	64	73	74	284	896
Paul Lawrie	71	68	73	72	284	896
Blaine McCallister	70	67	75	72	284	896

British Open Championship

Turnberry Hotel, Ailsa Course, Turnberry, Scotland
Par 35-35—70; 6,957 yards

July 14-17
purse, £1,100,000

	SCORES				TOTAL	MONEY
Nick Price	69	66	67	66	268	£110,000
Jesper Parnevik	68	66	68	67	269	88,000
Fuzzy Zoeller	71	66	64	70	271	74,000
Anders Forsbrand	72	71	66	64	273	50,666.67
Mark James	72	67	66	68	273	50,666.67
David Feherty	68	69	66	70	273	50,666.67
Brad Faxon	69	65	67	73	274	36,000
Colin Montgomerie	72	69	65	69	275	30,000
Tom Kite	71	69	66	69	275	30,000
Nick Faldo	75	66	70	64	275	30,000
Tom Watson	68	65	69	74	276	19,333.33
Frank Nobilo	69	67	72	68	276	19,333.33
Ronan Rafferty	71	66	65	74	276	19,333.33
Jonathan Lomas	66	70	72	68	276	19,333.33
Russell Claydon	72	71	68	65	276	19,333.33
Larry Mize	73	69	64	70	276	19,333.33
Greg Norman	71	67	69	69	276	19,333.33
Mark Calcavecchia	71	70	67	68	276	19,333.33
Mark McNulty	71	70	68	67	276	19,333.33
Peter Senior	68	71	67	71	277	12,500
Mark Brooks	74	64	71	68	277	12,500
Vijay Singh	70	68	69	70	277	12,500
Greg Turner	65	71	70	71	277	12,500
Loren Roberts	68	69	69	72	278	7,972.73
Tom Lehman	70	69	70	69	278	7,972.73
Peter Jacobsen	69	70	67	72	278	7,972.73
Andrew Coltart	71	69	66	72	278	7,972.73
Paul Lawrie	71	69	70	68	278	7,972.73
Bob Estes	72	68	72	66	278	7,972.73
Mike Springer	72	67	68	71	278	7,972.73
Craig Stadler	71	69	66	72	278	7,972.73
Ernie Els	69	69	69	71	278	7,972.73
Jeff Maggert	69	74	67	68	278	7,972.73
Terry Price	74	65	71	68	278	7,972.73
Lee Janzen	74	69	69	67	279	6,700

	SCORES				TOTAL	MONEY
Gary Evans	69	69	73	68	279	6,700
Mark Davis	75	68	69	67	279	6,700
Jose Maria Olazabal	72	71	69	68	280	6,100
Jean Van de Velde	68	70	71	71	280	6,100
Darren Clarke	73	68	69	70	280	6,100
Masashi Ozaki	69	71	66	74	280	6,100
David Gilford	72	68	72	68	280	6,100
Davis Love III	71	67	68	74	280	6,100
Seve Ballesteros	70	70	71	69	280	6,100
Domingo Hospital	72	69	71	68	280	6,100
Brian Marchbank	71	70	70	69	280	6,100
Howard Twitty	71	72	66	72	281	5,450
David Edwards	68	68	73	72	281	5,450
Jim Gallagher, Jr.	73	68	69	71	281	5,450
Greg Kraft	69	74	66	72	281	5,450
David Frost	70	71	71	70	282	4,925
Tsukasa Watanabe	72	71	68	71	282	4,925
Mats Lanner	69	74	69	70	282	4,925
Katsuyoshi Tomori	69	69	73	71	282	4,925
Tsuneyuki Nakajima	73	68	69	73	283	4,700
John Cook	73	67	70	73	283	4,700
Peter Baker	71	72	70	70	283	4,700
Brian Watts	68	70	71	74	283	4,700
Ross McFarlane	68	74	67	74	283	4,700
Robert Allenby	72	69	68	75	284	4,350
Gordon Brand, Jr.	72	71	73	68	284	4,350
Bernhard Langer	72	70	70	72	284	4,350
Per-Ulrik Johansson	73	69	69	73	284	4,350
Hajime Meshiai	72	71	71	70	284	4,350
Wayne Grady	68	74	67	75	284	4,350
Christy O'Connor, Jr.	71	69	71	73	284	4,350
Lennie Clements	72	71	72	70	285	4,050
Carl Mason	69	71	73	72	285	4,050
Steve Elkington	71	72	73	69	285	4,050
Mark Roe	74	68	73	70	285	4,050
Ruben Alvarez	70	72	71	72	285	4,050
Wayne Riley	77	66	70	73	286	3,900
*Warren Bennett	72	67	74	73	286	
Sandy Lyle	71	72	72	72	287	3,850
Colin Gillies	71	70	72	75	288	3,775
Craig Ronald	71	72	72	73	288	3,775
Joakim Haeggman	71	72	69	77	289	3,650
Ben Crenshaw	70	73	73	73	289	3,650
Craig Parry	72	68	73	76	289	3,650
Nic Henning	70	73	70	78	291	3,550
John Daly	68	72	72	80	292	3,500

Out of Final 36 Holes

Paul Way	73	71			144	
Mikael Krantz	70	74			144	
Costantino Rocca	73	71			144	
D.A. Weibring	72	72			144	
Jose Rivero	72	72			144	
Kevin Stables	74	70			144	
Howard Clark	71	73			144	
John Huston	71	73			144	
Paul McGinley	71	73			144	
Chris Gray	69	75			144	
Miguel Martin	69	75			144	

	SCORES		TOTAL
Eduardo Romero	73	72	145
Miguel Angel Jimenez	71	74	145
Gary Player	72	73	145
Stephen Robertson	75	70	145
Barry Lane	73	72	145
Jack Nicklaus	72	73	145
Tony Johnstone	75	70	145
Michael Campbell	72	73	145
*Lee James	75	70	145
Michael Clayton	71	75	146
Steven Richardson	69	77	146
Peter Mitchell	74	72	146
Fulton Allem	73	73	146
Mike Harwood	77	69	146
Andre Bossert	74	72	146
Bradley Hughes	72	74	146
Scott Simpson	73	73	146
Bruce Vaughan	69	78	147
Paul Curry	73	74	147
Andrew Magee	67	80	147
Lee Trevino	75	72	147
Sam Torrance	74	73	147
Kirk Triplett	71	76	147
Hiroshi Goda	71	76	147
Wayne Westner	73	74	147
Gabriel Hjertstedt	71	76	147
Craig Jones	71	76	147
Gary Emerson	75	73	148
Payne Stewart	74	74	148
Kenneth Walker	72	76	148
James Wright	71	77	148
Steen Tinning	75	73	148
Carlos Franco	72	76	148
Andrew Oldcorn	77	71	148
Paul Broadhurst	73	75	148
Jim McGovern	78	70	148
Gary Orr	76	72	148
Francis Quinn	77	71	148
Gil Morgan	73	76	149
Des Smyth	80	69	149
Jose Maria Canizares	80	69	149
Peter Smith	73	76	149
*John Harris	73	76	149
*Craig Evans	74	75	149
Ian Baker-Finch	73	77	150
Fredrik Lindgren	78	72	150
Keith Waters	75	75	150
Chip Beck	76	75	151
Corey Pavin	75	76	151
Carl Green	75	76	151
Pierre Fulke	77	75	152
Mark Mouland	76	76	152
Ian Woosnam	79	73	152
Phil Mickelson	78	74	152
Craig Cassells	77	75	152
Bob Charles	74	79	153
Rodger Davis	77	76	153
Anders Gillner	74	79	153
Paul Eales	76	78	154
Joe Higgins	78	76	154

	SCORES			TOTAL	
*Stephen Pullan	81	74		155	
Eduardo Herrera	77	79		156	
Andrew George	74	83		157	
Lee Fickling	80	80		160	

(Professionals who did not complete 72 holes received £600.)

Heineken Dutch Open

Hilversum Golf Club, Utrecht, Netherlands
Par 36-36—72; 6,704 yards

July 21-24
purse, £650,000

	SCORES				TOTAL	MONEY
Miguel Angel Jimenez	65	68	67	70	270	£108,330
Howard Clark	67	67	71	67	272	72,210
Peter Mitchell	65	67	70	71	273	40,690
Colin Montgomerie	68	65	73	68	274	27,593.33
John Huston	70	69	67	68	274	27,593.33
David Gilford	66	67	71	70	274	27,593.33
Bradley Hughes	68	71	68	68	275	16,753.33
Ernie Els	70	66	68	71	275	16,753.33
Mark Roe	68	70	69	68	275	16,753.33
Frank Nobilo	69	66	73	68	276	11,308
Richard Boxall	65	75	67	69	276	11,308
Derrick Cooper	71	67	71	67	276	11,308
Eduardo Romero	71	70	66	69	276	11,308
Peter O'Malley	71	70	69	66	276	11,308
Mike Harwood	70	69	68	70	277	8,343.13
Russell Claydon	67	74	69	67	277	8,343.13
Ruben Alvarez	71	67	69	70	277	8,343.13
Sam Torrance	72	68	69	68	277	8,343.13
Andrew Sherborne	68	75	70	64	277	8,343.13
Paul McGinley	69	71	66	71	277	8,343.13
Philip Walton	69	66	71	71	277	8,343.13
Jamie Spence	69	68	71	69	277	8,343.13
Gabriel Hjertstedt	66	70	72	70	278	7,020
Ian Woosnam	70	69	70	69	278	7,020
Jim McGovern	68	70	67	73	278	7,020
Paul Way	69	69	71	70	279	6,240
Jose Maria Olazabal	70	66	72	71	279	6,240
Mark Mouland	67	68	72	72	279	6,240
Jeremy Robinson	67	67	72	73	279	6,240
Paul Affleck	72	71	67	69	279	6,240
Peter Baker	70	67	71	72	280	5,275.83
Costantino Rocca	72	71	69	68	280	5,275.83
Jonathan Lomas	73	68	67	72	280	5,275.83
Ross Drummond	68	71	69	72	280	5,275.83
Wayne Westner	72	69	73	66	280	5,275.83
Rolf Muntz	67	67	74	72	280	5,275.83
Mike Hunter	70	71	70	70	281	4,680
Gordon Brand, Jr.	68	69	71	73	281	4,680
Per-Ulrik Johansson	71	69	72	69	281	4,680
Des Smyth	71	70	68	73	282	3,900
Rodger Davis	70	69	71	72	282	3,900
Jose Rivero	66	74	72	70	282	3,900
Ignacio Garrido	71	71	71	69	282	3,900
Ross McFarlane	71	67	75	69	282	3,900
Jeff Hawkes	70	68	74	70	282	3,900

		SCORES			TOTAL	MONEY
Stephen McAllister	70	72	73	67	282	3,900
Darren Clarke	68	69	71	74	282	3,900
Mark Davis	69	71	69	73	282	3,900
Vijay Singh	70	70	73	70	283	3,120
Phil Golding	71	71	70	71	283	3,120
Klas Eriksson	68	70	76	69	283	3,120
Peter Teravainen	69	70	71	74	284	2,600
Brian Barnes	70	68	74	72	284	2,600
Mats Lanner	74	69	71	70	284	2,600
Robert Allenby	70	73	73	68	284	2,600
Ove Sellberg	72	71	72	69	284	2,600
Paul Moloney	69	69	71	76	285	2,063.75
Domingo Hospital	70	71	73	71	285	2,063.75
Gary Evans	70	70	68	77	285	2,063.75
De Wet Basson	72	69	68	76	285	2,063.75
Jonas Saxton	67	71	77	71	286	1,531.86
Gary Orr	72	71	72	71	286	1,531.86
Joost Steenkamer	76	67	74	69	286	1,531.86
Wayne Riley	71	72	72	71	286	1,531.86
Vicente Fernandez	71	72	72	71	286	1,531.86
Andrew Oldcorn	70	71	74	71	286	1,531.86
David A. Russell	68	70	72	76	286	1,531.86
Roderick Watkins	70	73	74	70	287	971
Craig Cassells	72	71	74	71	288	967
Retief Goosen	69	72	72	75	288	967
Ian Palmer	71	72	73	72	288	967
Barry Lane	71	70	73	75	289	963
Jay Townsend	70	73	76	72	291	961
Gavin Levenson	70	71	79	72	292	959
Frederic Regard	71	71	69	82	293	957
Thomas Gogele	75	66	77	76	294	955

Scandinavian Masters

Drottingholm Golf Club, Stockholm, Sweden
Par 36-36—72; 6,842 yards

July 28-31
purse, £650,000

		SCORES			TOTAL	MONEY
Vijay Singh	68	67	69	64	268	£108,330
Mark McNulty	67	69	69	66	271	72,210
Per Haugsrud	70	66	68	68	272	33,573.33
Jesper Parnevik	69	71	65	67	272	33,573.33
Mark Davis	64	72	65	71	272	33,573.33
Mark Roe	66	72	64	71	273	22,750
Robert Karlsson	70	68	69	67	274	17,875
Sven Struver	70	65	70	69	274	17,875
Paul Curry	66	72	71	66	275	13,156.67
John Bland	68	70	70	67	275	13,156.67
Andrew Coltart	72	67	66	70	275	13,156.67
Scott Watson	70	68	70	68	276	10,526.67
Michel Besanceney	70	72	64	70	276	10,526.67
Colin Montgomerie	72	68	68	68	276	10,526.67
Brett Ogle	70	70	67	70	277	8,786
Peter O'Malley	69	67	72	69	277	8,786
Gordon J. Brand	70	70	71	66	277	8,786
Frank Nobilo	69	67	71	70	277	8,786
Steven Richardson	70	72	65	70	277	8,786
Steen Tinning	72	70	69	67	278	7,410

	SCORES				TOTAL	MONEY
Mike McLean	69	67	71	71	278	7,410
Lee Westwood	72	70	66	70	278	7,410
Bernhard Langer	67	74	69	68	278	7,410
Paul Affleck	64	72	75	67	278	7,410
Mike Harwood	68	71	69	71	279	6,435
Jamie Spence	68	73	70	68	279	6,435
Richard Boxall	72	70	70	67	279	6,435
Gavin Levenson	67	68	72	72	279	6,435
Pierre Fulke	67	68	73	71	279	6,435
Manny Zerman	71	67	71	71	280	5,499
Mike Clayton	67	73	72	68	280	5,499
Derrick Cooper	67	70	73	70	280	5,499
Joakim Haeggman	68	69	75	68	280	5,499
Per-Ulrik Johansson	72	69	70	69	280	5,499
Peter Mitchell	71	71	71	68	281	4,680
Chris Williams	71	69	71	70	281	4,680
Miguel Angel Jimenez	71	69	69	72	281	4,680
Silvio Grappasonni	70	71	68	72	281	4,680
Russell Claydon	70	72	68	71	281	4,680
Santiago Luna	74	67	69	71	281	4,680
Mikael Piltz	68	70	73	70	281	4,680
Diego Borrego	70	70	71	71	282	3,835
Adam Hunter	72	70	71	69	282	3,835
Olle Nordberg	71	70	71	70	282	3,835
Jeremy Robinson	70	67	72	73	282	3,835
Alberto Binaghi	68	73	71	70	282	3,835
Ignacio Gervas	71	71	70	70	282	3,835
John McHenry	68	74	70	71	283	3,120
Miguel Angel Martin	67	72	72	72	283	3,120
Mathias Gronberg	69	73	71	70	283	3,120
Jose Rivero	70	72	72	69	283	3,120
Gordon Brand, Jr.	70	70	71	72	283	3,120
Marc Farry	69	72	70	73	284	2,730
Jay Townsend	72	69	69	75	285	2,405
Ian Woosnam	71	71	72	71	285	2,405
Barry Lane	72	70	71	72	285	2,405
Thomas Levet	69	73	69	74	285	2,405
*Mikael Lundberg	71	67	71	76	285	
Paul Eales	69	70	78	69	286	2,080
David R. Jones	73	69	74	71	287	1,950
Andre Bossert	72	69	72	74	287	1,950
Fredrik Larsson	70	70	73	74	287	1,950
Mike Miller	68	74	71	78	291	1,820
David J. Russell	69	72	71	80	292	1,722.50
Ove Sellberg	71	71	74	76	292	1,722.50
Paul Lawrie	71	70	76	78	295	1,625

BMW International Open

St. Eurach Land-und, Munich, Germany
Par 37-35—72; 7,049 yards

August 4-7
purse, £525,000

	SCORES				TOTAL	MONEY
Mark McNulty	70	71	68	65	274	£87,500
Seve Ballesteros	69	68	72	66	275	58,250
Mark Roe	68	71	68	69	276	32,750
Darren Clarke	67	69	68	73	277	26,200
John Bland	71	72	67	68	278	20,250

		SCORES			TOTAL	MONEY
Jeremy Robinson	67	71	71	69	278	20,250
Derrick Cooper	72	69	70	68	279	11,147.14
Jeff Hawkes	71	70	71	67	279	11,147.14
Nicklas Fasth	67	73	68	71	279	11,147.14
Ross McFarlane	72	68	66	73	279	11,147.14
Costantino Rocca	73	71	70	65	279	11,147.14
Peter Mitchell	73	66	68	72	279	11,147.14
Sven Struver	73	70	67	69	279	11,147.14
Mark James	71	72	66	71	280	7,410
Andrew Collison	71	66	73	70	280	7,410
Anders Forsbrand	73	71	69	67	280	7,410
Bernhard Langer	68	68	71	73	280	7,410
Andre Bossert	74	67	70	69	280	7,410
Richard Boxall	71	73	68	69	281	6,080
Andrew Oldcorn	71	68	69	73	281	6,080
Juan Quiros	71	73	69	68	281	6,080
Andrew Coltart	74	69	68	70	281	6,080
Peter O'Malley	69	72	71	69	281	6,080
Roger Chapman	71	72	67	72	282	5,155.71
Andrew Murray	66	73	70	73	282	5,155.71
Domingo Hospital	68	70	71	73	282	5,155.71
Stephen McAllister	70	70	70	72	282	5,155.71
Howard Clark	69	70	74	69	282	5,155.71
Bradley Hughes	73	71	69	69	282	5,155.71
Paul Eales	77	66	67	72	282	5,155.71
Phillip Price	68	70	70	75	283	4,465
Santiago Luna	73	70	73	67	283	4,465
Glenn Ralph	73	66	70	74	283	4,465
Mike Clayton	75	68	69	71	283	4,465
Paul Affleck	71	72	68	73	284	3,915
Gary Orr	74	70	68	72	284	3,915
Ricky Willison	69	74	68	73	284	3,915
Retief Goosen	75	67	73	69	284	3,915
Carl Mason	73	70	70	71	284	3,915
Miles Tunnicliff	72	69	72	71	284	3,915
Paul Curry	71	72	69	73	285	3,255
Tony Johnstone	70	74	68	73	285	3,255
Andrew Sherborne	73	71	75	66	285	3,255
Paul Mayo	72	70	72	71	285	3,255
Steen Tinning	70	71	73	71	285	3,255
Michel Besanceney	72	70	74	69	285	3,255
Klas Eriksson	70	72	72	72	286	2,760
Martin Poxon	71	73	72	70	286	2,760
Mathias Gronberg	67	74	74	71	286	2,760
Mike McLean	73	69	76	69	287	2,430
Steven Bottomley	71	69	76	71	287	2,430
Stephen Hamill	73	69	74	71	287	2,430
Oliver Eckstein	69	74	72	73	288	2,100
Scott Watson	74	69	71	74	288	2,100
Mark Nichols	72	70	69	77	288	2,100
Russell Claydon	70	72	73	74	289	1,732.50
John McHenry	73	70	74	72	289	1,732.50
Brian Nelson	70	73	74	72	289	1,732.50
Phil Golding	71	71	74	73	289	1,732.50
Thomas Levet	67	73	73	77	290	1,525
Marc Farry	68	72	76	74	290	1,525
Simon Brown	72	72	74	74	292	1,450
Peter Teravainen	70	70	76	77	293	1,350
Pierre Fulke	70	73	79	71	293	1,350
David Curry	72	72	76	73	293	1,350

Hohe Brucke Austrian Open

Colony Club Gutenhof, Himberg, Germany
Par 36-36—72; 6,912 yards

August 11-14
purse, £250,000

	SCORES				TOTAL	MONEY
Mark Davis	68	69	69	64	270	£41,660
Philip Walton	68	65	69	70	272	27,770
Retief Goosen	68	72	66	67	273	15,650
Andrew Coltart	72	69	68	66	275	10,616.67
Michel Besanceney	69	68	69	69	275	10,616.67
Andrew Sherborne	73	65	66	71	275	10,616.67
Paul Mayo	71	68	69	69	277	6,875
Heinz P. Thul	69	69	69	70	277	6,875
Anders Sorensen	73	69	69	67	278	4,428.57
David A. Russell	70	72	69	67	278	4,428.57
George Ryall	68	71	70	69	278	4,428.57
Ronan Rafferty	70	70	69	69	278	4,428.57
Phil Golding	66	74	68	70	278	4,428.57
Paul Richard Simpson	71	66	70	71	278	4,428.57
Alexander Cejka	69	72	66	71	278	4,428.57
Chris Moody	68	69	73	69	279	3,447.50
John McHenry	71	68	69	71	279	3,447.50
Steve Jones	73	71	70	66	280	3,225
Iain Pyman	71	70	75	65	281	2,891.67
Stephen Hamill	70	71	71	69	281	2,891.67
Ross Drummond	71	70	71	69	281	2,891.67
Roger Chapman	71	66	73	71	281	2,891.67
Andrew Hare	67	73	70	71	281	2,891.67
Brian Barnes	68	72	68	73	281	2,891.67
Bill Malley	69	71	72	70	282	2,400
Peter Fowler	70	70	72	70	282	2,400
David Williams	71	70	71	70	282	2,400
Bradley Hughes	70	70	71	71	282	2,400
Thomas Levet	72	71	67	72	282	2,400
Paul Broadhurst	67	68	73	74	282	2,400
Mark Nichols	68	67	73	74	282	2,400
Dennis Edlund	74	71	68	70	283	1,975
Martin Poxon	70	71	72	70	283	1,975
Per Haugsrud	73	70	71	69	283	1,975
Adam Hunter	73	69	71	70	283	1,975
Massimo Scarpa	71	68	73	71	283	1,975
Steven Bottomley	67	72	72	72	283	1,975
Steve Van Vuuren	71	70	73	70	284	1,750
Diego Borrego	72	68	74	70	284	1,750
Brian Nelson	74	71	66	73	284	1,750
Jon Robson	69	72	72	72	285	1,600
Nick Godin	71	72	71	71	285	1,600
Nicklas Fasth	72	72	72	69	285	1,600
Mikael Piltz	67	76	70	73	286	1,400
Ricky Willison	72	69	73	72	286	1,400
Nic Henning	69	74	71	72	286	1,400
Antoine LeBouc	68	70	74	74	286	1,400
Jose Coceres	70	68	71	77	286	1,400
Paul McGinley	74	68	72	73	287	1,150
Manny Zerman	72	69	73	73	287	1,150
Adam Mednick	74	71	70	72	287	1,150
Stuart Little	71	74	72	70	287	1,150
Yago Beamonte	73	70	75	69	287	1,150
Miles Tunnicliff	74	70	72	72	288	925
Scott Watson	72	70	75	71	288	925

	SCORES				TOTAL	MONEY
Claude Grenier	74	70	73	71	288	925
Jacob Rasmussen	73	70	70	75	288	925
Keith Waters	71	74	69	75	289	725
Mikael Krantz	71	68	74	75	289	725
Mark Parker	72	71	72	74	289	725
Stephen McAllister	75	68	73	73	289	725
Andrew Collison	70	75	71	73	289	725
Ignacio Gervas	72	70	75	72	289	725
Gordon Manson	72	71	77	69	289	725
Chitprasong Jamnian	73	68	74	75	290	474.33
Ian Spencer	68	73	74	75	290	474.33
Johan Rystrom	70	74	73	73	290	474.33
David Ray	71	72	74	74	291	396
Jonathan Sewell	69	73	77	73	292	393
Carl Suneson	73	72	76	71	292	393
Glenn Ralph	73	72	73	75	293	390
*Markus Brier	72	72	76	76	296	

Murphy's English Open

Forest of Arden Country Club, Warwickshire, England
Par 36-36—72; 7,079 yards

August 18-21
purse, £600,000

	SCORES				TOTAL	MONEY
Colin Montgomerie	70	67	68	69	274	£100,000
Barry Lane	66	69	72	68	275	66,660
Retief Goosen	72	72	65	67	276	37,560
Gordon Brand, Jr.	69	70	70	68	277	27,700
Des Smyth	69	68	66	74	277	27,700
Mark Davis	72	70	66	71	279	18,000
Costantino Rocca	67	69	72	71	279	18,000
Andre Bossert	69	71	69	70	279	18,000
Sam Torrance	70	69	72	70	281	13,440
Gary Orr	70	70	70	72	282	9,917.14
Andrew Sherborne	68	70	71	73	282	9,917.14
Gary Evans	69	68	70	75	282	9,917.14
Ross Drummond	73	70	71	68	282	9,917.14
Ian Woosnam	68	70	72	72	282	9,917.14
Vicente Fernandez	69	71	69	73	282	9,917.14
Pierre Fulke	68	69	71	74	282	9,917.14
Iain Pyman	73	69	67	74	283	7,760
Greg Turner	72	72	71	68	283	7,760
Thomas Levet	71	71	71	70	283	7,760
Scott Watson	71	71	71	71	284	7,110
Tony Johnstone	77	69	70	68	284	7,110
Robert Allenby	69	71	70	75	285	6,480
Jamie Spence	72	74	70	69	285	6,480
Heinz P. Thul	73	71	71	70	285	6,480
Mike Miller	76	69	72	68	285	6,480
Rodger Davis	71	72	72	70	285	6,480
Phil Golding	67	76	73	70	286	5,850
Peter Hedblom	67	70	79	70	286	5,850
Sandy Lyle	70	74	75	68	287	5,160
Joe Higgins	75	71	71	70	287	5,160
Alberto Binaghi	72	70	72	73	287	5,160
Eoghan O'Connell	75	69	73	70	287	5,160
Keith Waters	72	72	71	72	287	5,160
Wayne Westner	69	72	72	74	287	5,160

	SCORES				TOTAL	MONEY
Ross McFarlane	72	74	72	70	288	4,200
Nicklas Fasth	67	76	74	71	288	4,200
David Gilford	70	76	73	69	288	4,200
Steven Richardson	72	74	72	70	288	4,200
Paul Affleck	71	73	71	73	288	4,200
Mike Clayton	72	72	70	74	288	4,200
Ignacio Garrido	71	75	73	69	288	4,200
Andrew Murray	71	74	69	74	288	4,200
Fredrik Larsson	72	71	75	70	288	4,200
Peter Mitchell	71	74	71	73	289	3,240
Paul Way	70	76	73	70	289	3,240
Eamonn Darcy	67	74	76	72	289	3,240
Steven Bottomley	74	72	72	71	289	3,240
Lee Westwood	69	70	71	79	289	3,240
Andrew Coltart	69	72	75	73	289	3,240
Phillip Price	71	71	72	75	289	3,240
Brian Marchbank	73	72	75	70	290	2,400
Pedro Linhart	72	73	76	69	290	2,400
Paul Richard Simpson	72	72	71	75	290	2,400
Ian Palmer	69	71	79	71	290	2,400
Paul Eales	75	71	69	75	290	2,400
Ian Spencer	73	73	71	73	290	2,400
David Williams	74	70	75	71	290	2,400
Andrew Oldcorn	71	73	71	76	291	1,830
Paul Mayo	72	71	75	73	291	1,830
John McHenry	74	72	72	73	291	1,830
Paul Moloney	71	73	75	72	291	1,830
Roger Chapman	75	71	76	70	292	1,590
Philip Parkin	68	75	76	73	292	1,590
Darren Clarke	73	73	72	74	292	1,590
Jean Van de Velde	74	72	72	74	292	1,590
Paul Broadhurst	74	72	75	72	293	897
Gavin Levenson	74	71	75	73	293	897
Chris Hall	73	72	79	69	293	897
Miguel Angel Jimenez	70	70	78	75	293	897
Johan Rystrom	74	71	77	72	294	892
Alexander Cejka	72	74	79	70	295	888
George Ryall	74	72	74	75	295	888
Frederic Regard	72	71	78	74	295	888
Martin Gates	75	71	73	77	296	884
Jose Maria Carriles	72	74	79	74	299	882
Mark Mouland	70	74	82	76	302	880
Paul Lawrie	73	71	76	84	304	878

Volvo German Open

Hubbelrath Golf Club, Dusseldorf, Germany
Par 36-36—72; 6,793 yards

August 25-28
purse, £650,000

	SCORES				TOTAL	MONEY
Colin Montgomerie	65	68	66	70	269	£108,330
Bernhard Langer	69	68	65	68	270	72,210
Phillip Price	65	67	67	72	271	40,690
Per-Ulrik Johansson	64	70	70	68	272	30,015
Ross McFarlane	68	65	67	72	272	30,015
Thomas Levet	63	72	67	71	273	21,125
Miguel Angel Jimenez	69	71	65	68	273	21,125
Gordon Brand, Jr.	67	68	72	67	274	16,250

	SCORES				TOTAL	MONEY
Vicente Fernandez	70	67	70	69	276	14,510
Mike Clayton	71	68	70	68	277	13,000
Wayne Westner	69	71	71	67	278	11,570
Andrew Bossert	67	68	75	68	278	11,570
Andrew Oldcorn	68	70	68	73	279	10,460
Paul Broadhurst	69	72	73	66	280	8,978.33
David Curry	71	71	70	68	280	8,978.33
Peter Mitchell	74	68	69	69	280	8,978.33
Greg Turner	66	70	70	74	280	8,978.33
Ronan Rafferty	68	70	69	73	280	8,978.33
Silvio Grappasonni	65	70	71	74	280	8,978.33
Brian Marchbank	71	71	68	71	281	7,312.50
David Gilford	73	67	71	70	281	7,312.50
Iain Pyman	69	72	67	73	281	7,312.50
Peter Teravainen	69	68	72	72	281	7,312.50
Gavin Levenson	68	69	72	72	281	7,312.50
Darren Clarke	71	71	70	69	281	7,312.50
Mathias Gronberg	66	74	73	69	282	6,337.50
Gary Evans	70	71	71	70	282	6,337.50
Chris Moody	70	71	70	71	282	6,337.50
Phil Golding	70	69	70	73	282	6,337.50
Martin Gates	67	70	74	72	283	5,427.50
Gary Orr	70	68	77	68	283	5,427.50
Joakim Haeggman	68	72	71	72	283	5,427.50
Adam Mednick	68	72	73	70	283	5,427.50
Eduardo Romero	68	73	68	74	283	5,427.50
Jay Townsend	74	68	69	72	283	5,427.50
Peter Hedblom	69	64	76	75	284	4,810
Tony Johnstone	69	73	70	72	284	4,810
Jamie Spence	72	70	73	69	284	4,810
Jean Louis Guepy	71	71	74	69	285	3,965
John Bland	71	69	71	74	285	3,965
Andrew Sherborne	71	68	73	73	285	3,965
Anders Sorensen	71	70	71	73	285	3,965
Lee Westwood	72	69	71	73	285	3,965
Eamonn Darcy	68	71	73	73	285	3,965
Mark Roe	71	67	73	74	285	3,965
Paul Curry	67	72	75	71	285	3,965
Steve Jones	69	71	71	74	285	3,965
Jose Rivero	69	69	74	73	285	3,965
Pierre Fulke	67	73	75	71	286	2,990
Manny Zerman	68	74	72	72	286	2,990
Scott Watson	73	68	76	69	286	2,990
Manuel Pinero	73	69	70	74	286	2,990
David A. Russell	70	70	74	72	286	2,990
Robert Karlsson	69	72	72	74	287	2,285.83
Russell Claydon	74	68	70	75	287	2,285.83
Robert Allenby	67	75	75	70	287	2,285.83
Gordon J. Brand	69	72	70	76	287	2,285.83
Christy O'Connor, Jr.	69	69	72	77	287	2,285.83
Ignacio Garrido	69	73	71	74	287	2,285.83
Mike Miller	71	69	69	79	288	1,852.50
Steve Bowman	69	69	75	75	288	1,852.50
Torsten Giedeon	68	73	75	72	288	1,852.50
Thomas Gogele	70	72	75	71	288	1,852.50
Jose Manuel Carriles	69	72	78	72	291	1,246.80
Mark Nichols	71	67	71	82	291	1,246.80
Ian Palmer	72	70	76	73	291	1,246.80
Pedro Linhart	69	71	77	74	291	1,246.80
Jeff Hawkes	68	73	75	75	291	1,246.80

	SCORES			TOTAL	MONEY
Anders Gillner	69	73	75	75	292	968
Massimo Scarpa	71	71	76	74	292	968
Simon Brown	69	72	78	74	293	965
Jose Coceres	71	71	73	79	294	963
Frederic Regard	69	69	76	83	297	961

Canon European Masters

Crans-sur-Sierre Golf Club, Crans-sur-Sierre, Switzerland
Par 36-36—72; 6,745 yards

September 1-4
purse, £668,000

	SCORES				TOTAL	MONEY
Eduardo Romero	64	68	66	68	266	£111,290
Pierre Fulke	70	65	65	67	267	74,150
Jean Van de Velde	68	68	67	66	269	34,513.33
Barry Lane	67	69	66	67	269	34,513.33
Sam Torrance	67	65	69	68	269	34,513.33
Nick Faldo	69	66	67	68	270	21,710
Martin Gates	69	65	70	66	270	21,710
Bernhard Langer	69	70	64	68	271	15,830
Adam Hunter	65	69	68	69	271	15,830
Per-Ulrik Johansson	69	68	67	68	272	12,380
Retief Goosen	68	69	67	68	272	12,380
Gordon Brand, Jr.	65	65	71	71	272	12,380
Peter O'Malley	70	69	69	66	274	9,446.43
John Bland	68	72	66	68	274	9,446.43
Miguel Angel Martin	69	69	68	68	274	9,446.43
Gary Orr	70	68	70	66	274	9,446.43
Santiago Luna	69	67	71	67	274	9,446.43
Sandy Lyle	68	67	72	67	274	9,446.43
Frederic Regard	70	65	72	67	274	9,446.43
Stephen McAllister	69	71	70	65	275	7,615
David Gilford	69	71	67	68	275	7,615
Seve Ballesteros	73	68	68	66	275	7,615
Thomas Levet	74	64	66	71	275	7,615
Massimo Scarpa	68	68	71	68	275	7,615
*Francisco Valera	67	71	68	69	275	
Anders Forsbrand	69	71	70	66	276	6,315
Robert Allenby	68	72	68	68	276	6,315
Domingo Hospital	72	69	69	66	276	6,315
Jeff Hawkes	70	68	69	69	276	6,315
Manuel Pinero	69	68	69	70	276	6,315
Peter Mitchell	70	67	67	72	276	6,315
Derrick Cooper	67	69	70	70	276	6,315
Andrew Sherborne	69	66	68	73	276	6,315
Paolo Quirici	70	69	70	68	277	4,805
Russell Claydon	70	69	68	70	277	4,805
Peter Teravainen	71	69	71	66	277	4,805
Robin Freeman	69	71	66	71	277	4,805
Michel Besanceney	70	71	67	69	277	4,805
Vicente Fernandez	68	70	69	70	277	4,805
Corey Pavin	70	67	69	71	277	4,805
Roger Chapman	69	68	69	71	277	4,805
Steen Tinning	69	68	71	69	277	4,805
Howard Clark	66	70	72	69	277	4,805
Ross McFarlane	70	66	70	71	277	4,805
Alexander Cejka	69	70	68	71	278	3,535.63
Des Smyth	72	67	69	70	278	3,535.63

	SCORES				TOTAL	MONEY
Stephen Ames	68	71	68	71	278	3,535.63
Wayne Westner	66	73	69	70	278	3,535.63
David J. Russell	72	69	70	67	278	3,535.63
Paul Curry	70	71	69	68	278	3,535.63
Andre Bossert	67	71	69	71	278	3,535.63
Philip Walton	67	70	72	69	278	3,535.63
Steven Bottomley	69	70	69	71	279	2,690
Silvio Grappasonni	69	72	70	68	279	2,690
David Curry	68	73	68	70	279	2,690
Jamie Spence	69	68	72	70	279	2,690
Sven Struver	69	67	71	72	279	2,690
Steven Richardson	69	70	72	69	280	2,235
Nicklas Fasth	71	68	71	70	280	2,235
Paul Mayo	71	68	75	67	281	1,752.75
Ignacio Garrido	70	69	67	75	281	1,752.75
Eoghan O'Connell	71	68	69	73	281	1,752.75
Ross Drummond	67	73	70	71	281	1,752.75
Fredrik Lindgren	68	73	71	69	281	1,752.75
Costantino Rocca	69	72	69	71	281	1,752.75
Marc Farry	69	69	73	70	281	1,752.75
Carl Mason	70	68	73	70	281	1,752.75
Raymond Burns	70	69	72	72	283	999
Olle Nordberg	71	69	74	69	283	999
Manny Zerman	69	71	75	69	284	995
Darren Clarke	66	69	77	72	284	995
Ralf Berhorst	69	72	74	72	287	992
Paul Moloney	72	67	75	75	289	990
David A. Russell	71	70	77	72	290	988
Wayne Riley	71	69	77	79	296	986

European Open

East Sussex National Golf Club, Uckfield, England
Par 36-36—72; 7,138 yards

September 8-11
purse, £600,000

	SCORES				TOTAL	MONEY
David Gilford	70	68	70	67	275	£100,000
Costantino Rocca	68	72	70	70	280	52,110
Jose Maria Olazabal	68	74	69	69	280	52,110
Colin Montgomerie	66	73	73	70	282	30,000
Howard Clark	71	68	74	71	284	21,466.67
Darren Clarke	71	74	71	68	284	21,466.67
Craig Cassells	72	73	69	70	284	21,466.67
Seve Ballesteros	68	75	72	70	285	15,000
Barry Lane	70	74	75	68	287	12,153.33
David J. Russell	74	74	70	69	287	12,153.33
Pedro Linhart	71	74	73	69	287	12,153.33
Anders Forsbrand	71	72	75	70	288	9,970
Frank Nobilo	68	74	71	75	288	9,970
Russell Claydon	67	77	74	71	289	8,134.29
Christy O'Connor, Jr.	73	74	78	67	289	8,134.29
Mark Roe	74	70	74	71	289	8,134.29
Ernie Els	72	74	73	70	289	8,134.29
Mike Clayton	74	74	73	68	289	8,134.29
Sam Torrance	75	73	71	70	289	8,134.29
Sandy Lyle	70	75	74	70	289	8,134.29
Santiago Luna	71	73	76	70	290	6,480
Greg Turner	76	70	74	70	290	6,480

	SCORES				TOTAL	MONEY
Ian Woosnam	75	70	76	69	290	6,480
Derrick Cooper	71	72	75	72	290	6,480
Mark Davis	76	67	73	74	290	6,480
Nicklas Fasth	75	72	71	72	290	6,480
David A. Russell	74	72	72	72	290	6,480
Paul McGinley	71	76	74	70	291	5,580
Paul Mayo	73	74	71	73	291	5,580
Andrew Murray	68	73	72	78	291	5,580
Mats Lanner	69	76	74	73	292	4,995
Vijay Singh	72	75	72	73	292	4,995
Mike McLean	76	70	72	74	292	4,995
Jose Manuel Carriles	71	75	74	72	292	4,995
Ronan Rafferty	73	75	71	74	293	4,620
Klas Eriksson	71	75	75	72	293	4,620
Mike Harwood	72	74	76	72	294	4,200
Retief Goosen	70	75	73	76	294	4,200
Tony Johnstone	73	70	80	71	294	4,200
Vicente Fernandez	73	75	75	71	294	4,200
Johan Rystrom	73	72	75	74	294	4,200
Paul Eales	73	73	77	72	295	3,480
Wayne Riley	72	74	79	70	295	3,480
Per-Ulrik Johansson	74	74	76	71	295	3,480
Ian Palmer	71	73	78	73	295	3,480
Marc Farry	72	75	74	74	295	3,480
Miguel Angel Martin	72	76	78	69	295	3,480
Jose Rivero	77	69	75	74	295	3,480
Steven Richardson	70	71	76	79	296	2,820
Gary Orr	73	73	79	71	296	2,820
Malcolm Mackenzie	75	73	71	77	296	2,820
Manuel Pinero	72	74	77	73	296	2,820
Robert Karlsson	72	75	76	74	297	2,340
Olle Nordberg	76	72	74	75	297	2,340
Steven Bottomley	78	70	75	74	297	2,340
Justin Hobday	72	73	77	75	297	2,340
Paul Curry	73	74	79	72	298	1,872
Martin Gates	73	75	78	72	298	1,872
Gordon Brand, Jr.	73	73	78	74	298	1,872
Robert Allenby	74	73	76	75	298	1,872
Steen Tinning	75	71	77	75	298	1,872
Peter Baker	73	73	78	76	300	1,680
Anders Sorensen	74	72	82	74	302	1,620
Phillip Price	71	77	76	79	303	1,560
Mark James	68	77	82	81	308	1,500

Dunhill British Masters

Woburn Golf & Country Club, Buckinghamshire, England
Par 34-38—72; 6,940 yards

September 15-18
purse, £650,000

	SCORES				TOTAL	MONEY
Ian Woosnam	71	70	63	67	271	£108,330
Seve Ballesteros	69	65	69	72	275	72,210
Colin Montgomerie	72	66	70	68	276	36,595
Bernhard Langer	71	69	65	71	276	36,595
Ernie Els	68	71	70	68	277	25,140
Jose Rivero	74	67	68	68	277	25,140
Eoghan O'Connell	71	69	70	68	278	16,753.33
Philip Walton	68	72	66	72	278	16,753.33

	SCORES				TOTAL	MONEY
Miguel Angel Martin	71	69	65	73	278	16,753.33
Martin Gates	67	70	72	70	279	12,046.67
Andrew Murray	67	69	72	71	279	12,046.67
Sam Torrance	70	70	68	71	279	12,046.67
Nick Faldo	71	74	70	65	280	9,983.33
Joakim Haeggman	72	73	70	65	280	9,983.33
Miguel Angel Jimenez	74	71	69	66	280	9,983.33
Roger Chapman	71	71	71	68	281	8,967.50
Jose Maria Olazabal	71	69	71	70	281	8,967.50
Russell Claydon	74	71	70	67	282	8,222.50
David Williams	74	70	69	69	282	8,222.50
Eduardo Romero	72	71	73	67	283	7,312.50
Barry Lane	70	74	71	68	283	7,312.50
Mark Roe	74	70	70	69	283	7,312.50
Wayne Riley	78	66	70	69	283	7,312.50
Phillip Price	73	72	67	71	283	7,312.50
Ian Palmer	67	74	69	73	283	7,312.50
Derrick Cooper	71	72	72	69	284	6,240
Andrew Oldcorn	70	74	72	68	284	6,240
Mark James	71	69	76	68	284	6,240
Greg Turner	72	66	74	72	284	6,240
Howard Clark	71	72	67	74	284	6,240
Mike Miller	70	73	73	69	285	5,481.67
Costantino Rocca	75	69	69	72	285	5,481.67
Gavin Levenson	71	69	72	73	285	5,481.67
Klas Eriksson	73	70	73	70	286	5,070
Mark Davis	70	75	73	68	286	5,070
David Gilford	72	72	71	71	286	5,070
Gary Orr	69	74	72	72	287	4,550
Mike Clayton	73	71	72	71	287	4,550
Ross Drummond	71	72	73	71	287	4,550
Alberto Binaghi	71	74	70	72	287	4,550
Paul McGinley	69	74	71	73	287	4,550
Stephen McAllister	73	71	75	69	288	4,095
Jonathan Lomas	73	70	71	74	288	4,095
Marc Farry	74	71	70	74	289	3,640
Paul Eales	73	70	74	72	289	3,640
Richard Boxall	70	70	77	72	289	3,640
Peter Teravainen	73	71	75	70	289	3,640
Jose Manuel Carriles	74	71	74	70	289	3,640
Peter Baker	72	71	73	74	290	2,990
Silvio Grappasonni	74	71	72	73	290	2,990
Des Smyth	76	69	73	72	290	2,990
John Bland	73	72	75	70	290	2,990
Santiago Luna	72	73	75	70	290	2,990
Paul Curry	72	72	73	74	291	2,600
Steve Bowman	67	78	75	74	294	2,405
Jeff Hawkes	72	73	75	74	294	2,405
Steen Tinning	71	72	75	77	295	2,145
David Ray	71	74	74	76	295	2,145
Paul Way	72	73	75	79	299	1,982.50
Bernard Gallacher	72	73	75	79	299	1,982.50

Trophee Lancome

St. Nom la Breteche, Paris, France
Par 35-35—70; 6,742 yards

September 22-25
purse, £600,000

	SCORES				TOTAL	MONEY
Vijay Singh	65	63	69	66	263	£100,000
Miguel Angel Jimenez	67	64	66	67	264	66,000
Seve Ballesteros	65	69	66	65	265	37,000
Colin Montgomerie	69	66	67	68	270	30,000
Jose Maria Olazabal	68	68	71	65	272	23,000
Barry Lane	71	68	66	67	272	23,000
Nick Faldo	68	71	66	68	273	15,350
Mark Davis	69	66	67	71	273	15,350
Frank Nobilo	68	68	70	67	273	15,350
Peter Mitchell	72	68	68	66	274	10,475
Lee Westwood	70	67	71	66	274	10,475
Howard Clark	69	67	70	68	274	10,475
Ian Woosnam	68	65	70	71	274	10,475
Joakim Haeggman	68	68	71	68	275	8,500
Gordon Brand, Jr.	69	69	66	71	275	8,500
David Gilford	69	69	67	70	275	8,500
Andrew Coltart	70	66	71	69	276	7,500
Sam Torrance	71	69	72	64	276	7,500
Eduardo Romero	72	65	70	69	276	7,500
Greg Turner	70	65	72	69	276	7,500
Costantino Rocca	70	67	71	68	276	7,500
Rodger Davis	69	71	68	68	276	7,500
Darren Clarke	72	69	68	68	277	6,800
Bernhard Langer	72	68	67	71	278	6,400
Stephen Ames	71	68	69	70	278	6,400
Sandy Lyle	73	72	68	65	278	6,400
Mike Harwood	70	72	67	70	279	6,000
Carl Mason	72	69	70	69	280	5,725
Wayne Westner	75	67	67	71	280	5,725
Gary Orr	69	72	72	68	281	5,275
Russell Claydon	71	67	72	71	281	5,275
Peter Baker	71	68	73	69	281	5,275
Des Smyth	73	70	69	69	281	5,275
Paul McGinley	72	68	73	69	282	4,600
Jose Coceres	72	71	73	66	282	4,600
Paul Eales	68	71	74	69	282	4,600
David J. Russell	71	69	68	74	282	4,600
Mark McNulty	74	69	69	70	282	4,600
Per-Ulrik Johansson	74	71	70	68	283	4,000
Jean Louis Guepy	71	72	72	68	283	4,000
Gary Player	70	70	72	71	283	4,000
Philip Walton	71	69	74	70	284	3,550
Mark James	75	69	70	70	284	3,550
Robert Allenby	72	72	70	70	284	3,550
Ronan Rafferty	69	72	74	69	284	3,550
Tony Johnstone	71	76	69	69	285	3,300
Paul Curry	72	71	74	69	286	3,200
Peter Hedblom	72	69	72	74	287	3,100
Mike Clayton	72	73	70	73	288	2,850
Paul Way	70	72	70	76	288	2,850
Jesper Parnevik	73	76	69	70	288	2,850
Jonathan Lomas	71	71	74	72	288	2,850
*Laurent Pargade	73	69	72	74	288	
*Greg Chalmers	77	70	69	72	288	
Thomas Levet	75	71	73	70	289	2,500

		SCORES			TOTAL	MONEY
Mark Roe	72	69	73	75	289	2,500
Gabriel Hjertstedt	74	72	69	74	289	2,500
Mats Lanner	74	73	74	69	290	2,300
*Stephen Gallacher	74	71	71	74	290	
Anders Forsbrand	73	64	81	73	291	2,150
Jean Van de Velde	75	72	73	71	291	2,150
Lee Trevino	76	73	71	72	292	1,950
Steven Richardson	72	75	71	74	292	1,950
Michel Besanceney	74	75	69	75	293	1,800
Arnold Palmer	74	79	77	72	302	1,700
Jean Garaialde	79	73	78	79	309	1,650
Retief Goosen	75	76	73	WD		1,550

Mercedes German Masters

Motzener See Golf & Country Club, Berlin, Germany
Par 37-35—72; 6,848 yards

September 30-October 3
purse, £625,000

		SCORES			TOTAL	MONEY
Seve Ballesteros	68	70	65	67	270	£104,125
Ernie Els	63	64	70	73	270	54,250
Jose Maria Olazabal	67	67	66	70	270	54,250
(Ballesteros defeated Els and Olazabal on first extra hole.)						
Vijay Singh	66	70	70	67	273	24,593.75
Nick Faldo	69	68	67	69	273	24,593.75
Sven Struver	67	70	70	66	273	24,593.75
Eamonn Darcy	70	69	66	68	273	24,593.75
Peter Mitchell	66	70	68	70	274	14,812.50
Eoghan O'Connell	67	72	68	67	274	14,812.50
Per-Ulrik Johansson	69	68	67	71	275	11,583.33
Pierre Fulke	69	71	68	67	275	11,583.33
Greg Turner	72	69	66	68	275	11,583.33
Adam Hunter	66	70	70	71	277	9,601.67
Russell Claydon	64	73	69	71	277	9,601.67
Miguel Angel Martin	68	71	70	68	277	9,601.67
Jean Van de Velde	69	68	70	71	278	8,262.50
Stephen McAllister	69	68	69	72	278	8,262.50
Jose Rivero	70	69	65	74	278	8,262.50
Rodger Davis	67	73	67	71	278	8,262.50
Peter Baker	66	70	69	74	279	7,120
Andrew Sherborne	70	68	72	69	279	7,120
Craig Cassells	71	70	68	70	279	7,120
David J. Russell	71	70	70	68	279	7,120
Sam Torrance	68	74	68	69	279	7,120
Santiago Luna	70	67	71	72	280	6,363.33
Thomas Gogele	69	70	68	73	280	6,363.33
Carl Mason	69	71	70	70	280	6,363.33
Stephen Ames	67	71	71	72	281	5,554.17
Jose Maria Canizares	71	69	72	69	281	5,554.17
Costantino Rocca	71	69	71	70	281	5,554.17
Mark James	71	71	72	67	281	5,554.17
Des Smyth	66	77	68	70	281	5,554.17
Peter O'Malley	71	72	66	72	281	5,554.17
Bernhard Langer	69	68	70	75	282	4,687.50
Magnus Sunesson	70	68	71	73	282	4,687.50
Stephen Richardson	66	72	71	73	282	4,687.50
Anders Forsbrand	68	72	73	69	282	4,687.50
Ian Woosnam	68	71	72	71	282	4,687.50

	SCORES				TOTAL	MONEY
Sandy Lyle	67	74	69	72	282	4,687.50
Heinz P. Thul	68	70	76	69	283	4,125
Mark Mouland	71	70	68	74	283	4,125
Jeremy Robinson	72	71	71	69	283	4,125
Paul Curry	70	70	76	68	284	3,625
Alberto Binaghi	67	73	72	72	284	3,625
Steen Tinning	68	72	72	72	284	3,625
Roger Chapman	70	71	67	76	284	3,625
Manny Zerman	68	74	75	67	284	3,625
Jose Manuel Carriles	71	68	73	73	285	3,000
Fredrik Lindgren	75	66	68	76	285	3,000
Pedro Linhart	72	69	72	72	285	3,000
Robert Lee	68	73	73	71	285	3,000
Marc Farry	68	74	70	73	285	3,000
Andre Bossert	67	71	76	72	286	2,312.50
Jamie Spence	70	69	73	74	286	2,312.50
Mats Lanner	71	69	70	76	286	2,312.50
Domingo Hospital	71	69	70	76	286	2,312.50
Mark Davis	70	71	69	76	286	2,312.50
David Curry	72	72	69	73	286	2,312.50
Paul Way	72	70	73	72	287	1,902.50
Wayne Riley	72	71	75	69	287	1,902.50
Silvio Grappasonni	73	69	75	71	288	1,750
Manuel Pinero	70	73	76	69	288	1,750
Miguel Angel Jimenez	75	69	71	73	288	1,750
Jose Coceres	66	72	77	75	290	1,268
Jeff Hawkes	71	73	72	74	290	1,268
Olle Karlsson	72	72	71	75	290	1,268
Richard Boxall	69	75	75	71	290	1,268
Ralf Berhorst	73	69	73	77	292	932
Gordon J. Brand	70	74	73	75	292	932

Alfred Dunhill Cup

Old Course, St. Andrews, Scotland
Par 36-36—72; 6,933 yards

October 6-9
purse, £1,000,000

FIRST ROUND

UNITED STATES DEFEATED JAPAN, 2-1
Nobuo Serizawa (J) defeated Tom Kite, 74-75; Curtis Strange (US) defeated Tomohiro Maruyama, 78-80; Fred Couples (US) defeated Yoshinori Mizumaki, 75-80.

NEW ZEALAND DEFEATED IRELAND, 2-1
Darren Clarke (I) defeated Frank Nobilo, 72-74; Greg Turner (NZ) defeated Paul McGinley, 72-77; Grant Waite (NZ) defeated Philip Walton, 80-81.

ENGLAND DEFEATED SPAIN, 3-0
Barry Lane (E) defeated Jose Rivero, 76-77; Howard Clark (E) defeated Miguel Angel Martin, 80-82; Mark Roe (E) defeated Miguel Angel Jimenez, 75-80.

AUSTRALIA DEFEATED FRANCE, 2-1
Steve Elkington (A) defeated Jean Van de Velde, 75-76; Jean Louis Guepy (F) defeated Robert Allenby, 77-78; Greg Norman (A) defeated Michel Besanceney, 72-76.

SOUTH AFRICA DEFEATED REPUBLIC OF CHINA, 2-1
Chen Tze Chung (Ch) defeated Wayne Westner, 83-84; Ernie Els (SA) defeated Yeh Chang Ting (81-83); David Frost (SA) defeated Chen Tze Ming, 76-77.

SCOTLAND DEFEATED PARAGUAY, 2-1
Angel Franco (P) defeated Gordon Brand, Jr., 74-79; Andrew Coltart (Sc) defeated
Raul Fretes, 78-78, first extra hole; Colin Montgomerie (Sc) defeated Carlos Franco,
78-79.

SWEDEN DEFEATED CANADA, 2-1
Gabriel Hjertstedt (Sw) defeated Dave Barr, 76-76, second extra hole; Ray Stewart
(Ca) defeated Jesper Parnevik, 76-77; Anders Forsbrand (Sw) defeated Rick Gibson,
81-85.

ZIMBABWE DEFEATED GERMANY, 2-1
Nick Price (Z) defeated Bernhard Langer, 76-78; Alexander Cejka (G) defeated Tony
Johnstone, 76-81; Mark McNulty (Z) defeated Sven Struver, 76-82.

SECOND ROUND

JAPAN DEFEATED NEW ZEALAND, 2-1
Nobuo Serizawa (J) defeated Greg Turner, 71-74; Grant Waite (NZ) defeated
Tomohiro Maruyama, 72-77; Yoshinori Mizumaki (J) defeated Frank Nobilo, 71-73.

IRELAND DEFEATED UNITED STATES, 2-1
Curtis Strange (US) defeated Paul McGinley, 74-76; Philip Walton (I) defeated Tom
Kite, 72-76; Darren Clarke (I) defeated Fred Couples, 71-74.

AUSTRALIA DEFEATED SPAIN, 2-1
Steve Elkington (A) defeated Miguel Angel Martin, 67-70; Jose Rivero (Sp) defeated
Robert Allenby, 67-69; Greg Norman (A) defeated Miguel Angel Jimenez, 70-72.

ENGLAND DEFEATED FRANCE, 3-0
Howard Clark (E) defeated Michel Besanceney, 73-73, second extra hole; Barry Lane
(E) defeated Jean Louis Guepy, 70-73; Mark Roe (E) defeated Jean Van de Velde,
73-76.

SCOTLAND DEFEATED REPUBLIC OF CHINA, 3-0
Gordon Brand, Jr. (Sc) defeated Chen Tze Chung, 70-75; Andrew Coltart (Sc) defeated
Yeh Chang Ting, 70-74; Colin Montgomerie (Sc) defeated Chen Tze Ming, 70-75.

SOUTH AFRICA DEFEATED PARAGUAY, 2-1
Wayne Westner (SA) defeated Raul Fretes, 69-73; David Frost (SA) defeated Carlos
Franco, 70-72; Angel Franco (P) defeated Ernie Els, 72-72, sixth extra hole.

GERMANY DEFEATED SWEDEN, 2-1
Bernhard Langer (G) defeated Gabriel Hjertstedt, 69-72; Alexander Cejka (G) defeated
Anders Forsbrand, 73-73, second extra hole; Jesper Parnevik (Sw) defeated Sven
Struver, 70-76.

CANADA DEFEATED ZIMBABWE, 2-1
Rick Gibson (C) defeated Tony Johnstone, 71-72; Mark McNulty (Z) defeated Ray
Stewart, 71-76; Dave Barr (C) defeated Nick Price, 68-69.

THIRD ROUND

UNITED STATES DEFEATED NEW ZEALAND, 3-0
Tom Kite (US) defeated Grant Waite, 69-71; Curtis Strange (US) defeated Frank
Nobilo, 69-70; Fred Couples (US) defeated Greg Turner, 72-74.

IRELAND DEFEATED JAPAN, 2-1
Yoshinori Mizumaki (J) defeated Philip Walton, 64-70; Paul McGinley (I) defeated
Tomohiro Maruyama, 70-72; Darren Clarke (I) defeated Nobuo Serizawa, 70-76.

FRANCE DEFEATED SPAIN, 2-1
Miguel Angel Jimenez (Sp) defeated Jean Louis Guepy, 73-77; Jean Van de Velde (F)

defeated Jose Rivero, 67-70; Michel Besanceney (F) defeated Miguel Angel Martin, 69-73.

ENGLAND DEFEATED AUSTRALIA, 3-0
Barry Lane (E) defeated Robert Allenby, 69-71; Howard Clark (E) defeated Steve Elkington, 65-68; Mark Roe (E) defeated Greg Norman, 69-72.

REPUBLIC OF CHINA DEFEATED PARAGUAY, 2-1
Raul Fretes (P) defeated Chen Tze Chung, 72-74; Yeh Chang Ting (Ch) defeated Angel Franco, 75-76; Chen Tze Ming (Ch) defeated Carlos Franco, 72-73.

SOUTH AFRICA DEFEATED SCOTLAND, 2-1
Andrew Coltart (Sc) defeated Wayne Westner, 70-72; Ernie Els (SA) defeated Gordon Brand, Jr., 68-70; David Frost (SA) defeated Colin Montgomerie, 71-74.

CANADA DEFEATED GERMANY, 2-1
Sven Struver (G) defeated Ray Stewart, 72-72, first extra hole; Rick Gibson (C) defeated Alexander Cejka, 69-73; Dave Barr (C) defeated Bernhard Langer, 69-70.

SWEDEN DEFEATED ZIMBABWE, 2-1
Tony Johnstone (Z) defeated Gabriel Hjertstedt, 70-73; Nick Price (Z) defeated Anders Forsbrand, 70-73; Jesper Parnevik (Sw) defeated Mark McNulty, 67-70.

SEMI-FINALS

UNITED STATES DEFEATED ENGLAND, 3-0
Tom Kite (US) defeated Mark Roe, 69-70; Fred Couples (US) defeated Howard Clark, 68-74; Curtis Strange (US) defeated Barry Lane, 70-71.

CANADA DEFEATED SOUTH AFRICA, 2-1
Ray Stewart (C) defeated David Frost, 70-75; Rick Gibson (C) defeated Wayne Westner, 70-74; Ernie Els (SA) defeated Dave Barr, 68-72.

FINAL

CANADA DEFEATED UNITED STATES, 2-1
Dave Barr (C) defeated Tom Kite, 70-71; Curtis Strange (US) defeated Rick Gibson, 67-74; Ray Stewart (C) defeated Fred Couples, 71-72.

	MATCHES WON	INDIVIDUAL GAMES WON (After Round 3)	PRIZE MONEY TEAM	PLAYER
GROUP 1				
United States	2	6	£150,000	£50,000
Ireland	2	5	45,000	15,000
Japan	1	4	25,500	8,500
New Zealand	1	3	19,500	6,500
GROUP 2				
England	3	9	95,000	31,666
Australia	2	4	45,000	15,000
France	1	3	25,500	8,500
Spain	0	2	19,500	6,500
GROUP 3				
South Africa	3	6	95,000	31,666
Scotland	2	6	45,000	15,000
Republic of China	1	3	25,500	8,500
Paraguay	0	3	19,500	6,500

	MATCHES WON	INDIVIDUAL GAMES WON (After Round 3)	PRIZE MONEY TEAM	PLAYER
GROUP 4				
Canada	2	5	300,000	100,000
Zimbabwe	2	5	45,000	15,000
Germany	1	4	25,500	8,500
Sweden	1	4	19,500	6,500

Toyota World Match Play Championship

Wentworth Club, Surrey, England
Par 434 534 444—35; 345 434 455—37—72; 6,957 yards

October 13-16
purse, £600,000

FIRST ROUND

Vijay Singh defeated Jesper Parnevik, 4 and 3
| Singh | 4 4 4 | 4 3 4 | 4 4 4 | 35 | 2 3 4 | 4 3 4 | 3 4 4 | 31 | 66 |
| Parnevik | 3 2 4 | 4 3 4 | 3 4 4 | 31 | 3 3 3 | 4 3 4 | 4 5 5 | 34 | 65 |

Match all-square
| Singh | 3 3 4 | 4 2 4 | 5 4 5 | 34 | 3 4 4 | 4 2 4 |
| Parnevik | 4 3 4 | 5 3 4 | 4 4 6 | 37 | 3 4 4 | 4 3 4 |

Colin Montgomerie defeated Yoshinori Mizumaki, 2 and 1
| Montgomerie | 4 3 3 | 4 3 5 | 4 4 3 | 33 | 3 4 4 | 3 3 5 | 4 5 4 | 35 | 68 |
| Mizumaki | 3 3 5 | 4 3 5 | 4 3 3 | 33 | 3 4 5 | 4 3 5 | 4 5 4 | 37 | 70 |

Montgomerie leads, 1 up
| Montgomerie | 4 3 4 | 4 3 4 | 5 4 4 | 35 | 3 4 4 | 3 3 5 | 4 4 |
| Mizumaki | 4 3 4 | 3 4 4 | 3 4 4 | 33 | 3 4 4 | 4 3 5 | 4 5 |

Seve Ballesteros defeated David Frost, 8 and 7
| Frost | 4 3 4 | 4 2 4 | 3 4 4 | 32 | 4 4 4 | 3 3 4 | 4 4 5 | 35 | 67 |
| Ballesteros | 4 3 3 | 4 2 3 | 3 4 4 | 30 | 3 3 4 | 4 3 4 | 4 4 4 | 33 | 63 |

Ballesteros leads, 4 up
| Frost | 3 3 5 | 5 3 4 | 4 4 4 | 35 | 3 4 |
| Ballesteros | 4 3 4 | 4 3 4 | 4 4 3 | 33 | 2 3 |

Brad Faxon defeated Ian Woosnam, 1 up
| Woosnam | 4 3 4 | 4 3 4 | 3 4 5 | 34 | 3 3 4 | 4 3 5 | 4 C 4 | X | X |
| Faxon | 4 3 4 | 4 3 4 | 4 4 4 | 34 | 4 3 4 | 3 3 4 | 4 W 4 | X | X |

Faxon leads, 2 up
| Woosnam | 4 3 4 | 4 3 4 | 4 4 W | X | 4 4 4 | 5 3 4 | 4 4 4 | 36 | X |
| Faxon | 3 3 5 | 4 3 4 | 4 4 C | X | 3 3 5 | 4 3 4 | 5 6 4 | 37 | X |

SECOND ROUND

Vijay Singh defeated Corey Pavin at 37th hole
| Pavin | 4 2 4 | 4 3 3 | 4 4 4 | 32 | 4 4 3 | 4 3 4 | 4 5 4 | 35 | 67 |
| Singh | 4 3 4 | 4 3 4 | 4 4 3 | 33 | 3 4 3 | 3 2 4 | 4 5 5 | 33 | 66 |

Singh leads, 1 up
| Pavin | 4 2 4 | 4 3 3 | 4 4 5 | 33 | 2 4 4 | 4 2 4 | 5 4 5 | 34 | 67 |
| Singh | 4 2 4 | 4 4 4 | 3 4 4 | 33 | 3 4 4 | 4 3 4 | 4 5 4 | 35 | 68 |

Match all-square
| Pavin | 5 |
| Singh | 4 |

Colin Montgomerie defeated Nick Faldo, 1 up
| Faldo | 4 3 5 | 4 3 4 | 4 4 4 | 35 | 3 3 3 | 4 4 4 | 4 4 4 | 33 | 68 |
| Montgomerie | 5 2 4 | 4 3 4 | 3 4 4 | 33 | 3 4 4 | 4 3 4 | 3 4 3 | 32 | 65 |

Montgomerie leads, 3 up

Faldo	4 3 3	3 3 4	3 3 5	31	3 4 5	4 3 4	4 4 4	35	66
Montgomerie	4 2 5	5 3 4	4 4 4	35	2 4 4	4 4 4	4 5 4	35	70

Ernie Els defeated Seve Ballesteros, 2 and 1

Els	4 3 2	4 2 4	4 4 4	31	2 4 4	W2 5	3 5 4	X	X
Ballesteros	4 3 3	5 2 4	4 4 4	33	2 3 4	C2 4	4 4 5	X	X

Els leads, 2 up

Els	4 3 4	3 2 4	4 4 4	32	3 4 4	5 4 4	4 4	
Ballesteros	4 2 4	4 2 4	5 4 4	33	2 5 4	4 2 5	3 5	

Jose Maria Olazabal defeated Brad Faxon, 6 and 4

Olazabal	4 3 3	4 3 4	5 4 3	33	3 4 4	4 3 3	4 5 4	34	67
Faxon	4 3 4	4 3 4	4 4 4	34	3 3 4	5 4 3	4 5 4	35	69

Olazabal leads, 2 up

Olazabal	4 3 3	4 4 4	4 4 4	34	3 4 W	4 3	
Faxon	3 3 4	5 4 4	4 4 4	35	3 4 C	5 C	

SEMI-FINALS

Colin Montgomerie defeated Vijay Singh, 1 up

Singh	3 3 4	4 3 4	4 4 4	33	3 4 5	4 3 5	4 5 3	36	69
Montgomerie	4 4 4	4 3 4	4 4 4	35	3 4 4	5 3 4	3 4 5	35	70

Match all-square

Singh	4 4 4	4 3 4	5 4 4	36	3 5 3	4 3 4	4 5 4	35	71
Montgomerie	4 3 4	4 2 4	5 4 4	34	4 5 4	4 3 4	4 4 4	36	70

Ernie Els defeated Jose Maria Olazabal, 2 and 1

Els	5 3 3	5 3 4	5 3 4	35	3 5 4	3 3 4	4 5 5	36	71
Olazabal	4 3 4	4 3 4	4 4 4	34	3 4 4	4 3 4	4 4 5	35	69

Olazabal leads, 2 up

Els	4 3 3	4 3 4	4 3 4	32	3 3 4	4 3 4	4 4	
Olazabal	3 2 4	5 3 4	4 4 4	33	3 4 4	5 3 4	4 5	

FINAL

Ernie Els defeated Colin Montgomerie, 4 and 2

Montgomerie	4 3 5	4 3 4	5 4 5	37	3 4 4	4 3 3	3 5 4	33	70
Els	4 3 3	4 3 4	4 4 4	33	3 6 4	4 3 3	4 5 5	37	70

Match all-square

Montgomerie	4 3 4	4 3 4	4 4 4	34	3 4 4	4 3 5	4	
Els	3 3 4	4 3 4	4 4 3	32	4 4 4	4 2 4	3	

THIRD-PLACE PLAYOFF

Jose Maria Olazabal defeated Vijay Singh, 2 and 1

Singh	4 3 4	4 3 3	4 4 4	33	4 4 4	4 3 4	4 5	
Olazabal	4 3 3	3 3 4	4 4 4	32	3 3 5	4 3 4	4 5	

PRIZE MONEY: Els £160,000; Montgomerie £90,000; Olazabal £60,000; Singh £50,000; Pavin, Faldo, Ballesteros, Faxon £35,000 each; Parnevik, Mizumaki, Frost, Woosnam £25,000 each.

LEGEND: C—conceded hole to opponent; W—won hole by concession without holing out; X—no total score.

Chemapol Trophy Czech Open

Marianske Lazne Golf Club, Czech Republic
Par 34-25—59; 5,645 yards

October 20-23
purse, £500,000

	SCORES				TOTAL	MONEY
Per-Ulrik Johansson	61	56	54	66	237	£83,330
Klas Eriksson	59	58	56	67	240	55,550
Russell Claydon	56	61	57	67	241	28,150
Frank Nobilo	54	59	57	71	241	28,150
Sven Struver	58	58	54	72	242	15,470
Joakim Haeggman	59	55	60	68	242	15,470
Darren Clarke	59	56	57	70	242	15,470
Jose Rivero	59	57	56	70	242	15,470
Sam Torrance	54	61	57	70	242	15,470
Christy O'Connor, Jr.	63	56	58	67	244	8,077.50
Eoghan O'Connell	58	59	59	68	244	8,077.50
Paul Eales	60	57	55	72	244	8,077.50
Alberto Binaghi	60	55	60	69	244	8,077.50
Jamie Spence	57	58	60	69	244	8,077.50
Robert Allenby	58	54	62	70	244	8,077.50
Barry Lane	59	55	60	70	244	8,077.50
Seve Ballesteros	62	56	56	70	244	8,077.50
Paul Lawrie	58	61	58	68	245	6,125
Silvio Grappasonni	58	57	60	70	245	6,125
Paul McGinley	60	54	59	72	245	6,125
Gordon Brand, Jr.	54	59	58	74	245	6,125
Paul Mayo	56	61	60	69	246	5,550
Mark James	63	58	55	70	246	5,550
Steven Richardson	57	59	58	72	246	5,550
David Curry	55	50	60	69	247	5,100
Gary Orr	59	61	54	73	247	5,100
Malcolm Mackenzie	57	61	55	74	247	5,100
Wayne Riley	61	60	58	69	248	4,500
Jeff Hawkes	59	61	59	69	248	4,500
Domingo Hospital	62	57	59	70	248	4,500
Jose Manuel Carriles	58	61	59	70	248	4,500
Stephen Ames	60	58	58	72	248	4,500
Bernhard Langer	59	58	62	70	249	3,850
David Ray	59	61	61	68	249	3,850
Jean Van de Velde	59	61	59	70	249	3,850
Anders Sorensen	59	59	60	71	249	3,850
Magnus Sunesson	59	61	58	71	249	3,850
Ross Drummond	62	56	57	74	249	3,850
Fredrik Larsson	60	61	60	69	250	3,450
Fredrik Lindgren	60	58	58	74	250	3,450
Adam Hunter	58	63	58	72	251	3,100
John McHenry	61	58	62	70	251	3,100
Miguel Angel Martin	63	59	59	70	251	3,100
Steen Tinning	59	62	57	73	251	3,100
Eamonn Darcy	60	60	56	75	251	3,100
Peter Baker	63	58	59	72	252	2,550
Anders Forsbrand	65	58	57	72	252	2,550
David A. Russell	64	57	61	70	252	2,550
Mark Mouland	60	61	62	69	252	2,550
Carl Mason	61	59	59	73	252	2,550
Richard Boxall	58	63	57	74	252	2,550
Sandy Lyle	61	61	59	72	253	2,150
Nicklas Fasth	61	62	59	71	253	2,150
Andre Bossert	60	59	61	74	254	1,900

	SCORES				TOTAL	MONEY
Manuel Pinero	61	62	58	73	254	1,900
Philip Walton	61	61	61	71	254	1,900
Andrew Murray	60	58	63	74	255	1,616.67
De Wet Basson	61	59	64	71	255	1,615.67
Marc Farry	63	59	62	71	255	1,616.67
Mats Lanner	62	58	63	73	256	1,500
Steven Bottomley	60	61	58	78	257	1,450
David R. Jones	60	61	61	76	258	1,325
Gavin Levenson	60	61	63	74	258	1,325
Andrew Sherborne	63	60	63	72	258	1,325
Peter Hedblom	62	61	64	71	258	1,325
Mike Miller	60	63	63	74	260	750
Pierre Fulke	61	57	63	80	261	748
Claude Grenier	58	63	65	76	262	745
Jiri Janda	61	61	65	75	262	745
Mike McLean	61	58	63	81	263	742
Thomas Gogele	65	58	WD			740

Volvo Masters

Valderrama, Sotogrande, Spain
Par 35-36—71; 6,819 yards

October 27-30
purse, £750,000

	SCORES				TOTAL	MONEY
Bernhard Langer	71	62	73	70	276	£125,000
Vijay Singh	71	70	70	66	277	65,175
Seve Ballesteros	69	67	68	73	277	65,175
Miguel Angel Jimenez	65	70	72	71	278	34,800
Colin Montgomerie	69	65	72	72	278	34,800
Mark McNulty	70	69	69	71	279	23,800
Costantino Rocca	69	72	67	73	281	23,000
Ian Woosnam	68	69	73	72	282	18,250
Jose Maria Olazabal	70	70	71	71	282	18,250
Frank Nobilo	70	69	73	71	283	15,500
Joakim Haeggman	71	71	69	73	284	13,850
David Gilford	70	74	69	71	284	13,850
Sven Struver	71	71	70	73	285	11,520
Mike Harwood	70	70	71	74	285	11,520
Howard Clark	71	71	70	73	285	11,520
Nick Faldo	74	70	71	70	285	11,520
Per-Ulrik Johansson	72	75	64	74	285	11,520
Robert Allenby	69	72	75	70	286	9,775
Paul Curry	70	68	73	75	286	9,775
Darren Clarke	74	68	71	73	286	9,775
Miguel Angel Martin	72	73	67	74	286	9,775
Paul Eales	69	72	72	74	287	8,900
Sandy Lyle	71	72	69	75	287	8,900
Mark Roe	74	73	71	69	287	8,900
Mark James	75	71	72	70	288	8,275
Sam Torrance	65	73	72	78	288	8,275
Jesper Parnevik	73	67	73	76	289	7,650
Tony Johnstone	67	71	74	77	289	7,650
Peter Mitchell	65	74	74	76	289	7,650
Peter Hedblom	71	70	75	74	290	7,200
Anders Forsbrand	73	66	75	77	291	6,816.67
Klas Eriksson	75	69	74	73	291	6,816.67
Mark Davis	74	68	73	76	291	6,316.67

		SCORES			TOTAL	MONEY
Pierre Fulke	68	71	79	74	292	6,425
Phillip Price	71	76	72	73	292	6,425
Greg Turner	75	70	69	79	293	6,050
Gary Orr	75	69	75	74	293	6,050
Paul Way	70	73	77	73	293	6,050
Barry Lane	72	71	71	80	294	5,750
Rodger Davis	71	74	75	75	295	5,525
Jonathan Lomas	71	73	79	72	295	5,525
Eduardo Romero	75	73	74	74	296	5,225
Paul McGinley	73	78	70	75	296	5,225
Carl Mason	73	74	76	74	297	4,850
Andrew Coltart	71	76	74	76	297	4,850
Russell Claydon	72	70	78	77	297	4,850
Gordon Brand, Jr.	74	69	79	76	298	4,550
Philip Walton	75	71	77	76	299	4,400
Ronan Rafferty	71	75	73	81	300	4,250
Jose Rivero	79	75	78	69	301	4,100
Gabriel Hjertstedt	77	75	76	74	302	3,950
Retief Goosen	79	74	75	76	304	3,800
Lee Westwood	76	76	76	78	306	3,650
Wayne Westner	84	73	73	82	312	3,500

Johnnie Walker World Championship

Tryall Golf & Beach Resort, Montego Bay, Jamaica
Par 35-36—71; 6,760 yards

December 15-18
purse, $2,500,000

		SCORES			TOTAL	MONEY
Ernie Els	64	64	71	69	268	$550,000
Mark McCumber	67	70	70	67	274	250,000
Nick Faldo	67	67	73	67	274	250,000
Brad Faxon	72	70	69	64	275	106,666.67
Paul Azinger	71	74	62	68	275	106,666.67
Ian Woosnam	70	68	69	68	275	106,666.67
David Gilford	71	64	73	68	276	80,000
Jeff Maggert	68	72	70	66	276	80,000
Bernhard Langer	70	70	68	68	276	80,000
Robert Allenby	69	71	69	68	277	68,000
Colin Montgomerie	67	74	67	69	277	68,000
Nick Price	71	67	68	72	278	63,500
Tom Lehman	69	65	75	69	278	63,500
David Frost	70	71	74	68	283	61,500
Seve Ballesteros	73	72	65	73	283	61,500
Tom Kite	71	73	68	73	285	60,000
John Huston	73	73	70	70	286	57,500
Craig Parry	72	71	69	74	286	57,500
Loren Roberts	68	71	76	71	286	57,500
Fred Couples	73	65	75	73	286	57,500
Larry Mize	70	78	74	69	291	55,000
Vijay Singh	75	75	73	69	292	54,000
Carl Mason	70	74	76	74	294	52,500
Fuzzy Zoeller	73	74	74	73	294	52,500

Asia/Japan Tours

Manila Southwoods Philippine Open

Manila Southwoods Golf Club, Manila, Philippines
Par 36-36—72; 7,044 yards

February 17-20
purse, $250,000

		SCORES			TOTAL	MONEY
Carlos Franco	72	69	68	71	280	$41,650
Sang Ho Choi	70	68	68	74	280	27,775
(Franco defeated Choi on first extra hole.)						
Colin Montgomerie	72	72	70	70	284	15,650
Andre Cruse	74	73	73	66	286	12,500
Aaron Meeks	76	68	72	72	288	8,950
Todd Hamilton	71	71	73	73	288	8,950
Mike Cunning	67	71	77	73	288	8,950
Prayad Marksaeng	75	73	73	68	289	5,170
Stephen Talbot	73	69	75	72	289	5,170
Marty Schiene	72	71	73	73	289	5,170
Raul Fretes	72	72	70	75	289	5,170
Jim Rutledge	69	70	74	76	289	5,170
Ken Mattiace	73	72	72	73	290	3,933.33
Craig Kanada	73	73	68	76	290	3,933.33
Frankie Minoza	71	71	69	79	290	3,933.33
Robert Meyer	72	72	77	70	291	3,179.17
Rob Moss	69	73	79	70	291	3,179.17
Anders Forsbrand	71	77	72	71	291	3,179.17
Hsieh Chin Sheng	68	77	72	74	291	3,179.17
Howie Johnson	70	74	73	74	291	3,179.17
Michael Blewett	67	72	74	78	291	3,179.17
Pete Izumikawa	77	72	75	68	292	2,569.44
Tom Brodersen	73	75	73	71	292	2,569.44
Bob Lendzion	74	75	69	74	292	2,569.44
Nico Van Rensburg	72	75	71	74	292	2,569.44
Lee Porter	71	72	75	74	292	2,569.44
Jerry Smith	73	74	70	75	292	2,569.44
Wen Ter Lu	72	70	75	75	292	2,569.44
Gerry Norquist	70	72	73	77	292	2,569.44
Chul Sang Cho	67	73	73	79	292	2,569.44

Kent Hong Kong Open

Royal Hong Kong Golf Club, Fanling, Hong Kong
Par 36-35—71; 6,552 yards

February 24-27
purse, $250,000

		SCORES			TOTAL	MONEY
David Frost	69	69	69	67	274	$41,650
Craig McClellan	70	67	70	67	274	27,775
(Frost defeated McClellan on first extra hole.)						
Barry Lane	68	70	67	70	275	14,075
Corey Pavin	68	70	70	67	275	14,075
Steve Flesch	67	69	70	70	276	9,675
Don Walsworth	70	72	66	68	276	9,675
Carlos Larrain	71	69	69	68	277	6,450

	SCORES				TOTAL	MONEY
Mike Tschetter	67	70	72	68	277	6,450
Gary Webb	66	71	69	71	277	6,450
Antonio Barcellos	66	73	71	68	278	4,415
Carlos Franco	69	74	69	66	278	4,415
Todd Hamilton	69	70	70	69	278	4,415
Tom Pernice	68	68	70	72	278	4,415
Jerry Smith	70	71	67	70	278	4,415
David Berganio	70	69	71	69	279	3,612.50
Jeff Maggert	66	71	71	71	279	3,612.50
Chen Tze Chung	66	68	75	71	280	2,952.77
Andre Cruse	68	72	71	69	280	2,952.77
Anders Forsbrand	69	74	71	66	280	2,952.77
Scott Frisch	74	69	69	68	280	2,952.77
Rick Gibson	70	72	69	69	280	2,952.77
Ralph Howe	69	69	69	73	280	2,952.77
Frankie Minoza	68	71	69	72	280	2,952.77
Lee Porter	69	70	71	70	280	2,952.77
Jean Van de Velde	67	74	69	70	280	2,952.77
Raul Fretes	71	66	69	75	281	2,537.50
Jeff Schmid	69	69	73	70	281	2,537.50
*Jun Chen	68	70	71	73	282	
Brandt Jobe	73	70	70	69	282	2,295.83
Philip Jonas	65	74	73	70	282	2,295.83
Pedro Martinez	71	70	72	69	282	2,295.83
Marimuthu Ramayah	67	73	70	72	282	2,295.83
Nobuhito Sato	69	71	70	72	282	2,295.83
Brian Watts	67	71	73	71	282	2,295.83

Classic Indian Open

Royal Calcutta Golf Club, Calcutta, India
Par 36-36—72; 7,102 yards

March 4-7
purse, $200,000

	SCORES				TOTAL	MONEY
Emlyn Aubrey	69	70	76	70	285	$33,320
Brandt Jobe	72	73	71	70	286	22,220
Lee Porter	72	76	70	69	287	9,500
Carlos Franco	71	72	74	70	287	9,500
Scott Frisch	72	76	69	70	287	9,500
Pedro Martinez	75	72	69	71	287	9,500
Rick Todd	76	74	70	69	289	4,870
Mike Tschetter	71	74	74	70	289	4,870
Gaurav Ghei	73	73	73	70	289	4,870
Steve Flesch	71	72	74	72	289	4,870
Kyi Hla Han	71	73	78	68	290	3,720
Young Il Kim	69	73	78	71	291	3,400
Kevin Baker	72	73	72	74	291	3,400
Tom Brodersen	74	75	72	71	292	2,895
Nobuhito Sato	71	73	76	72	292	2,895
Jim Rutledge	73	72	73	74	292	2,895
Mike Cunning	71	73	73	75	292	2,895
Dustin Phillips	77	73	74	69	293	2,325
Carlos Larrain	73	77	72	71	293	2,325
Marty Schiene	73	73	75	72	293	2,325
Ramnath	69	77	75	72	293	2,325
Raul Fretes	71	75	74	73	293	2,325
Stewart Ginn	70	73	77	73	293	2,325
Robert Meyer	71	73	75	74	293	2,325

	SCORES				TOTAL	MONEY
Todd Hamilton	73	71	73	76	293	2,325
Ralph Howe III	72	78	76	68	294	1,913.33
Feroz Ali	72	78	72	72	294	1,913.33
Ken Mattiace	73	75	72	74	294	1,913.33
Frank Edmonds	74	75	71	74	294	1,913.33
Max Stevens	75	74	70	75	294	1,913.33
Philip Jonas	76	72	69	77	294	1,913.33

Thai International Thailand Open

Tanah City Country Club, Bangkok, Thailand
Par 36-36—72; 6,907 yards

March 10-13
purse, $300,000

	SCORES				TOTAL	MONEY
Brandt Jobe	65	72	69	70	276	$49,980
Lee Porter	72	69	71	68	280	33,330
John Gould	68	68	76	71	283	15,500
Emlyn Aubrey	68	73	71	71	283	15,500
Carlos Franco	74	71	66	72	283	15,500
Don Walsworth	73	69	73	69	284	9,750
Steve Flesch	69	71	72	72	284	9,750
Jim Rutledge	72	74	70	69	285	6,204
Jerry Smith	71	73	71	70	285	6,204
Per Haugsrud	71	75	69	70	285	6,204
Gerry Norquist	69	70	74	72	285	6,204
Chris Gray	69	73	69	74	285	6,204
Steven Scahill	69	70	78	69	286	4,370
Mike Tschetter	71	76	70	69	286	4,370
Rob Moss	72	72	70	72	286	4,370
Eric Meeks	75	69	69	73	286	4,370
Pedro Martinez	73	72	68	73	286	4,370
Nico Van Rensburg	69	70	73	74	286	4,370
Ray Stewart	77	70	69	71	287	3,562.50
Kazunari Matsunaga	73	71	71	72	287	3,562.50
Philip Jonas	72	73	69	73	287	3,562.50
Tom Pernice	73	71	69	74	287	3,562.50
Gary Webb	73	70	73	72	288	3,174
Kyi Hla Han	72	74	70	72	288	3,174
Sang Ho Choi	68	74	73	73	288	3,174
Aaron Meeks	72	71	72	73	288	3,174
Boonchu Ruengkit	68	70	76	74	288	3,174
Dustin Phillips	73	73	70	73	289	2,820
John Clifford	70	73	72	74	289	2,820
Lin Keng Chi	71	71	73	74	289	2,820

Benson & Hedges Malaysian Open

Royal Selangor Country Club, Kuala Lumpur, Malaysia
Par 36-36—72; 6,941 yards

March 17-20
purse, $250,000

	SCORES				TOTAL	MONEY
Joakim Haeggman	71	67	72	69	279	$41,650
Frank Nobilo	72	70	69	68	279	21,712.50
Periasamy Gunasagaran	68	69	72	70	279	21,712.50

(Haeggman defeated Nobilo and Gunasagaran on eighth extra hole.)

	SCORES				TOTAL	MONEY
Bob Mattiace	70	69	72	69	280	11,550
Jim Rutledge	72	69	69	70	280	11,550
Boonchu Ruengkit	67	74	70	70	281	7,025
Mike Tschetter	71	67	71	72	281	7,025
Carlos Espinosa	67	73	69	72	281	7,025
Carlos Franco	70	65	73	73	281	7,025
Robert Meyer	71	67	74	70	282	4,825
Mike Cunning	70	69	70	73	282	4,825
Philip Jonas	68	72	70	73	283	4,141.67
Brandt Jobe	70	70	70	73	283	4,141.67
Nico Van Rensburg	73	67	68	75	283	4,141.67
Mark McNulty	73	72	71	68	284	3,443.75
Craig McClellan	66	71	75	72	284	3,443.75
Emlyn Aubrey	71	70	69	74	284	3,443.75
Michael Campbell	70	69	71	70	284	3,443.75
Johan Tumba	74	69	71	71	285	2,930
Jerry Anderson	72	71	71	71	285	2,930
Gerry Norquist	72	71	69	73	285	2,930
Antonio Barcellos	72	69	70	74	285	2,930
Marimuthu Ramayah	71	68	72	74	285	2,930
Rick Todd	69	71	75	71	286	2,575
Eric Meeks	68	76	71	71	286	2,575
Tom Brodersen	73	69	72	72	286	2,575
Lin Keng Chi	71	70	71	74	286	2,575
Per Haugsrud	73	67	69	77	286	2,575
Jack Kay, Jr.	73	72	71	71	287	2,210
Wayne Westner	73	69	72	73	287	2,210
Young Il Kim	70	72	71	74	287	2,210
Kyi Hla Han	71	68	72	76	287	2,210
Stewart Ginn	73	70	67	77	287	2,210

Sampoerna Indonesian Open

Damai Indah Golf & Country Club, Jakarta, Indonesia
Par 36-36—72; 7,186 yards

March 24-27
purse, $250,000

	SCORES				TOTAL	MONEY
Frank Nobilo	69	67	68	69	273	$41,650
Jerry Smith	68	72	70	66	276	27,775
Philip Jonas	68	71	70	68	277	15,650
Gary Webb	69	69	67	75	280	12,500
Robert Meyer	69	72	66	74	281	10,600
Jim Rutledge	73	69	73	67	282	8,125
Sam Torrance	67	72	70	73	282	8,125
Robert Allenby	70	72	67	74	283	6,925
Scott Frisch	70	69	71	73	283	6,925
Craig Reed	73	72	75	64	284	4,825
Steven Scahill	71	72	72	69	284	4,825
Michael Clayton	71	73	72	69	285	3,829.17
Nico Van Rensburg	72	74	68	71	285	3,829.17
Joakim Haeggman	71	70	70	74	285	3,829.17
Steve Flesch	68	74	70	73	285	3,829.17
Brandt Jobe	69	72	73	71	285	3,829.17
Kevin Wentworth	71	70	73	71	285	3,829.17
Marty Schiene	71	74	72	70	287	3,226
Ray Stewart	70	72	76	70	288	2,788.89
Kazunari Matsunaga	70	72	73	73	288	2,788.89
Rodrigo Cuello	70	74	72	72	288	2,788.89

	SCORES				TOTAL	MONEY
Daniel Chopra	70	76	68	74	288	2,788.89
David Podlich	69	71	72	76	288	2,788.89
Taichi Teshima	67	74	75	72	288	2,788.89
Emlyn Aubrey	74	70	70	74	288	2,788.89
John Kernohan	72	70	75	71	288	2,788.89
Carlos Larrain	74	72	73	69	288	2,788.89
John Clifford	76	66	76	71	289	2,068.18
Robert Farley	72	74	74	69	289	2,068.18
Matthew King	72	72	71	74	289	2,068.18
Jeev Milkha Singh	69	75	73	72	289	2,068.18
Norikazu Kawakami	69	76	71	73	289	2,068.18
Carlos Franco	69	73	75	72	289	2,068.18
Lin Keng Chi	72	70	75	72	289	2,068.18
Mike Cunning	71	74	70	74	289	2,068.18
Bob Mattiace	69	72	75	73	289	2,068.18
Scott Taylor	72	73	73	71	289	2,068.18
Brian Wilson	68	78	73	70	289	2,068.18

Sabah Masters

Sabah Golf & Country Club, Kota Kinabalu, Malaysia
Par 36-36—72; 6,968 yards

March 31-April 3
purse, $260,000

	SCORES				TOTAL	MONEY
Craig McClellan	75	71	71	67	284	$43,316
Kyi Hla Han	73	70	69	72	284	28,886
(McClellan defeated Han at second extra hole.)						
Rafael Ponce	72	73	69	71	285	14,638
Carlos Franco	72	74	66	73	285	14,638
Carlos Espinosa	74	71	71	70	286	10,062
Rob Moss	71	70	73	72	286	10,062
Mike Cunning	74	72	67	74	287	7,150
Don Walsworth	71	72	72	72	287	7,150
Stephen Talbot	74	69	75	70	288	5,512
Pedro Martinez	72	69	73	74	288	5,512
Jim Rutledge	74	71	74	70	289	4,326.40
Periasamy Gunasagaran	72	70	76	71	289	4,326.40
Nico Van Rensburg	76	70	71	72	289	4,326.40
Lee Porter	74	73	70	72	289	4,326.40
Jerry Smith	72	72	68	77	289	4,326.40
Per Haugsrud	74	72	71	73	290	3,484
Bob Mattiace	75	71	74	70	290	3,484
Peter Teravainen	72	70	73	75	290	3,484
Robert Farley	70	72	76	73	291	3,087.50
Philip Jonas	73	74	71	73	291	3,087.50
Gerry Norquist	75	71	74	71	291	3,087.50
Eric Johnson	70	73	75	73	291	3,087.50
Pete Izumikawa	75	72	74	71	292	2,888
Antonio Barcellos	74	76	70	73	293	2,639
Ray Stewart	73	71	71	78	293	2,639
Sangsui Net	75	73	70	75	293	2,639
Walter Hall	70	75	73	75	293	2,639
Eric Meeks	73	73	73	74	293	2,639
Marty Schiene	71	76	71	75	293	2,639
John Clifford	75	72	75	72	294	2,188.33
Max Stevens	74	75	71	74	294	2,188.33
Andre Cruse	77	73	72	72	294	2,188.33
Robert Pactolerin	71	77	73	73	294	2,188.33

	SCORES				TOTAL	MONEY
Tom Pernice	75	71	76	72	294	2,188.33
Rick Todd	68	78	72	76	294	2,188.33

Chin Fong Republic of China Open

Taiwan Golf & Country Club, Taipei, Taiwan
Par 36-36—72; 7,161 yards

April 7-10
purse, $300,000

	SCORES				TOTAL	MONEY
*Hong Chia Yuh	70	65	73	68	276	
Boonchu Ruengkit	70	70	69	68	277	$49,980
Chung Chung Hsin	73	68	69	71	281	22,370
Hsieh Chin Sheng	68	69	70	74	281	22,370
Kevin Wentworth	72	71	70	68	281	22,370
Lee Porter	73	74	65	70	282	12,720
*Yeh Wei Tse	73	72	67	71	283	
Raul Fretes	72	68	70	73	283	8,460
Tsao Chien Teng	69	70	70	74	283	8,460
Rick Todd	69	73	71	70	283	8,460
Mike Tschetter	71	69	72	71	283	8,460
Hsieh Yu Shu	72	69	72	70	283	8,460
Kawika Cotner	72	74	68	70	284	5,100
Chen Tsang Ter	69	72	72	71	284	5,100
Wang Ter Chang	69	71	72	73	285	4,460
Jim Rutledge	70	74	74	67	285	4,460
Pedro Martinez	74	68	75	68	285	4,460
Lu Chien Soon	72	70	71	73	286	3,685
Steve Flesch	70	71	71	74	286	3,685
Daniel Bateman	71	70	72	73	286	3,685
Lin Keng Chi	71	70	72	73	286	3,685
Brandt Jobe	71	71	72	72	286	3,685
Li Wen Sheng	71	70	74	71	286	3,685
Antonio Barcellos	70	74	69	74	287	3,210
Rafael Ponce	71	74	73	69	287	3,210
Scott Frisch	72	69	74	72	287	3,210
Yeh Chang Ting	67	72	78	70	287	3,210
Brian Wilson	67	78	67	76	288	2,737.50
Carlos Espinosa	75	71	70	72	288	2,737.50
Yu Chin Han	72	75	71	70	288	2,737.50
Darryl Donovan	72	70	72	74	288	2,737.50
Lin Chie Hsiang	71	72	72	73	288	2,737.50
Rodrigo Cuello	71	73	72	72	288	2,737.50
Chen Tse Ming	73	69	73	73	288	2,737.50
Jerry Smith	70	70	78	70	288	2,737.50

Maekyung Korean Open

Nam Seoul Country Club, Seoul, Korea
Par 36-36—72; 6,901 yards

April 14-17
purse, $350,000

	SCORES				TOTAL	MONEY
Jong Duck Kim	74	72	70	68	284	$58,310
Jim Rutledge	75	74	69	66	284	30,397.50
Mike Tschetter	70	73	73	68	284	30,397.50
(Kim defeated Rutledge and Tschetter at second extra hole.)						
Kwang Soo Choi	72	73	69	71	285	14,863.33

	SCORES				TOTAL	MONEY
Hsieh Yu Shu	70	66	74	75	285	14,863.33
Marty Schiene	72	73	71	69	285	14,863.33
Emlyn Aubrey	71	73	71	72	287	8,522.50
Wan Tae Kim	69	72	72	74	287	8,522.50
Myung Ha Lee	72	73	71	71	287	8,522.50
Carlos Larrain	75	72	69	71	287	8,522.50
Sang Ho Choi	72	75	71	70	288	6,136.66
Lee Porter	75	71	72	70	288	6,136.66
Oh Chul Kwon	73	70	71	74	288	6,136.66
Yoon Soo Choi	71	76	72	70	289	5,066.25
Per Haugsrud	79	71	69	70	289	5,066.25
Pete Izumikawa	71	72	76	70	289	5,066.25
Don Walsworth	77	71	72	69	289	5,066.25
Young Kun Han	69	75	70	76	290	4,287.50
Gary Webb	78	71	70	71	290	4,287.50
Rafael Ponce	72	73	75	70	290	4,287.50
Stephen Leaney	73	71	70	76	290	4,287.50
Tom Pernice	77	72	68	74	291	3,930
Philip Jonas	75	71	73	72	291	3,930
Brian Wilson	74	72	76	70	292	3,657.50
Antonio Barcellos	75	74	69	74	292	3,657.50
Carlos Espinosa	74	74	73	71	292	3,657.50
Aaron Meeks	75	72	72	73	292	3,657.50
Stewart Ginn	72	76	74	71	293	3,290
Max Stevens	74	76	71	72	293	3,290
Matthew King	76	72	71	74	293	3,290

Token Corporation Cup

Kedoin Country Club, Kagoshima
Par 36-36—72; 7,072 yards
(Fourth round cancelled — heavy rains.)

March 10-13
purse, ¥75,000,000

	SCORES			TOTAL	MONEY
Craig Warren	70	68	70	208	¥13,500,000
Masashi Ozaki	74	69	66	209	7,500,000
Brian Jones	70	69	71	210	5,100,000
Yoshitaka Yamamoto	69	74	68	211	3,100,000
Masahiro Kuramoto	70	72	69	211	3,100,000
Nobuo Serizawa	70	71	70	211	3,100,000
Harumitsu Hamano	73	71	68	212	2,062,000
Ken Kusumoto	73	69	70	212	2,062,000
Toshiaki Odate	72	70	70	212	2,062,000
Hisayuki Sasaki	71	68	73	212	2,062,000
Tomohiro Maruyama	75	72	66	213	1,278,000
Peter McWhinney	72	74	67	213	1,278,000
Chen Tze Chung	72	73	68	213	1,278,000
Daisuke Serizawa	69	75	69	213	1,278,000
Peter Senior	72	69	72	213	1,278,000
Shinji Ikeuchi	73	72	69	214	877,000
Eiichi Itai	75	70	69	214	877,000
Hajime Meshiai	73	70	71	214	877,000
Kazuhiro Takami	70	71	73	214	877,000
Yoshinori Ichioka	73	73	69	215	646,000
Toru Nakamura	74	71	70	215	646,000
Katsunari Takahashi	75	70	70	215	646,000
Akiyoshi Omachi	74	70	71	215	646,000
Yoshiyuki Ohmori	74	70	71	215	646,000

	SCORES			TOTAL	MONEY
Toshinori Horiki	72	72	71	215	646,000
Ryoken Kawagishi	74	70	71	215	646,000
Teruo Sugihara	75	68	72	215	646,000
Satoshi Higashi	73	69	73	215	646,000
Hirofumi Miyase	74	68	73	215	646,000
Takaaki Fukuzawa	72	75	69	216	477,000
Yoshinori Kaneko	72	75	69	216	477,000
Chen Tze Ming	76	70	70	216	477,000
Isao Aoki	74	71	71	216	477,000
Shigeru Kawamata	74	71	71	216	477,000
Mitsuo Harada	72	73	71	216	477,000
Todd Hamilton	76	69	71	216	477,000
Ikuo Shirahama	70	74	72	216	477,000
Hisashi Nakase	74	70	72	216	477,000
Hsieh Chin Sheng	73	71	72	216	477,000
Hideki Kase	74	69	73	216	477,000
Richard Backwell	74	69	73	216	477,000
Shigeki Maruyama	70	72	74	216	477,000

Daido Drinco Shizuoka Open

Shizuoka Country Club, Hamaoka Course, Shizuoka
Par 36-36—72; 6,902 yards

March 17-20
purse, ¥100,000,000

	SCORES				TOTAL	MONEY
Tsuneyuki Nakajima	71	71	69	69	280	¥18,000,000
Toru Nakamura	73	73	67	67	280	10,000,000
(Nakajima defeated Nakamura on first extra hole.)						
Peter Senior	71	72	69	69	281	6,800,000
Hiroshi Ueda	76	71	71	64	282	4,400,000
Hideki Kase	70	74	66	72	282	4,400,000
David Ishii	71	70	69	73	283	3,600,000
Peter McWhinney	77	68	71	68	284	2,750,000
Chen Tze Ming	74	74	68	68	284	2,750,000
Masanobu Kimura	74	68	74	68	284	2,750,000
Eiichi Itai	73	70	68	73	284	2,750,000
Nobuo Serizawa	73	69	73	70	285	2,000,000
Todd Hamilton	71	74	73	68	286	1,451,000
Tomohiro Maruyama	77	68	72	69	286	1,451,000
Brian Watts	73	70	74	69	286	1,451,000
Hisayuki Sasaki	72	70	74	70	286	1,451,000
Kiyoshi Murota	72	70	74	70	286	1,451,000
Masayuki Kawamura	75	71	70	70	286	1,451,000
Yoshinori Mizumaki	72	68	76	70	286	1,451,000
Noboru Sugai	75	71	76	65	287	915,000
Brian Jones	77	72	70	68	287	915,000
Wayne Smith	72	76	71	68	287	915,000
Teruo Sugihara	75	73	70	69	287	915,000
Hirofumi Miyase	74	75	69	69	287	915,000
Akiyoshi Omachi	70	73	74	70	287	915,000
Craig Warren	76	70	70	71	287	915,000
Yutaka Hagawa	74	70	72	71	287	915,000
Yurio Akitomi	74	74	70	70	288	780,000
Hsieh Chin Sheng	74	72	71	71	288	780,000
Eiji Mizoguchi	74	73	70	71	288	780,000
Takaaki Fukuzawa	69	73	80	67	289	685,000
Shoichi Kuwahara	76	73	72	68	289	685,000
Anthony Gilligan	74	72	74	69	289	685,000

	SCORES				TOTAL	MONEY
Yoshimi Niizeki	72	76	71	70	289	685,000
Hsieh Min Nan	75	71	71	72	289	685,000
Shinji Ikeuchi	73	73	68	75	289	685,000
Katsuyoshi Tomori	74	69	71	75	289	685,000

United Airlines KSB Sentonaikai Open

Kinojyo Golf Club, Okayama
Par 36-36—72; 6,948 yards

March 24-27
purse, ¥70,000,000

	SCORES				TOTAL	MONEY
Kazuhiro Takami	70	71	67	73	281	¥12,600,000
Yoshinori Kaneko	66	74	74	73	287	7,000,000
Kiyoshi Maita	67	76	76	69	288	3,360,000
Toshimitsu Izawa	77	70	70	71	288	3,360,000
Zaw Moe	70	74	73	71	288	3,360,000
Tsuneyuki Nakajima	72	70	73	73	288	3,360,000
Peter McWhinney	77	71	71	71	290	2,030,000
Craig Warren	74	74	70	72	290	2,030,000
Masanobu Kimura	70	75	72	73	290	2,030,000
Katsuyoshi Tomori	71	72	79	69	291	1,368,000
Jin Han Lim	71	76	74	70	291	1,368,000
Motomasa Aoki	73	74	72	72	291	1,368,000
Shigenori Mori	73	72	72	74	291	1,368,000
Brian Watts	71	73	77	71	292	1,050,000
Haruto Yamamoto	72	76	72	72	292	1,050,000
Stewart Ginn	75	77	74	67	293	795,000
Todd Hamilton	71	79	75	68	293	795,000
Seiji Ebihara	75	74	74	70	293	795,000
Shinji Ikeharu	73	73	76	71	293	795,000
Hisashi Nakase	73	78	69	73	293	795,000
Teruo Sugihara	74	76	74	70	294	658,000
Hsieh Chin Sheng	71	81	70	72	294	658,000
Kiyoshi Murota	70	80	72	73	295	616,000
Yoshitaka Yamamoto	72	76	77	71	296	581,000
Tetsu Nishikawa	73	77	75	71	296	581,000
Ken Mattiace	78	74	73	71	296	581,000
Toru Taniguchi	76	72	74	74	296	581,000
Shinji Kuraoka	76	75	76	70	297	532,000
Kinpachi Yoshimura	80	71	76	70	297	532,000
Chen Tze Ming	72	78	73	74	297	532,000

Descente Classic Munsingwear Cup

Century Miki Golf Club, Hyogo
Par 36-36—72; 6,958 yards

March 31-April 3
purse, ¥80,000,000

	SCORES				TOTAL	MONEY
Brian Watts	67	71	69	73	280	¥14,400,000
Hideki Kase	70	70	71	72	283	5,120,000
Frankie Minoza	70	70	71	72	283	5,120,000
Hisao Inoue	71	71	68	73	283	5,120,000
Tsukasa Watanabe	70	68	72	73	283	5,120,000
Samson Gimson	71	70	74	69	284	2,460,000
Teruo Sugihara	70	72	71	71	284	2,460,000
Tsuneyuki Nakajima	69	71	72	72	284	2,460,000

	SCORES				TOTAL	MONEY
Takaaki Fukuzawa	75	64	72	73	284	2,460,000
Katsuyoshi Tomori	72	69	71	73	285	1,564,000
Hirofumi Miyase	72	71	69	73	285	1,564,000
Tsuyoshi Yoneyama	71	66	73	75	285	1,564,000
Roger Mackay	70	70	69	76	285	1,564,000
Shoichi Kuwahara	72	71	71	72	286	992,000
Rick Gibson	74	70	69	73	286	992,000
Tomohiro Maruyama	69	69	74	74	286	992,000
Anthony Gilligan	73	68	71	74	286	992,000
Hsieh Chin Sheng	74	70	67	75	286	992,000
Teruo Nakamura	71	68	72	75	286	992,000
Kinpachi Yoshimura	70	68	73	75	286	992,000
Hisayuki Sasaki	72	69	75	71	287	724,000
Nobumitsu Yuhara	69	75	72	71	287	724,000
Toyotake Nakao	70	73	69	75	287	724,000
Saburo Fujiki	69	72	71	75	287	724,000
Shoichi Yamamoto	71	74	74	69	288	593,000
Masanobu Kimura	72	70	75	71	288	593,000
Toru Taniguchi	70	74	73	71	288	593,000
Seiki Okuda	72	72	73	71	288	593,000
Eduardo Herrera	71	74	71	72	288	593,000
Toshiaki Sudo	71	74	71	72	288	593,000
Hiroya Kamide	74	71	71	72	288	593,000
Kazuhiro Takami	70	72	73	73	288	593,000
Nobuo Serizawa	70	72	73	73	288	593,000
Yoshinori Mizumaki	72	71	72	73	288	593,000
Satoshi Higashi	76	69	68	75	288	593,000

Pocari Sweat Open

Hiroshima Hakuryuko Country Club, Hiroshima
Par 35-36—71; 6,780 yards
(First round cancelled — heavy rains.)

April 7-10
purse, ¥60,000,000

	SCORES			TOTAL	MONEY
Yoshinori Mizumaki	72	65	66	203	¥10,800,000
Tsukasa Watanabe	69	65	70	204	6,000,000
Masayuki Kawamura	69	70	67	206	3,480,000
Richard Backwell	70	69	67	206	3,480,000
Shigeki Maruyama	68	69	70	207	2,400,000
Teruo Sugihara	71	68	69	208	1,940,000
Hideto Shigenobu	67	71	70	208	1,940,000
Craig McClellan	68	68	72	208	1,940,000
Masanobu Kimura	69	71	69	209	1,311,000
Toshikazu Sugihara	69	71	69	209	1,311,000
Hideyuki Sato	70	69	70	209	1,311,000
Seiki Okuda	67	70	72	209	1,311,000
Mitsuo Harada	71	74	65	210	936,000
Hisashi Nakase	73	71	66	210	936,000
Shigeo Kinoshita	71	68	71	210	936,000
Takaaki Fukuzawa	74	70	67	211	702,000
Kiyoshi Murota	72	71	68	211	702,000
Hiroshi Goda	72	71	68	211	702,000
Brian Jones	72	68	71	211	702,000
Yoshinori Kaneko	71	71	70	212	524,000
Katsuyoshi Tomori	69	73	70	212	524,000
Kiyoshi Maita	69	73	70	212	524,000

	SCORES			TOTAL	MONEY
Shoichi Yamamoto	69	73	70	212	524,000
Tadami Ueno	71	70	71	212	524,000
Mitsutaka Kusakabe	72	69	71	212	524,000
Satoshi Higashi	70	70	72	212	524,000
Yoshinori Ichioka	70	70	72	212	524,000
Shoichi Kuwahara	68	68	76	212	524,000
Taisei Inagaki	74	71	68	213	417,000
Hiromichi Namiki	71	73	69	213	417,000
Tomohiro Maruyama	70	73	70	213	417,000
Kinpachi Yoshimura	72	71	70	213	417,000
Ryoken Kawagishi	71	70	72	213	417,000
Wayne Smith	70	71	72	213	417,000
Stewart Ginn	70	71	72	213	417,000
Takayoshi Nishikawa	72	67	74	213	417,000

Tsuruya Open

Sports Shinko Country Club, Yamanohara
Par 36-36—72; 6,842 yards

April 14-17
purse, ¥100,000,000

	SCORES				TOTAL	MONEY
Tsuneyuki Nakajima	68	70	70	71	279	¥18,000,000
Tsutomu Higa	71	68	73	67	279	10,000,000
(Nakajima defeated Higa on second extra hole.)						
Tsukasa Watanabe	70	72	69	69	280	5,800,000
Shigeki Maruyama	69	73	67	71	280	5,800,000
Akiyoshi Omachi	74	71	71	65	281	3,600,000
Toshiaki Odate	73	72	68	68	281	3,600,000
Kiyoshi Murota	69	69	71	72	281	3,600,000
Naomichi Ozaki	74	71	67	70	282	2,450,000
Kazuhiro Takami	73	71	66	72	282	2,450,000
Akihito Yokoyama	73	70	67	72	282	2,450,000
Chen Tze Chung	72	70	67	73	282	2,450,000
Yeh Chang Ting	66	72	78	67	283	1,568,000
Hsieh Min Nan	66	77	70	70	283	1,568,000
Toru Suzuki	70	72	70	71	283	1,568,000
Chen Tze Ming	73	67	71	72	283	1,568,000
Kinpachi Yoshimura	71	72	67	73	283	1,568,000
David Ishii	68	74	73	69	284	980,000
Anthony Gilligan	70	71	74	69	284	980,000
Fumiaki Matsutaka	74	71	70	69	284	980,000
Ryoken Kawagishi	71	74	68	71	284	980,000
Katsunari Takahashi	67	75	70	72	284	980,000
Yasunobu Kuramoto	70	75	67	72	284	980,000
Peter Senior	71	69	71	73	284	980,000
Richard Backwell	69	69	72	74	284	980,000
Saburo Fujiki	71	69	70	74	284	980,000
Tsuyoshi Yoneyama	73	69	73	70	285	800,000
Hisayuki Sasaki	72	73	69	71	285	800,000
Masanobu Kimura	70	71	70	74	285	800,000
Seiji Ebihara	76	68	75	67	286	712,000
Harumitsu Hamano	72	71	73	70	286	712,000
Todd Hamilton	69	74	72	71	286	712,000
Hiroshi Goda	70	72	72	72	286	712,000
Brian Watts	71	71	70	74	286	712,000
Teruo Sugihara	72	70	70	74	286	712,000

Dunlop Open

Ibaragi Golf Club, Ibaragi
Par 36-36—72; 7,134 yards

April 21-24
purse, ¥100,000,000

	SCORES				TOTAL	MONEY
Masashi Ozaki	67	68	70	69	274	¥18,000,000
Hsieh Chin Sheng	72	67	69	67	275	10,000,000
Frankie Minoza	69	69	66	74	278	6,800,000
Rick Gibson	70	70	72	69	281	3,900,000
Stewart Ginn	74	71	65	71	281	3,900,000
Masanobu Kimura	68	71	70	72	281	3,900,000
Katsunari Takahashi	71	68	69	73	281	3,900,000
Katsuyoshi Tomori	70	74	70	68	282	2,450,000
Teruo Sugihara	70	75	68	69	282	2,450,000
Dominique Boulet	69	73	70	70	282	2,450,000
Peter Senior	69	69	73	71	282	2,450,000
Yoshinori Kaneko	71	74	68	70	283	1,840,000
David Ishii	69	71	74	70	284	1,560,000
Tsukasa Watanabe	69	70	73	72	284	1,560,000
Robert Allenby	73	71	67	73	284	1,560,000
Yoshinori Mizumaki	72	72	71	70	285	1,136,000
Bradley Hughes	72	72	71	70	285	1,136,000
Steve Flesch	72	74	69	70	285	1,136,000
Brandt Jobe	69	73	71	72	285	1,136,000
Satoshi Higashi	71	71	70	73	285	1,136,000
Yoshitaka Yamamoto	71	71	74	70	286	892,000
Michael Clayton	73	72	71	70	286	892,000
Mike Cunning	74	69	72	71	286	892,000
Bob Mattiace	73	69	71	73	286	892,000
Tsuneyuki Nakajima	69	72	71	74	286	892,000
Seiki Okuda	73	73	71	70	287	800,000
Craig McClellan	73	72	72	70	287	800,000
Shinji Ikeuchi	71	71	70	75	287	800,000
Ken Kusumoto	70	76	74	68	288	712,000
Graham Marsh	74	72	73	69	288	712,000
Jerry Smith	72	73	73	70	288	712,000
Masahiro Kuramoto	76	68	73	71	288	712,000
Steve Flesch	73	73	71	71	288	712,000
Todd Hamilton	71	74	71	72	288	712,000

Chunichi Crowns

Nagoya Golf Club, Aichi
Par 35-35—70; 6,473 yards

April 28-May 1
purse, ¥120,000,000

	SCORES				TOTAL	MONEY
Roger Mackay	64	67	67	71	269	¥21,600,000
Naomichi Ozaki	65	70	66	70	271	12,000,000
Teruo Sugihara	69	70	68	65	272	8,160,000
Rick Gibson	69	72	69	65	275	4,680,000
Tomohiro Maruyama	67	69	73	66	275	4,680,000
Daisuke Serizawa	73	66	69	67	275	4,680,000
Lee Janzen	70	71	66	68	275	4,680,000
Hiroshi Makino	71	71	68	67	277	2,940,000
Kikuo Arai	71	65	73	68	277	2,940,000
Scott Simpson	68	69	71	69	277	2,940,000
Seiki Okuda	68	68	70	71	277	2,940,000

	SCORES				TOTAL	MONEY
Chen Tze Chung	69	73	69	67	278	1,881,000
Hsieh Chin Sheng	70	70	70	68	278	1,881,000
Peter McWhinney	67	71	71	69	278	1,881,000
Frankie Minoza	71	65	71	71	278	1,881,000
Tsukasa Watanabe	69	66	71	72	278	1,881,000
Katsunari Takahashi	70	74	70	65	279	1,344,000
Peter Senior	65	72	74	68	279	1,344,000
Hideto Shigenobu	72	69	70	68	279	1,344,000
Masashi Ozaki	70	68	72	70	280	1,128,000
Masanobu Kimura	67	68	74	71	280	1,128,000
Seiji Ebihara	73	66	70	71	280	1,128,000
Isao Aoki	68	69	72	71	280	1,128,000
Noboru Sugai	74	67	75	65	281	924,000
Ikuo Shirahama	72	70	71	68	281	924,000
Satoshi Higashi	69	70	73	69	281	924,000
Masayuki Kawamura	73	67	71	70	281	924,000
Toru Suzuki	71	69	71	70	281	924,000
Tsuneyuki Nakajima	67	72	70	72	281	924,000
David Ishii	70	70	69	72	281	924,000
Ryoken Kawagishi	69	72	68	72	281	924,000
Hajime Meshiai	73	66	70	72	281	924,000
Brian Watts	72	67	69	73	281	924,000

Fuji Sankei Classic

Kawana Hotel Golf Club, Shizuoka
Par 36-35—71; 6,694 yards

May 5-8
purse, ¥120,000,000

	SCORES				TOTAL	MONEY
Kiyoshi Murota	69	70	73	72	284	¥21,600,000
Nobuo Serizawa	73	73	69	73	288	12,000,000
Shigeki Maruyama	73	77	70	69	289	6,240,000
Frankie Minoza	71	70	72	76	289	6,240,000
Toshiaki Odate	71	66	73	79	289	6,240,000
Todd Hamilton	71	72	77	70	290	3,880,000
Katsumi Nanjo	69	76	73	72	290	3,880,000
Kiyoshi Maita	75	72	70	73	290	3,880,000
Nobumitsu Yuhara	71	69	77	74	291	2,760,000
Hajime Meshiai	71	73	72	75	291	2,760,000
Daisuke Serizawa	73	70	71	77	291	2,760,000
Katsuyoshi Tomori	73	75	74	70	292	1,881,000
Seiichi Kanai	72	72	76	72	292	1,881,000
Eduardo Herrera	72	71	76	73	292	1,881,000
Tetsu Nishikawa	74	70	75	73	292	1,881,000
Satoshi Higashi	72	73	72	75	292	1,881,000
Yoshinori Kaneko	71	70	78	74	293	1,392,000
Hiroshi Makino	71	70	76	76	293	1,392,000
Harumitsu Hamano	75	72	75	72	294	1,176,000
Hideki Kase	74	75	70	75	294	1,176,000
Eiichi Itai	68	77	73	76	294	1,176,000
Toru Nakamura	74	72	71	77	294	1,176,000
Katsuji Hasegawa	80	70	74	71	295	984,000
Katsunari Takahashi	76	71	76	72	295	984,000
Masahiro Kuramoto	71	75	76	73	295	984,000
Shoichi Kuwahara	75	72	74	74	295	984,000
Hsieh Chin Sheng	73	77	69	76	295	984,000
Masayuki Kawamura	71	74	73	77	295	984,000
Toshiaki Sudo	71	72	74	78	295	984,000

	SCORES				TOTAL	MONEY
Tadami Ueno	70	77	78	71	296	842,000
Kazuhiro Takami	74	75	75	72	296	842,000
Craig Warren	73	72	76	75	296	842,000
Teruo Nakamura	71	75	74	76	296	842,000
Richard Backwell	72	73	71	80	296	842,000

Japan PGA Championship

Gifu Lake Green Golf Club, Gifu
Par 35-36—71; 7,138 yards

May 12-15
purse, ¥100,000,000

	SCORES				TOTAL	MONEY
Hiroshi Goda	66	73	67	73	279	¥18,000,000
Masashi Ozaki	69	71	72	68	280	10,000,000
Noboru Sugai	71	71	74	69	285	5,800,000
Seiji Ebihara	67	72	72	74	285	5,800,000
Isao Aoki	70	70	74	73	287	4,000,000
Ryoken Kawagishi	78	69	71	70	288	3,233,000
Takaaki Fukuzawa	71	71	74	72	288	3,233,000
Todd Hamilton	75	68	71	74	288	3,233,000
Tetsu Nishikawa	72	71	71	75	289	2,300,000
Masanobu Kimura	69	69	75	76	289	2,300,000
Katsuyoshi Tomori	68	72	73	76	289	2,300,000
Wayne Smith	71	77	69	73	290	1,760,000
Hiroya Kamide	70	72	72	76	290	1,760,000
Yutaka Hagawa	67	78	73	73	291	1,380,000
Hirofumi Miyase	70	74	72	75	291	1,380,000
Yukiyoshi Idogi	69	70	77	75	291	1,380,000
Chen Tze Ming	70	73	70	78	291	1,380,000
Teruo Nakamura	75	68	75	74	292	986,000
Nobuo Serizawa	73	73	71	75	292	986,000
Rick Gibson	71	72	73	76	292	986,000
Hideto Shigenobu	75	67	74	76	292	986,000
Katsunari Takahashi	69	71	75	77	292	986,000
Richard Backwell	76	70	68	78	292	986,000
Frankie Minoza	74	74	72	73	293	810,000
Hideki Kase	70	72	78	73	293	810,000
Eiichi Itai	71	71	74	77	293	810,000
Shigeru Kawamata	69	73	74	77	293	810,000
Tsuneyuki Nakajima	76	65	74	78	293	810,000
Daisuke Serizawa	73	71	71	78	293	810,000
Toshiaki Odate	70	77	72	75	294	711,000
Hiroshi Makino	71	70	77	76	294	711,000
Atsushi Takamatsu	75	73	68	78	294	711,000
Satoshi Higashi	74	70	71	79	294	711,000

Pepsi Ube-Kosan Tournament

Ube Country Club, Yamaguchi
Par 35-36—71; 6,935 yards

May 19-22
purse, ¥80,000,000

	SCORES				TOTAL	MONEY
Tsuneyuki Nakajima	65	67	67	69	268	¥14,440,000
Tsukasa Watanabe	66	72	69	64	271	8,000,000
Samson Gimson	68	71	70	64	273	5,440,000
Saburo Fujiki	72	69	67	66	274	3,840,000

	SCORES				TOTAL	MONEY
Todd Hamilton	69	74	67	65	275	3,200,000
Tetsu Ouide	72	70	67	67	276	2,880,000
Hideyuki Sato	69	72	69	67	277	2,320,000
Shigenori Mori	70	70	68	69	277	2,320,000
Hideto Shigenobu	70	71	66	70	277	2,320,000
Katsuyoshi Tomori	68	72	72	66	278	1,564,000
Seiji Ebihara	69	70	69	70	278	1,564,000
Tsuyoshi Yoneyama	72	69	67	70	278	1,564,000
Brent Franklin	68	69	70	71	278	1,564,000
Atsushi Takamatsu	71	70	71	67	279	1,152,000
Kiyoshi Murota	71	68	68	72	279	1,152,000
Takaaki Fukuzawa	72	67	68	72	279	1,152,000
Yoshitaka Yamamoto	73	71	67	69	280	832,000
Shinji Ikeuchi	70	71	70	69	280	832,000
Mitsutaka Hikabe	72	72	67	69	280	832,000
Hiroshi Makino	72	70	67	71	280	832,000
Kinpachi Yoshimura	69	72	68	71	280	832,000
Nobuo Serizawa	68	68	72	72	280	832,000
Hisashi Nakase	68	72	76	65	281	680,000
Hiroshi Ueda	72	70	72	67	281	680,000
Zaw Moe	69	72	71	69	281	680,000
Hiroya Kamide	72	71	68	70	281	680,000
Masanobu Kimura	72	71	70	69	282	616,000
Tadaaki Matsutaka	76	67	69	70	282	616,000
Tadashi Ezure	69	74	69	70	282	616,000
Noboru Sugai	74	68	67	73	282	616,000

Mitsubishi Galant Tournament

Hokkaido Hayakita Country Club, Hokkaido
Par 36-36—72; 7,120 yards
(Second round cancelled — rain.)

May 26-29
purse, ¥75,000,000

	SCORES			TOTAL	MONEY
Katsuyoshi Tomori	69	66	70	205	¥13,500,000
Tsuneyuki Nakajima	71	68	72	211	7,500,000
Chen Tze Ming	68	70	74	212	5,100,000
Masashi Ozaki	70	72	71	213	3,600,000
Norikazu Kawakami	71	68	76	215	3,000,000
Hisao Inoue	73	67	76	216	2,700,000
Kazuhiro Takami	71	72	74	217	2,287,000
Ken Kusumoto	69	74	74	217	2,287,000
Masayuki Kawamura	74	74	70	218	1,381,000
Shoichi Yamamoto	73	75	70	218	1,381,000
Brian Watts	75	72	71	218	1,381,000
Kinpachi Yoshimura	71	76	71	218	1,381,000
David Ishii	73	73	72	218	1,381,000
Eduardo Herrera	68	76	74	218	1,381,000
Carlos Franco	70	73	75	218	1,381,000
Toru Taniguchi	72	69	77	218	1,381,000
Peter Senior	75	74	70	219	762,000
Anthony Gilligan	75	73	71	219	762,000
Tsukasa Watanabe	72	74	73	219	762,000
Shigenori Mori	73	73	73	219	762,000
Nobumitsu Yuhara	72	73	74	219	762,000
Katsunari Takahashi	73	71	75	219	762,000
Richard Backwell	72	72	75	219	762,000
Hisayuki Sasaki	77	71	72	220	607,000

	SCORES			TOTAL	MONEY
Toru Suzuki	75	73	72	220	607,000
Yoshimi Niizeki	72	76	72	220	607,000
Naoya Sugiyama	77	70	73	220	607,000
Masanobu Kimura	74	71	75	220	607,000
Chen Tze Chung	72	73	75	220	607,000
Wayne Smith	73	76	72	221	526,000
Shigeki Maruyama	72	76	73	221	526,000
Shoichi Kuwahara	77	71	73	221	526,000
Hisashi Terada	75	71	75	221	526,000
Hirofumi Miyase	74	71	76	221	526,000

JCB Sendai Classic

Omote Zoah Golf Club, Miyagi
Par 35-36—71; 6,645 yards

June 2-5
purse, ¥100,000,000

	SCORES				TOTAL	MONEY
Masahiro Kuramoto	71	65	67	68	271	¥18,000,000
Roger Mackey	70	68	68	67	273	8,400,000
Toshiaki Sudo	68	68	68	69	273	8,400,000
Tsuneyuki Nakajima	70	67	71	67	275	3,900,000
Frankie Minoza	67	69	70	69	275	3,900,000
Craig Warren	69	66	71	69	275	3,900,000
Shigenori Mori	71	68	67	69	275	3,900,000
Peter Senior	73	67	68	68	276	2,900,000
Minoru Hatsumi	68	74	67	68	277	2,600,000
Kiyoshi Maita	71	73	68	66	278	2,300,000
Nobuo Serizawa	71	71	72	65	279	1,640,000
Masashi Ozaki	71	70	72	66	279	1,640,000
Tetsu Nishikawa	68	73	70	68	279	1,640,000
Katsuyoshi Tomori	69	74	66	70	279	1,640,000
Toru Suzuki	70	73	65	71	279	1,640,000
Eiji Mizoguchi	67	73	67	72	279	1,640,000
Samson Gimson	70	71	73	66	280	1,090,000
Yoshinori Mizumaki	71	71	69	69	280	1,090,000
Kinpachi Yoshimura	68	70	72	70	280	1,090,000
Ken Kusumoto	68	67	73	72	280	1,090,000
Chen Tze Chung	69	72	70	70	281	920,000
Katsunori Kuwabara	71	70	70	70	281	920,000
Kiyoshi Murota	73	67	70	71	281	920,000
Harumitsu Hamano	69	71	72	70	282	860,000
Seiji Ebihara	67	75	73	68	283	800,000
Hisayuki Sasaki	70	72	71	70	283	800,000
Tsutomu Higa	72	66	73	72	283	800,000
Satoshi Higashi	71	72	68	72	283	800,000
Tomohiro Maruyama	73	70	66	74	283	800,000
Shigeki Maruyama	70	69	77	68	284	694,000
Shoichi Yamamoto	68	76	72	68	284	694,000
Seiki Okuda	72	73	69	70	284	694,000
Lin Chie Hsiang	67	71	76	70	284	694,000
Brian Jones	74	71	68	71	284	694,000
Tsuyoshi Yoneyama	71	71	67	75	284	694,000

Sapporo Tokyu Open

Sapporo Kokusai Country Club, Hokkaido
Par 36-36—72; 6,949 yards

June 9-12
purse, ¥100,000,000

	SCORES				TOTAL	MONEY
Yoshinori Mizumaki	65	70	68	74	277	¥18,000,000
Eduardo Herrera	71	73	65	69	278	10,000,000
Chen Tze Ming	71	66	69	73	279	6,800,000
Saburo Fujiki	72	69	68	71	280	4,800,000
Daisuke Serizawa	67	70	72	72	281	3,800,000
Craig Warren	71	65	72	73	281	3,800,000
Peter Senior	71	65	76	70	282	2,900,000
Kinpachi Yoshimura	71	68	70	73	282	2,900,000
Ikuo Shirahama	71	71	67	73	282	2,900,000
Brian Watts	68	71	71	73	283	2,046,000
Akiyoshi Omachi	70	70	70	73	283	2,046,000
Yoshimi Niizeki	67	67	74	75	283	2,046,000
Ken Kusumoto	70	73	72	69	284	1,620,000
Yoshitaka Yamamoto	71	67	71	75	284	1,620,000
Chen Tze Chung	70	66	75	74	285	1,270,000
Kouki Idoki	72	72	67	74	285	1,270,000
Peter McWhinney	68	71	71	75	285	1,270,000
Ryoken Kawagishi	70	71	69	75	285	1,270,000
Kohichi Suzuki	70	72	73	71	286	1,000,000
Katsuyoshi Tomori	71	69	73	73	286	1,000,000
Tadami Ueno	73	72	68	73	286	1,000,000
Katsunari Takahashi	72	70	74	71	287	875,000
Lin Chie Hsiang	70	73	72	72	287	875,000
Shinji Ikeuchi	69	72	71	75	287	875,000
Tsutomu Higa	71	71	67	78	287	875,000
Kiyoshi Murota	71	70	73	74	288	820,000
David Ishii	72	71	74	72	289	780,000
Seiji Ebihara	65	74	76	74	289	780,000
Shoichi Yamamoto	72	70	72	75	289	780,000
Kazuhiro Takami	71	70	74	75	290	720,000
Fumiaki Matsutaka	69	73	73	75	290	720,000
Eiji Mizoguchi	71	69	75	75	290	720,000

Yomiuri Open

Yomiuri Golf Member Course, Osaka
Par 36-35—71; 6,979 yards

June 16-19
purse, ¥100,000,000

	SCORES				TOTAL	MONEY
Tsukasa Watanabe	68	64	67	71	270	¥18,000,000
Anthony Gilligan	65	64	71	72	272	10,000,000
Tsuneyuki Nakajima	69	67	69	68	273	6,800,000
Mitsutaka Kusakabe	66	69	69	71	275	4,800,000
Frankie Minoza	71	69	71	65	276	3,800,000
Katsunari Takahashi	65	70	70	71	276	3,800,000
Shigeki Maruyama	70	69	67	71	277	3,050,000
Eduardo Herrera	64	73	69	71	277	3,050,000
Hideyuki Sato	72	71	66	69	278	2,300,000
Tetsu Nishikawa	68	70	70	70	278	2,300,000
Kouki Idoki	67	71	70	70	278	2,300,000
Nobuo Serizawa	69	73	69	68	279	1,760,000
Lin Chie Hsiang	67	69	72	71	279	1,760,000

		SCORES			TOTAL	MONEY
Saburo Fujiki	71	72	69	68	280	1,380,000
Tadami Ueno	72	68	70	70	280	1,380,000
Harumitsu Hamano	68	71	69	72	280	1,380,000
Yoshitaka Yamamoto	69	71	67	73	280	1,380,000
Akihito Yokoyama	69	71	72	69	281	1,030,000
Samson Gimson	69	71	70	71	281	1,030,000
David Ishii	72	68	70	71	281	1,030,000
Yoshinori Kaneko	71	69	67	74	281	1,030,000
Daisuke Serizawa	69	73	69	71	282	886,000
Chen Tze Chung	71	69	70	72	282	886,000
Vicente Fernandez	70	71	67	74	282	886,000
Kazuhiro Takami	66	74	74	69	283	780,000
Todd Hamilton	74	69	71	69	283	780,000
Peter McWhinney	72	71	70	70	283	780,000
Hirofumi Miyase	68	71	72	72	283	780,000
Ikuo Shirahama	70	70	71	72	283	780,000
Kohichi Suzuki	69	67	75	72	283	780,000
Richard Backwell	66	70	72	75	283	780,000

Mizuno Open

Tokinodai Country Club, Ishikawa
Par 36-36—72; 6,929 yards

June 23-26
purse, ¥100,000,000

		SCORES			TOTAL	MONEY
Brian Watts	68	68	73	71	280	¥18,000,000
Yoshinori Kaneko	67	75	70	68	280	7,200,000
Kohichi Suzuki	66	70	74	70	280	7,200,000
Eduardo Herrera	69	70	70	71	280	7,200,000
(Watts defeated Kaneko, Suzuki and Herrera on first extra hole.)						
Katsuyoshi Tomori	69	71	72	69	281	3,800,000
David Ishii	70	71	69	71	281	3,800,000
Richard Backwell	65	77	72	68	282	2,750,000
Shigeki Maruyama	71	71	71	69	282	2,750,000
Saburo Fujiki	69	68	75	70	282	2,750,000
Eiji Mizoguchi	72	70	68	72	282	2,750,000
Peter McWhinney	71	72	71	69	283	1,770,000
Hiroshi Goda	69	72	72	70	283	1,770,000
Kouki Idoki	70	70	73	70	283	1,770,000
Taisei Inagaki	70	72	71	70	283	1,770,000
Hiroya Kamide	69	73	73	69	284	1,097,000
Seiji Ebihara	69	72	73	70	284	1,097,000
Jin Han Lim	72	70	72	70	284	1,097,000
Toru Kihara	69	72	73	70	284	1,097,000
Chen Tze Chung	71	68	74	71	284	1,097,000
Seiki Okuda	67	70	75	72	284	1,097,000
Anthony Gilligan	69	66	76	73	284	1,097,000
Masanobu Kimura	69	70	71	74	284	1,097,000
Hisashi Nakase	70	70	70	74	284	1,097,000
Ken Kusumoto	69	72	71	73	285	860,000
Stewart Ginn	71	71	68	76	286	840,000
Craig McClellan	71	73	74	69	287	790,000
Wayne Smith	70	75	72	70	287	790,000
Hikaru Emoto	67	72	76	72	287	790,000
Kiyoshi Maita	68	74	71	74	287	790,000
Yohsuke Mizobuchi	70	70	77	71	288	720,000
Gregory Meyer	73	73	70	72	288	720,000
Yutaka Hagawa	66	76	71	75	288	720,000

PGA Philanthropy Cup

Golden Valley Golf Club, Hyogo
Par 36-36—72; 6,860 yards

June 30-July 3
purse, ¥100,000,000

	SCORES				TOTAL	MONEY
Todd Hamilton	74	69	68	67	278	¥12,600,000
Eiji Mizoguchi	70	69	72	67	278	7,000,000
(Hamilton defeated Mizoguchi on first extra hole.)						
Chen Tze Chung	68	72	73	66	279	3,360,000
Yoshinori Kaneko	71	73	68	67	279	3,360,000
Shigeki Maruyama	72	67	71	69	279	3,360,000
Teruo Sugihara	68	69	70	72	279	3,360,000
Lin Chie Hsiang	71	72	68	69	280	2,135,000
Richard Backwell	68	68	72	72	280	2,135,000
Anthony Gilligan	70	69	73	69	281	1,529,000
Katsunori Kuwabara	70	70	70	71	281	1,529,000
Shinji Kuraoka	67	71	71	72	281	1,529,000
Nobuo Serizawa	69	66	70	76	281	1,529,000
Hiroshi Goda	71	69	73	69	282	1,008,000
Frankie Minoza	68	72	71	71	282	1,008,000
Seiki Okuda	73	67	71	71	282	1,008,000
David Ishii	70	69	71	72	282	1,008,000
Yoshimi Niizeki	67	68	73	74	282	1,008,000
Brian Watts	66	71	77	69	283	784,000
Masahiko Akazawa	73	70	74	67	284	686,000
Katsuyoshi Tomori	68	74	72	70	284	686,000
Akiyoshi Omachi	68	74	72	70	284	686,000
Nobumitsu Yuhara	71	70	73	70	284	686,000
Roger Mackay	73	68	74	70	285	602,000
Tetsu Nishikawa	68	67	75	75	285	602,000
Kunihiko Masuda	72	71	67	75	285	602,000
Satoshi Higashi	72	71	75	68	286	532,000
Peter McWhinney	73	70	73	70	286	532,000
Toshiaki Odate	70	68	77	71	286	532,000
Ikuo Shirahama	72	72	69	73	286	532,000
Rick Gibson	73	66	73	74	286	532,000
Saburo Fujiki	67	70	74	75	286	532,000
Hirofumi Miyase	69	69	71	77	286	532,000

Yonex Open Hiroshima

Hiroshima Country Club, Hiroshima
Par 36-36—72; 6,865 yards

July 7-10
purse, ¥80,000,000

	SCORES				TOTAL	MONEY
Masashi Ozaki	68	74	67	65	274	¥14,400,000
Nobuo Serizawa	69	69	73	66	277	8,000,000
Yoshitaka Yamamoto	68	69	72	69	278	4,160,000
Samson Gimson	71	70	67	70	278	4,160,000
Toyotake Nakao	69	68	68	73	278	4,160,000
Craig Warren	73	71	66	69	279	2,720,000
Kouki Idoki	68	69	71	71	279	2,720,000
Shoichi Kuwabara	69	71	73	67	280	1,700,000
Tomohiro Maruyama	70	69	73	68	280	1,700,000
Stewart Ginn	73	67	71	69	280	1,700,000
Shoichi Yamamoto	72	72	67	69	280	1,700,000
Wayne Levi	72	70	69	69	280	1,700,000

	SCORES				TOTAL	MONEY
Todd Hamilton	71	68	70	71	280	1,700,000
Chen Tze Chung	72	70	67	71	280	1,700,000
Yutaka Hagawa	68	75	72	66	281	979,000
Richard Backwell	70	73	70	68	281	979,000
Seiki Okuda	69	73	69	70	281	979,000
Hajime Meshiai	72	69	69	71	281	979,000
Satoshi Higashi	67	73	69	72	281	979,000
Hiroshi Makino	71	71	72	68	282	739,000
Masayuki Kawamura	69	72	71	70	282	739,000
Nobumitsu Yuhara	69	70	73	70	282	739,000
Ikuo Shirahama	77	64	70	71	282	739,000
Shinsaku Maeda	66	73	70	73	282	739,000
Seiji Ebihara	70	70	75	68	283	608,000
Shigeru Kawamata	68	73	73	69	283	608,000
Akiyoshi Omachi	71	71	71	70	283	608,000
Toru Nakayama	70	70	73	70	283	608,000
Yoshinori Kaneko	70	70	72	71	283	608,000
Takaaki Fukuzawa	72	68	72	71	283	608,000
Gregory Meyer	69	74	69	71	283	608,000
Tsuyoshi Yoneyama	71	72	68	72	283	608,000
Ken Kusumoto	68	71	68	76	283	608,000

Nikkei Cup Torakichi Nakamura Memorial

Mitsui Kanko Tomakomai Golf Club, Hokkaido
Par 36-36—72; 7,007 yards

July 21-24
purse, ¥80,000,000

	SCORES				TOTAL	MONEY
Toru Suzuki	72	67	65	64	268	¥14,400,000
Katsunari Takahashi	67	70	67	69	273	8,000,000
Yoshitaka Yamamoto	71	69	66	68	274	4,160,000
Satoshi Higashi	70	67	65	72	274	4,160,000
Yoshinori Kaneko	71	68	62	73	274	4,160,000
Takaaki Fukuzawa	68	69	72	66	275	2,460,000
Nobumitsu Yuhara	68	68	71	68	275	2,460,000
Eiji Mizoguchi	68	69	69	69	275	2,460,000
Stewart Ginn	67	68	68	72	275	2,460,000
Hiroshi Ueda	69	71	68	68	276	1,840,000
Toru Murota	71	71	69	66	277	1,312,000
Toshinori Horiki	70	70	69	68	277	1,312,000
Masayuki Kawamura	68	70	70	69	277	1,312,000
Akihito Yokoyama	68	70	69	70	277	1,312,000
Harumitsu Hamano	65	72	68	72	277	1,312,000
Tsukasa Watanabe	70	68	66	73	277	1,312,000
Mitsutaka Kusakabe	69	71	69	69	278	851,000
Masanobu Kimura	71	67	70	70	278	851,000
Tsuyoshi Yoneyama	70	68	70	70	278	851,000
Hisayuki Sasaki	67	72	68	71	278	851,000
Kiyoshi Maita	70	66	69	73	278	851,000
Samson Gimson	71	70	73	65	279	682,000
Zaw Moe	63	72	75	69	279	682,000
Brent Franklin	69	68	73	69	279	682,000
Lin Chie Hsiang	70	72	67	70	279	682,000
Eiichi Itai	69	71	69	70	279	682,000
Hideto Shigenobu	70	68	70	71	279	682,000
Taisei Inagaki	68	74	70	68	280	616,000
Noboru Fujiike	71	69	71	69	280	616,000
Saburo Fujiki	72	70	70	69	281	548,000

	SCORES				TOTAL	MONEY
Daisuke Serizawa	68	70	73	70	281	548,000
Yutaka Hagawa	72	69	70	70	281	548,000
Motomasa Aoki	68	69	72	72	281	548,000
Ikuo Shirahama	69	66	73	73	281	548,000
Yurio Akitomi	68	68	72	73	281	548,000
Kazuhiro Takami	68	70	69	74	281	548,000

NST Niigata Open

Nakajyo Golf Club, Niigata
Par 36-36—72; 7,029 yards

August 4-7
purse, ¥60,000,000

	SCORES				TOTAL	MONEY
Pete Izumikawa	67	70	70	69	276	¥10,800,000
Kiyoshi Maita	70	72	66	70	278	6,000,000
Mitsutaka Kusakabe	69	70	68	73	280	4,080,000
Masayuki Kawamura	71	71	69	70	281	2,640,000
Hiroshi Ueda	66	73	71	71	281	2,640,000
Satoshi Higashi	72	70	71	69	282	1,752,000
Kohichi Suzuki	68	73	71	70	282	1,752,000
Shoichi Yamamoto	71	70	71	70	282	1,752,000
Yoshinori Kaneko	73	71	67	71	282	1,752,000
Seiji Ebihara	71	71	69	71	282	1,752,000
Gregory Meyer	72	73	70	68	283	1,152,000
Keiichiro Fukabori	70	71	71	71	283	1,152,000
Samson Gimson	73	73	69	69	284	936,000
Brad Andrews	72	70	72	70	284	936,000
Kazunari Matsunaga	67	72	72	73	284	936,000
Hiroya Kamide	69	69	69	78	285	792,000
Hisayuki Sasaki	73	71	72	70	286	598,000
Toshiaki Nakagawa	70	72	74	70	286	598,000
Kiyoshi Nomura	68	76	72	70	286	598,000
Hiroshi Goda	68	75	71	72	286	598,000
Hiromichi Namiki	69	76	69	72	286	598,000
Kenji Kawasaki	72	71	69	74	286	598,000
Shigenori Mori	72	71	68	75	286	598,000
S. Holmes	68	74	69	75	286	598,000
Daisuke Serizawa	71	75	72	69	287	468,000
Toshiaki Sudo	72	72	73	70	287	468,000
Jin Han Lim	70	72	74	71	287	468,000
Hideki Kase	72	73	70	72	287	468,000
Hirofumi Miyase	71	74	70	72	287	468,000
Kikuo Arai	71	72	72	72	287	468,000
Shigeru Kawamata	75	68	72	72	287	468,000

Acom International

Seve Ballesteros Golf Club, Ibaragi
Par 36-36—72; 6,806 yards

August 11-14
purse, ¥100,000,000

	POINTS				TOTAL	MONEY
Naomichi Ozaki	14	2	12	13	41	¥18,000,000
Masayuki Kawamura	4	6	8	17	35	10,000,000
Satoshi Higashi	22	-1	5	8	34	6,800,000
Hirofumi Miyase	18	4	6	5	33	4,133,000
Roger Mackay	8	12	7	6	33	4,133,000

		POINTS			TOTAL	MONEY
Brian Watts	5	9	5	14	33	4,133,000
Tsukasa Watanabe	6	3	13	9	31	3,200,000
S. Holmes	7	2	10	11	30	2,900,000
Kiyoshi Maita	11	8	3	7	29	2,600,000
Kazunari Matsunaga	10	6	6	6	28	2,150,000
Yasunobu Kuramoto	16	11	6	-5	28	2,150,000
Hisayuki Sasaki	7	13	4	3	27	1,760,000
Greg Turner	5	5	10	7	27	1,760,000
Masahiko Akazawa	5	8	5	7	25	1,500,000
Shoichi Kuwabara	13	-2	6	8	25	1,500,000
Hideto Shigenobu	5	2	10	7	24	1,213,000
Hiroya Kamide	11	5	6	2	24	1,213,000
Craig Warren	9	4	12	-1	24	1,213,000
Masanobu Kimura	8	8	-1	8	23	1,040,000
Hideyuki Sato	6	3	7	6	22	1,000,000
Isao Isozaki	12	-1	4	6	21	920,000
Hiroshi Makino	6	2	6	7	21	920,000
Ryoken Kawagishi	7	4	7	3	21	920,000
Yurio Akitomi	13	8	0	-1	20	850,000
Todd Hamilton	2	8	4	6	20	850,000
Yoshinori Kaneko	5	8	3	3	19	750,000
Nobuo Serizawa	2	12	3	2	19	750,000
Takaaki Fukuzawa	6	5	8	0	19	750,000
Nobumitsu Yuhara	8	0	5	6	19	750,000
Noboru Fujiike	6	1	4	8	19	750,000
Eiji Mizoguchi	5	3	4	7	19	750,000
D. Paul	6	5	4	4	19	750,000
Carlos Franco	8	0	7	4	19	750,000

Maruman Open

Narita Springs, Chiba
Par 36-36—72; 7,077 yards

August 18-21
purse, ¥120,000,000

		SCORES			TOTAL	MONEY
David Ishii	69	71	67	72	279	¥21,600,000
Hirofumi Miyase	71	71	68	69	279	10,080,000
Nobuo Serizawa	73	66	70	70	279	10,080,000
(Ishii defeated Miyase and Serizawa on first extra hole.)						
Yoshinori Kaneko	71	71	70	68	280	4,960,000
Nobumitsu Yuhara	73	65	72	70	280	4,960,000
Yutaka Hagawa	74	67	69	70	280	4,960,000
Daisuke Serizawa	70	71	69	71	281	3,300,000
Masayuki Kawamura	71	69	69	72	281	3,300,000
Masanobu Kimura	69	67	73	72	281	3,300,000
Richard Backwell	68	69	71	73	281	3,300,000
Craig McClellan	69	72	72	69	282	1,892,000
Chen Tze Chung	70	72	69	71	282	1,892,000
Futoshi Irino	70	68	73	71	282	1,892,000
Zaw Moe	70	67	73	72	282	1,892,000
Yurio Akitomi	70	70	68	74	282	1,892,000
Roger Mackay	71	70	66	75	282	1,892,000
Eiji Mizoguchi	68	69	70	75	282	1,892,000
Anthony Gilligan	66	75	73	69	283	1,162,000
Frankie Minoza	70	72	71	70	283	1,162,000
Seiji Ebihara	68	72	71	72	283	1,162,000
Toshimitsu Izawa	72	71	68	72	283	1,162,000

	SCORES			TOTAL	MONEY
Kazuhiro Takami	70	71	68 74	283	1,162,000
Katsuji Hasegawa	70	71	68 74	283	1,162,000
Carlos Franco	70	67	72 74	283	1,162,000
Stewart Ginn	69	74	71 70	284	972,000
Craig Warren	71	69	73 71	284	972,000
Lin Chie Hsiang	69	68	73 74	284	972,000
Saburo Fujiki	71	67	68 78	284	972,000
Satoshi Higashi	70	72	72 71	285	814,000
Hideto Shigenobu	71	72	71 71	285	814,000
Shigenori Mori	72	71	70 72	285	814,000
Yoshimi Niizeki	70	72	71 72	285	814,000
Eiichi Itai	71	69	71 74	285	814,000
Tadami Ueno	72	68	71 74	285	814,000
Brad Andrews	72	68	71 74	285	814,000
Hiromichi Namiki	68	71	72 74	285	814,000
Isao Isozaki	71	72	68 74	285	814,000
Kazunari Matsunaga	66	71	71 77	285	814,000

Hisamitsu KBC Augusta Tournament

Keya Golf Club, Fukuoka
Par 36-36—72; 7,144 yards

August 25-28
purse, ¥100,000,000

	SCORES			TOTAL	MONEY
Brian Watts	66	67	71 67	271	¥18,000,000
Masashi Ozaki	70	69	68 66	273	10,000,000
Hiroshi Ueda	69	70	69 67	275	6,800,000
Masayuki Kawamura	65	69	72 70	276	4,133,333
Hsieh Chin Sheng	69	72	63 72	276	4,133,333
Tadashi Ezure	66	70	68 72	276	4,133,333
Brent Franklin	69	72	66 70	277	3,200,000
Satoshi Higashi	69	69	61 69	278	2,900,000
Scott Simpson	70	70	72 67	279	1,996,666
Nobuo Serizawa	71	71	68 69	279	1,996,666
David Ishii	67	71	71 70	279	1,996,666
Katsunari Takahashi	67	73	69 70	279	1,996,666
Kiyoshi Maita	66	73	69 71	279	1,996,666
Jin Han Lim	65	69	71 73	279	1,996,666
Ryoken Kawagishi	72	68	71 69	280	1,224,000
Yasunobu Kuramoto	69	70	71 70	280	1,224,000
Chen Tze Ming	66	72	72 70	280	1,224,000
Yoshinori Kaneko	68	69	70 73	280	1,224,000
Tsuyoshi Yoneyama	67	68	70 75	280	1,224,000
Eiichi Itai	71	68	73 69	281	940,000
Anthony Gilligan	69	73	69 70	281	940,000
Kazuo Kaneyama	69	70	71 71	281	940,000
Hisashi Nakase	71	67	71 72	281	940,000
Katsuyoshi Tomori	73	70	71 68	282	780,000
Ken Kusumoto	70	70	73 69	282	780,000
Toshiaki Nakagawa	71	71	70 70	282	780,000
Chen Tze Chung	68	69	74 71	282	780,000
Zaw Moe	71	69	70 72	282	780,000
Kiyoshi Murota	69	70	70 73	282	780,000
Wayne Smith	73	69	67 73	282	780,000
Toshimitsu Izawa	69	68	71 74	282	780,000
Tsukasa Watanabe	70	67	70 75	282	780,000

Japan Match Play Championship

Nidom Classic Golf Club, Hokkaido
Par 36-36—72; 6,986 yards

September 1-4
purse, ¥80,000,000

FIRST ROUND

Hajime Meshiai defeated Kazuhiro Takami, 3 and 1
Shigeki Maruyama defeated Hirofumi Miyase, 1 up, 19 holes
Shinji Ikeuchi defeated Naomichi Ozaki, 1 up
Tetsu Nishikawa defeated Yoshitaka Yamamoto, 2 and 1
Todd Hamilton defeated Tsuyoshi Yoneyama, 2 up
Katsuyoshi Tomori defeated Hiroshi Makino, 3 and 2
Katsunari Takahashi defeated Shigeru Kawamata, 3 and 2
Tomohiro Maruyama defeated Saburo Fujiki, 1 up
Samson Gimson defeated Chen Tze Chung, 2 and 1
Ryoken Kawagishi defeated Toru Suzuki, 3 and 1
Seiki Okuda defeated Kohichi Suzuki, 2 and 1
Akiyoshi Omachi defeated Eiichi Itai, 3 and 2
Ikuo Shirahama defeated Tsukasa Watanabe, 3 and 1
Nobuo Serizawa defeated Masahiro Kuramoto, 4 and 3
Kouki Idoki defeated Yoshinori Mizumaki, 3 and 2
Kiyoshi Murota defeated Tateo Ozaki, 8 and 6

(Each losing player received ¥450,000.)

SECOND ROUND

Maruyama defeated Meshiai, 5 and 4
Ikeuchi defeated Nishikawa, 1 up, 19 holes
Hamilton defeated Tomori, 2 and 1
Takahashi defeated Maruyama, 1 up
Kawagishi defeated Gimson, 1 up, 20 holes
Okuda defeated Omachi, 3 and 2
Shirahama defeated Serizawa, 4 and 3
Murota defeated Idoki, 2 up

(Each losing player received ¥850,000.)

QUARTER-FINALS

Maruyama defeated Ikeuchi, 1 up
Hamilton defeated Takahashi, 1 up
Kawagishi defeated Okuda, 6 and 4
Shirahama defeated Murota, 3 and 2

(Each losing player received ¥1,600,000.)

SEMI-FINALS

Hamilton defeated Maruyama, 3 and 2
Shirahama defeated Kawagishi, 4 and 3

THIRD-FOURTH PLACE PLAYOFF

Kawagishi defeated Maruyama, 1 up, 19 holes

(Kawagishi received ¥6,000,000; Maruyama ¥4,500,000.)

FINAL

Hamilton defeated Shirahama, 8 and 7

(Hamilton received ¥25,000,000; Shirahama ¥12,500,000.)

Suntory Open

Narashino Country Club, Chiba
Par 36-36—72; 7,008 yards

September 8-11
purse, ¥100,000,000

	SCORES				TOTAL	MONEY
David Ishii	72	68	69	68	277	¥18,000,000
Hisayuki Sasaki	71	70	69	67	277	10,000,000
(Ishii defeated Sasaki on first extra hole.)						
Katsunari Takahashi	72	70	70	66	278	4,480,000
Naomichi Ozaki	71	71	68	68	278	4,480,000
Andrew Magee	73	68	68	69	278	4,480,000
Brent Franklin	67	71	70	70	278	4,480,000
Anthony Gilligan	70	70	67	71	278	4,480,000
Masashi Ozaki	72	68	66	73	279	2,750,000
Masayuki Kawamura	69	67	70	73	279	2,750,000
Tomohiro Maruyama	73	68	71	68	280	1,876,000
Saburo Fujiki	73	70	68	69	280	1,876,000
Seiichi Kanai	74	65	72	69	280	1,876,000
Yoshinori Mizumaki	69	72	69	70	280	1,876,000
Gregory Meyer	73	68	69	70	280	1,876,000
Hsieh Chin Sheng	70	71	72	68	281	1,186,000
Nobuo Serizawa	71	70	70	70	281	1,186,000
Nobumitsu Yuhara	72	65	74	70	281	1,186,000
Rick Gibson	71	70	69	71	281	1,186,000
Seiki Okuda	70	66	71	74	281	1,186,000
Bradley Hughes	67	71	68	75	281	1,186,000
Kouki Idoki	73	67	73	69	282	920,000
Ikuo Shirahama	72	69	69	72	282	920,000
Shigenori Mori	70	68	71	73	282	920,000
Wayne Smith	73	70	74	66	283	790,000
Teruo Sugihara	75	69	70	69	283	790,000
Yoshinori Kaneko	71	70	72	70	283	790,000
Eiji Mizoguchi	70	70	73	70	283	790,000
Akio Nakamura	74	70	69	70	283	790,000
Motomasa Aoki	71	67	75	70	283	790,000
Kikuo Arai	68	70	73	72	283	790,000
Toyotake Nakao	70	69	71	73	283	790,000

ANA Open

Sapporo Golf Club, Hokkaido
Par 36-36—72; 7,063 yards

September 15-18
purse, ¥100,000,000

	SCORES				TOTAL	MONEY
Masashi Ozaki	68	68	63	69	268	¥18,000,000
Kiyoshi Murota	69	71	67	70	277	10,000,000
Yoshitaka Yamamoto	68	76	67	67	278	6,800,000
Todd Hamilton	72	73	67	67	279	4,400,000
Eduardo Herrera	70	74	68	67	279	4,400,000
Naomichi Ozaki	74	70	68	68	280	3,075,000

		SCORES			TOTAL	MONEY
Wayne Grady	71	70	71	68	280	3,075,000
Masahiro Kuramoto	71	67	73	69	280	3,075,000
Lin Chie Hsiang	68	72	69	71	280	3,075,000
Anthony Gilligan	72	72	68	70	282	2,150,000
Tsuneyuki Nakajima	69	70	71	72	282	2,150,000
Hisayuki Sasaki	70	72	71	70	283	1,840,000
Hiroshi Makino	70	74	71	69	284	1,440,000
Andrew Magee	68	75	72	69	284	1,440,000
Masayuki Kawamura	70	73	71	70	284	1,440,000
Hajime Meshiai	66	74	73	71	284	1,440,000
Tsuyoshi Yoneyama	69	72	70	73	284	1,440,000
Masanobu Kimura	69	74	70	72	285	1,120,000
Peter McWhinney	70	72	73	71	286	1,000,000
David Ishii	70	73	71	72	286	1,000,000
Hsieh Chin Sheng	68	72	71	75	286	1,000,000
Daisuke Serizawa	72	73	70	72	287	864,000
Saburo Fujiki	71	71	72	73	287	864,000
Carlos Franco	71	71	72	73	287	864,000
Hiroshi Ueda	70	72	68	77	287	864,000
Atsushi Takamatsu	68	72	70	77	287	864,000
Shigeki Maruyama	70	74	75	69	288	722,000
Yoshinori Kaneko	72	74	72	70	288	722,000
Chen Tze Chung	71	75	70	72	288	722,000
Nobumitsu Yuhara	72	72	72	72	288	722,000
Hiroya Kamide	74	70	71	73	288	722,000
Tadashi Ezure	72	70	73	73	288	722,000
Frankie Minoza	70	75	69	74	288	722,000
Hikaru Emoto	73	71	70	74	288	722,000
Curtis Strange	73	70	69	76	288	722,000

Gene Sarazen Jun Classic

Rope Club, Tochigi
Par 36-36—72; 7,025 yards

September 22-25
purse, ¥110,000,000

		SCORES			TOTAL	MONEY
Carlos Franco	65	67	68	72	272	¥19,800,000
Tsuneyuki Nakajima	71	70	68	65	274	11,000,000
Naomichi Ozaki	72	69	68	67	276	5,720,000
Masashi Ozaki	72	66	70	68	276	5,720,000
Todd Hamilton	70	70	65	71	276	5,720,000
Nobumitsu Yuhara	69	71	68	69	277	3,960,000
Eiji Mizoguchi	69	71	72	66	278	3,355,000
Katsunari Takahashi	68	72	67	71	278	3,355,000
Ryoken Kawagishi	71	70	70	68	279	2,403,000
Seiki Okuda	68	73	69	69	279	2,403,000
Wayne Smith	71	68	70	70	279	2,403,000
Lin Chie Hsiang	69	64	73	73	279	2,403,000
Bradley Hughes	73	68	71	68	280	1,584,000
Kiyoshi Maita	73	71	67	69	280	1,584,000
Masayuki Kawamura	68	70	71	71	280	1,584,000
Hiroya Kamide	71	70	68	71	280	1,584,000
Samson Gimson	70	68	69	73	280	1,584,000
Chen Tze Chung	69	72	70	70	281	1,047,000
Hiroshi Makino	71	73	67	70	281	1,047,000
Yoshimi Niizeki	71	68	72	70	281	1,047,000
Yoshinori Kaneko	71	67	72	71	281	1,047,000

	SCORES				TOTAL	MONEY
Yoshinori Mizumaki	72	69	69	71	281	1,047,000
Craig Warren	73	69	68	71	281	1,047,000
Satoshi Higashi	72	69	68	72	281	1,047,000
Masahiro Kuramoto	69	69	70	73	281	1,047,000
Motomasa Aoki	71	70	73	68	282	869,000
Kiyoshi Murota	71	70	72	69	282	869,000
Rick Gibson	69	70	74	69	282	869,000
Eduardo Herrera	69	69	73	71	282	869,000
Hideto Shigenobu	72	72	71	68	283	763,000
Akihito Yokoyama	70	71	72	70	283	763,000
Shigeru Kawamata	71	70	72	70	283	763,000
Anthony Gilligan	70	71	71	71	283	763,000
Katsunori Kuwabara	72	67	72	72	283	763,000
Yuichi Takano	72	70	69	72	283	763,000

Japan Open Championship

Yokkaichi Country Club, Mie Prefecture
Par 35-36—71; 7,257 yards

September 29-October 2
purse, ¥100,000,000

	SCORES				TOTAL	MONEY
Masashi Ozaki	68	66	69	67	270	¥18,000,000
David Ishii	70	74	69	70	283	8,600,000
Hideki Kase	71	67	71	74	283	8,600,000
Katsuyoshi Tomori	74	66	73	71	284	5,100,000
Carlos Franco	68	74	76	67	285	4,100,000
Yoshinori Mizumaki	73	70	73	69	285	4,100,000
Tsuneyuki Nakajima	73	71	71	71	286	3,500,000
Frankie Minoza	76	71	68	72	287	2,800,000
Kazuhiro Takami	69	73	72	73	287	2,800,000
Todd Hamilton	72	72	66	77	287	2,800,000
Hiroshi Goda	71	75	74	68	288	1,754,000
Peter Senior	76	68	74	70	288	1,754,000
Masayuki Kawamura	74	72	70	72	288	1,754,000
Seiji Ebihara	72	71	72	73	288	1,754,000
Hiroshi Makino	72	71	72	73	288	1,754,000
Hisayuki Sasaki	75	70	72	72	289	1,310,000
Hideto Shigenobu	72	73	71	73	289	1,310,000
Kohichi Suzuki	71	74	76	69	290	1,009,000
Akiyoshi Omachi	76	69	74	71	290	1,009,000
Hidezumi Shirakata	73	74	72	71	290	1,009,000
Hsieh Min Nan	77	70	71	72	290	1,009,000
Shigeki Maruyama	74	71	72	73	290	1,009,000
Brian Watts	71	69	76	74	290	1,009,000
Yoshimi Niizeki	74	69	72	75	290	1,009,000
Daisuke Serizawa	74	72	73	72	291	854,000
Yoshinori Ichioka	72	74	73	72	291	854,000
Eiichi Itai	70	74	73	74	291	854,000
Ryoken Kawagishi	74	75	74	69	292	771,000
Tsukasa Watanabe	73	76	73	70	292	771,000
Nobuo Serizawa	72	73	76	71	292	771,000
Jim Rutledge	75	71	75	71	292	771,000
Craig Warren	76	69	75	72	292	771,000

Tokai Classic

Miyoshi Country Club, Aichi
Par 36-36—72; 7,089 yards

October 6-9
purse, ¥110,000,000

	SCORES				TOTAL	MONEY
Corey Pavin	68	69	68	72	277	¥19,800,000
Hsieh Chin Sheng	72	68	70	68	278	1,100,000
Akiyoshi Omachi	70	70	73	67	280	5,720,000
Vijay Singh	72	71	69	68	280	5,720,000
Hiroshi Ueda	71	68	68	73	280	5,720,000
Hisayuki Sasaki	69	67	75	70	281	3,960,000
Tsuyoshi Yoneyama	71	70	73	68	282	3,520,000
Brian Watts	70	73	71	69	283	3,190,000
Kazuhiro Takami	71	70	70	73	284	2,860,000
Shigenori Mori	72	71	71	71	285	2,365,000
Katsunari Takahashi	70	70	72	73	285	2,365,000
Kazunari Matsunaga	73	69	72	72	286	1,724,000
Bradley Hughes	72	73	69	72	286	1,724,000
Masanobu Kimura	70	74	69	73	286	1,724,000
Hideto Shigenobu	73	70	69	74	286	1,724,000
Teruo Nakamura	71	71	70	74	286	1,724,000
Ikuo Shirahama	72	73	72	70	287	1,276,000
Masahiro Kuramoto	73	71	72	71	287	1,276,000
Eiji Mizoguchi	73	72	73	70	288	1,037,000
Hideyuki Sato	75	70	73	70	288	1,037,000
Mitsunobu Hatsumi	74	74	69	71	288	1,037,000
Teruo Sugihara	72	71	72	73	288	1,037,000
Peter Senior	73	70	71	74	288	1,037,000
Yutaka Hagawa	73	70	71	74	288	1,037,000
Phil Mickelson	72	75	73	69	289	847,000
Stewart Ginn	75	72	72	70	289	847,000
Atsushi Takamatsu	74	73	72	70	289	847,000
Toshimitsu Izawa	74	73	71	71	289	847,000
Tadami Ueno	73	71	69	76	289	847,000
Jin Han Lim	72	73	68	76	289	847,000

Asahi Beer Golf Digest Tournament

Tohmei Country Club, Shizuoka
Par 35-36—71; 6,801 yards

October 13-16
purse, ¥150,000,000

	SCORES				TOTAL	MONEY
Eiji Mizoguchi	70	68	64	63	265	¥27,000,000
Stewart Ginn	66	69	67	68	270	12,600,000
Hiroshi Ueda	69	68	63	70	270	12,600,000
Peter Senior	67	68	70	66	272	6,200,000
Nobuo Serizawa	68	67	69	68	272	6,200,000
Masahiro Kuramoto	70	68	66	68	272	6,200,000
Hisayuki Sasaki	66	69	70	68	273	4,575,000
Hiroya Kamide	68	65	72	68	273	4,575,000
Hideto Shigenobu	69	69	70	67	275	3,277,000
Brian Watts	71	69	66	69	275	3,277,000
Pete Izumikawa	69	64	73	69	275	3,277,000
Kinpachi Yoshimura	69	69	68	69	275	3,277,000
Tsuneyuki Nakajima	70	70	70	66	276	2,250,000
Toru Suzuki	71	67	69	69	276	2,250,000
Masashi Ozaki	71	69	65	71	276	2,250,000

	SCORES				TOTAL	MONEY
Samson Gimson	68	69	66	73	276	2,250,000
Saburo Fujiki	70	72	69	66	277	1,635,000
Eiichi Itai	66	74	69	68	277	1,635,000
Toshiaki Sudo	71	68	68	70	277	1,635,000
Ken Kusumoto	66	71	70	70	277	1,635,000
Hideki Kase	73	68	70	67	278	1,302,000
Tsukasa Watanabe	71	66	73	68	278	1,302,000
Katsunari Takahashi	67	71	72	68	278	1,302,000
Masayuki Kawamura	66	71	72	69	278	1,302,000
Tadashi Ezure	71	69	69	69	278	1,302,000
David Ishii	69	68	69	72	278	1,302,000
Kazuhiro Takami	68	68	70	72	278	1,302,000
Hsieh Chin Sheng	70	70	72	67	279	1,110,000
Tsuyoshi Yoneyama	71	71	69	68	279	1,110,000
Shigenori Mori	69	71	70	69	279	1,110,000
Anthony Gilligan	69	70	66	74	279	1,110,000
Shigeru Kawamata	69	66	70	74	279	1,110,000

Bridgestone Open

Sodegaura Country Club, Chiba
Par 36-36—72; 7,110 yards

October 20-23
purse, ¥120,000,000

	SCORES				TOTAL	MONEY
Brian Watts	68	67	67	72	274	¥21,600,000
Mark Calcavecchia	72	70	69	66	277	12,000,000
Roger Mackay	67	71	72	68	278	8,160,000
Naomichi Ozaki	71	70	70	68	279	4,960,000
Hisayuki Sasaki	70	71	68	70	279	4,960,000
Nick Price	68	71	70	70	279	4,960,000
Shoichi Kuwahara	70	68	73	69	280	3,480,000
Toshiaki Odate	68	70	72	70	280	3,480,000
Masashi Ozaki	68	71	68	73	280	3,480,000
Teruo Sugihara	72	73	66	70	281	2,760,000
Hideki Kase	68	71	74	69	282	2,304,000
Yoshinori Mizumaki	70	74	67	71	282	2,304,000
Seiji Ebihara	72	70	73	68	283	1,664,000
Hiroya Kamide	74	72	67	70	283	1,664,000
Seiichi Kanai	71	71	71	70	283	1,664,000
Kouki Idoki	71	75	66	71	283	1,664,000
Masayuki Kawamura	70	68	73	72	283	1,664,000
Tsukasa Watanabe	69	69	70	75	283	1,664,000
Hirofumi Miyase	73	72	70	69	284	1,152,000
Hiroshi Ueda	71	74	69	70	284	1,152,000
Frankie Minoza	69	69	74	72	284	1,152,000
Chen Tze Ming	70	73	68	73	284	1,152,000
Mitsutaka Kusakabe	71	71	67	75	284	1,152,000
Richard Backwell	70	73	74	68	285	924,000
Eiji Mizoguchi	71	71	74	69	285	924,000
Anthony Gilligan	69	75	72	69	285	924,000
Akiyoshi Omachi	71	74	71	69	285	924,000
Hideto Shigenobu	73	72	71	69	285	924,000
Nobumitsu Yuhara	69	73	73	70	285	924,000
Rick Gibson	71	75	69	70	285	924,000
Wayne Smith	71	73	70	71	285	924,000
Daisuke Serizawa	67	74	72	72	285	924,000
Kiyoshi Maita	66	74	72	73	285	924,000

Philip Morris Championship

ABC Golf Club, Hyogo
Par 36-36—72; 7,176 yards

October 27-30
purse, ¥200,000,000

	SCORES				TOTAL	MONEY
Brian Watts	71	66	71	68	276	¥36,000,000
Masashi Ozaki	69	70	68	70	277	14,400,000
Naomichi Ozaki	68	66	73	70	277	14,400,000
Duffy Waldorf	70	68	68	71	277	14,400,000
Teruo Sugihara	68	70	70	71	279	8,000,000
Rick Gibson	69	71	70	70	280	6,466,000
Masahiro Kuramoto	69	67	70	74	280	6,466,000
Tsuyoshi Yoneyama	71	70	65	74	280	6,466,000
Hisayuki Sasaki	74	68	72	67	281	4,370,000
Pete Izumikawa	71	74	67	69	281	4,370,000
Toshimitsu Izawa	70	69	72	70	281	4,370,000
Harumitsu Hamano	70	68	71	72	281	4,370,000
Peter Senior	71	71	70	70	282	3,120,000
Lin Chin Hsiang	69	74	68	71	282	3,120,000
Yoshimi Niizeki	68	71	72	71	282	3,120,000
Shoichi Kuwabara	74	67	71	71	283	2,426,000
David Ishii	70	72	69	72	283	2,426,000
Kiyoshi Murota	66	75	70	72	283	2,426,000
Yoshinori Kaneko	71	70	73	70	284	1,886,000
Tomohiro Maruyama	73	70	70	71	284	1,886,000
Shigenori Mori	70	72	70	72	284	1,886,000
Yutaka Hagawa	72	68	72	72	284	1,886,000
Hideki Kase	72	69	70	73	284	1,886,000
Bob Gilder	70	71	69	74	284	1,886,000
Tsuneyuki Nakajima	73	72	71	69	285	1,620,000
Kiyoshi Maita	72	70	72	71	285	1,620,000
Saburo Fujiki	72	71	71	71	285	1,620,000
Hsieh Chin Sheng	74	71	66	74	285	1,620,000
Satoshi Higashi	72	72	73	69	286	1,406,000
Masanobu Kimura	71	75	70	70	286	1,406,000
Chen Tze Chung	72	70	74	70	286	1,406,000
Daisuke Serizawa	73	73	70	70	286	1,406,000
Wayne Smith	71	71	72	72	286	1,406,000
Carlos Franco	73	69	71	73	286	1,406,000
Tsukasa Watanabe	71	71	70	74	286	1,406,000

Daiwa International

Hatoyama Country Club, Mie Prefecture
Par 36-36—72; 7,146 yards

November 3-6
purse, ¥170,000,000

	SCORES				TOTAL	MONEY
Masashi Ozaki	65	72	70	63	270	¥30,600,000
Fuzzy Zoeller	74	73	70	68	285	17,000,000
Todd Hamilton	68	76	71	71	286	9,860,000
Eduardo Herrera	70	74	71	71	286	9,860,000
Chen Tze Ming	69	80	67	71	287	5,822,000
Masahiro Kuramoto	75	70	70	72	287	5,822,000
Craig Warren	74	73	68	72	287	5,822,000
Carlos Franco	73	72	70	72	287	5,822,000
Tsuneyuki Nakajima	70	76	74	68	288	3,910,000
Richard Backwell	74	72	71	71	288	3,910,000

	SCORES				TOTAL	MONEY
Peter McWhinney	69	76	69	74	288	3,910,000
Naomichi Ozaki	68	73	78	70	289	2,992,000
Katsuyoshi Tomori	72	73	70	74	289	2,992,000
Bob Estes	74	75	72	69	290	2,448,000
Masayuki Kawamura	72	78	69	71	290	2,448,000
Yoshinori Kaneko	71	78	70	71	290	2,448,000
Eiji Mizoguchi	70	79	72	70	291	1,904,000
Hisayuki Sasaki	71	74	71	75	291	1,904,000
Mike Reid	72	74	68	77	291	1,904,000
Tsukasa Watanabe	73	77	73	69	292	1,632,000
Seiji Ebihara	74	75	72	71	292	1,632,000
Tomohiro Maruyama	71	80	69	72	292	1,632,000
Lin Chie Hsiang	73	76	75	69	293	1,377,000
Masakazu Noritake	77	75	72	69	293	1,377,000
Kazuhiro Takami	73	78	72	70	293	1,377,000
Jeff Sluman	70	78	75	70	293	1,377,000
Masanobu Kimura	74	74	73	72	293	1,377,000
Kouki Idoki	73	76	71	73	293	1,377,000
Hisashi Nakase	70	73	76	74	293	1,377,000
Graham Marsh	71	75	73	74	293	1,377,000

Sumitomo Visa Taiheiyo Masters

Taiheiyo Club, Gotenba Course, Shizuoka
Par 36-36—72; 7,072 yards

November 10-13
purse, ¥150,000,000

	SCORES				TOTAL	MONEY
Masashi Ozaki	66	69	68	67	270	¥27,000,000
Bob Estes	68	67	72	68	275	15,000,000
Craig Parry	68	69	75	64	276	7,200,000
Kiyoshi Murota	71	68	70	67	276	7,200,000
Eiji Mizoguchi	70	67	71	68	276	7,200,000
Yoshinori Mizumaki	69	70	67	70	276	7,200,000
Tsuneyuki Mizumaki	67	71	73	66	277	4,350,000
Larry Mize	67	70	72	68	277	4,350,000
David Ishii	70	71	66	70	277	4,350,000
Todd Hamilton	69	70	71	68	278	3,450,000
Hideki Kase	75	69	69	66	279	2,760,000
Shigeki Maruyama	68	74	67	70	279	2,760,000
Eiichi Itai	70	69	67	73	279	2,760,000
Ikuo Shirahama	68	73	71	68	280	1,992,000
Phil Mickelson	69	71	72	68	280	1,992,000
Seve Ballesteros	73	69	70	68	280	1,992,000
Teruo Nakamura	72	69	68	71	280	1,992,000
Katsuyoshi Tomori	71	67	69	73	280	1,992,000
Nobuo Serizawa	73	70	70	68	281	1,470,000
Hiroshi Ueda	75	69	69	68	281	1,470,000
Masahiro Kuramoto	72	70	69	70	281	1,470,000
Billy Andrade	68	69	72	72	281	1,470,000
Masanobu Kimura	73	71	71	67	282	1,305,000
Jeff Sluman	69	69	74	70	282	1,305,000
Naomichi Ozaki	73	67	71	72	283	1,245,000
Shigenori Mori	68	72	70	73	283	1,245,000
Nobumitsu Yuhara	73	71	74	66	284	1,140,000
Mike Heinen	73	69	73	69	284	1,140,000
Saburo Fujiki	73	72	69	70	284	1,140,000
Anthony Gilligan	70	72	71	71	284	1,140,000
Isao Aoki	70	75	67	72	284	1,140,000

Dunlop Phoenix

Phoenix Country Club, Miyazaki
Par 36-36—72; 6,993 yards
(Second round cancelled — heavy rains.)

November 17-20
purse, ¥150,000,000

	SCORES			TOTAL	MONEY
Masashi Ozaki	67	69	65	201	¥27,000,000
Tom Watson	66	68	68	202	15,000,000
Scott Hoch	71	69	64	204	7,800,000
Nobuo Serizawa	69	66	69	204	7,800,000
Barry Lane	66	69	69	204	7,800,000
Larry Mize	68	71	66	205	5,100,000
Naomichi Ozaki	68	68	69	205	5,100,000
Isao Aoki	71	67	68	206	4,125,000
David Ishii	71	65	70	206	4,125,000
Yoshinori Mizumaki	69	70	68	207	2,932,000
Kouki Idoki	68	71	68	207	2,932,000
Tom Lehman	68	71	68	207	2,932,000
Miguel Angel Jimenez	72	67	68	207	2,932,000
Masanobu Kimura	70	71	67	208	2,250,000
Satoshi Higashi	67	71	70	208	2,250,000
Brian Watts	72	68	69	209	1,660,000
Eiji Mizoguchi	72	67	70	209	1,660,000
Ernie Els	66	73	70	209	1,660,000
Peter Senior	73	65	71	209	1,660,000
Larry Nelson	68	70	71	209	1,660,000
Costantino Rocca	71	66	72	209	1,660,000
Robert Allenby	72	71	67	210	1,280,000
Hiroshi Makino	70	72	68	210	1,280,000
Seve Ballesteros	71	71	68	210	1,280,000
Tetsu Nishikawa	70	70	70	210	1,280,000
Jose Maria Olazabal	69	70	71	210	1,280,000
Todd Hamilton	66	72	72	210	1,280,000
Samson Gimson	72	71	68	211	1,140,000
Masahiro Kuramoto	73	68	70	211	1,140,000
Jack Nicklaus	70	71	70	211	1,140,000

Casio World Open

Ibusuki Golf Club, Kaimon Course, Kagoshima
Par 36-36—72; 7,014 yards

November 24-27
purse, ¥150,000,000

	SCORES				TOTAL	MONEY
Robert Gamez	68	66	68	69	271	¥27,000,000
Scott Hoch	70	69	67	69	275	15,000,000
Jose Maria Olazabal	70	70	70	67	277	8,700,000
Eiji Mizoguchi	73	66	67	71	277	8,700,000
Brian Watts	69	73	71	65	278	5,700,000
Shinji Ikeuchi	70	65	64	69	278	5,700,000
Mitsutaka Kusakabe	73	70	69	67	279	3,900,000
Yoshimi Niizeki	70	74	67	68	279	3,900,000
Hsieh Chin Sheng	71	68	71	69	279	3,900,000
Satoshi Higashi	69	70	70	70	279	3,900,000
Wayne Smith	67	69	68	75	279	3,900,000
Richard Gibson	69	69	73	69	280	2,540,000
Hideki Kase	74	69	67	70	280	2,540,000
Masayuki Kawamura	68	70	71	71	280	2,540,000

	SCORES				TOTAL	MONEY
Joakim Haeggman	70	73	72	66	281	1,980,000
Tsuneyuki Nakajima	68	72	71	70	281	1,980,000
Yoshinori Kaneko	69	70	70	72	281	1,980,000
Kouki Idoki	73	69	72	68	282	1,386,000
Hiroshi Makino	73	69	72	68	282	1,386,000
Katsuyoshi Tomori	71	67	73	71	282	1,386,000
Ryoken Kawagishi	68	70	73	71	282	1,386,000
Akiyoshi Omachi	74	70	67	71	282	1,386,000
Tsuyoshi Yoneyama	69	70	71	72	282	1,386,000
Richard Backwell	71	69	70	72	282	1,386,000
Hideyuki Sato	70	72	68	72	282	1,386,000
Keith Clearwater	74	66	70	72	282	1,386,000
Ikuo Shirahama	69	70	70	73	282	1,386,000
Mike Reid	71	71	75	66	283	1,056,000
Todd Hamilton	73	69	72	69	283	1,056,000
Hiroya Kamide	69	72	72	70	283	1,056,000
Hisayuki Sasaki	71	64	77	71	283	1,056,000
Costantino Rocca	72	72	68	71	283	1,056,000
Hirofumi Miyase	74	69	68	72	283	1,056,000
Tom Lehman	70	72	69	72	283	1,056,000
Miguel Angel Jimenez	71	70	70	72	283	1,056,000
Saburo Fujiki	71	66	72	74	283	1,056,000

Japan Series Hitachi Cup

Yomiuri Member Golf Club, Hyogo
Par 36-35—71; 7,002 yards

December 1-4
purse, ¥100,000,000

	SCORES				TOTAL	MONEY
Hisayuki Sasaki	68	66	70	66	270	¥30,000,000
Naomichi Ozaki	62	66	69	74	271	15,000,000
Tsuneyuki Nakajima	68	70	67	67	272	7,500,000
Eiji Mizoguchi	64	70	70	71	275	5,500,000
Masayuki Kawamura	66	67	72	71	276	4,350,000
Yoshinori Kaneko	65	68	67	76	276	4,350,000
Brian Watts	71	69	71	66	277	3,200,000
David Ishii	68	71	71	67	277	3,200,000
Katsuyoshi Tomori	67	70	71	69	277	3,200,000
Hsieh Chin Sheng	73	68	66	72	279	2,500,000
Tsukasa Watanabe	69	69	73	69	280	2,250,000
Craig Warren	70	71	71	69	281	2,000,000
Masayuki Kuramoto	71	70	68	74	283	1,800,000
Nobuo Serizawa	72	72	71	69	284	1,500,000
Kazuhiro Takami	74	72	67	71	284	1,500,000
Toru Suzuki	68	71	69	76	284	1,500,000
Hiroshi Goda	71	73	69	72	285	1,250,000
Katsunari Takahashi	67	70	75	73	285	1,250,000
Kiyoshi Murota	71	71	72	73	287	1,150,000
Yoshinori Mizumaki	71	68	77	74	290	1,075,000
Hiroshi Ueda	72	72	71	75	290	1,075,000
Tomohiro Maruyama	71	72	73	76	292	1,000,000
Todd Hamilton	73	71	72	81	297	950,000
Pete Izumikawa	73	74	77	76	300	800,000

Daikyo Open

Daikyo Country Club, Okinawa
Par 36-35—71; 6,276 yards

December 8-11
purse, ¥120,000,000

	SCORES				TOTAL	MONEY
Hideki Kase	69	66	66	67	268	¥21,600,000
Masahiro Kuramoto	69	72	63	65	269	8,640,000
Ken Kusumoto	63	70	68	68	269	8,640,000
Seiji Ebihara	66	70	64	69	269	8,640,000
Hirofumi Miyase	66	66	70	68	270	4,800,000
Isamu Sugita	67	69	68	69	273	4,320,000
Hsieh Chin Sheng	68	71	68	67	274	3,660,000
Yoshitaka Yamamoto	66	67	71	70	274	3,660,000
Tomohiro Maruyama	67	70	66	72	275	3,120,000
Hiroya Kamide	70	72	70	64	276	2,580,000
Masanobu Kimura	68	71	70	67	276	2,580,000
Stewart Ginn	70	71	69	67	277	1,881,000
Kohichi Suzuki	70	71	68	68	277	1,881,000
Yoshinori Kaneko	68	70	70	69	277	1,881,000
Tadashi Ezure	70	68	69	70	277	1,881,000
David Ishii	68	67	71	71	277	1,881,000
Hiroshi Goda	72	68	72	66	278	1,197,000
Ryoken Kawagishi	73	70	69	66	278	1,197,000
Hiroshi Makino	70	69	73	66	278	1,197,000
Satoshi Higashi	73	69	68	68	278	1,197,000
Katsuyoshi Tomori	73	67	69	69	278	1,197,000
Eiichi Itai	68	73	68	69	278	1,197,000
Wayne Smith	71	70	67	70	278	1,197,000
Toshiaki Sudo	67	70	67	74	278	1,197,000
Peter McWhinney	70	73	69	67	279	960,000
Ikuo Shirahama	71	64	75	69	279	960,000
Masahiro Kawamura	67	74	67	71	279	960,000
Zaw Moe	69	67	69	74	279	960,000
Atsushi Takamatsu	67	68	70	74	279	960,000
Atsushi Ikehara	68	70	74	68	280	813,000
Rick Gibson	71	70	69	70	280	813,000
Kouki Idoki	71	68	71	70	280	813,000
Hideto Shigenobu	71	72	66	71	280	813,000
Jin Han Lim	70	70	68	72	280	813,000
Hiromichi Namiki	71	69	68	72	280	813,000
Richard Backwell	67	71	69	73	280	813,000
Seiki Okuda	70	68	68	74	280	813,000

Australasian Tour

AMP New Zealand Open

The Remuera Golf Club, Auckland, New Zealand
Par 34-37—71; 6,783 yards

January 6-9
purse, A$243,000

	SCORES				TOTAL	MONEY
Craig Jones	69	71	65	72	277	A$43,740
Frank Nobilo	68	68	72	70	278	24,786
Steven Conran	70	69	70	71	280	12,595.50
Tony Maloney	68	70	70	72	280	12,595.50
Zoran Zorkic	67	66	73	74	280	12,595.50
Evan Droop	69	73	70	69	281	8,748
David Iwasaki-Smith	65	76	74	67	282	6,864.75
Peter Fowler	72	69	72	69	282	6,864.75
Michael Long	71	69	69	73	282	6,864.75
Greg Turner	70	65	72	75	282	6,864.75
Grant Moorhead	66	72	72	73	283	5,346
Michael Campbell	73	69	71	71	284	4,455
Robert Willis	70	69	72	73	284	4,455
Chris Gray	69	71	68	76	284	4,455
George Serhan	74	71	72	68	285	3,136.72
Leith Wastle	69	69	77	70	285	3,136.72
Anthony Painter	68	71	76	70	285	3,136.72
David Diaz	69	71	73	72	285	3,136.72
John Senden	74	71	68	72	285	3,136.72
Jeff Senior	73	66	70	76	286	3,136.72
Mike Weir	71	73	71	71	286	2,502.90
Max Stevens	72	67	73	74	286	2,502.90
Craig Mann	70	73	71	73	287	2,253.82
David Smail	69	70	75	73	287	2,253.82
Rob Whitlock	66	70	78	73	287	2,253.82
Phillip Tataurangi	73	73	68	73	287	2,253.82
Jonathan Cresswell	77	70	71	70	288	1,846.80
Mark Allen	74	72	71	71	288	1,846.80
John Wade	71	73	73	72	289	1,652.40
Jeffrey Wagner	72	73	71	73	289	1,652.40
Matthew Lane	73	72	70	74	289	1,652.40

Optus Players Championship

Kingston Heath Golf Club, Melbourne, Australia
Par 36-36—72; 6,814 yards

January 20-23
purse, A$300,000

	SCORES				TOTAL	MONEY
Patrick Burke	69	67	72	72	280	A$54,000
Bradley Hughes	68	73	70	70	281	30,600
Ossie Moore	73	70	69	70	282	20,250
Craig Parry	72	70	72	69	283	10,600
Steven Conran	68	72	73	70	283	10,600
Phillip Tataurangi	69	75	69	70	283	10,600
Wayne Smith	66	77	69	71	283	10,600

	SCORES				TOTAL	MONEY
Leith Wastle	70	71	71	71	283	10,600
Peter Senior	70	73	68	72	283	10,600
Grant Moorhead	71	73	71	69	284	7,050
Robert Allenby	72	74	69	69	284	7,050
Anthony Gilligan	68	76	71	71	286	5,325
Russell Swanson	69	69	75	73	286	5,325
Tim Herron	67	75	72	72	286	5,325
Anthony Painter	64	78	69	75	286	5,325
David Iwasaki-Smith	69	73	74	71	287	4,110
Mark Allen	70	70	72	75	287	4,110
Paul Devenport	72	72	74	70	288	3,405
Michael Harwood	71	74	70	73	288	3,405
Matthew Lane	68	74	68	78	288	3,405
Andre Stolz	70	72	75	72	289	3,060
Michael Clayton	70	69	75	75	289	3,060
Simon Owen	70	72	69	78	289	3,060
Brad Andrews	70	77	76	67	290	2,617.50
Jim Kennedy	72	75	71	72	290	2,617.50
Robert Stevens	72	70	74	74	290	2,617.50
Jeff Senior	69	76	70	75	290	2,617.50
Brad King	72	76	72	71	291	2,085
Gavin Stratfold	71	71	76	73	291	2,085
Richard Backwell	73	73	74	71	291	2,085
Peter Fowler	73	73	70	75	291	2,085

Heineken Classic

The Vines Resort, Perth, Western Australia
Par 36-36—72; 6,720 yards

January 27-30
purse, A$350,000

	SCORES				TOTAL	MONEY
Michael Clayton	67	71	71	70	279	A$63,000
Wayne Smith	69	67	73	73	282	35,700
Patrick Burke	68	68	78	69	283	20,212.50
Robert Allenby	70	69	71	73	283	20,212.50
David Ecob	72	70	75	67	284	14,000
Chris Van Der Velde	67	72	73	73	285	12,600
Richard Green	70	70	75	71	286	10,675
Jeff Senior	71	77	70	68	286	10,675
John Senden	68	74	72	73	287	8,225
Rick Gibson	70	70	73	74	287	8,225
Tim Herron	70	70	70	77	287	8,225
Michael Campbell	73	67	78	69	287	8,225
Chris Gray	73	75	73	67	288	6,125
Peter Senior	74	68	72	74	288	6,125
Andre Stolz	75	70	75	69	289	4,665.50
Darren Barnes	69	73	73	74	289	4,665.50
John Wade	72	74	69	74	289	4,665.50
Michael Harwood	79	69	73	68	289	4,665.50
Martyn Roberts	79	69	70	71	289	4,665.50
Craig Parry	71	74	76	69	290	3,500
Arden Knoll	78	69	73	70	290	3,500
Rodger Davis	67	72	77	74	290	3,500
Jon Evans	76	70	73	71	290	3,500
Brad Andrews	72	70	76	72	290	3,500
Evan Droop	76	72	70	72	290	3,500
David Hill	75	70	75	71	291	2,632

	SCORES				TOTAL	MONEY
Stephen Collins	71	72	73	75	291	2,632
Graham Marsh	71	68	74	78	291	2,632
Bradley Hughes	74	71	74	72	291	2,632
Stephen Leaney	72	72	75	72	291	2,632

New South Wales Open

Manly Golf Club, Sydney, Australia
Par 36-36—72; 6,620 yards

February 3-6
purse, A$50,000

	SCORES				TOTAL	MONEY
Darren Chivas	73	71	69	70	283	A$9,000
David Ecob	75	71	68	70	284	5,000
Russell Swanson	75	71	67	73	286	2,937.50
Michael Campbell	70	72	70	74	286	2,937.50
David McKenzie	74	70	73	70	287	2,000
Grant Kenny	67	73	72	77	289	1,600
Gregory Hohnen	71	74	74	70	289	1,600
Steven Conran	74	71	72	72	289	1,600
Dean Wilson	75	76	65	74	290	1,168.75
Mike Weir	76	72	74	68	290	1,168.75
George Serhan	77	67	75	71	290	1,168.75
Daniel Motusenko	71	71	72	76	290	1,168.75
Robert Willis	70	76	71	74	291	709.38
Jeffrey Wagner	74	69	77	71	291	709.38
Andre Stolz	71	74	73	73	291	709.38
Ricky Schmidt	73	75	70	73	291	709.38
Khan Pullen	74	75	66	76	291	709.38
Paul Gow	68	77	72	74	291	709.38
Craig Cork	75	75	67	74	291	709.38
Gavin Coles	75	70	72	74	291	709.38
Anthony Summers	73	73	72	74	292	512.50
Neale Smith	73	72	76	71	292	512.50
Tim Herron	69	74	73	76	292	512.50
Darren Cole	73	75	72	72	292	512.50
Leonard Wade	76	70	76	71	293	450
Noel Ratcliffe	70	74	75	74	293	450
Peter Jones	73	72	70	78	293	450
David Snelling	74	74	74	72	294	375
Lucas Parsons	74	76	71	73	294	375
David Hill	74	75	71	74	294	375

Microsoft Australian Masters

Huntingdale Golf Club, Melbourne, Australia
Par 36-37—73; 6,955 yards

February 17-20
purse, A$750,000

	SCORES				TOTAL	MONEY
Craig Parry	74	70	70	68	282	A$135,000
Ernie Els	70	70	72	73	285	76,500
Peter Senior	73	71	74	68	286	43,312.50
Peter Teravainen	71	70	75	70	286	43,312.50
Wayne Smith	71	74	72	70	287	30,000
Robert Willis	74	72	73	69	288	23,250

	SCORES				TOTAL	MONEY
Michael Harwood	69	76	71	72	288	23,250
Wayne Grady	68	75	72	73	288	23,250
Lucas Parsons	74	71	71	72	288	23,250
Brett Ogle	73	70	74	73	290	16,750
Paul Devenport	72	76	71	71	290	16,750
Andre Stolz	73	75	73	69	290	16,750
Patrick Burke	69	71	76	75	291	11,760
Peter O'Malley	75	70	73	73	291	11,760
Russell Swanson	71	70	76	74	291	11,760
Richard Backwell	73	71	75	72	291	11,760
Simon Owen	70	72	76	73	291	11,760
Michael Clayton	72	75	75	70	292	8,334.37
Leith Wastle	71	71	79	71	292	8,334.37
Katsuyoshi Tomori	70	72	77	73	292	8,334.37
Greg Norman	73	74	68	77	292	8,334.37
Terry Gale	70	77	76	70	293	7,575
Nobumitsu Yuhara	73	75	73	72	293	7,575
Michael Campbell	73	75	76	70	294	6,345
Chris Gray	80	68	76	70	294	6,345
Anthony Painter	72	75	73	74	294	6,345
Greg Sweatt	67	76	77	74	294	6,345
Grant Kenny	65	78	72	79	294	6,345
Rodger Davis	70	74	80	71	295	4,890
Neale Smith	74	74	75	72	295	4,890
Richard Green	74	76	73	72	295	4,890
Gavin Stratfold	70	76	74	75	295	4,890
Jeffrey Wagner	73	72	73	77	295	4,890

Canon Challenge

Castle Hill Country Club, Sydney, Australia
Par 36-36—72; 6,716 yards

February 24-27
purse, A$300,000

	SCORES				TOTAL	MONEY
Peter Senior	68	67	72	69	276	A$54,000
Chris Gray	70	68	70	68	276	30,600
Stuart Appleby	71	69	73	67	280	14,362.50
Rob Whitlock	71	71	68	70	280	14,362.50
Simon Owen	68	72	69	71	280	14,362.50
Richard Green	73	71	64	72	280	14,362.50
Katsuyoshi Tomori	70	67	73	71	281	9,600
Michael Clayton	73	68	71	70	282	6,771.42
Dean Wilson	68	73	71	70	282	6,771.42
Robert Willis	70	69	73	70	282	6,771.42
Paul Devenport	71	70	69	72	282	6,771.42
Leith Wastle	69	71	70	72	282	6,771.42
Stephen Scahill	71	72	67	72	282	6,771.42
Gavin Stratfold	70	70	68	74	282	6,771.42
David Iwasaki-Smith	71	70	70	72	283	4,560
Anthony Painter	72	64	73	74	283	4,560
Wayne Dodd	72	73	71	68	284	3,528.75
Bradley Hughes	72	73	68	71	284	3,528.75
Hank Baran	68	74	68	74	284	3,528.75
Craig Jones	68	71	70	75	284	3,528.75
Anthony Gilligan	71	67	73	74	285	3,090
Peter McWhinney	69	72	68	76	285	3,090
John Senden	70	69	77	70	286	2,545.71

	SCORES				TOTAL	MONEY
Scott Laycock	69	74	73	70	286	2,545.71
Steven Conran	69	71	75	71	286	2,545.71
Brian Jones	70	73	72	71	286	2,545.71
Raymond Picker	69	72	73	72	286	2,545.71
Michael Long	73	71	69	73	286	2,545.71
Jon Evans	72	68	69	77	286	2,545.71
Darren Chivas	71	72	73	71	287	1,845
Martin Peterson	75	70	71	71	287	1,845
Jamie Taylor	72	71	71	73	287	1,845
Max Stevens	73	70	71	73	287	1,845
Tim Herron	72	68	72	75	287	1,845
Neale Smith	71	70	68	78	287	1,845

Foodlink Queensland Open

Windaroo Country Club, Beenligh, Queensland, Australia   October 20-23
Par 36-36—72; 6,850 yards   purse, A$200,000

	SCORES				TOTAL	MONEY
Lucas Parsons	66	72	75	69	282	A$36,000
Michael Campbell	68	77	66	73	284	20,400
Michael Clayton	70	72	75	70	287	11,550
Glenn Joyner	73	69	73	72	287	11,550
Shane Robinson	71	73	74	70	288	7,600
Robb MacDonald	76	71	70	71	288	7,600
Don Fardon	73	69	77	70	289	6,100
Russell Swanson	74	72	71	72	289	6,100
Grant Kenny	74	71	74	71	290	5,200
Glen Lilley	70	74	72	74	290	5,200
*Adam Levesconte	67	75	77	72	291	
*Chris Jones	69	72	73	77	291	
*Robert Brook	67	72	74	78	291	
David Hill	73	72	77	69	291	4,000
Jack O'Keefe	68	70	80	73	291	4,000
Krishna Singh	70	74	74	73	291	4,000
Shane Tait	72	76	73	71	292	2,698.57
Stephen Leaney	71	69	79	73	292	2,698.57
Rob Willis	71	74	74	73	292	2,698.57
David Iwasaki-Smith	69	72	77	74	292	2,698.57
Michael Etherington	70	77	71	74	292	2,698.57
Rob Whitlock	73	75	69	75	292	2,698.57
Neil Kerry	74	73	65	80	292	2,698.57
John Clifford	71	75	76	71	293	2,010
Peter Teravainen	71	71	76	75	293	2,010
Cameron Howell	73	75	70	75	293	2,010
Kevin Miskimins	69	75	74	75	293	2,010
Peter Lonard	73	73	77	71	294	1,635
Scott Laycock	76	71	74	73	294	1,635
Jeff Senior	70	76	73	75	294	1,635
Martyn Roberts	73	76	70	75	294	1,635

Epson Singapore Open

Tanah Merah County Club, Singapore
Par 36-36—72; 7,001 yards

October 27-30
purse, A$546,040

	SCORES				TOTAL	MONEY
Kyi Hla Han	67	69	68	71	275	A$98,287.20
Wayne Grady	68	70	69	69	276	55,696.08
Chris Gray	69	70	69	69	277	36,857.70
Michael Clayton	68	69	70	72	279	24,025.76
Hsieh Yu Shu	69	69	69	72	279	24,025.76
Stephen Leaney	68	67	72	73	280	19,657.44
Jack O'Keefe	71	68	71	71	281	14,743.08
David Iwasaki-Smith	71	68	70	72	281	14,743.08
Boonchu Ruangkit	72	71	67	71	281	14,743.08
Rob Willis	67	69	72	73	281	14,743.08
Andre Stolz	68	71	70	72	281	14,743.08
Robert Farley	71	69	71	71	282	10,374.75
Tom Pernice	72	69	68	73	282	10,374.75
Darren Cole	72	73	69	69	283	9,009.66
Michael Campbell	72	69	71	71	283	9,009.66
Prayad Marksaeng	72	71	71	70	284	6,538.82
Don Fardon	70	72	72	70	284	6,538.82
Mike Cunning	70	72	72	70	284	6,538.82
Grant Dodd	69	72	71	72	284	6,538.82
Patrick Burke	72	72	68	72	284	6,538.82
Carlos Larrain	70	70	70	74	284	6,538.82
Terry Price	73	69	72	71	285	5,515
Leith Wastle	71	71	71	72	285	5,515
Paul Moloney	71	70	74	71	286	4,619.49
Aaron Meeks	68	72	74	72	286	4,619.49
Mark Allen	71	73	73	69	286	4,619.49
Rob Whitlock	69	73	71	73	286	4,619.49
K. Kasyadi	73	67	71	75	286	4,619.49
David Hill	74	68	75	70	287	3,560.18
David Podlich	71	71	75	70	287	3,560.18
Max Stevens	71	73	70	73	287	3,560.18
Paul Devenport	72	69	72	74	287	3,560.18
Greg Sweatt	72	73	73	69	287	3,560.18

Alfred Dunhill Asian Masters

Bali Golf & Country Club, Bali, Indonesia
Par 36-35—71; 6,829 yards

November 3-6
purse, A$466,216

	SCORES				TOTAL	MONEY
Jack Kay	73	66	66	72	277	A$83,918.88
Patrick Burke	68	70	70	70	278	47,554.03
Vijay Singh	75	70	67	67	279	31,469.58
Colin Montgomerie	68	75	71	66	280	19,270.26
Terry Price	71	73	68	68	280	19,270.26
Craig Parry	70	67	71	72	280	19,270.26
Nico Van Rensburg	69	73	70	69	281	13,675.66
Michael Campbell	71	70	69	71	281	13,675.66
David Frost	70	70	70	71	281	13,675.66
Mike Cunning	67	74	71	70	282	10,956.07
Jong Duck Kim	74	69	70	69	282	10,956.07
Paul Devenport	70	73	73	67	283	8,858.10

	SCORES				TOTAL	MONEY
Jack O'Keefe	69	72	72	70	283	8,858.10
Terry Gale	67	76	75	66	284	6,750.80
Peter O'Malley	73	69	75	67	284	6,750.80
Tony Carolan	70	74	71	69	284	6,750.80
David Podlich	73	73	67	71	284	6,750.80
I. Ilyasak	70	71	70	73	284	6,750.80
Rob Willis	73	69	72	71	285	4,971.02
Max Stevens	70	72	70	73	285	4,971.02
Michael Clayton	71	71	71	72	285	4,971.02
Andre Stolz	69	73	66	77	285	4,971.02
Matthew King	71	74	73	68	286	4,324.15
Simon Owen	70	74	71	71	286	4,324.15
Hsieh Yu Shu	72	72	71	71	286	4,324.15
Glenn Joyner	73	70	71	72	286	4,324.15
Shane Tait	69	73	74	71	287	3,543.24
Russell Swanson	68	74	72	73	287	3,543.24
Mark Allen	71	74	74	69	288	3,100.33
Evan Droop	72	71	72	73	288	3,100.33
Tim Elliott	70	75	71	72	288	3,100.33
Shane Robinson	70	72	71	75	288	3,100.33

Victorian Open

Victoria Golf Club, Melbourne, Australia
Par 36-36—72; 6,801 yards

November 10-13
purse, A$200,000

	SCORES				TOTAL	MONEY
Patrick Burke	73	70	68	67	278	A$36,000
Rob Willis	69	69	70	72	280	16,950
Tim Elliott	70	71	70	69	280	16,950
Stuart Allenby	71	66	77	67	281	9,600
*Gary Simpson	68	71	70	73	282	
Robert Allenby	71	69	71	72	283	8,000
*Craig Spence	70	71	77	67	285	
Paul Moloney	73	70	74	68	285	6,200
Stephen Scahill	73	73	69	70	285	6,200
*Jarrod Moseley	73	71	71	70	285	
Mike Harwood	68	74	72	71	285	6,200
Andrew Bonhomme	71	72	71	71	285	6,200
Brad King	72	73	71	70	286	4,466.66
Wayne Riley	69	74	71	72	286	4,466.66
Matthew King	72	72	70	72	286	4,466.66
*Gavin Vearing	72	70	75	70	287	
Glen Lilley	75	69	73	70	287	3,013.33
Tony Christie	74	71	71	71	287	3,013.33
Richard Lee	75	71	70	71	287	3,013.33
Bradley Hughes	71	73	70	73	287	3,013.33
Terry Price	70	74	70	73	287	3,013.33
Peter Lonard	72	69	72	74	287	3,013.33
Matthew Ecob	74	71	72	71	288	2,250
Jack O'Keefe	69	73	77	70	289	2,000
Max Stevens	71	76	71	71	289	2,000
Andrew Gott	75	71	71	72	289	2,000
Evan Droop	75	68	71	75	289	2,000
Stuart Hendley	71	71	70	77	289	2,000
Jack Kay	72	71	69	77	289	2,000
Jon Evans	71	76	74	69	290	1,540

	SCORES	TOTAL	MONEY
Grant Dodd	74 74 71 71	290	1,540
George Serhan	70 72 75 73	290	1,540
Greg Sweatt	72 74 71 73	290	1,540

Reebok PGA Championship

New South Wales Golf Club, New South Wales, Australia
Par 36-36—72; 6,771 yards

November 17-20
purse, A$200,000

	SCORES	TOTAL	MONEY
Andrew Coltart	67 67 77 70	281	A$36,000
Terry Price	67 73 72 71	283	20,400
Mike Harwood	69 69 72 74	284	13,500
Grant Moorhead	67 73 73 72	285	8,800
Wayne Riley	70 71 72 72	285	8,800
Elliott Boult	64 71 78 73	286	6,466.66
Paul Moloney	69 71 73 73	286	6,466.66
Paul Devenport	66 69 73 78	286	6,466.66
Rodger Davis	67 76 71 73	287	4,933.33
Lucas Parsons	70 75 67 75	287	4,933.33
Lyndsay Stephen	73 72 67 75	287	4,933.33
Iain Pyman	70 73 76 69	288	3,416
Jack O'Keefe	71 74 71 72	288	3,416
Stuart Appleby	66 72 77 73	288	3,416
David Diaz	72 73 70 73	288	3,416
Stuart Bouvier	70 73 70 75	288	3,416
Tim Elliott	68 74 75 72	289	2,255
Jamie Taylor	68 68 80 73	289	2,255
Jeff Wagner	69 71 75 74	289	2,255
Jeff Woodland	69 74 72 74	289	2,255
Bradley Hughes	70 74 71 74	289	2,255
Stuart Hendley	71 70 71 77	289	2,255
Patrick Burke	68 70 76 76	290	2,000
Jim Kennedy	70 77 72 72	291	1,646.66
Peter Teravainen	69 76 72 74	291	1,646.66
Grant Dodd	71 73 72 75	291	1,646.66
Anthony Painter	73 68 73 77	291	1,646.66
Richard Lee	71 74 69 77	291	1,646.66
Retief Goosen	66 71 76 78	291	1,646.66
Rob Willis	68 75 75 74	292	1,300
Jean Van de Velde	70 73 73 76	292	1,300
Grant Waite	68 77 70 77	292	1,300

Heineken Australian Open

Royal Sydney Golf Club, Sydney, Australia
Par 36-36—72; 6,815 yards

November 24-27
purse, A$850,000

	SCORES	TOTAL	MONEY
Robert Allenby	70 70 70 70	280	A$153,000
Brett Ogle	69 68 70 74	281	86,700
Peter Baker	70 71 68 73	282	57,375
Brad Faxon	70 76 67 70	283	35,133.33
Gary Orr	76 68 68 71	283	35,133.33
Greg Norman	74 70 68 71	283	35,133.33

	SCORES				TOTAL	MONEY
*David Bransdon	69	73	70	72	284	
Paul Devenport	73	69	67	75	284	27,200
Wayne Grady	70	68	74	73	285	22,950
Lyndsay Stephen	73	69	70	73	285	22,950
Paul Moloney	70	72	70	73	285	22,950
Pierre Fulke	73	71	73	69	286	15,810
Mike Weir	76	69	69	72	286	15,810
Terry Price	71	71	70	74	286	15,810
Jeff Woodland	70	69	72	75	286	15,810
Mike Harwood	73	71	70	72	286	15,810
*Greg Chalmers	73	72	66	75	286	
Simon Owen	74	71	75	67	287	10,178.75
Peter O'Malley	75	72	70	70	287	10,178.75
Grant Waite	73	70	72	72	287	10,178.75
Michael Clayton	75	67	70	75	287	10,178.75
Andrew Bruyns	70	74	71	72	287	10,178.75
Craig Parry	70	69	72	76	287	10,178.75
Retief Goosen	73	71	74	70	288	8,245
Rob Whitlock	74	70	72	72	288	8,245
Grant Moorhead	73	72	71	72	288	8,245
Rob Willis	76	71	68	73	288	8,245
Jamie Spence	71	75	74	69	289	6,545
Jeff Wagner	71	73	72	73	289	6,545
Lee Westwood	75	71	68	75	289	6,545
Andre Stolz	71	71	70	77	289	6,545

Greg Norman's Holden Classic

Royal Melbourne Golf Club, Composite Course, Melbourne, Australia   December 1-4
Par 35-37—72; 6,994 yards   purse, A$700,000

	SCORES				TOTAL	MONEY
Anthony Gilligan	71	66	70	67	274	A$126,000
Paul Moloney	69	69	71	67	276	50,750
Greg Norman	71	67	69	69	276	50,750
Mike Calcavecchia	68	68	70	70	276	50,750
Peter Fowler	72	69	70	67	278	26,600
Lucas Parsons	71	71	69	67	278	26,600
Brett Ogle	72	67	72	69	280	21,350
Wayne Grady	71	70	70	69	280	21,350
*Gary Simpson	72	69	68	71	280	
Peter O'Malley	70	68	73	70	281	18,900
Brad Faxon	71	67	70	74	282	16,450
Glenn Joyner	73	65	69	75	282	16,450
*Greg Chalmers	71	73	70	69	283	
*David Bransdon	71	69	72	71	283	
Lennie Clements	70	70	70	73	283	12,833.33
Andre Stolz	71	69	70	73	283	12,833.33
Steve Rintoul	69	71	71	72	283	12,833.33
Robert Farley	71	71	73	69	284	9,695
Steve Conran	71	71	67	75	284	9,695
Robert Allenby	71	68	69	76	284	9,695
Terry Price	72	69	67	76	284	9,695
Craig Parry	70	70	73	72	285	7,371
Grant Kenny	74	72	73	68	285	7,371
Grant Waite	72	70	72	71	285	7,371
Neil Kerry	74	72	68	71	285	7,371

	SCORES				TOTAL	MONEY
Michael Clayton	72	70	70	73	285	7,371
Elliott Boult	77	68	71	70	286	6,107.50
Max Stevens	75	68	70	73	286	6,107.50
Peter Senior	74	69	69	74	286	6,107.50
Craig Jones	72	74	68	72	286	6,107.50

Air New Zealand-Shell Open

The Grange Golf Club, Auckland, New Zealand
Par 35-35—70; 6,533 yards

December 8-11
purse, A$244,050

	SCORES				TOTAL	MONEY
Shane Robinson	70	64	69	71	274	A$43,929
David McKenzie	70	74	65	66	275	24,893.10
Terry Price	69	69	72	66	276	10,270.43
Don Fardon	67	69	74	66	276	10,270.43
Peter Fowler	71	68	70	67	276	10,270.43
David Smail	74	63	71	68	276	10,270.43
Tony Christie	67	69	71	69	276	10,270.43
Lucas Parsons	64	70	68	74	276	10,270.43
Jack O'Keefe	71	69	69	68	277	6,589.35
David Podlich	70	73	67	68	278	5,450.45
Neale Smith	69	70	70	69	278	5,450.45
Andre Stolz	67	70	66	75	278	5,450.45
Greg Turner	69	71	73	66	279	4,270.87
Phillip Tataurangi	69	69	71	70	279	4,270.87
Craig Cassells	72	69	71	68	280	3,150.27
David Ecob	69	71	72	68	280	3,150.27
Gavin Stratfold	69	71	72	68	280	3,150.27
Grant Moorhead	73	67	71	69	280	3,150.27
Chris Taylor	71	69	71	69	280	3,150.27
Lennie Clements	69	69	71	71	280	3,150.27
John Senden	76	68	70	67	281	2,401.45
Richard Green	70	72	70	69	281	2,401.45
Michael Clayton	72	71	68	70	281	2,401.45
Grant Waite	68	70	71	72	281	2,401.45
Paul Devenport	68	74	67	72	281	2,401.45
David Diaz	69	73	72	68	282	1,717.50
Paul Gow	75	68	72	67	282	1,717.50
Craig Jones	70	72	68	72	282	1,717.50
Mike Weir	71	66	73	72	282	1,717.50
Matthew King	68	69	72	73	282	1,717.50
Jeff Woodland	70	70	69	73	282	1,717.50
Glenn Joyner	69	71	66	76	282	1,717.50
Patrick Burke	69	70	69	74	282	1,717.50

Schweppes Coolum Classic

Hyatt Regency Golf Course, Coolum, Queensland, Australia
Par 36-36—72; 6,918 yards

December 15-18
purse, A$200,000

	SCORES				TOTAL	MONEY
Michael Clayton	69	73	66	69	277	A$36,000
Andre Stolz	71	67	72	71	281	20,400
Jack O'Keefe	74	71	73	67	285	13,500

	SCORES				TOTAL	MONEY
Paul Moloney	71	75	71	69	286	8,266.66
Matthew Lane	73	67	72	74	286	8,266.66
Andrew Bonhomme	67	69	74	76	286	8,266.66
Don Fardon	71	71	71	74	287	5,650
Wayne Grady	68	74	72	73	287	5,650
David Podlich	68	74	73	72	287	5,650
David Diaz	68	73	70	76	287	5,650
Stuart Bouvier	69	71	73	75	288	4,200
Phillip Tataurangi	70	71	73	74	288	4,200
Stuart Appleby	71	72	74	72	289	3,600
Mike Harwood	73	71	75	71	290	2,788.33
Evan Droop	70	73	74	73	290	2,788.33
Jim Kennedy	69	70	78	73	290	2,788.33
Paul Devenport	74	72	72	72	290	2,788.33
Patrick Burke	68	74	74	74	290	2,788.33
Brad King	71	74	71	74	290	2,788.33
Rob Willis	72	72	76	71	291	2,093.33
Max Stevens	75	73	71	72	291	2,093.33
Neale Smith	69	72	74	76	291	2,093.33
Grant Kenny	70	74	72	76	292	2,000
David Hill	77	68	74	74	293	1,646.66
David Smail	71	68	81	73	293	1,646.66
Peter Senior	72	73	80	68	293	1,646.66
Grant Moorhead	69	69	80	75	293	1,646.66
Lucien Tinkler	70	72	76	75	293	1,646.66
Stephen Leaney	66	71	80	76	293	1,646.66
David Armstrong	74	73	73	74	294	1,230
Ben Jackson	69	74	77	74	294	1,230
Stephen Collins	76	69	74	75	294	1,230
Rodney Pampling	73	73	75	73	294	1,230
Mark Allen	75	71	72	76	294	1,230
Tony Carolan	71	69	71	83	294	1,230

African Tours

Bell's Cup

Fancourt Hotel & Country Club, George, South Africa
Par 36-36—72; 6,790 yards

January 6-9
purse, R525,000

	SCORES				TOTAL	MONEY
Tony Johnstone	65	68	68	70	271	R82,950
Ernie Els	66	65	72	71	274	48,352.50
David Frost	68	67	72	67	274	48,352.50
Ben Fouchee	68	66	68	73	275	25,777.50
Rodger Davis	69	69	70	68	276	20,133.75
Robbie Stewart	69	71	70	66	276	20,133.75
Ian Leggatt	63	70	74	70	277	15,487.50
Sam Torrance	69	71	71	67	278	12,915
Eric Woods	68	70	71	70	279	11,340
Tripp Isenhour	70	69	74	68	281	9,485
Bobby Lincoln	67	73	69	72	281	9,485
Roger Wessels	73	69	66	73	281	9,485
Wayne Westner	70	66	75	71	282	8,242.50
Sean Pappas	72	70	74	67	283	7,472.50
Deane Pappas	69	71	70	73	283	7,472.50
Fran Quinn, Jr.	69	68	72	74	283	7,472.50
Michael Archer	71	71	73	69	284	6,361.25
Hendrik Buhrmann	71	73	70	70	284	6,361.25
Scott Dunlap	67	69	75	73	284	6,361.25
Russell Fletcher	67	68	75	74	284	6,361.25
Ian Hutchings	69	69	72	74	284	6,361.25
Derek James	70	69	75	70	284	6,361.25
Retief Goosen	71	70	73	71	285	5,512.50
Philip Jonas	71	70	75	69	285	5,512.50
Desmond Terblanche	67	73	69	76	285	5,512.50
Mike Board	72	67	74	73	286	5,118.75
Stuart Hendley	71	73	71	71	286	5,118.75
Wouter Loots	72	72	71	72	287	4,725
Michael Mitchell	71	71	76	69	287	4,725
Omar Uresti	75	69	69	74	287	4,725

Lexington PGA Championship

Wanderers Golf Club, Johannesburg, South Africa
Par 35-35—70; 6,903 yards

January 13-16
purse, R575,000

	SCORES				TOTAL	MONEY
David Frost	64	67	65	63	259	R90,850
Nick Price	66	66	66	68	266	66,125
Wayne Westner	65	68	71	63	267	39,790
Ernie Els	68	67	66	67	268	28,232.50
Chris Davison	69	66	68	69	272	23,747.50
Tony Johnstone	65	71	71	67	274	18,658.75
Chris Williams	67	67	73	67	274	18,658.75
Russell Fletcher	66	74	67	68	275	13,282.50

	SCORES				TOTAL	MONEY
Roger Wessels	67	67	68	73	275	13,282.50
Ben Fouchee	68	69	71	68	276	11,270
Tripp Isenhour	68	68	70	71	277	9,947.50
John Restino	70	69	71	67	277	9,947.50
Ian Leggatt	71	68	67	72	278	8,548.33
Fran Quinn, Jr.	72	70	68	68	278	8,548.33
Ashley Roestoff	64	69	73	72	278	8,548.33
Allan Henning	69	68	72	70	279	7,791.25
Ian Hutchings	72	68	69	70	279	7,791.25
Andre Cruse	70	72	68	70	280	7,216.25
Retief Goosen	66	69	76	69	280	7,216.25
Raymond Burns	69	73	70	69	281	6,394
Wouter Loots	71	67	70	73	281	6,394
Sean Pappas	69	71	71	70	281	6,394
Greg Reid	69	68	71	73	281	6,394
Kevin Stone	73	68	71	69	281	6,394
Andre Bossart	72	67	70	73	282	5,778.75
Sammy Daniels	68	70	72	72	282	5,778.75
Hendrik Buhrmann	70	66	72	75	283	4,864.50
Mike Christie	68	72	70	73	283	4,864.50
Scott Dunlap	68	72	71	72	283	4,864.50
Jeff Hawkes	71	72	68	72	283	4,864.50
Stuart Hendley	69	71	73	70	283	4,864.50
Richard Kaplan	67	69	72	75	283	4,864.50
Brett Liddle	67	65	78	73	283	4,864.50
Brook Tully	69	70	72	72	283	4,864.50
Nico Van Rensburg	68	71	74	70	283	4,864.50
Bobby Verwey, Jr.	67	71	72	73	283	4,864.50

ICL International

Zwartkop Country Club, Verwoerdburg, South Africa
Par 36-36—72; 7,121 yards

January 20-23
purse, R500,000

	SCORES				TOTAL	MONEY
Nick Price	61	69	65	72	267	R79,000
David Frost	70	70	68	68	276	46,050
Bruce Vaughan	69	68	67	72	276	46,050
Andre Cruse	67	66	70	76	279	24,550
Ben Fouchee	69	70	71	72	282	19,175
Kevin Johnson	70	67	70	75	282	19,175
Hugh Baiocchi	70	70	72	71	283	13,525
Ashley Roestoff	70	70	75	68	283	13,525
Derek James	72	71	71	71	285	9,850
Scott Medlin	67	67	78	73	285	9,850
John Restino	70	72	71	72	285	9,850
Hendrik Buhrmann	74	71	72	69	286	7,662.50
Chris Davison	72	70	69	75	286	7,662.50
Jan Nel	69	69	75	73	286	7,662.50
Michael Scholz	73	70	73	70	286	7,662.50
Michael Archer	71	70	73	73	287	6,283.33
Wayne Bradley	71	73	70	73	287	6,283.33
Stuart Hendley	71	69	72	75	287	6,283.33
Ian Hutchings	68	75	72	72	287	6,283.33
Philip Jonas	73	71	73	70	287	6,283.33
Brook Tully	75	66	74	72	287	6,283.33
Derek Crawford	75	70	68	75	288	5,025

	SCORES				TOTAL	MONEY
Michael Green	73	72	72	71	288	5,025
Allan Henning	72	72	75	69	288	5,025
Bobby Lincoln	72	73	75	68	288	5,025
Brenden Pappas	73	72	70	73	288	5,025
Schalk Van Der Merwe	70	72	72	74	288	5,025
Neil Wallace	72	68	77	71	288	5,025
Chris Williams	70	75	70	73	288	5,025
James Becker	73	69	73	74	289	4,233.33
Don Gammon	69	69	72	79	289	4,233.33
Roger Wessels	71	69	76	73	289	4,233.33

Telkom South African Masters

Lost City Country Club, Sun City, Bophuthatswana
Par 36-36—72; 7,637 yards

January 27-30
purse, R575,000

	SCORES				TOTAL	MONEY
Chris Davison	69	74	68	70	281	R79,000
Bruce Vaughan	69	70	71	73	283	57,500
James Becker	71	67	77	71	286	29,575
James Kingston	75	69	69	73	286	29,575
Ian Hutchings	73	69	76	69	287	19,175
Kevin Johnson	74	71	70	72	287	19,175
Ian Leggatt	72	76	72	69	289	14,750
Tripp Isenhour	76	70	73	72	291	10,966.66
Brenden Pappas	75	68	74	74	291	10,966.66
Jeev Milkha Singh	69	72	74	76	291	10,966.66
John Bland	73	73	73	73	292	7,750
Philip Jonas	72	73	72	75	292	7,750
Richard Kaplan	73	69	74	76	292	7,750
Roger Wessels	72	71	77	72	292	7,750
Eric Woods	74	71	71	76	292	7,750
Zane Zwemke	74	72	72	74	292	7,750
Wallie Coetsee	73	73	72	75	293	6,058.33
Don Gammon	73	70	78	72	293	6,058.33
Robert Huxtable	73	72	76	73	293	6,058.33
Ashley Roestoff	75	72	71	75	293	6,058.33
Oyvind Rojahn	74	73	73	73	293	6,058.33
Robbie Stewart	73	75	74	71	293	6,058.33
Scott Dunlap	76	73	73	72	294	5,250
Sean Pappas	71	76	75	72	294	5,250
Omar Uresti	76	71	71	76	294	5,250
Michael Archer	74	72	76	73	295	4,800
Jannie Le Grange	70	76	73	76	295	4,800
Bobby Lincoln	71	73	73	78	295	4,800
Mark James	70	72	76	78	296	4,500
Mike Du Toit	70	76	76	75	297	4,200
Russell Fletcher	71	72	77	77	297	4,200
Ben Fouchee	76	72	76	73	297	4,200
Allan Henning	73	76	74	74	297	4,200

Hollard Insurance Royal Swazi Sun Classic

Royal Swazi Sun Golf Club, Mbabane, Swaziland
Par 36-36—72; 6,694 yards

February 3-6
purse, R400,000

	SCORES				TOTAL	MONEY
Omar Uresti	65	73	68	68	274	R63,200
Andrew Pitts	69	68	72	67	276	46,000
Wayne Westner	72	66	68	71	277	27,688
Scott Dunlap	69	71	66	72	278	18,080
Don Robertson	66	69	74	69	278	18,080
James Becker	71	68	67	73	279	12,980
John Bland	70	71	70	68	279	12,980
Michael Archer	68	69	71	72	280	8,773.33
Hugh Baiocchi	69	71	68	72	280	8,773.33
Tripp Isenhour	72	71	72	65	280	8,773.33
Phillip Hatchett	67	69	71	74	281	6,500
Kevin Johnson	72	69	71	69	281	6,500
Philip Jonas	67	71	70	73	281	6,500
Dave Schreyer	70	71	70	70	281	6,500
Michael Green	72	70	71	69	282	5,506.66
Ian Leggatt	77	67	69	69	282	5,506.66
Neil Wallace	70	72	71	69	282	5,506.66
Don Gammon	71	74	70	68	283	4,920
Greg Reid	67	69	76	71	283	4,920
Andrew Rice	71	70	72	70	283	4,920
Don Bell	71	71	71	71	284	4,500
Ian Hutchings	73	65	73	73	284	4,500
Duane Rock	75	70	68	72	285	3,960
Hendrik Buhrmann	71	72	70	72	285	3,960
Joe Dlamini	67	73	72	73	285	3,960
Oswald Drawdy	72	71	76	66	285	3,960
Nic Henning	70	74	70	71	285	3,960
Jimmy Johnson	69	70	72	74	285	3,960
Bobby Lincoln	69	73	72	71	285	3,960
Stuart Hendley	69	74	72	71	286	3,280
Richard Kaplan	72	69	73	72	286	3,280
Jannie Le Grange	72	69	70	75	286	3,280
Brett Liddle	68	73	72	73	286	3,280
Bruce Vaughan	73	72	74	67	286	3,280
Roger Wessels	72	74	70	70	286	3,280

Standard Chartered Kenya Open

Muthaiga Golf Club, Nairobi, Kenya
Par 36-35—71; 6,829 yards

February 3-6
purse, £70,000

	SCORES				TOTAL	MONEY
Paul Carman	67	70	68	71	276	£11,660
Glenn Ralph	69	67	69	71	276	7,770
(Carman defeated Ralph on fourth extra hole.)						
Mark Litton	67	73	71	68	279	3,925
Peter Harrison	69	71	70	69	279	3,925
Peter Njiru	70	68	71	71	280	2,970
Craig Maltman	72	68	70	71	281	2,725
Chris Platts	71	72	72	67	282	2,505
David Jones	69	74	69	72	284	2,310
Liam White	69	73	73	71	286	2,130

	SCORES				TOTAL	MONEY
*Jacob Okello	79	71	66	71	287	
Daniel Westermark	70	72	70	75	287	1,960
Chris Hall	70	72	72	74	288	1,805
Brendan McGovern	69	77	74	69	289	1,365
Steven Waltman	72	74	73	70	289	1,365
Ron Smith	74	70	75	70	289	1,365
Simon Hoffman	71	77	68	73	289	1,365
Michael Ingham	73	73	70	73	289	1,365
John Vingoe	74	73	72	71	290	980
Mike Williams	72	77	73	69	291	833
Gert Coetzee	73	74	73	71	291	833
Andrew Sandywell	74	71	74	72	291	833
Charles Farrar	68	75	72	76	291	833
John Harrison	73	72	69	77	291	833
John Ngugi	73	76	73	70	292	697.50
John Lower	74	70	75	73	292	697.50
Mbwana Juma	75	74	70	73	292	697.50
Miles Tunnicliff	72	73	73	74	292	697.50
Roger Winchester	72	73	75	73	293	623.30
John Kingori	70	74	76	73	293	623.30
Andy Rogers	70	74	69	80	293	623.30
Wayne Stephens	77	71	76	70	294	566.60
James Ngigi	77	69	73	75	294	566.60
Stuart Bannerman	72	73	71	78	294	566.60

Autopage Mount Edgecombe Trophy

Mount Edgecombe Country Club, Umhlanga, South Africa
Par 36-36—72; 6,759 yards

February 10-13
purse, R500,000

	SCORES				TOTAL	MONEY
Bruce Vaughan	72	70	70	63	275	R79,000
Tony Johnstone	68	71	68	68	275	57,500
(Vaughan defeated Johnstone on second extra hole.)						
Hugh Baiocchi	67	71	74	69	281	29,575
Philip Jonas	76	67	67	71	281	29,575
Ernie Els	71	72	73	67	283	17,700
Roger Wessels	68	74	74	67	283	17,700
Wayne Westner	73	70	68	72	283	17,700
Brett Liddle	74	70	71	70	285	12,300
Don Gammon	71	69	75	71	286	10,300
Retief Goosen	75	73	70	68	286	10,300
Chris Davison	73	67	73	74	287	8,125
Scott Dunlap	71	76	69	71	287	8,125
Bobby Lincoln	74	73	71	69	287	8,125
Sean Pappas	71	72	75	69	287	8,125
Mike Board	68	70	70	80	288	6,640
Ian Leggatt	70	70	73	75	288	6,640
Deane Pappas	72	73	73	70	288	6,640
John Restino	72	73	73	70	288	6,640
Schalk Van Der Merwe	64	72	75	77	288	6,640
Oswald Drawdy	74	73	72	70	289	5,560
Michael Green	71	73	76	69	289	5,560
Jimmy Johnson	74	74	72	69	289	5,560
Andrew Park	71	75	73	70	289	5,560
Andrew Pitts	73	72	73	71	289	5,560
Raymond Burns	71	73	71	75	290	4,800

	SCORES				TOTAL	MONEY
Kevin Johnson	73	73	70	74	290	4,800
Craigen Pappas	72	71	74	73	290	4,800
Greg Reid	76	73	72	69	290	4,800
Clinton Whitelaw	76	71	71	72	290	4,800
Ben Fouchee	73	75	74	69	291	4,250
Jeff Hawkes	71	75	74	71	291	4,250
Stuart Hendley	74	71	74	72	291	4,250

Hassan II Trophy

Royal Golf Dar-es-Salam, Rabat, Morocco
Par 36-37—73; 7,300 yards

November 2-5
purse, $402,000

	SCORES				TOTAL	MONEY
Martin Gates	68	67	75	69	279	$93,000
Robert Karlsson	70	72	68	72	282	49,500
Scott Gump	69	72	74	71	286	29,500
Wayne Westner	70	67	78	73	288	23,800
Jim Furyk	69	75	71	74	291	26,766
Howard Clark	72	70	78	70	291	26,766
Peter Fulke	69	75	71	76	291	26,766
Robert Chapman	70	74	75	73	292	11,500
Des Smyth	76	72	72	72	292	11,500
Scott Hoch	70	72	76	74	292	11,500
Peter Baker	69	75	75	74	293	9,516
Lee Westwood	71	75	76	71	293	9,516
Sandy Lyle	75	72	75	71	293	9,516
Gordon J. Brand	73	73	74	74	294	8,273
Mike Carnevale	72	72	75	75	294	8,273
Paul McGinley	73	70	76	75	294	8,273
Jean Van de Velde	73	73	74	75	295	7,270
Steve Brodie	72	72	77	74	295	7,270
Doug Tewell	68	77	73	77	295	7,270
Corey Pavin	71	74	77	74	296	6,510
Derrick Cooper	71	74	74	77	296	6,510
Mark Davis	73	71	83	72	299	6,120
David A. Russell	78	71	77	75	301	5,860
Bobby Casper	72	79	78	74	303	5,500
Mark Wurtz	78	76	76	73	303	5,500
Mohamed Makroune	75	78	76	77	306	5,100
Michel Besanceney	73	78	78	77	306	5,100
Robert Rafferty	74	76	81	76	307	5,000
Charles Coody	77	78	75	77	307	5,000
Moussa Fatmi	78	77	75	78	308	5,000

Zimbabwe Open

Royal Harare Golf Club, Harare, Zimbabwe
Par 36-36—72; 7,060 yards

November 17-20
purse, R350,000

	SCORES				TOTAL	MONEY
Chris Williams	65	68	70	69	272	R49,770
Andrew Pitts	67	67	68	70	272	36,225
(Williams defeated Pitts on first extra hole.)						
Mark McNulty	69	70	68	66	273	21,798

	SCORES				TOTAL	MONEY
Derek James	71	67	63	73	274	15,466.50
Hendrik Buhrmann	70	68	70	68	276	11,151
Adilson da Silva	68	74	65	69	276	11,151
Tony Johnstone	67	65	74	70	276	11,151
John Bland	73	67	70	67	277	6,325.20
Raymond Burns	70	70	69	68	277	6,325.20
Chris Davison	73	68	69	67	277	6,325.20
Ian Hutchings	67	68	70	72	277	6,325.20
Gavin Levenson	71	69	71	66	277	6,325.20
Steve Van Vuuren	69	69	71	69	278	4,945.50
Michael Archer	71	73	67	68	279	4,410
Jannie Le Grange	71	69	73	66	279	4,410
Warren Schutte	72	69	68	70	279	4,410
Desmond Terblanche	71	70	70	68	279	4,410
Malcolm Mackenzie	68	73	71	68	280	4,032
Wayne Bradley	72	70	70	69	281	3,727.50
*Mark Cayeux	69	71	69	72	281	
Michael Ure	73	70	70	68	281	3,727.50
Roger Wessels	72	72	67	70	281	3,727.50
Craig Kamps	70	68	68	76	282	3,496.50
Jaco de Witt	68	69	72	74	283	3,260.25
Nasho Kamungeremu	71	68	70	74	283	3,260.25
John Mashego	75	69	70	69	283	3,260.25
Andrew Park	72	71	72	68	283	3,260.25
Gerry Coetzee	70	74	69	71	284	2,882.25
Russell Fletcher	74	71	70	69	284	2,882.25
Jimmy Johnson	68	70	73	73	284	2,882.25
Don Robertson	69	70	73	72	284	2,882.25

Nashua Wild Coast Challenge

Wild Coast Country Club, Port Edward, South Africa
Par 35-35—70; 7,011 yards

November 24-27
purse, R500,000

	SCORES				TOTAL	MONEY
Hendrik Buhrmann	64	67	72	69	272	R118,500
Trevor Dodds	69	66	68	74	277	69,075
Ernie Els	69	66	70	72	277	69,075
Ian Palmer	73	67	70	72	282	33,900
Warren Schutte	70	67	73	72	282	33,900
Hugh Baiocchi	70	70	69	74	283	26,550
Mark McNulty	70	66	76	72	284	20,287.50
Andrew Pitts	69	71	71	73	284	20,287.50
Wouter Loots	72	70	71	72	285	15,450
Phil Simmons	66	74	72	73	285	15,450
Jeff Hawkes	68	68	71	79	286	12,975
Philip Jonas	70	64	73	79	286	12,975
Desmond Terblanche	71	64	72	80	287	11,400
Bruce Vaughan	69	73	72	73	287	11,400
Michael Archer	68	69	68	83	288	10,650
Todd Fanning	70	72	74	73	289	9,787.50
Derek James	72	69	69	79	289	9,787.50
John Mashego	71	70	75	73	289	9,787.50
Eoghan O'Connell	69	68	73	79	289	9,787.50
Don Gammon	74	69	72	75	290	8,340
Ian Hutchings	69	71	76	74	290	8,340
Noel Maart	69	70	73	78	290	8,340

	SCORES				TOTAL	MONEY
Nico Van Rensburg	72	69	79	70	290	8,340
Chris Williams	72	68	75	75	290	8,340
John Bland	76	67	71	77	291	6,890.62
Wayne Bradley	70	72	72	77	291	6,890.62
Raymond Burns	71	68	74	78	291	6,890.62
Brandon Goetals	69	71	73	78	291	6,890.62
Nic Henning	72	72	73	74	291	6,890.62
Don Robertson	67	71	76	77	291	6,890.62
Steve Van Vuuren	68	72	75	76	291	6,890.62
Roger Wessels	67	74	76	74	291	6,890.62

Nedbank Million Dollar Challenge

Gary Player Country Club, Sun City, Bophuthatswana
Par 36-36—72; 7,691 yards

December 1-4
purse, $2,510,000

	SCORES				TOTAL	MONEY
Nick Faldo	66	64	73	69	272	$1,000,000
Nick Price	71	66	70	68	275	250,000
Ernie Els	68	70	67	72	277	187,500
David Frost	73	67	71	66	277	187,500
Bernhard Langer	68	69	74	68	279	137,500
Tom Lehman	71	69	70	69	279	137,500
Seve Ballesteros	76	71	68	66	281	110,000
Mark McNulty	72	69	68	73	282	100,000
Corey Pavin	71	70	72	70	283	100,000
Hale Irwin	72	70	74	72	288	100,000
Colin Montgomerie	72	71	72	73	288	100,000
Vijay Singh	80	73	76	78	307	100,000

Senior Tours

Mercedes Championship

La Costa Country Club, Carlsbad, California
Par 36-36—72; 7,022 yards

January 6-9
purse, $500,000

	SCORES				TOTAL	MONEY
Jack Nicklaus	73	69	69	68	279	$100,000
Bob Murphy	71	70	67	72	280	60,000
Dave Stockton	67	72	69	75	283	48,000
Raymond Floyd	73	72	70	69	284	40,000
Jim Colbert	71	74	70	70	285	29,500
Lee Trevino	71	71	73	70	285	29,500
Bob Charles	70	72	73	71	286	24,000
Al Geiberger	72	73	71	72	288	21,000
George Archer	71	73	73	72	289	18,250
Simon Hobday	73	74	71	71	289	18,250
Jim Albus	73	75	70	73	291	15,250
Dale Douglass	71	69	74	77	291	15,250
J.C. Snead	78	72	70	72	292	13,000
Tom Wargo	73	75	72	72	292	13,000
Chi Chi Rodriguez	73	77	72	71	293	12,000
Bob Betley	75	74	75	73	297	11,500
Tom Shaw	78	79	70	73	300	11,000
Gibby Gilbert	76	78	76	74	304	10,500
Bob Wynn	77	74	77	77	305	10,000

Royal Caribbean Classic

Links at Key Biscayne, Key Biscayne, Florida
Par 36-35—71; 6,754 yards

February 4-6
purse, $800,000

	SCORES			TOTAL	MONEY
Lee Trevino	66	73	66	205	$120,000
Kermit Zarley	71	66	68	205	70,400
(Trevino defeated Zarley on fourth extra hole.)					
Bob Charles	70	67	70	207	52,800
J.C. Snead	71	66	70	207	52,800
George Archer	69	68	71	208	38,400
Simon Hobday	75	69	65	209	28,800
Bob Murphy	67	71	71	209	28,800
Tom Wargo	69	72	68	209	28,800
Tommy Aaron	69	71	70	210	20,000
Terry Dill	73	73	64	210	20,000
Gary Player	69	70	71	210	20,000
Chi Chi Rodriguez	70	70	70	210	20,000
Jim Albus	70	73	68	211	14,400
Gay Brewer	71	70	70	211	14,400
Jim Colbert	70	70	71	211	14,400
Gibby Gilbert	74	66	71	211	14,400
Rocky Thompson	71	72	68	211	14,400
Don Bies	72	69	71	212	11,280

	SCORES			TOTAL	MONEY
Charles Coody	73	68	71	212	11,280
Jim Dent	70	72	70	212	11,280
Richard Rhyan	73	72	68	213	9,600
DeWitt Weaver	74	70	69	213	9,600
Bruce Crampton	67	75	72	214	8,400
Dale Douglass	69	73	72	214	8,400
Mike Hill	71	70	73	214	8,400
Richard Bassett	68	73	74	215	6,800
Jim Ferree	72	69	74	215	6,800
Al Geiberger	73	70	72	215	6,800
Larry Gilbert	73	75	67	215	6,800
Roger Kennedy	72	72	71	215	6,800
Walter Zembriski	73	73	69	215	6,800
Butch Baird	74	71	71	216	5,280
Dick Goetz	74	69	73	216	5,280
Dick Hendrickson	70	74	72	216	5,280
Al Kelley	74	71	71	216	5,280
Calvin Peete	76	72	68	216	5,280
Tom Shaw	75	73	69	217	4,560
Tommy Aycock	74	74	70	218	4,080
Bob Dickson	77	72	69	218	4,080
Don January	73	74	71	218	4,080
Rives McBee	75	73	70	218	4,080
Jimmy Powell	71	72	75	218	4,080

Senior Grand Slam of Golf

Club Campestre de Queretaro, Queretaro, Mexico
Par 36-36—72; 6,700 yards

February 7-8
purse, $500,000

	SCORES		TOTAL	MONEY
Tom Shaw	70	69	139	$250,000
Jim Colbert	70	71	141	125,000
Tom Wargo	70	72	142	75,000
Jack Nicklaus	75	70	145	50,000

GTE Suncoast Classic

TPC of Tampa Bay, Lutz, Florida
Par 35-36—71; 6,638 yards

February 11-13
purse, $700,000

	SCORES			TOTAL	MONEY
Rocky Thompson	73	67	61	201	$105,000
Raymond Floyd	70	66	66	202	61,600
Lee Trevino	69	68	66	203	50,400
Orville Moody	66	69	70	205	42,000
Mike Hill	69	64	73	206	30,800
Richard Rhyan	70	70	66	206	30,800
Jim Colbert	68	74	65	207	25,200
George Archer	66	70	72	208	19,250
Bob Charles	71	70	67	208	19,250
Simon Hobday	71	66	71	208	19,250
J.C. Snead	71	71	66	208	19,250
Tom Wargo	71	70	68	209	14,233.34
Terry Dill	69	71	69	209	14,233.33

	SCORES			TOTAL	MONEY
Gary Player	75	66	68	209	14,233.33
Jim Dent	71	69	70	210	11,550
Dale Douglass	68	71	71	210	11,550
Gibby Gilbert	74	68	68	210	11,550
DeWitt Weaver	79	63	68	210	11,550
Richard Bassett	71	69	71	211	8,722
Charles Coody	71	71	69	211	8,722
Bobby Nichols	68	71	72	211	8,722
Randy Petri	72	68	71	211	8,722
Harry Toscano	70	72	69	211	8,722
Jim Albus	72	71	69	212	6,842.50
Harold Henning	71	68	73	212	6,842.50
Jay Sigel	71	70	71	212	6,842.50
Walter Zembriski	73	72	67	212	6,842.50
Bob Betley	74	69	70	213	5,425
Bruce Crampton	71	72	70	213	5,425
Larry Gilbert	74	68	71	213	5,425
Arnold Palmer	72	71	70	213	5,425
Chi Chi Rodriguez	68	74	71	213	5,425
Tom Shaw	70	72	71	213	5,425
Don Bies	75	66	73	214	4,305
Dick Goetz	68	76	70	214	4,305
Gene Littler	71	71	72	214	4,305
George Shortridge	73	72	69	214	4,305
Bob Dickson	70	75	70	215	3,640
Al Geiberger	75	69	71	215	3,640
Dick Hendrickson	77	67	71	215	3,640
Dave Stockton	71	70	74	215	3,640

IntelliNet Challenge

The Vineyards Golf & Country Club, Naples, Florida
Par 36-36—72; 6,682 yards

February 18-20
purse, $500,000

	SCORES			TOTAL	MONEY
Mike Hill	69	69	63	201	$75,000
Tom Wargo	71	65	68	204	44,000
George Archer	67	67	71	205	30,000
Dick Goetz	68	68	69	205	30,000
Dave Stockton	69	67	69	205	30,000
Simon Hobday	69	70	67	206	18,000
Jay Sigel	65	71	70	206	18,000
J.C. Snead	68	71	67	206	18,000
Bob Charles	71	67	69	207	13,500
Richard Rhyan	68	71	68	207	13,500
Tommy Aaron	68	70	71	209	11,000
Dale Douglass	72	70	67	209	11,000
Jerry McGee	72	68	69	209	11,000
Gibby Gilbert	72	70	68	210	9,500
Jim Albus	72	71	68	211	8,250
Jim Colbert	68	72	71	211	8,250
Graham Marsh	72	68	71	211	8,250
Lee Trevino	70	71	70	211	8,250
Tommy Aycock	72	72	68	212	6,412.50
Orville Moody	72	70	70	212	6,412.50
Gary Player	68	74	70	212	6,412.50
Chi Chi Rodriguez	71	73	68	212	6,412.50

	SCORES			TOTAL	MONEY
Miller Barber	74	70	69	213	4,485
Bruce Crampton	71	71	71	213	4,485
Terry Dill	73	72	68	213	4,485
Lee Elder	71	75	67	213	4,485
Jim Ferree	71	71	71	213	4,485
Bill Hall	70	73	70	213	4,485
Tommy Horton	73	72	68	213	4,485
Rocky Thompson	73	69	71	213	4,485
Bert Yancey	73	73	67	213	4,485
Walter Zembriski	68	72	73	213	4,485
Jim Dent	75	69	70	214	3,375
Larry Gilbert	72	71	71	214	3,375
Bob Dickson	71	73	71	215	2,880
Al Kelley	68	72	75	215	2,880
Tony Perla	70	71	74	215	2,880
Tom Shaw	75	69	71	215	2,880
DeWitt Weaver	74	72	69	215	2,880
Don Bies	72	72	72	216	2,150
Gay Brewer	74	76	66	216	2,150
Bob Brue	73	71	72	216	2,150
Dave Eichelberger	72	72	72	216	2,150
Robert Gaona	73	72	71	216	2,150
Larry Laoretti	74	72	70	216	2,150
Calvin Peete	72	72	72	216	2,150
Ben Smith	73	70	73	216	2,150
Harry Toscano	74	70	72	216	2,150

Chrysler Cup

TPC Club at Prestancia, Stadium Course, Sarasota, Florida
Par 36-36—72; 6,763 yards

February 25-27
purse, $600,000

INDIVIDUAL SCORES

	SCORES			TOTAL	MONEY
George Archer	68	63	72	203	$55,000
Simon Hobday	67	67	69	203	39,000
(Archer defeated Hobday on first extra hole.)					
Bob Charles	66	70	69	205	26,000
Tom Weiskopf	71	67	67	205	26,000
Bruce Devlin	65	71	71	207	18,333.34
Gary Player	73	67	67	207	18,333.34
Al Geiberger	70	71	66	207	18,333.34
Graham Marsh	69	68	71	208	16,000
Tommy Horton	68	69	72	209	13,000
Jim Colbert	70	71	68	209	13,000
Dave Stockton	69	72	68	209	13,000
Chi Chi Rodriguez	72	66	72	210	11,000
Mike Hill	70	71	70	211	10,000
Bruce Crampton	72	69	73	214	9,000
Miller Barber	70	71	77	218	8,000
Harold Henning	78	72	75	225	6,000

FINAL RESULTS: International 1,022 (-58), United States 1,024 (-56).

(Each member of the International team received $25,000; each member of the United
States team received $12,500.)

GTE West Classic

Ojal Valley Inn & Country Club, Ojal, California
Par 35-35—70; 6,190 yards

March 4-6
purse, $550,000

	SCORES			TOTAL	MONEY
Jay Sigel	70	66	62	198	$82,500
Jim Colbert	62	64	72	198	48,400
(Sigel defeated Colbert on fourth extra hole.)					
Larry Laoretti	65	68	66	199	36,300
Bob Murphy	67	66	66	199	36,300
Tom Wargo	66	64	70	200	24,200
Kermit Zarley	67	65	68	200	24,200
Jim Albus	65	66	71	202	17,600
Bruce Crampton	68	67	67	202	17,600
Simon Hobday	67	69	66	202	17,600
George Archer	67	70	66	203	12,650
Don Bies	69	66	68	203	12,650
Dale Douglass	69	66	68	203	12,650
Richard Rhyan	65	69	69	203	12,650
Charles Coody	68	65	71	204	10,175
Robert Gaona	67	67	70	204	10,175
Tommy Aycock	66	72	67	205	8,800
Gene Littler	65	70	70	205	8,800
Graham Marsh	69	67	69	205	8,800
Butch Baird	66	69	71	206	7,507.50
Dave Stockton	66	70	70	206	7,507.50
Rod Curl	69	69	69	207	6,256.25
Larry Gilbert	68	70	69	207	6,256.25
Randy Petri	73	67	67	207	6,256.25
Walter Zembriski	70	72	65	207	6,256.25
Jack Kiefer	71	68	69	208	5,243.34
Bob Betley	66	71	71	208	5,243.33
Chi Chi Rodriguez	70	68	70	208	5,243.33
Gary Player	68	70	71	209	4,455
Jimmy Powell	67	71	71	209	4,455
Bob Smith	72	66	71	209	4,455
DeWitt Weaver	68	72	69	209	4,455
Bob Goalby	69	70	71	210	3,630
Tommy Horton	73	69	68	210	3,630
Jim Jones	67	69	74	210	3,630
Orville Moody	73	72	65	210	3,630
Bert Yancey	70	69	71	210	3,630
Bob Brue	70	71	70	211	2,860
Bob Carson	76	67	68	211	2,860
Lou Graham	69	74	68	211	2,860
Dick Hendrickson	67	69	75	211	2,860
Rocky Thompson	70	70	71	211	2,860
Harry Toscano	72	68	71	211	2,860

Vantage at the Dominion

The Dominion Country Club, San Antonio, Texas
Par 36-36—72; 6,814 yards

March 11-13
purse, $650,000

	SCORES			TOTAL	MONEY
Jim Albus	68	67	73	208	$97,500
Graham Marsh	72	67	70	209	47,666.67

	SCORES			TOTAL	MONEY
Lee Trevino	71	69	69	209	47,666.67
George Archer	69	69	71	209	47,666.66
Rocky Thompson	71	69	70	210	31,200
Jim Colbert	71	70	70	211	22,100
Gibby Gilbert	71	67	73	211	22,100
J.C. Snead	71	70	70	211	22,100
Tom Wargo	70	71	70	211	22,100
Tommy Aaron	74	71	67	212	15,600
Dale Douglass	74	70	68	212	15,600
Dave Stockton	69	72	71	212	15,600
Don January	72	74	67	213	13,000
Jim Dent	71	70	73	214	11,700
Jerry McGee	74	70	70	214	11,700
DeWitt Weaver	72	73	69	214	11,700
Bob Betley	74	70	71	215	8,915.84
Gay Brewer	73	71	71	215	8,915.84
Simon Hobday	70	69	76	215	8,915.83
Jack Kiefer	71	69	75	215	8,915.83
Jimmy Powell	71	72	72	215	8,915.83
Kermit Zarley	70	73	72	215	8,915.83
Charles Coody	72	72	73	217	6,513
Larry Gilbert	74	70	73	217	6,513
Dave Hill	72	74	71	217	6,513
Ben Smith	75	69	73	217	6,513
Walter Zembriski	73	71	73	217	6,513
Terry Dill	70	75	73	218	5,265
Mike Hill	73	69	76	218	5,265
Orville Moody	75	69	74	218	5,265
Bruce Summerhays	73	73	72	218	5,265
Dick Goetz	76	72	71	219	4,387.50
Gary Player	73	71	75	219	4,387.50
Bob Reith	74	75	70	219	4,387.50
Chi Chi Rodriguez	73	73	73	219	4,387.50
Butch Baird	76	74	70	220	3,454.29
Dave Eichelberger	76	71	73	220	3,454.29
Snell Lancaster	79	71	70	220	3,454.29
Randy Petri	77	68	75	220	3,454.29
Fred Ruiz	75	74	71	220	3,454.28
Bob Wynn	71	76	73	220	3,454.28
Bert Yancey	72	76	72	220	3,454.28

Doug Sanders Celebrity Classic

Deerwood Country Club, Kingwood, Texas
Par 36-36—72; 6,659 yards

March 25-27
purse, $500,000

	SCORES			TOTAL	MONEY
Tom Wargo	71	66	72	209	$75,000
Bob Murphy	75	69	66	210	45,000
Chi Chi Rodriguez	69	69	73	211	37,000
Jimmy Powell	72	70	70	212	30,600
Mike Hill	74	70	69	213	24,600
George Archer	72	72	70	214	19,600
Bob Charles	70	69	75	214	19,600
Homero Blancas	72	69	74	215	15,600
Walter Zembriski	71	72	72	215	15,600
Jim Albus	70	73	73	216	13,100

	SCORES			TOTAL	MONEY
Dale Douglass	71	72	73	216	13,100
Tommy Aaron	69	73	76	218	11,600
Rocky Thompson	71	73	75	219	10,550
Charles Coody	72	73	75	220	9,300
Bruce Devlin	75	74	71	220	9,300
Dick Goetz	75	73	72	220	9,300
Babe Hiskey	71	74	75	220	9,300
Larry Gilbert	68	77	76	221	7,080
Harold Henning	71	77	73	221	7,080
Jerry McGee	73	76	72	221	7,080
Tom Shaw	72	73	76	221	7,080
J.C. Snead	72	71	78	221	7,080
Bob Betley	76	74	72	222	5,230
Billy Casper	72	75	75	222	5,230
Jim Dent	78	72	72	222	5,230
Gene Littler	74	70	78	222	5,230
Kermit Zarley	77	70	75	222	5,230
Miller Barber	77	71	75	223	4,350
Simon Hobday	76	76	71	223	4,350
Charles Sifford	77	73	73	223	4,350
Butch Baird	79	72	73	224	3,687.50
Gibby Gilbert	69	80	75	224	3,687.50
Orville Moody	72	77	75	224	3,687.50
Ben Smith	71	77	76	224	3,687.50
Bob Goalby	76	72	77	225	3,087.50
Dick Hendrickson	74	76	75	225	3,087.50
Jack Kiefer	76	74	75	225	3,087.50
Jim O'Hern	70	75	80	225	3,087.50
Gay Brewer	75	76	76	227	2,700
Don Massengale	79	76	72	227	2,700
Rives McBee	77	72	78	227	2,700

The Tradition at Desert Mountain

Desert Mountain Country Club, Scottsdale, Arizona
Par 36-36—72; 6,869 yards

March 31-April 3
purse, $850,000

	SCORES				TOTAL	MONEY
Raymond Floyd	65	70	68	68	271	$127,500
Dale Douglass	68	68	69	66	271	74,800
(Floyd defeated Douglass on first extra hole.)						
Jim Colbert	70	66	68	70	274	61,200
Jack Nicklaus	70	71	69	68	278	41,933.34
Jimmy Powell	67	69	72	70	278	41,933.33
Tom Weiskopf	68	70	70	70	278	41,933.33
Gibby Gilbert	66	69	73	71	279	28,900
Mike Hill	70	70	68	71	279	28,900
Isao Aoki	67	69	71	73	280	22,100
Dave Stockton	68	70	72	70	280	22,100
Tom Wargo	68	75	65	72	280	22,100
George Archer	70	70	70	71	281	17,283.34
Charles Coody	68	67	71	75	281	17,283.33
Simon Hobday	68	71	71	71	281	17,283.33
Jim Albus	73	70	67	72	282	14,875
Bob Charles	71	75	66	70	282	14,875
Jim Dent	71	69	72	71	283	12,388.75
Don January	67	77	73	66	283	12,388.75

	SCORES				TOTAL	MONEY
Calvin Peete	73	66	75	69	283	12,388.75
J.C. Snead	70	70	68	75	283	12,388.75
Dick Hendrickson	68	72	71	73	284	10,200
Lee Trevino	68	71	72	73	284	10,200
Larry Laoretti	69	74	69	73	285	9,137.50
Tom Shaw	67	78	70	70	285	9,137.50
Butch Baird	74	73	70	69	286	8,287.50
DeWitt Weaver	68	71	75	72	286	8,287.50
Larry Gilbert	75	70	73	69	287	7,225
Bob Murphy	73	69	74	71	287	7,225
Gary Player	70	71	72	74	287	7,225
Kermit Zarley	71	73	70	73	287	7,225
Jack Kiefer	69	72	78	69	288	6,247.50
Richard Rhyan	71	75	71	71	288	6,247.50
Bruce Crampton	73	75	73	68	289	5,482.50
Gene Littler	74	69	73	73	289	5,482.50
Graham Marsh	69	68	78	74	289	5,482.50
Walter Zembriski	73	71	73	72	289	5,482.50
Tommy Aycock	71	74	75	70	290	4,590
Dick Goetz	74	71	74	71	290	4,590
Larry Mowry	72	70	75	73	290	4,590
Chi Chi Rodriguez	70	73	72	75	290	4,590

PGA Seniors Championship

PGA National Golf Club, Palm Beach Gardens, Florida
Par 36-36—72; 6,718 yards

April 14-17
purse, $800,000

	SCORES				TOTAL	MONEY
Lee Trevino	70	69	70	70	279	$115,000
Jim Colbert	68	71	74	67	280	85,000
Raymond Floyd	69	69	69	75	282	57,500
Dave Stockton	70	69	71	72	282	57,500
Isao Aoki	71	71	75	66	283	32,500
Dale Douglass	70	71	70	72	283	32,500
Chi Chi Rodriguez	73	72	69	69	283	32,500
DeWitt Weaver	72	73	70	68	283	32,500
Jack Nicklaus	71	71	72	72	286	20,500
Bob Charles	69	74	71	73	287	16,500
Bob Murphy	69	75	73	70	287	16,500
Tom Wargo	72	80	70	65	287	16,500
Jay Sigel	72	71	74	71	288	15,000
Walter Zembriski	70	74	73	72	289	14,500
Tommy Aaron	71	70	75	74	290	13,250
Gene Borek	72	76	71	71	290	13,250
Mike Hill	78	72	70	70	290	13,250
J.C. Snead	74	70	75	71	290	13,250
Charles Coody	74	70	74	74	292	11,000
Dick Hendrickson	73	74	74	71	292	11,000
Gary Player	74	75	73	70	292	11,000
Art Proctor	72	74	74	72	292	11,000
Rocky Thompson	74	72	70	76	292	11,000
Kikuo Arai	72	71	74	76	293	8,500
Larry Gilbert	76	73	74	70	293	8,500
Bill Hall	72	77	74	70	293	8,500
Graham Marsh	75	73	71	74	293	8,500
Larry Ziegler	68	77	74	74	293	8,500

	SCORES				TOTAL	MONEY
Jim Dent	66	76	79	73	294	6,250
Gibby Gilbert	72	78	68	76	294	6,250
Simon Hobday	76	75	70	73	294	6,250
Jack Kiefer	73	74	69	78	294	6,250
Gay Brewer	73	73	75	74	295	5,000
Larry Laoretti	73	73	76	74	296	3,812.50
Rives McBee	75	75	74	72	296	3,812.50
Larry Mowry	70	68	85	73	296	3,812.50
Tom Weiskopf	75	73	77	71	296	3,812.50
Jim Albus	73	74	73	77	297	2,900
Masaru Amano	75	76	75	71	297	2,900
Hisashi Suzumura	75	75	74	73	297	2,900

Dallas Reunion Pro-Am

Oak Cliff Country Club, Dallas, Texas
Par 35-35—70; 6,579 yards

April 22-24
purse, $500,000

	SCORES			TOTAL	MONEY
Larry Gilbert	67	68	67	202	$75,000
George Archer	67	68	68	203	40,000
Rocky Thompson	68	67	68	203	40,000
Jack Kiefer	66	70	68	204	30,000
Bob Murphy	68	66	71	205	22,000
J.C. Snead	65	71	69	205	22,000
Chi Chi Rodriguez	67	68	71	206	16,000
Tom Shaw	70	71	65	206	16,000
Tom Wargo	69	67	70	206	16,000
Terry Dill	70	68	69	207	11,500
Dick Hendrickson	68	70	69	207	11,500
Joe Jimenez	71	70	66	207	11,500
Jerry McGee	66	66	75	207	11,500
Jim Albus	69	69	70	208	8,750
Bob Dickson	73	65	70	208	8,750
Robert Gaona	67	68	73	208	8,750
Simon Hobday	65	70	73	208	8,750
Jim Dent	69	70	70	209	6,630
Jim Ferree	69	72	68	209	6,630
Richard Rhyan	69	67	73	209	6,630
Dave Stockton	69	68	72	209	6,630
DeWitt Weaver	65	69	75	209	6,630
Jim Colbert	72	69	69	210	5,250
Dick Goetz	69	65	76	210	5,250
Jimmy Powell	69	69	72	210	5,250
Dick Lotz	68	73	70	211	4,550
George Shortridge	71	71	69	211	4,550
Robert Zimmerman	72	69	70	211	4,550
John Paul Cain	71	69	72	212	3,950
Rives McBee	71	68	73	212	3,950
Randy Petri	70	68	74	212	3,950
Tommy Aycock	72	67	74	213	3,300
Bill Hall	71	70	72	213	3,300
Marion Heck	69	73	71	213	3,300
Bob Smith	67	74	72	213	3,300
Bob Wynn	69	71	73	213	3,300
Richard Bassett	70	71	73	214	2,500
Bob Brue	68	74	72	214	2,500

	SCORES			TOTAL	MONEY
Bob Irving	74	70	70	214	2,500
Snell Lancaster	73	69	72	214	2,500
Orville Moody	72	74	68	214	2,500
Walter Morgan	73	72	69	214	2,500
Larry Mowry	70	73	71	214	2,500
Walter Zembriski	73	70	71	214	2,500

Las Vegas Senior Classic

TPC at Summerlin, Las Vegas, Nevada
Par 36-36—72; 6,963 yards

April 29-May 1
purse, $900,000

	SCORES			TOTAL	MONEY
Raymond Floyd	68	70	65	203	$135,000
Tom Wargo	71	67	68	206	80,100
Jim Dent	70	66	71	207	65,700
Larry Gilbert	66	73	70	209	54,720
Tommy Aycock	72	67	71	210	33,876
Jim Colbert	72	67	71	210	33,876
Jack Kiefer	68	70	72	210	33,876
Rocky Thompson	70	70	70	210	33,876
Kermit Zarley	66	72	72	210	33,876
George Archer	68	69	74	211	22,500
Chi Chi Rodriguez	73	65	73	211	22,500
Lee Trevino	72	67	72	211	22,500
Charles Coody	73	70	69	212	18,000
Rives McBee	72	69	71	212	18,000
Gibby Gilbert	70	71	71	212	18,000
Terry Dill	73	68	72	213	15,750
Jimmy Powell	71	70	72	213	15,750
Dave Stockton	72	70	72	214	14,400
Don Bies	75	68	72	215	13,500
Tommy Aaron	75	71	70	216	11,317.50
Tom Shaw	72	71	73	216	11,317.50
Jay Sigel	74	70	72	216	11,317.50
J.C. Snead	77	70	69	216	11,317.50
Larry Ziegler	70	73	74	217	9,630
Miller Barber	73	74	71	218	8,955
Jim Ferree	74	71	73	218	8,955
Jim Albus	76	70	73	219	7,830
Dale Douglass	72	73	74	219	7,830
Larry Laoretti	73	70	76	219	7,830
Don January	77	70	72	219	7,830
Gay Brewer	75	72	73	220	6,795
Mike Hill	76	71	73	220	6,795
Bob Murphy	70	76	75	221	6,390
Dave Hill	75	72	75	222	5,850
Bobby Nichols	74	70	78	222	5,850
DeWitt Weaver	73	76	73	222	5,850
Butch Baird	74	74	75	223	5,130
Harold Henning	78	70	75	223	5,130
Larry Mowry	73	74	76	223	5,130
Lou Graham	73	75	76	224	4,770

Liberty Mutual Legends of Golf

Barton Creek Country Club, Austin, Texas
Par 36-36—72; 6,777 yards

May 6-8
purse, $1,115,000

	SCORES			TOTAL	MONEY
					(Team)
Dale Douglass/Charles Coody	63	61	64	188	$200,000
Chi Chi Rodriguez/Jim Dent	63	63	63	189	82,500
Bob Murphy/Jim Colbert	65	61	63	189	82,500
Harold Henning/Graham Marsh	64	65	61	190	55,000
Lee Trevino/Mike Hill	65	62	64	191	45,000
Tom Wargo/Arnold Palmer	67	64	62	193	40,000
J.C. Snead/Gibby Gilbert	65	65	64	194	37,000
Simon Hobday/George Archer	64	65	66	195	34,000
Tom Shaw/Homero Blancas	67	64	65	196	32,000
Larry Mowry/Bert Yancey	65	65	67	197	28,000
Gene Littler/Don January	67	65	65	197	28,000
Larry Laoretti/Jim Albus	64	68	66	198	24,000
Lee Elder/Calvin Peete	67	65	67	199	22,000
Bruce Devlin/Don Bies	66	68	67	201	20,000
Joe Jiminez/Orville Moody	66	69	68	203	18,000
Bobby Nichols/Lou Graham	64	69	70	203	18,000
Miller Barber/Jim Ferree	65	70	69	204	15,000
Roberto De Vicenzo/Peter Thompson	70	67	67	204	15,000
Bob Toski/Mike Fetchick	68	69	69	206	12,000
Charlie Sifford/Bob Rosburg	69	69	68	206	12,000
Bob Goalby/Billy Maxwell	67	70	71	208	10,500
Billy Casper/Gay Brewer	71	70	69	210	9,500
Mason Rudolph/Dave Hill	73	70	68	211	9,000
Paul Harney/Mike Souchak	72	68	72	212	7,000
Lionel Hebert/Bill Collins	70	69	75	214	6,000
Doug Sanders/Dow Finsterwald	75	73	71	219	6,000

PaineWebber Invitational

TPC at Piper Glen, Charlotte, North Carolina
Par 36-36—72; 6,774 yards

May 13-15
purse, $750,000

	SCORES			TOTAL	MONEY
Lee Trevino	70	65	68	203	$112,500
Jim Colbert	68	70	66	204	60,000
Jimmy Powell	69	66	69	204	60,000
Graham Marsh	71	68	66	205	40,500
Jerry McGee	69	66	70	205	40,500
Butch Baird	66	70	70	206	30,000
Mike Hill	71	68	68	207	24,000
Dick Lotz	73	68	66	207	24,000
Larry Ziegler	68	68	71	207	24,000
Raymond Floyd	70	69	69	208	18,000
Larry Gilbert	69	68	71	208	18,000
Tom Shaw	67	69	72	208	18,000
Bob Dickson	68	69	72	209	13,875
Dale Douglass	67	71	71	209	13,875
Bobby Nichols	66	72	71	209	13,875
DeWitt Weaver	69	66	74	209	13,875
Jim Albus	75	69	66	210	11,275
Dick Hendrickson	71	67	72	210	11,275

	SCORES			TOTAL	MONEY
Larry Laoretti	74	67	69	210	11,275
Jim Dent	68	69	74	211	9,037.50
Bunky Henry	70	68	73	211	9,037.50
Bob Smith	69	70	72	211	9,037.50
Kermit Zarley	69	72	70	211	9,037.50
Tommy Aycock	72	72	68	212	6,703.13
Rives McBee	73	71	68	212	6,703.13
Orville Moody	73	70	69	212	6,703.13
Jay Sigel	68	73	71	212	6,703.13
Bob Brue	71	70	71	212	6,703.12
Charles Coody	73	68	71	212	6,703.12
Dave Stockton	73	65	74	212	6,703.12
Harry Toscano	69	72	71	212	6,703.12
Simon Hobday	71	71	71	213	5,400
Richard Rhyan	71	70	73	214	4,950
Ben Smith	69	69	76	214	4,950
Tom Wargo	71	72	71	214	4,950
Tommy Aaron	75	69	71	215	4,275
Terry Dill	74	71	70	215	4,275
Jim Ferree	75	67	73	215	4,275
Jack Kiefer	75	68	72	215	4,275
Bob Charles	71	72	73	216	3,675
Al Kelley	70	73	73	216	3,675
J.C. Snead	70	78	68	216	3,675
Bob Verwey	73	73	70	216	3,675

Cadillac NFL Classic

Upper Montclair Country Club, Clifton, New Jersey
Par 36-36—72; 6,816 yards

May 20-22
purse, $900,000

	SCORES			TOTAL	MONEY
Raymond Floyd	64	68	74	206	$135,000
Bob Murphy	70	69	68	207	72,000
Gary Player	71	67	69	207	72,000
Dave Stockton	72	70	68	210	48,600
Lee Trevino	70	69	71	210	48,600
George Archer	67	70	74	211	36,000
Walter Zembriski	70	72	70	212	32,400
Bob Charles	71	71	71	213	25,800
Jim Dent	70	75	68	213	25,800
Larry Gilbert	69	72	72	213	25,800
John Paul Cain	72	72	70	214	19,800
Chi Chi Rodriguez	73	72	69	214	19,800
Tom Wargo	70	73	71	214	19,800
Jim Albus	76	69	70	215	15,750
Gay Brewer	72	72	71	215	15,750
Graham Marsh	72	69	74	215	15,750
Rocky Thompson	76	68	71	215	15,750
Terry Dill	76	71	69	216	11,595
Dale Douglass	72	70	74	216	11,595
Dave Eichelberger	74	71	71	216	11,595
Larry Laoretti	74	66	76	216	11,595
J.C. Snead	72	73	71	216	11,595
Larry Ziegler	76	71	69	216	11,595
Jack Kiefer	74	72	71	217	9,225
Kermit Zarley	77	73	67	217	9,225

	SCORES			TOTAL	MONEY
Butch Baird	71	73	74	218	7,482.86
Miller Barber	73	72	73	218	7,482.86
Bobby Nichols	73	74	71	218	7,482.86
Jimmy Powell	75	73	70	218	7,482.86
DeWitt Weaver	72	74	72	218	7,482.86
Dick Goetz	75	69	74	218	7,482.85
Roger Stern	72	70	76	218	7,482.85
Isao Aoki	75	71	73	219	5,940
Bob Dickson	76	72	71	219	5,940
Quinton Gray	73	72	74	219	5,940
Tommy Aycock	76	74	70	220	5,062.50
Gene Littler	75	73	72	220	5,062.50
Rives McBee	72	78	70	220	5,062.50
Orville Moody	74	77	69	220	5,062.50
Tommy Aaron	71	74	76	221	4,230
Don Massengale	75	70	76	221	4,230
Jerry McGee	74	73	74	221	4,230
Bob Panasik	75	72	74	221	4,230
Tom Ulozas	77	72	72	221	4,230

Bell Atlantic Classic

Chester Valley Golf Club, Malvern, Pennsylvania
Par 35-35—70; 6,608 yards

May 27-29
purse, $700,000

	SCORES			TOTAL	MONEY
Lee Trevino	71	67	68	206	$105,000
Mike Hill	69	71	68	208	61,600
Tommy Aaron	71	68	71	210	50,400
Tom Wargo	68	72	71	211	34,533.34
Jim Dent	68	71	72	211	34,533.33
Chi Chi Rodriguez	69	71	71	211	34,533.33
Raymond Floyd	70	74	68	212	23,800
Jack Kiefer	74	67	71	212	23,800
Bob Murphy	71	71	71	213	18,900
Jimmy Powell	73	70	70	213	18,900
Bob Charles	70	73	71	214	15,400
Ben Smith	70	70	74	214	15,400
Larry Ziegler	68	72	74	214	15,400
Isao Aoki	72	73	70	215	13,300
Gary Player	71	74	71	216	12,250
Bert Yancey	72	72	72	216	12,250
Arnold Palmer	73	74	70	217	10,523.34
Tommy Aycock	74	72	71	217	10,523.33
Robert Zimmerman	71	75	71	217	10,523.33
Dave Eichelberger	76	74	68	218	8,015
Gibby Gilbert	76	69	73	218	8,015
Don January	69	72	77	218	8,015
Graham Marsh	73	75	70	218	8,015
Jerry McGee	75	70	73	218	8,015
Bobby Nichols	76	73	69	218	8,015
Billy Casper	76	70	73	219	6,230
Dave Hill	73	72	74	219	6,230
Dick Lotz	73	72	74	219	6,230
Jay Sigel	77	71	71	219	6,230
Bob Carson	75	74	71	220	5,162.50
Bob Dickson	71	73	76	220	5,162.50
Jay Hyon	73	72	75	220	5,162.50

	SCORES			TOTAL	MONEY
Walter Zembriski	74	74	72	220	5,162.50
Miller Barber	74	73	74	221	4,050
Terry Dill	76	73	72	221	4,050
Jim Ferree	74	71	76	221	4,050
Robert Gaona	74	72	75	221	4,050
Rives McBee	76	71	74	221	4,050
Orville Moody	77	74	70	221	4,050
Walter Morgan	75	72	74	221	4,050

Bruno's Memorial Classic

Greystone Country Club, Birmingham, Alabama
Par 36-36—72; 7,207 yards

June 3-5
purse, $1,000,000

	SCORES			TOTAL	MONEY
Jim Dent	66	68	67	201	$150,000
Larry Gilbert	67	66	70	203	73,333.34
Bob Charles	66	66	71	203	73,333.33
Kermit Zarley	67	68	68	203	73,333.33
Tommy Aaron	67	70	68	205	39,000
Jim Albus	64	71	70	205	39,000
George Archer	68	69	68	205	39,000
Dale Douglass	68	68	69	205	39,000
Simon Hobday	71	67	68	206	26,000
Jack Kiefer	69	67	70	206	26,000
Jay Sigel	67	68	71	206	26,000
Bob Murphy	69	69	69	207	22,000
Graham Marsh	68	70	70	208	18,500
Chi Chi Rodriguez	67	70	71	208	18,500
J.C. Snead	67	68	73	208	18,500
Rocky Thompson	72	67	69	208	18,500
Jim Colbert	73	69	67	209	15,500
Orville Moody	71	69	69	209	15,500
Tommy Aycock	70	69	71	210	13,650
Lee Trevino	69	69	72	210	13,650
Don Bies	74	69	69	212	11,100
Gibby Gilbert	71	72	69	212	11,100
Calvin Peete	70	68	74	212	11,100
Jimmy Powell	74	67	71	212	11,100
Walter Zembriski	73	70	69	212	11,100
Isao Aoki	71	70	72	213	8,900
Don January	71	71	71	213	8,900
Gary Player	72	70	71	213	8,900
Harry Toscano	69	71	73	213	8,900
Bob Brue	74	70	70	214	7,066.67
Dick Hendrickson	70	74	70	214	7,066.67
Mike Hill	75	68	71	214	7,066.67
Robert Rawlins	71	70	73	214	7,066.67
Gay Brewer	70	71	73	214	7,066.66
Dave Stockton	70	71	73	214	7,066.66
Butch Baird	76	67	72	215	5,850
Randy Petri	76	70	69	215	5,850
Rives McBee	73	70	73	216	5,100
Jerry McGee	74	72	70	216	5,100
Tom Wargo	73	75	68	216	5,100
Bert Yancey	77	69	70	216	5,100
Larry Ziegler	69	73	74	216	5,100

Nationwide Championship

Country Club of the South, Atlanta, Georgia
Par 36-36—72; 6,856 yards

June 10-12
purse, $1,150,000

	SCORES			TOTAL	MONEY
Dave Stockton	67	63	68	198	$172,500
Bob Murphy	67	64	68	199	101,200
Jim Albus	66	73	64	203	75,900
Jim Dent	72	64	67	203	75,900
Chi Chi Rodriguez	71	65	68	204	50,600
Lee Trevino	70	66	68	204	50,600
Jimmy Powell	70	67	68	205	39,100
Jay Sigel	70	67	68	205	39,100
Gibby Gilbert	65	73	68	206	31,050
Tom Wargo	70	68	68	206	31,050
Larry Gilbert	67	69	71	207	26,450
Tom Shaw	67	68	72	207	26,450
Bob Charles	68	72	68	208	23,000
Jim Ferree	70	69	70	209	21,850
Graham Marsh	67	69	74	210	20,700
George Archer	72	68	71	211	17,853.75
Marion Heck	72	69	70	211	17,853.75
Mike Hill	71	71	69	211	17,853.75
Gary Player	73	64	74	211	17,853.75
Don January	72	69	71	212	14,720
Kermit Zarley	77	68	67	212	14,720
Isao Aoki	74	70	69	213	11,313.13
Orville Moody	73	72	68	213	11,313.13
J.C. Snead	74	70	69	213	11,313.13
Rocky Thompson	76	70	67	213	11,313.13
John Paul Cain	69	72	72	213	11,313.12
Charles Coody	78	65	70	213	11,313.12
Dale Douglass	70	72	71	213	11,313.12
Jack Kiefer	71	72	70	213	11,313.12
Tommy Aaron	71	70	73	214	8,481.25
Bob Brue	76	71	67	214	8,481.25
Billy Casper	75	65	74	214	8,481.25
Walter Zembriski	74	70	70	214	8,481.25
Tommy Aycock	73	74	68	215	6,526.25
Don Bies	76	69	70	215	6,526.25
Bruce Devlin	66	75	74	215	6,526.25
Gene Littler	73	68	74	215	6,526.25
Rives McBee	73	72	70	215	6,526.25
Jerry McGee	73	70	72	215	6,526.25
Robert Rawlins	73	66	76	215	6,526.25
Ben Smith	71	72	72	215	6,526.25

BellSouth Senior Classic at Opryland

Springhouse Golf Club, Nashville, Tennessee
Par 36-36—72; 6,783 yards

June 17-19
purse, $1,050,000

	SCORES			TOTAL	MONEY
Lee Trevino	67	65	67	199	$157,500
Jim Albus	66	68	66	200	84,000
Dave Stockton	62	69	69	200	84,000
Gibby Gilbert	71	65	66	202	63,000

	SCORES			TOTAL	MONEY
George Archer	65	71	67	203	50,400
Tom Wargo	67	68	69	204	39,900
Raymond Floyd	70	66	68	204	39,900
Jim Dent	63	71	71	205	28,875
Graham Marsh	69	68	68	205	28,875
J.C. Snead	68	67	70	205	28,875
Larry Ziegler	68	69	68	205	28,875
Mike Hill	69	67	70	206	22,050
Rocky Thompson	67	69	70	206	22,050
Terry Dill	68	68	71	207	18,900
Bill Hall	66	69	72	207	18,900
Walter Zembriski	70	70	67	207	18,900
Calvin Peete	71	68	69	208	18,900
Bob Charles	68	70	72	210	14,358.75
Larry Gilbert	71	68	71	210	14,358.75
Ben Smith	72	68	70	210	14,358.75
Kermit Zarley	70	76	64	210	14,358.75
Tommy Aycock	69	71	71	211	10,797.50
Bob Brue	69	68	74	211	10,797.50
Charles Coody	70	72	69	211	10,797.50
Jerry McGee	70	73	68	211	10,797.50
Jimmy Powell	71	70	70	211	10,797.50
Tom Weiskopf	71	71	69	211	10,797.50
Tommy Aaron	74	68	70	212	8,505
Isao Aoki	71	73	68	212	8,505
Jim Colbert	68	70	74	212	8,505
Orville Moody	69	72	71	212	8,505
Jim Ferree	74	69	70	213	7,402.50
Gary Player	74	70	69	213	7,402.50
Dave Hill	73	72	69	214	6,930
Gaylord Burrows	72	71	72	215	5,820
Harold Henning	72	72	71	215	5,820
Simon Hobday	71	71	73	215	5,820
Al Kelley	73	74	68	215	5,820
Richard Rhyan	69	72	74	215	5,820
Jay Sigel	71	71	73	215	5,820
DeWitt Weaver	72	74	69	215	5,820

Ford Senior Players Championship

TPC of Michigan, Dearborn, Michigan
Par 36-36—72; 6,876 yards

June 23-26
purse, $1,400,000

	SCORES				TOTAL	MONEY
Dave Stockton	66	66	71	68	271	$210,000
Jim Albus	67	69	72	69	277	123,200
Isao Aoki	67	70	73	68	278	84,000
Raymond Floyd	72	68	71	67	278	84,000
Lee Trevino	66	69	74	69	278	84,000
Jim Dent	72	67	70	71	280	50,400
Harold Henning	69	67	74	70	280	50,400
Jack Nicklaus	68	72	73	67	280	50,400
Jay Sigel	67	71	73	70	281	39,200
Jerry McGee	69	69	74	70	282	32,200
Bob Murphy	69	68	73	72	282	32,200
Tom Wargo	70	73	71	68	282	32,200
Tom Weiskopf	65	71	74	72	282	32,200

	SCORES				TOTAL	MONEY
Jim Colbert	69	72	71	71	283	25,900
Graham Marsh	67	71	75	70	283	25,900
Larry Gilbert	72	67	74	72	285	21,735
Tom Shaw	67	78	71	69	285	21,735
J.C. Snead	71	68	76	70	285	21,735
Rocky Thompson	74	68	76	67	285	21,735
Dale Douglass	72	73	72	69	286	17,920
Walter Zembriski	68	71	75	72	286	17,920
George Archer	68	73	76	70	287	15,446.67
Dave Eichelberger	76	68	74	69	287	15,446.67
Dick Goetz	72	67	76	72	287	15,446.66
Gibby Gilbert	71	71	76	70	288	13,346.67
Kermit Zarley	68	75	76	69	288	13,346.67
Mike Hill	66	76	73	73	288	13,346.66
Simon Hobday	71	71	78	69	289	11,340
Mike Joyce	71	70	75	73	289	11,340
Jack Kiefer	72	70	73	74	289	11,340
Calvin Peete	71	71	72	75	289	11,340
Tommy Aaron	71	71	77	72	291	9,660
Bob Charles	68	76	75	72	291	9,660
Chi Chi Rodriguez	71	71	76	73	291	9,660
Butch Baird	75	71	75	71	292	8,225
Dave Hill	70	70	82	70	292	8,225
Larry Mowry	68	73	76	75	292	8,225
Harry Toscano	68	74	73	77	292	8,225
Doug Dalziel	75	70	75	73	293	7,140
Bruce Lehnhard	69	73	78	73	293	7,140
Rives McBee	70	70	76	74	293	7,140

U.S. Senior Open

Pinehurst Resort & Country Club, No. 2 Course,
Pinehurst, North Carolina
Par 35-36—71; 6,771 yards

June 30-July 3
purse, $800,000

	SCORES				TOTAL	MONEY
Simon Hobday	66	67	66	75	274	$145,000
Jim Albus	66	69	66	74	275	63,418.50
Graham Marsh	68	68	69	70	275	63,418.50
Dave Stockton	74	67	68	68	277	30,608
Tom Wargo	69	70	68	70	277	30,608
Tom Weiskopf	72	66	72	67	277	30,608
Bob Murphy	71	70	71	67	279	21,651
Jack Nicklaus	69	68	70	72	279	21,651
Jay Sigel	73	66	70	70	279	21,651
Isao Aoki	69	71	73	67	280	18,313
Lee Trevino	69	71	72	69	281	17,169
Raymond Floyd	69	68	74	71	282	16,044
Dave Eichelberger	74	72	69	69	284	14,280
Gary Player	72	67	73	72	284	14,280
Rocky Thompson	70	74	69	71	284	14,280
Mike Hill	72	68	70	75	285	12,760
Jim Ferree	71	75	69	71	286	11,429.33
DeWitt Weaver	74	73	70	69	286	11,429.33
Kermit Zarley	74	68	71	73	286	11,429.33
Jim Colbert	72	74	69	72	287	9,070
Bob Dickson	76	73	69	69	287	9,070

	SCORES	TOTAL	MONEY
Gibby Gilbert	73 73 68 73	287	9,070
Mike Joyce	74 73 69 71	287	9,070
Calvin Peete	73 70 72 72	287	9,070
Dale Douglass	72 68 74 74	288	7,287.50
Jimmy Powell	70 76 73 69	288	7,287.50
Jack Kiefer	69 75 71 74	289	6,589
Tommy Aycock	74 70 73 73	290	5,738.33
Larry Mowry	72 73 72 73	290	5,738.33
Larry Ziegler	71 76 75 68	290	5,738.33
*Johnny Stevens	75 71 74 70	290	
Terry Dill	70 74 72 75	291	5,050.25
Bill Hall	70 76 73 72	291	5,050.25
Chi Chi Rodriguez	70 76 76 69	291	5,050.25
Ben Smith	71 73 72 75	291	5,050.25
Charles Coody	74 73 73 72	292	4,292
Marion Heck	76 70 73 73	292	4,292
Bob Irving	76 72 74 70	292	4,292
Larry Laoretti	75 73 76 68	292	4,292
Bill McDonough	76 72 71 73	292	4,292
Bobby Nichols	76 73 75 68	292	4,292

Kroger Classic

Jack Nicklaus Sports Center, Mason, Ohio
Par 36-35—71; 6,628 yards

July 8-10
purse, $850,000

	SCORES	TOTAL	MONEY
Jim Colbert	66 64 69	199	$127,500
Raymond Floyd	68 68 65	201	74,800
Mike Hill	68 70 67	205	46,750
Bob Murphy	71 65 69	205	46,750
Rocky Thompson	66 70 69	205	46,750
DeWitt Weaver	65 71 69	205	46,750
Bob Charles	71 69 67	207	25,925
Jimmy Powell	71 71 65	207	25,925
J.C. Snead	68 70 69	207	25,925
Tom Wargo	68 70 69	207	25,925
Graham Marsh	67 70 71	208	19,550
Bert Yancey	71 67 70	208	19,550
Larry Gilbert	67 74 68	209	16,575
Kermit Zarley	64 72 73	209	16,575
Tom Weiskopf	69 73 68	210	15,300
Gibby Gilbert	71 67 73	211	12,424.17
Bill Hall	69 69 73	211	12,424.17
Marion Heck	72 71 68	211	12,424.17
Jerry McGee	70 71 70	211	12,424.17
Tom Shaw	66 75 70	211	12,424.16
Robert Zimmerman	69 70 72	211	12,424.16
Tommy Aycock	74 69 69	212	8,942
Gay Brewer	72 73 67	212	8,942
Charles Coody	67 71 74	212	8,942
Bob Dickson	71 73 68	212	8,942
Simon Hobday	69 74 69	212	8,942
Dave Eichelberger	70 72 71	213	7,565
Jack Kiefer	70 71 72	213	7,565
George Archer	72 74 68	214	6,885
Bob Smith	67 74 73	214	6,885

	SCORES			TOTAL	MONEY
Bob Brue	73	66	76	215	5,278.50
John Paul Cain	72	76	67	215	5,278.50
Jim Dent	73	72	70	215	5,278.50
Randy Glover	73	70	72	215	5,278.50
Dick Goetz	71	72	72	215	5,278.50
Tommy Horton	74	69	72	215	5,278.50
Orville Moody	69	76	70	215	5,278.50
Fred Ruiz	69	75	71	215	5,278.50
Jesse Vaughn	73	73	69	215	5,278.50
Larry Ziegler	73	68	74	215	5,278.50

Ameritech Open

Stonebridge Country Club, Chicago, Illinois
Par 36-36—72; 6,840 yards

July 15-17
purse, $650,000

	SCORES			TOTAL	MONEY
John Paul Cain	66	67	69	202	$112,500
Jim Colbert	67	67	69	203	60,000
Simon Hobday	66	69	68	203	60,000
Chi Chi Rodriguez	69	66	69	204	45,000
Jay Sigel	70	69	66	205	33,000
Harry Toscano	68	69	68	205	33,000
Tommy Aaron	72	67	67	206	22,875
Mike Hill	70	64	72	206	22,875
Tom Wargo	71	67	68	206	22,875
Tom Weiskopf	69	69	68	206	22,875
Jim Dent	71	71	65	207	17,250
J.C. Snead	65	70	72	207	17,250
Dave Eichelberger	70	69	69	208	13,875
Marion Heck	65	73	70	208	13,875
Jack Kiefer	74	66	68	208	13,875
Larry Ziegler	71	69	68	208	13,875
Tom Shaw	69	70	70	209	11,625
Ron Skiles	70	73	66	209	11,625
Dave Stockton	71	68	71	210	10,575
George Archer	70	72	69	211	8,000
Miller Barber	70	73	68	211	8,000
Bruce Crampton	71	71	69	211	8,000
Bob Dickson	70	72	69	211	8,000
Robert Gaona	72	72	67	211	8,000
Rives McBee	70	71	70	211	8,000
Jerry McGee	73	67	71	211	8,000
Orville Moody	72	72	67	211	8,000
Jimmy Powell	75	70	66	211	8,000
Jim Albus	70	72	70	212	5,925
Dick Goetz	70	74	68	212	5,925
Fred Ruiz	74	68	70	212	5,925
Jim Ferree	71	72	70	213	4,950
Bill Hall	70	72	71	213	4,950
Dick Hendrickson	70	71	72	213	4,950
Richard Rhyan	76	69	68	213	4,950
Robert Zimmerman	72	68	73	213	4,950
Gay Brewer	71	70	73	214	3,975
Bob Brue	70	71	73	214	3,975
Ken Harrelson	71	69	74	214	3,975
Larry Mowry	69	73	72	214	3,975
DeWitt Weaver	70	70	74	214	3,975

Southwestern Bell Classic

Loch Lloyd Country Club, Belton, Missouri
Par 35-35—70; 6,539 yards

July 22-24
purse, $700,000

	SCORES			TOTAL	MONEY
Jim Colbert	68	63	65	196	$105,000
Isao Aoki	69	64	65	198	56,000
Larry Gilbert	67	66	65	198	56,000
Graham Marsh	66	67	67	200	42,000
Dave Stockton	70	65	66	201	33,600
Larry Laoretti	69	66	67	202	28,000
Rocky Thompson	68	68	67	203	25,200
J.C. Snead	67	68	69	204	22,400
Kermit Zarley	69	69	67	205	19,600
Raymond Floyd	67	73	66	206	17,500
Bob Smith	69	69	68	206	17,500
Dale Douglass	70	71	66	207	13,066.67
Mike Joyce	68	72	67	207	13,066.67
Jimmy Powell	70	69	68	207	13,066.67
Richard Rhyan	68	71	68	207	13,066.67
Simon Hobday	71	66	70	207	13,066.66
Calvin Peete	67	68	72	207	13,066.66
Jim Albus	73	69	66	208	9,282
Bruce Crampton	70	67	71	208	9,282
Jerry McGee	73	66	69	208	9,282
Jay Sigel	72	69	67	208	9,282
Ben Smith	67	69	72	208	9,282
Tommy Aaron	70	66	73	209	6,710
Bob Dickson	71	69	69	209	6,710
Robert Gaona	71	70	68	209	6,710
Marion Heck	71	70	68	209	6,710
Larry Mowry	70	70	69	209	6,710
Bob Reith	73	63	73	209	6,710
Harry Toscano	68	70	71	209	6,710
Bob Brue	75	69	66	210	5,273.34
Homero Blancas	72	68	70	210	5,273.33
Charles Coody	70	70	70	210	5,273.33
Dick Hendrickson	70	66	75	211	4,515
Harold Henning	71	72	68	211	4,515
Joe Jimenez	70	69	72	211	4,515
Robert Zimmerman	70	67	74	211	4,515
John Paul Cain	71	70	71	212	3,710
Gibby Gilbert	71	70	71	212	3,710
Al Kelley	74	68	70	212	3,710
Dick Lotz	72	71	69	212	3,710
Bert Yancey	69	73	70	212	3,710

Northville Long Island Classic

Meadow Brook Country Club, Jericho, New York
Par 36-36—72; 6,775 yards

July 29-31
purse, $650,000

	SCORES			TOTAL	MONEY
Lee Trevino	66	69	65	200	$97,500
Jim Colbert	70	72	65	207	57,200
Jay Sigel	68	68	72	208	46,800
Isao Aoki	69	69	72	210	29,900

	SCORES			TOTAL	MONEY
Terry Dill	71	72	67	210	29,900
Jerry McGee	71	66	73	210	29,900
Jimmy Powell	66	73	71	210	29,900
George Archer	69	73	69	211	19,500
Harry Toscano	67	71	73	211	19,500
Jim Albus	68	74	70	212	14,430
Bob Dickson	67	73	72	212	14,430
Dave Eichelberger	71	70	71	212	14,430
Raymond Floyd	69	73	70	212	14,430
Tom Wargo	72	70	70	212	14,430
Bob Charles	74	70	69	213	9,815
Robert Gaona	71	70	72	213	9,815
Dick Goetz	72	71	70	213	9,815
Rives McBee	73	69	71	213	9,815
Bob Murphy	71	74	68	213	9,815
Richard Rhyan	72	71	70	213	9,815
Dave Stockton	74	71	68	213	9,815
Dale Douglass	73	71	70	214	7,003.75
Larry Gilbert	73	73	68	214	7,003.75
Joe Jimenez	74	72	68	214	7,003.75
Ben Smith	69	73	72	214	7,003.75
Charles Coody	73	74	68	215	5,785
Gibby Gilbert	72	70	73	215	5,785
Marion Heck	72	73	70	215	5,785
DeWitt Weaver	70	76	69	215	5,785
Gay Brewer	71	71	74	216	4,793.75
Walter Morgan	75	74	67	216	4,793.75
Jack Nicklaus	70	74	72	216	4,793.75
Bob Smith	74	72	70	216	4,793.75
John Paul Cain	74	71	72	217	3,913
Tony Jacklin	71	74	72	217	3,913
Dick Lotz	74	73	70	217	3,913
Fred Ruiz	72	71	74	217	3,913
Bert Yancey	74	74	69	217	3,913
Mike Joyce	77	72	69	218	3,315
Bob Panasik	74	72	72	218	3,315
Chi Chi Rodriguez	74	74	70	218	3,315

Bank of Boston Classic

Nashawtuc Country Club, Boston, Massachusetts
Par 36-36—72; 6,725 yards

August 5-7
purse, $750,000

	SCORES			TOTAL	MONEY
Jim Albus	67	66	70	203	$112,500
Bob Brue	67	73	65	205	60,000
Raymond Floyd	69	67	69	205	60,000
Mike Hill	73	68	66	207	37,000
Dick Lotz	74	67	66	207	37,000
Lee Trevino	70	67	70	207	37,000
Dave Stockton	72	68	68	208	25,500
Tom Wargo	68	70	70	208	25,500
Bob Charles	69	70	70	209	21,000
Butch Baird	70	67	73	210	18,750
Joe Jimenez	71	73	66	210	18,750
Isao Aoki	69	74	68	211	15,250
Bob Dickson	69	70	72	211	15,250

	SCORES			TOTAL	MONEY
Terry Dill	72	69	70	211	15,250
George Archer	70	74	68	212	13,125
Dave Eichelberger	68	75	69	212	13,125
Jim Colbert	72	69	72	213	10,931.25
Jerry McGee	72	72	69	213	10,931.25
Rocky Thompson	73	70	70	213	10,931.25
Walter Zembriski	71	71	71	213	10,931.25
Homero Blancas	69	72	73	214	8,125
Bruce Crampton	76	70	68	214	8,125
Dale Douglass	71	71	72	214	8,125
Gene Littler	73	71	70	214	8,125
Bob Murphy	74	69	71	214	8,125
DeWitt Weaver	69	71	74	214	8,125
Miller Barber	71	70	74	215	5,831.25
Charles Coody	70	73	72	215	5,831.25
Dick Goetz	69	75	71	215	5,831.25
Dick Hendrickson	68	74	73	215	5,831.25
Orville Moody	70	76	69	215	5,831.25
Bobby Nichols	73	69	73	215	5,831.25
Richard Rhyan	73	72	70	215	5,831.25
Robert Zimmerman	73	72	70	215	5,831.25
Richard Bassett	72	73	71	216	4,406.25
Rod Curl	72	71	73	216	4,406.25
Larry Gilbert	70	72	74	216	4,406.25
Chi Chi Rodriguez	72	73	71	216	4,406.25
John Paul Cain	75	71	71	217	3,450
Marion Heck	70	72	75	217	3,450
Jack Kiefer	77	71	69	217	3,450
Randy Petri	71	71	75	217	3,450
Jay Sigel	70	76	71	217	3,450
Ben Smith	74	74	69	217	3,450
Ken Still	70	73	74	217	3,450
Harry Toscano	73	70	74	217	3,450

First of America Classic

Egypt Valley Country Club, Ada, Michigan
Par 36-36—72; 6,673 yards
(Event shortened due to heavy rains.)

August 12-14
purse, $650,000

	SCORES		TOTAL	MONEY
Tony Jacklin	68	68	136	$97,500
Dave Stockton	67	70	137	57,200
Jim Albus	66	72	138	42,900
Lee Trevino	72	66	138	42,900
Harry Toscano	72	67	139	28,600
Tom Wargo	67	72	139	28,600
John Paul Cain	69	71	140	22,100
Jimmy Powell	66	74	140	22,100
Rod Curl	72	69	141	17,550
Larry Mowry	67	74	141	17,550
Isao Aoki	66	76	142	12,268.75
George Archer	68	74	142	12,268.75
Jim Colbert	71	71	142	12,268.75
Jim Dent	70	72	142	12,268.75
Don January	68	74	142	12,268.75
Joe Jimenez	72	70	142	12,268.75

	SCORES			TOTAL	MONEY
Bobby Nichols	71	71		142	12,268.75
Tom Weiskopf	70	72		142	12,268.75
Dave Eichelberger	74	69		143	8,099
Gibby Gilbert	70	73		143	8,099
Bob Goalby	68	75		143	8,099
Larry Laoretti	72	71		143	8,099
Richard Rhyan	69	74		143	8,099
Bob Dickson	69	75		144	6,077.50
Mike Hill	73	71		144	6,077.50
Graham Marsh	66	78		144	6,077.50
Rives McBee	72	72		144	6,077.50
Jerry McGee	73	71		144	6,077.50
Bob Panasik	75	69		144	6,077.50
Dick Hendrickson	71	74		145	4,304.45
Jack Kiefer	73	72		145	4,304.45
Bob Leaver	72	73		145	4,304.45
Robert Zimmerman	73	72		145	4,304.45
Gay Brewer	70	75		145	4,304.44
Bob Brue	74	71		145	4,304.44
Robert Gaona	73	72		145	4,304.44
Marion Heck	71	74		145	4,304.44
Bob Smith	71	74		145	4,304.44
Larry Gilbert	72	74		146	3,185
Dick Goetz	70	76		146	3,185
Fred Ruiz	72	74		146	3,185
Rocky Thompson	70	76		146	3,185
DeWitt Weaver	72	74		146	3,185

Burnet Classic

Bunker Hills Golf Club, Coon Rapids, Minnesota
Par 36-36—72; 6,894 yards

August 19-21
purse, $1,050,000

	SCORES			TOTAL	MONEY
Dave Stockton	68	66	69	203	$157,500
Jim Albus	69	66	69	204	92,400
George Archer	67	69	73	209	53,760
Jim Dent	68	72	69	209	53,760
Dave Eichelberger	71	72	66	209	53,760
Larry Gilbert	69	73	67	209	53,760
Chi Chi Rodriguez	73	67	69	209	53,760
Dale Douglass	73	69	68	210	30,100
Tom Weiskopf	67	74	69	210	30,100
Kermit Zarley	70	75	65	210	30,100
John Paul Cain	70	73	69	212	22,312.50
Dick Hendrickson	70	75	67	212	22,312.50
Jerry McGee	72	72	68	212	22,312.50
Walter Zembriski	73	66	73	212	22,312.50
Isao Aoki	76	71	66	213	18,375
Bob Brue	69	72	72	213	18,375
Tommy Aaron	75	69	70	214	14,847
Miller Barber	71	70	73	214	14,847
Graham Marsh	73	71	70	214	14,847
Bob Smith	68	74	72	214	14,847
Tom Wargo	74	71	69	214	14,847
Don Bies	74	69	72	215	9,880.50
Bob Charles	73	70	72	215	9,880.50
Harold Henning	78	66	71	215	9,880.50

	SCORES			TOTAL	MONEY
Simon Hobday	72	73	70	215	9,880.50
Dick Lotz	71	76	68	215	9,880.50
Rives McBee	71	73	71	215	9,880.50
Richard Rhyan	68	77	72	215	9,880.50
Tom Shaw	72	75	68	215	9,880.50
Terry Small	70	75	70	215	9,880.50
Larry Ziegler	70	71	74	215	9,880.50
Dick Goetz	72	71	73	216	6,930
Ben Smith	71	69	76	216	6,930
Lee Trevino	73	71	72	216	6,930
DeWitt Weaver	73	72	71	216	6,930
Tony Jacklin	71	74	71	216	6,930
Bruce Crampton	72	73	72	217	5,460
Bob Dickson	74	73	70	217	5,460
Bobby Nichols	71	71	75	217	5,460
Jay Sigel	71	76	70	217	5,460
J.C. Snead	71	75	71	217	5,460
Ken Still	73	70	74	217	5,460

Franklin Quest Championship

Park Meadows Country Club, Park City, Utah
Par 36-36—72; 7,026 yards

August 26-28
purse, $500,000

	SCORES			TOTAL	MONEY
Tom Weiskopf	68	67	69	204	$75,000
Dave Stockton	68	66	70	204	44,000
(Weiskopf defeated Stockton on first extra hole.)					
Jack Kiefer	68	69	68	205	33,000
Bob Murphy	69	66	70	205	33,000
Jim Albus	71	67	69	207	22,000
George Archer	72	66	69	207	22,000
Tommy Aaron	70	68	70	208	16,000
Tony Jacklin	71	67	70	208	16,000
Jay Sigel	69	69	70	208	16,000
Bob Smith	71	72	67	210	13,000
Charles Coody	69	69	73	211	10,300
Dave Eichelberger	72	71	68	211	10,300
J.C. Snead	71	70	70	211	10,300
Harry Toscano	72	68	71	211	10,300
Tom Wargo	70	71	70	211	10,300
Simon Hobday	74	71	67	212	7,308.34
Don January	73	70	69	212	7,308.34
Dale Douglass	72	71	69	212	7,308.33
Bill Hall	74	68	70	212	7,308.33
Larry Laoretti	71	71	70	212	7,308.33
Orville Moody	71	70	71	212	7,308.33
Gay Brewer	70	68	76	214	5,387.50
Bob Brue	70	67	77	214	5,387.50
Robert Gaona	71	70	73	214	5,387.50
Babe Hiskey	77	69	68	214	5,387.50
Tom Shaw	75	69	71	215	4,650
Bruce Summerhays	72	72	71	215	4,650
Bob Dickson	73	70	73	216	3,875
Dick Lotz	70	70	76	216	3,875
Rives McBee	72	70	74	216	3,875
Jerry McGee	74	70	72	216	3,875
DeWitt Weaver	76	69	71	216	3,875

	SCORES			TOTAL	MONEY
Robert Zimmerman	71	71	74	216	3,875
Richard Rhyan	73	75	69	217	3,225
Fred Ruiz	73	72	72	217	3,225
Terry Dill	73	73	72	218	2,760
Al Kelley	74	69	75	218	2,760
Gary Player	77	71	70	218	2,760
Ben Smith	73	73	72	218	2,760
Larry Ziegler	75	72	71	218	2,760

GTE Northwest Classic

Inglewood Country Club, Seattle, Washington
Par 36-36—72; 6,455 yards

September 2-4
purse, $550,000

	SCORES			TOTAL	MONEY
Simon Hobday	70	69	70	209	$82,500
Jim Albus	66	75	68	209	48,400
(Hobday defeated Albus on first extra hole.)					
Tony Jacklin	67	73	71	211	33,000
Larry Laoretti	72	70	69	211	33,000
Jay Sigel	72	68	71	211	33,000
Babe Hiskey	69	75	68	212	19,800
J.C. Snead	73	70	68	212	19,800
Dave Stockton	74	71	67	212	19,800
Butch Baird	72	72	69	213	14,850
Dave Eichelberger	68	72	73	213	14,850
Rod Curl	72	68	74	214	10,685.72
Don January	73	71	70	214	10,685.72
Bob Reith	72	71	71	214	10,685.72
Homero Blancas	70	70	74	214	10,685.71
John Paul Cain	69	75	70	214	10,685.71
Richard Rhyan	68	76	70	214	10,685.71
Robert Zimmerman	70	72	72	214	10,685.71
Bob Dickson	73	69	73	215	7,293
Bob Irving	68	74	73	215	7,293
Dick Lotz	70	71	74	215	7,293
Ben Smith	71	72	72	215	7,293
Bob Smith	71	75	69	215	7,293
Dale Douglass	76	69	71	216	5,511
Graham Marsh	71	73	72	216	5,511
Bob Murphy	74	70	72	216	5,511
Ed Sneed	71	72	73	216	5,511
Kermit Zarley	73	75	68	216	5,511
Bruce Crampton	71	72	74	217	4,565
Rives McBee	73	69	75	217	4,565
Tom Shaw	73	74	70	217	4,565
Jim O'Hern	72	72	74	218	3,630
Arnold Palmer	70	75	73	218	3,630
Ken Still	72	73	73	218	3,630
Rocky Thompson	73	67	78	218	3,630
Harry Toscano	74	74	70	218	3,630
Tom Wargo	68	81	69	218	3,630
Ted Wurtz	73	73	72	218	3,630
Lee Elder	70	75	74	219	2,860
Joe Jimenez	73	74	72	219	2,860
Mike Joyce	73	73	73	219	2,860
Walter Zembriski	72	74	73	219	2,860

Quicksilver Classic

Quicksilver Golf Club, Pittsburgh, Pennsylvania
Par 36-36—72; 6,907 yards

September 9-11
purse, $1,050,000

	SCORES			TOTAL	MONEY
Dave Eichelberger	71	67	71	209	$157,500
Homero Blancas	71	71	69	211	84,000
Raymond Floyd	69	72	70	211	84,000
Bob Dickson	69	72	71	212	51,800
Chi Chi Rodriguez	72	71	69	212	51,800
Tom Wargo	73	70	69	212	51,800
Jim Colbert	69	72	72	213	33,600
Jay Sigel	73	71	69	213	33,600
Dave Stockton	71	70	72	213	33,600
Jim Albus	70	71	73	214	22,575
Isao Aoki	73	70	71	214	22,575
Jim Dent	74	70	70	214	22,575
Simon Hobday	72	71	71	214	22,575
Graham Marsh	71	68	75	214	22,575
J.C. Snead	72	69	73	214	22,575
Tommy Aaron	73	72	70	215	16,301.25
George Archer	72	72	71	215	16,301.25
Larry Gilbert	75	70	70	215	16,301.25
Rives McBee	72	72	71	215	16,301.25
Miller Barber	72	68	76	216	12,327
Jerry McGee	74	70	72	216	12,327
Jimmy Powell	72	73	71	216	12,327
Ed Sneed	70	73	73	216	12,327
DeWitt Weaver	72	71	73	216	12,327
Don Bies	74	68	75	217	9,791.25
Jim Ferree	75	74	68	217	9,791.25
Mike Hill	70	74	73	217	9,791.25
Tony Jacklin	76	70	71	217	9,791.25
Dale Douglass	73	73	72	218	7,938
Jack Kiefer	74	70	74	218	7,938
Orville Moody	71	71	76	218	7,938
Walter Morgan	72	72	74	218	7,938
Richard Rhyan	77	71	70	218	7,938
Bob Carson	74	76	69	219	6,321
Terry Dill	74	71	74	219	6,321
Marion Heck	77	71	71	219	6,321
Joe Jimenez	70	74	75	219	6,321
Larry Laoretti	70	74	75	219	6,321
Bob Charles	70	78	72	220	5,460
Bruce Crampton	74	73	73	220	5,460

Bank One Classic

Kearney Hill Links, Lexington, Kentucky
Par 36-36—72; 6,798 yards

September 16-18
purse, $550,000

	SCORES			TOTAL	MONEY
Isao Aoki	69	64	69	202	$82,500
Chi Chi Rodriguez	71	68	66	205	48,400
Gay Brewer	68	69	70	207	33,000
Jim Dent	69	72	66	207	33,000
Jack Kiefer	69	67	71	207	33,000

	SCORES			TOTAL	MONEY
Jim Albus	66	68	74	208	18,700
Dave Eichelberger	68	71	69	208	18,700
Jimmy Powell	66	68	74	208	18,700
DeWitt Weaver	67	69	72	208	18,700
Larry Gilbert	72	67	70	209	13,200
Rives McBee	69	70	70	209	13,200
Tom Wargo	69	69	71	209	13,200
George Archer	69	67	74	210	10,450
Dick Hendrickson	68	72	70	210	10,450
Jerry McGee	74	70	66	210	10,450
Mike Hill	68	68	75	211	9,350
Charles Coody	68	71	73	212	8,525
George Shortridge	72	71	69	212	8,525
Terry Dill	71	70	72	213	7,053.75
Dale Douglass	67	72	74	213	7,053.75
Lee Trevino	73	68	72	213	7,053.75
Larry Ziegler	69	74	70	213	7,053.75
Jim Colbert	73	74	67	214	5,637.50
Orville Moody	71	67	76	214	5,637.50
J.C. Snead	73	70	71	214	5,637.50
Walter Zembriski	71	72	71	214	5,637.50
Tommy Aaron	71	72	72	215	4,565
Tommy Aycock	70	75	70	215	4,565
Bob Carson	71	72	72	215	4,565
Larry Mowry	73	68	74	215	4,565
Gary Player	72	72	71	215	4,565
Gary Cowan	72	70	74	216	3,547.50
Bill Hall	76	71	69	216	3,547.50
Marion Heck	71	71	74	216	3,547.50
Tony Jacklin	72	71	73	216	3,547.50
Bob Thatcher	76	68	72	216	3,547.50
Harry Toscano	71	73	72	216	3,547.50
Miller Barber	72	71	74	217	2,860
Dave Hill	70	73	74	217	2,860
Calvin Peete	72	69	76	217	2,860
Richard Rhyan	72	70	75	217	2,860

Brickyard Crossing Championship

Brickyard Crossing Golf Club, Indianapolis, Indiana
Par 36-36—72; 6,721 yards
(First round cancelled — rain.)

September 23-25
purse, $700,000

	SCORES		TOTAL	MONEY
Isao Aoki	66	67	133	$105,000
Jimmy Powell	68	66	134	56,000
Tom Wargo	66	68	134	56,000
Jim Dent	65	70	135	32,200
Dave Eichelberger	71	64	135	32,200
Simon Hobday	66	69	135	32,200
Graham Marsh	66	69	135	32,200
Jerry McGee	70	66	136	22,400
Larry Gilbert	65	72	137	19,600
Bob Murphy	69	69	138	17,500
J.C. Snead	67	71	138	17,500
Homero Blancas	71	68	139	13,440
Jim Ferree	69	70	139	13,440
Mike Hill	66	73	139	13,440

	SCORES			TOTAL	MONEY
Dave Stockton	72	67		139	13,440
Larry Ziegler	71	68		139	13,440
Terry Dill	70	70		140	10,202.50
Jack Kiefer	70	70		140	10,202.50
Calvin Peete	68	72		140	10,202.50
Walter Zembriski	68	72		140	10,202.50
Jim Albus	68	73		141	6,930
John Paul Cain	71	70		141	6,930
Dale Douglass	68	73		141	6,930
Dick Goetz	71	70		141	6,930
Harold Henning	70	71		141	6,930
Rives McBee	71	70		141	6,930
Walter Morgan	70	71		141	6,930
Chi Chi Rodriguez	73	68		141	6,930
Jay Sigel	69	72		141	6,930
Tom Weiskopf	68	73		141	6,930
Bob Carson	69	73		142	4,935
Pat O'Brien	70	72		142	4,935
Tom Shaw	72	70		142	4,935
George Shortridge	69	73		142	4,935
George Archer	69	74		143	3,880
Jim Colbert	71	72		143	3,880
Tony Jacklin	71	72		143	3,880
Larry Laoretti	70	73		143	3,880
Bobby Nichols	71	72		143	3,880
Bob Reith	71	72		143	3,880
Harry Toscano	67	76		143	3,880

Vantage Championship

Tanglewood Park, Clemmons, North Carolina
Par 36-36—72; 6,680 yards

September 30-October 2
purse, $1,500,000

	SCORES			TOTAL	MONEY
Larry Gilbert	66	66	66	198	$225,000
Raymond Floyd	70	64	65	199	132,000
Jim Dent	66	66	69	201	99,000
Dave Stockton	63	74	64	201	99,000
Calvin Peete	72	66	66	204	66,000
Tom Wargo	70	66	68	204	66,000
George Archer	68	72	65	205	45,750
Jim Colbert	68	70	67	205	45,750
Dick Goetz	68	69	68	205	45,750
Jimmy Powell	69	66	70	205	45,750
Bob Charles	69	65	72	206	31,875
Bob Dickson	71	69	66	206	31,875
Mike Hill	66	68	72	206	31,875
J.C. Snead	70	66	70	206	31,875
Isao Aoki	67	67	73	207	25,500
Dave Eichelberger	66	68	73	207	25,500
Gary Player	66	71	70	207	25,500
Tommy Aycock	71	69	68	208	21,150
Bob Murphy	64	72	72	208	21,150
DeWitt Weaver	69	68	71	208	21,150
Jim Albus	69	69	71	209	16,650
Charles Coody	74	69	66	209	16,650
Jack Kiefer	72	69	68	209	16,650
Graham Marsh	72	68	69	209	16,650

	SCORES			TOTAL	MONEY
Lee Trevino	69	70	70	209	16,650
Tommy Aaron	69	69	72	210	14,250
Homero Blancas	71	66	74	211	12,175
Babe Hiskey	73	68	70	211	12,175
Don January	68	71	72	211	12,175
Jerry McGee	72	72	67	211	12,175
Larry Mowry	67	73	71	211	12,175
Rocky Thompson	70	70	71	211	12,175
Miller Barber	67	73	72	212	9,250
Tony Jacklin	72	68	72	212	9,250
Orville Moody	69	71	72	212	9,250
Richard Rhyan	72	69	71	212	9,250
Chi Chi Rodriguez	71	70	71	212	9,250
Ben Smith	69	71	72	212	9,250
John Paul Cain	73	68	72	213	7,200
Terry Dill	72	71	70	213	7,200
Jay Sigel	74	70	69	213	7,200
Bob Smith	70	70	73	213	7,200
Kermit Zarley	70	74	69	213	7,200
Walter Zembriski	70	70	73	213	7,200

The Transamerica

Silverado Country Club, Napa, California
Par 35-37—72; 6,632 yards

October 7-9
purse, $600,000

	SCORES			TOTAL	MONEY
Kermit Zarley	70	68	66	204	$90,000
Isao Aoki	69	72	63	204	52,800
(Zarley defeated Aoki on first extra hole.)					
Gary Player	68	68	70	206	36,000
J.C. Snead	71	69	66	206	36,000
Dave Stockton	71	69	66	206	36,000
Butch Baird	65	71	71	207	18,600
Bob Brue	68	69	70	207	18,600
John Paul Cain	69	69	69	207	18,600
Jim Dent	68	72	67	207	18,600
Jack Kiefer	70	69	68	207	18,600
Jay Sigel	67	69	71	207	18,600
Tommy Aycock	68	68	72	208	11,850
Orville Moody	73	66	69	208	11,850
Tom Shaw	70	67	71	208	11,850
Tom Wargo	73	67	68	208	11,850
Dick Hendrickson	71	70	68	209	9,036
Dick Lotz	70	69	70	209	9,036
Jimmy Powell	69	70	70	209	9,036
Bruce Summerhays	70	73	66	209	9,036
Robert Zimmerman	72	69	68	209	9,036
Jim Albus	72	69	69	210	7,000
Bob Charles	71	68	71	210	7,000
Don January	72	69	69	210	7,000
John Brodie	72	71	68	211	5,485.72
Gibby Gilbert	72	71	68	211	5,485.72
Simon Hobday	71	71	69	211	5,485.72
Larry Laoretti	69	72	70	211	5,485.71
Rives McBee	74	68	69	211	5,485.71
Jerry McGee	71	70	70	211	5,485.71
Bob Smith	65	74	72	211	5,485.71

	SCORES			TOTAL	MONEY
Homero Blancas	69	70	73	212	4,320
Bob Murphy	73	72	67	212	4,320
Walter Zembriski	73	68	71	212	4,320
Bob Carson	71	71	71	213	3,690
Dave Eichelberger	73	72	68	213	3,690
Bill Hall	69	73	71	213	3,690
Ed Sneed	69	75	69	213	3,690
Don Bies	77	67	70	214	3,000
Charles Coody	72	71	71	214	3,000
Bruce Devlin	72	71	71	214	3,000
Al Geiberger	70	72	72	214	3,000
Harry Toscano	75	69	70	214	3,000
Larry Ziegler	72	69	73	214	3,000

Raley's Gold Rush

Rancho Murieta Country Club, Rancho Murieta, California
Par 36-36—72; 6,685 yards

October 13-16
purse, $650,000

	SCORES			TOTAL	MONEY
Bob Murphy	69	71	68	208	$97,500
Dave Eichelberger	68	69	71	208	57,200
(Murphy defeated Eichelberger on fifth extra hole.)					
Jim Albus	69	72	69	210	42,900
J.C. Snead	71	76	63	210	42,900
Bob Charles	71	72	69	212	26,866.67
Larry Gilbert	69	74	69	212	26,866.67
Al Geiberger	72	69	71	212	26,866.66
Gary Player	72	71	70	213	20,800
Tommy Aycock	69	75	70	214	16,250
Bob Dickson	71	72	71	214	16,250
Chi Chi Rodriguez	70	70	74	214	16,250
Dave Stockton	70	75	69	214	16,250
Jim Colbert	75	73	67	215	12,025
Raymond Floyd	71	73	71	215	12,025
Dick Lotz	70	73	72	215	12,025
Kermit Zarley	73	71	71	215	12,025
Don Bies	70	76	70	216	9,473.75
Simon Hobday	68	74	74	216	9,473.75
Orville Moody	71	75	70	216	9,473.75
DeWitt Weaver	72	73	71	216	9,473.75
Miller Barber	75	72	70	217	7,393.75
Jim Dent	72	73	72	217	7,393.75
Jimmy Powell	71	74	72	217	7,393.75
Tom Wargo	71	71	75	217	7,393.75
George Archer	73	73	72	218	6,061.25
Terry Dill	69	76	73	218	6,061.25
Dale Douglass	74	77	67	218	6,061.25
Jerry McGee	75	74	69	218	6,061.25
John Paul Cain	72	74	73	219	5,265
Larry Mowry	76	71	72	219	5,265
Isao Aoki	73	75	72	220	4,485
Gibby Gilbert	67	78	75	220	4,485
Jack Kiefer	73	75	72	220	4,485
Ken Still	73	76	71	220	4,485
Harry Toscano	75	73	72	220	4,485
Homero Blancas	75	74	72	221	3,454.29
Larry Laoretti	73	77	71	221	3,454.29

	SCORES			TOTAL	MONEY
Richard Rhyan	72	77	72	221	3,454.29
Ben Smith	69	78	74	221	3,454.29
Charles Coody	75	72	74	221	3,454.28
Marion Heck	73	73	75	221	3,454.28
Tom Shaw	71	76	74	221	3,454.28

Ralph's Classic

Rancho Park Golf Course, Los Angeles, California
Par 36-35—71; 6,307 yards

October 20-23
purse, $750,000

	SCORES			TOTAL	MONEY
Jack Kiefer	69	65	63	197	$112,500
Dale Douglass	70	67	61	198	66,000
Jim Colbert	68	67	66	201	54,000
Jim Dent	68	63	71	202	30,500
Tony Jacklin	65	72	65	202	30,500
Bob Murphy	68	69	65	202	30,500
Jimmy Powell	67	69	66	202	30,500
Ben Smith	71	68	63	202	30,500
Kermit Zarley	68	68	66	202	30,500
Dick Lotz	68	68	67	203	17,250
Bobby Nichols	64	71	68	203	17,250
Jay Sigel	70	68	65	203	17,250
J.C. Snead	68	67	68	203	17,250
Tommy Aaron	71	68	65	204	13,125
Don Bies	69	68	67	204	13,125
Dave Eichelberger	70	62	72	204	13,125
Larry Gilbert	68	69	67	204	13,125
George Archer	74	67	64	205	9,662.50
Bob Charles	69	68	68	205	9,662.50
Raymond Floyd	69	70	66	205	9,662.50
Al Geiberger	70	69	66	205	9,662.50
Joe Jimenez	68	71	66	205	9,662.50
Tom Weiskopf	70	68	67	205	9,662.50
John Paul Cain	68	70	68	206	6,558.34
Dave Stockton	68	70	68	206	6,558.34
DeWitt Weaver	67	70	69	206	6,558.34
Jim Albus	69	68	69	206	6,558.33
Charles Coody	70	68	68	206	6,558.33
Chi Chi Rodriguez	70	66	70	206	6,558.33
Tom Shaw	68	69	69	206	6,558.33
George Shortridge	70	65	71	206	6,558.33
Harry Toscano	67	69	70	206	6,558.33
Bob Dickson	70	64	73	207	4,950
Gary Player	70	70	67	207	4,950
Bob Wynn	70	70	67	207	4,950
Harold Henning	71	65	72	208	4,218.75
Don January	70	70	68	208	4,218.75
Jerry McGee	71	66	71	208	4,218.75
Tom Wargo	67	72	69	208	4,218.75
Isao Aoki	68	71	70	209	3,450
Miller Barber	69	71	69	209	3,450
John Brodie	73	69	67	209	3,450
Bob Brue	67	73	69	209	3,450
Terry Dill	69	72	68	209	3,450
Dick Hendrickson	68	69	72	209	3,450

Hyatt Regency Maui Kaanapali Classic

Royal Kaanapali Country Club, Maui, Hawaii
Par 35-36—71; 6,590 yards

November 4-6
purse, $550,000

	SCORES			TOTAL	MONEY
Bob Murphy	62	67	66	195	$82,500
Jack Kiefer	66	66	65	197	48,400
Dale Douglass	68	66	65	199	39,600
George Archer	70	65	65	200	33,000
Larry Mowry	68	65	68	201	26,400
Jerry McGee	66	64	72	202	22,000
Homero Blancas	71	65	67	203	17,600
Harry Toscano	70	67	66	203	17,600
Tom Wargo	68	64	71	203	17,600
Gibby Gilbert	70	67	68	205	13,200
Larry Gilbert	70	67	68	205	13,200
Rocky Thompson	67	69	69	205	13,200
Jim Dent	69	69	68	206	10,725
Dave Stockton	68	68	70	206	10,725
Tommy Aycock	70	69	68	207	9,625
Bill Hall	69	69	69	207	9,625
Tommy Aaron	68	67	73	208	7,136.25
Jim Albus	70	69	69	208	7,136.25
Don Bies	70	68	70	208	7,136.25
Dave Eichelberger	69	68	71	208	7,136.25
Babe Hiskey	71	66	71	208	7,136.25
Joe Jimenez	69	71	68	208	7,136.25
Gary Player	70	68	70	208	7,136.25
Tom Weiskopf	70	65	73	208	7,136.25
DeWitt Weaver	70	69	70	209	5,243.34
Dick Goetz	69	67	73	209	5,243.33
Don January	70	67	72	209	5,243.33
Richard Bassett	71	70	69	210	4,455
Jim Colbert	74	67	69	210	4,455
Gary Groh	69	67	74	210	4,455
Mike Joyce	72	70	68	210	4,455
Marion Heck	71	70	70	211	3,712.50
Tony Jacklin	71	70	70	211	3,712.50
Jay Sigel	69	68	74	211	3,712.50
Ben Smith	71	67	73	211	3,712.50
Butch Baird	75	71	66	212	2,866.88
Dick Lotz	72	71	69	212	2,866.88
Bob Panasik	74	69	69	212	2,866.88
Ed Sneed	72	72	68	212	2,866.88
Bruce Crampton	73	68	71	212	2,866.87
Bob Dickson	69	71	72	212	2,866.87
Jimmy Powell	70	68	74	212	2,866.87
Chi Chi Rodriguez	69	72	71	212	2,866.87

Golf Magazine Senior Tour Championship

The Dunes Golf & Beach Club, Myrtle Beach, South Carolina
Par 36-36—72; 6,815 yards

November 10-13
purse $1,350,000

	SCORES				TOTAL	MONEY
Raymond Floyd	67	73	67	66	273	$240,000
Jim Albus	64	71	66	72	273	141,000

(Floyd defeated Albus on fifth extra hole.)

	SCORES				TOTAL	MONEY
Jay Sigel	69	72	71	63	275	115,000
Jim Dent	71	69	70	67	277	96,000
Tom Wargo	67	74	70	68	279	77,000
Dave Stockton	69	73	71	67	280	64,100
Tommy Aaron	73	72	69	67	281	57,700
Mike Hill	68	73	71	70	282	48,100
Jerry McGee	69	74	71	68	282	48,100
Rocky Thompson	65	70	75	73	283	41,700
Bob Charles	70	77	67	71	285	38,500
Graham Marsh	72	72	71	71	286	32,633.34
George Archer	69	75	74	68	286	32,633.33
Jimmy Powell	70	74	74	68	286	32,633.33
Gibby Gilbert	72	74	71	70	287	28,100
Simon Hobday	72	73	72	70	287	28,100
Dale Douglass	73	72	70	73	288	25,700
Jack Kiefer	74	76	73	66	289	23,350
DeWitt Weaver	69	76	76	68	289	23,350
J.C. Snead	76	74	70	70	290	20,550
Kermit Zarley	72	74	71	73	290	20,550
Dave Eichelberger	71	75	73	73	292	18,600
John Paul Cain	73	77	71	72	293	17,300
Larry Gilbert	74	73	74	72	293	17,300
Tom Weiskopf	76	78	73	67	294	16,400
Jim Colbert	76	74	78	68	296	15,500
Chi Chi Rodriguez	73	74	77	72	296	15,500
Bob Murphy	69	80			WD	

Diners Club Matches

PGA West, Jack Nicklaus Course, La Quinta, California December 8-11
Par 36-36—72; 6,546 yards purse, $2,100,000

FIRST ROUND

Jack Nicklaus and Arnold Palmer defeated Simon Hobday and Tom Weiskopf, 1 up.
Jim Dent and Chi Chi Rodriguez defeated Jim Colbert and Larry Murphy, 5 and 4.
Larry Gilbert and Gibby Gilbert defeated Jim Albus and Tom Wargo, 1 up.
Raymond Floyd and Dave Eichelberger defeated Dave Stockton and Al Geiberger, 5 and 3.

(Losers in first round received $15,000 each.)

SECOND ROUND

Nicklaus and Palmer defeated Dent and Rodriguez, 4 and 3.
Floyd and Eichelberger defeated L. Gilbert and G. Gilbert, 3 and 2.

(Losers in second round received $35,000 each.)

THIRD ROUND

Floyd and Eichelberger defeated Nicklaus and Palmer, 19 holes.

(Winners in third round received $125,000 each; losers received $50,000 each.)

European Seniors Tour

St. Pierre Classic

St. Pierre Golf and Country Club, Chepstow, England
Par 35-36—71; 6,785 yards

May 13-15
purse, £50,000

	SCORES			TOTAL	MONEY
Tommy Horton	71	71	70	212	£8,330
Brian Huggett	73	70	72	215	5,550
Neil Coles	71	71	74	216	3,130
David Butler	75	67	76	218	2,310
John Morgan	73	73	72	218	2,310
David Snell	71	73	75	219	1,945
Liam Higgins	75	71	74	220	1,590
Malcolm Gregson	69	78	73	220	1,590
Brian Waites	73	75	72	220	1,590
Rafe Botts	73	75	72	220	1,590
John Fourie	73	74	74	221	1,235
Norman Drew	74	75	72	221	1,235
Jimmy Kinsella	74	71	77	222	936.67
Phil Ferranti	74	72	76	222	936.67
Peter Green	71	74	77	222	936.67
Hedley Muscroft	77	74	72	223	770
Renato Campagnoli	74	76	73	223	770
John Hamilton	74	74	76	224	677.50
Joe Carr	75	77	72	224	677.50
Stuart Murray	72	77	75	224	677.50
David Jimenez	72	77	75	224	677.50
Ross Whitehead	77	73	75	225	620
Roger Fidler	77	73	75	225	620
George Will	76	75	74	225	620
Lionel Platts	76	74	78	228	590
Marcel Vercruyce	72	78	78	228	590
Peter Butler	79	73	76	228	590
Richard Emery	75	75	79	229	565
Tony Grubb	80	73	76	229	565
Tony Coveney	76	76	78	230	550

La Manga Club Spanish Open

La Manga Golf Club, Cartegena, Spain
Par 36-36—72; 6,674 yards

May 20-22
purse, £100,000

	SCORES			TOTAL	MONEY
Brian Huggett	72	74	69	215	£16,660
David Snell	69	78	68	215	8,680
Malcolm Gregson	73	77	65	215	8,680
(Huggett defeated Snell and Gregson on first extra hole.)					
Chick Evans	71	73	72	216	4,620
Brian Waites	72	72	72	216	4,620
Tommy Horton	71	75	71	217	3,735
Antonio Garrido	71	74	72	217	3,735
John Morgan	70	76	73	219	3,046.67
Michael Murphy	72	74	73	219	3,046.67

	SCORES			TOTAL	MONEY
Tony Coveney	77	71	71	219	3,046.67
Hugh Inggs	74	72	74	220	2,470
David Jimenez	74	73	73	220	2,470
Alberto Croce	70	78	73	221	1,760
Vincent Tshabalala	72	77	72	221	1,760
Renato Campagnoli	72	76	73	221	1,760
Gordon Gray	75	74	72	221	1,760
Jose Maria Roca	77	74	70	221	1,760
Frederick Boobyer	73	73	76	222	1,275
David Talbot	77	71	74	222	1,275
Bobby Verwey	74	73	76	223	1,133.33
Francisco Abreu	78	74	71	223	1,133.33
Michael Thomas Hoyle	79	74	70	223	1,133.33
Rafe Botts	74	79	72	225	1,030
John Fourie	76	69	80	225	1,030
Bob Thatcher	72	81	73	226	965
Derek Craik	74	76	76	226	965
Terry Squires	73	77	77	227	862
Roberto Bernardini	75	76	76	227	862
Bryan Carter	77	74	76	227	862
Keith MacDonald	77	75	75	227	862
Tony Grubb	79	75	73	227	862

D-Day Open

Omaha Beach Golf Club, Bayeux, France
Par 36-36—72; 6,614 yards

June 8-10
purse, £50,000

	SCORES			TOTAL	MONEY
Brian Waites	69	66	71	206	£8,330
Antonio Garrido	72	69	71	212	5,550
Tommy Horton	72	73	68	213	2,815
Tony Grubb	71	69	73	213	2,815
Phil Ferranti	72	72	70	214	2,032.50
John Morgan	72	72	70	214	2,032.50
Liam Higgins	73	68	74	215	1,790
Michel Damiano	72	73	71	216	1,650
Renato Campagnoli	73	73	71	217	1,520
Jose Maria Roca	76	73	69	218	1,290
David Butler	75	70	73	218	1,290
David Jimenez	77	71	70	218	1,290
Alberto Croce	74	71	74	219	985
Jean Garaialde	73	73	73	219	985
Hedley Muscroft	72	72	76	220	840
Bernard Hunt	76	70	75	221	753.33
Terry Squires	75	74	72	221	753.33
John Fourie	77	74	70	221	753.33
David Talbot	77	74	71	222	690
Roberto Bernardini	74	76	73	223	650
Peter Butler	77	74	72	223	650
David Snell	74	76	74	224	625
Malcolm Gregson	75	72	77	224	625
John Hamilton	78	76	71	225	605
Frederick Boobyer	76	74	75	225	605
Hugh Boyle	78	73	75	226	585
Bryan Carter	76	72	78	226	585
George Will	73	78	76	227	560
Ramon Sota	76	74	77	227	560
Vincent Tshabalala	76	75	76	227	560

Northern Electric Seniors

Slaley Hall Golf & Country Club, Hexham, England
Par 36-36—72; 6,435 yards

June 24-26
purse, £50,000

	SCORES			TOTAL	MONEY
John Morgan	74	71	74	219	£8,330
Bernard Hunt	70	76	73	219	5,550
(Morgan defeated Hunt on sixth extra hole.)					
Tommy Horton	76	72	72	220	2,815
Liam Higgins	73	71	76	220	2,815
John Fourie	72	74	76	222	2,120
Malcolm Gregson	77	73	74	224	1,945
David Butler	79	73	73	225	1,720
David Snell	77	77	71	225	1,720
David Talbot	75	73	78	226	1,347.50
Brian Huggett	76	74	76	226	1,347.50
Bobby Verwey	76	74	76	226	1,347.50
Michael Murphy	74	74	78	226	1,347.50
Brian Waites	76	74	77	227	985
Peter Butler	75	76	76	227	985
David Huish	73	75	80	228	775
Neil Coles	77	77	74	228	775
Chick Evans	73	75	80	228	775
Tony Grubb	79	77	72	228	775
Joe Carr	80	73	77	230	663.33
Terry Squires	76	77	77	230	663.33
Hedley Muscroft	73	78	79	230	663.33
Frederick Boobyer	77	77	77	231	625
Bryan Carter	76	77	78	231	625
Rafe Botts	79	70	73	232	595
Frank Hill	79	76	77	232	595
Hugh Boyle	78	73	81	232	595
Vincent Tshabalala	77	79	76	232	595
Phil Ferranti	71	75	87	233	565
Roger Fidler	77	79	77	233	565
Alberto Croce	74	77	83	234	547.50
David Jimenez	75	77	82	234	547.50

Tandem Open

Stockley Park Golf Club, Heathrow, England
Par 36-36—72; 6,548 yards

June 30-July 2
purse, £52,000

	SCORES			TOTAL	MONEY
Malcolm Gregson	69	67	69	205	£8,330
John Morgan	71	70	65	206	4,340
Liam Higgins	70	67	69	206	4,340
Renato Campagnoli	69	73	66	208	2,500
David Jimenez	67	72	71	210	2,120
Phil Ferranti	68	72	72	212	1,867.50
John Fourie	71	73	68	212	1,867.50
Alberto Croce	69	73	71	213	1,650
Brian Waites	75	69	70	214	1,460
David Butler	69	71	74	214	1,460
Jimmy Kinsella	68	75	72	215	1,290
Bobby Verwey	71	75	70	216	1,180
Chick Evans	77	68	72	217	985

	SCORES			TOTAL	MONEY
Hugh Boyle	69	75	73	217	985
Peter Blaze	69	73	76	218	840
David Talbot	75	75	70	220	737.50
Antonio Garrido	73	77	70	220	737.50
Neil Coles	74	76	70	220	737.50
Bernard Hunt	76	71	73	220	737.50
Tony Grubb	76	73	72	221	643.33
Vincent Tshabalala	75	75	71	221	643.33
Derek Craik	75	73	73	221	643.33
Richard Emery	74	76	72	222	615
Roger Fidler	69	80	73	222	615
David Snell	76	72	75	223	600
Michael Murphy	77	72	75	224	580
Bryan Carter	71	79	74	224	580
Frederick Boobyer	75	75	74	224	580
Terry Squires	76	74	75	225	546
Rafe Botts	76	77	72	225	546
Roberto Bernardini	76	72	77	225	546
Austin Skerritt	76	75	74	225	546
Brian Huggett	76	74	75	225	546

Seniors British Open

Royal Lytham & St. Annes Golf Club, Lancashire, England
Par 36-36—72; 6,673 yards

July 20-23
purse, £220,000

	SCORES				TOTAL	MONEY
Tom Wargo	73	68	68	71	280	£36,650
Bob Charles	70	69	72	71	282	18,905
Doug Dalziel	75	66	71	70	282	18,905
Gary Player	73	69	71	74	287	10,165
Brian Huggett	78	68	70	71	287	10,165
John Morgan	71	73	71	73	288	7,150
Arnold Palmer	69	74	71	74	288	7,150
Tommy Horton	71	72	71	75	289	5,500
Billy Dunk	73	69	74	74	290	4,665
Liam Higgins	69	75	76	70	290	4,665
Bobby Verwey	72	72	78	69	291	3,920
Christy O'Connor	73	72	71	75	291	3,920
Renato Campagnoli	74	73	74	72	293	3,380
Michel Damiano	71	72	71	79	293	3,380
Antonio Garrido	70	73	74	76	293	3,380
John Fourie	76	75	70	73	294	2,910
Allan Henning	71	72	73	78	294	2,910
Frank Rennie	76	73	71	74	294	2,910
Vincent Tshabalala	71	72	76	75	294	2,910
Gary Cowan	71	75	77	73	296	2,571.67
Alberto Croce	69	76	74	77	296	2,571.67
Bernard Hunt	76	76	73	71	296	2,571.67
David Butler	78	74	74	71	297	2,375
Roland Stafford	72	76	76	73	297	2,375
Ramon Sota	71	76	78	72	297	2,375
Malcolm Gregson	78	75	73	72	298	2,147.50
Brian Waites	72	73	76	77	298	2,147.50
Arne Dokka	74	75	79	70	298	2,147.50
David Creamer	74	72	77	75	298	2,147.50
Arthur Proctor	73	74	74	78	299	1,985

Lawrence Batley Seniors

Woodsome Hall Golf Club, Huddersfield, West Yorkshire, England   July 27-29
Par 35-35—70; 6,096 yards   purse, £65,000

	SCORES			TOTAL	MONEY
John Morgan	67	65	70	202	£10,170
Jose Maria Roca	69	69	68	206	6,800
Tommy Horton	69	68	70	207	3,445
Peter Butler	71	64	72	207	3,445
Brian Waites	71	68	69	208	2,208
Alberto Croce	66	72	70	208	2,208
Brian Huggett	70	72	66	208	2,208
David Butler	67	71	70	208	2,208
Liam Higgins	69	69	70	208	2,208
Bernard Hunt	71	69	69	209	1,566.67
Roger Fidler	71	68	70	209	1,566.67
Neil Coles	68	72	69	209	1,566.67
Bobby Verwey	71	70	69	210	1,280
Malcolm Gregson	69	71	71	211	1,120
John Fourie	70	74	69	213	990
David Talbot	68	71	74	213	990
David Huish	72	72	70	214	875
Bryan Carter	74	71	69	214	875
David Snell	75	69	70	214	875
Michael Murphy	70	76	69	215	795
Terry Squires	70	72	73	215	795
Hedley Muscroft	75	70	71	216	738.75
Vincent Tshabalala	71	73	72	216	738.75
Denis Hutchinson	74	71	71	216	738.75
Doug Dalziel	78	69	69	216	738.75
Joe Carr	73	72	72	217	700
Renato Campagnoli	71	72	74	217	700
David Jimenez	71	74	73	218	685
Ross Whitehead	73	73	73	219	675
Tony Grubb	71	76	73	220	655
Frederick Boobyer	72	73	75	220	655
Rafe Botts	71	72	77	220	655

Forte PGA Seniors Championship

Sunningdale Golf Club, Sunningdale, Berkshire, England   August 5-7
Par 35-35—70; 6,341 yards   purse, £75,000

	SCORES			TOTAL	MONEY
John Morgan	68	68	67	203	£12,500
David Creamer	70	66	69	205	8,330
Renato Campagnoli	72	69	65	206	4,700
Terry Fine	69	68	70	207	3,760
Alberto Croce	67	70	72	209	3,050
Antonio Garrido	70	72	67	209	3,050
Tommy Horton	68	71	71	210	2,585
Neil Coles	70	68	72	210	2,585
Bernard Hunt	71	70	70	211	2,280
Malcolm Gregson	71	71	70	212	2,015
Joe Carr	72	72	68	212	2,015
Peter Butler	71	70	72	213	1,537.50
David Huish	72	67	74	213	1,537.50

	SCORES			TOTAL	MONEY
Roger Fidler	73	69	71	213	1,537.50
Francisco Abreu	74	68	71	213	1,537.50
Brian Huggett	70	74	70	214	1,105
Andrew Gauld	75	68	71	214	1,105
Jose Maria Roca	71	75	69	215	933.33
Brian Waites	73	73	69	215	933.33
Norman Drew	73	71	71	215	933.33
Hugh Boyle	70	72	74	216	805
Mike Ingham	70	72	74	216	805
Phil Ferranti	70	73	73	216	805
Paul Barkhouse	70	72	74	216	805
Tony Grubb	70	75	72	217	700
Tony Coveney	71	77	69	217	700
Michael Murphy	71	73	73	217	700
Manuel Cabrera	73	74	70	217	700
Peter Headland	71	76	71	218	630
David Butler	72	71	75	218	630
John Fourie	73	73	72	218	630

Belfast Telegraph Irish Senior Masters

Malone Golf Club, Belfast, Northern Ireland
Par 36-35—71; 6,358 yards

August 12-14
purse, £60,000

	SCORES			TOTAL	MONEY
Tommy Horton	68	71	69	208	£9,665
Renato Campagnoli	67	70	71	208	6,430
(Horton defeated Campagnoli on second extra hole.)					
Malcolm Gregson	70	69	72	211	2,790
Liam Higgins	70	70	71	211	2,790
Antonio Garrido	73	70	68	211	2,790
Peter Butler	73	69	69	211	2,790
Bobby Verwey	71	69	72	212	1,900
Bob Charles	70	71	71	212	1,900
Brian Huggett	70	71	71	212	1,900
John Morgan	74	69	70	213	1,525
Brian Waites	69	72	72	213	1,525
Jose Maria Roca	72	72	70	214	1,310
Ramon Sota	71	71	73	215	1,115
Hugh Boyle	74	70	71	215	1,115
Roger Fidler	75	72	69	216	945
Bryan Carter	77	72	68	217	810
Bernard Hunt	76	72	69	217	810
Terry Squires	75	70	73	218	702
David Butler	76	72	70	218	702
Joe Carr	77	72	69	218	702
Rafe Botts	73	73	72	218	702
Hugh Inggs	74	70	74	218	702
Tony Grubb	71	77	71	219	640
Bob Thatcher	73	72	74	219	640
Chick Evans	75	69	75	219	640
David Snell	69	72	79	220	615
Vincent Tshabalala	74	73	73	220	615
Dave Marr	70	77	75	222	595
Bobby Browne	76	72	74	222	595
David Jimenez	76	73	74	223	580

Joe Powell Memorial Classic

Collingtree Park Golf Club, Northampton, England
Par 36-36—72; 6,692 yards

August 23-25
purse, £52,000

	SCORES			TOTAL	MONEY
Liam Higgins	70	70	70	210	£8,330
Malcolm Gregson	71	71	72	214	5,550
Neil Coles	69	72	75	216	3,130
Brian Huggett	71	77	69	217	2,500
John Morgan	74	73	71	218	2,032.50
Norman Drew	74	71	73	218	2,032.50
Alberto Croce	71	74	74	219	1,530
Bryan Carter	75	73	71	219	1,530
Bobby Verwey	72	74	73	219	1,530
Tommy Horton	75	73	71	219	1,530
Terry Squires	71	78	70	219	1,530
Francisco Abreu	72	76	72	220	1,180
Hugh Boyle	74	76	71	221	985
Brian Waites	68	75	78	221	985
Renato Campagnoli	74	74	74	222	815
Tony Grubb	77	75	70	222	815
Peter Butler	66	80	77	223	735
Ramon Sota	72	77	74	223	735
Vincent Tshabalala	72	78	74	224	655
Christy O'Connor	77	72	75	224	655
Rafe Botts	73	77	74	224	655
Derek Craik	73	75	76	224	655
David Huish	76	77	73	226	620
Denis Hutchinson	74	77	76	227	595
Hugh Inggs	78	76	73	227	595
David Snell	77	79	71	227	595
Peter Blaze	73	80	74	227	595
Ross Whitehead	74	78	76	228	556.25
Hedley Muscroft	76	75	77	228	556.25
Roberto Bernardini	75	76	77	228	556.25
Michael Murphy	76	77	75	228	556.25

Shell Scottish Seniors Open

Royal Aberdeen Golf Club, Aberdeen, Scotland
Par 35-35—70; 6,372 yards

September 2-4
purse, £100,000

	SCORES			TOTAL	MONEY
Antonio Garrido	66	68	67	201	£16,660
Neil Coles	73	65	68	206	8,680
Renato Campagnoli	72	68	66	206	8,680
Brian Huggett	66	73	69	208	4,376.67
Tommy Horton	69	70	69	208	4,376.67
Malcolm Gregson	70	70	68	208	4,376.67
Doug Dalziel	64	70	75	209	3,440
Brian Waites	69	70	70	209	3,440
Gordon Gray	74	68	69	211	3,040
Vincent Tshabalala	71	69	72	212	2,690
David Jimenez	71	72	69	212	2,690
John Morgan	69	72	72	213	2,052.50
Frank Hill	73	71	69	213	2,052.50
John Fourie	75	69	69	213	2,052.50

	SCORES			TOTAL	MONEY
Francisco Abreu	72	75	66	213	2,052.50
Michel Damiano	71	70	73	214	1,420
Alberto Croce	71	72	71	214	1,420
David Huish	69	74	71	214	1,420
Bobby Verwey	75	68	72	215	1,240
Bernard Hunt	69	72	75	216	1,092
Hugh Inggs	70	73	73	216	1,092
Michael Murphy	68	76	72	216	1,092
Liam Higgins	77	68	71	216	1,092
Frederick Boobyer	73	76	67	216	1,092
David Snell	69	73	75	217	920
Mike Ingham	74	69	74	217	920
Hedley Muscroft	71	74	72	217	920
Bob Thatcher	69	77	71	217	920
Peter Butler	74	73	70	217	920
Austin Skerritt	73	70	75	218	810
Roger Fidler	76	68	74	218	810
Frank Rennie	73	72	73	218	810

Zurich Senior Pro-Am: Lexus Trophy

Breitenloo Golf Club, Breitenloo, Switzerland
Par 36-36—72; 6,698 yards

September 22-24
purse, £47,000

	SCORES			TOTAL	MONEY
Liam Higgins	67	66	67	200	£7,850
Antonio Garrido	68	64	71	203	5,200
Neil Coles	67	68	71	206	3,000
Brian Huggett	68	69	70	207	2,320
Malcolm Gregson	72	69	68	209	2,020
Tony Grubb	75	71	66	212	1,720
John Morgan	73	70	69	212	1,720
Alberto Croce	76	70	67	213	1,380
Ramon Sota	72	68	73	213	1,380
Chick Evans	73	67	73	213	1,380
Francisco Abreu	73	74	68	215	1,080
Bobby Verwey	74	70	71	215	1,080
John Fourie	75	70	71	216	920
Joe Carr	71	74	71	216	920
Tommy Horton	72	70	74	216	920
David Butler	73	72	72	217	823.33
Renato Campagnoli	70	73	74	217	823.33
Peter Gill	73	70	74	217	823.33
David Snell	74	71	73	218	780
Roberto Bernardini	75	72	73	220	720
Norman Drew	74	74	72	220	720
Brian Waites	74	75	71	220	720
Vincent Tshabalala	74	72	74	220	720
Hugh Inggs	72	70	78	220	720
Terry Squires	70	77	74	221	660
Hugh Boyle	76	72	74	222	640
Roger Fidler	73	76	73	222	640
Bryan Carter	76	73	73	222	640
Hugh Jackson	75	72	76	223	620
Richard Emery	73	75	76	224	610

Japan Senior Tour

American Express Grand Slam

Oak Hills Country Club, Kurimotomachi
Par 36-36—72; 6,657 yards

March 25-27
purse, ¥60,000,000

	SCORES			TOTAL	MONEY
Lee Trevino	70	68	69	207	¥9,000,000
Gary Player	72	69	73	214	4,200,000
Masaru Amano	70	73	72	215	3,300,000
Hisashi Suzumura	74	73	69	216	2,100,000
Tom Weiskopf	71	71	74	216	2,100,000
Haruo Yasuda	71	69	76	216	2,100,000
Art Proctor	79	68	70	217	1,340,000
Bill Hall	70	72	75	217	1,340,000
Kikuo Arai	74	69	74	217	1,340,000
Shozo Miyamoto	73	73	72	218	1,020,000
Hsieh Min Nan	75	71	72	218	1,020,000
Bob Dickson	73	71	74	218	1,020,000
Graham Marsh	71	72	76	219	930,000
Jay Sigel	70	73	76	219	930,000
Mitsuhiro Kitta	72	78	70	220	891,000
Fujio Kobayashi	76	72	72	220	891,000
Rod Curl	75	74	72	221	846,000
Kiyokuni Kimoto	75	72	74	221	846,000
Kesahiko Uchida	70	75	76	221	846,000
Ed Sneed	76	73	73	222	774,000
Shichiro Enomoto	77	70	75	222	774,000
Katsumi Jomura	73	73	76	222	774,000
Seiichi Kanai	77	69	76	222	774,000
Norihiko Matsumoto	71	74	77	222	774,000
Bill Kennedy	72	76	75	223	720,000
Takahiko Hori	76	74	74	224	690,000
Bob E. Smith	76	76	72	224	690,000
Chen Chien Chung	69	78	77	224	690,000
Eleuterio Nival	75	77	72	224	690,000
Takuo Terashima	75	75	75	225	618,000
Al Kelley	74	75	76	225	618,000
Bob Menne	75	76	74	225	618,000
Akio Toyoda	73	78	74	225	618,000
Gary Groh	77	75	73	225	618,000
Shigeru Uchida	77	75	73	225	618,000
Terry Dill	71	81	73	225	618,000
Billy Dunk	71	74	80	225	618,000

TPC Starts Senior

Garden Golf Club, Ibaragi-shi
Par 36-36—72; 6,585 yards

April 7-10
purse, ¥50,000,000

	SCORES				TOTAL	MONEY
Seiichi Kanai	72	69	69	72	282	¥7,500,000
Hsieh Min Nan	68	71	69	74	282	3,625,000

	SCORES				TOTAL	MONEY
Hiroshi Ishii	69	71	70	72	282	3,625,000

(Kanai defeated Hsieh and Ishii on first extra hole.)

	SCORES				TOTAL	MONEY
Ichiro Teramoto	73	69	71	71	284	2,250,000
Bob E. Smith	75	68	71	71	285	1,750,000
Shigeru Uchida	73	70	72	71	286	1,125,000
Ryosuke Ota	69	70	75	72	286	1,125,000
Kikuo Arai	67	74	72	74	287	925,000
Fujio Kobayashi	71	73	72	71	287	925,000
Masaru Amano	73	71	74	71	289	825,000
Shoji Kikuchi	68	77	70	74	289	825,000
Hideo Jibiki	73	74	71	71	289	825,000
Haruo Yasuda	75	73	71	70	289	825,000
Tetsuhiro Ueda	76	72	72	70	290	693,750
Ichiro Togawa	73	74	74	69	290	693,750
Norihiko Matsumoto	70	73	72	75	290	693,750
Billy Dunk	73	70	74	73	290	693,750
Ichio Sato	75	77	70	70	292	612,500
Hideyo Sugimoto	71	73	74	74	292	612,500
Seiji Ogawa	75	72	73	73	293	540,000
Isao Matsui	72	75	70	76	293	540,000
Yoshihiro Takada	76	75	70	72	293	540,000
Inatoshi Yoshikawa	73	74	74	73	294	515,000
Akio Toyoda	77	72	75	70	294	515,000
Hisashi Suzumura	75	73	74	73	295	490,000
Nariaki Wakisaka	74	74	74	73	295	490,000
Eleuterio Nival	80	74	72	69	295	490,000
Kesahiko Uchida	79	74	70	73	296	465,000
Chen Ching Po	74	77	73	72	296	465,000
Kenji Ueda	76	76	71	74	297	431,000
Koichi Okuno	74	73	77	73	297	431,000
Tadashi Kitta	74	75	75	73	297	431,000
Mitsuhiro Kitta	76	77	70	74	297	431,000
Takuo Terashima	72	72	77	76	297	431,000
Masayoshi Toda	77	76	74	70	297	431,000

Daiichi Seimei Cup

Tomisato Golf Club, Sanbu-shi, Chiba
Par 36-36—72; 6,444 yards

May 20-22
purse, ¥50,000,000

	SCORES			TOTAL	MONEY
Hiroshi Ishii	71	68	64	203	¥7,500,000
Eleuterio Nival	70	68	69	207	3,500,000
Hsieh Min Nan	72	69	68	209	2,375,000
Haruo Yasuda	70	66	73	209	2,375,000
Ryosuke Ota	70	71	69	210	1,625,000
Billy Dunk	66	75	69	210	1,625,000
Shigeru Uchida	73	70	68	211	1,175,000
Chen Ching Po	67	72	72	211	1,175,000
Shinzo Arai	73	70	69	212	913,333
Kikuo Arai	71	73	68	212	913,333
Akio Toyoda	70	69	73	212	913,333
Masaru Amano	71	71	71	213	769,000
Chen Ching Po	70	74	69	213	769,000
Hisashi Suzumura	71	68	74	213	769,000
Norihiko Matsumoto	71	70	72	213	769,000
Hsiung Kuo Chie	67	72	74	213	769,000

	SCORES			TOTAL	MONEY
Seiichi Kanai	67	79	68	214	705,000
Yasuo Kuninaka	71	74	69	214	705,000
Fujio Kobayashi	69	70	75	214	705,000
Namio Takasu	69	75	71	215	667,500
Masaharu Oshima	67	74	74	215	667,500
Hsieh Yung Yo	71	71	74	216	630,000
Teruo Suzumura	73	70	73	216	630,000
Bob E. Smith	71	73	72	216	630,000
Sadao Ogawa	70	74	73	217	600,000
Hirokazu Seto	69	76	73	218	580,000
Tetsuhiro Ueda	68	76	74	218	580,000
Yoshio Hagino	72	71	75	218	580,000
Shoji Kikuchi	72	73	74	219	550,000
Takaaki Kono	72	77	70	219	550,000
Ichiro Teramoto	72	75	72	219	550,000

Mizuno Senior Classic

Daei Country Club, Katori-shi, Chiba
Par 36-36—72; 6,440 yards

May 27-29
purse, ¥30,000,000

	SCORES			TOTAL	MONEY
Tetsuhiro Ueda	69	69	66	204	¥4,500,000
Hiroshi Ishii	70	68	68	206	1,875,000
Ichiro Teramoto	68	68	70	206	1,875,000
Kikuo Arai	69	70	69	208	1,050,000
Kesahiko Uchida	71	69	68	208	1,050,000
Teruo Suzumura	69	68	71	208	1,050,000
Seiichi Kanai	71	71	67	209	558,750
Shoji Kikuchi	73	67	69	209	558,750
Kiyokuni Kimoto	74	68	67	209	558,750
Hideo Jibiki	72	69	68	209	558,750
Shigeru Uchida	72	68	69	209	558,750
Masaharu Oshima	71	70	68	209	558,750
Ryosuke Ota	69	68	72	209	558,750
Mitsuhiro Kitsuta	68	70	71	209	558,750
Haruo Yasuda	71	69	70	210	445,500
Billy Dunk	71	70	69	210	445,500
Takeo Abe	68	72	72	212	409,500
Masao Kikuchi	69	72	71	212	409,500
Fujio Kobayashi	71	68	73	212	409,500
Hiroshi Tahara	72	68	72	212	409,500
Yoshihiro Takada	70	69	73	212	409,500
Masami Nishiyama	73	68	71	212	409,500
Shichiro Enomoto	74	70	69	213	361,800
Hsieh Min Nan	73	72	68	213	361,800
Inatoshi Yoshikawa	73	72	68	213	361,800
Norihiko Matsumoto	73	71	69	213	361,800
Hsu Chie San	71	74	68	213	361,800
Hisashi Suzumura	71	72	71	214	339,000
Hsiung Kuo Chie	71	71	72	214	339,000

Japan PGA Senior Championship

Shimoakima Country Club, Annaka-shi, Gunma
Par 36-36—72; 6,548 yards

June 2-5
purse, ¥50,000,000

	SCORES				TOTAL	MONEY
Shigeru Uchida	66	71	74	70	281	¥7,500,000
Fujio Kobayashi	72	72	70	69	283	3,500,000
Masaru Amano	70	71	69	74	284	2,375,000
Seiji Ogawa	68	72	76	68	284	2,375,000
Ichiro Teramoto	71	72	68	74	285	1,587,500
Akio Toyoda	70	76	67	72	285	1,587,500
Hsieh Min Nan	72	73	68	73	286	1,150,000
Hideo Jibiki	71	73	71	72	287	950,000
Hsu Chie San	73	69	72	73	287	950,000
Mitsuhiro Kitsuta	71	71	72	74	288	771,250
Mitoshi Tomita	74	73	70	71	288	771,250
Hsiung Kuo Chie	75	72	70	71	288	771,250
Eleuterio Nival	76	72	68	72	288	771,250
Kikuo Arai	75	74	69	71	289	700,000
Shoji Kikuchi	73	69	75	72	289	700,000
Seiji Katayama	72	75	68	74	289	700,000
Teruo Suzumura	74	71	68	77	290	655,000
Yoshihiro Takada	73	68	74	75	290	655,000
Norihiko Matsumoto	70	73	73	74	290	655,000
Haruo Yasuda	75	73	72	71	291	602,500
Hiroshi Ishii	70	73	73	75	291	602,500
Takuo Terashima	74	73	71	73	291	602,500
Yoshio Hagino	75	71	68	77	291	602,500
Bob E. Smith	75	73	71	73	292	565,000
Seiichi Kanai	73	77	71	72	293	535,000
Fukuji Kikuchi	75	74	75	69	293	535,000
Ryosuke Ota	76	73	72	72	293	535,000
Hisashi Suzumura	73	75	76	69	293	535,000
Masayuki Imai	71	75	73	75	294	485,000
Takaaki Kono	75	71	73	75	294	485,000
Seiichi Sato	74	73	70	77	294	485,000
Yoichi Miyashiro	73	73	74	74	294	485,000
Tetsuhiro Ueda	74	72	78	70	294	485,000
Masaharu Oshima	71	71	77	75	294	485,000

Komatsu Open

Sahara Springs Country Club, Sawara-shi, Chiba
Par 36-36—72; 6,571 yards

June 10-12
purse,¥30,000,000

	SCORES			TOTAL	MONEY
Ryosuke Ota	68	72	68	208	¥4,500,000
Masaru Amano	69	71	69	209	1,650,000
Seiji Ogawa	66	70	73	209	1,650,000
Billy Dunk	69	70	70	209	1,650,000
Isao Matsui	70	70	71	211	900,000
Hiroshi Ishii	68	72	71	211	900,000
Norihiko Matsumoto	69	69	73	211	900,000
Sadao Ogawa	71	69	72	212	600,000
Shigeru Uchida	68	73	71	212	600,000
Hsiung Kuo Chie	71	72	69	212	600,000
Mitsuhiro Kitsuta	72	69	72	213	495,000
Art Proctor	73	68	72	213	495,000

	SCORES			TOTAL	MONEY
Haruo Yasuda	71	78	65	214	471,000
Shoji Kikuchi	75	69	71	215	454,500
Namio Takasu	71	72	72	215	454,500
Seiichi Sato	72	72	72	216	441,000
Shinzo Arai	68	74	75	217	418,500
Hiroshi Kaihata	68	76	73	217	418,500
Takaaki Kono	72	71	74	217	418,500
Hsu Chie San	70	72	75	217	418,500
Masayuki Imai	72	76	70	218	378,000
Ichio Sato	71	71	76	218	378,000
Hsieh Min Nan	77	71	70	218	378,000
Shori Miura	74	73	71	218	378,000
Seiji Katayama	74	70	74	218	378,000
Yasuo Kuninaka	69	75	75	219	339,000
Fujio Kobayashi	75	70	74	219	339,000
Ryokichi Jibiki	74	72	73	219	339,000
Chen Ching Po	71	75	73	219	339,000
Inatoshi Yoshikawa	70	70	79	219	339,000
Takuo Terashima	73	73	73	219	339,000

HTB Senior Classic

Chitose Kuko Country Club, Hokkaido
Par 36-36—72; 6,666 yards

July 1-3
purse, ¥30,000,000

	SCORES			TOTAL	MONEY
Masaru Amano	67	67	74	208	¥4,500,000
Kikuo Arai	70	72	67	209	1,875,000
Seiji Ogawa	70	69	70	209	1,875,000
Haruo Yasuda	69	70	71	210	1,200,000
Shigeru Uchida	68	70	73	211	1,050,000
Kiyokuni Kimoto	69	70	74	213	825,000
Namio Takasu	68	71	74	213	825,000
Hiroshi Ishii	71	71	72	214	558,000
Masaharu Oshima	72	69	73	214	558,000
Mitsuhiro Kitsuta	69	72	73	214	558,000
Mitoshi Tomita	70	69	75	214	558,000
Hsiung Kuo Chie	72	71	71	214	558,000
Fujio Kobayashi	72	69	74	215	460,000
Kunio Koike	73	74	68	215	460,000
Matsumoto Norihiko	73	68	74	215	460,000
Hiroshi Kaihata	72	73	71	216	441,000
Kesahiko Uchida	72	69	76	217	423,000
Shoji Kikuchi	71	70	76	217	423,000
Teruo Suzumura	71	72	74	217	423,000
Sadao Ogawa	75	70	73	218	387,000
Hiroshi Tahara	71	73	74	218	387,000
Tetsuhiro Ueda	72	77	69	218	387,000
Ryosuke Ota	73	72	73	218	387,000
Eleuterio Nival	73	71	74	218	387,000
Akio Toyoda	75	73	71	219	351,000
Mitsuo Hirukawa	71	74	74	219	351,000
Billy Dunk	74	70	75	219	351,000
Art Proctor	69	76	74	219	351,000
Yoshihiro Takada	73	72	75	220	336,000
Kiyoshi Oko	72	76	73	221	324,000
Hisashi Suzumura	73	73	75	221	324,000
Yoshio Hagino	75	73	73	221	324,000

Tokyu Senior Cup

Grand Oak Golf Club, Hyogo
Par 36-36—72; 6,684 yards

September 23-25
purse, ¥30,000,000

	SCORES			TOTAL	MONEY
Norihiko Matsumoto	65	67	70	202	¥4,500,000
Yoshihiro Takada	70	68	69	207	2,100,000
Haruo Yasuda	69	69	70	208	1,300,000
Teruo Sugihara	69	70	69	208	1,300,000
Hsiung Kuo Chie	68	73	67	208	1,300,000
Seiichi Kanai	68	70	71	209	770,000
Kenji Ueda	70	71	68	209	770,000
Ichiro Teramoto	69	69	71	209	770,000
Mitsuhiro Kitsuta	72	68	70	210	570,000
Teruo Suzumura	71	65	74	210	570,000
Kenji Takeda	74	71	66	211	495,000
Hisashi Suzumura	69	72	70	211	495,000
Seiji Ogawa	68	70	74	212	455,250
Kiyokuni Kimoto	68	70	74	212	455,250
Hsieh Yung Yo	72	72	68	212	455,250
Shigeru Uchida	73	68	71	212	455,250
Masao Kikuchi	69	74	70	213	427,500
Izuru Taka	69	69	75	213	427,500
Yasuo Kuninaka	70	70	74	214	405,000
Fujio Kobayashi	70	70	74	214	405,000
Seiji Katayama	72	73	69	214	405,000
Shoji Kikuchi	70	71	74	215	373,500
Takahiko Hori	70	70	75	215	373,500
Masaharu Oshima	73	73	69	215	373,500
Billy Dunk	69	69	77	215	373,500
Masaru Amano	72	74	70	216	336,000
Kesahiko Uchida	69	72	75	216	336,000
Kiyoshi Oko	72	70	74	216	336,000
Ichio Sato	74	71	71	216	336,000
Ryosuke Ota	70	71	75	216	336,000
Hsu Chie San	73	74	69	216	336,000
Art Proctor	69	73	74	216	336,000

Nagoya TV Cup

Hananoki Golf Club, Mizunami-shi, Gifu
Par 36-36—72; 6,695 yards

October 21-23
purse, ¥40,000,000

	SCORES			TOTAL	MONEY
Seiichi Kanai	72	70	65	207	¥6,000,000
Hsiung Kuo Chie	70	69	69	208	2,800,000
Haruo Yasuda	74	70	66	210	2,200,000
Kikuo Arai	72	73	66	211	1,300,000
Seiji Ogawa	69	72	70	211	1,300,000
Mitsutaka Kono	68	74	69	211	1,300,000
Teruo Suzumura	71	72	68	211	1,300,000
Shigeru Uchida	72	74	66	212	800,000
Izuru Taka	71	71	70	212	800,000
Eleuterio Nival	74	70	68	212	800,000
Tadashi Kitsuta	71	72	71	214	660,000
Billy Dunk	71	72	71	214	660,000
Kesahiko Uchida	73	72	70	215	594,666
Ichio Sato	71	74	70	215	594,666

	SCORES			TOTAL	MONEY
Hsieh Min Nan	73	73	69	215	594,666
Tetsuhiro Ueda	74	70	71	215	594,666
Koichi Okuno	73	69	73	215	594,666
Mitsuhiro Kitsuta	72	68	75	215	594,666
Takahiko Hori	73	71	72	216	534,000
Hiroshi Ishii	70	77	69	216	534,000
Yoshihiro Takada	72	73	71	216	534,000
Ichiro Teramoto	72	73	71	216	534,000
Yasuo Kuninaka	74	73	70	217	492,000
Takuo Terashima	75	72	70	217	492,000
Ichiro Togawa	74	70	73	217	492,000
Sadao Ogawa	74	71	73	218	452,000
Hsieh Yung Yo	72	73	73	218	452,000
Mitsuo Hirukawa	74	73	71	218	452,000
Norihiko Matsumoto	76	73	69	218	452,000
Hsu Chie San	73	73	72	218	452,000
Art Proctor	74	72	72	218	452,000

Ho-Oh Cup

Ho-Oh Golf Club, Ohta-shi, Gunma
Par 36-36—72; 6,546 yards

October 28-30
purse, ¥35,000,000

	SCORES			TOTAL	MONEY
Seiichi Kanai	66	67	69	202	¥5,250,000
Ichiro Teramoto	70	64	69	203	2,450,000
Masaru Amano	68	68	68	204	1,925,000
Hiroshi Ishii	65	69	71	205	1,312,500
Ryosuke Ota	68	69	68	205	1,312,500
Seiji Ogawa	68	70	68	206	962,500
Hsieh Yung Yo	65	71	70	206	962,500
Masayuki Imai	68	69	70	207	735,000
Billy Dunk	64	71	72	207	735,000
Hsieh Min Nan	66	73	69	208	595,000
Mitsuhiro Kitta	68	72	68	208	595,000
Bob E. Smith	69	70	69	208	595,000
Kiyokuni Kimoto	71	72	66	209	542,500
Hsiung Kuo Chie	70	69	70	209	542,500
Shigeru Uchida	72	69	69	210	514,500
Teruo Suzumura	70	71	69	210	514,500
Yoshio Hagino	70	70	70	210	514,500
Hirokazu Seto	68	72	71	211	493,500
Mitsuo Hirukawa	69	73	70	212	483,000
Isao Matsui	70	72	71	213	462,000
Seiji Katayama	69	72	72	213	462,000
Yoshihiro Takada	75	71	67	213	462,000
Shinzo Arai	74	71	69	214	435,750
Yuji Ogawa	71	71	72	214	435,750
Fujio Kobayashi	70	70	75	215	406,000
Tetsuhiro Ueda	70	73	72	215	406,000
Norihiko Matsumoto	72	71	72	215	406,000
Hahn Chang Sang	73	73	69	215	406,000
Eleuterio Nival	70	76	69	215	406,000
Takaaki Kono	71	70	75	216	374,500
Chen Chien Chung	74	71	71	216	374,500
Masaharu Oshima	74	71	71	216	374,500
Hsu Chie San	72	70	74	216	374,500

Asahi Kokusai Vintage Classic

Hamamura Onsen Golf Club, Tottori
Par 72; 6,576 yards

November 4-6
purse, ¥30,000,000

	SCORES			TOTAL	MONEY
Haruo Yasuda	71	66	70	207	¥4,500,000
Kikuo Arai	72	67	69	208	2,100,000
Fujio Kobayashi	68	70	71	209	1,425,000
Hsieh Min Nan	71	67	71	209	1,425,000
Mitoshi Tomita	71	70	71	212	1,050,000
Hiroshi Ishii	71	70	72	213	900,000
Seiji Ogawa	71	70	73	214	558,750
Tetsuhiro Ueda	74	72	68	214	558,750
Mitsuhiro Kitsuta	70	71	73	214	558,750
Yoshihiro Takada	71	75	68	214	558,750
Ichiro Teramoto	74	66	74	214	558,750
Hsu Chie San	69	73	72	214	558,750
Billy Dunk	73	73	68	214	558,750
Bob E. Smith	73	75	66	214	558,750
Hideo Chibiki	72	70	73	215	441,000
Hsiung Kuo Chie	76	69	70	215	441,000
Art Proctor	77	71	67	215	441,000
Masaru Amano	73	71	72	216	414,000
Hirokazu Seto	74	69	73	216	414,000
Mitsuo Hirukawa	74	70	72	216	414,000
Hiroshi Kaihata	74	73	70	217	387,000
Seiji Katayama	75	71	71	217	387,000
Teruo Suzumura	73	74	70	217	387,000
Namio Takasu	74	74	70	218	364,600
Masami Nishiyama	75	70	73	218	364,600
Isao Matsui	73	73	73	219	348,000
Akio Toyoda	74	75	70	219	348,000
Eleuterio Nival	74	74	71	219	348,000
Hiroyuki Nagai	72	76	72	220	330,000
Shigeru Uchida	72	76	72	220	330,000
Hisashi Suzumura	76	73	71	220	330,000

Japan Senior Open

Nara Kokusai Golf Club, Nara
Par 72; 6,808 yards

November 24-27
purse, ¥50,000,000

	SCORES				TOTAL	MONEY
Isao Aoki	71	69	72	67	279	¥7,500,000
Mitsuhiro Kitsuta	68	68	71	73	280	3,500,000
Gary Player	73	74	67	70	284	2,750,000
Seiichi Kanai	78	67	72	70	287	2,000,000
Hsieh Min Nan	77	69	71	71	288	1,750,000
Haruo Yasuda	73	74	70	72	289	1,287,500
Norihiko Matsumoto	73	69	74	73	289	1,287,500
Kikuo Arai	72	75	71	73	291	950,000
Hsiung Kuo Chie	72	73	71	75	291	950,000
Teruo Suzumura	78	68	73	73	292	800,000
Seiji Ogawa	76	72	71	74	293	790,000
Fujio Kobayashi	72	71	72	79	294	760,000
Ichiro Teramoto	74	77	69	75	295	725,000
Hsu Chie San	76	74	73	72	295	725,000

	SCORES				TOTAL	MONEY
Ryokichi Chibiki	78	74	72	72	296	685,000
Ryosuke Ota	69	74	77	76	296	685,000
Bob E. Smith	76	75	75	70	296	685,000
*Tetsuo Miura	77	73	72	74	296	
Hideo Chibiki	76	73	74	74	297	647,500
Billy Dunk	77	74	73	73	297	647,500
Hisashi Suzumura	74	75	75	74	298	625,000
Yasuo Kuninaka	78	77	70	74	299	595,000
Hiroshi Ishii	70	74	71	75	299	595,000
Mitsuo Hirukawa	74	77	75	73	299	595,000
Tetsuhiro Ueda	76	75	71	78	300	565,000
Kesahiko Uchida	79	71	73	78	201	520,000
Ichio Sato	77	74	77	73	201	520,000
Isao Matsui	74	76	76	75	201	520,000
Shigeru Uchida	76	76	76	75	201	520,000
Koichi Okuno	74	75	76	76	201	520,000
Ichiro Togawa	76	76	73	76	201	520,000
Akio Toyoda	81	73	74	73	201	520,000

Ryokuei Group Cup

Onahama Springs Hotel & Golf Club, Iwaki-shi, Fukushima
Par 72; 6,404 yards

December 2-4
purse, ¥40,000,000

	SCORES			TOTAL	MONEY
Hsieh Min Nan	70	67	72	209	¥6,000,000
Seiichi Kanai	72	68	71	211	2,800,000
Sadao Ogawa	68	75	72	215	2,200,000
Masaru Amano	67	79	70	216	1,300,000
Kikuo Arai	69	74	73	216	1,300,000
Fujio Kobayashi	72	77	67	216	1,300,000
Teruo Suzumura	73	69	74	216	1,300,000
Shigeru Uchida	74	74	69	217	840,000
Kunio Koike	74	74	69	217	840,000
Art Proctor	69	74	75	218	720,000
Shozo Miyamoto	74	73	72	219	660,000
Hsiung Kuo Chie	71	78	70	219	660,000
Izuru Taka	73	75	72	220	628,000
Ryokichi Chibiki	76	75	70	221	600,000
Isao Matsui	73	75	73	221	600,000
Billy Dunk	74	76	71	221	600,000
Hideo Chibiki	75	73	74	222	564,000
Masaharu Oshima	74	78	70	222	564,000
Akio Toyoda	71	74	77	222	564,000
Katsuji Murakami	78	72	73	223	528,000
Shunji Kanazawa	76	74	73	223	528,000
Ichiro Teramoto	74	77	72	223	528,000
Kesahiko Uchida	76	73	75	224	487,000
Seiji Ogawa	71	77	76	224	487,000
Hiroshi Tahara	70	77	77	224	487,000
Bob E. Smith	72	76	76	224	487,000
Seiichi Sato	75	75	75	225	452,000
Ryosuke Ota	72	80	73	225	452,000
Mitsuhiro Kitsuta	78	75	72	225	452,000
Norihiko Matsumoto	78	70	77	225	452,000

Women's Tours

HealthSouth Palm Beach Classic

Wycliff Golf & Country Club, Lake Worth, Florida
Par 36-36—72; 6,334 yards

February 4-6
purse, $400,000

	SCORES			TOTAL	MONEY
Dawn Coe-Jones	67	69	65	201	$60,000
Lauri Merten	71	67	64	202	37,237
Laura Davies	69	65	69	203	27,173
Lisa Walters	66	68	70	204	21,134
Dottie Mochrie	70	67	69	206	17,108
Jan Stephenson	70	68	69	207	14,089
Julie Larsen	71	69	68	208	11,170
Pat Bradley	68	69	71	208	11,170
Robin Walton	71	70	68	209	8,527
Cindy Figg-Currier	70	69	70	209	8,527
Tracy Kerdyk	68	70	71	209	8,527
Hiromi Kobayashi	72	71	67	210	6,662
Nancy Ramsbottom	70	71	69	210	6,662
Dana Dormann	69	71	70	210	6,662
Muffin Spencer-Devlin	73	71	67	211	4,692
Hollis Stacy	71	72	68	211	4,692
Barb Thomas	69	73	69	211	4,692
Jane Geddes	71	70	70	211	4,692
Jackie Gallagher-Smith	71	70	70	211	4,692
Danielle Ammaccapane	70	71	70	211	4,692
Kristi Albers	70	71	70	211	4,692
Leigh Ann Mills	68	72	71	211	4,692
Amy Read	72	67	72	211	4,692
Jenny Lidback	70	69	72	211	4,692
Joan Pitcock	69	70	72	211	4,692
Barb Mucha	72	72	68	212	3,324
Elaine Crosby	73	70	69	212	3,324
Missie McGeorge	70	72	70	212	3,324
Beth Daniel	75	66	71	212	3,324
Missie Berteotti	70	71	71	212	3,324
Eva Dahllof	70	70	72	212	3,324
Kim Williams	69	71	72	212	3,324

Hawaiian Open

Ko Olina Golf Club, Kapolei, Oahu, Hawaii
Par 36-36—72; 6,216 yards

February 17-19
purse, $500,000

	SCORES			TOTAL	MONEY
Marta Figueras-Dotti	68	70	71	209	$75,000
Jane Geddes	69	70	71	210	46,546
Vicki Fergon	69	74	69	212	27,256
Tracy Kerdyk	70	71	71	212	27,256
Val Skinner	67	71	74	212	27,256
Sherri Steinhauer	71	73	69	213	11,377

	SCORES			TOTAL	MONEY
Joan Pitcock	72	71	70	213	11,377
Jenny Lidback	71	72	70	213	11,377
Beth Daniel	72	70	71	213	11,377
Marianne Morris	71	71	71	213	11,377
Yuko Moriguchi	71	70	72	213	11,377
Muffin Spencer-Devlin	68	73	72	213	11,377
Kathryn Marshall	71	69	73	213	11,377
Nina Foust	68	71	74	213	11,377
Dottie Mochrie	72	74	68	214	6,457
Lauri Merten	74	71	69	214	6,457
Michelle McGann	72	73	69	214	6,457
Kris Monaghan	72	72	70	214	6,457
Sally Little	69	73	72	214	6,457
Liselotte Neumann	68	74	72	214	6,457
Laura Davies	74	72	69	215	4,532
Michele Redman	72	73	70	215	4,532
Lisa Walters	71	74	70	215	4,532
Cindy Figg-Currier	73	71	71	215	4,532
Mary Beth Zimmerman	72	72	71	215	4,532
Toshimi Kimura	73	70	72	215	4,532
Kristi Albers	71	72	72	215	4,532
Barb Thomas	71	71	73	215	4,532
Brandie Burton	71	71	73	215	4,532
Ayako Okamoto	69	73	73	215	4,532
Dana Dormann	71	70	74	215	4,532
Betsy King	71	68	76	215	4,532

Chrysler-Plymouth Tournament of Champions

Grand Cypress Resort, Orlando, Florida
Par 36-36—72; 6,424 yards

March 2-5
purse, $700,000

	SCORES				TOTAL	MONEY
Dottie Mochrie	72	75	71	69	287	$115,000
Lauri Merten	71	78	70	70	289	62,250
Nancy Lopez	75	72	69	73	289	62,250
Meg Mallon	75	76	71	68	290	41,000
Kristi Albers	75	77	70	69	291	33,100
Missie Berteotti	75	74	72	71	292	27,200
Dana Dormann	75	76	71	71	293	20,500
Donna Andrews	72	77	71	73	293	20,500
Betsy King	72	71	74	76	293	20,500
Laura Davies	73	76	72	74	295	16,350
Kelly Robbins	74	78	73	71	296	13,741
Danielle Ammaccapane	75	76	74	71	296	13,741
Florence Descampe	73	76	72	75	296	13,741
Sherri Steinhauer	77	76	74	70	297	11,662
Dawn Coe-Jones	73	74	73	77	297	11,662
Kris Tschetter	72	79	74	73	298	10,116
Patty Sheehan	72	78	74	74	298	10,116
Judy Dickinson	74	78	71	75	298	10,116
Jane Geddes	75	78	76	70	299	8,746
Val Skinner	78	76	74	71	299	8,746
JoAnne Carner	77	77	73	72	299	8,746
Brandie Burton	75	78	69	77	299	8,746
Pat Bradley	77	77	72	74	300	7,808
Cindy Schreyer	76	79	76	70	301	7,419

	SCORES				TOTAL	MONEY
Tammie Green	75	79	75	72	301	7,419
Shelley Hamlin	79	79	72	72	302	6,952
Kris Monaghan	76	77	76	73	302	6,952
Marta Figueras-Dotti	79	80	72	72	303	6,254
Helen Dobson	74	81	73	75	303	6,254
Helen Alfredsson	73	81	73	76	303	6,254
Barb Mucha	74	76	77	76	303	6,254

Ping/Welch's Championship

Randolph Park Golf Course, Tucson, Arizona
Par 35-37—72; 6,222 yards

March 10-13
purse, $425,000

	SCORES				TOTAL	MONEY
Donna Andrews	66	68	69	73	276	$63,750
Judy Dickinson	71	71	69	68	279	34,217
Brandie Burton	69	68	69	73	279	34,217
Michelle McGann	72	70	69	69	280	20,316
Sherri Steinhauer	66	70	72	72	280	20,316
Lauri Merten	73	70	67	71	281	13,793
Jan Stephenson	67	72	71	71	281	13,793
Helen Alfredsson	74	71	68	69	282	10,051
Dale Eggeling	71	72	67	72	282	10,051
Dana Dormann	67	74	67	74	282	10,051
Amy Alcott	69	72	69	73	283	8,165
Alice Miller	72	71	73	68	284	6,882
Katie Peterson-Parker	70	73	71	70	284	6,882
Jodi Figley	72	73	67	72	284	6,882
Tina Barrett	68	72	70	74	284	6,882
Val Skinner	69	73	71	72	285	5,599
Melissa McNamara	69	70	72	74	285	5,599
Cindy Rarick	68	71	71	75	285	5,599
Elaine Crosby	73	70	70	73	286	4,747
Annika Sorenstam	68	75	69	74	286	4,747
Amy Benz	69	72	71	74	286	4,747
Meg Mallon	72	68	72	74	286	4,747
Michele Redman	70	71	69	76	286	4,747
Beth Daniel	71	73	70	73	287	3,930
Danielle Ammaccapane	72	70	72	73	287	3,930
Suzanne Strudwick	74	69	70	74	287	3,930
Jane Geddes	69	73	71	74	287	3,930
Dottie Mochrie	70	70	73	74	287	3,930
Muffin Spencer-Devlin	71	72	74	71	288	3,417
Hollis Stacy	72	72	70	74	288	3,417
Missie Berteotti	73	70	70	75	288	3,417

Standard Register Ping

Moon Valley Country Club, Phoenix, Arizona
Par 36-37—73; 6,495 yards

March 17-20
purse, $700,000

	SCORES				TOTAL	MONEY
Laura Davies	69	72	66	70	277	$105,000
Beth Daniel	71	71	70	69	281	56,359
Elaine Crosby	73	69	66	73	281	56,359

	SCORES				TOTAL	MONEY
Alice Ritzman	70	72	71	70	283	30,527
Hiromi Kobayashi	70	70	72	71	283	30,527
Kelly Robbins	68	70	71	44	283	30,527
Brandie Burton	71	69	72	72	284	20,782
Michelle McGann	75	68	72	70	285	16,555
Terry-Jo Myers	71	72	71	71	285	16,555
Dottie Mochrie	72	70	70	73	285	16,555
Lisa Walters	73	70	71	72	286	12,856
Dale Eggeling	72	72	67	75	286	12,856
Kim Saiki	72	73	70	72	287	9,598
Stephanie Maynor	72	72	71	72	287	9,598
Missie McGeorge	71	71	71	74	287	9,598
Nancy Lopez	75	65	73	74	287	9,598
Donna Andrews	71	71	70	75	287	9,598
Cindy Schreyer	69	70	72	76	287	9,598
Caroline Keggi	67	72	72	76	287	9,598
Connie Chillemi	68	70	73	76	287	9,598
Trish Johnson	74	72	68	74	288	7,408
Val Skinner	68	73	73	74	288	7,408
Alison Nicholas	73	71	69	75	288	7,408
Pearl Sinn	69	77	75	68	289	6,621
Annika Sorenstam	72	70	77	70	289	6,621
Meg Mallon	72	75	68	74	289	6,621
Kathryn Marshall	73	73	74	70	290	5,882
Kristi Albers	73	73	72	72	290	5,882
Amy Benz	73	72	71	74	290	5,882
Martha Nause	70	74	71	75	290	5,882

Nabisco Dinah Shore

Mission Hills Country Club, Rancho Mirage, California March 24-27
Par 36-36—72; 6,446 yards purse, $700,000

	SCORES				TOTAL	MONEY
Donna Andrews	70	69	67	70	276	$105,000
Laura Davies	70	68	69	70	277	65,165
Tammie Green	70	72	69	68	279	47,553
Jan Stephenson	70	69	70	71	280	36,985
Michelle McGann	70	68	70	73	281	29,940
Gail Graham	73	71	71	68	283	21,251
Kelly Robbins	73	70	69	71	283	21,251
Brandie Burton	73	73	65	72	283	21,251
Hollis Stacy	72	72	70	70	284	15,674
Nancy Lopez	68	72	73	71	284	15,674
Meg Mallon	72	75	69	69	285	12,064
Liselotte Neumann	76	71	68	70	285	12,064
Dana Dormann	73	71	70	71	285	12,064
Dale Eggeling	71	71	71	72	285	12,064
Kris Monaghan	70	76	70	70	286	9,862
Vicki Fergon	69	74	72	71	286	9,862
Lauri Merten	74	74	71	68	287	8,982
Nancy Scranton	75	70	69	73	287	5,982
Beth Daniel	76	72	70	70	288	7,204
Jane Geddes	70	77	71	70	288	7,204
Pat Bradley	71	75	71	71	288	7,204
Caroline Keggi	72	73	72	71	288	7,204
Chris Johnson	74	73	69	72	288	7,204

	SCORES				TOTAL	MONEY
Patty Sheehan	73	71	72	72	288	7,204
Dottie Mochrie	74	73	68	73	288	7,204
Ayako Okamoto	69	74	72	73	288	7,204
Missie McGeorge	72	71	70	75	288	7,204
Tina Tombs	73	74	72	70	289	5,670
Sherri Turner	72	74	71	72	289	5,670
Val Skinner	72	72	72	73	289	5,670
Missie Berteotti	71	73	72	73	289	5,670

Atlanta Championship

Eagle's Landing Country Club, Stockbridge, Georgia
Par 36-36—72; 6,241 yards

April 15-17
purse, $650,000

	SCORES			TOTAL	MONEY
Val Skinner	70	68	68	206	$97,500
Liselotte Neumann	69	67	71	207	60,510
Beth Daniel	69	70	70	209	44,156
Judy Dickinson	67	70	73	210	34,344
Debbie Massey	72	72	67	211	23,331
Helen Alfredsson	68	74	69	211	23,331
Dottie Mochrie	71	69	71	211	23,331
Patty Sheehan	73	71	68	212	12,989
Nancy Scranton	71	73	68	212	12,989
Michele Redman	74	68	70	212	12,989
Page Dunlap	71	71	70	212	12,989
Kristi Albers	71	71	70	212	12,989
Melissa McNamara	69	72	71	212	12,989
Jane Geddes	69	72	71	212	12,989
Karen Lunn	72	74	68	214	7,735
Mardi Lunn	74	71	69	214	7,735
Betsy King	72	73	69	214	7,735
Michelle Estill	70	75	69	214	7,735
Deb Richard	74	68	72	214	7,735
Nancy Lopez	69	73	72	214	7,735
Cindy Rarick	66	76	72	214	7,735
Nicky Le Roux	69	72	73	214	7,735
Brandie Burton	69	72	73	214	7,735
Chris Johnson	70	70	74	214	7,735
Meg Mallon	70	75	70	215	5,658
Vicki Fergon	75	69	71	215	5,658
Lori Garbacz	75	67	73	215	5,658
Sherri Turner	72	70	73	215	5,658
Lauri Merten	71	71	73	215	5,658
Laura Davies	72	69	74	215	5,658

Sprint Championship

Indigo Lakes Golf & Tennis Resort, Daytona Beach, Florida
Par 36-36—72; 6,355 yards

April 28-May 1
purse, $1,200,000

	SCORES				TOTAL	MONEY
Sherri Steinhauer	68	68	67	70	273	$180,000
Kelly Robbins	68	68	70	68	274	111,711
Barb Bunkowsky	68	72	68	70	278	81,519

	SCORES				TOTAL	MONEY
Beth Daniel	71	71	72	67	281	63,404
Alicia Dibos	66	76	70	70	282	51,326
Florence Descampe	74	70	71	68	283	36,431
Chris Johnson	68	75	72	68	283	36,431
Tammie Green	71	71	70	71	283	36,431
Martha Nause	71	75	72	66	284	23,550
Dottie Mochrie	68	73	74	69	284	23,550
Dawn Coe-Jones	72	71	71	70	284	23,550
Judy Dickinson	69	71	71	73	284	23,550
Sally Little	68	72	70	74	284	23,550
Nancy Harvey	72	73	71	69	285	16,665
Helen Alfredsson	73	73	69	70	285	16,665
Vicki Goetze	72	71	72	70	285	16,665
Patty Sheehan	76	71	67	71	285	16,665
Trish Johnson	67	68	75	75	285	16,665
Dale Eggeling	72	71	75	68	286	13,032
Kristi Albers	71	73	73	69	286	13,032
Tina Barrett	74	68	74	70	286	13,032
Karen Lunn	73	74	68	71	286	13,032
Susie Redman	69	74	72	71	286	13,032
Michelle McGann	68	68	73	77	286	13,032
Deb Richard	74	71	73	69	287	9,922
Muffin Spencer-Devlin	75	72	70	70	287	9,922
Stephanie Maynor	73	74	70	70	287	9,922
Maggie Will	73	72	72	70	287	9,922
Brandie Burton	73	74	69	71	287	9,922
Janice Gibson	72	71	73	71	287	9,922
Dana Dormann	72	71	72	72	287	9,922
Val Skinner	70	72	72	73	287	9,922
Hollis Stacy	69	72	73	73	287	9,922

Sara Lee Classic

Hermitage Golf Club, Old Hickory, Tennessee
Par 36-36—72; 6,290 yards

May 6-8
purse, $525,000

	SCORES			TOTAL	MONEY
Laura Davies	65	70	68	203	$78,750
Meg Mallon	65	70	69	204	48,873
Deb Richard	71	71	64	206	35,664
Dina Ammaccapane	71	68	69	208	22,895
Amy Benz	67	71	70	208	22,895
Jane Crafter	64	72	72	208	22,895
Betsy King	71	71	67	209	14,661
Rosie Jones	70	71	68	209	14,661
Danielle Ammaccapane	69	75	66	210	11,183
Tammie Green	71	70	69	210	11,183
Gail Graham	73	64	73	210	11,183
Val Skinner	73	69	69	211	8,453
Barb Mucha	68	73	70	211	8,453
Beth Daniel	68	72	71	211	8,453
Alice Ritzman	67	72	72	211	8,453
Michelle McGann	69	74	69	212	6,736
Julie Larsen	68	74	70	212	6,736
Dottie Mochrie	70	71	71	212	6,736
Lauri Merten	69	71	72	212	6,736
Michele Redman	74	70	69	213	5,573

	SCORES			TOTAL	MONEY
JoAnne Carner	72	72	69	213	5,573
Tina Barrett	71	73	69	213	5,573
Pat Bradley	68	76	69	213	5,573
Alicia Dibos	69	73	71	213	5,573
Shirley Furlong	75	71	68	214	4,268
Missie Berteotti	72	74	68	214	4,268
Muffin Spencer-Devlin	70	75	69	214	4,268
Martha Nause	70	75	69	214	4,268
Dana Dormann	71	73	70	214	4,268
Amy Read	69	75	70	214	4,268
Sherri Steinhauer	70	73	71	214	4,268
Judy Dickinson	74	68	72	214	4,268
Donna Andrews	73	68	73	214	4,268
Nanci Bowen	70	69	75	214	4,268

McDonald's LPGA Championship

Du Pont Country Club, Wilmington, Delaware
Par 35-36—71; 6,386 yards

May 12-15
purse, $1,100,000

	SCORES				TOTAL	MONEY
Laura Davies	70	72	69	68	279	$165,000
Alice Ritzman	68	73	71	70	282	102,402
Elaine Crosby	76	71	69	67	283	54,660
Pat Bradley	73	73	70	67	283	54,660
Hiromi Kobayashi	72	73	71	67	283	54,660
Liselotte Neumann	74	73	67	69	283	54,660
Sherri Steinhauer	75	70	72	68	285	27,676
Amy Alcott	71	75	70	69	285	27,676
Beth Daniel	72	74	68	71	285	27,676
Patty Sheehan	72	68	72	73	285	27,676
Dottie Mochrie	68	78	70	70	286	20,203
Meg Mallon	71	71	69	75	286	20,203
Val Skinner	74	69	72	72	287	18,266
Juli Inkster	69	76	74	69	288	16,051
Dana Dormann	71	76	71	70	288	16,051
Chris Johnson	70	74	73	71	288	16,051
Barb Mucha	73	74	75	67	289	12,257
Nanci Bowen	73	75	73	68	289	12,257
Tammie Green	71	76	74	68	289	12,257
Donna Andrews	73	76	69	71	289	12,257
Betsy King	74	73	71	71	289	12,257
Missie McGeorge	75	71	70	73	289	12,257
Kris Monaghan	72	72	72	73	289	12,257
Mardi Lunn	70	75	70	74	289	12,257
Robin Walton	70	70	75	74	289	12,257
JoAnne Carner	73	75	74	68	290	9,907
Michelle McGann	70	76	75	69	290	9,907
Jenny Lidback	73	73	74	71	291	8,460
Missie Berteotti	75	70	75	71	291	8,460
Gail Graham	73	71	76	71	291	8,460
Brandie Burton	76	70	73	72	291	8,460
Ayako Okamoto	74	72	73	72	291	8,460
Jennifer Wyatt	72	74	73	72	291	8,460
Tina Barrett	73	77	68	73	291	8,460

Lady Keystone Open

Hershey Country Club, Hershey, Pennsylvania
Par 36-36—72; 6,338 yards

May 20-22
purse, $400,000

	SCORES			TOTAL	MONEY
Elaine Crosby	69	72	70	211	$60,000
Laura Davies	70	71	71	212	37,237
Val Skinner	70	71	72	213	24,153
Betsy King	70	70	73	213	24,153
Noelle Daghe	69	74	71	214	13,384
Tina Barrett	75	67	72	214	13,384
Missie McGeorge	74	68	72	214	13,384
Missie Berteotti	66	75	73	214	13,384
Laurie Brower	76	69	70	215	7,862
Donna Andrews	73	72	70	215	7,862
Denise Baldwin	74	69	72	215	7,862
Jan Stephenson	72	71	72	215	7,862
Pearl Sinn	70	72	73	215	7,862
Dawn Coe-Jones	73	74	69	216	5,455
Juli Inkster	73	73	70	216	5,455
Marianne Morris	73	73	70	216	5,455
Martha Nause	70	76	70	216	5,455
Michelle Estill	70	76	70	216	5,455
Annika Sorenstam	72	70	74	216	5,455
Danielle Ammaccapane	75	71	71	217	4,353
Michele Redman	74	71	72	217	4,353
Lenore Rittenhouse	72	72	73	217	4,353
Amy Read	76	67	74	217	4,353
Dottie Mochrie	74	72	72	218	3,744
Cathy Johnston-Forbes	73	73	72	218	3,744
Robin Walton	72	72	74	218	3,744
Brandie Burton	69	73	76	218	3,744
Pat Bradley	73	73	73	219	3,204
Robin Hood	71	75	73	219	3,204
Cindy Figg-Currier	79	66	74	219	3,204
Pamela Wright	73	72	74	219	3,204
Janet Anderson	72	73	74	219	3,204

Corning Classic

Corning Country Club, Corning, New York
Par 36-36—72; 6,070 yards

May 26-29
purse, $500,000

	SCORES				TOTAL	MONEY
Beth Daniel	67	71	71	69	278	$75,000
Stephanie Farwig	68	71	69	71	279	40,256
Nancy Ramsbottom	64	71	71	73	279	40,256
Kelly Robbins	75	71	68	67	281	20,065
Tammie Green	72	73	67	69	281	20,065
Colleen Walker	71	70	68	72	281	20,065
Martha Nause	68	69	72	72	281	20,065
Donna Andrews	72	71	70	70	283	12,454
Deb Richard	71	71	71	70	283	12,454
Chris Johnson	72	73	73	66	284	9,668
Laura Davies	70	74	68	72	284	9,668
Pat Bradley	65	73	70	76	284	9,668
Sherri Turner	69	75	70	71	285	8,086

	SCORES				TOTAL	MONEY
Mary Beth Zimmerman	69	73	71	72	285	8,086
Dawn Coe-Jones	72	72	74	68	286	6,492
Missie McGeorge	69	72	77	68	286	6,492
Shelley Hamlin	72	72	73	69	286	6,492
Becky Iverson	70	74	73	69	286	6,492
Alison Nicholas	73	73	70	70	286	6,492
Joan Pitcock	70	74	71	71	286	6,492
Janet Anderson	70	76	73	68	287	5,045
Lori West	72	73	74	68	287	5,045
Michelle McGann	71	73	74	69	287	5,045
Annika Sorenstam	74	71	71	71	287	5,045
Amy Benz	65	78	72	72	287	5,045
Jane Crafter	70	71	72	74	287	5,045
Page Dunlap	70	77	72	69	288	3,821
JoAnne Carner	71	73	75	69	288	3,821
Pamela Allen	72	71	74	71	288	3,821
Stephanie Maynor	71	72	74	71	288	3,821
Laurie Brower	75	72	69	72	288	3,821
Laurie Rinker-Graham	70	71	75	72	288	3,821
Lisa Kiggens	69	72	75	72	288	3,821
Jean Zedlitz	72	73	70	73	288	3,821
Ellie Gibson	69	75	71	73	288	3,821
Sherri Steinhauer	71	72	72	73	288	3,821

Oldsmobile Classic

Walnut Hills Country Club, East Lansing, Michigan
Par 36-36—72; 6,166 yards

June 2-5
purse, $600,000

	SCORES				TOTAL	MONEY
Beth Daniel	67	63	70	68	268	$90,000
Lisa Kiggens	68	69	67	68	272	55,855
Amy Benz	68	67	70	68	273	40,759
Meg Mallon	68	66	72	69	275	31,702
Tania Abitbol	72	69	67	69	277	23,398
Donna Andrews	70	69	68	70	277	23,398
Marianne Morris	68	70	69	71	278	17,813
Sherri Turner	72	69	70	68	279	15,700
Dottie Mochrie	71	72	69	68	280	13,435
Colleen Walker	75	67	68	70	280	13,435
Michele Redman	71	69	74	67	281	9,228
Robin Hood	72	71	70	68	281	9,228
Elaine Crosby	74	69	69	69	281	9,228
Kris Tschetter	71	70	69	71	281	9,228
Helen Alfredsson	69	72	69	71	281	9,228
Hollis Stacy	72	68	70	71	281	9,228
Nancy Ramsbottom	68	68	74	71	281	9,228
Sherri Steinhauer	69	70	69	73	281	9,228
Jane Geddes	71	71	72	68	282	6,195
Betsy King	71	71	71	69	282	6,195
Rosie Jones	74	69	69	70	282	6,195
Leigh Ann Mills	72	69	71	70	282	6,195
JoAnne Carner	70	74	67	71	282	6,195
Chris Johnson	73	69	69	71	282	6,195
Alice Ritzman	71	71	69	71	282	6,195
Juli Inkster	73	70	66	73	282	6,195
Deborah Vidal	71	69	69	73	282	6,195

	SCORES			TOTAL	MONEY
Katie Peterson-Parker	72	68	71	72	283	5,152
Penny Hammel	72	71	73	68	284	4,627
Barb Bunkowsky	73	70	70	71	284	4,627
Cathy Johnston-Forbes	72	70	71	71	284	4,627
Pamela Allen	72	68	72	72	284	4,627
Barb Mucha	72	72	67	73	284	4,627

Minnesota LPGA Classic

Edinburgh USA Golf Course, Brooklyn Park, Minnesota   June 10-12
Par 36-36—72; 6,141 yards   purse, $500,000

	SCORES			TOTAL	MONEY
Liselotte Neumann	68	71	66	205	$75,000
Hiromi Kobayashi	72	70	65	207	46,546
Sherri Steinhauer	72	70	66	208	33,966
Amy Alcott	71	69	69	209	26,418
Katie Peterson-Parker	72	71	68	211	21,386
Julie Larsen	70	73	69	212	17,612
Kelly Robbins	71	78	64	213	11,447
Terry-Jo Myers	73	71	69	213	11,447
Michelle McGann	72	72	69	213	11,447
Deb Richard	71	73	69	213	11,447
Val Skinner	70	73	70	213	11,447
Caroline Pierce	71	68	74	213	11,447
Cindy Figg-Currier	70	79	65	214	7,008
Jodi Figley	74	70	70	214	7,008
Jane Geddes	67	77	70	214	7,008
Chris Johnson	70	72	72	214	7,008
Rosie Jones	69	73	72	214	7,008
Jane Crafter	73	68	73	214	7,008
Beth Daniel	70	71	73	214	7,008
Shelley Hamlin	75	71	69	215	5,535
Jody Anschutz	69	77	69	215	5,535
Tina Barrett	70	74	71	215	5,535
Kim Bauer	77	71	68	216	4,811
Mary Beth Zimmerman	72	75	69	216	4,811
Kris Tschetter	70	75	71	216	4,811
Kathy Guadagnino	72	72	72	216	4,811
Joan Pitcock	73	75	69	217	3,852
Martha Nause	76	71	70	217	3,852
Dana Dormann	75	72	70	217	3,852
Lisa Kiggens	71	74	72	217	3,852
Nina Foust	73	71	73	217	3,852
Barb Thomas	69	75	73	217	3,852
Marianne Morris	76	67	74	217	3,852
Nancy White	73	70	74	217	3,852
Stefania Croce	72	71	74	217	3,852

Rochester International

Locust Hill Country Club, Pittsford, New York
Par 35-37—72; 6,162 yards

June 16-19
purse, $500,000

	SCORES				TOTAL	MONEY
Lisa Kiggens	67	69	71	66	273	$75,000
Dawn Coe-Jones	69	67	71	67	274	46,546
Betsy King	66	68	72	69	275	33,966
Patty Sheehan	67	72	67	71	277	26,418
Kelly Robbins	68	69	73	69	279	19,499
Kristi Albers	69	68	69	73	279	19,499
Tammie Green	71	70	69	70	280	13,963
Michele Redman	68	67	71	74	280	13,963
Hollis Stacy	71	70	71	69	281	10,659
Helen Alfredsson	69	70	70	72	281	10,659
Barb Bunkowsky	72	67	68	74	281	10,659
Marta Figueras-Dotti	69	72	69	72	282	8,328
Laurie Brower	66	73	71	72	282	8,328
Nancy Ramsbottom	68	71	69	74	282	8,328
Dale Eggeling	70	69	73	71	283	6,902
Joan Pitcock	68	69	73	73	283	6,902
Dottie Mochrie	69	70	69	75	283	6,902
Nancy Lopez	71	72	74	67	284	5,938
Jane Geddes	74	69	72	69	284	5,938
Susie Redman	68	73	72	71	284	5,938
Colleen Walker	68	71	72	73	284	5,938
Leigh Ann Mills	71	70	72	72	285	5,099
Missie McGeorge	74	70	68	73	285	5,099
Rosie Jones	72	71	67	75	285	5,099
Heather Drew	75	69	71	71	286	4,454
Kim Cathrein	72	69	73	72	286	4,454
Sally Little	74	69	70	73	286	4,454
Amy Alcott	70	71	72	73	286	4,454
Shelley Hamlin	68	71	74	73	286	4,454
Vicki Goetze	67	74	76	70	287	3,412
Tina Barrett	73	71	72	71	287	3,412
Sherri Steinhauer	73	70	73	71	287	3,412
Allison Finney	73	70	73	71	287	3,412
Val Skinner	74	71	69	73	287	3,412
Jenny Lidback	72	71	71	73	287	3,412
Michelle McGann	73	67	72	75	287	3,412
Jan Stephenson	72	68	72	75	287	3,412
Janet Anderson	68	73	70	76	287	3,412
Nina Foust	71	69	71	76	287	3,412

ShopRite Classic

Greate Bay Country Club, Somers Point, New Jersey
Par 36-35—71; 6,235 yards

June 24-26
purse, $500,000

	SCORES			TOTAL	MONEY
Donna Andrews	67	66	74	207	$75,000
Michelle Estill	67	77	65	209	46,546
Caroline Pierce	70	69	71	210	24,845
Kim Saiki	68	71	71	210	24,845
Dottie Mochrie	69	68	73	210	24,845
Barb Bunkowsky	67	69	74	210	24,845

	SCORES			TOTAL	MONEY
Janet Anderson	71	70	70	211	13,250
Pat Bradley	67	74	70	211	13,250
Helen Alfredsson	71	68	72	211	13,250
Meg Mallon	74	68	70	212	9,644
Sally Little	68	73	71	212	9,644
Judy Dickinson	68	72	72	212	9,644
Alicia Dibos	71	73	69	213	6,709
Julie Larsen	71	72	70	213	6,709
Elaine Crosby	70	73	70	213	6,709
Jodi Figley	69	74	70	213	6,709
Val Skinner	69	73	71	213	6,709
Amy Alcott	69	73	71	213	6,709
Jenny Lidback	68	72	73	213	6,709
Nancy Harvey	67	72	74	213	6,709
Sherri Steinhauer	68	70	75	213	6,709
Connie Chillemi	70	76	68	214	4,441
Vicki Fergon	74	71	69	214	4,441
Hollis Stacy	72	73	69	214	4,441
Jean Zedlitz	74	70	70	214	4,441
Juli Inkster	70	73	71	214	4,441
Marty Dickerson	69	74	71	214	4,441
Carolyn Hill	68	74	72	214	4,441
Dale Eggeling	72	69	73	214	4,441
Missie McGeorge	66	75	73	214	4,441
Jennifer Wyatt	71	68	75	214	4,441
Betsy King	67	71	76	214	4,441

Youngstown-Warren Classic

Avalon Lakes Golf Course, Warren, Ohio
Par 36-36—72; 6,308 yards

July 1-3
purse, $550,000

	SCORES			TOTAL	MONEY
Tammie Green	67	69	70	206	$82,500
Colleen Walker	68	69	71	208	51,201
Kim Shipman	69	69	71	209	33,211
Dottie Mochrie	68	70	71	209	33,211
Barb Bunkowsky	74	68	68	210	18,404
Betsy King	70	71	69	210	18,404
Katie Peterson-Parker	69	71	70	210	18,404
Jean Zedlitz	68	71	71	210	18,404
Jenny Lidback	71	72	68	211	10,424
Kelly Robbins	70	73	68	211	10,424
Patty Sheehan	72	70	69	211	10,424
Laura Baugh	71	69	71	211	10,424
Donna Andrews	71	69	71	211	10,424
Val Skinner	69	71	71	211	10,424
Caroline Keggi	68	77	67	212	7,250
JoAnne Carner	72	71	69	212	7,250
Janice Gibson	72	69	71	212	7,250
Muffin Spencer-Devlin	69	72	71	212	7,250
Nancy Lopez	71	69	72	212	7,250
Barb Mucha	71	74	68	213	5,265
Lenore Rittenhouse	75	69	69	213	5,265
Michele Redman	74	69	70	213	5,265
Caroline Pierce	72	70	71	213	5,265
Alicia Dibos	73	68	72	213	5,265

	SCORES			TOTAL	MONEY
Michelle McGann	71	70	72	213	5,265
Connie Chillemi	71	70	72	213	5,265
Cindy Figg-Currier	72	68	73	213	5,265
Nancy Ramsbottom	71	69	73	213	5,265
Cathy Johnston-Forbes	69	71	73	213	5,265
Elaine Crosby	72	67	74	213	5,265

Jamie Farr Toledo Classic

Highland Meadows Golf Club, Sylvania, Ohio
Par 34-37—71; 6,319 yards

July 8-10
purse, $500,000

	SCORES			TOTAL	MONEY
Kelly Robbins	69	70	65	204	$75,000
Tammie Green	66	71	67	204	46,546
(Robbins defeated Green on first extra hole.)					
Meg Mallon	67	70	69	206	33,966
Kris Tschetter	68	71	69	208	26,418
Beth Daniel	71	71	67	209	15,750
Michelle Estill	71	70	68	209	15,750
Judy Dickinson	70	71	68	209	15,750
Dottie Mochrie	69	70	70	209	15,750
Lauri Merten	66	71	72	209	15,750
Dawn Coe-Jones	71	71	68	210	9,662
Kim Williams	68	72	70	210	9,662
Amy Alcott	66	72	72	210	9,662
Tracy Kerdyk	73	71	67	211	7,034
Robin Walton	72	72	67	211	7,034
Terry-Jo Myers	73	69	69	211	7,034
Hiromi Kobayashi	70	72	69	211	7,034
Jane Geddes	70	70	71	211	7,034
Caroline Pierce	70	68	73	211	7,034
Deb Richard	68	70	73	211	7,034
Becky Iverson	71	71	70	212	5,561
Barb Mucha	68	74	70	212	5,561
Lori West	69	70	73	212	5,561
Stephanie Farwig	72	73	68	213	4,383
Heather Drew	74	70	69	213	4,383
Karen Lunn	73	71	69	213	4,383
Nanci Bowen	73	70	70	213	4,383
Patty Sheehan	72	71	70	213	4,383
Kathy Postlewait	72	71	70	213	4,383
Pamela Wright	70	73	70	213	4,383
Hollis Stacy	72	70	71	213	4,383
Jenny Lidback	70	70	73	213	4,383
Penny Hammel	70	69	74	213	4,383

JAL Big Apple Classic

Wykagyl Country Club, New Rochelle, New York
Par 35-36—71; 6,095 yards

July 14-17
purse, $650,000

	SCORES				TOTAL	MONEY
Beth Daniel	70	69	66	71	276	$97,500
Laura Davies	71	69	70	66	276	60,510
(Daniel defeated Davies on first extra hole.)						

	SCORES				TOTAL	MONEY
Nancy Ramsbottom	67	74	72	65	278	39,250
Nancy Bowen	68	70	72	68	278	39,250
Pat Bradley	70	67	72	70	279	27,801
Missie Berteotti	70	71	67	72	280	22,895
Chris Johnson	73	68	73	67	281	19,297
Alicia Dibos	77	68	69	68	282	16,190
Michele Redman	69	71	71	71	282	16,190
Helen Alfredsson	73	72	69	69	283	11,736
Meg Mallon	74	70	67	72	283	11,736
Lisa Kiggens	71	67	71	74	283	11,736
Dale Eggeling	69	68	72	74	283	11,736
Juli Inkster	72	69	67	75	283	11,736
Allison Finney	74	68	71	71	284	9,192
Alison Nicholas	72	69	71	72	284	9,192
Michelle McGann	73	70	71	71	285	7,561
Judy Dickinson	70	72	72	71	285	7,561
Annika Sorenstam	74	69	70	72	285	7,561
Amy Alcott	72	68	72	73	285	7,561
Denise Baldwin	72	70	69	74	285	7,561
Laurel Kean	71	70	68	76	285	7,561
Sally Little	67	73	69	76	285	7,561
Sherri Turner	72	71	75	68	286	5,985
Tracy Kerdyk	74	71	69	72	286	5,985
Kristi Albers	73	67	73	73	286	5,985
Kris Tschetter	72	72	68	74	286	5,985
Michelle Estill	70	70	70	76	286	5,985
Nancy Lopez	73	73	70	71	287	4,771
Kelly Robbins	73	73	70	71	287	4,771
Rosie Jones	71	74	71	71	287	4,771
Jill Briles-Hinton	71	73	72	71	287	4,771
Joan Pitcock	73	73	69	72	287	4,771
Julie Larsen	72	69	74	72	287	4,771
Tina Barrett	72	71	71	73	287	4,771
Trish Johnson	68	69	74	76	287	4,771

U.S. Women's Open

Indianwood Golf Club, Lake Orion, Michigan

Par 35-36—71; 6,244 yards

July 21-24

purse, $850,000

	SCORES				TOTAL	MONEY
Patty Sheehan	66	71	69	71	277	$155,000
Tammie Green	66	72	69	71	278	85,000
Liselotte Neumann	69	72	71	69	281	47,752
Tania Abitbol	72	68	73	70	283	31,132
Alicia Dibos	69	68	73	73	283	31,132
Meg Mallon	70	72	73	69	284	21,486
Amy Alcott	71	67	77	69	284	21,486
Betsy King	69	71	72	72	284	21,486
Kelly Robbins	71	72	70	72	285	16,445
Donna Andrews	67	72	70	76	285	16,445
Helen Alfredsson	63	69	76	77	285	16,445
Lauri Merten	74	68	75	69	286	12,805
Dottie Mochrie	72	72	71	71	286	12,805
Lisa Grimes	72	73	69	72	286	12,805
Judy Dickinson	66	73	73	74	286	12,805
Michelle Estill	69	68	75	74	286	12,805
Laura Davies	68	68	75	75	286	12,805

	SCORES				TOTAL	MONEY
Michelle McGann	71	70	77	69	287	10,202
Juli Inkster	75	72	69	71	287	10,202
Beth Daniel	69	74	71	73	287	10,202
Joan Pitcock	74	72	67	74	287	10,202
Stephanie Maynor	73	70	76	69	288	9,011
Lisa Walters	72	73	72	71	288	9,011
Sherri Steinhauer	68	72	74	74	288	9,011
Kris Tschetter	71	73	72	73	289	8,089
Deb Richard	68	74	72	75	289	8,089
Pat Bradley	72	69	70	78	289	8,089
Pamela Wright	74	65	71	79	289	8,089
Karen Lunn	72	72	77	69	290	7,371
Vicki Goetze	71	73	73	73	290	7,371

Ping/Welch's Championship

Blue Hill Country Club, Canton, Massachusetts
Par 36-36—72; 6,137 yards

July 28-31
purse, $450,000

	SCORES				TOTAL	MONEY
Helen Alfredsson	70	68	70	66	274	$67,500
Pat Bradley	67	71	72	68	278	36,230
Juli Inkster	68	69	72	69	278	36,230
Sherri Steinhauer	74	69	72	65	280	21,511
Pearl Sinn	70	69	73	68	280	21,511
Alice Miller	74	69	71	67	281	13,661
Melissa McNamara	68	70	73	70	281	13,661
Gail Graham	72	70	68	71	281	13,661
Robin Walton	70	69	72	71	282	10,642
Judy Dickinson	71	71	72	69	283	8,695
Lauri Merten	70	71	72	70	283	8,695
Annika Sorenstam	70	68	71	74	283	8,695
Colleen Walker	71	73	73	67	284	6,476
Chris Johnson	72	72	71	69	284	6,476
Sherri Turner	73	70	70	71	284	6,476
Marta Figueras-Dotti	72	71	70	71	284	6,476
Alice Ritzman	73	71	68	72	284	6,476
Julie Larsen	70	71	71	72	284	6,476
Dale Eggeling	74	72	71	68	285	4,819
Jennifer Wyatt	73	72	72	68	285	4,819
Dottie Mochrie	72	72	71	70	285	4,819
Shelley Hamlin	72	71	72	70	285	4,819
Vicki Goetze	72	71	72	70	285	4,819
Katie Peterson-Parker	74	69	71	71	285	4,819
Barb Thomas	71	73	68	73	285	4,819
Dina Ammaccapane	75	69	75	67	286	3,804
Marty Dickerson	73	72	72	69	286	3,804
Denise Baldwin	73	70	72	71	286	3,804
Allison Finney	70	71	74	71	286	3,804
Martha Nause	72	73	69	72	286	3,804
Michelle Bell	71	74	67	74	286	3,804

McCall's Classic at Stratton Mountain

Stratton Mountain Country Club, Stratton Mountain, Vermont
Par 36-36—72; 6,087 yards

August 4-7
purse, $500,000

	SCORES				TOTAL	MONEY
Carolyn Hill	69	72	65	69	275	$75,000
Nancy Ramsbottom	69	69	70	70	278	46,546
Pat Bradley	73	73	71	66	283	27,256
Deb Richard	71	69	74	69	283	27,256
Joan Pitcock	73	68	68	74	283	27,256
Dottie Mochrie	73	69	72	70	284	16,228
Kris Tschetter	70	69	72	73	284	16,228
Nancy Lopez	72	70	72	71	285	11,825
Donna Andrews	68	71	73	73	285	11,825
Betsy King	64	73	72	76	285	11,825
Michelle McGann	76	72	70	68	286	8,093
Cathy Johnston-Forbes	72	70	74	70	286	8,093
Amy Benz	73	71	71	71	286	8,093
Cindy Rarick	69	73	72	72	286	8,093
Caroline Pierce	69	71	74	72	286	8,093
Page Dunlap	68	71	71	76	286	8,093
Meg Mallon	75	70	74	68	287	6,289
Jenny Lidback	73	75	69	70	287	6,289
Gail Graham	75	65	73	74	287	6,289
Vicki Fergon	69	75	75	69	288	5,035
Lisa Kiggens	70	77	71	70	288	5,035
Kim Saiki	75	70	71	72	288	5,035
Val Skinner	73	71	72	72	288	5,035
Nancy White	70	73	73	72	288	5,035
Sherri Turner	74	72	69	73	288	5,035
Deborah Vidal	71	71	72	74	288	5,035
Shelley Hamlin	71	69	71	77	288	5,035
Kim Cathrein	73	74	71	71	289	3,980
Penny Hammel	73	72	72	72	289	3,980
Hiromi Kobayashi	70	76	70	73	289	3,980
Sally Little	74	68	74	73	289	3,980
Michelle Bell	71	70	73	75	289	3,980

Children's Medical Center Classic

Country Club of the North, Beavercreek, Ohio
Par 36-36—72; 6,319 yards

August 12-14
purse, $350,000

	SCORES			TOTAL	MONEY
Maggie Will	70	70	70	210	$52,500
Jill Briles-Hinton	68	72	70	210	28,179
Alicia Dibos	67	72	71	210	28,179
(Will defeated Briles-Hinton and Dibos on second extra hole.)					
Tracy Kerdyk	74	69	68	211	16,731
Beth Daniel	70	70	71	211	16,731
Judy Dickinson	69	75	68	212	12,328
Deb Richard	73	73	67	213	8,805
Ellie Gibson	70	72	71	213	8,805
Rosie Jones	68	73	72	213	8,805
Shelley Hamlin	72	68	73	213	8,805
Lisa Kiggens	70	73	71	214	6,222
Michele Redman	70	71	73	214	6,222

	SCORES			TOTAL	MONEY
Barb Thomas	68	72	74	214	6,222
Jean Zedlitz	72	70	73	215	5,283
Cindy Rarick	71	70	74	215	5,283
Kim Saiki	74	72	70	216	4,314
Alice Miller	70	75	71	216	4,314
Penny Hammel	75	69	72	216	4,314
Jennifer Wyatt	72	71	73	216	4,314
Kim Williams	73	69	74	216	4,314
Janice Gibson	66	74	76	216	4,314
Susan Thielbar	77	71	69	217	3,551
Denise Baldwin	73	72	72	217	3,551
Chris Johnson	72	71	74	217	3,551
Jane Crafter	74	75	69	218	2,845
Hollis Stacy	75	73	70	218	2,845
Marianne Morris	74	74	70	218	2,845
Carolyn Hill	77	70	71	218	2,845
Mary Beth Zimmerman	76	71	71	218	2,845
Juli Inkster	72	75	71	218	2,845
Loretta Alderete	73	73	72	218	2,845
Colleen Walker	71	75	72	218	2,845
Kim Cathrein	75	69	74	218	2,845
Katie Peterson-Parker	71	71	76	218	2,845

Chicago Challenge

White Eagle Golf Club, Naperville, Illinois
Par 36-36—72; 6,256 yards

August 18-21
purse, $500,000

	SCORES				TOTAL	MONEY
Jane Geddes	68	69	68	67	272	$75,000
Robin Walton	72	70	68	65	275	40,256
Dale Eggeling	70	67	71	67	275	40,256
Judy Dickinson	70	70	71	67	278	26,418
Cathy Johnston-Forbes	69	70	71	69	279	17,947
Brandie Burton	71	72	66	70	279	17,947
Janice Gibson	70	67	71	71	279	17,947
Missie McGeorge	69	71	69	71	280	12,454
Margaret Platt	69	70	69	72	280	12,454
Michelle McGann	68	71	74	68	281	9,650
Katie Peterson-Parker	65	72	75	69	281	9,650
Deb Richard	72	68	71	70	281	9,650
Hollis Stacy	68	72	73	69	282	7,556
Lynn Connelly	71	71	69	71	282	7,556
Dina Ammaccapane	71	70	70	71	282	7,556
Becky Iverson	71	71	67	73	282	7,556
Alice Ritzman	74	67	71	71	283	6,423
Kim Shipman	70	69	72	72	283	6,423
Kelly Robbins	69	73	74	68	284	5,244
Terry-Jo Myers	71	72	71	70	284	5,244
Juli Inkster	70	70	74	70	284	5,244
Kim Williams	71	69	73	71	284	5,244
Barb Mucha	69	70	74	71	284	5,244
Beth Daniel	72	68	72	72	284	5,244
Michelle Estill	70	67	75	72	284	5,244
Kristi Albers	70	71	69	74	284	5,244
Shelley Hamlin	73	70	72	70	285	3,926
Tina Barrett	73	70	72	70	285	3,926

	SCORES				TOTAL	MONEY
Leigh Ann Mills	73	70	71	71	285	3,926
Sherri Turner	74	70	69	72	285	3,926
Meg Mallon	71	71	71	72	285	3,926
Lisa Walters	70	71	72	72	285	3,926
Amy Alcott	67	73	73	72	285	3,926
Kathryn Marshall	71	66	76	72	285	3,926

du Maurier Ltd. Classic

Ottawa Hunt Club, Ottawa, Ontario, Canada   August 25-28
Par 36-36—72; 6,400 yards   purse, $800,000

	SCORES				TOTAL	MONEY
Martha Nause	65	71	72	71	279	$120,000
Michelle McGann	66	71	71	72	280	74,474
Liselotte Neumann	70	67	71	73	281	54,346
Jane Geddes	74	67	70	72	283	34,888
Meg Mallon	70	72	68	73	283	34,888
Betsy King	67	69	74	73	283	34,888
Dawn Coe-Jones	72	70	71	71	284	20,128
Marianne Morris	69	72	70	73	284	20,128
Judy Dickinson	72	68	70	74	284	20,128
Kelly Robbins	66	70	73	75	284	20,128
Vicki Fergon	72	68	75	70	285	14,223
Sherri Steinhauer	68	72	73	72	285	14,223
Patty Sheehan	71	71	68	75	285	14,223
Amy Alcott	73	70	72	71	286	12,076
Dottie Mochrie	67	74	72	73	286	12,076
Jane Crafter	71	74	75	67	287	9,862
Page Dunlap	72	69	75	71	287	9,862
Alice Ritzman	76	70	68	73	287	9,862
Rosie Jones	73	70	70	74	287	9,862
Jenny Lidback	70	72	71	74	287	9,862
Alicia Dibos	71	71	70	75	287	9,862
Sally Little	74	72	73	69	288	7,348
Missie Berteotti	70	72	73	73	288	7,348
Brandie Burton	71	74	69	74	288	7,348
Barb Bunkowsky	74	69	71	74	288	7,348
Kim Williams	67	74	73	74	288	7,348
Karen Lunn	70	73	70	75	288	7,348
Annika Sorenstam	72	67	73	76	288	7,348
Nancy Lopez	67	70	75	76	288	7,348
Leigh Ann Mills	66	72	70	80	288	7,348

State Farm Rail Classic

Rail Golf Club, Springfield, Illinois   September 3-5
Par 36-36—72; 6,403 yards   purse, $525,000

	SCORES			TOTAL	MONEY
Barb Mucha	67	69	67	203	$78,750
Kim Shipman	68	67	69	204	48,873
Gail Graham	70	66	69	205	31,701
Suzanne Strudwick	69	66	70	205	31,701
Lori West	70	69	67	206	15,630

	SCORES			TOTAL	MONEY
Hiromi Kobayashi	69	70	67	206	15,630
Michelle McGann	70	68	68	206	15,630
Meg Mallon	66	72	68	206	15,630
Stephanie Farwig	66	70	70	206	15,630
Kristi Albers	66	70	70	206	15,630
Allison Finney	70	71	66	207	9,334
Dottie Mochrie	69	69	69	207	9,334
Patty Jordan	69	68	70	207	9,334
Ellie Gibson	71	71	66	208	7,132
Becky Iverson	72	68	68	208	7,132
Pat Bradley	69	71	68	208	7,132
Vicki Goetze	71	68	69	208	7,132
Chris Johnson	66	71	71	208	7,132
Laura Davies	65	66	77	208	7,132
Kim Williams	73	70	66	209	5,286
Kris Tschetter	69	71	69	209	5,286
Janice Gibson	69	71	69	209	5,286
Judy Dickinson	68	71	70	209	5,286
Vicki Fergon	66	73	70	209	5,286
Cindy Figg-Currier	71	67	71	209	5,286
Betsy King	69	69	71	209	5,286
Val Skinner	66	70	73	209	5,286
Annika Sorenstam	71	69	70	210	4,178
Barb Thomas	69	71	70	210	4,178
Karen Lunn	67	73	70	210	4,178
Barb Bunkowsky	68	71	71	210	4,178
Lauri Merten	70	66	74	210	4,178

Ping-Cellular One Championship

Columbia Edgewater Country Club, Portland, Oregon
Par 36-36—72; 6,317 yards

September 9-11
purse, $500,000

	SCORES			TOTAL	MONEY
Missie McGeorge	72	69	66	207	$75,000
Betsy King	71	70	69	210	46,546
Cindy Rarick	72	71	68	211	30,192
Allison Finney	71	69	71	211	30,192
Sally Little	70	74	68	212	14,886
Donna Andrews	73	69	70	212	14,886
Elaine Crosby	72	68	72	212	14,886
Ellie Gibson	68	72	72	212	14,886
Chris Johnson	72	67	73	212	14,886
Val Skinner	67	72	73	212	14,886
Patty Sheehan	72	75	66	213	9,607
Denise Baldwin	71	74	69	214	8,600
Amy Alcott	70	68	76	214	8,600
Joan Pitcock	72	73	70	215	6,695
Laura Davies	72	73	70	215	6,695
Annika Sorenstam	71	74	70	215	6,695
Dawn Coe-Jones	76	68	71	215	6,695
Karen Lunn	73	69	73	215	6,695
Robin Walton	70	71	74	215	6,695
Rosie Jones	71	69	75	215	6,695
Pat Bradley	70	77	69	216	4,578
Tammie Green	75	71	70	216	4,578
Dina Ammaccapane	74	72	70	216	4,578

	SCORES			TOTAL	MONEY
Helen Alfredsson	75	70	71	216	4,578
Amy Benz	73	72	71	216	4,578
Hollis Stacy	71	74	71	216	4,578
Dale Eggeling	76	68	72	216	4,578
Jane Geddes	74	70	72	216	4,578
Lisa Kiggens	74	70	72	216	4,578
Sherri Turner	73	70	73	216	4,578
Judy Dickinson	71	71	74	216	4,578
Noelle Daghe	72	69	75	216	4,578

Safeco Classic

Meridian Valley Country Club, Kent, Washington
Par 36-36—72; 6,234 yards

September 15-18
purse, $500,000

	SCORES				TOTAL	MONEY
Deb Richard	71	68	70	67	276	$75,000
Tammie Green	72	69	69	67	277	32,079
Rosie Jones	70	69	70	68	277	32,079
Michelle Estill	68	70	69	70	277	32,079
Chris Johnson	68	71	67	71	277	32,079
Vicki Fergon	72	68	68	71	279	15,179
Betsy King	69	68	70	72	279	15,179
Annika Sorenstam	67	72	66	74	279	15,179
Kelly Robbins	73	68	68	71	280	11,196
Juli Inkster	71	68	69	72	280	11,196
Vicki Goetze	71	70	73	67	281	9,570
Patty Sheehan	72	71	71	68	282	8,311
Donna Andrews	72	69	71	70	282	8,311
Susie Redman	71	71	67	73	282	8,311
Brandie Burton	69	71	74	69	283	6,884
Liselotte Neumann	74	71	68	70	283	6,884
Elaine Crosby	72	68	68	75	283	6,884
Helen Alfredsson	74	72	68	70	284	6,172
Sherri Steinhauer	74	71	67	72	284	6,172
Dottie Mochrie	74	72	70	69	285	5,129
Sherri Turner	71	73	72	69	285	5,129
Michele Redman	71	68	76	70	285	5,129
Dawn Coe-Jones	70	72	72	71	285	5,129
Julie Larsen	70	73	69	73	285	5,129
Beth Daniel	71	72	68	74	285	5,129
Alison Nicholas	70	68	68	79	285	5,129
Barb Mucha	74	73	72	67	286	3,993
Missie McGeorge	78	69	69	70	286	3,993
Lauri Merten	71	70	74	71	286	3,993
Amy Alcott	75	69	70	72	286	3,993
Michelle McGann	70	74	70	72	286	3,993
Pamela Wright	73	70	71	72	286	3,993
Colleen Walker	69	74	67	76	286	3,993

Heartland Classic

Forest Hills Country Club, St. Louis, Missouri
Par 36-36—72; 6,350 yards

September 30-October 2
purse, $500,000

	SCORES				TOTAL	MONEY
Liselotte Neumann	70	71	67	70	278	$75,000
Elaine Crosby	71	71	69	70	281	40,256
Pearl Sinn	67	70	72	72	281	40,256
Sherri Turner	73	72	71	67	283	23,902
Deb Richard	71	70	68	74	283	23,902
Chris Johnson	77	71	68	68	284	16,228
Jane Geddes	70	73	70	71	284	16,228
Joan Pitcock	73	74	73	65	285	13,083
Cindy Schreyer	73	71	76	66	286	9,812
Carolyn Hill	74	72	72	68	286	9,812
Gail Graham	72	71	72	71	286	9,812
Nanci Bowen	71	71	73	71	286	9,812
Colleen Walker	71	70	73	72	286	9,812
Betsy King	73	69	75	71	288	6,943
Julie Larsen	73	68	75	72	288	6,943
Missie Berteotti	75	72	68	73	288	6,943
Dottie Mochrie	71	73	71	73	288	6,943
Meg Mallon	69	75	69	75	288	6,943
Brandie Burton	74	72	75	68	289	5,912
Donna Andrews	76	71	70	72	289	5,912
Annika Sorenstam	73	74	72	71	290	5,189
Dale Eggeling	71	76	70	73	290	5,189
Nancy Ramsbottom	71	74	72	73	290	5,189
Dawn Coe-Jones	71	74	72	73	290	5,189
Mary Beth Zimmerman	74	76	70	71	291	4,579
Shelley Hamlin	78	71	68	74	291	4,579
Pat Bradley	71	73	72	75	291	4,579
Alicia Dibos	77	72	72	71	292	4,050
Nancy Lopez	74	72	74	72	292	4,050
Marta Figueras-Dotti	74	73	71	74	292	4,050
Lynn Connelly	72	75	69	76	292	4,050

World Championship of Women's Golf

Naples National Golf Club, Naples, Florida
Par 36-36—72; 6,346 yards

October 14-16
purse, $425,000

	SCORES				TOTAL	MONEY
Beth Daniel	68	70	71	65	274	$105,000
Elaine Crosby	70	66	69	72	277	55,000
Laura Davies	68	73	67	71	279	35,000
Liselotte Neumann	71	67	72	70	280	22,500
Dottie Mochrie	67	69	73	71	280	22,500
Helen Alfredsson	71	72	68	71	282	18,000
Donna Andrews	69	71	73	70	283	16,000
Sherri Steinhauer	67	71	75	70	283	16,000
Martha Nause	73	72	67	71	283	16,000
Val Skinner	69	69	75	71	284	14,000
Meg Mallon	72	74	70	72	288	13,700
Betsy King	71	72	75	74	292	13,400
Patty Sheehan	75	69	78	72	294	13,100

	SCORES				TOTAL	MONEY
Kelly Robbins	73	71	76	75	295	12,750
Hiromi Kobayashi	72	79	73	72	296	12,340
Tammie Green	75	72	75	77	299	12,085

Solheim Cup

The Greenbrier, White Sulphur Springs, West Virginia   October 21-23
Par 36-36—72; 6,400 yards

FIRST DAY
Foursomes

Dottie Mochrie and Brandie Burton (USA) defeated Liselotte Neumann and Helen Alfredsson (Europe), 3 and 2.
Annika Sorenstam and Catrin Nilsmark (Europe) defeated Beth Daniel and Meg Mallon (USA), 1 up.
Dale Reid and Lora Fairclough (Europe) defeated Tammie Green and Kelly Robbins (USA), 2 and 1.
Laura Davies and Alison Nicholas (Europe) defeated Donna Andrews and Betsy King (USA), 2 and 1.
Patty Sheehan and Sherri Steinhauer (USA) defeated Pam Wright and Trish Johnson (Europe), 2 up.

United States 2, Europe 3

SECOND DAY
Fourballs

Mochrie and Burton (USA) defeated Davies and Nicholas (Europe), 2 and 1.
Daniel and Mallon (USA) defeated Nilsmark and Sorenstam (Europe), 6 and 5.
Reid and Fairclough (Europe) defeated Green and Robbins (USA), 4 and 3.
Andrews and King (USA) defeated Johnson and Wright (Europe), 3 and 2.
Neumann and Alfredsson (Europe) defeated Sheehan and Steinhauer (USA), 1 up.

United States 5, Europe 5

THIRD DAY
Singles

Alfredsson (Europe) defeated King (USA), 2 and 1.
Mochrie (USA) defeated Nilsmark (Europe), 6 and 5.
Daniel (USA) defeated Johnson (Europe), 1 up.
Robbins (USA) defeated Fairclough (Europe), 4 and 2.
Mallon (USA) defeated Wright (Europe), 1 up.
Nicholas (Europe) defeated Sheehan (USA), 3 and 2.
Burton (USA) defeated Davies (Europe), 1 up.
Green (USA) defeated Sorenstam (Europe), 3 and 2.
Steinhauer (USA) defeated Reid (Europe), 2 up.
Andrews (USA) defeated Neumann (Europe), 3 and 2.

FINAL RESULTS: United States 13, Europe 7

JC Penney Classic

Innisbrook Hilton Resort, Tarpon Springs, Florida
Ladies: Par 36-35—71; 6,394 yards
Men: Par 36-35—71; 7,054 yards

December 1-4
purse, $1,200,000

	SCORES				TOTAL	MONEY (Each)
Marta Figueras-Dotti/Brad Bryant	64	70	62	66	262	$150,000
Helen Alfredsson/Robert Gamez	66	64	64	68	262	73,000
(Figueras-Dotti and Bryant defeated Alfredsson and Gamez on fourth extra hole.)						
Beth Daniel/Davis Love III	65	65	65	68	263	48,000
Amy Alcott/Robin Freeman	65	66	64	69	264	36,500
Kelly Robbins/Dan Pohl	67	66	65	67	265	21,500
Colleen Walker/Lee Janzen	68	67	63	67	265	21,500
Dottie Mochrie/Dave Stockton, Jr.	66	69	62	68	265	21,500
Dana Dormann/Fred Funk	65	68	64	68	265	21,500
Laura Davies/David Feherty	66	65	70	65	266	12,000
Lisa Kiggens/Jim Furyk	67	67	66	66	266	12,000
Deb Richard/Mike Heinen	67	70	64	66	267	9,167
Vicki Goetze/Steve Stricker	65	69	67	66	267	9,167
Martha Nause/Dicky Pride	66	67	67	67	267	9,167
Dale Eggeling/Jim McGovern	66	68	68	66	268	7,500
Pat Bradley/Bill Glasson	69	70	64	65	268	7,500
Elaine Crosby/Ed Humenik	67	69	64	68	268	7,500
Rosie Jones/Mark Carnevale	70	66	68	67	269	5,167
Donna Andrews/Mike Hulbert	66	68	67	68	269	5,167
Barb Mucha/Glen Day	69	65	67	68	269	5,167
Debbie Massey/Mark McCumber	68	67	66	68	269	5,167
Jan Stephenson/Curt Byrum	67	68	66	68	269	5,167
Michele Redman/Guy Boros	67	69	65	68	269	5,167
Betsy King/Rick Fehr	68	72	64	65	269	5,167
Liselotte Neumann/Tony Jacklin	68	64	66	71	269	5,167
Jane Crafter/Steve Jones	68	66	64	71	269	5,167
Brandie Burton/Billy Mayfair	68	69	66	67	270	4,300
Jane Geddes/Brian Claar	64	68	68	70	270	4,300
Chris Johnson/Neal Lancaster	65	68	66	71	270	4,300
Judy Dickinson/Jay Sigel	65	71	67	68	271	4,000
Michelle Estill/Donnie Hammond	72	70	61	68	271	4,000
JoAnne Carner/Jim Albus	64	68	70	70	272	3,800
Val Skinner/Mike Standly	71	69	65	68	273	3,600
Carolyn Hill/Michael Bradley	71	71	65	66	273	3,600
Dawn Coe-Jones/Brian Henninger	69	72	67	65	273	3,600

Diners Club Matches

PGA West, Jack Nicklaus Course, La Quinta, California
Par 36-36—72; 6,546 yards

December 8-11
purse, $2,100,000

FIRST ROUND

Kelly Robbins and Tammie Green defeated Martha Nause and Pat Bradley, 2 and 1.
Laura Davies and Mardi Lunn defeated Donna Andrews and Michelle McGann, 1 up.
Beth Daniel and Meg Mallon defeated Patty Sheehan and Nancy Lopez, 6 and 5.
Dottie Mochrie and Juli Inkster defeated Liselotte Neumann and Jane Geddes, 3 and 2.

(Losers in first round received $15,000 each.)

SECOND ROUND

Robbins and Green defeated Davies and Lunn, 2 and 1.
Mochrie and Inkster defeated Daniel and Mallon, 4 and 2.

(Losers in second round received $35,000 each.)

THIRD ROUND

Robbins and Green defeated Mochrie and Inkster, 2 and 1.

(Winners in third round received $125,000 each; losers received $50,000 each.)

Women's European Tour

Ford Classic

Woburn Golf & Country Club, Milton Keynes, England
Par 37-37—74; 6,103 yards

April 21-24
purse, £100,000

	SCORES				TOTAL	MONEY
Catrin Nilsmark	73	68	73	70	284	£15,000
Trish Johnson	74	70	73	71	288	8,575
Joanne Morley	73	69	77	69	288	8,575
Laura Davies	74	73	71	71	289	5,400
Suzanne Strudwick	74	72	72	72	290	3,580
Amaia Arruti	75	71	72	72	290	3,580
Annika Sorenstam	73	71	73	73	290	3,580
Mardi Lunn	72	70	75	74	291	2,246.66
Sally Prosser	73	73	74	71	291	2,246.66
Jean Bartholomew	70	78	71	72	291	2,246.66
Kathryn Marshall	75	76	73	69	293	1,840
Federica Dassu	72	72	77	73	294	1,626.66
Karen Lunn	76	74	75	69	294	1,626.66
Alison Nicholas	72	75	75	72	294	1,626.66
Penny Grice-Whittaker	79	75	73	68	295	1,480
Caroline Hall	72	74	76	73	295	1,480
Susan Moon	74	73	75	74	296	1,420
Susan Hodge	75	75	72	75	297	1,340
Mette Hageman	69	75	75	78	297	1,340
Julie Forbes	76	72	76	73	297	1,340
Laurette Maritz-Atkins	76	75	72	76	299	1,240
Gillian Stewart	73	78	74	74	299	1,240
Patti Rizzo	78	75	76	70	299	1,240
Karine Espinasse	76	76	77	71	300	1,135
Dale Reid	73	75	78	74	300	1,135
Corinne Soules	75	77	76	72	300	1,135
Pamela Wright	73	76	75	76	300	1,135
Shani Waugh	73	75	72	81	301	1,045

	SCORES				TOTAL	MONEY
Lora Fairclough	75	73	83	70	301	1,045
Diane Barnard	80	75	72	75	302	955
Catherine Panton-Lewis	75	76	73	78	302	955
Laura Navarro	76	74	74	78	302	955
Sarah Bennett	79	71	75	77	302	955

Ladies Open Costa Azul

Montado and Aroeira Golf Courses, Lisbon, Portugal
Par 36-36—72
(Third and fourth rounds cancelled — rain.)

May 19-22
purse, £50,000

	SCORES		TOTAL	MONEY
Sandrine Mendiburu	70	70	140	£7,500
Lora Fairclough	70	71	141	5,075
Federica Dassu	69	74	143	2,517.50
Tracy Hammond	72	71	143	2,517.50
Joanne Morley	73	70	143	2,517.50
Helen Wadsworth	70	73	143	2,517.50
Sarah Nicklin	71	73	144	1,500
Claire Duffy	72	73	145	1,123.33
Susan Hodge	74	71	145	1,123.33
Laura Navarro	72	73	145	1,123.33
Regine Lautens	74	72	146	920
Marie Laure de Lorenzi	77	70	147	792.50
Laurette Maritz-Atkins	76	71	147	792.50
Veronique Palli	74	73	147	792.50
Lisa Hackney	75	72	147	792.50
Corinne Dibnah	76	72	148	672.14
Karine Espinasse	73	75	148	672.14
Catrin Nilsmark	75	73	148	672.14
Sally Prosser	74	74	148	672.14
Shani Waugh	76	72	148	672.14
Mette Hageman	79	69	148	672.14
Cathy Stolz	76	72	148	672.14
Penny Grice-Whittaker	77	72	149	605
Maureen Madill	75	75	150	567.50
Allison Shapcott	75	75	150	567.50
Caroline Hall	74	76	150	567.50
Morag Wright	73	77	150	567.50
Liz Weima	74	77	151	500
Isabella Maconi	73	78	151	500
Valerie Michaud	77	74	151	500
Jacqueline Brown	76	75	151	500
Evelyn Orley	78	73	151	500

Evian Masters

Royal Golf Club, Evian, France
Par 36-36—72; 5,832 yards

June 9-12
purse, £232,500

	SCORES				TOTAL	MONEY
Helen Alfredsson	71	73	73	70	287	£34,875
Sarah Gautrey	73	71	77	69	290	19,936.87
Lora Fairclough	68	72	77	73	290	19,936.87

	SCORES				TOTAL	MONEY
Florence Descampe	73	74	72	72	291	12,555
Trish Johnson	72	71	74	77	294	8,997.75
Vicki Goetze	74	73	73	74	294	8,997.75
Tracy Hanson	72	73	73	77	295	5,998.50
Kathryn Marshall	72	75	77	71	295	5,998.50
Sandrine Mendiburu	74	72	74	75	295	5,998.50
Laura Davies	76	75	70	75	296	4,309
Sally Prosser	71	75	71	79	296	4,309
Loraine Lambert	71	76	73	76	296	4,309
Suzanne Strudwick	75	74	73	75	297	3,611.50
Catrin Nilsmark	74	74	74	75	297	3,611.50
Laura Navarro	74	77	74	72	297	3,611.50
Penny Grice-Whittaker	73	78	72	75	298	3,255
Karina Orum	77	76	72	73	298	3,255
Amaia Arruti	73	76	75	74	298	3,255
Lisa Hackney	76	77	75	70	298	3,255
Estefania Knuth	74	73	77	75	299	2,917.87
Carin Hjalmarsson	74	73	79	73	299	2,917.87
Isabella Maconi	76	74	75	74	299	2,917.87
Patricia Meunier	71	76	75	77	299	2,917.87
Corinne Dibnah	72	73	77	78	300	2,673.75
Debbie Dowling	78	71	77	74	300	2,673.75
Evelyn Orley	75	78	73	74	300	2,673.75
Karine Espinasse	79	74	75	73	301	2,534.25
Susan Hodge	74	76	74	78	302	2,464.50
Alison Nicholas	76	73	79	75	303	2,290.12
Gillian Stewart	77	73	76	77	303	2,290.12
Xonia Wunsch-Ruiz	76	75	79	73	303	2,290.12
Shani Waugh	80	74	76	73	303	2,290.12

OVB Damen Open

Golf Course Europa-Sportregion Zell am See, Salzburg, Austria   June 16-19
Par 37-36—73; 6,015 yards   purse, £100,000

	SCORES				TOTAL	MONEY
Florence Descampe	70	70	69	68	277	£15,000
Tracy Hanson	70	69	66	72	277	10,150
(Descampe defeated Hanson on second extra hole.)						
Loraine Lambert	71	64	71	73	279	7,000
Malin Burstrom	71	71	69	71	282	4,820
Shoko Yamamoto	70	72	70	70	282	4,820
Lisa Hackney	68	72	74	69	283	3,500
Karine Espinasse	75	72	70	67	284	2,580
Gillian Stewart	69	74	71	70	284	2,580
Karina Orum	69	73	73	69	284	2,580
Janice Arnold	73	70	70	72	285	1,853.33
Jean Bartholomew	70	65	75	75	285	1,853.33
Helen Wadsworth	70	76	68	71	285	1,853.33
Patti Rizzo	74	70	69	73	286	1,465.71
Jennifer Allmark	70	73	75	68	286	1,465.71
Laree Sugg	68	72	74	72	286	1,465.71
Patricia Meunier	73	74	71	68	286	1,465.71
Petra Rigby	71	71	74	70	286	1,465.71
Michelle Dobek	71	74	71	70	286	1,465.71
Sandrine Mendiburu	70	71	74	71	286	1,465.71
Susan Moon	71	72	71	73	287	1,285

	SCORES				TOTAL	MONEY
Evelyn Orley	72	72	71	72	287	1,285
*Heidi Klump	73	71	70	73	287	
Kristal Parker	70	70	74	74	288	1,225
Sarah Gautrey	75	70	69	74	288	1,225
Debbie Dowling	73	73	73	70	289	1,135
Dale Reid	70	72	74	73	289	1,135
Susan Hodge	71	72	72	74	289	1,135
Joanne Morley	72	73	69	75	289	1,135
Maureen Madill	68	73	73	76	290	970
Penny Grice-Whittaker	71	75	72	72	290	970
Trish Johnson	73	71	71	75	290	970
Laurette Maritz-Atkins	73	74	72	71	290	970
Sally Prosser	74	71	71	74	290	970
Mette Hageman	74	72	71	73	290	970
Julie Forbes	71	70	74	75	290	970

BMW European Masters

Golf du Bercuit, Brussels, Belgium
Par 38-35—73; 5,953 yards

June 23-26
purse, £160,000

	SCORES				TOTAL	MONEY
Helen Wadsworth	69	66	70	73	278	£24,000
Tracy Hanson	69	69	70	73	281	16,240
Laura Davies	69	70	72	72	283	9,920
Annika Sorenstam	71	70	71	71	283	9,920
Sally Prosser	70	73	72	70	285	6,192
Karina Orum	66	75	73	71	285	6,192
Susan Hodge	73	71	70	72	286	4,800
Corinne Dibnah	72	74	68	73	287	3,432
Trish Johnson	73	71	71	72	287	3,432
Susan Moon	76	73	69	69	287	3,432
Estefania Knuth	71	72	70	74	287	3,432
Marie Laure de Lorenzi	69	75	72	72	288	2,552
Florence Descampe	70	71	74	73	288	2,552
Joanne Morley	71	72	74	71	288	2,552
Lora Fairclough	74	66	73	75	288	2,552
Patti Rizzo	75	68	73	73	289	2,178.66
Shani Waugh	72	74	74	69	289	2,178.66
Amaia Arruti	76	71	71	71	289	2,178.66
Caroline Hall	74	71	75	69	289	2,178.66
Laura Navarro	74	71	70	74	289	2,178.66
Shoko Yamamoto	71	73	74	71	289	2,178.66
Alison Nicholas	69	75	71	75	290	1,936
Dale Reid	70	76	73	71	290	1,936
Corinne Soules	73	73	71	73	290	1,936
Gillian Stewart	69	73	74	75	291	1,816
Sarah Gautrey	78	72	73	68	291	1,816
Lisa Hackney	70	75	77	70	292	1,720
Evelyn Orley	75	69	76	72	292	1,720
Karen Davies	75	73	72	73	293	1,624
Wendy Doolan	72	78	72	71	293	1,624

Hennessy Cup

Golf und Landclub, Cologne, Germany
Par 36-36—72; 6,119 yards

June 30-July 3
purse, £220,000

	SCORES				TOTAL	MONEY
Liselotte Neumann	69	71	72	65	277	£33,000
Alison Nicholas	69	71	67	71	278	22,300
Kristal Parker	70	72	68	69	279	15,400
Annika Sorenstam	71	73	69	68	281	10,610
Helen Alfredsson	71	70	69	71	281	10,610
Pamela Wright	70	69	70	74	283	7,700
Karen Lunn	67	71	72	75	285	6,050
Shani Waugh	73	72	71	69	285	6,050
Dale Reid	74	68	70	74	286	4,675
Gillian Stewart	70	75	72	69	286	4,675
Corinne Dibnah	72	73	73	69	287	3,816.66
Karen Pearce	72	72	75	68	287	3,816.66
Tracy Hanson	76	70	70	71	287	3,816.66
Laura Davies	71	72	74	71	288	3,380
Karina Orum	72	76	70	70	288	3,380
Amaia Arruti	74	73	71	70	288	3,380
Estefania Knuth	74	72	71	72	289	3,220
Susan Moon	72	76	71	71	290	3,020
Catrin Nilsmark	72	76	71	71	290	3,020
Sarah Gautrey	73	76	71	70	290	3,020
Caroline Hall	70	73	74	73	290	3,020
Marie Laure de Lorenzi	73	75	72	71	291	2,743.33
Karine Espinasse	75	73	71	72	291	2,743.33
Laura Navarro	74	73	70	74	291	2,743.33
Debbie Dowling	81	67	74	70	292	2,440
Loraine Lambert	71	71	75	75	292	2,440
Julie Forbes	75	75	75	67	292	2,440
Lora Fairclough	75	70	70	77	292	2,440
Helen Wadsworth	71	73	71	77	292	2,440
Penny Grice-Whittaker	70	75	72	76	293	2,160
Trish Johnson	71	76	73	73	293	2,160

Irish Holidays Open

St. Margaret's Golf & Country Club, Dublin, Ireland
Par 36-36—72; 6,049 yards

July 28-31
purse, £70,000

	SCORES				TOTAL	MONEY
Laura Davies	70	72	69	71	282	£10,500
Carin Hjalmarsson	72	75	70	73	290	6,002.50
Helen Wadsworth	72	71	75	72	290	6,002.50
Federica Dassu	70	71	77	73	291	3,374
Caroline Hall	72	74	69	76	291	3,374
Sofia Gronberg Whitmore	72	72	73	75	292	2,100
Catrin Nilsmark	72	76	72	72	292	2,100
Evelyn Orley	76	73	70	73	292	2,100
Corinne Dibnah	69	77	75	72	293	1,568
Karine Espinasse	72	71	75	76	294	1,297.33
Cindy Figg-Currier	75	73	71	75	294	1,297.33
Rachel Hetherington	72	73	72	77	294	1,297.33
Karen Lunn	71	74	75	75	295	1,087.33
Karen Pearce	71	74	73	77	295	1,087.33

		SCORES			TOTAL	MONEY
Sarah Gautrey	72	76	71	76	295	1,087.33
Patti Rizzo	70	70	74	82	296	994
Karina Orum	73	75	72	76	296	994
Franca Fehlauer	73	75	74	74	296	994
Shani Waugh	79	73	71	74	297	924
Sarah Bennett	75	75	72	75	297	924
Janice Arnold	74	77	74	73	298	847
Tracey Craik	77	69	75	77	298	847
Allison Shapcott	74	71	77	76	298	847
Loraine Lambert	73	74	75	76	298	847
Julie Forbes	71	77	73	77	298	847
Gillian Stewart	72	77	74	76	299	742
Karen Davies	75	75	73	76	299	742
Liz Weima	72	78	77	72	299	742
Patricia Meunier	69	75	79	76	299	742
Laura Navarro	74	77	74	74	299	742

Skoda Scottish Open

Dalmahoy Hotel Golf & Country Club, Dalmahoy, Scotland
Par 36-36—72; 6,202 yards

August 4-7
purse, £75,000

		SCORES			TOTAL	MONEY
Laura Davies	69	69	68	72	278	£11,250
Karina Orum	68	70	71	70	279	7,610
Jane Geddes	71	68	71	70	280	4,650
Laura Navarro	73	69	70	68	280	4,650
Helen Alfredsson	70	73	68	70	281	3,180
Federica Dassu	70	70	71	71	282	2,250
Penny Grice-Whittaker	70	69	73	70	282	2,250
Liselotte Neumann	68	72	71	71	282	2,250
Alison Nicholas	72	72	69	71	284	1,520
Dale Reid	69	70	72	73	284	1,520
Wendy Doolan	69	75	72	68	284	1,520
Trish Johnson	73	75	66	71	285	1,248.50
Karen Pearce	72	73	71	69	285	1,248.50
Karen Lunn	68	72	72	74	286	1,143.50
Carin Hjalmarsson	69	71	75	71	286	1,143.50
Patti Rizzo	74	74	70	69	287	1,065
Sarah Gautrey	71	71	75	70	287	1,065
Loraine Lambert	72	73	73	69	287	1,065
Corinne Dibnah	71	69	72	76	288	990
Shani Waugh	69	78	67	74	288	990
Karine Espinasse	72	73	73	71	289	929
Pamela Wright	74	71	75	69	289	929
Lisa Hackney	70	74	72	73	289	929
Diane Barnard	76	73	73	68	290	848.50
Catrin Nilsmark	72	74	71	73	290	848.50
Estefania Knuth	67	73	75	75	290	848.50
Nicola Moult	74	73	72	71	290	848.50
Julie Forbes	74	74	72	71	291	768
Sara Robinson	72	69	74	76	291	768
Evelyn Orley	72	73	73	73	291	768

Weetabix Women's British Open

Woburn Golf & Country Club, Milton Keynes, England
Par 38-35—73; 6,258 yards

August 11-14
purse, £335,000

	SCORES				TOTAL	MONEY
Liselotte Neumann	71	67	70	72	280	£52,500
Dottie Mochrie	73	66	74	70	283	27,250
Annika Sorenstam	69	75	69	70	283	27,250
Laura Davies	74	66	73	71	284	14,625
Corinne Dibnah	75	70	67	72	284	14,625
Cindy Figg-Currier	69	74	68	74	285	10,750
Helen Alfredsson	71	76	71	68	286	9,250
Tracy Hanson	74	73	66	74	287	8,000
Suzanne Strudwick	71	71	71	75	288	6,250
Val Skinner	77	71	66	74	288	6,250
Caroline Pierce	70	75	71	72	288	6,250
Hiromi Kobayashi	73	73	69	74	289	5,100
Sarah Gautrey	69	74	72	75	290	4,800
Tania Abitbol	76	68	75	72	291	4,526.66
Penny Grice-Whittaker	77	72	72	70	291	4,526.66
Marnie McGuire	71	73	78	69	291	4,526.66
Sofia Gronberg Whitmore	71	69	74	78	292	4,100
Li Wen Lin	73	70	73	76	292	4,100
Jane Geddes	74	72	72	74	292	4,100
Estefania Knuth	78	69	72	73	292	4,100
Pamela Wright	68	75	78	72	293	3,740
Karen Pearce	70	74	75	74	293	3,740
Kris Tschetter	68	76	75	74	293	3,740
Kay Cockerill	71	77	73	73	294	3,425
Amy Alcott	74	74	75	71	294	3,425
Betsy King	73	74	69	78	294	3,425
Alice Ritzman	69	76	75	74	294	3,425
Susan Moon	72	78	74	71	295	2,930
Alison Nicholas	72	73	70	80	295	2,930
Dale Reid	76	72	75	72	295	2,930
Mardi Lunn	73	75	75	72	295	2,930
Kathryn Marshall	76	72	75	72	295	2,930
Lora Fairclough	75	72	72	76	295	2,930
Susan Redman	74	71	76	74	295	2,930

Trygg-Hansa Open

Haninge Golf Club, Stockholm, Sweden
Par 37-36—73; 6,188 yards

August 18-21
purse, £100,000

	SCORES				TOTAL	MONEY
Liselotte Neumann	69	67	71	67	274	£15,000
Corinne Dibnah	71	70	69	68	278	10,150
Annika Sorenstam	73	73	72	66	284	7,000
Helen Alfredsson	74	72	70	69	285	5,400
Sofia Gronberg Whitmore	71	72	72	71	286	4,240
*Sofie Eriksson	71	70	74	73	288	
Alison Nicholas	73	71	73	72	289	3,500
Susan Moon	73	72	77	68	290	2,580
Kristal Parker	73	68	74	75	290	2,580
Joanne Morley	71	71	74	74	290	2,580
Janice Arnold	70	73	71	77	291	1,920
Dale Reid	73	74	74	70	291	1,920

	SCORES				TOTAL	MONEY
Sally Prosser	70	73	78	71	292	1,595
Jennifer Allmark	77	74	70	71	292	1,595
Karina Orum	73	74	74	71	292	1,595
Lora Fairclough	71	75	73	73	292	1,595
Federica Dassu	74	73	71	75	293	1,380
Marie Laure de Lorenzi	70	78	76	69	293	1,380
Debbie Dowling	75	73	71	74	293	1,380
Muffin Spencer-Devlin	73	73	72	75	293	1,380
Wendy Doolan	72	75	74	72	293	1,380
Penny Grice-Whittaker	74	75	75	70	294	1,210
Anna Oxenstierna	72	77	70	75	294	1,210
Gillian Stewart	74	74	71	75	294	1,210
Sophie Gustafson	77	71	75	71	294	1,210
Kimberly Cayce	74	73	73	74	294	1,210
Diane Barnard	72	75	75	73	295	1,090
Patricia Meunier	71	75	76	73	295	1,090
Lisa Hackney	76	76	76	67	295	1,090
Julie Forbes	75	73	75	73	296	1,030

Waterford Dairies English Open

Tytherington Club, Manchester, England
Par 36-36—72; 5,896 yards

September 1-4
purse, £60,000

	SCORES				TOTAL	MONEY
Patricia Meunier	73	74	70	71	288	£9,000
Marie Laure de Lorenzi	78	69	72	71	290	5,145
Corinne Dibnah	75	73	67	75	290	5,145
Lora Fairclough	73	71	71	76	291	3,240
Shani Waugh	71	77	70	74	292	2,544
Franca Fehlauer	73	72	73	75	293	2,100
Janice Arnold	74	74	77	69	294	1,800
Diane Barnard	76	75	74	70	295	1,287
Sofia Gronberg Whitmore	75	70	71	79	295	1,287
Loraine Lambert	75	76	73	71	295	1,287
Myra McKinlay	75	73	72	75	295	1,287
Susan Moon	71	73	76	76	296	957
Joanne Furby	77	74	73	72	296	957
Liz Weima	74	76	72	74	296	957
Joanne Morley	73	75	70	78	296	957
Debbie Dowling	76	73	72	76	297	852
Karine Espinasse	75	73	74	75	297	852
Alison Nicholas	71	74	80	72	297	852
Gillian Stewart	75	71	72	80	298	772.50
Rachel Hetherington	77	75	73	73	298	772.50
Julie Forbes	77	73	71	77	298	772.50
Sara Robinson	76	79	72	71	298	772.50
Penny Grice-Whittaker	75	74	76	74	299	699
Xonia Wunsch-Ruiz	76	72	72	79	299	699
Helen Wadsworth	75	75	74	75	299	699
Valerie Michaud	76	78	72	73	299	699
Debbie Petrizzi	71	78	74	77	300	636
Jennifer Allmark	78	71	75	76	300	636
Laura Navarro	76	72	74	78	300	636
Rica Comstock	77	75	74	75	301	573
Sally Prosser	74	69	80	78	301	573
Susan Hodge	75	73	73	78	301	573
Lara Tadiotto	74	73	82	72	301	573

Sens Dutch Open

Rijk van Nijmegen, Groesbeek, Netherlands
Par 36-36—72; 5,856 yards

September 9-11
purse, £55,000

	SCORES			TOTAL	MONEY
Liz Weima	74	68	72	214	£8,250
Sofia Gronberg Whitmore	72	74	70	216	5,580
Janice Arnold	74	72	72	218	2,768.75
Rachel Hetherington	73	75	70	218	2,768.75
Joanne Morley	73	74	71	218	2,768.75
Catriona Matthew	74	71	73	218	2,768.75
Catrin Nilsmark	76	71	72	219	1,512.50
Loraine Lambert	73	72	74	219	1,512.50
Susan Elliott	76	73	71	220	1,165
Laura Navarro	76	72	72	220	1,165
Corinne Dibnah	71	76	74	221	979
Dale Reid	78	72	71	221	979
Maureen Madill	76	71	75	222	854.33
Gillian Stewart	74	75	73	222	854.33
Isabella Maconi	72	75	75	222	854.33
Karine Espinasse	74	76	73	223	770
Regine Lautens	72	79	72	223	770
Sally Prosser	73	77	73	223	770
Valerie Michaud	73	78	72	223	770
Marjan de Boer	76	75	73	224	689.50
Nicola Buxton	78	76	70	224	689.50
Maria Bertilskold	73	74	77	224	689.50
Sandrine Mendiburu	73	75	76	224	689.50
Sarah Nicklin	72	78	75	225	615.40
Karina Orum	80	72	73	225	615.40
Wendy Doolan	73	75	77	225	615.40
Patricia Meunier	75	76	74	225	615.40
Petra Rigby	76	73	76	225	615.40
Debbie Dowling	77	71	78	226	525.83
Catherine Panton-Lewis	74	78	74	226	525.83
Jill Kinloch	74	74	78	226	525.83
Shani Waugh	79	75	72	226	525.83
Sarah Gautrey	75	76	75	226	525.83
Julie Forbes	77	76	73	226	525.83

BMW Italian Open

Lignano Golf Club, Lignano Sabbiadoro, Italy
Par 36-36—72; 6,112 yards

September 22-25
purse, £70,000

	SCORES				TOTAL	MONEY
Corinne Dibnah	73	67	71	66	277	£10,500
Dale Reid	73	68	70	66	277	7,105
(Dibnah defeated Reid on second extra hole.)						
Susan Moon	70	69	72	67	278	4,900
Lora Fairclough	67	71	71	70	279	3,780
Sarah Nicklin	72	69	69	70	280	2,968
Kristal Parker	74	69	70	68	281	2,450
Marie Laure de Lorenzi	70	71	72	69	282	1,925
Allison Shapcott	72	72	69	69	282	1,925
Debbie Petrizzi	75	71	69	68	283	1,568
Janice Arnold	70	72	76	66	284	1,220.80

		SCORES			TOTAL	MONEY
Karina Orum	77	68	71	68	284	1,220.80
Catriona Matthew	73	73	68	70	284	1,220.80
Pernilla Sterner	71	73	68	72	284	1,220.80
Evelyn Orley	74	69	72	69	284	1,220.80
Sofia Gronberg Whitmore	76	73	69	67	285	1,022
Gillian Stewart	74	73	70	68	285	1,022
Helen Hopkins	75	71	72	67	285	1,022
Rachel Hetherington	74	70	73	69	286	952
Joanne Morley	74	69	72	71	286	952
Debbie Dowling	73	69	76	69	287	868
Maureen Madill	69	71	73	74	287	868
Susan Hodge	70	72	73	72	287	868
Estefania Knuth	73	70	74	70	287	868
Federica Dassu	78	70	70	70	288	794.50
Kimberly Cayce	71	72	72	73	288	794.50
Tina Yarwood	67	76	74	72	289	742
Patti Rizzo	75	70	71	73	289	742
Cindy Figg-Currier	73	73	75	68	289	742
Karine Espinasse	76	71	71	72	290	637
Xonia Wunsch-Ruiz	73	71	71	75	290	637
Wendy Dicks	75	74	71	70	290	637
Wendy Doolan	75	75	70	70	290	637
Natascha Fink	74	70	74	72	290	637
Maria Bertilskold	75	69	73	73	290	637
Valerie Michaud	71	74	74	71	290	637

La Manga Club Spanish Open

Hyatt La Manga Golf Resort, La Manga, Spain　　　　　September 29-October 2
Par 36-36—72; 6,164 yards　　　　　　　　　　　　　　　purse, £60,000

		SCORES			TOTAL	MONEY
Marie Laure de Lorenzi	71	72	68	71	282	£9,000
Sofia Gronberg Whitmore	68	69	73	72	282	6,090
(De Lorenzi defeated Gronberg Whitmore on second extra hole.)						
Karina Orum	70	72	70	72	284	4,200
Trish Johnson	72	70	73	70	285	3,240
Debbie Dowling	72	73	71	70	286	2,322
Loraine Lambert	72	76	69	69	286	2,322
Dale Reid	73	70	73	71	287	1,650
Lara Tadiotto	72	70	73	72	287	1,650
Amaia Arruti	73	72	71	72	288	1,216
Lora Fairclough	77	72	69	70	288	1,216
Lisa Hackney	73	73	71	71	288	1,216
Kristal Parker	72	74	69	74	289	976
Patricia Meunier	70	75	71	73	289	976
Laura Navarro	78	72	69	70	289	976
Nicola Moult	75	72	71	72	290	876
Petra Rigby	71	77	71	71	290	876
Sandrine Mendiburu	69	74	72	75	290	876
Janice Arnold	75	69	74	73	291	804
Julie Forbes	77	73	66	75	291	804
Catriona Matthew	71	77	74	69	291	804
Penny Grice-Whittaker	75	74	73	70	292	744
Catherine Panton-Lewis	75	72	74	71	292	744
Sally Prosser	73	73	74	72	292	744
Debbie Petrizzi	75	75	72	71	293	672

	SCORES				TOTAL	MONEY
Catrin Nilsmark	70	80	69	74	293	672
Mette Hageman	72	72	75	74	293	672
Isabella Maconi	70	76	76	71	293	672
Anna Radford	76	71	74	72	293	672
Diane Barnard	74	73	74	73	294	591
Corinne Dibnah	77	74	70	73	294	591
Alison Nicholas	75	74	73	72	294	591
Susan Hodge	71	77	72	74	294	591

Var Open de France Feminin

Golf de Saint Endreol, La Motte, France
Par 36-36—72; 5,454 yards

October 13-15
purse, £55,000

	SCORES			TOTAL	MONEY
Julie Forbes	73	70	70	213	£8,250
Dale Reid	72	69	72	213	4,715
Suzanne Strudwick	73	66	74	213	4,715
(Forbes defeated Reid and Strudwick on second extra hole.)					
Marie Laure de Lorenzi	69	74	72	215	2,970
Valerie Michaud	71	72	74	217	2,330
Maureen Madill	70	75	73	218	1,925
Gillian Stewart	71	73	75	219	1,512.50
Pernilla Sterner	73	78	68	219	1,512.50
Kitrina Douglas	71	75	74	220	1,004.33
Alison Nicholas	73	74	73	220	1,004.33
Sally Prosser	71	76	73	220	1,004.33
Jennifer Allmark	72	71	77	220	1,004.33
Joanne Morley	72	73	75	220	1,004.33
Sandrine Mendiburu	75	71	74	220	1,004.33
Tina Yarwood	72	73	76	221	803
Karina Orum	73	71	77	221	803
*Maitena Alsuguren	73	77	71	221	
Alison Brighouse	74	72	75	221	803
Xonia Wunsch-Ruiz	73	74	75	222	737
Emma-Jane Smith	72	76	74	222	737
Sarah Bennett	71	78	73	222	737
Federica Dassu	74	76	73	223	640
Debbie Dowling	73	81	69	223	640
Karine Espinasse	75	79	69	223	640
Laurette Maritz-Atkins	74	74	75	223	640
Axelle Semo	72	74	77	223	640
Asa Gottmo	72	78	73	223	640
Laura Navarro	71	74	78	223	640
Veronique Palli	76	74	73	223	640
Debbie Petrizzi	74	77	73	224	542.50
Lara Tadiotto	76	75	73	224	542.50
Patricia Meunier	74	75	75	224	542.50
Anna Radford	73	73	78	224	542.50

Princess Lalla Meriem Cup

Royal Golf Dar-es-Salam, Blue Course, Rabat, Morocco
Par 36-37—73; 6,150 yards

November 3-5
purse, FF250,000

	SCORES			TOTAL	MONEY
Gillian Stewart	69	74	67	210	FF50,000
Karina Orum	71	71	75	217	35,000
Joanne Morley	73	75	70	218	25,500
Carin Hjalmarsson	77	73	70	220	20,000
Susan Hodge	75	76	72	223	15,000
Karine Espinasse	71	78	75	224	12,000
Shani Waugh	75	77	73	225	11,250
Diane Barnard	76	74	75	225	11,250
E. Berthet	75	71	80	226	10,000
Helen Wadsworth	76	78	72	226	10,000
Allison Shapcott	76	77	74	227	10,000
Xonia Wunsch-Ruiz	77	77	73	227	10,000
Patricia Meunier	79	78	71	228	10,000
Regine Lautens	74	83	73	230	10,000
Veronique Palli	79	79	78	236	10,000

Women's Australasian Tours

Thailand Open

Thana City Golf & Country Club, Bangkok, Thailand
Par 36-36—72; 6,905 yards

January 13-15
purse, $89,086

	SCORES			TOTAL	MONEY
Laura Davies	70	70	66	206	$13,500
Mardi Lunn	72	71	70	213	9,000
Young Mi Lee	74	71	70	215	6,750
Alison Munt	74	73	70	217	5,400
Carin Hjalmarsson	70	72	76	218	3,780
Amy Childers-Dubois	76	73	70	219	2,790
Diane Barnard	75	74	70	219	2,790
Mariko Watanabe	74	75	70	219	2,790
Debbi Miho Koyama	74	74	72	220	2,115
Fukumi Tani	74	75	71	220	2,115
Shani Waugh	73	71	77	221	1,615
Jennifer Steiner	74	73	74	221	1,615
Kim Lasken	70	73	78	221	1,615
Tomoe Fumihira	73	74	74	221	1,615
Sarinee Kasemsual	72	73	77	222	1,435
Sally Prosser	71	76	75	222	1,435
Lisa Hackney	77	74	71	222	1,435

	SCORES			TOTAL	MONEY
Wendy Doolan	71	77	74	222	1,435
Mary Grace Estuesta	73	73	77	223	1,255
Regine Lautens	76	75	72	223	1,255
Karen Davies	75	72	76	223	1,255
Fusako Nagata	77	74	72	223	1,255
Lora Fairclough	72	74	78	224	1,120
Helen Wadsworth	75	75	74	224	1,120
Kay Cornelius	73	78	74	225	1,008
Caroline Hall	74	77	74	225	1,008
Li Wen Lin	70	81	74	225	1,008
Tracy Hanson	73	78	75	226	819
Karen Weiss	74	78	74	226	819
Susan Shapcott	71	79	76	226	819
Sarah Nicklin	77	75	74	226	819
Debbie Dowling	75	74	77	226	819
Patricia Meunier	71	76	79	226	819

Malaysian JAL Open

Bukit Jambul Country Club, Penang, Malaysia
Par 36-36—72; 5,977 yards

January 20-22
purse, $85,312

	SCORES			TOTAL	MONEY
Jae Sook Won	75	75	70	220	$12,750
Tracy Hanson	75	73	74	222	8,500
Karen Weiss	77	74	74	225	5,737
Young Mi Lee	77	76	72	225	5,737
Mitsuyo Hirata	77	73	76	226	3,570
Kim Lasken	77	74	76	227	2,635
Li Wen Lin	76	75	76	227	2,635
Lora Fairclough	81	74	72	227	2,635
Sally Prosser	76	75	77	228	1,861
Nancy Kessler	76	78	74	228	1,861
Shani Waugh	81	74	73	228	1,861
Helen Wadsworth	73	77	79	229	1,525
Lisa Hackney	79	74	76	229	1,525
Mardi Lunn	74	80	76	230	1,398
Deborah Petrizzi	75	79	76	230	1,398
Junko Kitajima	78	76	76	230	1,398
Susan Shapcott	82	75	73	230	1,398
Liz Earloy	78	75	78	231	1,206
Carin Hjalmarsson	77	77	77	231	1,206
Mariko Watanabe	73	82	76	231	1,206
Alison Munt	78	79	74	231	1,206
Isabella Maconi	79	79	73	231	1,206
Diane Barnard	77	77	78	232	1,058
Karen Davies	82	72	78	232	1,058
Karine Espinasse	77	78	78	233	899
Debbi Miho Koyama	82	84	77	233	899
Laree Pearl Sugg	76	81	76	233	899
Mary Grace Estuesta	81	77	75	233	899
Jennifer Steiner	77	81	75	233	899
Feng Tseng Hsiu	79	73	82	234	724
Janet Soulsby	77	78	79	234	724
Juline Forbes	81	79	74	234	724
Tomomi Masuda	78	82	74	234	724
Mayumi Ishii	83	78	73	234	724

Indonesian Open

Bali Handara Kosaido Country Club, Bali, Indonesia
Par 36-36—72; 6,153 yards

January 27-29
purse, $79,200

	SCORES			TOTAL	MONEY
Tracy Hanson	71	70	71	212	$12,000
Jae Sook Won	75	69	68	212	7,000
Sally Prosser	73	66	73	212	7,000
(Hanson defeated Won and Prosser on second extra hole.)					
Janet Soulsby	73	70	70	213	4,080
Young Mi Lee	71	71	71	213	4,080
Mardi Lunn	71	72	71	214	2,720
Lora Fairclough	75	69	71	215	2,480
Kim Lasken	71	72	73	216	2,120
Helen Wadsworth	71	71	74	216	2,120
Fukumi Tani	76	73	68	217	1,532
Diane Barnard	71	75	71	217	1,532
Debbie Dowling	72	73	72	217	1,532
Carin Hjalmarsson	70	72	75	217	1,532
Karen Weiss	75	71	72	218	1,296
Mette Hageman	74	72	72	218	1,296
Alison Munt	71	74	73	218	1,296
Lisa Hackney	75	70	73	218	1,296
Mary Grace Estuesta	72	72	74	218	1,296
Isabella Maconi	73	75	71	219	1,116
Susan Shapcott	74	73	72	219	1,116
Karen Davies	73	73	73	219	1,116
Mitsuyo Hirata	73	71	75	219	1,116
Wendy Dicks	76	74	70	220	956
Li Wen Lin	76	73	71	220	956
Debbi Miho Koyama	70	77	73	220	956
Regine Lautens	72	73	75	220	956
Elizabeth Bowman	70	79	72	221	732
Xonia Wunsch	72	76	73	221	732
Kiyoe Yamazaki	73	74	74	221	732
Maria Bertilskold	74	73	74	221	732
Deborah Petrizzi	74	73	74	221	732
Jean Bartholomew	74	73	74	221	732
Wendy Doolan	75	71	75	221	732
Mariko Watanabe	80	65	76	221	732

Republic of China-Taiwan Open

Chang Gung Golf Club, Taipei, Taiwan
Par 36-36—72; 6,215 yards

February 3-5
purse, $110,388

	SCORES			TOTAL	MONEY
Karen Weiss	74	71	68	213	$16,500
Carin Hjalmarsson	78	72	64	214	11,000
Tsai Li Hsiang	77	69	69	215	8,250
Lora Fairclough	78	69	70	217	6,600
Helen Wadsworth	79	67	72	218	4,600
Li Wen Lin	72	73	74	219	3,550
Young Mi Lee	78	71	70	219	3,550
Lisa Hackney	75	71	74	220	2,733
Janet Soulsby	75	73	72	220	2,733
Wu Ming Yueh	79	72	69	220	2,733

	SCORES			TOTAL	MONEY
Fusako Nagata	77	69	76	222	1,950
Susan Shapcott	78	71	73	222	1,950
Karen Davies	79	72	71	222	1,950
Huang Yueh Chin	78	73	71	222	1,950
Tracy Hanson	78	71	74	223	1,675
Sarah Nicklin	78	71	74	223	1,675
Chen Li Ying	76	74	73	223	1,675
Cheng Mei Chi	81	69	73	223	1,675
Mary Grace Estuesta	77	73	73	223	1,675
Debbie Dowling	78	74	71	223	1,675
Wendy Doolan	80	70	74	224	1,433
Nancy Kessler	80	71	73	224	1,433
Fukumi Tani	79	74	71	224	1,433
Huang Bie Shyun	79	73	73	225	1,275
Jean Bartholomew	78	76	71	225	1,275
Shani Waugh	76	75	75	226	1,125
Sally Prosser	79	73	74	226	1,125
Regine Lautens	77	78	71	226	1,125
Debbi Miho Koyama	81	74	71	226	1,125
Mariko Watanabe	78	72	77	227	928
Chang Mei Chu	76	76	75	227	928
Xonia Wunsch	77	76	74	227	928
Tomoe Fumihira	83	70	74	227	928
Lisa Grimes	78	77	72	227	928

Holden Australian Open

Royal Adelaide Golf Club, Adelaide, South Australia
Par 38-36—74; 6,290 yards

December 8-11
purse, A$200,000

	SCORES				TOTAL	MONEY
Annika Sorenstam	68	72	72	74	286	A$30,000
Rachel Hetherington	73	72	74	72	291	20,000
Jane Crafter	76	74	73	69	292	11,000
Kris Tschetter	72	71	75	74	292	11,000
Alicia Dibos	73	73	75	73	294	8,000
Barb Bunkowsky	74	73	74	74	295	7,600
Jennifer Sevil	73	74	71	78	296	6,800
Kathryn Marshall	80	69	71	77	297	6,000
Lori Garbacz	78	73	75	72	298	4,400
Alison Nicholas	73	77	76	72	298	4,400
Amy Fruhwirth	79	74	73	72	298	4,400
Tracy Hanson	80	73	70	75	298	4,400
*Kate Macintosh	68	76	79	75	298	
Valerie Michaud	79	77	72	71	299	2,986.66
Jennifer Wyatt	73	74	79	73	299	2,986.66
Karina Orum	74	73	79	73	299	2,986.66
Evelyn Orley	79	72	73	76	300	2,580
Dale Reid	75	78	70	77	300	2,580
*Tanya Holl	75	74	73	78	300	
*Allison Wheelhouse	75	79	74	73	301	
Lynette Brooky	80	74	72	75	301	2,400
Sherrin Smyers	77	73	76	76	302	2,200
Marianne Morris	78	74	74	76	302	2,200
Corinne Dibnah	76	73	76	77	302	2,200
Jennifer Allmark	76	78	76	73	303	1,960
*Simone Williams	74	79	75	75	303	

	SCORES				TOTAL	MONEY
Mardi Lunn	75	73	77	78	303	1,960
Joanne Mills	80	73	70	80	303	1,960
Christine Greatrex	81	74	79	70	304	1,640
Shani Waugh	75	81	75	73	304	1,640
*Anne-Marie Knight	74	77	76	77	304	
Karrie Webb	81	71	78	74	304	1,640
Lynn Connelly	75	76	76	77	304	1,640
Caroline Hall	75	75	76	78	304	1,640

Alpine Australian Ladies Masters

Royal Pines Resort, Queensland, Australia

Par 36-37—73; 6,153 yards

December 15-18

purse, A$250,000

	SCORES				TOTAL	MONEY
Laura Davies	64	68	73	67	272	A$37,500
Karrie Webb	67	70	70	69	276	25,000
Jane Crafter	69	66	74	72	281	15,000
Annika Sorenstam	69	68	73	72	282	12,500
Kathryn Marshall	69	69	76	69	283	9,750
Marianne Morris	69	70	72	72	283	9,750
Corinne Dibnah	67	70	74	73	284	8,000
Patricia Meunier	69	69	73	73	284	8,000
Kris Tschetter	71	68	74	72	285	6,750
Tracy Hanson	69	69	74	74	286	5,750
Nancy Harvey	72	74	74	67	287	4,300
Lori Garbacz	69	70	76	72	287	4,300
Alison Nicholas	68	72	75	72	287	4,300
Franca Fehlauer	70	76	68	73	287	4,300
Michelle Estill	76	71	71	70	288	3,316.66
Alison Munt	71	70	75	72	288	3,316.66
Muffin Spencer-Devlin	73	68	73	74	288	3,316.66
Janet Soulsby	73	70	74	72	289	3,000
Wendy Doolan	73	71	77	69	290	2,850
Shani Waugh	72	72	77	70	291	2,550
Evelyn Orley	72	68	77	74	291	2,550
Alicia Dibos	73	70	73	75	291	2,550
Joanne Mills	70	72	72	77	291	2,550
Kristal Parker-Gregory	70	69	72	80	291	2,550
Valerie Michaud	72	72	74	74	292	2,250
Malin Burstrom	73	75	74	71	293	1,908.33
Dale Reid	67	75	78	73	293	1,908.33
Caroline Hall	72	74	73	74	293	1,908.33
Florence Descampe	72	75	72	74	293	1,908.33
Kim Cathrein	70	71	77	75	293	1,908.33
Lynn Connelly	72	68	75	78	293	1,908.33

Japan LPGA Tour

Daikin Orchid

Ryukyu Golf Club, Okinawa
Par 36-36—72; 6,252 yards

March 4-6
purse, ¥60,000,000

	SCORES			TOTAL	MONEY
Akiko Fukushima	71	70	72	213	¥10,800,000
Ayako Okamoto	70	73	74	217	4,800,000
Hiromi Takamura	69	74	74	217	4,800,000
Kaori Higo	72	76	70	218	1,800,000
Yoko Morioka	75	72	71	218	1,800,000
Ae Sook Kim	74	72	72	218	1,800,000
Junko Yasui	73	72	73	218	1,800,000
Akemi Yamaoka	72	73	73	218	1,800,000
Kayoko Ikoma	73	69	76	218	1,800,000
Yuri Kawanami	67	75	76	218	1,800,000
Wu Ming Yueh	76	69	74	219	1,320,000
Fuki Kido	71	72	76	219	1,320,000
Young Mi Lee	73	70	76	219	1,320,000
Mayumi Murai	77	71	72	220	972,000
Rie Fujiwara	75	72	73	220	972,000
Mariko Ohtani	71	75	74	220	972,000
Toshimi Kimura	77	69	74	220	972,000
Yuko Moriguchi	76	73	72	221	607,000
Miki Oda	77	72	72	221	607,000
Nayoko Yoshikawa	74	74	73	221	607,000
Miyuki Shimabukuro	75	73	73	221	607,000
Huang Yueh Chin	69	75	77	221	607,000
Aiko Hashimoto	71	73	77	221	607,000
Cheng Mei Chi	75	73	74	222	555,000
Li Wen Lin	72	75	75	222	555,000
Atsuko Hikage	75	73	75	223	525,000
Rie Mitsuhashi	72	76	75	223	525,000
Marnie McGuire	74	74	75	223	525,000
Yukiyo Haga	75	73	75	223	525,000
Aki Nakano	75	72	76	223	525,000
Aki Takamura	73	74	76	223	525,000
Jeong Soo Kim	72	74	77	223	525,000

Chiyoda Ladies

Zaronbai Country Club, Miyazaki
Par 36-36—72; 6,211 yards
(Second round cancelled — heavy rains.)

March 11-13
purse, ¥50,000,000

	SCORES		TOTAL	MONEY
Wu Ming Yueh	68	71	139	¥6,750,000
Mayumi Murai	71	70	141	3,375,000
Keiko Suzuki	73	69	142	1,515,000
Jae Sook Won	71	71	142	1,515,000
Yuka Irie	70	72	142	1,515,000

	SCORES			TOTAL	MONEY
Hiromi Takamura	70	72		142	1,515,000
Sadae Kumagai	70	72		142	1,515,000
Yuko Saitoh	72	71		143	1,012,500
Ikuyo Shiotani	72	72		144	931,250
Kikuko Shibata	72	72		144	931,250
Yuko Nakamura	71	73		144	931,250
Mayumi Hirase	73	72		145	668,125
Shin Sora	75	70		145	668,125
Yuko Moriguchi	72	73		145	668,125
Toshimi Kimura	77	68		145	668,125
Akemi Yamaoka	72	73		145	668,125
Akiko Fukushima	71	74		145	668,125
Young Mi Lee	73	73		146	396,250
Huang Yueh Chin	72	74		146	396,250
Fukumi Tani	71	75		146	396,250
Aiko Hashimoto	74	73		147	346,875
Hiromi Hirakata	74	73		147	346,875
Suzuko Maeda	73	74		147	346,875
Kumiko Hiyoshi	71	76		147	346,875
Nayoko Yoshikawa	71	76		147	346,875
Jeong Soo Kim	69	78		147	346,875
Kaori Harada	73	75		148	322,500
Mariko Watanabe	75	73		148	322,500
Mariko Ohtani	73	75		148	322,500
Michiko Hattori	76	72		148	322,500
Ae Sook Kim	73	75		148	322,500
Huang Bie Shyun	72	76		148	322,500

Saishunkan Ladies

Takayubaru Country Club, Kumamoto
Par 36-36—72; 6,329 yards

March 18-20
purse, ¥60,000,000

	SCORES			TOTAL	MONEY
Ikuyo Shiotani	71	72	71	214	¥10,800,000
Kaori Harada	68	71	76	215	5,400,000
Akiko Fukushima	68	69	79	216	4,200,000
Junko Yasui	71	74	73	218	2,250,000
Yuka Irie	71	71	76	218	2,250,000
Fuki Kido	71	74	74	219	1,710,000
Yuko Moriguchi	74	71	74	219	1,710,000
Ae Sook Kim	72	73	75	220	1,590,000
Yuko Nakamura	75	69	76	220	1,590,000
Michiko Hattori	75	75	71	221	1,455,000
Ray Bell	75	71	75	221	1,455,000
Ok Hee Ku	73	77	72	222	1,123,200
Hiroko Inoue	75	73	74	222	1,123,200
Huang Yueh Chin	71	75	76	222	1,123,200
Akemi Yamaoka	73	72	77	222	1,123,200
Aiko Hashimoto	69	74	79	222	1,123,200
Aki Takamura	76	74	73	223	741,000
Kikuko Shibata	75	72	76	223	741,000
Norimi Terazawa	77	74	73	224	565,500
Mayumi Hirase	77	74	73	224	565,500
Toshimi Kimura	74	79	71	224	565,500
Huang Bie Shyun	70	74	80	224	565,500
Yukie Ueki	76	74	75	225	519,000

	SCORES			TOTAL	MONEY
Hiromi Takamura	72	77	76	225	519,000
Miyuki Shimabukuro	72	77	76	225	519,000
Hisako Higuchi	74	77	74	225	519,000
Chikayo Yamazaki	75	73	77	225	519,000
Atsuko Hikage	77	72	76	225	519,000
Fumiko Muraguchi	76	76	73	225	519,000
Natsuko Noro	72	74	79	225	519,000

Kibun Classic

Arashiyama Country Club, Saitama
Par 37-37—74; 6,484 yards

April 1-3
purse, ¥50,000,000

	SCORES			TOTAL	MONEY
Woo Soon Ko	73	74	74	221	¥9,000,000
Norimi Terazawa	76	72	74	222	4,500,000
Nayoko Yoshikawa	73	74	76	223	3,600,000
Chikayo Yamazaki	78	73	73	224	1,733,000
Yukie Ueki	73	74	77	224	1,733,000
Chieko Nishida	71	75	78	224	1,733,000
Yuko Saitoh	75	76	74	225	1,295,000
Mitsuyo Hirata	75	75	75	225	1,295,000
Hisako Higuchi	75	74	76	225	1,295,000
Akiko Fukushima	73	75	77	225	1,295,000
Toshimi Kimura	74	73	78	225	1,295,000
Junko Kitajima	79	73	74	226	1,062,000
Kumiko Hiyoshi	75	74	77	226	1,062,000
Kaori Higo	74	76	77	227	871,000
Fumiko Muraguchi	76	72	79	227	871,000
Ae Sook Kim	75	72	80	227	871,000
Michiko Hattori	75	76	77	228	592,000
Fuki Kido	73	77	78	228	592,000
Michiko Okada	75	75	78	228	592,000
Junko Yasui	72	75	81	228	592,000
Megumi Matsuo	75	76	78	229	485,000
Miyuki Shimabukuro	73	77	79	229	485,000
Ikuyo Shiotani	71	74	84	229	485,000
Nobuko Kizawa	75	77	78	230	456,000
Kayo Mochizuki	76	76	78	230	456,000
Huang Yueh Chin	73	77	80	230	456,000
Aki Takamura	72	78	80	230	456,000
Marnie McGuire	71	79	80	230	456,000
Suzuko Maeda	77	72	81	230	456,000
Elizabeth Wilson	74	75	81	230	456,000
Yuko Moriguchi	73	75	82	230	456,000

Mitsukoshi Cup

Segovia Golf Club, Ibaragi
Par 36-36—72; 6,091 yards

April 7-10
purse, ¥60,000,000

	SCORES				TOTAL	MONEY
Yuko Moriguchi	76	72	69	70	287	¥10,000,000
Akiko Fukushima	69	76	73	69	287	5,400,000
(Moriguchi defeated Fukushima on fourth extra hole.)						

	SCORES				TOTAL	MONEY
Ikuyo Shiotani	69	76	73	73	291	4,200,000
Shin Sora	78	74	73	68	293	2,060,000
Fuki Kido	75	72	75	71	293	2,060,000
Jae Sook Won	75	73	71	74	293	2,060,000
Ray Bell	77	74	71	72	294	1,620,000
Fukumi Tani	67	77	76	74	294	1,620,000
Suzuko Maeda	76	76	68	74	294	1,620,000
Yukie Ueki	79	72	72	72	295	1,500,000
Aiko Hashimoto	75	78	71	72	296	1,227,600
Nayoko Yoshikawa	75	76	74	71	296	1,227,600
Chieko Nishida	74	75	74	73	296	1,227,600
Ayako Okamoto	73	77	73	73	296	1,227,600
Young Mi Lee	71	76	74	75	296	1,227,600
Fumiko Muraguchi	74	75	77	71	297	781,500
Fusako Nagata	71	76	74	76	297	781,500
Aki Takamura	73	76	72	76	297	781,500
Ritsu Imahori	72	72	75	78	297	781,500
Miyuki Shimabukuro	78	73	75	72	298	579,000
Ae Sook Kim	74	74	77	73	298	579,000
Natsuko Noro	72	74	77	75	298	579,000
Toshimi Kimura	72	80	71	75	298	579,000
Michiko Hattori	70	77	74	78	299	564,000
Tamayo Ueda	77	74	75	74	300	549,000
Kumiko Hiyoshi	77	74	77	72	300	549,000
Man Soo Kim	73	79	77	71	300	549,000
Kaori Higo	74	78	73	75	300	549,000
Marnie McGuire	76	73	76	76	301	503,142
Mariko Ohtani	75	75	76	75	301	503,142
Mayumi Murai	76	77	74	74	301	503,142
Hiromi Takamura	75	76	76	74	301	503,142
Jeong Soo Kim	75	76	78	72	301	503,142
Nobuko Kizawa	75	75	73	78	301	503,142
Junko Yasui	73	74	76	78	301	503,142

Kenshoen Ladies

Dogo Golf Club, Ehime
Par 36-36—72; 6,211 yards

April 15-17
purse, ¥50,000,000

	SCORES			TOTAL	MONEY
Ikuyo Shiotani	71	79	79	209	¥9,000,000
Aki Nakano	71	70	70	211	4,500,000
Jae Sook Won	70	74	68	212	2,875,000
Toshimi Kimura	72	72	68	212	2,875,000
Man Soo Kim	69	73	71	213	1,600,000
Akiko Fukushima	71	73	70	214	1,425,000
Norimi Terazawa	69	70	75	214	1,425,000
Ok Hee Ku	74	79	72	215	1,325,000
Aki Takamura	70	73	74	215	1,325,000
Aiko Hashimoto	71	73	72	216	1,175,000
Kikuko Shibata	68	75	73	216	1,175,000
Sadae Kumagai	72	70	74	216	1,175,000
Huang Bie Shyun	73	73	71	217	985,000
Mariko Ohtani	74	71	72	217	985,000
Minako Wada	72	75	71	218	614,000
Kumiko Hiyoshi	75	73	70	218	614,000
Elizabeth Wilson	75	71	72	218	614,000

	SCORES			TOTAL	MONEY
Akane Ohshiro	75	71	72	218	614,000
Mariko Watanabe	72	72	74	218	614,000
Yuko Saitoh	74	70	74	218	614,000
Mayumi Murai	74	70	74	218	614,000
Hisako Higuchi	76	71	72	219	460,000
Fumiko Muraguchi	73	73	73	219	460,000
Fuki Kido	75	71	73	219	460,000
Hiromi Hirakata	73	74	73	220	430,625
Mitsuyo Hirata	71	75	74	220	430,625
Suzuko Maeda	75	72	73	220	430,625
Miyuki Shimabukuro	71	77	72	220	430,625
Akemi Yamaoka	74	72	74	220	430,625
Kasumi Adachi	76	73	71	220	430,625
Ayako Okamoto	78	72	70	220	430,625
Junko Yasui	75	75	70	220	430,625

Nasu Ogawa

Nasu Ogawa Golf Club, Tochigi
Par 36-36—72; 6,091 yards

April 22-24
purse, ¥50,000,000

	SCORES			TOTAL	MONEY
Marnie McGuire	70	69	71	210	¥9,000,000
Ikuyo Shiotani	71	69	71	211	4,500,000
Young Mi Lee	72	75	67	214	2,416,666
Miyuki Shimabukuro	72	72	70	214	2,416,666
Yuko Moriguchi	73	69	72	214	2,416,666
Norimi Terazawa	72	73	70	215	1,400,000
Akane Ohshiro	70	74	71	215	1,400,000
Kumiko Hiyoshi	74	69	72	215	1,400,000
Toshimi Kimura	69	76	71	216	1,241,666
Nayoko Yoshikawa	75	70	71	216	1,241,666
Ae Sook Kim	70	73	73	216	1,241,666
Shin Sora	72	74	71	217	1,062,500
Kikuko Shibata	70	74	73	217	1,062,500
Aki Takamura	71	75	72	218	758,000
Takako Matsuo	71	76	71	218	758,000
Chieko Nishida	73	72	73	218	758,000
Sheree Higgens	71	73	74	218	758,000
Ray Bell	72	71	75	218	758,000
Huang Yueh Chin	71	75	73	219	485,000
Rie Mitsuhashi	72	72	75	219	485,000
Maumi Ishii	70	76	74	220	442,500
Mariko Ohtani	73	73	74	220	442,500
Chikako Matsuzawa	75	71	74	220	442,500
Fuki Kido	76	71	73	220	442,500
Jae Sook Won	71	73	76	220	442,500
Akemi Yamaoka	73	71	76	220	442,500
Chihiro Nakajima	74	70	76	220	442,500
Mayumi Hirase	69	71	80	220	442,500
Junko Yasui	73	73	75	221	399,166
Aiko Hashimoto	73	73	75	221	399,166
Fusako Nagata	72	73	76	221	399,166
Nobuko Kizawa	75	74	72	221	399,166
Kaori Higo	75	74	72	221	399,166
Huang Bie Shyun	74	75	72	221	399,166

Satake Japan Classic

Hiroshima Country Club, Hiroshima
Par 36-36—72; 6,195 yards

April 29-May 1
purse, ¥50,000,000

	SCORES			TOTAL	MONEY
Chieko Nishida	72	74	72	218	¥9,000,000
Akiko Fukushima	72	75	72	219	3,416,666
Laura Davies	72	71	76	219	3,416,666
Miyuki Shimabukuro	70	75	74	219	3,416,666
Kumiko Hiyoshi	75	75	71	221	1,450,000
Jae Sook Won	73	75	73	221	1,450,000
Aki Takamura	76	72	73	221	1,450,000
Mayumi Murai	70	80	72	222	1,350,000
Aki Nakano	75	79	69	223	1,241,666
Wu Ming Yueh	72	76	75	223	1,241,666
Fuki Kido	74	72	77	223	1,241,666
Toshimi Kimura	73	76	75	224	1,100,000
Ok Hee Ku	76	75	74	225	985,000
Hiromi Hirakata	78	77	70	225	985,000
Mariko Ohtani	77	76	73	226	758,333
Yuri Kawanami	77	75	74	226	758,333
Aiko Hashimoto	75	77	74	226	758,333
Suzuko Maeda	77	76	74	227	493,571
Chihiro Nakajima	73	80	74	227	493,571
Chikako Matsuzawa	74	79	74	227	493,571
Mitsuyo Hirata	76	75	76	227	493,571
Hisako Higuchi	68	83	76	227	493,571
Miki Oda	75	76	76	227	493,571
Marnie McGuire	77	74	76	227	493,571
Keiko Suzuki	80	73	75	228	452,500
Aiko Takasu	76	79	73	228	452,500
Hiromi Takamura	76	77	76	229	430,000
Junko Yasui	75	78	76	229	430,000
Yuko Saitoh	73	81	75	229	430,000
Liselotte Neumann	78	74	77	229	430,000
Chikayo Yamazaki	79	72	78	229	430,000
Tokiko Hashimura	77	74	78	229	430,000

Gunze World Cup

Tokyo Yomiuri Country Club, Inagi-shi
Par 36-36—72; 6,387 yards

May-5-8
purse, ¥60,000,000

	SCORES				TOTAL	MONEY
Jae Sook Won	75	68	73	71	287	¥10,800,000
Kumiko Hiyoshi	78	69	72	71	290	4,800,000
Yuko Moriguchi	76	72	71	71	290	4,800,000
Young Mi Lee	74	74	75	68	291	2,250,000
Mitsuyo Hirata	78	69	73	71	291	2,250,000
Mayumi Hirase	77	71	74	70	292	1,710,000
Woo Soon Ko	73	72	75	72	292	1,710,000
Fuki Kido	75	73	74	71	293	1,440,000
Nayoko Yoshikawa	76	70	75	72	293	1,440,000
Stefania Croce	75	72	73	73	293	1,440,000
Michiko Hattori	76	72	72	73	293	1,440,000
Akemi Yamaoka	76	69	74	74	293	1,440,000
Vicki Goetze	72	76	70	75	293	1,440,000

	SCORES				TOTAL	MONEY
Kaori Higo	74	73	76	71	294	964,500
Toshimi Kimura	78	73	73	70	294	964,500
Akiko Fukushima	77	73	72	72	294	964,500
Wu Ming Yueh	77	71	71	75	294	964,500
Junko Yasui	75	71	72	77	295	696,000
Mayumi Murai	75	76	72	73	296	580,000
Marnie McGuire	75	71	73	77	296	580,000
Shin Sora	75	70	70	81	296	580,000
Yuka Irie	75	72	76	74	297	543,000
Annika Sorenstam	76	75	72	74	297	543,000
Aki Nakano	74	71	77	75	297	543,000
Karen Lunn	74	74	73	76	297	543,000
Jane Geddes	74	73	73	77	297	543,000
Suzuko Maeda	75	74	71	77	297	543,000
Keiko Arai	76	75	73	74	298	489,750
Cheng Mei Chi	72	78	74	74	298	489,750
Ikuyo Shiotani	73	75	74	76	298	489,750
Sadae Kumagai	76	74	72	76	298	489,750
Michiko Okada	74	71	76	77	298	489,750
Fukumi Tani	70	73	78	77	298	489,750
Megumi Matsuo	79	70	72	77	298	489,750
Kaori Harada	72	72	75	79	298	489,750

Yakult Ladies

Fukuoka Kokusai Country Club, Fukuoka
Par 36-36—72; 6,221 yards

May 13-15
purse, ¥60,000,000

	SCORES			TOTAL	MONEY
Kaori Higo	70	69	72	211	¥10,800,000
Suzuko Maeda	70	72	70	212	4,100,000
Nayoko Yoshikawa	68	71	73	212	4,100,000
Hisako Takeda	71	67	74	212	4,100,000
Kumiko Hiyoshi	70	72	71	213	1,710,000
Ok Hee Ku	69	71	73	213	1,710,000
Jae Sook Won	71	69	73	213	1,710,000
Hiromi Takamura	70	69	74	213	1,710,000
Hiroko Inoue	70	71	73	214	1,560,000
Mitsuyo Hirata	72	73	70	215	1,365,000
Mayumi Hirase	70	73	72	215	1,365,000
Huang Bie Shyun	68	73	74	215	1,365,000
Fuki Kido	70	71	74	215	1,365,000
Aki Takamura	70	74	72	216	1,036,000
Ritsu Imahori	74	70	72	216	1,036,000
Fusako Nagata	74	70	72	216	1,036,000
Michiko Hattori	71	74	72	217	673,200
Tamayo Ueda	71	73	73	217	673,200
Woo Soon Ko	71	72	74	217	673,200
Shoko Yamamoto	70	72	75	217	673,200
Ikuyo Shiotani	71	70	76	217	673,200
Hisako Higuchi	71	76	71	218	570,000
Norimi Terazawa	69	74	75	218	570,000
Aki Nakano	74	70	74	218	570,000
Miyuki Shimabukuro	70	76	73	219	546,000
Aiko Hashimoto	71	74	74	219	546,000
Kazue Sada	72	72	75	219	546,000
Mariko Ohtani	71	71	77	219	546,000

	SCORES			TOTAL	MONEY
Ray Bell	74	66	79	219	546,000
Fumiko Muraguchi	71	76	73	220	504,000
Yukie Ueki	74	73	73	220	504,000
Aiko Takasu	74	72	74	220	504,000
Hitomi Notsu	71	73	76	220	504,000
Li Wen Lin	75	69	76	220	504,000

Chukyo TV Bridgestone

Kasugai Country Club, Aichi
Par 36-36—72; 6,307 yards

May 20-22
purse, ¥50,000,000

	SCORES			TOTAL	MONEY
Akemi Yamaoka	75	72	67	214	¥9,000,000
Ok Hee Ku	71	72	72	215	4,500,000
Fumiko Omata	73	75	70	218	2,175,000
Aiko Hashimoto	72	75	71	218	2,175,000
Woo Soon Ko	73	73	72	218	2,175,000
Hiromi Takamura	73	71	74	218	2,175,000
Akiko Fukushima	75	76	68	219	1,375,000
Kikuko Shibata	71	74	74	219	1,375,000
Miyuki Shimabukuro	77	71	72	220	1,300,000
Kaori Higo	73	77	71	221	1,212,500
Mayumi Murai	75	76	70	221	1,212,500
Minako Wada	78	73	71	222	906,666
Toshimi Kimura	78	73	71	222	906,666
Keiko Suzuki	76	73	73	222	906,666
Fuki Kido	73	75	74	222	906,666
Jae Sook Won	73	74	75	222	906,666
Fukumi Tani	72	73	77	222	906,666
Nayoko Yoshikawa	74	75	74	223	514,285
Hisako Higuchi	73	75	75	223	514,285
Chikayo Yamazaki	76	76	71	223	514,285
Rie Mitsuhashi	75	73	75	223	514,285
Megumi Matsuo	77	70	76	223	514,285
Natsuko Noro	76	71	76	223	514,285
Yukiyo Haga	69	76	78	223	514,285
Yuka Irie	75	74	75	224	470,000
Ray Bell	75	75	75	225	439,444
Ae Sook Kim	73	78	74	225	439,444
Jeong Soo Kim	77	73	75	225	439,444
Shin Sora	76	75	74	225	439,444
Junko Kitajima	75	77	73	225	439,444
Hiroko Inoue	75	77	73	225	439,444
Elizabeth Wilson	77	72	76	225	439,444
Hisako Takeda	76	76	73	225	439,444
Mariko Watanabe	70	77	78	225	439,444

Toto Motors

Toto Hanno Country Club, Saitama
Par 36-36—72; 6,185 yards

May 27-29
purse, ¥50,000,000

	SCORES			TOTAL	MONEY
Jae Sook Won	73	70	68	211	¥9,000,000
Kumiko Hiyoshi	71	71	70	212	4,500,000
Aiko Hashimoto	71	70	72	213	2,875,000
Akemi Yamaoka	73	68	72	213	2,875,000
Mayumi Hirase	72	73	69	214	1,450,000
Michiko Hattori	70	69	75	214	1,450,000
Fuki Kido	75	66	73	214	1,450,000
Chieko Nishida	74	72	69	215	1,350,000
Elizabeth Wilson	74	71	71	216	1,241,666
Hiromi Takamura	72	72	72	216	1,241,666
Aiko Takasu	74	71	71	216	1,241,666
Keiko Arai	73	70	74	217	1,100,000
Young Mi Lee	74	73	71	218	713,333
Huang Bie Shyun	74	73	71	218	713,333
Megumi Matsuo	72	76	70	218	713,333
Fukumi Tani	73	73	72	218	713,333
Suzuko Maeda	73	76	69	218	713,333
Aki Takamura	73	72	73	218	713,333
Chihiro Nakajima	74	71	73	218	713,333
Aki Nakano	74	71	73	218	713,333
Mariko Ohtani	72	72	74	218	713,333
Tomoe Fumihira	73	73	73	219	470,000
Nayoko Yoshikawa	72	74	73	219	470,000
Mayumi Murai	72	73	74	219	470,000
Minako Wada	73	72	74	219	470,000
Shin Sora	69	75	75	219	470,000
Kikuko Shibata	73	72	75	220	455,000
Kaori Harada	71	76	74	221	423,125
Hiroko Inoue	71	77	73	221	423,125
Kaori Higo	72	76	73	221	423,125
Keiko Suzuki	74	74	73	221	423,125
Rie Fujiwara	71	74	76	221	423,125
Junko Yasui	76	73	72	221	423,125
Akane Ohshiro	76	73	72	221	423,125
Nobuko Kizawa	75	69	77	221	423,125

Mitsubishi Electric Ladies

Kita-Rokko Country Club, Hyago
Par 37-36—73; 6,297 yards

June 3-5
purse, ¥50,000,000

	SCORES			TOTAL	MONEY
Suzuko Maeda	74	69	68	211	¥9,000,000
Aiko Hashimoto	70	71	73	214	4,500,000
Jae Sook Won	71	72	72	215	3,600,000
Mayumi Murai	74	73	69	216	1,733,333
Fuki Kido	73	72	71	216	1,733,333
Toshimi Kimura	72	69	75	216	1,733,333
Nayoko Yoshikawa	72	75	70	217	1,350,000
Chieko Nishida	75	69	73	217	1,350,000
Akane Ohshiro	74	71	72	217	1,350,000
Li Wen Lin	73	75	70	218	1,099,000

	SCORES			TOTAL	MONEY
Kumiko Hiyoshi	74	72	72	218	1,099,000
Fukumi Tani	74	71	73	218	1,099,000
Wu Ming Yueh	73	72	73	218	1,099,000
Norimi Terazawa	72	70	76	218	1,099,000
Huang Yueh Chin	73	75	71	219	711,250
Mitsuyo Hirata	74	72	73	219	711,250
Yuko Moriguchi	73	73	73	219	711,250
Woo Soon Ko	75	71	73	219	711,250
Tokiko Hashimura	73	75	72	220	466,666
Yuka Irie	77	71	72	220	466,666
Young Mi Lee	74	73	73	220	466,666
Miyuki Shimabukuro	73	73	74	220	466,666
Huang Bie Shyun	72	73	75	220	466,666
Akemi Yamaoka	74	70	76	220	466,666
Bie Mitsuhashi	75	73	74	222	429,285
Hiromi Takamura	74	75	73	222	429,285
Yuko Saitoh	76	72	74	222	429,285
Kasumi Adachi	74	73	75	222	429,285
Kaori Higo	73	77	72	222	429,285
Ae Sook Kim	77	73	72	222	429,285
Akiko Fukushima	69	74	79	222	429,285

Suntory Ladies Open

Arima Royal Golf Club, Hyogo
Par 36-36—72; 6,212 yards

June 9-12
purse, ¥50,000,000

	SCORES				TOTAL	MONEY
Akemi Yamaoka	67	66	70	72	275	¥9,000,000
Ikuyo Shiotani	70	72	68	71	281	4,500,000
Mayumi Hirase	75	70	69	71	285	2,020,000
Aki Takamura	70	70	73	72	285	2,020,000
Yuko Moriguchi	68	69	74	74	285	2,020,000
Akiko Fukushima	70	67	74	74	285	2,020,000
Huang Bie Shyun	68	73	71	73	285	2,020,000
Mayumi Murai	68	72	75	72	287	1,300,000
Toshimi Kimura	70	70	75	72	287	1,300,000
Jae Sook Won	73	71	66	77	287	1,300,000
Nayoko Yoshikawa	72	74	70	72	288	1,175,000
Fukumi Tani	70	71	73	75	289	1,062,500
Chikayo Yamazaki	73	71	69	76	289	1,062,500
Suzuko Maeda	70	75	70	75	290	900,000
Junko Yasui	72	72	71	75	290	900,000
Chieko Nishida	70	72	76	73	291	710,000
Wu Ming Yueh	73	71	72	75	291	710,000
Midori Wakaura	73	70	76	73	292	515,000
Yuka Irie	75	69	74	74	292	515,000
Hiromi Takamura	73	70	73	76	292	515,000
Miyuki Shimabukuro	73	70	70	79	292	515,000
Aiko Hashimoto	73	74	73	73	293	462,500
Mitsuyo Hirata	72	71	75	75	293	462,500
Aiko Takasu	75	72	71	75	293	462,500
Yuko Saitoh	75	71	70	77	293	462,500
Fumie Furayama	74	73	75	72	294	428,750
Miki Oda	72	73	76	73	294	428,750
Keiko Suzuki	76	69	76	73	294	428,750
Reiko Kashiwado	70	74	76	74	294	428,750

	SCORES			TOTAL	MONEY
Hisako Kawaguchi	74	72 74	74	294	428,750
Huang Hui Fan	71	75 73	75	294	428,750
Keiko Arai	70	74 72	78	294	428,750
Kaori Harada	70	74 70	80	294	428,750

Dunlop Twin Lakes Ladies

Twin Lakes Country Club, Gunma

June 16-19

Par 36-36—72; 6,240 yards

purse, ¥50,000,000

	SCORES				TOTAL	MONEY
Toshimi Kimura	68	72	67	77	284	¥9,000,000
Michiko Hattori	70	76	73	71	290	4,000,000
Akiko Fukushima	72	72	68	78	290	4,000,000
Man Soo Kim	72	74	72	73	291	2,250,000
Mariko Ohtani	72	75	71	74	292	1,425,000
Ok Hee Ku	74	74	70	74	292	1,425,000
Marnie McGuire	72	72	70	78	292	1,425,000
Mitsuyo Hirata	72	69	73	78	292	1,425,000
Miyuki Shimabukuro	71	74	75	73	293	1,206,250
Rie Mitsuhashi	71	73	75	74	293	1,206,250
Akemi Yamaoka	72	74	73	74	293	1,206,250
Aiko Hashimoto	73	70	73	77	293	1,206,250
Ayako Okamoto	72	68	77	77	294	985,000
Keiko Suzuki	68	76	70	80	294	985,000
Nobuko Kizawa	68	77	74	76	295	756,666
Cheng Mei Chi	76	69	73	77	295	756,666
Wu Ming Yueh	74	74	70	77	295	756,666
Fukumi Tani	75	72	73	76	296	680,000
Reiko Kashiwado	75	74	68	80	297	490,000
Yumiko Akagi	72	72	67	86	297	490,000
Fusako Nagata	74	76	72	76	298	460,000
Yuka Irie	74	74	74	76	298	460,000
Ae Sook Kim	75	73	73	77	298	460,000
Kumiko Fuchi	75	73	72	78	298	460,000
Chie Yoshida	70	73	76	79	298	460,000
*Harumi Sakagami	72	73	72	82	299	
Megumi Matsuo	74	73	75	78	300	437,500
Hiromi Kobayashi	72	78	73	77	300	437,500
Hisako Takeda	77	70	74	79	300	437,500
Mayumi Murai	70	72	77	81	300	437,500

Japan Women's Open Championship

Musashi Country Club, Saitama

June 23-26

Par 36-36—72; 6,366 yards

purse, ¥60,000,000

	SCORES				TOTAL	MONEY
Michiko Hattori	69	76	71	71	287	¥10,800,000
Hiromi Kobayashi	73	71	74	72	290	6,000,000
Kaori Higo	74	72	76	69	291	4,320,000
Kaori Harada	75	69	74	74	292	3,060,000
Toshimi Kimura	70	71	75	77	293	2,580,000
Huang Yueh Chin	75	71	75	73	294	2,220,000
Aiko Hashimoto	73	76	71	74	294	2,220,000

	SCORES				TOTAL	MONEY
Fuki Kido	72	70	80	73	295	1,860,000
Ayako Okamoto	72	72	78	74	296	1,470,000
Hiromi Takamura	74	74	74	74	296	1,470,000
Ikuyo Shiotani	71	69	78	78	296	1,470,000
Akane Ohshiro	72	75	77	73	297	1,134,000
Miyuki Shimabukuro	75	77	74	72	298	1,002,000
Akiko Fukushima	71	74	77	76	298	1,002,000
Huang Bie Shyun	72	78	77	72	299	792,000
Ok Hee Ku	73	76	77	73	299	792,000
Akemi Yamaoka	69	76	77	77	299	792,000
Wu Ming Yueh	71	73	76	79	299	792,000
Marnie McGuire	75	75	77	73	300	621,000
Woo Soon Ko	72	78	77	73	300	621,000
Junko Yasui	73	77	76	74	300	621,000
Mayumi Hirase	69	75	79	77	300	621,000
Suzuko Maeda	75	77	77	72	301	540,500
*Huang Yu Chen	78	74	76	73	301	
Misayo Fujisawa	75	75	75	76	301	540,500
Yuka Irie	67	78	76	80	301	540,500
Hiromi Hirakata	72	76	73	80	301	540,500
*Atsuko Kikuchi	78	74	80	70	302	
Hisako Higuchi	73	79	80	70	302	495,000
Nayoko Yoshikawa	77	72	78	76	303	478,000

Tohato Ladies

Oak Village Golf Club, Chiba
Par 36-36—72; 6,147 yards

July 1-3
purse, ¥50,000,000

	SCORES			TOTAL	MONEY
Ayako Okamoto	73	71	70	214	¥9,000,000
Hiromi Takamura	72	70	72	214	4,500,000
(Okamoto defeated Takamura on first extra hole.)					
Ok Hee Ku	71	71	73	215	3,500,000
Chieko Nishida	73	69	74	216	2,250,000
Yuka Irie	71	77	69	217	1,500,000
Jae Sook Won	75	73	72	220	1,375,000
Aiko Takasu	72	74	74	220	1,375,000
Young Mi Lee	75	72	73	220	1,375,000
Kaori Higo	74	70	75	220	1,375,000
Ray Bell	78	74	69	221	1,212,500
Wu Ming Yueh	75	71	75	221	1,212,500
Huang Yueh Chin	75	75	72	222	1,025,000
Chikako Matsuzawa	69	78	75	222	1,025,000
Norimi Terazawa	72	74	76	222	1,025,000
Sanae Suzuki	74	78	71	223	747,500
Marnie McGuire	75	77	71	223	747,500
Rie Mitsuhashi	77	74	72	223	747,500
Mayumi Hirase	73	76	74	223	747,500
Fuki Kido	71	77	76	224	550,000
Megumi Matsuo	71	80	74	225	495,000
Junko Yasui	74	78	74	226	480,000
Hisako Takeda	76	76	74	226	480,000
Toshimi Kimura	73	78	75	226	480,000
Ae Sook Kim	79	76	71	226	480,000
Yuri Kawanami	75	75	76	226	480,000
Michiko Hattori	77	75	75	227	451,666

	SCORES			TOTAL	MONEY
Suzuko Maeda	75	77	75	227	451,666
Ikuyo Shiotani	76	78	73	227	451,666
Woo Soon Ko	78	73	76	227	451,666
Nobuko Kizawa	77	78	72	227	451,666
Hiromi Hirakata	75	75	77	227	451,666

Toyo Suisan Ladies

Kosaido Sapporo Country Club, Hokkaido   July 8-10
Par 36-36—72; 6,412 yards   purse, ¥50,000,000

	SCORES			TOTAL	MONEY
Hiromi Takamura	69	68	72	209	¥9,000,000
Kumiko Hiyoshi	67	68	76	211	4,500,000
Mayumi Murai	73	71	71	215	2,875,000
Jae Sook Won	70	73	72	215	2,875,000
Misayo Fujimura	72	70	74	216	1,450,000
Aiko Takasu	69	72	74	216	1,450,000
Man Soo Kim	68	73	75	216	1,450,000
Li Wen Lin	73	72	72	217	1,350,000
Suzuko Maeda	70	76	72	218	1,275,000
Ritsu Imahori	73	73	72	218	1,275,000
Miyuki Shimabukuro	72	75	72	219	1,025,000
Fuki Kido	74	73	72	219	1,025,000
Huang Bie Shyun	72	73	74	219	1,025,000
Akane Ohshiro	70	74	75	219	1,025,000
Aki Takamura	74	74	71	219	1,025,000
Akemi Yamaoka	71	74	75	220	687,500
Yuko Moriguchi	73	74	73	220	687,500
Rie Fujiwara	73	72	75	220	687,500
Fukumi Tani	73	71	76	220	687,500
Nayoko Yoshikawa	70	77	74	221	495,000
Ray Bell	72	74	75	221	495,000
Toshimi Kimura	70	74	77	221	495,000
Woo Soon Ko	73	73	76	222	471,500
Ae Sook Kim	75	72	75	222	471,500
Hisako Higuchi	73	72	77	222	471,500
Nobuko Kizawa	76	72	74	222	471,500
Reiko Kashiwado	72	72	78	222	471,500
Yuki Ueko	72	75	76	223	439,000
Hiromi Hirakata	68	77	78	223	439,000
Junko Yoshida	74	73	76	223	439,000
Ikuyo Shiotani	73	75	75	223	439,000
*Chika Aritoh	71	72	80	223	
Michiko Okada	70	72	81	223	439,000

Resort Trust Cleanup Ladies

Maple Point Golf Club, Yamanashi   July 15-17
Par 36-36—72; 6,268 yards   purse, ¥50,000,000

	SCORES			TOTAL	MONEY
Feng Tseng Hsiu	70	73	70	213	¥9,000,000
Reiko Kashiwado	68	78	70	216	3,416,666
Kaori Harada	73	71	71	216	3,416,666

	SCORES			TOTAL	MONEY
Natsuko Noro	74	69	73	216	3,416,666
Fusako Nagata	73	73	71	217	1,375,000
Junko Yasui	69	75	73	217	1,375,000
Kaori Higo	71	72	74	217	1,375,000
Aiko Takasu	72	71	74	217	1,375,000
Aki Takamura	72	69	76	217	1,375,000
Wu Ming Yueh	68	73	76	217	1,375,000
Fukumi Tani	71	75	72	218	1,137,500
Hisako Kawaguchi	71	74	73	218	1,137,500
Tatsuko Morimoto	75	74	70	219	897,500
Chikayo Matuszawa	75	70	74	219	897,500
Miki Oda	71	73	75	219	897,500
Mayumi Ishii	70	74	75	219	897,500
Hiroko Inoue	74	75	71	220	530,000
Aiko Hashimoto	72	75	73	220	530,000
Michiko Hattori	72	74	74	220	530,000
Cheng Mei Chi	72	73	75	220	530,000
Akane Ohshiro	70	75	75	220	530,000
Huang Bie Shyun	70	73	77	220	530,000
Chieko Nishida	68	74	78	220	530,000
Ikuyo Shiotani	70	75	76	221	455,000
Shin Sora	74	75	73	222	452,500
Rie Mitsuhashi	73	75	74	222	452,500
Akemi Yamaoka	71	75	76	222	452,500
Huang Yueh Chin	67	76	79	222	452,500
Mayumi Yamada	75	73	75	223	428,750
Woo Soon Ko	75	72	76	223	428,750
Sadae Kumagai	74	72	77	223	428,750
Mariko Ohtani	69	75	79	223	428,750

Katokichi Queens Cup

Takamatsu Grand Country Club, Kagawa
Par 36-37—73; 6,325 yards

July 22-24
purse, ¥50,000,000

	SCORES			TOTAL	MONEY
Ikuyo Shiotani	68	74	71	213	¥9,000,000
Kazumi Takada	75	70	71	216	4,500,000
Miyuki Shimabukuro	70	74	73	217	3,500,000
Aiko Hashimoto	75	73	70	218	1,541,666
Junko Yasui	73	73	72	218	1,541,666
Kumiko Hiyoshi	70	76	72	218	1,541,666
Michiko Hattori	73	73	72	218	1,541,666
Chieko Nishida	72	73	73	218	1,541,666
Yuko Saitoh	72	72	74	218	1,541,666
Misayo Fujisawa	71	75	73	219	1,137,500
Michiko Okada	74	72	73	219	1,137,500
Megumi Matsuo	72	73	74	219	1,137,500
Keiko Arai	71	73	75	219	1,137,500
Masumi Inaba	73	77	70	220	851,666
Woo Soon Ko	72	75	73	220	851,666
Mitsuyo Hirata	72	75	73	220	851,666
Ok Hee Ku	73	76	73	222	538,000
Mariko Ohtani	75	74	73	222	538,000
Akemi Yamaoka	71	76	75	222	538,000
Sheree Higgens	71	74	77	222	538,000
Huang Hui Fan	73	68	81	222	538,000
Chikayo Yamazaki	72	77	74	223	442,000

	SCORES			TOTAL	MONEY
Nayoko Yoshikawa	76	73	74	223	442,000
Kasumi Adachi	75	74	74	223	442,000
Aiko Takasu	71	79	73	223	442,000
Mayumi Ishii	73	75	75	223	442,000
Natsuko Noro	74	76	73	223	442,000
Chihiro Nakajima	75	75	73	223	442,000
Huang Yueh Chin	74	74	75	223	442,000
Miki Oda	76	75	72	223	442,000
Marnie McGuire	74	78	71	223	442,000

SC Ladies

Kosaido Saitama Golf Club, Chichibu, Saitama
Par 36-36—72; 6,291 yards

July 29-31
purse, ¥50,000,000

	SCORES			TOTAL	MONEY
Yoko Moriguchi	67	72	71	210	¥9,000,000
Aiko Hashimoto	67	70	73	210	4,500,000
(Moriguchi defeated Hashimoto on second extra hole.)					
Cheng Mei Chi	68	72	71	211	2,875,000
Akemi Yamaoka	66	72	73	211	2,875,000
Toshimi Kimura	70	68	74	212	1,500,000
Nayoko Yoshikawa	74	71	69	214	1,400,000
Keiko Suzuki	72	72	70	214	1,400,000
Aki Takamura	71	71	72	214	1,400,000
Haruni Hyodoh	71	73	71	215	1,241,666
Ae Sook Kim	72	71	72	215	1,241,666
Li Wen Lin	69	73	73	215	1,241,666
Nicole Lowien	71	76	69	216	912,500
Rie Mitsuhashi	72	73	71	216	912,500
Mayumi Ishii	72	72	72	216	912,500
Miyuki Shimabukuro	73	71	72	216	912,500
Yoko Morioka	73	70	73	216	912,500
Chikako Matsuzawa	72	68	76	216	912,500
Tomiko Ikebuchi	72	74	71	217	555,000
Kaori Imai	70	75	72	217	555,000
Ray Bell	70	75	72	217	555,000
Fukumi Tani	71	71	75	217	555,000
Misayo Fujisawa	71	75	72	218	485,000
Fumiko Omata	73	73	72	218	485,000
Huang Bie Shyun	71	74	73	218	485,000
Miki Matsuzawa	73	73	73	219	472,500
Chen Yueh Shuang	74	74	71	219	472,500
Marnie McGuire	70	76	74	220	450,000
Yukiyo Haga	75	72	73	220	450,000
Junko Yoshida	74	73	73	220	450,000
Hiroko Inoue	73	75	72	220	450,000
Huang Yueh Chin	75	69	76	220	450,000
Sadae Kumagai	73	70	77	220	450,000

Asahi Kokusai Ladies

Asahi Kokusai Hamamura Onsen Golf Club, Tottori
Par 36-36—72; 6,362 yards

August 5-7
purse, ¥50,000,000

	SCORES			TOTAL	MONEY
Young Mi Lee	68	69	71	208	¥9,000,000
Ikuyo Shiotani	68	69	72	209	4,000,000
Hiromi Hirakata	74	66	69	209	4,000,000
Jae Sook Won	72	70	70	212	2,250,000
Ayako Okamoto	73	70	70	213	1,475,000
Junko Yasui	67	75	71	213	1,475,000
Aki Nakano	72	72	70	214	1,325,000
Chieko Nishida	72	71	71	214	1,325,000
Hiromi Takamura	70	72	72	214	1,325,000
Fuki Kido	69	72	73	214	1,325,000
Michiko Hattori	70	74	71	215	1,137,500
Suzuko Maeda	73	70	72	215	1,137,500
Akiko Fukushima	77	69	70	216	985,000
Keiko Arai	70	73	73	216	985,000
Akane Ohshiro	75	71	71	217	712,500
Kaori Harada	73	72	72	217	712,500
Cheng Mei Chi	70	74	73	217	712,500
Michiko Okada	74	71	72	217	712,500
Yoshiko Mizunaga	74	72	72	218	468,571
Yukiyo Haga	70	75	73	218	468,571
Yoshiko Masuda	74	73	71	218	468,571
Miki Oda	72	73	73	218	468,571
Mayumi Hirase	72	73	73	218	468,571
Hisako Higuchi	74	70	74	218	468,571
Aiko Hashimoto	70	71	77	218	468,571
Ok Hee Ku	73	74	72	219	442,500
Natsuko Noro	74	74	71	219	442,500
Hitomi Notsu	75	71	74	220	417,500
Yuko Motoyama	71	76	73	220	417,500
Kumiko Fuchi	72	75	73	220	417,500
Yuka Irie	76	71	73	220	417,500
Keiko Suzuki	75	74	71	220	417,500
Mayumi Murai	71	73	76	220	417,500

NEC Karuizawa 72

Karuizawa 72 Golf Club, Kitasaku, Nagano
Par 36-36—72; 6,437 yards

August 12-14
purse, ¥60,000,000

	SCORES			TOTAL	MONEY
Mayumi Hirase	68	69	74	211	¥10,800,000
Ayako Okamoto	69	74	68	211	5,400,000
(Hirase defeated Okamoto on first extra hole.)					
Akiko Fukushima	70	77	68	215	2,424,000
Michiko Hattori	69	74	72	215	2,424,000
Young Mi Lee	71	72	72	215	2,424,000
Nayoko Yoshikawa	70	72	73	215	2,424,000
Ikuyo Shiotani	70	72	73	215	2,424,000
Mitsuyo Hirata	69	78	69	216	1,590,000
Aiko Hashimoto	71	73	72	216	1,590,000
Akane Ohshiro	73	72	72	217	1,455,000
Huang Bie Shyun	76	69	72	217	1,455,000

	SCORES			TOTAL	MONEY
Yuko Moriguchi	72	75	71	218	1,177,500
Yuka Irie	71	75	72	218	1,177,500
Akemi Yamaoka	73	71	74	218	1,177,500
Mariko Ohtani	69	73	76	218	1,177,500
Sadae Kumagai	74	74	71	219	710,400
Tomiko Ikebuchi	76	72	71	219	710,400
Megumi Matsuo	71	75	73	219	710,400
Ray Bell	73	73	73	219	710,400
Tokiko Hashimura	75	71	73	219	710,400
Cheng Mei Chi	72	77	71	220	555,000
Suzuko Maeda	71	75	74	220	555,000
Yukiyo Haga	76	71	74	221	546,000
Ritsu Imahori	75	74	73	222	525,000
Woo Soon Ko	76	73	73	222	525,000
Kiyoe Yamazaki	75	74	73	222	525,000
Matsuko Moro	72	75	75	222	525,000
Tatsuko Morimoto	73	73	76	222	525,000
Reiko Kashiwado	69	75	78	222	525,000
Misayo Fujisawa	73	76	74	223	480,000
Kaori Higo	76	72	75	223	480,000
Masako Ichiguchi	72	75	76	223	480,000
Kayoko Ikoma	75	72	76	223	480,000
Aiko Takasu	72	72	79	223	480,000

Itoki Classic

Glen Oaks Country Club, Katori-gun, Chiba
Par 36-36—72; 6,301 yards
(Third round shortened to nine holes — heavy rains.)

August 19-21
purse, ¥50,000,000

	SCORES			TOTAL	MONEY
Ayako Okamoto	66	68	38	172	¥9,000,000
Mayumi Hirase	75	67	33	175	4,500,000
Sadae Kumagai	70	70	38	178	2,416,666
Yuko Moriguchi	69	71	38	178	2,416,666
Mitsuyo Hirata	72	67	39	178	2,416,666
Yoko Kobayashi	72	71	36	179	1,425,000
Mayumi Murai	71	71	37	179	1,425,000
Ikuyo Shiotani	71	73	36	180	1,235,000
Junko Yasui	74	70	36	180	1,235,000
Akane Ohshiro	70	71	39	180	1,235,000
Akiko Fukushima	69	72	39	180	1,235,000
Aki Nakano	69	69	42	180	1,235,000
Yukie Ueki	72	73	36	181	723,125
Aiko Takasu	69	75	37	181	723,125
Chikako Matsuzawa	71	73	37	181	723,125
Sheree Higgens	73	71	37	181	723,125
Jae Sook Won	71	72	38	181	723,125
Chieko Nishida	71	72	38	181	723,125
Keiko Arai	71	72	38	181	723,125
Woo Soon Ko	71	71	39	181	723,125
Hisako Higuchi	72	74	36	182	435,000
Aki Takamura	72	74	36	182	435,000
Kasumi Adachi	75	71	36	182	435,000
Ray Bell	73	73	36	182	435,000
Hiromi Hirakata	74	72	36	182	435,000
Ae Sook Kim	74	72	36	182	435,000

	SCORES			TOTAL	MONEY
Fuki Kido	77	68	37	182	435,000
Suzuko Maeda	70	74	38	182	435,000
Miki Oda	71	73	38	182	435,000
Mitsuko Hamada	75	70	38	183	380,000
Chihiro Nakajima	75	71	37	183	380,000
Natsuko Noro	75	71	37	183	380,000
Yukiyo Haga	73	73	37	183	380,000
Michiko Hattori	70	74	39	183	380,000
Mieko Nomura	73	70	40	183	380,000

Goyo Kensetsu Cup

Tomisato Golf Club, Chiba
Par 36-36—72; 6,126 yards

August 26-28
purse, ¥60,000,000

	SCORES			TOTAL	MONEY
Chikako Matsuzawa	70	66	73	209	¥10,800,000
Akemi Yamaoka	70	72	68	210	4,100,000
Kaori Higo	72	70	68	210	4,100,000
Suzuko Maeda	69	66	75	210	4,100,000
Hisako Takeda	72	71	70	213	1,770,000
Miki Oda	72	68	73	213	1,770,000
Feng Tseng Hsiu	71	74	69	214	1,620,000
Michiko Okada	76	68	70	214	1,620,000
Kumiko Hiyoshi	68	73	73	214	1,620,000
Chihiro Nakajima	70	75	70	215	1,365,000
Akiko Fukushima	73	71	71	215	1,365,000
Junko Yasui	71	71	73	215	1,365,000
Fuki Kido	69	72	74	215	1,365,000
Mitsuyo Hirata	70	75	71	216	1,050,000
Huang Bie Shyun	71	74	71	216	1,050,000
Akane Ohshiro	73	71	72	216	1,050,000
Jae Sook Won	73	73	71	217	650,000
Fumiko Muraguchi	73	73	71	217	650,000
Mariko Ohtani	71	74	72	217	650,000
Chieko Nishida	75	70	72	217	650,000
Hiromi Takamura	69	75	73	217	650,000
Miyuki Shimabukuro	69	74	74	217	650,000
Hisako Higuchi	73	71	73	217	650,000
Ritsu Imahori	72	70	75	217	650,000
Nayoko Yoshikawa	74	67	76	217	650,000
Ray Bell	71	76	71	218	552,000
Aiko Takasu	72	72	74	218	552,000
Mayumi Ishii	73	70	75	218	552,000
Ok Hee Ku	72	71	75	218	552,000
Cheng Mei Chi	75	67	76	218	552,000

Fuji Sankei Classic

Five Hundred Club, Shizuoka
Par 36-37—73; 6,520 yards
(First round cancelled — heavy rains.)

September 2-4
purse, ¥45,000,000

	SCORES		TOTAL	MONEY
Huang Yueh Chin	69	71	140	¥8,100,000
Young Mi Lee	71	70	141	3,075,000
Fuki Kido	70	71	141	3,075,000
Nayoko Yoshikawa	69	72	141	3,075,000
Huang Bie Shyun	73	69	142	1,282,500
Kumiko Hiyoshi	72	70	142	1,282,500
Ae Sook Kim	71	71	142	1,282,500
Yuko Moriguchi	71	71	142	1,282,500
Ayako Okamoto	74	69	143	1,147,500
Hisako Higuchi	73	70	143	1,147,500
Reiko Kashiwado	75	69	144	956,250
Marnie McGuire	72	72	144	956,250
Junko Yasui	69	75	144	956,250
Akane Ohshiro	70	74	144	956,250
*Chika Aritoh	69	75	144	
Fukumi Tani	74	71	145	559,500
Aki Nakano	74	71	145	559,500
Jae Sook Won	73	72	145	559,500
Miki Oda	75	70	145	559,500
Yukiyo Haga	72	73	145	559,500
Michiko Hattori	72	73	145	559,500
Suzuko Maeda	71	74	145	559,500
Ray Bell	71	74	145	559,500
Yukie Ueki	70	75	145	559,500
Miyuki Shimabukuro	73	73	146	409,050
Yuko Saitoh	73	73	146	409,050
Takako Matsuo	74	72	146	409,050
Kaori Harada	74	72	146	409,050
Chikako Matsuzawa	74	72	146	409,050
Toshimi Kimura	73	73	146	409,050
Mariko Ohtani	73	73	146	409,050
Matsuko Hamada	72	74	146	409,050
Akemi Yamaoka	72	74	146	409,050
Ok Hee Ku	71	75	146	409,050

Japan LPGA Championship

Hodaka Country Club, Nagano
Par 36-36—72; 6,472 yards

September 8-11
purse, ¥65,000,000

	SCORES				TOTAL	MONEY
Kumiko Hiyoshi	69	77	78	71	285	¥11,700,000
Mayumi Hirase	70	76	66	75	287	5,850,000
Aiko Hashimoto	69	74	71	72	288	3,900,000
Michiko Hattori	74	73	68	74	289	2,177,500
Chikako Matsuzawa	74	71	73	72	290	1,917,500
Jae Sook Won	74	69	69	78	290	1,917,500
Feng Tseng Hsiu	73	73	75	70	291	1,755,000
Chihiro Nakajima	72	74	73	72	291	1,755,000
Fuki Kido	69	75	70	77	291	1,755,000
Akiko Fukushima	74	70	74	74	292	1,592,500

	SCORES				TOTAL	MONEY
Aki Nakano	70	74	73	75	292	1,592,500
Yuko Moriguchi	73	76	73	71	293	1,300,000
Ae Sook Kim	77	70	74	72	293	1,300,000
Mariko Ohtani	72	77	71	73	293	1,300,000
Mayumi Murai	72	74	73	74	293	1,300,000
Akemi Yamaoka	71	73	71	78	293	1,300,000
Keiko Suzuki	71	74	71	77	293	1,300,000
Mitsuko Hamada	71	76	76	71	294	720,200
Megumi Matsuo	72	72	75	75	294	720,200
Hisako Higuchi	73	75	71	75	294	720,200
Yuri Kawanami	76	73	69	76	294	720,200
Kaori Higo	72	70	73	79	294	720,200
Yuko Saitoh	74	75	75	71	295	585,000
Fukumi Tani	73	73	75	74	295	585,000
Chikayo Yamazaki	71	75	73	76	295	585,000
Yuko Motoyama	75	73	71	76	295	585,000
Yukiyo Haga	71	76	71	77	295	585,000
Suzuko Maeda	76	73	74	79	296	526,500
Huang Bie Shyuñ	73	74	75	74	296	526,500
Tatsuko Morimoto	76	71	74	75	296	526,500
Sheree Higgens	74	72	72	78	296	526,500

Kosaido Asahi Cup

Chiba Kosaido Country Club, Chiba
Par 36-36—72; 6,183 yards

September 16-18
purse, ¥60,000,000

	SCORES			TOTAL	MONEY
Ayako Okamoto	71	70	70	212	¥10,800,000
Woo Soon Ko	68	70	75	213	5,400,000
Tracy Hanson	72	73	69	214	4,200,000
Junko Yasui	71	74	70	215	2,250,000
Kikuko Shibata	71	72	72	215	2,250,000
Huang Bie Shyun	72	73	71	216	1,650,000
Ikuyo Shiotani	70	74	72	216	1,650,000
Nicole Lowien	74	70	72	216	1,650,000
Akemi Yamaoka	71	72	73	216	1,650,000
Wu Ming Yueh	74	72	71	217	1,365,000
Yoko Kobayashi	71	74	72	217	1,365,000
Hiromi Takamura	72	72	73	217	1,365,000
Mitsuko Hamada	71	73	73	217	1,365,000
Feng Tseng Hsiu	73	76	69	218	783,000
Michiko Hattori	74	75	69	218	783,000
Aiko Takasu	75	74	69	218	783,000
Miki Oda	74	74	70	218	783,000
Fusako Nagata	73	73	72	218	783,000
Cheng Mei Chi	75	70	73	218	783,000
Yuka Irie	73	71	74	218	783,000
Ritsu Imahori	69	74	75	218	783,000
Toshimi Kimura	74	73	72	219	526,000
Masumi Inaba	76	71	72	219	526,000
Hiromi Hirakata	75	72	72	219	526,000
Keiko Arai	72	74	73	219	526,000
Yuko Saitoh	76	70	73	219	526,000
Marnie McGuire	75	70	74	219	526,000
Kayoko Yamaguchi	74	74	72	220	471,428
Kayoko Ikoma	74	74	72	220	471,428

	SCORES			TOTAL	MONEY
Aki Nakano	76	72	72	220	471,428
Natsuko Noro	71	75	74	220	471,428
Kaori Harada	76	70	74	220	471,428
Young Mi Lee	74	71	75	220	471,428
Ok Hee Ku	75	70	75	220	471,428

Miyagi TV Cup

Hananoyashiro Golf Club, Miyagi
Par 36-36—72; 6,233 yards
(Tournament shortened to 27 holes — rain.)

September 23-25
purse, ¥37,500,000

	SCORES		TOTAL	MONEY
Jae Sook Won	69	34	103	¥6,750,000
Ikuyo Shiotani	69	35	104	3,375,000
Toshimi Kimura	71	34	105	2,156,000
Ae Sook Kim	71	34	105	2,156,000
Aki Nakano	72	34	106	1,087,000
Keiko Arai	72	34	106	1,087,000
Hiromi Hirakata	71	35	106	1,087,000
Mitsuyo Hirata	73	34	107	975,000
Miki Oda	72	35	107	975,000
Wu Ming Yueh	69	38	107	975,000
Akiko Fukushima	72	36	108	796,000
Fukumi Tani	72	36	108	796,000
Fumiko Omata	72	36	108	796,000
Akemi Yamaoka	71	37	108	796,000
Chikayo Yamazaki	74	35	109	591,000
Hiromi Takamura	72	37	109	591,000
Woo Soon Ko	72	37	109	591,000
Junko Yasui	76	34	110	371,000
Huang Yueh Chin	75	35	110	371,000
Natsuko Noro	75	35	110	371,000
Fuki Kido	74	36	110	371,000
Suzuko Maeda	73	37	110	371,000
Hisako Higuchi	73	37	110	371,000
Fusako Nagata	72	38	110	371,000
Ritsu Imahori	72	38	110	371,000
Hiroko Inoue	72	38	110	371,000
Kiyoe Yamazaki	72	38	110	371,000
Marnie McGuire	70	40	110	371,000
Mitsuko Hamada	74	37	111	332,000
Mariko Watanabe	74	37	111	332,000
Aki Takamura	73	38	111	332,000

Yukijirushi Tokai Classic

Ryosen Golf Club, Mie
Par 36-36—72; 6,225 yards

September 30-October 2
purse, ¥60,000,000

	SCORES			TOTAL	MONEY
Michiko Hattori	70	73	69	212	¥10,800,000
Fuki Kido	71	74	68	213	4,800,000
Mitsuko Hamada	69	73	71	213	4,800,000
Suzuko Maeda	72	74	69	215	2,080,000

	SCORES			TOTAL	MONEY
Jae Sook Won	67	76	72	215	2,080,000
Marnie McGuire	71	73	71	215	2,080,000
Aki Nakano	71	73	72	216	1,650,000
Hisako Higuchi	65	77	74	216	1,650,000
Junko Yasui	72	75	70	217	1,530,000
Ray Bell	71	74	72	217	1,530,000
Natsuko Noro	73	77	68	218	1,230,000
Kumiko Hiyoshi	72	76	70	218	1,230,000
Nicole Lowien	70	77	71	218	1,230,000
Sheree Higgens	71	74	73	218	1,230,000
Toshimi Kimura	72	71	75	218	1,230,000
Kaori Higo	69	71	79	219	960,000
Michiko Okada	72	76	72	220	735,000
Reiko Kashiwado	70	76	74	220	735,000
Akiko Fukushima	73	73	74	220	735,000
Miyuki Shimabukuro	72	73	75	220	735,000
Misayo Fujisawa	74	75	72	221	585,000
Mayumi Murai	74	75	72	221	585,000
Akemi Yamaoka	71	76	74	221	585,000
Ok Hee Ku	71	74	76	221	585,000
Mayumi Hirase	73	77	72	222	546,750
Yukie Ueki	72	77	73	222	546,750
Shin Sora	74	75	73	222	546,750
Woo Soon Ko	71	76	75	222	546,750
Yuri Kawanami	70	77	75	222	546,750
Wu Ming Yueh	72	75	75	222	546,750
Ikuyo Shiotani	72	75	75	222	546,750
Hiroko Inoue	70	73	79	222	546,750

Takara World Invitational

Caledonian Golf Club, Chiba
Par 36-36—72; 6,222 yards

October 6-9
purse, ¥65,000,000

	SCORES				TOTAL	MONEY
Mayumi Hirase	68	71	67	72	278	¥11,700,000
Liselotte Neumann	69	65	75	71	280	5,850,000
Brandie Burton	72	70	73	71	286	4,550,000
Mayumi Murai	73	72	73	71	289	2,253,333
Michiko Hattori	74	68	74	73	289	2,253,333
Mitsuko Hamada	69	73	71	76	289	2,253,333
Huang Bie Shyun	73	75	71	71	290	1,787,500
Miyuki Shimabukuro	74	70	72	74	290	1,787,500
Florence Descampe	73	71	73	74	291	1,690,000
Vicki Goetze	70	75	73	74	292	1,625,000
Toshimi Kimura	72	76	74	71	293	1,430,000
Akiko Fukushima	72	73	72	76	293	1,430,000
Junko Yasui	66	78	73	76	293	1,430,000
Helen Alfredsson	73	75	75	71	294	1,107,166
Young Mi Lee	77	72	71	74	294	1,107,166
Kaori Higo	71	73	76	74	294	1,107,166
Sherri Steinhauer	72	78	73	72	295	802,750
Woo Soon Ko	71	75	73	76	295	802,750
Aiko Hashimoto	74	74	76	72	296	630,500
Michiko Okada	75	77	70	74	296	630,500
Mitsuyo Hirata	74	73	76	74	297	586,625
Aki Nakano	75	76	72	74	297	586,625

	SCORES				TOTAL	MONEY
Misayo Fujisawa	74	73	75	75	297	586,625
Hiromi Hirakata	74	71	76	76	297	586,625
Yuko Moriguchi	71	77	78	72	298	556,833
Aki Takamura	72	75	78	73	298	556,833
Yuri Kawanami	79	75	76	74	298	556,833
Mieko Nomura	76	76	73	74	299	539,500
Kaori Harada	78	73	77	72	300	533,000
Shin Sora	72	79	75	75	301	500,500
Chihiro Nakajima	75	75	75	76	301	500,500
Yuko Motoyama	79	73	71	76	301	500,500
Ikuyo Shiotani	72	73	76	80	301	500,500

Fujitsu Ladies

Hamono Golf Club, Chiba
Par 36-36—72; 6,369 yards

October 14-16
purse, ¥60,000,000

	SCORES			TOTAL	MONEY
Kikuko Shibata	72	71	70	213	¥10,800,000
Aki Nakano	71	71	72	214	3,535,000
Chikayo Yamazaki	72	69	73	214	3,535,000
Shin Sora	70	71	73	214	3,535,000
Akane Ohshiro	69	70	75	214	3,535,000
Mayumi Murai	71	68	76	215	1,710,000
Tomiko Ikebuchi	73	68	74	215	1,710,000
Woo Soon Ko	73	73	70	216	1,620,000
Miki Oda	70	73	74	217	1,447,500
Junko Yasui	68	74	75	217	1,447,500
Akiko Fukushima	71	72	74	217	1,447,500
Miyuki Shimabukuro	69	72	76	217	1,447,500
Sheree Higgens	75	74	69	218	1,017,600
Aki Takamura	74	73	71	218	1,017,600
Yuko Moriguchi	73	72	73	218	1,017,600
Young Mi Lee	70	73	75	218	1,017,600
Fusako Nagata	71	70	77	218	1,017,600
Misayo Fujisawa	78	71	70	219	546,000
Suzuko Maeda	76	73	70	219	546,000
Ritsu Imahori	73	74	72	219	546,000
Huang Bie Shyun	75	72	72	219	546,000
Yuko Saitoh	71	75	73	219	546,000
Ray Bell	73	73	73	219	546,000
Kaori Shimura	70	75	74	219	546,000
Chieko Nishida	74	72	73	219	546,000
Ok Hee Ku	69	75	75	219	546,000
Feng Tseng Hsiu	73	71	75	219	546,000
Aiko Hashimoto	73	71	75	219	546,000
Wu Ming Yueh	67	74	78	219	546,000
Jae Sook Won	72	77	71	220	450,000
Mitsuyo Hirata	75	74	71	220	450,000
Toshimi Kimura	71	75	74	220	450,000
Yukie Ueki	75	71	74	220	450,000
Hiromi Takamura	72	74	74	220	450,000
Mayumi Hirase	71	74	75	220	450,000
Ikuyo Shiotani	72	73	75	220	450,000

Nichirei International

Ami Golf Club, Ibaragi-ken
Par 36-36—72; 6,337 yards

October 28-30
purse, US$618,750

FINAL RESULTS: United States 22½, Japan 13½

TEAM MATCHES

United States 10½, Japan 7½.

INDIVIDUAL MATCHES

Woo Soon Ko (Japan) defeated Martha Nause, 70-72.
Donna Andrews (US) defeated Young Mi Lee, 66-73.
Toshimi Kimura (Japan) defeated Helen Alfredsson, 77-78.
Aiko Hashimoto (Japan) defeated Alicia Dibos, 70-71.
Judy Dickinson (US) halved with Fuki Kido, 70-70.
Dottie Mochrie (US) defeated Nayoko Yoshikawa, 67-70.
Kumiko Hiyoshi (Japan) defeated Val Skinner, 73-76.
Nancy Ramsbottom (US) defeated Akemi Yamaoka, 73-75.
Yuko Moriguchi (Japan) defeated Alice Ritzman, 69-77.
Meg Mallon (US) defeated Kaori Higo, 70-73.
Beth Daniel (US) defeated Chieko Nishida, 71-72.
Tammie Green (US) defeated Suzuko Maeda, 73-74.
Sherri Steinhauer (US) defeated Mayumi Hirase, 71-77.
Elaine Crosby (US) defeated Akiko Fukushima, 70-75.
Hiromi Kobayashi (US) defeated Jae Sook Won, 71-73.
Rosie Jones (US) defeated Ikuyo Shiotani, 71-75.
Michelle McGann (US) defeated Michiko Hattori, 66-76.
Jane Geddes (US) halved with Ayako Okamoto, 72-72.

(Each U.S. player received US$22,000; each Japanese player US$12,375.)

Toray Japan Queens Cup

Oak Hills Country Club, Chiba
Par 35-36—72; 6,056 yards

November 4-6
purse, ¥67,960,000

	SCORES			TOTAL	MONEY
Woo Soon Ko	65	71	70	206	¥10,290,000
Betsy King	67	67	72	206	6,386,000
(Ko defeated King on first extra hole.)					
Nancy Lopez	67	71	69	207	4,660,000
Helen Alfredsson	70	68	70	208	2,991,000
Val Skinner	70	68	70	208	2,991,000
Julie Larsen	66	72	70	208	2,991,000
Hiromi Kobayashi	72	68	69	209	1,915,000
Laura Davies	67	69	73	209	1,915,000
Jane Geddes	68	68	74	210	1,622,000
Sherri Steinhauer	70	68	74	212	1,449,000
Kaori Higo	70	75	68	213	1,152,000
Michiko Hattori	71	73	69	213	1,152,000
Meg Mallon	69	74	70	213	1,152,000
Nayoko Yoshikawa	72	70	71	213	1,152,000
Alicia Dibos	70	68	75	213	1,152,000
Carolyn Hill	73	73	68	214	834,000
Aiko Hashimoto	71	74	69	214	834,000
Katie Peterson-Parker	70	74	70	214	834,000

	SCORES			TOTAL	MONEY
Michelle Estill	71	71	72	214	834,000
Nancy Ramsbottom	70	71	73	214	834,000
Annika Sorenstam	68	73	73	214	834,000
Rosie Jones	72	69	73	214	834,000
Wu Ming Yueh	74	71	70	215	655,000
Joan Pitcock	71	74	70	215	655,000
Vicki Fergon	72	71	72	215	655,000
Dawn Coe-Jones	67	73	75	215	655,000
Elaine Crosby	70	70	75	215	655,000
Barb Mucha	74	72	70	216	533,000
Michele Redman	72	74	70	216	533,000
Huang Yueh Chin	73	72	71	216	533,000
Amy Benz	75	70	71	216	533,000
Ayako Okamoto	76	68	72	216	533,000
Mayumi Hirase	72	72	72	216	533,000
Deb Richard	72	69	75	216	533,000

Itoen Ladies

Great Island Course, Chosei, Chiba
Par 36-36—72; 6,215 yards

November 11-13
purse, ¥60,000,000

	SCORES			TOTAL	MONEY
Laura Davies	64	66	71	201	¥10,800,000
Mayumi Murai	67	69	66	202	5,400,000
Nayoko Yoshikawa	69	66	71	206	4,200,000
Hiromi Takamura	69	72	69	210	2,250,000
Mayumi Hirase	69	70	71	210	2,250,000
Kaori Higo	69	66	76	211	1,740,000
Kaori Harada	71	73	69	213	1,590,000
Shin Sora	73	68	72	213	1,590,000
Marnie McGuire	71	69	73	213	1,590,000
Akiko Fukushima	68	72	73	213	1,590,000
Akane Ohshiro	68	74	72	214	1,224,000
Suzuko Maeda	70	71	73	214	1,224,000
Aki Takamura	71	70	73	214	1,224,000
Tomiko Ikebuchi	68	72	74	214	1,224,000
Hiromi Kobayashi	69	70	75	214	1,224,000
Akemi Yamaoka	72	72	71	215	849,000
Yukie Ueki	70	72	73	215	849,000
Chikako Matsuzawa	69	76	71	216	603,000
Hisako Higuchi	70	75	71	216	603,000
Ae Sook Kim	73	69	74	216	603,000
Aiko Hashimoto	71	70	75	216	603,000
Nicole Lowien	68	76	73	217	531,000
Aki Nakano	72	72	73	217	531,000
Young Mi Lee	72	72	73	217	531,000
Ayako Okamoto	73	72	72	217	531,000
Junko Yasui	72	74	71	217	531,000
Helen Alfredsson	70	72	76	217	531,000
Kayo Yamada	68	74	75	217	531,000
Fumiko Muraguchi	73	69	75	217	531,000
Cheng Mei Chi	73	72	74	219	480,000
Mitsuko Hamada	74	71	74	219	480,000
Kayoko Motoki	73	71	75	219	480,000
Fukumi Tani	71	71	77	219	480,000
Miki Oda	72	75	72	219	480,000

Daio Seishi Elleair Open

Elleair Golf Club, Matsuyama, Ehime
Par 36-36-72; 6,276 yards

November 18-20
purse, ¥60,000,000

	SCORES			TOTAL	MONEY
Mayumi Hirase	71	70	70	211	¥10,800,000
Nayoko Yoshikawa	73	70	70	213	4,800,000
Michiko Hattori	71	71	71	213	4,800,000
Huang Bie Shyun	70	74	70	214	2,700,000
Nicole Lowien	74	72	69	215	1,800,000
Hiromi Kobayashi	74	71	71	216	1,650,000
Shin Sora	70	74	72	216	1,650,000
Aiko Hashimoto	72	72	72	216	1,650,000
Kumiko Hiyoshi	70	72	74	216	1,650,000
Natsuko Noro	73	74	70	217	1,275,000
Yuko Moriguchi	72	73	72	217	1,275,000
Ray Bell	72	72	73	217	1,275,000
Marnie McGuire	72	71	74	217	1,275,000
Miyuki Shimabukuro	71	71	75	217	1,275,000
Yuri Kawanami	71	71	75	217	1,275,000
Hiromi Takamura	74	73	71	218	758,400
Kaori Harada	75	73	70	218	758,400
Toshimi Kimura	72	72	74	218	758,400
Aiko Takasu	73	71	74	218	758,400
Aki Takamura	73	71	74	218	758,400
Rie Fujiwara	73	74	72	219	573,000
Hiroe Tani	74	74	71	219	573,000
Megumi Matsuo	75	71	73	219	573,000
Ikuyo Shiotani	74	72	73	219	573,000
Jae Sook Won	75	70	74	219	573,000
Norimi Terazawa	72	68	79	219	573,000
Chikayo Yamazaki	71	77	72	220	549,000
Fumiko Omata	72	72	76	220	549,000
Ayako Okamoto	73	74	74	221	537,000
Yukie Ueki	72	71	78	221	537,000

Meiji Nyugyo Cup

Aoshima Golf Club, Miyazaki
Par 36-36—72; 6,311 yards

November 25-27
purse, ¥50,000,000

	SCORES			TOTAL	MONEY
Mayumi Hirase	68	70	70	208	¥9,000,000
Aiko Hashimoto	71	71	70	212	4,500,000
Kumiko Hiyoshi	77	69	69	215	2,750,000
Marnie McGuire	70	70	75	215	2,750,000
Ikuyo Shiotani	70	76	70	216	1,700,000
Chikako Matsuzawa	70	73	73	216	1,700,000
Ayako Okamoto	68	74	75	217	1,500,000
Michiko Hattori	71	72	74	217	1,500,000
Miyuki Shimabukuro	70	74	74	218	1,350,000
Mayumi Murai	75	74	70	219	1,250,000
Suzuko Maeda	75	72	73	220	1,175,000
Woo Soon Ko	73	72	75	220	1,175,000
Aki Takamura	73	78	70	221	1,050,000
Nayoko Yoshikawa	68	82	71	221	1,050,000
Mitsuyo Hirata	75	71	75	221	1,050,000
Huang Bie Shyun	72	78	72	222	900,000

	SCORES			TOTAL	MONEY
Yuko Moriguchi	71	76	75	222	900,000
Junko Yasui	78	70	74	222	900,000
Aiko Takasu	73	73	77	223	743,750
Fuki Kido	75	72	76	223	743,750
Chieko Nishida	74	70	79	223	743,750
Akiko Fukushima	73	72	78	223	743,750
Ok Hee Ku	77	72	75	224	637,500
Aki Nakano	71	76	77	224	637,500
Wu Ming Yueh	74	73	77	224	637,500
Toshimi Kimura	72	75	77	224	637,500
Young Mi Lee	74	78	73	225	562,500
Akemi Yamaoka	76	74	75	225	562,500
Kaori Higo	77	76	73	226	525,000
Norimi Terazawa	77	77	73	227	450,000
Ray Bell	78	77	72	227	450,000
Akane Ohshiro	74	76	77	227	450,000
Kikuko Shibata	73	77	77	227	450,000
Huang Yueh Chin	73	75	79	227	450,000

Mizuno Ladies Open

Kumamoto Chuo Country Club, Kikuchi, Kumamoto
Par 36-36—72; 6,274 yards

December 2-4
purse, ¥60,000,000

	SCORES			TOTAL	MONEY
Mitsuyo Hirata	69	67	71	207	¥10,800,000
Nayoko Yoshikawa	67	70	73	210	4,800,000
Aiko Hashimoto	70	68	72	210	4,800,000
Mayumi Murai	68	71	73	212	2,700,000
Akiko Fukushima	72	71	71	214	1,770,000
Kumiko Hiyoshi	71	71	72	214	1,770,000
Marie Laure de Lorenzi	70	73	72	215	1,650,000
Akemi Yamaoka	72	70	73	215	1,650,000
Junko Yasui	70	75	69	216	1,530,000
Miyuki Shimabukuro	71	70	75	216	1,530,000
Miki Oda	73	73	71	217	1,410,000
Aki Takamura	71	76	71	218	1,185,000
Cheng Mei Chi	71	74	73	218	1,185,000
Kaori Higo	71	73	74	218	1,185,000
Nicole Lowien	66	75	77	218	1,185,000
Natsuko Noro	70	77	72	219	758,400
Hiromi Kobayashi	73	74	72	219	758,400
Michiko Hattori	68	77	74	219	758,400
Huang Bie Shyun	67	76	76	219	758,400
Aiko Takasu	68	74	77	219	758,400
Yukiyo Haga	74	73	73	220	567,000
Jae Sook Won	75	72	73	220	567,000
Akiko Ogawa	74	74	72	220	567,000
Marnie McGuire	72	77	71	220	567,000
Ok Hee Ku	71	74	75	220	567,000
Ray Bell	74	75	71	220	567,000
Michiko Ogawa	72	73	75	220	567,000
Huang Hui Fan	72	71	77	220	567,000
Mayumi Hirase	73	73	75	221	520,800
Tokiko Hashimura	77	72	72	221	520,800
Young Mi Lee	69	76	76	221	520,800
Fumiko Muraguchi	74	75	72	221	520,800
Ae Sook Kim	73	72	76	221	520,800